The Cuban Revolution

By the same author

The Spanish Civil War

Cuba: The Pursuit of Freedom

The Cuban Revolution

Hugh Thomas

HARPER & ROW, PUBLISHERS

NEW YORK, HAGERSTOWN, SAN FRANCISCO, LONDON

This is a shortened version of *Cuba: The Pursuit of Freedom.*

ISBN 0-06-014277-4

LIBRARY OF CONGRESS CATALOG CARD NUMBER: 75-25068

77 78 79 80 81 10 9 8 7 6 5 4 3 2 1

DEDICATION

'Yet, Freedom! yet, thy banner, torn, but flying,
Streams like the thunder-storm *against* the wind.'

Byron, *Childe Harold*

CONTENTS

PLATES

Acknowledgements for the Plates

Acknowledgements and thanks for permission to reproduce the photographs are due to Ampliaciones y Reproducciones MAS for plates 3c and 4b; Sr Guillermo Cabrera Infante for plate 2a; United Press International Inc. for plates 2b and 8b; Associated Press Ltd for plate 3a; Pix Photography for plates 1a, 1b and 6; Camera Press Ltd for plates 3b and 10b; the Keystone Press Agency for plates 4a, 7, 10a and 11b; United Press International Ltd for plates 8a; 11a and 12; and Photo Pic (France) for plate 9.

MAPS

All the maps were drawn by William Bromage

ACKNOWLEDGEMENTS

This book owes a great deal to many Cubans and others who in some cases have become friends. In the latter part of the book many of these have given actual historical evidence. Some of these informants remain anonymous for the purposes of their own safety or comfort, even though the anonymous reference, 'private information', may be irritating to the reader. However, I should like to thank them all for their assistance though probably few of them will entirely approve what I have written. When in Cuba, I should add, I have had the assistance of the press department of the Foreign Ministry and I am grateful to them.

I must also thank Mr Theodore Draper for most generously making available to me his own collection of Cuban newspapers, interviews and manuscript sources, in particular the unpublished memorials and papers of Dr Justo Carrillo, Sr Mario Llerena, Sr Raúl Chibas and Sr Luis Simón. This material, now deposited in the Hoover Library of War, Revolution and Peace, at Stanford, was originally intended for a book on the coming of the Cuban Revolution which was never written. Mr Cass Canfield, Jr, of Harper & Row is in many ways the godfather of the book and I thank him for his valuable advice over several years.

Mr Theodore Draper, Mr Robin Blackburn, Dr Eric Jones, Dr E. A. Smith, Dr Alastair Hennessy, Mr Stephen Clissold, Dr Felipe Pazos, Dr Javier Pazos, Sr Guillermo Cabrera Infante, Sr Luis Anguilar Leon, Professor Arthur Schlesinger Jr and Lord Gladwyn all read part of the book in proof or MSS and made many valuable suggestions; I am very grateful to them. I am particularly grateful to Sr Cabrera Infante who is such a mine of information on so many aspects of Cuban history. Finally, I thank Mrs Hugh Pennant Williams, Mrs Janet Cory and Miss Griselda Grimond who typed the book at different stages and did much other work.

Hugh Thomas
London, April 1970

PREFACE

This paperback edition contains roughly one-half of the text of my larger work, *Cuba: The Pursuit of Freedom,* a history of Cuba from 1762 to the present. This edition covers the period from 1952. I hope that the present edition will make this part of the study more accessible, in terms of length and price, than the complete book.

This edition does not include the appendices, glossary, bibliographical note or general bibliography available in the original edition to which the reader may wish to refer. The index includes those entries referring to this part of the complete work. The maps and photographs in the original edition covering this section are included. I have made no revisions or corrections: time and other work has not allowed this, and also, in general, I believe the main facts and judgments continue to be valid.

ABBREVIATIONS

The following abbreviations are used:

Foreign Relations:	Foreign Relations of the U.S. (State Department Papers published annually)
HAHR	: Hispanic American Historical Review
HAR	: Hispanic American Report
PP	: Parliamentary Papers (Commercial and consular reports)
PRO	: Public Record Office, London
WB	: World Bank (i.e. International Bank for Reconstruction and Development) Report on Cuba, 1952

The first reference to a work gives author, full title, and place and date of publication. Full references can be discovered thereafter by consulting the Bibliography (page 1579) in *Cuba: The Pursuit of Freedom*.

INTRODUCTION

General Batista overthrew the democratic government of Cuba on 10 March 1952. The *coup* was easy: Batista and a few fellow officers took over the military barracks in Havana and the President, Carlos Prío, fled by car from the capital a few hours later. One member of the President's bodyguard was killed.

This event occurred three weeks before the presidential elections in which Batista was a candidate, though, by all good estimations, he was running third to two other candidates, that of the Ortodoxos (headed by Dr Roberto Agramonte), and that of the Auténticos (headed by Dr Aurelio Hevia), the party of the outgoing President Prío.

The electoral system in Cuba which was thus rudely pushed aside had never worked well, nor had Cuba under its democratically elected presidents been a happy republic. President Prío and his immediate predecessor, Dr Ramón Grau San Martín, for example, had failed to deal with two main problems of public life: one, corruption, which extended even to those who worked in the presidential office; and secondly, political gangsterism, which dominated the University and affected both the police and the junior ranks in all political parties. The corruption had characterised Cuba for generations, even when it was a colony under Spain from 1511 until 1898.

The gangsterism was a direct inheritance of the struggle of numerous student and other groups in the 1930s against the then dictator General Machado: Machado was overthrown in 1933, with the help of the United States, but his enemies remained active and kept their arms. Yet there were some who traced the gangsterism to the times of Spain, too, for the Spanish colony had been overthrown, and the independent republic begun, when rebels who, of course, like all rebels, had started life as private persons, had risen against the Spanish regime. Thus the origins of this *coup d'état* of 1952, which led to the capture of power by Fidel Castro in 1959 and to the subsequent Cuban revolution, can be traced a long way back in the history of this island which Columbus, when he discovered it in 1493, found the most beautiful place he had ever seen.

The Cubans in 1952 were more white than black in colour,[1] the whites being mostly Spanish in origin. Many of those of Spanish blood had come into the country in the twentieth century, that is to say, since independence. The blacks were the descendants of the slaves brought in between the sixteenth and the nineteenth centuries from Africa, mostly during the hundred years between 1770 and 1870, when the slave-powered sugar plantations (and coffee plantations for a time) were developing so fast. About half the blacks were reckoned by the Cubans as 'mulatto', and most of those were descended from irregular unions between masters and slaves. While slavery had only ended in Cuba in the 1880s, there had been, however, many freed negroes since an early time—as a result of the purchase of freedom or the granting of freedom by indulgent masters.

There were some other elements in the Cuban population: Some Chinese, descendants of those imported into the island in the nineteenth century when the price of slaves went too high. These were well established in a number of minor crafts near Havana, such as (as in the U.S.A.) laundries and market gardens. Then there were an unknown (since uncounted) number of persons with recognisable South American Indian features. The island had been occupied by several thousand of these Arawaks when Columbus discovered it and, though they were diminished by disease and ill treatment during the early days of the Spanish conquest, their blood ran in the veins of many old nominally 'white' Cuban families. Finally, there were the descendants of English, U.S. and French families, who had come to Cuba for commercial reasons and settled there.

The main Cuban crop had been for several generations sugar cane and, indeed, except for a short period during the second Cuban war of Independence in the 1890s, Cuba had been since the 1830s the largest sugar exporter in the world. She was also the largest overall producer, though, for a time, between 1890 and 1914, that position had been held by Germany, whose sugar beet production had then been enormous. By the 1950s Cuba was producing a tenth of world sugar while a hundred years before she had been responsible for a third.

During the early days of nominal independence, between 1898 and 1933, U.S. interests had dominated the sugar industry. But since 1933 this role had been much reduced, the Cuban entrepreneur Julio Lobo having led the day in a re-'Cubanisation' of sugar interests. Still, some 35% of Cuban sugar production was in U.S. hands, and that stake in the economy, together with interests in land, public utilities and other industries, made the U.S. an overwhelmingly

---

[1] See below, p. 335, for discussion of the official figures.

powerful force in the land. That was enhanced by an arrangement whereby the U.S. bound themselves to buy a regular, large percentage of Cuban sugar at above the world price in order to guarantee a regular supply in all circumstances: the price was fixed well above the world one in order to avoid undercutting U.S. sugar beet producers whose lobby was powerful enough in Washington to ensure this favourable treatment.

Other Cuban products included the world-famous tobacco of Havana, winter fruit and vegetables for export to the U.S. east coast, some beef and coffee, and a little nickel, iron and copper. By and large, however, Cuba was a single crop sugar economy and Cuban society prospered or did badly in direct relation to the rise or fall of world sugar prices. During the world wars, for example, allied demand for safe supplies of sugar created enormous fortunes in Cuba while the depression of the 1930s affected Cuba more than any other South American country.

The long-standing emphasis on sugar in Cuba is difficult to judge easily: on the one hand it enabled Cuba to make use of modern technology very soon after the innovation concerned—the steam engine, the vacuum pan, the railway, for example, were all used in Cuba before they were employed in Spain. Sugar also ensured that the island benefited from a large U.S. investment in the last years of the nineteenth century and the first years of this. Primarily for this reason the island in the 1920s was far and away the richest tropical country anywhere, with a *per capita* income equivalent to that of Ireland, two-thirds that of Britain and a half that of the U.S.A. But the emphasis on sugar prevented the development of a diversified agriculture, tied the country commercially to the U.S. and maintained, after sugar had ceased to develop fast, the economy in a somewhat stagnant state: very well off in the 1920s for a South American country, Cuba was still among the top two or three of those countries in living standards in 1950. But she was still at much the same level in 1950 as she had been in 1925, for population had increased while sugar production had not gone up, thanks to a change in the character of world demand rather than to any lack of possibilities for expansion in the island.

This stagnation of the economy had led to a widespread sense of frustration throughout Cuban society. There was an equally widespread desire to rejuvenate the country and many hoped that the Ortodoxo party would carry out this reformation. This party had been founded by Eduardo Chibás in 1947 as a protest against corruption. In 1950 Chibás killed himself, and by 1952 its leaders were unimpressive. The Ortodoxos had admittedly formulated a promising programme of recovery: an end to gangsterism and corruption,

diversification of agriculture, a school- and hospital-building programme to try and redress the imbalance between town and country,
foreign loans to secure new industries to cut down the chronic under-
and unemployment, and so on. It was an ambitious platform, though
it might very well not have been put into practice had the Ortodoxos
won. For, as most Cubans well new, similar programmes had featured
in other reformist parties' ideas since independence—indeed, had
featured in the programmes of the independence parties themselves
while Spain was still in control.

This national, reformist tradition was one of the strongest cur-
rents of opinion in the country, even though it was usually misunderstood or neglected by both North Americans and Spaniards
who thought more highly of the economic or political benefits their
countries could offer. Still, the minor planters and the slaves who had
fought the first war of independence thought almost as much in terms
of freedom from the dominance of an overpowerful oligarchy and the
emancipation of slaves as they did in respect of freedom from Spain.
José Martí, the brilliant writer who organised the second and ultimately successful war of independence, already saw in the U.S. the
'colossus of the north' as he put it, a new menace to Cuban freedom,
though he also recognised the vitality, originality and power of the
unique North American experience. (Martí died in action in 1895,
a long-mourned martyr and hero to successive generations.)

Subsequently, dissident movements, which formed whenever governments seemed in decline—which they often were—frequently took
upon themselves the colouring of radical nationalism.

The political system as well as the economy of Cuba had been
strongly affected by the U.S. since in the end it had been U.S. intervention at the end of the second Cuban war of independence that had
finally ensured the withdrawal of Spain. A U.S. military government
had run Cuba between 1898 and 1902 and the U.S. only withdrew in
the latter year on the condition, written into the new Cuban constitution, that she should return if there seemed to be disorder in the
island and on certain other conditions. This was the so-called Platt
Amendment, named after Senator Platt, who introduced the wording
into the U.S. Senate. In 1906, the U.S. invoked this clause after a
Cuban civil war did indeed seem to be brewing and remained till
1909. From then on, Cuba was nominally independent, but the U.S.
threatened to intervene several times and that almost had the effect
of real intervention. In 1912, the U.S. marines landed in order to put
down a rebellion of ex-slaves in East Cuba and again in 1917, they
landed in order to ensure sugar supplies in the penultimate year of
the first world war.

This continuous U.S. presence, benevolent though it often set out to be, paternalist though it usually was in practice, fatally delayed the achievement of political stability in Cuba. True, the Liberal party which gave Cuba her first and fourth presidents after 1909 (Gómez from 1909 to 1913, Machado from 1925 to 1933) did achieve a solid national backing, but that party collapsed when Machado illegally extended his term of office with U.S. connivance. The other political parties, such as the conservatives headed by the second president, Menocal (1913–1919), were often merely a conglomeration of sugar interests.

The fall of Machado in the depths of the depression offered Cuba one new chance. But the revolution of 1933, which started with high hopes, collapsed into a fragmentation of authority. Only the army was able to restore government. This was the first opportunity of Fulgencio Batista, who, then a mere sergeant stenographer, carried out his first *coup d'état* only a few weeks after Machado had fled. To begin with, Batista was allied with nationalist forces such as professional groups and students: subsequently, with the encouragement of the U.S. special ambassador, Sumner Welles, he moved towards an orthodox conservative position. He ensured the downfall of one progressive government and acted as the strong man behind several presidents (Mendieta, Mariano Gómez, Laredo Bru) until, with a new constitution in 1940, he stood himself for and won the democratic presidency.

The achievement of the constitution of 1940 was one further good opportunity for the Cubans to establish political viability. There was a general amnesty for all past political crimes, including those committed under the dictator Machado. The economy was recovering, thanks to the war and to new demands for sugar. The era of the Popular Front and the German attack on Russia even made it possible for the small Cuban Communist party to collaborate in Batista's government: two communists became ministers. Batista also gave the system a boost by voluntarily standing down from the presidency in 1944, and watching his own candidate being beaten by Dr Ramón Grau San Martín. But as the *coup* of 1952 showed, that modesty could not be counted upon indefinitely.

Batista was an attractive man, with some black and some Chinese blood. In his early days, he showed many indications of possessing a strong social conscience. He had proved a successful and popular president of Cuba during the second world war and was far the best known Cuban leader internationally. Power and popularity had, however, gone to his head, and in 1952 he wished to return to the presidency mostly for ignoble motives—the accumulation of money and the enjoyment of comfort in grand style.

BOOK ONE

The Struggle
1952 - 9

CHAPTER 1

Batista

In the spring of 1952 the Cuban political system, such as it was, had already been tortured to death. The accumulated follies of fifty years were bearing their rotten fruit. The overthrow of Prío passed easily, the scarcely melancholy cry of *'Prío sale!'* (Prío quits!) echoing throughout the cigar-smoking and rum-drenched streets of old Havana. The prostitutes of Virtue Street knew that the substitution of Batista for Prío in the National Palace would make little difference to them. But Batista's easy triumph spelled tragedy to those who hoped, through the constitutional process enshrined in 1940 and through the Ortodoxo party, to create by the next elections a new Cuba, a decent and happy country. For all interested in political decency Batista's *golpe* in 1952 was intolerable, an event comparable in the life of an individual to a nervous breakdown after years of chronic illness. Thus to men of the generation of the directors of the Agricultural and National Banks, Carrillo and Pazos, this event represented, at the least, a new monstrous interruption in their careers, already gravely injured by the interruptions of the 1930s, of the *Machadato* and afterwards under Batista in his first incarnation. To such people, often temperamentally sensitive, it seemed the final insult that *Time* magazine, the dream machine of the north, should in April for the first time feature Cuba on its cover with a specially effulgent representation of the head of Batista, the Cuban flag behind him spread like a halo, accompanied by the bright comment, 'Cuba's Batista: he got past Democracy's sentries'.[1]

The stamp of acceptance had indeed by this time been given to Batista. On 12 March Elliott Roosevelt, son of Franklin, visited Batista on behalf of a television company.[2] On 23 March the Ortodoxo politicians made a vain appeal to the OAS and to the UN for help.[3] But on 27 March Willard Beaulac, the U.S. ambassador in Havana, visited the new Foreign Minister, Campa, to give U.S. recognition. A less official, but no less welcome and significant move, was a visit by officials of the United States Steel Co. to Ernesto de la Fe, Minister of Information, to say that U.S. capital 'responded favourably' to U.S.

---

[1] *Time*, 9 April 1952.
[2] *Bohemia*, 13 March 1952.
[3] The Ortodoxo politician, Buenaventura Dellundé, went to the U.S. on behalf of their cause to see John Dreir, U.S. ambassador to the OAS.

recognition of Batista; U.S. capital, they assured the minister, could supply Cuba with whatever was needed. On the other hand, the *chargé d'affaires* at the embassy on 10 March itself later assured Carlos Hevía the Auténtico candidate for the presidency that if Prío had held out in any part of the island, the U.S. would not have recognized Batista.[4]

But what was this new government, how was it sustained? The government itself was made up of loyal Batista men or opportunists. On the other hand there is some evidence to suggest that Batista did his best to get Carlos Saladrigas or Emeterio Santovenia or Jorge García Montes to take over the presidency: the last named refused by saying, 'Batista has caught a lion by the tail, let's see how it will escape.'[5] Batista declared that he was loyal to the 1940 Constitution, but that he had nevertheless suspended constitutional guarantees, as well as the right to strike. In April however he proclaimed a new constitutional code of 275 articles, *estatutos de gobierno*, claiming that the 'democratic and progressive essence' of the 1940 Constitution was preserved in the new law. But rights of speech, of assembly and of press could be automatically suspended at any time for forty-five-day periods. New elections would be held, but not before November 1953, eighteen months ahead. Until then, all parties would be suspended, and it was suspected that they would only be reorganized on Batista's terms. The old Congress also was suspended, though congressmen were to draw their salaries for another six months. For the time being the premiership and vice-premiership would be abolished. Batista would govern as president. There would also be an eighty-member *consultative council* to take the place of the legislature, since Batista knew that the old assembly would not support him. Batista's old friend, Carlos Saladrigas, the ex-ABC ex-premier of 1940–4 and his unsuccessful presidential candidate in 1944, would become president, and Oscar García Montes, another old crony, vice-president. This group of legislators would hold at least fifteen sessions a month and be paid $30 per session they attended, though not more than $600 in all.

Batista was full of promises: he would honour international agreements: guarantee all lives and property; fulfil public works contracts (the new president of the development commission, the sugar administrator Amadeo López Castro, said that all projects already begun would be finished in six months). The economy would be strengthened through foreign investments. Cuba would send men to Korea 'if needed', and build 12,000 houses. 'The people and I are the dictators,' Batista explained.

[4] HAR, December 1952. López Fresquet, 31. Ambassador Beaulac told the author that he had been apprised of the imminence of a *coup* by the U.S. businessman, Hodges.
[5] José Suárez Núñez, *El Gran Culpable* (1963), 9.

The conventional *bourgeoisie* rallied quite quickly round the new regime. Batista's past democratic record did not make it far-fetched to suppose that ultimately some constitutional restoration would be achieved. The ex-mayor of Havana, Castellanos, offered to collaborate. The Veterans' Association (a shadow of its once powerful political force), the Bankers' Association, and the Asociación de Colonos y Hacendados (*colonos* and sugar planters) offered co-operation. The CTC gave practical co-operation. A circular from the National Federation of Sugar Workers asked members to 'maintain cordial relations' with the new government.[6] Many isolated Labour leaders – such as Pascasio Linares, Jesús Artigas, Calixto Sánchez (textile, medicine and airway workers' leaders, respectively) – denounced the regime; they were in the minority. Within a few weeks even some parties which had backed Prío or contributed to his cabinets, such as the Democrats and Radicals, were scurrying round to Batista. Marta Fernández de Batista began to make gifts to charity in the style of Evita Perón, stretching out the hand of a First Lady in the hope of soothing disturbed political sensibilities.

But it immediately became clear even to old admirers of Batista that in the years of exile the ex-sergeant had changed. He was far lazier than he had been in the 1940s. He spent an inordinate amount of time in peripheral matters such as the punctuation of a letter, the correct tying of a tie, and changing his clothes. He was fascinated by the private life of his opponents or even of ordinary people in Cuban society and spent hours listening to their tapped telephone conversations: in particular the correspondence of Aureliano Sánchez Arango obsessed him. He ate sumptuously. He spent hours playing canasta with his military friends and hours watching horror films.[7] He seemed more snobbish than he had been before, cultivating the friendship of the heirs of the old Cuban oligarchy and inviting them to splendid banquets even if he knew from their tapped telephones or their intercepted letters that they opposed him. It was popularly suggested that 'Batista worked sixteen hours a day'. This was quite false.

Some new arrangement of public force was judged necessary and the pay of the army was increased. There were a large number of shifts in the disposition of both police and military commands: in April the new police chief, Brigadier Rafael Salas Cañizares (who had taken over the radio station on 10 March), announced openings for 2,000 more men in the police: all police would get new weapons, new cars, new motor cycles. The rank and file of both army and police accepted

[6] HAR, May 1952, 23.
[7] This description derives from the interesting book by his press secretary, Suárez Núñez, *El Gran Culpable*, 11.

the new regime with satisfaction even if they had been mostly recruited under Grau and Prío.[8]

But one beneficial consequence of the *Batistato* was the virtual demise of private political gangsterism. Policarpo Soler was allowed to leave Cuba for more promising shores – Spain and later the Dominican Republic. Rolando Masferrer, the MSR chief, now a senator, was willing to throw in his hand with Batista, and became a pillar of the regime though he retained a considerable private army in Santiago. The truth was that the abolition of political life partly meant the abolition of the violence and the opportunities for corruption which went with it, while the old members of UIR, MSR and ARG took up positions as defenders or opponents of Batista. In a way Batista's *golpe* formalized gangsterism: the machine gun in the big car became the symbol not only of settling scores but of an approaching change of government.

The opposition to Batista was slow to gather shape but it never really died. For the next six and a half years, though Batista was always apparently confident in the Capitol, there was never an occasion when it could be said, 'Cuba is at peace'.

The Auténticos were divided, their followers almost equally furious with Prío as with Mujal. Mujal replied to an attack by Varona with the evasion that the Auténticos had failed to represent the interests of the workers. The Ortodoxos meantime refused to accept their dissolution: Carlos Márquez Sterling, on their behalf, denounced the idea of taking part in elections in 1953.[9] They tried, unsuccessfully, to expel the mayor of Camagüey for swearing allegiance to the new government. On 6 April the Ortodoxo presidential candidate, Agramonte, and several others (Márquez Sterling, Manuel Bisbé, and Luis Orlando Rodríguez), were taken with Pardo Llada before Colonel Cruz Vidal, the new chief of the SIM (the special political police).[10] Cruz Vidal threatened them, accusing them of plotting with the students, but let them go. By this cat-and-mouse procedure, the police and the administration kept the Ortodoxos on the hop. A lack of robustness as well as opportunity on the part of Agramonte and the leaders restrained them from action. Nor were the Communists an effective centre of opposition. Rebuffed by all other parties in the election campaign before the *golpe*, the leaders of course denounced Batista but were slow to do anything more: Marinello, who was still the party's

---

[8] To Batista's surprise, according to Suárez Núñez, 19.

[9] Carlos Márquez Sterling (born 1899), son of Manuel Márquez Sterling (see *Cuba: The Pursuit of Freedom*, p. 674); lawyer, diplomat, representative, 1936–48.

[10] Cruz Vidal, a special follower of Batista, had become sergeant, lieutenant and captain in swift succession between September and December 1933; he was retired from the army in 1944, and now at the age of forty-six had been recalled to the colours to head this investigation squadron.

formal president, merely assured a visiting U.S. historian that the party would probably not resume its old alliance with Batista, though they did have some friendships which he believed might be useful to him.[11] For a few weeks, Batista and the Communists held back in their attitudes to each other: several Communists remained in the Ministry of Labour and in other posts in the administration, whilst others were newly appointed. Cuban-Russian diplomatic relations admittedly were interrupted, after a Russian diplomatic courier's bags were inspected in Havana: the Cubans refused to apologize and Russia broke off relations. But the Communists remained free and well-considered. Some went abroad, most remained. Communist magazines and newspapers still circulated. The historian, Portell Vilá, now an Ortodoxo, even complained that while Communist newspapers such as *Hoy* could easily be bought, he, Portell Vilá, could not be heard on the radio.[12] This ambivalent situation persisted, though in May the police raided Communist headquarters in Havana and forty-three branch offices to prevent any demonstration on Guiteras's anniversary – a curious move since no such demonstration would have been then likely by the party, whose leaders hated Guiteras dead as they had hated him alive.

As usual the Church in Cuba was as ambiguous as the Communists: Cardinal Arteaga congratulated Batista, and other bishops backed him. Two or three opposed and a Franciscan priest, Fr Bastarrica, publicly denounced the *golpe*, as did several prominent Catholic lay leaders, such as Andrés Valdespino, president of Juventud Católica, and Angel del Cerro. In June a Catholic Action meeting at Guanajay was broken up by the police. It became clear that while some members of the hierarchy and the regular clergy would tolerate the new order only too easily, most Catholic laymen and priests would not. Communists and Catholics separately showed themselves ambiguous.[13]

The students provided Batista's main source of worry. Anxious for their own future, many had been thwarted by the *golpe* of the fine future which must have awaited them in Auténtico or Ortodoxo governments. They felt strongly on the issues involved, and demanded the dismissals of professors who had accepted jobs with Batista – such as Carrera Justiz, the new Minister of Communications, and Saladrigas, the president of the new legislature. Batista let it be known that he would give $M10 to build a new 'Ciudad Universitaria' with boarding houses for the students; they replied heroically, '*La Universidad ni se vende ni se*

[11] Alexander, 293.
[12] *Bohemia*, 7 April 1952.
[13] So much for the often quoted remarks of Dr Magiot in Graham Greene's *The Comedians* (1966): 'Catholics and Communists have committed great crimes but at least they have not stood aside . . . and been indifferent' (p. 312).

rende.' On 2 April the police found out that the student leaders were planning a massive demonstration for the following Sunday, at which a copy of the 1940 Constitution would be symbolically buried. Four of them were arrested and taken personally before Batista.

Batista said ingratiatingly, if royally, 'We have an enormous desire to talk with you.'

Alvaro Barba replied, 'Fine, but first we want to know why we have been detained.'

Batista denied that they had been detained. He said that he wished that he could describe the chaos which had existed before 10 March. Prío had been planning a *coup*. Another student, Robledo, spoke of the military *golpe*. Batista interrupted to explain that he had not carried out a *golpe* but a revolutionary movement, to avoid a civil war.

Baeza: 'Yes, a *madrugonazo*!'

Batista: 'No, no, not a *madrugonazo*,[14] but a *madrugón*.'

The student Baeza answered that it might have been a fresh spring morning for Batista but it had not been so for him. Batista said that he needed the co-operation of all Cubans to reorganize the institutional life of the nation, and that the students could not bury the Constitution, because it had not died.

'Precisely,' returned Barba, 'it has been murdered.'

Batista appealed to the need to maintain public order.

Robledo asked, 'But General, are you going to ban all opposition?'

'Opposition is a necessity,' replied Batista, charmingly, 'a constructive opposition is more beneficial to the government than a good minister. This is why I admire you so much . . . if I were a student, I would be in the FEU doing what you do . . . I am not against this demonstration for itself [i.e. the burying of the Constitution] but against the professional agitators who will make capital out of the occasion . . .'

But the students said that they would have to persist in their plan: 'General, we must continue this till the end.'

'Then Colonel Salas [the police chief] will have to act,' said Batista, who thereupon let them free.[15]

The students had every intention of carrying out their plans. On 4 April at three o'clock in the afternoon the chief of the university police, always a key figure, telephoned the FEU leaders and said that two armoured lorries were on their way. Alvaro Barba said, 'Comrades, we must advance the hour of the burial to avoid being shut up in here.' So immediately, instead of waiting for 4 p.m., two hundred

---

[14] There have been so many early morning *golpes* in Latin American history that the Spanish word for a very early rising or an early bird, *madrugón* has received the suffix *-azo*, from *cuartelazo* (a military *coup d'état*), to indicate a rising at dawn against the government.

[15] *Bohemia*, 6 April 1952.

students stood by while their leaders solemnly interred the 1940 Constitution before the bust of Martí at the corner of 25th and Hospital streets. This act of opposition was thus brought to a triumphant conclusion.

The next month, on 20 May, the students staged a massive demonstration to commemorate the fiftieth anniversary of Cuban independence. The meeting was held on the stone staircase, the famous *escalinata*, on the way up to the university: Barba and Mañach, the writer, defended the Constitution in impassioned speeches. 'Cuba can live without meat, water, even dancing,' proclaimed Mañach, 'but not without liberty.' There were cries of 'Chibás, Chibás, Chibás', and demands that the U.S. should boycott the regime.[16] The students, secure in the sanctuary of their autonomous university, were thus able to maintain a front of hostility. In June they proposed that the solution to the political problem in Cuba should be the resignation of Batista, followed by a provisional presidency, to be appointed, as Grau had been in 1933, by the FEU till elections were held. Students called on the public (usually through loudspeakers) to reject Batista's Constitution and swear support of the 1940 Constitution.

With the legislature dormant, there remained only one institution which reflected representative opinion – the municipalities or the mayoralties. Here all stood or fell by what happened in Havana. The Havana municipal council included several prominent citizens some of whom, like the historian Portell Vilá, had tried unsuccessfully to build up Cuban politics from that level. On the municipal council there was also César Escalante, a Communist of long standing and of *bourgeois* origins, brother of the editor of *Hoy*, Aníbal Escalante. Here if anywhere a stand might perhaps still be made. All the elected councillors refused to swear the Batista statutes. But a few weeks later César Escalante was arrested with Nila Ortega, leading a demonstration outside the city hall. Portell Vilá was stopped by Lieutenant Chorro, armed with a machine gun. He was never able to return.[17] Thereafter opponents of Batista did not go to Havana or any other city hall.

By midsummer Batista had thus survived the storms which had followed his insolent capture of power in March. In June he tried to define to the country more precisely why he at least thought he should remain in the President's Palace: he made three speeches, explaining that his 'liberation movement' had made an end of a disastrous regime of disorder, anarchy, concupiscence, vice, venality and ineptitude; and that he, Batista, needed time to study the 'tremendous problems' facing Cuba. Violence, he explained, derived from the opposition; he

[16] *Ibid.*, 22 May 1953.
[17] Evidence of Herminio Portell Vilá.

personally had ended gangsterism as well as suppressing smuggling and bribery, and allowing the reorganization of government departments. He promised agrarian reform, public beaches, public works, cheap housing, honest government and educational reforms (a 'school wardrobe' for school children). Constantly, he blamed Prío for all shortcomings. On 4 July Batista told the *Havana Post* that his revolution was intended to 'eliminate the cancer which was consuming the vital organs of the nation' – that is, the conspirators and gangsters of the past. As an earnest of its high intentions, the government had decided to revive the Grau case once again; and both Grau and his Minister of Agriculture, Germán Álvarez Fuentes, were brought up on a new charge and forced to deposit $40,000 to enjoy provisional liberty.[18] Other 'cancers', however, still flourished. *Botellas* (sinecures) increased. In the countryside landowners connected with the regime or the army were able to do much as they liked, living outside the law: thus in Oriente some landowners were able to take over the property of peasants by sheer force of arms: in the *hacienda* Arroyo del Medio, in Mayarí Arriba, seven families were evicted, their houses wrecked, and 700 *caballerías* taken over in mid-1953 by a certain Baldomero Casas and his nephew Álvaro;[19] while from the very beginning every public work contract, of which there were many, brought its 30 per cent commission to various secretaries and assistants of the President and thence to Batista's bank account.[20] On 14 June the students took advantage of another famous anniversary, Maceo's birthday, to march up the Prado in Havana making protest, in elaborate mourning for the recently dead horse 'Caporal' which had belonged to Eddy Chibás. That night a U.S. Embassy official did a disproportionate amount of harm to Cuban–U.S. relations by drunkenly driving his car into the police across red lights, and, when finally captured, by announcing, 'I am a North American citizen and no authority of a country of Indians can detain me.'[21]

The Auténticos began a lengthy attempt to lure the Ortodoxos into collaboration, proposing a 'civic front' of resistance to Batista. The Ortodoxos were, however, themselves divided in this matter – Mañach and Márquez Sterling leading those in favour of an alliance. But, alas, while the Auténticos, in their humiliation, were surprisingly united, the Ortodoxos were proudly split. The heritage of Chibás had many heads. What did Agramonte stand for, what did Márquez Sterling, and what about 'Millo' Ochoa?

Another movement altogether was being formed by Dr Rafael

[18] HAR, July 1952.
[19] *Revolución*, 27 January 1959, 5.
[20] Suárez Núñez, 21.
[21] *Bohemia*, 29 June 1952.

García Barcena, one of the most attractive and intelligent of the generation of 1933, who as professor of the Escuela Superior de Guerra (a post given to him by Grau) had already tried to form a conspiracy of officers against Prío, and who now prepared a gathering of liberal officers against Batista. García Barcena, noted for his anti-Communism and his nationalism, had some almost Fascist characteristics – particularly a reliance on demagogy and eloquence and a personal clique of devoted friends (without ideology but with loyalty to him), desiring power though lacking administrative experience. His movement, the Movimiento Nacional Revolucionaria (MNR), gathered momentum among students and younger professional people in Havana for a time. It seemed to satisfy their demands for 'action', rather than discussions of ideology. The only other movement was led by Prío's Minister of Education, Sánchez Arango, whose organization, the triple A (a codeword, nicknamed Amigos de Aureliano Arango), represented the most respectable of those who were actually trying to do something more than talk.

García Barcena's was an interesting movement. Mario Llerena, one of its central committee members, who had at first been impressed by García Barcena himself because of his 'charming personality', and 'sympathised right away with his idea of organising armed action against the Batista government', later 'came to realise that the MNR was not entirely democratic':

> Two of the members of the central committee betrayed a definite fascist mentality. Another . . . was, as it turned out later, a Marxist. García Barcena himself, while looking and sounding like a true freedom-loving man, was somewhat lax and sceptical in regard to democratic procedure. Whether he felt the same way about the democratic philosophy itself I never knew. His immediate political objective seemed to amount to something like a moral, constructive dictatorship.[22]

The MNR was indeed one of the many tributary movements of what ultimately became Castroism, or, as it was later re-christened, Cuban Communism, both so far as its ideology and its intellectual approach is concerned and in respect of its actual membership.

There were meantime constant arrests: Jorge Agostini, for a time chief of Prío's secret service, was accused of arms smuggling; Hevia, the Auténtico presidential candidate in March, was for a time imprisoned on a trumped-up charge of gangsterism. The secretary-general of the Transport Workers, Marco Antonio Hirigoyen, was arrested for the murder in a gang battle in 1947 of Manuel Montero Castillo, a tramway

[22] Mario Llerena, Memoir (unpublished MSS), p. 3.

worker; his lawyers, Arnaldo Escalona (a Communist)[23] and Jesús Rolando Valera, were detained too.

Batista and those around him were thus shown to be nervous, insecure and suspicious, even by their own definition, of many whom they should have sought to placate. The top ranks of the military were from the start disgruntled: the chief of staff, Tabernilla Dolz, was at odds with the Minister of Defence, Nicolás Hernández ('Colacho'); the chief of police, Salas Cañizares, took orders not from the Ministry of the Interior nor the head of the army, but only from Batista. Soon the army was dominated by a net of intrigue and distrust, exacerbated by Tabernilla's recall of all officers dismissed by Grau in 1944–5, who were given their back pay over seven or eight years as well. Tabernilla was concerned to establish a network of officers loyal to him – an activity which made enemies not only of the professional group of officers, the *puros*, who had joined since 1945 but of those – the *tanquistas* – who had begun the conspiracy against Prío and who now were increasingly disillusioned, having hoped for a tougher, stricter and more puritanical regime. The only real protests were made by the articulate but relatively small professional middle class. As for the masses, unawakened, their imaginations concentrated on the lottery and on the harvest, and their long unsatisfied thirst for a miraculous cure of their ills seemed briefly assuaged by the extraordinary success of a self-styled faith healer, a singer named Clavelito, who would appear either in life or on the wireless armed with a glass of water and bring almost immediate healing to all disease. The programme was so successful that Unión Radio, which refused to ban Clavelito's programme, was eventually suspended.

The largest sugar harvest in Cuban history had meantime been reaped. Its size was due to excessive sowing in the first days of the Korean War as well as to the coincidence of specially good weather. Restriction of the harvest was politically unpopular; hence Prío had shrunk from it. Nor did Batista's government face the problem: by March, indeed, it would have been difficult to restrict the harvest fairly. There was a feeling that the larger the surplus, the larger the quota would be at the next world conference (planned for 1953). Yet as production went up, prices, partly for that reason, partly due to the decline of world tension after Korea, went down. The government decided finally to keep back 1·7 million tons as a reserve to be sold over the next five years and to restrict the next year's harvest. This plan was vigorously attacked by, among others, Lobo, the biggest Cuban mill owner.

The summer was full of plots and rumours as this great harvest came

[23] His wife was director of the Escuela Normal in Havana. Longstanding party members, the Escalonas were examples of the best sort of progressive and humane Cubans.

in. The chief of police accused nearly every politician of some sort of plot during August: a meeting in Santiago commemorating the anniversary of the death of Chibás was broken up by the arrest of Roberto Agramonte, with Raúl Chibás, Eddy's brother, Luis Conte Agüero and Luis Orlando Rodríguez, all Ortodoxo writers and leaders. Ochoa too was once again arrested on a charge of using television to incite the public to revolt. Tried and found guilty, he refused to pay a fine and so remained in prison. On 17 August a new and sinister event occurred, intolerably reminiscent of the era of Machado: a leading opposition half-Chinese journalist, Mario Kuchilán, who worked on the paper *La Calle*, was called out of his house in Havana at about nine o'clock in the evening, pushed into an Oldsmobile, driven into the Country Club district and beaten, the blows being punctuated with demands for news of the whereabouts of Aureliano Sánchez Arango. Kuchilán escaped alive and got home. The Journalists' Association demanded a seventy-two hour strike of newspapers. The Information Minister, Ernesto de la Fe, blandly said that the Legión Caribe, Prío's famous democratic international squadron, must be responsible. Batista himself spoke of this 'indescribable brutality', and let it be understood that he personally thought the attack had been framed by his enemies to discredit the regime. He said he would fight *gangsterismo* everywhere, 'even in the circle of my friends'. Some attempt was made to carry this into effect: police who beat two photographers for trying to photograph others while being beaten up were suspended. There was also an amnesty cutting sentences for minor offences by a third; but this was, of course, an attempt to please, not to make political concessions.

In October the new Batista constitutional code was published: anyone wishing to organize a party had to gather 5,000 signatures and, after January 1953 parties could act normally, preparing for the elections in November 1953. There would be nine senators for each province, six for the party or *bloc* which gained a majority of votes there, and three for the minority or runner-up. Parties which had been dissolved in March could reorganize themselves providing they could boast 6% of the electorate. The president would be elected by direct vote, and would take office in May 1954. There would be one member of the House of Representatives for each 45,000 inhabitants, each to serve four years. Half would be renewed every two years. Political meetings could be held, provided that those who requested them 'observed the law'. They also had to 'recognise and respect' the existing government and to refrain from inflammatory statements.[24]

All parties of the opposition found this too insulting to take much

[24] HAR, November 1952.

notice of: besides, they had other plans. $240,000 to buy arms for action against Batista were stolen from the friends of Prío in a hotel at Fort Worth, Florida: about half of this sum was later found in a thermos flask in Texas. Another incident occurred in New York State, where police discovered $10,000 worth of arms for Cuba. The Auténticos' hand, mildly fortified by the adherence of an old enemy leader from the Liberals, Eduardo Suárez Rivas, and by some co-operation between Varona and Grau, was once more stretched out to the Ortodoxos. It remained unclasped. Among the Ortodoxos, Agramonte and Ochoa were still at loggerheads, and on 7 October, Agramonte challenged Ochoa to a duel over this very question of alliance with the Auténticos. After elaborate preparations, made in the full glare of public knowledge, the duel was called off. Ochoa resigned his position in the movement and then withdrew his resignation.

There was of course widespread disillusion with this prevaricating and ineffective Ortodoxo leadership; some members of the Young Ortodoxos joined the Communist Youth (Juventud Socialista).[25] Still the press (to which, of course, many political leaders contributed as individuals) remained the most important institution of critical comment and opposition. On 14 October 1952 most of the leading newspapers demanded immediate elections and announced that Cuba was in economic and political peril; and it was in *Bohemia* that Agramonte on 10 November dispatched an open letter to Batista:

> If our country which was born with the most generous democratic ideals, in a heroic fight against abuse and despotism, has to return to the dark and sombre days of the *Machadato*, the fault will be yours, General Batista . . . I accuse you, Fulgencio Batista, of being the great obstacle for the happiness of the poor crushed Cuban people.[26]

And it was in *Bohemia* also that Dr Pelayo Cuervo revealed curious details of the new regime; how interesting, he pointed out, that Francisco Blanco, manager of Batista's own sugar *central*, *Washington*, had paid $M24 to Dr Jorge Barroso, the Sugar Board chief, and how almost every morning Blanco went to visit Amadeo López Castro, the government's representative at the committee on sugar sales. Was it as a result of this that the Vendedor Único, the single Cuban selling agency, dominated by Blanco, had been set up?

Nothing happened to Pelayo Cuervo for the moment. But Batista made an effort to tighten censorship. Grau meantime continued to keep the Auténticos in the same fissiparous condition as the Ortodoxos

[25] Raúl Castro, *Fundamentos*, June–July 1961, 8–9.
[26] *Bohemia*, 16 November 1952.

by claiming to be their new leader through getting 12,300 signatures in his support.

The first martyr in the struggle against the new dictatorship came on 15 January 1953, when a student named Batista (Rubén Batista) was shot when taking part in a banned student procession in memory of Mella; he later died. 'The blood of good men does not flow in vain,' announced with bravura the student leader Barba at the funeral. Another demonstration shared in by all classes occurred at the centenary of the death of Martí on 28 January. On 10 March there were riots inspired by the students in protest against the first anniversary of the *golpe*. As expected, Batista made a speech, only promising, however, maintenance of high police and army salaries. He accused Prío and his brother of stealing $M20 from the Treasury: they replied from Mexico that it had been lent to them. Batista also announced that Prío could return when he wished. Prío said that he would not dream of doing so until Batista had left.

In April 1953 more serious events occurred. On Easter Sunday Professor García Barcena's MNR finally took action and a large group of students and lecturers, armed with knives and guns, marched on Campamento Columbia with a plan to try to persuade the military there to rise against Batista.[27] The government was appraised of the plot and was ready. All were arrested, as were García Barcena and José Pardo Llada, who had been on the movement's fringes. A week later the police dispersed two hundred students who had gathered to place a wreath on the tomb of Rubén Batista. There was also a demonstration at the Medical School, where two students were shot and ten others beaten by the police. On 14 April the university was summarily closed by its council (dominated by Batista men), but even so the police had to arrest another 175 students, including thirty-two girls, at the Faculty of Arts on 23 April. On 27 April García Barcena and sixty-nine others were tried, García Barcena having been tortured so vilely that his spirit and any political career that he might have had were finished; even so he was sentenced to two years' imprisonment and twelve others were given provisional terms of one year. His movement collapsed.[28] Resignations followed from the medical faculty. When the university was reopened, the students went on strike. In May Pelayo Cuervo made another violent attack on Batista in *Bohemia*, saying that the only way to oust him was through force of arms. He also accused

[27] The Central Committee of the MNR had been divided between 'electoralists' and 'insurrectionists'; the latter won.

[28] And his followers, young men such as Armando Hart, Faustino Pérez, Manuel Fernández, Frank País, Mario Llerena – all future followers of Castro to one point or another – had to seek another star. García Barcena obtained liberty on the undertaking that he would do no more against the regime – which undertaking he fulfilled.

officers in the new army of the old crime of swindling the lottery. He was arrested and charged with inciting a revolt.

The atmosphere was thus everywhere warming up. No doubt this was responsible for at least a degree of agreement being reached at last by the Ortodoxos and Auténticos on some sort of common action. Prío and Ochoa signed an agreement at Montreal by which they undertook to aim to restore the 1940 Constitution. They called for a new provisional government, as well as a committee to coordinate action. But this was all that occurred, either in Montreal or in subsequent meetings at the Hotel Plaza in New York and the Ritz Carlton, and not all the leading Ortodoxos signed: Cuervo after all was in prison, Agramonte was being accused of *colaboracionismo* – i.e. considering taking part in the 1954 elections, while Prío was criticized from the left of the Ortodoxos as interested only in restoration, not renewal (*restauracionismo*).[29] Despite this, the situation, violent and unpromising though it might remain, was better in July 1953 from the point of view of the opposition than it had been for some time. Meanwhile, a new grouping, *Acción Libertadora*, was formed in May under the leadership of the ex-head of the agricultural development bank, Carrillo, with the backing of some students such as Barba and Baeza, some trade unionists such as Calixto Sánchez, and some professional men.

[29] The Montreal document was signed by Prío, Ochoa, Varona, Parda Llada, Alonso Pujol, Isidoro Figuera, Hevia, José Manuel Gutiérrez and Eduardo Suárez Rivas.

CHAPTER 2

Fidel Castro: Childhood and Youth

In the early summer of 1953 the historian of Cuban–U.S. relations, Portell Vilá, was sitting in a bar in Havana when a young ex-pupil of his at the university passing by told him that he was planning an attack on the Moncada barracks at Santiago de Cuba, a gloomy pile named after a Negro commander in the war of 1895. Portell Vilá tried to dissuade the conspirator but he was adamant, explaining how he had the arms, the volunteers, and the enthusiasm, and how the attack would be a great moral blow against the regime.[1]

The ex-pupil was Fidel Castro Ruz, then just under twenty-seven years old,[2] and at that time a member of the left wing of the Ortodoxos, known for his energy and gift of language. His character since that time has become widely known, but while few have been so vilified few have also been so praised. It is desirable therefore to gain some impression of his earlier life and experiences.

Castro's father, Angel Castro, like the father of so many Cubans, had come from Galicia in north-west Spain, with the Spanish army at the time of the Spanish-American war. He was a strong man, in physique and in character, willing to do anything, suited to do well out of the general social collapse that attended the end of Spanish rule and the coming of the Americans and the independent Republic. He worked on the United Fruit Company railway in 1904, and otherwise as a day labourer near Antilla,[3] but despite this (or perhaps because of it) he always had a violent hispanic antipathy towards the North Americans, who, he thought, rightly, had cheated the Spaniards out of victory over the Cuban rebels: an odd origin, but no doubt genuine, for his son's similarly hispanic dislike of the Monster of the North.[4] By one means or

---

[1] Portell Vilá, evidence to the author. There are already several lives of Fidel Castro. The most favourable is that by Herbert Matthews, *Castro, a Political Biography* (London, 1969), and the most hostile are the works of his old friend, Luis Conte Agüero, *Los Dos Rostros de Fidel Castro* (Mexico, 1960), and a new edition, *Fidel Castro, Psiquiatría y Política* (Mexico, 1968). Castro's autobiography, long expected, has yet to appear.

[2] Castro was born on 13 August 1926, despite rumours that he was actually born a year later.

[3] According to a vice-president of the United Fruit Company to the author, Angel Castro had been a checker of sugar and had been charged with systematic theft, though the charge was dropped.

[4] A rather wild but suggestive biographical article by Julio del Mar in *El Diario de Nueva York*, 20 July 1962, hints that Castro's family were *integristas*, i.e. Right-wing Carlists, in politics: The village from which they came was Lanteira (Lugo).

another Angel Castro accumulated money enough to buy land, and later succeeded in expanding it, by what means is somewhat speculatory. He appears to have been able to profit by the revolution of 1917 through looking after United Fruit Company property and increasing his own estate at the cost of the company. He worked, perhaps not always honestly, but anyway no less so than, say, H. E. Catlin, or Perceval Farquhar. He hacked his farm out of forest, perhaps sometimes on moonless nights, perhaps by stealing title deeds. His son admitted that Angel Castro paid 'no taxes on his land or income'.[5] His farm, a mixed farm but one which grew cane, lay at a village named Birán near Mayarí, twenty miles inland, in a countryside which till the twentieth century had remained unsubdued, virgin soil; the region had, however, been opened up by the Antilla railway and by the foundation in 1901 and 1904 of the United Fruit Company's great sugar mills, *Boston* and *Preston*. Mayarí, the municipality, increased in population ten times between 1899 and 1953; the village and surroundings of Birán, a United Fruit Company town in every respect, increased no less than sixteen times in the same period, from 529 to 8,305.[6]

The land lying round the Bay of Nipe is among the most beautiful in Cuba. The town of Mayari, inland from the centre of the bay, is old; that of Antilla, on the west, is twentieth-century, being founded as the northern end of the Cuban railway system. The river Mayarí meanders into the bay, its banks being one of the oldest tobacco regions of Cuba, though latterly neglected. However, in the twentieth century there was some diversification of agriculture in the neighbourhood: some cattle, even some corn. Once there had been two small sugar mills in the valley. In the twentieth century the whole area was dominated by four great U.S. companies – not just the United Fruit, but also the Dumois–Nipe Company,[7] the Spanish–American Iron Company and the Cuba Railroad Company.[8] Beyond was forest, except where men such as Angel Castro had carved a *colonia*.

Few places in Cuba were quite so dominated by the North American presence. The United Fruit Company's employees had a polo club, swimming pools, shops for U.S. goods. Even the post office and rural guard headquarters were on company land. The company had its own force of twenty field soldiers, licensed to bear arms. At both *Boston* and *Preston* there were schools and hospitals, and every possible amenity. From Antilla to New York the Munson line maintained a fortnightly service. Only a few miles along the coast were the Nicaro nickel deposits, developed in the Second World War – probably the most

[5] Lee Lockwood, *Castro's Cuba, Cuba's Fidel*, 25.
[6] See Census of 1899, 189, and census of 1953, 193.
[7] Bananas, grapefruit, oranges, sugar cane.
[8] The Nipe Bay Co. in which the *Preston* was vested, was owned by the UFCO.

valuable industrial plant in Cuba, with an estimated capital of $M85. It was owned by the U.S. government itself and was not now working. At Felton, the Spanish–American Iron Company also presided for years over deposits which, at the time, it was uneconomic to mine.[9] Work had gone on at Felton from 1908 till 1917, and then closed.[10]

In 1953 the municipality of Mayarí had a working population of 24,000, of which 15,000 were engaged in agriculture, 3,000 in manufacture, and nearly 2,000 in shopkeeping or some kind of trading.[11] There were about twice as many white as black or mulatto (54,000 to 27,000).[12] Under 250 (1% of the adult population) had attended a university course. 30,000 out of a total population of nearly 70,000 over six years old had not even made the first grade in education. It was therefore a poor area; Castro himself said that most of his companions at the village school went barefoot.[13] Very few of Mayarí's 15,000 houses had lavatories, baths or showers.[14] Fourteen per cent of the people were said to be unemployed or 'looking for a job'.[15]

Angel Castro's *hacienda*, Manacas, grew to about 10,000 acres and dominated the surrounding area.[16] According to his daughter Juana, it employed 500 men.[17] Though the farm produced mixed crops its main activity was growing sugar cane to be sold to the *Central Miranda* ten miles to the south. In the 1950s its quota was about 18,000 tons of cane a year.

Angel Castro made two marriages. By the first, a school teacher – most school teachers in Cuba were women – there were a son and a daughter (Pedro Emilio and Lidia; the former became an Auténtico politician, the latter married an army officer). Afterwards, the great sugar boom during the First World War brought many living in Pinar del Río or Matanzas eastwards in search of work, amid the crashing trees of East Cuba and the foundation of new sugar principalities. Among them was Lina Ruz González, a girl from Pinar del Río who worked for a time as a cook in Angel's house and later (while the first

[9] The Spanish–American Iron Co. was a subsidiary of Bethlehem Steel.
[10] *Cf.* description in Wright, 494–501; World Bank, 211, 996–7; Jenks, 292.
[11] Census of 1953, 193.
[12] More Negroes were 'urban' than 'rural'.
[13] Letter, qu. Robert Merle, *Moncada, premier combat de Fidel Castro* (1965), 342.
[14] Census of 1953, 248. B. Goldenberg, *The Cuban Revolution and Latin America* (1965), 148 says Castro's house did not have a bathroom or an indoor lavatory.
[15] Census of 1953, 160. In 1899 the population of the municipality of Mayarí reached 8,504; in Birán, the second *barrio* in the district, where Angel Castro eventually placed his farm, 529 (Census of 1899, 189). In 1907 Mayarí reached 17,628 and Birán 2,280; Mayarí reached 45,126 in 1931, Birán 3,787. By 1943 Mayarí had a population of 61,172 and Birán 4,505 (Census of 1943, summary, i.e. Birán doubled in size between 1943 and 1953).
[16] Lee Lockwood (*Castro's Cuba, Cuba's Fidel*, 25), has a story of Fidel and Raúl Castro disputing, in May 1965, how many *caballería* of land their father owned. The above is a rough calculation.
[17] *Life*, 28 August 1964.

wife still lived) gave Angel Castro five more children: Ramón, Fidel, Juana, Emma and Raúl. It does not seem, however, that Angel Castro ever settled down with one woman.

The early lives of men who become famous are often shrouded in

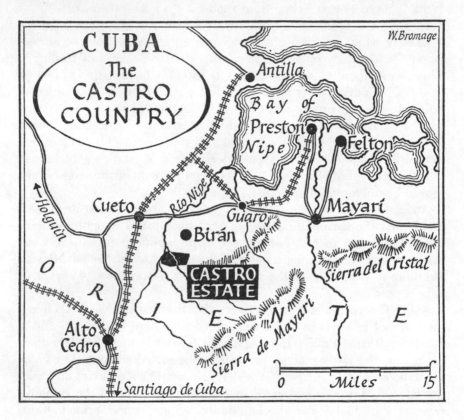

myth; that of Castro is more obscure than usual due to the break that he made afterwards with his upbringing and with his parents' world. In some ways, of course, his parents did not have a world: they were both *nouveau*, both in different ways ambitious and greedy, both restless and insecure, he an immigrant from Spain and a self-made rich man, she an internal immigrant from the country of tobacco, both now living in the profitable but savage sugar territory of Oriente, where the few villages were formless shanty gatherings without traditions or churches, where bandits of various types persisted into the 1950s and where the dominant institution was the United Fruit Company's mills with their private railways, their wharves and their seemingly insatiable demands on the soil.

It is easy to picture the exciting childhood led by the Castro family – fishing, hunting, shooting, surrounded by dogs. The atmosphere in the household was evidently savage: Angel, reticent, violent, hard-working, and rich, resembling *le père* Grandet, though more generous with money, or the father of Cirilo Villaverde, the novelist, who is described as having 'neither time nor inclination to talk with his sons':[18] no emphasis on comfort: poverty and squalor nearby, unredeemed by even the minor advantages that long traditions may bring. Castro's mother liked money and possessions; thus in 1957, after her husband was dead, she visited Mexico when her son was fighting a guerrilla war in the hills of Cuba. She complained to a group of Castro's supporters that her cane fields had been burned, and she had spent $26,000 having them weeded. She asked for it to be arranged that her crop should be left alone, though she did not help her cause when she explained that Batista's soldiery dropped in to see her for coffee.[19]

However it was accumulated, Angel Castro's fortune enabled him to circumvent the depression. In the early 1930s he began to consider the question of the education of his second family,[20] who previously had only been to the hardly existent local school. He called on the college of La Salle in Santiago de Cuba, directed by the Marianist brothers, where many upper-class boys of Oriente went: the registrar insisted on baptism and confirmation, and also on his religious marriage to his new wife, since the first wife had now died. This was arranged by the bishop of Camagüey, Enrique Pérez Serantes, from Galicia like Angel Castro, and an old friend.[21] Ramón, Fidel and later Raúl then went to the Colegio La Salle, later to the Colegio Dolores, Santiago, and after to Belén, the famous Jesuit school in Havana – an educational path which had been followed twenty years before by Eddy Chibás. It is perhaps possible to trace in Castro's father's hostility to legal forms in both property and personal relations his son's lack of interest in constitutionalism, bureaucracy and formality of any kind.

The Jesuit education made a strong impression on Castro. He became known there as a debater and athlete, and as the owner of an excellent memory. He gained a prize in 1943–4 as Cuba's best all-round school athlete. Here again myth takes over: 'He had many heroes during his boyhood and youth . . . Lenin, Hitler, José Antonio Primo de Rivera . . . Mussolini . . . Perón . . . He knew the speeches of José Antonio by memory . . . He knew *Mein Kampf* and also Lenin's *What is to be Done?*'[22] Thus one recollection; and it is clear from the internal evidence of Castro's speeches that José Antonio was an inspiration to

[18] In *Nota Biográfica* to the 1941 edition of Cecilia Valdés.
[19] Casuso, 131.
[20] i.e. by Lina Ruz de Castro.
[21] This derives from a reliable source, an attorney who watched the Castro estates grow.
[22] José Antonio Rasco to Daniel James, *Cuba: the First Satellite in the Americas* (New York, 1961), 34. Also told to me by Portell Vilá.

him. 'The first time I heard of him was when he wrote to President Roosevelt asking for $20 and congratulating him on his victory in 1940. The State Department's answer was posted up on the door, giving thanks and regrets that no money could be sent.'[23] One school contemporary commented: 'The Jesuits were training him to be the white hope of the right.' School stories are not easy to disentangle. One priest, Fr Jean Marie Ramousse, who claimed to have taught him at La Salle, said that though Castro worked quite hard in the classes, outside he was 'insupportable', being always surrounded by a gang of followers and eventually he was removed to the Jesuits who, the Marianists supposed, could do better with him.[24] Evidently, though, he was not an insistent rebel, accepting much of his conventional education with a good grace. His brother Raúl is perhaps a reliable witness here: 'He succeeded in everything. In sport, in study. And every day he fought. He had a very explosive nature. He defied the most powerful and the strongest and when he was beaten he began again the next day. He never gave up.'[25] At least it is evident that Castro seemed then strong, ambitious, well read; a host of historical allusions crop up all the time in his later revolutionary speeches. It also seems that so far as the family was concerned Castro was rebellious: in 1940, aged thirteen, he tried to organize a strike of sugar workers against his father; when he was eighteen there were many quarrels, Castro calling his father to his face 'one of those who abuse the powers they wrench from the people with deceitful promises'.[26] Even so, he continued to expect and to receive financial support from his father.[27] He was following partly, perhaps, his elder brother, Pedro Emilio, who had broken with the father in 1940 and denounced him over the radio in Santiago as a thief, and partly perhaps a Spaniard named Salazar, a teacher, hired as a tutor by Mayarí families and a survivor of the Spanish Civil War. Pedro Emilio was by the 1950s a minor Auténtico politician in Oriente.[28]

Castro's early impressions and ambitions were mostly therefore formed by conditions in Oriente province, the most savage part of Cuba, where gun-law often reigned; the area where the U.S. influence was strongest and most brutally exercised; where the doctors, teachers, dentists and indeed all social professions were least

[23] Told me by a school friend of Castro's at Colegio Dolores, Santiago.

[24] Fr Ramousse, *Bohemia Libre*, 3 September 1961.

[25] To Robert Merle (Merle, *op. cit.*, 90).

[26] But Juana Castro (*Life*, 28 August 1964) says that Castro never showed interest in the *guajiros* on their own father's farm; he is alleged even to have criticized his father for over-generosity to these peasants. This is not very reliable evidence.

[27] See comment by the Wohlstetters, *Controlling the risks in Cuba* (Adelphi Papers (Institute for Strategic Studies) April 1965), 7. See also the somewhat unreliable article by Emma and Lidia Castro, as told to Michael Erice, '*Vida de Fidel Castro*', *El Diario de Nueva York*, 22 April–1 May 1957.

[28] *Cartas del Presidio*, 32.

numerous in proportion to the population. Castro could have known little of Matanzas or Pinar del Río (save through his mother), the old sugar and tobacco areas. Nor could the memory of slavery have been a dominant one among those who were living around him. Many Spanish rather than explicitly Cuban traditions came to him either through his father, or perhaps through the Spaniard Salazar, or the Jesuits: thus he is found saying, as he watched the elections of 1954 from prison: 'what good luck to watch the bulls from the good seats':[29] Cuba of course had no bullfights after 1898.

At the same time his curious family background was certainly unrestful and insecure: the Balzac-like father, like so many characters out of those Latin-American novels which Anglo-Saxons and Europeans find difficult to read; the wildness of the family plantation; the link which the family had perforce with the *Central Miranda*, the medium-size U.S.-owned mill to which the Castros sent their sugar; the fact indeed that this mill had been founded in the great boom of 1917, and was an efficient mill, with its high yield[30] and increasing production from an increasing number of *colonia* – in 1958 there would be 374 *colonia*, in 1937, 73;[31] the fact that Castro's father had not only fought for the Spaniards (against Martí, Maceo, Gómez) but had worked for the United Fruit Co.; the intellectual agility prized by the Jesuit schools; and the disputes within the Castro family; all these influences blended to create the mercurial but forceful character which Fidel Castro now proceeded to display.[32]

Castro went to the University of Havana in October 1945, in a car given to him by his father.[33] He appeared from the beginning possessed with desire to triumph at all costs and always over the most heavily weighted odds. Within a week of the beginning of the term at the university Professor Portell Vilá, the same who saw him in July 1953, was greeted by a porter who said: 'Don't you know there are no students, everyone has gone to watch the fight – the President of the FEU [Student Federation] has been challenged by a freshman, Fidel Castro.'[34] The pattern became settled: Castro drove a bicycle hard into a brick wall to prove to onlookers he had the willpower to do something they would never do.

Castro chose to study law without much more appreciation of what

[29] *Loc. cit.*
[30] In 1937 its yield was 14·54%, higher than anywhere else in Oriente.
[31] *Anuario Azucarero*, 1937, 1959.
[32] An ex-police officer of President Prío, Salvador Díaz Versón, claims that Castro was recruited as a Soviet agent in 1943 by the Russian diplomat Bashirov. See his article in *El Mundo* (Miami), 9 December 1961. No one who has known Castro at any time could believe this.
[33] Juana Castro, *Life*, 28 August 1964.
[34] Evidence of Professor Portell Vilá.

it would lead to than many English students who choose that faculty.[35] In 1961 he said, 'I ask myself why I studied law. I don't know. I attribute it partly to those who said "He talks a lot, he ought to be a lawyer". Because I had the habit of debating and discussing, I was persuaded I was qualified to be a lawyer.'[36] But he was a student who 'never went to lectures, never opened a book except just before examinations';[37] 'how often have I not regretted that I was not made to study something else.'[38]

From the beginning at the university, in fact, Castro spent his time in political activity. For his first two years he was elected 'class delegate' in the Law School – partly at least as a result of his athletic prowess at school. Among his friends were Alfredo Guevara and Leonel Soto, already members of the Communist youth, the first being then president of the Social Sciences Faculty Students and secretary of the FEU in 1948, the latter president of the School of Philosophy and Letters. Castro entered politics at the university as he had been athletically active at school, because it was 'the favourite hobby or obsession. It was the anteroom to power . . . There was nothing odd or unusual about this. The political atmosphere in the University was so charged and pervasive that many were caught up in it.'[39] Thus from 1946 onwards Castro belonged to the millenarian minority of the population of Cuba, phrasing heroic slogans, recalling past heroes, an active political minority: it is as a representative of the law faculty in September 1946, supporting Chibás and in January 1947, criticizing Grau's 're-electionism', that Castro first appears as a politician.[40] In this speech, Castro is found talking of the *'pléiade'* of students who faced the dictatorship (of Machado).[41] From the second term of his university career, Castro had also, like most of his fellow student leaders, a connection with at least two of the revolutionary organizations which dominated university politics and threatened national affairs.

His university career was, therefore, already extraordinary, and it became more so. Castro himself later spoke of the time in fairly candid terms:

The political atmosphere in the University of Havana had been contaminated by the national disorder. My impetuosity, my desire

[35] Theodore Draper is scornful of Castro's decision to read law. 'He chose a field of study in which the standards were notoriously low, the pressure to study minimal and his future profession already over-crowded.' (*Castroism: theory and practice* (1965), 114.)
[36] *Revolución*, 10 April 1961.
[37] *Ibid.*, 7 March 1964.
[38] *Ibid.*, 14 March 1964.
[39] Comments of Fructuoso Pérez.
[40] Conte Agüero, 457.
[41] *El Mundo*, 17 January 1947, and 17 July 1947.

to excel fed and inspired the character of my struggle. My straight-forward character made me enter rapidly into conflict with the *milieu*, the venal authorities, the corruption and the gang-ridden system which dominated the university atmosphere. The pressure groups of corrupt politicians made the gangs threaten me and led to a prohibition on my entering the University. This was a great moment of decision. The conflict struck my personality like a cyclone. Alone, on the beach, facing the sea, I examined the situation. Personal danger, physical risk made my return to the University an act of unheard-of temerity. But not to return would be to give in to threats, to give in before bullies, to abandon my own ideals and aspirations. I decided to go back and I went back . . . *with arms in my hand* . . .[42] Naturally I did not find myself fully prepared to understand ex-actly the roots of the profound crisis which disfigured the country. This resulted in my resistance being centred on the idea of personal valour.[43]

Reading between the lines, it is clear that Castro must have indeed been threatened, that perhaps to begin with against his will he joined in the extraordinary gang warfare in which against his better judgement he excelled. It should be remembered too that the 'action groups', though they had degenerated into *gangsterismo*, were not even in 1948 wholly bereft of idealism and political romanticism.

The two groups with whom Castro was in any way implicated were, first, Rolando Masferrer's MSR, and the UIR, led, until his murder, by Emilio Tró, the police boss of Marianao. The revolutionary violence which characterized the students who had overthrown Machado never lost its fundamentally romantic appeal. The future leader of the Cuban socialist revolution was blooded in politics during the machine-gun and big car era in the time of Grau and, whatever part he personally played it is evident that he learned much about the nature of Cuban political institutions, their feebleness, their susceptibility to violence and their corruption.[44] On the other hand, though Castro used all the action groups, he failed to be elected either president of the Law Students or president of the FEU.

Elections in student politics at Havana were often settled by fists, guns and kidnappings. Some shootings were attributed to Castro. Thus in December 1946 Leonel Gómez, president of the Student Federation at the (first) Havana High School, and a member of the UIR, was wounded in Rionda Street. This attack had apparently been

---

[42] Author's italics.
[43] Remarks to Gloria Gaitán de Valencia, *América Libre* (Bogotá), 22–8 May 1961.
[44] This is well put by Suárez, *Cuba: Castroism and Communism* (MIT Press, 1967), 18.

engineered by Manolo Castro, the president of the Students' Union, since Gómez had bragged that he was going to enter the university and take over power there. At this time Fidel Castro was anxious to gain the confidence of Manolo Castro in order to help him in his own university ambitions, and (according to another student who was wounded)[45] Fidel Castro and some others were apparently responsible for the shooting.

When still a friend of Manolo Castro, Fidel Castro also took part in the abortive invasion of the Dominican Republic organized by the MSR and other 'action groups' in the summer of 1947.[46] Castro was placed in command of a group of Dominican exiles;[47] but since he was the only member of the UIR on this expedition he was in a delicate position. When the expedition was called off the participants were mostly arrested. Castro was among those who escaped; he swam, carrying an Argentinian sub-machine gun and a pistol, across the Bay of Nipe, known to be infested with sharks, but arrived safely at his father's farm.[48]

By this time, however, it had become clear that Manolo Castro was not going to help Fidel Castro much in his quest for university political leadership, and so he joined his enemies, the UIR, the action group led by Emilio Tró until his death in open battle in Marianao at the hands of Manolo Castro's friends, the Salabarrías. At the same time, through a friendship with Enrique Ovares, Manolo Castro's successor as president of the students' union, Fidel Castro succeeded in being nominated as president of one of the university specialist committees on legal affairs.

In the autumn of the same year, with a group of students (financed by Chibás), Castro went on a wild expedition to Manzanillo to bring back to the students of Havana, as a symbol of a new revolt, the bell which Céspedes had rung as a tocsin in 1868 – which the owners, the surviving veterans of 1898 in the town, had refused to present to the city of Havana.[49] On 12 February 1948 he was involved in a famous clash with the police outside the university in protest again at the invasion of university autonomy.[50] Ten days later, on 22 February 1948, Manolo Castro, State Secretary of Sports, president of the FEU some time before, 'handsome as a picture postcard but a paranoiac', the virtual tyrant of the university, a close friend of the Education Minister Alemán and other Auténtico leaders, was lured out of a cinema (of which he was part-owner) and shot down. Fidel Castro was accused of

[45] Fernando Freyre.
[46] See the author's *Cuba: The Pursuit of Freedom* (Harper & Row, 1971), p. 755.
[47] Rolando Masferrer, in a letter to Theodore Draper.
[48] The shark swim is confirmed by Juan Bosch, the Dominican commander who attempted to dissuade him (memorandum of Juan Bosch).
[49] Evidence of Max Lesnick.
[50] *Hoy*, 13 February 1948.

being implicated in this assassination. He was arrested at the airport, appeared before a judge and had his passport removed.[51] It seems probable that Castro did not participate in the attempt itself nor did he fire a shot in the next street to distract attention, as alleged, but that he was present at the meeting of the UIR which agreed to undertake the attempt.[52] The evidence, however, is inconclusive. The UIR was a group given to black humour – the killers each received engaging nicknames such as Billykin, Bright Eyes, Patachula – and the idea of one Castro killing another would have appealed to the then leader, Justo Fuentes, a Negro gangster and part-time student. It is not a matter on which Fidel Castro has bothered to dwell much in his speeches. (Manolo Castro was, of course, avenged in 1949 by the assassination of Justo Fuentes.[53])

This was certainly the most sensational act of the political gang warfare to date. (Fidel Castro as a suspect told the judge in March that he believed that some of Manolo Castro's friends were out to kill him.) It would not be out of character if Fidel Castro had been involved, and in equity it is not inappropriate to add that in some ways Manolo Castro deserved his fate. Castro gave later an analysis of this stage in his career:

> Without experience but full of youthful rebelliousness, [he had fought] against the imperium of Mario Salabarría . . . This evil which culminated in *autenticismo* had its origins in the resentment and hatred which Batista sowed during [his first] eleven years of abuses and injustices. Those who saw their comrades assassinated wished to avenge them, and a regime which was incapable of imposing justice, permitted vengeance. The blame lies not with those young men who, distracted by their natural anxieties and by the legend of a heroic epoch, desired to make a revolution which had not been achieved, at a moment when it could not be done. *Many of those who, victims of illusion, died as gangsters, would today be heroes.*[54]

On another occasion he remarked, 'When the worst is enthroned, a pistol at his belt, it is necessary to carry pistols oneself in order to fight for the best.'[55]

[51] *Noticias de Hoy*, 21 March 1948 (the Communist paper). Manolo Castro's friend, Carlo Puchol Samper, was also killed, and others.

[52] Evidence of Enrique Barroso. Osvaldo Soto (then president of the Law School students) says that Castro invited him and another student (Benito Besada) to a café that night and left a few minutes after arriving (Soto memorandum).

[53] Manuel Corrales, who is believed to have accompanied Manolo Castro from the cinema into the street on this occasion, was appointed by Castro in 1959 to the Cuban delegation to UNESCO. Those who appeared before a court accused of the crime were Fidel Castro, Justo Fuentes, Pedro Mirassón, Armando Galí Menéndez and Gustavo Ortiz Faes.

[54] *Bohemia*, 25 December 1955 (author's italics).

[55] '*Cuando lo peor está entronizado con la pistola al cinto, para luchar por lo mejor hay que portar la pistola también.*' (Remark to Carrillo, September 1955, Carrillo MSS, *Información Histórica*, 8.)

Whatever Castro's part in the death of Manolo Castro, a month later he was implicated in a still more sensational event – the famous 'Bogotazo', as it is now known. Here again rumour and fear have fed fantastically on tragedy: here those who find comfort in seeing themselves threatened by a single, centrally directed minority conspiracy allow Fidel Castro to appear on the scene for the first time, outrageously garbed, the assassin of the Americas, professional subverter of private enterprise.

In April 1948 a Pan-American Conference had been arranged to be held in Bogotá, the capital of Colombia, to reform the old Pan-American Union of American states into a more closely knit organization, the Organization of American States (OAS). General Marshall would arrive representing the U.S. and all other American states would be represented by Foreign Ministers.

A protest to coincide with this assembly was planned by Cuban and Argentinian students, with a sprinkling of others from other parts of Latin America. The fares of many students, including those of the student delegation from Cuba, were paid by Perón, the Argentinian dictator, anxious to make trouble for the U.S. in Latin America.[56] Perón also desired an attack on British imperialism to try to force Britain to return the Falkland Islands to him. Among those asked from Cuba were the president and the secretary of the FEU, Enrique Ovares and Alfredo Guevara (the Communist leader in the University of Havana), along with Castro, representing the law faculty of the University of Havana, and Rafael del Pino, a Cuban-American who registered every year as a student but did not attempt much to study, also like Castro a member of UIR. Their meeting at Bogotá was to prepare for a full meeting inaugurating a new inter-American student organization to be held in the autumn, in which Castro had always been interested.[57] Both Communists and Peronists throughout South America collaborated in these student plans.

Castro and del Pino arrived in Bogotá on 29 March 1948, armed with various documents including a letter of introduction from Rómulo Betancourt, the Venezuelan Social Democrat president whom they had visited en route.[58] During the next week they had discussions with other student leaders in Bogotá; on 3 April the Pan-American meeting

[56] Evidence of Max Lesnick, president of Ortodoxo Youth, in letter dated 20 August 1963 to Draper. The Peronist representative in the University of Havana was Santiago Tourino and, according to Carlos Reyes Posada (*El Espectador*, Bogotá, 10 December 1961), the chairman of the Argentinian Senate Foreign Relations Committee, Diego Molinari, visited Havana in February 1948 to arrange the Cuban delegation's expenses.

[57] 'When we were still on good terms with him during his second year . . . we asked him why he wanted to be President of the Law School . . . he would always say that time was running out, that his true ambition was not merely to be president of the FEU but to organize a Federation of Latin American students which would be a tremendous political instrument in South America.' (Memorandum of Fernando Freyre.)

[58] *La República* (Bogotá, 21 January 1959), in *Communist Threat to the Caribbean*, 277.

began and the two groups – the established world of statesmen and diplomats and the new world of placeless and ambitious students – swung towards each other, and clashed for the first time, though gently, as if irregulated pendulums. At a public ceremony in the Teatro Colono attended by the most prominent members of Colombian society and the government, leaflets were dropped in thousands from the balconies, attacking U.S. colonialism. Many of these leaflets were printed in Havana and some were dropped by Castro and del Pino. Interrogated, these two students were ordered to report to the police two days later: when they did not do so, their hotel rooms were searched and more so-called Communist leaflets were found. On 6 April both were taken to the police headquarters and ordered to cease 'actos hostiles'.

On 9 April the worlds of statesmen and students clashed again, much more severely. At about 1.20 p.m. the much-loved Colombian Liberal demagogue Jorge Eliécer Gaitán, the Chibás of Colombia it might be argued, was murdered, in the course of a demonstration, by a lunatic, Juan Roa Sierra.[59] Gaitán had been the great hope for Colombian social reform. His speeches had roused the masses of Colombia and, if he were not precisely a democrat in the European tradition ('there are roads more advisable than those of the ballot boxes' was one of his more famous remarks), he had a generous heart.[60] His death cast Bogotá into a spasm of fury and fear: Roa Sierra was lynched. Processions were formed, rioting began and, by the evening, Bogotá was out of control. Shops were looted, and burned, police stations blown up, and there was much sporadic firing and fighting. Police gave arms to rioters anxious to overthrow the government. The Communists tried to seize advantage of the confusion, but failed. For several days the violence continued, an earthquake uncontrolled and undirected, resembling the tragic week of Barcelona of 1909, though estimates of the numbers killed in Bogotá reached 3,000, far higher than had occurred in Spain. Afterwards, as usual in such circumstances, scapegoats were sought. General Marshall and the majority of the statesmen attending the Pan-American Conference blamed the Communists. The U.S. ambassador to the U.N., Pawley, a veteran anti-Communist who was in Bogotá,[61] later recalled: 'We had information that there was a Cuban there, a very young man who appeared to us not to be the real threat.' Later, he said that he heard a voice on the radio just after Gaitán's

[59] That Roa Sierra was the sole assassin is accepted in the report by the Scotland Yard chief, Sir Norman Smith, who says that Roa's motives derived from Gaitán's reiterated refusal to receive him.
[60] See La Nueva Prensa (Bogotá), 6–9 April 1963, for Gaitán's programme.
[61] William D. Pawley (born 1896), founder of Cubana Airlines, businessman, ambassador to Peru and Brazil; in 1949 he took over the Havana Trolley Co., and in 1950–1 founded Havana's Autobuses Modernos.

murder: 'This is Fidel Castro from Cuba. This is a Communist revolution. The President has been killed, all the military establishments in
Colombia are now in our hands, the Navy has capitulated to us and this
Revolution has been a success.'[62] This report must surely have owed
much to imagination. But the Colombian chief of police, Alberto Niño,
also later claimed that Castro and del Pino were Communist agents
sent in to organize the riots and others have claimed that Castro killed
thirty-two people in these days.[63] A guest at the Hotel Claridge heard
Castro and del Pino boasting about their success: Castro is even
believed to have shown Colombian detectives a pass book which
identified himself as 'Grade I agent of the Third Front of the U.S.S.R.
in South America'.[64] Another, perhaps more reliable report described
how the two Cubans arrived at their hotel on 9 April 'bringing a large
quantity of arms and staying there for many hours, talking on the
phone, in English, with various people.'[65] It is true that Castro did get
involved in the riots, but obscure how much fighting he did; it is evidently incorrect to suppose that Castro was the agent of the riots, and
it is not a subject upon which he, usually garrulous, has enlightened the
world. Castro had a *rendezvous* with Gaitán about the hour of his death
but he apparently wished to ask advice about booking a theatre for a
meeting.[66] On 13 April Castro and Rafael del Pino were taken to the
Cuban Embassy by an Argentinian secretary of embassy, and the ambassador, Dr Guillermo Belt, an old ABC leader, gave them sanctuary
and enabled them to return to Havana in a cargo plane.[67]

These events of course made an impression on Castro: the crowds,
the violence, the destruction, the oratory of Gaitán and his magnetic
personality – Castro met him before 9 April – all played their part.[68]
He commented later that the Colombian masses failed to gain power
'because they were betrayed by false leaders'.[69] Doubtless he felt as
Napoleon did when observing the Swiss guards fighting to the last man

---

[62] *Communist Threat*, 724–5.

[63] *Antecedentes y secretos del 9 de Abril.*

[64] *Ibid*, 278.

[65] Report by Sir Norman Smith of Scotland Yard, as reported in *El Tiempo* (Bogotá), 12
April 1961.

[66] Comment of Gloria Gaitán de Valencia in *América Libre*, 22 May 1961.

[67] The author has encountered no evidence that, as argued by his enemies, Castro's life was
spared on the intervention of the Russian ambassador. There were other scapegoats. Thus:
'Romulo Betancourt headed a plot against the Nation on April 9 . . . it was prepared in the
city of Havana.' See *El Siglo* (Bogotá, 2 July 1948), qu. *Communist Threat*, 278. A Colombian
detective claimed to have seen Castro with Roa Sierra on the morning of the 9th (*La República*,
Bogotá, 10 April 1961). See also Francisco Sandiño Silva, *La Penetración Soviética en América y el
9 de Abril* (Colección *Nuevos Tiempos*, Bogotá, 1949).

[68] '*Tuve oportunidad de oír a Gaitán. Su voz, su personalidad impresionante, y el movimiento popular
vigoroso que acaudillaba, lucía como la salvación de ese gran pueblo colombiano. Por eso lo asesinaron . . .*'
(interview with Gaitán's daughter, *América Libre*, 22 May 1961).

[69] *Ibid.*

at the Tuileries: that these 'masses' could win when they were well led.

On return from Bogotá, Castro for a time turned to a conventional life. He married, when just twenty-two, Mirta, sister of Rafael Díaz Balart, a friend in the law faculty at the university, also of the UIR, of the same age as himself. The Díaz Balart family disapproved of the engagement, but the marriage occurred on 10 October 1948, the day of the inauguration of Prío as president. For the rest of that year and till 1952 Castro was a member of Chibás's Ortodoxo party, which he had formally joined in 1947. Indeed, he had been to its foundation meeting in Havana in May 1947. He followed Chibás with immense enthusiasm, regarding him as the man of the future, and seems to have dropped what little feeling for Marxism he may have had: maybe the absence in Moscow of his university Communist friends, Soto and Alfredo Guevara, helped. He also dropped out of the action group UIR, after another fracas in the university resulting in an armed attack on a member of the university police, Sergeant Fernández Cabral[70] and a final fling at his old enemy Masferrer in 1949 in which one man was killed.[71] Justo Fuentes, the UIR leader, meantime was killed when leaving the radio station COCO on which he and Fidel Castro had a daily programme: Fidel Castro did not reach the station that day and so escaped. At the same time, in the first two years of marriage, he worked, and graduated as a doctor of law in 1950.

There was one other interesting incident. Batista returned to Cuba after the election of 1948, and one of his friends, Leopoldo Pío Elizalde, hearing of Castro as an exceptionally promising and wild student, thought that he might draw him into Batista's new Partido de Acción Unitaria. According to Pío Elizalde, Castro said that he personally had no animosity against Batista, that his father knew him and owed him gratitude, but that for 'generational reasons' he could not link himself politically to the ex-president. If Batista had come back with insurrectionary (*golpista*) intentions, he could count on him. Pío Elizalde then primly told Castro that Batista expected to get back to power by vote (*con las urnas*).[72]

This curious tale is so fully in character that it is difficult not to accept it: Castro has so evidently believed in insurrection rather than election campaigns. Pío Elizalde told Batista, and some months later

[70] See *Hoy*, 8 July 1948, and *El Mundo*, 7 July 1948. Fernández Cabral was one of Salabarría's men and was shot by the UIR including José de Jesús Ginjaume who claimed to have been in the house of the Minister of Education at the time.

[71] Castro was accused, along with surviving members of the Acción Revolucionaria Guiteras and UIR, such as 'Billykin' (Guillermo García Riestra), Rafael del Pino (his collaborator at Bogotá), José de Jesús Ginjaume, etc.

[72] '*Si Batista ha regresado de Daytona con una intención golpista, que cuente conmigo*', L. Pío Elizalde, *La Tragedia de Cuba* (1959), 225-6.

Castro's brother-in-law, Rafael Díaz Balart, who had joined Batista from the UIR, persuaded Castro to visit Batista in his estate, *Kuquine*. The two then talked in the library on 'literary and historical themes without the host giving [Castro] a chance to begin a political discussion'.[73]

On this period of his life Castro later remarked, perhaps forgetting, certainly rationalizing:

At the time I passed the baccalaureat I was a political illiterate. My first contacts at the university with middle class economics showed me some of its contradictions and I got to know some revolutionary ideas . . . Afterwards, naturally, [there was] University politics. We [that is, himself or perhaps himself and his intimates] began at that time to have our first contacts with the communist manifesto, with the works of Marx, Engels, Lenin. This was a very clearly defined stage of development. Of course, many of the things which we did at the university were not devised by us, certainly not. When we left the University, I myself particularly, we were already greatly influenced [by Marxism]; I am not going to say I was already a Marxist–Leninist; possibly I had two million petty *bourgeois* prejudices . . . At best I can say that if I had not had all those prejudices I would not have been in a condition to make a contribution to the Revolution in the way I have now been able to . . .[74]

A little later, in an interview with an American journalist, Castro said that his 'first questionings of an economic and social kind arose when I was a student . . . [The] problems posed by overproduction and the struggle between the workers and the machines . . . aroused my attention extraordinarily.'[75] Castro explained that he had read as far as page 370 in *Das Kapital* at this period[76] and had 'studied' the Communist manifesto and some of the works of Marx, Engels and Lenin:[77] but page 370 is not so very far in most editions of *Das Kapital* and it is perhaps unexpected to hear that 'the Marxist point of view . . . captivated me and awakened my curiosity'.[78]

All this surely was to say at some length that at the university Castro was influenced in a modest and superficial way by Marxism and nationalism. By the former he perhaps meant no more than that he

---

[73] *Loc. cit*; Batista gave himself a guarded account of the meeting saying he had avoided talking of political matters because he knew of Castro's '*antecedentes gangsteriles*' (*Respuesta*, 325). To Suárez Núñez (*El Gran Culpable*, 12), Batista said, 'I had to tell Díaz Balart not to bring Fidel Castro to my house because he was a *pistolero*'.

[74] Castro speech, 2 December 1961 (*Obra Revolucionaria*, 1961, No. 46, p. 38).

[75] Lockwood, 138. (This was in 1965.)

[76] *Obra Revolucionaria*, 1961, No. 46, p. 35.

[77] *Loc. cit.*

[78] Lockwood, 139.

heard for the first time the theory that society is divided into antagonistic classes. Yet if he only got to page 370 in *Das Kapital*, he seems to
have reached further in Thiers's and Jaurés's histories of the French
Revolution and also Macchiavelli and Malaparte's *Technique of the
Coup d'Etat*. Later on, he was anxious to give the impression that he had
been a good revolutionary for as long as possible. It would be appropriate to point out that several of Castro's contemporaries at the university
regarded him as 'a power-hungry person, completely unprincipled,
who would throw in his lot with any group he felt could help his political
career',[79] and not long before the famous confessional speech of December 1961, quoted above, Castro explained that 'the knowledge gained
from a revolutionary work, from . . . Marx or . . . Lenin cannot be the
same when we read it without having any experience of government . . .
we once read them [i.e. Marx and Lenin] for general interest, for curiosity. . . .'[80] Yet one further comment might be suggested: the culmination of his university experiences and those of his childhood appear for
whatever reason – a desire to carry on a student tradition of tyrannicide,
revolution and insurrection, an identification conscious or unconscious
with the seething crowds in Bogotá, a challenge to his father or a pursuit
of intellectual systemization – to have led him to what he would later
refer to as the 'vocation of revolution'. 'What made us revolutionaries?'
he demanded rhetorically in 1961, and answered, first, the vocation
of 'being a revolutionary':[81] and perhaps revolution for revolution's
sake, not any particular revolution.

Afterwards anyway his life seems to have been ever preoccupied
with politics. He hardly became at all involved in the career of the law.
Though he worked in a law firm named Azpiazu, Castro and Resende,
his clients were mostly few and poor. One case only caught public
attention: at a student meeting called to protest against an increase in
bus fares a police lieutenant, Salas Cañizares (afterwards chief of
Batista's police) hit a young worker, who later died of his wounds.
Castro volunteered to act as prosecutor. Meantime, it seems that
money was short: he recalled later that milk was often short for his
son, that the electricity company cut off his light, that he could not
find an apartment and that he was always in debt, when not to the
grocer, to the butcher.[82] He was anxious to stand for Congress, but
his old history teacher, Portell Vilá, refused to champion him, on
the grounds that he associated with the left wing of the Ortodoxos.[83]

[79] From a memorandum by Fernando Freyre, a fellow law student.
[80] Speech at 1st National Congress of Responsables del Trabajo de Orientación Revolucionaria, *Revolución*, 11 November 1961, 8.
[81] *Obra Revolucionaria*, 2 December 1961.
[82] *Ibid.*
[83] Evidence of Dr Portell Vilá, repeated by him in *Avance* (Miami), 5 January 1962.

An active member of the Ortodoxo party, he carried out in 1950 a famous raid on Prío's villa, where he took compromising photographs afterwards published in the newspaper *Alerta*.[84] In the 1952 election campaign, Castro, having specifically denounced his old friends in the political gangster groups in *Alerta*,[85] spoke on behalf of the senatorial aspirations of Chibás's old friend Leonardo Fernández Sánchez and was himself later nominated, under the sponsorship of the mulatto editor of *Alerta*, Vasconcelos, as Ortodoxo candidate for the House of Representatives for one of the Havana municipalities. He later explained, not entirely convincingly, that, though he had been thinking of using parliament . . .

> as a point of departure from which I might establish a revolutionary platform . . . I didn't believe that my programme could be realized in a legal, parliamentary way . . . already I believed then that I had to do it in a revolutionary way . . . once in parliament I would break party discipline and present a programme embracing practically all the measures that later on were contained in our Moncada programme and which [after the Revolution were] . . . turned into laws.[86]

He added also (but this was in 1965) that to gain power he would need the support of a section of the army.

Castro's writings at this time often appeared in *Alerta*, whose editor, Vasconcelos, can, despite his own ambiguous past,[87] be considered one of his mentors. In June 1951 we hear of an attack by him on *latifundistas* and a demand for 'justice for the workers and Cuban peasantry';[88] in November 1950 came a demand for the independence of Puerto Rico and a statement that 'the students of Cuba are united against the tyrants . . . of America'.[89] A week before Batista's *golpe*, Castro accused Prío of distributing $18,000 a month to action groups – to one of which at least he had himself once belonged but which he now castigated: 'The mystique and past struggles gave [these groups] access to the organs of propaganda . . . young men attracted by a false concept of heroism and of the revolution . . . The regime degenerated and all those organisations sooner or later lost . . . their ideological concept . . . But the apparatus of terror and death cannot be sustained without vast financial means.' Castro's speech before the Tribunal de

---

[84] *Mártires del Moncada*, 90.
[85] 28 January 1952.
[86] Lockwood, 140.
[87] An opponent of Machado, he was later persuaded to join Machado as a diplomat and acted as a spy for the government on Cuban exiles in Europe (see Conte Agüero, *Eduardo Chibás*, 343–4). He had also had a similar career with respect to Batista.
[88] *Alerta*, 6 June 1951.
[89] *Ibid.*, 4 March 1952.

Cuentas, making detailed accusations against President Prío for financing the *grupos de acción*, reads well, a long and sustained philippic by an apparently highly articulate patriot.[90] On the other hand, it would seem that he really attacked the groups led by El Colorado and Masferrer, not UIR.

It was in this mood that the *golpe* of the *sunsundamba* of 10 March found him. On that day, he was at the university and helped to distribute arms to the students and others with them.[91] Several days later, he distributed a manifesto entitled *Zarpazo*,[92] which, while challenging Batista in vigorous terms, is significant as Castro's first independent political statement:[93] it ended with a call to struggle: '*La hora es de lucha*; to live in chains is to live in shame!' It called on Cubans to restore the constitution of 1940.[94] His own response to this injunction was first to write a personal letter warning Batista of the dire consequences of his action, second to file a suit with the court of Constitutional Guarantees demanding Batista's punishment for crimes against the Constitution. No one listened, though these acts gave publicity to Castro's somewhat new-found devotion to the old constitution.

Castro was now a politician without a platform as well as a lawyer without clients,[95] although his brother-in-law, Díaz Balart, who had become a supporter of Batista, tried unsuccessfully to persuade him to back the *cuartelazo*.[96] He was nearing thirty, his father was still vaguely supporting him, his marriage was not very successful (though he had had a son, Fidelito, in September 1949). Something had to be done if the chance of a political career was not to slip through his fingers. He had a reputation already as a man who loved risks: one who wished to assert his quality and his individuality in a world where other politicians seemed powerless. He had already, as he had always had since the university, a group round him who regarded him as a leader, who either discounted or even admired his exhibitionist side; a Negro admirer once described how Castro ate enormously, and thought, 'This *blanco* eats like a *negro*.'[97] He always had fine thoughts (in his mind): 'Those who march towards death with the smile of supreme happiness on

[90] *Ibid.*
[91] C. Franqui, *Le Livre des Douze* (1965); also article by José Rebellón, *Revolución*, 24 July 1962.
[92] The word means the blow of a wild cat's paw.
[93] See Castro's speech in Venezuela in 1959; in 1960 he referred to it as his '*primer manifiesto*' (*La Calle*, 30 March 1960).
[94] Full text republished in Castro's speech at Matos trial (*Revolución*, 20 December 1959).
[95] In 1943 there were 6,000 lawyers in Cuba, plus 625 judges and 1,300 involved in some side of legal work – i.e. a total of about 8,000 persons living off the law, or one per 900 of the population.
[96] Evidence of Raúl Martínez Arará. Díaz Balart had been for a time secretary of the Juventud Ortodoxo of Banes, but had moved over to Batista about a year before the *golpe de estado*.
[97] Merle, 143.

their lips embraced by the call of duty.'[98] '[Men] not born to resign themselves to the hypocritical and miserable life of these times', a sentence which recalls some of the better passages in the works of José Antonio Primo de Rivera. His reading and his language were full of 'the manly thoughts which agitate unquiet souls'.[99] At the rally on 28 January 1953 to commemorate the centenary of Martí's birth, Castro had led, he said, 'an erect group of ex-students and others in military style parade'[100] – again, an expression which perhaps owed something to José Antonio.[101]

Fidel Castro in 1953 was a restless and energetic nationalist with a sound education behind him. Although it doubtless misses the point to charge so ardent a patriot with insincerity, he was able to deceive, though often, like Lloyd George, the first person he deceived was himself.[102] He found it impossible to fit in with García Barcena, Sánchez Arango and Carrillo, the only politically promising groups of the years 1952–3. He revelled in action and in crowds and sometimes seemed to regard politics, even violence, as hunting carried on by other means. He had as strong a sense of humour as of history but he lacked magnanimity, and while he might enjoy laughing at others, he rarely did so at himself. He had evident gaps in his imagination; for instance, he had never had anything yet to say on the problem of the Negro in Cuba, and he had only a sporadic economic understanding. His closest followers, however, already regarded him as a potential saviour of the nation. His chance might come in certain extreme circumstances which in their turn could only be achieved by the maintenance in power of Batista, the increase in support of Batista by the business community and, despite this, the collapse of Batista at Castro's own hands. Western countries, recalling the experience of Lenin, have come to expect from revolutionary leaders a consistency and a ruthless integrity which they would not demand from more conventional leaders; Castro, with his many changes of mind and of front, may have been a man almost incapable of consistency, therefore difficult for conventional Liberals or Conservatives to understand. Obviously, power meant much to him: before 1952 Alfredo Guevara had done his best to convert Castro to Communism. Castro allegedly replied gaily, 'I'd be a Communist if I were Stalin'.[103]

---

[98] *Cartas del Presidio*, 18.

[99] *Ibid.*, 19.

[100] Raúl Castro, *Fundamentos*, June–July 1961, 10–11.

[101] For what it is worth, Pardo Llada later said that he found Primo de Rivera's complete works in Castro's camp in the Sierra Maestra (*Bohemia Libre*, December 1961).

[102] There were other aspects of Castro's character which recall Lloyd George: c.f. F. E. Smith's remark, 'The man who enters into real and fierce controversy with Mr Lloyd George must think clearly, think deeply and think ahead. Otherwise he will think too late.'

[103] *Sería comunista si yo fuera Stalin.* (Private Information.)

At the beginning of this second *Batistato*, Castro's idea probably was, as he said himself:

Not to organise a movement but to try to unite all the different forces against Batista. I intended to participate in that struggle simply as one more soldier. I began to organise the first action cells, hoping to work alongside those leaders of the [Ortodoxo] party who might be ready to fulfil the elemental duty of fighting against Batista . . . But when none of these leaders showed that they had the ability, the resolution, the seriousness of purpose or the means to overthrow Batista it was then that I finally worked out a strategy on my own.[104]

[104] Lockwood, 141.

CHAPTER 3

Moncada: the Idea

By the middle of 1953 Castro was the centre of a group of young men, and a few women, whose aim was to carry on the struggle against Batista with greater energy than the conventional politicians. Those who had any formal political loyalty were, like Castro himself, members of the Ortodoxo Youth Movement, though these were in a minority. By accident of acquaintance, the Pinar del Río section of the Juventud Ortodoxia was, however, captured by Castro, and its leader, José Suárez, brought in to Castro's group a number of friends who lived near him in Artemisa. Hence Artemisa, a town founded by Arango in 1803 on the main highway to the west, became by chance a stronghold of followers of Castro. The meetings of these men at Artemisa took place in the masonic lodge because one of the Members (the printer Ponce) was a Mason: the others were not.[1]

Those who followed Castro in 1953 were almost entirely men of the lower middle class or working class.[2] Few were students, and only a small minority had been to the university.[3] Out of 150 or so who took part in the attacks on the barracks, most were factory workers, agricultural workers and shop assistants. Four only seem to have been directly involved in the sugar industry, and there was one schoolboy. The others worked in a wide diversity of professions: there was one watchmaker, a teacher, a taxi-driver, a doctor, a dentist, a bookshop assistant, a chimney sweep, three carpenters, a butcher, an oyster seller and a male nurse.[4] Only one or two appear to have been unemployed. Nearly sixty came from Havana and twenty-four from

[1] Franqui, 16. There were some others who had been active in the Masonic movement.
[2] To Lockwood, Castro said that 90% of his followers were 'workers and farmers' (p. 146). He seems to have been right.
[3] Herbert L. Matthews (*The Cuban Story* (1961), 144) thus errs in speaking of Castro's followers as then 'nearly all university students'. At Moncada the explicitly 'university group', four students of Havana led by the wooden-legged 'Patachula', son of a rich advocate of Havana, and an ex-member like Castro of the UIR, withdrew at the last minute. Castro himself, his brother Raúl, Dr Muñoz, Jesús Montané (in 1953 an accountant at General Motors in Havana) and Miret were apparently the only members who had completed a higher education. Raúl de Aguiar, Hector de Armas and Lester Rodríguez could still be regarded as students. Abelardo Crespo was a part-time student. Gustavo Arcos, often listed as a student, was in fact a shop assistant in the Calle Muralla, having come to Havana to study but having failed.
[4] See Appendix XI of *Cuba: The Pursuit of Freedom* for detailed analysis.

Artemisa or Guanajay. Few came from the province of Oriente. Of the *habaneros*, however, about twenty-five had been born elsewhere in the island and like so many citizens of the capital had migrated there since. Of those whose ages are known, eleven were under twenty, fifty-two between twenty and thirty, seventeen in their thirties, five over forty. A large number had been active in one branch or other of the Ortodoxo Youth. Judging from photographs, it would seem that a maximum of twenty-five might have had some Negro or Indian blood, mostly Negro, but this may be to over-estimate the right number. A few – perhaps twenty – were married. So far as can be seen none of these men had been associated with Castro in his gangster days in the university and none except Castro had been a member of UIR or MSR except for the so called 'Patachula'.

These men were in fact mostly camp-followers of industrial civilization and some had direct experience of U.S. firms – Santamaría had worked at the *Central Constancia* owned by the U.S. Cuban–American Co., Montané worked as an accountant in General Motors, and 'Nico' López in the Nela milk factory. They came together under Castro partly fortuitously (he was friend of a friend) or because he evidently had gifts at least for gang leadership. Some of the Artemisa group had been part of García Barcena's movement for a few months.[5] Ernesto Tizol had tried unsuccessfully to lead his own group before.[6] Montané and Santamaría had run a clandestine political news letter, *Son Los Mismos*, before Castro had joined them and founded *El Acusador*. Tasende had been somewhat involved with Castro since the days of Cayo Confites,[7] while two of Castro's followers, the Gómez brothers, had been cooks at the Jesuit school of Belén and had followed him, in all the vicissitudes of his career, ever since:[8] these two had been political 'militants' since the struggle against Machado, when they had been in the ABC. Castro's movement in 1953, then, was the merger of several small groups, each following a minor leader who in turn accepted Castro as the over-all chief. They had little ideology save hostility to Batista, though in most of the leaders the notion of revolution, patriotic and social, burned fiercely, if vaguely. Several of the older of these men had made the far from untypical intellectual journey from support of the Auténticos to the Ortodoxos and then, with disillusionment, to Castro.

One group almost unrepresented among Castro's followers was the Juventud Socialista, the Communist Youth movement. On the contrary, while some members of the Ortodoxo Youth were joining Castro,

[5] See statements made by Angel Eros in the magazine *Cuba*, March 1965, 3.
[6] Tizol to Merle, Merle, 87.
[7] *Mártires del Moncada* (1965) p. 90.
[8] *Ibid.*, 222. The Colegio Belén is now (1967) called after these revolutionary cooks and is known as Gómez Brothers Technical Institute.

others, as an alternative, were moving towards the Communists.[9] Castro's younger brother Raúl was among these, though he only left the university in 1953 and had little political experience with the Ortodoxos behind him. He visited the World Youth Congress at Vienna in February 1953. Afterwards he went to Bucharest and Prague as well as Paris. Travelling home with a Russian and two young Guatemalan Communists, he solicited entry to the Communist Youth on his return to Havana in June 1953 (after a few days in gaol for having Communist literature on him).[10] But Raúl Castro was not a supporter of his brother's movement till July 1953. When he joined in, he did so on brotherly rather than ideological grounds, as he was not a leader, and he did not tell the Communist party what he was doing.[11] Fernando Chenard, the photographer, had also once been a member of Juventud Socialista, but he was now thirty-four and an Ortodoxo.[12] One man, José Luis López, who followed Castro in 1953, had voted Communist in the past and accordingly had had difficulties with his employers.[13] The only member of the Cuban Communist party was Luciano González Camejo, a forty-year-old sugar mechanic from Bayamo.[14] Some of the other Fidelistas of 1953 may have had philo-Communist outlooks in the sense that they were vaguely familiar with Communist textbooks; among these were the Santamaría brother and sister, 'Nico' López and Ramiro Valdés, but none of these had formal relations with the party.[15]

These men had as yet no name (though for a time they were referred to as the Youth of the Centenary – that is, of José Martí's birth), calling themselves simply the Movement.[16] Castro provided them with arms, bought by well-wishers (the Ortodoxo leaders refused to help). Castro apparently only received $140 instead of the $3,000 from his father he had demanded.[17] Cuba was never short of guns, particularly the university, and many of the hangers-on of one or another of the old

[9] See article by Raúl Castro, *Fundamentos*, June–July 1961.

[10] Merle, 121. Fidel Castro confirmed this to Lee Lockwood in 1965: 'Raúl completely on his own . . . had joined the Communist Youth' (Lockwood, 144). Raúl Castro himself attributed his early radicalism to the fact that when he got home from his vacations, he saw that of 'thousands of peasants, the only ones who could study were those of my family' (*Obra Revolucionaria*, 1960, No. 2, p. 3).

[11] Lockwood and Merle, *loc. cit.* Raúl Castro had had a childhood which contrasted with that of Fidel Castro: his break with religion at the Colegio Dolores, for instance, seems to have been more anguished than his brother's. He was less successful, being less strong and prominent physically; he took up a totally hostile attitude to Belén and left when quite young to work in the estate office at Birán, afterwards joining the law faculty at the University of Havana.

[12] Merle, 154.

[13] Merle, *op. cit.*

[14] *Mártires del Moncada*, 164.

[15] Martínez Arará's evidence.

[16] Raúl Castro, *Fundamentos*, June–July 1961, 11.

[17] Martínez Arará's evidence: he and Castro visited Castro's father at this time.

gangster groups had all sorts of weapons for sale. By late 1952 there were a number of young women also attached to the Castro group.[18]

Castro was nominally still an Ortodoxo, but he did not consult with the Ortodoxo leadership in deciding what to do. He had already expressed his personal dissatisfaction, indeed, with the Ortodoxos, in his mimeographed sheet, *El Acusador*:

Whoever thinks that up to now everything has been done well, that we have nothing with which to reproach ourselves, such a man is one very tender to his conscience. These sterile fights which followed the death of Chibás, these colossal commotions for reasons scarcely ideological, but of a purely egoistical and personal nature, even now resound like bitter hammer blows in our conscience. This most funereal proceeding of going to the public tribunal to elucidate Byzantine[19] quarrels was a grave symptom of indiscipline and irresponsibility. Unexpectedly, there came the *golpe* of 10 March. One might have hoped that such a grave happening would eradicate from the party the petty rancours and the sterile private empire-building . . . [but] the stupid quarrels returned. The madness of the idiots did not give heed that the doorway of the Press was too narrow to enable a full attack on the regime but on the other hand it was all too broad for an attack on the Ortodoxos themselves . . . nevertheless the immense mass of the Ortodoxo party is ready, more so than ever, demanding sacrifice . . .

Those who have a traditional concept of politics feel themselves pessimists in the present situation. But those who in contrast have faith in the masses, those who believe in the indestructible force of great ideas, will not be affected by the vacillation and gloom of the leaders. For this vacuum will soon be filled by tougher men from the ranks. The moment is revolutionary, not political. Politics means the consecration of the opportunism of those who have means . . . Revolution opens the way to true merit – to those who have valour and sincere ideals, to those who carry their breast uncovered, and who take up the battle standard in their hands. To a revolutionary party there must correspond a young and revolutionary leadership, of popular origin, which will save Cuba.[20]

Stirring words such as these had of course often appeared on the

---

[18] Before 26 July 1953 there would appear to have been six – Haydée Santamaría, Melba Hernández, Elda Pérez, Natividad ('Naty') Revuelta, Elisa Dubois, and an 'old Spanish revolutionary', Josefa. Natividad Revuelta, of good family, was married to a prosperous doctor and worked for a U.S. oil company.

[19] A favourite adjective with Castro (as with other Cuban political orators): for instance, he repudiated the Sino-Soviet breach as such in 1965.

[20] Qu., Raúl Castro, *Fundamentos*, June 1961, 8–9.

lips of Cuban politicians: a speech by Grau or Laredo Bru, Gómez or even Machado or the young Batista would hardly have been complete without them. The political thought was scarcely detailed, and the sentiments would have been little different if they had been expressed by Eddy Chibás.

There was, however, a difference. The project which Castro had in mind was a desperate one, an attack on two barracks in Oriente, at Santiago and at Bayamo. The purpose of this was primarily to capture an arsenal, to arm his movement for future exploits. If he won, he hoped to arm many volunteers from the ranks of anti-Batistianos in Santiago. Santiago was after all far from Havana: the barracks had normally a thousand men who might just be overwhelmed by a hundred if taken by surprise.[21]

There was also another purpose: the attack might lead to a spectacular and heroic success which could spark off a popular rising everywhere in Oriente – 'to light the flame of a general rising in the country: to be the initiators'.[22] This attempt had a certain affinity, conscious or unconscious, with the old anarchist idea of propaganda of the deed, a single act which would lead, if not to the millennium, at least to revolution. Castro was not an anarchist by traditional standards but his methods had affinities with anarchism, as was his expectation that the country would fall into the hands of revolution by a single act. Also, unconsciously Castro's movement took for its colours the black and red of the anarchist flag.

Oriente, of course, was the old traditional centre of Cuban revolution, in 1868 and 1895. Castro wished naturally to gain prestige for himself as a major revolutionary leader by a sensational gesture. The allegation that he met with the Communist party in order to plan an attempt on Batista's life seems to be certainly false.[23] Castro was probably further from the Communists than he had been at any time since arriving at the university: and afterwards the Communist party dismissed the attack on the Moncada barracks as futile.[24] It is true that Castro now lived in a circle which regarded it as ignorant not to read Lenin; Abel Santamaría, one of his followers with whom he really discussed matters, was 'an impassioned reader of Lenin and Soviet revolutionaries', according to his sister, and at the Moncada carried a

[21] This is the case put forward by Merle, 102–3.
[22] Martínez Arará's comment.
[23] The full range of fancy is shown in Nathaniel Weyl, *Red Star over Cuba* (1960), 122, allegedly basing himself on reports of Batista's new anti-Communist investigation and police force, Buró de Represión Actividades Comunistas (BRAC). But BRAC was not founded till 1954.
[24] See below, p. 56. Juan Almeida later said, however, of this stage of Castro's life that he always carried a book by Lenin about with him: 'a blue book with a portrait of Lenin on the front' (Franqui, 15).

book of Lenin's with him;[25] but this is indeed far from saying that they were Communists, for Santamaría was also, like Castro, 'a fanatic of Martí'.

The theoretical ideas of Castro and his friends in 1953 can be gauged most exactly from the proclamation to be read after the capture of the radio station:

> The Revolution declares its firm intention to establish Cuba on a plan of welfare and economic prosperity that ensures the survival of its rich subsoil, its geographical position, diversified agriculture and industrialisation . . . The Revolution declares its respect for the workers . . . and . . . the establishment of total and definitive social justice, based on economic and industrial progress under a well-organised and timed national plan . . . The Revolution . . . recognises and bases itself on the ideals of Martí . . . and it adopts as its own the revolutionary programme of Joven Cuba, the ABC Radical and the PPC [Ortodoxos] . . . The Revolution declares its absolute and reverent respect for the Constitution which was given to the people in 1940 . . . In the name of the martyrs, in the name of the sacred rights of the fatherland . . .[26]

Castro also had ready to play a recording of Chibás's last speech.[27]

Was this the real programme of Castro's movement on 26 July 1953? If so, what are we to make of his self-questioning in December 1961: 'Did I believe in [Marxism] on the 26th of July [1953]? I believed on the 26th of July. Did I understand it as I understand it today after ten years of struggle? No, I did not understand it as I understand it today . . . There is a great difference. Did I have prejudices? Yes, I had prejudices; yes I had them on the 26th of July.'[28] The truth though is that Castro was in no way a Marxist in 1953, even if he had some superficial knowledge of those matters. He did, perhaps, have slightly more radical views than he gave out, yet if the previously described programme was actually to be implemented, the changes in Cuba's condition would be radical: 'The ideals of Martí'? 'Joven Cuba' – Guiteras's old programme? In fact, any of these, if precisely defined, might result in perhaps not a Communist revolution, but one certainly more 'revolutionary' than that in Mexico under Cárdenas. It may very well be that, as Martínez Arará recalled, there was 'never any type of ideological discussion', but this comment need only apply to Martínez Arará.

[25] Ibid., 69; Obra Revolucionaria (1961), No. 46, 35.
[26] As qu., Du Bois, 34; complete text in Bohemia, 15 February 1959. Conte Agüero (Los dos rostros de Fidel Castro (1960) says that it was written by Raúl Gómez García.
[27] So Castro himself said, History will absolve me (1961).
[28] Obra Revolucionaria, loc. cit.

Castro explained[29] later that he had in fact five revolutionary laws which would have been immediately proclaimed had he conquered the barracks:

First, a restoration of the 1940 Constitution, and, until elections, the Revolutionary Movement – that is, he and his friends, presumably – would have itself assumed all legislative, executive and judicial powers, except the power to modify the Constitution. There was, of course, a contradiction here since the Constitution of 1940 naturally divided these powers. This law would have meant too that Castro would have immediately either seized power from his nominal Ortodoxo leaders or that they would have been impressed into the revolutionary movement. (This was roughly what occurred when finally Batista withdrew in 1959.)

Second, all property 'not mortgageable and not transferable' would be handed over to planters, sub-planters, squatters or others who had less than 150 acres. The State would pay the old owners on the basis of rent which they would have received over ten years. This would, of course, have been a genuine if somewhat conventional land reform. In 1946 there had been 140,000 farms of this size in Cuba out of a total of 160,000, or about 80% of the farms.[30]

Third, workers and employers would have been able to share a third of the profits of all sugar mills and other 'large' non-agricultural concerns. Such a profit-sharing scheme fitted in more with Chibás's ideas than with any other intellectual ancestor.

Fourth, sugar colonos would receive henceforth a minimum quota of about 450 tons of cane a year and the colonos would have a right to 55% of the total production. This was a sugar reform law of a modest kind in the tradition of Batista's laws of the late 1930s. There were about 50,000 colonos in 1950.[31]

Fifth, all land illegally obtained and all other property or cash obtained by fraud would be confiscated.

Castro added that these laws would be followed by further laws for agrarian and educational reform, by the nationalization of the utilities and the telephones, and even by a refund of some of what had been paid to these U.S. owned companies in the past. There would also be a housing reform. The agrarian reform would reflect the Constitution of 1940 in that a maximum area of land would be indicated for each agricultural project. Measures would be adopted to make land 'tend to revert to the Cubans', though this was a general tendency anyway

[29] In the pamphlet based on his speech in his own defence at his trial in September. I have assumed that the main parts in the pamphlet were included in the speech; but that the general language and argument of the pamphlet should be considered later.

[30] See Agricultural Census of 1946. No later figures available.

[31] World Bank, 798.

since 1934. Small farmers working on rented land would receive that land as owners. Castro spoke of these as numbering 100,000, showing that he included all squatters, share-croppers and sub-renters. Swamp would be filled in, there would be reafforestation and the establishment of centres of research. Agricultural cooperatives would be encouraged, to help the use of costly equipment, cold storage and scientific farming generally. These cooperatives were intended to help individual land-owners; they did not foreshadow any nationalization of land.

The educational reform he envisaged seems to have meant an increase of pay to teachers. Rural teachers would have free travel and every five years all teachers would have a sabbatical six months, to keep up to date in their subjects at home or abroad. An 'integral reform' of education was intended, but nothing more specific than this was mentioned.

The housing reform would involve a cut in rent of 50%. Tax exemptions on owner-occupied houses; triple taxes on rented homes; slum clearance and redevelopment with 'multiple dwelling buildings' – all aimed to create and to encourage the ownership of one's own house or flat.

These different projects would be financed by the end of corruption and the end of the purchase of expensive armaments. There was also a plan to 'mobilize all inactive capital', estimated at $M500, for the industrialization of the country. Details of this topic, and of the manner of nationalization of the utilities and telephone company were not provided. There was no mention of compensation, except to those whose lands were being given to small farmers.

This programme could not in itself be described as supporting any single political philosophy, though it was evidently close to the ideas of Chibás. It concentrated on the aspects of Cuban society which Castro himself knew – farming and education, housing and social conditions. The plans must have been Castro's own, and it seems likely that he did not consult anyone. None of the distinguished economists such as Cuervo or Pazos who were connected with the Ortodoxo movement was consulted. The idea of the division of land, the *repartimiento* beloved of the Spanish anarchists of the 1920s, would of course have led to the increase of the number of plots beyond an economically desirable point. Small estates, even of 150 acres, are not easier to run than large, particularly if they produce sugar. Indeed, what seems surprising is the modesty of Castro's approach towards the sugar problem. Workers' shares in profits; encouragement of Cuban ownership (already increasing); guaranteed 55% *colono* participation in cane production (already normal); movement towards a *colonia* between 150 acres and (say) 1,000 acres – all this was scarcely radical, and by itself would not have fulfilled the demand that Cuba should become internationally independent. There was no mention of nationalization of the sugar industry – a measure which might certainly have been justified by its curious structure and the extent to which the nation depended on it. The English Labour party, for instance, would have placed that demand high on a list of prescriptions. Any social democratic economist, on the other hand, would have been doubtful about the proposed 50 % cut in rents, the tax exemptions on owner-occupier houses and the increased taxes on rented houses: these measures would all be ones which would antagonize the *bourgeoisie*, without in themselves leading to a larger number of houses available.

Later on, Castro implied that these proposals of 1953 contained less radical views that he had actually had at that time. In 1961 he said in a famous speech:[32]

> People have asked me if my thinking at the time of Moncada was what it is today. I have replied 'I thought very much then as I think today' . . . Whoever reads what we said on that occasion will see very many fundamental things of the Revolution . . . That is a document further written with care. It was written with a care adequate to express a series of fundamental points, avoiding at the same time making commitments which would limit the field of action within the Revolution . . . That is, one had to try and make the movement the most broad-based as possible. If we had not written this document with care, if it had been a more radical programme (even though it is certain that many people were a trifle sceptical of programmes and did not pay them much attention) the revolutionary movement of struggle against Batista could not afterwards have acquired the breadth that it afterwards did and which made victory possible. Anyone reading the manifesto, the speech of that occasion, will understand our fundamental ideas. There are certain things, like various pledges which we made on that occasion, such as the increase to the *colonos* (at least 55 % of the quota) . . . and which, afterwards, in certain conferences of *colonos*, were pointed out to me: they said *Bueno*, and aren't you going to mention the increase. I told them: Yes, but in that period we could not think of what we can talk of today and we have converted these *colonos* into proprietors of lands and that is much more than to have conceded them an increase in the proportion of sugar in the quota. Some pledges of that time were made simply with the concern of not harming the breadth of the revolutionary movement.[33]

On the other hand, some devoted supporters of Castro at that time and

[32] 2 December 1961.
[33] *Obra Revolucionaria*, 1961, No. 46, 34–5.

since believe that 'the Revolution . . . is always the same as that which we directed at Moncada'.[34]

In addition to this reform programme, Castro and his comrades were suffused by an heroic picture of their own actions in the tradition of the Cuban revolution against Spain: Castro made much of the cry of Yara and Baire, of Martí and Maceo; Castro might know something of Marx, might regard those who did not know Lenin as ignoramuses, but he evidently knew Martí much better. Like others before him, he saw himself indeed as Martí, the young man who forced the different groups opposed to Spain into a single movement, the man of heroic phrases as well as deeds, speaker and soldier, enemy of tyrants *par excellence*, incorruptible renewer. Castro embarked on the Moncada attack without indeed a very carefully worked-out ideology, only a desire to overthrow the 'tyrant' Batista and also move on to destroy the whole rotten society, the institutionalized, 'normal' violence of old Cuba of which Batista was a symptom not a cause. The 'Hymn of Liberty',[35] composed a few days before the attack on the Moncada barracks, with its emphasis on liberty, not bread or gold, made the point despite its English seaside rhythm.[36]

THE HYMN OF THE 26 JULY

Marchando vamos hacia un ideal	Marching towards an ideal
Sabiendo que vamos a triunfar	Knowing very well we are going to win;
Además de paz y prosperidad	More than peace and prosperity
Lucharemos todos por la libertad.	We will all fight for liberty.
Adelante Cubanos!	Onwards Cubans!
Que Cuba premiara nuestro heroismo	Let Cuba give you a prize for heroism.
Pues somos soldados	For we are soldiers
Que vamos a la patria a liberar	Going to free the country
Limpiando con fuego	Cleansing with fire
Que arrase con esa plaga infernal	Which will destroy this infernal plague
De gobernantes indeseables	Of bad governments
Y de Tiranos insaciables	And insatiable tyrants
Que a Cuba han sumido en el mal.	Who have plunged Cuba into evil.

[34] Haydée Santamaría, in Franqui, 54.

[35] Afterwards, 'Hymn of 26 July'.

[36] Composed by the mulatto singer Agustín Díaz Cartaya, who took part in the Bayamo attack (*Revolución*, 26 July 1963). The similarity with 'We do like to be beside the seaside' is marked.

La sangre que en Cuba se
  derramó
Nosotros no debemos olvidar
Por eso unidos debemos
  estar
Recordando a aquellos
Que muertos están.

El pueblo de Cuba
Sumido en su dolor se siente
  herido
Y se ha decidido
A hallar sin tregua una
  solución
Que sirva de ejemplo
A esos que no tienen compasión
Y arriesguemos decididos
Por esta causa dar la vida:
Que viva la Revolución!

The blood which flowed in
  Cuba
We must never forget
For that reason we must stay
  united
In remembrance of those
Who died.

The Cuban people
Drowned in grief feels itself
  wounded
And has decided
To pursue without respite a
  solution
Which will serve as an example
To those who don't have pity
And we risk, resolved
For this cause to give our life:
'Long live the Revolution!'

CHAPTER 4

Moncada: the Fight

Castro's plan, worked out in the offices of Abel Santamaría at Sosa brothers, in Havana,[1] was to attack two military barracks in Oriente, the Moncada barracks at Santiago and the Bayamo barracks. The main force of his supporters, 134 men, would attack at Santiago: 28 would fall on Bayamo.[2] The men would force entrance by surprise, capture the barracks and distribute arms to other volunteers who, it was supposed, would then crowd to their support. The attack would occur at dawn. The date, 26 July, was suitable because it coincided with the carnival at Santiago. Many soldiers, including the officers, would be going to the public dances of the carnival on the night of 25 July, and might be expected to be unready for fighting at 5.30 a.m. on 26 July. Castro had secured the use of a farm near Siboney as a base and several rooms had been rented in Santiago itself.

The attack was, of course, an act of war. Castro was outnumbered by about ten to one (the barracks held about 1,000 soldiers) but he banked on surprise, confusion and superior morale among his men. (Castro had apparently visited his brother-in-law, Rafael Díaz Balart, the sub-secretary for the Interior, a week before, to make sure that the police suspected nothing of his plans.)[3] Castro's armaments were limited to three U.S. army rifles, six old Winchester rifles, one old machine gun and a large number of game rifles. 'I awaited my rifle as if it had been a Messiah,' Almeida said ten years later, 'when I saw it was a 0·22, I froze.'[4] There were also some revolvers and a certain quantity of ammunition. Some small arms had been bought from soldiers, and so had about one hundred military uniforms; others had been made.[5] Castro himself spoke of the expedition as costing less than $20,000,[6] which appears to have been the sum collected by his followers beforehand,[7]

[1] In Consulado, No. 9.

[2] Castro speaks of 27 at Bayamo. (*History will absolve me*, 25.) Martínez Arará, the commander at Bayamo, has 28.

[3] Martínez Arará's evidence (Raúl Martínez Arará was present at Castro's talk with Díaz Balart and Orlando Pietra on 19 or 20 July).

[4] Franqui, 18.

[5] Merle, 111–13, has interesting details.

[6] *History will absolve me*, 44.

[7] Merle, 102. Martínez Arará said that some $3,000 of the money was obtained by Santamaría by means of a fraudulent signature on a cheque drawn on his firm, Sosa Bros. But this cheque seems to have been cashed nevertheless after the revolution.

of which the arms cost $5,000, the rifles costing $80 each.[8]

Nine volunteers fell out through fear, at the last minute; these included some of the few students in the expedition. Others of the group were vaguely religious and visited the Virgin del Cobre on the eve of the fight, though fortuitously. Most had driven down from Havana in cars, while some had come by train or *guagua*. Only six knew precisely what was afoot before the hour of combat,[9] and few knew each other.[10] One man at least (Almeida) thought they were going to the carnival at Santiago, as a prize for successes at earlier weapon training.[11] Others appear to have been only told that they were going to embark on some more intense shooting practice.[12] The farm at Siboney was attended by two women, Melba Hernández and Haydée Santamaría, the *fiancées* of two of the combatants, Jesús Montané and Boris Santa Colona. In his harangue of encouragement before they set out, Castro seems to have dwelt particularly on the 'historic' importance of their exploit more than the social and political.[13] Several of the participants clearly envisaged that they would be killed,[14] and one participant, Dr Muñoz, is understood to have told Castro that it was a crime to deceive so many men into so perilous an enterprise.[15]

Night of Carnival turned to revolutionary dawn: at 5.30 a.m. twenty-six cars bearing a hundred and eleven men (all dressed as sergeants) and two women drove into Santiago from Siboney. Castro was in the second car. The next car contained Raúl Castro, who, with ten men,[16] was supposed to take over the Palace of Justice overlooking the barracks; from the roof he would be in an excellent position to give covering fire to his brother in the central courtyard of the barracks. Another three cars contained Abel Santamaría, Castro's second-in-command, the two women and Dr Muñoz, twenty-two men in all.[17] They would take the civil hospital nearby and be available to treat the wounded. One car had a puncture and was left behind. According to Castro himself, 'Due to a most unfortunate error, half our forces – and the better armed half at that – went astray at the entrance to the city

---

[8] Marta Rojas, *Verde Olivo*, 29 July 1962.

[9] Merle, 143, says these were Castro, Santamaría, Alcalde, Tizol, Tasende and Guitart. Martínez Arará claims, no doubt rightly, he also knew everything.

[10] Thus the printer José Ponce remarked, 'There were so many unknown faces. No one really knew each other.' Franqui, 13.

[11] *Ibid.*, 17.

[12] Martínez Arará's evidence.

[13] Almeida in Franqui, 18.

[14] *Cf. ibid.* 54–5.

[15] Martínez Arará's evidence. Another account makes Gustavo Arcos, a young shop assistant, say the same thing.

[16] Castro, *History will absolve me*, 23.

[17] *Ibid.*, 23–5, speaks of 'Santamaría and 21 men'. Merle speaks of 20 men at the hospital and six at the law courts (p. 167).

and were not on hand to help us at the decisive moment.'[18] But the group of university students who had withdrawn at the last minute had been ordered by Castro to follow the motorcade; they moved up into the middle in a Chrysler and it was they who diverted several cars from the route to Moncada.[19]

The first car halted at the gate of the barracks. Six men[20] got out and their leader, Guitart, called on the sentry to 'make way for the general'. The three sentries, deceived by the sergeants' uniforms, which they 'did not recognize but which they momentarily assumed were those of a military band', presented arms, and these weapons, Springfield rifles, were seized from them. The rebels then burst into the barracks upstairs, pushing the sentries before them. Outside, Castro in the second car had been held up by two unexpected encounters: two soldiers with machine guns and an armed sergeant. Castro ran his car against the machine gunners and the sergeant fled. But he could clearly give the alarm. Following previous orders, once Castro's car stopped, the men in the following cars all leapt out and attacked the buildings to their left. Castro tried unsuccessfully to regroup his men. Inside the barracks, the men of the first car, having bewildered a dormitory of undressed soldiers, found themselves cut off, and, having shot down a number of sergeants, as well as the officer of the day, Lieutenant Morales, withdrew. The alarm being given, a general fusillade followed from the first floors into the street. The attackers protected themselves behind parked cars. What precisely occurred in any such event is bound to be a matter of controversy afterwards: another account has it that Castro drove his car on to the pavement, hitting the kerb violently, and so attracting the attention of the guard who thereupon shot at and wounded Gustavo Arcos.

The other two sections of the attack in Santiago had been successful; Raúl Castro captured the almost unguarded Palace of Justice, and Abel Santamaría the Civil Hospital, with no losses to themselves or to the army. But this meant little while the advantage of surprise at Moncada had been lost and when the attack had turned into an uneven battle between one hundred men armed with sporting guns and one thousand well-armed soldiers, rallied by Major Morales, a brother of the dead officer of the day. Castro quickly gave the order to retire, and he and his men did so, leaving behind some wounded and some others to be captured. As usual in such circumstances there were later allegations that the leaders fled first. Raúl Castro and the victors of the Palace of Justice also withdrew, but those in the Civil Hospital did not know

[18] *History will absolve me*, 23.
[19] Merle, 254.
[20] José Suárez, Ramiro Valdés, José Luis Tasende, Rigoberto Corcho, Carmelo Noa and Renato Guitart.

of the order to retreat and afterwards hid, disguised as patients, in the hospital itself. At this stage it seems that Castro had lost only two men killed[21] and one mortally wounded;[22] the army had lost three officers and sixteen men killed.[23] Both sides had a substantial number of wounded. The battle had lasted about one hour.

At Bayamo also the attack failed, horses apparently giving the alarm. The leader, Raúl Martínez Arará, delayed in giving the order for withdrawal, but the battle nonetheless lasted only fifteen minutes.[24] It was an even more complete fiasco than Moncada. It is clear that there had been some political dispute and argument among the Bayamo fighters, several disapproving of Fidel Castro as leader.[25] Six were killed.

The aftermath of the attacks on the barracks had crucial consequences for the history of Cuba. Some, such as Martínez Arará of the Bayamo attack, escaped to foreign embassies. Perhaps eighty of the original 160 rebels were captured either on 26 July or in the following days; most of these who were captured the first day or two were murdered. Those who, like Castro himself, managed to hold out a few days in the forests, escaped this death. But altogether sixty-eight prisoners appear to have been killed, including even three young men (the 'Almendares' group of Víctor Escalona) who had withdrawn from the attack at the last minute. Most of these prisoners were beaten with rifle butts before being shot and some were tortured in other ways. Some died during the course of brutal treatment. Three prisoners at Bayamo were dragged along for miles behind a jeep. The two women, Haydée Santamaría and Melba Hernández, were not themselves tortured; but Abel Santamaría, the brother of the former and *novio* of the latter, was apparently tortured to death in their hearing, as was Boris Santa Colona, Haydée Santamaría's *novio*. Thirty-two prisoners survived to be brought to trial while forty-eight escaped altogether, returning to Havana by bus or escaping to friends' houses.[26]

This brutality was initially a spontaneous reaction of frightened and angry soldiery, backed by their NCOs. The accusations later made by Batistiano officers of brutality on the part of the rebels (such as knifing patients in the military hospital) appear false.[27] The com-

[21] Gildo Fleitas and Guillermo Granados.

[22] Rigoberto Corcho.

[23] *Avance*, 27 July, speaks of 16 soldiers dead. The most immediate press reports seem in the circumstances the most likely.

[24] See Merle, 213–15.

[25] Evidence of Martínez Arará, who adds, '*casi todos los compañeros de mi grupo sentían cierta repugnancia por Fidel Castro*'. This may have been an afterthought.

[26] An incomplete list of killed first appeared in *Revolución*, 15 January 1959, 14. In 1967 Castro argued (at the first conference of the Latin American Solidarity Organisation) that the attack was a mistake and that he should have embarked on guerrilla warfare at the start.

[27] The commander of the military hospital said at the trial of some of the rebels that no one was killed there except one patient who rashly put his head out of the window.

manders of the Moncada barracks (Colonel del Río Chaviano and Captain Pérez Chaumont), also frightened and also angry, with the scent of rum and cigars from the carnival still in their nostrils and no doubt heavy hangovers, arriving on the scene of battle after the last shot had been fired, not only made no attempt to restrain the brutalities but encouraged them and afterwards helped cover them up.[28] The military intelligence (SIM) at Moncada, under Captain Lavastida, also took a prominent part in the repression. A few doctors and officers (such as Captain Tamayo, Major Morales and Lieutenant Sarriá) tried to save several lives and did so. But this was hard since in so doing they themselves risked ill treatment.

Finally, this brutality was underwritten by the government itself though the governor of Oriente, Pérez Almaguer, later said that Batista did not know what was being done in his name.[29] On 26 July the cabinet hastily approved a decree suspending Article 26 of the Prison Statute making the prison officers responsible for the lives of their prisoners. Batista himself and the officer corps were evidently as frightened and as angry as the soldiery and their officers. If rebels could make an onslaught on the second biggest barracks in Cuba, who was safe? The government panicked, the army throughout the island was placed on the alert, and hundreds of people were detained. Since some *Fidelistas* were known to be wounded, anyone with a wound, even from a road accident, was in danger of interrogation and ill treatment. A Santiago citizen whose arm was in plaster was for that reason taken to Moncada and badly beaten.[30] This ruthless and reckless behaviour caused public opinion to forget entirely the doubtful morality of the original attack.

The Moncada attack occurred at a bad moment in the life of Batista's administration since the intrigues and struggles in the armed forces had been almost uncontrolled: Tabernilla as chief of staff was more and more unpopular but more and more ambitious, now seeking to arrange the ruin of three ministers – Nicolás Hernández, Ramón Hermida and Pablo Carrera Justiz, who had been architects on the civilian side of the 10 March plot. He had already successfully disposed of the able General García Tuñón, who had been Hernández's own candidate for the chief army command, to be military attaché in Chile; another disappointed *Batistiano*, Colonel Lambea, had pulled a pistol on Tabernilla in his office and been disposed of to a similar job in Costa Rica; an unconditional friend, Ugalde Carrillo, had been given the important post of command of the SIM, and two of Tabernilla's sons, 'Wince' and

---

[28] The governor of Oriente province, Waldo Pérez Almaguer, who tried unsuccessfully to stop the bloodshed and who visited the barracks early in the morning of 26 July, confirms the personal responsibility of Del Río Chaviano (*La Calle*, 3 June 1956).

[29] *Ibid.*, 3 June 1955.

[30] Merle, 249.

'Silito', had been promoted beyond all possible deserts; while other representatives of the Tabernilla faction had been given command of the rural guard up and down the island. These appointments had naturally antagonized the rest of the civil and military administration, particularly the officers who had manned the 10 March plot and who had been excluded from the benefits in a signal manner: they had after all many of them quite serious if autocratic desires for the regeneration of the country, and were affronted by the use to which Tabernilla's men put their power, in particular by the network of protection rackets and gambling dens which they had organized throughout the country. One minister, Ernesto de la Fe, had had an open scene with Batista on this matter, pointing out to the president that the military commands in all the six provinces were held by intimate friends of Tabernilla[31] and saying that the government could only hold its backing in public opinion by getting rid of these men as of the chief of police, Salas Cañizares, and the head of the SIM, Ugalde Carrillo.[32]

Batista had then agreed at least to make an inquiry into these charges and appointed Colonel Fermín Cowley to investigate. Cowley had confirmed them while Colonel Barrera, a member of the 10 March group, had told Batista of a particularly scandalous instance of the misuse of power, whereby Ugalde Carrillo was using his influence in the rural guards to force a lorry company to sell out to a friend of his for an absurdly low sum; the rural guards were forcing the lorries to stop, subjecting them to all sorts of delays and thereby causing the company to lose the confidence of their customers. Batista had just agreed that as a result of all these charges, there should be a general reorganization of the military commands when the Moncada crisis began.[33]

The attack was something bigger than even the gangster attack on the police headquarters of Marianao in 1948; any army would have reacted fairly strongly. But the savagery of the repression exceeded normal expectations. The consequences were critical. The facts of torture and murder became quickly known, both through gossip and afterwards, despite censorship, through the press: *Bohemia* published on 2 August a large number of photographs of bodies, many dressed up in clean clothes after being killed, to give an impression that they had been killed in fighting.[34] Before then a meeting had occurred between several Santiago notables – the bishop (Angel Castro's old friend, Pérez Serantes), the rector of the university, a judge, a large department store owner, Enrique

---

[31] Colonels José Fernández Rey, Dámaso Sogo (Soguito), Pilar García, Aquilino Guerra, and Alberto del Río Chaviano, in the provinces running west to east.

[32] Barrera Pérez, *Bohemia Libre*, August 1961. Barrera was present at the interview.

[33] *Loc. cit.*

[34] These photographs were taken by one of a group of journalists to whom Colonel del Río Chaviano spoke on the day of the attack on the Moncada barracks.

Canto – with Batista's principal secretary, Morales del Castillo.[35] The notables demanded an end to the massacre of prisoners, and Batista shortly gave the proper order. Pérez Serantes gave a press conference announcing the agreement, but in setting out himself (with Judge Subirats and Enrique Canto) for La Gran Piedra, a mountain where Castro was thought (rightly) to be hiding, he showed his lack of faith in the regime's word: his intention was personally to find those who surrendered and hand them over to the army. The bishop drove, and then walked, several hours over the mountainside, calling through a megaphone that he guaranteed the lives of those who surrendered. Though unsuccessful immediately, his gesture led to the surrender of several rebels; shortly after, Castro was himself captured by the humane army lieutenant, Sarriá, with two followers, while sleeping.[36]

Officials of Batista's regime had thus swung backwards to the era of Machado and of Spain, equalling or even exceeding in their be-haviour the worst excesses of those dark days. Partly, no doubt, they saw in Castro and his friends the outriders of a movement which threatened them personally: they had a real interest in serving the regime and, being poor and ill-educated, they reacted in the most brutal way possible. It is also clear that they would not have so acted had it not been for their presumption that their superior officers would not cause them to bear responsibility for their actions: the Cuban army, first, partook of the easy-going character of Cubans in general, so that indiscipline was normal: many officers acted in all matters as if they owned private fiefs. The officers also served a regime from which they hoped much. The condition of the law and its relation to the administra-tion was such that there was only a remote chance that they would be faced with charges as a result. Indeed, some were promoted.[37] Recalling atrocious precedents, insecure, hating a revolt which seemed led by middle-class people more than they would have hated a working-class explosion, they did not scruple to react in a way which seriously affected Cuba for years to come.

The commander in Santiago was Alberto del Río Chaviano, then thirty-eight, commander of the Maceo Regiment No 1, who had entered the army at eighteen in November 1933, presumably attracted by the prospects apparently opening up after the sergeants' revolt of September. In 1938 he entered the cadet school; while there, he had led the cadets loyal to Batista in opposition and protest to the attempted Pedraza golpe in 1941. He remained in the army during the Auténtico governments, and indeed had on that account been briefly detained on

---

[35] Usually in Cuba a member of the cabinet.
[36] See Fidel Castro's account, La Calle, 30 May 1955.
[37] Bohemia, 2 August 1953.

10 March 1952. But, due to his friendship with General Tabernilla, his brother-in-law, he was soon released, promoted and sent back to an active command in Santiago. The SIM commander, Captain Lavastida, had been only a sergeant at Camagüey before 1952[38] and owed his promotion to his knowledge of the drug traffic. Captain Pérez Chaumont, under thirty, known as '*Ojos Bellos*', who shot many prisoners on the outskirts of El Caney, had already in the last few years made enough out of protection rackets to buy a $100,000 house in Miramar, near Santiago.

A number of leading Communists were also arrested at this time. These included Lázaro Peña, Blas Roca, Carlos Rafael Rodríguez and others who chanced to be in Santiago at the time in order to celebrate Blas Roca's birthday. This always sounded suspicious, and their presence has been naturally used further to implicate Castro with long-standing Communist associations: Blas Roca, after all, lived in Havana and his home town was Manzanillo. But their presence was fortuitous. They 'knew nothing of the Moncada plan'[39] and actually most of the party leaders left the town on 25 July. Afterwards they repudiated the attack on the Moncada:

> We repudiate [they said] the Putschist methods, peculiar to *bourgeois* factions, of the action in Santiago de Cuba and Bayamo, an adventurist attempt to capture the two military headquarters. The heroism displayed by the participants in this action is false and sterile, as it is guided by mistaken *bourgeois* conceptions. But even more we repudiate the repression directed by the government with the revolt as a pretext . . . The entire country knows who organised, inspired and directed the action against the barracks and that the communists had nothing to do with it. The line of the Communist party and of the masses had been to combat the Batista tyranny seriously and to unmask the *putschistas* and adventurers as being against the interests of the people. The Communist party poses the necessity of creating a united front of the masses against the government, for a democratic way out of the Cuban situation, restoration of the constitution of 1940, civil liberties, general elections, and the establishment of a National Democratic Front government, with a programme of national independence, peace, democracy, and agrarian reform.[40]

[38] Merle, 256.
[39] Carlos Rafael Rodríguez to the author, June 1966.
[40] *Daily Worker* (New York), 5 and 10 August. The statement could not be published in Havana. It is interesting to compare this attitude with that of the established Communist parties towards the guerrilla struggles in the 1950s: thus the Communist leader in Ceylon Sanmugathasan said that Guevara in Bolivia failed because his method was 'the romantic and petty bourgeois ideology which places its main reliance on a band of swashbuckling "Three Musketeers" type of bravados who one expected to perform miraculous feats against terrific odds'. (*Ceylon Daily News*, 5 November 1967.)

Moncada had found Batista at Varadero beach. He gave no sign of concern but showed himself a great deal to the crowd, appearing on television, giving prizes at a regatta, claiming later he knew himself to be a target for an assassin. On 2 August he arrived in Santiago to commiserate with the soldiers. Constitutional guarantees were suspended. On the 6th a more vigorous public order law was decreed, aimed specially at the press. As a result the press all but dried up. Batista also rearranged his cabinet to give an impression at least of vitality: and to the newly created Transport Ministry went Castro's father-in-law.[41] But there were no changes in the army command. Batista went back on his plan to weaken the empire of Tabernilla, thinking it best in these abnormal circumstances to keep such commanders as there were where they were.[42] Nor were there any changes in the police command who despite their obsession with the telephone calls of the opposition, had failed to predict this event.

In October Castro and his comrades were tried. An attempt was made either to poison Castro or to prevent him from appearing by alleging that he was sick. In the event he appeared, on 21 September and 16 October (on the first occasion as a witness), and made a brilliant speech in his own defence.[43] He was sentenced to fifteen years' imprisonment, Raúl Castro to thirteen years, others to lesser terms. The case against the Communists was dismissed.[44]

The consequences on public opinion of Moncada and its aftermath were considerable. Had it not been for the repression, the Moncada attack would doubtless have been dismissed as one more wild and semi-gangster incident in the life of Fidel Castro. The repression and the trial made Castro appear henceforth something of a hero. Professional, catholic, liberal or middle class opinion was outraged. A Santiago judge on 27 July telephoned Andrés Domingo, Batista's presidential secretary, and asked 'Are you trying to revive the epoch of Machado

[41] The new ministers were: Rafael Díaz Balart (Transport); Gustavo Gutiérrez (Finance); José E. Olivella (Health); Rafael Guas Inclán (Communications); Santiago Rey (without Portfolio); Radio Cremata Valdés (Secretary of the Consultative Council); César Camacho Govani (Chairman of Social Security); Marino López Blanco (in charge of United Railways). Arsenio González remained at the Ministry of Labour – a lawyer who had been the Communists' adviser in their struggles against Prío; he was said to be a Communist himself, by, for example, R. J. Alexander.

[42] Barrera Pérez, *Bohemia Libre*, August 1961.

[43] Roughly, one may assume, similar to the text of the pamphlet, *History will absolve me*. But see below, p. 62.

[44] See description, *Bohemia*, 22 May 1955. The judges were A. Nieto Piñeiro Osorio, Juan Francisco Mejías Valdivieso and Ricardo Díaz Oliveira. Present also were three journalists and fifty soldiers. Others imprisoned at the time of Moncada were also put at liberty, these were Dr 'Millo' Ochoa, Dr O. Alvarado and R. Arango Alsina, of the Ortodoxos; Ordoqui and Lázaro Peña, Communists; and Auténticos – Aracelio Azcuy, Roberto García Ibáñez, Sergio Mejías, José Manuel Gutiérrez, Arturo Hernández Tellaheche and Luis Casero (*ibid.*, October 1953).

with all these assassinations?'[45] Professional people in Santiago, people who had either seen or had met someone who had seen something of what happened, turned almost without exception away from Batista. The part played by the bishop, Pérez Serantes, was also important, both for the Church and for the upper class Catholics: if Castro's life could be saved by the bishop, then his cause seemed almost respectable. For Castro himself, the attack had overwhelming consequences: exposure to the imminent threat of death, the death of so many of his associates, led by him into an action of his planning, both isolated him from other young Ortodoxo leaders and heightened his own sense of mission. Afterwards, it seemed symbolic that the first peasant he should meet in the Sierra Maestra should have been an old woman who apparently recalled helping the *mambises* of the war of independence. At the end of his period of hiding he was toying with the idea of moving up into the Sierra Maestra on the other side of Santiago. The future seemed to have no alternative except further action, 'the continuance of the struggle'. On the other hand, the morale of Batista's army sank lower, not only because of the widespread hostility to the treatment by Río Chaviano of the prisoners but because of his happy acceptance of the role of hero and victor in this contest: so much so that he began to persecute the real victor, Major Morales, and sent him under guard to Havana as an enemy of the people.[46]

[45] Baudilio Castellanos to Merle (Merle, 282).
[46] Barrera Pérez, *Bohemia Libre*, 6 August 1961. For Pérez Serantes's account, see Herbert Matthews, *Castro*, 61.

CHAPTER 5

Indian Summer

In October 1953, ten days after the trial of the survivors of Moncada, Batista announced that there would be general elections a year later, on 1 November 1954. All parties would have till February 1954 to register. Censorship was soon lifted and on 28 October the ninety-day decree suspending civil rights came to an end. Batista coyly refused to say whether he would be a presidential candidate: 'The grapes are still green,' he told audiences, usually whipped up by Díaz Balart, Castro's brother-in-law, and still youth leader of Batista's movement. Other crowds cheered Señora de Batista, shouting on her public appearances as if she were indeed Evita Perón: '*Marta del pobre, Marta del Pueblo*'.[1] Marta Batista went to Washington, where she was received by Mrs Eisenhower and Secretary Hobby of the Department of Health, Education and Welfare. With Prío forced to register as an agent of a foreign political party, the star of Batista seemed to be rising. Indeed, the regime seemed outwardly solid and self-confident, lapped in the arms of U.S. acceptance, its enemies in gaol or in exile. The new ambassador, Arthur Gardner, was a vigorous and unashamed friend of both the regime and of Batista. Gardner, an appointee of the new President Eisenhower (who had been inaugurated six months before Moncada, in January 1953), had been Assistant Secretary of the Treasury under President Truman, 1947–8: as such, it had fallen to him to receive the news of the arrival at Miami of Grau's Minister of Education, Alemán, with $M20 of Cuban government funds[2] in his suitcase. Perhaps this experience caused him to look on the Auténticos and politicians of the old order with special suspicion, and to regard Batista as the saviour which Cuba needed. Amiable and agreeable, he gave Batista much self-confidence, though the *New York Times* correspondent, Mrs Phillips, noted that his fulsome admiration for the general sometimes caused its object some embarrassment.[3]

---

[1] She was Batista's second wife, having married him in November 1945; he divorced his first wife, Elisa Godínez, in October 1945. By her he had had three children – Mirta Caridad, Fulgencio and Elisa Aleida. By Marta, he had Jorge (born 1942), Roberto (born 1947), Carlos Manuel (born 1950), Fulgencio José (born 1953). He also recognized in his will an illegitimate daughter Fermina Lázara, born 1935 (*cf.* will published in *Revolución*, 24 January 1959). He was evidently a generous father and treated all his children, of both marriages, with equal generosity.

[2] Evidence of Ambassador Gardner.

[3] R. H. Phillips, *Island of Paradox*.

A big sugar conference had meanwhile been successfully held in London, binding its seventy-eight national participants for five years to keep to certain quantities in the world market. Cuba received $2\frac{1}{4}$ million tons or slightly under half the whole free market (40%) over and above her sales to the U.S. However some exporting countries (India, Indonesia, Peru) did not sign the convention. Nor were the importing countries constrained to restrict their imports in the same way as the exporters had to restrict theirs. Yet the Cuban share was, of course infinitely superior to that handed out in 1937 (940,000 tons), and the 1954 harvest was fixed firmly at $4\frac{3}{4}$ million tons; most people believed that, despite the long-term uncertainty – could the standard of living be maintained unless sugar production went up steadily? – the government had done well.

Gardner's arrival in Havana coincided with a firmer hand towards the Communists than Batista had hitherto ventured towards his old friends. On 10 November the Communist party was outlawed. Its appendages, such as the newspapers *Hoy* and *Ultima Hora*, the Federation of Democratic Women, and the youth movement Juventud Socialista, were banned. The weekly magazine *Carta Semanal* and the theoretical monthly *Fundamentos* continued to be produced, however, and were sold, the former at least quite easily, though under the counter. Batista and his ministers, in fact, maintained a deliberately agreeable and relaxed attitude to the Communists, at least towards those with whom they had once had dealings: Ramón Vasconcelos, for instance, the journalist and afterwards Minister of Communications, concerned himself with the interests of Negro Communist leaders. There was not much persecution of any of them except that they were occasionally detained and questioned on their arrival from Mexico, Prague or elsewhere. Fabio Grobart, for so long *éminence grise* of the Communist party, left Cuba in this period, profiting thereby since he was able to refresh his views in the relatively new atmosphere in Moscow which opened up after Stalin's death.[4] The Cuban Communists in general were in semi-retirement during most of these years, recovering their health and energies, and so preparing themselves effectively for the future. Blas Roca, the old secretary-general, was ill and day-to-day control rested in the hands of a five-man junta composed of Carlos Rafael Rodríguez, Aníbal Escalante, Lázaro Peña, Manuel Luzardo and Severo Aguirre.[5]

---

[4] Luis Serrano Romayo told Alexander that Grobart had already left in the time of Prío (Alexander, 293).

[5] Evidence in Marquitos trial, 1964. Some isolated Communist party members, however, were later persecuted by the police: thus a young Negro athlete Chicqui Hernández was murdered later in the 9th police station, and José María Pérez, the Communist transport workers' leader, disappeared without a trace. Some students or ex-students such as Valdés Vivo and Leonel Soto were brutally tortured.

Their policy eddied between different aims. Some Communists expected that Batista would over-reach himself and so create an acute crisis from which they would profit. Some seem to have expected that, with Stalin dead, a Soviet–U.S. *rapprochement* was possible, in turn making possible a renewed deal between themselves and Batista, perhaps leading to their capture of power through Batista rather than against him. The inaction necessitated by this policy was as early as 1953–4 resented by younger members of the party, members of Juventud Socialista, and particularly by its members who had been contemporaries of Fidel Castro or his brother Raúl – himself, after all, a member, if then an errant one, of Juventud Socialista – at the university.

Fidel Castro, on the other hand, now in prison in the Isle of Pines, was still closely linked to the Ortodoxos – perhaps closer to them than he had been at Moncada. On 12 December 1953, in a letter to an old friend, the journalist Luis Conte Agüero, the secretary-general of Ortodoxo youth in the beginning, he wrote:

If our revolutionary effort had triumphed, our plan was to put power in the hands of the most fervent Ortodoxos. Our triumph would have meant the immediate rise to power of Ortodoxia, first provisionally, afterwards via general elections . . . so inevitable was this that despite our failure, our sacrifice has strengthened the cause of the ideals of Chibás . . . speak to Agramonte, show him this letter, express to him our most loyal sentiments towards the most pure ideals of Chibás.[6]

Castro was bitter about the role of the Communists:

We would never have had . . . inappropriate and sterile theories about a *putsch* or a revolution, at the very moment when it was right to denounce monstrous crimes . . . do you think, Luis, that we would have called a *putsch* your effort to raise the Maceo Regiment on the morning of March 10?[7]

Immediately after this letter, a pamphlet on its general lines was prepared by Luis Conte Agüero, Melba Hernández (freed after the Moncada trial) and other supporters of Castro in Havana, with Castro's aid from prison. They followed the outlines of Castro's speech in self defence in Santiago, and it was in that form that the pamphlet was eventually published. Nevertheless, the feel, the mood, even on occasion the language and allusions echo more the letter of 12 December 1953.

[6] L. Conte Agüero, *Cartas del Presidio* (1959), 20–1. 'Our' meant 'my'. Castro early adopted this royal first person plural which he would use afterwards in speeches though in his speech at the trial he spoke of 'History' absolving 'me' not 'us', a *personalismo* which was at the time resented by his friends.

[7] Conte Agüero, *Cartas del Presidio*, 22.

The pamphlet was clearly based on the letter. An edition prepared in 1964 argued that it was a 'reconstruction' of the speech made 'little by little' without apparently the shorthand notes of what was said being available.[8]

Whether written at this time or not, this famous pamphlet began as a speech in self-defence: 'Never has a lawyer had to practise his profession under more difficult conditions . . . As attorney for the defence I have been denied even a look at the indictment . . . As the accused, I have been for the past seventy-six days shut away in solitary confinement.'[9] The speech was carefully formal, appealing to precedent, looking back at the past as if there had indeed been a time in Cuba when law and liberty had marched together. Thus we hear of a right 'sanctified by long tradition in Cuba', namely that of an accused's right to plead in his own defence, and:

> Once upon a time there was a Republic. It had its constitution, its laws, its civil rights, a president, a Congress and law courts. Everyone could assemble, associate, speak and write with complete freedom. The people were not satisfied with the government officials at that time but . . . had power to elect new officials and only a few days remained before they were going to do so . . . There existed a public opinion both respected and heeded: all problems of common interest were freely discussed . . . the whole nation throbbed with enthusiasm . . . they felt confident that no one would dare commit the crime of violating their democratic institutions. They desired a change for the better . . . and they saw all this at hand.[10]

This indeed was an extravagant over-romanticism of the age of Prío, to highlight the monstrosity of Batista's regime, with which Chibás for one would not have agreed.

Castro attempted too to depict Batista not only as a tyrant but as the

[8] See appendix to 1964 edition (Havana, *Ediciones Política*) of speech, and article by Francisco de Armas in *Hoy*, 21 July 1963, 2–3. The information derived from Melba Hernández. But shorthand notes taken by the *Bohemia* reporter Marta Rojas must have been available (*cf.* Merle, 333, and Draper's comments, *Castroism*, 5). The pamphlet was first circulated in June 1954, when it said that 'A group of Cuban intellectuals . . . have decided to publish the complete text of Dr Fidel Castro's defence plea'. But see also the version given by Castro to Robert Taber in a foreword to the New York edition in the spring of 1957: Castro spoke of 'a "little book" that he had written several years before . . . He showed obvious pleasure and no little pride in describing the ingenuity with which while in solitary confinement and under close guard . . . he had set down his thoughts invisibly in lime juice between the lines of ordinary letters'. 'You would be surprised how much trouble it was. I could write for only twenty minutes or so each evening at sunset when the sun slanted across the paper . . . to make the letters visible.' (p. 7). This last account perhaps owes something to romantic imagination.

[9] Dr Paglieri of Santiago was not allowed to visit Castro in gaol except once with a SIM sergeant present.

[10] *Ibid.*, 16.

worst dictator in all Cuba's history, or indeed in Latin American history.

> *Monstrum horrendum* . . . a man named Batista . . .[11] The man who encouraged the atrocious acts in Santiago . . . has not even human entrails . . .[12] has furthermore, never been sincere, loyal, honest or chivalrous for a single minute of his public life . . .[13] Only one man in all these centuries has stained with blood two separate periods of our historic existence and has dug his claws into the flesh of two generations of Cubans . . .[14] That grip, those claws, were familiar: those jaws, those death-dealing scythes, those boots . . .[15]

Castro did not omit, either, to revive memory of the murders of officers after the surrender of the Hotel Nacional in 1933 and of Blas Hernández and others, after the surrender of Fort Atarés the same year.[16] Batista, he said, was not content with 'the treachery of December 1933, the crimes of March 1935 and the $M40 fortune that crowned his first regime'.[17]

Revolutionary appeals were almost non-existent:

> The *people* means the vast unredeemed masses, to whom all make promises and whom all deceive; we mean the people who yearn for a better, more dignified and more just nation; who are moved by ancestral aspirations of justice, for they have suffered injustice and mockery, generation after generation; who long for great and wise changes in all aspects of their life . . .[18]

The speech spoke of '700,000 Cubans without work'[19] – a rough approximation of numbers of unemployed during the dead season; of 500,000 farm labourers inhabiting miserable shacks;[20] of 400,000 industrial labourers and stevedores whose pension funds had been stolen and whose life was otherwise intolerable – again, perhaps an overstatement; there were 275,000[21] supposed to be involved in manufactures (not including sugar). Builders (50,000)[22] and transport workers (75,000)[23] might bring the total up to 400,000. Not all these

[11] *Ibid.*, 18.
[12] *Ibid.*, 49.
[13] *Loc. cit.*
[14] *Loc. cit.*
[15] *Ibid.*, 62.
[16] *Ibid.*, 48.
[17] *Ibid.*, 49.
[18] *Ibid.*, 33–4.
[19] *Ibid.*, 34.
[20] Possibly an exaggeration, since the 1953 census makers thought there were only 118,000 houses in really bad condition (Census, p. 212). The number of agricultural labourers in 1953 totalled 510,016.
[21] Exact number 272,569.
[22] 51,263.
[23] 76,378.

people's lives were intolerable and not all of their pension funds had been stolen. Castro also spoke of 100,000 small farmers working land which was not their own, 200,000 peasant families without an acre of land, much good but uncultivated land, 30,000 underpaid teachers, 20,000 small debt-ridden businessmen, 10,000 young professionals – all fairly accurate approximations. He contended that 85% of small farmers paid rent and lived under the threat of being dispossessed, that over half the best cultivated land belonged to foreigners, while in Oriente the United Fruit Company's lands and the West India Sugar Corporation joined the north with the south coast.[24]

Castro pointed out what he judged the anomaly of exporting sugar in order to import sweets, hides to import shoes, iron to import ploughs. He urged the planned manufacture of steel, paper and chemicals, and the improvement of cattle food and grain products, to compete with Europe in cheese, condensed milk, wine and oil, and with the U.S. in tinned goods. Tourism should bring 'an enormous revenue'. But, said Castro, 'the capitalists insist that the workers remain under a Claudian yoke; the state folds its arms and industrialization can wait for the Greek Calends.'[25] This was Castro's only reference to 'capitalism' or indeed his only use of the jargon of Marxism or the class war.

Castro also launched a general attack on inadequate schooling, health, child welfare, and rural unemployment, while complaining that the rich could buy as much justice as they wanted, 'like Balzac's taillefer'. Cuba, he said, could easily feed a population three times as great – 'markets should be overflowing with produce ... all hands should be full, all hands should be working'. What seemed to him intolerable was that '30% of our farm people cannot write their names and that 99% of them know nothing of Cuba's history' – a somewhat curious bracketing.

Initially there was a series of legal arguments based on Cuban law, and upon historical arguments about the morality of the overthrow of tyrants: the authority of Montesquieu, John of Salisbury, St Thomas, Luther, Melanchthon, Calvin, Milton, Locke, Rousseau and Tom Paine were invoked for rebellion; the American, English and French revolutions were mentioned, as well as the Cuban leaders of 1868–98 (Agramonte, Céspedes, Maceo, Gómez and Martí). Always there was a hint of the role played by fighting: Maceo was quoted as saying liberty is 'not begged for but won with the blow of a machete'.[26]

Finally came the rhetorical conclusion:

[24] The West India Sugar Corporation, which had just over one million shares in 1957, had $M35 worth of land in the Dominican Republic also, according to a Dow Jones estimate in 1957 (*Havana Post,* 1 May 1957).
[25] *Op. cit.,* 38.
[26] 77.

I know that imprisonment will be as hard for me as it has ever been for anyone – filled with cowardly threats and wicked torture. But I do not fear prison, just as I do not fear the fury of the miserable tyrant who snuffed life out of seventy brothers of mine. Sentence me, I don't mind. History will absolve me.

Thus in the winter of 1953–4 Castro and his friends out of prison were at work on an eloquent denunciation of the regime, supported by a multiplicity of historical and social arguments, which was not only an attack on the Batista government but more profoundly was an attempt to plant a land-mine beneath the entire structure of Cuban society as it was then organized. The statistics were loosely gathered but roughly accurate and the drive of the pamphlet's social demands chiefly reflected Castro's own knowledge of the countryside of Oriente. There was as ever lacking any mention of racial intolerance; indeed, it would have been possible to have read *History will absolve me* without knowing there were Negroes at all in Cuba. But Castro knew that Batista was quite popular among Negroes and mulattoes. He gave consistent support to various Afro-Cuban cults. Several of his own black or mulatto followers had been taunted by their black soldier captors at the time of Moncada for following a white leader against Batista, the friend of the Negroes. Some soldiers had shown genuine surprise that there were any 'black revolutionaries'. A Negro brick-layer, Armando Mestre, maltreated by the police at Moncada, was told 'You a revolutionary, you? You don't know that Negroes can't be revolutionaries? Negroes are either thieves or partisans of Batista, not revolutionaries.'[27] When Lieutenant Sarriá and his men came upon the sleeping Castro and his two followers, their shout was, 'They are white!', '*Son Blancos,*' as if proof that they were revolutionaries, not *guajiros* or workers.[28]

Three further points might be made about this famous statement: first, there was no major attack on the U.S. – indeed, Castro spoke less violently of the 'colossus of the north' than most Cuban nationalist politicians of the previous fifty years; second, unlike the rhetorical statements of his fellows in Cuban politics, the speech included a considerable panoply of statistical material; and third, much of this statistical material seems from internal evidence to have come from a famous popularizing work, *Los Fundamentos del Socialismo*, by the secretary general of the Cuban Communist party, Blas Roca.[29]

With every month after Moncada, and despite Castro's literary activities, Batista improved his position. The man in the street told

[27] Almeida to Francqui, 18.
[28] See Merle, 268.
[29] I am indebted for this last point to Mr Robin Blackburn.

himself that political gangsterism and graft had been reduced. Labour relations seemed good and the foreign exchange situation excellent. An occasional ugly incident could be ignored if it remained unexplained – such as the mysterious murder of Mario Fortuny, a journalist who had worked with Sánchez Arango in the Ministry of Education. There were anyway fewer political murders than in the days of the Auténticos. In December the regime received a fillip from the arrest of ex-President Prío in Florida, on charges of violating the U.S. Neutrality Law of 1939. Released on a $50,000 charge, he was arraigned on 14 December with various followers, finger-printed and sent for trial. Such events might cause merriment to Batista. They exacerbated U.S. relations with the opposition. Jorge Mañach sent an open letter to Eisenhower accusing him of intervening in Cuban affairs.

But in the army the animosities and intrigues continued. General del Río Chaviano, it will be remembered, had sent Major Morales, the real victor of Moncada, back to Havana under lock and key, as a conspirator: but Morales had successfully got a letter to Batista explaining the truth of the matter, adding that del Río Chaviano was running a big gambling and protection racket in Santiago, that there were almost daily drunken orgies in the barracks, and that he had made vast profits from smuggling; he added too that if on investigation these things were not found to be true, he personally would shoot himself in Batista's presence. Batista did make an investigation. Morales was freed and became head of the Cuban military archives but nothing was done to del Río Chaviano; the scandals associated with Tabernilla and the officers so well placed and so near to him continued.

The reason for this was that Tabernilla's eldest son, the young Lieutenant 'Silito', had successfully manœuvred his way from being simply a military aide of the president to being his chief secretary, securing the dispatch of Dr Raúl Acosta Rubio who had held this post for years, including during the time when Batista was in exile, to the appointment of Cuban minister to Honduras. This had led to various changes and promotions in the military commands, designed to establish further Tabernilla in a powerful position.

In January 1954 an embarrassing event occurred: Grau San Martín announced his candidacy in the Batista presidential elections for November. He was naturally criticized, even by his relations, for deigning to collaborate with the new constitutional laws – a criticism in no way removed by Batista's 'pledge' that the old constitution would be restored piecemeal after the elections, beginning with the articles that dealt with local government.[30] The articles on the Congress

---

[30] Several supporters of Grau left him, among them Primitivo Rodríguez, Hugo Alvarez, Edgardo Buttari and Antonio Fernández Macho.

would apply after January 1955, when that body would meet again. The whole constitution would function after the new president had taken office on 20 February 1955.

The Communists were not among those groups who trifled to register for the elections. They urged their followers to back Dr Grau San Martín and later explained:

We said to the masses: since we have to vote, let us vote against Batista's tyrannical and anti-popular government. We explained publicly that Grau could not supply any solution; that we were not calling for a vote for him but for a vote against Batista, though the only way possible to vote against Batista . . . was to mark a cross against Batista's name. The slogan of the negative vote [Blas Roca self-importantly added] had profound repercussions amongst the masses. Under that slogan . . . the masses of all tendencies and parties of the opposition united . . . the meetings that Grau called in the election campaign became against those who called them, militant mass demonstrations against the tyranny.[31]

The nation was thus faced by the bizarre alliance of the Communists and Auténticos, with Ortodoxos holding aloof. Whether as a result or not, only 210,000 registered for Grau: and only 20,000 for the single splinter group of the Ortodoxos who were interested in participating. Nearly 1·7 million allegedly registered for the pro-Batista parties,[32] but the chances of this being in any way a truthful reflection of Batista's following are remote; the total electorate in mid-1954 did not attain 2,800,000.

Raúl Chibás, Eddy's brother, finally took over the leadership of the Ortodoxos in February, as a compromise leader. Another letter from Castro in prison, this time to Melba Hernández, should be judged against this background.

One should not abandon propaganda for one moment because it is the soul of all struggles [he wrote in February], ours must have its own style and adjust to circumstances. We must continue ceaselessly denouncing the assassinations. Mirta [his wife] will speak to you of a document of decisive importance for its ideological content and for its tremendous accusations [i.e. the 'speech', *History will absolve me*] . . . whatever happens a demonstration on the university *escalinata* is

[31] Blas Roca at the 8th Congress of the PSP in 1960, 35-6.
[32] Batista's PAP: 945,555
 Liberals: 279,542
 Democrats: 250,190
 Radicals: 211,058.

essential . . . Gustavo Arcos[33] must speak with the FEU leaders about it.

Secondly, we must co-ordinate the work between our people here and abroad. Prepare to this end . . . a voyage to Mexico to meet there with Raúl Martínez [the Bayamo leader] and Lester Rodríguez.[34] We must arrange with great care whatever proposition may be made for co-ordination with other groups, lest they simply make use of our name, as Pardo Llada[35] has been doing . . . It is preferable to go alone . . . you keep the flag flying until the *muchachos* now in prison come out . . . To know how to wait, said Martí, is the great secret of success.

Thirdly, show much guile [*mano izquierda*] and smiles to everybody. Follow the same course which we followed in the trial: defend our points of view without wounding others. We will have time later on to trample underfoot all the cockroaches . . . Accept all sorts of help, but, remember, trust in no one. Mirta has instructions to help you with all her soul.[36]

A little later, on 15 April 1954, he wrote:

With what joy would I bring revolution to this country from top to bottom . . . I would be disposed to draw on me the hate and ill will of one or two thousand people, among them some relations, half my friends, two-thirds of my colleagues, and four-fifths of my old comrades at university . . . Have you noticed the number of invisible links which a man who is anxious to live in accord with his ideas must break? What makes me suffer most, is to think that if all the generous men there are on earth were to respond to our appeal, all the charlatans, parasites, mediocrities, and egoists of every kidney would vanish at once.[37]

Castro was thus able to communicate easily with his co-conspirators. Letters flowed regularly. He was able also to read extensively in prison: books flowed in all the time. He read *Les Misérables*, and, though contrasting the novel unfavourably with *Le 18 Brumaire de Louis Bonaparte*, admitted that 'the phrases of Hugo . . . remind me of our own speeches, full of poetic faith in liberty, and holy indignation against outrages . . .'[38]

Back in Havana meantime Sánchez Arango, the most active of Prío's old lieutenants, and believed to be in exile, was discovered in the

[33] One of the Moncadaistas then free. Afterwards Cuban ambassador to Belgium, and apparently in confinement since 1966.

[34] Another Moncadaista from Santiago, also escaped without arrest.

[35] The Ortodoxo radio writer.

[36] Conte Agüero, *Cartas del Presidio*, 37–8.

[37] Qu. Merle, 347–8.

[38] Qu. *ibid.* (date, 1 March 1954).

Country Club district of Havana. Pursued by police, he took refuge in the Uruguayan Embassy, with various followers, mostly ex-officials of the Ministry of Education such as Carlos Enrique Alfonso Varela or Guillermo Barrientos and Prío's ex-Communications Minister, Sergio Mejías. He was later allowed to go abroad. A list of Aureliano's followers fell into the hands of the police: the simply named Asociación de Amigos de Aureliano (AAA) seemed larger than had been anticipated and a curious panic overcame the police for some months. Still, Batista continued to treat his opponents warily: thus in May an amnesty was offered to all exiles except to those who had taken part in the attack on the Moncada, but at the same time, due to 'hemispheric anxiety', Batista declared a new anti-Communist decree by which Communist activity in any form was declared a sufficient cause for dismissal from, for instance, the Civil Service, the universities, and the Labour unions. But this seemed a mere token act of solidarity with the U.S. at the moment when the latter was about to commit itself to the overthrow of the Guatemalan government of Colonel Arbenz.[39] About this time too there came the more serious foundation of a special committee of the Ministry of War to 'fight' the Communists, the Buró de Represión a las Actividades Comunistas (BRAC). This owed much to U.S. representations: the U.S. ambassador, Arthur Gardner, regarded himself as 'the father of the BRAC';[40] Batista had promised Foster Dulles that he 'would organize an effective agency to cope with Communist activities in Cuba'; and Allen Dulles, the new director of the Central Intelligence Agency, had a long conversation with Batista about this time, being 'not unfavourably impressed': the U.S., according to Allen Dulles, helped Batista's intelligence organization, though quite soon it declined in quality,[41] and for the next two years 'most of the money' meant for the BRAC 'never reached the proper destination'.[42]

In June 1954 Castro's *History will absolve me* finally appeared as a pamphlet and circulated clandestinely. In two more letters written in that month, from his sunless cell, to Conte Agüero, Castro further explained how he read all day; how his only companions were the bodies of fellow prisoners who had mysteriously died and were hanging on the other side of his cell: but even these, he added with a somewhat self-defeating excess of drama, he could not see because of a wall separating him from them; the theme of the seventy prisoners killed in Moncada recurred; he recalled again 'the beloved and unforgettable shape of the masses of our party, always vibrant and enthusiastic . . . the soul incarnate of the great leader' (Chibás); while praising some

[39] This was done by clandestine support to Guatemalan exiles.
[40] In a conversation with the author, 1962.
[41] These words were also in a conversation with the author in 1962.
[42] Lyman B. Kirkpatrick, *The Real CIA* (1968), 157.

Ortodoxo leaders, he denounced others who were prostituting Ortodoxia, 'landowners, millionaires and exploiters of the peasants' – what
were they doing inside a party whose first duty was social justice? With
increasing bitterness he referred to the Auténticos' disputes with
Batista as a battle between the robbers of yesterday against the robber
of today. There was more than ever about the importance of 'principles'.
'All will save themselves if they save their principles: from the deepest
dregs of corruption will come more purified and clean the ideal re-
deemer; sacrifice is now our only duty.' During some months he was
treated very harshly in gaol but this ceased after the representations of
the richest of his fellow prisoners, Enrique Sánchez del Monte, who
threatened to cut off his monthly bribe to the governor if they did not
cease.[43]

Castro now became far more famous than he had been when free.
In the elections of 1954 he was already an unseen candidate, the spirit
of liberty incarcerated and of Martí reincarnated. Among those who
sang, revived and warmed the flame of hope was Carlos Puebla, a
mulatto, who nightly, with elegiac grace, aroused memories and
expectations in *La Bodeguita del Medio*, a Bohemian restaurant off the
Plaza de la Catedral, his songs becoming famous throughout Cuba:

Los caminos de mi Cuba	The roads of my Cuba
Nunca van a donde deben.	Never lead where they should.

Castro found himself increasingly critical of other groups: the
College of Lawyers he found too weak; the students (FEU) were
behaving badly; the main body of the Ortodoxo youth movement (led
by Max Lesnick and Omar Borges) had denounced Castro's movement
as destructive; he was furious that his wife, Mirta, should have accepted
a pension from the Ministry of Information, thanks to the influence of
her brother Rafael, under-secretary at the Ministry of the Interior.[44]
(Castro's marriage was clearly heading for breakdown, the test being his
instructions to his wife to withstand the pressure of her powerful and
politically successful family, while her husband was in prison.)

On 26 July 1954, a year after the attack on Moncada, Castro received
a visit from Hermida, Minister of the Interior, and two other *Batistiano*
ministers, Gastón Godoy and Marino López Blanco. Hermida said:

Castro, I want you to know that I am not your personal enemy, I am
simply an official filling the task of being Minister of the Interior.
You are here because the tribunals, not I, sentenced you. My task

---

[43] Sánchez was in gaol for the murder of the son of Joaquín Martínez Sáenz, who had been
killed by two gunmen hired by Sánchez in mistake for the father, whom Sánchez believed to be
the lover of his wife.
[44] Conte Agüero, *Cartas del Presidio*, 43 ff.

is simply to watch over the conduct of the prisons, always fulfilling the President's wishes . . . Batista is a very fair man, I have never in twenty years seen him insult anyone, nor even raise his voice: I realise I am not myself quite the same and people say I am a little brusque . . . Major [to the officer in attendance], treat them chivalrously, for they are gentlemen.

Castro listened in silence and said:

I, for my part, have never considered the struggle as a personal quarrel but a struggle against a ruling political system. [He added] I have been placed on the offensive by your declarations which leave my integrity in doubt. If an alleged intimate of mine is one of the high officials of the regime and these officials, without my wish or knowledge, make representations to this circumstance to attack my home and family . . .

The minister interrupted and said:

Look Castro, I know that the guilty one is Rafaelito[45] who always behaves as an irresponsible infant. I assure you on my honour that I have never had the intention of angering you and that the note you mention was altered and appeared in a different form from what I made. As for your name, what doubt can there be? There is no one in Cuba who has a more clearly defined position than you. Don't be impatient, I myself was a political prisoner in the years '30 and '31. I placed myself many times in the Country Club to make an assassination attempt on Machado or Ortiz. You are a young man, be calm, all these things will pass.

'Very well, Minister,' answered Castro, 'I accept your explanation . . . I recognize that you anyway have been very correct.'[46] When Castro's brother-in-law Díaz Balart heard of the visit, he violently criticized Hermida, protesting against such intercourse with the 'promoter of the murderous attack against the Army'. The letter was published, with the result that both Díaz Balart and Hermida had to resign.

In midsummer 1954 the Grau cause in the elections began to prosper when all but the most faithful Prío wing of the Auténticos began to support the old fox. People began to remember how ten years before they had taught their parrots to say *Viva Grau San Martín*, even in remote places.[47] The Ortodoxos were once again in difficulties. Raúl Chibás proved himself more ineffective than had been supposed and Márquez Sterling could not be prevented from entering to run in the

[45] i.e. Díaz Balart.
[46] Conte Agüero, *Cartas del Presidio*, 49–57.
[47] Nelson, 13.

election. Agramonte pursued private squabbles, challenging Aureliano Sánchez Arango to a duel for 'defaming the memory of Chibás'. Batista finally announced, as everyone expected, that he would himself run as president, taking Guas Inclán, son of old General Guas Pasquera of the war of independence, as his vice-president. These two were the 'unanimous' candidates of the four government parties (PAP, Liberals, Democrats, Radicals). He started off his election campaign by announcing that bonds reaching $M350 would be issued to finance a huge public works programme. The situation seemed more and more like the days of Machado; for few doubted that this money would find its way into the hands of government members.

On 14 August Batista, as incumbent president, stepped down to run in the election campaign and his faithful secretary, Andrés Domingo took over temporarily with a cabinet similar to that before. The same day another letter came out of the Isle of Pines to Luis Conte Agüero from Fidel Castro: the tone was again different – as different from the letters in June as those were from the letters in December and the spring; Castro had evidently thought a good deal about the question of revolutionary leadership:

> I believe fundamentally that one of the biggest obstacles preventing the integration of the [opposition] . . . is the excessive number of *Personalismos* and the ambitions of groups and . . . *caudillos* . . . the [situation] . . . makes me remember the efforts of Martí to join all worthy Cubans in the struggle for independence . . . perhaps for this reason, the chapters I most admire in the history of Cuba are not so much the proud moments of battle . . . as that gigantic and heroic enterprise of uniting the Cubans for the struggle . . . I must in the first place organise the men of the 26th of July and unite, into an unbreakable bundle [*haz*], all the fighters, those in exile, those in prison, those free, who together amount to over eighty men implicated in the same historic day of sacrifice. The importance of such a perfectly disciplined nucleus contributes incalculable strength to the . . . formation of *cadres* of struggle for civil or insurrectional organisation. From then . . . a great civic-political movement must count on the necessary force to capture power, either by pacific or revolutionary paths, or run the risk of being beaten, like Ortodoxia, only two months before the election.[48]

This suggests that Castro was no longer regarding himself as an Ortodoxo; already he was contrasting his own behaviour with that of the Ortodoxos: he would not make Ortodoxia's mistakes: he could therefore not be an Ortodoxo. He continued:

[48] Conte Agüero, *Cartas del Presidio*, 60.

Conditions indispensable for the integration of a true civil movement are: ideology, discipline, leadership. All are desirable, but leadership is essential. I don't know if it was Napoleon who said that one bad general counts more in battle than twenty good ones. One cannot organise a movement in which everyone believes they have a right to make public declarations without consulting anyone. Neither can one expect anything of an organisation full of anarchic men who at the first difficulty take the path they think best, unsettling and destroying the vehicle. The organisation and propaganda apparatus must be so powerful that it implacably destroys anyone who tries to create splits, *camarillas*, schisms, or to rise against the movement . . . The programme must contain a full, concrete and acceptable exposition of the social and economic problems which face the country, so that a truly new and improving message can be taken to the masses. I know that not even God could create in a single day all the marvels of the world but from the first moment the masses must feel that the foundations of marvels exist. Above all . . . our energies must not be invested uselessly, improvising and amalgamating instead of creating and founding, a thing which . . . did not happen with Ortodoxia.[49]

It is clear from other letters that Napoleon, Julius Caesar ('a true revolutionary', in contrast with Cicero, the incarnation of oligarchy), and Plutarch's *Lives* were all on Castro's mind in 1954.[50] The overwhelming impression from his writings of this period is his desire to identify himself with the world historical process, his own position expressed in nineteenth-century romantic terms.

Batista was meanwhile staging a lavish electoral campaign, of which the most typical incident was the anecdote of how he had found a wounded crane in 1939, how he helped it and saved its life, but how it died after he went elsewhere; Cuba, said Batista, resembled this crane (*grulla*) and now he was bringing it back to life. The image caught on and the cry *Viva la grulla* was echoed everywhere by his supporters. He accumulated large sums of money given to him by companies and private supporters: according to his own youth leader Suárez Núñez, he personally made nearly $M12 out of the election.[51] The Communists continued to support Grau . . . Blas Roca later recalled: 'The meeting at Santiago [on 24 October 1954] was memorable . . . For twenty-four hours the party recovered its legality and, with the masses, became masters of the streets . . . Faced with the threat of an avalanche of

[49] *Ibid.*, 60–2.
[50] See Merle, 344–5.
[51] Suárez Núñez, 17.

negative votes, the Government found itself impelled to change the rules of the election and to call on Mujal to control the masses.'[52] The meeting in Santiago was however chiefly memorable for the fact that the crowd shouted Fidel Castro's name when Grau appeared.[53]

The government had in fact determined all along to control the election boards. Grau demanded equal representation with the government representatives. Refused, he demanded a postponement. This was not granted. Grau then withdrew from the election, to the annoyance of the Communists who accused him of surrendering to the pressure of 'Yankee imperialists'.[54] Batista accused Grau of being 'conspiratorial'. Agramonte praised him.[55] Batista next took what seemed the final step of outlawing the Communists completely; but in practice most Communists could carry on their work in the normal way: César Escalante thus continued to live at his wife's *crèche*; Carlos Rafael Rodríguez and Aníbal Escalante remained at large.

On 1 November the elections finally took place. Batista was returned as president without opposition, with only half the electorate voting, though to vote was nominally compulsory. Some Auténticos won seats in the House of Representatives and the Senate and so took the minority seats in the legislature – 18 out of 54 in the Senate, 16 out of 114 in the House of Representatives. Grau himself was understood to have received one out of six votes, even though he announced himself not to be taking part.

Castro's reaction to the election was blunted since his divorce from Mirta was then coming through, and, busy reading and studying, he allowed it to pass without comment. His chief anxiety was that his son had to sleep under the same roof as his in-laws, the Díaz Balarts, and 'receive on his innocent cheeks the kisses of these miserable Judases . . . I presume they know that for me to abandon this child they would have to kill me . . . I lose my head when I speak of these matters'.[56]

The new Congress assembled, with the Auténticos in their seats (only two of them accepted Grau's request to boycott it).[57] In February 1955 Batista was duly inaugurated, an event crowned with the capture and killing of a famous gangster of the old days, a friend of Prío's, Orlando León Lemus (*el Colorado*). There was a new ministry, though the names contained no surprises: Saladrigas was Foreign Minister and Jorge García Montes (vice-president of the Consultative

[52] Roca, VIIIth Congress, 35–6.
[53] Castro listened to the radio from prison. (Letter to his sister, in Conte Agüero, *Cartas del Presidio*, 63.)
[54] *Loc. cit.*
[55] Phillips, 241.
[56] Letter to his sister, in Conte Agüero, *Cartas del Presidio*, 65–6.
[57] HAR, February 1955. They were José Miguel Morales and Francisco Grau Alsina.

Assembly from 1953–5) was prime minister. Aurelio Fernández Concheso, a familiar face from the 1940s when he had been ambassador in the U.S. (1940–4), cropped up as Minister of Education: in the interim he had been a supreme court judge. One 'new' face was Raúl Menocal, Minister of Commerce, son of the old president and mayor of Havana during Batista's first period of office. The Interior Ministry was taken by Santiago Rey, Minister without Portfolio since Moncada, a man who had served Batista as he had served Prío before, opportunistically. Santiago Verdeja, Minister of Defence, and chief therefore of the armed forces except the police, was an ex-Menocalista; he was a doctor by profession, had been a representative from 1917–25 and had spent many months in La Cabaña in the last years of Machado: Ramón Vasconcelos, the journalist who had been in Prío's cabinet and resigned, and had afterwards been Fidel Castro's sponsor on the newspaper *Alerta*, joined Batista as Minister of Communications – a bizarre transformation of a somewhat discredited politician who had begun his career as a diplomat under Machado. The faithful provisional president, Andrés Domingo y Morales del Castillo, returned to the secretaryship of the cabinet. Ministers without Portfolio included Batista's old friend, the sugar chief Amadeo López Castro, president of the Development Commission, and Dr Jorge Barroso, the sugar stabilization board's chief.[58]

Constitutional government was now allegedly restored. Batista told Congress, 'We want amnesty and we want peace,' though there could be no amnesty while terrorism continued. There was still incessant turmoil at the university, and bombs appeared sporadically all over the island, placed either by Castro's friends or Prío's: the ex-mayor of Santiago, Luis Casero, was arrested after a bomb explosion in late February 1955 in Santiago. The Ortodoxos, seemingly uniting behind Raúl Chibás, were less active than the Priístas. It was to Prío in Miami that in March several congressmen of Batista's packed legislature, Conrado Bécquer, a sugar workers' leader (an Auténtico opportunist), with Jorge Cruz, Conrado Rodríguez, also of the sugar union, and Alejandro Jiménez went to discuss the political situation, asking him not to return without guarantees of pardon for all political prisoners. But in April there was a growing feeling in all sections of opinion in favour of an amnesty.

Batista believed that his position was so strong that he could afford

[58] Complete list: Prime Minister, Jorge García Montes; Minister of State, Saladrigas (C); Education, Fernández Concheso; Labour, Suárez Rivas (J); Finance, Justo García Rayneri; Agriculture, Fidel Barreto; Defence, Santiago Verdeja Neyra; Health, Armando Coro; Interior, Santiago Rey; Justice, Camacho; Commerce, Raúl Menocal; Communications, Ramón Vasconcelos; Public Works, Nicolás Arroyo; Transport, Mario Cobas; Ministers without Portfolio: José Pardo Jiménez, Amadeo López Castro, Jorge L. Barroso, Julia Elisa Consuegra, José Pérez González; Secretary of the Presidency, Andrés Domingo y Morales del Castillo.

this: Justo Carrillo's Acción Libertadora, with Sánchez Arango's organization the only effective opposition group with links with the old regime, disintegrated at the end of 1954. There was an air of prosperity in Cuba, brought on after an agreement to sell reserve sugar in the U.S.S.R., sustained by the feeling that the elections had brought a period of uncertainty to an end. Cuban and U.S. promoters were discussing the idea of a cross-Cuba canal to cut the distance between Cuba and the Panama Canal – to spare ships a 'detour of 400 miles'. The plan was criticized by Liberals such as Mañach as likely to lead to still greater U.S. control over the economy, but the economic advantages seemed strong, and there appeared a good chance that the idea would prosper. A ferry from Key West to Cárdenas was opened, being immediately successful. Vice-President Nixon came to give the regime his blessing in February in the course of a Central American goodwill tour, and in April Allen Dulles of the CIA came to place his stethoscope to the Cuban 'security organization'. He said somewhat mysteriously that the U.S. was seriously preoccupied by the problem of Communism in Cuba.[59] Batista's public works programme was beginning and there was a great leap forward in private building in Vedado. A new organization for constitutional development, headed by Mañach, was formed with Luis Botifoll, Rufo López Fresquet, Justo Carrillo, Pardo Llada and Vicente Rubiera. A letter from Castro to Conte Agüero in March 1955 assured the democratic opposition that Castro and his group held to their principles. Even so, in mid-April Batista relaxed, and declared an amnesty. All political prisoners would come out in May. This was Batista's greatest error of judgement.

[59] Evidence of Allen Dulles.

CHAPTER 6

The Civic Dialogue

On 15 May 1955 Castro and his brother with eighteen followers left the Isle of Pines under the amnesty law. There were scenes of rejoicing at reunions with families, and Castro was welcomed by the National Committee of Ortodoxos. To *Bohemia* he announced:

I do not have . . . the intention of creating a new political party. We do not abandon our plans of maintaining and cooperating with the (Ortodoxo) party . . . We consider it a good thing that Dr Raúl Chibás has been named as leader, though we cannot say that he has great political experience . . . All of us must unite under some flag . . . All [Ortodoxos] are necessary in this struggle, all have the same advanced ideological conception. And if there exists ideological unity, why need we continue divided? [He added] The amnesty is the result of an extraordinary popular mobilisation, backed splendidly by the Cuban press, which has gained the most glittering of victories.

To Agramonte and Raúl Chibas, Castro explained, 'What Cuba needs is decent politicians . . . Great economic and social reform is needed.'[1]

Castro repeated his opposition to any break with the Ortodoxos in an interview with Carlos Franqui, then a reporter on the periodical *Carteles*.[2] In his last weeks in prison, he had been preoccupied with the aim of getting representatives of the opposition youth (such as Conte Agüero) heard and seen on television.[3] In a letter to Conte Agüero himself, he argued that Christ's reply to the Pharisees as to the relation between God and Caesar was bound to make him unpopular with one of the two; 'thus today [the regime] is trying to ruin our prestige with the people or to leave us in prison.'[4] He appeared preoccupied with whether further armed action against Batista was desirable. He quoted Martí: 'Anyone is a criminal who promotes an avoidable war; and so is he who does not promote an inevitable civil war.' Compromise would always be rejected, though genuine constitutional guarantees could make violence unnecessary.[5] Castro saw his movement already as the

---

[1] *Bohemia*, 22 May 1955.
[2] Qu., Conte Agüero, *Cartas del Presidio*, 91.
[3] Letter to Mañach, 17 February 1955 (*Ibid.*, 71–3).
[4] *Ibid.*, 83.
[5] *Ibid.*, 85.

'spiritual sons of the Titan of Bronze' (that is, Maceo):[6] what room was there for him among the meek and mild Ortodoxos?

But where did Castro fit in? Not with some of the old members even of his own organization, such as the leader of the Bayamo attack in 1953, Martínez Arará, who saw him the day he returned; Castro criticized Martínez's relations with Carlos Prío;[7] nor with the students, who in the years since he had left the university had built up their own organization and their own leaders. Castro and his comrades, admittedly, were welcomed home formally by a meeting of students on 20 May at the university. The police moved in, led by two already notorious police captains, Colonel Carratalá and Lieutenant Esteban Ventura. The electricity of the university was cut off, and the police prevented the meeting being held in the famous *escalinata*, but it nevertheless continued.[8] Even so, the students did not need Castro as their leader: they already had their own, such as José Antonio Echevarría, the strongest candidate for the presidency of the FEU in the autumn, a youth from Cárdenas, a solid courageous and respectable character, though perhaps not of wide intelligence and gifts, known as '*Manzanita*' (little apple). He was an intellectual, later forced to play the role of a man of action, for which he was not fitted.[9] He was a Catholic and honest, and his arrival at the university had coincided with, or led to, a marked change in the moral attitude to politics in the university. Earlier in May he had been involved in riots at a meeting commemorating the death of Guiteras. He and four others had been wounded at Matanzas. The university had protested and been closed for two days.[10]

Castro had nothing directly to do with these events in the university. None of the university leaders were his followers, though Echevarría and Javier Pazos had links with the Ortodoxos. Of Echevarría, Castro later remarked:

Really between him and me there was always a great current of friendship, understanding, sympathy: he was a *muchacho* outstanding

[6] *Ibid.*, 86.
[7] Martínez Arará's evidence. The two met several times more between then and early July.
[8] *Bohemia*, 28 May 1955.
[9] Comment of Dr Herminio Portell Vilá.
[10] Echevarría's campaign for the presidency of FEU was the central question in the university in mid-1955. His opponent was Leonel Alonso, a Matancero of humble social origins who had worked his way to the university and was backed by the traditional Auténtico Priísta group, led by Hidalgo Peraza. Voting as usual was by faculties and the vote finally split 6 to 6. A progressive socialist group led by Javier Pazos, the son of Prío's director of the National Bank, moved over from Alonso to back Echevarría, securing a more extreme man, René Anillo, into the FEU as secretary. In the past, in the time of Castro, gangsterism would no doubt have settled the affair; one group would have bribed, kidnapped or even physically injured the other. The acute political crisis had led to the end of this bellicose and corrupt atmosphere within the university.

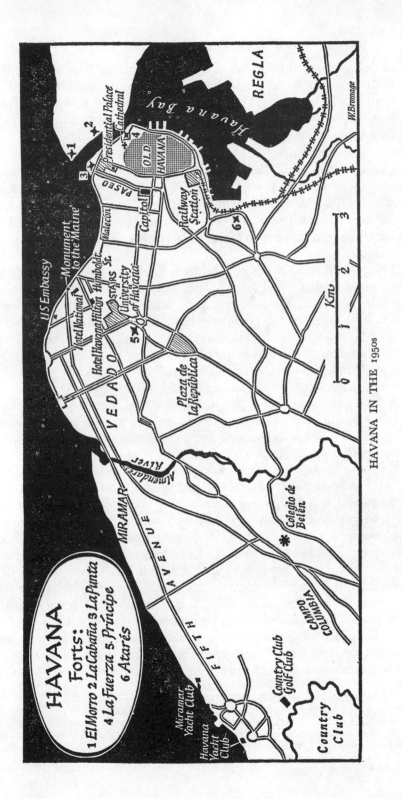

HAVANA IN THE 1950s

in decisiveness, enthusiasm and valour . . . [but] we at that time would scarcely enter the University because there were some FEU leaders who thought that history was going to repeat itself and that they were going to be everything in the future, and only they: they believed themselves the eldest sons of the Revolution.[11]

But he had more success with the student leaders of the University of Santiago, a group of men evidently out of sympathy on personal grounds with those in Havana, and who had been for a time attached to García Barcena and then to one or two other minuscule groups.[12] Those men, Frank País and Pepito Tey (the president of the FEU in Oriente) went to Havana to meet Castro and reached an understanding with him.

The general atmosphere in Havana in mid-1955 was, however, antipathetic to Castro. Having staked all on the politics of action and, if need be, violence, the amnesty itself and the mood of compromise which it had created played against him. There was widespread feeling among Ortodoxos and middle-class professional Cubans that negotiations with Batista were both possible and really the only viable way ahead. Castro was temperamentally and psychologically opposed to this approach; nor could he forget, and his followers would not let him forget, the sixty-eight prisoners murdered after Moncada. Even with a moderate Catholic Action group which was prepared to countenance military action Castro could not cooperate since he wished to be the chief of any united movement.[13]

Within a fortnight of being let free Castro had published an article in *Bohemia* entitled, 'You Lie, Chaviano', a direct attack on the colonel in command in Santiago two years before,[14] making effective play with the sixteen-to-one proportion of killed to wounded, a proportion never obtained in wars of the past. Early in June Congressman Waldo Pérez Almaguer, Batista's governor in Oriente in 1953, followed with a denunciation in the newspaper *La Calle*, that Río Chaviano had definitely himself ordered the execution of over thirty prisoners caught after Moncada. The editor of *La Calle*, Luis Orlando Rodríguez, Castro's new sponsor in the Cuban press, was taken into custody (on the orders, as it happened of Ramón Vasconcelos, the minister who had been Castro's previous sponsor in journalism before 1952), but even so, Chaviano was transferred, though he did make a response also in *La*

---

[11] Castro in his speech at Marquitos's trial, March 1964.

[12] These were Acción Libertadora and Acción Nacional Revolucionaria.

[13] Mario Llerena MSS, p. 18, describes the abortive negotiations between Castro on the one hand and Llerena (ex-member of García Barcena's MNR), Andrés Valdespino, and Amalio Fiallo – the last two being Catholic Action leaders. All of these collaborated eventually with Castro in the 26 July Movement, but went into exile afterwards.

[14] *Bohemia*, 29 May 1955.

Calle. A day or two later came a new murder: Jorge Agostini, ex-chief of the presidential secret police under Grau and Prío, had been in exile since 1952, and returned, hoping to profit under the amnesty. He was arrested. He was then either summarily shot or shot while trying to escape, more likely the first since twenty-one bullets were later found to have been fired, apparently under the orders of Julio Laurent, chief of Naval Intelligence.[15]

In a matter of weeks Castro decided to go to Mexico and to form there a trained and disciplined group to provide the backbone of a guerrilla troop to try to overthrow Batista by force – by, as he supposed then, some new dramatic strike. The police in Havana were probably preparing an attack on him, as became well known; according to one account, a car riddled with bullets already existed – ready for his body to be found within (killed 'fighting the police', as Agostini had been killed).[16] Castro's decision to go to Mexico appears to have been taken by him alone without consultation with the Ortodoxo leaders. His brother Raúl (who had recently been falsely accused of arson) had indeed preceded him. Before Castro left Havana he held a meeting on 19 July of his friends and supporters whom he would leave behind and it is perhaps appropriate to think of this meeting as inaugurating what afterwards became the 26 July Movement as an organization separate from Ortodoxia: for the time being, however, Castro refrained from defining his differences with the old movement of Chibás (anyway these were less differences of ideology or political aims than of method and tactics).[17]

The friends whom Castro left behind him consisted, first, of a few old comrades of the Moncada such as Haydée Santamaría, Pedro Miret and Lester Rodríguez, and one or two friends of these such as Aldo Santamaría, Haydée's brother, and the Ameijeiras brothers whose elder brother Juan Manuel had died after the Moncada attack: but these old comrades were in the minority. Most of the members of the 26 July Movement were new adherents of Castro, having until very recently been adherents of Professor García Barcena's Movimiento Nacional Revolucionario; they were looking for a new leader committed to the idea of revolutionary action against Batista now that the professor (who had also been released in the amnesty) had showed that he was no longer to be counted upon to this end. They included not only the leaders of the Santiago students, Pepito Tey and Frank País, the Baptist schoolmaster (with whom Lester Rodríguez, of the Moncada,

---

[15] See *Havana Post*, 22 February 1956; and for Castro's attack on the regime as a result, *La Calle*, 11 June 1955.

[16] Almeida in Franqui, 21; see *La Calle*, 4 June 1955, where Castro made the accusation at the time.

[17] René Ray Rivero, *Libertad y revolución* (1959), 11–12.

would work in Santiago), but also men such as Faustino Pérez – a Presbyterian chemist – Armando Hart, a law student who had defended García Barcena, and Enrique Oltuski, son of a Polish immigrant, who were to be the main organizers of the 26 July Movement in Cuba itself (for most of the years of struggle against Batista) until 1959. One new adherent at this time was at least for Castro an old acquaintance: this was Carlos Franqui, who had taken part in the abortive attack on the Dominican Republic in 1947 in the 'Cayo Confites' expedition. Franqui, an ex-Communist, was a journalist on the magazine *Carteles* and, having previously been the animator of several anti-Batista news-sheets, now organized the 26 July cyclostyled weekly, *Revolución*.[18]

Although Hart and Faustino Pérez became Castro's chief lieutenants later on, it was the Santiago group headed by Tey and País that seemed to count most with Castro at this moment, and Castro nominated País as his head of all 'action groups' in Cuba, when leaving the island himself.[19] This was chiefly because País already had, in the remains of the Oriente section of García Barcena's movement and of his own Acción Revolucionaria Oriente, the skeleton of an organization.

In Mexico Castro found a number of young Cubans together with some older exiles. One centre was the house in Pedregal de San Angel of Orquídea Pino, a beautiful Cuban singer married to a distinguished Mexican engineer, Alfonso Gutiérrez. There Castro and his friends began to prepare their next move and also to think more of their general ideology.

Mexico in 1955 was still run by the Institutional Revolutionary Party (PRI). The president, Adolfo Ruiz Cortines, was an austere book-keeper who attempted almost successfully to establish a thrifty government after the magnificences of his predecessor the expansionist, tireless and ambitious Miguel Alemán. Ruiz Cortines maintained the independence of Mexico in foreign affairs and the traditional hostility towards Fascism or any form of it, such as that expressed by Franco's Spain. Diplomatic relations with the exiled Spanish Republican government remained and there were many Spanish exiles and their families. The Communist party legally flourished, if without hope of gaining an electoral victory. Mexico City was a natural centre of political discussion and even conspiracy covering much of Latin America.

[18] Franqui had been a member of Juventud Socialista and afterwards worked for *Hoy* which 'seemed to him to deviate from the socialist line'. According to what he is believed to have told Mario Llerena (MSS, p. 5), he left the Communist party because of general disillusionment with their conduct and tactics.

[19] The 26 July committee left behind in Cuba were Aldo Santamaría, Manuel Cueto, Ricardo González, Maximo Reyes, Universo Sánchez, Ayán Rosell, Santiago Riera, Efraín Alfonso, Osvaldo Rodríguez, Haydée Santamaría, Carlos Franqui, Enrique Hart, Pedro Miret, Frank País, Vilma Espín, Carlos Chaín, Carlos Iglesias, and Quintín Pino (list in René Ray, 11–12).

In this volatile atmosphere Castro thrived. Under the influence of her *Batistiano* brother, his wife had now completed divorce proceedings so that he was now in a sense married only to the Revolution. He and his friends attached themselves early to Spanish Republicans such as the sculptor and frame-maker Víctor Trapote, a Catalan whose daughter married one of Castro's closest followers, Ramiro Valdés, a student from Artemisa and a Moncada veteran.[20] Trapote's studio became another centre of meetings for the 26 July Movement.[21] In August 1955 Castro sent back to Havana (by the hands of Ondina Pino, sister of Orquídea, in a hollowed-out copy of Garcilaso's *History of the Incas*) a document for the 'militants' of the Ortodoxo party entitled *Manifiesto No. 1*. Prefaced by quotations from Martí and Maceo, this followed roughly the line of *History will absolve me*, containing a fifteen-point programme of reforms to be carried out within the spirit of 'our advanced' Constitution of 1940. That old anarchist dream – 'distribution of land among peasant families' – reappeared as the first point; nationalization of public services, mass education, and industrialization figured importantly; but while there was an assurance that the 26 July Movement was led by 'new men without compromises with the past', Castro insisted that he was still an Ortodoxo and spoke of the pure principles of Chibás: 'We do not constitute a tendency within the party; we are the revolutionary apparatus of Chibásismo.'[22] Certainly all close followers of Castro appear still to have been Ortodoxos in outlook. Thus the early adherents in Mexico were Fernando Sánchez Amaya, who had been living there before Castro arrived; Pedro Miret, the ex-Moncadaista, engineering student and cartographer, who arrived from Havana; Juan Manuel Márquez, Ortodoxo ex-city counsellor for Marianao who had been beaten up by the police in Havana in June. The housing for these early Fidelistas was partly arranged by 'a Cuban long resident in Mexico', in a rather military style, all acknowledging the leadership of a *responsable de casa*. Five to ten people lived in each house. But as early as September 1955 Batista's secret service chief, Colonel Orlando Piedra,[23] arrived in Mexico, and a curious cat-and-mouse game of observation and betrayal began which was to last for over a year in Mexico City and its surroundings.

Back in Cuba the democratic mellowing of the regime continued. On 11 August 1955, Prío (who had been covered by the same amnesty as Castro) nerved himself to come home. Accompanied by much enthusiasm, he went first to the Hotel Nacional, then to his famous farm,

[20] Afterwards Minister of the Interior in Cuba.
[21] Discussion with Trapote, August 1962.
[22] *Manifiesto Numero 1 del 26 de Julio al Pueblo de Cuba*, August 1955. See Draper, *Castroism*, 10; and Conte Agüero, *Dos Rostros*, 104–7.
[23] Colonel Orlando Piedra Negueruela, chief of Buró de Investigaciones.

La Chata where a great rally of his supporters, old friends and place-men, assembled eagerly. There was a call for the mending of relations with Grau, and Prío said he would henceforth oppose Batista only through the ballot box. In September Prío was found working on 'a programme to attract the whole nation', although he said that he himself would not run in any election. On 1 October he addressed a large audience, perhaps 50,000, in the large square facing Havana's Ward Line piers. The critical point in his speech was a denunciation as illegal of all governmental acts carried out since 1952. Another big meeting followed in Santa Clara, but Prío failed to make much head-way in uniting the opposition, though he somewhat disturbed the government: 'The only solution with Prío is to kill him, kidnap him or expel him from Cuba,' General Tabernilla said to Batista, who knew better and said, 'Pancho, you know nothing about this sort of thing, you are mad.'[24]

The most favourable chance for uniting the opposition was a new movement formed specifically with that aim in view, the Sociedad de Amigos de la República (SAR: Society of Friends of the Republic). The moving spirit of this group was Cosme de la Torriente, then aged eighty-three, survivor of all the turbulent events in the history of the independent Cuban Republic; of the war against Spain; of Wood's and Estrada Palma's administrations; Foreign Minister under Menocal and Mendieta; leader of the Cuban delegation to the League, and, since 1938, retired, directing the Revista de la Habana.[25] In mid-October he sought an interview with Batista to try to persuade him there and then to hold elections. But Batista refused, on the grounds that De la Torriente had no status and no standing to make such demands. De la Torriente decided to hold a mass meeting in Prío's style, and, miraculously, the other opposition leaders decided to do nothing until then.[26]

The meeting was held on the waterfront on 19 November, the purpose being to force new elections during the course of 1956. All the opponents of Batista except the Communists were present. The crowd filled the space between the Alameda de Paula and the Customs House. The platform was remarkable for its catholicity. Apart from the venerable Don Cosme there was also present the young José Antonio Echevarría, newly elected president of the students (FEU); Raúl Chibás, president of the Ortodoxos; Carlos Prío; Grau San Martín; Dr Miró Cardona, president of the Bar Association; Pardo Llada, the radio commentator; Amalio Fiallo (of the Radical party), José Andreu (Democrat) and

[24] Suárez Núñez, 68.

[25] See Cosme de la Torriente, *Cuarenta años de mi vida* (1940).

[26] See the excellent summary of this period in *Hispanic American Report*, November–December 1955.

Rogelio Pina, the secretary of the newly formed SAR. The 26 July Movement did not take part and indeed had tried to dissuade the Ortodoxos from so doing.[27] The meeting marked a high point in the history of the democratic opposition. But afterwards nothing happened. Batista was secure in his palace, and amiably told newspapermen that such meetings were good for the country. He refused to discuss the idea of elections until 1958: though he would on the other hand be prepared to talk to Don Cosme.[28]

The renewed inaction brought new student riots, in both Santiago and Havana. Sorties against the police were made under the pretext of honouring martyrs. Many students were arrested, many wounded, some beaten up, some tortured; and on 10 December Raúl Cervantes, president of the Ortodoxo youth, was shot dead by police in Ciego de Avila. On 16 December the Rector of Havana University, Dr Clemente Inclán, a paediatrician, successfully persuaded the FEU to cease demonstrations and to return to work at least for a time. But the student leaders, headed by Echevarría, founded a new organization, the Directorio Revolucionario, whose aims were to gather together all interested in fighting against Batista – workers as well as students.[29] The end of student protest furthermore was followed almost immediately by protests from the sugar workers, for economic purposes. Wage agreements had for several years provided that if the average price of sugar exceeded the average for the preceding year, bonuses based on the excess would be paid. In 1955 prices were such that workers expected a small bonus at Christmas. But the Sugar Institute had included in their calculations a 350,000-ton allotment of reserve sugar withdrawn from current stocks for sale in 1956, at an artificially chosen price of 2·77 cents per pound. The sugar leaders claimed the ultimate price of 5 cents.

In consequence Cuba was faced in mid-December by a 500,000-man labour strike beginning on 26 December. This threatened to paralyse the entire sugar harvest due to begin on 1 January. The Communists and the newly formed Directorio Revolucionario (with as yet unknown membership) supported the strike, as well as some Mujalistas, and at least one Communist striker, Bernardo Carreras, was killed by the army with

[27] Raúl Chibás, Memoirs, MSS, p. 34.

[28] HAR, December 1955. Daniel James says that an attempt was made to break up this meeting by the Communist party. He cites Flavio Bravo, later a critical figure in Castro's regime, as a leading figure in this attempt. Of this there is no other evidence. (See James, 95.)

[29] The relationship between FEU and Directorio Revolucionario was described in a supplement to *Alma Mater* (undated): 'The FEU because of its special character is an academic organization ... The Directorio Revolucionario is the instrument created, inspired and originated by the FEU ... to vertebrate the student body in an organized manner in its typically revolutionary work.'

rifle butts at Palos.[30] Some members of Castro's organization left behind in Cuba also participated, at their head David Salvador, a sugar workers' leader in Las Villas who had joined the 26 July Movement in Santiago.[31] Salvador, like many of Castro's early supporters, had already had a chequered career having been a Communist from 1939 to 1946, an Auténtico and Ortodoxo, and a backer of Aureliano Sánchez Arango's Triple A (1952-5). He now became for a time co-ordinator of the 26 July Movement in Havana.

Batista finally decided in favour of Labour on 30 December. But several sugar union officials tried to use this opportunity to capture control of their Labour organization from José Luis Martínez, the sugar workers' leader, and indirectly from Mujal. They refused to order their followers back to work after Batista's settlement, and sought to hold a plenary meeting of sugar workers in opposition to the established leaders. The rebels were immediately suspended and Martínez took over their offices by force. The sugar leaders in Congress, Conrado Bécquer, Conrado Rodríguez, and Jorge Cruz, thereupon went on a hunger strike at the House of Representatives. This strike was only ended after 168 hours by the intervention of Cardinal Arteaga. Bécquer did not return to his post as vice-secretary-general of the FNTA, and radio programmes which backed his action were suspended.[32]

Faced with these industrial difficulties Batista finally agreed to see Don Cosme de la Torriente. He did so on 29 December and again on 10 January. In the meantime there were certain bomb explosions, presumably let off by students or by the 26 July Movement, in Santiago. Six people were injured. Newspapers such as *Diario de la Marina* and *Información* denounced these activities: 'A noble, generous and valiant people who love peace cannot at any moment nor under any circumstances give their backing to any infamous delinquent who places a bomb . . . we must do everything possible to wipe out useless terrorism and terrorists' and 'We cannot permit the Martian gestures just started to fail without making ourselves accomplices of an unpardonable civil cowardliness'.[33] The Martian gestures were Don Cosme's offers at compromise.

Batista had now been in power again for nearly four years. In that time many people had become committed to him. He enjoyed the sympathy of many North Americans, not only the ambassador. The few bombs exploding in back streets and Castro's activity in Mexico seemed like freak hailstorms, disagreeable, inexplicable but unimportant

---

[30] Roca, VIIIth Congress, p. 24.

[31] David Salvador, born Ciego de Avila, 1923: secretary-general of the Cuban trade unions, 1959-60; in prison since 1960.

[32] *Havana Post*, 27 January 1956.

[33] 'Martian', of course, in Cuba means pertaining to José Martí.

and soon forgotten. Articles describing the health of the Cuban economy often appeared in the U.S. press: tourism in 1955 had been higher than ever before; the $M34 expansion of the U.S. government's Nicaro nickel plant was estimated as one quarter complete; car sales in 1955 were expected to be up 20% over 1954; Havana bank clearings on 1 December 1955 were 15% ahead of figures registered the previous year. Both national income and national output were 7% over 1954.[34] At the same time, a building boom was under way in Havana. Private building permits granted in 1955 in Havana province rose to 3,400 compared with 2,376 in 1952.[35] Many nineteenth-century houses in the Vedado were being torn down and in their place skyscrapers, such as the FOCSA apartment building and the Havana Hilton, were going up. Havana was being transformed. Another centre of new building was the Plaza de la República, on the south, inland side of Havana, where some ministries were being moved from the old city. Plans were under way for even more lavish and grandiose hotels such as the Capri and the Riviera. Gambling was taking on a new lease of life, with a large number of casinos opening. Pornographic films could now be seen in the Shanghai cinema. The *Havana Post* described Cuba as bidding for the title of 'The Las Vegas of Latin America'.[36] The old Hotel Nacional opened a casino in early 1956. Eartha Kitt, Maurice Chevalier, Lena Horne, and Nat King Cole appeared incessantly in Havana bars and night clubs. Fulgencio Batista, moving agreeably between the presidential palace and Campamento Columbia, with occasional visits to his old estate, Kuquine, handing out toys on the Día de Reyes, could have been forgiven if he concluded his position to be strong, and his crown firmly placed. 'The future looks fabulous for Havana,' said Wilbur Clark, a prince of croupiers, who had come from Las Vegas to operate a new casino at the Hotel Nacional.

When Batista saw Don Cosme on 10 January, he proposed that all future negotiations should be carried out by teams representing the two sides: Don Cosme agreed to consider this but, as Batista perhaps guessed would occur, he took a long time to consult everyone who wished to be consulted. Many tried to persuade Don Cosme that Batista was stalling and that he would in the end make no real concession, and certainly refuse any election in 1956. The Directorio Revolucionario, the new opposition force founded by the student leader Echevarría, in its first manifesto threw doubt on the political possibility of a real dialogue. The 26 July Movement did the same in more violent terms. The most persuasive force was nevertheless the writer (and ex-ABC

---

[34] See article by Ruth McCarthy, *Miami Herald*, 4 January 1956.
[35] U.S. Dept of Commerce, *Investment in Cuba* (1956), 98.
[36] See article, *Havana Post*, 19 January 1956.

member), Jorge Mañach, and he urged dialogue; and eventually at the end of January 1956 a committee representing each side was set up. Batista's men were the mayor of Havana, Pozo; the president of the Senate, Anselmo Alliegro; and various ministers (López Castro, Godoy, Álvarez, and Rey). Don Cosme's men were three Priístas (Tony Varona, Félix Lancís, Pablo Balbuena); and three Grauistas (Eduardo Suárez Rivas, Antonio Lancís and Miguel Hernández Bauzá). The Ortodoxos were Manuel Bisbé, Pelayo Cuervo and Dr Eduardo Corona. Others included the Movimiento de la Nación (Luis Botifoll, editor of *El Mundo*, José Pardo Llada and Enrique Huertas, a doctor); and various members of the amorphous Democratic party (Lincoln Rodón, Carlos Peláez, and Wilfredo Figueras).

The meetings began in March.

This *Diálogo Cívico* represented what turned out to be the last hope for Cuban middle-class democracy. But Batista clearly felt himself far too strong to have to make any concession. The *Havana Post*, expressing the attitude of the U.S. business community, after a survey of the four years of Batista's second reign, alluded to the disappearance of gangsterism and said: 'All in all, the Batista regime has much to commend it.'[37] But it was not only U.S. circles which backed the regime: all 'respectable' Cubans, such as read the *Diario de la Marina*, condemned student political militancy ('it is the university which is spoiling everything'). The opposition's demand for elections in 1956 was not acceptable; there could be nothing before November 1958.[38] On 11 March, in a radio and television speech, Batista publicly ridiculed Don Cosme's demands as absurd and on the 12th Don Cosme called a halt in all negotiations. A mood of doubt and depression swung over the political scene once more. Castro cleverly took the opportunity to issue from Mexico a new announcement separating himself from the Ortodoxos for good. This launched a catalogue of insults against the 'bad faith of the *políticos*', 'the intrigues of the incapable', 'the envy of the mediocre', 'the cowardice of the vested interests'. The latter suggested that under the guise of supporting the Constitution of 1940, Castro always had an inclination to break out of the bounds of normal democratic politics. Nevertheless he still held on to the father figure of Eddy Chibás. He broke with the Ortodoxo leaders but not the *'masas Chibásistas'*. He said that his movement was the 'revolutionary organization of the humble, for the humble, by the humble . . . the hope of renewal for the working class'. The 26 July Movement, he said, is a warm invitation to close ranks, extended

---

[37] *Ibid.*, Editorial, 19 March 1956, 4.
[38] Batista, *Cuba Betrayed*, 35, said that no decision was reached because of the opposition's demand for the immediate resignation of the government.

with open arms, to all the revolutionaries of Cuba, without petty party differences.[39]

His move was also prompted by a sudden revival of torturing and cruelty by the special police (SIM). In February there were three cases of atrocious police behaviour, firstly the case of a twenty-three-year-old student member of the Ortodoxos, Evélida González (a secretary of Castro's friend, Conte Agüero), secondly, that of a member of the Priísta youth organization, Antonio López Camejo; and thirdly, the case of José Carballo García who was beaten up in Las Villas. All were tortured by police agents to get information, the former on the interesting question of the relation between the 26 July Movement and the Ortodoxos. The revival of this behaviour by the *Batistiano* police left a dark stain and Batista's 'personal assurance' that the torturers would be discovered carried no conviction; the impression was that the police were out of control whenever they wished to be.[40]

[39] *Bohemia*, 1 April 1956.
[40] See *Havana Post*, 9–10 February, 1956, 12. Señorita González explained that her chief torturers were women, one black, one white.

CHAPTER 7

Castro in Mexico

Castro's movement in Mexico had had many ups and downs since its provisional establishment there the preceding summer. There were financial problems: Castro travelled to Miami and to New York in the autumn of 1955 in search of promoters, but his only big source of income was none other than ex-president Prío, always anxious to have his finger in almost any opposition activities. At the end of September, Castro met the ex-president of the Development Bank under Prío, Justo Carrillo, at Mérida, Yucatán; Carrillo was at this time working, as Castro must have known, with a group of left-wing officers to overthrow Batista by *golpe de estado*; and Castro asked him for the mayoralty of Havana after Batista's defeat if Carrillo should triumph.[1] Carrillo promised him instead 'a job in which you can apply all your energy, achieve a function of high usefulness and convert yourself into a constructive representative of your generation'.

Other sympathizers who gave money at this stage included Venezuelan exiles such as Romulo Betancourt, and some Mexicans. Castro also raised some money through appeals at meetings in the U.S., organized usually by Ortodoxo exiles. He appointed Juan Manuel Márquez as his representative in Miami, and from Miami brought back a military instructor in the shape of Miguel Sánchez, known as El Coreano, because, though a Cuban, he had fought in the U.S. army in the Korean war.[2] Another military instructor was an old Cuban-Spaniard, Alberto Bayo.

Bayo was born in Cuba, son of a Spanish officer and a mother from Camagüey, and joined first the Spanish army, and then its air section, sided with the Spanish Republic in the civil war and led the famous but unsuccessful expedition to Majorca in the summer of 1936: later he led guerrilla expeditions in Castille. A man of varied experience, he fought in the Moroccan wars as well as the civil war; he founded the first civil air school in Spain, and wrote books about whatever he had done, not to speak of novels, poetry and technical handbooks. Probably it was this considerable knowledge of the world and of past conflict

---

[1] Carrillo MSS, p. 7.
[2] F. Sánchez Amaya, *Diario del Granma* (1959).

that commended Bayo to Castro.[3] In the past he had been a Mason and a Socialist, and had been refused admittance to London by a prejudiced immigration officer.[4] Due to that and other accidents in the course of the Spanish Civil War he had developed a not unjustifiably hostile and jaundiced view of the role of England in contemporary international affairs.[5] Though he had begun the Spanish war as a Socialist of the Right, by the end he was to be found among Negrín's supporters, partly because he had been aide to Prieto in his most pessimistic period. Afterwards in Mexico, as director of the School of Military Aviation or as president of the Casa de la Democracia Española, Bayo had invariably taken a Popular Front line, and in the previous fifteen years at least once trained young Spanish Communists as *guerrilleros* to return to Spain.[6] Bayo was one of those whom the Spanish war had convinced that the Communists were often more resolute and brave than others;[7] but he had not kept his instructions for them, since he also helped to train a group of young anti-Communist fighters against the Somozas, the dictators of Nicaragua.

Bayo, El Coreano and a Cuban named José Smith began the preliminary military training of Castro's men in the autumn of 1955 at a firing range, Las Guamitas, in Santa Fe, a suburb of Mexico City. Castro attempted to establish military discipline, keeping the recruits in houses under the orders of a commander. But there came a serious setback when a number of the group (Cándido González, Montané, Máximo Celaya) were arrested for illegal holding of firearms and held in the Pocito prison, when they underwent the normal disagreeable, brutal treatment of Mexican prisons.[8]

The Mexican and *Batistiano* police[9] probably collaborated in this action: there was at least one attempt on Castro's life, no doubt by a Batista agent, in the style of Magriñats murder of Mella. A cache of arms which Castro kept in Sierra Madre Street, in the agreeable suburb of Lomas de Chapultepec, was confiscated. After this, Castro resolved to find a more remote place for training and set up a new base at the farm *Santa Rosa*, borrowed from a certain Señor Rivera (a survivor

[3] Castro first met Bayo in July 1955 (Alberto Bayo, *Mi Aporte a la Revolución Cubana* (1960), 15).

[4] See Bayo, *Mi Desembarcó en Mallorca* (1944), 298-9.

[5] e.g. the attempted espionage of the then Wing-Commander R. V. Goddard and Squadron Leader Pearson in 1938 (Bayo, *ibid.* 327-35).

[6] *Ibid.*, 352-3.

[7] 'I am not a Communist even though I admire them and I believe them to be admirable people' (Bayo, *Mi Desembarcó*, 126).

[8] See Oscar Lewis, *The Children of Sánchez* (1961); Sánchez Amaya, 16-17.

[9] Sánchez Amaya speaks of Colonels Cartaya and Maymir of the SIM as being on the trail. However, Colonel Cartaya, at least, suffered from too close contact with the revolutionaries, for on his return to Cuba he was submitted for eleven days to torture and left the 5th Police Station of Havana with six broken ribs. See his statement to *Revolución*, 24 January 1959, 8.

of Pancho Villa's army) on misleading assumptions,[10] in the Chalco district, twenty miles outside Mexico City. Here an even more rigid life was instituted. Passports were confiscated. Trainees were not allowed off the ranch except at specified hours. Sex life was controlled.[11] Letters to Cuba were kept to a minimum. Bayo successfully persuaded Castro to abandon the idea of frontal attack for guerrilla war – an idea which he had at first found repugnant. Discussion with unknown people was forbidden. The men of the 26 July Movement left *Santa Rosa* in batches. Early on, political instruction as well as military training began, though it seems that this was not much more than discussion led by certain prominent members of the group, such as the recorder of property, Dr Electro Pedrosa, Fernando Sánchez Tamayo, Universo Sánchez or Antonio López. None of these had either advanced or coherent political ideas. On the other hand, Bayo talked a great deal about the Spanish war, filling the minds of the young revolutionaries with heroic memories of past tragedies and betrayals.[12]

In the autumn of 1955 Castro was still empirical in what precisely his little force was striving for: for example he seems to have had conversations with some of the Cuban Communists in Mexico at that time, such as Joaquín Ordoqui, Lázaro Peña and Blas Roca. But a conversation is not a conversion. A number of his followers in the Moncada attack, such as Mario Dalmau, Calixto García and 'Ñico' López, had been in exile in Guatemala where some had worked with the revolutionary government until its overthrow in mid-1953 and therefore, when they arrived in Mexico, contributed a new bitterness and probably a new hostility to the U.S. More important from the point of view of what eventually occurred was Castro's meeting in late 1955 with Ernesto Guevara, known as 'Che'[13] Guevara, an Argentinian then aged twenty-six, a medical graduate of the University of Buenos Aires.[14]

Guevara came from a *bourgeois* family in Rosario, the second city of Argentina: his father, Ernesto Guevara Lynch, for a time ran a *mate* farm at Alta Gracia, near Córdoba, and both he and his wife Celia de la Serna (who owned the farm) were active in left-wing politics. His father had Irish blood through his mother, whilst his own mother was Spanish in origin. His family was Catholic but did not go to church

---

[10] See Bayo, 66–7.
[11] Daniel James says he saw receipts, etc., for budgets of this enterprise, covering, for example, $10,000 a month for training, $7,500 a month for food, $4,800 a month for propaganda, etc.
[12] *Cf.* Bayo, *passim*.
[13] 'Che' is the diminutive or affectionate for 'you' in Argentina, though he appears to have been called this from his middle twenties only, in Guatemala to begin with.
[14] In 1967 Castro said that he met Guevara in 'July or August 1955' (*Granma*, weekly edn, 29 October 1967), but this was probably a bit early. See Ricardo Rojo, *Che Guevara*, Paris, 1969, 66, where the meeting is described as late November. Guevara was born 14 July 1927.

much, though his sisters had been confirmed. Guevara *père* had taken part in anti-Perón plots and assisted Paraguayan revolutionaries.[15] Suffering from asthma from early in life, the son spent much time away from school, being educated partly by his mother and his four brothers and sisters. This goaded him into further study, at first in engineering. The family moved to Buenos Aires in 1944 but apparently went downhill financially.

Entering the university as an engineer, Guevara changed to medicine. An obituary notice remarked that 'interest in Baudelaire as well as sports tempered him both spiritually and physically'. Like Baudelaire, he had no ear for music. He worked for a while as assistant to Dr Salvador Pissani, an Argentinian heart specialist who specialized in allergies, with whom he was co-author of one or two scientific papers. As a student he travelled a good deal in Argentina, Peru and Chile, on bicycle and on foot, and he also visited Colombia and Venezuela. He seems to have had no contact with the Argentinian Communists[16] but his political interests appear to have been awoken by what he had seen in the rest of South America. Also, he had had several friends who were children of Spaniards exiled by or killed in the Spanish Civil War. The role of such politically aware children of Spain cannot be overestimated in discussing the Latin-American revolutionary experience. For a time he was engaged to a rich girl from Córdoba, but on graduation in March 1953, Guevara started again to travel, with a large library accompanying him; at first deciding to work in the Venezuelan leper hospital of Cabo Blanco where a student friend was already established, he was persuaded by an Ecuadorian lawyer, Ricardo Rojo, that 'Guatemala was the place to see' because of the revolutionary government there. On the way, he was arrested in Peru, and stayed some time in Ecuador and Panama where he wrote a number of semi-archaeological articles to pay his fare to Guatemala.

In Guatemala Guevara volunteered as a doctor in tropical diseases, in the jungle, but was unable to qualify quickly enough. He lived in Guatemala City and made his living 'selling things in rural areas'.[17] He met Antonio (Ñico) López, one of Castro's Moncada adherents and then an exile. Shortly, however, the Guatemalan government was overthrown as a result of the conspiracy of the U.S. Central Intelligence Agency and some right-wing Guatemalan officers. Guevara, taking refuge in the Argentinian Embassy, tried to be sent to the 'front' but

[15] Letter from him to Mario Llerena, Llerena MSS, 266–7.

[16] A friend of his youth, Fernando Barral, did join the Argentinian Communist Youth in 1946 but in an article in *Granma* (weekly edition, 29 October 1967), Barral said that it was precisely from then on that he ceased to see Guevara. Both Barral and Guevara were for a time attached to Guevara's cousin Negrita Córdoba, whose father was a *comunizante* poet.

[17] From an obituary by his first wife in *Granma*, 29 October 1967.

failed; but he apparently went on duty against air raids, tried to encourage the Guatemalans to fight, and by his own account 'saved lives and transported weapons'. He eventually left Guatemala for Mexico by means of the Argentine Embassy.

Guevara came out of his experience in Guatemala immensely hostile to the U.S., its final destroyer. He had not been to the U.S., but from that time regarded with suspicion anyone who had merely lived there for any length of time.[18]

In Mexico City Guevara worked as a street photographer, in company with another exile from Guatemala, 'El Patojo', Julio Cáceres,[19] whom he had met *en route*. Perhaps through the influence of Lombardo Toledano, Guevara got a job in Mexico City in the allergy ward at the general hospital: he also did some lecturing at the university. Afterwards, he went to work at the Institute of Cardiology, on the recommendation of Dr Concepción Palacios.

In late 1955 Guevara was a revolutionary but not necessarily a Marxist, if by that is understood simply a view that the changing means of production are the fathers to political change. On the other hand, he believed in the perfectibility of man, he despised the profit motive and thought that it could be quickly eradicated. According to a Cuban, Mario Dalmau, whom he met in Guatemala, he had 'read' everything written by Marx and Lenin, and had with him a complete library of their works. He was 'a complete Marxist'.[20] To his wife, Hilda Gadea, a Peruvian and an Aprista (whom he left behind in Lima), he appeared as a puritanical, intelligent and practical man who had already experienced one revolution and how it had failed: through the government failing to destroy the army and through the U.S. intervention from outside. He already believed in the purgative effects of revolution as such, believing (as he later put it) that 'revolution cleanses men, improving them as the experimental farmer corrects the defects of his plant'.[21] On the other hand, he was able to classify himself a few years later as a Trotskyist or an ex-Peronist and, though this was at a time when he was about to begin to use the Communists in Cuba, he may have been telling the truth.[22] Perhaps the explanation of his character is

[18] Seven years later, however, he apparently admitted that 'the model whom we must cite as closest [to] the man most resembling man of the future society [is] the North American . . . the product of a developed economy, of modern technology, of abundance . . . A revolutionary Cuban, Vietnamese, or Algerian of today [is] less like the man who is going to shape the Communist society than a Yankee . . . we men are children of the economic métier. But should this truth be told?' (S. Cazalis, *La República* (Caracas), February 1966).

[19] Ernesto (Che) Guevara, *Pasajes de la Guerra Revolucionaria*, 123; Hilda Gadea, article in *Granma*, 29 October 1967 (weekly edition).

[20] Mario Dalmau, *Granma*, 29 October 1967. This story about the books is borne out by the stories in *Bohemia*, July 1956, on the occasion of Guevara's arrest.

[21] Guevara, *op. cit.*, 124.

[22] To Luis Simón, in September 1958 (Luis Simón, MSS).

to be found in his ambiguous family, where extreme Left sentiments were combined with *haut-bourgeois* living, an extremely frequent phenomenon in Latin countries, and one which must greatly irritate those brought up in it; in addition the family was, though *bourgeois*, declining and Guevara's mother was evidently a stronger influence than his father.

In November 1955 Guevara met Castro, and the two talked for a long time one night in the house of a Cuban exile, María Antonia González de Paloma, in the Lomas de Chapultepec, whence, for a few hours at dawn, Mount Popocatépetl can be seen.[23] Guevara saw Castro as possessing the characteristics of a 'great leader', such as perhaps in his wanderings he had been seeking.[24] In 1962 Guevara described himself as being from the first drawn to Castro as a romantic adventurer who, however, had the courage to risk death for a noble cause.[25] He enrolled in Castro's army, as a doctor and as a *guerrillero*. As such, he was very successful at the *Santa Rosa* estate, far the most intelligent of the pupils of Colonel Bayo,[26] though he was evidently always antimilitary in an orthodox sense.[27]

Perhaps under the influence of this new friendship Castro wrote an article which appeared in *Bohemia* on 25 December 1955. This once again criticized those who in Cuba 'did nothing' against Batista, denounced the Auténticos and proclaimed its author free of all public corruption: '*Contra mundum*' seemed his battle-cry (though this was a moment when there did, on the contrary, seem to be a chance of negotiation between Batista and Don Cosme de la Torriente). In February a Havana Urgency Court formally ordered Castro's arrest.[28] Nevertheless Castro waited till the *Diálogo Cívico* had collapsed before writing on 19 March a public resignation from the Ortodoxos. He also announced the formation of the 26 July Movement as a separate one from Ortodoxia, as it had in reality always been; and he denounced the *Diálogo Cívico* as playing into Batista's hands. His own goals, he said, remained the same: 'For the Chibásist masses, the 26 July Movement is not distinct from Ortodoxia'.[29]

---

[23] In his letter of farewell to Castro in 1965 Guevara recalled this meeting: 'At this moment I remember many things – when I met you at María Antonia's house, when you suggested my coming, all the tensions involved in the preparations.' (Castro speech, 3 October 1965, Cuban Embassy, London, Inf. Bull. No. 97, p. 13.) The house is Amparán, No. 49.

[24] '*Tiene las características de gran conductor*' (*Verde Olivo*, 9 April 1961).

[25] *Bohemia*, 30 November 1962.

[26] 'Guevara overtook all the others because of his great learning and dedication to study and observation.' (Bayo, 76.)

[27] *Cf.* his remark in 1963 to the journalist Cazalis at a detention camp at Guahanacabibes: 'No, no, not One! Two! Three! Four! Military discipline makes me vomit.' (*La República*, Caracas, February 1966.)

[28] *Havana Post*, 4 February 1956.

[29] Du Bois, 121–4. See also Draper, *Castroism*, 10–11.

It hardly seems possible that Castro had already decided on what line he would follow if he gained power, since the capture of power seemed infinitely remote. In early 1956 he was merely one among many Cuban exile and opposition leaders, even if he was younger, more determined, more optimistic and indeed more politically subtle than the others. Even the guerrilla tactics and the military training at the farm *Santa Rosa* were based more on the experience of Spain than of China: Guevara later said that he and his friends only knew of Mao's book of guerrilla warfare after they had reached the Sierra Maestra, and he later spoke of Bayo as '*el maestro*', so far as the guerrillas were concerned. As for Castro himself, the older Cuban exile Teresa Casuso described him as he seemed to her, a little later, on the edge of strife, among a group in a prison yard in Mexico:

> Tall and clean-shaven, and with close-cropped chestnut hair, dressed soberly and correctly ... standing out from the rest by his look and his bearing ... He gave one the impression of being noble, sure, deliberate, like a big Newfoundland dog ... eminently serene ... He gave me a greeting of restrained emotion, and a handshake that was warm without being overdone. His voice was quiet, his expression grave, his manner calm, gentle ... he had a habit of shaking his head like a fine thoroughbred horse ... His basic point, the fixed star, was 'the People' ... Fidel showed that he had read a great deal of José Martí who seemed indeed to be the guiding spirit of his life ... The plans he revealed seemed beyond his reach and I felt a kind of pity for this aspiring deliverer who was so full of confidence and firm conviction and I was moved by his innocence ... [yet] I could not give myself up to the intense admiration which he inspired in his group of young men ... Fidel and his band of young men seemed to me to be a lost cause.[30]

Castro's letter of resignation from the Ortodoxos hardly had much effect, for one reason above all: other plotters were at work. During the early part of 1956 a series of conspiracies were made to overthrow Batista, partly from Cuba itself, partly from the neighbouring dictatorship, the Dominican Republic, where Leonidas Trujillo, the Benefactor on high heels, still ruled implacably as he had done for a quarter of a century.

Cuban-Dominican relations had never been very good, at least since the abortive Cayo Confites expedition of 1947. Batista tried to differentiate himself from his fellow dictator, and indeed there was a gap between them: Batista clearly was a dictator who wished always to be loved, a democratically elected president: Trujillo did not mind being

[30] Casuso, 92 ff.

feared. Batista was less himself a torturer than a weak man surrounded by cruel ones whom he could not control. Bad relations between the two governments were exacerbated by the murder in Havana in January of a Dominican democratic exile, 'Pipi' Hernández, then a foreman at the Havana Hilton under construction in Vedado. It seemed clear that he had been murdered by agents of Trujillo, and, a few days later, several gangsters who had been associated earlier with the action groups of the 1940s were implicated. Among these was most important, a group led by N. Nasser, who had assaulted the Royal Bank of Canada, and Vizoso, an extortionist killed in a gun battle with the police.[31] In February counter-allegations began to implicate Batista's chief of staff and old friend General Tabernilla in plots against the Dominican Republic,[32] while the Ortodoxo chief, Pelayo Cuervo, in March accused other army leaders in Cuba of taking Trujillo's money and support in plotting against the government. On 12 March Trujillo carried out one of his biggest crimes – the kidnapping and eventual murder of Jesús Galíndez, leader of the Basque Nationalists in the Spanish Civil War and afterwards professor in Santo Domingo and in New York. Galíndez was kidnapped in New York, when preparing to publish an authoritative attack on Trujillo, and flown to Santo Domingo apparently by a young U.S. pilot, Gerald Murphy, a friend of various anti-Batista union leaders in Cuba such as Cálixto Sánchez.[33] The truth of this disgraceful affair has never been fully brought to light. There were various notes sent, rumours of war, complaints to the OAS, between Cuba and the Dominican Republic, and, in a jumpy mood, the SIM tried to round up all known enemies of the government, at least those on the right or gangster wing.

This nervousness on the part of the SIM was further encouraged by the appearance in Masferrer's journal, *Tiempo en Cuba*, on 18 March, of a report of a conspiracy led by Policarpo Soler, the Auténtico gangster who had been in Santo Domingo since 1952. Among those arrested were Cándido de la Torre, ex-city councillor; Hirigoyen, the bus workers' leader; Menelao Mora, an ex-Auténtico deputy; Echevarría, the student leader; and several Spanish exiles such as Carlos Gutiérrez Menoyo, Daniel Martín and Ignacio González. The SIM also made a bid to lay hands on several political gangsters such as the famous *el Extraño*. On 20 March a number of others involved with these plotters

[31] See *Havana Post*, 17 January 1956. One of the arrested murderers, Félix Oscar Gaveria Guerra, had been a policeman in De la Fé's ministry. Others involved were Ulises Sánchez Hinojosa and Rafael Eugenio Grafta (see *ibid.*, 28 February 1956). *El Caribe*, 12 August 1956, stated that Sánchez Hinojosa had returned from Cuba, after an 'intelligence mission', to rejoin the police in Santo Domingo.

[32] See *ibid.*, 15 February 1956.

[33] For the Galíndez case, see Ornes, *Pequeño Tirano del Caribe*; Bosch; Galíndez; and Basaldúa's tribute to Galíndez, Pedro de Basaldúa, *Jesús de Galíndez* (?1960).

were arrested, such as the head of the national lottery under Prío, Colonel Artigas, who had unwisely returned to Cuba; Prío's ex-secret service chief, Eufemio Fernández; and ex-congressman Esteva Lora.[34]

After these arrests a group of intelligent younger officers known as the *Puros*,[35] headed by the military attaché in Washington, Colonel Ramón Barquín, decided to make a long prepared strike against Batista. These men, though opposed to Batista and Batista's new establishment of officers, were not senior enough to have suffered in the general purge of the army of Prío's time. All had entered the army well after the revolution of 1933, were real professional men, and therefore had no hates or loyalties deriving from that time. Some of the *Puros* had been closely attached to the Ortodoxos before 10 March. Prío indeed had feared them, and by carefully removing them from central commands (it had been he who had appointed Barquín to Washington), had helped to make the way easier for Batista. Since then, the *Puros* had kept in touch with García Barcena and with the Ortodoxos. In April 1955 Barquín and Colonel Manuel Varela Castro, who commanded the Cuban tank regiment, took the lead of a number of young officers, among whom Majors Borbonnet and José Orihuela were prominent.[36] The plotters intended to take command of Campamento Columbia in orthodox *pronunciamiento* style. They planned not to kill Batista, but to put him on an aeroplane heading for the U.S.[37] They were, however, betrayed on 3 April 1956 by one of their number, the officer who was then the commander in La Cabaña and they and a large number of other officers only vaguely connected with them were arrested.[38]

This *golpe*, however unsuccessful, nevertheless marked a serious crisis for the Batista regime. Another group of army officers had taken shape with the nickname of *tanquistas*, men who wished to change Cuba from the limping democracy that it was even under Batista into the tougher totalitarian system which prevailed in the Dominican Republic. These were the men who had planned the *golpe* of 10 March, but had failed

---

[34] See *Havana Post*, 20 March 1956, and 21 March 1956.

[35] The name (signifying a cigar in Spanish and purer than pure in Cuban) was given to them contemptuously by Grau and it stuck.

[36] Others named were: Captains Ernesto Despaigne, Hugo Vázquez, José C. Ramos Avila, and Mateo Travieso (all of infantry); Lieutenants Manuel Villafaña and Réné Travieso (of the air force); and Lieutenant Guillermo J. Morales (*Havana Post*, 5 April 1956). See also Batista, *Cuba Betrayed*, 46. Barquín, *Bohemia* (8 February 1959), admitted that a number of Ortodoxos and like-minded men backed him: León Reduit, Vicente León, Justo Carrillo, Felipe Pazos, Diego Vicente Tejera, Fernando Leyva, Roberto Agramonte and Raúl Chibás. None of these was tried and only Carrillo was closely involved. He had been responsible for the selection of thirty-five to forty university trained young men to lead the police in Cuba after the success of the *golpe*.

[37] See Havana press, 10 and 11 April 1956, for trial report.

[38] Carrillo, MSS, p. 11.

to profit from it. In touch with Trujillo's army, they wanted to force Batista to carry through a totalitarian revolution, or else to abandon power to them. They were in touch too with Ernesto de la Fe and Senator Rolando Masferrer, the ex-leader of the MSR, and by now leader in Santiago of a large private army, *los Tigres*, trained (though inadequately) to carry out his merest whim. The *tanquistas'* plan was to stimulate disorder (even helping groups such as Castro's, which they hated) in order to justify their *golpe*, and their removal of constitutionalism. Batista would either have to be the figurehead or go. Thus the *tanquistas* spread a good many of Trujillo's arms about Cuba during early 1956, not really caring who had what, some going to Priístas, some to Castroists, while the *tanquistas* themselves held on to the tanks. But the defeat of the Puros' conspiracy not only revealed how badly the officers in Cuba were divided but gave such power to the Tabernillas that Batista was virtually their prisoner for the next two years. The *tanquistas* probably also helped *el Extraño* to get his hands on new caches of ammunition. But they clearly underestimated both the popularity of Batista in the rank and file of the army and the political guile of the dictator.[39]

Among the by now innumerable little groups in Cuba with gun-happy but patriotic and socially conscious *caudillos* was one surrounding Reynol García, an ambitious but unimportant Auténtico,[40] eager to make an attack on the government. What followed is hard to disentangle. Batista apparently prepared a trap for García in order to restrain the *tanquistas*. García was in his turn persuaded that if he arrived at the Goicuría barracks at Matanzas, the men would come over to him. He drove there with about a hundred men,[41] but he and nine others were killed, many wounded. At least one was killed after surrender[42] – a fact which was bitterly denounced. Prío, Varona and other Auténtico leaders were seized and questioned. Constitutional guarantees were suspended. Batista claimed that the opposition as a whole was now willing to kill innocent soldiers in its avid pursuit of power. He was thus able to assure the *tanquistas* that he was going to follow a tough policy at the same time as indicating that in difficult times like these it would be better to remain with the old leather-jacketed leader, the saviour of *la grulla*.[43] The suspension meant censorship, but in succeeding weeks the Cubans heard much in the press about captures of arms and further

---

[39] See the article by Javier Pazos, *Cambridge Opinion* (1963), 20.
[40] Ex-chauffeur to Aureliano Sánchez Arango.
[41] Some being Castro followers such as Israel Escalona, Julio César, Ernesto Carbonell, Casanova 'El guaguo'.
[42] See *Time*, 14 May 1956. *Life* magazine had photographs.
[43] Justo Carrillo, who was then with Castro in Yucatán, reports that Castro regarded this attack as opportunistic and irresponsible (MSS, p. 27). See *Havana Post*, 30 April 1956.

failures to catch *el Extraño*. Prío, blamed for Reynol García's attempt, was dispatched by Batista back to Miami, where he was nevertheless held before being allowed in[44] – administrative errors spoiling further the poor standing of the U.S. government with the Cuban opposition. It was not till June that Prío received permission to stay in the U.S.

The summer saw the climax of Batista's war of nerves with Trujillo. The Cuban Senate had empowered Batista to break relations with the Dominican Republic whenever he wanted. The Cuban police had claimed that Prío's contacts with Trujillo had been cemented by some of the men arrested in March, such as the Auténtico politician Menelao Mora, and Batista declared the Dominican minister *persona non grata*. Captain Esteban Ventura, the indefatigable police agent, found another cache of arms near Prío's farm. Policarpo Soler was charged with being concerned in June. Batista's aim was to implicate all his enemies with Trujillo, thereby making them seem, in the face of international public opinion, to be gangsters and gangsters based abroad, but this was difficult since it had already been his plan to involve Fidel Castro's group with the Communists. In late June yet another 'plot' was unearthed to kill Batista, this time affecting the Cuban matador, José Sánchez, again with the same old gangster names allegedly among his backers. Cuba, beneath a surface of prosperity, was a centre of warring gangs of gunmen, policemen, ex-ministers, officers, students, all out for 'supreme power', none collaborating genuinely with or 'implicated with' each other: thus, in Costa Rica, Eufemio Fernández's gang apparently betrayed some of Castro's supporters, and prevented them getting visas for Mexico, even though Fernández's backer Prío was then helping Castro.[45]

Castro's friends had now been training at the *Santa Rosa* farm for nine months. Castro himself kept in touch with all political groups; thus on 29 April he met Justo Carrillo in Tapachula, on the Guatemala-Mexican border, and while exchanging views about the *Puros'* plot, accepted $5,000 from him and the Montecristi movement. In addition Castro received money from López Vilaboy, president of Cubana Airways and a comrade of Batista – a gift he only accepted for lack of other help.[46] New waves of young men had come to join him, among them a group of ex-Moncada men from Costa Rica, where they had been in refuge. One of these was a well known gangster, Trujillo's

[44] *Havana Post*, 10 May 1956.
[45] Franqui, 23.
[46] Carrillo, MSS, 18–19. Carrillo criticized this and Castro replied that '*no tenía un centavo*' and therefore had had to. According to Carrillo, Castro spent some of the money he brought on a present for a girl: but, as Carrillo points out, Castro was usually forgiven for that sort of thing.

confidant, the hatchet-man Ricardo Bonachea; he turned out to be an informer. Probably in consequence the Mexican police, no doubt with Cuban police assistance, discovered their lair. Castro, Bayo, Guevara and twenty-one others were arrested on 24 July on charges of preparing an attack on another country.[47] A vast cache of arms was also captured. Mexican police, again in connivance with the Cuban SIM, apparently accused Castro of being in relation with the Communists in Mexico, saying that a visiting card of a Soviet official (Nikolai Leonov) had been found in his pocket and argued that he had had persistent contacts with the Cuban Communist Lázaro Peña, and with Lombardo Toledano. These allegations were reported in *Bohemia* in an article by a Spanish Mexican, Luis Dam. From prison on 3 July, Castro formally denounced the charges of being a Communist as 'absolutely fantastic'.[48] He also wrote a reply which appeared in the next week's issue of *Bohemia*. The whole incident, he charged, derived from a plot by the Batista regime and the U.S. Embassy. He added:

> What moral right on the other hand, does Señor Batista have to speak of communism when he was the presidential candidate of the Communist party in the elections of 1940, when his electoral slogans hid behind the Hammer and Sickle, when his photographs hung next to those of Blas Roca and Lázaro Peña, and when half a dozen of his present ministers and confidential collaborators were outstanding members of the Communist Party.[49]

To Justo Carrillo in April, Castro had said: 'The Communists will never be in a majority though their strength will grow in this struggle; afterwards . . . you will be important in the government; you also, like I, will prevent them from dominating.'[50]

Castro continued to attack the Communists, and they attacked him in reply. Some time earlier a young Negro student, Walterio Carbonell, was expelled from the Communist party for sending a telegram congratulating Castro: the party added, for good measure, 'The

[47] They were: Ciro Redondo, Universo Sánchez, Ramiro Valdés, Cálixto García, Oscar Rodríguez, Celso Maragoto, Alberto Bayo (*fils*), Jimmy Hutzel, María Antonia González, Almeida, Rolando Santana, Ricardo Bonachea López, Arturo Chaumont, Reinaldo Benítez, Luis Crespo, Tomás Electo Pedrosa, Agueldo Aguiar, Eduardo Roig, José Raúl Vega, Horacio Rodríguez and Víctor Trapote (a Spanish-Mexican painter). (*Bohemia*, 8 July 1956.) Julio Díaz, Cándido González and Alfonso Celaya had already been arrested (*Bohemia*, 15 July 1956, 85).

[48] See *Havana Post*, 4 July.

[49] *Bohemia*, 15 July 1956. Draper rightly comments that it is hard to imagine a Communist, open or concealed, defending himself by reminding the Communists of their old friendship with the dictator. (See *Castroism*, 28 ff.) Batista himself said that rumours of ex-President Cárdenas's support for the plotters was absurd, since he and Cárdenas were great friends (see *Havana Post*, 20 September 1956).

[50] '*Ud. también, como yo, va a impedir que ellos dominen*' (Carrillo, MSS, p. 18).

party rejects this kind of adventurist action which serves only to immolate dozens of young people in ruin ... those who are attempting to involve the newspaper *Hoy* with a filthy provocation ... entangling it in the adventure of Castro and his group.'[51] Ironically, within a few weeks, Castro found himself having to write another letter of self-defence, this time against the argument that he was allied with Trujillo.[52]

On 24 July the Mexican police released Castro and his friends on the condition that they left Mexico.[53] Castro was now in fact anxious to return to Cuba to resume the conflict; he had already issued a promise to be either dead or back by the end of 1956. Final training now continued in Mexican apartments, not Santa Rosa, in the Lomas de Chapultepec, the house of the Cuban exile Teresa Casuso, widow of the poet de la Torriente Brau, killed in the Spanish war, which was used as an arms store.[54] In August, by arrangement with Teresa Casuso, Castro swam across the Río Grande to meet, on the advice of Justo Carrillo, the newly-exiled Prío at Reynolo near the border. Prío agreed to back Castro with $100,000, of which the first $50,000 arrived within a few weeks.[55] Castro's cause prospered more, since he now had money not only to buy arms but also to bribe the Mexican police to keep away,[56] although he was hard put to rival Batista's resources for the same activity. In September, Castro also reached an agreement of collaboration in the so-called 'pact of Mexico', with the students' president and leader of the Directorio, Echevarría, though when Castro apparently suggested an alliance with the Cuban Communists, Echevarría vigorously refused and the matter was dropped as was any suggestion that the Directorio should place itself under Castro's lead.[57] Both Echevarría and Castro renounced any collaboration with Trujillo. But Prío was financing another expedition (with Eufemio Fernández and others) in the Dominican Republic, and Castro had to work hard to get his own

[51] Qu., S. Casalis (Siquitrilla), *La República* (Caracas), 4 February 1965. Carbonell was later (1967) imprisoned by Castro for trying to organize a Cuban version of the Black Power movement.

[52] See Du Bois, 27–33.

[53] *Havana Post*, 25 July 1956. Twenty minor members were allowed out in early July: the last three to go out were Castro, Universo Sánchez and Ciro Redondo.

[54] Casuso, 105. Teresa Casuso describes how at this time Castro made a new offer of marriage to a beautiful Cuban, was accepted, but finally dropped – leaving Castro once more affianced only to Revolution. Teresa Casuso first met Castro and his friends in prison which she visited.

[55] Carrillo, MSS, p. 21. This was September. Present with Castro were Juan Manuel Márquez, Montané, Melba Hernández, and Rafael del Pino (Du Bois, 134). The other $50,000 was a long time coming.

[56] Casuso, 112.

[57] Evidence of Dr Primitivo Lima of the Directorio. There were 'other differences of a doctrinal character'. The Directorio undertook to kill an important member of Batista's regime but when they did so, Castro formally disassociated himself.

movement started first 'so as not to be confused with those others',[58] at a moment when Prío was in touch with him too.

Back in Havana, the *Diálogo Cívico* seemed to have foundered. Pardo Llada fended off a challenge to a duel from the Speaker of the House, Godoy. The usual animosities among the Ortodoxos persisted: Raúl Chibás resigned from the Ortodoxo leadership, out of disagreement with Emilio Ochoa over plans to commemorate the death of Eddy Chibás, and what power there was in the movement seemed now to lie with Luis Conte Agüero, the radio commentator and Castro's old friend, who had become Ortodoxo secretary-general. The 26 July Movement in Havana was busy not only with sabotage and occasional terrorism but also trying to work out a coherent dogma – a sure sign of intellectual ambiguity – by establishing a commission to this effect.[59] In union politics, Conrado Bécquer and Conrado Rodríguez defeated the Mujalistas in their election, though Mujal, becoming more and more a grand defender of the established order, himself retained control of the CTC. Batista seemed on top of the *tanquistas* and the Tabernillas on top of him. He had just received a new supply of arms from the U.S., 'to help democracy in Cuba', as part of the 1952 agreement and, in July and August with, first, examinations and then holidays, the students were relatively quiet – apart from an incident on 10 September when Echevarría's second-in-command at the university, Fructuoso Rodríguez, led a group of student gunmen (including Echevarría's old opponent Leonel Alonso) into the TV Channel 2 Station. However, in October, a gratuitous act of violence occurred in Santiago when a former police captain, Arsenio Escalona, who was believed to be in sympathy with the opposition, was beaten, tortured and thrown into Santiago Bay. The chief of naval intelligence, Captain Alejandro García Olayón, was accused, but left undisturbed. The clouds of barbarism seemed to be indeed gathering when, with this crime unpunished, an attack was launched by several students of Echevarría's group, led by Juan Pedro Carbó Serviá, a medical student who had become prominent in the campaign between Echevarría and Alonso, together with Rolando Cubela, another middle-class student. These two and others attacked a group of policemen and officers of Batista's army in the early hours of 28 October, a Sunday morning, as they left the night club Montmartre in the Vedado. Killed immediately was Colonel

[58] 113. See Salas Cañizares's statement, in *Havana Post* (11 August 1956). In September, meantime, a meeting occurred in Mexico of the Congress for Cultural Freedom. The Cuban delegation included the Ortodoxo, Mario Llerena, and Raúl Roa, professor at Havana, and one of the leaders of the generation of 1933, who was reluctant to meet Castro since he associated him with the UIR and MSR of the late 1940s.

[59] Mario Llerena, MSS (14). Llerena says that he and Oltuski were the main members of the commission which was also occasionally attended by Carlos Franqui and once by Armando Hart.

Blanco Rico, the thirty-six-year-old chief of military intelligence, and wounded were Colonel Marcelo Tabernilla (son of the chief of staff) and his wife. Another officer's wife was slightly injured. The bleeding and bejewelled women reeled into mirrors in the foyer which, in their fright, they took for open space.[60] Carbó Serviá and Cubela fled through the casino to escape through the service entrance.

This attack was made by the students in order to draw the attention of the Cuban-American Press Association, then meeting in Havana, to the existence of disorder. Ironically, alas, the gunmen chose to kill almost the only prominent member of Batista's police who opposed torture during interrogation. Also the attack seems to have been carried out almost by accident: Carbó and Cubela were anxious to kill any important functionary of the Batista government and they saw Blanco Rico by accident. Had he not recognized them, they might not have fired.[61]

The aftermath was bloody. The police naturally went to work to find the killers and at noon the next day General Salas Cañizares and Colonel Orlando Piedra, with some men, went to the Haitian Embassy in Miramar, for what reason never became clear. The Haitian ambassador and his staff were at lunch. Within the Embassy were a number of Cubans who had taken sanctuary there, on the normal understanding prevalent in Spanish America that they would receive sanctuary. Most had been present several days; the others had arrived at 4 a.m. that day. Carbó Serviá and Cubela were not there. The police knocked at the door and firing began: who fired first is not clear. The police then entered the Embassy, breaking the sanctuary rule, shooting dead several of the refugees, capturing others and killing them afterwards: ten were killed. The police lost nobody, though General Rafael Salas Cañizares was wounded, and died on 31 October, with Batista and the prime minister, García Montes, at his bedside, not to speak of his three brothers, two colonels and a lieutenant. Six of the ten civilians killed had apparently been Auténticos, who had taken part in the attack on the Goicuría barracks in April. Two others had been involved in an attempt on Masferrer in Santiago; the other two appear to have been students.[62] According to one source close to Batista, the death of Salas Cañizares did not much sadden the president since it enabled him to get his own hands on the ex-police chief's gambling protection income – reputedly $730,000 a month.[63]

---

[60] *Excelsior* (Mexico), article by Aldo Baroni. See *Havana Post*, 30 October 1956; *New York Times*, 29 October 1956.

[61] Private information. See *Havana Post*, 1 December 1956, for identification of these two, after their escape, by Armando de Cárdenas. He alleged that they had been helped to get away by Prío's nephew, Dr Fernando Prío.

[62] See *Havana Post*, 31 October 1956. Salas Cañizares was succeeded by Colonel Hernando Hernández.

[63] Suárez Núñez, 25.

Daily the press carried stories about the activities of Prío or Castro, Sánchez Arango, or the gangsters of Santo Domingo who, it was believed, were about to strike at any moment. An ugly consciousness of the imminence of violence settled over the island. In Castro's case these apprehensions were real. Having failed to obtain a Catalina flying boat or a U.S. naval crash boat, he had now procured a 58-foot yacht, the *Granma*, bought with Prío's money from an American couple named Ericson; it cost $15,000.[64] On to this he could place nearly one hundred people, and he could sail it from Tuxpan to Oriente, where sixty years before Martí had landed. On 2 November the newspaper *Alerta* published an exclusive interview with Castro in which he declared himself ready to enter Cuba at all costs – a fact interesting not only for itself, but for the suggestion it made that Castro still had some communication with his old friend the editor of *Alerta*, Ramón Vasconcelos, despite the fact that he had entered Batista's government.

In mid-November, just before the 26 July Movement was about to set off, a large cache of arms was captured by the Mexican police in Teresa Casuso's house. She, Pedro Miret and Ennio Leyva, who had been looking after these supplies, were arrested. Castro had this time apparently been betrayed by Rafael del Pino, his old companion at Bogotá, and one of his closest companions in the meantime; they had collaborated together in an attempt on Masferrer's life too, in the 1940s. Guilty or not, Del Pino had left the 26 July Movement before this disaster and was always blamed afterwards.[65] Batista, as a matter of fact, knew everything that was going on in Mexico, and according to one source he had turned down both an offer to murder Castro and to burn the boat in which he proposed to embark for Cuba.[66]

These events led Castro to move as quickly as possible on to Cuba. His organizer in Cuba, the Baptist school teacher Frank País, had come to Mexico a few weeks before to coordinate (and incidentally warn against) a rising in Santiago at the end of November, the moment when Castro planned to land (Melba Hernández had also returned from Cuba with the same message). On 21 November Castro himself was given three days by the Mexicans to leave Mexico City. He and most of his men did so, going to Vera Cruz, some leaving without training of any kind,[67] and only the leaders knowing exactly what they were going to do.

[64] Martínez Arará erroneously states it as $20,000.
[65] HAR, XII, 431. Goldenberg evidence *re* Masferrer; Du Bois, 13; Casuso, 117. After he was suspected, Del Pino was sent by Castro to Ciudad Victoria where a group of Cubans had been sent under Faustino Pérez. Del Pino stole a pistol and left for the U.S. whence he only returned in 1959 to lead an abortive expedition against Castro and to receive a thirty-year sentence.
[66] Suárez Núñez, 35.
[67] Bayo, *Mi aporte*, p. 163.

Before they left Castro had no time to prepare any new manifesto.[68] His ideas no doubt were much as they were when he wrote to Melba Hernández, on 4 October:

The 26th of July [Movement] is constituted free of hate for anyone. It is not a political party, but a revolutionary movement. Its ranks are open to all Cubans who sincerely desire to re-establish political democracy and to implant social justice in Cuba. Its leadership is collective and secret, formed by new men of strong will who bear no responsibility for the past. The Cuban Revolution will achieve all reforms within the spirit and practice of our enlightened Constitution of 1940, without depriving anyone of what he legitimately possesses and indemnifying any interest that is injured . . . The Cuban Revolution will punish with a firm hand all acts of violence committed against the tyranny and will repudiate and repress all manifestations of ignoble vengeance inspired by hate or base passions.[69]

On 19 November Castro told a reporter from *Alerta* that he would be willing to desist from any invasion if Batista would accept a seven-point programme including Batista's own resignation, general elections within ninety days, a break of diplomatic relations with Trujillo, and amnesty for political prisoners.[70] One Havana intellectual who had met him in late summer 1956 thought that 'the possibility of [Castro] taking a too radical course did not cross my mind. On the contrary, my worry was that he might slide down the easy slope of traditional politics'.[71] In this mood, uncommitted, on 25 November the *Granma* sailed. Castro had crossed the Rubicon, emulating his hero Caesar as well as Martí. Ahead of him in Cuba, the only force making for peace, the Society of Friends of the Republic, remained inactive, due to the intransigence of Batista, and to the illness of Don Cosme de la Torriente. The future could hold only violence.

As often in the history of Cuban revolutions, this action contrasted with short-term prospects for prosperity. Ever since 1948 Cuba had made efforts not to maintain but to increase her share in the U.S. sugar market. These had failed. In 1956 the U.S. introduced new changes to her sugar law by which her domestic producers won most of the market created by enlarged demand in the U.S. (itself the product of increased population) and also shared out any deficit among them.

[68] The document dated November 1956 entitled *Nuestra Razón*: *Manifiesto-Programa*, was in fact not written (by Mario Llerena) until mid-1957. See Draper, *Castroism*, 12.

[69] As qu., James, 528.

[70] See *Havana Post*, 20 November 1956.

[71] Llerena, MSS, p. 27. Llerena adds, however, that he personally then told Castro that 'the 26th of July Movement . . . should let itself off from whatever ties it might still have with political organizations of the past'. Castro then said, 'We'll come to that . . . but at the beginning we cannot put every card on the table.'

But the immediate effects of this were overcome by the revision of the 1953 convention, in order to increase Cuban participation in the world market by 150,000 tons (though not her share, which dropped from 41·7% to 40·9%), and by the Suez crisis in October. The consequences of this were to raise sugar prices advantageously in the winter of 1956–7 and to promise well for 1957. There was also in this winter a drop in European and Russian beet production.[72] Thus Castro's revolution began in earnest at the moment when, as in 1895 at the time of Martí's landing in Cuba, the short-term prospects for Cuban sugar capitalism were promising.

[72] *Cf. Estudio*, 98–9.

CHAPTER 8

The Granma and the Sierra Maestra

The *Granma* left Tuxpan, Mexico, in the night of 24–5 November 1956, with eighty-two men on board.[1] As at Moncada, the majority were white Cuban townsmen, though more of them had a higher education than at Moncada.[2] Twenty out of the eighty-two had taken part in the attack at Moncada or Bayamo in 1953. There were four non-Cubans on board – Guevara, from Argentina; Gino Doné, an Italian;[3] Guillén, a Mexican; and the pilot Ramón Mejías del Castillo ('Pichirilo'), a Dominican who had been on the abortive Cayo Confites expedition. One Guatemalan, Julio Cáceres, a friend of Guevara's, was turned down because Castro did not want a 'mosaic of nationalities'.[4]

Castro, supreme commander, took the rank of major. There were beneath him three platoons of twenty-two men each under 'captains' Raúl Castro, Juan Almeida and José Smith.[5] Guevara was in charge of health. The captain of the ship was an ex-captain in the Cuban navy, Onelio Pino, seconded by ex-Lieutenant Roberto Roque.[6]

The expedition set off in high spirits, though some friends in Mexico refused to take part on the grounds that it was doomed.[7] They had on board two anti-tank guns, thirty-five rifles with telescopic sights, fifty-five Mendoza rifles, three Thompson light machine guns and forty light hand machine gun pistols. The voyage took seven days due to ill-direction: sea-sickness and overcrowding lowered the euphoria, but by 1 December

---

[1] It is no doubt a misprint that caused Guevara to speak of '83' people on board (see *Geografía de Cuba*, 574), though it is an odd error to have made; the same error, rather curiously, was made by 'General' Bayo, in his enumerated list of men on the *Granma*; he reckoned the pilot, Mejías del Castillo, twice (*Mi Aporte a la Revolución Cubana*, 167–9). Photographs of most of the *Granma* men were published in *Revolución*, 2 December 1959.

[2] Guevara was misleading when he said in 1960 that 'none of the first group who arrived in the *Granma* . . . had a past of worker or peasant' (*Obra Revolucionaria*, No. 24, 16 September 1960, 21).

[3] Erroneously referred to by Guevara as 'Lino' in his book.

[4] Guevara, *Pasajes*, 122.

[5] Castro's headquarters was composed of: Juan Manuel Márquez, Faustino Pérez, Antonio López, Jesús Reyes, Cándido González, Onelio Pino, Roberto Roque, Jesús Montané, César Gómez, Ramón Mejías del Castillo, and Rolando Moya (Sánchez Amaya evidence, as qu., *Revolución*, 26 January 1959). The three platoons were divided into three sections commanded by a lieutenant and a sergeant.

[6] Pino was the brother of Orquidea Pino, married to the Mexican oil engineer, Alfonso Gutiérrez, in whose house, in El Pedregal de San Angel, Castro and his friends often met.

[7] e.g. The Spanish painter, Víctor Trapote, father-in-law to Ramiro Valdés.

when the *Granma* approached the south-west corner of Oriente province, enthusiasm returned. On 30 November the men on board heard by radio the news of the rising against Batista in Santiago, led by Frank País, to coordinate with the *Granma*'s arrival.[8] None of the force had had much to do with the Communist party except for 'Ñico' López who had visited Communist exiles in Mexico, such as Ordoqui.

Frank País, then aged twenty-four, assisted by several veterans of the Moncada attack, such as Haydée Santamaría and Lester Rodríguez, had prepared this rising with care and much intelligence. His organization in Santiago was far the best of the 26 July Movement's agencies in Cuba, and he had also had success in establishing cells in other nearby cities of Oriente.[9] He had had much success too in attracting the middle-class youth of Santiago to the revolutionary cause, including many girls, among them Vilma Espín, an engineering student, daughter of the Bacardi lawyer in the city, who on return from studying in the U.S. saw Castro in Mexico and acted as a messenger for the movement.[10] As has been seen, Frank País was actually opposed to a rising in Santiago or in Cuba generally at the end of November and, before he told Castro this, he had put his point of view to a meeting of the 26 July provincial leaders in Havana in August. But they, though disposing of less strength and less men than País, were more foolhardy than he and he was over-ruled.[11] Action being decided upon, País made every precaution and procured a great quantity of arms – some of them coming from Trujillo by, no doubt, an error on the part of Dr Eufemio Fernández who had a shipment of *matériel* landed in the wrong place in Oriente.

Despite, however, País's visit to Castro in early November, communications and orders for the coordination of the activities of the 26 July Movement were confused. Having heard that Castro would arrive '*una noche sin luna del mes de noviembre*', there was nearly a mobilization on 15 November, a very dark night. However, on 27 November Duque de Estrada, the propaganda secretary in Santiago, received a telegram from Mexico: 'Book you asked for is out of print. Editorial Divulgación.' This meant that the rising was to be timed seventy-two hours after this.

País and his organization now carried out far the most effective strike

---

[8] Sánchez Amaya, 35; Pablo Díaz, *Bohemia*, 3 December 1961, gives another account.

[9] The 26 July in Oriente was organized as follows: Treasurer, Dr María Antonia Figueroa; Propaganda, Gloria Cuadras; *Sección Obrera*, Ramón Alvarez; *Acción*, Frank País, with Pepito Tey his deputy; provincial co-ordinator, Lester Rodríguez; professionals, Dr Baudilio Castellanos; secretary of demonstrations and propaganda, Arturo Duque de Estrada. There were some ten cells in Santiago with eight or ten men in each (Arturo Duque de Estrada, *Revolución*, 30 July 1963).

[10] She later married Raúl Castro.

[11] Vicente Cubillas, 'Los Sucesos del 30 de Noviembre de 1956', *Bohemia*, 6 December 1959.

yet against the Batista regime:[12] País, an amateur soldier who had once desired to enter the military academy,[13] showed great talent for military leadership in arranging what was in effect a series of morale-raising commando raids. At dawn on 30 November 1956 perhaps three hundred young men in olive green uniforms with 26 July red and black armbands, attacked the police headquarters, the Customs House and the harbour headquarters. (They had got some of the arms by raiding the Shooting Club of Santiago, and some from the Triple A organization.) The Customs House was successfully set on fire, the other two captured.[14] At the same moment another group of *fidelistas* fell on the Boniato prison and freed several political prisoners there.[15] A number of policemen and soldiers were killed. País then withdrew, leaving the city in a state of panic. The next day he struck again, with eighty-six men,[16] setting fire to the harbour headquarters, capturing public buildings and bringing civil life to a standstill. Batista suspended guarantees in this and in three other provinces and sent reinforcements of 280 well-trained men by airlift to Santiago under Colonel Pedro Barrera, a career officer who had helped plan the *golpe* of 10 March. A small group of the 26 July men were eventually caught and isolated in the chief secondary school, but the rebels were allowed to escape through a back door; faced by absurd odds, the rebellion died. In fact, País had really controlled the city on 30 November and 1 December and perhaps a mortar differently directed would have led to the fall of Moncada.[17] At the same moment, a vigorous demonstration of exiled Cubans of the Club Patriótico paraded before the U.N. building in New York.[18] There were also successful commando raids in Guantánamo, where Julio Camacho had bought or stolen arms from the U.S. base. He and thirty men took the Ermita barracks without difficulty because there

[12] Much of this derives from evidence of his brother Agustín País, to Raúl Chibás, in Chibás MSS. According to Chibás, País rejected one man, Luis Clergé, from joining the 26 July Movement on the ground that he was a '*simpatizante comunista*' but when he insisted he was not, he was given '*tareas subalternas*'.

[13] According to Vilma Espín, *Revolución*, 17 January 1959, 16. She went on: 'His ideas were always revolutionary. In the system of Martí, he found a fertile inspiration. He was a complete Martian.' He had been a full-time revolutionary since January.

[14] The different columns were led by: Jorge Sotús and Antonio Roca (Policía Marítima); Pepito Tey and Otto Parellada, plus 45 men (Policía Nacional); Instituto de Santiago (50–100 men under Lester Rodríguez, veteran of Moncada); railway line – Enzo Infante, Tara Dimitro and Agustín País; 10–20 *francotiradores* under Emiliano Díaz, near the Moncada barracks; and other groups led by Agustín Navarrete, and the Céspedes brothers.

[15] These included Captain Braulio Coronú, an ex-enemy of Castro in 1953; Carlos Fonseca; and Orlando Benítez.

[16] The estimate of Representative Miguel de León Royas was 500. Chibás has 300 (MSS) for the first day. Robert Taber, *M26, The Biography of a Revolution* (1961), gives 86 (p. 75). (See *Havana Post*, 4 December 1956.)

[17] See Barrera Pérez, *Bohemia Libre*, 13 August 1961; Pazos, *Cambridge Opinion*, 21; Taber, 70–4; *Verde Olivo*, 16 December 1962.

[18] *Havana Post*, 4 December. Its leader was Arnaldo Barrón.

was no one there. They gave it up when the army arrived. The Labour leaders, Louit and Antonio Torres, carried out a twenty-four-hour general strike at the same time.[19]

The Santiago rising, however, brought three deaths among the Fidelistas – Pepito Tey (País's second-in-command and ex-president of the students in Oriente), Otto Parellada (telephone worker, who had tried unsuccessfully at the last minute to join in at Moncada), and Antonio Alomá (an office worker), but it had rubbed home to the army that basically the sons of the middle class were in opposition, and that their parents would, even if they had not taken part, at least not give them up.[20] Not only fathers but also strangers sheltered revolutionaries whom they had never seen before, and hid their guns.[21]

On 2 December, rather late for coordination, the *Granma* reached Cuba, though not before the naval second-in-command, ex-Lieutenant Roque, had fallen overboard and had to be picked up.[22] The omen was bad. The *Granma*, instead of beaching at Niquero at a good landing stage where waiting friends could immediately have assisted them (and where they were expected), was forced because of delays to hit land at the Playa de los Colorados, near Belic; and this was not land but swamp, overhung with thick undergrowth, swarming with little crabs. The men had been originally to land at dawn on 30 November at Niquero. The group would take Niquero and advance on Manzanillo, while the uprising broke out at Santiago. Then there would follow sabotage and agitation to culminate in a general strike.[23] None of this was now possible. It was even impossible to get all ammunition and weapons on land. The becalmed yacht was seen from the air by a fighter, a naval frigate appeared and there was some machine-gunning in the void. An 'irresponsible comrade' led them the wrong way.[24] At last, after three hours, the column reached hard ground. A peasant, Angel Pérez, invited the rebels to share his food, but when they were about to eat, they heard firing. They moved on inland and, on the first day after landing, did not eat at all.[25] One group became temporarily lost. Still they pressed on. They saw various peasants, some of whom gave blessings to the Virgen del Cobre for them.[26]

The next two days, 2 and 3 December, the little army pressed on towards the Sierra through cane fields attached to Julio Lobo's *central Niquero*. They lacked provisions, their boots were new, and they

[19] Vicente Cubillas, 'Los Sucesos del 30 de Noviembre', *Bohemia*, 6 December 1959.
[20] See León Rojas, *Havana Post*, *loc. cit.*
[21] Franqui, 155.
[22] Sánchez Amaya, 53–4; Guevara, *loc. cit.*
[23] Faustino Pérez, *Bohemia*, 11 January 1959.
[24] Guevara, *loc. cit.*
[25] Faustino Pérez's account in René Ray, *op. cit.*, 25.
[26] Sánchez Amaya, 54.

foolishly sucked cane stalks to combat thirst. The lost group rejoined the main body; where were they going, what were they going to do? To establish a base in the hills, as Castro had contemplated after the failure of Moncada? And then? Who knew? Meantime, Havana was full of rumours. It was said that Fidel Castro had landed with forty men, had been attacked and had been killed. The United Press correspondent in Havana, Francis McCarthy, reported Castro killed, and confirmed the error later by saying that this was clear from passport and documents found on the body.[27] Mario Llerena gave $5 to the presumed widow of Faustino Pérez.[28] Batista on the other hand publicly denied that Castro had left Mexico.[29]

The people in Havana were next told by their morning papers that rebels in the hills numbered anything from 'forty-nine to two hundred', and that one thousand troops were looking for them; but Castro's sisters, Emma and Lidia, in Mexico, with a carelessness and exuberance over figures that might have been envied by Las Casas, were claiming their brother was in Camagüey with over 50,000 men.[30] In fact, the government's reaction was that when the local commander at Manzanillo, Caridad Fernández, had informed the commander in Oriente, Díaz Tamayo, the latter had reported to Tabernilla in Havana, and Tabernilla, instead of sending locally based Oriente men against Castro, had sent a crony of his, Captain Juan González; González had at first confined himself to an effective defence of the barracks at Manzanillo, in the hope that they would be attacked.[31] There was then a confusion between Fernández and González, resulting in the death of some soldiers by accident and the appointment of Colonel Cruz Vidal to succeed González.

Castro was in fact betrayed. The party's guide left them on the morning of 5 December and went to the nearest rural guard post.[32] On that day none of the expedition could walk any further. All lay up in a canefield at a place named Alegría de Pío, not far from the Sierra.

At nearly four o'clock in the afternoon of 5 December the rebels were in consequence surprised on the edge of the canefield. Some aircraft had flown overhead and their noise concealed that of the army's aproach. Castro's men imagined that the shooting derived from one of their own patrols. The firing increased. A unit of the army under the command of Cruz Vidal was in fact less than a hundred yards away. The 26 July men returned fire. Great confusion followed, and Castro

[27] See *Havana Post*, 4 December 1956.
[28] Llerena, MSS, p. 35.
[29] *Loc. cit.*
[30] *Havana Post*, 5 December 1956.
[31] Barrera Pérez, *Bohemia Libre*, 16 August 1961.
[32] Guevara, *Pasajes*, 8.

and his headquarters' staff withdrew. Almeida, in command of one platoon, could not find anyone to give orders.[33] The withdrawal did not become general till about six o'clock. Castro attempted to re-group on the other side of the boundary line of the canefield, but too late. The army either set the canefield alight or it became alight due to incendiary bombing. Several men of the 26 July surrendered, to be immediately shot. Others were maltreated, though not as badly as were the prisoners of Moncada. A total of twenty-four seem to have been killed either in the fight or immediately after.[34] Some were captured but survived, to be tried later. Others escaped, some wounded, in separate little groups, all making for the jungle-covered mountains. They left apparently only one man killed on the other side.[35]

Two of the group who were taken prisoner, Mario Fuentes and José Díaz, gave to Colonel Ramón Cruz Vidal, the army commander, and then to the rest of Cuba, a description of the expedition:[36] the former even accused Castro of wounding him for wishing to surrender.

The men fleeing from Alegría de Pío found it hard to re-assemble. Some did not wish to do so; a peasant of the neighbourhood, Guillermo García, found some 'flying like rabbits'; one (unarmed) man wept, 'Why did I come?' (his wife was peacefully in Mexico).[37] Several groups made their way to safety for the time being; one was led by Guevara (wounded), and consisted of the mulatto Almeida, Ramiro Valdés, an older Spaniard 'veteran of the Spanish war', Rafael Chao, and Reinaldo Benítez;[38] Sánchez Amaya led another, consisting of six men.[39] Fidel Castro was with two others only, Universo Sánchez and Faustino Pérez.[40] Raúl Castro found himself with Efigenio Ameijeiras, Ciro Redondo and René Rodríguez.[41] Camilo Cienfuegos wandered round with 'Pancho' González and Pablo Hurtado.[42] Finally there was a group consisting of Calixto Morales, Calixto García, Carlos Bermúdez, Julio Díaz and Luis Crespo,[43] who later

[33] Sánchez Amaya, 65–73; Guevara, *Pasajes*, 9.

[34] *Cf.* the list in *Bayo*, 167.

[35] *Havana Post*, 7 December 1956.

[36] *Ibid.*, 8 December 1956.

[37] G. García to Franqui (Franqui, 71).

[38] Guevara, *Pasajes*, 10–11; Guillermo García speaks of finding Almeida, Che, Chao and 'Pancho' Gonzáles (Francqui, 71).

[39] Norberto Godoy, Enrique Camara, René Heinte, Mario Chaves, J. Capote and Raúl Suárez (Sánchez Amaya, 74 ff.).

[40] Faustino Pérez and René Ray, 28. *Cf.* U. Sánchez in Franqui, 39 ff.

[41] René Rodríguez, *Verde Olivo*, 2 December 1962. Ameijeiras said that a sixth member of this group was César Gómez; he gave himself up (Franqui, 3).

[42] Guevara, *Souvenirs de la Guerre Révolutionnaire*, 40 (this French edn, ed. Maspero, 1967, is more complete than the Havana edition of these memoirs, *Pasajes*). Guillermo García says that Cienfuegos came separately with Reinaldo Benítez and 'Aguilasta' (?) and another peasant who worked with him and later joined. Fajardo omitted Cienfuegos from the list.

[43] Faustino Pérez, *loc. cit.* Pérez actually said Raúl Díaz. See Crespo's account in *Revolución*, 23 July 1962.

joined Guevara. Thirteen men also gathered under Juan Manuel Márquez.

Of these groups, Sánchez Amaya and his friends wandered desperately in the forest for several days, thirsty and hungry, before reaching the sea; three gave themselves up and were killed; the other four made their way to Niquero and eventually to Havana.[44] Juan Manuel Márquez and his group gave themselves up and were mostly shot.[45] Despite napalm bombing of the forests, those still at large were facing the enemies of nature as much as Colonel Cruz Vidal. José Ponce drank his own urine.[46] Desperately, these survivors sought something edible among the trees, but found nothing except an occasional parasite plant, in which there was a residue of water. They ate herbs, occasional raw corn, or crabs.[47] Guevara attempted to draw water from a rock with his asthma apparatus and he and his group narrowly avoided asking for succour at a house where the health of Batista's army was being drunk.[48] Castro, alone with his two men, sucked cane stalks[49] and remained several days hidden in a cane field. They got some food from a peasant and carried enough away to keep them for a day or two. One peasant bought them food gratuitously and one of his sons, Guillermo García, joined them and led them towards the Sierra Maestra.[50] They were hidden for some days in the farms of Marcial Averiches and Mongo Pérez, brother of Cresencio Pérez, a lorry driver on Lobo's estate (uncle of García), who backed Castro, who had been looking for Castro for days and who now helped with his sons to gather together the remnants of the *Granma* men. Thus Raúl Castro's group of five men was able to meet with Castro on 17 December near the farm of Hermes Caldero.[51] Eventually, Almeida's group too discovered the whereabouts of Castro, and, leaving most of such arms as they had preserved, moved towards that place on 19 December. Guevara with his group were directed to Castro by several peasants, including an Adventist, Argelio Rosabal, Carlos Mas, and others.[52] The remaining Fidelistas in the

---

[44] Sánchez Amaya, *loc. cit.*
[45] Du Bois, 142–3.
[46] Franqui, 35.
[47] Guevara, in Núñez Jiménez, 575.
[48] Guevara, *Souvenirs*, 42.
[49] Universo Sánchez to Franqui, 42.
[50] To Lee Lockwood in 1965, Guillermo García (then a major) recalled 'I met Fidel for the first time on the twelfth of December ... Fidel said "Are we already in the Sierra Maestra?" I said, "yes." "Then the revolution has triumphed," he said.' (Lockwood, 52.)
[51] Franqui, 37, 75. Caldero is now a major in the Army. He was afterwards a guide in the Sierra.
[52] Guevara, *Souvenirs*, 43–4. Guevara's group consisted in the end of 'Pancho' González, Ramiro Valdés, Almeida, and himself, with Cienfuegos, Chao and Benítez following some way behind. Pablo Hurtado, who had originally been with Guevara, stayed behind ill at one of the peasants' houses being exhausted by the days of marching, and the hunger and thirst. He afterwards gave himself up.

Sierra thus came together. Cresencio Pérez was a curious figure to find later established as one of the founding fathers of the successful revolution, since he was a bandit more than a radical, a common criminal believed to have committed murder and reputedly father of eighty illegitimate children up and down the Sierra Maestra.

This re-assembly was chiefly due to the help of Cresencio Pérez and various men who worked with him, such as Guillermo García, and Manuel Fajardo, who also did much collecting together of rifles and other weapons. There were apparently fifteen of Castro's original followers together: Fidel and Raúl Castro, Guevara, Universo Sánchez, Faustino Pérez, Ramiro Valdés, Efigenio Ameijeiras, Camilo Redondo, Armando Rodríguez, René Rodríguez, Reinaldo Benítez, Calixto García, Calixto Morales, Chao ('veteran of the Spanish war') and Morán 'El Gallego'.[53] Castro then addressed these men, 'With the same vehemence which he would have done before a large political audience in the Central Park in Havana. He assured them that they had triumphed in the first stage of this adventure. He communicated to them that he did not have the least doubt that in the long run victory would be theirs . . . all left convinced of the strength of their position and the confidence of obtaining victory in a long run or the short . . .'[54]

---

[53] Carlos Bermúdez and 'Pancho' González seem to have dropped out at the last minute. It is remarkable how none of the participants who have written of these events agree on the exact names of those taking part. There may at one moment in early December have been only twelve men in the Sierra around Fidel Castro, as invariably argued since, no doubt to suggest Christ-like parallels, but this could only have been for a very short time before the survivors of the disaster at Alegría de Pío had caught up with one another. Camilo Cienfuegos in an interview published in *Revolución*, 4 January 1959, spoke of 'only eight men being left' after Alegría de Pío. Ameijeiras in another interview published 8 January 1959 said, 'of the eighty-two men who embarked on the *Granma* there remained not twelve – as Batista said – but nine' (*Revolución*, 8 January 1959). Castro himself spoke of twelve men several times in his speech of 8 January 1959 at Campamento Columbia (*Discursos para la Historia* (1959), 16) and this number crops up in the Circular de Organización by the National Directorate of the 26 July Movement of 18 March 1958. Castro also mentions it in his denunciation of the Miami group (see e.g. the version in Guevara's reminiscences, 227). Guevara in an account of the battles of the Sierra published in 1960, in the *Geografía de Cuba* by Antonio Núñez Jiménez (575), spoke of 'some seventeen' men reunited in early December and, a few lines later, a *quincena* – 'about fifteen'. Universo Sánchez, one of the men with Castro all the time after Alegría, repeated that there were twelve in 1963 (Franqui, 38). Faustino Pérez, in an account to René Ray, listed sixteen by name: these were Fidel and Raúl Castro, Guevara, Faustino Pérez, himself, Valdés, Sánchez, Ameijeiras, Armando Rodríguez, René Rodríguez, Cienfuegos, Almeida, Calixto García, Calixto Morales, Benítez and Julio Díaz (Ray, 28). To these however should be added the names of Redondo, Chao and Morán while that of Raúl Díaz should be omitted (see Guevara, *Pasajes*, 23). But the number of twelve has taken a firm hold over the Revolution's mythology and Carlos Franqui has even written a book, *Cuba: Le Livre de Douze*. In mid-February, at the time of the visit of Herbert Matthews, there probably were twelve *Granma* men for several weeks – since Faustino Pérez, René and Armando Rodríguez, Calixto García, Calixto Morales and Benítez had by then left; see below, p. 919. But several peasants were by then an integral part of the Movement.
[54] This is the account of Universo Sánchez as related to or by, Raúl Chibás (MSS), which I have preferred to other accounts of this occasion.

Back in Havana, the varying stories told of their fortunes in the Sierra had a curiously mixed effect. Was Castro dead or alive? Some Liberals, for instance a mother of four young sons in Havana, were secretly pleased at the United Press news that Castro was dead: sad for Cuba, she thought, but perhaps good for her and the lives of her sons.[55] The papers were as usual full of comforting statements by *Batistiano* businessmen and politicians describing good economic prospects: good production and investment levels everywhere.[56] Yet political confidence was weak: the death of the aged Don Cosme de la Torriente on 8 December symbolically removed, a week after Castro landed in Oriente, the strongest protagonist of a policy of compromise.[57] The regime and the opposition drifted daily further apart. During December the rumours that Castro was still alive began to trickle into Havana. A legend grew: Castro's survival from yet another terrible clash suggested a myth of immortality. As yet nothing was clearly known. The members of the 26 July Movement in Havana and Santiago knew nothing for certain, though they not unnaturally suspected that since the army had not exhibited Castro's body, he must be alive – a feeling of confidence which increased when Batista himself began to throw doubt on the idea that Castro had even left Mexico. Who therefore would not take the risk and go and join him: *Con Fidel en las montañas*?

Castro and his reunited followers had in truth moved further and further away from Alegría de Pío, being continually helped by Cresencio Pérez, another of whose cattlemen, Manuel Fajardo, joined Castro at this time, with the peasant Guillermo García.[58] According to one account Cresencio Pérez offered Castro a hundred men but Castro rejected them because they had no arms and accepted provisionally only fifteen, most of whom were for the time being only auxiliary or half-time helpers.[59] The slightly enlarged group marched at night and slept by day. Discussion was intense, Castro taking great interest in everything said and seen.[60] Guevara later recorded:

> Hunger, what is truly known as hunger, none of us had ever known before and then we began to know it . . . and so many things became very clear [i.e. about the condition of the peasants]. We who in the beginning punished severely anyone who took any animal from a rich farmer, one day took ten thousand head of cattle and we said

[55] A remark to me of Sra Sara de Pazos.
[56] See below, p. 123, for more detailed inquiry.
[57] Not long before he died, Haydée Santamaría, on behalf of Castro, had visited him and asked him for 'one more patriotic gesture' by committing suicide (evidence of Elena Mederos).
[58] Franqui, 77.
[59] Faustino Pérez, *Bohemia*, 11 January 1959.
[60] Guevara in *Geografía*, 576.

simply to the peasants, 'Eat.' And the peasants, for the first time in many years, and some for the first time in their lives, ate beef.[61]

This was therefore a formative period for the revolutionaries, and they learned much about the country where they had already begun a revolution. Before, Castro and his men

... did not know a single peasant in the Sierra Maestra and, further, the only information we had of [it] ... was what we had learnt in geography books ... [We] might have known that the [rivers] Cauto, Contramaestre and Yara rose there – but what we knew of the Yara was the song and nothing more ... [nevertheless] the bands of rebels immediately met with support from large numbers ...[62]

By now indeed the problem of food supplies was almost solved, since Cresencio Pérez and his comrades knew peasants who could sell or give a modest food supply, and who could tell them where to find water or where to get natural supplies.

What did we meet in the Sierra Maestra? [Castro later went on in describing these days.] We met there the first peasants who wished to join us, some very scattered workers [*salteados*]. First the disappointments, the dispersion; some peasants helped us to regroup the remains of these forces. This group ... helped us meet each other in the Sierra ... What was the situation of the greater part of peasants at that moment? First, a great terror of the Army ... second, they could scarcely know that our group of badly dressed, hungry men, with very few arms, could defeat a force which moved in lorries, trains, aeroplanes ... We had often to move ... without being seen by the population ... because always in a township ... of 100 people ... there was a *Batistiano* ... and then the army would come in.[63]

---

[61] *Obra Revolucionaria*, No. 24 of 1960 (24 September 1960), 21.
[62] *Ibid.*, No. 46 of 1961, 17. The song runs:

> Por la orilla floreciente
> Que baña el río de Yara
> Donde dulce fresca y clara
> Se desliza la corriente
> Donde brilla el sol ardiente
> De nuestra abrasada zona
> Y un cielo hermoso corona
> La selva, el monte y el prado
> Iba un guajiro montado
> Sobre una yegua trotona.

[63] *Loc cit.*

It should be appreciated that it was clearly necessary for the rebels to buy the help of some of the peasants, and not inexpensively. Thus Faustino Pérez told Carrillo on 24 December 1956 that 'to attract peasants it was necessary to pay double the value of everything they bought from them . . .'[64]

The area of the Sierra Maestra is the wildest part of all Cuba. It includes the highest mountains of the island, including Pico Turquino, the Blue Mountain, which rises to 8,600 feet. It is an area of great beauty which has often inspired poets. Manuel Navarro Luna, for example, in his *Poemas Mambises* twenty-five years before, has written:

> The Blue Mountain
> And River Cauto!
> Sinews of the eternity
> Which begat us . . .
> The Mountain warms us with its great heart
> Splendid son of excellence and infinity . . .

This is the southernmost part of Cuba, and its vegetation and altitude resemble less Cuba than the other more hilly islands of the Antilles, of whose central range the Sierra Maestra is topographically the continuation; this range is indeed a contrast with the rest of the island. These mountains are wooded, the vegetation ranging from coarse cactus on the lower and dryer slopes to beautiful rain forests of tree ferns on the higher ones. The Sierra runs along the coast, to which its slopes descend precipitously, though interrupted by a curious natural terracing, each step being some 600 feet or more. The coast itself is indented, though without the offshore keys which lie off the north and south-west coasts of Cuba. The Sierra Maestra is about a hundred miles in length and twenty to thirty miles or so at its widest. The area is bounded by the sea in the south, the coastal plain of Niquero–Campechuela–Manzanillo in the west, and the central highway in the north and east, though in practice the mountains continue northwards as far as the Río Cauto and its valley. In the east also the mountains continue, becoming known as the Sierra del Cobre, the copper mountains, before falling to the central highway again and to Santiago and its bay.

The Sierra Maestra was a poor area. From time immemorial these lands had both belonged to a small group of families and had been neglected. Boundaries were obscure. Most of those who actually lived there were squatters without title or security to their land: these *precaristas* represented only 8% to 10% of the farmers of Cuba, but over

[64] Carrillo, MSS, p. 32.

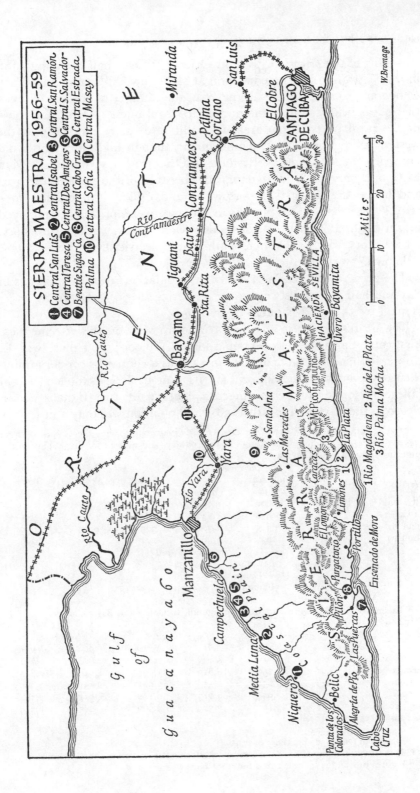

SIERRA MAESTRA · 1956–59

① Central San Luis ② Central Isabel ③ Central San Ramón
④ Central Teresa ⑤ Central Dos Amigos ⑥ Central S. Salvador
⑦ Beattie Sugar Co. ⑧ Central Cabo Cruz ⑨ Central Estrada
Palma ⑩ Central Sofía ⑪ Central Masay

W. Bromage

O R I E N T E

S I E R R A   M A E S T R A

Gulf of Guacanayabo

Miranda
San Luis
Palma Soriano
El Cobre
SANTIAGO DE CUBA
Contramaestre
Río Contramaestre
Baire
Jiguaní
Sta. Rita
Bayamo
Río Cauto
Río Cauto
HACIENDA SEVILLA
Bayamita
Uvero
Mr. Pico Turquino
Santa Ana
Las Mercedes
Caracas
La Plata
Yara
Río Yara
Manzanillo
El Plátin
Campechuela
Media Luna
El Lomón
Limones
Purgatorio
Epillón
Las Vueltas
Portillo
Ensenada de Moro
Niquero
Belic
Alegría de Pío
Punta de los Colorados
Cabo Cruz

1 Río Magdalena 2 Río de La Plata
3 Río Palma Mocha

Miles
0   10   20   30

two-fifths of the *precaristas* were in Oriente.[65] Over half the population in the Sierra had had no education at all.[66] Few children of school age were going to school.[67] In all the area, the number of consensual marriages was nearly double the number of legal ones.[68] About half those in the rural parts of the area were illiterate, more especially at the western, Niquero end.[69] Unemployment, though high, apparently did not reach the levels found elsewhere in Oriente: 4% in Bayamo, 8% in El Cobre, only 1·4% in Jiguaní, but (because of the mills in the area and hence the seasonal opportunities and difficulties) in Niquero – 16%.[70] The majority of persons in the area were, of course, employed in agriculture. Nearly all the houses were *bohíos*, with earth floors; refrigerators, running water, baths and electric light were almost unknown.[71]

The area was increasing rapidly in population: thus the districts of Bayamo had grown between 1943 and 1953 by 60%, Cobre by 25%, Jiguaní by 35% and Niquero by over 30%.

The nearest towns to the Sierra Maestra were in the extreme east. First came Santiago with a population of 160,000; then there was El Cobre, founded by the Spaniards in 1558 as a centre for copper mining (hence the name) and known for its famous black wooden Virgin (allegedly found in the seventeenth century by two Indians and a Negro in the Bay of Nipe). In 1958, its population was only a little over

[65] Agricultural Census of 1946. See Draper for discussion, though the Census of 1953 suggests that 45·7% of those with houses in the country paid no rent for them. Thus in the total rural area the situation was:

	Total houses	Own houses		Rented	No rent	Others
		Both house and land	House only			
Bayamo	15,999	5,890	3,704	772	5,461	172
El Cobre	6,576	1,850	1,247	83	3,067	329
Jiguaní	9,214	3,315	1,715	375	3,337	472
Niquero	8,598	736	7,069	221	374	198

	Not declared
Bayamo	334
El Cobre	70
Jiguaní	99
Niquero	163

[66] Taken from census figures for Niquero, Jiguaní, El Cobre and Bayamo.

[67] Thus:

	Age 5-9		Age 10-14		Age 15-19	
	At school	Not at school	At school	Not at school	At school	Not at school
Bayamo	5,591	17,290	8,813	11,192	1,943	12,849
El Cobre	1,737	5,654	2,558	3,991	531	3,989
Jiguaní	3,028	8,944	4,717	6,140	901	7,104
Niquero	1,430	10,161	2,369	7,360	445	6,559

(Census of 1953, 116–117.)

[68] Figures in *ibid.*, 50.

[69] Figures in *ibid.*, 150; i.e. those over 10.

[70] *Ibid.*, 168; i.e. many of these were employed during the harvest in the sugar mills.

[71] Figures in *ibid.*, 247; *ibid.*, 251–2 for rural houses.

2,500. Palma Soriano, with 25,500 people, had had in 1860 160 sugar mills, though in the 1950s there were merely three. Between these were Jiguaní, an eighteenth-century Indian foundation, with 7,000 people, and Baire, the starting point of the 1895 revolt, with 4,000. Bayamo, 50 miles west, had 20,000. Manzanillo, on the coast, 30 miles beyond Bayamo, had over 40,000. Niquero, with its sugar mill,[72] was an old town founded in 1571, down the coast towards the point where the *Granma* came ashore; it had a population of little more than 7,000. Campechuela, between Niquero and Manzanillo, had 5,000 people. A little to the north of Niquero was Media Luna with its sugar mill *Isabel*, employing 3,000, and controlling nearly 70,000 acres. The western coast of the Sierra broadened to a plain of about thirty miles in the Manzanillo–Bayamo area. Along that coast, in the two municipalities, there were in fact six sugar *centrales*. Along the south coast was Pilón, also with a sugar mill,[73] with 2,500 people, but otherwise in the area of the Sierra Maestra there was no other place with a population larger than 1,000. Communications in the Sierra Maestra were bad. They consisted chiefly of long forest paths which the sun never reached.

Race in the 1950s seems to have been fairly balanced between black and white.[74] Niquero, with nominally the most white people in the area, was oddly enough the least literate. At the same time, many of those in the northern part of the area, especially those living round Jiguaní, had Indian blood, or perhaps were entirely Indian: the Yara valley is the most strongly Indian area left in Cuba and, interestingly enough, it claims to be the least race conscious.[75]

The sugar mills in the Niquero district were Cuban-owned, *Niquero* and *Pilón* belonging to Julio Lobo. Much of the eastern section of the Sierra Maestra consisted of *latifundios* such as the huge Hacienda Sevilla, owned by the Lebanese Babun brothers, cement makers and exporters of cedar and mahogany.[76] Such cultivation as there was was confined to the line of the rivers. Coffee was extensively grown and there were a number of charcoal burners whose economic position was highly precarious. The lower stretches at the eastern end of the Sierra produced vast stores of honey. On the extreme west of the area, near

[72] It employed 4,000 workers.
[73] Employing 1,650, with lands of 136 caballería and milling another 377.

[74]

	White	Black	Mixed	Yellow
Bayamo	52,538	9,968	33,598	20
El Cobre	8,983	10,357	18,590	224
Jiguaní	35,239	3,362	15,379	15
Niquero	31,923	3,861	19,750	15

[75] See comments by Núñez Jiménez, *Geografía*, 562; visited by the author in 1961.

[76] *Cf.* evidence in Playa Girón trial given by sons of one of the Babuns, Omar, Lancelot and Santiago, who joined the invading force in 1961, having worked before 1959 in Guatemala (*Playa Girón: Derrota del Imperialismo*, 4 vols (1961), IV, 124–33). The Babuns sold this estate in late 1957 for $M1 (see Lazo, 138).

Cabo Cruz, there were estates belonging to the old Céspedes family. Large estates also belonged to the Beattie Sugar Company, to Lobo's big New Niquero Sugar Company, to various members of the Castillo family, and to the Cape Cruz Company (which controlled the *central Pilón*). The large estates were run by *mayorales*, whose main task was to try to restrict the persistent diminution of these lands of their employers by the *precaristas* – a task which led to perpetual gunfights and occasional deaths; the *mayorales* might burn down the *precaristas*' house who in turn might respond by murder. Each side had its known leaders and gangs of followers. Many regarded the Sierra Maestra as the last refuge for escaping criminals and in many ways indeed it resembled the Wild West before the American Civil War.

Such was the region into whose most remote fastnesses Cresencio Pérez, for years a leader with his sons of the *precaristas*, began on 25 December 1956 to lead Castro's men. A few days before, one member of the party, the Baptist student Faustino Pérez, left the Sierra with two peasant guides (Quique Escalona and Rafael Sierra) for Havana to establish contact with and reorganize the town supporters of the movement, to confirm that Castro was in fact still living,[77] and to try to ensure that all available arms in Havana and other cities were in fact sent to the Sierra – an instruction upon which Castro had continually to insist but which was not quickly enacted.[78] He had arrived by Christmas.

[77] Faustino Pérez, in René Ray, *op. cit.* Faustino Pérez came from a Protestant lower middle-class family in Las Villas, and had been in charge of the dispensary next to the first Presbyterian church in Havana where he had stored explosives for the MNR movement before joining Castro. See also another Pérez account in *Bohemia*, 30 November 1962.

[78] See discussion in Régis Debray, *Révolution dans la Révolution?* (1967), 77–8.

CHAPTER 9

Herbert Matthews goes to the Sierra

Christmas Day 1956 was greeted traditionally by Habaneros; newspapers were full of advertisements for presents from El Encanto, the big department store: for $36 flights to Miami ('55 minutes of sheer pleasure, 5 swift flights daily'). Rancho Luna Restaurant, 'typically Cuban country-style thatched *bohío*', told its sophisticated clients that 324,000 chickens had been eaten there in the last three years. Americans bade farewell to various 'integral' members of their community and their assiduous wives (active members of the American Club, Rovers' Club, Women's Club and the 'egregious Book and Thimble' society). The 'lovely family of Mr and Mrs John Albert Ferreira, Sr, of *central Agramonte*, would pass Christmas at the home of their son-in-law and daughter, Mr and Mrs Clarence Bonstra, in Country Club'. 'The Great Christmas Story of Old' was told anew in pageant to hundreds of Americans and Cubans. The *Havana Post*, recalling the crises of Suez and Hungary during 1956, alluded to 'revolutionaries in Oriente', whom the armed forces were 'hoping to dominate with a minimum of loss of life', and announced confidently that 'even if we are forced to a military decision with Communist Russia, our strength in the final analysis will be our faith in Christ'. *El Mundo* said that 'terrorism and sabotage are to be condemned at all times but even more so now at Christmas time'. 'Choose Irish linen as a lasting and lovely souvenir of your Cuban pleasant vacation' carolled one advertisement, and 'Greetings in the name of Hatuey, the finest Cuban beer', exclaimed another.

But the spirit of Christmas, over-worked ghost of affluent societies, was in truth weak. Faustino Pérez, arriving in Havana from the Sierra, received $1,000 from Justo Carrillo for the Movement on Christmas night.[1] The 26 July Movement planned to strike during the holiday and a number of bombs went off, causing a blackout on Christmas Eve in several towns of Oriente. Batista's army also struck: Colonel Fermín Cowley, commander at Holguín in northern Oriente, and, like so many of Batista's supporters, a cell member of ABC in the early 1930s,[2] gave orders for a number of reprisals. Twenty-two men accordingly were

---

[1] Justo Carrillo, MSS, p. 32.
[2] Phillips, 333. He had also been Batista's investigator in the case of corruption by Tabernilla, etc.

killed in different parts of Oriente, some members of the 26 July Movement, some Ortodoxos, some Auténticos – all members of the opposition.[3] Two were hanged and their bodies left on trees outside Holguín.

The scandal was great. Newspaper proprietors of leading papers called on all to 'preserve society', not excluding from condemnation the 'violent repression' of terrorism, and offering to mediate.[4] But this had no effect. New Year's Eve was the signal for further violence: the 26 July placed bombs in several public places; leading members of the 26 July Movement carefully laid bombs in the huge Tropicana night club, blowing off the arm of a seventeen-year-old girl, injuring the daughter of an ex-police chief, Martha Pino Donoso, and causing other damage.[5] Bombs were set off in Santiago. The army killed at least another three people in Oriente and two in Las Villas.[6]

At this time among the leaders of the 26 July Movement in Havana was Javier Pazos. He and others, children of the men of the revolution in 1933, such as Leila Sánchez and Raulito Roa (children of Aureliano Sánchez Arango and Raúl Roa), with others such as the surrealist painter Manuel Couzeiro, the law student leader Marcelo Fernández and Luis de la Cuesta, were prominent members of a group of young intellectuals in their twenties accustomed to meet in the committee rooms of the Cuban chapter of the Congress for Cultural Freedom, then headed by Mario Llerena, an older and more experienced political writer. The movement of these people towards Castro in 1956 had been one of the 26 July Movement's most important intellectual accretions to date.[7]

The tragic events of the New Year did not seem to trouble the mayor of New York, Robert Wagner, who passed the New Year in Havana. 'Such visits as yours contribute very substantially,' Batista assured him in English, 'to the good relations between our countries'. Mutual expressions of esteem and good jokes accompanied Mayor Wagner on his way to Varadero.[8] Isolated events of this sort might not have had much consequence, and even an accumulation of them, under the persuasion of Batista's public relations chief, Chester Arthur, are hard to pin down to any specific consequence. But they continued to give the impression that official North America was intimate with official Cuba: the enemies of the latter began easily to seem the enemies of the former. If Mayor Wagner seemed happy to receive the Order of Céspedes at the

[3] See names in *Havana Post*, 27 December 1956.
[4] See papers, 29 and 30 December.
[5] Evidence of Javier Pazos. See also *Havana Post*, 2 January 1957 and 4 January 1957.
[6] See *ibid.*, 2 January 1957.
[7] Llerena, MSS, 39–40; evidence of Javier Pazos.
[8] *Havana Post*, 2 January 1957.

hands of President Batista it seemed inevitable that Mayor Wagner should approve of President Batista. The U.S. assistant secretary of commerce, General Thomas Wilson, was happily present when Wagner received his decoration. The same point seemed hammered home even further with the award of the Cuban military medal to Colonel Isaacson, retiring head of the U.S. military mission. North Americans were not alone in these visits: Yael, daughter of General Dayan of Israel, had exchanged a Hebrew Bible for a pure silk Cuban flag with General Tabernilla in October 1956.[9]

The same moral applied when it became known that U.S. investment in late 1956 was on a high level; a total of $M357 new private investments were made in the years 1952 to 1957.[10] Texaco and Shell had invested in Cuba $M40 in 1956. Some such investments were made with joint Cuban and U.S. capital and as usual it was difficult sometimes to know which was which. Some Cuban firms had U.S. investors, some U.S. firms Cuban shareholders. Cuba still represented a far too tempting field for U.S. business: the Cuban economy in January 1957 was at record level, while the average Cuban income per head had risen to $400, or a total of $M2,400 – a near *per capita* maximum for Latin America. National credit stood high, due to recent prompt repayments of loans. Building in Havana and nearby, public and private, radiated its usual wild but unreliable air of well-being. North American investors did not observe that the political crisis had worsened while the dictatorship masked the effects of it. In January, furthermore, it seemed that the fears of the traditional weapon of cane-burning by Castro's men or others during the harvest had proved groundless. Gangsterism had declined, while U.S. brokers noted with satisfaction that Batista's relations with Trujillo had improved. The Cuban Minister of Agriculture even approvingly visited a livestock exhibition in Santo Domingo so there were fewer fears now of an invasion from gangsters based there. Castro's rebellion, if indeed it survived at all,[11] seemed, in Wall Street, in no way likely to pose an economic threat. U.S. business continued to hold conventions in Havana, the businessmen finding the high life, the brothels and the blue films even more exciting than what was available in Pittsburgh, and superficially more exciting than even the old days in Havana: the new hotels had an incomparably gilded luxury and splendour. Cuban ministers continued to be received in Washington: Santiago Rey, the Defence minister, went there in January 1957 as an official guest. He and other Cuban ministers absorbed without much

[9] *Ibid.,* 3 January 1957.

[10] HAR, January 1957. Britain too was involved. The *Board of Trade Journal* in January assured British investors that excellent opportunities lay ahead in Cuba.

[11] The Mexican paper, *Ultimas Noticias,* stated that Castro had returned to Mexico on 5 January.

difficulty the most slipshod of U.S. politicians' stock denunciations of Communism, and denounced Castro, Prío, even Trujillo and other enemies, regularly as 'communistic'.[12]

But the Cuban police did not behave as if it had conquered its enemy. On 2 January, while the nation had still not digested the vile Christmas and New Year news, four youths – one of whom, William Soler, was only fourteen years old – were found killed in an empty building site in Santiago. They had apparently been arrested as suspects for the 26 July activities over the holidays and been tortured. In consequence, on 4 January a procession of five hundred women, headed by the mother of Soler, dressed in black, moved slowly through the streets of Santiago with a banner: '*Cesen los asesinatos de nuestros hijos!*', 'Stop the murders of our sons.' The press leaders' offers of mediation were supported by all varieties of persons – presidents of the coffee merchants, Rotarians, Freemasons, chambers of commerce, the Havana University Council – most of whom coupled their appeals for mediation with a denunciation of terrorism. However, the vice-president, Guas Inclán, rather spoiled the impression by welcoming the press bloc's attempt and saying that its chief, Cristóbal Díaz, was 'a successful businessman and a friend of President Batista'.[13]

Sporadic violence continued. Bombs were placed at least once a week somewhere in Cuba during January 1957. Arrests were frequently made and what happened to those held was not always clear. The house of Colonel Orlando Piedra, chief of the SIM, in 5th Avenue, Miramar, was fired on from a moving car on the night of 13 January. Castro's mother appears at this point to have appealed to Batista to save her son's life by letting him and his friends escape to an embassy.[14] On 15 January constitutional guarantees (already suspended in Oriente) were dropped throughout the island.[15]

Castro's force, regrouped in the Sierra, still about twenty men, now reappeared. On 14 January it had reached the river Magdalena, where the men washed and prepared for an attack on La Plata barracks at the mouth of the little river of that name.[16] At this point they apparently had twenty-three weapons – nine rifles with telescopic lenses, five semi-automatic rifles, four rifles with bolts, two Thompson machine guns,

---

[12] The *Havana Post*, a typical expression of the views of the U.S. colony in Cuba, reported as late as 16 February 1957 that 'McCarthy is a controversial figure but he is also a U.S. Senator and a patriotic citizen'.

[13] *Ibid.*, 6 January 1957. Cristóbal Díaz (born 1894) was an architect and owner of *El País*. He was also founder of Radio Habana.

[14] Army statement, 1 March 1957.

[15] This involved the appointment of censors to cover each paper. See list in press, 16 January 1957. The *Havana Post* and, one may assume, the U.S. colony in general approved, denouncing terrorism and saying that it must be Communist inspired and not the work of the known opposition leaders (see *Havana Post*, 16 January 1957).

[16] Guevara, 12.

two machine pistols and one 16-bore air gun.[17] Several more peasants had become loosely attached to them (Edward Díaz, Manuel and Sergio Acuña).[18] They had as a guide a peasant named Melquíades Elías. During the day they met two peasants, relations of the guide, one of whom as a precaution they held prisoner. On 15 and 16 January they carefully watched the barracks, and took two more prisoners, one of whom said that there were fifteen soldiers within. Another told them details of the local land-holding – how the Laviti family held a huge semi-feudal estate maintained against *precaristas* by three notorious tough *mayorales*.

Soon afterwards one of these agents, 'Chicho' Osorio, *mayoral* of the El Macho estate, approached on a mule, accompanied by a little black boy, and drunk.[19] Universo Sánchez called on Osorio to halt in the name of the rural guard: Osorio immediately answered 'Mosquito' – the password.[20] Castro was able to persuade him that he was himself colonel of the army looking for the rebels. Osorio told Castro how sluggardly the troops were in the barracks at La Plata and gave a good deal of other information, including the opinion that if Castro were caught he would be immediately murdered. Castro then placed his men ready for a night attack on 16–17 January, and divided his men into four groups, led respectively by Julio Díaz, Castro himself, Raúl Castro and Juan Almeida. At the moment the attack began, 2.40 a.m. on 17 January 1957, 'Chicho' Osorio, the unjust steward, was shot, still drunk.[21]

The principle of the attack was, in the dark, to fire a heavy volley from several sides and then to demand surrender. With the barracks surprised, this worked well: several houses at the side of the barracks were also set on fire by Guevara and Lucio Crespo. The Fidelistas afterwards stormed the place and the soldiers surrendered. Altogether 1,500 rounds had been fired.[22] The Batistianos had lost two dead, and five wounded; three prisoners were taken. Another crooked steward, Honorio, and the other soldiers fled. Castro lost no one. He ordered

---

[17] *Loc. cit.*

[18] Colonel Barrera, the Batistiano commander, later fairly accurately referred to the Acuñas as famous bandits, along with Julio Guerrero and Chico Mendoza, the latter being a semi-bandit leader and who however fought the *precaristas* on behalf of the proprietors.

[19] The accusation later lodged against Osorio was that he had used the government's anxiety after the landing of the *Granma* to dislodge various peasants on the pretext that they were Fidelistas (see Castro, *Discursos para la historia*, 25; Castro on Television, 9 January 1959).

[20] Franqui, *loc. cit.*

[21] This was the occasion of which Castro later spoke to the journalist Jules Dubois: 'When we arrived at the Sierra Maestra we executed a ranch foreman who had accused tenant farmers of being pro-rebel and who had increased holdings of his landlord from ten acres to four hundred by taking the land of those whom he denounced.' (Jules Dubois, *Fidel Castro: rebel – liberator or dictator?* (1959), 145). In a denunciation of the 26 July for 'atrocities', two farmers later spoke of 'Chicho' as an 'army guide'. (See *Havana Post*, 19 June 1957.)

[22] Guevara, 17. *Cf.* Franqui, 32–3.

the barracks to be burned. Three of the wounded soldiers died. The others were left behind in the care of prisoners when the Fidelistas returned to the jungle.

This victory enabled Castro to add to his supplies Springfield rifles, a new Thompson machine gun, a few thousand rounds, and various cartridge belts, firewood, clothes, food and knives. One of the prisoners later joined Castro's forces. Castro freed all the army's peasant prisoners and made off towards the next river, the Palma Mocha, a few kilometres nearer the Pico Turquino. On their way they observed the melancholy sight of an exodus of peasants from the hills. The previous day the overseer and the rural guard had told the *precaristas* of the region that the air force was going to bomb the Sierra in order to get rid of the rebels, and they should leave if they valued their lives. Since the government did not know that the Fidelistas were in the region and since there was no air attack the next day, this was evidently an attempt by the overseers to drive away the peasants in their own interests.[23]

> Almost every group of peasants whom we met [Castro recalled five years later] had some complaint. Naturally, we began a political attempt to win over the peasants ... They worked in the plain fifteen days, gathered fifteen or twenty pesos, bought salt and a little fat and then returned to their little coffee farms with them. The Agricultural Bank only gave money for credit to peasants who were already well off. When the rural guard passed by such peasants' houses you can be certain that at the very least he helped himself to a fine chicken; and the merchants who sold foods to the peasants sold dear. There were no schools.[24] These were the conditions that we met in the Sierra – the objective conditions ... [of revolution].

On 19 January, meanwhile, the press carried the false news that 'eight rebels and two members of the armed forces had been killed in a clash at La Plata'.[25] On 1 March, however, the army announced that in fact twelve men had been killed in this fight – while 'forty rebels' also had been killed, and twenty prisoners taken afterwards:[26] that is, rather more than double the total number of rebels at large were said to have been casualties – a useful criterion, no doubt, to judge the claims of other governments in similar wars.

Castro was in fact now heading northwards towards a small stream known as Arroyo del Infierno. Calculating that the army would pursue him, he prepared a simple ambush, though the effect was nearly spoiled by Guevara, who, wearing a Batistiano uniform captured at La Plata,

[23] Guevara, 17–18; Castro, 2 December 1961, *Obra Revolucionaria*, No. 46 of 1961, 22.
[24] This was definitely the case in respect of this area.
[25] *Havana Post*, 19 January 1957.
[26] *Ibid.*, 2 March 1957.

was fired on by Cienfuegos. Eventually a small troop of Batistianos, part of a patrol led by Lieutenant Sánchez Mosquera (as part of a recent new command of 100 men under Major Casillas) appeared, looking at two *bohíos* in the centre of a glade in which Castro's men had specifically avoided sheltering – remembering how Castro himself had been caught in a *bohío* after Moncada in 1953. Castro fired the first shot and killed one man, and three more Batistianos were also killed, one by Guevara. Afterwards both sides withdrew, the Fidelistas capturing one rifle, a Garand and a cartridge belt. This limited success taught Castro to attempt to attack vanguards of patrols, for 'without a vanguard there can be no army'.[27] The Fidelistas discovered later that Sánchez Mosquera had also shot a Negro peasant who had refused to act as their guide.[28]

Castro next returned south-west, to where they had been before La Plata, in the region of a densely wooded hill known as Caracas. They found the situation changed, for the army had since been through and Major Casillas had driven out many *precaristas*. Castro found only empty *bohíos*. He was rejoined at this point by a peasant, Eutimio Guerra, who had acted as a guide earlier, and after La Plata had gone down from the hills to visit his mother. In truth, he had been captured by the army and had agreed, for a fee of $10,000 and an army rank, to kill Castro. He was a well-known bandit leader, like Cresencio Pérez a defender of the *precaristas* against the *mayorales* and their henchmen.[29]

At this moment there was some despondency among the Fidelistas: various members of the party were demanding that they should be allowed to go into the cities. Castro announced a death penalty for insubordination, desertion and defeatism. Guevara drily commented that, as yet, the rebels lacked 'a spirit forged in struggle and . . . a clear ideological conscience'.[30] All had been demoralized by the appearance over their heads the day before of a squadron of fighters which machine-gunned the forest close to them. They had not known that Eutimio Guerra was actually in one aeroplane, directing the attack.[31] In these circumstances, Castro took the critically dangerous but actually funda-mental decision, in late January, to send René Rodríguez to Havana to tell his followers in the capital that he would be willing to see a

---

[27] Guevara, 91.
[28] *Ibid.*, 18–20; Núñez Jiménez, 576–7, for his earlier account. Barrera Pérez, on the other hand, then the commander in the Sierra Maestra, said that he lost no men during his time in command from 29 January to 16 April. This must be false.
[29] Barrera Pérez, *Bohemia Libre*, 20 August 1961. Barrera Pérez says that Guerra told Casillas that Castro's forces were divided into two – one led by the Castros, of 120 men, the other led by Guevara, of 80. Nothing could be further from the truth and Guerra probably helped Castro by this misinformation far more than he harmed him.
[30] Guevara, 24.
[31] Barrera Pérez confirms (*loc. cit.*).

foreign press correspondent, for with the Cuban press under censorship there would be no point in seeing a Cuban.[32]

The air attack had caused depression and dispersion of the Fidelistas. One peasant, Sergio Acuña, the bandit, abandoned the group, while his brother, Manuel, with Calixto García and Calixto Morales, became for a time separated from the main column. Fortunately, on the same day, 1 February, about ten new followers from Manzanillo led by Roberto Pesant successfully reached Castro. Surgical instruments and clothes were soon brought from Manzanillo, though one of the new men was quickly killed in some sporadic firing, from Sánchez Mosquera's forward patrol – the first death on Castro's side since Alegría de Pío. The column moved back towards the stream El Ají, seeking always territory which they knew, in order to establish contact with the *precaristas* and to be in a favourable position to receive help, men and supplies, from Manzanillo. Some more *precaristas* joined, among them a forty-five-year-old illiterate, Julio Zenón Acosta, who became what Guevara called the revolution's first pupil in education: Guevara taught him the alphabet.[33]

This group brought the news that Sergio Acuña, who had deserted a few days before, had returned to his home, had boasted of his activities as a *guerrillero* and had been betrayed. He had been beaten and then shot by Corporal Roselló, and his body hanged. This, commented Guevara, taught the column 'the value of cohesion and the uselessness of trying individually to flee the collective destiny'. There was afterwards a purge of the unreliable or exhausted, and the 'Spanish veteran', Chao, Reinaldo Benítez and Edward Díaz were sent away from the Sierra, while Ramiro Valdés and Ignacio Pérez, Cresencio's son (like his father a leader of *precaristas*), also went away temporarily to care for their wounds: Chao had lost faith in the enterprise, saying that the rebels had embarked on 'a phenomenal folly'.[34]

A curious little biblical story now occurred. The traitor Eutimio Guerra, back in the fold, claimed that he had known from a dream that an air raid on the woods was about to happen. A discussion followed as to whether dreams could in fact evoke the prediction of such events. Guevara, part of whose daily task was 'to make explanations of a political or cultural nature', patiently explained that it was impossible, but some – among them the illiterate Acosta – stuck firmly to a physiological interpretation. A few nights later Guerra made his bid to kill Castro. He complained he had no blanket, and asked Castro to lend him one (the nights at that time were cold). Castro replied that

[32] Matthews, 19, 21.
[33] Guevara, 31–2.
[34] Franqui, 71.

they had better share the same one. Castro and the traitor, armed with a 0·45 pistol, lay down then under the same blanket. But Castro was also guarded by three others and Eutimio Guerra spent the whole night fingering his pistol unable to make up his mind when to shoot.

Though vacillating in his mission, he was not, however, without audacity; the following day, he predicted, according to his famous dream foresight, that the Loma del Duro (to which Castro was now close) would be shot up by Batistiano aeroplanes. He was delighted when this turned out to be the case. The Castro supporters were dispersed for several days – the peasant Labrador, Armando Rodríguez and six of the last Manzanillo party were either lost or, despairing, abandoned their place. A day or so later a peasant boy was captured who said that he had talked with Eutimio at Captain Casillas's headquarters. Castro moved his camp, which only shortly afterwards was shot up, Acosta being killed. Suspicions about Eutimio Guerra grew, though nothing could be done, since for three days the Fidelistas were divided. Reunited on 12 February, but with some more losses, the Fidelistas still only numbered eighteen.[35] In the next day or so they moved towards the plain, and in the farm La Montería a meeting was held with representatives of some Fidelistas in the cities – Haydée Santamaría and Armando Hart from Havana, Frank País, Celia Sánchez and Vilma Espín from Santiago. (Women had been specially chosen for this rendezvous as it was supposed that they would have a better chance of getting through the army's barriers.)[36] País had previously been trying to persuade Castro to go abroad in order to rally the revolutionary forces there; but his mind was changed by Castro's determination, confidence and energy.[37]

It was a few days after this that Castro's rebellion became well known in North America. Castro was aware of the important part played by the North American press in the war of independence.[38] Certainly the request carried to Havana by René Rodríguez, for a foreign correspondent to go to the Sierra, was an intelligent one. The moment was propitious. The executions by the army at Christmas had tipped the balance among many professional people in Havana, including many Ortodoxos, who were increasingly prepared to take Castro seriously as a force maintaining the prestige of the opposition by actually fighting Batista. Typical Ortodoxos who changed their position included Raúl Chibás, until recently their nominal leader, who met Frank País in Santiago on

[35] See below, p. 133.
[36] Guevara, 37, 38. *Cf.* Haydée Santamaría and Celia Sánchez in Franqui, 60.
[37] Haydée Santamaría in *ibid.*
[38] This is suggested by Herbert Matthews, in quoting from Máximo Gómez, 'Without a press we shall get nowhere.'

28 January and returned to Havana to try and organize a 'Civic Resistance', on the model of that existing in Santiago, harking back to the cellular organization of the ABC in the struggle against Machado. Ignacio Mendoza, an Ortodoxo leader who had been leader of the bomb placers in the fight against Machado, and a member of a noted Havana legal and commercial family, became a leader in Havana of the struggle against Batista. Mendoza, a broker of respectability, seemed above suspicion.[39] The Civic Resistance was supposed to be an independent non-political secret organization composed of middle and upper-class people regardless of party; in fact, it was from the start a front organization for the 26 July Movement in the cities, and a means of getting supplies and money;[40] on the other hand many of those who worked in it thought that they were doing so in order to avoid actually joining the 26 July Movement which they judged too extreme.[41]

Enrique Oltuski, a youthful engineer, once a supporter of García Barcena, became the Havana head of the Civic Resistance; he had joined Castro in mid-1955.[42] Raúl Chibás found that within a month he had gained $1,000 mostly from persons contributing $1 each, as agreed, paying by cells of ten.[43] Another prominent man who began to collaborate with the 26 July Movement in these weeks was Felipe Pazos, Cuba's leading economist and a governor of the National Bank under Prío. His son had been active in the struggle against Batista from the end of 1955 and, as with many Cubans, the son apparently drove the father to enter the movement for which he was already risking his life. Like Mendoza, Pazos had been in the struggle against Machado, and a member of the Student Directorate in 1933. Although Pazos could not himself boast a large following, his acceptance of the 26 July Movement was indicative of the political development of the Cuban middle class.

The Pazos family had secured the success of Castro's request for a foreign journalist in the Sierra. Felipe Pazos went to the office of the *New York Times*, whose correspondent, the intrepid Mrs Ruby Hart Phillips, herself a veteran of the Machado struggle, arranged that Herbert Matthews, a senior editor on the *New York Times* experienced in Latin American affairs, who had extensively covered the Spanish Civil War, should come from New York to try to see Castro.[44] Though fifty-seven years old, he was intrepid: twenty years before, Hemingway

[39] *Cf.* Jules Dubois, 257.

[40] This was the description given of the Civic Resistance by Armando Hart to Mario Llerena (Llerena, MSS, p. 46).

[41] This was the comment of Raúl Chibás (MSS).

[42] *Revolución*, 20 January 1959.

[43] The system of the Civic Resistance was that no one knew more than ten members of the organization; each head of a cell only knew his superior, etc.

[44] Herbert Matthews (born 1900), in U.S. army 1918; with *New York Times*, 1922-66.

had described him as 'brave as a badger'. Matthews, with his wife for a cover, was escorted to Manzanillo by Javier Pazos and Faustino Pérez. Pazos himself said later, 'I must confess that within myself I had doubts about Fidel's presence in the Sierra until we saw him'.[45] Batista meantime on 12 January had announced that there was 'absolute peace throughout Cuba', except for a few bombs thrown by Communists whose 'identity had been perfectly defined'.[46]

Leaving his wife at the house of Pedro and Ena Saumell, two Manzanillo school teachers and supporters of Castro, Matthews set off into the Sierra on 15 February and met Castro at dawn on 17 February.

He had driven with Pazos and some others much of the way, but walked the last stretch.[47] He was much impressed: 'The personality of the man is overpowering. It was easy to see that his men adored him . . . Here was an educated, dedicated fanatic, a man of ideals, of courage and of remarkable qualities of leadership . . . one got a feeling that he is now invincible.' The significance of the interview was considerable. First, Matthews created for North Americans the legend of Castro, the hero of the mountains, 'of extraordinary eloquence', 'a powerful six-footer, olive-skinned, full-faced, with a shapely beard. He was dressed in an olive grey fatigue uniform and carried a rifle with a telescopic sight of which he was very proud . . .' 'a great talker who dealt fairly with the peasants, paying for everything they ate'. For the next three years Fidel Castro was, much to his surprise and even for a time his anger, a North American hero.

Second, the interview exaggerated the number under Castro's leadership. Castro said that Batista worked 'in columns of 200; we in groups of ten to forty', although 'I will not tell you how many we have, for obvious reasons . . .' 'They had had many fights and inflicted many losses,' Matthews reported; he described Castro as saying, 'We have been fighting for seventy-nine days now and are stronger than ever . . . the soldiers are fighting badly; their morale is low, ours could not be higher.' Matthews reported that Castro's men had over fifty telescopic rifles, while Castro left the clear impression that his original eighty-two of the *Granma* had been a hard core which since had been greatly added to: they had 'kept the government at bay while youths came in from other parts of Oriente'. In fact, Raúl Castro kept passing in front of Matthews with the same men, and the impression was left that Castro himself was 'in another camp' for much of the time;[48] Castro then had

[45] Matthews, *The Cuban Story*, 23.
[46] *Havana Post*, 12 January 1957.
[47] Matthews, *op. cit.*, 26, 27; Felipe Guerra (who accompanied the mission) wrote an account in *Bohemia*, 6 June 1964.
[48] Franqui, 59.

only eighteen followers.[49] Castro could, it is true, also rely on Cresencio Pérez, his sons and several other peasants such as Manuel Acuña, temporarily absent but who had at one time or another been with him.[50] Matthews specifically said that in Oriente 'thousands of men and women are heart and soul with Fidel Castro and the new deal for which they think he stands'; these were sympathizers, but sympathizers who might be called to arms. The truth was that Castro was increasingly gaining the confidence of *precaristas* and their leaders through such men as Pérez, against the large and small landowners, who believed that the presence of Batista's army and the existence of a war situation might help them to dispose of the *precaristas* for ever. This 'revolutionary' attitude on the part of the *precaristas* was increased when Lieutenant Casillas drove out the peasants from the region of Palma Mocha: the leaders of the *precaristas* found collaboration with the new force in the Sierra more and more necessary (Casillas was a thug; he kept a box full of human ears to show to favoured visitors; he liked fighting and once told a guest that after the battles were over in Cuba he would not stay in a land of peace but leave for Columbia and fight for Colonel Pérez Jiménez.)[51] Yet Castro so influenced Matthews both by his character and his energy that Matthews asked him 'about the report that he was going to declare a revolutionary government in the Sierra'. 'Not yet,' he replied, 'the time is not ripe. I will make myself known at the opportune moment.'[52]

Matthews's article on his visit to the Sierra was published on 24 February and immediately made of Castro an international figure. Since the censorship was by chance lifted in Cuba the very next day, the news that Castro was alive became known quickly in Cuba also. The imprecise overestimate of the size of Castro's forces helped to attract urban Cubans to his cause. It was supposed that Castro was winning, that Batista's reports could not any more be relied on, and that his side was therefore the right side to be on; Castro's morale was raised. The morale in Batista's army was further depressed, and afterwards, when the Minister of Defence, Santiago Rey, denied both that Matthews could have penetrated the army's ring round the Sierra and that Castro was alive, the government was made ridiculous, since Matthews next published a photograph that he had taken of himself with Castro.

[49] Raúl Castro, Ameijeiras, Redondo, Morán, Crespo, Almeida, Julio Díaz, Universo Sánchez, Cienfuegos and Guevara, of the original *Granma* group; Fajardo, Guillermo García and Ciro Frías of the *precaristas*; Pesant, Motolá, Yayo, Echevarría of the Manzanillo reinforcements; together with the treacherous guide Guerra.

[50] Soon after Matthews's visit, Morán, Raúl Díaz, Gil and Sotolongo rejoined (ex-*Granmaistas*).

[51] See Barrera Pérez, *Bohemia Libre*, 16 August 1961. For Casillas, the author has had private information.

[52] Qu. from Matthews's article in *New York Times*, 24-6 February 1957.

Castro deceived Matthews about the size of his forces but not much about his political aims. 'The 26th of July Movement talks of nationalism, anti-colonialism, anti-imperialism,' Matthews wrote. 'These views he must have heard from Javier Pazos and people like him whom he met in Havana. Also in Havana, he obtained the 26 July Movement's clandestine tabloid, *Revolución*, in which, in an article entitled 'Necessity of Revolution', the word 'socialism' appeared.[53] To Matthews, Castro, however, said: 'You can be sure that we have no animosity towards the United States and the American people ... we are fighting for a democratic Cuba and an end to the dictatorship. We are not anti-military ... for we know the men are good and so are many of the officers.' 'Anti-imperialism' and even 'democratic' might of course mean anything. It is clear that Matthews himself saw Castro as a social democrat; but it is not of course certain that that was how Castro saw himself. The precise nature of Castro's political purposes in February 1957 is indeed hard to estimate, since, as has been suggested, Castro himself has given so many discordant versions of his political education. It would be wisest to assume that this education was under way rather than complete. Guevara, the most politically sophisticated of the group suggests in his account of the campaign in the Sierra that even he was open to influence by outside people such as País, the Santiago leader; País, he tells us, was anyway instrumental in making him clean his rifle more efficiently.[54] Yet Guevara and Raúl Castro were, with Castro himself, the only ones in the Sierra at this moment who had had a higher education. Their influence must have been the dominant intellectual ones on Castro, while Castro himself, as we have seen, was not a man of fixed or coherent ideological point of view, or of firmly held opinions. Even so, it would be wrong to overestimate how far Guevara and Raúl Castro influenced Castro. The opportunities of political discussion were not limitless, and all three were preoccupied by problems of survival, battle and the search for food. Fidel Castro was without doubt the dominant individual in the Sierra. His childhood and youth had prepared him for this sort of struggle, perhaps indeed only for this sort of struggle. His programme as described in an early issue of *Revolución*, in February 1957, has the stamp of authenticity, both in its vagueness, its rhetoric and its yearning patriotism:

The Revolution is the struggle of the Cuban nation to achieve its

---

[53] Most of the article was taken from Mario Llerena's pamphlet, *Nuestra Razón* (p. 23), not yet published; but Franqui, who had commissioned the pamphlet, had changed 'social justice' to 'socialism'. This word, together with the use of the word by Castro in the Sierra, had led Matthews to argue that Castro never changed his mind (*The Cuban Story*, 79–80). The point was also seized on by W. A. Williams (*The U.S., Cuba and Castro*, 77–9).

[54] *Pasajes*, 38.

historic aims and realise its complete integration. This integration consists in the complete unity of the following elements: political sovereignty, economic independence, in particular a differentiated culture. The Revolution is not exactly a war and an isolated episode. It is a continuous historic process which offers distinct moments or stages. The conspiracies of the last century, the wars of '68 and '95, the repression of the 1930s and today the struggle against the Batista terror are parts of the same . . . Revolution [which] . . . is struggling for a total transformation of Cuban life, for profound modifications in the system of property, and for a change in institutions . . . The Revolution is democratic, nationalist and socialist.[55]

As to the vexed and intriguing question of the relation between the 26 July Movement and Communism at this time, Blas Roca, the Communist secretary-general, said in 1960:

As soon as the first combat groups were established in the Sierra we tried to give them all possible aid. One outstanding, widely publicised case was a letter we sent to all the opposition parties shortly after the *Granma* landing, asking them to hold back the murderous hand of the government and prevent it from using superior force to exterminate Fidel Castro and his comrades.[56]

About six months later, in September 1957, the New York *Daily Worker*, the Communist paper of the U.S., was found complaining that the Cuban Communists were not getting enough credit for their support of the rebels.[57] But in reality, only four days after the publication of Castro's interview with Matthews, the Cuban Communist party made clear their 'radical disagreement with the tactics and plans' of Fidel Castro;[58] despite his 'valour and sincerity', they believed armed action to be wrong. They deplored terrorism, sabotage, and the burning of sugar cane. Though they admitted that the 26 July Movement 'came closest' to the Communists' 'strategic conception', it had not yet taken a strong enough line against 'imperialist domination' – that is, against the U.S. A month later Juan Marinello, then president of the Communists, wrote to Matthews, by then established on a pinnacle of fame as the interpreter of Cuba to North America, that the Communist party was opposed to the policy of 'the armed struggle' as such. It supported elections, forced on by such classic methods as strikes, popular demonstrations and civil protests. A Popular Front ought to be formed to

[55] Qu. Matthews, 79.
[56] Speech at 8th Congress of PSP.
[57] *Daily Worker*, 22 September 1957.
[58] *Carta del Comité Nacional del Partido Socialista Popular al Movimiento 26 de julio*, qu. Draper, *Castroism*, 29–30.

include not only workers and peasants but 'Cuban petty *bourgeoisie*' and 'national *bourgeoisie*'.[59] Thus, although the Communists might later claim that they had helped the 26 July Movement, at the time they differed from them upon a fundamental question of tactics; and, though tactical, it was the same sort of question which led to the open rift between Russia and China in 1959–60, or between Castro and the Latin American Communists in 1967.

There was clearly some dissension among the Communists. Both the youth movement, centred on Havana University, and some younger members of the party proper – particularly those such as Alfredo Guevara or Leonel Soto who had been university contemporaries of Castro – were doubtful of the desirability of placing all their bets on winning an electoral or constitutional struggle; already some such people saw in the Chinese road to power through armed struggle the only hope for triumph in Latin America; they were already distrustful of Soviet policies leading towards peaceful co-existence with the U.S. and the world of capitalism.[60]

The weeks after Matthews's report in the Sierra were not immediately successful for Castro. The false guide, Eutimio Guerra, was finally accused of treachery. He broke down, demanded to be killed, and only asked that his sons should be cared for; he was shot, a thunderstorm preventing the shot being heard.[61] Another dubious supporter, Morán, 'El Gallego', succeeded in leaving the group by shooting himself in the leg and so being allowed to stay behind.[62] Three old supporters of Castro, *Granma* men who had hidden, rejoined.[63] But the total force still numbered only about twenty, and morale was low. There was nothing to do till 5 March when they were due to meet new reinforcements being sent up from Santiago by Frank País. Guevara had a recurrence of asthma and had to be left behind for several days.[64] It rained heavily. Castro's boots were worn through. The force depended for food on purchases from a peasant named Emiliano and his son Hermes, in the valley Las Mercedes. Hermes was captured and gave Castro's position away. In a hurried escape, Guevara's asthma nearly prevented him leaving. Harsh days continued. A new attack at Altos de Merino followed, and a new dispersion – twelve men got away with Castro, six with Ciro Frías, who shortly was himself killed. On Batista's side, in yet another change of appointments, Major Barrera Pérez, the

[59] The letter is in Columbia University Library. See comments by Draper. *op. cit.*, 30–1; and Matthews, 51–2.
[60] Based on private discussions.
[61] Guevara, 40.
[62] Afterwards he joined Batista and was killed in Guantánamo.
[63] Raúl Díaz, Gil, Sotolongo.
[64] *Cf.* Ameijeiras, in Franqui, 119–20.

same who had established order in Santiago in November, was given the command in Oriente with 1,430 men, including a headquarters company, three infantry companies and one company of mountain troops with a battery of mountain artillery, an engineer corps, and a communications and transport group.[65]

Castro's group was late for its rendezvous with País's force but Jorge Sotús, the leader of that troop, consisting of some fifty men, managed nevertheless to get through alone to Castro and explain that he too was delayed, since Barrera Pérez had been holding the road too well. The rebels seemed in a tight corner and they could not even count on the support of all those *precaristas* whom they knew.[66] But some of the Batista forces were still incurring the further hatred and anger of the *precaristas* through arbitrary atrocities; in particular the navy (to whom part of the task of reducing Castro and re-establishing order had been allocated) was implicated. Thus the frigate *José Martí* was patrolling the coast from Cabo Cruz to Santiago; a lieutenant on board observed the naval intelligence chief, Laurent, and his henchman, García Olayón, in the act of burning the houses of peasants in the neighbourhood of Pilón. Some were drowned; countryside merchants met the same fate.[67]

These actions were opposed by the army colonel in charge, Barrera and his staff, and he and his aides sent a plan for an effective operation in the Sierra, which included a single command, the dismissal of the naval tyrants previously named and a rehabilitation scheme for the *precaristas*; as a consequence three of Batista's ministers, Dr Pardo Jiménez, Salas Humara and Fidel Barreto, arrived at the Sierra Maestra and a beginning was made: houses began to be built, medical services were embarked upon, and plans for schools laid, with a census of children. A free kitchen was set up at Colonel Barrera's command post where as many as three hundred persons a day were fed. Within a matter of weeks the army believed that it was beginning to wean away the affections of the *precaristas*, highly suspicious as most of them were at heart of both Castro and Batista.[68] By late March Barrera was in a position to contemplate the second part of his plan which was to construct an impenetrable line through which Castro's group could neither be reinforced nor supplied.

[65] After a survey by General Cantillo. The commanders were Barrera, chief of operations; Colonel Casasús, second in command; naval advisor, Major Rodríguez Alonso; legal advisor, Captain Evaristo Cordero; section 1, Captain Ricardo Grao; section 2, Major Joaquín Casillas Lumpuy; section 3, Captain Julio Castro Rojas; section 4, Lieutenant Fernando Ball Llovera.

[66] See Guevara in Núñez Jiménez's *Geografía*, 576. However, four new men did join in early March.

[67] Letters of Lieutenant Santa Cruz, U.S. Congressional Record, 20 March 1958, qu. Taber, 169. Also, see Barrera Pérez, *Bohemia Libre*, 13 August 1961, where he describes the interrogation of a survivor of one of the *noyades*.

[68] *Ibid.*, 20 August 1961; Suárez Núñez, 88-9.

CHAPTER 10

The Attack on the Palace

Even after the landing of the *Granma*, much of the sabotage outside the Sierra had been the work of people not part of Castro's movement. The Havana university students and the Directorio Revolucionario had been fairly active, despite some controversy over the use of violence between the latter's leader, Echevarría, and its 'intellectual leader', Jorge Valls, and despite the fact also that the university had been closed in late November. Also active had been a strong Priísta opposition group headed by Carlos Gutiérrez Menoyo, a thirty-three-year-old Spanish exile who had been in both the French resistance and the U.S. army. In 1957 he owned a grocer's shop in Havana. Associated with him in political gangsterism were several others of the same background, such as Ignacio González, also a Spaniard, who had been briefly arrested and then released in the preceding December. Though these were essentially Prío's men, they also had connections with the gangsters based on the Dominican Republic and through them even with Trujillo himself, from whom they got arms. Gutiérrez Menoyo had been a part of the famous Cayo Confites expedition. One man involved with them was Ricardo Olmedo, who had participated in a famous armed attack on the Royal Bank of Canada in 1948. Another, Ramón Alfaro, had had convictions for other than political activities.

These groups did not see eye to eye with Castro's 26 July Movement, although the Directorio Revolucionario had concluded an agreement with Castro in Mexico the previous summer,[1] and although, through its link with the Resistencia Cívica (in the process of formation by Raúl Chibás in Havana on the lines of País's movement in Santiago), the 26 July Movement's appeal was being widened. For some time anyway Gutiérrez, Menelao Mora, Echevarría and their friends had been actively but separately preparing an attack on Batista himself – a plan apparently devised in the first place by a comrade of Gutiérrez Menoyo, also a Spanish Republican, Daniel Martín Labandero, who had been caught and shot the previous autumn, escaping from the Principe prison.[2]

[1] See above, p. 102.
[2] According to Samuel B. Cherson, 'José Antonio Echevarría: Héroe y Mártir', *Bohemia*, March 1959, plans for the attack on Batista's life had been laid in 1955 and at least once in 1956.

The Directorio Revolucionario's links with Prío, meantime, grew closer during the winter of 1956–7, though Prío's money had also been made available to Castro. The decision to attack the palace was given extra weight by the publicity gained by Castro after his interview with Matthews: the other conspirators felt that time was no longer on their side.

At all events, in late February a plan even more dramatic than Castro's attack on the Moncada barracks was devised by the activist section of the Directorio, led by Echevarría, and Carlos Gutiérrez Menoyo, who broke relations with Prío and effectively joined Echevarría.[3] Another ex-Priísta, Menelao Mora, an ex-congressman in the Auténtico interest (earlier a member of the ABC), who had been president of the Havana bus company, Omnibus Aliados, also played a major part, bringing with him a number of personal followers. Menelao Mora had broken with Prío over the bus company, whose concession Prío, when still president, had given to Autobuses Modernos. Afterwards he joined Sánchez Arango for a time, but he always wished to strike out on his own and did so, having apparently organized 1,000 men in Havana in mid-1955.[4] Alberto, the son of Menelao Mora, then at the university, was a member of the Directorio, though a leftist one, while Menelao's brother Cándido had joined Batista and was now a representative in the assembly.[5] Some Auténticos involved, such as Segundo Ferrer, who had been in both Grau's and Prío's Secret Service, took this opportunity to join the Directorio.[6] The 26 July Movement was not at the beginning asked by anyone to help or to collaborate in any way. (It is of interest that, when the idea of an attempted assassination of Batista was put to Castro in 1955 by Justo Carrillo, he had vigorously opposed it: he was against personal attacks of that nature.[7]) The Communists were also aloof; they regarded the Directorio as 'a group of gangsters combined with elements of Prío, Aurelianismo and . . . Trujillismo'.[8] The Directorio was indeed explicitly anti-Communist and specifically refused membership to those it thought 'red' – wisely, for at least one of those who applied was Marcos Armando Rodríguez, who, though a friend of Jorge Valls, was trying to ingratiate

---

[3] Cf. Taber, 104; and Faure Chomón in La Sierra y el Llano (Havana, 1960), 110.

[4] Enrique Rodríguez Loeches, Bohemia, 15 March 1959.

[5] In 1961 Cándido Mora would be one of the oldest members of the Bay of Cochinos expedition. See below, 582. Alberto became a minister under Castro.

[6] Cuba, March 1964, 13.

[7] Carrillo, MSS, p. 25. This was at the Tapachula meeting. Castro explained his position on the grounds that 'It would not carry us to power but power would go to a reactionary military junta'.

[8] Letter from Marcos Armando Rodríguez to Joaquín Ordoqui, Hoy, 21 March 1964; César Gómez, in 1957 secretary of the Communist Youth, made play later with a photograph which showed a young Communist, Fulgencio Oroz, alongside Echevarría (ibid., 25 March 1964, 8).

himself with the Juventud Socialista, the Communist Youth, which he had also wished to join.[9] Faure Chomón,[10] one of the leaders of the Directorio, later claimed that its magazine, *Alma Mater*, 'often included quotations from Lenin',[11] and certainly its founder, Carlos Franqui, had been a Communist until the winter of 1946–7. But the general attitude of the Directorio was anti-Communist, democratic, middle class, and basically Catholic despite what has sometimes been suggested since.

The attack on Batista's palace was planned to be a shock attempt by about a hundred men to break through the presidential guards by sheer weight of numbers. They would shoot their way up to Batista's apartments on the first floor and kill the dictator. In the meantime José Antonio Echevarría and some others would capture Havana radio and announce the end of the tyranny. The detailed plans were worked out by Gutiérrez, with Menelao Mora and, for the Directorio, Faure Chomón and Fructuoso Rodríguez, who were too well known by the police to move freely.[12] On 9 March fifty men gathered in an apartment rented by Carlos Gutiérrez and awaited the call. The Russian poet Yevtushenko, in his autobiography, chose to write, having been told it by a Cuban:

> Each had his favourite occupation – one was reading, another writing poetry, others were playing chess. Among the revolutionaries were two painters, a realist and an abstract artist. They painted, arguing furiously (though, in view of the special conditions, in whispers) and very nearly came to blows. But when the final instructions arrived, both the realist and the abstract painters went to fight for the future of their country and were killed together.[13]

Of course, by no means all the men engaged in this assault were heroes or idealists; several were merely gun-happy men who relished the thought of a dramatic fight. The total force numbered nearly eighty, including most of the Directorio, except the pacifist Valls wing; several members of the 26 July Movement joined in of their own accord – some of them members of the original Artemisa Fidelistas of the days of the Moncada.[14] At the last minute on the morning of the attack, Javier Pazos, the 26 July leading representative in Havana, was asked if the

[9] This seems the only explanation of the conduct of this unhappy individual whose treachery and tragic end is chronicled later.

[10] Previously known as 'Chaumont'.

[11] *Hoy*, 21 March 1964.

[12] Evidence of Julio García Olivera, *Cuba*, March 1964.

[13] Yevtushenko, *A Precocious Autobiography*, 121. These were Luis Gómez Wangüemert and José Briñas – though in fact the first survived.

[14] See interview with Angel Eros, *Cuba*, March 1964. Eros, however, already called himself a member of the Directorio Revolucionario.

Fidelistas would join; he refused.[15] Castro apparently did not know what was going on. Listening to a wireless in the Sierra he could only tell his companions, 'Something big is going on in Havana.'[16] This was in fact a brave but rash frontal attack on the palace.

Since the forces were so large it was inconceivable that the plan would not be betrayed by someone; and in fact Batista had, on the 11th, got to know what was afoot through intercepted telephone calls.[17] His reaction, according to himself, was to ask the SIM chief, Colonel Piedra, to pass a message via Cándido Mora, the politician with the seat in the rump House of Representatives, to his brother, Menelao.[18] But this message was apparently not made explicitly clear. At all events, the rebels struck immediately after lunch on 13 March, with Batista's forces prepared for some sort of attack, though the details were not certain. Batista, whiling away the tedium of his tyranny reading *The Day Lincoln was Shot*, did not know on which day the attack would come and he had not imagined that it would be in broad daylight.[19]

The attack was in two waves. The first, led by Gutiérrez Menoyo, with Faure Chomón of the Directorio as his second-in-command, was composed of fifty men armed with sub-machine guns, twelve carbines, and a number of 0·45-calibre pistols. These men drove to the palace in a Buick sedan (four men), a Ford (four men) and a lorry labelled 'Fast delivery' (forty-two men).[20] All were in shirt sleeves, Batista having banned anyone going into the palace so dressed. The second wave was led by Ignacio González, with twenty-six men. Echevarría and Rodríguez Loeches, an ex-member of Masferrer's MSR, were to take over Radio Reloj, the somewhat absurd Havana radio station (which became very successful by broadcasting the time every minute, with news and advertisements in between), and announce that Batista was dead. As usual in Cuban revolutionary developments, the protagonists had a high sense of history: 'That morning we were Destiny,' recalled Chomón.[21] 'We knew that this attack ... was a highly historic enterprise which would free our people. We were going to give the world an impressive example.'

The first car arrived just before the palace at 3.20 p.m. Gutiérrez and three men[22] shot the traffic policeman[23] and, firing sub-machine

[15] Evidence of Javier Pazos.
[16] Ameijeiras, in Franqui, 131. On the other hand, Dr Lima says that he had known of, and encouraged, the attack in a letter to Echevarría before it occurred.
[17] Suárez Núñez, 72.
[18] Batista, *Cuba Betrayed*, 59.
[19] Batista to Edward Scott of the *Havana Post*, in *Havana Post*, 14 March 1957.
[20] *Cuba*, March 1964, 7.
[21] Franqui, 97.
[22] José Luis Goicoechea, José Castellanos, and Luis Almeida.
[23] Goicoechea to Franqui, 109.

guns, ran to the main entrance. About twelve surprised soldiers who were there fell dead, were wounded or fled. Though delayed by traffic, often a snag in street fighting in the twentieth century, the two other vehicles in the first wave arrived safely, but they were fired on from many quarters, including by a 0·30-calibre machine-gun on the church of San Angel. The men from the cars of the first wave ran to the palace; perhaps ten were shot down *en route*, but a group of nine men led by Menelao Mora reached the palace and quickly made their way up to the second floor of the palace on its left wing. Others kept on the ground floor. Gutiérrez, with four men, was on the left wing and destroyed the telephone switchboard with a grenade. They arrived at Batista's dining-room, and shot their way into the presidential offices, throwing grenades ahead of them and killing two men by Batista's desk. Not finding Batista, they realized that he had gone up to the 'presidential suite' on the next floor. Unfortunately for them they could not find the staircase upwards, though they had got from Prío careful plans of the palace.

The attackers then realized that Batista had concentrated his defences on the top floor, for from there rifle and machine-gun fire, directed by Batista himself, was beginning to dominate the courtyard and the forecourt of the palace. A telephone rang. Gómez Wangüemert answered: 'Yes it is true, the palace has fallen. Batista is dead. We are free.' Meantime some of Mora's group had become dispersed, while the whole second wave of the attack, under Ignacio González, had not arrived at all, since once the firing had begun, the palace was surrounded by a huge army of policemen and soldiers, almost giving the impression that it was they who were doing the attacking. Tanks even had begun to move towards the palace. Echevarría had captured the radio station and broadcast an excited message: 'People of Havana! The Revolution is in progress. The presidential palace has been taken by our forces and the Dictator has been executed in his den!' But after he had blown up the central control panel in the radio station, Echevarría was shot dead in the street by police. Meanwhile, the men on the second floor of the palace continued to fire and to throw grenades upwards, but, eventually, they retreated. Most (including Mora and Gutiérrez) were killed on the marble staircase. Only three of the men who had penetrated into Batista's offices actually escaped alive from the palace.[24] Firing continued much of the afternoon, soldiers shooting indiscriminately and wounding several bystanders. The little park near the palace seemed to run with blood. Most of the buildings nearby were chipped with bullets.

---

[24] This account derives chiefly from Luis Goicoechea. Goicoechea's story is graphically told in Taber, 110–22, and in *Cuba*, March 1965, where there are other stories by participants. See also Batista, *Cuba Betrayed*, 59.

In this contest, thirty-five rebels and five members of the palace guard were killed. One American tourist was accidentally killed. Afterwards, an unknown number of students, boys, odd suspects and members of the opposition, were rounded up and eventually shot – many, as usual, being tortured. The Ortodoxo ex-Senator Pelayo Cuervo, nominal president of the Ortodoxo party, was found murdered on the edge of a lake in the Country Club next morning. Apparently the police had thought, on the basis of papers found on Echevarría's body, that Cuervo would have become provisional president if the attack had succeeded, and had let themselves run riot. The executioner was Sergeant Rafael Linares.[25] Batista himself accused Prío of providing the arms, and told reporters that he had definite evidence that international Communism was heavily involved – though the Communists had held aloof.[26]

The attack on the palace was foolhardy. Castro was surely correct, if tactless, in saying that it constituted 'a useless expenditure of blood'. Its chances of success were remote. The third floor of the palace was only approachable by a lift, and therefore the attackers could never have got up there if the lift was, as it was, at the top. No provision had been made for the aftermath or for a successful hiding place for the attackers in the event of failure. If, however, the 'second wave' had arrived the attack might just have terrified the defenders into flight. Thus, as can be expected, the survivors felt full of rancour towards those who did not help them; they may have fought in the Spanish war but that was a long time ago, commented Chomón.[27] The 26 July Movement helped to pick up the wounded and Javier Pazos gave up to Chomón, Gutiér-rez's second-in-command, his hiding place. The 26 July also captured a lorry-load of arms which had not been used and hid them in the apartment of a minor member of their movement, 'Barba Roja' Piñeiro, who was conveniently married to an American; they afterwards found their way to the Sierra.[28]

The aftermath of the attack on the palace had two characteristics; first, the sympathy which the business world, the upper classes in general, and foreign commercial interests showed towards Batista was remarkable. The leaders of all these communities called on Batista during the next few weeks to condemn the attack; so did the National Association of Sugar Mill Owners, the CTC (Mujal), the Veterans of

[25] Jules Dubois, 155.

[26] *Havana Post*, 14 March 1957. These days show Batista in the full flood of an anti-Communism which would have seemed extravagant even to McCarthy – verbally at least: on 9 March he has assured the Chicago journalist Dubois that the Communist Castro had killed six priests with his teeth at the Bogotazo.

[27] Franqui, 106.

[28] Javier Pazos's evidence. Piñeiro later became Castro's chief of counter-intelligence, afterwards vice-minister of the Interior. One member of the Directorio, Dr Lima, however, later accused the 26 July Movement of stealing the arms (Lima memorandum, p. 4).

The Moncada attack:
1*a* Fidel Castro (left) and other prisoners
 b The barracks afterwards

2 a The Sierra Maestra
  b The Rebels in their stronghold: Raúl Castro, Juan Almeida, Fidel Castro,
     Ramiro Valdés, Ciro Redondo

the War of Independence, the Cuba Banking Association, the Insurance Companies, American and Spanish businessmen, property owners, coffee and cattle-breeders' associations, rice growers, cigarette and cigar manufacturers, even fishermen.[29] On 1 April the leading banks and bankers of Cuba, headed by Víctor Pedroso, Alex Roberts (Banco Caribe) and Martínez Sáenz, the president of the National Bank, called.

Most unsuccessful attempts at assassinations do good to the intended victim but in this case the advantage to the regime was enormous; Batista felt himself supported on every hand by all that was best in Cuban public and commercial life. He had never received such an overwhelming endorsement. A very large number greeted Batista on 7 April when he addressed the crowd – perhaps approaching the 250,000 which he claimed – in the square before the palace. The majority of these supporters no doubt regarded the attack on the palace as gangsterish as much as political, the latest in an endless series of outrages: to find Ricardo Olmedo, who had taken part in the attack on the Bank of Canada in 1948, among those involved, confirmed them in these views. The known participation of friends of Aureliano, Eufemio Fernández, the students and the 26 July Movement did not enhance, in public estimation, the reputation of any of these groups.[30]

The second consequence was heightened repression. The police maintained their search for the participants and made many arrests. On 19 April, Captain Esteban Ventura, of the police, and his men, were, due to the treachery of Marcos Armando Rodríguez, a university colleague of the students involved, able to corner and kill, in an apartment in Humboldt Street, four of the surviving leaders of the students: Fructuoso Rodríguez, who had succeeded Echevarría outside the radio station on 13 March;[31] José Westbrook, also 'a veteran of the radio station'; José Machado ('Machadito'); and Juan Pedro Carbó Serviá, who had been into the palace itself with Gutiérrez. Carbó had been one of the assassins of Colonel Blanco Rico in the night-club the previous autumn. The treachery of Rodríguez became afterwards a *cause célèbre* in revolutionary Cuba, due to his support afterwards by powerful Communist friends to whom he is believed later to have confessed the whole crime in Mexico.[32] At the time of his treachery, he was

[29] See Batista, *Cuba Betrayed*. Castro later commented bitterly on this 'contemptible procession of representatives of the upper classes ... all the *haute-bourgeoisie*, its lumpenist [!], gangsters, mujaliestas ... I assure you that none of this class visited the palace after the passage of a revolutionary law. None.' (*Obra Revolucionaria*, 1961, No. 46, p. 24).

[30] Though it might be argued, as Professor Dumont did of the Columbian banditry, that the gangsterism of Cuba '*se purifie en se politisant*' (*Cuba*, 9).

[31] It seems only too possible that, as Fructuoso Rodríguez's father told a judge later, the student leader was in fact alive when he reached the first aid post, and was afterwards killed. (See *Havana Post*, 27 April 1957.)

[32] The Communists were Joaquín Ordoqui and Edith García Buchaca, to whose house in Mexico Rodríguez often repaired when in exile 1957-9.

not, however, a Communist party member and his motives appear to have been primarily personal rather than political – a dislike of the activist wing of the Directorio, possibly a hatred of violence itself, probably jealousy, a desire to be important, and perhaps a continuing desire to try to please the Communist Youth leaders (who had continued to rebuff him even though he had been for a time their informer) by the destruction of their rivals who indeed might in the end have turned out anti-Communists.[33] It is clear that he did not do it for money and equally clear that the Communists to whom he later confessed did not take a very serious view of his treachery.

The burial of these four students, all Catholics, in the Colón cemetery, was attended by large crowds. Protests were widespread but it speaks harshly for the regime that four young men could be in effect executed without trial, without any reprimand for Captain Ventura and without much disapproval of him in the *haute-bourgeois* and commercial worlds. Imperceptibly Cuban society was disintegrating towards the same situation as occurred in the late 1920s and early 1930s, where police violence was condoned. The death of Dr Pelayo Cuervo served as a notice to all members of the opposition that they could count on no guarantees and made them more likely than ever to countenance Castro and the armed struggle.

The attack on the palace did not prevent new visits from distinguished North Americans; within a week Admiral Burke, chief of naval operations, came to receive an order of Cuban naval merit from Batista; Kansas businessmen continued to fly in for conventions. But 'normality' was increasingly absent; men were constantly arrested, for setting fire to canefields, for being suspected of bomb placing, even for collecting money in memory of José Antonio Echevarría. The secondary schools of Cuba were closed for one week by government order, and for another week after the deaths in Humboldt 7. In the continued atmosphere of agitation, Batista banned the half-term elections due for Congress in 1957, only permitting the establishment of a congressional committee to 'spend twenty days taking testimony from the political parties', including from the 26 July, and then 'work out a solution' for the future. This had little success though it heard a number of political opposition leaders such as Grau, Varona, Pardo Llada and Alonso Pujol.

The guerrilla 'war' might be the only heroic aspect of Cuban life in the spring of 1957, but there was nevertheless no revolutionary demand

[33] See the author's article in the *New Statesman*, 29 May 1964. The original police statement said that there were six students in the apartment and that Marquitos and Eugenio Pérez Cowley had been there and escaped (see *Havana Post*, 23 April 1957). Another account by one closely involved is *El Crimen de Humboldt 7*, by Enrique Rodríguez Loeches, *La Sierra y el Llano*, 143–65). Ventura, incidentally, in *his* book (p. 251) admitted that there was a betrayal but makes other accusations of identity.

from all sections of the nation. Thanks to the Suez crisis, sugar prices were high. The 1957 harvest was large, the crop had been declared free of control, and there was an unusual sale of 15,000 tons to the U.S.S.R. in April, causing much speculation which itself kept prices up. By April it was evident that there would be no difficulty in disposing of a substantial harvest, and the only question remaining was how much would be available, sixty-four mills having still to grind, and sixty-four having finished. Some cane was burned by Castro in Oriente but not enough to make an appreciable difference to the harvest. It was 1870–4 all over again. The guerrilla war and political activity was thus waged in the face of the economic situation in more ways than one, just as Martí's revolt against Spain had been: 1894 and 1957 were alike in being excellent years for the economy. 1957 also saw a number of important steps towards that reasonable diversification of the economy which had been urged for a long time by the World Bank and others: typical were the big paper mills established at the *central Trinidad* and at *central Morón*, using *bagasse*. A $M25 Shell oil refinery was inaugurated by Batista on 30 March. In April bulldozers were at work on a motorway to link the recently completed Via Blanca to Varadero with the Central Highway. A new suburb, Havana del Este, was taking shape. The *Hispanic American Report*, the best U.S. review of Latin American events at that time and usually criticized for its radical politics, commented:

> Economic stability and progress continued unabated. The Government continued heavy spending on public works, new buildings were going up everywhere, new investments . . . continued at an accelerated pace, *per capita* income was the highest ever recorded . . . government revenues were running $M21 ahead of the previous year.[34]

The only serious effect of the near-civil war was on the tourist trade,[35] but, even so, big hotels continued to be put up: the Havana Hilton was opened in April with a party attended by half of Batista's cabinet;[36] and the Capri and the Habana Riviera hotels, huge luxurious castles, were also under way – the Capri with a swimming pool on its roof on the twenty-fifth floor.

[34] HAR, May 1957.
[35] A protest appeared in *Havana Post*, 28 March 1957.
[36] *Ibid.*, 6 April 1957.

CHAPTER 11

War in the Sierra (March–May 1957)

On 16 March Castro had received his first large reinforcement in the Sierra – fifty men from Santiago under Jorge Sotús.[1] These recruits seemed unpromising to those who had already lasted out in the Sierra for three months. Guevara complained that they were unused to having only one meal a day and that they brought with them all manner of useless things. All were exhausted from their journey from Manzanillo. Only thirty were armed, though they did have two old machine guns. They had been brought part of the way by a local rice grower, Hubert Matos, an important sympathizer who would figure in a *cause célèbre* two and a half years later. Sotús, who had led the attack on the Santiago Maritime police headquarters on 30 November 1956 had given himself the rank of captain; and he had named five lieutenants commanding ten men each.[2] Among this group were three young Americans – Charles Ryan, Victor Buchman and Michael L. Garney – sons of North Americans working in Guantánamo. They had set out in the hope of adventure, but two left before seeing action.

Relations between the new arrivals and the veterans of three months were bad. Sotús, a 'prosperous warehouse owner's son',[3] despite his eminent part in Frank País's battle of Santiago had not proved himself as a guerrilla leader and he had difficulties with Castro. The united force was reorganized in three companies under Sotús,[4] Raúl Castro[5] and Almeida,[6] while special vanguard and rearguard units were placed under Cienfuegos with four men and Ameijeiras with three men. A small headquarters unit under Castro himself comprised Ciro Redondo, Manuel Fajardo, Crespo, Guevara as doctor, and Universo Sánchez as chief of staff. This reorganization gave little responsibility in practice to the new recruits. A small inner council directed affairs, including Castro, the three company commanders, with Ciro Frías, Guillermo

---

[1] Taber gives 58 (p. 102); Guevara has 'about 50' (48).

[2] Hermo, Domínguez, René Ramos Latour ('Daniel'), 'Pedrín' Soto, who had escaped from the *débâcle* after the *Granma*, and a Santiago student named Peña.

[3] Taber, 72.

[4] Under Sotús were three lieutenants, Ciro Frías, Guillermo García and René Ramos Latour, who had come up with Sotús.

[5] Under Raúl Castro were three lieutenants, Julio Díaz, Ramiro Valdés (who rejoined, after his wound, after 24 March), and 'Naño' Díaz.

[6] Lieutenants Hermo, Guillermo, Domínguez and Peorín.

García, Cienfuegos, Fajardo and Guevara. Cooking, medicine, and provisioning was henceforth done in platoons rather than centrally. Already the outlines of an army were being drawn, about eighty strong though with rather fewer than that number of weapons. Each man was supposed to make for himself a hammock of sacking, though some canvas hammocks were also available. The company commanders sought to accustom the new recruits to the rigours of the mountains by marching and counter-marching, rather than, as suggested by the intemperate Guevara, attacking the nearest post to test them in the struggle.[7] They marched eastwards, finding as before among the peasants 'first a great terror of the army; [and] second, how it was [still] hard for them to realize how a badly dressed and badly armed group such as ourselves could defeat the army'.[8] Relations between the *precaristas* who had joined the column, and the people of the plain were not always good. For instance, the peasants were outraged one night by the eating of a horse.

On 30 March, meantime, Batista once more announced that Castro was not in the Sierra and that he had not been seen since 'he shot some soldiers sleeping' at La Plata. A few days later the army carried an aeroplane load of eighty journalists across the Sierra, to demonstrate that there was 'no one there'. Colonel Barrera's plans were now beginning to bear fruit; some of the *precaristas* had rallied to the army, though the scheme of attempting to insulate Castro from succour by a '*barrida*' was a somewhat defensive one: the field operation under Barrera having been placed under Major José Cañizares, with the mountain artillery, the naval units assigned, a squadron of bombers and a battalion of infantry.[9] This force was indeed perfectly adequate to keep the rebels from increasing their forces, though neither Cañizares nor Barrera supposed that Castro had so few men. By early April it seemed to them that their mission was completed, and Colonel Barrera, the inspiration of this stage of Batista's counter-offensive, could be recalled; according to him, he had lost only one man and that as a result of a shooting accident.[10] On return to Havana Barrera Pérez made a full report to Batista who congratulated him on his success. But this report did Barrera no good, since it immediately brought the jealousy of General Tabernilla's apparatus of intrigue and misrepresentation: it was put abroad by the chief of staff and his cronies that Barrera had attempted the rehabilitation of the *precaristas* in order to get in touch with the enemy: and that his failure to capture Castro was because he was secretly in

[7] Guevara, 49–51.

[8] Castro's speech, December 1961, *Obra Revolucionaria*, No. 46, p. 18.

[9] Composed of three companies under Captains Merob Sosa, Juan Chirino, and Raúl Sáenz de Calahorra. The air squadron was under Colonel Félix Catasús.

[10] He was recalled on 16 April (*Bohemia Libre*, 20 August 1961).

contact with him. For the time being Barrera successfully stood up to these insinuations in La Cabaña, while his activity in the Sierra, 'mopping up' the remains of the rebels, as it was supposed, was given over to the bloodthirsty Major Casillas, who had been in the area off and on since December. Before leaving, Barrera had in fact told the journalists who visited the Sierra that there was only a band of outlaws (not Castro) there, 'with harems of five women each'. The commander produced a number of *precaristas* who proclaimed themselves grateful to the army, and he said that, in addition to his 550 officers and men, he had at least 250 informers and government agents among the peasants and farmers of the area. He was accurate in his statement that there had been no action in the Sierra since 9 February,[11] but it was of course an error to withdraw the special troops which Barrera had with him, leaving the field to Casillas and conventionally trained men.

By mid-April 1957 the rebels had returned to the neighbourhood of the Pico Turquino. The *precaristas* García and Frías played a big part at this time, moving backwards and forwards across the jungle carrying news and food. The house of the priest of Manzanillo, Fr Antonio Albizú, became a rendezvous for messengers. There were still no engagements with the army. The rebels spent weeks establishing lines of contact with the peasants, identifying those who could be trusted, those who might serve as messengers, those who would give honest information and who would know places where permanent bases could be safely established and where food could be permanently provided or stored. This spring campaign – though it scarcely merits the name – was of the greatest importance in the future. One of Castro's followers from the plain was Celia Sánchez, daughter of a dentist on Lobo's plantation at Pilón.[12] From her the news came that (on the initiative of Hart and the 26 July organization in Havana) two new North American journalists, one with a television camera, were ready to visit the rebels. The idea was accepted by Castro, and Lalo Sardiñas, a commercial traveller from near the sugar mill *Estrada Palma*, transported into the hills Robert Taber and Wendell Hoffman, of the Columbia Broadcasting System.[13] With them came Marcelo Fernández, son of a Cárdenas grocer who had been president of the Engineering School at the University of Havana, as an English interpreter. The two Americans remained several days, and the

---

[11] See *Havana Post*, 13 April; E. Scott's column on 14 and 16 April; cf. Guevara, 54; HAR, September 1957.

[12] She was an eccentric woman in her thirties and Lobo had built her on the estate a dovecote where she could 'sleep, write or dream'. She later became Castro's secretary and his most faithful aide.

[13] A key part in the reception of these journalists was played by the Rev. Raúl Fernández Ceballos, pastor of the First Presbyterian Church in Havana, a preacher of predominantly left-wing views who afterwards remained in the 1960s a vigorous supporter of the revolution.

interview ultimately took place on top of the Pico Turquino. In the interview Castro gave an impression of moderation as strong as that he had given to Matthews: he said that he normally opposed bloodshed but that he wished to create an atmosphere where the government would have to fall; he requested that the U.S. should send no more arms to Batista; he was fighting for the restoration of the Constitution of 1940.[14] Shown in May, as 'The story of Cuba's Jungle Fighters', the film proved that, contrary to the statements of Colonel Barrera, Castro was certainly still in the Sierra. New recruits continued to arrive, some such as El Vaquerito, 'the little cowboy', from Morón (Camagüey), with no political ideas and the intention only of having a marvellous adventure – to whom Guevara, as political conscience of the group, had necessarily to give lessons; or the farm labourer and builder who had taken the bus from his home in Pinar del Río to join Castro to fight for a better world against the one which seemed to have so persecuted him.[15] The mere movement through the Sierra in these months was enough to show the revolutionary torch and, the legend being created, *precaristas*, after the brief Barrera experiment was over, once again began to approach the rebels as their friends. But treachery and the trial and afterwards execution of informers was still fairly frequent, as the guerrilla war became blended with older internecine blood feuds.

The experience of dealing with the peasants, with their ailments and their malnutrition, evidently affected the political views of the rebels. Guevara noted: 'In these activities there began to take shape in us the consciousness of the need for a definitive change in the life of the people. The idea of agrarian reform was born and that of communion with the people ceased to be theory, being converted into a definite part of our being.'[16] This may overstate the matter. Guevara had worked, if only for a short time, in the Guatemalan revolutionary Institute of Agrarian Reform. His experience was such that he needed less further education of this sort than he said; and his temperament was such that he preferred to teach others, rather than receive lessons, even from experience. Castro had been talking about the need for a radical change in society for a long time and, whatever importance is given to his later reinterpretation of his youth, he had clearly known of the existence of schemes to change society. But even Guevara's 'Marxism' was probably theoretical. Castro had said so many things, and had changed his mind so often, that, as with the Scriptures, almost any interpretation could have been based on them. Anything he had said would have been changed as a result of his experiences in the Sierra. But this does not

[14] See *Life*, 27 May 1957.
[15] This was the later Major Antonio Sánchez Díaz ('Piñares'). See his account in *Verde Olivo*, 12 May 1963. He was killed in Bolivia in 1967 with Guevara under the pseudonym 'Marcos'.
[16] Guevara, 65.

mean that his 'communion with the people' was not real and that it did not mark a definite change in the 'actualization' of his political activity. Guevara added: 'The guerrilla and the peasant became joined into a single mass, so that (and no one could say at which moment precisely of the long march it occurred) we became part of the peasants.' These judgements seem romantic, but they doubtless represent a true picture of what Guevara, the political teacher of new recruits, himself thought about the Sierra's importance.[17] In Guevara's conversations with a peasant named Banderas, afterwards killed, who fought in order to work with more land than he had, there were also clear foretastes of the revolution's own controversial socialization of land.[18]

The march eastwards continued and what happened in the next few weeks was a good illustration of the tactics of guerrilla action. At Pino del Agua, the rebels captured a mounted Batistiano corporal known to have many crimes to his discredit since the days of Machado. Castro resisted demands for his execution, since it was his policy to treat captives in the opposite manner to the way of the Batistianos. He and his horse were held prisoner by recruits, while the main body pressed on to see if an important cargo of arms had arrived at the appointed place despite the detention of the messenger.[19] But in fact the arms were brought in a yacht belonging to the Babun family, a large timber firm and ship-builders of Santiago – three machine guns on tripods, three Madison machine guns, nine M1 carbines, ten Johnson automatic rifles, and 6,000 rounds.[20] The Babun family were great friends of Batista and the military leaders. but one of their employees, Enrique López, an old friend of the Castro brothers, was of some assistance to the rebels in getting food in this area. At this time, due to further recruitment of *precaristas*, and the return of various old friends such as Cresencio Pérez, total rebel numbers in the Sierra approached 150. But, due to the usual lack of physical preparation on some of the recruits' part, lack of persistence, or irritation with the horse-fly, many asked permission to return to their homes: 'Our struggle against lack of moral, ideological and physical preparation of the combatants was daily.' On 23 May Castro disbanded a whole squadron, leaving a total force of 127 men, eighty of whom were well armed, who were accompanied for a time by a U.S. journalist and secret agent, Andrew St George,[21] of Hungarian birth, who apparently returned to Washington to report that

[17] All this was still in respect of May 1957.
[18] See Guevara, 90.
[19] These were arms unused in the attack on the palace and sent up to the Sierra by Javier Pazos by means of a young Santiago recruit, Carlos Iglesias (known as 'Nicaragua').
[20] Guevara, 71.
[21] Mario Lazo, *Dagger in the Heart*, 235. Guevara regarded St George as a FBI spy, and, in a series of articles about Guevara's activities in Bolivia (*Sunday Telegraph*, 7 July 1968), St George was described as having done 'a spell in the U.S. military intelligence service'.

Castro was 'an ego-maniac and emotionally unstable but not a Communist'.

The 'guerrilla war' had still been quiet since February, and the irritation and even bewilderment of Batista and his officers at the world-wide interest in Castro can be readily understood. Now a new action was decided on: the discussion reveals the level at which events still were being enacted. Guevara merely desired, for instance, to capture a military lorry; Castro decided, however, on an attack on the military post of El Uvero, then ten miles away, placed similarly to the barracks of Plata, on the sea, and on the Babún brothers' estate. The rebels were helped greatly by Hermes Caldero, son-in-law of the administrator of the region. Two spies sent by Major Casillas were shot on 27 May; they had first revealed that the army knew of Castro's proximity to the post. A careful study was made of the surroundings. The rebels made the march to it at night down the roads built for their woodcutters by the Babuns. According to Colonel Barrera Pérez the employees of the region, on Castro's orders, gave a fiesta to the local soldiery the night before so that they would face an attack drunk and dazed; but of this no mention occurs in 'revolutionary history'.[22]

The orders for the attack were simply to surround the post on the three sides away from the sea, and then fire continuously at it. The living quarters where there were women and children were to be spared. The wife of the administrator of the estate knew of the imminent attack but did not leave because of not wishing to rouse suspicion. Rebel platoons commanded by Jorge Sotús, Guillermo García, Juan Almeida, Castro, Raúl Castro, Cienfuegos and Ameijeiras, got into position; Cresencio Pérez commanded the road towards Chivirico to prevent reinforcements. Guevara operated a machine gun. Eighty men entered into action, the remainder apparently staying in the hills.

The barracks were held by fifty-two men, commanded by Lieutenant Carrera, a somewhat aged officer in his fifties who had been in the army since 1922. The action, supposed to begin before dawn, began in fact only at daylight. Castro opened the firing, with his famous rifle with the telescopic lens; the barracks replied. One of the early shots broke the telephone exchange, and cut off the post from the possibility of communication. The advance then began, in bad conditions for the attackers, because of a lack of cover. Several men were wounded and some killed. Almeida overwhelmed the advance post in the direct path, with several wounded and one dead, and the ex-*precarista* Guillermo García did the same on the flank. The rebels prepared to storm the barracks after about three hours, with only some sporadic firing continuing. The rebels advanced, took over the living quarters

[22] Barrera Pérez, *Bohemia Libre*, 20 August 1961.

and captured the barracks' doctor, who showed himself incapable of action.[23]

In this contest, the fiercest which the rebels had yet fought, six attackers were killed – Julio Díaz (of the *Granma*); a guide, Eligio Mendoza; Moll; Emiliano Díaz (from the Santiago recruits), Vega and 'El Policía' an aide to Sotús. Two men were very badly wounded. The army had fourteen killed, nineteen wounded (amongst them Lieutenant Carrera) and fourteen captured, while six escaped. One North American, Charles Ryan, fought for Castro.

After the contest, the rebels drew back to the mountains, carrying with them all possible supplies and medicaments in one of Babun's lorries. They took with them the fourteen prisoners, whom they later freed (after 'indoctrination', according to Colonel Barrera Pérez), and four of their own wounded, but left behind their two very badly wounded. It seemed impossible to move them, and the remaining Batistianos gave their word that they would be honourably treated. Leal, in fact, was sent to the Isle of Pines; Cilleros died on the way to Santiago. The other wounded men were escorted by Guevara in a column following behind the rest, going slowly and narrowly escaping capture, but aided by peasants and by a *mayoral* of the Peladero estate owned by a Santiago lawyer, José Pujol. The *mayoral* Sánchez was later caught and tortured brutally by the army, though he was, in the eyes of Guevara at least, an orthodox *mayoral*, faithful to his master, 'racist' and contemptuous of his peasants.[24]

This action heightened the morale of the rebels and gave them the feeling that they could master any of the little barracks near the Sierra.

Batista made no further attempt for the time being to cope with Castro in the only manner by which guerrilla forces can in fact be met, as suggested, for example, in the English campaign against guerrilla forces in Malaya in the 1950s, the most successful anti-guerrilla campaign of recent times. In Malaya the English decided on a full attempt to enmesh the Communist guerrillas of Chin Peng, blocked roads, and moved all scattered villagers into well-guarded compounds, echoing Weyler's camps, though they gave to those who were moved a new home and a new cash resettlement. Food was sealed, rationed and accounted for. These measures were accompanied by a general amnesty, a cash reward for surrender, and a rehabilitation programme including a monthly cash allowance during 'de-indoctrination' and preparation for a new job. There were also psychological appeals, protection against terrorism, generous aid for education, medical assistance and public

[23] See description of this battle in *Verde Olivo*, 2 June 1963, where the defeated Lieutenant Carrera exchanged memories with Ameijeiras; Guevara, 79, also has a rebel account.

[24] Guevara, 90. Sánchez was betrayed by peasants in August. *Cf. Havana Post*, 13 August 1957.

works. The English army in Malaya, interestingly enough, was smaller than Batista's in Cuba, consisting of 15,000 regular army and marines, but they were accompanied by 150,000 police and 250,000 volunteer home guards. The guerrilla forces were on the other hand far larger than Castro's at any stage, numbering 15,000 at their peak – and as Major Peterson of the U.S. marines thoughtfully put it, the rebellion was wiped out at a cost of £30,000 per guerrilla. Even so, some 1,000 or so guerrillas – more than Castro had at any stage in 1957 – were believed to be in action on the Thai border after the emergency was nominally declared at an end in 1960.

It would have been impossible for Batista to have emulated these methods completely, as men as intelligent as Barrera Pérez or Cantillo knew. His army of 40,000 was incomparably inferior to the English army of 15,000. So was his police. He could not rely on any organized voluntary help of any kind at any time. Maybe even allowing for the smaller number of rebels, £30,000 ($80,000) would have been too much per head though throughout 1957 with 150 rebels to destroy, this would have cost roughly only $M12, a sum which Batista could certainly have raised, perhaps out of his own pocket. But Batista certainly could not have attempted the mixture of toughness and magnanimity which characterized the approach of the English. Not only was he incapable of this, but the army was completely hamstrung by the evil genius of General Tabernilla and his cronies. Batista had never allowed himself to be influenced by the few intelligent officers who did exist in the Cuban army. The U.S. officers in Cuba as part of the military mission seem to have told him nothing. The small size of Castro's forces also placed Batista in a quandary: to concentrate an immense effort on the Sierra Maestra would explicitly contradict his argument that the rebels were being beaten. The problem of urban terrorism was also lacking in Malaya. In general, Batista's government showed itself incapable of dealing with a resolute, progressive revolutionary guerrilla force, with considerable peasant backing, once it had become firmly established.

These facts did not mean that by mid-1957 the regime was doomed to fall. Guerrilla forces had been maintained in China, Colombia or Guatemala for many years without achieving a national victory. The reasons for Batista's fall did not lie in the Sierra. The field of struggle was in Havana, and in Santiago, and in Washington as well. The role played by the government of the U.S. in the next eighteen months was ambivalent and extraordinary, even if in the end unsatisfactory both to Batista and to Castro.

CHAPTER 12

The U.S. enters the Controversy

The attack on El Uvero came as a shock to Batista and, despite the protest of Tabernilla, it caused him to send back Colonel Barrera Pérez as field commander in the Sierra.[1] The month of May had been a time of difficulty: bombs went off incessantly. They were even set off in schools to try to keep children from taking their end of year examinations. Secondary schools spontaneously went on continuous strikes. There were frequent civilian casualties. On the day of the El Uvero attack itself, an immense explosion in Havana cut off telephone, electricity, gas and water for over fifty homes. The cost was $375,000, which the government was undecided whether to blame on Castro or their electoral enemies. Arrests also continued (among them Armando Hart and Carlos Franqui, of the Havana leadership). Captain Esteban Ventura, chief of police of the 5th Precinct, became in the public mind almost what Arsenio Ortiz had been in the era of Machado: a legendary death-dealer. Bombs were aimed to kill police chiefs, as in Machado's day. On 11 May, Batista met almost for the first time opposition from the law: at a trial in Santiago of a hundred Fidelistas, some survivors of the *Granma*, the presiding judge, Manuel Urrutia, declared that all should be acquitted. Batista, furious, foolishly allowed his Minister of Justice to enter a plaint against Urrutia (it was later dropped) and against the prosecutor, who had not asked for sentence. It was of small matter that the other two judges sent the *Granma* men to prison for varying periods of up to eight years: a judge had defied the government, and even the Conservative *Diario de la Marina*, which had always condemned terrorism, called on Batista to act according to the Constitution and hold elections. But Batista continued to refuse to put forward the date of elections any day before June 1958.

There was also trouble from the Electrical Workers' Union. Angel Cofiño, its leader, one of the few Cuban leaders who could have been regarded as a Social Democrat – he had been a Communist till 1941 – was dismissed in April, by Mujal, from his position on the executive of the CTC, on the suspicion that he was involved in sabotage against the government. Most electrical workers then went on strike to force Mujal to restore Cofiño. Many towns were partly or completely cut off from

---

[1] Barrera Pérez was nominated to go back on 9 June.

electricity or gas. The telephone union also walked out in sympathy. In consequence, Batista took the extreme step of temporarily nationalizing the electrical industry, and appointed an intervener, as Prío had done in the case of the railways in 1949. Several electrical union leaders were arrested. Cofiño then ordered his men back to work after deciding that the strike was not serving any useful end. He himself left Cuba, ostensibly to represent the country at the ILO in Geneva. Cofiño's conduct, however, as later became clear, was not irreproachable; his relations with Batista's government were far from unfriendly and those with the opposition were devious.[2]

The government's position meantime was curious. On the one hand Batista had the explicit and personal support of leaders of industry and of commerce, given at a series of ceremonies after his escape from assassination in March; and these men, and their U.S. colleagues so closely connected with them, continued to evince optimism about the state of the economy. The prosperity was indeed striking. Development seemed to be going ahead on every hand – a dry dock was planned for Havana; the Antilles Steel Company was expanding; the first quarter of 1957 showed new high levels of employment. Salaries were high, and reserves at $M476, were 9% higher than in 1956. The sugar chief Barreto explained that even the forty-five Oriente sugar mills (which then ground a fifth of the sugar in Cuba) had had a full harvest. The situation resembled 1870 more than 1895, though the old *Tinguaro* mill at Matanzas was seriously damaged on 26 May by a bomb, when it had only eight days more to grind, and the *Andorra* mill in Pinar del Río was similarly damaged, some sacks of sugar being destroyed. At the same time as the prosperity the threats to Batista grew daily. The movement towards sympathy with Castro mounted even among the opulent middle classes; and in the course of 1957 even the biggest sugar baron of all, Julio Lobo, gave the opposition $50,000.[3]

The constant attacks by the government leaders and their friends on Castro and the saboteurs as 'Communists' were beginning to have a life of their own: egged on by the BRAC,[4] Batista had for some months been sanctioning the dismissal of workers under a decree of 1955 if they proved to be Communists. In May 1957 he began, perhaps with reluctance, to take steps against Communist leaders – not because they had individually or as a party done anything to threaten him but because of the pressure of his own propaganda. Thus on 17 May Ursinio Rojas,

[2] See discussion of his case after the revolution, *Revolución*, 25 January 1959, 16.
[3] Carrillo MSS, p. 35. This money, obtained by Justo Carrillo and Rufo López Fresquet, was paid half to the 26 July Movement's treasurer Julio Duarte, and half to Carrillo's own, Montecristo movement. Lobo himself has, however, explained to the author that he never gave this money for Castro's movement.
[4] The Anti-Communist Bureau.

who had been the Communist secretary-general of the sugar workers till 1948, was arrested in Havana on the ground of helping Angel Cofiño and the electrical workers, a charge which scarcely carried weight since Cofiño and the Communists had been on atrocious terms since the former left the party in the 1940s. In this month also the Cuban Communist party, through its Havana City branch, and through Labour (particularly in the disturbed electrical union), began to make its first move towards the 26 July Movement – a gesture not reciprocated and which at the time led to very little. Yet within a few weeks, two members of Juventud Socialista, the Communist youth – Hiram Prats and Pablo Ribalta – were dispatched to the Sierra Maestra. Ribalta, a strong and handsome Negro, had worked for some years at the headquarters of the International Union of Students in Prague and in October 1956 had visited China as a member of the delegation of the World Federation of Democratic Youth.[5] Prats, who had gone to the university in 1950, had been a member of Juventud Socialista since 1955; in 1957 he was president of the Young Communists' committee in the engineering school. These two joined Guevara – who formed a separate unit operating independently under Castro in July.[6] At the same time the Batistiano police began to treat Juventud Socialista more toughly than before, almost as much as it treated the 26 July and the Directorio: one member, Armando Mirabal, for instance, died after being beaten without revealing the names of his colleagues.[7]

The 26 July were, however, far from seeing eye to eye in these days with Juventud Socialista, at least outside the Sierra. Later in the year, Javier Pazos and Armando Hart shared a cell in prison, and the discussion turned to whether or not the Communist party should be allowed to function legally after the victory. Pazos thought yes; Hart the scion of a prominent Catholic family, thought no.[8]

From now on bombs and Molotov cocktails, arbitrary police executions and arrests leading to permanent disappearances were an essential part of the Cuban scene. Some of these bombs were laid by individuals wishing to assert themselves in the 'struggle'. Most were laid as part of the general programme of Civic Resistence, which had by this time abandoned its original policy of non-violence for sabotage, as a result

[5] Evidence of Carlos Zayas, a Spanish Democratic Socialist who was with him in China. After the Revolution, Ribalta became Cuban ambassador to Tanzania – a delicate post.

[6] *Hoy*, 25 March 1964 (Valdés Vivo's evidence at Marquito's trial; Hiram Prats's evidence.) Carlos Rafael Rodríguez in conversation with the author in June 1966 confirmed Ribalta's stay in the Sierra from 'late 1957'.

[7] *Ibid.*, Valdés Vivo evidence. Faure Chomón, no friend to the Communist party, referred to Mirabal in 1964 as 'a real Communist', who died fighting the tyranny.

[8] After the revolution, Pazos became an exile, and Hart became one of the eight-member Communist party politburo, secretary-general to the Latin American revolutionary organization and Minister of Education.

of a visit paid in mid-1957 by one of Castro's lieutenants, Iglesias ('Nicaragua').[9] Branches collected money, and distributed propaganda, flags and black and red arm bands. Sabotage was in the hands of a specific group in each branch, some of them being, like Ignacio González or Merced María Díaz Sánchez, veteran bomb layers of the 1930s; thus, when Señorita Díaz Sánchez, who worked in the Ministry of Public Works, was found injured in an explosion at the Havana Woolworth store in August, she was found to be an ex-member of Joven Cuba and to have laid bombs against Batista as early as 1936.[10] Manuel Ray, the architect, became chief of the Havana underground in mid-1957.

The bomb layers were of every age and every background; consider, for instance, the list of persons arrested on 15 August 1957: Francisco Pérez Rivas, aged twenty-seven, employee of Mendoza y la Torre, accused of distributing literature and placing bombs; María Urquiola Lechuga, aged forty-three, with no profession given, who owned the apartment where the bombs in this particular *cache* were found; Mercedes Urquiola Lechuga, her sister, aged twenty-seven, employed in the National Paper Company, accused of placing bombs and *petards*; José Manuel Alvárez Santa Cruz, student, aged seventeen, resident of the El Sevillano suburb, accused of placing bombs; Francisco Miares Fernández, aged eighteen, art student, resident of El Sevillano, accused of placing bombs given to him by two others; Manuel de Jesús Alfonso Gil, aged fifteen, resident of La Víbora, accused of selling 26 July bombs; Enrique Delgado Mayoral, aged eighteen, resident of the La Víbora suburb, employee of RCA laboratories, accused of bomb placing and bomb selling; Eliecer Cruz Cabrera, aged eighteen, student, accused of participating in a terrorist plot; Eladio and Ignacio Alfonso Carrera, aged sixteen and nineteen, accused of recruiting for the 26 July Movement; José Herrera León, aged sixteen, gardener, accused of placing bombs for a payment of $5; Ubaldo Fiallo Sánchez, aged twenty, a travelling drug salesman; Antonio Fernández Segura, aged thirty-five, dock employee; Jorge Alvarez Tagle, aged nineteen, employee of Richmond Company; Juan Fernández Segura, aged thirty-eight, labourer; Francisco Gómez Bermejo, aged seventeen, dock employee; Pastor Valiente Hernández, aged thirty-eight; Norberto Belanzoarán López, aged twenty-four. In the Señoritas Urquiola apartment were found: 15 *petards*, ready for action; two jars of phosphorus; one large time bomb; 24 Molotov cocktails; 15 gallons of gasoline mixed with oil; six 0·32-calibre Colt revolvers and ammunition.[11] The support given by

[9] For 'Nicaragua's' mission, see Llerena MSS, 58.
[10] *Havana Post*, 13 August 1957. Aged 53, she later died.
[11] *Ibid.*, 16 August 1957.

many teachers to the rebellion meant not only that their pupils followed them but that both had access in the science laboratories to the materials of explosion – as in the case of Eriberto Marbán, teacher at the Víbora Institute, who confessed on 27 August to having taught others to make weapons from materials in the laboratories.

A large number of Catholics and many priests in Oriente were now active members of the 26 July. In the course of the summer, Fr Guillermo Sardiñas climbed the Sierra to become, with permission of the coadjutor bishop of Havana, chaplain to the rebel army. Another priest, Fr Chelala, became treasurer of the movement in Holguín. The national treasurer, Enrique Canto, was a leading Catholic layman. Only the bishops and the regular clergy remained suspicious or divided, though both the bishops of Santiago and Matanzas never wavered in their hostility to the dictatorship. Protestant pastors such as the Rev. Fernández Ceballos were active in Havana. A labour organization depending on the Movement had also been founded, led at first by a bank workers' leader, Aguilera and then by David Salvador, the ex-Communist sugar worker from Las Villas.[12]

1957 was the first year of General Eisenhower's second term as president of the United States. It was a sluggish if, in retrospect, a happy time. The interviews between Castro and, first, Matthews and then Taber and Hoffman had created great interest in the U.S. Castro seemed a hero, a legend, a T. E. Lawrence of the Caribbean. The *New York Times* took a consistently interested and moderate position; for instance, a leader on the Humboldt 7 affair, doubtless written by Matthews, strongly denounced the 'harsh military dictatorship'. As in the 1870s, 1890s and 1930s, Cuban exiles were resourceful in demonstrations and in collecting money. From mid-1957 an agent of the 26 July operated in the Cuban Embassy in Washington, and a young economist, Ernesto Betancourt, was a registered 26 July agent in Washington. A similar organization existed in Mexico nominally headed by Pedro Miret and Gustavo Arcos, veterans of the Moncada attack, though, in the manner usually associated with exile movements, criticized by some other exiles, among them Castro's sisters who thought they were taking too much limelight. But the normal neighbourliness of U.S.–Cuban relations continued: *Time-Life* executives held their egregious conferences in Cuba; the Hedges family, half American, half Cuban, continued on excellent personal terms with the dictator, expressing in this intimacy the general approval felt by most American businessmen for the regime. Batista himself kept receiving U.S. honours of one kind or another – on

---

[12] See Carlos Rodríguez Quesada, *David Salvador*, 10. His deputies were Octavio Louit, a railwaymen's leader, and Reinol González, a bank employees' leader and a prominent member of the Catholic Workers' Youth.

18 May he became an honorary citizen of Texas. In return, he continued to distribute Cuban honours to resident or visiting U.S. officers or government officials. The U.S. military mission seemed to be frequent visitors to 'their Cuban opposite numbers'. Photographs showing U.S. colonels embracing General Tabernilla or Batista himself occurred often enough for the Cuban public to assume that the two countries were the close allies the statesmen of both said that they were.

The U.S. ambassador in Cuba, Arthur Gardner, had from the start closely identified himself with this position. He had suggested to Batista that the FBI or CIA should send up a man to the Sierra to kill Castro; Batista answered: 'No, no, we couldn't do that: we're Cubans.'[13] In his four years in Cuba Gardner had become a close friend of Batista's; he believed 'I don't think we ever had a better friend . . . It was regrettable, like all South Americans, that he was known – although I had no absolute knowledge of it – to be getting a cut . . . in almost all the things that were done. But . . . he was doing an amazing job.'[14]

In the spring the question of Gardner's replacement arose, not, so far as can be seen, from any dissatisfaction felt by the Secretary of State, John Foster Dulles, with his services, but because such a question was bound to arise after a new presidential term had begun. It was contemplated that one of the intellectual stars of the American foreign service, the admirable Charles Bohlen, then ambassador in Moscow, should go to Havana. It would have been a wise choice. Bohlen however went to Manila. Instead, the appointment in Havana went to Earl Smith, an investment broker, Yale 1926, colonel in the air force in the Second World War and on the War Production Board, then aged fifty-four, with no political experience of any sort. Gardner did not want to move: he went direct to Eisenhower, saying that 'Batista would be very upset as he, Gardner, was so close to Batista and that it would be a sign we were changing our policy towards Cuba and acknowledging the rightness of the criticism of himself.'[15] But Gardner had sent in a *pro forma* resignation after Eisenhower's re-election. This was taken out and accepted, to the ambassador's annoyance, on 14 May.

The ambassador returned to Washington. As in every other Cuban civil war, in 1868–78 and 1895–8, the situation there was critical. Gardner thought that the State Department had changed sides, and was supporting the cause of Castro against Batista. The assistant secretary in charge of the Latin American Department, Roy Rubottom, a

[13] Gardner to the author.
[14] Gardner evidence to Senate Internal Security Sub-Committee.
[15] Matthews, 68. Dulles told this to Herbert Matthews.

Texan ex-naval officer, had several times visited Havana during the Gardner era: 'My wife and I,' Gardner complained three years afterwards, 'would ask him questions whether he didn't agree with us and he would never answer ... He favoured Castro. There is no question about it.'[16] Rubottom, outside the easy-going, deceptively appealing Havana commercial belt which in the 1950s as in the 1850s had such a debilitating effect on all who experienced it, was disturbed at police torturing in Havana; as a Democrat, he had high hopes of the opposition. His chief, the ubiquitous U.S. diplomat of the 1940s and 1950s, Robert Murphy, took a stronger view; he believed Batista was a 'gorilla'.[17]

At the Caribbean desk in the State Department, meantime, a new appointment had been made: a man who later would, more than Rubottom, become a sacrificial scapegoat for U.S. anxiety in Cuba – William Wieland, then aged fifty, who had spent twelve years in Havana between 1925 and 1937. Wieland's father died young and his mother had married again, a Cuban, Manuel Montenegro, and for a time Wieland had gone under that name when a child. He had worked in Havana, first for the General Electric and Cuban Electric Companies, afterwards for the *Havana Post*, during the revolution of 1933. He met Sumner Welles and later, in 1941, 'when he had worked some years for the Associated Press', Welles secured his entry into the State Department. Afterwards, he had been in various U.S. legations in Latin America, including that at Bogotá in 1947 during the Bogotazo. By experience he was thus well suited to the task of being the Cuban specialist in the State Department during a revolutionary period.

His views were, however, curiously difficult to estimate; granted that he was unjustly persecuted by the Senate Internal Security Sub-Committee and its special counsel J. G. Sourwine, Wieland appears to have changed his mind several times. 'I was never an admirer of Castro,' he told his taunters in 1960, 'I became convinced that he was a mentally sick man, completely obsessed with his own ego, and unscrupulously ambitious',[18] but at the same time William Pawley, another businessman ambassador, though of tougher mettle than Smith or Gardner, recalled that when they were both at Rio de Janeiro, he 'got him out [because] he was much too far to the Left'.[19] At the time of his appointment Wieland, like Murphy and Rubottom, was a firm opponent of Batista. This view was apparently shared by those members of the CIA in Washington who specialized on Cuba, such as Colonel J. C. King (later head of the CIA's Latin American section), and even

---

[16] Gardner evidence.
[17] So he told Gardner.
[18] *Communist Threat*, 670.
[19] *Ibid.*, 672.

more so by those who were in the Embassy at Havana, particularly its second-in-command.[20]

Such was the ambivalent atmosphere in Washington when Earl Smith took up his appointment as ambassador to Havana. Before going to Havana Smith consulted a fellow businessman and diplomat, Robert Hill, then concerned with the Department's relations with Congress, previously vice-president of Grace Shipping Lines and ambassador in Central America. Hill, who had just been appointed U.S. ambassador to Mexico, said to Smith, 'I am sorry you are going to Cuba ... You are assigned to Cuba to preside over the downfall of Batista. The decision has been made that Batista has to go.' Hill urged Smith to take with him to Havana a minister whom he could trust, and made some suggestions, but none would accept the job. One at least of them told Hill privately, 'I don't want to go to Havana because Castro is coming to power.' 'It was my judgement,' Hill said later, 'at that time that Castro was being assisted into power and that there had been some activity along the corridors of the Department to support his cause.'[21] But Smith persevered. Wieland suggested he should see Herbert Matthews – a sensible idea but one which later almost cost him his job.[22] Smith anyway saw Matthews, who told him that he thought Batista 'a ruthless and corrupt dictator ... who would soon fall, and that it would be in the best interest of Cuba and ... the world ... if Batista were removed'.[23] Matthews also urged Smith to travel in the rest of Cuba as soon as possible, and go outside Havana.

Smith, of good connections in the U.S., had known Cuba as a tourist for many years. Though he had had no diplomatic experience and owed his embassy to his contribution to Republican funds – he had been Republican leader in Florida since 1952 – he had 'long wanted' this job.[24] He was 'an old friend' of Cubans such as Raúl Menocal, then a minister, and Miguel Tarafa, a sugar king.[25] He was sworn as ambassador on 13 June. The wife of his Palm Beach companion, Senator John Kennedy of Massachusetts, was among the little group who attended the ceremony. But in order not to give the impression that his appointment would mean anything in the way of intervention by the U.S. or a change of policy he did not actually install himself in Cuba till mid-July. The stage was now set for a chapter bizarre even in the history of diplomacy.

[20] See Smith's testimony. For King see the testimony of Willauer and Gardner (ibid. 678). Lyman Kirkpatrick, The Real CIA, 157, describes how he secured Ambassador Gardner's reluctant agreement to allow the CIA to enter into contact with the opposition in 1956.

[21] Hill testimony, Communist Threat, 807–8.

[22] See Wieland, ibid.

[23] Smith testimony, ibid., 682–3. Matthews notes in his book (71) this testimony to be accurate.

[24] Earl T. Smith, The Fourth Floor (1962), 4.

[25] Havana Post, 18 July 1957. See also, ibid., 20 July 1957.

CHAPTER 13

Miami and Santiago

On 25 May 1957 a little group of men sailed out of Miami under the ex-leader of the Havana airport workers, Calixto Sánchez, who had been implicated in the attack on the palace in March and had apparently felt guilt at not having progressed further.[1] These were Prío's men. They had landed near Mayarí, in Oriente, Castro's home territory, and were swiftly tricked into surrender. Sixteen men, including Sánchez, were shot by the local lieutenant of police.[2] This was a serious setback to the hope Prío still cherished of putting forward an effective rival to Castro among the revolutionary opposition. A few days before, too, the most famous of Prío's gangster friends, El Extraño, had been arrested in Costa Rica with two companions, for planning to assassinate the democratic President Figueres; El Extraño said he had been offered $200,000 by Trujillo to kill Figueres. A case was mounted against him, he remained in prison, and one more Cuban gangster of the old time disappeared, at least for the time being. The ground was becoming clearer and clearer for the opposition to unite behind Castro in the Sierra.

In these circumstances and following the attack at El Uvero, Batista began a new policy towards the rebels. In June Colonel Barrera had been sent back to his battlefield of limited success earlier in the year, establishing a command post at the sugar mill *Estrada Palma*. He had devised a plan whereby he and his aides, Sánchez Mosquera, Moreno Bravo and Merob Sosa, would pursue the different rebel columns, when Díaz Tamayo was suddenly dismissed from command in Oriente and succeeded by an unconditional friend of General Tabernilla, Rodríguez Avila. He gave quite new orders for the evacuation of all the peasant families in the Sierra, so as to establish a zone which would be completely banned to all except the army. The army would shoot at sight without troubling to see whether the peasant concerned was a friend or a foe. The air force would also be able to bomb the jungle indiscriminately.

---

[1] Sánchez was an Auténtico who had joined Carrillo's Acción Libertadora and then Menelao Mora. On the day of the attack on the palace he did not appear and afterwards left Cuba with the help of Mujal, an old friend. In Miami he was regarded as a traitor and he gained the help of Prío to save his face (evidence of Suárez to Draper).

[2] Two members of the group, Lázaro Guerra Calderón and Mario Rodríguez Arenas, were captured and described how they had lived in the Dominican Republic till the attack.

At the same time, new plans had been decided upon by the 26 July Movement. June in the Sierra was passed in recuperation. The battle at El Uvero had been the first contest won by the rebels in which they had had serious casualties. The treatment of the wounded occupied a section of the force, under Guevara, for several weeks. Moving slowly back towards the heart of the Sierra, behind the main column, Guevara's force had gone up and down in size as different groups of peasants rallied to it and then dropped out; others came from the cities, and then returned there, unable to stand the hard conditions. Two Batistiano ex-soldiers joined Guevara but they significantly found the going too rough and went down again. It was not till late in June that the groups rejoined: the whole rebel force now reached about two hundred.[3] Batista's decision to change the nature of the war enlarged the area of free movement of the rebels. There was now almost a true '*territorio libre*' with a rough repair shop, a hospital, a shoe and leather factory, an armoury with an electric saw, and an ironmonger charged to refill brass grenades. There were bread ovens, and later, schools and a lecture hall. All such places were in danger from time to time, though several remote valleys such as that of La Mesa, were never reached and remained an invulnerable centre of these activities till the end of the war.[4]

If little new fighting occurred in the Sierra for a time, it was a period of much political manœuvring. Nearly every civic and social group in each province was writing to the government to protest against arbitrary arrests and against the continuance of military operations in the Sierra. Thanks to Suez and failures in the European and Russian beet fields the harvest had sold splendidly, and 1957 looked like being one of the best years of the Cuban economy. A meeting of the ecclesiastical hierarchy resulted in pleas for peace from Cardinal Arteaga, archbishop of Havana, and the bishop of Pinar del Río (Aurelio Díaz). Mgr Pérez Serantes, bishop of Santiago, made a similar plea.[5] The regular Ortodoxos and Auténticos dropped out of Batista's parliamentary commission, but the Congress nevertheless passed 'constitutional reforms' which included the provision for holding presidential elections on 1 June 1958, and the inauguration of a new president on 24 February 1959. Grau, Ochoa's branch of the Ortodoxos and four other groups of the centre opposition formed an alliance and proposed that the senior Supreme Court judge should take over as provisional president with elections within ninety days; but Grau also let it be known that he would take part in Batista's 1958 elections. Such ambivalence prevented any

---

[3] Guevara, 100.
[4] Núñez Jiménez, 577.
[5] *Havana Post*, 1 June 1957.

chance, always remote, that this new political alignment might be taken seriously.

Prío, damped by the failure of his last military expedition, that of the *Corinthia*, was reduced to the expedient of writing to Batista from Miami begging him to leave: Batista's answer was to stage a mass demonstration of parties backing him to open the 1958 election campaign in Santiago. But only about 5,000 came, most of these, it was thought, government employees, with sporadic rioting on the edges and some shooting. A similar meeting, by Senator Masferrer in Chivirico on the Sierra Maestra coast between Santiago and El Uvero, was also unsuccessful as a rallying point for the regime, though Masferrer, trying to outbid Castro, promised in a grandiose way to give land to the peasants.

Batista had several times said that he would not stand at the 1958 elections both because the Constitution forbade it and because he thought he had done his bit. Who would stand? The vice-president, Guas Inclán said that he hoped Castro would take part in the 1958 general elections. Ochoa, resident of the 'registered Ortodoxos', agreed to participate, as did Márquez Sterling, another dissident Ortodoxo. Both these ex-disciples of Chibás thereby dissociated themselves from the mass of his following, as from Castro. Various attempts began to be made to get these moderate opposition parties together with a single 'front'.

The 26 July Movement was also busy. In Mexico, a document described as a 'manifesto'[6] was published ostensibly containing Castro's views in November 1956; it had in fact been written by Mario Llerena, without direct contact with Castro. No doubt it reflected what many of the younger followers of Castro now believed: the Ortodoxos were no more 'than a curious psychological phenomenon lacking their own ideology and programme; only Chibás's personality had given them cohesion'; and Chibás was dead. The 26 July preferred to avoid abstract formulae or preconceived blueprints. 'The ideology of the Cuban Revolution must be born from Cuba's own roots and the condition of the people and of the race. It will not be . . . something imported from other latitudes.' But the 26 July Movement considered the 'Jeffersonian philosophy still valid' and subscribed fully to the 'Lincoln formula'. Yet it was also 'necessary to see that the dividends of the utilities, land and mines went to the country, not abroad'. Economic planning would free the nation from the evils of monoculture, such as the privileged monopolies, and the *latifundios*. (There was criticism of 'foreign bases' (such as Guantánamo).) A hopeful if mysterious sentence referred to the 26 July Movement's desire to reach a state of solidarity and harmony

---

[6] *Nuestra Razón: Manifiesto-Programa del Movimiento 26 de Julio. Cf.* Pedrero, 89–130. Llerena (MSS 93–5) discusses.

between capital and labour in order to raise productivity. Although the document did not mention the Constitution of 1940, there would be a representative government based on the genuine expression of popular will, and a new electoral code. The whole document might be regarded as roughly expressive of a social democratic movement in Europe, though it was more of a constitutional guide than an election programme.[7]

This and similar programmes caused more and more professional men to join the 26 July Movement, among them the outstanding young engineer, Manuel Ray, president of the Civil Engineers' Association. Ray, a graduate in 1946, had worked in the State Development Commission in the days of Prío and had recently been the engineer of the tunnel linking Vedado with Miramar in Havana. Sympathetic to the Ortodoxos, he nevertheless took a slightly different position; on 1 May 1957 he spoke with Raúl Chibás and then joined the Civic Resistance Movement. At that time he knew very little about Castro, as did most of that movement. He 'did not quite know Castro's programme' and had known Raúl Chibás 'only as a football leader at school'. Essentially non-political, he had wanted to become president of the Civil Engineers in order to destroy its corruption.[8]

So far Castro had avoided giving his name to any programme since he had arrived in the Sierra: indeed his remarks to Matthews, Taber and Andrew St George were all that had come out of the Sierra. He never commented on 'Nuestra Razón', and his lieutenants such as Hart and Marcelo Fernández avoided full endorsement of it. But having aroused expectation among the professional middle class this doctrinal silence could not last. In early July Raúl Chibás and Felipe Pazos, the titular Ortodoxo leader and the most distinguished economist in Cuba, made their way up to the Sierra. Chibás says that he went to the Sierra as a gesture, a commitment of maturity to the armed struggle.[9] On 12 July, after some days of discussions, a general manifesto was issued, signed by Castro, Chibás and Pazos. Most of it was written by Castro.[10] It called all Cubans to form a civic revolutionary front to 'end the regime of force, the violation of individual rights, and the infamous crimes of the police'; the only way to settle the peace of Cuba was free elections and a democratic government; the rebels were, the manifesto

---

[7] Llerena had, it appears, struck out of the text any mention of totalitarian Communism, on the suggestion of Faustino Pérez who had told him that some of those in the hills would find this unwelcome; he had included the radical section of the document on the advice of Marcelo Fernández (Llerena MSS, p. 44). Armando Hart wrote later that the document contained 'the thought of the Movement even though ... it could be amplified' (letter, 15 October 1957).
[8] Evidence to the author of Manuel Ray, Puerto Rico, 1963.
[9] Chibás MSS.
[10] Ibid.

insisted, 'fighting for the fine ideal of a Cuba free, democratic and just'. There would be an absolute guarantee of press freedom and free elections in all the trade unions. A request to the U.S. was framed for a suspension of arms shipments in Cuba during the civil war, and also a rejection of foreign intervention or mediation. A military junta to replace Batista would be unacceptable. Instead, there would be an 'impartial' non-political provisional president, and a provisional government would hold elections within a year of getting office; elections would be held according to the Constitution of 1940 and the Electoral Code of 1943.

The economic side of the programme was written by Castro on the basis of notes taken by a young lawyer, Baudilio Castellanos, at Santiago, from lectures given by Pazos himself and his colleague, Regino Boti, a clever young economist, the son of a patriarchal poet of Guantánamo.[11] The proposals included a demand for the suppression of gambling and corruption; for agrarian reform, leading to the distribution among landless workers of uncultivated lands; for the increase of industrialization; and for the conversion of tenant farmers and squatters into proprietors. Existing owners would be compensated. There was nothing about nationalization of public utilities, nothing about the collectivization of land nor certainly of industry. It was a document somewhat less radical than that written by Llerena in Mexico, less radical also than Castro's own statements in Mexico, certainly less radical than the proposals in *History will absolve me*,[12] and less radical than Pazos's lectures themselves as embodied in a note current in Mexico in 1956 and worked on by Castro.[13] According to Guevara, Castro 'tried to make more explicit some of the declarations on agrarian reform' but he could not break the united front of the two others;[14] but the others present dispute the truth of this contention.[15]

Was this manifesto a deception? Guevara later commented explicitly:

> We were not satisfied with the compromise, but it was necessary; it was progressive at that moment. It could scarcely last beyond the moment when it marked a break in the development of the revolution[16] ... we knew it was a minimum programme, a programme which limited our effort, but ... we knew that it was not possible to realise our will from the Sierra Maestra and that we had to reckon,

[11] Pazos's evidence. Castellanos later became Cuban ambassador to France (1967).
[12] Text in Jules Dubois, 166–72.
[13] Guevara, 103.
[14] Llerena read this, but in the late summer of 1956 in Mexico City.
[15] Chibás (MSS), who says that Castro 'never tried to express different thoughts from those which we all signed in common'.
[16] *No podía durar más allá del momento en que significara una detención en el desarrollo revolucionario.*

during a long period, with a whole series of 'friends' who tried to use
our military strength and the great confidence which the people
already had in Fidel Castro, for their own macabre purposes, and ...
to maintain the dominion of imperialism in Cuba, through its
imported *bourgeoisie*, so tightly linked with North American masters
... This declaration for us was only a short pause in the journey,[17]
we had to continue our fundamental task of defeating the enemy on
the field of battle.[18]

Some of Castro's explanations of 1961 presumably apply to this
epoch: 'It is undeniable that if when we began to be strong we had been
known as people of very radical ideas, the social class which is now
making war on us would have done so then' – that is, the professional
middle class which afterwards turned in its majority away from Castro.[19]

In view of such remarks it would be appropriate to conclude that
Castro's drafting and signature of the 'Pact of the Sierra' involved
dissimulation; that probably as a result of his experiences in the Sierra
itself and the influences to which he had been subject there (such as
those of Guevara and his brother) he had already determined to attempt
a more radical reconstruction of society than he had envisaged at the
time of the Moncada attack or even the landing of the *Granma*; that
although there was as yet no alliance, and scarcely actual contact with
the Communist party of Cuba, nor even its youth movement, Fidel
Castro, presumably through his brother Raúl, knew of the changing
policies of those groups themselves which could later prepare the way
for sympathy. But Castro's own thinking, like that even of Guevara,
was in evolution; maybe he made in those days private commitments to
Guevara and Raúl Castro, which he afterwards fulfilled; but he could
have still deceived them or broken with them as he did others. In 1957
Castro was preoccupied with overthrowing Batista; and he did not
seem particularly to care with whom he made an alliance, what he said,
or what commitments he undertook to serve that end. The future, after
the victory, could look after itself, an attitude held by nearly all combatants in nearly all wars.

That the 26 July Movement's political aims were in the process of
change is shown by an article attributed (apparently falsely) to Castro
in the magazine *Cuba Libre*, published in San José, Costa Rica, in
August 1957, in which provisions for the nationalization of electricity
and the telephone system and the 'final solution of the land problem'
(including the expropriation of plots over 170 acres) were both included.

This manifesto of the Sierra signed, it was sent back to Havana by the

[17] *Un pequeño alto en el camino.*
[18] Guevara, 103–5.
[19] *Obra Revolucionaria*, 1961, No. 46, 17.

hands of a loyal peasant of the region, El Trolinero, and published in *Bohemia*. At the same time Castro's scheme for the establishment of a regular government in the Sierra foundered.[20] Two of the Ortodoxo splinter groups (those led by Manuel Bisbé in Havana, and Agramonte in Mexico) gave full support to it; two (those which followed Márquez Sterling and Ochoa) did not, nor did any other opposition group: 'What's the point of substituting one *de facto* government for another?' was their attitude.

Earl Smith meantime arrived in Havana on 15 July.[21] He found the capital calm, but outside the atmosphere was one of terror. There was near-open war in Santiago between the 26 July and the police. The plan of the 26 July Movement was to provoke universal disruption in the cities of Oriente and in the countryside by strikes and terrorism, and then to strike at the main public buildings in the cities, thereby winning control of the province. Jeeps and cars carrying soldiers or police were constantly attacked; and, always, a large percentage of those who were arrested turned out to be very young, even schoolboys. On 7 July an eight-year old girl was arrested placing a bomb in Guantánamo. The old gangsters of the days of Prío had thus given way to idealistic gunmen in their teens or even younger. It was as if delinquency had been articulated into street fighting, though sometimes 26 July Movement flags would appear on top of buildings rather than bombs beneath them – on the new FOCSA building in Vedado, or the television tower. But it was much harder to coordinate all these activities. Maybe there was some settling of private scores; what, for instance, really lay behind the murder of Daniel Sánchez, school bus driver of Santiago, found with the label 'Traitor to the 26 July' in the street on 6 July?

Batista tried to answer all this with pleas for 'electoralism'; the choice was between bloodshed and elections – his elections, that is, of 1958. He appealed to the 'genuine' opposition of Grau San Martín, Pardo Llada, and Ochoa, to continue to compete in his elections. On 4 July he issued a stirring statement recalling Jefferson and Washington. This had no effect save perhaps among the U.S. community who, once again, mouthed Roosevelt's old dictum about Trujillo. On 24 July Smith gave his first press conference: 'Our two nations I feel will always be the closest of friends and allies in the common fight against Communism.'[22] He also praised BRAC – unwisely, since BRAC had recently confounded Communists with all members of the opposition. But, he added, 'we have nothing substantial to make us believe', that Castro's

[20] See letter of refusal to countenance such an idea by Justo Carrillo, dated 27 June.
[21] Smith, *The Fourth Floor*, 8.
[22] *Ibid.*, 11–12.

movement 'is red-inspired'.[23] He came, he said, as an observer; and in this spirit he decided to follow Herbert Matthews's advice and get out of Havana as soon as he could, to see something of the country. The following week he announced that he would go to Oriente and visit Santiago, the U.S. base at Guantánamo and the U.S.-owned Moa Bay and Nicaro properties, the largest single U.S. concerns in the island.

Santiago had had a harsh July. There were even rumours that U.S. citizens were thinking of withdrawing altogether. 26 July Movement flags had often appeared. There had been much shooting. Schools had been burned. Molotov cocktails were used frequently by the 26 July Movement. On 26–27 July, the anniversary of the Moncada attack, the police were said to have arrested 200 people, many in Santiago. All this was, of course, a deliberate plan to destroy ordinary life in Oriente as much as possible prior to an attempted mass attack on public buildings. On 30 July, the day before Smith was due to set out, the main 26 July organizer in Santiago, Frank País, then still aged only twenty-three, was shot down in the Callejón del Muro in Santiago by the police chief of Santiago, Colonel José Salas Cañizares and one of his henchmen, 'Mano Negra'. País had been identified some weeks before as a main police quarry, and had been on the run, though remaining in the city. His brother José had been killed at the government demonstration in June. País had been hiding in the shop of Raúl Pujol, an ironmonger, who had been one of the chief suppliers of the rebels, and who was also killed.[24] One more political crime had been committed, one more execution without trial. The consequences were, however, unusual. The entire 26 July Movement of Santiago attended País's lying-in-state in the house of his *novia*, América Telebauta. The police refrained, however, from any action. The next day an immense demonstration of women gathered in the centre of Santiago to protest. Ostensibly arriving to shop, they gathered in the main square at the moment when Earl Smith, General Eisenhower's ambassador, was to be officially received.[25]

It was a successful demonstration. Smith drove into the city in an eight-car motorcade. Women dressed in black ran to greet him shouting 'Libertad! Libertad!' At the town hall huge crowds gathered. The Smiths went inside the hall and the police brought water hoses to press the women back, and arrested about forty. The main square was in confusion at the moment Smith came out. The police attempted desperately

[23] *Ibid.*

[24] Two men, a lieutenant of police and a soldier, Ortiz Guirado and Alvarez Echevarría, were tried for their part in the murder in July 1965 (*cf. Hoy*, 16 July 1965). Colonel Ventura, *Memorias*, 86, accused two prominent Castro followers Armando Hart and Haydée Santamaría, of betraying País to Colonel Faget of the BRAC but this is inconceivable.

[25] País was succeeded as 'national chief of the militias' by René Ramos Latour ('Daniel'), a worker in Nicaro, who had spent some time in the Sierra, and who had been active throughout Cuba raising money and collecting arms.

to beat back the women with a violence that outraged Smith. He saw women being knocked down and thrown into the police wagon. One woman successfully handed him a letter demanding a reconsideration of U.S. policy of support for Batista. In the afternoon, the ambassador gave a press conference and announced that 'excessive police action is abhorrent to me. I deeply regret that my presence in Santiago . . . may have been the cause of public demonstrations . . . I . . . trust that those held by the police have been freed.'[26] Afterwards, while País's body was escorted by a huge procession to the cemetery, Smith tactfully laid a wreath on Martí's grave.

These actions by Smith made an excellent impression among the Cuban opposition and on their friends in the U.S. The *New York Times* praised him. The friends of Batista denounced him, accusing him of undiplomatic behaviour. Against this charge Smith was defended by the Secretary of State, Dulles. Many now supposed that Smith would bring a new policy to Cuba: but in fact the State Department had merely instructed him 'to alter the prevailing notion in Cuba that the American Ambassador was intervening on behalf of the government of Cuba to perpetuate the Batista dictatorship'[27] – that is, he was to try to be neutral.

There was some coordination between the protests in Santiago and events in the Sierra. After the emissaries from the plain had left, Castro had reorganized his followers. Raúl Castro and Guevara both now commanded separate columns, with the rank of major. Guevara ceased to be doctor to the rebels, his place being taken by a new recruit from the plain, Dr Sergio del Valle. But these separate columns did not act in a new theatre of war; Castro resisted the demands from the plain that a 'second front' should be opened up – especially after the failure of a minor attempt to do so in the north near *central Miranda*.[28] The rebels were still troubled by desertions and one young peasant had recently been shot accordingly. On 26 July a group led by the peasant Guillermo García fell on the *central Estrada Palma*, the nearest sugar mill to the Sierra on the Manzanillo side, and withdrew after causing damage and casualties.[29] On 31 July Guevara's column tried to attack a small military post in the copper mining district, Bueycito, where he believed that Major Casillas would be found visiting a mistress. The column travelled in three lorries, fell on the barracks at night, and engaged in firing for only a few minutes before it surrendered; six Rural Guardsmen were wounded, one rebel killed and three wounded;

[26] Smith, *The Fourth Floor*, 21.
[27] *Ibid.*, 20.
[28] Guevara, 105–6.
[29] *Bohemia*, 30 July 1957. See also *Havana Post*, 29 July. In fact Guillermo García was after this disciplined for insufficient powers of command (see Chibás MSS).

the rebels burned the barracks, seized a Browning machine gun and other things useful to them, and took away as prisoners the sergeant in command and a spy named Orán, to act as hostages against reprisals in the village, but both were later freed. They also blew up a bridge, the dynamiter being a farmer in the village, Cristóbal Naranjo, who then joined the rebels. The village gave the rebels beer and fruit juices.[30]

On the plain, meantime, the País funeral procession was succeeded by a strike, long prepared, but only now enacted – following naturally from the closing of the shops in Santiago during the funeral and demonstrations. The police tried to force the shops to reopen, but the strike lasted five days. The Nicaro nickel plant was also closed. This was of course a part of the rebels' ambitious overall plan. The following week the strike spread through the island, in Havana affecting bus drivers and bank clerks. The government responded by arresting as many members of the 26 July Movement as they could. In Holguín, Colonel Cowley shot nine people in the streets during a power cut. There was, however, little coordination of the strikes and when Havana returned to work on 6 August, Oriente, licking its wounds, also went back. Constitutional guarantees were once more suspended. At least locally the Communists seem to have backed the strike where possible.[31]

From this time on it would be correct to assume that Cuba was in the same state of civil war as existed in, say, Cyprus or Malaya during the emergency, and the manner in which it was fought resembled the conditions whereby an imperial power attempted by the use of police methods to put down a revolt in which the rebels could count on the sympathy of large sections of the population of all classes. The police continued to kill men but each death created ten new supporters of the revolt. Beyond the horizon too there loomed the unpredictable power of the U.S., for so long the arbiter of Cuban destinies. It was inconceivable that the U.S. could remain merely an observer. Her army and navy continued to be ranged beside Batista, their white uniforms resplendent next to his in hundreds of photographs of innumerable friendly gatherings. Her businessmen continued only too friendly with the regime; the funeral of the textile and rayon magnate, Dayton Hedges, in June, had been attended by Batista and most of his cabinet; Hedges's sons, Dayton Jr. and Burke, were among Batista's closest friends. By late 1957 it seemed even to middle class professional men that the struggle not only resembled a struggle against an old imperial power but in fact *was* one; a few individuals, like the apparently

[30] See *Havana Post*, 3 August 1957.
[31] *Cf.* Blas Roca to the 8th Congress of the Communist Party (*The Cuban Revolution* (1961), 8).

progressive Earl Smith or Matthews[32] or enlightened men in the CIA or State Department, could not atone for the silence of thousands of businessmen, soldiers and tourists; silence surely meant commitment; and commitment, enmity – an enmity which seemed bereft of disguise in Oriente where the first battalion in search of Castro was composed of men trained in the U.S. and which used 'the most modern U.S. weapons'. Ambassador Gardner, when leaving in June, had announced that the U.S. had no intention of intervening in Cuba; some newspapers gave this statement a headline; Batista's hand went quickly to his scabbard, denouncing the very idea that such a project could even be considered and arguing that it was poor taste of the editors to use such a headline from a remark by an old friend of Cuba out of context. But clearly it suggested an anxiety not far below the surface: who would provide the mediation, and when? For some weeks Batista and his ministers implied that the opposition was seeking to do this. But more extreme Americans accepted Batista's evaluation of Castro: thus Spruille Braden, the ex-ambassador in Havana, progressive in the 1940s but now in the 1950s, through the turn of emotions during the age of McCarthy, a member of the far Right, wrote in *Human Events* on 17 August 1957 that Castro 'is a fellow traveller, if not a member of the Communist party and has been so for a long time . . .'.[33] The game of accusations and counter-accusations had begun.

[32] Not surprisingly, Cuban journalists were annoyed at the ease with which U.S. journalists seemed to have got to the Sierra, and they had not. See protest by the Cuban College of Journalists, June 1957.

[33] Qu., *Communist in the Caribbean*, 248. Mario Lazo, the Cuban lawyer who advised the U.S. Embassy in Havana, went to New York in August 1957 to try to get the *New York Times* to stop supporting the rebels. At a discussion with the ex-ambassador to Cuba, Guggenheim, at which Batista's ambassador to Washington, Arroyo, was present, Guggenheim explained, 'You must get Batista to call for elections before any change can be expected.' (Lazo, 116–17.)

CHAPTER 14

The Naval Mutiny at Cienfuegos

Castro, Raúl Chibás and Pazos had denounced in the manifesto of the Sierra any idea that a section of the armed forces themselves might help towards the overthrow of Batista. They had criticized Barquín's *coup*. Of course if such a *coup* were to occur, it would prejudice Castro's own chances of attaining power. Thus Barquín was for Castro a dangerous rival. But in September a section of the navy in Cienfuegos made a serious attempt to overthrow the regime through the naval officers quartered there, in collaboration with the 26 July Movement, the Auténticos, and others.

The plan resembled most of those enacted by Cuban revolutionaries: a shock attack, surprise in overcoming numbers, afterwards improvisation. The situation in Cienfuegos favoured such action. But unlike the attack at Moncada, men inside the barracks played a key part in the attack; and again, unlike Moncada, the U.S. Embassy had been informed; indeed, according to the U.S. Ambassador, the second-in-command of the CIA (William Williamson) at the U.S. Embassy had told the conspirators that any government set up as a result of a successful rising would be recognized by the U.S.[1] Smith knew nothing of the CIA man's activities, though he did know of the projected revolt.

The 26 July Movement had had for some months a following among the younger officers of the navy, many of whom deeply resented the barbarous killer Laurent, chief of naval intelligence, and his henchmen. At the end of May a group of young civilian 26 July men in Cienfuegos had been arrested and tortured.[2] This was the signal for a new and ambitious plan to take over the naval base. The leader of the 26 July Movement in Cienfuegos, Emilio Aragonés, of a good family in the town, met Javier Pazos, temporarily head of the Havana underground. He co-ordinated the plan with Santiago and with Castro. Pazos took 'all the guns in Havana to Cienfuegos'. Aragonés, however, did not shine as an organizer and many of these were not used.[3] But the naval conspirators did not rely entirely on Castro's movement, since several had links with Carrillo's Montecristi, Prío and the Auténticos. Carrillo

---

[1] Smith testimony to Senate Internal Security Sub Committee; see Suárez Núñez, 75.
[2] René Ray, 33.
[3] Pazos's evidence.

had spent his share of Julio Lobo's $25,000 on this venture.[4] Nor was the scheme limited to Cienfuegos. The plan contemplated that as a key to the situation, the cruiser *Cuba* would be seized and with other ships then in Havana Harbour, would train her big guns on Campamento Columbia, and the Morrow and Príncipe castles, and then capture the city with naval manpower and the Havana underground. Other ports were implicated. In the pressure of conspiracy, men became committed to increasingly lavish schemes. Details were forgotten. The day before the attack was due, 5 September, the naval officers in Havana decided that they were not ready. An attempt was made to postpone all action, successfully in the case of Mariel and Santiago. But the 26 July Movement gave the order to go ahead in Cienfuegos.[5]

The attack on Cienfuegos was led by a cashiered naval lieutenant, Dionisio San Román, who had previously served in Cienfuegos and who in 1956 played a minor part in the Barquín conspiracy. Twenty-eight conspirators within the base were headed by Santiago Ríos, a petty officer. Their task was to capture the naval base at night, arrest the officers and open the gates to San Román and the Auténtico conspirators, led by Miguel Merino and Raúl Coll. Many of the married officers and men slept in the town, so that there were only about a hundred and fifty men sleeping at the base. At dawn, Ríos and four enlisted men took over the armoury and the main gatehouse. The sentry at the armoury and several of the men at the gate joined the rebellion, the others were locked up. All the inner security posts were also seized. By 5.30 a.m. the base was in rebel hands, though Colonel Roberto Comesañas, the commander, still slept. San Román came in from the town and woke and arrested the commander. A hundred and fifty members of the 26 July Movement arrived, with about fifty Auténticos. All received arms.

Officers and men began to arrive from the town. Each was quickly given the choice of being arrested or joining the rebellion. Six officers and most of the men took the second choice, while eighteen officers were arrested.

The rebellion was now led into the city; cries were heard of *Viva Cuba Libre! Viva la Revolución! Viva la marina de guerra! Viva San Román!* At 8 a.m. a rebellious lieutenant of the harbour police took over the maritime police headquarters and killed the superintendent, Major Cejas. The Cienfuegos military commander, Major Eugenio Fernández, was arrested at the headquarters of the Guardia Rural. All that remained was the police headquarters, which was surrounded by rebels. The

[4] Carrillo MSS, p. 35.

[5] Carrillo, who was involved in this from Havana, suggested that Faustino Pérez in Havana gave the order to go ahead knowing that there was only a slender chance of success – on the ground that Castro wished his possible rivals in the opposition, the Barquinistas, better dead.

Rebel Commanders:
3a Raúl Castro and 'Che' Guevara
 b Guevara later, as a Minister
 c Camilo Cienfuegos

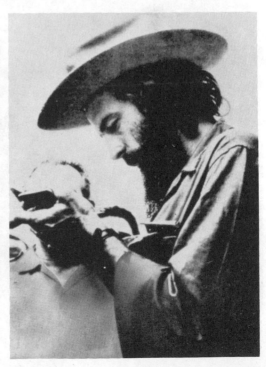

The Honeymoon period,
abroad and at home:

4a Castro says goodbye to Vice-President Nixon, Washington, April 1959
 b The first cabinet after the fall of Batista: Robert Agramonte, Armando Hart
   Cepero Bonilla, José Míro Cardona (Prime Minister), Luis Buch, Manue
   Fernández, Angel Fernández, Manuel Ray, Faustino Pérez, Julio Martíne
   Páez

police commander, Major Ruiz, telephoned for help from Havana, and tried to cause delay. A cannonade followed. The police surrendered, and were all driven as prisoners to the naval base. By this time, of course, the city knew of the attack. But, though many shops were shuttered, the pavements and balconies were crowded with onlookers. Cienfuegos, except for the Guardia Rural base on the Santa Clara Road, had been captured. Many doubtful or hesitant supporters of the ' rebels put on the red and black 26 July arm bands or the orange Auténtico bands.

The freedom of Cienfuegos lasted only a morning. In the afternoon, Colonel Cándido Hernández drove in from Santa Clara at the head of motorized infantry. They were ambushed in the Parque Martí and many were killed or wounded – including the colonel, who was wounded and his son, who was killed. But, shortly, B-26 bombers, supplied by the U.S. as part of the U.S.–Cuban military programme, began to move over the city, dropping a few bombs and also machine-gunning the naval base and the rebels' defence posts. Tank and armoured regiments, also equipped with recent U.S. material, appeared from Havana. The city was given over to street fighting in which the rebels stood no chance. They should, no doubt, have withdrawn to the Sierra Escambray after their initial victories, but these had been too complete for such a course to be regarded as other than a retreat. The rebel commanders also had not anticipated such a heavy response, since they had assumed that there would also be fighting at Havana. The use of the tanks, armoured cars and B-26 bombers was technically a breach of the U.S.–Cuban arms understanding since it specifically forbade the use of these weapons except in agreement and in defence of the hemisphere. As a result there was no plan for a prolonged defence. Isolated groups fought on hopelessly throughout the evening and the night. By nightfall, however, the naval base was once more in government hands and by the next day the last rebels, holding out in the police headquarters, had been overwhelmed.

Sixty-seven rebels surrendered to the naval commander, Colonel Comesañas, and were later sent for trial. A few rebels, such as the 26 July chief, Aragonés, and naval lieutenant Julio Camacho, escaped from the city. Most prisoners were shot, including about thirty who surrendered in the police headquarters, and forty in the San Lorenzo school under one of the bravest of the rebels, Lieutenant Dimas Martínez. Naval intelligence, led by Captain García Olayón, searched houses; anyone who seemed to betray signs of having participated – possession of arms, wounds, blood on clothes and even, according to one allegation, the mere fact of youth – was dragged out and shot. San Román was captured, tortured for months, and killed – of course, without trial.[6] Allegations were later made by the secretary-general of the World Medical Association that two hundred wounded were buried alive;[7] though such figures are perhaps exaggerated, the reality was higher than the figures, of between forty and fifty, given by Batista himself. The armed forces had twelve men killed, according to the army.[8] Probably four hundred rebels in all took part in the action, and perhaps as many as three hundred were killed.[9] It was the largest action in the civil war so far. Cienfuegos was cut off for several days – but the press played down the part of the reinforcements: the average Cuban would have supposed that the rising had been defeated by the naval base itself.

There were important consequences. The government's use of the bombers, tanks and armoured cars could not be concealed from the U.S. Embassy or military mission; accordingly it was asked to explain. 'We did not get that satisfaction from them,' William Wieland said some years later. Further, in the coming weeks, 'the entire hemispheric defence unit supplied with U.S. grant equipment was eventually . . . scattered in combat areas throughout the Eastern part of the island. This was done without seeking our prior agreement.'[10] As time passed with still no adequate explanation, the progressive group in the State Department, headed by Rubottom and Wieland, began to speculate whether this was not a reason for ending arms shipments to Batista. This move was being pressed strongly by supporters of Castro and Prío in the U.S. and during the winter it became the main question at issue in U.S.–Cuban relations.

The role of the new U.S. ambassador, Earl Smith, now became decisive. Smith's stand against police brutality in Santiago had won him great prestige among the opposition. The ABC colony disapproved and even condemned Smith's games of golf with such moderate members of the opposition as Luis Machado, Prío's ambassador to the U.S., or Joaquín Meyer, director of the Office of Economic Affairs under Prío and later a Cuban director of the World Bank. Batista's ex-prime minister, García Montes, refused to attend a dinner for Smith at the French Embassy. In fact Smith had little sympathy for the opposition. In his first weeks he may have been influenced by officials such as the political officer, John Topping, a Liberal, and by the CIA representatives – not only by the 'No. 2 man' (whose role at the Cienfuegos rising

[6] René Ray, 34–7.

[7] Medical News, January 1958; article by Dr Louis Bauer.

[8] Havana Post, 8 September 1957. The best account in English is that in Taber, 173–81. Cf. E. Morello, New York World Telegram, and Jules Dubois, Chicago Tribune, who were both there. See also the account by Carlos Franqui read on Radio Rebelde, 5 September 1958, and reprinted in Revolución, 26 January 1959, 11.

[9] This is the figure given by Smith, 31.

[10] Wieland evidence, Communist Threat, 541.

came out during the trial of the sixty-seven rebels) but also the head of the CIA in Havana, whom Smith regarded as a 'Fidelista'. Smith asked him to investigate Communist strength in Cuba, but he seems to have refused and, walking out of Smith's office, muttered: 'We don't care what you think.'[11] This man was shortly moved on but other members of the U.S. Embassy (many of them being new) remained hostile to Batista; and the question of arms deliveries hung on all winter, exacerbated by such incidents as the new arrest in Miami of Priístas with arms *caches*, and the feeling that, as even Grau had said, by merely recognizing Batista, the U.S. exercised a type of intervention. In general, however, the Embassy was wary of Castro himself. As Democrats, they would have liked an alternative to Castro as a successor to Batista; but, hostile to the idea of intervention, they shrank from any positive action to unseat Batista. The arms embargo seemed then the most positive form of negative action.

The belief (unsubstantiated, to be sure) that Castro, in pressing on with the rising in Cienfuegos, had been preoccupied by a treacherous desire to see his rivals, the Barquinistas, killed, led the leader of the Montecristi group, Carrillo – previously a supporter, though a sceptical one, of Castro – into an attempt to stage a *golpe de estado* on the Isle of Pines, where Barquín was still incarcerated.[12] Carrillo received a promise of help from the vice-president of Argentina, Admiral Rojas, and from the president of Honduras – neither of them fulfilled; the provisional president of Venezuela, Admiral Larrazábal, an old friend of Barquín's in Washington, also promised help.

In the Sierra the Cienfuegos affair was preceded by a clash at a hill known as Hombrito, between Guevara's column and an army group led by Major Merob Sosa, which was halted; and it was followed by an attack by Castro at Palma Mocha in the Cuevas zone where four veteran Fidelistas were killed but where fifty-seven Batistiano soldiers also died.[13] This attack was almost the last occasion when the Batistiano army entered the Sierra. By this time the able Colonel Barrera Pérez had once again been dismissed from his command as a result of intrigues of General Tabernilla and morale was low since he was replaced by none other than the incapable and cruel braggart Alberto del Río Chaviano of Moncada fame.[14]

Was there in fact a chance of a democratic solution without Castro?

[11] Smith, 34.

[12] Carrillo recorded, 'Here was revealed the aspiration of the 26th July Movement towards totalitarian power and the moral attitude of its leaders, capable of sending to their death hundreds of men to avoid the triumph of a different faction, with the result that the failure of the *golpe* of September produced the fall of tens of officials of the Army, the Navy and the Air Force.' (MSS, 37.)

[13] Guevara, 120. 'Veteran' means in this instance that they had been in the Sierra six months.

[14] Barrera Pérez, *Bohemia Libre*, 27 August 1961.

In purely political terms it seemed possible. Batista himself was no doubt genuine in his statement that he would not run in the 1958 elections. What he wanted now was less love from history but respectability before it. He wished to hand over his system to his successor so that eventually the whole opposition would be implicated in it. But who would be his successor? His brother Panchín? That would smack too much of the Dominican Republic, where Héctor Trujillo was now president while power remained with the general, his brother. López Castro, the development board chief? The prime minister Rivero Agüero? But these had no independent political backing without Batista himself. Such successors would have been swept away by either a Castro–Ortodoxo military victory or, more likely, a tougher military dictatorship under one of the generals or police chiefs. Elections were still, however, a year away and Batista resolutely refused to hold them earlier, partly because to do so would admit the illegality or provisional nature of the system, partly because if he were to consolidate the system he needed time. At this stage, in the early autumn of 1957, many people or parties were suggesting that they might still collaborate with him to the extent of taking part in his elections. Batista himself was making elections the main drive of his policy:

> Nothing will deprive the people of the path to the polls, [he said on 4 September] no one will make us back down . . . the balance of bank clearings for the first six months of the year demonstrate the increasing economic power of the country. Foreign investors whom some have tried to scare away continue to announce new investments.

It was true. Hardly a day in early 1957 passed without some new investment by a large U.S. company. A heavy new programme of investment at Moa Bay was begun. In September Langbourne Williams, president of the Freeport Sulphur Co., the owner of Moa Bay, after an interview with Batista said that construction would begin immediately; Moa Bay was believed to represent the best source of new nickel in the free world,[15] cobalt being a specially high percentage.[16]

The question was now posed whether the 26 July Movement would make any compromise. Castro believed that he was strong enough to refuse to do so, and to ignore completely, for instance, the fact that Grau, the foremost opposition leader of the Centre, claimed to have 300,000 voters registered for him. In the autumn of 1957 there were a few minor actions in the Sierra such as that of Pino del Agua of 10 September,[17] but Castro was given all the time he needed to consolidate his position.

---

[15] HAR, October 1957 and May 1953.
[16] See *Havana Post*, July 1957.
[17] Guevara, *Souvenirs de la Guerre*, 148–9.

A few actions, such as the murder of fifty-three peasants at Oro de Guisa by the army, merely redounded to Batista's discredit.[18] Peasants began to feel that it was wiser to be in the Sierra with Castro than in their own homes and risk death from Río Chaviano.[19] Government and rebels, police and bomb-layers stepped up their war of nerves. Many peasants who had worked with Castro were betrayed by Leonardo Baró. An endless procession of young men followed each other into the underground and many into prison. A doctor, Jorge Ruiz Ramírez, was murdered after trying to treat a youth for gun wounds received in a clash with the police. The Cuban Medical Association made a new protest and more doctors became sympathetic to Castro merely by turning away from Batista. The assistant editor of Masferrer's *Tiempo en Cuba*, Luis Manuel Martínez, was shot in Havana by the 26 July Movement. In October bombs destroyed Radio Oriente. A curfew was imposed in Santiago and as usual on such occasions the bodies of several youths were found hanging. The whole of Oriente lay under military control, the army being responsible for the north, the navy for the south. Traffic was limited. A price of $100,000 was set on Castro's head. Earl Smith, becoming rapidly less inclined to believe the State Department or his own embassy advisers, telegraphed Allen Dulles, head of the CIA, recommending the placing of an agent with Castro in the Sierra 'to discover the extent of Communist control' in the 26 July Movement. Apparently this could not be done and anyway the CIA in Cuba itself remained favourable to, rather than opposed to, the 26 July,[20] even though relations with the rebels were not improved by the grant of the U.S. Legion of Merit to Colonel Carlos Tabernilla. A big assignment of arms went to Batista from New Jersey in November and a U.S. civilian agent arrested thirty-one Cubans in Florida, led by César Vega,[21] with arms for Castro. Various U.S. right-wing men urged that any embargo on arms to Batista would 'lead to Communist control'.[22] As if to answer such complaints, the *Daily Worker* argued that the Cuban Communists were not receiving adequate credit for their support of the rebels and that U.S. newspapers wanted to hide the fact.[23] In October the Soviet government made its first direct allusion to the struggle in Cuba, when its ECOSOC delegate attacked Batista's

---

[18] The army announced that fifty-three revolutionaries had been killed. Castro, on Radio Rebelde, 21 August 1958, qu. Jules Dubois, 297.

[19] The comment of Barrera Pérez, *Bohemia Libre*, 6 September 1961.

[20] Smith, 35. Lyman Kirkpatrick, however, implies that agents were successfully placed in the Sierra (*Real CIA*, 159), but perhaps he means simply Andrew St George, who was back in the U.S. by now.

[21] He was betrayed by an agent of Masferrer's, Ariel Ajo, later arrested in 1959 by the revolutionary government (*Revolución*, 26 January 1959, 31).

[22] e.g. Braden.

[23] See article by Harold Philbuch, *New York Tribune*, 22 September 1957.

as a 'terrorist government that strangles and tortures its people'.[24] This was certainly true; and however many Batistianos may have been killed by the rebels, there appear to have been no instances of torture by them.

Exile activity continued in the U.S. in the early winter, with uncertainty about Castro's plans; was the 26 July Movement simply an offshoot of the Ortodoxo party? Had the Ortodoxo party merely joined the 26 July? Which, after the death of País, actually constituted the Central Committee of the 26 July Movement? Felipe Pazos, Lester Rodríguez (a Moncada man from Santiago), Mario Llerena and Luis Morán (a Santiago lawyer who had defended several *Granma* prisoners at their trial in May) spoke for the 26 July Movement at a general meeting of seven opposition groups, at Miami, in the house of Lincoln Rodón, who had been president of the Cuban House of Representatives until 1952. Present also, among others, were Agramonte and Bisbé for two of the Ortodoxo groups; Prío, Varona, Hevía and Carlos Maristany of the Auténticos;[25] Ramón Prendes for the remains of the FEU; Faure Chomón, second-in-command in the attack on the palace, for the Directorio Estudiantil, recently reformed separately from the FEU; and Angel Cofiño, with Hirigoyen, for the trade union opposition.[26] These men established what they called a council (junta) of National Liberation, including representatives of all the opposition except the Communists, Grau's Auténticos and those electionist Ortodoxos who followed Ochoa or Márquez Sterling. 'Tony' Varona, Prío's last premier (in exile since September), was named president, the Ortodoxo Bisbé became secretary, while the national committee consisted of all 26 July men – Mario Llerena (propaganda), Lester Rodríguez, Franqui (organization), and Raúl Chibás (finance) – the latter having now divested himself of the cloak of Ortodoxia. The new council declared first that the 'struggle' should be continued till democratic rule was restored, and that a general election should be held 'as soon as possible', in any case not more than eighteen months ahead. The Constitution of 1940 would be restored. The only economic point was that 'new sources of employment should be created, as well as higher standards of living'.[27] Since Prío financed not only the two Auténtico groups but the students, the Labour unionists and even to some extent the 26 July Movement, he was inevitably the centre of attention and reputed to be the main organizer.

[24] HAR, November 1957.

[25] Actually divided by now into two – the PRC or Auténtico party people; and the OA (Organización Auténtica), a more activist branch of the former, led by Maristany, who had been Prío's Minister of Communications.

[26] Directorio Obrero Revolucionario (DOR).

[27] Full text and commentary in Jules Dubois, 188–90, and Wieland, 579–86. *Cf.* Rodríguez Loeches, for the Directorio's point of view, 21.

This declaration had a good effect in the U.S. But Pazos and the two other 26 July men had not discussed these questions with Castro; indeed, Pazos had technically no real right to commit the 26 July Movement save that he was, with Chibás, now its best known backer. News of the Miami Pact reached Castro only through the *New York Times*. Comprehensibly, this infuriated Castro, less for its contents than for the fact that it was realized without himself. Nevertheless, to begin with, the National Directorate of the 26 July Movement responded with some caution to Pazos and Lester Rodríguez, saying that the agreement of Miami seemed to 'look like the clever political trickery of certain discredited leaders of the opposition'. It was only when the Junta in Miami reproduced all the familiar difficulties and confusions of democratic politics that the attitude of Castro hardened. At one point in November the letters from Armando Hart, the secretary of organization of the National Directorate, to Mario Llerena, representative of the 26 July Movement in Miami, seemed to be demanding the dissolution of the Miami Junta and its replacement by a national committee of non-partisan people: 'The military, the banks, big insurers, the sugar mill owners' would be canvassed for support of just such a body.[28] Llerena thought this impossible and, in a letter of 26 November to Hart he pointed to the necessity for the central committee to decide if they were going to break with the Junta or not. Finally, on 14 December, after a success by the rebels at Veguitas where a two-hundred-strong force inflicted a hundred and seventy casualties on a column of three hundred soldiers of Batista,[29] Castro dispatched a four thousand word letter to the Council of Liberation denouncing it:

> For those who are fighting against an Army incomparably greater in number and arms, with no support for a whole year apart from the dignity with which we are fighting for a cause which we love sincerely ... bitterly forgotten by fellow countrymen who, in spite of being well provided for, have systematically ... denied us their help, the Miami Pact was an outrage. The 26th of July had not authorised anyone to sign. Prío had refused them arms, how could they now sit down at a conference table with them?

Castro criticized the omission in the Miami Pact of any declaration against foreign intervention – 'clear evidence of a lax kind of patriotism and of a cowardice that are self-denouncing'.[30] He also denounced the omission of any consideration of the army: 'Let us have no military

[28] All this derives from Llerena's MSS. It has never been clear who precisely formed part of the Dirección Nacional but at this time it appears to have been Hart, Faustino Pérez and Castro.
[29] Taber, 197.
[30] The manifesto of the Sierra Maestra had included this.

junta ... let the people govern ... let the soldiers go back to their barracks.' Though there should be 'complete constitutional normality', the future president 'should not be limited in his free power of appointment'.[31] Cubans would, of course, have to fight 'other Caribbean dictators'. 'The new Government will be governed by the Constitution of 1940, will assure all the rights therein recognized and will stay clear of all political partisanships ...' Political parties would have only one right in the 'provisional period – freedom to organize, within the liberal framework of our Constitution and to take part in the general elections'. Finally, the provisional president would not be Pazos or anyone at Miami – but Judge Urrutia, the magistrate who had found that the *Granma* expeditionaries had behaved constitutionally in trying to overthrow Batista by force. This was a clever move: Urrutia had been on the Bench for thirty-one years, and was politically a moderate. He was put forward by Castro not as a strong man but deliberately as a man without qualities, who would prevent any more dangerous candidate (such as Pazos) from getting in instead.[32] Urrutia was at that time still in Cuba and, after discussions by letter with Mario Llerena, had been approached (only on 26 November) on Castro's behalf by Armando Hart and Luis Buch, who at that time could travel fairly easily between the U.S. and Cuba since his political activities were not well known. Hart and Buch asked Urrutia if he would take part in a five-man government of Cuba in exile. Urrutia agreed, asking 'time to obtain my retirement benefits' from the magistracy, and on 23 December arrived in Miami.[33] He had not had time to become absorbed in exile intrigues before. About Christmas time, Luis Buch and Raúl Chibás brought Urrutia a clear offer to be the 26 July candidate for the presidency, in the form of a letter from Armando Hart. (Hart himself had actually already said in a private letter to Llerena in Miami that he would really have preferred Castro himself as the provisional president.)[34]

Hart's letter was, as usual, couched in grandiose terms ('Destiny has reserved for me the honour of writing these lines'). The 26 July, he said, was 'a youthful movement which is sacrificing everything for the sole honour of being faithful to the tradition of Mambí'. Difficulties in Miami, that perennial problem in Cuban history, as yet made a

---

[31] It was presumably this phrase that struck the State Department Cuban chief, Wieland, as presenting a 'pretty hair-raising picture of a dictatorship' (Wieland, 579).

[32] Other candidates were Dr Gelasio Pérez, of the Cuban Medical Association, García Barcena and Carrillo. Urrutia, then aged 56, was born in Yaguajay (Las Villas), graduated 1923, judge of Jiguaní 1928. As a judge in Matanzas he had in 1933 saved the lives of two men pursued by Machado's police, and therefore himself had to hide in Havana. His father had been a major in the war of Independence. (*Revolución*, 4 January 1958.)

[33] Manuel Urrutia Lleó, *Fidel Castro & Company, inc.: Communist tyranny in Cuba* (1964), 7–10.

[34] Letter of Hart to Llerena, 19 November 1957.

government-in-exile 'inappropriate'. Nevertheless, Urrutia would remain 'the candidate of the people'. The 26 July Movement admitted that it might act alone and apart from the rest of the opposition: 'Alone we began and alone we may have to continue, because we must finish this crusade that represents the last historic possibility for Cuba to be preserved as a sovereign and independent nation.' Hart added:

> The struggle for national independence is more impassioned than ever before since, unless this process is successful, for small, politically disintegrated, socially immature and economically poor countries, perhaps one of the imperialisms now competing for the world will devour us completely and extinguish all hope of Cuba's occupying that position of which the liberators dreamed.[35]

Urrutia, flattered, believed that his acceptance would help the unification of the whole opposition. He did not appreciate that the old parties wanted other candidates. It is hard, on the other hand, to believe that he could have taken Hart's letter seriously: for the full realization of its terms implied a clash with the U.S., to which it is clear he was opposed. But it soon became obvious that, in the words of Mario Llerena to Marcelo Fernández in the Sierra in a letter in early January, the new president-elect was a man of 'unheard-of *naïveté*'.[36]

These developments had destructive effects. Castro (whose letter of 14 December arrived at Miami about 30 December)[37] demanded the withdrawal of the 26 July Movement from the Council of Liberation. Pelayo Cuervo's son Orlando resigned as chairman of the Miami 26 July group, expressing confidence in Pazos. The Ortodoxos, Bisbé and Agramonte, withdrew too. The council foundered. The reconstituted Directorio Estudiantil begged Castro to reconsider. So did Prío. Varona said that his group would accept Urrutia as provisional president but that they could not agree that the 26 July Movement should command the army and be responsible for order during the provisional period. That might mean continued military rule. Castro's reply was merely that his was the way to 'the destruction of tyranny'; Prío, he said, now counted for little in Cuba. Pazos and others left the 26 July, Chomón denounced Castro and prepared to organize his own invasion of Cuba, but the showdown increased rather than ended the fragmentation of the opposition; all over the U.S. and Central America were hundreds of groups and leaders each claiming to represent 'Fidel'.[38]

[35] Letter in Urrutia, 8–10. The translation has been modified.
[36] Llerena to Fernández, 6 January 1958, Llerena MSS.
[37] Llerena MSS, p. 160.
[38] Thus in New York there were three separate groups headed by the ex-*Granma* Negro, Pablo Díaz; by Angel Pérez Vidal; and by Arnaldo Barrón. In Miami Lester Rodríguez, Mario Llerena, Jorge Sotús and others were rivals for Fidel's affection more than his delegates.

Castro had already called for the destruction of the 1958 sugar harvest: 'Either Batista without *zafra* or *zafra* without Batista'; 'After the tyrant is in the tomb . . . we shall have a *zafra* of liberty.' A single-page pamphlet had been distributed to sugar workers, giving instructions for setting fire to cane, and including a suggestion for a rat to be tied to a gasoline-soaked sponge. Batista countered this scheme with a general permission for grinding to begin in December. More army units were dispatched towards the cane fields. Many fires did break out. The army was permitted to fire on all suspicious people. Mujal called on workers to 'stand guard against the torch'.

Arrests, deaths and bombs continued daily during November and December. The most sensational event was the assassination of the hated Colonel Fermín Cowley, commander in the Holguín district, in a hardware shop. He had been responsible for killing many 26 July men the previous December. His death predictably was followed by the murder of six men, all innocent, in reprisal, two weeks after. On 16 December the Auténtico Senator Conrado Rodríguez wrote to Godoy, president of the Senate, protesting against the deaths of five hundred Cubans in attempting to crush the opposition; Castro, calling in the hills for more personal assassinations such as that of Cowley, spoke of three thousand having been killed.[39] The unrest was spreading at last to Labour. A Mujalista dock workers' leader, Navea Arambarri, was found murdered, allegedly for anti-Communism. It was hardly surprising that in the course of this winter Mujal, still secretary-general of Labour, moved over more and more towards overt identification of the Labour movement with the regime. The Ministry of Labour announced that absenteeism would be regarded as an 'anti-government act'. Mujal tried to quell menaces of a general strike by the opposition with remarks that 'as long as I live there will be no general strike'. Union Labour had benefited from rising minimum wages, he trumpeted; what earthly need was there to strike?[40] And indeed, despite murder and bloodshed, 1957 had been a record year. Total income from sugar was $M680, $M200 more than in 1956 and higher than any sum achieved since 1952. New investments of foreign capital in 1957 totalled $M200. Bonuses for Christmas were numerous. Money flowed throughout the island. Professional gangsters swarmed the new hotels of Havana. The murder of the gangster Anastasia in Chicago was linked with an attempt by him to capture Meyer Lansky's gambling business in Havana.[41] It was also hard to separate 'gangsterdom from revolutionary ardour; thus when in December Earl Smith, the U.S. ambas-

---

[39] HAR, January 1958.
[40] *Cf. ibid.*, November-December 1958.
[41] *Ibid.*, January 1957.

sador, received news through the U.S. Embassy in Ciudad Trujillo that 'Communist members of the Castro revolution were plotting my assassination', it was doubtful whether the Communists (who had shown hitherto little interest in violent action) or the Auténticos were really at the root of things. Smith himself was now no longer doubtful about the regime; Batista dined with him and his wife in December while the Democrat aspirant to the presidency, Senator John Kennedy, stayed in the embassy for Christmas.[42]

The size of Castro's forces was still being exaggerated by visitors, above all by North Americans. Thus Charles Ryan, who had gone up to the Sierra in March, had descended in October with the news that there were 1,000 men; a journalist for the *New York Herald Tribune*, Donald Hogan, spoke of 2,000 men, half of them well equipped.[43] None of these figures was true. At the end of the year Castro still had less than 300 men under arms.

[42] Smith, 222.
[43] *New York Herald Tribune*, 15 November 1957.

CHAPTER 15

The Arms Embargo

Castro had now been in the Sierra for over twelve months. Instead of being a hunted fugitive, he commanded a guerrilla army which could roam at will over nearly all the territory south and west of the *Carretera Central* in Oriente – almost 2,000 square miles. Within this region an elaborate system of maintenance and supply had been organized, based on the connivance of friendly peasants. Much merchandise came up on mules from Manzanillo, Bayamo and other places. There were also now quite elaborate factories in the heart of the Sierra: to the shoemakers and gun repairers a small cigar factory had been added, along with a butcher's shop, a bomb factory and hospitals. But there was still a great shortage of arms – only very few consignments got through, apart from the large quantity after the failure of the attack on the palace. Raids continued along the outlying areas, particularly near Manzanillo, farm machinery was destroyed, rice and cane fields were burned.[1] Westwards in Camagüey private aircraft were used to drop phosphorus on to cane fields.

In the Sierra itself the revolutionary army was increasingly preoccupied with what might be regarded as a second stage in its development: problems of discipline both in the army itself and among the peasants. Many of the latter, as Guevara later explained,[2] were alternatively suspicious and afraid, and also sometimes cynically opportunistic. Guevara commented: 'The execution of anti-social individuals who profited from the situation of force established in the country was, unhappily, not rare in the Sierra Maestra.'[3] There were numerous minor incidents, some causing unnecessary deaths, as when Captain Lalo Sardiñas shot an insubordinate peasant by mistake.[4] Numerous bandits took over sections of the so-called *territorio libre*. Shootings of treacherous peasants or bandits or marijuana smugglers (such as the Chinese bandit

---

[1] In one of these a *Granmaista*, Ciro Redondo, was killed, but, in general, casualties were slight.

[2] Guevara, 171 ff.

[3] *Ibid.*, 152.

[4] *Ibid.*, 154. On this occasion, Lalo Sardiñas was tried by majority vote: 70 voted for his death, 76 for a different punishment. 146 *guerrilleros* took part in this vote. Afterwards, several who were defeated in this vote withdrew.

Chang) were frequent, for the simple reason that the rebel army had no prison.[5]

In the big cities sabotage continued unabated, despite many arrests. Engineer Ray took over from Engineer Oltuski the leadership of the Havana Civic Resistance.[6] More than ever arrests resulted in the final disappearance of the man arrested – for instance, in Guanajay, Luis Enrique Álvarez was tortured so badly on 6 January, under the orders of Major Pérez Pantoja,[7] that he died. Some were thrown into the sea with weights – in the style of Machado.[8] The Esso gas storage depot was blown up in January, damaging the Havana water main. A building company was also attacked, and 280 lbs of dynamite with eighteen electric detonators disappeared. On 15 January a military bulletin from Campamento Columbia spoke of twenty-three rebels being killed in an 'encounter' at Los Hombritos; in fact they were prisoners taken from Boniato gaol and shot.[9] Two men fortunate to escape death were the prominent 26 July men of Havana, Javier Pazos and Armando Hart (arrested for the second time), along with Antonio Buch, information chief of the 26 July in Santiago. Typically, the Buch family – Luis Buch was chief of the Civic Resistance in Santiago – protested not to any Cuban institution, but to the *New York Times*; and that newspaper made a protest which may have helped stave off possible death.[10] The continual atrocities practised by the police did not, however, restrict the activities of the saboteurs; indeed, quite the contrary, they stimulated the desire for vengeance, and thrilled yet more and more young men and women anxious to recreate in reality the dangerous excitements of the cinema. The concept of 'revolution' rather than 'revolt' gathered more and more friends.

There were of course many who were anxious to end the increasingly acute political crisis, above all the North American business community, and the ABC colony in general. Prominent among these was Earl Smith. He held worried meetings with the nuncio, Mgr Centoz, and with other 'neutral' individuals, such as Guillermo Belt, ex-ambassador and ex-treasurer of ABC in the 1930s, or Luis Machado, ex-ambassador to the U.S.[11] But these neutral gentlemen were not in touch with the revolutionary forces. Machado, for instance, was the legal adviser

[5] An Auténtico lawyer, Humberto Sorí Marín, who had come to the Sierra after disputes on the plain, took part in these judgements. He later became Minister of Agriculture, quarrelled with Castro, fled to the U.S., returned as a conspirator and was shot in April 1961.

[6] *Revolución*, 20 January 1959. Oltuski (whose job had been transferred to Sta. Clara) went to Las Villas.

[7] Pérez Pantoja was himself executed after Batista's defeat.

[8] See letter of Luis Quintal Herrera, *ibid.*, 16 January 1959, 4.

[9] Taber, 199.

[10] Matthews, 62.

[11] Smith, *The Fourth Floor*, 31.

of Irénée du Pont, the millionaire of Varadero beach.[12] Such men would point out that, whatever the political situation, the economy could hardly be better. They were right. Smith was thus ill-prepared for the description of the economy made by Wieland in a State Department paper in early January which suggested that the country was in ruins. Wieland also proposed that the U.S. should put pressure on Batista's administration to speed its final downfall. Topping, head of the embassy's political division, helped Wieland prepare an Embassy memorandum with the same message. Smith set off angrily to Washington, paying his own fare since Assistant Secretary of State Rubottom, evidently reluctant to meet the ambassador, desperately said that the Department had no funds for the journey.

On arrival at Washington, Smith said that Batista would restore constitutional guarantees in Cuba, providing that, despite the misuse of grant-in-aid equipment at Cienfuegos, the U.S. assured him the delivery of twenty armoured cars which he had ordered. This arrangement was to be a secret, but since by this time Castro had an agent (the assistant military attaché Saavedra) in the Cuban Embassy in Washington, the news soon reached the Sierra Maestra in naturally more elaborate terms: Castro was thus found telling the journalist Homer Bigart (of the *New York Times*), that Batista had undertaken to restore civil liberties in return for U.S. action against revolutionary groups in the U.S.[13] But though Prío was indeed once again indicted before a Federal jury for planning an arms delivery to Cuba from Miami,[14] Castro's informant had garbled the information. He did, however, get accurate news of another development: Earl Smith gave a press conference in Washington in which he said that he did not think 'the U.S. government' would ever be able 'to do business with Fidel Castro', because Castro, he thought, would neither honour international obligations nor maintain law and order.[15] This naturally became known too.

Smith was not alone in making these judgements. Wieland was visited in Washington in January by General García Tuñón, one of the ablest of Batista's generals dismissed by Tabernilla, who tried to persuade the State Department that the best replacement for Batista would be a military junta composed of various officers, including himself, Barquín, and some of the more intelligent and humane of Batista's officers, such as Cantillo.[16] Wieland himself, however, in an unguarded

[12] *Cf. Bohemia*, 27 July 1952; *Havana Post*, 12 September 1957.
[13] *New York Times*, 25 February 1958. On 9 January Castro appointed Mario Llerena and Raúl Chibás as chairman and treasurer respectively of the Cuban Committee in exile which he recognized as the sole representatives of the 26 July in the U.S.
[14] This time he chose to go to gaol with his comrades, who could not raise bail.
[15] Smith, *The Fourth Floor*, 60.
[16] *Communist Threat*, 857-8.

moment, confided to a journalist[17] in words which afterwards haunted him:

> I know Batista is considered by many as a son of a bitch ... but American interests come first ... at least he is our son of a bitch,[18] he is not playing ball with the Communists ... On the other hand, Fidel Castro is surrounded by commies. I don't know whether he is himself a communist ... [But] I am certain he is subject to communist influences.[19]

Wieland's own comment later on was:

> Our problem ... was a desire to see an effective solution to Cuba's political strife that would ensure a democratic transition and the support of the ... bulk of the Cuban people [and] that would have eliminated any major threat from the violence which was at that time being waged by the Castro forces ... Castro at that time was still a small figure in the east ... We were not thinking of dictating on the type of government ...[20]

Batista himself was still keeping up his old programme – elections in the summer, with himself not a candidate. He did say, however, that he would afterwards be eligible to be chief of staff of the army. It was reasonable to suppose, therefore, that the presidency of Andrés Rivero Agüero (who would be the government candidate) would simply be a cover for a prolongation of the Batista era, a return to the era of the presidents *fainéants* of the 1930s. In February the Allied Professional Institute charged that the preparations being made for the elections included 'the most scandalous frauds in the history of Cuba', and argued that elections should not be held while Cuba was in civil war. These charges were the occasion for the withdrawal from the contest of Pardo Llada – 'never a serious candidate' – leaving only Grau and Márquez Sterling of the opposition in the running.

A bizarre proposal next came from Castro, sent through the Liberal congressman for Manzanillo, Manuel de Jesús León Ramírez. Castro undertook to agree to elections supervised by the OAS, provided Batista withdrew all military forces from Oriente. He also told Homer Bigart that after all he would not insist on Urrutia as president. This was news to Urrutia, who learned (at second hand) that the suggestion of his candidacy would only operate 'in the case of a revolutionary triumph'.[21] Batista regarded Castro's proposal as a sign of weakness, and rejected it.

---

[17] Shaffer, of *Newsweek*.
[18] This phrase of course echoes Roosevelt's about Trujillo.
[19] Wieland hearing, 1–4.
[20] *Ibid.*, 540–6.
[21] *Cf.* Urrutia, 12–18; and Meneses, *Fidel Castro*, 64.

A possible split in the 26 July Movement was therefore avoided; Raúl Chibás said that Castro's statements must have been misinterpreted because there could be 'no political solution where Batista presides over an election'.[22] Castro himself reaffirmed support for Urrutia,[23] in a letter to him on 9 March. But this modest gesture towards 'electoralism' was without doubt a possible opportunity for compromise and one rejected by the government.

Immediately afterwards, there was renewed activity on all sides, New guerrilla groups appeared in northern Oriente, and plans were made for the establishment of a second guerrilla force permanently in that region. On 16 February 1958, Castro destroyed a small garrison at Pino del Agua, killing ten, and capturing an officer,[24] an engagement which Guevara describes as marking the end of 'the long period of consolidation' of the *guerrilleros*. After this date it began to be evident to all the people of the hills that Castro and his men were there to stay and that therefore they had nothing to gain in the long run from working with Batista's army.[25] From all provinces there were reports of killing and sabotage, bodies being found hanging outside several towns. The presidents of the three student federations (Havana, Santiago and Las Villas) all declared that no students would go back to work until there was peace. Sabotage of railways reached such a pitch that timetables in East Cuba were changed daily and soldiers accompanied all trains. There were fires in harbours and warehouses, stores and schools. In Havana the 26 July Movement raided the central clearing bank and destroyed $M16 worth of cheques. On 23 February the Argentinian racing motorist, Fangio, was kidnapped from his hotel as propaganda to prevent him taking part in the race the next day. He was returned afterwards. At the race itself, a car skidded and, driving into the crowd, killed six and wounded fifty. The government accused the 26 July Movement of pouring oil on the course; the charge was denied, but the affair was never fully solved.[26] The leader of the kidnappers, Oscar Lucero, was later caught, tortured and murdered.[27]

Meantime a new expedition of guerrilla fighters composed of men of the Directorio had landed on the north coast of Cuba at Playa Santa Rita near Nuevitas, and made their way slowly south-west into the Escambray mountains; it had been a 'question of honour' for them to land before the first anniversary of the attack on the palace. Fifteen men and a woman left Miami on 31 January and arrived at 10.30 p.m.

[22] *Carteles*, 5 March 1958.
[23] Urrutia, 16.
[24] Taber, 207–8.
[25] Guevara, *Souvenirs*, 172–3.
[26] Batista, *Cuba Betrayed*, 70.
[27] *Revolución*, 19 January 1959.

on 8 February,[28] aiming to achieve, like Castro, what Chomón had called a *'mañana esplendorosa* for our country'. Like Castro, they used a U.S. owned boat, the *Thor II*, which belonged to Alton Sweeting of Miami. They reached the Sierra on 13 February. (A number of anti-Batistianos of various political affiliations had been in these hills since mid-1957 – Rafael López Cárdenas, for instance.)[29] The Directorio had with them fifty Italian carbines, two English Sten machine guns, a Thompson, two Springheeds, one Garand, two M3s and one M1, with five Remington semi-automatic rifles with telescopic lenses.[30] Several local members joined, including Ramón Pando, the secretary of the Directorio in Las Villas. By 17 February there were already twenty-nine rebels in the second front of Escambray, in three columns; they had attacked a military post at Cacapual, Banao, and killed three men.[31] On 19 February, however, their advance guard met ten soldiers, and were dispersed. Pando, Edelmira and their guide were caught and murdered on the orders of Captain Mirabal, chief of police at Sancti Spiritus. After further skirmishes on the slopes of the hill Diana, they eventually moved on towards the site of the old Indian city of Cubanacán, where they stayed several days surrounded by rats. On 24 February they issued a new manifesto setting out their aims:

> We won't be . . . the people to make false promises . . . we are fighting to abolish in our country the idea of youth without education, men

[28] They were: Alberto Mora (son of the deputy Menelao Mora, killed in the attack on the palace), Eduardo García Lavandero, Carlos Montiel, Julio García, Faure Chomón, Alberto Blanco, Raúl Díaz Argüelles, Rolando Cubela, Antonio Castell, Enrique Rodríguez Loeches, Carlos Figueredo, Guillermo Jiménez, García Olivera, Luis Blanco, Ramón Pando (who joined them on arrival), Gustavo Martín and Esther Martín (Rodríguez Loeches, 50).

[29] *Revolución*, 15 January 1959.

[30] Also 11,000 cartridges for the carbines, 2,000 for the M1, 2,000 30·06 calibre and 5,000 calibre 0·45; three walkie-talkie sets, 65 uniforms, three tents, 'soda syphons, knapsacks, nylon pillows, lanterns, etc.' (Rodríguez Loeches.)

[31] The three columns were:

A	B	Advance Guard
Cubela	G. Lavandero	Ramón Pando
Darío Pedroso	Chomón	Willie Morgan (an American)
Pablo Machín	Luis Blanco	Artola
'Cárdenas'	Armando Fleites	Ramiro Camajuaní
Rodríguez Loeches	Eloy Gutiérrez Menoy (brother of	Edelmira
Carlos Figueredo	the leader of the 13 March	Faustinito (guide)
Julio García Clirera	attack)	
plus seven others	Ivan Rodríguez	
	Oscar Ruiz	

Of this group of young men, Cubela and Gutiérrez Menoyo were in years to come to be imprisoned for trying to murder Castro. Fleites fled to the U.S. in early 1961. Willie Morgan was shot for counter-revolutionary activities in 1961. Pando, Edelmira and Faustinito were killed within a month of their arrival. On the other hand, Chomón has been a Cuban minister since 1960; Machín is a major in charge of a factory and Rodríguez Loeches was an ambassador. Carlos Figueredo and Julio García both worked under Castro for the Ministry of the Interior.

without work ... We don't limit ourselves to re-establish ... the social guarantees systematically ignored by the dictatorship. We must ensure work to every Cuban, knowing that our country has the necessary conditions for economic development ... This proclamation, though specifically directed to Cuba, we extend to the American continent. The Directorio ... advocates the creation of a confederation of American Republics, such as demanded by Miranda and Bolívar ...[32]

But alas, matters went badly, the two groups became separated, and Chomón and his group went off for a time to Havana. Gutiérrez Menoyo held on grimly with a handful of men in Escambray,[33] and when Chomón returned he established himself independently in a different command.

Castro was being less histrionic. To Andrew St George, once again in the Sierra, he remarked in January: 'I have personally come to feel that nationalization is at best a cumbersome instrument. It does not seem to make the state stronger yet it enfeebles private enterprise ... foreign investments will always be welcome ... here.'[34] This was an appropriate thing to say to St George who on his own account was an agent of U.S. military intelligence. On 21 February Castro issued from the Sierra his first administrative decree, to apply a scheme of criminal jurisdiction to the *territorio libre* over which he now had control.[35] Henceforth he acted as if he were the *de facto* ruler of part of Oriente. Already he had a newspaper, *Cubano Libre*, run at first by two *guerrilleros*, and later by the Ortodoxo, Luis Orlando Rodríguez, and later still by Carlos Franqui. On 24 February a radio station began operating from the Sierra: *Aquí Radio Rebelde transmitiendo desde la Sierra Maestra en Territorio Libre de Cuba!*[36]

At this time, too, it appears that the cautious Cuban Communist party at long last also decided to support the idea of 'armed struggle' in cities and in the countryside – to back, that is, the very cause which they had previously denounced as Putschist.[37] A resolution supporting Castro seems to have been passed in February by the party leadership. Several

---

[32] Rodríguez Loeches, 72–84.
[33] *Ibid.*, 94–7.
[34] A Visit with a Revolutionary, *Coronet*, February 1958.
[35] Text in González Pedrero, 133–6.
[36] Jules Dubois, 212. Its news bulletins were written by Carlos Franqui, and others in the organization were Ricardo Martínez, Orestes Valera, Violeta Casals and Jorge Mendoza (René Ray, 60).
[37] Aníbal Escalante, *Fundamentos*, August 1959; Carlos R. Rodríguez, *Hoy*, 15 April 1959, 3. A decision was certainly taken but only after controversy. Carlos Rafael Rodríguez later said that he had personally got in touch with Haydée Santamaria, as representive of the 26 July Movement in Havana in August 1957 after the murder of Frank País in Santiago. See C. R. Rodríguez, *La Revolución y el transición*.

members of the Communist Youth (such as Prats[38] and Ribalta) had been in the Sierra in 1957. At least one peasant, a certain Conrado, who was a member of the Communist party, had been in contact with Guevara since mid-1957.[39] It is also clear from Guevara's writings that he had been in contact with the Communists in early 1958, for he tells us how he had upbraided a local party leader. 'You are capable of creating units who allow themselves to be martyred in the obscurity of a dungeon ... but not of creating units able to take a machine gun nest by assault.'[40] A member of the party proper, Osvaldo Sánchez Cabrera, visited Castro's headquarters as a go-between.[41] Carlos Rafael Rodríguez later spoke of 'public' instructions to Communist members to join Castro in February 1958.[42] However there was as yet no explicit alliance, only contact; and even that was lacking between the party on the one hand and, on the other, the Civic Resistance and the 26 July Movement in Havana.

It is possible indeed that the Communists would not have taken this decision had they not themselves begun to bear the brunt of attacks by Batista's police. The development of civil war and the propaganda need to identify the rebels as Communists, made it increasingly difficult for the regime to restrain itself from making attacks on known Communists – if not on the national leaders at least on local militants. Thus the police in Yaguajay, in the north of Las Villas, began wantonly to persecute various Communists. Over twenty members of the party in that area – the centre of three sugar mills (*Narcisa, Victoria, Nela*) – had their houses burned. Police ill-treatment occurred in other parts of the province. Yaguajay was, however, the most outrageous instance, chiefly because the Communists were specially strong in the union movement – they claimed 30 % of the workers at the *central Narcisa* – and also among small farmers who had formed a league to resist dislodgement. The consequence was that the police literally drove the local Communists into a state of semi-rebellion, leading to the formation of a guerrilla group to which a Havana Communist, Félix Torres, was dispatched as commander. Another guerrilla group, an offshoot of the Directorio, refused the Communists entry, and, within a few months, Torres was leading his own Communist guerrilla force of fifty men, known as the Máximo Gómez column.[43]

At the same time that the Communists began to go over to the

[38] National organizer of Juventud Socialista.
[39] Guevara, p. 158.
[40] Guevara p. 178.
[41] *Verde Olivo*, 22 January 1961, and 2 July 1961; *Hoy*, 4 January 1964. (He was killed in an air crash in 1961.) *Cf.* comments by Draper, *Castroism*, 31.
[42] In *Hoy*, 15 April 1959. Suárez (58) discounts this.
[43] See letter of Félix Torres to Aldo del Valle, 9 January 1965, qu. *Hoy*, 20 July 1965.

revolutionary cause, another institution roused itself from an even stuffier lethargy: the Church decided at the end of February to take a hand in the Cuban political crisis. This derived from pressure from below: for instance, four young Catholics of the University of Villanueva were killed by the police on their way to join the rebel army.[44] On 10 February Father Angel Gaztelu, priest of the Church of the Holy Spirit in Havana, condemned the regime harshly in the course of a sermon. A similar statement was issued by Acción Católica, and the Catholic weekly *La Quincena* began also to denounce the regime. Conservative opponents of Batista had for some time hoped the Church would give leadership. The *Diario de la Marina*, the main Catholic paper, indeed attributed the political crisis to the decay of the upper class and of Catholic morality. On 1 March the Cuban bishops, headed by Cardinal Arteaga and the nuncio Mgr Centoz, called on the government to bring peace through the formation of a government of national unity, and on the revolutionaries to abandon sabotage and' terrorism. A 'commission of harmony' was proposed, to consist of Raúl de Cárdenas, an aristocrat who, having been a deputy since 1911, had been vice-president both under Grau and in 1933; Gustavo Cuervo Rubio, vice-president and Foreign Minister during the Second World War, being now Señora Batista's gynaecologist; Víctor Pedroso, the bank president; and a Negro priest, Father Pastor González.

The government sought to prevent any publication of this unwelcome plan in the Havana press, but it soon transpired that some of the bishops, including Pérez Serantes of Santiago (who had instigated the scheme), had wanted a stronger call, including one to Batista to resign; others, such as the bishops of Camagüey and Cienfuegos, were opposed; the actual document therefore was a compromise such as Pérez Serantes, for one, did not really approve.[45]

It had, however, an immediate effect: On 3 March Batista's Foreign Minister, Dr Güell, told Earl Smith that his master would be pleased to invite the OAS, U.N. and the world's press to the Cuban elections. Batista also began to prepare a new ministry, selecting Dr Emilio Núñez Portuondo,[46] the ambassador at the U.N., to be at its head – a move clearly calculated to please the U.S. since Portuondo had been well known and popular there. Batista announced that he would be glad to see the Church's harmony group. This was nicely timed, since opinion in the U.S. government was hardening over the question of the supply of arms to Batista. The Cubans' use of grant-in-aid equipment against

[44] *Revolución*, 11 January 1959. Their re-burial in 1959 was attended by the Nuncio.
[45] See Dewart, 109–11. The letter was published by *Bohemia*, 18 January 1959.
[46] Emilio Núñez Portuondo (born 1898), son of the revolutionary General Núñez; lawyer and adviser to railways; Representative and Senator. He was brother to Ricardo Núñez Portuondo, the physician who was a presidential candidate in 1948.

the rebels was raised in the Senate Foreign Relations Committee on 5 March and Rubottom temporized.[47] The Embassy had in fact protested to Batista and received no quick answer. On 6 March it became clear that Núñez would only accept the premiership on the condition that the U.N. supervised the elections. The same day a full protest by thirteen judges against the regime of force showed the premier-designate the magnitude of the difficulties before the regime. Accordingly, he did not form a government after all, and on 12 March the old Foreign Minister, Dr Güell, took over with an administration scarcely different from its predecessor. On 9 March Castro, though tacitly acknowledging the bishops' good intent, had announced that he would not receive the Church's harmony commission because it was too much in favour of Batista – a fair comment on Cuervo and Pedroso, though not on Father González nor on Cárdenas.[48] Castro was now in the middle of what was described as a 'reunion of the National Directorate in the Sierra Maestra', taking place between 7 and 10 March discussing the persistent rumours in late February of a compromise with the regime. The National Directorate pointed out to all its provincial representatives that this – reflected in the interviews with Homer Bigart in the *New York Times* – was purely a 'tactical manœuvre'.[49]

The difficulties were now mounting on every side for Batista. On 11 March a courageous Havana magistrate, Alabau Trelles, agreed to indict police Colonel Ventura and the naval intelligence chief Laurent for the murder of four youths. A serious crisis could not be avoided. On 12 March Batista once again suspended civil rights and reimposed press and radio censorship. The indictment was quashed by the Minister of Justice and Alabau fled to the U.S. The hated Colonel Pilar García then became chief of police. The toughening up was everywhere evident. 75,000 secondary school children were now on strike. All schools were closed. Ambassador Earl Smith was visited by the only electoralist Ortodoxo, Márquez Sterling, along with Mario Lazo, the lawyer who inspired the Havana Hilton; both agreed that there was a case for the postponement of elections till November, with the inauguration of a new president in February 1959; Márquez Sterling confirmed Smith's own view when he agreed that 'Castro would be ten times worse than Batista'.[50]

Castro followed his rejection of the bishops' plan with a new manifesto

[47] Wieland, 541.

[48] Castro's reply in full was published in *Revolución*, 26 July 1962.

[49] *Circular de Organización*, dated Santiago de Cuba, 18 March 1958, which adds that both Castro and the National Directorate considered this to have been a mistake. But Raúl Castro left the Sierra Maestra for northern Oriente with his troop on 10 March.

[50] Smith, *The Fourth Floor*, 81. Lazo was always closely connected with the U.S. government and the CIA, as can be seen from Lyman Kirkpatrick's *The Real CIA*, 179.

from the Sierra[51]; there was mention of that ancient bludgeon, 'the general revolutionary strike, to be seconded . . . by military action'. The 26 July Movement in Havana was in fact preparing such an action. Castro repeated (a warning to the U.S.) that strikes and war would be prolonged if a military junta should take over from Batista. Then came some confident demands: all highway and railway traffic should be halted throughout Oriente. As from 1 April payment of taxes to the State, provincial or municipal authorities, should be suspended. If payments were made, they would be declared null and void and have to be paid again to the new provisional government (headed by Urrutia). All those who remained after 5 April in offices of trust in the executive branch of the government would be judged guilty of treason. Officers and men who continued in the armed services after 5 April would be dismissed. Anyone who afterwards joined the armed services would be judged a criminal. Judges should resign if they wished to continue to practise after the victory of the revolution. The country as a whole should consider itself in a state of total war against the tyranny. Finally, 'Column 6 of the rebel forces under Major Raúl Castro . . . had invaded the north part of Oriente [with fifty men][52] . . . the whole nation is determined to be free or perish.'[53] At this point Castro had under his own command in fact only 100–120 men, excluding those with his brother and Almeida[54] – scarcely more that is than six months before. It is not clear how many supporters he had in the plain, but it is fairly evident that these far outdistanced that number: the organization being carefully established with sub-sections in all parts of Cuba[55] each with separate instructions for each month: thus in March action committees were supposed to unleash total war in Oriente, and extend armed action to Las Villas and Pinar del Río; the workers' committees were supposed to constitute a workers' front as 'flag of struggle'; and the resistance sections, whose tasks were to establish relations with Civic Resistance movements, had among other things to take action around the judicial persons to see that they resigned as demanded in the statement of 12 March.[56]

[51] Worked out by the National Directorate of the Movement, according to a letter of Marcelo Fernández to Mario Llerena of 30 March, and signed by Castro as 'Comandante jefe de las fuerzas armadas' and Faustino Pérez as 'delegado nacional'. Among those present was Major René Ramos Latour, who had succeeded País as chief of action in Santiago (See Verde Olivo, 10 May 1963, article by Major Lussón).

[52] Obra Revolucionaria, 1961, No. 46, 12. His mission was to harass transport and disrupt communications. A column under Almeida with 35 men had gone East.

[53] Tr. in Jules Dubois, 240.

[54] 'There remained forces which in conjunction were no more than 120 men. Less even. There were less than 100 men in the Sierra.'

[55] The sub-sections were Acción; Finanzas; Obreras; Propaganda; Resistencia; and Organización.

[56] From 'Plan de Trabajo para el mes de marzo', Circular de Organización, 18 March.

On 13 March Batista received Earl Smith at the Villa Kuquine. Seated in his study surrounded by its familiar busts of Lincoln, Batista told the ambassador he would accept 'all reasonable requests' by the Church's commission of harmony;[57] he would investigate allegations of brutality made against Captain Sosa Blanco and others; he would accept all suggestions for elections; and he could afford an amnesty to all revolutionaries providing they left their arms behind. He himself would stand down on 24 February 1959, and thereafter enjoy, as he hoped, an honourable retirement.[58] But the following day, Smith was assured by Raúl de Velasco, president of the Cuban Medical Association and chairman of the Civil Co-ordinating Committee (the most respectable of the civilian peace making groups), that elections would be no problem if Batista handed over to a neutral government; there could be no peaceful solution with Batista or his own designated successor in office.[59] As if to confirm that point of view, Raúl Menocal, Minister of Commerce until the recent cabinet reshuffle, narrowly escaped murder by the 26 July on 13 March: and even while Smith was speaking to Velasco, the most critical decision of the war had just been taken, symptomatically, in Washington: the U.S. suspended shipment of 1,950 Garand rifles due for shipment to Cuba and already on the New York dockside. This was in effect a U.S. embargo on arms to Batista; no more arms officially were sent except for some rockets in exchange for previously supplied defective items.[60]

No step by Castro could have so disheartened Batista. His old friends were seen to be deserting him. A position of neutrality, Batista complained to Smith, operated 'against the constitutional regime of Cuba'. The embargo in effect gave belligerent status to 'extremist groups'. Smith needed no persuasion on this subject. He bitterly opposed this embargo, and left no doubt even with Batista that he was convinced Castro's movement was 'infiltrated with communism'.[61] Very soon an emissary came to Smith from Mujal to say that if the U.S. attitude was changing towards Cuba, he, Mujal, would like to know, since he would not be likely to stand firm behind Batista: the trade unions were a non-party organization.

Smith, beset on all sides, said that the U.S. could not intervene and

[57] Bishop Müller of Matanzas had visited Batista after the compromise document had been issued and called on him to resign – an appeal which got nowhere.

[58] Smith, *The Fourth Floor*, 83.

[59] *Ibid.*, 86–7.

[60] Though Smith and others later blamed Wieland, there is no doubt that he was not alone in recommending the action; it was the general action of the Department. See Wieland evidence, 42. Urrutia, Raúl Chibás and Angel Santos Buch (later director of Civic Resistance, Havana) had called on Wieland just before (Urrutia, 17).

[61] Batista, *Cuba Betrayed*, 96.

he could not in any way anticipate his government's behaviour.[62] He asked the Department of State at least to deliver twenty armoured cars previously requested; the same day (18 March) he lunched with Herbert Matthews, prowling around Havana for the *New York Times*, and Matthews said that even the embassy's demands for elections constituted intervention.

Velasco's committee, meanwhile, encouraged, like all the opposition, by the U.S. action, issued a new call to Batista to resign, and for the formation of a neutral government which would annul all political condemnations since 1952. Miró Cardona, the lawyer, believed to be the author of this document, was forced to hide, disguised as a priest: from a sanctuary in the Uruguayan Embassy he wrote a report to the Havana Bar directors saying that, since Batista's regime was illegal, it could not call for elections.[63]

The inflammatory situation meant that Batista had little choice save to postpone elections, as Márquez Sterling had argued, from June until November. To save face he publicly also cancelled the order for armoured cars from the U.S. Smith begged the State Department that before banning all arms shipments he should at least suggest to Batista that he might merely absent himself during the elections, while a provisonal government and the army supervised the poll. Again, the State department refused Smith's recommendation as constituting intervention. Matthews, on the other hand, still in Havana, was now speaking of Castro, as St George and other journalists had before him, in heroic terms: 'The most remarkable and romantic figure . . . in Cuban history since José Martí.'[64] Castro needed this sort of backing then in propaganda almost as much as he needed arms; and the two matters were interconnected, since so much of his arms came from the U.S., bought with contributions from well-wishers in that country. Thus on 27 March the U.S. coastguards caught up with $20,000 worth of arms on a yacht, *El Orión* belonging to Arnaldo Barrón (one of the splinter group leaders of the 26 July Movement in New York), with thirty-six men 'bound for Cuba';[65] such setbacks were compensated by the arrival of a large replenishment of arms brought by air from Costa Rica by a pilot, Pedro Díaz Lanz, who afterwards in 1959 would become briefly and sensationally head of the Cuban air force. The new government of Venezuela also made a gift of $50,000 to Urrutia for the 26 July Movement,[66] and the 26 July Movement in Santiago

[62] Smith, *The Fourth Floor*, 102.
[63] *Cf.* Jules Dubois, 229-33.
[64] Matthews, 70.
[65] He had been expelled from the 26 July and was perhaps hoping to work his passage back.
[66] Urrutia, 17. The dictator Jiménez had been overthrown in January.

had a considerable propaganda success in storming the Boniato barracks.[67]

The American ambassador now became, as at all previous moments of trouble in Cuba since 1902, the repository of confidences, hopes and fears; a Labour leader, Serafín Romualdo, told him he was afraid of being seen with Batista; the president of the Catholic university at Las Villas said that the Church urged U.S. intervention,[68] presumably occupation. At the Havana Biltmore Club, Smith told the British ambassador, Fordham,[69] that the U.S. hoped in a case of emergency that the two of them would act as if they were Siamese twins.[70] He hoped no doubt that the Anglo-Saxons would stand together.

[67] This operation was led by the then *jefe de acción* in Santiago, Belarmíno Castilla, one of the officers of the rebel army who did best in Cuba under the Revolution: he later (1966) became chief of staff and a member of the central committee of the Cuban Communist party.

[68] Smith, *The Fourth Floor*, 96–7, 103.

[69] Alfred Stanley Fordham (born 1907), married to a Peruvian; Eton and Trinity, Cambridge; previous posts, partly U.S. consular, partly Latin American, Stockholm and Warsaw, afterwards knighted.

[70] Smith, *The Fourth Floor*, 103.

CHAPTER 16

The Strike of 9 April

Castro had publicly announced that a general strike would soon be called, but the government did not know when. Much was left to chance. The plan was that the 26 July Movement and Civic Resistance in Havana would call for the strike and, except in various concerns where they were strong, trust to luck that the call would be respected. The director and coordinator was Faustino Pérez, the member of the National Directorate who had survived from the *Granma* and gone down to Havana to assure Castro's supporters that all was well.[1] He did not, of course, have the backing of the bulk of the unions, nor of the Communists, the only opposition group with any real following in organized labour. The Communists had been prepared to join the strike committees, but they were rejected.[2] On 28 March Castro, however, wrote from the Sierra proposing that all groups of the opposition, including the Communists, should participate; the strike committee in Havana felt, however, that the idea was too difficult to achieve at that late hour.[3] There was already much doubt and suspicion between the rebels of the hills and those of the plain, many of whom regarded Castro as a would-be *caudillo* and his followers as militarists.[4] At the same time the organization of the strike was left entirely to the 26 July action committees, without any real contact with labour. The strike committee in Havana, the key area, was in the end composed of Pérez, Manuel Ray (the engineer), David Salvador (who had since mid-1957 been at the head of the 26 July's labour organization), Dr Fernández Ceballos (head of the Cuban evangelical churches), Carlos Lechuga (an Ortodoxo journalist), and Dr Eladio Blanco (a fashionable physician). None of these men was in favour of alliance with the Communists, less on doctrinal grounds than because of the damage such an alliance might have

[1] See above, p. 122. It is obscure whether Castro really wanted this strike, and it has been said, without evidence, that Faustino Pérez, then effectively in control of the 26 July Movement outside the Sierra, brought pressure on him to call it.

[2] Strike committees at national, provincial and municipal levels would consist of six people – a 26 July coordinator; an action and propaganda leader, both representatives of the 26 July Movement; a workers' representative, from the 26 July workers' front organization; and representatives of the Civic Resistance and of the students.

[3] Evidence of Manuel Ray; *cf.* Jules Dubois, 246, and Jacques Arnault, *Cuba et le Marxisme* (1963), 77. This was the first occasion that Castro showed himself willing to collaborate with the Communists.

[4] See Guevara, 180.

done to their cause among liberal opinion, which regarded the Communists of Cuba as not so much menacing as, in view of their past relation with Batista, simply untrustworthy. On 4 April Urrutia and Llerena (on behalf of the 26 July in exile) announced openly that they repudiated all collaboration with the Communists.[5]

The Communists themselves later extensively discussed this strike, saying:

[It could] with armed support from the Sierra have led to the defeat of the tyranny, if it had been developed in the correct way ... The general strike was sabotaged by various elements [that is, the Civic Resistance], even though all elements were there for its ... triumph ... We had correctly planned in advance for the prospect that the masses would struggle on under the tyranny till they reached the phase of armed struggle ... But over a long period we did not take practical steps to promote these ends ... That was our failure.

The Communists nevertheless welcomed the strike 'as a step towards organization of the masses and away from excessive reliance on heroic but indecisive guerrilla warfare, futile bombing and sabotage'.[6] But Castro later castigated the 'premature' launching of the general strike due to 'an erroneous appreciation of the objective conditions'.[7]

The Civic Resistance's instructions for the strike read:

As soon as you get the order to strike, sabotage your work and leave the place with your fellow workers ... Listen to the guidance given by 26 July radio stations. Do not use buses driven by police or strike-breakers. Proprietors of businesses which remain open will be considered as collaborators of the dictatorship. Block the streets with junk, garbage cans, bottles, etc.; assemble Molotov cocktails; Liberty or Death.

Faustino Pérez took the opportunity to assert publicly:

[The] present revolutionary movement is far from being Communist ... We ... shall repeat as often as necessary that our leader [Castro] will not be part of the provisional Government ... The provisional Government will hold national elections within the shortest possible time ... We shall create a climate of confidence and security for the investment of national and foreign capital necessary for our industrial development.[8]

[5] Urrutia, 19.
[6] U.S. *Daily Worker*, 7 May 1958, qu. R. Scheer and M. Zeitlin, *Cuba: An American Tragedy*, rev. edn. (1964), 127.
[7] *Obra Revolucionaria*, 1961, No. 46, 12.
[8] Jules Dubois, 249.

The strike was in fact much more of an urban uprising than a withdrawal of labour and should be classed as such. Its leaders were men who were already somewhat suspicious of Castro and of his reliance on Guevara and Raúl Castro.

Batista seemed confident. He told a U.S. journalist, Skelly, that in any strike Castro did not have a chance of victory.[9] He was right. When 9 April came, there was a good deal of confused violence but most shops were open, as were most factories and the harbour. Neither the CTC nor the Communists took any notice of the 26 July's calls and the transport system therefore worked normally. Some electric companies were sabotaged, some buses overturned, two big shops were attacked, but the Havana electricity supply was left alone, though that had been supposed to signal the beginning of the strike. About twenty civilians were killed, as were three policemen, but probably another eighty revolutionaries were shot. There were rumours in Havana that the strike was a provocation by Batista to uncover strongholds of opposition: and many workers who had struck in the morning went back to work in the afternoon. In Santiago, where a similarly abortive attempt was made, thirty were killed, many by Masferrer's private army of thugs, the rest by police. It was a bloody day but not a very successful one for the forces of protest.[10]

Afterwards came recriminations: the Communists blamed the 'unilateral call' of Faustino Pérez and the national directorate of the 26 July movement.[11] Carlos Rafael Rodríguez, the most intelligent of the Communist leaders, hoped that the failure of the strike would convince Castro of the need to include supporters of Grau and Prío in a future government and to subdue any anti-U.S. propaganda.[12] A few weeks later the Communists spoke of Castro's movement as composed of 'those who count on terroristic acts and conspiratorial *coups* as the chief means of getting rid of Batista'. Faustino Pérez did not mention the Communists in his explanation of the failure of the strike, but instead spoke of 'certain tactical factors inspired by our desire to avoid great torrents of blood so as not to add extra grief to what the people have already suffered . . .'[13]

The failure of this strike reduced Castro's prestige considerably. Sabotage and terrorism declined and in May even tourists began to return to Cuba.[14] Batista, cock-a-hoop, succeeded in getting five plane-

---

[9] *Miami News*, 4 April 1958. Skelly, who had lived in Oriente, knew the Castro family well as a child.

[10] *Cf.* Jules Dubois, 253; Taber, 238; Rodríguez Quesada, *Salvador*, 10.

[11] Draper, *Castro's Revolution* (1962), 12-13. Carlos Rafael Rodríguez, *France Nouvelle*, 17-22 July 1958.

[12] To Claude Julien of *Le Monde*; *cf.* Julien, *La Révolution cubaine* (1961).

[13] Qu. Jules Dubois, 258.

[14] HAR, June 1958.

loads of rifles from the Dominican Republic. Outside Havana there was little revolutionary activity. The statue of the patron of Artemisa, Saint Mark, was taken from its place in the church to avoid the holding of the carnival there in late April.[15] But few followed Castro's adjurations of March to public servants to break with the regime. Only twenty-six aircraft pilots resigned. Most people continued to pay as many taxes as they had ever done. The chief of the Central American Bureau of the CIA called on Ambassador Smith and comfortingly said that he quite agreed with the Ambassador's appreciation of Communist dangers in Cuba.[16] On the day that the Communists issued their denunciation of Faustino Pérez, Smith was busy noting more 'reports of Communist support for the 26 July'. The latest, he said, as if that settled the matter, came from J. Edgar Hoover.[17] Smith was also busy organizing the defence of the Guantánamo water supply, which was outside the base area. It was agreed that if Cuban troops had to withdraw (for use elsewhere) U.S. marines could step in. Smith's relations with Batista were never better.

Efforts to reach a compromise were still going on, but the bishops were the only optimists. The nuncio, Mgr Centoz, asked whether the U.S. could not intervene to force a truce. Smith said that was impossible. Could the U.S. provide Bishop Müller (the new coadjutor on his way to Oriente to try to see Castro) with a U.S. naval helicopter? That too would constitute intervention.[18] Bishop Müller nevertheless set off. At the end of the month (with little or no activity from Castro or anywhere else) the episcopacy demanded a specifically neutral government whose leaders would be ineligible for future office. The episcopacy would choose the prime minister. But Batista was now far less worried than he had been in March. The harvest was almost in: 4·5 million tons of sugar, and the effects of sabotage once more almost negligible. Substitutes for U.S. arms were being found. The 26 July Movement in Havana was hurt by the breaking of the strike. Faustino Pérez, though at large, was being hunted everywhere and went to the Sierra. He was replaced as national coordinator of the Movement by Marcelo Fernández. David Salvador was transferred from labour activities to reorganize the Havana underground. Ray remained head of the Civic Resistance.

The failure of the strike led directly to two separate developments. First Castro, as Carlos Rafael Rodríguez had hoped, went out of his way to issue soothing statements for the benefit of public opinion in the

---

[15] It was returned in January 1959, having been held by the cardinal archbishop of Havana. Cf. Revolución, 24 January 1959.

[16] Smith, The Fourth Floor, 34.

[17] J. Edgar Hoover (born 1895), born Washington; George Washington University; director of FBI since 1924; put his name on the cover of many books.

[18] Smith, The Fourth Floor, 126.

U.S. In mid-May he gave an interview to Jules Dubois in which he said:

> Never has the 26 July talked of Socialism or of nationalizing industries
> ... we have proclaimed from the first that we fought for the full
> enforcement of the Constitution of 1940 [whose provisions] establish
> guarantees, rights and obligations for all elements who have a part
> in production – including free enterprise and invested capital.[19]

He similarly began to promote discussions abroad for a new unification of the opposition, to take the place of the unhappy council of the previous November. This was helped by the establishment on 29 April of a direct radio telephone between the Sierra Maestra and Caracas, Venezuela. But also, and unknown to the rest of the opposition or to his own followers who were negotiating with other members of the opposition, he began to look with more sympathy on the idea of formal collaboration with the Communist party.

It is instructive that Castro took this new step at a time when his brother, the 'more radical' Raúl (as he later described him), was away in Northern Oriente. On 20 April Raúl Castro had written his first dispatch to his brother. He had been away then over a month, since 10 March, travelling partly by jeep, partly on foot. He was accompanied by Manuel Fajardo, Ciro Frías and Efigenio Ameijeiras of the old guard, though after a few days he had reached territory of Mayarí, which was familiar to him from childhood. He had with him a priest too, Fr Antonio Rivas, of Santiago, and indeed his good relations with the Church were such that Fr José Chabebé broadcast secret messages to him on his weekly radio programme from Santiago.[20] By 16 March Raúl Castro was in the Sierra Cristal. There he established relations with a number of other rebels – Captain Demetrio Montseny ('Villa'), Raúl Menéndez Tomasevich, whom he promoted to captain, and the 26 July leader in Guantánamo, 'Toto' Lara. Some of these previously existing units were Communists.[21] Raúl Castro also took over a group of some two hundred 'musketeers':[22]

> Good boys most of them from that zone, but living a fantasy of a
> revolution in various camps, with jeeps ... eating free in a farm with
> cooks and everything; the people provided everything for them and
> all they did was to drive like mad chickens with all the vehicles they

[19] Jules Dubois, 263.
[20] Dewart, 108.
[21] Aníbal Escalante, *Hoy*, 28 June 1959, notes, 'The communist campesinos...were of great help in the formation of the 2nd Front, Frank País.'
[22] These included Lieutenant Vicente Rudea, Sub-Lieutenant Jesús Alejandro Chuchú, Argelio Campos and Captain Julio Pérez.

had from side to side . . . The *responsables* had among them 1,000 pesos in the treasury . . . I told these gentlemen that we were staying there.[23]

Afterwards Raúl Castro purged this guerrilla band – though there were at least two other rebel groups in the area – two hundred men under Armando Castro (no relation), and thirty under ex-sergeant Wicho. Raúl Castro established in this remote area a public works corps (with tractors to make new roads), a bomb factory under Gilberto Cardero, with an American, Evans Russell, working beneath him, a health unit, headquarters, and even a temporary air base. Raúl Castro showed powers of organization not suspected by those who had previously seen him under the shadow of his brother. The steadily growing force was divided into companies led by Ameijeiras, Manuel Fajardo, and Frías, the first of these being attended by a bodyguard who, due to their wild appearance, were called Mau Maus. There was a successful attack on 8 April on the barracks of Ramón de las Yaguas.[24] Several villages were taken and though afterwards, as usual, most were evacuated, one or two such as Felicidad de Yateras remained permanently in their hands. They were soon joined by a mutinous group of Batista's soldiery under a Sergeant Zapata, and Lieutenant Carlos Lite ('Pepecito'). In this wild area there was almost total breakdown of law; had it indeed ever existed? The revolution caught all ages: one boy of ten killed a soldier, seized his rifle and then marched to the Sierra to place himself under Raúl Castro's orders.[25]

In mid-April Raúl Castro dispatched Ciro Frías with a small group of his followers – Company E – to the east of the city of Guantánamo.[26] But this force was beaten off and Frías killed in an attack on the barracks of Initas with a garrison of seventeen men, between Baracoa and Guantánamo, on the south-east coast. Immediately a new attack was ordered – Ameijeiras, with Félix Peña (who succeeded Frías) and Fajardo, would attack the barracks at Jamaica, in the Yateras area; Raúl Castro himself would attack the barracks at the *central Soledad*. These attacks also were unsuccessful. A third attack at the naval barracks at Caimanera did better. This brought the rebels close to the U.S. base at Guantánamo Bay. The essential achievement of Raúl Castro, however, was less in actual attacks, though this kept the army in a state of nerves, than in his success in unifying the many rebel bands who were at work

[23] See article by Lios Pavón, *Verde Olivo*, 24 March 1963.

[24] Raúl Castro, in *Revolución*, January 1959.

[25] *Ibid.*

[26] Captain Ciro Frías, Lieutenant Jesús Soto Mayor, Juan Carlos Borgés, Gerardo Reyes (Yayo) – all with Garands; Nano Pérez and Echevarría, with Johnsons; Floirán Piña with a *mirilla*; Conrado Díaz, with a Springfield; Moralitos, with a Browning machine rifle; and Labrada and Lite, with short arms. Frías was in command, Carlos Lite his second-in-command.

in the area, due to his possession of superior discipline and morale, with a civil organization including a legal adviser (Augusto Martínez Sánchez, a lawyer from Holguín), as well as a priest. By the end of April an Amazon group had been sent up from the city of Guantánamo, and supplies were also assured from that and other towns. All five companies were well organized over Eastern Oriente, with effective civilian backing.[27] Raúl Castro's headquarters lay at Monte Rus, two hours from Guantánamo. The regulations against pillage had almost abolished the incipient banditry of the region. By midsummer there were perhaps 1,000 ex-bandits or free rebels (*escopeteros*) over whom Raúl Castro had more or less established his leadership.[28]

If Castro was to draw nearer the Communists in mid-1958, he was also being more and more actively supported by the Church. Raúl Castro's contacts with the priests in Santiago were matched by chaplaincies held in both Fidel Castro's and Almeida's groups; Fidel Castro soon had a Protestant as well as a Catholic chaplain. In Havana a priest, Father Madrigal, had become treasurer of the 26 July; the church of Father Boza Masvidal became another centre of activity after the death of several young Catholics at police hands in April. The nuncio, Mgr Centoz, had taken a protest signed by many priests on that occasion to Batista, who, however, had refused to see him.[29] Lay Catholic leaders continued active on a far grander scale than the Communists.

Castro was by no means yet the only opponent in the field against Batista. His most formidable rival was Barquín, still in prison but with both his own group of officers (describing themselves as the 4 April Movement, from the date of their abortive *golpe* in 1957) and the Montecristi Movement, led by Justo Carrillo, working for his release by means of a *golpe* on the Isle of Pines. Carrillo had the promised support of the provisional president of Venezuela, Admiral Larrazábal, for his scheme;

[27] Company A: Menéndez Tomasevich – Alto Songo
Company B: Ameijeiras – Guantánamo
Company C: Julio Pérez – Sagua y Mayarí
Company D: Fajardo – Yateras
Company E: Peña – Baracoa, east of Guantánamo
[28] The source for this account, Raúl Castro's diary published in *Revolución*, 26–29 January 1959. See also the article by his aide, José Caussé, in *Verde Olivo*, 24 March 1963. A later reorganization placed all Raúl Castro's men in the columns led by Majors Lussón, Belarmino Castilla and Peña, and finally at the end of the war there was a fourth, under Major Iglesias ('Nicaragua'). Except for Peña who died suddenly in 1959, these remained the pillar of the revolutionary army in the 1960s. Thus these commanders and Captains Jiménez Lage, Filiberto Olivera, Colomé ('Furry') Pepito Cuza, Samuel Rodiles and Félix Lugano (Pilón), have in the main been the revolutionary commanders of the new Cuban army and of these commanders, seven (Lussón, Colomé, Jiménez Lage, Olivera, Fajardo, Menéndez Tomasevich and Ameijeiras) were on the first central committee of the new Cuban Communist party in 1965.
[29] *Bohemia*, 18 January 1959.

Venezuela would make available aircraft painted in the colours of the Dominican Republic; but in order to receive this, Carrillo had to secure the approval or the blind eye of the U.S. Carrillo then flew to Washington where he saw General Darcey, chief of the U.S. delegation on the Cuba–American Defence Board. Carrillo, still recalling what he believed to be the treachery of the 26 July Movement over the Cienfuegos rising,[30] described to Darcey the situation which would face the U.S. if Castro won, 'even without yet believing that Castro would convert himself into a direct agent of Moscow'. He told Darcey: 'The greater delay in the triumph of the revolution the more radical it would be', that this radicalism would lead to some anti-Americanism, since the U.S. arms embargo on Batista had been counter-balanced by the maintenance of the military mission, by such things as U.S. decorations to Tabernilla, or by the delivery of arms ordered before the embargo; he added that if the army of Batista was quite overcome by Castro the latter would substitute the Army of Cuba by the rebel army and that the very least evil to befall the U.S. would be that in future, 'the U.S. could not count on the Cuban Army . . . as she had been able to do in the First and Second World Wars'.[31]

Darcey said that he could not possibly approve Carrillo's use of Venezuelan aeroplanes and that the U.S. desired to prevent rather than to provoke disturbances in the Caribbean and advised Carrillo to try to found a militant Catholic movement to fight Batista.[32] Thus Carrillo was once more thwarted in his plan to free Barquín and create in him a military counterweight to Fidel Castro in the ranks of the Cuban opposition. Larrazábal eventually gave arms to the anti-Batista opposition in Cuba, but he did so only in November and then directly to the 26 July.[33]

[30] See above, 178 fn. 5.
[31] Carrillo MSS, 38–9.
[32] Loc. cit.
[33] Ibid. The arms were taken to the Sierra in the same aeroplane which carried Luis Buch and 'President' Urrutia.

CHAPTER 17

Batista's 'Big Push' of May 1958

On 24 May Batista launched against the Sierra Maestra the only major offensive of the war: *operación verano*. Seventeen battalions had been concentrated, each with a tank company; there was aerial and naval support; and the Rural Guard.[1] The commanders were Generals Cantillo and del Río Chaviano. These two officers were hardly on speaking terms and their personal animosity accounts for much of their subsequent failure. Their aim was to advance into the Sierra with an overwhelming mass of men, cut Castro off from supplies, and, by reducing the territory in which he operated to a few square miles, prepare the way for a final assault.

For weeks it was impossible to know what was going on. Even within the Sierra news was difficult to get at. The Batistiano army advanced with difficulty but sureness, along the foothills, mostly in the north of the front. Castro brought back all his men (until then grouped in little sub-columns), from the south.[2] The army columns were insistently ambushed and their losses were considerable, particularly from mines carefully laid by Castro, but for twenty-five days the officers drove their men on with energy and some zeal. Cantillo on the other hand had been somewhat dismayed by Batista's instruction that a quarter of the available men should be kept to guard the coffee crop and the sugar *centrales* of the region.[3]

Radio Rebelde appealed for doctors and some new ones rallied to the cause.[4] Castro later recalled that his difficulties were increased because he was now less mobile than before; he had a network of workshops and an elaborate system of communications. There was even a cigar factory.[5] 'We had therefore to reunite all our forces, except those in Santiago, to resist the enemy offensive; [but] we scarcely had three hundred

---

[1] Barrera Pérez, *Bohemia Libre*, 27 August 1961.

[2] Castro's commanders were previously: Column 3, Almeida (Cobre); Column 2, Cienfuegos (centre); Column 4, R. Valdés (E. Turquino); Column 7, Crecensio Pérez (east of Sierra); Column 8, Guevara; Column 1, H.Q., Castro himself. These were drawn back to guard along all the entrances to the Sierra (Núñez Jiménez, 582).

[3] Suárez Núñez, 96.

[4] *Cf.* interview with Dr Raúl Trilla Gómez, in *Revolución*, 26 January 1959, 8.

[5] Guevara, 176.

men, of whom sixty were very badly armed . . .'[6] Almeida's column near Santiago and a patrol under Cienfuegos near Holguín were recalled.

In mid-June Batista's army was advancing in two directions, from the north and south, the latter being left unguarded. Two battalions under, respectively, Colonel Sánchez Mosquera and Major Menéndez Martínez, advanced from the mines of Bueycito, crossed the main range of the Sierra and moved on towards Santo Domingo. On 19 June these forces successfully reached Las Vegas de Jibacoa, Santo Domingo and Navajal. A day or two later they passed Gaviro and so surrounded the Sierra at the peak San Lorenzo. In north and south the army had penetrated in depth. Between the two advance guards there remained only four square miles of territory left undisputedly to Castro; 'Our territory was reduced and reduced until we could not reduce any further.'[7] But by this time the morale of the army was drooping. Many of the men, untrained for this sort of territory, were exhausted. There was a pause for consolidation at this extreme point of penetration; Navajal, where Major Quevedo had brought the 18th Battalion, advancing from the mouth of the River Plate,[8] and Merino, where Major Suárez Zoulet had penetrated with the 19th Battalion. On 29 June Sánchez Mosquera's 11th Battalion, which was resting in a valley at Santo Domingo, was surrounded on three sides by Castro's riflemen. Sánchez Mosquera had nearly 1,000 men, Castro still less than 300. But in the next three days' sporadic fighting, Sánchez Mosquera's force was decimated. Many prisoners were taken and barely a third escaped alive. Sánchez Mosquera was himself wounded and the short-wave radio equipment of one of his companies fell into Castro's hands, along with the army code and many arms.[9] The main reason was that the 'combat intelligence' of Castro's forces was immensely superior to that of the enemy – 'Batista's forces could not go a yard without a perspiring runner arriving a few minutes later to tell Castro of it.'[10]

The consequences of this setback were extraordinary. Batista's High Command, now a demoralized gaggle of corrupt, cruel and lazy officers without combat experience, began to fear total extinction from an enemy of whose numbers and whereabouts they knew nothing accurate,

[6] *Obra Revolucionaria*, 1961, No. 46, 12. On 9 January 1959 Castro said that he had 300 rifles (*Revolución*, 10 January 1959) but Guevara (*Souvenirs*, 197) says only 200 rifles in good condition. Taber comments that it was Castro's policy to lead Batista's army into the mountains 249).

[7] *Obra Revolucionaria*, 1961, No. 46, 12.

[8] La Plata.

[9] For all this, see Castro's own account on Radio Rebelde, 18 August 1958, qu. Núñez Jiménez, 578–82; Taber, 263–4.

[10] Dicky Chapelle in F. M. Osanka, ed., *Modern Guerrilla Warfare*, (1962), 320.

perhaps even believing some of their own communiqués which described hundreds of rebels being killed. The extent of Sánchez Mosquera's defeat was exaggerated. The advance was halted. At the same moment the rebel army launched a series of counter-attacks on all the exposed and most advanced positions; new combats followed at Merino, El Jigüe, Santo Domingo, Las Vegas de Jibacoa and Las Mercedes. To avoid being cut off the army attempted to withdraw. Some deserted (for instance, thirty out of eighty on 24 July at El Cerro). The air force failed to distinguish between Batistianos and rebels and some of the former were killed by napalm bombing. Fear of the rebels meant that instead of sending tanks forward to protect the infantry, the infantry was sent ahead to guard tanks and then mown down.

Within the next month almost the entire army withdrew from the Sierra Maestra. The High Command panicked. The withdrawal became so general that little resistance was offered. Minor advances were ordered, based on fallacious map-reading. Castro's capture of the enemy's code enabled him not only to discover army movements but even to give misleading orders (including to the air force).[11] Communications between the different columns barely existed. By the beginning of August, not merely Sánchez Mosquera's 11th Battalion but also Major Menéndez's 22nd Battalion and Major Suárez Zoulet's 19th had been destroyed as a fighting force. The 18th Battalion collapsed, partly due to lack of food and drink, partly because Castro entered into contact with Major Quevedo, whom he had known at the university and who afterwards joined the rebels. Several other units suffered serious losses. The gain in arms to the rebels was large: a 14-ton tank, twelve mortars, two bazookas, twelve machine guns on tripods and twenty-one rifle machine guns, 142 Garand rifles, 200 Cristóbal machine guns. Total rebel losses were 27 killed and about fifty wounded; those killed included five officers (nearly 20% – a high percentage, though in small-scale war of this sort not surprising). The rebels took 433 prisoners, of whom 422 were turned over to officials of the Red Cross and twenty-one to the army itself; none was maltreated.[12] 117 were wounded, of whom two died. The care with which these men were treated was exemplary even if that treatment served a political purpose, for it contrasted so strongly with treatment of prisoners captured by Batista that it inflicted another blow to army prestige. The army had till this point taken no prisoners at all. Castro justified this unusual but wise method:

War is not a mere question of rifles, bullets, cannon and aeroplanes. This belief has been many times one of the causes of the failure of

[11] The code was not changed till 25 July, being captured on 29 June. After that another code was also captured.

[12] See article on Red Cross, in *New York Times Magazine*, 25 August 1963.

tyrannies ... Since January 1957 ... some six hundred members of the armed forces ... have passed into our hands ... none have been killed ... while torture and death has been the certain fate awaiting every rebel, every sympathiser, even every suspect who fell into enemy hands. In many cases unhappy peasants have been assassinated to add to the number of bodies with which to justify the false news of the chief of staff ... more than six hundred defence-less citizens, in many cases far from any revolutionary activity, have been assassinated [by the army].[13] In these twenty months of campaign, killing has made nobody stronger. Killing has made *them* weak; refusing to kill has made *us* strong ... only cowards and thugs murder an enemy when he has surrendered ... the rebel army cannot carry out the same tactics as the tyranny which we fight ...'

It naturally cost the rebels less to send back the prisoners than to maintain them. Given, said Castro, the existing economic conditions and unemployment they would never lack men to fight for the army ... but 'victory depends on a minimum of men and a maximum of morale'.[14] This impression was confirmed by a clever U.S. journalist expert in guerrilla war, Dicky Chapelle, who later wrote that this handling of prisoners was an 'expression of utter contempt for the fighting potential of the defeated [which] had an almost physical impact'.[15]

News of these victories by Castro was concealed by the Batistiano High Command, and on two successive nights – 18 and 19 August – Castro broadcast on Radio Rebelde and gave as full details as he could of the encounters, in the eloquent accomplished language that became so familiar to Cuban audiences later: he paid special attention to the army, denouncing the High Command and General Cantillo, who he said belonged 'among the cowards who have contemplated with indifference – the rosary of corpses which his colleagues Chaviano, Ventura, Pilar García and others have left in the streets and cities of Cuba ...' In contrast, he stretched out his hand towards younger officers, 'who have in these months of war earned our gratitude. They are not corrupted, they love their career and their Service. For many of them, the War which has entangled them is absurd ... but they obey orders.' He cleverly contrasted them with the higher ranks, those who had made themselves millionaires by the exploitation of gaming, by vice protection and other crooked practices. He spoke of a possible *golpe* by the army; if this was the work of opportunist military men anxious to save their fortunes and to seek the best possible way out for the *camarilla* of the tyranny,

13 A guess no doubt.
14 Speech on Radio Rebelde, quoted in Núñez Jiménez, *Geografía*, 578–92.
15 Osanka, 329. Mrs Dicky Chapelle was killed in Vietnam.

We are resolutely against . . . For . . . the sacrifices *which have been made and the blood which has been shed cannot be made to leave things more or less as they were, so repeating the story which followed the fall of Machado.* If the military *golpe* is the work of honest men and has a sincerely revolutionary purpose, a peaceful solution will then be possible on just and beneficial bases. Between the armed forces and the Revolution, whose interests are not and never must be antagonistic, the problem of Cuba may be resolved. We are at war with the tyranny, not the armed forces . . . The dilemma for the Army is clear . . . either take a step forward, shaking off this corpse of the Batista regime . . . or commit suicide as an institution. Those who today save the Army will not be able to save it within a few months. If war continues another six months the Army will totally disintegrate . . .

Then Castro told the army what they could do to achieve peace: the arrest of Batista, of the politicians of the regime, and 'of all officers who have permitted torture. Afterwards there would be removal from the armed forces of all political issues so that they could never end up again as the instrument of any *caudillo* or political party.' There was also a quotation from Maceo ('The revolution will go on while a single injustice remains'), and a rousing peroration.[16] Batista on the other hand gave out an anodyne communiqué saying that army patrols had liquidated an enemy which then took to flight.[17]

Batista's offensive, important though it was for the war, was overshadowed in the minds of many by the tactics of Raúl Castro on the northern coast of Cuba in June and July. The most serious incident of the summer had probably been the murder by the police of the two Giral sisters of Santiago, after an attempt on the Minister of Defence, Rey; and an attempt on Batista by a fifteen-year-old boy. On 26 June two hundred members of the 26 July under Raúl Castro came down from the Sierra Cristal on to Moa Bay and kidnapped ten U.S. citizens and two Canadians who were working there, including the head of the mineral engineering department at the University of Minnesota. Forty miles to the south Desmond Elsmore, field superintendent of the *Ermita* sugar mill, was also taken. On 27 June Richard Sargent, Canadian manager of the *Isabel* sugar mill, was captured, and twenty-seven U.S. sailors and marines were kidnapped when they were returning on a Cuban bus from an outing near Guantánamo. On 30 June the general manager and one other executive of Nicaro were kidnapped. The same day a letter reached Ambassador Smith from Raúl Castro saying that the captives would be released on the condition, first, that

[16] Qu. Núñez Jiménez, *Geografía*, 592-4.
[17] Suárez Núñez, 97.

the U.S. cease shipment of *all* military equipment to the government of Cuba – including spare and defective parts in previously supplied weapons; second, that the U.S. would cease assisting the Cuban government aircraft with fuel from the Guantánamo base; and third, that the U.S. would obtain an assurance from Batista that Cuba would not use U.S. military equipment against Castro.[18] Finally, in early July four United Fruit Company men and two officials were kidnapped.

These acts naturally angered the U.S. government. Senators Knowland and Styles Bridges demanded that if the men were not given up within forty-eight hours, 'effective help would be given to Batista'. John Foster Dulles told a press conference that the U.S. could 'not be blackmailed into helping the rebels'. The State Department denied that it was fuelling Cuban aircraft and that it was supplying arms to Batista, but made no reference to the third rebel demand.

Whatever the truth, Batista was now in considerable difficulties. He could not dislodge Castro, so he could not guarantee the return of the prisoners. Ambassador Smith believed that he would have allowed U.S. marines to land to do so. Smith, the navy and others in Washington also desired this: indeed the navy recommended 'an immediate intervention in Cuba of divisional size'. The State Department correctly argued that to enter Cuba would be much easier than leaving, while to intervene militarily might not save the lives of the marines.[19]

In the end, the prisoners were released with no concessions wrung from the U.S., save that the rebels in the Sierra Cristal would enjoy two or three weeks' freedom from air attack. The 26 July obtained maximum publicity for the release of the captives, who had been well treated, though subjected to long cross-examination by Vilma Espín, the young Santiago 26 July girl who had been in the Sierra Cristal since March. The effect of these kidnappings was to lose some of the good will that Castro had garnered in the U.S. But Castro won another victory when, in late July, Cuban troops were withdrawn from guarding the U.S. Guantánamo water supply at Yateras. U.S. troops took over. Castro protested. The U.S. withdrew and Cubans returned.[20]

While this important offensive and these kidnappings were continuing in the Sierra there had been a number of critical changes in the plain between the supporters of Castro and the rest of the anti-Batistiano opposition. After the strike of April there had been a time of relative calm in much of Cuba outside the Sierra. Ray and Faustino Pérez, directors of activity in Havana, had successfully evaded the police to

[18] Smith, *The Fourth Floor*, 142.
[19] R. D. Murphy, *Diplomat among Warriors* (1964), 456.
[20] *Ibid*, 458.

get to the Sierra in order to confer with Castro in mid-June, but on 17 June they received news that almost all of the executives of the Civic Resistance and 26 July in Havana had been arrested or had had to leave the country. Ray and Pérez returned quickly to Havana without seeing Castro. They found their organization almost leaderless, and many groups had lost touch with each other.[21] By this time the Communists in Havana, rebuffed by the Civic Resistance, had begun negotiating an agreement with the 26 July in the labour field. The 26 July Movement, for its part, knew from the experience of April that if it wanted any union or labour action, support would have to be obtained from some organization with strength there. The Communists were the only possibility.[22] On 5 June Carlos Rafael Rodríguez sent an article to *La France Nouvelle* (Paris) making clear that negotiations had at least begun:[23] Rodríguez also wrote that day to the French journalist Claude Julien explaining that the need was still to draw into the opposition alliance people such as Prío and Grau, forming a coalition that 'would go beyond the limits of anti-imperialism'.[24]

No important developments occurred for a few weeks and, presumably as a threat, the Communist party itself brightly came out on 28 June with an appeal for 'honest and democratic' elections – an apparent new retreat away from the policy of Castro. In consequence Ray, on behalf of the Civic Resistance, told the Communists that in these circumstances, they could contribute nothing to the struggle.[25] The Communists then began to organize new groups of partisans in Camagüey, Escambray and even Pinar del Río.[26] Raúl Castro kept in touch with the Communists in Havana, since at the end of June he sent 'Pepe' Ramírez, a Communist sugar workers' leader, to report to the Politburo in Havana in person about the kidnappings of U.S. businessmen, and early the following month Carlos Rafael Rodríguez, on behalf of the Communist central committee, made his way up first to see Raúl Castro in the Sierra Cristal and then to the Sierra Maestra.[27] For some days Fidel Castro (who appears not to have expected the visit) was either too busy, too preoccupied with the war or too cautious to see him. Rodríguez later recalled: 'In the Sierra Cristal, where Raúl Castro was in command, there was nothing but understanding for the Communists. But

[21] Ray to the author.
[22] Ursinio Rojas, Communist trade union leader, later said negotiations began in June and July (*Fundamentos*, March 1959).
[23] *La France Nouvelle*, No. 664, 17 July 1958.
[24] Julien, 123.
[25] Ray to the author.
[26] Arnault, 78.
[27] *Hoy*, 11 January 1959; Rodríguez confirmed to the author in June 1966 that he went up to the Sierra at that time. Rodríguez got his chance of going to the Sierra since Castro had invited all revolutionary parties to consult with him and only the Communists and Directorio took advantage of the opportunity.

when I got to Fidel in the Sierra Maestra, the understanding had changed to suspicion.'[28]

In Caracas, meantime, all opposition groups, apart from the Communists and the two 'electoral' parties (Grau's and Márquez Sterling's) met once more, and this time, on 20 July, a genuine pact was made by them with the 26 July Movement, all the organizations represented forming a 'Junta of Unity' or 'Frente Cívico Revolucionario Democrático'. Present were many men who had taken a personal part in the struggle and others who had always operated in exile, union leaders and students. The list was impressive: Prío, Miró Cardona (the lawyer of the Civic Dialogue); Varona; Rodríguez Loeches and Orlando Blanco (for the Directorio Revolucionario); David Salvador (26 July); Pascasio Linares, Lauro Blanco, José María Aguilera and Angel Cofiño – all trade union leaders, members of the United Labour Front; José Puente and Omar Fernández, leaders of the FEU; Gabino Rodríguez Villaverde, for the Barquinista officers (the 4 April Movement); Justo Carrillo, the economist now at the head of the Catholic Democratic Montecristi Movement; Lincoln Rodón, speaker of the House of Representatives in 1952, for the Democratic party; Angel María Santos Buch, the exiled leader of the Civic Resistance; and, finally, José Llanusa[29] on behalf of Fidel Castro, whose signature had been previously obtained and with whom contact was maintained by radio. It appears that Castro insisted on being paid another $44,000 by Prío before he would sign.[30] The pact demanded 'a common strategy to defeat the dictatorship by armed insurrection', a brief provisional government 'that will lead ... to full constitutional and democratic procedures; [and] a scheme to guarantee punishment of the guilty ... the rights of workers, the fulfilment of the international commitments ... as well as the economic and political progress of the Cuban people'.[31] The distinguished lawyer Miró Cardona was nominated to be coordinator of the Frente, and Castro was named commander-in-chief of the forces of the revolution. Judge Urrutia was designated 'President of Cuba in arms'.

This pact naturally gave a respectable and hopeful front to the opposition in general, but in reality it merely meant a temporary end to internecine squabbling, rather than a common strategy, and there was a good deal of quarrelling immediately afterwards, particularly over a 'theft' of

[28] See interview with Rodríguez by Gianni Corbi, in *L'Espresso* (Italy), 26 January–23 February 1964, and his evidence in the Marquitos trial, *Hoy*, 25 March 1964.

[29] Later chief of sports in Castro's revolutionary government and Minister of Education. Llanusa, pushed by Haydée Santamaría de Hart, began to be prominent in April.

[30] Evidence of Primitivo Lima (Directorio representative, Caracas). Prío promised another $6,000 to the Caracas pact alliance which was not paid.

[31] As qu. Jules Dubois, 280.

arms from the Directorio by the 26 July Movement: what had been intended for the Sierra Escambray, went to Raúl Castro in the Sierra Cristal.[32] Further, the nomination of Castro as commander-in-chief did not prevent the other groups maintaining their own operations, but it did enable Castro to demand more vigorously that those who wished for direct action should go and enrol themselves under his command in the Sierra Maestra.

[32] Evidence of Primitivo Lima. Gabino Rodríguez, the Barquinista representative, gave evidence that the money raised by the Frente was only enough to finance a small propaganda office and send a delegate to Geneva to the Red Cross (Gabino Rodríguez evidence).

CHAPTER 18

The Collapse

In August 1958, after the final withdrawal of the army, Castro fixed his headquarters near La Plata, some few miles inland from the sea, on a river of that name. Three new operations were planned. Castro and the main force would attempt the encirclement of Santiago; Guevara would set off westwards to the province of Las Villas with 148 men (Column No. 8, Ciro Redondo) to cut systematically all means of communication between the two ends of the island and to establish Castro's authority over those guerrillas still active in the Escambray – the Directorio being now once more under Faure Chomón, who had returned from Havana the previous month.[1] Cienfuegos with eighty-two men would move on to Pinar del Río (at the head of Column No. 2, Antonio Maceo). Castro appointed Guevara to be commander of all the opposition units in Las Villas (towns included) and gave him the power to collect taxes, apply the new Penal Code and inaugurate agrarian reform. It remained to be seen whether the Directorio would accept these impositions. Nor was the Directorio the only organization active in Escambray, since there was also a group of semi-gangsters who had split off from it, known as 'the Second Front of Escambray', apparently stimulated to do so by Prío. These were led by a brother of the Spaniard involved in the attack on the palace, Gutiérrez Menoyo.[2] Then there was also in Las Villas Félix Torres's 'Máximo Gómez' column of Communists, now sixty-five strong.[3]

Guevara and Cienfuegos left at the end of August, on foot, after their lorries had been destroyed in an air raid,[4] the former accompanied by an old Communist of Santa Clara, Armando Acosta, who, though he had left Santa Clara only a few weeks before, returned with the rank of captain and the pseudonym 'Rodríguez'.[5]

Meantime, from La Plata, Castro continued to negotiate both with

---

[1] See Guevara, in *Verde Olivo*, 5 October 1960. For Chomón's return, see Rodríguez Loeches, 99. The minutes of the Commissions of Cooperation and Coordination of the Caracas Frente (which I have seen) are full of quarrels as to the exact proportion between the effort to be spent on the Sierras de Escambray and Oriente.

[2] Primitivo Lima alleges that Prío encouraged the 'Second Front' to leave the Directorio.

[3] *Hoy*, 20 July 1965.

[4] Guevara, *Souvenirs*, 198.

[5] Evidence of Carlos Rafael Rodríguez to the author; memorandum of a 26 July leader in Las Villas, Joaquín Torres.

Communists and with all other members of the opposition. Carlos Rafael Rodríguez left the Sierra on 10 August,[6] with what he anyway later claimed was a verbal acceptance by Castro of the idea of unity between Fidelistas and Communists; and at least one more Communist, Luis Mas Martín, a member of Juventud Socialista when Castro had been at the university, came up to the Sierra and thereafter stayed at headquarters as the party's representative.[7] In 'the plain', that is, in Havana, Carlos Rafael Rodríguez met the local representatives of the parties which had signed the Caracas pact and told them, to their surprise, that Castro had become convinced that the Communists ought to join in with them, at least in the labour section which was designed to transform the opposition in that department. A meeting was held in Havana of the Caracas pact parties and all resisted the idea, the 26 July representative, Delio Gómez Ochoa, being specially hostile to the plan, despite Carlos Rafael Rodríguez's claims about Castro's views. Carlos Rafael Rodríguez then decided to go up again to the Sierra Maestra, as he was sure that Castro would disapprove what the Caracas junta had just done.[8] But then two further approaches by the Communists – this time by Marinello, the Communist president – were rejected, again with Gómez Ochoa intervening 'in an almost violent manner'.[9] Gómez Ochoa, who had left the Sierra for Havana on 23 May (that is, long before Carlos Rafael Rodríguez's first visit to the hills), was an Ortodoxo student of diplomatic law at the University of Havana, the son of a landowner, and a passionate anti-Communist and enemy of Raúl Castro. It cannot be quite excluded that Castro dispatched him as his representative in Havana to represent the right wing of the 26 July Movement at a moment when in fact he was himself opening negotiations with the Communist party.[10] Negotiations even over Labour unity with the Communists therefore remained incomplete, with Carlos Rafael Rodríguez again in the Sierra: this time however, he remained there,[11] establishing himself not at Castro's headquarters but in another camp nearby at Las Vegas. He was accompanied by a well-known Communist sugar workers' leader, Ursinio Rojas.

Shortly afterwards there was a definite agreement about the right of

[6] Evidence of Carlos Rafael Rodríguez to the author.

[7] *Hoy*, 15 January 1959.

[8] Letter from Angel dei Cerro (Montecristi representative at these discussions) to Theodore Draper, 2 September 1962.

[9] Manuel Ledón evidence. This said, however, it is clear that some members of the 26 July Movement in Havana were in favour of an arrangement with the Communists – in particular Ricardo Alarcón, the leader of the students' branch of the 26 July Movement (in 1969 Cuban Ambassador to the U.N.).

[10] See Luis Simón (MSS, p. 254). Simón accompanied Gómez Ochoa from the Sierra to the plain in May and back again in October.

[11] Evidence of Carlos Rafael Rodríguez to the author, June 1966.

Communists to join the rebel army.[12] Delio Gómez Ochoa was then withdrawn from Havana to the Sierra and replaced by Marcelo Fernández, a more diplomatic spirit, and negotiations for an agreement on Labour unity went ahead faster. Fernández in later years was able to live down a strong conservative and anti-Communist period in 1959, to join in 1965 the new central committee of the Cuban Communist party. But relations between Castro and Rodríguez were not close. Rodríguez appears again to have been kept waiting for several days before being received by Castro,[13] and it seems improbable that any general political agreement, verbal or written, was reached between them as to the nature of Cuba after the victory. One member of the Directorio Revolucionario, Manuel Ledón, writing of the efforts made in Havana in August 1958 to achieve unity among the opposition groups in consequence of the Pact of Caracas, said that none now showed any concern with anything save getting rid of Batista: the clear assumption was that there would be a return to the Constitution of 1940, but no more.[14]

A critical meeting from the point of view of the negotiations on Labour unity occurred now in the zone controlled by Raúl Castro – the venue being selected because of the difficulties in getting to the Sierra Maestra. A large cortège of hardened Labour leaders – David Salvador, Jesús Soto, Octavio Louit (Cabrera), Conrado Bécquer and Ñico Torres – made the journey to the Sierra Cristal, where they were received by Raúl Castro, who harangued them on the need for unity with the Communists; and in the event such was the prestige of this young *guerrillero* that he got his way despite the fact that nearly all of these men had been for years rivals to and even enemies of the Communists.[15]

Castro, sensing victory, after the repulse of the army moved more and more into the role of a political rather than a guerrilla leader. Already in the early summer he had imposed a levy of 15 cents on each 250-pound bag of sugar produced in sugar mills. This levy was often paid, in Oriente, even by U.S. owned mills. In September came a request to the public to boycott fiestas, the lottery, and the newspapers, and to purchase only necessities. Castro also appealed to all to give any help to rebels that they could.

He now seemed for the first time to be giving thought to the nature of the future regime: the head of the Havana Civic Resistance, Manuel

[12] *Cf.* Blas Roca, VIIIth Congress speech, p. 38; *Hoy*, 11 January 1959.
[13] Ray to author.
[14] Manuel Ledón evidence.
[15] Memorandum of Joaquín Torres, of the 26 July Movement, also present. Present on Raúl Castro's side were the lawyers Martínez Sánchez ('a sort of major-domo') and Lucas Morán. The house where the meeting was held was nicknamed 'the Palace of Justice'.

Ray, visited him in September (meeting him for the first time). Castro asked Ray to work out a scheme for agrarian reform. Ray, impressed with Castro, agreed that the army should be purged after a victory and that the rebel army should take over its functions. But they disagreed over the size of the army – Castro being clearly interested, according to the recollection of Ray, in a large force.[16] Castro also wanted a boarding school for 20,000 rural children in each province. The Havana underground had been worried about the influence of Guevara and Raúl Castro in the Sierra, but at this time neither was with Castro. Raúl Castro had just completed another spectacular *coup*, by rescuing a prominent 26 July leader from Santiago, Carlos Iglesias ('Nicaragua'), from an Oriente train.[17]

Guevara had already on 7 September, with his column, crossed the Jobabo river into Camagüey and, moving along the south coast of the island, clashed with the army near Santa Cruz del Sur, where a captain under him, Marcos Borrero, was killed.[18] This expedition to Las Villas was carried out in conditions as bad as those of the early days in the Sierra: Cienfuegos, in a report written in October, spoke of:

Forty days of march, often with the south coast and a compass as the only guide. During fifteen days we marched with water and mud up to the knees, travelling by night to avoid ambushes . . . during the thirty-one days of our journey across Camagüey we ate eleven times. After four days of famine we had to eat a mare . . . Almost all our animals were left in the marsh.[19]

As leader, Guevara showed himself as parsimonious and ascetic as any of his followers, thereby noticeably differentiating himself from Castro in the Sierra, who had usually lived well when he could.[20]

The two columns, Guevara's and Cienfuegos's, sometimes moved together in the earlier stages – as in their skirmish at Santa Cruz del Sur – afterwards separately, occasionally dispensing justice[21] or brushing with guards, but otherwise pressing on as fast as possible. Only one serious

[16] Ray to the author. Though Ray was pleased with these talks, the emphasis on a large army left a definite memory. Karl Meyer of the *Washington Post* recalls that in an interview in September Castro seemed preoccupied by the hemispheric significance of his struggle against the army. To stage a successful revolution against the army seemed to him, rightly, to be, not only remarkable from Cuba's point of view but from all Latin America's. (Meyer to author.)

[17] See the accounts by the attacking commander, Captain Raúl Menéndez Tomasevich and 'Nicaragua', in *Revolución*, 13 August 1962.

[18] Jules Dubois, 305.

[19] Report in Franqui, *L'Histoire des Douze*, 136-7; *Verde Olivo*, 29 October 1961.

[20] Luis Simón MSS, 279-80 (Simón encountered the columns near Manzanillo).

[21] Cienfuegos had two men, Máximo Quevedo and Edel Casañas, shot for looting. Franqui, 239.

setback occurred when, on 27 September, a group of Guevara's column under Captain Jaime Vega was caught and butchered by the army Sergeant Otaño.[22] Guevara received the assistance in Camagüey of the local Communists, who had offered him a mimeographical apparatus and propaganda leaflets: a member of the 26 July Movement, Joaquín Torres, told him at Guasimal, in the foothills of the Escambray mountains, that his organization could supply all this too. But Guevara, though appearing to accept these arguments, continued to use the Communists.[23]

Batista's government reacted slowly to the possibility, not yet of defeat, but of a prolongation of war. Like most Cuban rulers before him, Batista placed the blame on the U.S.; not only was the U.S. helping the rebels through denying him arms, but they were guilty of negligence in letting the rebels get arms.[24] In the U.S. itself the exiles were still, however, condemning the Eisenhower administration as committed to Batista; the military mission remained, for instance, necessitated by 'hemispheric defence'.[25] Further, in September, the U.S.'s ally, England, agreed to sell Batista fifteen Sea Fury fighters. Castro telegraphed the English prime minister, Harold Macmillan, in the name of liberty, to prevent the sale. Macmillan would not be drawn; there was no objection to the sale. When these were delivered, the rebel headquarters issued 'Law 4: against English aggression'. A plan was put forward to confiscate English companies' property; all good Cubans were asked to boycott English goods.

The situation in the cities was calmer but the police responded to what action there was with more savagery than ever. Thus, after two bombs exploded in Havana in August, seven youths were found hanging the next day. The inspector-general of the CIA, Kirkpatrick, complained to the Minister of Defence about the tortures practised by the BRAC, the anti-Communist bureau which was practically a branch of the CIA, but to no effect.[26] A little crisis involved the famous black Virgin of Regla, patron saint of sailors; two boys stole it and apparently dropped it in their flight. The rumour spread, however, that the police substituted a false, smaller one. The police became so disturbed that the traditional fiesta of 8 September was banned, while the rebels tried to keep the people away from all fiestas. In September there was sabotage at Havana airport of perhaps $M2 to $M3 worth of merchandise, and six

[22] The rumour is widespread in exile circles that the Batistiano local commander, Colonel Dueñas, was given $100,000 to permit Guevara to cross Camagüey on the condition that he crossed to the south.

[23] Memorandum of Joaquín Torres. (Not to be confused with the Communist Félix Torres.)

[24] In a note of 28 August. But on 9 September the U.S. seized the *Harpoon*, with one and a half tons of ammunition.

[25] *Cf.* Jules Dubois, 312–13.

[26] Kirkpatrick, *The Real CIA*, 175.

armed men set off a bomb destroying a transmitting station for Circuito Nacional Cubano at Havana, and also Radio Aeropuerto. Visitors to the cities continued to be amazed at the extent to which the middle classes, rotarians and professional people, were even more behind Castro, particularly in Santiago where smart residential districts such as Vista Alegre or the Country Club seemed embattled fortresses of the 26 July Movement.

At long last, indeed, in the autumn of 1958, the war began to make its mark on the economy.[27] By November there was a strong downward trend in all sales. Shop owners reduced their stock and turnover to a minimum.[28] There were many arrests, among them leaders of the 26 July such as Salvador and Louit in Havana, so that Manuel Ray was effectively in charge of all underground activity in the cities of the island. Two more kidnappings of Americans (Texaco employees) by Castro kept up the tense expectancy, even though they were quickly released. A U.S. transport took off fifty-five U.S. citizens from Nicaro, a confession of lack of trust in the Batista government's ability to keep order. The State Department mildly said that 'the U.S. might have to take action' if kidnapping did not cease, and Castro denounced Smith and Batista severally for trying to provoke U.S. intervention.[29] On 21 October a DC 3 with twelve passengers was hijacked when *en route* to Miami and forced to land in the Sierra Maestra.

Castro did not confine his activities to a war of nerves. In October the negotiations with the Communists for labour unity were concluded with the formation of a loose coalition, to be known as Frente Obrero Nacional de Unidad (FONU).[30] No one attributed much importance to this; it seemed merely a temporary tactical alliance. A member of the Montecristi Movement recalls that 'the Communists presented themselves with an exquisite urbanity and humility'. They asked to join the Frente but they agreed that they should be left to join the workers section. Here among the workers, they could count on 'some slight strength'.[31] Some old members of the Communist-dominated CTC (such as Alfredo Rancaño, of the waiters and 'gastronomic' workers, or José Miguel Espino, a railway leader) took positions in the new Labour organization. In fact, however, the FONU was scarcely in existence even by 1 January 1959 when Batista fell. More important seemed the text of a decree of agrarian reform to be applied after the victory – Law 1 of the Sierra Maestra. The essence of this law was that all those with

[27] See Batista, *Cuba Betrayed*, 76, for the president's reaction.
[28] HAR, December 1958.
[29] Smith, *The Fourth Floor*, 150–1.
[30] Apparently on 15 October (see article by Carlos Castañeda in *Bohemia Libre*, 16 October 1960).
[31] Andrés Suárez to Draper, 17 September 1962.

less than 150 acres would be guaranteed. All who had less than 60 acres would receive land, while those with large idle estates would be compensated if they were taken away. State land and Batista's lands would be divided up among peasants. There was thus no mention of cooperatives (as had been promised in *History will absolve me*) or indeed any effort at communal or collective holdings. The agrarian reform would be essentially the *repartimiento*, division of land, ancient ideal of the rural anarchists.[32] At the same time, a further law announced that those who took part in Batista's elections on 3 November would be sentenced to thirty years in prison or to death; and indeed within the next few weeks a prominent Batistiano politician in Camagüey, Aníbal Vega, was 'executed' by local 26 July men as an earnest of this intention.

A visit to Castro's camp in the Sierra in the autumn showed that the *'comandancia'* was now quite formally organized. Celia Sánchez, the dentist's daughter from Pilón, was firmly installed as Castro's secretary and she efficiently controlled his time and the people who visited him. The female group known as the 'battalion Mariana Grajales', led by Olga Guevara, served as the personal staff to the commander. Others in perpetual attendance included the organizers of Radio Rebelde (Franqui, Valera, Violeta Casals). Faustino Pérez lived in a nearby hut. Father Guillermo Sardiñas moved about as chaplain attempting on Castro's orders to regulate the inevitable sexual licence by marriages, without much success. Even a somewhat hostile observer, Luis Simón (who visited the *'comandancia'* in October), however, thought that this 'moral disintegration', as he called it, did not exceed the limits usually reached by regular armies.[33] Carlos Rafael Rodríguez and Luis Mas Martín, the two political representatives of the Communist party, did not play any military or indeed any other part in the activities of the Sierra; they behaved more as political refugees, like José Parda Llada (near whom they lived), than political organizers, who were being put up in the Sierra by Fidel Castro's permission. They had no hand in dealing with new recruits (Aldo Santamaría's responsibility); with the peasants, who preoccupied Faustino Pérez; or with economic matters, then principally dealt with by the Auditor-General, Sorí Marín. According to Luis Simón, Rodríguez 'read constantly a work of U.N. statistics and another by Raúl Presbisch.[34] He played chess badly but lost with elegance'.[35]

[32] Those consulted on this law in the Sierra were, apparently, Humberto Sorí Marín, Faustino Pérez, Angel M-Luis Rodríguez, Carlos Rafael Rodríguez, Luis Mas Martín, Carlos Franqui, Orestes Valera, Jorge Mendoza, Efrem González, and others (Luis Simón MSS, 150A).
[33] *Ibid.*, p. 265.
[34] The president of ECLA.
[35] Simón MSS, p. 266.

By the middle of October Guevara and Cienfuegos had arrived in the mountainous region of Las Villas.³⁶ Guevara had now 142 men in place of 148.³⁷ Aided by deserters from the army and by local 26 July men in the places which they passed, they travelled along much the same route as that followed by Maceo and Máximo Gómez in 1896. On arrival on 14 October in Las Villas, Cienfuegos linked forces with Félix Torres, the Communist commandant of the Yaguajay region who had taken the usual rank of major.³⁸ Félix Torres's sixty-five men were now organized into three platoons, but he immediately 'put himself at [Cienfuegos's] orders' and took part in an exchange of gunfire with an army group numbering perhaps 450.³⁹ Torres had also had further difficulties with a Directorio commander 'Diego', who had instructed the peasants with whom he came into contact not to help Torres since they were Communists – though one or two members of the 26 July Movement did in fact join Torres.⁴⁰ As elsewhere, women helped, above all with communications. Pastor González, shoemaker of Jarhaueca, was the centre of communication of arms, news, clothes and also men;⁴¹ the priest of Yaguajay, Fr Modesto Amo, also assisted and even on occasion accompanied these forces.⁴²

Guevara on arrival was also surprised to receive a letter from one of the leaders of the wilder Directorio splinter group, the Second Front of Escambray, Jesús Carreras, telling him that he could not go up into Escambray without first consulting him on his movements.⁴³ Guevara took no notice and advanced to the hills near Sancti Spiritus, establishing his base on the top of Monte del Obispo, and there waiting for new supplies of boots, that essential demand of guerrilla war. Guevara had an interesting, confused and unfriendly conversation with 'Major' Carreras, who was half drunk and therefore easy to mislead, and another with his colleague, 'Major' Peña, 'famous in the region for his forays behind cattle' who emphatically forbade Guevara to attack Guisa de Miranda, which 'was in his zone'. The 26 July coordinator in the province, Enrique Oltuski, came up from Trinidad to try to mediate and to meet Guevara, and went on to see Cienfuegos to the north. The Communists, Waldo Reina and Armando Acosta, also carried up a large cargo of provisions to Cienfuegos, and afterwards another Com-

---

³⁶ Guevara, *Souvenirs*, 201 (on October 16).

³⁷ *Revolución*, 15 January 1959.

³⁸ See *Obra Revolucionaria*, 1962, No. 10, 22; Guevara's interview in *O Cruzeiro Internacional*, 16 July 1964; Cienfuegos in Franqui, 136.

³⁹ *Revolución, Supplement* October 1961; *Hoy*, 8 October 1963.

⁴⁰ See Torres's letter to Del Valle, previously dated. Diego was 'Major' Víctor Manuel Paneque.

⁴¹ See letter of Wilfredo Velázquez to Del Valle, *Hoy*, 21 July 1965.

⁴² *Revolución*, 3 January 1959, commemorating this column's victorious entry into Havana.

⁴³ See Aldo Isidrón del Valle, *La Batalla de Santa Clara*, extracts in *Hoy*, 16 July 1965.

munist, Manuel del Peso, did the same.[44] Guevara also met some Directorio commanders including Chomón and Cubela though the former refused to make any agreement with the Communists in the province, since he recalled only too well their attacks upon him in the university as 'a gangster of the Revolution'. Chomón feared 'a trap of Castro's' to make him change his principles.[45] Guevara decided, wisely, that unity could only be effectively achieved by means of joint attacks on the enemy. Armando Acosta, becoming Guevara's chief aide, helped establish rebel headquarters on a peak known as Caballete de Casa. The work began of attempting to cut off the roads connecting the west with the east of the island. Some of the disaffected Directorio troops (under Gutiérrez Menoyo) were sent on one side. Major Víctor Bordón's group, which had been holding out in Matanzas since late 1956 and which had joined Guevara on arrival,[46] was purged by Guevara and Bordón was demoted to captain. Cienfuegos in the meantime busied himself with collective reading sessions, studying Martí's works and 'everything which related to General Maceo', these being read out by Cienfuegos himself in a deep voice.[47] He showed no eagerness to press on to Pinar del Río. More and more rallied to the cause, peasants, urban workers and women too. By November the agrarian reform was already being applied. Thus the lands of the farm *La Diana,* near Banao, belonging to the governor of Las Villas, Segundo Enríquez, were divided up among the peasants of the region, two cabs each.[48] Meanwhile, the local 26 July leaders had been increasingly angered by Guevara's reliance on Communists and complained through their own organization to the then national coordinator, Marcelo Fernández. Fernández, with Joaquín Torres and Oltuski, the Las Villas leaders, visited Guevara and made their complaints in no uncertain terms. Guevara replied that he was not obliged to insist on any political affiliation and that any Cuban could join his forces; finally, in the course of a heated argument, Guevara said that between him and the 26 July Movement there was a political chasm (*abismo político*) and that if in these moments they were united in the struggle against Batista, sooner or later they would end by going separate ways.[49] But, meantime, a first meeting had taken place

[44] In 1965 Cuban military attaché in Moscow.

[45] Evidence of Manuel Ledón. Chomón suggested a pact on a national level, causing '*un estallido de violencia*' in Fidel Castro.

[46] *Revolución*, 8 January 1959.

[47] Major Gálvez, in *Hoy*, 16 July 1965.

[48] *Hoy*, 16 July 1965.

[49] '*que si en esos momentos estábamos unidos en la lucha contra Batista, tarde o temprano terminaríamos per separarnos*' (memorandum of Joaquín Torres, present at this meeting). Of those present at this meeting, instructively, Marcelo Fernández was in 1968 a member of the central committee of the Cuban Communist party (and an opponent of Guevara's policies of excessive centralization); Oltuski worked still then in the Institute of Agrarian Reform; and Torres was in exile.

between the Directorio and the Communists in Havana: Alberto Mora, son of Menelao Mora who had been killed in the attack on the Palace, met Ramón Nicolau, a veteran Communist leader from Holguín.[50]

Batista's presidential election was duly held. On its eve Foster Dulles visited a Cuban Embassy reception in Washington, thereby giving his *imprimatur* to at least the process. But it had become clear that the only opposition candidate of any status, Márquez Sterling, had no hope – both through the certain knowledge that the ballots would be rigged and that he personally would not carry enough votes. There was a strong swing away from the electoral idea. The result was a foregone conclusion; Batista's candidate, Rivero Agüero, was elected. A self-made man who had come up with Batista – an orphan, he had worked in the fields at the age of seven[51] – his success might in normal times have been hailed as yet one more Horatio Alger success story, like Batista's own. These were not normal times. Few noticed his victory. Few believed that if he were to take over on 24 February as planned there would be any difference in the regime. Few believed that he would take over. He was not however fairly elected. The *New York Times* correspondent estimated that only 30 % voted, and that in some places the poll was as low as 10 %.[52] In fact, an entirely bogus set of election papers had been printed and marked by the army and distributed long before election by the air force, the printer receiving the sum of $40,000: it was one of the most perfectly executed frauds perpetrated, even in Cuba.[53] This fraud was the last straw even for Earl Smith who henceforth believed that Batista could not be allowed to remain and that every effort should be made by his government to find a replacement.[54] In west Cuba, the atmosphere was tense, but not violent. Well armed police and soldiers guarded the 8,500 polling stations. In Oriente there were massive abstentions, due to Castro's threats. In Las Villas, Guevara and Cienfuegos did their best to prevent the arrival of voting urns. Grau, who trailed third behind Rivero and Márquez Sterling, petitioned the Supreme Court to annul the elections because of fraud. The Cuban House of Representatives declared the elections

---

[50] Evidence of Guillermo Cabrera Infante who arranged the meeting, Mora arriving in an expensive *dril cien* suit, the veteran Communist expressing hatred for a recent Directorio terrorist attack in Mariano. The meeting was held in the beautiful house of Nicasio Silverio.

[51] Born Banes, Oriente; orphaned at ten; went aged 15 years to Santiago, illiterate; worked at night at University of Havana; afterwards lawyer; backed by Carlos Manuel de la Cruz; entered Ministry of Health, 1934; political secretary to Batista; director of Coffee Institute; sub-secretary of Agriculture; Minister of Agriculture, 1940; Minister of Education, 1952; prime minister, 1957-8. He was, though blue-eyed and fair-skinned, a half-brother of Castro's erstwhile Ortodoxo friend, Luis Conte Agüero, an octaroon.

[52] Phillips, 381.

[53] Suárez Núñez, 50.

[54] Evidence of Earl Smith, January 1969.

valid; again, few noticed. The fate of Cuba was being decided else-where.

Still, about 15 November Rivero Agüero, as president-elect, called on Ambassador Smith and told him that he was studying how to achieve a peaceful solution to Cuba's political problems, which would probably be supported by 90% of the people. He, like Smith, realized that Castro would oppose any peaceful formula, but thought he could gather support elsewhere. Ambassador Smith then went to the U.S. After giving a ball at the Waldorf Astoria – a charity occasion for the Florence Pritchett Smith scholarship for commercial design – he went to Washington on 23 November.[55] He urged the State Department to honour Rivero's appeal for U.S. backers. Rubottom and Wieland said that there was no solution possible in Cuba through U.S. aid. They did not wish to support or stimulate the Church's effort at reconciliation, and they did not think that any of the civil and military would associate themselves with the president-elect. Smith said that he had now realized that Batista could not last, since the economy was declining, bridges were being blown up, and so on. The Under-Secretary of State, Murphy, asked Smith if Castro's movement could be regarded as Communist and Smith said that he could convince any jury that it was.[56] In the end Smith went back to Havana, being told to ascertain if Rivero Agüero had any chance of devising a solution such as he had suggested, with the backing of the main elements of the opposition. But it transpired that Rivero had merely reverted to Batista's old position of an indefinite reliance on force.[57]

This failure did lead to new action in the U.S. A few days later a meeting was held in a house in Miami belonging to William Pawley, ex-ambassador and businessman (founder of Cubana Airlines in the 1920s). At this meeting there were present Deputy Assistant Secretary of State Snow,[58] Assistant Secretary Henry Holland,[59] and Colonel J. C. King, in command of the Latin American section of the CIA.[60] There was discussion: 'What do you do about this Cuban problem?' Pawley said that 'everything we were doing was wrong. I told them that we should now, to try to save the peace, see if we can go down there to get Batista to capitulate to a caretaker government unfriendly to him but satisfactory to us, whom we could immediately recognise and give military assistance to in order that Fidel Castro should not come to

[55] Smith, *The Fourth Floor*, 214.
[56] *Ibid.*, 160–1.
[57] Wieland evidence, 661–2, 545–7.
[58] Afterwards ambassador in Burma.
[59] He had been head of the Latin American division of the State Department in 1954 during the Guatemalan *coup*, to which he was privy, though he had opposed it.
[60] Pawley evidence to Senate Internal Security Sub-Committee, *Communist Threat*, 738.

power.' The next day they all went up to Washington and had talks at the CIA and Department of State. Pawley was then 'selected to go to Cuba to talk with Batista to see if I could convince him to capitulate, which I did'.[61]

But before Pawley arrived on this somewhat desperate and unconventional mission, events had begun to move fast. Though the activities of the resistance in Havana had been kept to a minimum, partly by the capture of the Auténtico representative in Havana (who gave away information under torture), partly by the insistence by Castro on the dispatch of arms to the Sierra, there had been some isolated incidents at the end of November, such as the seizure of yet another aeroplane, full of tourists bound for Varadero from Miami, by an unofficial Castro supporter, of whom nothing was known, resulting in the death of the crew and of ten passengers, which plunged into the Bay of Nipe. Castro, who had moved his headquarters to La Miel from La Plata,[l] had planned an attack on the village of Bueycito, but the garrison withdrew before the attack; the rebels moved on towards Guisa, by-passing Bayamo, aiming to concentrate their forces over Santiago. An ex-schoolmaster and rice grower, Hubert Matos, with 245 men, and Almeida, with 350, began to invest that city. Rumours of an attack on the city were widespread, and there were innumerable bombings. There were also several minor clashes in the Guantánamo area.[62] At Guisa Castro faced 5,000 men of Batista's with 200 *guerrilleros*, of whom 100 were new to the combat.[63] Batista's commanders were beginning to despair: 'Our Army, tired and decimated by two years of fighting without relief, had completely lost its combat power. Desertions to the enemy increased daily. We lacked reserves and a great part of the officers confined in the barracks maybe [were] . . . in contact with the enemy.' The prospect of Batista's own abandonment of power in February caused further demoralization. Surrender of one or two officers such as Major Quevedo to Castro and two others (Villamil and Ulbino León) to Guevara, caused alarm out of all proportion to the damage caused. Several officers were arrested and gaoled by Batista for fear that they were about to act against him.[64] Raúl and Fidel Castro joined forces, but the different sections of Batista's kingdom seemed out of touch with each other, and all out of touch with Havana.[65] More and more people went to the Sierra Maestra and, often through

[61] *Ibid.*, 739; Kirkpatrick, *The Real CIA*, 178-9, refers.
[62] E.g. that described by Dicky Chapelle (*cf.* Osanka, *Modern Guerrilla Warfare*, 325).
[63] Debray, *Révolution dans la révolution*, 58.
[64] They were: Pedro Castro Rojas, José Rodríguez San Pedro, José Viamontes Jardines, Eugenio Menéndez, Félix Gutiérrez Fernández and José Robles Cortés.
[65] *Cf.* letter from General Silito Tabernilla to Batista, 13 February 1959, qu. Batista, *Cuba Betrayed*, 104-5, fn.

opportunism, effectively joined with the 26 July Movement even though until then they had been active in other organizations. Batista seemed to place all hope in an abrogation of arms embargo, but in an interview after his return from Washington, Smith left him in no doubt of the 'unpleasant' atmosphere in Washington.[66] About the beginning of December Smith saw a group of local business-men who mostly thought Batista could not last till the end of his term, perhaps not even past 1 January, unless the U.S. gave him support. These men argued that the 26 July was 'Communist-dominated', and the Esso representative, G. W. Potts, said that a recent 26 July statement seemed very similar to one by the Arbenz government in Guatemala. Everyone thought that the best idea was for the U.S. to support a military junta. Smith, reporting all this, suggested that Rivero Agüero should be persuaded to take over control immediately, with U.S. support for the formation of a national unity government.[67] On 5 December Kenneth Redmond, president of the United Fruit Com-pany, telegraphed Dulles to help to save the sugar crop in Oriente: the rebels had cut off water to the United Fruit's *Preston* mill because of the company's refusal to pay 15 cents tax on every 250-pound bag of sugar.[68]

Batista made a number of desperate changes of command. Cantillo was named chief of operations in Oriente and Del Río Chaviano (whom he hated beyond reason and who had remained at the headquarters in Santiago) was transferred to Las Villas. Colonel Pérez Coujil took over in Camagüey from Colonel Dueñas. In Oriente Colonels Suárez Susquet and Sánchez Mosquera tried to keep their troops mobile. Even so more of the officers went over to Castro, particularly Captains Dinaz and Oquendo, who had been held in Jibacoa. Palma Soriano fell without a fight. By the beginning of December the government still held Santiago, Bayamo, Holguín and the other big towns; but outside these Castro seemed in control of southern Oriente. By 7 December the arrival of a transmitter had enabled him to be in radio communication with Cien-fuegos in Las Villas. He could thus learn that on 1 December Guevara had finally reached a successful agreement with the Directorio; a pact signed by Guevara and Cubela (following conversations in which Chomón had also taken part for the Directorio and Ramiro Valdés for the 26 July) spoke of full agreement, full collaboration for military purposes, and agreement by the Directorio with Castro's agrarian reform.[69] But it did not speak of Guevara's or Castro's command over

[66] *Ibid.*, 96.
[67] Smith, *The Fourth Floor*, 162–3.
[68] HAR. It was a telegraph like this, perhaps also from Redmond, which alerted Dulles to the situation in Guatemala in 1954. Dulles had once been legal adviser to the United Fruit Company.
[69] *Cf. Hoy*, 17 July 1965.

the Directorio; that matter remained for later consideration. Meantime, the few representatives of the Directorio in Havana had received orders to go to Las Villas.[70] With this agreement behind them, the rebels put one army detachment to flight beyond Santa Lucia, so leaving Guevara free to blow up the bridge where the central highway crossed the River Tuinicú. By now Guevara's subordinate Captain José Silva controlled the road from Trinidad to Sancti Spiritus; the main railway was damaged at two points.

Pawley saw Batista for three hours on 9 December – Ambassador Smith (who was not informed) having flown to Washington. Pawley offered Batista the chance to live again at Daytona Beach. He suggested that a new provisional government for Cuba might be composed of Colonels Barquín and Borbonnet, General Díaz Tamayo and Pepe Bosch of the Bacardí family.[71] The trouble was, Pawley said, that he had no authority to say the U.S. would definitely carry out their side of the bargain, only that 'I will try to persuade the U.S. government'. Anyway, Batista refused, saying to an aide that he had had a mind to 'kick out this Pawley'.[72]

The following day Smith, in Washington, saw his State Department colleagues and Allen Dulles; he received instructions to disabuse Batista of any idea that Rivero Agüero might receive the backing of the U.S. government. So Smith went back once more to Havana and told the Foreign Minister, Dr Güell, 'It is my unpleasant duty to inform the President of the Republic that the U.S. will no longer support the present government of Cuba and that my government believes that the President is losing effective control'; Güell said that Batista would see Smith in a few days.[73]

At this point Batista made a last effort to rally his army. Ten companies of a hundred men each were sent to Santa Clara, reinforced by three battalions of 400 men each. Their mission was partly to prevent bridge destruction. The key point in this defence system was an armoured train prepared by Western Railways under Colonel Rosell y Leyva.[74]

About the middle of December Batista brought all the commanders of the armed services together to Ciudad Militar. It became clear that the president was contemplating some sort of desperate action. He told his followers: 'We should try and change the administration ... [and]

[70] Evidence of Manuel Ledón.
[71] Robert Murphy told Smith that Cantillo and Sosa would be part of the junta.
[72] *Communist Threat*, 739; Kirkpatrick, 179. Suárez Núñez, 105. Later Batista regretted not accepting Pawley's plan and said he would have done so if he had known that the U.S. government really backed the emissary (Lazo, 162-3).
[73] Smith, *The Fourth Floor*, 170.
[74] Batista, *Cuba Betrayed*, 99.

meet frequently, and discuss every new event.' Despite agreement on secrecy General Tabernilla, Batista's *bête noire*, and the real author of the army's defeat, talked to a large number of officers. Batista sent for him and Tabernilla said, 'The soldiers are tired and the officers do not want to fight. Nothing more can be done.' Already, in fact, General Cantillo, the commander in Oriente, on Tabernilla's instructions, was preparing for negotiations with Castro. General Tabernilla told his son, 'Silito' Tabernilla (still Batista's private secretary), to tell the president this news; 'Silito' could not bring himself to do so and merely pledged his loyalty to the president 'unto death'.[75] On 17 December Smith finally saw Batista and said on instructions that the State Department believed that Batista could no longer maintain effective control in Cuba and that it would avoid a great deal of bloodshed if he were to retire.[76] Batista replied that without him no military junta could survive; without him the army would collapse. Could the U.S. intervene to stop the fighting? Smith said that that was unthinkable. Batista asked if he could go to Florida to visit his home at Daytona Beach. Smith suggested Spain instead, and asked if he thought he could control the situation till February; Batista said it would be difficult since the U.S. had refused him arms in his hour of need. He ran through many possible solutions, as if distracted. No doubt by this date he had decided to leave Cuba;[77] and within forty-eight hours, anyway, he is found asking the head of the air force ('Wince', or Brigadier Carlos Tabernilla) how many seats he could ensure on an aeroplane at a moment's notice.[78] Smith afterwards regarded his action in this interview as being tantamount to an instruction to Batista to leave.[79] By this time even the business community in Havana seems to have agreed with Julio Lobo: 'We didn't care who overthrew Batista providing someone did.'[80]

Pawley's mission to Batista, however, was not the only activity in which the CIA was engaged in December 1958 so far as Cuba was concerned. Justo Carrillo was still hoping to realize his plan of achieving the release of Colonel Barquín and by now he and an aide, Dr Andrés Suárez, having failed to receive help from Argentina, Venezuela and Honduras, were at last in touch with the CIA – or rather one of its representatives named Beardsley in Havana, and Robert Rogers in Miami. This project was for once not rejected and must have been under consideration by the CIA in Washington while Pawley was in Havana.[81]

[75] Batista, *Cuba Betrayed*, 99.
[76] *Communist Threat*, 687.
[77] Smith, *The Fourth Floor*, 171–3.
[78] Suárez Núñez, 107. This was apparently on 20 December.
[79] Evidence of Earl Smith.
[80] Evidence of Julio Lobo.
[81] Justo Carrillo MSS, p. 44.

CHAPTER 19

How Batista Fell

The night after this interview with Smith, Batista met with his generals who, it transpired, were hoping to hear that the president was giving up the fight. Batista in fact wanted to make preparations to prevent the 'total disintegration of his troops'. The generals 'told me how strange it was that military units were being continually surrendered without combat to an enemy who, in number and military capacity, could not possibly possess the strength necessary to immobilize the army'.[1] Castro's forces were indeed operating at this time steadily but menacingly along the *Carretera Central*, upon which Contramaestre had been taken by Major Francisco Cabrera. This meant that Santiago was cut off by road – less an overwhelming strategic blow than a psychological one. The capture of this small town, the first place of over 1,000 persons to fall to the rebels, had a decisive effect upon Batista's administration. Refugees began to flee into Santiago, while Batista's air force with some reluctance and incompetence bombed the villages taken by Castro. Colonel Sánchez Mosquera was bogged down and all but surrounded. He himself was wounded. In Las Villas the army was if anything in an even greater disarray than in the east. Guevara's successes and the increasing demoralization of the enemy led to a decision to order Cienfuegos to remain with his column in Las Villas rather than, as was anticipated, to advance Maceo-like to Pinar del Río. Cienfuegos would aid Guevara to cut the island in half there and then. On 18 December Guevara captured Fomento, and on 21 December attacked Cabaiguán and Guayos to the east of that town some ten miles short of Sancti Spiritus;[2] Captain Bordón received the latter's surrender and on the 22nd, Cabaiguán surrendered too, to Major Cubela.[3] On 22 December Cienfuegos in the north of the province launched a full-scale attack on Yaguajay near the sea, while Guevara turned towards Havana to attack the road junction of Placetas, which, being almost deserted, he captured with its 30,000 inhabitants.[4]

[1] Batista, *Cuba Betrayed*, 103.

[2] Guevara, *Souvenirs*, 203.

[3] Bordón had been in the Sierra Escambray for almost two years before Guevara arrived there, in command of local 26 July forces operating *por la libre*. On Guevara's arrival he had been demoted but now was restored. Cubela was a leader of the Directorio.

[4] *Cf.* 'Diario de Guerra', in Núñez Jiménez, 500. In an interview in *Revolución* on January 4 1959 Cienfuegos said that he captured 250 men and 375 rifles.

All this military activity in the centre of the island took Batista completely unawares. The brilliance of Guevara's military leadership, with the audacity of Castro's original strategic idea of sending him to the centre of the island and not making himself known till then, was made very clear. Batista later accused two of his officers, Major González Finalés and Lieutenant Ubineo León, of letting Guevara pass through their sectors for a cash payment.[5] But even if that were the case – for which there is no evidence – it would hardly argue that the army was in a fit state. On 20 December he refused an offer from Trujillo to land 2,000 'fresh men' in the Sierra Maestra and another 2,000 in Santa Clara; 'I do not wish to treat with dictators,' he told Trujillo's emissary, Colonel Estévez Maymir, the Cuban military attaché in St Domingo.[6]

The last twitching reactions of Batista to what seemed the possibility of defeat finally began. He appointed his oldest comrade, General Pedraza, the chief of staff dismissed in 1940, to succeed Del Río Chaviano in Las Villas, and transferred the latter to Oriente. But Tabernilla persuaded the president that it would be best to have Pedraza at headquarters and so Colonel Casillas Lumpuy was brought back from the Isle of Pines to the command in Santa Clara. From the nature of these appointments it would seem that Batista was making a serious effort to regain the initiative which he had incredibly lost to so small a group of opponents. Meantime among his officers a *coup* was prepared to stave off Castro's victory. The scheme was that General Cantillo would take over in Oriente, while Commodore Carrera, General Del Río Chaviano and Colonel Rosell, then in command nominally of the armoured train at Santa Clara, would also take part. Colonel Barquín, still in prison, would be approached to take over Las Villas, while the command at Campamento Columbia would be given to one of the officers associated with him in his unsuccessful *golpe* of 1956. The military chiefs of Camagüey and Holguín (Colonels Pérez Coujil and Ugalde Carrillo) would be captured or killed if they refused to join in. Batista would be put on to an aeroplane to the U.S. along with the Tabernillas.[7] Barquín, who was then in prison, apparently accepted, sending his graduation ring as token of his agreement. It is evident that a number of officers, such as Colonel Rosell, regarded Barquín not just as a man of compromise but as the one officer who could defeat Castro. Action was planned for 26 December. Then General Del Río Chaviano decided that it would be more appropriate to bring in the Tabernillas and inform them of the role allotted to them. Meantime neither the U.S. Embassy nor Batista was informed of what was happening. Batista himself was seeing his

[5] Batista, *Cuba Betrayed*, 86, fn.
[6] Suárez Núñez, 108.
[7] See Barrera Pérez, *Bohemia Libre*, 3 September 1961; and Colonel Rosell's *La Verdad*, 31 f.

usual group of bishops who told them that 'any sacrifice would be worth-while if it ended terrorism'; and indeed the civil war was far from lost, if only Batista could have brought himself to admit that a civil war, properly speaking, was in existence.

His generals still believed that they had the situation in control. Tabernilla, independently of Batista, dispatched General Cantillo to Oriente to try to discuss an armistice with Castro. Tabernilla had by then been told by Del Río Chaviano of the plan for a military *golpe*, and himself determined to try a modified version of it. During 22 December Batista, however, having received news of these moves, confronted Tabernilla and, in an interview that night, gave Cantillo permission to proceed to Oriente to do what he could with Castro; Cantillo, coming out of Batista's office, remarked to Batista's military secretary, still 'Silito' Tabernilla, 'Silito, every time I read a life of a great man, I skip the last pages because the end is always disagreeable.'[8] On 23 December at another meeting Tabernilla told Batista bluntly that he considered the war lost. He had received news that the city of Guantánamo was then surrounded by forces coming down from the hills under Juan Almeida, the mulatto singer who commanded what was described as the 'Tercera Frente Oriental'. The same day some of Guevara's forces, led by the Communist, Armando Acosta, reached the outskirts of Sancti Spiritus, upon which the 115,000-strong town surrendered without a battle. No spirit of resistance reigned in the city administration, and apart from the police there was no effective force there able to resist even a small number of men. In Oriente the next day (Christmas Eve), Cantillo (having given $10,000 each to Colonels Ugalde Carrillo and Jesús María Salas Cañizares, and $15,000 to Colonel Pérez Coujil)[9] successfully arranged through Father Guzmán, a priest of Santiago, a meeting with Castro at the Oriente sugar mill (which had once belonged to the Chibás family). Also present were Majors Sierra Talavera and José Quevedo. Cantillo, who arrived and left by helicopter, promised that the army would rise before 3 p.m. on 31 December and prevent Batista's escape.[10] According to one eye-witness of this meeting, every-thing was agreed between the two, except that Castro wished that the army officers of the Barquín group should be held in prison.[11] On Christmas Day Cantillo returned from Santiago by air to Havana. He was immediately confronted by Batista who carried out a clever inquiry

---

[8] This is Cantillo's and Suárez Núñez's account (p. 99), but Batista afterwards denied that he gave such permission to Cantillo. But the above appears to be correct.

[9] *Ibid.*, 110. As bribes to leave the country.

[10] Castro gave his account of this meeting in his speech of 2 January. (*Revolución*, 3 January 1959.) *Cf.* also *Discursos para la Historia*, 23. It is doubtful if Cantillo would agree with Castro's account.

[11] Carrillo evidence.

of him. Cantillo said that Tabernilla had insisted that he seek out Castro. Batista, not hearing exactly what had transpired at the meeting at the sugar mill, told Cantillo that he would be prepared to hand over power to a junta of officers headed by Cantillo as a gesture to the Cuban nation and to leave on 26 January. [12]

Castro passed Christmas with his brother Ramón at Marcané, near the *Alto Cedro* sugar mill; but Guevara was attacking Remedios near the north coast and commanding the main northern approach to Santa Clara, the capital of the province of Las Villas. Remedios fell on the 26th, its commander, Captain Guerrero, surrendering 150 large weapons. The same day Caibarién, a few miles further down the sea coast itself, also fell. The naval captain, Luis Aragon, who was in command there, offered no resistance. This cut off Santa Clara from reinforcement on the north and on the south.[13] Guevera moved next into position to attack Santa Clara. But perhaps an attack of this magnitude would not be needed. On the 28th Castro received an ambiguous note from Cantillo saying that, though 'the situation was developing favourably', it would be best to delay action till 6 January at least. Cantillo was vacillating. Castro said that it was impossible to wait, accused Cantillo of treachery, and continued his own build-up of forces around Santiago. But Castro did not expect Batista to collapse so fast as he now did.[14]

On 29 December Ambassador Smith, isolated by events whose direction he greatly disliked, apparently in ignorance of the intrigues which had been going on in the capital as of the battles elsewhere, was called on by the two Generals Tabernilla, father and son, together with Del Río Chaviano. Tabernilla *père* said that in his opinion the army would not fight any more and that the government could not last. He, Tabernilla, was anxious, however, to save Cuba from 'chaos, Castro and communism'. He proposed a military junta comprising Generals Cantillo, Sosa de Quesada (a Prústa officer), García Casones (an air force officer) and some naval officer; would the U.S. recognize such a government? Smith said that unfortunately he could only do business with Batista. He asked whether Tabernilla had talked with Batista? Yes, came the reply, but Batista had no plan. He had indeed asked Tabernilla to 'come up with a plan'. Smith sent back Tabernilla to talk again with Batista.[15]

Batista was, in fact, planning to leave, either as he had told Cantillo,

[12] Batista, *Cuba Betrayed*, has a slightly different version, but this is that of Colonel Barrera Pérez (*Bohemia Libre*, 3 September 1961).

[13] 'Diario', Núñez Jiménez, 500.

[14] So he admitted later in Washington to the ex-president of Ecuador, Galo Plaza whom both he and Batista had accepted as mediator earlier. (Evidence of Sr Galo Plaza.) See Castro speech, *Revolución*, 4 January 1959.

[15] *Communist Threat*, 709; Smith, *The Fourth Floor*, 177.

on 6 January or earlier. His children secretly left Havana on the 29th for the U.S. He had already burned much of his private correspondence and other documents.[16] He had arranged aeroplanes. In taking this decision Batista was thinking only of himself and a few close followers. He was making no provision for the thousands of Cubans who had worked with him and whose fortunes and in many cases whose lives depended on him. He had already a list of people who would be allowed to escape with him. Castro, meantime, had entered into correspondence by messenger with the commanding officer of Santiago, Colonel Rego, who had been part of Cantillo's conspiracy.[17] Guevara had already attacked Santa Clara. On the other hand most local political leaders and mayors had already abandoned their posts, and with their families were making essential journeys abroad for reasons of health.

Guevara travelled on 28 December from the coast at Caibarién along the road to Camajuaní and thence by small roads to reach the University of Santa Clara, on the outskirts of the town, at dusk. There he divided his forces (which numbered about 300)[18] into two. The southern column was the first to meet the defending forces (commanded for the last two or three days by Colonel Casillas Lumpuy). An armoured train, on which the colonel greatly relied, steamed along to the foot of the hill Capiro, at the north-east of the city, establishing there a command post. Guevara dispatched a small force under an eighteen-year-old, Captain Gabriel Gil, to capture the hill, using mostly hand grenades, and hidden from the train by the hill itself.[19] The defenders of the hill withdrew with surprising speed and the train was then withdrawn too towards the middle of the town. The morale of the defenders was shown to be very low. Guevara successfully mobilized the tractors of the School of Agronomy at the university to raise the rails of the railway. The train was therefore derailed. The officers within tumbled out and were immediately attacked. They asked for a truce. At this, the ordinary soldiers of the army began to fraternize with the rebels, saying that they were tired of fighting against their own people. Shortly afterwards the armoured train surrendered and its 350 men and officers were transported as prisoners. The train became a base for further attack. There was also fighting inside the city, between the police and the Civic Resistance. This grew in intensity during 31 December. Batista's air force – the usual B-26s and British Sea Furies – dropped bombs on the parts of the city occupied by Guevara, but only a few civilians were killed.

[16] Suárez Núñez, 116.

[17] Rego understood Castro's first note as a demand for surrender (see *Revolución*, 4 January 1959).

[18] Castro, on 18 October 1967 (*Granma*, weekly edition., 29 October 1967).

[19] Gabriel Gil had been in the *Granma*. Lost after Alegría de Pío, he had rejoined Castro in the Sierra in February 1957.

The Batistianos held out in five main centres – the Leoncio Vidal barracks; the central police station; the provincial government buildings; the Palace of Justice; and the Grand Hotel. The Palace of Justice was defended by two tanks. These were attacked by an eighteen-year-old rebel captain, Rogelio Acevedo.[20] Three men who stood beside the tanks were wounded. The Palace of Justice fell soon after, along with the provincial government and Grand Hotel. The police station was stormed by a suicide squadron led by the young rebel captain 'Vaquerito' ('the little cow-boy'),[21] who was killed in the assault. The commanding Batistiano, Colonel Cornelio Rojas, a septuagenarian, ordered resistance to the last man, but he was nevertheless captured and the police station fell.[22] Aeroplanes as ever moved in to attack the posts where the rebels triumphed, and night fell on the last day of 1958 with Colonel Casillas Lumpuy still holding half the city, with five hundred men, though many of them were contemplating desertion.[23] There were desperate telephone calls by Batista to Colonel Casillas in Santa Clara; and over the line also came news of disputes between Colonels Casillas and Fernández Suero, who had fallen back on military headquarters. 'The last time we spoke to them,' Batista recalled later, 'their words were practically unintelligible, they had become hoarse with yelling to make their orders understood above the tumult' – the noise being compounded by the shouting of 'undisciplined personnel' and indiscriminate shooting. The 'heroic defender of this redoubt', as Batista described Casillas, proceeded to arrest the 'seditious' Major Suárez Fowler who had urged the combatants to lay down their arms.[24] About 9 p.m. the chief of staff, General Rodríguez Avila, advised Batista that in his opinion Las Villas could not be held. At 10 p.m. General Cantillo advised the same in respect of Oriente. Batista, then at the Finca Kuquine, thereupon ordered his government and the military commanders to meet him at Campamento Columbia to say good-bye to the old year. This was normal and no one thought much of the invitation. Another meeting was at that same time being held in the

[20] Later one of the stalwart officers of the revolution. In 1965 member of the Central Committee of the Cuban Communist party.

[21] Roberto Rodríguez, of very small build, aged about twenty; he was a Camagüeyano from Morón. Guevara speaks of him as a youth of extraordinary 'alegría', 'amazingly mendacious', who always decorated truth with fantasy, but who was nevertheless astoundingly brave.

[22] He was uncle to Masferrer, and was summarily tried and shot within forty-eight hours. He requested permission to command the firing squad; it was granted.

[23] Account in Revolución, 4 January 1959. Núñez Jiménez, 'Diario de Guerra', in Geografía, 502–3; Isidoro del Valle, Hoy, 18 July 1965. Somewhat unfortunately, as W. Lederer pointed out, A Nation of Sheep (1961), 138, Associated Press reported on 1 January from Havana that when the year had ended, the rebel threat had 'faded in a storm of Government firepower' and that Government troops 'hammered retreating rebel forces around Santa Clara . . . and drove them eastwards out of Las Villas'.

[24] Batista, 123.

Pentagon at Washington, at which Admiral Burke, chief of naval staff, with some support from Allen Dulles and Robert Murphy, argued that 'Castro was not the right man' for Cuba and that some action should be taken there to prevent him capturing power. The discussion lasted till 2 a.m., but nothing could be decided, and indeed what could have been at that late hour, other than an immediate intervention by the marines?[25]

The men of Batista's regime and their wives gathered at the military headquarters. In a confused gathering there were to be seen relations of Batista, military men, politicians, Batista's wife; José Luis del Pozo, mayor of Havana; ministers such as García Montes or Santiago Rey; Andrés Rivero Agüero, 'president-elect'; Anselmo Alliegro and Gastón Godoy, chairmen respectively of the Senate and of the House of Representatives. While most of these men nervously drank coffee, Batista saw the chiefs of staff in an inner room. These officers agreed that they could not last any longer and Batista went through a charade of handing over power to Cantillo who thus held in his hands the keys of incompatible intrigues, one with his brother officers, one with Castro, and both impossible to coordinate with one another. Afterwards, Batista came out and spoke to each group separately, saying he was resigning 'to avoid more bloodshed'. To the inner group of his intimate friends he proposed seats on aeroplanes which would leave for the U.S. or elsewhere in the course of the night. Meantime he asked Anselmo Alliegro, as president of the Senate, to designate the oldest judge on the Supreme Court (Carlos Manuel Piedra) as provisional president. Piedra, who was present, accepted, and General Cantillo took over from Rodríguez Avila as chief of staff. Batista then formally resigned and at 3 a.m. he flew out of the military airfield, accompanied by forty people, among them his wife and his son Jorge; Gonzalo Güell and his wife; Andrés Rivero Agüero; Gastón Godoy; Generals Rodríguez Avila, Rodríguez Calderón, and Rojas, and Colonels Orlando Piedra and Fernández Miranda. They headed not for the U.S. but for the Dominican Republic.[26] According to Castro, they took with them $M300 or $M400[27] but Batista and his followers already had money abroad and it does not appear that they had time to gather much cash. Batista's brother 'Panchín', governor of Havana, flew out of Havana with forty-six people later in the night, including ministers and police officers. Masferrer, warned by telephone, at the same time quietly left Santiago by yacht. Other flights followed, to New Orleans, or to Jacksonville (the Tabernillas and Pilar García).[28] Not only politicians fled, but also

[25] Admiral Burke to the author, 26 December 1962.
[26] Batista, *Cuba Betrayed*, 137.
[27] Speech, 1 January, *Revolución*, 4 January.
[28] Batista was afterwards refused permission to seek asylum in the U.S.

men such as Meyer Lansky, the gambler. Once the leading Batistianos had escaped, a message was passed to Radio Caracas in Venezuela, with whom they were on good relations and from that centre the world heard the news.

It is of course obscure to what extent Batista had enriched himself. His press secretary in exile and one who was for a time youth leader of his party estimated his fortune in 1958, as $M300, mostly invested abroad in Switzerland, Florida, New York or Mexico.[29] Certainly his income from protection money must have been quite considerable, though the estimated $M1·28 made each month out of this had to be divided among a lot of people.

Cantillo, now chief of staff, and on 1 January 1959 in effective command of the west of Cuba, then called a meeting of officers and told them the news, which rapidly spread throughout Havana and then the island. Cheering crowds came out into still dark streets. Judge Piedra, with other judges of the Supreme Court, and other prominent citizens such as Núñez Portuondo, Cuervo Rubio and Raúl de Cárdenas, read aloud in the presidential palace a cease-fire for the army and called upon Castro to do the same. But this shadow government had no backing. Pandemonium grew during the morning and supporters of Castro or of the Directorio began to appear in the streets, in uniform, announcing that they would keep order, as Batistiano officers and police disappeared, either flying abroad (aeroplanes continued to fly all morning), moving into foreign embassies or simply seeking other hiding. Most of the leaders of Batista's repression had escaped in the course of the morning. About noon the airport was declared closed for outgoing traffic, though by then most of the biggest targets for revolutionary revenge, such as the naval intelligence chief, Laurent, or Colonel Ventura of the political police, had escaped. Others, such as Major Jacinto Menocal, had killed themselves.[30] At Santa Clara meantime Colonel Casillas, the defender of the barracks, had learned the news of Batista's flight with fury. Quickly dressing in civilian clothes, he and Colonel Fernández Suero fled after handing over command to their subordinate, Colonel Hernández. At this moment, just after dawn, Guevara sent in a three-man peace mission demanding surrender.[31] The Batista soldiery once more demanded fraternization. Colonel Hernández asked for a truce. In the course of the discussion a telephone call came from Cantillo in Campamento Columbia. The peace mission refused to accept Cantillo as

[29] Suarez Nunez, 26. A more modest estimate was that given in the Daily Mail, 11 December, 1969: 'more than £40M'.

[30] Revolución, 4 January 1959.

[31] Núñez Jiménez, Rodríguez de la Vega, and Lieutenant Ríos. Dr Núñez Jiménez, a distinguished geographer, had only joined Guevara on Christmas Eve. He was the author of a famous outline economic geography of Cuba.

chief of staff. It being then 1.30, p.m. they announced that hostilities would begin again, at 2.15. After discussions, the Batistiano army surrendered unconditionally in Santa Clara before that time. By then, Major Bordón had caught Colonel Casillas; afterwards he was shot, while trying (genuinely, it seems) to escape.[32] Santa Clara having fallen, Castro ordered Guevara to move on to Havana. He himself, who heard the news of Batista's escape at the *central América*,[33] was both furious and surprised. He placed the full blame on Cantillo, and ordered a general advance on Santiago. But an assault was not necessary. Colonel Rego had decided to surrender (the two communicated through a Baptist minister), and flew by helicopter to Castro's headquarters to do so. Castro spoke with Rego's officers, told them that he knew that not all the officers of Batista's army were assassins, and persuaded all either to join him or to give up their arms. Two frigates also surrendered. It appears that the commanders in Santiago thought that their attitude would save the army from dissolution,[34] and Castro also promised that Colonel Rego would become chief of staff of the Cuban army.

By that time however, Colonel Barquín, leader of the 'Liberal' officers of the 1956 *coup*, had reappeared in Havana, having been flown there by a Colonel Carrillo from prison in the Isle of Pines.[35] It appears that he owed his release to the somewhat delayed intervention of the CIA, who on 30 December had dispatched a man, with the backing of Justo Carrillo, to offer the head of the prison $100,000 to release this prisoner.[36] General Cantillo, realizing the impossibility of forming a junta of compromise, now handed over command to Barquín, with whom he had been in contact since 20 December. Barquín therefore proclaimed himself chief of the armed forces in Havana. He ordered some of his co-conspirators in 1956 to similar positions (Borbonnet to the first infantry division, Varela to La Cabaña, Villafaña to the air force, Andrés González to the navy). But being himself at this time a member of the 26 July Movement and therefore in touch with its leaders of the Havana underground, he also arrested Cantillo and telephoned Castro in Santiago to ask when Judge Urrutia should take over as head of state. He thus subordinated himself to the 26 July Movement and without an effort gave up what chance there was of a government of the centre.

---

[32] Núñez Jiménez, *Geografía*, 502-3. Some doubt hangs over the precise fate of Casillas, since, in *Revolución*, 5 January, it is reported he was shot after court martial.

[33] As he said in a speech at Camagüey, *Revolución*, 5 January.

[34] Cf. Castro's speech, *ibid.*, 4 January 1959.

[35] Not Justo Carrillo, but a cousin of his.

[36] Carrillo's negotiations with the CIA, begun in early December, had finally resulted in this rather than the more spectacular *golpe de estado* in the Isle of Pines which he had earlier designed. That this sum was offered to the prison commander is made quite clear from the Carrillo MSS, which describe the discussion between Carrillo and Willard Hubert Carr of the CIA on 30 December.

As he spoke, outside in the streets there was some looting. Casinos were invaded. The offices of Masferrer's *Tiempo en Cuba* were smashed. The newspaper *Alerta* was taken over by 26 July men. The Shell Petroleum headquarters was also smashed – the supposition being widespread that the president of the Cuban Shell office had been responsible for sending the Sea Furies and some tanks from England. Some parking meters (particularly unpopular because their profits had gone to a small group in the regime) and public telephones were broken. The houses of Ventura and Pilar García were sacked. The remaining officers and men in Havana who had belonged to Batista's army waited without knowing what would happen. Old residents in Havana wondered bitterly whether the bloody scenes at the overthrow of Machado would be repeated.[37] But Castro made an urgent broadcast from Santiago appealing to people not to take the law into their own hands, and with the 26 July men and the Directorio moving everywhere into police stations, there was a remarkable absence of such violence. Nevertheless, the general strike called by both Castro and the Communists persisted – the first success and indeed the first sign of life of FONU, the anti-Batistiano Labour front.

Colonel Barquín in Campamento Columbia probably could not have maintained himself apart from the 26 July Movement and Castro, nor did he seem seriously to have wanted to do so. Armando Hart and Quintín Pino of the 26 July Movement were with him at Campamento Columbia. Nevertheless, had Barquín so desired he could have made matters extremely difficult for Castro. But he soon found that the rebel army was in control of most of Cuba and in his first statement he recognized 'the heroic efforts of the Army of Liberation'. Nor apparently, and surprisingly, was there any attempt by the U.S. Embassy to try to persuade him to remain in command; he received only two telephone calls from Ambassador Smith in the course of his time at Colombia: the first asked for a safe-conduct for Trujillo's ambassador in Cuba, Porfirio Rubirosa; the second asked that the normal Latin American right of asylum in foreign embassies would be guaranteed.[38]

In the night of 1 to 2 January the decisive military event occurred.

Guevara arrived in Havana with his men, and went straight to La Cabaña and took over command from Colonel Varela at 4 a.m.[39]

[37] Phillips, *Cuban Dilemma.*

[38] Barquín to Meyer. Seventy-seven people took advantage of this last. They included politicians such as Miguel Angel Campa, Anselmo Alliegro, Santiago Rey, López Castro, Guas Inclán, Raúl Menocal, Carlos Saladrigas (Jun.,) Justo Luis Pozo, Octavio Montoro, Dámaso Sogo and Leopoldo Pío Elizalde; trade unionists such as Mujal; and some thugs such as Calviño (see list in *Revolución,* 10 January 1959, 11).

[39] Núñez Jiménez, 504; *Revolución,* 3 January 1959.

Camilo Cienfuegos, with Victor Bordón and about 700 men, entered Campamento Columbia and took over from Barquín.[40] Majors Cubela and Chomón, for the Directorio, occupied the presidential palace. In a less publicized military manœuvre Armando Acosta, who now suddenly appeared with the rank of 'Major', Guevara's Communist party aide from Escambray, took command at the old fort of La Punta, immediately opposite La Cabaña on the west side of the harbour of Havana. Meantime, Miró Cardona, the secretary of the alliance of the Caracas Pact, Agramonte, the Ortodoxo candidate in the 1952 general elections, with two members of the 26 July Movement (Llanusa and Haydée Santamaría), flew from Miami to Cuba, not to take over power in Havana but to an airport near the Sierra Maestra. On 2 January Havana members of the Directorio and 26 July followers patrolled the streets, and even Ambassador Smith gave a grudging cheer: 'Under the circumstances, they remained in remarkable control.'[41] No shot was fired, and here as elsewhere the 26 July and Batista's men were shortly seen fraternizing.

Castro had meantime arrived in Santiago, accepted the surrender of the town, and late on the night of 1–2 January, in a speech to a huge crowd, declared that Santiago, 'bulwark of liberty', would become the new capital of Cuba. He announced that 'the people had elected' Judge Urrutia provisional president; he spoke of the forthcoming revolution; and gave some account of his negotiations with Cantillo and Colonel Rego. To those members of the army not guilty of 'war crimes', he extended the hand of peace.[42] All over Cuba the local 26 July forces (or mixed 26 July and Directorio Estudiantil) were busy occupying administrative buildings, police and radio stations, telephone exchanges, barracks, and local trade union buildings. There was everywhere some looting of houses of Batista's officials, but no bloodbath. Symbolically, in view of the as usual ambivalent role played by the U.S. in Cuban revolutionary development, a U.S.-born major, Willie Morgan, of dubious antecedents at home, led Directorio forces to occupy Cienfuegos.[43]

On 2 January the 26 July Movement had called for a general strike to mark the end of the old regime, and in Havana and most cities this was fairly complete. In Havana the rebel trade union FONU, now in

---

[40] *Revolución*, 3 January, speaks of some 4,000!

[41] Smith, *The Fourth Floor*, 321.

[42] In *Revolución*, 3 and 4 January 1959.

[43] Cuban embassies abroad were also taken over; in Washington, for instance, the 26 July representatives, Ernesto Betancourt and Emilio Pardo (minister), took over from Batista's ex-minister Arroyo. Later in the day ex-ambassador to Cuba Arthur Gardner telephoned to enable Arroyo's belongings and dog to be taken away. Teresa Casuso took over in Mexico. Similar scenes occurred all over the world, though in some places (e.g. Germany) the ambassador (Adolfo Caval) immediately joined the Castro movement.

offices lent them by the Freemasons, formed with difficulty and Communist backing during the previous October, called for mass demonstrations. David Salvador came out of gaol to head it as secretary-general.[44] The rebel committees in all unions came out into the open. A meeting was held at the Parque Central addressed by a series of workers' leaders, some new, some old.[45] A *guaracha* dancer in the crowd sang:

> *Ya ya ya ya, te ganaste la guerra*
> *Gánate ahora la paz*
> *Que el que haya sido cruel*
> *Tenga su justicia honrada.*[46]

The old CTC leaders compromised with Batista, Mujal at their head, had fled to hiding, Mujal himself being in the Uruguayan Embassy. The speakers at the FONU meeting talked chiefly of freeing the CTC from corruption.

In the next few days all the unions reformed themselves with new leaders. Militants of the 26 July and Directorio took over as *de facto* police. Offices of newspapers which had backed Batista were occupied. Exiles began to return from Miami, Mexico and the rest of Latin America, including many Prústas, and Castro's nine-year-old son. Not all were well received; the old gangster González Cartas, '*El Extraño*', went straight to La Cabaña. There was a little further shooting in Havana, one *miliciano* being shot up by a Ventura policeman.

Another inevitable process was, however, beginning. Hour by hour, ex-Batista soldiers, policemen, officers and *esbirros*, *políticos* and civil servants, were rounded up and jailed to await trial. Civic bodies from the Masons to the Spanish exile colony, the Chamber of Commerce and the sugar planters, all those who had so recently fawned on Batista, testified their support of the revolution. New rebel columns continued to arrive, some of them small groups who had held out for months as

---

[44] *Revolución*, 7 January, p. 2.

[45] Others on the first CTC executive were Wifredo Rodríguez, radio and television workers' leader; Alfredo Rancaño, the 26 July Movement's man in the gastronomic workers' union, but also a Communist; Octavio Louit, railway workers' leader from Guantánamo, who had been badly tortured by Batista; José Miguel Espino, transport workers' union, a Communist, probably since the 1930s; Orlando Blanco, of the Directorio, who also made a speech 'full of revolutionary concepts and generous human wisdom'; Rodrigo Lominchar, ex-Prústa congressman and sugar workers' leader, arrested in 1957 for planning the 'torch policy'; Jesus Soto, 26 July man from Escambray; and David Salvador, the 26 July Movement's general union chief (*Revolución*, 3 January 1959). These and other men established themselves in commissions controlling all the old CTC federations. The order calling off the strike on 5 January was signed by Livio Domínguez, Néstor Pinelo, Antonio Delgado, Patricio Durán, Alfredo Rancaño, Guido Guirado, Eduardo García, Narciso Sastre, Manuel Solaún and Carmen Martha Milla. (*Revolución*, 5 January 1959, p. 2.)

[46] Ya ya ya ya, you've won the war
Now you must win the peace;
He who has been so cruel
Let him have his just reward.

saboteurs in Havana or Matanzas, such as 'Majors' Sanjenís and Paneque. The Directorio meantime was still in control of the presidential palace, and it began to be a question of whether they might not refuse to move to make way for Urrutia. After all, they had attacked it two years before. Now they felt it was theirs. Their secretary-general, Faure Chomón, complained publicly that Castro had set up a provisional government in Santiago without the consent or advice of the other revolutionary groups. Cienfuegos, newly appointed by Urrutia chief of the armed forces of land, sea and air in Havana province, glowered from Columbia.

On 2 January the previously clandestine 26 July newspaper *Revolución* appeared publicly. It was thought to be the voice of Castro, though for a time it was merely the voice of the 26 July in Havana. On 5 January it had been taken over from its clandestine directors by Carlos Franqui, the director of Radio Rebelde in the Sierra, the ex-Communist who had helped Castro in newspapers and radio since 1955. *Revolución*, in these first days after Batista's flight, set the pace of things: on the 4th a photograph of Castro was underwritten 'The Hero-Guide of Cuban Reform. May God continue to illuminate him'. Across the pages of *Revolución*, on television and on radio, and soon across the island, a veritable series of legendary heroes, seemingly larger than life, were made to stride across Cuba – the 'glorious Major Cienfuegos'; the 'incomparable Che'; 'Ramirito' (Ramiro Valdés), all referred to by their Christian names. Here clearly was a nation which hungered at least for heroism.

Castro himself was moving slowly up to Havana, delayed by cheering crowds anxious to see him for the first time. He set off from Santiago on 1 January but by the 4th he had only reached Camagüey. There were speeches there, and at Holguín. No doubt he was consciously keeping Havana waiting, to draw out their enthusiasm for as long as possible, to win the rest of the country as if on an election tour; also, as he explained in Camagüey, he had to 'organize the revolutionary forces' on his way westwards – to make appointments, that is. He left his brother Raúl in command of Oriente, along with a twenty-four-year-old civilian aide, Carlos Chain. Guevara and Cienfuegos flew to confer with Castro on 2 and 5 January. Castro's delay too helped create a public for Cienfuegos. Hundreds of people saw him in person at Columbia, thousands saw him on Havana Television. The easy manners of this guerrilla chief made Batista's old barracks seem alive for the first time. Cienfuegos let out parrots from their cages at Columbia, saying to the reporters who were inevitably present, 'these also have a right to liberty.'[47] Even Ambassador Smith, who had to visit Cienfuegos on

[47] *Revolución*, 5 January.

behalf of his old friends of the old regime, found him 'courteous if aloof'.[48] Bearded men went in and out of Cienfuegos's office, rifles tossed backwards and forwards. Guevara in La Cabaña, a formidable presence, allowed Cienfuegos the headlines and maintained a discreet silence while ordering a prescription. Cienfuegos symbolized the rebel warrior who, Havana found to its surprise, behaved impeccably. The *barbudos*, as they became known, did not drink, did not loot, conducted themselves as if they were saints. No army had ever behaved like this in Havana.

The spirit of dissension was kept alive by the Directorio Revolucionario. On 4 January the 26 July Movement had to make a formal request to the Directorio to leave the presidential palace before Urrutia arrived. Since their secretary-general, Chomón, was not there, they asked for more time. Cienfuegos contemplated reducing the Palace by force. Chomón came back and the palace was finally handed over to Urrutia (whom the Directorio accepted with shouts of 'Long Live the President'),[49] but on the 6 January Chomón was found telling a large meeting, with Urrutia present, on the famous *escalinata* of the university, that the Directorio felt itself profoundly preoccupied; unity had made the revolution and the triumph belonged to everyone not simply one group; but the Directorio had no jobs in the government. The question of the Directorio's future remained unresolved. They even began to accumulate and seize arms.

Castro finally arrived in Havana on 8 January. His triumph was complete. Havana went out to cheer. Television cameras covered the route of entry. Placards were inscribed: *'Gracias Fidel'*. Castro's column of cars, jeeps, tanks and lorries drove slowly in from the east, and stopped at the presidential palace. Castro talked to President Urrutia, and indeed to those old hands Prío and Varona, who had arrived from Miami. Behind him walked armed and bearded men, who were also cheered. Castro carried his famous rifle with the telescopic lens. He addressed the crowd from the palace terrace. Even Mrs Phillips, who had over a quarter of a century seen so many changes of government in Cuba, was moved: 'As I watched Castro I realised the magic of his personality ... He seemed to weave a hypnotic net over his listeners, making them believe in his own concept of the functions of Government and the destiny of Cuba.'[50] He criticized the idea of having a presidential palace, though 'the Executive had to be somewhere' and, since there was no money for another palace, 'we are going to try to arrange that the people have an affection for this building ... what however is the

[48] Smith, *The Fourth Floor*, 202.
[49] Urrutia, 31.
[50] Phillips, *Cuba Island of Paradox*, 406.

emotion of the leader of the Sierra on entering the palace? ... exactly equal to what I feel on entering any other building in Cuba.' Afterwards he asked the crowd to open a file to let him pass through, without needing soldiers to help him do so.[51] He moved to Campamento Columbia, cheered all the way by crowds almost hysterically happy at seeing him. In this fortress he made a longer speech, with television in attendance.

It was not entirely a speech of rejoicing:

Apparently peace has been won yet we ought not to feel ourselves so optimistic. While the people laugh today and are happy, we are preoccupied ... Who can be 'the enemies of the revolution ...' We ourselves the revolutionaries ... who might turn out to be like the many revolutionaries of the past, who walked about with a 0·45 pistol and terrorised people. The worst part of the revolution against Machado was that afterwards gangs of revolutionaries roamed around fighting each other.

Castro half suggested that the Directorio Estudiantil (who had taken arms from Campamento Columbia two days before) was spoiling to be one of these gangs.[52] But this was perhaps the only precise statement in the speech. For the rest, it almost seemed as if William Jennings Bryan had returned. An Hispanic Bryan, a young strong tall no doubt military Bryan, but Bryan-like in his hypnotic effect on the immense audience, who on the other hand felt once more in their optimism that José Martí had really reappeared. As Castro began to speak two white doves were released by someone in the crowd; one of them alighted on Castro's shoulder: symbol and omen of peace.

[51] Text in *Discursos para la Historia*, tomo I, 5–6.
[52] Text in *ibid.*, 7–18.

BOOK TWO

Victory : L'Illusion Lyrique
1959

'The one thought that did not occur to anyone in the houses was that the Old World had not been crushed by its enemies but had killed itself.'

CESARE PAVESE, *The House on the Hill*

CHAPTER 20

Springs of Victory

What had happened? A heroic epic? The band of hunted men in the Sierra at the end of 1956 seemed to have turned, two years later, into an army large enough to beat the army of the nation, to expel the tyrant, to set the people free. The rebels were apparently young men, their leader thirty-two, many of the others in their twenties or even younger, a generation unstained by previous political failure, steeled by war. Many of the new leaders (though not the most important of them) came from fairly humble origins. For an emotional, generous and optimistic people such as the Cubans, Castro's capture of power, with its air, self-conscious no doubt but irresistible, of re-enacting the wars of independence, redeeming Martí's failure and Céspedes's before that, gave a superb thrill of self-congratulation and pleasure. For much of both South and North America, weary of the seemingly endless if often worthy steppes of the Eisenhower era, Castro's victory also afforded a moment of romance, a splash of sunlight, the echo of an heroic age long before even Martí – the era of the conquistadors.[1] For a few weeks Castro was to Eisenhower's America what Lawrence of Arabia had been to England during the First World War. This popular success, national and international, helped Castro from the moment of victory to ignore his allies, to forget the 'pact of Caracas' and to let it be assumed that he alone had won the war.

Castro's hold over the Cubans was established within a few days of Batista's flight to such an extent that, while before 1 January he had only a handful of followers, within weeks many thousands believed that he could do no wrong. He was their liberator, not merely from Batista, but from all old evils. Mothers of men who had died in the struggle trooped to see him. Occasionally after years of struggle and disappointment, and for many reasons, peoples decide to place their collective will-power in the hands of a single man. Ever since the death of Martí, the Cubans had been searching for such an individual. Now they believed they had found one. This was not Caribbean Bonapartism. Rather it resembled the belief that so many had had a few years before in Clavelito, the miraculous broadcaster who cured disease by his voice,

---

[1] Thus *El Independiente* of Caracas, 'In truth Fidel Castro has revived with his glorious epic a concept of heroism little known in our time' (as qu. in *Revolución*, 26 January 1959).

Cuba is a country where politics, magic and religion are neighbouring provinces, sometimes without boundary lines. At the same time Victory inspired throughout society a spirit of civic virtue never previously encountered in Cuba. Cubans had had little to believe in. Customs and institutions which, in more stable countries, act as a brake on the ambitions of single men and on the emotional expectations of masses, in Cuba had scarcely existed either during modern industrial society or in the slave society which had preceded it.

Some of these judgements about Castro's movement were well based: Castro and his men had always been few and they had been brave. Most had social consciences. They had triumphed over overwhelming odds. Many of their comrades had been cut down or brutally tortured. Though many believed that they were living an epic, self-consciousness has often been the mark of real heroes. Let there be honour where honour is due. But the defeat of Batista was not due only to the vanquishing of the army in the field, and the exploits of Castro's rebel army: indeed, the only serious battles fought in the civil war were those of Santa Clara and those which led to the defeat of the army's offensive in the summer of 1958. But even here the scale of combat was small – six rebels being killed[2] in Guevara's army at Santa Clara, forty in the battles leading to the defeat of Batista's offensive in 1958. Such a dearth of pitched engagements is typical of guerrilla warfare, but in fact even the number of guerrilla engagements was small. The scale of operations was far smaller than, say, the Malayan conflict, though the Batista air force had attempted in late 1958 to destroy towns held by rebels such as Sagua de Tanamo. Castro operated as much as a politician seeking to influence opinion as he did as a guerrilla leader seeking territory. The Cuban civil war had been really a political campaign in a tyranny, with the campaigner being defended by armed men. His first concern had been to establish himself in an intractable territory; this he accomplished, though he had hardly really done so till early 1958.[3] At the same time and, perhaps more important, by the skilful use of the foreign press – no Cuban journalists went to the Sierra Maestra before mid-1957[4] – he established a name which became known in North and South America (but particularly North) as much as in Cuba itself. In January 1959 Guevara said, 'At that time the presence of a foreign journalist, American for preference, was more important for us than a military

---

[2] *Revolución*, 14 January 1959.

[3] A point made firmly by Régis Debray in *Révolution dans la Révolution*; which as earlier indicated was read and apparently revised by Castro: '*Ce n'est qu'au bout de 17 mois de combats continuels, en avril 1958, que les rebelles installèrent une base guérillera au centre de la Sierra Maestra*', (64).

[4] The first were Eduardo Hernández of the newsreel *Noticuba* and Agustín Alles of *Bohemia* (*cf. Revolución*, 14 January 1959).

victory.'[5] By early 1957 Castro had thus become a battle standard of opposition, a point of reference around which the opposition in the rest of the country and in exile could rally, even if from a distance.

Here Batista played into Castro's hands, though indeed the very forces which destroyed him (division and politicking in the army) had also brought him to power in 1952. The Cuban army and police – the two were closely connected at officer level – had greatly suffered from political division, ever since the Sergeants' Revolt of 1933. Batista's personal cronies, the men of 4 September 1933, headed by Tabernilla, who were kept out of most commands during the Auténtico period, returned in 1952. With their sons, brothers and other adherents, they kept all the commands to themselves. Not only the Auténtico officers (hardly a disadvantage to any armed forces)[6] but the younger career men, professionals without politics, had been thrust on one side; and even the supporters of Batista in 1952 were divided two years later; there were, for instance, those *tanquistas* who had wished to establish, with or without Batista, some sort of military authoritarian regime, possibly, similar to that in the Dominican Republic; there were also in Batista's regime several policemen, such as Carratalá or Ventura, who became commanders either in name or in fact, because of the nature of the armed civil war in the cities. There was social resentment among junior officers, especially those who wanted to go to senior officers' clubs and could not.[7]

Discipline among officers is bad if promotion derives overtly from favouritism. If there is indiscipline among officers, that of the ranks will be worse. Batistiano NCOs sought to ingratiate themselves with commanders by excess of zeal and brutality, knowing from experience that ingratiation with these officers led to results. Cowardly actions by privates led on occasion to promotions to corporalcies and sergeantcies. Officers regarded commands merely as means of enrichment by the use of intimidation. The army was rotten and became more so as time went on; at the same time there was an increasing gap between the reality of what was happening in Oriente and public announcements about it. Batista's officers, both of the police and of the armed services, spent their leisure at casinos or night clubs and enriched themselves by exacting protection money and other graft. Also, as during the first period of Batista's power, the army was the most favoured of institutions.

---

[5] Guevara's talk to *Nuestro Tiempo* Association, 27 January 1959, in *Oeuvres Révolutionnaires, 1959–1967* (1968), 25.

[6] They vanished from military or political life without a murmur, and with scarcely a trace (for example, see the list of senior officers in *Bohemia*, 3 August 1952), displaced by Batista's *madrugón*. Not one of them ever played a major part in politics again or indeed was ever heard of.

[7] e.g. Lieutenant Barrera to Ameijeiras, *Verde Olivo*, 12 May 1963.

New barracks for enlisted men, new clubs, new houses for officers, new military hospitals, were constantly built. In both periods, too, soldiers assumed many of the tasks normally conducted by the Ministries of Public Works, Health, Education, Labour, and the Interior; although rotten, the army was all-pervasive. Yet the ordinary soldier was ill-paid; he received a mere $30 a month; and by late 1958 it was almost impossible to secure recruits.

Batista's losses in the war against Castro were probably no more than 300 men.[8] But several officers (Villafaña, González Finales, Ubineo León, Quevedo, Oquendo, Durán Batista, Braulio Coronú) defected to Castro in late 1958. There was always some secret support for Castro in the armed services, particularly the navy, though, after the revolution of Cienfuegos, conspirators were somewhat cowed. One officer who had worked as second-in-command of Batista's military intelligence was a Castro spy.[9] By late 1958 the disillusion of junior officers with their leaders was widespread. Nor was the army well armed: the artillery batteries were the same make of Schneiders which defended Verdun; the coastal batteries were ancient Spanish, of Ordóñez make; the rifles were in many instances 1903 models.

Castro's task in the struggle was both to create in Cuba a situation of civil war, so that Batista's regime would become overtly identified with the army, and then to drive this army, forced into such prominence, to disintegrate or destroy itself through its own weaknesses, divisions, jealousies and errors. This he did and at the same time forced the Cubans to hate Batista, as a Cuban psychologist once commented;[10] this is doubtless a more explicit way of saying, as Guevara did in his subsequent manual on guerrilla warfare, 'one does not necessarily have to wait for a revolutionary situation: it can be created'.[11]

Morale in Batista's army declined further after the U.S. arms embargo. Until then, Batista could suggest in a hundred small ways that behind him stood if need be the armed might of the world's most powerful country. This impression was carefully fostered by visits from U.S. generals, admirals and politicians, and by frequent photographs in the press of officers of the U.S. military mission with Batista or Tabernilla. Batista's American press adviser, Edward Chester, assured these impressions wide currency. After the arms embargo, a pillar fell away from the *amour propre* of the regime; the government's dismay communicated itself to the army. A further blow was given to morale when in 1958, after much expectation, a Chief of Staff and central headquarters were

---

[8] Colonel Carrillo told a U.S. Senate Internal Security Sub-Committee in 1959 that his losses were 200 to 300 in fourteen months (*Communist Threat*, 361).

[9] Earl Smith, 202.

[10] To the author in 1961.

[11] Guevara, *Guerrilla Warfare*, 111. Trans. J. P. Morray (1961).

created. This supreme command was given to the discredited General Tabernilla, with promotions at the same time to a large number of other unpopular and discredited officers; when complaints became impossible to staunch, Batista resorted to promotions *en masse* of all officers.[12] Finally, Batista's own laziness and weakness damaged morale more than anything else: the president played canasta when he should have been making war plans; as his press secretary put it in exile, 'Canasta was a great ally of Fidel Castro'.[13] Quite apart from the issue of morale, Batista spent a lot of time dealing with his many private affairs, his foreign fortunes and their disposition, leaving himself too little time for affairs of state.[14] So too did Tabernilla: Julio Lobo relates that when Tabernilla billeted his men at the *central Pilón*, he was required to submit three invoices for goods supplied from the mill store, for the benefit of Tabernilla's private account.[15]

Castro's aim continued to be not to engage in combat but to maintain himself in being, occasionally raising morale in the cities and among his own men by some carefully planned and publicized assault on a well-selected outpost. The only way for the army to fight this elusive enemy would have been, as previously suggested, a painstaking system such as was constructed by the English in Malaya. Batista was incapable of this, and indeed any regular army, with traditions of discipline however bad, is always at a disadvantage compared with a little group such as Castro's. The small numbers of Castro's army was an advantage. When in midsummer 1958 Batista at last brought himself to admit the seriousness of the challenge to him and launched a major attack on the Sierra, the spirits of his comparatively large force were very low. Too many men were left to guard sugar mills. Officers showed themselves interested only in killing peasants. Different columns failed to communicate with others and let themselves be dealt with individually by Castro. The Cuban army, after all, had no experience, and therefore no traditions, of combat; the wars of independence had been fought by amateurs before the army was founded. No regiments had battle-honours, none had captured flags to flaunt in regimental chapels. Further, the army in 1957–8 was mostly untrained for jungle or guerrilla war while Castro's propaganda – both respecting his methods of war and his political aims – appealed strongly to the rank and file.

Guevara and Cienfuegos carried the war to Las Villas, where the Directorio Revolucionario had hung on through 1958 in conditions similar to Castro's in the Sierra Maestra the year before, though with less attractive and less gifted leaders. There were also the Communist

[12] Colonel Barrera Pérez, *Bohemia Libre*, 3 September 1961.
[13] Suárez Núñez, 11.
[14] *Ibid.*, 26.
[15] Evidence of Julio Lobo, 10 November 1968.

band led by Torres, an independent 26 July group under Víctor Bordón and the semi-banditry of the 'Second Front of Escambray'. These had done little before Guevara and Cienfuegos arrived in October 1958 – though almost as much as Castro had in his first six months in the Sierra. The new arrivals transformed the situation in Las Villas and indeed the war. Guevara's qualities of leadership turned out scarcely less than those of Castro himself, though they were more analytical and less intuitive. In addition, his arrival in Las Villas coincided with the adhesion of the Communist party to the revolutionary cause: this meant that the Communists of Las Villas, already under arms, were ready to give him every support. Perhaps they would have supported any leader of the 26 July – for instance, they backed Cienfuegos (who was less politically minded) as much as they did Guevara – but Guevara's political inclinations at the least helped effective collaboration. By December 1958 the province of Las Villas was in revolutionary tumult, a threat posed to communications with Oriente, the island perhaps cut in two; and in the middle of the month Guevara began his brilliant final campaign.

At the end of 1958 the rebel army was a heterogeneous group of about 3,000 at most, many of them civilian camp followers. In mid-1958 there had been a mere 300, and probably there were only about 1,500–2,000 persons in arms against Batista in early December, so that most of those who were in the fight at the end were recent recruits. Perhaps 200 were non-Cuban (North or South American); about 1 in 20 were women. The women were non-combatants except for the afterwards famous *Batallón Femenino*, which only suffered one casualty – one girl wounded.[16] These figures include those in Las Villas under Cienfuegos, Guevara and the Directorio. The youngest officer, Enrique Acevedo, was sixteen.[17]

The basic unit by late 1958 was a platoon of forty, commanded by a lieutenant, and the platoons, as usual, were grouped in companies led by captains. There were no formal NCOs, though some non-officers were given posts of responsibility. All could become officers. The highest ranked commanders were majors, of which by the end of 1958 there were perhaps forty. No one was paid.

By 1958 the rebels were usually fed regularly – usually rice with some

[16] Figure given by Castro in the third week of December 1958 to the U.S. correspondent Dicky Chapelle (Osanka, 327), and I have kept to it despite some claims to the contrary, e.g. Cienfuegos told *Revolución* (8 January 1959) that he reached Havana with about 7,000 men (*ibid.*, 13 January 1959). Goldenberg (*The Cuban Revolution and Latin America*, 162) says that he was told in February 1959 that there were 803 'officially recognized' soldiers of Castro in December. Javier Pazos prominent in the 26 July Movement in Havana and in the Sierra for a time, speaks of '2000, well-armed rebels' when Batista fled (*Cambridge Opinion*, February 1963). This is also Karol's (*Les Guerrilleros au pouvoir*, Paris 1970, 167 fn. 1).

[17] *Ibid.*, 7 January 1959.

beef; they had much better clothes, shoes and blankets than in 1957. Probably 85% of the weapons used had been captured[18] and indeed before April 1958 the quantity of arms brought to the Sierra from the cities was almost negligible: one large consignment after the failure of the attack on the palace, one flown in from Mexico in March. This was despite Castro's personal and constant insistence that the cities should dispatch arms to the Sierra as their first priority. By late 1958 the rebels had a few dozen jeeps, all captured, and some lorries.

At the end of the war, perhaps half the rebel army were squatters or field hands from coffee or sugar estates in the Sierra Maestra. Most of the others were town workers of some sort, though some were agricultural workers from other parts of Cuba.[19] Most of those who joined Castro in 1958 received some basic training in a remote part of the Sierra. All knew that if captured they would probably be killed, tortured, or both. This fear prevented them from going home while Batista continued in power. The leaders were exemplary. As well as Castro, Guevara, for instance, was regarded as first in the fight, first to help a wounded man, first to make sacrifices. The progressive views of the commanders were also a help to discipline: a Catholic, Israel Pérez Ríos, for instance, spoke of Guevara as an 'excellent man, a universal figure; his ideas are of such a wonderful humanity, and even though things have been said to attack his personality . . . I can assure you that his ideas derive from a generous heart'. Men felt the same of Cienfuegos: 'He was not a chief, he was a friend, a guide for us all; for the soldiers he was a father, teaching all, treating us with affectionate sincerity and teaching us to be human, so much so that he even insisted that prisoners should eat first.'[20]

The commander-in-chief (he signed himself as such on 1 January 1959) was of course Fidel Castro. His chief lieutenants were Guevara (in command in Las Villas) and Raúl Castro in command on the north coast of Oriente, based on the Sierra Cristal (the 'Second Front Frank País'). Camilo Cienfuegos, commander of the Antonio Maceo column in the north of Las Villas, was of equal rank, as was the mulatto Juan Almeida, commander of the Third Front (East) – that is, the region of Guantánamo. All these, including Castro, had the rank of major.

The rebel army by late 1958 was not only a fighting force. It included a large administration for the control of the *territorio libre* in Oriente: a secretariat, with branches in several different places; and sub-sections dealing with justice, health, education, even industry. In overall control of administration (with headquarters at La Plata) at the end of the

---

[18] Dicky Chapelle in Osanka, 334.
[19] For example, Universo Sánchez. Robin Blackburn in *'Prologue to the Cuban Revolution'* (*New Left Review*, October 1963), estimated 75% peasants.
[20] See reminiscences of these men in *Revolución*, 7 January 1959.

war was Faustino Pérez, the *Granma* medical student who before the unsuccessful strike of April had been commander of the 26 July underground movement in Havana and had afterwards come to the Sierra. The secretary-general of administration was René Ray, brother of the architect who commanded the civil resistance in Havana. The Justice Department was headed by Dr Humberto Sorí Marín. He, like Pérez and Ray, had worked in the Havana underground and previously had been an Auténtico. In command of the Health Department was Dr René Vallejo, a doctor from Manzanillo; of the Education Department, Rodolfo Fernández; of the Industry and Repair Department, José Pellón; and of personnel, Jorge Ribas, an engineer. In truth the rebel army, in its administration, its sheer size, and its varied activities was coming more and more to resemble a regular army and, in the end, no doubt, would have been compelled to fight in a regular style.

But as well as the war in Oriente and Las Villas, there was the civic resistance in the towns. These men and women suffered most from the repression. However many people were in truth killed in the civil war, the men or women, boys or girls of the cities accounted for most of the perhaps 1,500 to 2,000 casualties.[21] The significance of the Civic Resis-

[21] The numbers are not easy to estimate. In late 1957 Senator Conrado Rodríguez spoke of 300 being killed, promptly countered by Castro as being 5,000. In August 1958 Castro spoke of more than 6,000 being killed. Some time in late 1958, Grau San Martín spoke of 20,000 having been killed. The figure was quoted by the *New York Times* correspondent, but Batista denied it as grossly exaggerated. However, the number of 20,000 stuck and was afterwards widely used. It is doubtful if any of these estimates was more than a guess. The only list of the dead occurred in *Bohemia*, 11 January 1959 and afterwards in subsequent issues. This amounts to:

Rebels	429
Batistianos	153
In skirmishes killed by government	18
„ killed by rebels	85
„ killed by unknown	24
Terrorist bombs	25
Executed by 26 July (spies, etc.)	12
	746
Civilians killed, Santiago, July 1953	48
Attack on palace, March 1957	30
Naval revolt, Cienfuegos	62
Goicuría barracks, 1956	12
	152
GRAND TOTAL	898

My instinct is to suppose these figures roughly accurate. On the other hand they must ignore many peasants killed by the Army in Oriente – and that would probably raise the total by at least another few hundred. Definite figures will probably never be found but it is difficult to believe that more than 2,000 Cubans died between 1952 and 1958 as a direct consequence of the political crisis in Cuba and the Civil War. Nevertheless the figure 20,000 was being used within days of Batista's flight. *Revolución*, on 2 January, spoke of 'a hundred heroes and tens of thousands of dead'. *Cf.* Lazo, *Dagger in the Heart*, 124–5.

tance can hardly be exaggerated. No doubt it would not have got under way had it not been for Castro's presence in the hills. No doubt too the Civic Resistance by themselves could not have forced Batista to flee, but their continual activity and courage tied down police and soldiers and demoralized the government when they might have pooh-poohed the existence of Castro in the Sierra. The later contempt of Guevara and other revolutionaries[22] for these guerrillas of the plain (*llano*) was enormous, but scarcely just or appropriate, even though many of the leaders of the plain afterwards became politically eclipsed.[23]

Castro's presence in the hills, however, helped the disintegration of all other political opposition to Batista. Batista himself gave the *coup de grâce* in 1952 to the old political system of Cuba. Just as the 'system' of the early years of the Republic had been destroyed by one of its founders, General Machado, so the 'system' which arose out of the revolution of 1933 was destroyed in 1952 by Batista, the outstanding revolutionary of 1933, although the Auténtico failure to realize the promise of the system had helped it, like Batista's army, to die within itself.

The civil war of 1956–8 had polarized Cuba: by December 1958 the struggle resembled a single combat, between Batista and Castro. Auténticos such as Grau, Prío and Varona; Ortodoxos such as Ochoa, Agramonte, Bisbé and Márquez Sterling; Saladrigas or Martínez Sáenz, the old leaders of ABC, all these were pushed aside. Politicians of the older parties, such as Liberals (the first party of the early days of the Republic), who had in any way served Batista, were at the very least ruined. This ruin involved many politicians who had served Cuba, and themselves, during the previous twenty-five years. (Martínez Sáenz, who had served as president of the National Bank from 1952 to 1959 was soon arrested, along with Dr Ernesto Saladrigas and other politicians of Batista's days who had injudiciously remained in Cuba, such as Ernesto de la Fe, or Emeterio Santovenia.) In short, over the years, Batista had completed what administrative corruption, *gangsterismo*, mass unemployment and economic stagnation had begun: 'the Cuban people had completely lost faith in the men who had been ruling them but being a people of great vitality did not resign themselves to a mere vegetable life, and kept in their souls an enormous potential of faith and hope, afterwards mobilized by Castro'.[24]

---

[22] Such as Régis Debray, in *Révolution dans la Révolution*, 76 ff.

[23] *Cf.* Guevara, *Guerilla Warfare*. Debray's comments are concerned with the value of these experiences from the point of view of the future in South America. Experiences elsewhere, such as Aden, Cyprus, Ireland and the Resistance in Europe, would suggest that urban guerrillas may both be directed effectively from the city and be the decisive reason for the failure of the authorities against whom the rebellion is directed. Castro seemed to agree when in 1967 he encouraged Stokely Carmichael and the Negroes of North America to destroy the hearts of U.S. cities.

[24] Felipe Pazos, speech to Club de Leones, San Juan (Puerto Rico), 29 March 1961.

As with the Army, Castro had only to remain aloof, unbending, inscrutable in prison or in the hills, for the old political parties to kill themselves. Some Auténticos were discredited not only through the ill memory of their own days of power but because they had collaborated with Batista to a lesser or greater extent, as members of the official opposition with seats in the legislature, or as opposition candidates in the elections of 1954 or 1958. Grau was the most exposed in this respect, and indeed would figure in January among a list of professors of the university – he had retained his professorship in the medical faculty – to be purged. Others, through private squabbles, had lowered their prestige. Prío was the president whom Batista had displaced but he made no move to reassume power, to nominate himself as the legal president, and no one proposed the plan on his behalf. On 4 January he issued a declaration saluting the new revolutionary government and the revolution itself in 'this new era of democracy and liberty'.[25] He gave no support at all to the idea that the war had been won by a coalition in which he had played a part.

The Ortodoxos had also squabbled bitterly and fatally. In 1952 there had been one Ortodoxo party, loosely led by Eddy Chibás's lieutenant, Agramonte. Now in 1959 there were at least four such parties. While their divisions had weakened the old parties, so too had their failure to play a militant part in the physical struggle against Batista.

There had been, it is true, Auténticos in the attack on the palace, in the naval revolution at Cienfuegos, and of course in some of the attacks sponsored by Prío (such as Cándido González's attack on the north coast). But still the leaders had not been involved. Prío had sent expedition after expedition to its death in Cuba while himself remaining peacefully in Miami; Menelao Mora, the ex-Auténtico senator who died in the attack on the palace, had severed relations with Prío before the attack; while Ortodoxos who had taken part in the fight against Batista had rallied specifically to Castro's movement. Thus Felipe Pazos and Raúl Chibás were members of the 26 July, Chibás being now a 'major' and wearing a beard. Thus Agramonte was to become Foreign Minister in the first revolutionary government, Bisbé ambassador to the U.S.

Auténticos and others from older parties were discredited even if they had not taken part in Batista's regime. They were men who, like the country itself, had become adjusted to disorder and abnormality and the permanent political crisis of old Cuba. Many of them were excluded from participation in any future government by the decree of the Sierra (which now had the force of law) that banned all who had taken part in any of Batista's elections from public life for thirty years. The war

25 *Ibid.*, 5 January 1959.

indeed not only destroyed the administration, it destroyed the system which had preceded the administration; and no one heard any more of the Pact of Caracas or other wartime agreements. A slogan of Castro's in 1958 had demanded a struggle against 'the 10th March [1952] without a return to the 9th': a slogan which, as will be seen, had plenty of backing.

CHAPTER 21

Castro and the Americas in 1959

What or who was the victor? Castro had, of course, influences around him. Those who had been with him through the struggle in the Sierra were those to whom he listened. These voices, however, did not all sing the same song. Some, such as those of Juan Almeida, of Celia Sánchez, the doctor's daughter from Pilón, or Efigenio Ameijeiras, the new police chief, felt loyalty to him as a leader *tout court* and would probably have followed whatever policy he decided on. Others had views of their own: Raúl Castro and Guevara doubtless put the extreme view, not necessarily that of Marxism or Communism but that the choice for Cuba lay between two extremes: either to permit the North-Americanized *bourgeoisie* (among whom would be classified most of the old Ortodoxo leaders) to spoil the prospects of social revolution, or institute a dictatorship of the proletariat. This choice was probably laid before Castro at the beginning of his time in office and the evidence suggests that beneath the rhetoric of those days he was coolly attempting to decide in which direction to go; the known comforts, and the possible intellectual corruption of the first alternative, the risky unknown of the second. Even in allegedly ideological matters such precise decisions are usually, where politicians are concerned, matters of calculation. But Guevara and Raúl Castro, as the most prominent commanders, had throughout had much influence on Castro. Their siren voices were balanced by neither the non-Communists nor anti-Communists. Yet even Guevara's voice in 1959 did not speak unambiguously. He was not a Communist and had never been a party member.[1] In 1964 he was asked whether in the Sierra Maestra he had foreseen that the Cuban Revolution would take so radical a direction as it by then had. Guevara answered:

Intuitively I felt it. Of course the direction, and the very violent development of the revolution could not have been foreseen. Nor was the Marxist-Leninist formulation foreseeable ... We had a more or less vague idea of solving problems which we clearly saw affected the

[1] See above, 93. Early in January he denied specifically again that he was a Communist (*Revolución*, 6 January 1959).

peasants who fought with us and the problems we saw in the lives of the workers.[2]

Somewhat earlier he had explained, 'We were only a group of combatants with high ideals and little preparation . . . we had to change the structures and we began the changes without a plan.'[3] A Spanish journalist present in the Sierra overheard Castro upbraiding Raúl Castro for exchanging letters with Guevara on political philosophy, the latter 'disagreeing with many of the premises of Marxism'.[4]

As to Castro's views in 1958–9, Guevara answered in 1964:

> I knew he was not a Communist but I believe I knew also that he would become a Communist, just as I knew then that I was not a Communist, but I also knew that I would become one within a short time and that the development of the Revolution would lead us all to Marxism-Leninism. I cannot say that it was a clear or conscious knowledge but it was an intuition, the consequence of a . . . careful assessment of the development of the attitude of the U.S. . . . and the way in which [the U.S.] acted at that time . . . in favour of Batista.[5]

This vague statement by an often candid politician is perhaps as close as it is possible to apprehend Guevara's state of mind about 1 January 1959. But at the end of that month Guevara, in a talk to the *Nuestro Tiempo* Association – an intellectual group in Havana partly composed of Communists – launched most of the ideas which he afterwards developed into a fairly consistent philosophy: he explained how the rebels in the Sierra had become converted by the needs of the peasants to the idea of agrarian reform; how the experience of the Sierra proved that 'a small group of resolute men' can conquer a regular army and how this offered an example to the rest of Latin America, whose other peoples should also seek to free themselves in the same way; and how the rebel army would henceforth be the main agent of social reform in Cuba ('our first instrument of struggle . . . the avant-garde of the Cuban people'); and how ultimately the entire Cuban people should transform themselves into a guerrilla army.[6] These thoughts were put forward less dogmatically than was afterwards Guevara's custom, and he recalled that the Constitution provided for agrarian reform, suggesting that here at least the aim of the revolution should be to fulfil the Constitution. Nevertheless, one must assume that it was of this sort of

---

[2] Lisa Howard, ABC Television interview, 22 March 1964 (interviewed in February).
[3] Speech in Algiers, 13 July 1963 (*Hoy*, 16 July 1963).
[4] Enrique Meneses, *Fidel Castro*, trans. J. Halcro Ferguson (1968), 62.
[5] Lisa Howard, ABC, 22 March 1964.
[6] In a lecture, 'Social Role of the Rebel Army', published in Guevara, *Oeuvres Révolutionnaires*, 22–32.

idea, couched presumably in more forthright style, that Guevara spoke to Castro in their many talks. The agrarian reform envisaged by Guevara at this stage seemed however to be less collectivist in principle than still based on the old idea of the division of large estates, coupled with some form of tariff policy which would encourage a large home market.

As for Raúl Castro it is true that he had been a member of the Communist Youth; but he had not been an orthodox one; he had always been influenced by his brother more than by his party friends; further, he had now acquired power in his own right and did not desire to share it. He was evidently an extremist but was not necessarily one subservient to any party line.[7] His apparent difference with Guevara over details of Marxism speaks for itself.

The only commander of the rebel army who rivalled Guevara and Raúl Castro in rank and fame was Cienfuegos; for a time, indeed, Cienfuegos (the son of Spanish anarchists), with his open, jovial manner and warm smile, bid fair to become almost as popular as Castro himself. Castro later spoke of him as 'a pure revolutionary soul, Communist timber . . . as can be seen from his books, his writings, his unitary spirit, expressed in his letters where he speaks of Félix Torres [the Communist of Yaguajay], when he met him in Las Villas'.[8] Most people, however, had different judgements; 'definitely anti-Communist, not simply neutral';[9] 'a childlike fellow, always playing with guns'.[10] But Cienfuegos' influence on Castro was slight: and Castro said later that he might have been removed from his command because of his 'low political level'.[11] Cienfuegos came to prominence in the last three months of the war; his campaign in Las Villas had been far less well conducted than Guevara's. Guevara and Raúl Castro were more intimate comrades, though it is necessary to recall the former's delphic comment when, six years later, he left Cuba: 'My only serious failing was in not having confided more in you from the first moments in the Sierra Maestra and not having understood quickly enough your qualities as a leader and a revolutionary.'[12] It should also be recalled that Raúl Castro had been away from Castro's side in the Sierra almost since March 1958, and Guevara had been away since September.

[7] The conversation reported by R. López Fresquet, *My Fourteen Months with Castro* (1966), 162, is of interest here.

[8] *Obra Revolucionaria*, 1962 No. 10, 22 (26 March 1962).

[9] Evidence of Javier Pazos.

[10] Evidence of Raúl Chibás; López Fresquet, 58, calls him 'gay, happy-go-lucky, adventuresome'. Others point out that Cienfuegos was much under the influence of his brother Osmani, later an important figure during Cuba's Communist stage, who had been already in touch with Cuban Communists in Mexico.

[11] *Revolución*, 28 March 1962, 6.

[12] Letter to Castro of 1 April 1965. I assumed that this was genuine. For contrary comment see A. de la Carrera, in *The New Leader*, 25 October 1965, and S. Casalis, in *La República*.

Further, there was the paradox that the most anti-Communist of the 26 July members (such as the ex-Communist Franqui, the National co-ordinator Marcelo Fernández or Faustino Pérez in Havana) were also anti-U.S. and hostile to the Communists for being conservative, oppor-tunistic, *embourgeoisé*, and insufficiently critical of the colossus of the north.

Castro's appeal as the rebel chief was heightened by his eloquence. This became apparent to a wide audience for the first time in his speech at Céspedes Park in Santiago on the night of 1 January. He spoke simply but romantically, in a classical manner, at immense length, and without notes. His tall figure and dignified, youthful, but grave face, regular features with a beard, was a commanding one to those who saw him speak in the flesh. The effect was scarcely less on the wider audiences of television. Even in this first speech he touched the later familiar note of the wise counsellor, the father as well as the rebel; the eloquence was warm, comprehensible, geared to sustain the heroic epic of the revolu-tionary war:

> What greater glory than the love of the people? What greater prize than these thousands of waving arms, so full of hope, faith and affection towards us? Never have we let ourselves be carried away by vanity or by ambition, because, as our Apostle [Martí] said, all the glories of the world vanish like a grain of maize; there is no satisfac-tion and no prize greater than that of fulfilling our duty, as we have been doing up to now, and as we shall always do, and in this I don't speak in my name, I speak in the name of the thousands and thous-ands [a perhaps pardonable exaggeration] of combatants who have made victory possible: I speak of the . . . respect due to our dead, the fallen, who will never be forgotten . . . this time it will not be pos-sible to say, as on other occasions, that we will betray our dead, because this time the dead will continue in command. Physically, Frank País is not here, nor many others, but they are here spirit-ually – and only the satisfaction that their death was not in vain can compensate for the immense emptiness which they left behind them.[13]

Castro's political attitudes in January 1959 however were probably not quite clear even to himself. In a famous speech three years later he spoke surely a little too precisely on the subject:

> I believe absolutely in Marxism! Did I believe on 1 January [1959]? I believed on 1 January [1959] . . . Did I understand as well as today . . . no I did not . . . Could I call myself a faultless revolutionary on

[13] *Revolución*, 5 January 1959, 4.

1 January? No, I could not even then call myself an 'almost faultless revolutionary'.[14]

But which politician tells the truth three years later about his beliefs three years before? Can one demand greater consistency from revolutionaries than from liberals? When Castro spoke in this manner, he had engaged in a close alliance with the Communist party, by whom he was then in danger of being enveloped. For tactical reasons, he was seeking to prove his revolutionary worth. To Herbert Matthews in 1963 Castro said, 'At the time of the Moncada, I was a pure revolutionary but not a Marxist revolutionary. In my defence at my trial I outlined a very radical revolution but I thought then that it could be done under the Constitution of 1940 and within a democratic system. That was the time when I was a Utopian Marxist'.[15] Javier Pazos, an ex-Marxist ten years younger than Castro, and an urban plotter on Castro's staff in late 1957, commented in 1962: 'The Fidel Castro I knew in the Sierra Maestra ... was definitely not a Marxist. Nor was he particularly interested in social revolution. He was above all a political opportunist – a man with a firm will and an extraordinary ambition.'[16] A Spanish journalist recalled hearing Castro in the Sierra saying: 'I'm not breaking my neck fighting one dictatorship to fall into the hands of another', since he hated 'Soviet imperialism as much as Yankee imperialism'.[17] Other comments might be chosen, made by Castro himself and by others, to suggest the difficulty of making a judgement. On the other hand, several years later he was asked by an intimate how he would have managed in Cuba had it not been for the Soviet Union. He drew a cloud of smoke from his cigar and after due reflection remarked: 'I would have played with the national bourgeoisie for ten years but in the end it would have been the same thing'.[18] If Castro was already toying in January with taking Cuba into the Communist camp, his motives perhaps derived from a passion to enact the most difficult, heroic and independent role he could devise, rather than through conviction that the Marxist view of history was correct.

Those who knew Castro when young agree that he had always a

[14] *Obra Revolucionaria*, 1961 No. 46, 35.

[15] Herbert Matthews, *Return to Cuba*, 1964, 11. If words mean anything this suggests that Castro changed from 'pure revolutionary' to 'Utopian Marxist' between July and October 1953. But then, words do not always mean anything.

[16] *New Republic*, 2 November 1962.

[17] Meneses, 62.

[18] Reported by one who was there. Such *ex-post facto* remarks may not of course contain the truth. But Carlos Rafael Rodríguez, the experienced Communist representative with Castro in the Sierra Maestra later recalled a conversation with Castro in 1958, in the Sierra, during which Castro said that one of the defects of the Communist party's programme was that it defined too clearly the aims of the Revolution and so alerted the enemy. (C. R. Rodríguez, *La Revolución Cubana y el período de Transición*, Havana, mimeographed 1966, II, 37.)

passion for an historic role, for cutting a figure on the Latin American political scene which would echo the liberators Bolívar or San Martín. To cut a dash is so universal a desire in political life that no one should be surprised to discover it among the Cubans.

The experiences of the years of struggle, combined with Castro's own mercurial temperament, led him to see this role as that of the revolutionary leader *par excellence* – and the rebel of all America too: on 1 January in Santiago he explained that 'the eyes of all America' were on Cuba, that Cuba deserved to be one of the first countries of the world through its 'valour, intelligence and firmness'. What sort of revolution? Perhaps this was of less importance. Above all, 'the Revolution' had to be carried through to its most extreme point. Thus a letter in 1958 from Luis Buch (of the 26 July Movement in Santiago) to Armando Hart, then in prison, says: 'Justo Carrillo is a revolutionary and desires a moderate revolution: not what we are planning.'[19] 'The Revolution' would realize the dreams of Céspedes, Maceo and Martí, and, though many Cuban politicians had mouthed such aspirations before, Castro's personality, comparative youth and previous experiences made him psychologically insistent that this time there should be no compromise. 'The dead of the three wars of Independence will now mingle in their dust with those of 1956–9'. But times had changed, Martí's message might have to be re-interpreted. This was, after all, to be, according to Castro, 'a Revolution of the whole people'. The disillusions of the past, of 1898 and 1933, caused Castro, a link in a long chain, to be inevitably more radical. In the same first speech in Santiago on the night of 1 January he told his audience, 'The Revolution is now beginning. The Revolution will not be an easy task ... but in this initial stage especially, full of danger.' But it would not be what happened in 1895–8, 'when the Americans intervened at the last minute and prevented Calixto García from being present at the fall of Santiago'. Nor would it be as in 1933 when first Carlos Manuel de Céspedes, then Batista, came to betray 'the Revolution', nor as in 1944 when 'those who arrived in power turned out to be thieves'. Judge Piedra, whom Cantillo had tried to make president, had also had the Christian names Carlos Manuel; but there would be 'no new Carlos Manuel'.[20] The revolution would not come in a day, but it would be achieved eventually. For the first time the Republic would be really free – 'the first time in four centuries'.[21]

What did 'the Revolution' mean? Members of the 26 July Movement

---

[19] Carrillo MSS (the letter was copied to the Montecristi movement).

[20] *Revolución*, 3 January 1959. The imagery of 1898 and 1933 was persistently used by other orators, for example Armando Hart, at the University on 6 January. At least once the 'betrayal' of the Spanish Republic, by Chamberlain, was cited in January as an example to avoid (28 January 1959).

[21] *Ibid.*, 4 January 1959.

always suggested that they were aware of the long 'revolutionary' past; they spoke of 'revolutionary obligations' and 'revolutionary duties' as if the adjective covered known and fully acceptable goals long ago worked out. But in his Santiago speech, Castro mentioned little specific save a plan for a school for 20,000 peasant children in the Sierra Maestra, a project which had been on his mind at least since he left Mexico.[22] On 5 January, in Camagüey, he said 'we have fought so that there will never again be censorship'[23] – a view to which he returned in Havana. On 6 January, at Matanzas, he was more explicit: 'We are going to attack illiteracy, graft, vice, gambling and disease'. The people of Cuba would save themselves morally.[24] In a letter from the prison of Principe in mid-1958, Armando Hart, who was of course pre-eminent in the 26 July Movement, had taken part in García Barcena's precursor, and who was furthermore of a Catholic, middle-class family, had written:

> I have here made concrete the two aspects of all revolutionary conduct: indoctrination of the *militancia* about where we are going, how we are going, and what we are, for the attainment of a greater integration and a full and comprehensible understanding of all the real forces which compose the community . . . so that we all are able to play our proper role in the full development of the revolution . . . if we do not triumph it will be because we do not have the right historical moment . . . [The letter closed] without more than a revolutionary embrace to all the comrades.[25]

The opaque vagueness about aims concealed, however, resolution about methods. In 1961 Castro was asked by a journalist whether, when in the Sierra Maestra, he had imagined that the revolution 'would assume the aspect that it presently has'. Castro replied, 'We knew what kind of revolution we desired . . . and that that revolution would advance as rapidly as the objective conditions of its development would permit. We wanted to give to our people the maximum of justice and well-being.'[26] From what Castro later said of his opinions in 1958–9, from his later views, and from consideration of his past, it is clear that Castro in January 1959 was a radical nationalist, willing or anxious to use 'revolutionary' methods to obtain his ends, but uncertain of the precise nature of those ends, of their practicality and of the wisest way of

[22] Llerena MSS, 30, recalls a conversation about 'school cities' in Mexico in 1956. This later matured as the City School Camilo Cienfuegos.

[23] *Revolución*, 5 January 1959.

[24] *Ibid.*, 7 January 1959.

[25] Letter to Quintín Pino, 25 July 1958 (Carrillo archives).

[26] *Revolución*, 13 May 1961. He added, 'we will continue advancing the revolution for as long a time as our forces and the circumstances permit us to do it.'

going about realizing them. He was more 'extreme' than he had made himself out to Herbert Matthews and Andrew St George in the Sierra Maestra and his experiences in the Sierra had deepened his self-confidence and his ambition. He was not a Communist in the sense of being a secret party member or a man much influenced by Marx's writings. On the contrary, he was already more 'revolutionary', genuinely nationalistic, unconventional, ambitious and audacious than the Cuban Communist party, which he regarded with almost the same suspicion that he looked on the other, rather similarly organized Communist parties of Latin America, during the late 1960s. Indeed, his ambition was too great, his temperament too quixotic to enable him to submit to the discipline and higher authority such as Communism regards as necessary; and the name, though not the policy, of his first political grouping in the late 1940s – *Unión Insurreccional Revolucionaria* – would have been quite appropriate for his inner group of followers in 1959.[27]

There was always in this undefined addiction to revolution for its own sake a certain Garibaldian romanticism as expressed particularly in the revolutionary slogans and catchwords – thus quite soon Castro ended his speeches with the slogan *Patria o Muerte* (in place of *Victoria o Muerte*), *Venceremos*! (Fatherland or Death, we shall conquer): a direct echo of the Risorgimento, even though they also echoed the epoch of the War of Independence (Mambí mottoes were *Independencia o Muerte* from 1895 to 1898 and *Patria y Libertad*, after 1902 – a slogan still seen on Cuban coins). It is almost as if Castro and his colleagues were in love with the concept of revolution, or with the word.[28] But then had this not been the tone of Cubans since at least 1895? Martínez Ortiz, in his history of the first years of Cuban independence, is found assuring his readers that the new municipal Council of Havana in 1899 was composed of 'revolutionaries of good stock', though these included Alfredo Zayas[29]; Horacio Ferrer, who was secretary of war in Céspedes's 'liberal' government in 1933, was described as 'a revolutionary who sweetens and enhances the significance of that word', in the preface to his autobiography.[30] Chibás described himself as a 'revolutionary' from his twentieth year and Grau had conceived his government in 1933 as such; 'we are the only pure revolutionaries in Cuba, doctor', Justo Carrillo had said of himself and the students to Grau in December 1933, when the latter's regime seemed to be crumbling.

---

[27] See the study of Castro by Carlos Diago in *Cambridge Opinion*, February 1963.
[28] *Cf.* Namier: 'The term was still current by force of ideological and linguistic survival; for ideas outlive the conditions which gave them birth and words outlast ideas.' (*England in the Age of the American Revolution*, 2nd edn, 4.)
[29] Martínez Ortiz, I, 35.
[30] Ferrer, *Con el rifle al hombro*, xi.

Indeed Chibás's use of the word explains much; he termed his democratic Left organization 'Izquierda Revolucionaria'; and in an article in 1937 he explained that 'Revolution is not a synonym for violence. Terrorists and extremists have never made any Revolution in any part of the world but on the contrary have frustrated many'.[31]

Further, though it might seem to outsiders that the concept of 'Revolution' was immature or absurd, or both, it was evidently an indigenous one, unlike that of 'democracy' or 'constitution': it was a concept linking the Cuba of 1959 with that of 1868, comprehending the struggle for freedom by slaves, by *criollos* against Spaniards, by Cubans against the U.S.; 'nothing more idiotic can be imagined than the attempt to establish a liberal government under Spanish laws', General Wood had said; but nevertheless Cuba in the twentieth century was an old and quite different culture from that of the U.S., and however weak it might seem to Americans of Wood's generation, something of that culture survived – or at least people hoped it did, or hoped to make it do so. The North Americans' effort to impose their own values, however superior, on Cuban ones, however 'decadent' was almost certain to falter.[32] And, despite vagueness about what the revolution meant, the nation soon heard of counter-revolutionaries – for instance 'the Cantillo group'; listening to Castro's speech at Campamento Columbia, the Cubans heard of 'enemies of the revolution' for the first time.

But the concept of 'the Revolution', however explained, was fundamental: people had talked of Revolution so much for twenty-five years that Castro was able ultimately to cause international upheaval by merely carrying out what his predecessors among reformist politicians in Cuba said they had already done themselves.[33] Before 1959 Castro had no ideology, even if perhaps he coveted one privately. All was vague, if heroic. Both he and the leaders of the 26 July generally had certain general ideas of nationalism and of social reform, but there was no explicit programme. When the revolution had to be defined, it divided.[34] Like all revolutions, its vision of the Utopian future was sustained by a view of the past.[35]

In fact by January 1959 Castro had already spoken of a number of goals. There had been the 'Fundamental laws' of the Moncada speech, and most recently the Caracas manifesto. There had been several other

[31] Conte Agüero, *Chibás*, 236.

[32] See Henry Wriston, in John Plank's *Cuba and the U.S.*, 38.

[33] Mario Llerena put this well, in *Bohemia Libre*, 20 January 1963: 'The people of Cuba were familiarized with the idea of the word 'Revolución'. . . . For thirty years they knew nationalist slogans and social achievements.'

[34] Thus Castro: 'As the Revolution becomes more defined, as the Revolution advances . . . progresses ideologically, the number of persons who can fit within the Revolution becomes reduced.' (Speech, *Revolución*, 11 November 1961).

[35] See C. A. M. Hennessy, 'The Roots of Cuban Nationalism', *International Affairs*, July 1963.

policy documents and many near-commitments to journalists, some dealing with personal matters, some public. None of these had been worked out in much detail, most were tactical compromises to gather more support. In 1961 Castro said to a North American:

Sometimes in the mountains, between fighting, I'd think of what would happen when we won, how we would have a new party and fight for the people's needs ... and it was all silly. Once we won, we had the power to do things; we didn't need party politics ... in the Sierra ... we could only think of politics in the old way, without realizing that it was not such a good way ... [He added] I'm a middle-class man with middle-class ideas, many ideas learned in school and never matched against life'.[36]

Castro told Karl Meyer in September 1958 that he personally was not interested in belonging to a revolutionary government.[37] He repeated this in a letter written to Colonel Rego Rubido on 31 December: 'Personally, power does not interest me.'[38] In his first speech at Santiago he said, 'Let no one think that I have pretensions to go above and beyond the President of the Republic', adding, 'fortunately we are immune to ambitions and vanities'.[39] These statements were either deceptions or self-deceptions, unless (which is not inconceivable, though improbable) he was so bowled over by the nature of his public backing in the next few weeks as to change his mind.[40]

If Castro coveted power, and if, once obtained, he like most other politicians would not give it up without a struggle, and if he was certain to use that power in a revolutionary style, the U.S. would inevitably be implicated. For so long the U.S. ambassador had been at least the second strongest man in Cuba. The U.S. regarded Cuba as in some ways her closest foreign friend. The economies of Cuba and the U.S. were really one. In 1959, the value of U.S. investment in Cuba was still greater than it was in any other Latin American country save for Venezuela, and, on a *per capita* basis, the value of U.S. 9nterprises in Cuba was over three times what it was anywhere else in Latin America. However, apart

---

[36] Carl Marzani, 'Fidel Castro: a Partisan View', *Mainstream*, May 1961.

[37] Evidence of Karl Meyer.

[38] *Revolución*, 4 January 1959.

[39] *Ibid.*, 5 January 1959.

[40] For instance, in April 1961 on a film for *Radio télevision française*, Castro said: 'I must admit that we [i.e. himself] really believed for a time that it would be possible to leave the power to others: we were a little ... utopian. In the first days after victory, we kept away from the government altogether and took no part in the decisions of the Council of Ministers ...' (qu. Dewart, 82). Celia Sánchez remarked to Herbert Matthews later 'we could not know that when victory came we and the 26 July Movement would be so strong and popular. We thought we would have to form a government with Auténticos, Ortodoxos and so forth. Instead, we found that we could be the masters of Cuba.' (Herbert Matthews, *Castro, A Political Biography*, London, 1969, 100.)

from sugar they were in utilities, and these were, or seemed to be, monopolies, and therefore also seemed to be identified with the government or at least regulated by it. These facts, combined with the U.S. Government's continued lease of the base at Guantánamo, meant that a political explosion was always near or could be made to be. They also meant that the U.S. businessmen, mill-owners and planters, would expect to appeal to the Embassy of the U.S.[41] The intimate association of U.S. and Cuban commercial interests made all Cuban governments of concern to the U.S. Castro was, however, determined from the start to avoid fitting into the familiar pattern of the progressive Latin American leader who, after a year or two of verbose power, becomes a docile puppet of Washington.[42] He was also, almost from the start, hostile to the grouping of 'Liberal' Caribbean leaders, such as Figueres of Costa Rica, Muñoz Marín of Puerto Rico, or Betancourt of Venezuela. Maybe it was a question of age. These men seemed to Castro, perhaps were, rather patronizing, in welcoming him as a junior member to the club which they had founded.

Eisenhower's America also expressed itself patronizingly. The difference in temperament between Eisenhower and Castro could hardly have been greater. But differences in temperament need not necessarily cause national quarrels. The two men themselves never met. The tension which later grew between Castro's Cuba and Eisenhower's U.S. had deeper roots. First, Castro's Cuba aspired to heroism and to an epic identity. Eisenhower's realm was comfortable. Castro's own temperament required tension, probably demanded an enemy; if possible a situation where he could pose, or remain, as the rebel chief embattled, surrounded by enemies (hence the very early allusions to enemies of the revolution, or counter-revolutionaries). Further, as two years later he himself suggested,[43] the kind of revolution which he had in mind, even in January 1959, had a definite use for an enemy, for an opponent who could be used, by playing on nationalism, to seal national differences. Thirdly, the relations of Cuba and the U.S., anyway since 1898, had been of a classic ambiguity.[44] Many Cuban intellectuals had looked forward for years to a day of reckoning. They read the books or lectures of Herminio Portell Vilá, Ramiro Guerra or Fernando Ortiz, castigating U.S. diplomacy or the sugar society which the U.S. seemed to sustain, and dreamed of vengeance. To choose to be free meant for

[41] See Leland Johnson, 'U.S. Business Interests in Cuba and the Rise of Castro', *World Politics*, April 1965. These matters are also explored below, on page 390.

[42] See below, 428.

[43] Two years later Castro stated baldly (*Obra Revolucionaria*, 25 January 1961, 6):, *Una Revolución que no fuese atacada, en primer lugar no sería, positivamente, una verdadera revolución. Además, una revolución que no tuviera delante un enemigo, correría el riesgo de adormecerse.'*

[44] 'Almost unbearable burdens' was the phrase of Theodore Draper, Castro's most intelligent critic in the U.S.

many Cubans, and above all for Castro, to act in a way most calculated to anger the U.S.[45]

Cuban intellectuals were also aware of the cultural threat of the U.S., just as Canadians had been a few years before, at the time of the Massey report, just as in the late 1960s other and grander countries, even in the Old World, became so. These feelings seem not to have been those of the mass: North Americans had always been more popular in Cuba than in Mexico or other countries. The revolutionaries, however, were suspicious of the U.S., not only because of the remote but also the recent past: the identification of the official U.S., through its ambassadors and its colonels of the military mission, with Batista; the use of U.S.-made bombs in the civil war; the failure of North Americans in Cuba to remark the police tortures and atrocities – precisely as had occurred in the days of Machado; all this assured that relations between the revolutionary and Eisenhower governments would be likely to be cool anyway at first. Castro only mentioned the U.S. once in his first, Santiago, speech (to point out their role in preventing the Cubans from getting the benefit of their 'victory' in 1898). He also said, gratuitously, that when 'the hour' came there would not be 4,000 but 400,000 Cubans ready to defend their liberties, if need be.[46] His silence on the subject was ominous, as was the extreme, exclusive nature of his patriotism: if Cuba had been unhappy in the past, who was more to blame than the U.S.? Revenge often plays a major part in the decisions of private life. Who can be surprised if it also does in public matters?

Many Cubans had in the past thought vaguely and disconnectedly about the U.S. as did Castro: in a sense, Castro made them live up to, or down to, these thoughts. Secondly, Castro had no plan.[47] If an opportunist, as Javier Pazos claimed, he was an inspired one, intuitively capable of seizing the right moment and wringing from it all the advantages. It is impossible to believe that in January 1959 his mind was made up to create, say, in Cuba a Communist state; impossible too not to believe that he was going to press far whatever he did. Like most Cubans, Castro did not seem to be personally anti-American; but he saw in a challenge to the U.S. one way to assert the idea at least of freedom; maybe the easiest way. To challenge the U.S. and withstand

[45] In 1969 the Communist leader, Carlos Rafael Rodríguez was asked: did the U.S. push Castro into Communism? 'No. Fidel always had a radical idea of the sort of revolution which he desired. But you might say that the U.S., by its actions, accelerated events in the Cuban Revolution.' Conversation with the author, January 1969.

[46] *Revolución*, 5 January 1959.

[47] These two last comments echo A. J. P. Taylor's comment on Hitler and the Germans in their relations to the Jews in *The Origins of the Second World War*. On the other hand it is doubtless true that, because of the much reduced economic role of the U.S. in Cuba since 1933, 'anti-imperialist tendencies in the upper and middle classes were weaker than they had been a generation before'. (Goldenberg, *The Cuban Revolution and Latin America*, 13.)

her rage: to avenge General Shafter's insult to General Calixto García in 1898; to avenge Sumner Welles's less studied insult to Grau San Martín in 1933; was not this the only way whereby, by antique instinct an honourable Cuban could find freedom?

The only real Cuba remained after all a rebel Cuba. Always in the past when rebels had captured power, they had become a new cause for protest. The only honourable national identity which the Cubans could disentangle from the last tumultuous hundred years was that of rebellion. Castro, the rebel incarnate who hardly ever again was seen dressed other than in the olive green uniform of the rebel of the Sierra, consciously or unconsciously appreciated that the only way of maintaining the integrity of both his rebellion and of the long tide of rebellions which preceded it, was to continue the rebellion, not now against Batista but against the ambiguous unpredictable colossus of authority who had been for so long Batista's friend, the U.S.: his first finance minister, López Fresquet, remarked, 'Castro planned to socialize Cuba. He believed that this would automatically alienate the U.S. He therefore gave up the hope of American friendship from the start.'[48] But did he not in fact desire first to 'alienate' the U.S. and then plan to socialize Cuba in consequence? Castro's desire to challenge the U.S., if not his hatred of it, appears deeply based.[49] In June 1958, Castro had written, after a bomb had dropped on a peasant's house, 'I swore to myself that the Americans were going to pay dearly for what they were doing. When this war is over, a much wider and bigger war will begin for me: the war that I am going to launch against them. I am saying to myself that is my true destiny.'[50]

The century-old anxiety was exacerbated by the contemporaneous one of the Eisenhower administration. Dulles was still Secretary of State in January 1959. For him and for the Administration generally, neutralist governments had been distrusted as much as outright enemies. Dulles and his brother Allen, still head of the CIA, had presided over the destruction of the Arbenz regime in Guatemala. Guevara had been present at the climax of that counter-revolution. He, Castro and their lieutenants knew that when it came to almost any reform there would be those in the U.S. who would demand 'action' (the marines or the CIA) to overthrow the Cuban government. He knew that 'Revolution', involving anything like the nationalization of U.S. property – an irresistibly attractive course for a Latin American revolutionary leader in power – would cause such voices to be widely listened to. He believed

---

[48] López Fresquet, 167.

[49] *Cf.* Philip Bonsal, 'Cuba, Castro and the U.S.', *Foreign Affairs*, January 1967: 'It was not Castro's predilection for Communism but his pathological hatred of the American power structure as he believed it to be . . . in Cuba that led him eventually into the Communist camp.'

[50] Quoted Herbert Matthews, *Castro, a political biography*, 107.

perhaps that there was a risk of some sort of tension with the U.S. whatever he did in the direction of reform.

He was, as it happened, partly misinformed. The U.S. no longer opposed neutralism *tout court*. Conservatives in the State Department, in business, and in other government agencies were less well placed in 1959 than in 1954. Among many North American government employees (Wieland, Rubottom, Philip Bonsal, in particular) there was a strong desire to help a reforming government in Cuba. These men were critical of, even hostile to, the businessmen who had been ambassadors in Cuba since 1952. The U.S. had at the turn of 1958–9 no policy towards Cuba or really towards Latin America. Attacks on Vice-President Nixon had suggested that something was wrong, but it was unclear what. There were so many other problems. Castro, who had been for so long hidden from the world, did not know quite how untypical Ambassador Smith was. Ironically, Ambassador Smith was right in his judgement that the Castro regime would turn out to be Communist; a greater irony was that the tendency of men such as Gardner and Smith to see Communists behind every bush helped to make that regime welcome Communism.

There was one other no less important element in the argument. A strong democratic and constitutional regime would by the nature of things have received much support from the enlightened section in the government of the U.S.; aid, technical assistance, investment would have poured in; no doubt the Cuban standard of living would have gone up; no doubt most Cubans, above all most middle-class Cubans, but much of the working class too, would have enjoyed a better life; but it would not have been a Cuban life; it would have been a department of U.S. life, with all its *splendeurs et misères*. Perhaps Castro subconsciously appreciated that here was a last chance of affirming an insular individuality, partly hispanic, partly African, at all events not North American.

Was there any principle involved in the U.S. judgement of whether a regime in another country was good or bad at that time? Perhaps that would have been too strong a word, for the U.S., from habit, regarded the western hemisphere quite differently from the way it regarded Europe or Africa. There, one-party states, even Communist states might be tolerated, even traded with. Those countries were the sphere of influence of others, the Truman doctrine notwithstanding – though even there, in the first moments of the power of an ideologically reprehensible government, the U.S. government would not have 'stood idly by'. Latin America and the Caribbean were a different matter. Since the 1820s and the still far from musty Monroe doctrine, the notion of a state actively hostile to the U.S. in the western hemisphere was barely conceivable.

It was certainly something to be avoided at all costs. The principle of freedom was not the main one, unless that were defined as the system of economic free enterprise. Diplomacy was not dictated by the commercial interests of the U.S. in Latin America, though evidently, since those interests were large, that was a factor. Diplomacy was dictated by friendship or enmity, 'our son of a bitch' against their *enfant de miracle*.

Cuba was a special case. The long years of political, economic, social and cultural dominance of the U.S. in Cuba made many North Americans who went to Cuba – perhaps most of them – patronizing. Havana had been for so long the place for the good time, the prostitute, and the cigar, the blue film, the daiquirí at Sloppy Joe's or the Florida Bar, the quick win at the roulette table. 'Best place to get drunk', Errol Flynn wrote on a menu at the Bodeguita del Medio, a famous restaurant near the cathedral. So many North Americans indeed had had such a good time in Cuba that it never occurred to them that these associations could be humiliating to Cubans. In addition they knew nothing of the far from negligible intellectual life of Cuba. Their history books did not mention José Martí, nor even their encyclopaedias. For North Americans, the Cuban War of Independence was a forgotten prologue to the Spanish American War, and even historians believed that the U.S. Army doctors, Walter Reed and William Gorgas, had alone discovered the cause of yellow fever without help from the Cuban doctor, Carlos Finlay. In 1956 there were two major rows between the U.S. and Cuba even under Batista, one when the winner of the television game, the $64,000 question, won the prize for saying that Walter Reed and not Carlos Finlay had found the cure for yellow fever, one when the Hollywood film 'Santiago' made Martí and Maceo absurd. These tactless and ignorant attitudes resembled British views of Arab or Egyptian nationalism. They marked the conduct of U.S. politicians and diplomats as well as businessmen and tourists and were themselves reflected in Cuban intellectual life.[51]

Finally, and again this was peculiar to Cuba, the commercial relations between Cuba and the U.S. were open to every misunderstanding, and had so been since the Commercial Treaty of 1904, whose essential outlines were renewed in 1934: Cuba could indeed sell a great deal of sugar to the U.S. at very favourable prices. This arrangement not only made it more difficult for Cuba to diversify her production but also enabled U.S. companies to flood Cuba with a vast range of cheap and sometimes pointless goods, the sale of which by North American methods of advertising further debilitated the cultural life of the Cubans.

[51] See essay by D. C. Corbitt and José R. Machado, *The Vindication of Carlos Finlay as an element in U.S.-Cuban relations*, published in R. F. Smith, *Background to Revolution*, New York 1966, 74.

In the previous fifteen years the relations between the U.S. and Latin America had changed in many ways, but above all in the contrasts now even more sharply poised: U.S. power was the greatest in the whole world, not merely in the western hemisphere. Her standard of living was outrageously high in comparison with that in Latin America, which in some countries had even dropped in comparison with the 1920s. Her military forces were so well equipped and so numerous as to be quite out of the class of the other nations of the western hemisphere. The alliances which she had bilaterally made in the hemisphere had enabled some of the old successor nations of the Spanish empire to change their armies and police from ragged barefoot gangs of thugs into skilled and sophisticated twentieth-century praetorians, making governments stronger, and increasing the availability of weapons throughout the continent.[52] Unique source of firepower – no other nation in the Americas had an armament industry on anything like such a scale – the U.S. was also by now by far the greatest source of investment. Long past were the days when England could compete.

The wealth, though not necessarily the standard of living, of Latin America had increased. In Venezuela there were oil millionaires, but oil had not greatly improved the lives of workers in the Orinoco valley. During the 1950s, commodity prices had slumped so that the increase of production brought no help. In the same period the U.S. drew out of Latin America more profits than she invested – as was the case in respect of underdeveloped nations generally. Latin Americans also drew money out of their own countries faster than it was put in,[53] partly because of the well intentioned U.S. policy of encouraging social reform.

The general policy of the U.S. had perceptibly changed with the economic changes. Roosevelt's Good Neighbour policy, with its affirmation of non-intervention, had made for the U.S. many friends in Latin America. But now these friends were themselves old or dying. Radicals though they may have been in the 1930s, they were now preservers of the *status quo*; and that *status quo*, that definition of the relationship between the U.S. and Latin America, was more and more expressed less in living bonds, than in legal or diplomatic ones. 'Except for the Export-Import Bank,' Arthur Schlesinger noted, the Good Neighbour policy 'lacked an economic dimension'.[54] Yugoslavia, he pointed out, a Communist country, received more economic aid

[52] During the missile crisis of 1962 for instance, Castro castigated the U.S. for the fact that Batista's bombs were U.S.-made (*Obra Revolucionaria*, 1962, No. 31, 10). But the vast majority of arms in Latin America are U.S.-made. Certainly most of Castro's were in the Sierra Maestra, apart from a few old German and English guns.

[53] René Dumont (*Cuba, Socialisme et Développement* (1964)) estimated there was $M20,000 deposited in Latin American accounts in Switzerland.

[54] Schlesinger, *A Thousand Days* (English ed., 1967), 155.

between 1945 and 1960 than all South and Central America. There was another point: North American reformers, pragmatic, liberal and to a large extent successful, did not live in the same intellectual tradition as the rhetorical, schematic, romantic, system-loving hispanic Americans in the south. South Americans have been accustomed, like all patriarchal societies in decline, to see societies in terms of political clashes between classes; classifications of societies into landowners, capitalists, working class and peasants merely seem old-fashioned, even a trifle insulting in the North, which had never been patriarchal. Despite the new and sophisticated interest in Latin America in Washington since Vice-President Nixon's disastrous journey there in the spring of 1958, it was hard to see how the South could be for the North of America anything other than an enemy or a colony. At the same time, all Cuban intellectuals, in addition to their schematic view of their society, had at the back of their minds a large fund of anti-U.S. emotions, partly obsolete, partly superficial which, deriving from the era of the Platt Amendment or from Sumner Welles's Cuban posting in 1933, were nevertheless an important part of their rhetorical culture.

CHAPTER 22

L'Illusion Lyrique

'A decent moment': thus Ernest Hemingway with customary understatement on Cuba in January 1959, 'after a period of violent readjustment'. There would now, he added, be a peaceful government.[1] The flight of a tyrant, the defeat of his minions, the capture of power by young men, the miraculous culmination of a brave gesture, the attention of the world; an honest army guarding public buildings; great projects for reform ahead; young men ready for any job, any undertaking, whatever their experience or lack of it: these things gave Cuba in early 1959 an extraordinary mood of hope, confidence, enthusiasm, comradeship. Certain companies such as José Bosch's Bacardí Rum Company and the Hatuey Beer Company offered to pay their annual taxes in advance.

The new government was the first reason for enthusiasm. No one knew the provisional president, Judge Urrutia; but he appeared nevertheless the ideal chief magistrate, a good judge, conventional maybe but a man who, if a test came, would act decisively, even bravely. The prime minister, Miró Cardona, it seemed, was a man of much the same kidney; a respectable and intelligent lawyer who also had refused to bow to the dictator; as dean of the College of Lawyers he had been, with de la Torriente, the moving spirit of whose Civic Dialogue and he had been the secretary-general nominally supposed to co-ordinate the work of the Frente formed by the Pact of Caracas. The first cabinet of the Revolutionary Government (as it was named) was divided between men who were of the same age and background as these two and those who, much younger, were followers of Castro; in the first group, Agramonte, the Ortodoxo presidential candidate in 1952, became Foreign Minister; Rufo López Fresquet, an economist and tax expert who had been columnist on economics for the *Diario de la Marina*, technical adviser to the Finance Minister under Grau, and manager of the industrial division of the Development Bank under Prío, became Finance Minister;[2] Cepero Bonilla, also an economist and journalist, became Minister of Commerce; Angel Fernández, another middle-class lawyer,

---

[1] Hemingway (then in the U.S.) had lived off and on in Cuba for years, at Cojímar where he said twelve boys had been tortured and killed by Batista's police (*Revolución*, 23 January 1959).

[2] See López Fresquet, 8; López Fresquet had been in private practice under Batista and had worked in the Resistencia Cívica. He had been offered the Finance Ministry in early 1958.

friend of Urrutia's, became Minister of Justice, his under-secretary, Yabur, being an old collaborator of Manolo Castro in the university and a minor Ortodoxo politician; Luis Orlando Rodríguez, once secretary-general to the Auténtico Youth Movement, and the leader of the anti-Communist university group, familiarly known as El Bonche Universitario, and then an Ortodoxo, who had joined the 26 July Movement and gone to the Sierra to edit *Cubano Libre*, after his newspaper, *La Calle* (which had sponsored Castro in 1955), had been closed, became Minister of the Interior and henceforth wore a tailored uniform and shining boots; and Manuel Fernández, ex-follower of Guiteras in the 1930s, member of Joven Cuba, and in the 1950s of García Barcena's MNR, a romantic revolutionary, became Minister of Labour; a little younger was Regino Boti, an economist, son of a well-known patriarchal poet of Guatánamo, co-author with Felipe Pazos of the revolution's only existing economic plan, who returned from ECLA[3] to become Minister of Economics; while Elena Mederos, the only woman in the government, was a tireless social worker who became Minister of Social Welfare. Associated too with this group were other prominent men such as Felipe Pazos and Justo Carrillo, who returned to be presidents of the National and the Development Banks respectively, posts which they had held under Prío, and resigned at Batista's *golpe*. Pazos had gone through, in company with Raúl Chibás, the bizarre controversy with Castro at Miami: but in the euphoria of victory such events were temporarily forgotten. Emilio Menéndez, one of the few judges who had clean hands in the Batista era, took over as president of a new Supreme Court. Ernesto Dihigo, a noted lawyer and once Prío's Foreign Minister, became ambassador to the U.S. Manuel Bisbé, leader, like Agramonte, of one sect of the Ortodoxos, became ambassador to the U.N. The adherence of all these men made the government resemble, in one way, the sort of cabinet that Agramonte might have appointed had he been elected President in 1952: decent men, for the decent time.

Their '*bourgeois*' nature, however, hid the fact that they ruled over a vacuum. Foreign governments assumed that, since they were men of the middle class, their government would also be middle class; and Urrutia certainly settled in quickly to the agreeable tasks of a Cuban president in the old style, his day spent receiving journalists and old friends, the grand master of the Masonic Lodge, priests and bishops, ex-president Prío, and occasionally the new ministers. He used the language of revolution, but then so had others before him. Urrutia's own initiative, however, was limited to a proposal to end gambling and brothels.[4] He was not a hard-working man.

[3] The U.N. Economic Commission for Latin America.
[4] Proposed in a press conference at midnight on 7 January.

In contrast to Urrutia and the middle-aged ministers there were the Fidelistas and the active members of the rebel army or the Civic Resistance. Both leaders of the Civic Resistance in Havana became ministers – Faustino Pérez, the Baptist ex-medical student, with his long and varied work for the cause, from García Barcena's MNR and the *Granma* onwards, became the minister charged to look after property confiscated from Batista and his friends – such as the Villa Kuquine and the *central Washington* which had been Batista's, the Cubana and Q. Airlines which had belonged to José Villaboy and José Iglesias respectively; and Manuel Ray, the brilliant engineer of the Almendares tunnel who, never apprehended, led the campaign of sabotage in Havana in 1958, became Minister of Public Works and so was immediately responsible for the restoration of the bridges, railways, roads and other public enterprises which had been destroyed or harmed in the war, particularly in Oriente. The first national co-ordinator and organizer of the 26 July Movement, Armando Hart (son of a judge who was now Vice-President of the Supreme Court), who had first come to public notice when as a student he provoked a turmoil at a television programme on which Jorge Mañach was speaking, had been a member of García Barcena's MNR before joining Castro in 1955, and became at twenty-eight the new Minister of Education.[5] The new Ministers of Defence and Agriculture, Augusto Martínez Sánchez and Humberto Sorí Marín, had been lawyers and advocates advising respectively Raúl Castro and Fidel Castro in the Sierra Cristal and Sierra Maestra; the latter had been earlier an Auténtico. The Minister of Communications, Enrique Oltuski, son of Russian-Jewish refugees, had been organizer of the 26 July Movement in Las Villas; he, like Hart, was still in his twenties and had studied engineering in the University of Miami, Florida. The Minister of Health, Dr Martínez Páez, had directed one of the hospitals in the Sierra Maestra, while the Secretary to the Cabinet – always an important post – was Luis Buch, a lawyer of a Liberal Santiago family who had headed the Civic Resistance in Santiago, and who had acted innumerable times as a courier between Havana and Miami. All these seemed honest, intelligent, peaceful, literate and literary people such as have too seldom dignified the bloody scramble of hispanic politics.

Castro was a member of the government as commander-in-chief of the rebel army, but he did not come to cabinet meetings in early January. Yet from the start he acted as a kind of extra chairman of the government, his intimates in the cabinet, such as Hart and Martínez Sánchez, holding unofficial meetings with him in the suite at the

[5] His brother, Enrique, had been blown up by a bomb which he was making.

Havana Hilton, where he spent most of his time.[6] But few members of the cabinet, even those of the 26 July Movement, knew him well; Ray, for instance, had met him twice in the Sierra; Agramonte could only remember him from those ambivalent days in the Ortodoxo movement. With Sorí Marín and Martínez Páez, companions during part of 1958 in the Sierra, he was on distant terms. As for his own position before the possibilities of power, Castro told watchers of French television in 1961, 'We [or I, as others would have said] kept away from the government altogether and took no part in the decisions of the Council of Ministers. We had no doubt that the people responsible would take the elementary measures that the people were expecting.'[7]

To begin with, Castro's absence from the business of government had no consequences, beneficial or damaging. The cabinet sat most of the time, often till far into the night, attempting to establish continuity of administration. 'At no time,' the Finance Minister recalled, 'was a general government policy outlined ... the major part of each Cabinet session,' he added, 'was spent in the preparation of a new constitution.'[8] They had too to make many appointments. The upper ranks in most government departments had either fled or had to be purged. Heroes of the revolution took over everywhere as administrators, sometimes on their own insistence. But usually the new ministers managed to avoid the grossest follies: López Fresquet kept two-thirds of the old officials in the Treasury and managed to persuade Castro that a certain major who desired the job as director of motor taxes was unsuitable.[9] Ministers had vast patronage. Catholic ministers such as Sorí Marín appointed Catholics, rationalists appointed rationalists, men of steel named men of steel, Savonarolas named Savonarolas. At the same time each ministry was busy unearthing *botelleros*, the sinecures, and – it often turned out to be the same persons – the corrupt officials: 800 *botelleros* left the Treasury, 300 the customs department, 265 the transport commission, 580 the health department.[10] Doubtless many of these were ex-gangsters who had received jobs from Prío in an attempt to end

---

[6] Later, Castro remarked that at this time 'we were very ignorant of governmental problems. That is, we were ignorant about the governmental apparatus and how it functioned ... We saw the problems of the Revolution through a series of concepts and fundamental ideas'. (*Revolución*, 4 October 1961, 8.) López Fresquet, Minister of Finance, recalled (41) that these ministers, 'whenever presenting a project for consideration by the Cabinet, declared that they had previously discussed it with Castro.'

[7] Hervé Chaigne, OFM, in 'La Révolution Cubaine: Miroir de notre temps' (*Frères du Monde*, 1962 No. 3, qu. Dewart, 82). To Lockwood, Castro once again said, 'when we were fighting the Revolutionary war, and making plans for a government that would replace Batista, I didn't plan to occupy the office of Prime Minister or President or any similar position.' (*Castro's Cuba*, 172.)

[8] López Fresquet, 42.

[9] *Ibid.*, 75.

[10] *Revolución*, 19, 24, 26 January 1959.

gangsterismo. Each day in the press new accounts of graft were unearthed: cheques, shares, deals of all sorts belonging to Batista or his family and friends were published with relish by the revolutionary newspaper *Revolución*, followed by other newspapers – less enthusiastically, since the financial connections of many respectable journalists and newspapers with the old regime were also embarrassingly revealed. Thirty-six of the forty Supreme Court judges were dismissed and the newly appointed judges then purged the lower ranks of the judiciary: some 20% of the bench were in consequence dismissed for collaboration with the old regime, while one of the outstanding younger teachers, Mirta Rodríguez, who had played a big part in sabotage against Batista, demanded a full-scale purge of school teachers, employees of the Ministry of Education, and even of pupils. Purges were also demanded in the University, which did not therefore re-open immediately.

One problem which was solved more quickly than was supposed likely was that of the Directorio Revolucionario. There had been real fear of fighting between them and the 26 July Movement. On 9 January, the day after Castro's arrival in Havana, swayed by Castro's eloquence and by its success among the populace, they began to hand back arms. But Chomón, their leader, accompanied this gesture by saying that Castro had had no right to set up Santiago as the capital. Castro, in a television interview on the night of 9 January, replied by trying to divide Chomón from other leaders, such as Cubela, or from the ghost of the dead Echevarría; 'I always thought that the Revolution ought to make a single movement. Our thesis is that this group or that should not make a revolution, but the people.'[11] No one, however, wanted more bloodshed, at least not immediately. A group of Cuban mothers asked to be allowed to go to the university where the Directorio's arms were accumulated: they had had enough of fighting. This offer reached Castro when on television – a fact which raises doubt whether it was quite so spontaneous as it seemed. *Revolución* commented: 'Fidel inclined his head, shut his eyes briefly, shifted his position, opened his eyes and said: "this shows that public opinion is an irresistible force in a democracy"'.[12] On 13 January, Castro and the Directorio met, and after much argument, Castro, confident in the public backing that his rule enjoyed, soon persuaded the Directorio to lay down their arms. The Directorio bowed, essentially, to the pressure of events. In a few weeks their leading members accepted minor government posts – Cubela went to Prague as military attaché and much later, when Cuba restored diplomatic relations with the U.S.S.R., Chomón became

[11] *Discursos para la Historia*, 20.
[12] *Ibid.*, 22.

ambassador.[13] This difficulty was thus easily overcome; but the difficulty itself was one reason why even Miró Cardona the prime minister, fatally for himself, did not insist on calling a meeting of all those parties and groups who had taken part in the Pact of Caracas.

Revelation, accusation and punishment were the first business of the revolutionary government. True, there were many other promises, hopes, expectations and plans. Others besides President Urrutia hoped that the National Lottery would be converted into a national savings institute. Vice would certainly be eliminated – though the disappearance of Batista's police meant that much of its economic backing anyway collapsed. Plans for the eradication of illiteracy would be pressed. A plan for national industrialization would be prepared. The universities would reopen, though purged, just as the schools had already reopened. The government would surely cut electricity and telephone costs. There would be an agrarian reform, and even the Association of Sugar Colonos, hastily changing from their flattery of Batista, demanded that it should be really effective. Castro, it was true, had in the past mentioned so many separate schemes for agrarian reconstruction (and indeed one based on the idea of the *reparto*, or division of the large estates, had already begun to be applied in parts of Las Villas and Oriente) that it was unclear what precisely such a reform would be, but few doubted that it would convert small tenant farmers into proprietors;[14] that it would insist on the effective use of cultivable but uncultivated land; and that it would carry into effect strictures on *latifundios* contained in the 1940 Constitution. In consequence, embarrassing salutes to the revolution from all sections in society continued for many days. They read like comic epitaphs in old churches: 'To the glorious rebel army. Just as yesterday we were at your side in the mountains ... today we are with you to consolidate the fatherland. National Association of Coffee growers.' Freemasons and Veterans of 1898, department stores and textile firms, insurance companies and bankers saluted the revolutionary government with fervour. Men such as Víctor Pedroso, aristocrat, banker and insurer, gave his tribute to Urrutia as he had given it less than two years before to Batista, after the attempt on the palace. Many surprising people put on 26 July armbands. Meanwhile, early in January buildings and institutions began to be known by names of dead revolutionaries; the technological institute of Ceiba del Agua thus became the Escuela Tecnológica Juan Manuel Márquez.

But the government's main problem for the first weeks was that of

---

[13] The fate of these two was contrasting: Cubela, after being the agent responsible for the destruction of the University of Havana in 1960, was tried and imprisoned for thirty years in 1966 for planning to murder Castro; Chomón was a minister in Castro's government for many years, and in 1965 a member of the Secretariat of the Cuban Communist party.

[14] Castro's own words in January, *Discursos para la Historia*, 20.

arrest and retribution. How could this be done? Batista's leading policemen had either fled, or were in hiding, or had been arrested by the army. But by no means the entire police force was arrested. Those against whom no charges of murder, torture or other misconduct could be preferred, remained in their places: 'All who had a worthy and decorous record would be confirmed.' Over them, however, was quickly – that is, within a week of 1 January 1959 – laid a new skeleton of police command under, first, the leading organizer of sabotage ('Action Chief') in Havana, Aldo Vera and, after Castro arrived at the capital, under Castro's faithful friend of the *Granma* days, the 'hero of a hundred fights', the ex-chauffeur Efigenio Ameijeiras, two of whose brothers had died in the fight against Batista, one after Moncada.[15] Ameijeiras organized the system of police command to put it firmly under men of the 26 July, and he himself said plainly that he was acting under the orders not of Luis Orlando Rodríguez, the Minister of the Interior, traditional minister of police, but of the commander-in-chief, Castro himself.[16] At first Ameijeiras accepted the *status quo*, confirming as the new police in different districts those members of the underground who had actually occupied the various police headquarters; at the end of January, out of the nineteen police stations of Havana, however, only four remained in the same hands as at the beginning: the new commanders were chiefly Sierra Maestra combatants.[17] Ameijeiras was twenty-seven. He had a close personal relationship with Castro and, being without political ideology, was prepared to follow Castro anywhere. 'Capable and very brave, up to a certain point a born leader' was one judgement of him; 'he can treat his men fantastically well'.[18] The uniform of the police was quickly changed to remove the old image of the force so disastrously well-known previously. The police were also given a pay rise. Nevertheless, even in quite high ranks prominent members of the Batistiano police were still found: thus Colonel Ledón became chief of the traffic police in Havana.[19]

There was also the army. Castro began by continuing the line of his statements in the Sierra: apart from 'war criminals' the old army would be merged with the new. On 4 January Cienfuegos spoke to old

---

[15] According to Colonel Esteban Ventura, *Memorias* (1960), 35, Ameijeiras had been in gaol on a morals charge in 1955 and had had other criminal activities to his account, under the alias 'Jomeguía'.
[16] Castro, visiting national police headquarters on 9 January, assured journalists that the army would 'cease all police activities shortly'.
[17] *Cf.* lists in *Revolución*, 27 January. Among those who found themselves in command was Ricardo Olmedo (of the 11th station), who had taken part in the famous attack on the palace but before that in the even more famous assault on the Royal Bank of Canada in 1949.
[18] Javier Pazos to the author.
[19] *Revolución*, 28 January 1959, *tránsito*. Some police officers had secretly sided with the rebels – such as Gabriel Abay. According to J. P. Murray (*The Second Revolution in Cuba*, New York 1962, 35) some 1,100 'rebel soldiers' were brought into the police.

and new officers and men of both parties: 'We shall blend these two armies into one single army – the army which will in truth defend national interests, the army which will sustain our rights and the democracy of the nation.' The new government had no rancour against the old officers and men.[20] But two days later after a talk with Castro at Camagüey Cienfuegos had changed his tune: 'It is necessary to reorganize the armed forces with men loyal to the Revolution, and not accomplices of tyranny.'[21] On 9 January, Castro, in his first speech at Campamento Columbia, said that the president had specifically asked him 'to reorganize the army'.[22] Castro said that 'the country needed an army', because 'the enemy has taken millions of pesos which can be used against the Revolution', and because Trujillo has always had hostile sentiments against Cuba: 'The country cannot be left unarmed.' Castro, however, also said that he personally wished to command 'the best column of the nation, that is the people'.[23] No one saw in this a foreshadowment of a militia. 'We have shown that ... it was false ... [to say] that a revolution could not be made against a modern army [and] without a total economic crisis.'[24] On 22 January he described a journalist who had asked him to abolish the army as an anarchist.[25] By this time, several officers of the intermediate school, democratic men of the old army, had been whisked to one side. The pivotal figure, Barquín, had become head of the military academies. Borbonnet, Barquín's chief follower who had been for a few hours in command at La Cabaña on 1 to 2 January, took over the nominal post of commander of tanks. Colonel Rego Rubido, the 'honourable' and 'worthy' commander in Santiago whom Urrutia actually made chief of the army staff, was appointed military attaché in Brazil. On 14 January, meanwhile, the first military-cultural school to 'raise the cultural level of the rebel army' was inaugurated at La Cabaña by Guevara.[26]

The provincial military commands of the island naturally went to trusted members of the rebel army – Raúl Castro in Oriente, Hubert Matos in Camagüey, Calixto Morales in Las Villas, Dermitio Escalona in Pinar del Río, and William Gálvez in Matanzas. Pedro Díaz Lanz, a commercial airline pilot who had flown arms into the Sierra from Central America, a less 'revolutionary' individual, became chief of the small air force; he was the son of an army officer tried by Machado. Colonel Rego Rubido's post as chief of army staff was taken by

---

[20] *Ibid.*, 5 January.
[21] *Ibid.*, 8 January.
[22] *Discursos para la Historia*, 16.
[23] *Ibid.*, 20.
[24] Castro to journalists, *Revolución*, 23 January 1959, 13.
[25] *Ibid.*, 23 January, 15.
[26] *Ibid.*, 15 January. See below, 300, for the significance of this.

Cienfuegos. Some of the soldiers of the old regime were freed, but few were integrated into the new army. With officers it was a little different: at headquarters Colonel Tomás Arias became director of personnel (G.1.); Major Quevedo became director of logistics (G.4); Captain Yañes Pelletier, the mulatto officer who saved Castro's life after Moncada, became his bodyguard.[27]

On the other hand, 145 ex-soldiers were imprisoned in the Príncipe Havana on 19 January, along with about 30 police and 25 civilians.

This new army soon appeared to be essentially the executive of the regime. Thus in Matanzas Major Gálvez settled a labour dispute in both the Rayon Works and the famous old *central Tinguaro*, which now belonged to Julio Lobo.

These forces of order, the new army, the half-new police, were the authority for the regime's policy of retribution, the vexed question of punishment for war crimes. The extent and horror of the Batista era became apparent only after it had ended. Bodies and skeletons, torture chambers and tortures, were discovered and photographed in the press. Those whose sons or brothers, husbands or *compañeros* had vanished came forward to demand revenge. Few of the assassins had taken steps to conceal their identify. Day after day after 1 January there were arrests. The laws dictating such steps were the decrees issued by Castro and his legal advisers in the Sierra Maestra: these had called on officers of the armed services to resign their commissions; on politicians to refuse collaboration with any elections; and had promised punishment of those who had committed crimes even on governmental orders. In that sense, therefore, the men of Batista's Cuba had been fully warned, and the law had been enacted prior to the offence; in that sense, too, as the advocates of the revolutionary regime, Castro included, pointed out, the Cuban war trials were legally superior to the Nuremberg trials: 'Those who applauded the Nuremberg tribunals cannot oppose our courts martial,' argued *Revolución* on 13 January.

There were other less legalistic arguments. The Foreign Minister, Agramonte, argued to the ambassadors and journalists who came to see him that the trials were dictated by the fear that relations of the dead or ill-treated would otherwise take the law into their own hands, as had occurred after the flight of Machado. Concern with the historical parallel was indeed an important point. There was anxiety lest, as had occurred in 1933–4, the successful revolution should spawn endless minor gangster forces roaming violently across the country. In the event, there was little private settling of scores, an almost unparalleled development in such situations in Cuba; and one has only to think of the end of the occupation of France to realize the extent of this achievement

[27] Significantly, however, old officers continued to draw their pensions.

by the Cubans, one of the most trigger-happy nations in the world. The only qualification that might be made to this judgement was the treatment of the hundred or so prisoners who seem to have been shot by Raúl Castro's men as soon as they reached Santiago.[28]

The ensuing trials of war criminals were conducted by tribunals composed of two or three members of the rebel army, an assessor, and perhaps a respected local citizen.[29] There was a prosecutor and a defence counsel. The trials conducted immediately after 1 January were drumhead courts martial, and perhaps one hundred or so officers or policemen suffered execution as a result up and down the country.[30] By 10 January however, regular tribunals had been set up, and from then on, as seems clear from the press accounts, the trials were fair in the sense that a genuine effort was made to establish the guilt or the innocence of the accused. A number confessed guilt. Once the truth was established, circumstances were not of course propitious for moderate sentences: every day new pictures of decomposed bodies or accounts of atrocities appeared in the newspapers. Even so, by no means all those who were convicted were shot; a first cousin of Batista's, Lieutenant Zaldívar, received a year and a half at Manzanillo for ill-treatment of prisoners.[31] Some got longer terms of imprisonment; others were released after examination without trial. By 20 January probably just over 200 men had been shot, all for murder of prisoners or for torture.[32] Some, such as the police agent Cara Linda, known for tortures in Caibarén, escaped after capture and lived on for some time a semi-gangster life in the country.[33] Many of those who were shot richly deserved it, by most criteria. Had they been imprisoned and afterwards let out, there would certainly have been some private acts of vengeance. Most of these men were corporals, sergeants or junior officers. General

[28] For what seems a genuine account see remarks of Father Jorge Bez, chaplain of the Catholic Youth in Santiago, to James Monahan and Kenneth Gilmore. (*The Great Deception*, New York, 1963, 27.)

[29] In *Santiago*: Major Belarmino Castilla; Captain Ayala and Captain Oriente Fernández, Dr Concepción Alonso and Jorge Serguera, Prosecutor. *Santa Clara*: Captain Orlando Pantoja (aide to Guevara in Escambray, ex-clerk in Contramaestra), Humberto Jorge Gómez, Delia Gayoso, Hornaldo Rodríguez, José Galbán del Río. *Havana* (Cabaña), investigations: Captain Antonio Llibre, Aníbal Sotolongo, José M. Duque de Estrada, Juan Rivero. Of these judges, Castilla became chief-of-staff of the Cuban army in 1966, Ayala was in 1962 chief interrogator of the political police (G.2.), Oriente Fernández a prominent aide of Castro's throughout the 1960s dealing with building projects, Serguera an ambassador and chief of radio and television in 1968, Pantoja was killed in Bolivia with Guevara, and Llibre was always on the General Staff.

[30] For instance, 'Judged in summary court martial, condemned and executed, were various agents of the SIM who tortured and murdered many people in Santa Clara – Montano, Alba Moya, Barroso, Sergeant la Rosa and a civilian spy named Villalta . . .' (*Revolución*, 4 January 1959).

[31] *Ibid.*, 22 January 1959.

[32] *Ibid.*, 19 January, speaks of 207 as having been shot.

[33] Cara Linda was not killed till 1962 (*ibid.*, 24 July 1962).

Cantillo, about to be shot without trial on 5 January for allowing Batista to escape, escaped death due to the intervention of Earl Smith and of the Brazilian ambassador, Vasco da Cunha.[34]

These trials were, however, unfair in the sense that as usual in such circumstances the powerful men got away and the little ones only were left to pay the price: Masferrer was in Florida – arriving on 6 January in his yacht with $M17, immediately impounded – but his chauffeur was awaiting trial in Santiago. The police chief, Colonel Ventura, too was in the U.S. but his private secretary was in Havana gaol. Some ex-ministers – including Santiago Rey the nominal chief, as Defence Minister, of all these men – were in foreign embassies, protected by the law of asylum, later to be escorted to flight by air, their last memory of Cuba the shouts of 'Traitor – thief – assassin' ringing from the crowd.

These Cuban war trials had scarcely opened than they began to be denounced in the U.S. Two important critics were Senator Wayne Morse and *Time* magazine. This led to a certain tension between Cuba and the U.S. when the revolutionary government was less than a fort-night old while the transcript of an exchange between Secretary of State Dulles and the Senate Foreign Relations Committee on 14 January shows that the State Department was thinking of some kind of pressure to bring on Cuba, 'to ensure a government of law and order and justice'.[35]

Ambassador Smith had by this time left Havana and resigned,[36] and the embassy was left with a *chargé d'affaires*; the U.S. recognized the new regime on 7 January, recalling no doubt the recriminations following their refusal to recognize Grau in 1933. Other countries fol-lowed suit.

Castro hardly mentioned the U.S. in his first speeches at Santiago or Havana. On 9 January he was asked if he knew that the U.S. had offered aid to reconstruct the country. All aid, he replied, would be welcome.[37] Did Castro know that the U.S. government was offering to withdraw her military mission? If the Cuban government asked for withdrawal, the mission would have to leave. That was not a prerogative of the U.S. but of Cuba. In addition, what use had the military mission been to Batista? Had they advised how to lose the war? 'If they are going to teach us that, it would be better that they teach us nothing.' Wars incidentally were won when one fought for a just and honourable cause.[38] On 13 January, Castro alluded to Senator Wayne Morse's castigation of the war trials:

[34] Earl Smith, 202–3.
[35] See discussion in W. A. Williams, *The United States, Cuba and Castro* (New York, 1962, 37).
[36] Under-Secretary Herter asked him to resign (Smith, 186).
[37] *Discursos para la Historia*, 27.
[38] *Revolución*, 10 January.

The Cuban revolution is already receiving criticisms ... from the U.S. ... There are interests, there are companies, who are afraid that some immoral concessions may be taken from them. The same with the military mission ... They cannot say that we are Communists, because, if so, they would have to say that the entire Cuban people is Communist. That would be absurd.[39]

In the same speech he said, 'The Platt Amendment is finished. I consider it an injustice to have imposed it on the generation who fought for independence.' But the *Daily News* of New York chose this moment to carry an article saying that the Platt Amendment should be restored.[40]

The criticisms of Senator Morse, in particular his suggestion that the U.S. should consider reprisals such as cutting off the sugar quota or freezing Cuban assets, caused great anger, backed by a wealth of historical allusion, evidently easily brought to Cuban lips: where had been the protests against Batista's atrocities? Had not the same occurred during 1895–8, when the 'interested neighbour' intervened at the point of Cuban victory, despite having been silent over Weyler's *reconcentrados*? And in 1933? Had not Batista strong links with the international press? So, this leading article of *Revolución* proclaimed, there would be a great public meeting, at five in the evening – the hour of García Lorca's death (another young man killed, the leader implied, due to external neglect) – to protest.[41] From this moment on Cubans heard daily in the press of an 'insidious campaign from abroad' against the revolution. The Associated Press was the special target of criticism, because of its past close relationship with Batista's government and the embarrassing revelation that its recent Havana correspondent, José Arroyo Maldonado, had been in receipt of a *botella* from the National Lottery of $71 a month. Castro said on television that he wanted the best relations with the U.S. but that he could not adopt an attitude of submission towards that country. 'I am not selling myself to the U.S., nor shall I receive orders from them.' Raúl Castro in Santiago said that he failed to see how the U.S. could complain about the executions when the U.S. had sold weapons to Batista 'to decimate the population of Cuba.'[42] Criticism began to be levied at Batista's concessions to the U.S. to develop Moa

---

[39] *Ibid.*, 14 January, 2.

[40] Qu., *ibid.*, 16 January, 14.

[41] *Ibid.*, 16 January 1959. The author was Guillermo Cabrera Infante, then just under thirty, and a man who later became one of the most successful modern Cuban novelists with *Así en la paz como en la Guerra*, and *Tres Tristes Tigres*. Cabrera was son of a Communist from Gibara who had worked on *Carteles* with Carlos Franqui in the 1950s and helped prepare the underground *Revolución*. From 1959 to 1961 he was director of the semi-independent *Lunes de Revolución* and afterwards was cultural attaché of the Cuban Embassy in Brussels. He now lives in London and is a prominent critic of the lack of intellectual freedom in Cuba.

[42] *Revolución*, 16 January, 8.

Bay. Worse, four members of the U.S. Embassy turned out to be honorary members of the hated SIM.[43] Nor was it simply Castro and his brother who spoke in uncompromising tones. President Urrutia said explicitly that he supported Castro in everything he had said.

Some slight efforts were made to heal these opening breaches. Paul Hellman, leader of the U.S. Chamber of Commerce, called on the Minister of Trade. The U.S. Embassy denied that the government had had anything to do with development at Moa. But information embarrassing to the U.S. continued to appear. The SIM were proved to have had special relations with the FBI and there were suggestions (never in fact sustained) that Ernesto de la Fe, Batista's first information minister in 1952, had even received a salary from the FBI. Several 'war criminals' – including the hated policemen Ventura, Pilar García and Carratalá – had taken refuge in the U.S. Castro demanded their extradition. In tones increasingly bitter, he told a group of U.S. journalists on 15 January that if the U.S. did not like what was being done in Cuba they could send the marines and then there would be '200,000 dead gringos'.[44] On 16 January at a speech by Chibás's grave he turned the metaphor upside down and said that if the marines came there would be six million dead Cubans.[45] In another speech the same day, he accused the U.S. of wishing to castrate the revolution: for the first time a Cuban government was in power which did not receive orders from abroad. Once more Castro gave his hearers some history, presented a little more harshly than before: the Platt Amendment had been 'a shame and a humiliation'; in 1933 the U.S. had bought Batista. The world had to know that Cuba 'knows how to defend herself. We are a small people but proud . . .' 'If they wish good relations with the people of Cuba, the first thing they must do is to respect our sovereignty. The criminals [during the civil war] were not the Cubans but those who did not speak a single word while the population of Cuba was being massacred.'[46] Guevara at La Cabaña went further: Wall Street always fought against peoples' struggles for freedom, as had occurred in the case of Guatemala. Similar aggression was being prepared against Cuba.[47] Swords, of course, were not yet drawn in January. Castro only mentioned U.S. economic interests, not the government. But yet, as he himself said, there was already tension, already the heavy air of imminent thunder. At the end of the month, the U.S. military mission would be finally withdrawn.

[43] See membership cards photographed, *loc. cit.*
[44] Phillips, *Cuban Dilemma*, 28.
[45] *Discursos para la Historia*, 30.
[46] *Revolución*, 17 January 1959.
[47] *Ibid.*, 20 January 1959.

CHAPTER 23

First Shadows

Questions naturally arose quite early about the Communists. After all, the Cuban Communist party, if its prestige was not high, had at least survived the Batista era. On 2 January Guevara told a North American Communist, Joseph North, that in the new Cuba the Communist party would behave and conduct itself like all other parties.[1] Guevara, however, hotly denied to a journalist from his native Argentina that the 26 July Movement had anything to do with Communism;

> We are democratic men, our movement is democratic, of liberal conscience, and interested in all American cooperation. It is an old trick of dictators to call people Communists who refuse to submit to them. Within a year and a half a political force will be organized with the ideology of the 26 July Movement. Then there will be elections and the new party will compete with these other democratic ones.[2]

Guevara had in fact soon after arriving in Havana dispatched one of his officers, the geographer, Dr Núñez Jiménez, to capture the files and documents of the BRAC, the anti-Communist police and research bureau set up by Batista and U.S. Ambassador Gardner, and inspected and reorganized by Lyman Kirkpatrick of the CIA.[3] Its director, Colonel Faget, had escaped to Miami, but his deputy, Captain Castaño, was arrested.[4] On 6 January a decree abolished all political parties for the time being. The Communists officially were therefore just where the Auténticos were.[5] Little was heard of the Communists' role in

---

[1] Joseph North, *Cuba: hope of a hemisphere* (1961), 26.

[2] *Correo de la Tarde*, 5 January, qu. *Revolución*, 5 January. This would appear to have been one of the few lies told by Guevara: usually he was candid.

[3] Evidence of Máximo Ruiloba to the Senate Internal Security Committee, *Communist Threat*, 525.

[4] Castaño was later shot on the charge of having violated '*una dama revolucionaria*'. He was an able official who talked seven languages (see Barrera Pérez, *Bohemia Libre*, 3 September 1961).

[5] According to Daniel James, José Ignacio Rasco interviewed Castro on 6 January for *Información*, at Santa Clara. After an affectionate discussion of their schooldays together, Rasco asked about 'Communist infiltration'. Castro, furious, allegedly turned the question immediately aside and talked of 'Yankee imperialism' and how he, anyway, was not going to be 'another Yankee lackey'. Daniel James, *Cuba: The First Soviet Satellite in the Americas* (1961), 107.

the Sierra, or Las Villas, meagre though this had been: Félix Torres, Armando Acosta, Pablo Ribalta, Hirán Prats, did not figure among 'the heroes of the Revolution', though in fact they and others had played a certain limited part.[6] On 9 January Cienfuegos told a reporter that he personally had only known three men with Communist ideology in the Sierra but that the Communist party would have rights to organize themselves like all other democratic parties providing that they did not represent the interests of a foreign power.[7] Public anxiety about Guevara's politics was temporarily allayed by the arrival in Havana of Guevara's respectable parents, though Ernesto Guevara, Sr, said that the liberation of Cuba should be an example to other countries.[8]

The Communist party at the end of 1958 was indeed in an odd position. In the struggle against Batista it had played a less prominent part than the Catholic laity. As late as April 1958 it had been ready to act directly contrary to the 26 July Movement in the general strike. Afterwards the leadership had committed itself to an alliance with Castro, sending one of its most enlightened members, Carlos Rafael Rodríguez, to the Sierra. The party directorate in Las Villas established close relations with Guevara and Cienfuegos when it arrived there in October. The same month the party labour leaders had entered into an alliance with the 26 July labour section. All these were of course recent events and possibly only tactical arrangements which might not outlast the victory: indeed the labour arrangements did not do so. In November 1958 the party thought that the disunity of the opposition made the overthrow of Batista improbable in the near future and therefore was still hoping for 'a democratic coalition government'[9] while the actual party members who now began to appear among the clandestine groups of the opposition were 'friendly, humble almost suppliant and asked for nothing but the opportunity to be of assistance', since they believed that the rebellion led by Castro had 'an outside chance of succeeding – but no more than that'.[10] The Communist Youth Movement had sent two members to the Sierra to represent it with Castro in 1957, and there were other isolated individuals who joined the rebel cause. None of this amounted to much. It did, however, enable the Communist party to greet the victory with satisfaction and to come out from the era of the dictatorship not so discredited as it would have been had Batista fled, say, a year before. Its moral position, for instance, was somewhat

[6] Though on 9 January Major Torres's men gave up their arms (*Revolución*, 10 January, 3) and a feast was held on 12 January for Armando Acosta.

[7] *Revolución*, 10 January 1959.

[8] *Ibid.*

[9] Message to the Chilean Communist party, quoted Luis E. Aguilar, *Marxism in Latin America* (New York, 1968), 42–3.

[10] Alfredo Sánchez, *Cambridge Opinion*, February 1963. Sánchez was in 1958 in the Havana underground.

superior to that of the bishops, who as a body had not committed themselves either way before 1 January 1959.

The party thus survived intact. Since it had not been allowed to take part in any of Batista's elections it was not prevented from taking part in public activity by any decree of the Sierra. At the beginning of 1959 it was the only party with a well-established organization throughout the island: it had probably about 17,000 members.[11] If so, it was presumably exceeded in numbers by the 26 July Movement, but that was an amateurish movement without an ideology, an alliance more than a party,[12] an organization to which, in the month before Batista's final flight, large numbers of people nominally members of other political groups had attached themselves informally, by the mere fact of telling others or even themselves that they were members of the movement. Whatever happened, therefore, the Communist party of Cuba would be able to play a major part in post-Batista Cuba. In 1947, after all, it had won 120,000 votes and before that, for ten years, the Communists had run the unions with competence. In 1959, all their most prominent leaders had taken part in the Revolution of 1933.

Further, the discredit with which the Communist party had to cope can be exaggerated. Its collaboration with Batista in the war and with Grau was a long time ago. The party's passive line throughout most of Batista's second reign was in fact more damning during the heady days of victory. Where had most party secretaries been in the epic days of Moncada or the *Granma*? 'Under the bed,' as Castro said later.[13] To balance this they could only say that they had consistently opposed the U.S., Batista's chief backer, until near the end. They had some other assets. They could boast that alone of the old parties they were relatively honest.[14] The handsome Negro, Lázaro Peña, for instance, when secretary-general of the unions before 1947, had been reputed to hand back $500 out of his $600 monthly salary. Many of Cuba's best writers were either Communists or sympathizers, from Nicolás Guillén, an eloquent

[11] This was the estimate of General Cabell of the CIA in November 1959. Other evidence suggests the same. See *Cuba: The Pursuit of Freedom*, 756. Other figures are discussed by Andrés Suárez (*Cuba: Castroism and Communism*, trans. J. Carmichael and E. Halperin (1967), 16), who believes that these figures were excessive. In 1946 the party had claimed 150,000 affiliates. Out of those who could be identified — admittedly a mere 77,000 — 64% were white and 36% black or mixed; 42% were industrial workers, 9% peasants, and 12% middle class people — artisans, merchants, professional men, employers or students.

[12] I have been unable to find any accurate figures or even estimates of members of the 26 July before 1959. In *Cuba et le Marxisme*, 103, Arnault says that there were 400 members in Havana. Andrés Suárez (33) thinks this an exaggeration. Carrillo says they had $M3 in their treasury on 1 January 1959.

[13] In his speech on 27 March 1962. See below, 601.

[14] For instance, even Mario Lazo, a strongly anti-Communist lawyer, recorded the Communists he knew to be 'men of financial integrity, highly intelligent, and fanatically devoted to their Marxist beliefs' (Lazo, 241).

mulatto poet in the tradition of his friend García Lorca, to Manuel Navarro Luna, poet of Manzanillo. These men linked the Cuban Communists with the great international leftist cultural tradition, with the Spanish war (to which Guillén had gone, though as a 'cultural combatant'), with Pablo Neruda and Rafael Alberti and the rest. Some of their leaders, such as Rodríguez, or Fabio Grobart, were men of ability. Among their followers were many well-intentioned social reformers. All the leaders had a long experience of politics and probably the discredit which reflected on the party for its unswerving support of Moscow, including Stalin, for twenty-five years was balanced by the continuity of the leadership. Further, Blas Roca had successfully survived the crisis of 'de-Stalinization' in 1956; he had travelled to China in 1957 and experienced what he would refer to as 'the human qualities of Mao-Tse-tung' at first hand.[15] Rodríguez and Marinello had been members of the cabinet in the war, the first Latin American Communists to enter a cabinet. Finally, the fact that Batista had described his opponents as Communists assisted that party. They were given an importance to which they had perhaps never even aspired. On 8 February 1959 *Bohemia* published a long article by Francisco Parés (a Spanish Civil War exile in Cuba) which effectively pointed out that the Communists were 'the one [party] afloat'. He added, 'the Fidelismo of Fidel is not enough to ensure the survival of Fidelismo', an astute prediction.

Hoy, the Communist newspaper, meantime appeared again for sale publicly for the first time since 1953, with Carlos Rafael Rodríguez, one of the pentarchs of the Communist party during the era of Batista, as editor. On 1 January, the Havana Communists had moved into the old workers' palace, headquarters of the CTC, which they had built under Grau. They soon, however, gave way to the FONU. They also took over a number of small gambling places, broke the equipment, and hung signs outside saying that the Communist party branch had been set up there. In Havana, the Communists seized the political headquarters of Alberto Salas Amaro, a minor presidential candidate in 1958, as party headquarters there.[16] Meetings began to be held, though cautiously, and their first big gathering was in memory of the old poet-hero of 1933, Martínez Villena – always sure of sympathy beyond the ranks of party members. Indeed, the memory of Martínez Villena and of Mella was one of the party's strongest appeals. In all these weeks there was such confusion that Castro, at the very least, did not seem to care what the Communists did. But they were of course the only organized party, and the only group at all who bothered to publish in early January a new manifesto: that of 6 January, that is before Castro had reached Havana,

[15] See Roca's interview in *Hoy*, 6 May 1959, and his article of 4 September 1959, on Mao's *'calidad humana'*.
[16] Phillips, *The Cuban Dilemma*, 38–9.

which consisted of four points: to convert the rebel army into the nucleus of the army of the future; to promulgate nationally the agrarian reform decree of October; to seek new markets for Cuban goods in eastern Europe; and to restore the Constitution of 1940.[17]

Behind the scenes, the party was trying already to consolidate its position in one section of the army. Guevara had brought a number of Communists with him from Las Villas. Although no publicity was given to these men, one or two received, or seized, in the first confused moments of the breakdown of power, strategically sensitive posts; thus Armando Acosta, the Communist leader of Las Villas, who had been a right-hand man of Guevara's in the battle of Santa Clara and who had helped Cienfuegos with food, found himself commander of La Punta, the old fortress on the Havana side of the harbour, opposite El Morro and La Cabaña.[18] Such a post may have been no more than was due to Acosta as a man of ability, but that could hardly be said of some other appointments made under, or by, Guevara at La Cabaña; within a few weeks Marcos Armando Rodríguez, afterwards famous as the traitor of Humboldt 7, who had recently succeeded in joining the Communist party, appeared as 'an instructor' at La Cabaña.[19] Further, Acosta soon took over 'cultural activities' at La Cabaña, which meant that he was in control of military education and leisure, a post which he naturally filled with dogmatic enthusiasm. Several Communists found jobs under him, among them Alberto Lavandeyra, brought up in France and with experience of the Revolution in Guatemala, and Ramón Nicolau, commissar of the Cubans who fought in the Spanish Civil War and the 'contact' between the Communists and the Directorio in 1958. Without doubt, these appointments at La Cabaña were the beginning of Communist influence in the Rebel Army.[20] This was admittedly the beginning of a process, not its end; nor is it precisely clear whence the initiative came – presumably from Guevara. But it should be assumed that the Communists in the army, however few they were, took every opportunity, from the first day after the victory, to improve and extend their influence. From the beginning of January they praised the revolutionary victory. *Pravda* hailed the Cuban revolution on 3 January: 'The Cuban people have drunk the dregs of bitter suffering and cannot be frightened off. The patriots have the [task] . . . of carrying the liberation through to the end.' But from another quarter there were already doubts: a U.S. diplomat, William Bowdler, second

---

[17] *Hoy*, 6 January 1959.
[18] *Revolución*, 5 January 1959.
[19] *Hoy*, 25 March 1964.
[20] Others who found jobs at La Cabaña at this time were intellectual friends of the Communists, such as the future propaganda film-maker, Santiago Alvarez, Antonio Massip (who had been director of *World Student News* in Prague) and Julio García Espinosa.

secretary at the embassy in Havana, had decided by 16 January 1959 that 'the Communists were being given a position everywhere',[21] and while the first Communist statement after Batista's flight, that of 6 January, was very moderate, the 'Theses on the Present Situation' published on 11 January seemed rather stronger.[22]

What happened in the army could have occurred in the unions. But here there was a tradition of anti-Communism. Everyone knew where they were. The 26 July Movement had a strong organization throughout organized labour. Hence by the end of January even the Communists who had been part of the Labour alliance (FONU), formed in October 1958, found themselves formally expelled from the FONU's new, smaller directorate.[23] They had not lost all following, since they controlled some unions – the dockworkers for instance, and the gastronomic workers – and since, as later transpired, some Labour leaders nominally neutral (such as Soto or Aguilera) were in fact willing to be sympathetic towards them. But they had nevertheless received a defeat and the new Minister of Labour, Manuel Fernández, was a known social democrat. Old Communist Labour leaders such as Lázaro Peña were either still in exile or needed time to readjust themselves to the circumstances.

On 16 January, before Chibás's grave, Castro himself formally denied that he was a Communist – an appropriate place since Chibás had always been an enemy of Communism.[24] His praise of Chibás seemed to confirm this. One man surely could not serve both Chibás and Marx. Castro repeated this denial on 22 January in a press conference.[25]

If Communists helped each other on to positions of influence, so too did the Catholics and others: thus the Minister of Agriculture, Sorí Marín, a Catholic ex-Auténtico, appointed young Catholics such as Manuel Artime and Rogelio González Corzo to command the Rural Commandos and to be Director of Agriculture.

On 9 January, the day after he arrived in Havana, Castro had said that elections would be held 'in a space of fifteen months, more or less':

The political parties will be organized inside eight to ten months. In the first three months of the liberation it is a crime to thrust the

[21] Bowdler to the author in 1962.
[22] *Hoy*, 11 January 1959.
[23] This was composed of nine members, not twenty-one. These were José Pellón, Conrado Bécquer (previously treasurer of the sugar workers), Antonio Torres, José de Jesús Plana, Jesús Soto and José María Aguilera. Salvador's deputies in the underground, Octavio Louit and Reinol González, were secretary of organization and of international relations respectively. Antonio Torres had been Louit's aide in the general strike in Guantánamo on 30 November 1956.
[24] *Discursos para la Historia*, 30.
[25] *Revolución*, 23 January, 13.

people into politics. It is better to work furiously[26] to reconstitute the nation . . . Rarely in Latin America have there been revolutions which are not merely *coups d'état*.

Would the Constitution be adjusted? 'The moment a provisional president was put in power marked an adjustment.'[27] Two days later, Castro was interviewed again, this time by CBS television: would the Student Directorate take part in the forthcoming elections? 'Naturally,' said Castro, 'if we do not give liberty to all parties to organize themselves we will not be a democratic people. We have fought to give democracy and liberty to our people.' What guarantees were there that elections would be held? 'Public opinion . . . our word . . . our intentions . . . because we are disinterested . . . because it is obvious that we have nothing to gain in not having elections.'[28] It was, of course, already known that Castro wished to create 'a model people of America'.[29] At the Club de Leones on 13 January he was pressed a little on these topics; would there be any constituent assembly before the elections? 'The problem here was not of substituting the existing Constitution but of adjusting it; therefore it would be negative to speak of a constituent assembly.' Should there be a provisional legislative assembly to help with the heavy burdens of the Council of Ministers? 'The provisional government would be short-lived and would . . . put everyone to work. Our revolution is genuinely Cuban, genuinely democratic.'[30] Two days later the prime minister, Dr Miró Cardona, explained that the Constitution of 1940 had been 'actualized' by the revolution. This later seemed to mean, however, that several articles of the Constitution would be revised. For example, Article 21 causing penal laws to be retroactive if they favoured the accused was suspended to exclude collaborators of the 'tyrant'. Article 25 which banned the death penalty was amended to provide precisely that punishment for Batistianos and others. Confiscation of Batistianos' property was to be permitted.[31] These constitutional revisions were, of course, by decree. Only the prime minister, Miró, seems to have protested. But his request to be allowed to resign in protest against moves that he rightly considered had totalitarian implications was brushed aside by his colleagues, and he did not persevere.[32]

By this time the cabinet, sitting almost continuously and at all hours of the night, had approved, among other appointments, a minister to

[26] The word Castro used was *febrilmente*.
[27] *Discursos para la Historia*, 27.
[28] CBS, TV interview, 11 January, qu. Léo Sauvage, *L'Autopsie du Castroisme* (1962), 74.
[29] He said this in the national police headquarters on 10 January 1959.
[30] *Revolución*, 14 January 1959.
[31] *Ibid.*, 16 January.
[32] *Diario de la Marina* (Miami), 12 November 1960.

'consider the authority of the Laws of the Revolution' – that is, the nature of the Constitution.[33] This post went to Osvaldo Dorticós Torrado, a forty year-old Cienfuegos lawyer and from one of the families who had founded Cienfuegos, distantly linked by blood to the nineteenth-century millionaire Tomás Terry – and also, more closely, to an old Auténtico, Pedro López Dorticós, one of the officials of Batista's BANFAIC, recently arrested. Dorticós had had a flirtation with the Communist party in his youth and had once been private secretary to Juan Marinello, the literary president of the Communists. But that was long ago; Marinello was a figurehead; and now Dorticós, Commodore of the Cienfuegos Yacht Club, lawyer to big Cienfuegos companies, president of the National College of Lawyers, appeared the most *bourgeois* of the new ministers. His part in the 26 July Movement in Cienfuegos had been small.[34]

Those Liberals who were well placed in Urrutia's provisional government unfortunately could not sustain their high principles. Although this can be chiefly explained by the policy, the power and the character of Castro, they prepared the way for their destruction themselves. First, Urrutia agreed with Castro that there should be no elections for eighteen months. Until then there would be government by decree. This decision seems to have been contested by nobody. One of the first decrees issued by the cabinet was the dissolution of Batista's Congress. Another was the dissolution of all past criminal tribunals. A third was a decree abolishing political parties: thus, trumpeted *Revolución*:

> We finish with all the vices of the past, all the old political games. The triumph of the Revolution cannot give a green light to the petty interests of the opportunists of all time. Let the figureheads who did not participate in the revolutionary struggle ... not be permitted any opportunity to betray the Revolution with their capacious hypocrisy. Worthy men who belong to definite political parties already have posts in the ... provisional government ... The others ... would do better to be silent.[35]

A fourth decree banned all candidates in the elections of 1954 and 1958 from political life. Some, such as Dr Fidel Núñez Carrión or Alberto Salas, were arrested for venturing to take part in these elections: the former had aspired to be mayor of Havana in 1958, and the latter to be president. Other decrees of early January froze the bank accounts of all civil servants under Batista and stopped any outstanding large cheques

[33] This was on 10 January.
[34] See below.
[35] *Revolución*, 7 January 1959, 7.

drawn during the Batista era.[36] These decrees were concerned with the destruction of the past and the removal of corruption: the Batista bank accounts seemed outrageous to those who followed, and every form of state interference seemed desirable to prevent anyone who was believed to have robbed the State profiting from his thefts.

Yet why was it thought there should be no elections for eighteen months? Why did Agramonte and Urrutia, Pazos and Miró Cardona, accept this delay? Both Urrutia and Miró Cardona explained at the time that there would have to be changes in the Constitution of 1940 to take into account the change of power from illegality to legality.[37] Why did the rest of liberal Cuba accept that delay without thought, welcoming, with *Revolución*, the extinction of the political parties? Because, like Castro himself, and like, no doubt, the masses, if their views could have been effectively sounded, they were ready to reject politics. Even ex-President Prío and Agramonte, the Ortodoxo presidential candidate of 1952, seemed prepared, even anxious, to submit to a 'national guide and leader' such as Castro – already referred to as the '*máximo líder*' in January; they, too, wanted to purge Cuba, not rebuild the old institutions. All were happy in the 26 July Movement, which had never been and was never to become a political party.

Castro in these first days of victory was indeed almost the only person who dared to say that 'the right of dissent and to make opposition' was an inalienable right. 'We are not trying to make the 26 July Movement into a single totalitarian party,' he told listeners in Las Villas on 6 January.[38] In most of his statements however, he tried to place his revolution against the background of all Latin America: thus on 22 January, to an audience of journalists, some of them Latin American, he explained that 'a dream he had in his heart [*sic*] was that one day Latin America would be entirely united in a single force, because we have the same race, language, feelings [*sentimientos*].'[39] Nevertheless Castro was also a patriot of an extreme, almost extravagant kind: 'It would be difficult to find a people so noble, so sensitive, humane, as this; you cannot see a *corrida de toros* here, because the people would rise against it.'[40] When he said 'America', he meant South America too.

> We have above all the interests of our country and of our America ...
> We are defending the interests of our peoples, we want political and economic independence and [desire] that exploitation cease and that

[36] Other decrees suspended for thirty days the guarantee against removal of the judiciary, expelled Barroso from the sugar stabilization institution, removed various state stipends given to journalists, etc.

[37] *Revolución*, 15 January 1959.

[38] *Ibid.*, 7 January 1959, 1.

[39] *Ibid.*, 23 January 1959, 14.

[40] *Ibid.*, 15. He said nothing of cockfights, which the people would doubtless rise up to keep. Some like cocks, some bulls.

regimes of social independence are established within the broadest frame of human liberties. This is the philosophy of the 26 July Movement ... the day [that liberty is no longer maintained] we shall resign ... The day the majority is against us we shall resign ...'[41]

All these themes were welded together in a series of speeches by Castro at the end of January. A huge meeting was held on 22 January in front of the presidential palace to support the government in its policy towards 'war crimes'. The crowd was, if anything, larger than that which greeted Castro on 8 January. Banners announced 'Cuban women demand execution of murderers'; 'For revolutionary justice'; and 'Extradite the lackeys of tyranny'. Some of these were in English, presumably for the benefit of the U.S. reporters who had hurried to Havana. Other banners recalled Nuremberg. Castro, on a specially constructed presidential tribune, was surrounded by most of his more prominent followers. His speech was essentially a denunciation of the U.S. for venturing to criticize the war trials when few had criticized the atrocities under Batista. But it was also a successful test of his strength. Thus he asked all who agreed with revolutionary justice to raise their arms: of course everyone did. Castro commented: 'Gentlemen of the diplomatic corps, gentlemen of the press of the whole continent, the jury of a million Cubans of all ideas and all social classes has voted.'[42]

Castro made eloquent play with the fear which had been expressed in the press that he might be assassinated: but 'the destiny of peoples cannot depend on one man ... because ... behind me come others more radical than I ... and [therefore] assassinating me would only fortify the revolution'. He thereupon named his brother, the mysterious, physically almost child-like Raúl, as second-in-command of the 26 July Movement, to succeed him if he should die. He demanded of the U.S. the extradition of war criminals who had gone there. He justified the executions by quoting, rather obviously perhaps, from the Bible: 'He who kills by the sword ...' He explained that the 26 July Movment had killed no innocent people, unlike the U.S. whose actions in Hiroshima and Nagasaki, as was well known, had been committed to save North American lives. Cuba had no hostile sentiment towards the U.S. but he believed that in the U.S. there were anti-Cuban interests, 'interests who fear the revolution'.[43] This speech suggested that Castro was either afraid of intervention by the U.S. or that he was already teasing himself and Cuba with the idea of it, to boost national morale and unity, a unity which would be behind himself and his victory. The criticisms of the war trials he attributed to an 'organized campaign of

[41] Remarks made on 23 January.
[42] *Discursos para la Historia*, 37.
[43] *Ibid.*, 44.

criticism'; he left his hearers vague as to who was responsible, but suggested that they worked through AP or UPI.[44] He seemed also to be developing the idea of a fully independent Cuba, perhaps neutral internationally (though this idea had yet to be fully explored), and behind him was clearly the memory of Martí. To journalists, on the same day as this speech, he said explicitly that 'the interests' which were attacking the executions wished in fact to crush the revolution.[45] On 22 January a Mexican asked him what he would do if the U.S. were to impose an economic blockade on Cuba and whether the 'powerful U.S. interests' which were already attacking the Cuban revolution might decoy the 26 July Movement into the murderous morass of the cold war. Castro said firmly:

> We have to try at all costs to avoid world problems coming to convert our ideals into a scenario for that struggle. Certainly various mono-polistic interests . . . arrange matters by trying to obtain from govern-ments which they can suborn all manner of privileges, and some of them often can count on the backing of the public power of the U.S. . . .'

What would happen if such companies in the future tried to paralyse the revolution completely? The Cuban people would have to defend themselves as circumstances dictated. Castro's belief was that this situation was not going to occur. 'I really am not afraid of falling into the orbit of international Communism. What are we doing to defend the revolution? Have we sought support from Communism? No, we have sought the backing of public opinion of the peoples of America.'[46]

Faced with so many criticisms, the Cuban government decided to stage the first major war trial in Havana in public, in the large sports stadium. The accused were Major Jesús Sosa Blanco, Colonel Grau and Colonel Morejón; the council of war, Humberto Sorí Marín (Minister of Agriculture), Catholic lawyer and Advocate-General in the Sierra; Major Universo Sánchez (a Granmaista); and Raúl Chibás.[47] The sports stadium was unfortunately filled with a furious and yelling crowd, as well as three hundred Cuban and foreign journalists. The crowd inter-rupted evidence by shouting 'Bandit', 'assassin', 'thug'. Sosa Blanco, the first to be tried, conducted himself with cynicism, gaiety and some dignity before what he himself termed 'a Roman circus'. Careful examination of witnesses was impossible in that atmosphere. No doubt Sosa Blanco was guilty, as many people testified, of many deaths in Oriente province in 1957–8. He had burned 200 houses at Levisa, some

[44] Interview in *Revolución*, 23 January ,14.
[45] *Ibid.*, 23 January.
[46] *Ibid.*, 15.
[47] Of these it is worth noting that the first was later himself executed for treason within two years and the last is an exile. Universo Sánchez is an unimportant army officer (1970).

being full of people. He had killed nine members of the Argote de Céspedes family in El Oro de Guisa on 10 October 1957. The widow of a peasant swore that Sosa Blanco had shot her husband before her eyes. A man said he had seen Sosa Blanco shoot nineteen workers in Minas de Ocujal. That he had committed some, at least, probably most, of these crimes, seemed beyond question, though no evidence other than hearsay evidence was in fact produced. Some of the crimes had occurred before the first 'law' emanating from the Sierra Maestra, in February 1958, which promised justice to the members of Batista's army who carried out murders. But what was the status even of that law? These points were made by the defending counsel, Captain Aristides da Costa, who also said that in war these things did happen: one side killed the other. These points were dismissed, and Sosa Blanco was condemned to death.[48] This trial, intended to be a proof to the rest of the world of the integrity of revolutionary justice, was in fact the worst advertisement for it possible. The U.S. press agreed with the defendant that the trial was a circus.

On 22 January Castro left for Venezuela, to attend celebrations there on the first anniversary of the expulsion of the dictator, Pérez Jiménez, and to thank the 'sister republic' for her aid in the Cuban struggle. President-elect Betancourt was then still the hero of the Left in Venezuela as well as of the centre. A huge multitude greeted him, proving beyond doubt that he had a following on a continental scale. Castro replied by giving a victory sign in the style of Churchill.

Castro made a number of speeches in Caracas. Once more he denied that the revolution in Cuba was Communist. To the Venezuelan Congress, he gave the assurance: 'In Cuba we shall have also a congress within two years.' Visas between Cuba and Venezuela would be abolished. A Venezuelan military mission would be invited to instruct the new Cuban army. The Organization of American States would be filled with democrats, the dictators would be expelled.[49] A common market was possible in Latin America; perhaps a common passport; and 'the U.S. will have to adapt itself to Latin American politics, will not always be defending the interests of monopolies'. The 26 July Movement would of course become a political party, for political parties would not be permanently abolished in Cuba, new ones would be founded, though the old *politiqueros* would have to go. He, Castro, did not aspire to the presidency of Cuba. Indeed he was thinking of making a journey round South America, partly to stop 'the calumnies of some monopolistic sectors interested in maintaining their privileges in Cuba, partly to sow the seeds of unity in the countries of Latin America in

[48] A fairly full report of the trial appeared in *Revolución* in January 1959.
[49] *Discursos para la Historia*, 46–9.

defence of their common interests'. Castro left Caracas, undertaking that a mission would soon be sent to Venezuela to co-ordinate a common policy with President-elect Betancourt. So far so good.

In fact Castro had a somewhat bizarre conversation with President Betancourt. They talked alone, though surrounded at a distance by guards, in a large patio. Castro came straight to the point: he told Betancourt he was thinking of 'having a game with the gringos'. If necessary, would Betancourt help him out with a loan of $M300 and with oil? Betancourt, taken aback, gave a discouraging reply:[50] he was interested himself in evolution not revolution.[51]

At the same time the candid Guevara, still merely the commander at La Cabaña, was hinting that his own political programme would give serious reasons for disquiet to any capitalist as to his ultimate motives. In his speech on 27 January he was explaining that the rebel army, the 'vanguard of the Cuban people', was the 'primary instrument of struggle'; the entire nation should be turned into a guerrilla army.[52]

A lyric spirit survived in Cuba for many months after these remarks, and few foreigners left the island without being entranced by the nobility, the vigour and the charm of the revolutionaries; but from the very beginning of 1959 there were those who wondered precisely what would happen. To many people the month of January 1959 in Havana was a unique moment of history, golden in promise, the dawn of a new age; great projects had already been begun; however, in a way that most of them scarcely appreciated, it was also the end of an old world.

[50] Evidence to the author by Betancourt. See also Betancourt's article in *The Reporter*, 13 August 1964. As Mrs Phillips points out (*The Cuban Dilemma*), Castro used the word 'gringo' for North American on another occasion in January 1959, an odd usage by a Cuban; for Cubans usually say 'Yankee', and Castro did himself usually. It was presumably a calculated attempt to talk in the language of South Americans or Mexicans.

[51] See Tad Szulc, 'Exporting the Cuban Revolution', in J. Plank, ed. *Cuba and the U.S.*, *Long Range Perspectives* (1967), 78 and 88. This rebuff substantially affected Castro's attitude to Betancourt afterwards.

[52] Guevara's talk to the *Nuestro Tiempo* Association in Havana. For text, see Guevara, *Oeuvres Révolutionnaires*, 23–32, or Gregorio Selser, *La Revolución Cubana* (1960), 427 ff. As it happened, Roca chose 27 January also to expand on his 'New Theses' of 11 January. Reading between the lines it is evident that there was a clash between Guevara and the Communists, the latter being outflanked by the former.

BOOK THREE

Old Cuba at Sunset

'I don't understand why it should have been the Cubans. They are all so individualistic and they had the highest standard of living in Latin America.'

LUIS SOMOZA OF NICARAGUA TO NICHOLAS WOLLASTON

CHAPTER 24

The Island

There were now between six and six and a half million Cubans, about the same number as there were Englishmen at the time of Albemarle's capture of Havana in 1762, or North Americans during Jefferson's presidency.[1] At 132 to the square mile, the density of population was $2\frac{2}{3}$ times that of the U.S.,[2] and the fourth biggest in Latin America.[3] The population had doubled twice since 1899, when density had been 32 to the square mile, and was now growing at 2 to 3% a year – a high figure but substantially lower than say Brazil or Mexico, being close to the level of North West Europe in the 1880s. Most Cubans had been country-dwellers until about 1930; most lived in towns or villages afterwards.[4] The 'urban' population seems to have been 57% in 1953, 55% ten years before, 51% in the last years of Machado. Cuba was no longer primarily an agricultural country; but nor, in terms of workers, had it been so since the beginning of the century.[5]

In comparison with other countries nearby, Cuba was exceeded in population by Mexico (32 million), by Colombia (13 million), and of course by the U.S. while Venezuela, with more inhabitants than Cuba in 1900, was behind in 1958, at 6·3 million. The six central American states, lying between Mexico and Colombia, together totalled only 11 million.[6] Haiti and the Dominican Republic, the two republics on

---

[1] The last census was in 1953 when the population was said to have been 5,829,092. Estimates for 1958 vary from the National Bank's 6,136,000 to the National Economic Council's 6,563,000.

[2] (131·8), 1953 figures.

[3] Haiti, El Salvador and the Dominican Republic had more people per square mile.

[4] But a 'town' was a place only 150 people in size, according to census definition, and which had access to services such as electric light and medical service. Thus, by definition, the country was less well off than the town. The 1931–43 definition was whether one lived in a house with a number and in a street. 1899–1919 used to define a town as over '1,000 strong'. But 1931–43 gave much the same proportion as that of 1953.

[5] According to their respective censuses, Argentina has an urban population of 62·5% Canada 64%, Chile 62%, the U.S. 64%. Different criteria for these surveys make any absolute comparison impossible.

[6]
Guatemala	3,546,000
El Salvador	2,434,000
Honduras	1,828,000
Nicaragua	1,378,000
Costa Rica	1,076,000
Panama	995,000

(*Statistical Yearbook UN*, 1961)

Hispaniola, numbered 3·5 million and 2·8 million, respectively. Puerto Rico had 2 million. The other islands of the Caribbean, French, Dutch, English and North American, did not together make up 4 million: the English islands totalled 3 million, the French, 500,000. The three Guianas reached 700,000, the Bahamas 45,000.

As for the rest of South America, Argentina, Brazil and Peru were of course all substantially larger than Cuba, having 20 million, 60 million, and 10 million people, respectively. Chile was only slightly larger (7 million). The others were smaller.[7] All Latin America and the Caribbean, Mexico included, comprised about 190,000 million, a figure only slightly above the U.S. In 1900 the U.S. had totalled 76 million; Latin America and the Caribbean under 30 million.

Within Cuba, the families in the country had usually more children than those in the town.[8] The size of families was slowly decreasing, but numbers were in fact still higher than in 1899–1907 when there had been so much more disease.[9] 80,000 women were believed to have had ten or more children,[10] and 660 had twenty or more children, of whom 250 lived in Oriente; interestingly enough, well over half these, nearly 400, were reckoned as white.[11]

The drop in the number of births during the war of independence between 1895–1898 could plainly be seen. No doubt in 1958 the virtual non-existence of men in their early sixties was a cause of extra instability in society: where would England be without those solid citizens, the elderly men in a hurry, retired from their professions, but still enthusiastic to bear responsibility, public and private, without payment?

The growth of Cuban towns in the twentieth century had been swift. In 1899 there were five cities with populations of over 25,000; in 1958, twenty-one. Cities with over 8,000 totalled sixteen in 1899, forty-six in 1958. The biggest rise was that of Havana's suburb-city Marianao, from the 'pretty little Cuban village' of a mere 5,000 (visited by Samuel Hazard) in 1899 to over 200,000 in 1958 – the second biggest city in

[7] Ecuador 4 million
 Uruguay 2·7 „
 Paraguay 1·7 „
[8] Census of 1953, xxix. 217 and 318, respectively per 100 women of 15 years or over, were the precise figures.
[9] Size of families: (Census of 1953, xxxvii; ibid., 1919, 381):
 1899 4·8
 1907 4·8
 1919 5·7
 1931 5·20
 1943 5·18
 1953 4·86
[10] Census of 1953, 67. Precise figures, 81,430 and 2,000,106.
[11] Precise figures, 657,245 and 377.

Cuba, if reckoned separately from Havana. In 1958 Havana and Marianao together totalled over 1,000,000, compared with under 250,000 in 1899.

As in most of South America, big cities grew faster than small ones: under a quarter of the population in 1907 lived in cities of over 25,000;[12] in 1953, well over half.[13] In 1953 a third of the population lived in the four cities larger than 100,000.[14] Compared with Havana and its neighbour, the cities of Oriente increased less swiftly, but nevertheless continuously, especially Holguín and Guantánamo.

Agricultural families of course continued to live chiefly in separate farmsteads, not, as in Spain, in villages, for villages were places rather for merchants, wholesalers and professional people. Farmers and labourers would go to the village to get their letters, usually addressed care of a shopkeeper, since there was no free postal delivery: they went to 'town' in fact several times a week, for supplies or social activities, sometimes to take part in the nightly *paseo* up and down the squares with the town-dwellers.

The construction of the towns did not now follow the strict patterns of the conquistadors. Houses were often built along the main road, with only one or two back streets, usually not paved. All pavements were narrow. Houses might have a porch supported by pillars, Greek in inspiration if stone, square if they were frame houses. Most houses in towns were however made of wood with a tile or metal roof. Nearly all would be one storey high. The small towns of Cuba, without the charm of the cities, nor the excitement, but also without immediate access to the country, were in many ways the most depressed parts of the island.

By 1958 between a half and two-thirds[15] of the houses of Cuba had electric light, but only 9% of rural ones, compared with 87% of urban. Of all the houses or flats, between a third and a half had been built since 1945; about a third between 1920 and 1945; and the rest, less than a quarter, before 1920. About nine-tenths of the rural houses and about two-thirds of the urban ones had probably been built since 1920.[16] Over a quarter of the houses were said to have been built with

[12] 21·4%.
[13] 58%.
[14] 35%.
[15] 58% in 1953.
[16] In 1953, 34·5%, 39·8% and 25·7%; adjusted to take into account building since 1953. Figures in 1953 were:

$$312,382: \text{before 1920}$$
$$483,635: \text{1920–45}$$
$$418,589: \text{since 1945}$$
$$41,988: \text{undeclared}$$

1,256,594

masonry and cement, though only 1% of those in the country. Two-thirds of the rural houses were still *bohíos* of palm and wood, with earth floors.[17] Though unhygienic, they were cool and, from the outside, beautiful. Half the Cuban houses had two to three rooms, 13% only one room, 17% five or more. 85% of rural houses had to use river water. 43% of urban houses, and only 3% of country ones had internal lavatories. Over half of the rural houses lacked all lavatory arrangements, giving a national fraction of just under a quarter. 15% of town houses, 1% of country houses, had baths.[18] All these low figures nevertheless represented marked advances over the situation fifty years before: in 1899, half the population had no lavatory arrangements. 1,300 houses in 1953 were declared worth $40,000, of which 1,100 were in Havana province. The average value was $1,000.[19] All houses were, of course, privately built, though the State had sometimes intervened in the regulation of rents and leases. Many members of the *bourgeoisie* had their savings invested in property; indeed, most of those who had savings had it so invested – a fact which affected all proposals of the revolutionary government of 1959 to cut rents. Rented houses added up to just over a third of the total houses – constituting the largest single source of revenue of the Cuban middle class.[20] A little under a quarter of the houses were lived in by squatters, or tied farmers, or in some other way occupied without payment of rent.[21] In towns, rented property amounted to over half the total,[22] but only 5% in the country, where nearly half were squatters,[23] compared with a tenth in the towns.[24]

In 1953 a sixth of the population lived in Havana.[25] It was a larger capital city in proportion to total inhabitants than any other in the world save the equally top-heavy London and Vienna.[26] Havana had sucked dry the province around it so that the density of population of those who lived on farms in the province of Havana was relatively small, in 1943 less than the national average.[27] Well over half[28] those

---

[17] Census of 1953, xliii.
[18] *Ibid.*, xliv–xv; c.f. *U.N. Demographic Yearbook 1958–9;*
[19] See Census of 1953 302. 1,306, 1,101 and $1,060 were the precise figures.
[20] 36·4%.
[21] 22·8%. 3·6% were unoccupied.
[22] 55%.
[23] 46%.
[24] 9%. Census, 253. In Pinar del Río, 70% of rural houses were occupied without rent, 65·6% in Matanzas, 62% in Camagüey. In 1943 statistics had been rather different. In towns, 124,931 families owned their houses; 4,240 were buying them on a mortgage; and 358,933 rented theirs. In the country, 129,926 owned their own farm; 2,097 had it on a mortgage; 227,403 rented it. (Census of 1943, 1010–11). 75,004 were unknown (squatters).
[25] Census of 1953.
[26] Census of 1943, 724.
[27] 22·9 national average; Havana in 1943, 18·4% (Census of 1943, 731).
[28] 221,455.

employed in services,[29] well over half[30] those employed in utilities,[31] and over half [32]of those employed in building were in Havana.[33] Sugar mills apart, perhaps three-quarters of the industrial investment in Cuba was in the region of Havana.

The traveller's first sight of Havana on arrival by sea remained what it had always been: a broad harbour, commanding buildings on either side, a multitude of ships, his views overlaid no doubt by the sentiment that Havana had been for longer than any city in the New World a centre of pleasure. To those who lived there, Havana cast a spell as great in the 1950s as in any earlier time, but now however there were at least four Havanas.

First, there was the old city, unchanged since the mid-nineteenth century, narrow streets, two-storey buildings, sometimes huge Spanish doors giving on to courtyards. Being near the docks, the old city remained the centre of business and it was, as always, the centre of restaurants, night life and brothels. The Presidential Palace remained in the old city, though other government departments had begun to be taken out of the centre to Batista's gaunt new buildings clustered round the Plaza de la República. The old city already had a serious traffic problem – exacerbated in the public mind by parking meters introduced in 1957 and which were, rightly, believed to be a means whereby various officials made money for themselves. The exodus of the richer families towards Miramar, on the North American model, lowered the rents, and the tone, of the old city. On the border of the old city was Chinatown, full of restaurants, more brothels and night clubs, some where blue films (since the mid 1950s) could be found cheaply. Some of the eighteenth-century palaces were crumbling, others were used by companies or embassies. In this respect, Havana resembled other Spanish-American capitals such as Lima or Mexico City. The prostitutes on the streets such as Virtudes or even the Prado were so numerous as to resemble a cattle market.[34] The Prado, with a double line of laurels, led up the centre of the old city, lined also with bootblacks, waiting taxis and beggars. These last were estimated to number about 5,000.[35] The gangster and brothel underworld of Havana under Batista was intimately connected with the police, and most night clubs paid protection money to some police officer or other. Most of this part of the city was held on leases which, though nominally monthly, were in

[29] Out of 395,904.
[30] 4,939.
[31] Out of 8,439.
[32] 34,617.
[33] Out of 65,292.
[34] One report estimated that in February 1958 11,500 in Havana earned their living as prostitutes (qu. Yves Guilbert, *La poudrière Cubaine: Castro l'infidèle* (1961), 35).
[35] W. MacGaffey and C. R. Barnett, *Twentieth-century Cuba* (1965), 144.

fact indefinite. Tenants who prospered might very well lay marble floors without any fear of being turned out. Rents could be raised but only within certain limits if the property in question was pre-1939.

The second Havana was Vedado, the fashionable suburb of the early years of the century but now the real centre of the city. Here Batista's building boom had had most effect. To the old Hotel Nacional, reconstructed after the battle in 1933 and redecorated in the 1950s, had been added several more glittering hotels such as the $M14, thirty-storey Havana Riviera, built by a group of North Americans apparently implicated in the murder of the Chicago gangster Anastasia; the $M5½ Capri, with a swimming pool on top of its twenty-two storeys; and the Havana Hilton, run by the Hilton chain on behalf of the Restaurant Workers' Union, which had invested $M24 of their pension funds in it. All these had casinos of astonishing luxury and splendour (being built by investors seeking gaming profits). All had several restaurants and bars. They were essentially an extension southwards of the plush hotels of Miami Beach. In them music was kept up endlessly over loud-speakers and, weekly, more and more well-known performers came from the U.S. to the cabarets. There were other new buildings, too, such as the even taller FOCSA building, a smart apartment block. Sheltering at the foot of these peaks lay many elegant villas, some embassies, some government departments, some still in the hands of the rich families who had built them during the early 1900s. It was in this part of Havana that the creeping 'Floridization' of the country was most visible.

A long broad avenue skirted the coast, the Malecón, which had begun to be built in the days of General Wood, offering splendid views, carrying the tourist or the gangster, the revolutionary or the sugar broker from the pillared arcades of old Havana past the remains of the old fort La Punta, as far as the Hotel Havana Riviera's bizarre blue pleasure-dome, passing on the way monuments to the students shot by the Spaniards in 1871, to the dead of the *Maine*, to Maceo and to Martí. The streets of Vedado, like the old city, were laid out on the gridiron pattern, but more irregularly, with variations due to ancient watercourses, paths or other boundaries.

Vedado had been extended on the west by a tunnel under the River Almendares, begun in 1950 by the engineer Manuel Ray, who showed his mastery also of conspiracy and sabotage in the year the tunnel was opened. The extension led to the most modern of the suburbs of Havana, Vedado's own successor as the home of the gracious, a huge area known as Miramar and, beyond, the even more gracious zone known as 'El Country Club'. This soft suburb had been constructed in the great days of *vacas gordas* during the 1920s and linked Havana with what had once been the separate township of Marianao. Miramar, and El Country Club even more, was a place of large comfortable houses, leafily set in their own grounds, to each house a royal palm and a hibiscus, with garages and outhouses, Havana's Wimbledon or Chevy Chase, though on a more exotic scale. The coastal frontier of Miramar was dotted with famous clubs and hotels with their private beaches – Havana Miramar Yacht Club, Hotel Commodore Yacht Club, Havana Biltmore Yacht Club, Copacabana Hotel Club. There stood too the 'largest theatre in the world', El Blanquita. El Country Club boasted above all, of course, the club after which it was named: there business men and politicians drank rum and Coca-cola (*Cuba Libre*), played golf, rode and behaved like gentlemen. Miramar or El Country Club was the home of the ABC colony, as Vedado had been thirty years before. It was the site of Tropicana, 'largest night club in the world', where Javier Pazos's famous bomb had exploded among the high heels on New Year's Eve, 1956. Not far, also, to the south-west of Miramar, lay the army head-quarters, Batista's favourite Campamento Columbia, with its airfield and its modern barracks. There was also the Colón cemetery where the marble vaults of the rich were fitted with lifts, air conditioning and telephones.[36]

The fourth and last Havana was the zone where most Habaneros lived, though there was not much remarkable about it. It was a large, dirty, dusty region behind Vedado and Old Havana, much of it slum, though most of it dating from the twentieth century, with some quarters, such as Pogolotti (called after the developer) conscious efforts at slum replacement by the creation of explicit working-class areas. None of this was picturesque; it was inadequately served by *guaguas*, full of frustration, steamily hot in summer, but noisy and animated at all times. It was a territory of crime, factories, tenements, small cinemas and cock-pits.[37]

Havana's several skins caused it to seem comparable to most cities of the rich and developed world rather than to the capitals of poor countries. There were a large number of little squares, most of them adorned with statues of Martí or some other hero. But contrasts were more extreme even than in Naples. Anxiety over traffic existed alongside beggars. There were eighteen daily papers, thirty-two radio stations, and five television centres; the city was so spread out as to demand car travel; air-conditioning had arrived on a large scale in hotels, businesses, restaurants, and many private houses, causing the breezy sections such as Vedado or Miramar to appear doubly enticing. But this contrasted with the slums, also doubly. Havana made other Caribbean capitals, such as Kingston, Jamaica, or San Juan, Puerto Rico, seem provincial:

[36] Robin Blackburn, *Prologue to the Cuban Revolution.*

[37] The nearby towns of Guanabacoa, Santiago de las Vegas, and Regla were also classified for administrative purposes in the metropolitan area of Havana. The first and last of these were centres of *santería*.

but the standard of living in the Cuban countryside lagged behind the levels in those islands.

Santiago, the second city of Cuba after Havana, with a population of 180,000, also contrasted with it. Its centre remained Spanish-colonial. No new North American architecture disturbed its agreeable symmetry. Its university, much less politically disturbed than Havana's, had almost as good a name. Its inhabitants regarded themselves as superior to those of Havana, and many were. It rejoiced in a tradition of rebellion. Its Spanish accent was specially eccentric, due to a mixture of bastard French deriving from the emigrants from Haiti, partly to the admixture of African words (some frenchified themselves). It had a pronounced black majority.[38]

A quarter of the people in Havana were born outside the province. In the other provinces the number of internal immigrants was negligible. For the first time in Cuban history too, immigration from abroad was no longer important. Over a million and a quarter immigrants, mostly Spaniards, had entered the island between 1902 and 1930, but afterwards the numbers were small.[39] By 1953 the number of persons born beyond Cuba was only 4% of the total (compared with 12% in 1919). Almost half of the 230,000 who were foreign-born lived in Havana province,[40] but many of these people had become nationalized and in 1953 only 150,000[41] were actually foreign citizens. Of these, men outnumbered women by over 50%[42] and half of these were Spanish.

The high percentage of 'foreigners' had dropped, due to lack of immigration during the depression and afterwards due to governmental nationalization policy, which caused the repatriation of many non-Cuban West Indians. Another factor was a change in the nationality law in 1940, whereby Cuba, following the U.S. in this as in everything, considered all those born in her territory, even from foreign parents, as Cuban, unless at twenty-one they renounced this and chose the nationality of the father.

Partly as a result there were now only half as many Spaniards in Cuba

---

[38] The population of other cities in 1953 were: Camagüey 110,000, Matanzas 64,000, Santa Clara 77,000, Cienfuegos 58,000, Guantánamo 64,000, Cárdenas 44,000, Pinar del Río 40,000, Sancti Spiritus 38,000.

[39] 1,280,000. *Investment in Cuba*, 177.

[40] Census of 1953, xxxiv. Foreigners (i.e. born abroad)

1953	230,431
1943	246,551
1931	436,897
1919	339,082
1907	228,741
1899	172,535

[41] 149,327.

[42] 102,612 men to 46,715 women. 74,561 were Spanish, 6,503 U.S., 27,543 Haitian (nearly all in Oriente or Camagüey), 14,421 'English' – mostly Jamaican, and also mostly in the east.

THE ISLAND · 319

as there had been even ten years before. Many workers had gone back to Spain during the depression and then, due to Spain's own condition and Cuba's new nationalistic laws, there was no chance of return. Some immigration had derived from refugees of the Spanish Civil War – radicals, technicians, men of experience: these (and here Cuba resembled many South American countries) were an important and often explosive little group afterwards. There were a number of clubs for Spaniards, particularly the old regional ones such as the Centro Asturiano or *central Gallego* in old Havana, both founded in the 1880s. These were much the most effective co-operative bodies in Cuba, owning clinics and hospitals, whose separate identity had in the past indeed given rise to acute political tension. Spanish working class immigrants continued to be called Gallegos even though many did not come from Galicia. The Cubanization law of 1934 had driven many Spaniards out of industrial jobs to become taxi drivers, servants, waiters. Spaniards still dominated the Church, which was therefore the more ineffective.[43]

There were about 16,000 Chinese in Cuba, almost all male, as in the past: half were in Havana province, many of them market gardeners.[44] In Havana the Chinese had a monopoly over laundering, and there was also Chinatown. The Chinese population not surprisingly was decreasing, though Chinese marriages with white or black had been common and those half-yellow, half-white usually regarded themselves (and were so regarded) as white. The Chinese were held to be homosexual by many – again scarcely surprisingly.[45] There were several Chinese clubs, and the Kuomintang had a branch. The Chinese themselves, on the other hand emphasized the part played by Chinese in the war of independence and in other struggles.[46]

8,000 Jews were supposed to live in Cuba, 5,000 in Havana. Many came from East Europe after the First World War. About three-quarters were engaged in small retail trades. A Jewish Chamber of Commerce and other Jewish commercial associations existed in Havana, and the Havana Jews had been important during the formation of the Cuban Communist party.[47]

6,500 U.S. citizens were formally residents of Cuba but many more lived there for short periods. There were in addition a group of English and Canadian businessmen, all together forming an important community. Most were executives, others owned property inland. They lived at Vedado, Miramar, latterly in El Country Club, in attractive modern

---

[43] See below, 345.
[44] Census of 1953, 89.
[45] Ortiz, *Negros Esclavos*, 12.
[46] See, for instance, Juan Jiménez Pastrana, *Los Chinos en las Luchas por la Liberación Cubana, 1847–1930*, a revolutionary account.
[47] See *Cuba: The Pursuit of Freedom*, 577.

houses, almost always with servants. They would be seen most often at the Country Club itself, the Havana Yacht Club, the Miramar Club, centres of cocktails known by their English names. Many ABC women belonged to a Women's Club, concerned with good works, or the Mothers' Club, where there were tea dances for children. The Women's Club met at a building built by the Masons, where the Little Theatre and th Choral Society presented their productions.

The ABC colony exercised an influence disproportionate to its numbers. Because of the wealth of the countries from which they came, and their self-confidence, they set the tone of upper-class social life. The Cuban upper middle class was imitative and easily copied U.S. modes of behaviour. All rich Cubans had money in North America, most had been educated there or would send their children to be educated there, many looked on North America as their social guarantor: some were really more North American than Caribbean. In return, North Americans who lived in Cuba a long time became gradually Cubanized, their fates entangled with Cuba's.

The Cubans, however, modelled their eating habits on Europe, not the U.S.: two meals a day, one at noon, one at night. Small cups of delicious coffee were also drunk at all hours in offices, in little screws of paper. Mutton or lamb being unknown, the Cubans ate beef or veal, sometimes pork. Most meat was sold fresh without refrigeration and supplies were therefore unsteady. Native pigs gave pork, but little ham, bacon or lard. Cuban bread traditionally resembled Spanish, but by the 1950s the vile U.S. style was being introduced, particularly in the Havana district, where there was modern machinery, including meaningless wrapping equipment. There happily remained, however, many Cuban bakeries, since the old Cuban loaf was not easily mechanized.

The Cuban dishes *par excellence* were still chicken with rice (much rice was usually imported till the 1950s) and soup of black beans (also about half imported). Rice was in great demand, but since so much was imported from the U.S. (before the war, from the East) it was expensive. Plantains – banana vegetables – were used both green and ripe, sometimes cooked as chips. Other vegetables often used were sweet potato (*boniato*), malanga, yucca, yam and some ordinary potatoes. Green vegetables were mostly unknown and fruit was not much eaten.

The Cubans were fairly abstemious. The upper classes drank whisky, brandy and a little French or Spanish wine. The rest drank rum, *aguardiente* and local gin or beer. Coca-cola, Pepsi-cola, Canada Dry ginger ale, were as well-known in Cuba as in the U.S.: all these had Havana subsidiaries. Exquisite *refrescos* (pineapple juice, cane juice, even banana juice) were often drunk. More soft drinks were drunk in the 1950s than ever before. Bottled waters were popular because of vague inherited doubts about the purity of ordinary water, now rarely justified save in inland Oriente.

Cuba ate a good deal of sugar: her consumption per head of 50 kilos[48] a year was only exceeded by England, Australia and Denmark; it was higher than that of the U.S. (48 kilos). In comparison, Indians ate only 10 kg, Italy 15, Mexico 31, France 29. But only at rather low levels can consumption of sugar per head be regarded as an index of the standard of living.[49] In Cuba sugar was often eaten raw, before refining. Many rural families ate vast quantities of cane in the dead season, when they had no money to buy other food. The Cuban consumption of sugar was in 1958 not much above what it had been in 1938[50] and probably higher in the 1920s than in the 1950s.

Consumption of meat seems to have been about 65 lbs to 70 lbs a year, in comparison with 85 lbs in the late 1940s, and about half that of the U.S.[51] The average Cuban's daily consumption of 2,740 calories was adequate, but that did not take into account the high starch consumption and low share of the average person in lower-class Havana and Oriente.

By most criteria, Cuba was now one of the better off countries in Latin America. Income per head lay between $350 and $550 a year, probably nearer the higher figure.[52] The only Latin American countries which definitely exceeded these figures were Argentina and Venezuela.[53] These figures prove little; first they are probably inaccurate;[54] second, even if true they tell little of the nature of the country, its injustice or its poverty in the terms most people think of such matters. The English drank five and a half million bottles of champagne in 1963–4.[55] This could be held to mean that 'every other family had a bottle' whereas that would be an inaccurate picture of the champagne habits of the English. So it is with these Cuban figures. What point is

[48] 1956.

[49] Consumption figures of exporting countries are rather unreliable, but, according to Vitón and Pignalosa, Jamaica took only 33 kg per head, the Dominican Republic 24, and Brazil 36. Cuba clearly ate more sugar than any other major exporting country. Russian consumption figures are also high.

[50] 37 kg.

[51] *Investment in Cuba*, 74; Coléou, *L'élévage et les producteurs*, 68. H. T. Oshima, *A new estimate of the national income and product of Cuba in 1953* (Food research studies, Vol II, No. 3, Stanford, 1961), 219, said 66·1 lb.

[52] No statistics of underdeveloped countries are reliable. These statistics (precise figures being $433 and $544) are those of the National Bank of Cuba and those in Oshima (117). Felipe Pazos, director of the National Bank of Cuba 1950–52 and again in 1959, accepted Oshima's estimate (*Cambridge Opinion*, February 1963).

[53] U.N. Statistical Yearbook.

[54] The GNP figures from which these were obtained vary in different texts. Thus for 1958 Banco Nacional: $M2,738; Oshima: $M3,305; U.N. (Statistical Yearbook, 1961, 486): $M2,397.

[55] *Times*, 20 November 1965.

there in taking an average between the millionaire's income and the beggar's? Distribution of income is the test. However, even if these figures were accurate, they would mean that Cuba, richest pearl of the Antilles, was poorer than Greece, though probably richer than Spain, at that time. The U.S., Cuba's nearest neighbour (except for Haiti and Jamaica), probably had in 1957 an income per head of $2,572.[56] So it would be right to consider Cuba a poor country, indeed one where, though even supposing the national wealth was justly spread, poverty could be regarded as a dominant fact of life; not though in the same category of poverty as India, Mexico, Bolivia or Haiti.[57] Calculations about incomes also give inaccurate pictures of standards of living since they omit not only regional variation but questions such as leisure or climate, which are not only important but have financial implications.[58] At the same time, it does not seem that even by the debauched standards possible the national income rose much in the 1950s. Incomes, according to the National Bank, rose from $206 a year in 1945 to $344 in 1951, and with various ups and downs climbed to $356 by 1958. The average income between 1952 and 1958 must have been about $334; between 1947 (after which prices seem relatively stable) and 1951, $306. These facts indeed offer a good example of how easy it is to prove anything with figures: between 1947–50 and 1951–8 the average income might be said to have gone up 9%, and between 1951 and 1958 it perhaps went up 4% or under 0·5% a year. Supposing these figures correct, incomes in real terms were not much higher than they had been in the early 1920s. Admittedly, from 1929 till the war there had been a slump in sugar and other prices, and that had caused a severe drop in incomes.[59]

The general experience of the Cuban Republic indeed was that incomes were not expected to go up, but rather to remain the same, or maybe drop and then rise again; and that in terms of buying power the peak of all time was the end of the First World War.

These statistics are the explanation of Cuba's economic organization. Cuban society was less underdeveloped than stagnant. Fewer children proportionately of school age went to school in the 1950s than in the 1920s.[60]

[56] *Historical Statistics of the U.S.A.*, 139.
[57] Even if the highest of these figures is taken as accurate – $550 – then the last time the U.S. had such a figure was in 1934–5.
[58] See K. Silvert, 'A hemispheric perspective', in Plank, *op. cit.*, 132–4.
[59] The World Bank reported in 1950 (7): 'In the past decade *per capita* real income has risen 30%. But this [about $300] is only slightly above that of the early 1920s.' During the 1950s there was evidently a small superficial rise in real *per capita* incomes. (For comparison with 1929 figures, *c.f.* World Bank, 38; also, comment in D. Seers, ed., *Cuba, the economic and social revolution* (1964), 12 and 391, and Draper, *Castroism*, 99–100).
[60] See Ch. 28.

No new sugar mills had been built since the 1920s. (Admittedly, there had been too many founded very quickly before.)[61] The main income of the country depended therefore on a crop whose structure had been settled twenty-five years before. People talked as if they regarded over-coming the effects of the slump and returning to the *status quo* – just as, in the middle ages, men were fascinated by the vision of *Roma antiqua*, not of the future. Despite the modern buildings in Havana which caught the eye, Cuba was essentially an old society barely maintaining herself, and perhaps affected adversely by the knowledge that in existing world conditions her main product, sugar, could not hope to be sold to more countries than already bought it.[62] The consequences of economic stag-nation were greater since the population went up by 2·3 % between 1943 and 1953, and the rate of increase was probably higher after 1953.

The difficulty of knowing who had what is the chief characteristic of most material on old Cuba at this, its sunset hour. Thus there was one physician per 1,000 people and one dentist per 3,000, compared with 1,900 and 20,000 respectively in Mexico.[63] But though the doctors in Cuba had increased in number by over 50 % between 1943 and 1953, the history of the Republic suggests a greater proportion of doctors – in 1943 more than half – were in Havana or its neighbourhood.[64] Havana had also 600 dentists out of 1,000; 650 nurses out of 900; 400 chemists out of 660; and even 130 vets out of 200. Clustered round the capital, with high standards specially noticeable in serving the ABC colony, this relatively large number of doctors available to the better-off no doubt exacerbated rather than soothed social tension.

Statistics apart, however, the organization of health did make medicine available to most people except during very bad times. Each of the country's 126 *municipios* (roughly equivalent to counties in the U.S.) employed one doctor to give medical attention. He charged a nominal fee while attention at his clinic or in the hospital was free. In 1934 this worked out in the country as one physician for each 13,000 of the population and one free hospital bed for each 1,700. In comparison, in Havana there was in the same year one poor relief doctor for each 3,000 people and one hospital bed per 180 people: and these figures take no account of the many rich who sought private medicine. The discrepancy between town and country therefore could not be greater.[65]

[61] See Ch. 29.
[62] Explained more fully below; see Ch. 29.
[63] Draper, *Castroism*, 100, qu. *Statistical Abstract of Latin America, 1962.*
[64] i.e. province. 1943 was the last census year for which statistics were available by province.
[65] *Problems of the New Cuba,* 119.

Everything requires qualification. Many poor people would go to Havana, if they could, for medical attention. Bribery and influence secured prior attention in many municipal clinics. In very poor times, as during the depression, the indigent would be unable to afford the journey to the doctor or even his nominal fee if they got there. The debility of the public service, if less notable than in respect of education, affected the medicine services severely. Many poor people would go to herb-doctors or medicine men. The lunatic asylum at Mazorra near Havana was particularly scandalous, patients being treated callously while the Director was a political appointee interested primarily in his salary (under Batista the Director even seems to have made money by selling the land on which the asylum had been built). Equipment of every sort was lacking.

But all in all Cuban health steadily improved throughout the history of the Republic. The main killers of the past, tuberculosis, typhoid and malaria, decreased substantially. There was no smallpox epidemic after 1897 and no outbreak of yellow fever after 1905. Infant mortality had dropped enormously, even since the 1930s. Thus in 1958 the figure of infant deaths was about 35 per thousand, while in the five years 1928–32 it had been on the average 111: the equivalent, incidentally, to the present difference between the black population of South Africa and the whites. It was therefore appropriate that Aníbal Escalante, a Communist leader for many years and one who must have seen the changes for the better that had occurred since he entered politics, should write in 1961: 'Cuba is one of the countries (of Latin America) where the standard of living of the masses was particularly high', and went on to criticize the argument that Revolution is the more likely in countries where the misery is greatest.[66]

Cuba's proximity to the U.S. meant that it was easy for her citizens to lay hands on many items frequently regarded as indices of social advance. Thus Cuba had more telephones per head than any other Latin American country except Argentina and Uruguay;[67] more wirelesses than any except Uruguay;[68] and far more television sets than any other Latin American country:[69] Cuba indeed had more television sets per head than Italy, a dry statistic but through them Castro turned the country aflame. In respect of cars per head, she ranked above all Latin

---

[66] *Verde Olivo*, 30 July 1961.

[67] 26 per 1,000. *Cf.* Argentina 60, Uruguay 50, U.S. 381, U.K. 144.

[68] Cuba 194 per 1,000, Argentina 159 per 1,000, Uruguay 261 per 1,000, U.S. 945 per 1,000.

[69] Cuba 56 per 1,000, Argentina 19 per 1,000, Italy 43 per 1,000. In 1953 the census proclaimed that Cuba had 78,931 television sets; by 1959 these increased to about 360,000 to 400,000 (Census of 1953, 253; UNESCO, *Basic Facts*, 166). There appear to have been 4,500,000 television sets in Latin America in the early 1960s, so Cuba probably had a tenth of them, a larger share than any other country.

American countries except Venezuela.[70] Havana in 1954 is believed to have bought more Cadillacs than any other city in the world.[71] These interesting facts, however, merely show that for Cuba, unlike most of the rest of Latin America except Mexico, transport costs from the U.S. were small and there was no problem of foreign exchange. The dollar and peso remained interchangeable and Cuba's exports to the U.S. always covered her purchases. The existence of wirelesses and television sets on this scale, by laying the apparent facts of North America's faintly absurd riches before large and often neglected audiences, doubtless whetted appetite for change. Alas, no figures exist for the imports of guns and revolvers into Cuba; but, like other U.S. manufactured goods, they were in constant supply.

[70] i.e. passenger cars: 25 per 1,000 inhabitants, 29 in Venezuela. All these figures derive from *UN Statistical Year Book, 1960–3*. Draper, in a similar analysis, has slightly different figures, taken from *Statistical Abstract for Latin America, 1960*. Robin Blackburn pointed out (*loc. cit.*) that the television sets of Cuba compensated Castro for the lack of an organized party.

[71] Ruiz, *Cuba, The Making of a Revolution*, 9.

CHAPTER 25

The Class Structure of Cuba

The structure of class in Cuba at the end of the 1950s was naturally stained by the hectic political events of the last three generations. The eighteenth-century *criollo* aristocracy had, during the golden age of sugar during the mid-nineteenth century, been largely displaced by adventurous capitalist immigrants from northern Spain. These in their turn had been wrecked in the 1880s and 1890s by the European sugar beet revolution, by the wars of independence, and by the challenge of technology made possible by North American capital. In the twentieth century, as has been seen, North Americans dominated the economic life of the country, despite a Cuban recovery of many sugar mills after 1934. These changes at the top of society, caused by the rapacious demands of sugar, brought shudders and cracks to the rest of the community, though in some ways the life of the sugar worker changed less than that of anyone else during the twentieth century: no new machinery was introduced which compared in its effect with the changes of the nineteenth century, and the life of the cane-cutter with his *machete* had changed much less than that of the Havana businessman, or even the Havana factory worker.

The size of the different sectors in Cuban society is not very easy to estimate, but at the bottom of the social scale there seem to have been some 200,000 families of peasants, of which 140,000 at least were very poor, owning, renting or 'squatting' on not much more than one *caballería* of land.[1] Some squatters (*precaristas*) became cane-cutters during the harvest. Many small farmers lived in very precarious circumstances, despite laws introduced since 1934, which were designed to help them – and in many cases did. In the Sierra Maestra, for instance, there was a state of half civil war long before Castro set up camp there in 1956, between landlord's agents and *precaristas* and, in disturbed times armies or landlords often treated peasants with complete callousness. Thus in the 1950s Benito Taboada Bernal, being friendly with Batista's president of the Senate, Anselmo Alliegro, took over with

---

[1] The size of the farm is not a good guide to wealth, since a tobacco grower with one *caballería* (33 acres) was of course rich in comparison with a farmer who planted a *caballería* of cane.

impunity over 1,000 *caballería* of land belonging to small farmers near Baracoa.[2]

Alongside this large peasant population, there were in Cuba some 600,000 rural workers, of whom well over half were cane-cutters, only employed fully during harvests. Some of these naturally had a few chickens and a little land of their own. Unlike the days of slavery, these workers were clearly differentiated from the 100,000 or so workers on sugar mills, the aristocrats of the labour force, well organized and dominant in the union system both under the Communists (before 1947) and with Mujal (after 1947). Next in social status came the 400,000 or so families of the Cuban urban proletariat, also well organized in unions. Alongside them were to be found perhaps 200,000 petty bourgeois families, street vendors, waiters, servants, dancers, parasitic in the sense that they lived off the rich or the tourists, uncertain in number since many were seasonally unemployed.

Finally, there was a large class of permanently or partially unemployed, half of them perhaps living in the shanty towns which were a characteristic of Havana or of Santiago as of most Latin American cities and perhaps one-half would-be rural workers, or at least countrymen. This group perhaps numbered 650,000, or a third of the labour force in some months of the year, such as May and June and September and October, though the figure may have dropped to about 400,000 or even below in the rest of the year.[3]

By the criteria used most often, Cuba had in the 1950s a large middle class: 53,000 persons had gained a university degree or diploma, just under 70% men; 86,000 were classified as professional or technical men – half that number being teachers;[4] another 90,000 were executives or directors of companies. There were 6,000 civil servants. As for what is usually referred to, inaccurately, slightingly, but nevertheless usefully, as 'the lower middle class', there were about 140,000 office workers and 120,000 salesmen.[5] In addition there were in the 1950s the enormous number of 185,000 officials, either national or local, 11% of the total population in employment, and most of

[2] Dr Carlos Rafael Rodríguez commented later that 'after 1952 all signs of legality vanished in the countryside' (Carlos Rafael Rodríguez, *La Revolución Cubana y el Período de Transición*, University of Havana mimeographed, folleto II). This is an excellent study, full of useful information.

[3] I have here largely followed the figures of Dr Carlos Rafael Rodríguez, *op. cit.* Slightly different figures are given by Robin Blackburn in *Prologue to the Cuban Revolution*. Both, however, base their estimates on the report of the *Consejo Nacional de Economía* of 1958. That document actually estimated overt unemployment at 361,000 unpaid workers (i.e. those who worked free for relations or parents) at 154,000, and partially unemployed (i.e. those who worked less than thirty hours a week) at 150,000.

[4] Census of 1953, 123–4.

[5] Census of 1953, 204–5.

them ill-paid, corrupt and the creatures of one or other of the leading politicians.[6]

To the size, intelligence and resilience of this Cuban middle class, many writers have paid special tribute.[7] That it was large is certain. But nevertheless, it had several unique characteristics which differentiated it from other middle classes in Latin America. First, it was not flanked by powerful landowners or by an upper class. The Cuban aristocracy had disintegrated during the sugar crisis between the two wars of independence. Old families such as the Calvos, Montalvos, and Pedrosos, remained, but not as latifundistas, the owners of half a province such as persisted in nearly all the rest of Latin America.[8] No descendant of an original grantee from the Spanish Crown owned a sugar mill in the 1950s. Instead, the largest and most productive estates were the property of companies, now mostly in name Cuban, but in the recent past mostly North American. Some aristocrats (Agramontes, Betancourts) held large cattle ranches in Camagüey, but these were not the greatest in the island. Others held cane *colonia*, sometimes being rich men: the list of big *colonos* in 1959 included a Zulueta, several Sotolongos, and an Iznaga. Others still more typically were in Havana, doubtless living well on stocks or high incomes, but essentially business men: such a one was Víctor Pedroso, president of the Bankers' Association and also of the Havana Yacht Club. Naturally, this section of society mixed extensively with the U.S. community: appropriately Elena Montalvo, descendant of all the oligarchy of the nineteenth century, married the elder son of Dayton Hedges, the textile millionaire; but if successful North Americans got their wives from the old Cuban families, the old Cuban families often got their standards, their dress, their drinks (as well, of course, as cars, telephones, radios and refrigerators) from the U.S. As the poet Pablo Armando Fernández put it to a North American traveller, 'Even our bad taste was imported'.[9] Other aristocrats had sunk rather lower: thus the Marqués de Almeiras was an employee at the Emergency Hospital, Havana.[10] In general, however, whereas, elsewhere in Latin America, rich business men made themselves landowners, in Cuba landowners made themselves, if they could, into businessmen. This is not to say that there were no rich in Cuba, of course; indeed, though it is hard to prove statistically, there were

[6] World Bank, 453. 80% of the national budget was spent on salaries in 1950, less later.

[7] Thus Gino Germani, in *Social Aspects of Economic Development in Latin America* (Paris UNESCO), 229, says Cuba had 22% in the middle and upper strata. Carlos María Raggi Ageo, *Materiales para el estudio de la clase media en la América Latina*, II, 79, said in 1950 that 33% (at least) of the economically active Cubans were middle class. Draper discusses the subject in *Castroism*, 76 ff., and Felipe Pazos, in *Cambridge Opinion*, February 1963.

[8] Except in Mexico and Bolivia.

[9] Warren Miller, *Ninety Miles from Home* (New York, 1961, 32).

[10] *Havana Post*, 15 September 1957. He was Abelardo de Zuazo.

probably more Cuban millionaires per head of population than any-where south of Dallas – millionaires in dollars, too, not Mexican *pesos* or Venezuelan *bolívarés*. But they were rich as capitalists, not men of land, though they might buy country estates as symbols of prestige and keep them half uncultivated. They were men of Havana, not of the country – a fact which lessened the likelihood of regional hostility towards a government (one of the chief difficulties in other parts of Latin America: thus in Mexico even the left wing ex-President Cárdenas was the master of his own province). They had also been implicated in all the political and commercial booms and eclipses of the last fifty years; they had no Olympian prestige, no social standing beyond politics.[11] The foremost North American student of Cuban society before revolution indeed concluded that there was no national middle class in Cuba.[12] He was right, in the sense that they were 'upper' not 'middle'. His belief was that Cuban society, despite settlement of the island a century before permanent white settlement in North America, had never articulated itself. In fact, there had once been a certain society worthy of the name – that of the oligarchy of the early nineteenth century. This had been ruined by technological change, war and revolution. Also, though firm after its fashion, it had been based on slavery and, even more artificial, the slave trade. That world had vanished along with the *volante*, the liveried *calesero*, the fast slave ships with their raking masts, that had so entranced Theodore Canot in Havana harbour. The old order changed but gave place to nothing new. From the 1880s onwards Cuba was a society of adventurers. Political independence brought interludes of hectic prosperity, never freedom from unrest. Wealth was made by speculation. North Americans burst into the country in the good times, and broke out again in the bad. Poor men became rich, the rich poor. The Dance of the Millions in 1920 and the depression of 1929–33 affected the Cuban middle class almost as severely as the collapse of the mark and the depression did the German middle class. Though the urban *bourgeoisie* of Havana was stratified into classes distinguished by numerous symbols of status, there was much social mobility. The more intelligent the observer, the more bewildered he became. Meantime, the bottom third of society, maybe the bottom half, was the unintegrated black or mulatto world, a world still half subconsciously longing for the unobtainable 'Guiné', the dream world of Africa, where

> All live happy
> A-dancing in de patios

[11] This argument has also been developed in a contribution by the author, 'Middle Class Politics and the Cuban Revolution', in *The Politics of Conformity in Latin America*, ed. Claudio Véliz (Oxford University Press (1967).
[12] Lowry Nelson, 139.

Where all God's children
Ain't sol' fuh money.[13]

Perhaps the survival of the Negro world, the actual expansion of 'criminal anthropology' (as whites from Castile referred to Afro-Cuban ritual), exacerbated the tendency for two classes, one rich, one poor.

The second characteristic of the Cuban middle class was its peculiar frustration. Relatively prosperous, as was evident to any casual visitor to Havana, the middle class of the 1950s was strongly affected by the stagnation in the economy, so that everywhere there seemed a lack of opportunities – political, social, and also, partly because of the labour laws, economic. The frustration was specially strongly felt by young men just leaving the University, and indeed in some ways the middle class in Cuba felt more acutely frustrated than did the workers. Young men were specially pleased to find in the U.S. a kind of perfect scapegoat, while Batista's dictatorship, relatively kid-gloved to begin with, but becoming needlessly cruel and superficial, acted as a catalyst to all these feelings.

The shifting character of the middle class is well illustrated by the most unsteady rise in the number of servants: in 1899 there were over 40,000 servants.[14] Most were black;[15] over 6,000 were under fifteen; half the male servants and two-thirds of the women were illiterate. By 1907 (a lean year) the number of servants had fallen slightly.[16] Native Cubans were exceeded by white foreigners, mostly Spaniards.[17] Between a third and a half were in the city of Havana. By now half could read, and most of those in Havana could do so.[18] Twelve years later, in the golden days of sugar production just after the First World War, servants had doubled, to over 80,000.[19] Over half were now male, and now over half were white.[20] In 1943, after the depression, the servant force had dropped back to the same in numbers as in 1907 – a little over 40,000,[21] half being black or mulatto. The foreign white had dropped to about 3,500,[22] even though the Cubans' Alien Labour law had forced some Spaniards into domestic service. Over half were in

[13] Castro Alves, the 'poet of the slaves', qu. C. M. Lancaster, 'Gourds and Castanets', *Journal of Negro History*, vol. 28, 78 (January 1943).
[14] 41,464 according to the census.
[15] Census of 1899, 463: 11,289 male and 17,390 female, to 3,171 and 4,267 native white; 4,197 and 1,150 foreign.
[16] 39,312.
[17] Census of 1907, 545.
[18] *Ibid.*, 566.
[19] 83,157. Census of 1919, 145.
[20] Foreign whites (chiefly Spaniards) numbered 21,000 and Cuban white 25,000. 1,500 boys and 2,000 girls were under fifteen. Over half could read.
[21] 43,795.
[22] Census of 1943, 1114.

Havana.[23] The average wage was under $30 a month.[24] Ten years later, thanks to the post-war prosperity, servants again numbered over 70,000, an increase of well over half since 1943.[25]

The professional middle classes in Cuba were, as in most other places, less than half the total group who can be described as the *bourgeoisie*:[26] thus in 1953 there may have been about 20,000 schoolteachers together with about 40,000 others who could conceivably have been so regarded. The nearly 100,000 business men, merchants, bankers, other administrators or directors of enterprises had committed themselves deeply to Batista as they had to all previous regimes except Grau's. There was hardly a commercial body which had not visited the national palace in 1957 to express its congratulations to Batista on his escape from assassination at the hands of a group which, if not now precisely in power, was nevertheless closely associated with it.[27] In 1958, some prominent business men (such as Vilaboy, of Cubana Airways, or the Shell Manager) fled. Several were imprisoned, perhaps to be tried, perhaps not. Others changed their politics hastily and congratulated the revolutionary government, assuring them of their support in large advertisements in newspapers. But the business community was diminished in the public mind. Some rich men such as Pepín Bosch of Bacardí had supported Castro and others (along with the North American-owned Telephone Company) paid their taxes in advance to assist the new government. This availed them little. Along with news of atrocities[28] there also became known in January 1959 documentary evidence of all sorts of corrupt practices: most striking, perhaps, was the revelation of how some employees of the Telephone Company had managed to escape criticism when it raised prices in 1957:

> There is a simple reason why the larger sections of the press are not complaining. They received their regular contribution . . . in addition to the above-board advertising, thus getting paid more than double. So the only dissatisfaction came from *Bohemia*, the newspapers *Excelsior* and *El País*, and José Pardo Llada, the wireless commentator.[29]

[23] 23,260. *Ibid.*, 1120.

[24] *Ibid.*, 1205.

[25] 71,561. Thanks to the decline in the detail and quality of information given in the Census of 1953 in comparison with 1943, it is not clear how these were divided. Maybe I have shown excessive credibility in accepting these figures. They seem, however, *vraisemblable* in view of other evidence.

[26] e.g. in the U.S. professional, technical and kindred persons numbered five million; managers, officials and proprietors (except farmers) numbered 5·2 million (*Hist. Stat.*, 75).

[27] See above, 147.

[28] The exaggeration of the numbers killed had the political effect of blackening the regime of Batista and its collaborators even further – which was its intention: 'What were they doing when Batista was murdering our sons?' The exaggeration does not mean, of course, that the question was not pertinent.

[29] A photocopy of this document was printed *in extenso* in *Revolución*, 18 January 1959.

This clear alienation of the business world at the start of 1959 had a historical background. There had always been a tendency among Cuban captains of industry to regard politics and government as something to be left on its own, to be ignored as a creative force if at all possible; there were traces in this of the old Spanish situation where creoles were excluded by law from a leading part in government. Although sugar developers of the nineteenth century needed the Spanish government to guarantee the continuance of the slave system by force, no doubt they also found the Spanish regime useful, since it enabled them to abdicate political duties and responsibilities. For much of Cuban history under the Republic, the Cuban *entrepreneur* looked on politics rather as U.S. men of business did in the thirty years following the Civil War. In a sense, they were right. Cuban politics in the twentieth century were at least as poor-spirited as those of the U.S. in the age of Blaine. Julio Lobo refused the secretaryship of the Cuban Treasury under Grau San Martín on the ground that the administration was corrupt. If they could not keep out, business men tried simply to secure that government held the ring to enable them to prosper. Power, they appreciated, lay in New York, not Havana.

Many 'Cuban' business men were North Americans. Many merchants were still Spaniards, as they had been at the start of the century. Such 'foreigners' (as they were referred to in law, though everyone knew that that phrase meant North American or Spanish citizens) could not take part in politics. This in turn had counter-productive consequences. The holding of large sections of capital in a country by foreigners deprives that country of the effects of their power. They are powerful but they cannot as foreigners be responsible.[30]

Typical perhaps of the Cuban-U.S. relation was the Hedges family, already mentioned; the father, Dayton Hedges, son of a New York farmer and a small contractor in Long Island before 1914, came to Havana in the boom years, in 1919. He bought up electrical businesses, made a success of them and sold out to the Cuban Electrical Company in 1928. With the capital so adroitly gathered, he established a large cattle estate and his famous textile business. He also began to grow cotton, which had been neglected in Cuba for a century. He received various Cuban honours, such as the Order of Céspedes, and founded a golf tournament with his name – for the American and English Club. Grateful workers financed a bust of him in marble at the textile factory. In the 1940s he was rich enough to found a big rayon factory in Matanzas. One of his sons married Elena Montalvo, another had been twice

[30] Robin Blackburn therefore concluded (*Prologue to the Cuban Revolution*) that there was in Cuba no 'national bourgeoisie', alluding to the variety of racial and national origins of the major entrepreneurs.

president of the American Club, and a daughter had married a Cuban engineer working in her father's firm. The family were intimate friends of Batista. One village changed its name to Dayton Hedges, and Hedges also founded a model village for his workers where no rent was paid. He was followed as president of the Rayon and Textile Companies by his two sons. When Dayton Hedges died in 1957 his funeral was attended by Batista, most of his cabinet and the British and U.S. ambassadors; although Dayton's sons were in fact Cuban, one of *their* sons was nevertheless a U.S. marine and both were educated in U.S. schools. Later Burke Hedges, the younger son – 'Burkie Boy' to his friends – became Batista's ambassador to Brazil. The total Hedges fortune in Cuba amounted to $M35 in 1958–9.[31]

Cuba in general lacked, apart from the Spanish clubs, the solid voluntary institutions, the benevolent societies and the independent groups of middle-class worthies which characterize North America and Europe and help greatly in limiting executive power. But there were some professional groups of importance, such as the freemasons. The Havana Lodge was supposed to be the biggest in Latin America. It was a powerful and dignified group of business companions, perhaps 50,000 strong,[32] all more or less rationalist. Some of its leaders still believed that in being anti-Catholic they were being revolutionary. They recalled with complacency their *confrère*, Martí, and their heroic role as a division of the rationalists of Spain in the last days of the Inquisition. The Grand Master, Carlos Piñeiro, had founded a big technical college, the so-called Universidad José Martí, in Havana. Like the Baptists, their links with North America were close. There was an English-speaking lodge in Havana, founded during the U.S. military occupation. In the 1950s, the Masonic Temple held few secrets. Like the masons of continental Europe, they rejected the idea of 'The Grand Architect'. Their headquarters were of use even in the struggle against Batista: for instance, the group of Ortodoxo youth who provided the backbone of revolutionaries at Moncada had been wont to meet in the Freemason's Hall at Artemisa. In January 1959, the lodge Hijos de América demanded that the masons of the world unite to back the revolution,[33] but the masons, unlike the workers, had much to lose. This appeal signified merely an alignment with the *status quo*. They had not thereby saved themselves from charges of collaboration with the tyrant.

There were other professional associations. Any job demanding a university degree meant that the holder joined a special college (*colegio*) which tried to maintain standards. 203 colleges guaranteed middle-class

[31] *Havana Post*, 5 June 1957.
[32] H.A.R., xv, 805.
[33] *Revolución*, 26 January 1959.

professional practice with as much energy as they could. In the disturbed political atmosphere, which had lasted as long as anyone could remember, these colleges often became involved in politics. The College of Lawyers (of which Miró Cardona, the new prime minister, was Dean) and the College of Journalists were constantly asked to 'take a stand': so were the colleges of dentists, doctors, vets, architects, all men of good will. They often did, but they did not take to the hills. Since a policy of war had in 1959 conquered, the standing of these professional groups was automatically diminished. They had some heroes to offer in the new epic age now beginning but even a man such as Pelayo Cuervo, killed by the Country Club lake, was tarnished by the accusation of compromise with the old political parties and the belief that he would have accepted something short of Batista's unconditional surrender. 'All that was best in Cuban public life' died with Pelayo Cuervo; and the Country Club lake was a sadly appropriate spot for such a departure.

CHAPTER 26

Black Cuba

In the 1950s the Negro or mulatto population was described as being under one-third of the total; an accurate figure is hard to give, since in 1953 the identification of this or that individual by the curious and misleading euphemism 'coloured' was left to the innumerators, whereas in previous censuses account was taken of the declarations made by the persons concerned. Presumably, therefore, the identification was inaccurate. At least one other published estimate suggested that as many as half of the total were 'Negroid' and another 20% really mulatto,[1] an estimate with which many intelligent observers would agree. These included Fernando Ortiz, the Afro-Cuban folklorist.[2]

OFFICIAL FIGURES FOR BLACK CUBA 1899–1953

		% of total population
1899	505,443	32·1
1907	608,967	29·7
1919	784,811	27·2
1931	1,179,106	27·2
1943	1,225,271	25·6
1953	{ 725,311 Negro 843,105 mulatto } 1,568,416 Total	27·2

However misleading the official figures may be, in comparison with whites there was a drop in the black or mulatto population between 1931 and 1943, due partly to the repatriation of over half the Jamaican or other West Indian labourers who had come to Cuba in the good times of the past,[3] partly to the effects of the depression which hit the poorest Cubans hardest (and probably more of these were black than white). The drop in the early years of the Republic was due to the Spanish immigration. The decline in that immigration, as well as the general recovery of prosperity after the Second World War, accounts

---

[1] MacGaffey and Barnett, 28. See also Goldenberg, 131.
[2] In conversation with the author, July 1966.
[3] 56%. Census of 1943, 741.

for the rise of the black or mulatt o percentage between 1943 and 1953. On the other hand the official figures, which must represent something of the truth, suggest that the 'white' population increased four times, the black or mulatto population three times.

Again according to the official figures, the Negro population dropped from 15% of the total in 1899 to 10% in 1943, and rose again to 12% in 1953, whereas the mulatto population fell from 17% in 1899 to 14·1% in 1953.[4] These changes can scarcely be accurate, given the alterations in methods of examination, but they are all that exist. There was obviously intermarriage between black and white, but more usually between white men and black girls. The voluptuous mulatto remained a symbol for sexual desirability; but marriage between white girls and black or mulatto men was relatively rare. The social area where the races mixed most freely was that of prostitution, habitual criminality, drug trafficking, gambling and superstition.[5] The mixture of Chinese and *mulata* produced offspring of very special beauty.

At the beginning of the century, about twenty municipalities of Cuba had formally a black or mulatto majority of the population, and these remained apparently the most non-white areas. There was little change in fact in the general geographical distribution of the Negroes during the early history of the Republic. This immobility of the black population is one of the many aspects of the matter where Cuba contrasted with the U.S.: the U.S. Negro had little part in the great expansion to the west in the nineteenth century, but moved much in the twentieth.

On paper, even Oriente formally had a majority of white people. Havana province had a total of 350,000 Negro or mulatto people in 1953, or a fifth of the total number; three-fifths[6] of the black population as a whole were considered 'urban' – slightly more, that is, than the national percentage.[7] The birth rate appears to have been higher among whites than coloured. But mulattoes, in Cuba as elsewhere, sought to pass themselves off as 'white' once they got to the towns, and often succeeded, particularly if they became well off.

It is impossible to resolve exactly how (and if so to what extent) the black or mulatto population suffered economically in comparison with whites. In some districts with a theoretically mostly Negro population, the majority in all school ages did not go to school. But in the Oriente towns of Caney and Guantánamo, both of which had a black or mulatto majority, most of those aged ten to fourteen went to school, and

[4] See Census of 1953, 49. Negro population rose from 235,000 to 725,000; mulatto from 270,000 to 840,000.
[5] Ortiz, *Negros Esclavos*, 11.
[6] 943,983.
[7] 'White' figures were 2,365,759 (57·5%) to 1,878,197

in Santiago a majority of those aged five to fourteen. Proximity to a city, more than race matters, determined this. There was little formal difference between predominantly Negro towns in Oriente and nearby mainly 'white' communities; while Santiago, a predominantly black city, resembled Camagüey, predominantly 'white', in the level of school attendance.[8] The only district even in Oriente which seems to have had an illiterate majority was Niquero, in the south-west, which was mainly white.[9] This was because many workers there were recently arrived sugar workers. Black and white illiteracy seems to have been much the same. In the late 1930s a quarter of students were black or mulatto – doubtless an underestimate.[10]

On paper, half the Cuban black or mixed population lived in Oriente,[11] the poorest province. They had not always done so, but then Oriente had not always been the province with the largest population, and it was natural that, in the early years of the century, the opening up of Oriente should attract a great immigration of labour. By the 1950s, however, the vast majority of Cubans were where they were because they had been born and brought up there.[12] Anyone, black or white, living in Oriente, had, again on paper, a less good chance of a good life than anyone living in Havana (schools, doctors, hospitals and so on being far less provided for), only 5,000 people out of the total population[13] having had any higher education. For educational and economic reasons alone it was not surprising to find black people poorly represented among the prestigious middle-class professions.[14] Even there, however, the situation had changed greatly since the beginning of the century. In 1943 there were 560 black or mulatto lawyers – a large number in comparison with the three or four in 1899–1907; 424 doctors were black or mulatto, a fifth of the total in the country, compared with 10 out of 1,000 in 1899–1907. There were also 3,500 teachers, compared with about 16,000 white teachers, though the black ones were more regular attenders than the whites. Negroes were well represented among musicians, painters and others involved in the arts. In 1943 workers on the average received less if black than if white: 46% of black workers got under $30 a month compared to 37% of white, while 43% of white got between $30 and $60 compared to 41·4% of black. There might be little in that but 6% of white workers got over $100 and only 2½% of black.

[8] See Census of 1953, 117–18.
[9] Though the sugar mill workers at Niquero from the manager down were all black or mulatto (evidence of Julio Lobo).
[10] *Problems of the New Cuba*, 32.
[11] 732,696 out of 1,568,416.
[12] See above, p. 336.
[13] 1,797,606.
[14] We have to make do with 1943 statistics in these matters.

In some professions, the black or mulatto population was well established. As in the early part of the century, they dominated laundering, sewing, shoemaking, woodcutting, and tailoring. They were on a level with whites among barbers, bakers, carpenters, coopers, and blacksmiths. They held their own, in terms of their percentage of the population, among tobacco workers. They also represented a majority of the servant population, partly out of tradition, partly because those with servants liked to imitate the North American deep South. In unskilled work, the black or mulatto population did more than its fair share – 26% – of mining, building and industrial activities,[15] but had slightly less than its percentage in agriculture.[16] It would be correct to assume, no doubt, that as in 1900, racial distinction in the country was still the superficial visible symbol of a distinction which in reality was based on the ownership of property.[17]

The Constitution of 1940 barred all race discrimination. This worked reasonably well. The situation was described by Castro in a press conference on 23 January 1959 when he said, in reply to a North American journalist, that 'the colour question' in Cuba did not exist in the same way as it did in the U.S.; there was some racial discrimination in Cuba but far less; the revolution would help to eliminate these remaining prejudices; on this topic, Castro added delphically, 'Our thoughts are the thoughts of Martí.'[18] This was Castro's first comment of any sort on the question of race, though, later on, the Cuban revolution would emphasize race questions harshly. Castro might also have gone on to say that, in so far as it did exist, racial discrimination was chiefly a middle-class phenomenon. The Cuban middle class was always rather

[15] In 1943, the professional breakdown* of black or mulatto to white persons had been:

	Black or mulatto	White
Agriculture, cattle, fishing	23·0	77·0
Mining	33·0	67·0
Construction	44·2	55·8
Manufactures and mechanical industries	35·9	64·1
Transport and communications	22·9	77·1
Commerce	15·9	84·1
Banks and finance	9·2	90·8
Domestic and personal services	46·9	53·1
Recreation and other services	39·7	60·3
Professional services	14·5	85·5
Government	19·3	80·7
Various services	28·0	72·0
Industrial and commerce unclassified	26·5	73·5
Average	25·9	74·1

*Corrected from Census of 1943, 786

[16] The Agricultural Census of 1946 did not make any allusion to the question of colour, so we know nothing about the size of farms in this period.

[17] Williams, *Race Relations in Caribbean Society*, qu. above, p.431

[18] *Revolución*, 23 January 1959. Martí's views were expressed in the Manifesto of Montecristi.

conscious of North American habits. Such racial discrimination as there was appears to have been imitative of North America rather than to have sprung from anything special to Cuban circumstances. In the smarter hotels of Havana, frequented by the American business community,[19] racial prejudice was yet another example of the way that some Cubans were always exiles, even in Havana. There was a half racial, half class colour bar in those streets where the upper class walked in the evenings. In the tobacco industry Negroes were cigar-makers and strippers but not sorters or trimmers.[20] Segregation was most remarked in Camagüey, least so in Oriente. No doubt there was segregation in certain enterprises, and a committee for rights of Negroes had been set up in 1934. There were also clubs for mulattoes and Negroes alone, in addition to the religious groups.[21] Relations between Negroes and mulattoes were ambivalent: one proverb ran: 'One Negro may hurt another; a mulatto will do worse.' Fights between black and white on racial grounds were rare, though some seem to have occurred from time to time; for instance in Trinidad in 1934.[22] That racial prejudice in old Cuba was not overwhelming is suggested by the fact that Castro never mentioned the matter in any of his speeches or programmes before the revolution. To read *History will absolve me* would suggest that Castro was addressing a racially homogeneous nation.

This silence on Castro's part was in fact denounced by militant Cuban Negroes. Some years later, a Cuban Negro Communist of Chinese views, Carlos Moore, criticized Castro as an upholder of white Castilian upper-class ways, and claimed that Castro's alleged improvement in racial harmony was a fraud.[23] The question is more complicated. (One Negro commented in the mid-1960s, 'Before the Revolution the only time I remembered I was black was when I had a bath; now I am reminded of it every day'.[24]) In general, since the mysterious and unsuccessful 'Negro revolution' of 1912, Negroes had not played a prominent part in public life. One or two minor politicians had been mulatto, such as Vasconcelos (a minister under both Prío and Batista and Castro's earliest political sponsor) but none had been as prominent, in the second era of Cuba's history as a Republic, as Morúa Delgado or Juan Gualberto Gómez had been in the first. In Grau's time there were five black or mulatto senators out of fifty, twelve representatives out of 127.

[19] See above, p. 319.

[20] *Problems of the New Cuba* (1935), 32.

[21] Discussed below.

[22] Grant Watson dispatch, 12 January 1934. This was apparently a consequence of Negroes pushing their way into that section of Central Park, Trinidad, habitually reserved to whites.

[23] *Présence Africaine*, November 1965.

[24] Evidence of a Bayamés. On the other hand, Víctor Franco among others reports a comment, 'I wasn't a man before. I was a nigger.' (Víctor Franco, *The Morning After*, 63.) The author has met Cuban Negroes who have said or implied both.

Two prominent generals of Prío's day, Hernández Nardo and Quere-
jeta, were Negroes. Locally, black or mulatto politicians were often successful: for instance, Justo Salas, a Negro, became mayor of Santiago
in the 1940s with votes from the (white) *bourgeois* district against black
votes for his white opponent. Negroes also rose to important positions in
the trade union movement, particularly among the Communist trade
unionists: Lázaro Peña, about to reappear on the political scene,
Aracelio Iglesias, the dockers' leader murdered in 1948, and Jesús
Menéndez, murdered in 1947, were the outstanding ones. The chief
exception was Batista, apparently a mulatto with Chinese blood. He
was the Cuban politician who appealed most to the black population,
precisely because he was a man from outside conventional politics, outside conventions, and because his lower-class origins, his apparent
sympathy with the masses, made him popular. Batista supported and
contributed to the *santería* and ñáñigo rites, whose initiates regarded him
as almost one of themselves, particularly in the city of Trinidad.[25] Indeed,
Batista paid 'out of his own money' for a big reunion in the summer
of 1958 for all the prominent *Santeros* (priests) of Guanabacoa, at which
many cocks and goats were sacrificed to appease the 'demons of war'.

Batista's army and police were full of Negroes and mulattoes. Yañes
Pelletier, the officer who arrested Castro in 1953 after Moncada, was
black. In 1943 (the latest year for which even doubtful statistics are
available), just under one-third of the army was allegedly black or
mulatto, just over what seems to have been the national proportion.[26]
In contrast, most active radicals or progressives were middle-class
whites. About a dozen of Castro's followers at Moncada were black or
mulatto,[27] but this was an exceptional event in Cuban revolutionary
history. Batista's soldiers openly said that it was a disgrace to follow a
white such as Castro against a *mestizo* such as Batista. When Captain
Yañes came on Castro hiding asleep in a *bohío*, it will be recalled that
the soldier who found them cried: '*Son blancos!*' 'They are white!'
Some Negroes even owed their lives at that time to the fact that they
were black.[28] It is not clear how many of the rebel army in the Sierra
were black but a majority certainly were not, and Almeida, a mulatto,
was the only officer of importance who was. The black population
as such never rallied to Castro before 1959. He appeared just another
middle-class white radical, with nothing to say to them.

The alienation of the black community from the revolutionaries and

[25] I am indebted for this comment to Sr Cabrera Infante.
[26] 4,039 Negroes or mulattoes to 14,637 white. There were 947 police of African origin to
5,492 hispanic.
[27] See analysis in appendix XI to *Cuba: The Pursuit of Freedom*.
[28] *Cf.* Merle, *Moncada*, 264, 268. There seem to have been about a dozen Negroes or
mulattoes at Moncada.

conventional politics had really lasted throughout the Republic. Perhaps they were less without means to rise to higher goals, as Lowry Nelson says, than without aspirations to do so. Like all the Caribbean Africans, the Cuban Negroes were still coping, not always satisfactorily, with the heritage of the forced migration of their ancestors, and of slavery itself. This heritage had meant above all the destruction of the family, the substitution (in some cases) for many generations of the Master for the Father, except in his strictly biological function.[29] The Cuban Negroes were still in some respects demanding real emancipation. Their task of adjustment may have been made easier by the fact that African ceremonies and religions sometimes blended effectively with Catholic festivals,[30] though the task of self-articulation may have been more difficult than in the English West Indies, where the white population was insignificant. It was certainly different. Since race is so much a problem of noticeable physical attributes, the predominantly sallow-skinned Spaniards, with their strong draughts of Moorish and Jewish blood, probably blended more easily, at least with mulattoes, than did the pink or beige Anglo-Saxons, Celts, Germans and Slavs who constitute the majority in the U.S.[31] There was no Cuban society for the advancement of coloured people, though in the 1930s some Negro Communists had argued for an autonomous Negro state in Oriente.

Cuban Negroes were not, however, living in a private world of their own. Their world extended outwards to embrace, if not politics, at least painting and music. If a country is measured by its arts, Cuba was over half Negro. African rhythms, echoes of ceremonies forgotten or practised still in secrecy, dominated Cuban popular music and poetry. The dances, for which the Cubans were as famous internationally as their cigars or sugar, were mostly African: the conga, rumba, mambo and finally the pachanga, were all direct popularizations of religious dances. They were not, however, entirely African and in fact their blend of African and Spanish, with some North American and French influences, was their distinctive contribution. Much Cuban music derived from the 'love affair of African drums and Spanish guitar', as Fernando Ortiz put it, echoing the carnival dances of Negroes at Catholic festivals before they were banned. By 1958 the old white Spanish dances, such as the *habanera* or *bolero*, had almost vanished. The best Cuban musicians, such as Brindis de Salas or José María Jiménez, were black. Nicolás Guillén,[32] the best Cuban poet, himself a mulatto, tried to catch in his poetry the

[29] I am indebted to Dr Sherlock for this point.
[30] See *Cuba: The Pursuit of Freedom*, p. 517, for further discussion.
[31] Even pure Castilians are of course darker than Anglo-Saxons.
[32] Born 1904 in Camagüey, published *Motivos de Son* (1930), *Sóngoro Cosongo* (1931), *West Indies Ltd* (1934), etc.

rhythm of the songs of Cuba as his master, García Lorca, did in Spain. Wilfredo Lam, half Chinese, half Negro,[33] in his jungle paintings, was partly an intellectual explorer but partly a mediator between a West already modishly searching for new dreams among primitive things and the African and West Indian worlds of green shadow and magic. The same sort of work was done in sculpture by Teodoro Ramos Blanco. Of course there were very few good Cuban artists who were untouched. The best Cuban novelist, probably the best novelist in South America, Carpentier, used *negrismo* in his *Ecue Yamba-O*, and his marvellous novel *The Kingdom of this World* is a brilliant evocation of Negro feelings during the Haitian revolution[34]. Guillén believed that in Cuba a real mulatto culture (which he named *negri-blanca*) was already, uniquely, in existence.

Artists in Cuba itself were in fact specifically mediators between black and white. So too were the folklorists, among whom Fernando Ortiz, the inspiration of Afro-Cuban studies for half a century and grand prosecutor of sugar monoculture, was the acknowledged master. His books too were an exploration: they awoke middle-class white Cubans to the beliefs, habits and myths of the African Cubans, weakening their fear and ignorance. It was hard to distinguish Afro-Cuban religion from lower-class Catholicism. Upper-class Catholics still referred to Afro-Cuban activities as witchcraft (*brujería*) – the word used by the Afro-Cuban population itself for bogus behaviour at rites. Other more timid writers described the development of Cuban Negroes as 'evolutionary disaster', or as inferior because their languages had no grammar.

The Africans introduced words as well as dances. A little Yoruba or Efik from Nigeria, some Fon from Dahomey, could be heard in Cuba, but the use of African languages was on the whole confined to religions, and, like the Sephardic Jews who lived so long in Arab countries, the Cuban Africans otherwise spoke the language of their adopted country, with different dialects.

The nature of Afro-Cuban religions appears to have become more closely identified than ever with Roman Catholicism since the Negro revolution of 1912. Catholicism was regarded by Africans increasingly as a Spanish version of the African *Santería*, the cult of *orishas*, dead great men. The black or mulatto middle class had become assimilated by white Spanish society except on the occasions of participation in

[33] Born 1902 in Sagua la Grande, son of Yam Lam and Serafina Castilla; educated at the Academia de S. Alejandro, Havana, and Spain; first exhibition Madrid, 1927; Paris, 1939; New York, 1942. Lived most of his life in Paris.

[34] Alejo Carpentier, born 1904, editor of *Carteles*, 1924-8, imprisoned by Machado; in Paris, 1933-9, and in Venezuela, 1945-59. He was the son of a French architect who went to Cuba in 1902.

Abakuá or *santería*, which therefore became more of a contrast with ordinary life. Changó, god of war, and St Barbara remained an uneasy identification, living in a ceiba tree of the acacia family (the only tree never uprooted by hurricanes), dressed alternately as man and woman; St Peter was still Elegua, destiny in a more malevolent dress, and also known as *El Dueño de los Caminos*, Master of the Paths. Destiny or Orumila, St Francis, was believed to have 200–300 *santeros* (*babalaôs*) in Havana alone – part-time, of course – ministering to his needs: white cocks and palm nuts at regular intervals and in special combinations. Madonnas as ever appeared sometimes with tribal marks. God himself, or Olofí, son of the Earth, a shadowy Holy Ghost rather than a Lord of Hosts, played little part. White people continued to go to these celebrations: senators, politicians and mayors would often make obeisance to these curious deities: '*Yo no creo pero lo repito*' ('I do not believe but I repeat the ritual') was a frequent explanation. One Cuban at least out of four had gone at one time or another to some such fiesta.[35]

There was much interchange between the different Africans, including the Cubans, Haitians and Jamaicans who had come for work in the 1920s or before and also in the 1940s. Some Yorubas, however, feared the Haitians' Voodoo. Haitians were thought to order Zombies to chase chosen victims 'at all hours, with a burning candle':[36] Voodoo had of course a nineteenth-century basis in Cuba as well. The ñáñigos were the most secretive of these groups: membership guaranteed a place in the next world only if kept secret. (They had been banned for a time after 1902 but Menocal allowed them to come back as part of an electoral deal.) Ñáñigos were feared by the whites: white nannies would explain to the children of the rich that, if they were bad, ñáñigos would come looking for little white boys.

The black population in Cuba therefore lived still partly in a mysterious dream world, hispanized or North Americanized to some extent, which whites could visit but never really incorporate into their own affluence or poverty. This went ill, inevitably, in a country where materialism had utterly displaced religion. The Communist party, despite its important following among Negroes, criticized the African cults as non-productive and anti-social, but without effect: it was true, however, that the African religions were fundamentally conservative and immobile, if vital: innovations in ceremony were rare except that it seems that during the twentieth century the stones upon which the cocks were sacrificed in Yoruba cults came to have greater and greater significance. These stones, hidden behind a curtain in the lower part of

[35] Catholic Action survey, 1958, qu. B. Macoin, *Latin America, the 11th Hour*, New York, 1962, 69.
[36] MacGaffey and Barnett, 209.

the altar, were supposed to have all sorts of magical powers once they had been baptized in blood. On the other hand, it is clear that this was not a wholly modern development since the most powerful stones, which were supposed to be able to walk, grow and bear children, were said to have been brought from Africa by the slaves.[37]

[37] See W. R. Banscom, 'The Focus of Cuban *Santería*', *South Western Journal of Anthropology*, VI, Spring 1950, quoted R. F. Smith, *Background to Revolution*, New York, 1966.

CHAPTER 27

The Church

The Church emerged from the age of Batista with more credit than most supposed possible: Bishop Pérez Serantes was, of course, one of Castro's oldest friends, and the bishops had interceded for peace. Nevertheless the Church remained a Spanish institution with little hold among even white workers, less among black.[1] The Church was an institution of the upper class. The Negro transposition of African rituals and gods into Catholic guises left the Church as such by the way. The situation remained in 1958 as it was earlier in the century: there were few churches in the country; such country churches as there were were poor; attendance in the cities was confined to conventional white families of Spanish outlook, often women only;[2] there were many foreign (Spanish) priests, and a tradition, dating from the wars of independence, of siding with conservative opinion. Those wars had been so long as to make the Church's identification with Spain almost impossible to sever. The Spanish conservative newspaper, the old *Diario de la Marina*, was strongly clerical.

The separation of Church from State by the U.S. in 1900 had had the effect of alienating the Church still further from the country. When Spain fell the Church fell too, to be discredited so much as to be almost a laughing stock. The Church lost its subsidy from the government, losing still more revenue when civil marriage was made possible after 1902, and compulsory after 1918. Since the mid-nineteenth century, there had been no monastic lands. After the Second World War, several sugar mills began to assume the burden of paying priests' salaries and ordinary parish expenses. This subsidy from private enterprise further removed the Church from the masses, though the bishops themselves claimed they did not know of priests acting as agents of exploitation, only of their taking the side of strikers.[3]

Martí, a Mason and an agnostic, had been excommunicated. The

[1] The international church seemed to have been bowled over by Castro as much as North American opinion. Thus *Il Quotidiano*, whose views were syndicated throughout the world, assured its readers that Castro was 'not red', was a believer, and so could not have any indulgence towards an ideology of materialism (2 January 1959).

[2] Angel del Cerro, in *Ha Comenzado la Persecución Religiosa?* (supplement to *Cuadernos*, March–April 1961), estimated that 10% of the Cuban population practised Catholicism to some degree and 80% would accept it nominally: the latter figure is open to doubt.

[3] Open letter of the Cuban bishops to Castro, 4 December 1960.

fact that he was known as El Apóstol was an almost open insult. The Church was also thought to be corrupt. Its attraction for women caused it to be associated sometimes with effeminacy. Priests with mistresses were respected. Priests working in parishs theoretically numbered 784 in 1953, but may have been fewer in practice.[4] This meant that there were 7,500 Cubans to each priest, or much more than was the case in say Chile or Venezuela (2,750 and 4,350 to the priest respectively). Supposing all were working, however, this in proportion was less than forty years before.[5] The shortage of priests was acknowledged but nothing was done. About two-thirds were Spanish, though only two bishops (including the popular Pérez Serantes, of Santiago) were Spanish. The primate, Cardinal Arteaga, was a native of Camagüey. If those in religious orders were included, the proportion of Spaniards to Cubans rose to four to one. The social origin of the few Cuban priests was chiefly upper class. There were no seminaries or houses of study in Cuba. Hence, candidates went abroad. The Christian Brothers, established about 1900, were mostly French in origin.

If the Church itself was less influential than in many Latin American countries, it could not be shaken off altogether. It had been in Cuba too long; too many Cubans had been brought up nominally Catholic; it permeated attitudes, even of rationalists. Carnivals in honour of local saints persisted, as in Spain, even if the Negroes or mulattoes converted these occasions scandalously. Cities and citizens were called after saints. Religious instruction might be banned in State schools, but still the Church schools remained excellent – particularly (as in Spain) secondary schools. The Church sponsored many welfare efforts and for many years the Sisters of Charity ran the girls' reformatory with sensitivity and efficiency. The number of Catholic schools rose during the Republic. In 1946 a Catholic university – the only private university –

---

[4] Census of 1953, 204.

[5] NUMBER OF PRIESTS IN CUBA

	Camagüey	Havana	City of Havana	Matanzas	Oriente	Pinar del Río	Santa Clara	Total
1899	16	117	89	44	36	20	50	283
1907	32	163	125	34	69	24	58	380
1919	100	374	269	81	165	34	126	880
1931	Not available							
1943	271	1,214		254	462	324	522	3,047*
1953	Not available							784

*Priests, social workers, etc.

(Compiled from Censuses of 1899, 1907, 1919, 1943, 1953.)

was founded: Santo Tomás de Villanueva. Catholic Action began to be active in the 1930s and in the 1940s a Christian Social Democrat movement was founded with an active youth movement.

In the 1950s the political crisis forced the Church to new activity. Neutrality became difficult, though not impossible. Batista continued to receive the tacit acceptance of bishops till the end, for reasons, it was argued, not totally unrelated to the justly famous largesse of Batista's second wife.[6] The revolutionaries of Castro's age criticized the Church as being Falangist, a charge true only in a few minor cases. The Church on the other hand had always denounced Communism; in early 1957 the Catholic *Diario de la Marina* said that 'the failure of religious conviction in general and the abandonment of Catholic principles in politics, economics and conduct is the underlying cause of the crisis' in Cuba. The *Diario* implied that the revolutionaries were Communists. But soon most of the Catholic laity backed Castro. Juventud Católica and other Catholic lay leaders took a strong line. Of the hierarchy Cardinal Arteaga congratulated Batista on taking power, and always preferred diplomacy to commitment, but himself did not escape a blow from a political policeman who afterwards went off with $30,000 in church funds. Of the other bishops, Cienfuegos supported Batista and, possibly sharing in the regime's spoils, fled to the U.S. on 1 January 1959; Matanzas (Alberto Martín Villaverde) was as vigorously opposed; Camagüey (Carlos Riu Anglés) thought it his and the Church's duty to be silent; Santiago (Pérez Serantes) had backed Castro from the beginning and indeed saved his life after Moncada: Pinar del Río was vacant and, as the diocesan administrator (Evelio Díaz) was also co-adjutor to the cardinal in Havana, he committed himself no further than his master.

The secular clergy almost all opposed Batista. Many were arrested. Some were tortured. Priests acted as treasurers to the 26 July Movement and at the very end of December several leading progressive priests were trying to get the hierarchy to issue a joint pastoral letter condemning the government. Was a Catholic renaissance now at hand?

Some thought so. The correspondent of *The Times* in Havana in January 1959 was persuaded that Castro was an ascetic and devout Catholic.[7] His deception was no doubt a mark of the time, possibly explained by a remark of Castro's that he favoured religious instruction in state schools.[8] Many churchmen reacted enthusiastically to Castro's triumph. Pérez Serantes appeared in public with Castro in Santiago. Mgr Roas of the Church of El Caney said, 'God has blessed this

[6] Dewart, 98.
[7] *Times*, 2 January 1959.
[8] Dewart, 143.

revolution, because its principles and ideals are in accord with God's word.'[9] The auxiliary bishop of Havana and Ignacio Biaín, the director of *La Quincena*, the leading church magazine (which had been attacking Batista since March 1958), supported the revolutionary tribunals.[10] Castro himself gravely said that the 'Catholics of Cuba have lent their most decided cooperation to the cause of liberty'.[11] So be it. The future therefore might not be dark.

Protestantism had a toe in Cuba too, perhaps 85,000 strong.[12] During the U.S. occupation of the turn of the century, forty Protestant denominations, from Southern Baptist to episcopal, swept in, establishing missions, schools, hospitals. Like the Communists, they depended at times on foreign support in order to survive. This enabled them to offer 'free religion', whereas the Catholics, with different financial arrangements depended on marriages and christenings for income. Even the Protestants concentrated on towns, though particularly on the less well off in Havana. Two North American writers argued that their activity in the country was hampered by the 'contrast between peasant living standards and even the humblest standard acceptable to a missionary accustomed to life in the U.S.'![13] The U.S. Baptists might be soldiers of Christ but they were not His *guerrilleros*. Nor did any Protestant fit in easily with any typical Cuban festival. Their relations with the U.S. were not, however, held much against them, and Protestants in general, with their high moral code and marmoreal concept of living, backed the revolution in the 1950s at least as much the Catholics did.

[9] *Revolución*, 15 January 1959, 15.
[10] *Ibid.*, 19 January 1957.
[11] *Bohemia*, 18 January 1959.
[12] *H.A.R.*, xvi, 257.
[13] MacGaffey and Barnett, 204.

CHAPTER 28

Education

About a million Cubans or nearly a quarter of the population over ten were officially believed not to be able to read or write. Further, the proportion of illiterates in 1953 was even officially higher – 23·5 % instead of 22 % – than in 1943. The overall impression is that, while in the thirty years of the Republic there was a swift advance in education as in other matters, this had come to a full stop. Perhaps, however, illiteracy had fallen by 1958 to about 20 %;[1] it was higher among men than women,[2] though paradoxically school attendance was higher among boys than girls: perhaps this is explained by the fact that boys left school earlier than girls to begin work. Also, even working-class girls had more time than their brothers, for there was no tradition of labour in the fields or factory by girls. and rural illiteracy was undoubtedly much greater than the official figures.

Most other countries of Latin America had far less impressive figures. Haiti was almost 90 % illiterate, Bolivia and Guatemala nearly 70 %, Venezuela, Brazil and the Central American countries (except Costa Rica and Panama) about 50 % illiterate. Only Chile, Argentina and Uruguay were more literate than Cuba.

The great Constitution of 1940 had provided that education be compulsory for children between six and fourteen in the *escuela primaria elemental*.[3] At fourteen, children could if they desired, go to the *escuela primaria superior* for two years.[4] Like many other parts of the Constitution, this programme was not fulfilled. In 1953 44 % of the six to fourteen year olds (547,000 children) were reported as not going to school. In Oriente, non-attendance rose to 60 %, compared with 33 % in Havana province. Taking the 630,000 country children as a whole, under 40 % went to school; and in Oriente only just over a quarter of country children went. But nearly three-quarters of the town children (600,000 in total) went to school.[5]

As for secondary schooling, in 1953, out of a total population (of those between fifteen and nineteen years of age) of 558,000, only 92,000 (17 %

[1] Estimate of *Estudio*, 826.
[2] 26% of men, 21% of women were illiterate.
[3] Grades 1 to 6.
[4] Grades 7 to 8.
[5] Census of 1953, 119.

or less) attended.[6] Thirty per cent of the teenage population of Havana might go to a secondary school, but only 7 % of rural teenagers went to school.[7] For the twenty-one secondary schools were all in towns and there was no free transport. There were admittedly some state boarding schools but nothing like enough. All in all, only one in ten Cuban children between thirteen and eighteen went to school.

Primary school pupils customarily attended for four hours, either in the morning or the afternoon. In some places, this dropped to two hours.[8] Here the situation was worse in the 1950s than it had been sixty years before when $5\frac{1}{2}$ hours' work was frequent, in one long and no doubt often distressing session.[9] Some of the syllabuses were absurdly North Americanized: 'What is the odd man out in this list: ROCKS, FOX, COCKS, SOCKS, LOCKS? The translation was direct: 'PEÑAS, ZORRO, GALLOS, CALCETINES, CERRAJAS'.[10] Nor was much attention paid to the special needs of rural areas. Children in the country usually got an urban education which was more than usually useless to them.[11]

Children who did not go to school spent their days running errands, carrying baskets, collecting salvage and stealing. Lowry Nelson in 1945 commented:

> Almost the entire childhood population in the lower-class urban families might be classified as 'neglected' in a better regulated society ... [but] this underdeveloped urban group is necessary to the upper class. What the latter would do without them is hard to imagine. They would have difficulty surviving![12]

Many of those who were with Castro at Moncada probably came from this section of society.[13] Juvenile crime had been high throughout the history of the Republic, often with boys belonging to gangs led by older men who taught them to rob and who beat them, à la Dickens, if they brought back nothing.

The consequences of this worsening situation had led to an increase in private education. Thus in 1925–6 there were 30,000 pupils in

[6] This may be an exaggerated figure, since El Mundo in an estimate qu. by World Bank (p. 413) said at the end of 1950 the figure only reached 54,000, of whom 20,000 were in private schools.

[7] Census of 1953, xxxviii–xxxix. Detailed figures, ibid., 99. See ibid. 1118 for discussion of Negro towns.

[8] E.g. the instance in Florida, qu. by World Bank, 415–18.

[9] Census of 1899, 581. The size of classes does not seem to have been so outrageous a problem as the others. Thus, though some teachers in the country might have 120 pupils, in towns 35 was common.

[10] Seen by the author in the Ministry of Education, 1962.

[11] Some schools had changed in this respect: for example the school at Florencia which had instruction in agriculture. But it all depended on the teacher.

[12] Nelson, 186–7.

[13] See the author's Cuba: The Pursuit of Freedom, Appendix XI.

private primary schools, in 1950, 90,000. Due to the half-day session and the lack of confidence in teachers, even poor people had begun to stint themselves to put children in private schools. In the country itinerant private teachers often spent two hours or so at each of three different houses per day.[14] In a medium-sized municipality with a population of 50,000 such as Florida (Camagüey), there were 23 state schools (seven of them kindergartens) in the town area, and 25 schools, in the country with 27 teachers; there were also 35 to 45 private schools, only five of which were registered with the Ministry of Education, charging from 50 cents to $2 per pupil per month.

It would be a brave man who named the number of Cuban teachers, despite a formal enumeration of 36,000 in 1953.[15] Many of these, however – perhaps a quarter – were temporarily or permanently retired. In the years under Grau and his supremely corrupt Minister of Education, Alemán, the scandal of idle teachers grew. Grau and Alemán made a massive appointment of teachers simply for cash.

Education was excessively centralized. Though boards of education had once been elected – indeed, the first elections ever held in Cuba were for education boards – the minister now appointed provincial school superintendents, who named boards of education and teachers in each of the municipalities.[16] Books, supplies and salaries were dispatched monthly from the capital even to Santiago. A corps of inspectors also set out from Havana.[17] Maybe such centralization need not have been a source of bad education. But unfortunately the Constitution of 1940 had provided, out of good intentions, that the Education Ministry's budget should never be less than that of any other department, save in an emergency. This made the ministry a centre of graft second to none, exacerbated by the fact that teachers were appointed for life: another well-intentioned provision which led to corrupt practice, since they received full salaries whether teaching or not. There were 'specialists' in music or art or English with no knowledge. Inspectors were also often both incompetent and corrupt. Promotion depended on political patronage or seniority. This too increased the desire of teachers to go to Havana. One observer wrote:

If you take the early morning train from Havana to Matanzas you will notice well-dressed people who get off a few at a time, at each

[14] The World Bank calculated $M8 to $M10 spent on private education per year in 1950 (415).

[15] World Bank. By a ludicrous provision of the Constitution (art. 52), 'the annual salary of a primary teacher was not in any case to be less than one millionth part of the total national budget'.

[16] World Bank. Out of 628 schools built under Grau, Sánchez Arango alleged that only 37 were placed according to need.

[17] World Bank, 423.

stop all the way along the line. These are teachers living in Havana and going out by train to their teaching posts. They hate their jobs, hate the towns where they teach, hate the pupils and the parents. Whenever they can say they are ill they do not go. They do everything they can to get transferred to Havana.[18]

Few school buildings were owned by the State; most were given free by individuals, some were rented. This meant that most Cuban schools were not built as schools and that the State paid $240,000 annually for school buildings. Most buildings consisted of a single room, where the same teacher had to teach all classes. Only rarely did country schools serve as centres of community cooperation or do anything to meet the needs of any adult education. Of course variations abounded. We hear of children having to walk three miles to school, of teachers saying that in ten years they had received no books from the government, that the few in use were bought by them out of their own salary, that as supplies for the new school year, they had had twenty-four pencils and a small pad. Sometimes the initiative of parents was considerable; fathers might buy pencils or build roofs or provide furniture.[19] Many schools, however, were badly placed. Sanitation might be good, where schoolmasters made a strong personal effort and lived near the school; and many sugar mills built good schools.

The increasing emphasis on private education was one cause of increased social tension, reflecting the dilemma of 'private wealth and public squalor' also evident in the U.S. For some of the private schools, such as the Jesuit schools of Belén to which Chibás and Castro went, or the Ruston Academy in Havana, gave admirable educations.

Thus the overall situation of education in Cuba, about the time of Batista's *golpe*, was dispiriting. The sociologist Nelson, writing in 1945, thought that little progress had been made since 1907.[20] The World Bank, a rather conservative source, thought that Cuba's educational system had 'steadily deteriorated over a period of years'.[21] In 1925 Cuba had been at the top among Latin countries in percentage of children enrolled in school. By 1950 she had been surpassed by several. The Bank went on with a carefully calculated attribution of the blame to 'political influence and patronage', and gave the warning that unless

[18] See article by Gonzalo del Campo, *Trimestre*, VII, No. 1 (January–March 1949). A similar point was made to Lowry Nelson by the agricultural inspector of Cienfuegos: 'The chief obstacle is the teachers who are so young when called upon to teach in these (remote) places. They manoeuvre in order to be transferred, or abandon the schools for military service, since poor communication prevents them from going to town as frequently as they wish and they do not care to take up the rustic life.' (Nelson, 267.) Mr Max Nolf was told in 1962 that 6,000 teachers left Cuba between 1959 and 1962.
[19] World Bank, 421.
[20] Nelson, 238–9.
[21] World Bank, 403–4, 409.

this were removed there were 'grave doubts whether Cuba will be able to provide the soundly educated adaptable human reserves which are essential to the success of her future development'.

During the seven years of the second *Batistato* there were some administrative reforms: for instance, rural education was placed under a special division of the ministry. 500 new teachers were appointed for rural areas. About a thousand new schools were set up in the country. There were several new technical establishments. The Ministers of Education were less corrupt than Alemán, though they were inferior to Sanchez Arango. But after Batista fled, it was found that there were still a thousand *botelleros* in the Ministry of Education.[22] Twenty per cent of the educational budget was absorbed (in 1955) by the central administration.[23] There was talk of reorganization of the primary schools in 1956. But in general, Batista's achievements were modest. In 1958 as in 1953, according to Batista's census of that year, there had been over 700,000 children between five and fourteen who were at school, nearly 700,000 not.[24] In general, the educational situation in Cuba in 1958 was probably at least no better than in 1952: a social survey conducted in 1956[25] among peasant families suggested that in the whole country about 45% had never been to school and, of those who had been, nearly 90% had not got beyond the third grade. Batista was thus a good deal less successful than Machado in his schools policy.

The situation of Cuban education was further unbalanced since, while her primary school attendance record placed her below most countries of Latin America,[26] her secondary education record, if low in real terms, placed her among the leaders: 12% of those between fifteen to nineteen were at school in Cuba, and over 4% of those between twenty and twenty-four were engaged in higher education. Such statistics are typical. Cuban education was ambiguous. In some sections of society Cuba was as bad as Asia, in some as good as New York. The shiftlessness and the drive by teachers to get to town, suggest that the educators were almost as rootless as those they taught. But Cuba could have afforded better than this. The position was bad enough to cause the parents of such children, themselves unschooled, to back any revolutionary cause which promised change.

[22] *Revolución*, 21 January, 1959.

[23] Seers, 173.

[24] Calculations from Census of 1953, 99. There is more than the usual amount of doubt about these figures. Ministry of Education files in Havana caused Richard Jolly to give state primary school attendance as 616,606, on 227 of *Cuban Economic and Social Revolution*, and 642,834 on 174. Private primary school attendance was 100,000 to 120,000. Of course 1958 was a troubled time.

[25] By the Agrupación Católica Universitaria, qu. Seers. Cf. Census of 1953.

[26] Argentina was 88%, Chile 85%, Uruguay 89%, Latin American average: 64%. UNESCO, *Projector Principal de Educación Boletín Trimestral*, No. 14 April–June 1962, 146, qu. Seers.

Cuba had now four universities – three state (Havana; Santiago, founded 1949; Las Villas, founded 1952) – and one private (Santo Tomás de Villanueva).[27] There had been no regular courses since November 1956. In 1953–5, 20,000 were enrolled in the state universities, 500 at Santo Tomás. The majority of undergraduates were preoccupied with arts or social subjects; out of 17,500 undergraduates at Havana, 1,500 only were involved in science. After the endless struggles of the 1920s and 1930s, Havana University was now autonomous and independent from ministerial control, like those of Mexico and other great Latin American institutions. The University of Havana had about 450 dons, most of whom had outside jobs as well or did journalism in order to supplement low salaries.

A Cuban of the old regime might argue that there was no point in learning to read in Cuba since there was little to read, and indeed very few books were published and most of those at the author's expense. Nor could the old Cuban press lift its head high in the weeks after January 1959. As earlier suggested, embarrassing revelations appeared frequently of dealings with the old regime, particularly over the Cuban Telephone Company's increase of prices. The only criticism had come from *Bohemia*, the newspapers *Excelsior* and *País*, and José Pardo Llada, the wireless commentator. Distributor of the bribes, it appeared, was Ichaso, of the *Diario de la Marina*, the oldest and most respectable of Cuban papers. Ichaso had been often a collaborator of *Bohemia* and was a member of the generation of 1923 at the university. More than fifty other journalists were quickly purged by the College of Journalists. But there was worse to come: on 29 January a full list was published of the most prominent journalists who were regularly bribed by the old regime, together with a list of their bribes. In effect these people received pay for non-existent government jobs. Nearly all the respectable news-papers had fatally compromised themselves, less by taking Batista's side than by at one time or another criticizing the politics of action: *Información*, *El Mundo*, and *Diario de la Marina*, all criticized 'terrorism'. One good source suggested that at the end of 1958 Batista was paying out to the press $450,000 a month for bribes.[28] Batista himself had bought the newspaper *Pueblo* and the weekly *Gente*, as well as the wireless chain Circuito Nacional Cubano, and the transmitter La Voz del Indio.[29]

Admittedly, Cuba had between sixty and seventy newspapers – eighteen well-established dailies in Havana alone – some of which were read daily (because of the good railways) throughout the island. The

[27] There were several private colleges and many technical schools and colleges including a school of agriculture in each province and schools of arts and crafts.
[28] Suárez Núñez, 30.
[29] *Loc. cit.*

twenty-eight main newspapers claimed a circulation of 580,000.[30] It is probable, however, that this figure was no higher, at least per head, than it had been in the 1950s.[31] Newspapers were exempt from corporate income tax and from duties on import of raw materials; and the government paid higher prices for advertisements than private business; and the papers concerned depended on the government more and more.

Several of the papers of the 1920s had vanished in the revolution of 1933, but the old *Diario de la Marina*, founded in 1832, remained, Catholic, Conservative, Spanish, and still in the hands of the Rivero family. *El Mundo*, founded in 1901, also survived – many of its shares being held by Prío, who in the 1950s sold them to Batista[32] – but both these two old papers were outstretched in circulation by recent foundations such as *El País*, *Prensa Libre* and *Excelsior*, which used subscription lotteries to boost circulation. Immediately after 1 January 1959, the Castroist *Revolución* and the old Communist paper *Hoy* reappeared. The American colony's *Havana Post* went on, though it was a superficial paper; there were many others catering for special interests such as the small anarchist group's *El Libertario*.

The magazines of Cuba were important. *Bohemia*, edited by a liberal, Miguel Angel Quevedo, had a circulation of 250,000,[33] much of it abroad: it was the most prominent weekly of hispanic America. It had been consistently hostile to Batista, and had given a platform to all Batista's opponents and greatly helped the revolutionary cause. Despite its consistently pro-U.S. line in matters such as the Cold War, it was the great liberal magazine of the Spanish Caribbean and helped too to persuade many people that Castro's cause was that of Jefferson.

[30] *Investment in Cuba*, 89.
[31] *Cf.* Chapera, 598.
[32] López Fresquet, 21.
[33] *Bohemia*, 1 November 1952.

CHAPTER 29

Sugar

The world now ate[1] 50 million tons of sugar a year, twice as much as ten years before and six times as much as in 1900.[2] Since world population had barely doubled since 1900,[3] the average man thus ate three times as much sugar as in 1900.[4]

The increase of sugar eating in the ten years before 1958 had been greater than that of any other food. Most of this increase had been in Latin America, the Middle East and Africa, which were now reaching the levels attained by western Europe a century before, though England's consumption of sugar per head in 1858 was higher than the world average of 1958.[5] Latin America, without much rationing in the Second World War, increased its sugar eating a good deal between 1938 and 1948. After 1948 there was rapid growth in Africa and the Near East, and, after 1952, Asia began to go through the same experience, though starting from a level which was only half that of before the war, due to the spoilations of war in the Far East. China continued to have the lowest consumption per head – about 1 kilo per head of population before 1939, 1 kilo still in 1954, perhaps 1½ kilos in 1958. The advanced countries had, however, reached a plateau: thus U.S. consumption had not risen from its level of 50 kilos a head in the 1920s, though it had doubled in the first quarter of the century.

Prices were everywhere artificial. A bricklayer[6] would have to work

[1] Either directly or in manufactured food. The use of sugar industrially for products which did not end up as food was negligible. In low consumption countries the use of sugar in manufactured forms was negligible. In the U.S. and Great Britain, however, household consumption was respectively just under and just over 50% of the sugar consumed (Viton and Pignalosa, 15). But see the comment by Mr (now Sir) P. Runge in *ibid.*, 16, fn. 7.

[2] 1898–1900:   8,139,000 tons.
   1948–1950:   28,640,000 tons.
   1951–1958:   47,135,000 tons.

[3] 1898–1900:   1,470,000 tons.
   1948–1950:   2,440,000 tons.
   1951–1958:   2,800,000 tons.

[4] 1898–1900:   5·5 kg
   1948–1950:   11·7 kg
   1951–1958:   15·4 kg

(i.e. consumption had increased in 1958 64% since 1948–50. If China, Russia, Pakistan and India were left out, the average consumption would have been 26 kg.)

[5] England's sugar consumption in 1859 was 15·8 kg (*British Historical Statistics*, 356).

[6] Thought by the ILO to be the largest and most homogeneous group for wage statistics available in a large number of countries.

in England twenty minutes to earn enough for a kilo of sugar, in the
U.S. four minutes only, in Thailand over two hours.[7] Factors other than
price and income affect sugar consumption; but colder countries, contrary to myth, do not consume more sugar. In general, in 1958–9,
the prospect was that tropical or semi-tropical countries would continue to demand more sugar; and within ten years the world seemed
likely to need at least 70,000,000 tons or almost half as much again as in
1958.

Despite this unfolding market, the production of sugar in Cuba had
been more or less static and was likely to remain so. First of all, at least
eight important countries which had once imported all their sugar had
begun their own production. Thus while in 1948 only five countries,
apart from Cuba, produced over a million tons of sugar a year,[8]
twelve did so in 1958.[9] Much of this increase was in beet sugar. The beet
production in 1958 of the U.S., for instance, was two-thirds greater
than it had been in 1948. U.S. cane, in Louisiana chiefly, had also
slightly increased.[10] Puerto Rico had also greatly exceeded her quota of
sales to the U.S. and had secured a permanent increase in her quota.

Cuba had already been shielded from the full effects of these developments. Hence the Korean crisis of 1950 caused the U.S. to buy an extra
600,000 tons at a time when there was a risk of a big surplus.[11] The Suez
crisis had raised prices in 1957. Cuba continued to produce mostly 'raw
sugar', that is, 96% pure sugar but with a thin layer of molasses and
some other impurities. A few mills, however, did do their own refining,
thus carrying the process from the cane to 100% pure sugar; much of
this was sold in Cuba itself.

A further point was that the sugar market of the world was really by
now rigidly divided into a number of consuming leagues, controlled
respectively by the U.S., France, England and Russia. There was
admittedly also a further 'free' world market outside these leagues, but
this only constituted a fifth of the total production of sugar. An International Sugar Council, with headquarters in London, devotedly circulated statistical material, but did little more. The English, French and
Russian consumers kept themselves to themselves. The U.S. league,
however, was open to the English and French suppliers. Cuba was still
far the largest exporting country, the U.S. the largest consuming one.
The quota afforded the Cubans by the U.S. depended on, first, the
previous estimate by the U.S. Secretary for Agriculture of the likely

[7] Viton and Pignatosa, 21.
[8] Brazil, India, Puerto Rico, Russia and the U.S.
[9] Argentina, Australia, Brazil, France, West Germany, India, Italy, Mexico, Philippines,
Poland, Russia and the U.S.
[10] Figures in U.N. Statistical Yearbook for 1961, 195. *Cf.* W.B., 712.
[11] World Bank, 506.

CUBA

SUGAR

IN 1959

Mills—▲

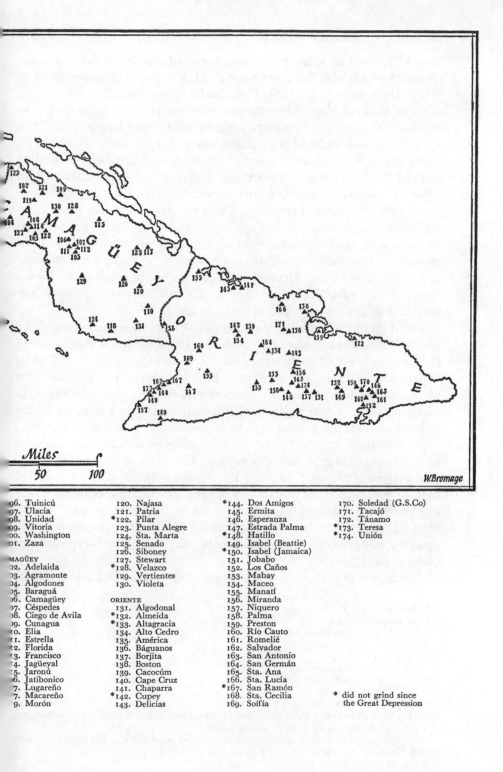

Miles
50   100

W.Bromage

total U.S. need of sugar in the year; second, on the deficits of other countries which also had fixed quotas. Thus if the Philippines failed to deliver their share to the U.S., Cuba had a chance of selling more.

From time to time international conferences were held to try to regulate the small but profitable jungle outside these leagues. But from 1944 till 1953 there had been no restriction of sugar production, and in Cuba every mill produced what it could. The huge harvest of 1952 marked the end of expansion. Instead of trying to dispose of the surplus sugar at low prices, Batista's government kept back 1,750,000 tons to try to save the prices. Thereafter, Cuba restricted her own production and accepted an international policy of restriction.[12] At the London conference in 1953 Cuba received an export quota of $2\frac{1}{4}$ million tons, rather less than half the world export total.[13] In 1958, another sugar conference was held at Geneva and another five-year agreement fixed Cuba's share of the 'free' market at 2·4 million tons, or what had become a little over one-third of that market.[14]

The difficulty of making any substantial increase in her share of the international market was one reason for the undoubted stagnation of Cuban sugar, with its debilitating consequences for the whole of Cuban society and the economy generally. But there were also reasons from within Cuba: first the artificial hindrances to further development, to mechanization or rationalization, imposed by law in deference to the unions; second, the bizarre system of agriculture based on the *colonos*.

No new sugar mill had been built for thirty years and none could be by law; nor could any mill be destroyed. Could the country even maintain present standards? In 1955 the National Bank of Cuba believed that, to give the Cuban population in 1965 the standard of living which she had reached in 1947, there would have to be a sugar crop of over nine million tons, to be valued at nearly $M800:[15] a prophecy which assumes importance when considering the actual achievements of Cuba in the 1960s.

The actual organization of the sugar industry in Cuba was indeed

[12] See above, 16. *Cf. Estudio*, 922.
[13] Or 41%. Others got:

Dominican Republic }	600,000 tons
Formosa	
Peru	280,000
Czechoslovakia	275,000
Indonesia	250,000
Poland	222,000
U.S.S.R.	200,000

(H.A.R., September 1953.) Cuba had asked for $2\frac{1}{2}$ million tons and might perhaps have got it if the organizations had not been in such a hurry.

[14] *Cf. Estudio*, 991–2. 1953–8 were referred to as 'years of restriction'. But in fact the years of real 'freedom' were far away, in the 1920s.

[15] Qu., *Investment in Cuba*, 7.

far from rational. Little had been done to develop the possible sugar industry by-products such as molasses (the residue containing no crystallizable sugar, used both in rough form as treacle and when refined as rum) or bagasse (cane waste) upon which industries could have been built. Bagasse can be used for hardboard, for paper-making, or for fencing, but most bagasse was used as fuel, often, once the harvest was under way, the main fuel. There had been little research into these matters, merely prophecy. The cane used in Cuba was now mostly of a variety brought from Java in the 1920s,[16] itself the successor of the old Crystallina, another Javanese plant,[17] and Otaheite. Cuba had never financed an effective national research station to breed varieties of cane which would be best for Cuban conditions. Only one interesting variety[18] had been bred in Cuba. An industry which had been for many years pre-eminent in the world should certainly have set aside the small percentage necessary for adequate national experiment. The Cuban Sugar Research Foundation at Jovellanos only received about $60,000 to $80,000 a year.[19] It still awaited payment of special taxes levied for its upkeep since 1941.[20] Yield of Cuban sugar per acre compared badly with most other countries. This was partly because, admittedly, the specially favourable soil in Cuba made it possible to rely on the same plant lasting longer than elsewhere though there was a big contrast in yields of sugar cane between first and later crops. (The first, plant, cane, often yielded thirty-five tons of sugar an acre, the second, ratoons, less, so that the average for all cane[21] was between sixteen and twenty tons.) This naturally compared ill with more intensively producing countries such as Hawaii (where research had always had a high priority), Peru and Indonesia,[22] but was somewhat compensated by the still relatively low price of land and by the high sugar content taken from the cane – at between 13% and 15%, the highest in the world.[23]

[16] Proefstation Oest Java (POJ), 2878.
[17] Crystallina, still used by 90% of Cuban cane planters in 1931.
[18] Media Luna 3/18 produced by Dr Ricardo Beattie at the *central Isabel*, Media Luna.
[19] 1½% of gross receipts would at the lowest reckoning have given an annual income of $M3·9.
[20] See more about this in Ch. 47.
[21] Say, 20% plant cane, 80% ratoons.
[22] Average yield respectively 206, 155, and 90 tons per hectare. Other yields in the 1950s were:

British Guiana:	90 tons	Jamaica:	59 "
Barbados:	87 "	Mexico:	55 "
Formosa:	70 "	U.S.A.:	53 "
South Africa:	70 "	Fiji:	47 "
Australia:	62 "	Trinidad:	47 "
Mauritius:	61 "	Brazil:	41 "
Puerto Rico:	61 "	Argentina:	34 "

(*FAO World Sugar Economy in Figures*).

[23] Núñez Jiménez, 227.

There had been some slight mechanization of the agricultural side of the sugar industry: for dragging cane to its point of shipment to the mill, the ox had now been largely replaced by the tractor.[24] Tractors were also used to weed and prepare land for cane. 'In some cases an operation with tractors is completed in ten days by ten workers when it took a hundred men three months to do it before.'[25] But further mechanization was made impossible by the law. Fertilization or fumigation by air were forbidden. The use of the continuous centrifugal by which the entire sugar-making operation might be made to work at the touch of a button (as occurred in Louisiana) was banned. Planting and cutting was still done by hand, mostly because of the hostility of unions to mechanization. Thus Julio Lobo had imported an experimental cane-cutting machine which remained in bond in the customs house for five years and eventually was returned to Louisiana when the authorities finally refused it entry.[26] But in nearly all Cuba except Oriente cutting of cane by machine was perfectly feasible – as indeed was shown during the 1968 sugar harvest when one-fifth of the total harvest was done by machine.[27] Loading at ports was also by hand – ten days being sometimes spent in work which probably could have been done in twenty hours with bulk shipping.[28]

The Institute of Sugar Stabilization had since 1931 been the directing force of the industry.[29] An autonomous institution, though always influenced by the government, it recommended the total amount of sugar to be produced each year and its division among the different mills. Its director, appointed by the president, was thus a powerful man, the maker and breaker of fortunes and often subornable by bribes. The Institute also regulated wages, the number of workers to be employed and whether any account should be taken of possible mechanization. Government was therefore much involved in this industry. Given its power, the institute could intervene, under a government willing to be corrupted, to create riches. One such example occurred during the record year in 1952. The sugar market in Cuba was then dominated by

[24] There were 1,888 tractors in Cuba in 1946, nearly 15,000 (all North American) in 1958 (*Estudio*, 1011). Over 90% of the cane land was prepared by tractor and 80% of cane carried in lorries.

[25] World Bank, 55.

[26] Evidence of Julio Lobo, Madrid, 9 November 1968.

[27] This admittedly is a controversial question. For the widespread use of the cane-cutting machine, doubtless much levelling of land and perhaps a less sinuous plant may be necessary. Castro in a speech on 2 January 1969 suggested that in the future cane would only be grown on flat land and during 1969–70 new items of machinery have begun to change the old picture.

[28] *Nuestra Industria*, qu. Reuters, Havana, 7 November 1962. Some attempt at bulk-shipping was imposed on the reluctant Cuban labour authorities since Tate & Lyle, a major shipper, had re-equipped their vessels for bulk-shipping. But the regulations even for this were highly restrictive.

[29] See the author's *Cuba: The Pursuit of Freedom*, p. 562.

two big speculations: one by Francisco Blanco, administrator of Batista's mill *Washington*, an able and elderly man of experience, and the other by the great pluralist holder of many mills, Julio Lobo. Blanco had available between 300,000 and 150,000 tons of sugar, whose price was threatened by the decline in the world market. A national sugar-selling organization was appointed. It was finally agreed that 1¾ million tons of surplus sugar should be sold over the next five years and that the market would, in the meantime, be kept down.[30] At the International Sugar Council in 1953, the Cuban representatives were instructed to sign anything provided that they reached agreement fast, since Batista had this substantial surplus to dispose of himself; and these men did accept a figure for the quota considerably lower than might otherwise have been obtained.[31]

Despite stagnation of production, there had been two important changes in the industry during the quarter-century between the two revolutions of 1933 and 1959. First, there was an increase in the number of cane-growing *colonia*. Thus in 1899 there had been 15,000 cane *colonia*, feeding just over 200 *centrales* with cane;[32] in 1936, 28,000, or not quite twice as many: in 1950 there were 40,000, and in 1958 there were 68,000, or an increase of 50% in eight years.[33]

These changes, however, meant less of a revolution in land-holding than might appear: first, many separate *colonia* were in fact owned by the same man, family or company; for the sugar law of 1937 had intervened in favour of the *colono* against the *central*, giving him permanency of tenure, regulating his rights, compelling mill-owners to share both powers and profits with *colonos* and workers, increasing mill costs, and laying substantial taxes on 'administration cane', and so mill-owners themselves got round this law, buying land, perhaps from themselves, perhaps openly under their own name, or under the cover of nominees such as their wives or daughters.[34] Still, the number of real owners substantially increased, chiefly through subdivision among families, but also from the formation of new *colonia* during 'free' harvests, from the recognition of the right of sub-*colonos* to call themselves *colonos*, and perhaps most of all from the improved conditions for all following the law of 1937.

While in the past many *centrales* had depended on their own 'admini-

[30] See article by Pelayo Cuervo, in *Bohemia*, 1 December 1952.
[31] Evidence of Julio Lobo, 10 November 1968.
[32] 15,521 to be precise. The 1899 figure may be an underestimate, since the census did not take account of those who claimed title to estates.
[33] World Bank, 198, for 1950; *Anuario Azucarero* of 1959 for 1958, and *ibid.* of 1937 for 1936 (28,486 to be precise); Census of Cuba for 1899, 524. The Cuban agricultural census of 1946 (referring to facts of 1944) speaks of 29,100 farms devoted primarily to cane. The big expansion, as can be seen, came immediately after the war.
[34] Evidence *inter alia* of Julio Lobo.

stration cane', by the 1950s many depended only on *colonos*, some being tenants, others being proprietors.[35] This explains the drop in the land nominally owned by *centrales* between 1936 and 1958.[36] There were, however, some mills such as the *centrales Niquero* and *Cabo Cruz*, where the owner (in this case Lobo) did control all the lands, by dint however of buying up or out the *colonos*. These mills became technically very proficient, providing for several years the highest yields in Cuba and offering an example from which other mills began to profit.[37]

The *colonos* which were attached to the new mills of Oriente or Camagüey rented almost all their land at low rates; those in the old centre of sugar in Matanzas or Santa Clara might have once had mills on their land, or were perhaps the owners outright. Some *colonos* were rich. But only about a hundred produced over 500,000 arrobas each of cane (compared with nearly 1,200 who had so done in 1939).[38] The list included many names famous in the past history of the Cuban oligarchy who had given up grinding in the 1880s: thus a Céspedes sold cane to the *central Sofía* near Bayamo; Betancourts, Alfonsos, and Agramontes were active in central Cuba, an Iznaga still sold to Atkins's old mill *Soledad,* a Rionda operated at *Tuinicú,* and there were also Sotolongos, and Beltrans de la Cruz. But the largest *colonia* were companies.[39] In 1950, the World Bank Mission to Cuba had thought that 15 % of *colonia* were owned by rich persons or firms, 70 % by middle-class people, and another 15 % by poor persons.[40] In the next eight years, the poor became more numerous.[41] Many of these last were nevertheless people of old families. Thus in Matanzas there were families who spoke impeccable Spanish and who were completely white but who nevertheless had never been as far as the main road.

The *colonos* still received in payment a percentage of the cane which they had delivered in sugar. This *arrobaje* varied from about 48 % to 46 % of the cane according to the average yield of the mill. Mills paid *colonos* at a ten-months' average price, not, as before 1948, a fifteen-day one. Payment also varied according to the tenure of the *colono*. Those who

[35] See Nelson, 121.

[36] In 1936, 236,437 cabs were controlled by *centrales*, of which 171,160 were owned; in 1958, the figures were 177, 427·5 and 124,667 respectively. (*Anuario Azucarero*; *cf.* figures in *Estudio*, 651, for 1939.) See *Problems of the New Cuba*, 269–80.

[37] Evidence of Julio Lobo.

[38] See list in *Anuario Azucarero* of 1959, 115 ff; for 1939, see Guerra, *La Industria Azucarera de Cuba*, 1940.

[39] Castro's family estate, run by his brother Ramón Castro, then had an *arrobaje* of 1,640,000 *arrobas* of cane delivered to the *central Miranda*.

[40] World Bank, 198.

[41] Census of 1943, 267. The larger *colonia* tended to be in the east part of the island, the smaller in the older areas of the west. Thus in the 1952 harvest the average *colono* in Camagüey produced 230,000 *arrobas* of cane, in Oriente 150,000 *arrobas*; in Matanzas, Havana and Las Villas the average was about 50,000. Well over half the *colonos* in 1952 (38,000 out of 62,000) produced under 30,000 *arrobas* of cane (*ibid.,* 1009).

rented their land from sugar *centrales* and those who owned land both used this system which, however theoretically fair, tied all *colonos* to their *central*, upon which they depended for transport for grinding, as well as, often, for credit. The system also meant that growers of good and bad cane received the same amount of sugar as each other; quantity, not quality, gave results.[42]

The whole system indeed was awkward and unprofitable. The *colonos* were one more hindrance against the introduction of mechanization. Their reluctance to collaborate also made scientific farming difficult, for example, to try to plant early and late maturing sugar cane in different places around the mill. *Colonos* were also reluctant even to invest in lorries to carry the cane to the mill. One experiment in re-organization was however carried out during the 1950s by Julio Lobo and other sugar mill owners in the province of Matanzas. Different *colonia* were exchanged between mill owners so that at least the most extreme illogicalities, whereby cane might have to be taken twenty miles to a traditional *central* instead of the nearest one, were avoided.[43] This rationalization worked well and began to be copied elsewhere. But this did not remove the *colono* completely, and it is difficult to avoid the conclusion that either the land had to be nationalized or most of it had to be bought up by the *central* for any improvement in agriculture to be possible – either capitalism or socialism was feasible, that is, but not neo-feudalism.

The second big change in the structure of Cuban sugar in the years since the depression was the relative U.S. withdrawal from ownership, primarily due to dislike of Cuban labour conditions but also to the general restrictions on expansion. This began with the sale in 1934 of the enormous Cuba Cane Corporation, which had been begun to exploit the favourable opportunities for sugar in the First World War. North American banks also gradually withdrew from the ownership of sugar mills. One businessman in 1950 commented that he and most of his colleagues 'admit that it is still worth operating in Cuba. But there is certainly far less scope for large profits'.[44] Batista's labour laws, the policy of Cubanization and the Sugar Law of 1937, had all done their work. The consequence was that even in mills nominally owned by U.S. companies, Cuban shareholders were sometimes prominent, sometimes even pre-eminent.[45] Thus Lobo for a time had a controlling interest in Cuban Atlantic, and Batista also had a 10 % to 15 % share in that company.[46] Lobo had too a 25 % interest in the West Indies Sugar

[42] *Cf.* the details in *Estudio*, 648.
[43] Evidence of Julio Lobo.
[44] Qu., World Bank, 822.
[45] *Estudio*, 1273.
[46] Evidence of Julio Lobo, 10 November 1968.

Company and Falla Gutiérrez had substantial shares in Punta Alegre, both nominally U.S. companies.

The Cuban Atlantic Gulf Sugar Company, with nine mills in Las Villas, Camagüey and Matanzas, was now the biggest company in Cuba. Its total output in 1937 was almost half as much again as any other single company.[47] It later bought the big Hershey mill near Havana as well, and in the 1950s owned over 600,000 acres,[48] but sold off the Hershey estates in 1958 to Julio Lobo, a deal which was skilfully made operative on 31 December 1958, the day Batista left Cuba.[49] Lobo was at that time a passionate opponent of Batista and so had looked to the future with confidence.[50] (Cuban Atlantic had not known that they were selling to Lobo and they, in particular their manager Francisco Blanco, an old enemy of Lobo, were furious.)

Afterwards in importance came the Cuban-American Sugar Company, and then the famous United Fruit Company. The former had six mills including the huge *Chaparra* and *Delicias*, close to each other on the north coast of Oriente near Puerto Padre, where Columbus landed on his first voyage. *Chaparra*, begun in 1901 under the future President Menocal, had a capacity in 1958 of a tenth of the entire Cuban crop, due in part to its use of the first 12-roller mills, the most important recent technological improvement. Even larger so far as its use of labour was concerned was *Delicias*, built a few miles to the east in 1911. A short time later, Congressman Hawley, the founder of these mills, had bought and restored Diago's old mill, *Tinguaro*, and another Matanzas estate, *Merceditas*. Later still, the Apezteguía's record-breaking mill of the 1890s, *Constancia*, in Cienfuegos, also fell into the hands of Cuban-American who, by the 1950s, owned over 300,000 acres (though they sold off *Tinguaro* to Lobo).[51] The United Fruit Company owned only two mills, *Boston* and *Preston*, but also 280,000 acres; they were reckoned as being together worth $M38 and their annual Cuban payroll was $M10 and 40,000 men.[52]

The most obvious disadvantage, so far as Cuba was concerned, of this still substantial North American holding was that these mill owners would always vote, in the mill owners' association, according to the interests of their shareholders or banks rather than of Cuba.[53] On the other hand, a firm such as United Fruit did make available to employees

---

[47] 1,650,299 sacks. *Anuario Azucarero*, 1937, 45.

[48] 18,510 *caballería*. Núñez Jiménez, 235.

[49] See *Fortune*, April 1963. The broker was Loeb Rhodes.

[50] Evidence of Julio Lobo.

[51] 10,722 cabs. Núñez Jiménez, 235. See Jenks, *op. cit.*, 253, for Cuban-American.

[52] Ruby Hart Phillips, *The Cuban Dilemma*, New York, 1962, 185–8, and Mario Lazo, *The Dagger in the Heart*, 50. For their colonization scheme of 1928, when they moved some 14,000 Cubans from West Cuba to their estates, see *Problems of the New Cuba*, 285.

[53] Comment of their colleague Julio Lobo to the author.

high standards of education and health and entertainment, and such new technological improvements or chemical possibilities as were possible even to talk about in the curious state of Cuban labour relations.

Far the biggest Cuban concern was the large series of interests represented by Lobo, who possessed fourteen mills. Like Tomás Terry in the nineteenth century, Lobo was of Venezuelan origin, though the Lobos were originally Sephardic Jews from Curaçao.[54] In 1959 he was reckoned as controlling almost 1,000,000 acres.[55] Lobo had an admirable record for honesty (the revolutionary government confirmed it on minute examination of his books) and good treatment of his workers. He had, in 1959, as has been seen, only recently bought the large Hershey interests.[56] His efforts at rationalization and modernization were persistent if often thwarted.

Lobo had also in 1959 wide interests in hotels (he financed the building of the Capri and the Riviera hotels), banking, radio networks and shipping as well as his enormous sugar holdings. He was the largest art collector in Cuba and his collection of Napoleonic relics was the biggest outside France. His wealth derived partly from his father Heriberto who fled to Havana after the revolution in Venezuela in 1902 and entered into partnership in Havana with a Spaniard, Galbán, as a private banker and importer – much as the Drakes had started in the 1790s. Julio Lobo began to work in the firm in 1919, a graduate of Louisiana State University (then almost exclusively a sugar institute) and though Galbán retired, the Lobos and then Lobo alone kept the old name – the Galbán Lobo trading company – and the old offices in old Havana. The Lobos sold out most of their non-sugar interests in 1946, by which time (exactly as with the great merchants of the nineteenth century) Julio had moved into the sugar business himself, accumulating eleven mills by 1952, mostly bought from North Americans.[57] The Lobos had also done specially well during the Dance of the Millions when they had wisely sold at the right time. Julio Lobo survived an attempt on his life in 1946 by Eufemio Fernández and the ARG, who had unsuccessfully demanded $50,000 protection money from him. In the 1950s he again accumulated non-sugar interests of consequence. He lived partly in Havana and partly at his favourite mill *Tinguaro*, the Diagos' construction of the 1840s which he had re-equipped as well as he could, given the labour laws, and there his daughter – by a Montalvo – was

[54] For Lobo, see *Fortune*, November 1958, and *Life en Español*, 3 November 1958.

[55] 405,000 hectares, with a total production of 540,000 tons, valued at about $M50 a year. Of these however only about 200,000 acres were cultivated, or cultivable.

[56] He bought Hershey for $M25 on 31 December, 1958.

[57] Lobo bought his first mill in 1926 (*Escambray*), but entered more fully into mill ownership in 1939–40.

suitably christened in cane juice. There too he held literary parties in what he believed to be the 'Cliveden' of Cuba. Lobo, a genius in finance, was primarily non-political and believed 'we didn't care who overthrew Batista so long as someone did'.[58] He sold annually between 35 % and 50 % of Cuban sugar and 60 % of the refined sugar sold to the U.S. He also sold half the raw sugar produced by Puerto Rico, as well as much of the Philippine production. His position in the U.S., as in the Cuban sugar market, was dominant and feared. His fortune was estimated at $M85 in the 1950s by a knowledgeable New York banker.[59] He had contributed neither to Castro nor to Batista and the former had accordingly burned his cane fields.

Next after Lobo among the non-North Americans came the heirs, children and grandchildren, of the Spaniard Laureano Falla Gutiérrez, representing nearly 300,000 acres, under the name of Administración de Negocios Azucareros.[60]

Although sugar was still the industry *par excellence* of Cuba, and although Cubans had come back into the field as proprietors in the last few years, the sugar industry still seemed in some respects a foreign enterprise, a great international exhibition set up on Cuban soil, with foreign capital, foreign machinery and sometimes, as in the 1920s, even foreign workers. In the 1880s and 1890s foreign capital had reorganized Cuban sugar along its present lines. Even with the slow Cubanization of the twenty years before 1959, New York banks continued to finance the sugar warehouses in Cuba and the shipping of it to the U.S. not to speak of holding it in warehouses there, prior to sale.[61] The great U.S. *central*, a magnificent monument of capitalism on the surface, seemed indeed a representation of the 'Colossus of the North' itself, as in the poem by Agustín Acosta:

> While oxen slowly move on
> The old carts creak . . . creak
> They go towards the nearby colossus of steel
> They go towards the North American mill
> And as if complaining as they draw near
> The old carts creak . . . creak.[62]

[58] A remark to the author, 9 November 1968.
[59] *Fortune, op. cit.*
[60] This firm had invested about $M40 abroad for fear lest a revolution should come again as had occurred in 1933. Other important Cuban firms in the last period were Gómez Mena, previously Spanish, (with 6,312 cabs); Manuel Azpuru (2,579 cabs), Manuel Luzárraga (1,571), and García y Díaz (2,248). The Rionda family, still ran the *Manatí, Francisco, Tuinicú* and *Elia* sugar mills as well as extensive commercial interests; but technically these mills were considered U.S. and by now the Riondas were almost completely North American.
[61] W.B., 584.
[62] The author of this poem (written in 1926) afterwards became secretary to the presidency

The number of active mills remained much the same throughout the history of the Republic. A hundred out of the 161 mills existing in 1958 had been founded in the nineteenth century. Though the total number of mills had risen (during the First World War) for a time to almost 200, after the depression they never exceeded 161, a figure which stayed constant between 1946 and 1958. The twentieth-century mills in general survived, those that failed during the depression being chiefly the old ones of Matanzas and Santa Clara – only twelve new mills failed, compared with over 100 old ones.[63] The cane cut in Matanzas in 1959 was slightly less than that cut there a hundred years before.[64] The mills varied greatly in size – ranging in capacity from about 5,000 to 170,000 tons of sugar. Their total value was estimated in 1950 as between $M750 and $M1,000.[65] By any reckoning the big Cuban sugar mills constituted one of the most remarkable networks of capital investments in the world, with their great rollers which were fed in the harvest with a continous supply of cane day and night, and their great chimneys towering over the *batey*, the schools and chapels, the *barracones* for temporary workers, the shops, *bodegas*, houses for managers, and even sports grounds and golf courses.

Sugar was grown on a little over a quarter of all Cuban farms but only for 18% of the farmers was it the major source of income. These, however, were the biggest farms.[66] Two-thirds of agricultural incomes derived from sugar. Nearly half the irrigated area grew cane,[67] while cane covered over a quarter of the total area of the country, or $7\frac{1}{2}$ million acres. But probably not more than four million acres was in sugar production in any single year.[68] The rest was held in reserve. Half a million workers were employed by the industry in harvest time,

[63] In 1899 there were 62 mills in Matanzas, in 1939–58 only 23–4; in 1899 there were 73 mills in Santa Clara, after 1939 only 50. About half the old mills of Oriente collapsed but a nearly equal number of new ones were built there so that in 1899 there were 42 mills and in 1958, 40. In Camagüey 22 new mills had been founded, compared with only three in 1899 – of which one failed; there were thus 24 mills in that province in 1958.

[64] *Cf.* Moreno Fraginals, 65.

[65] World Bank, 795 and 194–5.

[66] Cane covered 60% of the cultivated area. These figures derived from the Agricultural Census of 1945, thirteen years old; but there is nothing else (W.B. 88, 104). Núñez Jiménez (*Geografía*, 226) speaks of 55% of the cultivated area.

[67] World Bank, 109: 45%.

[68] 3.9 million in 1953, 3 million in 1955 (*Investment in Cuba*, 32).

under Mendieta and a senator during the first Batista epoch for Matanzas. The labour laws, of course, favoured oxen against lorries.

> Mientras lentamente los bueyes caminan
> Las viejas carretas rechinan . . . rechinan
> Van hacia el coloso de hierro cercano
> Van hacia el ingenio norteamericano
> Y como quejandose cuando a él se avecinan
> Las viejas carretas rechinan . . . rechinan.

nearly 400,000 as cane cutters, the rest in the mills: this accounted for a third of those gainfully employed in the country.[69] The cane cutters were tough and professional and well-organized in unions. Their work though not heavy was tedious and in neglected fields exasperating.[70] Sugar mills operated a rail mileage almost double the public system, while, in 1950, 80% of the tonnage of the leading public railways derived from hauling cane. Half of Cuba's electric power generating capacity was controlled by sugar mills.

The precise role of sugar in the economy is elusive. Thus between a quarter and a third of national income derived from sugar: a high proportion, but still suggesting that Cubans did some other things.[71] These figures do not show how far the whole economy depended on exports, and exports of course did depend on sugar; thus in the forty years before Batista's final overthrow, sugar accounted for 82% of Cuban exports.[72] Also, in the years since the depression, Cuba had in some ways become more, not less, sensitive to price fluctuations deriving from sugar: several laws in the interests of humanity had tied the wages of many non-sugar workers, and also many ordinary prices, to the price of sugar. These covered railway freight rates, rents on sugar lands, taxes paid by the sugar industry, many leases and even interest rates on mortgage loans.[73] The improved labour conditions which had secured a more fair distribution of incomes since 1933 meant that any change in exports would be likely to cause greater changes in economic activity than before. Thus during the 1950s at least as much as in the past, 'all commitments made in Cuba – no matter how well the risk [seemed] . . . to be spread [were] in fact commitments which depended upon the fate of sugar in the international markets'.[74] When sugar prices were good, no other enterprise in Cuba was so rewarding. When they were bad, most other activities suffered at the same time. To many Cuban investors, other forms of investment seemed less attractive than sugar in good times and almost as risky in bad. Any investment in Cuba depended directly or indirectly on sugar; why not therefore invest

[69] Cf. Hugo Vivó, El empleo y la población activa de Cuba (1950). Carlos Rafael Rodríguez, April 1963, qu. Hispanic American Report, XVI, 349, said that the cane cutters never numbered less than 375,000. In the war years, 1941–3, the average sugar labour force was 500,000, getting probably $1·00 a day in 1941 in harvest time and 80 cents a day out of harvest; in 1942–3 these wages had risen to $1·53 in harvest and $1·00 out (Census of 1943, 261). But one must doubt whether there was any real fulfilment of the latter figure. According nevertheless to the official statistics, a total of $23,377,022 was paid in wages and salaries in the sugar industry in 1940, $27,191,091 in 1941, $40,472,169 in 1942.

[70] Problems of the New Cuba, 286.

[71] Revista del Banco Nacional, September 1955, qu. Investment in Cuba, 6.

[72] Núñez Jiménez, 227. Tobacco accounted for another 10%.

[73] The sugar law of 1937 provided that daily wages should be, in the harvest, the equivalent of 50 lbs of sugar; but they were not to exceed 96 cents and not to drop below a minimum of 80 cents. (Minimum wages rose to $2·88 a day by 1947.)

[74] World Bank, 571.

directly in it? The dominance of sugar was a leading reason why diversification was hard. Experience – the name which the Cubans gave to the two world wars, the depression, Korea, Suez – impressed on Cubans of all walks of life that good and bad times in Cuba depended on good and bad times in the world outside. War rather than peace still brought prosperity. Nothing which Cuba could do at home was so important to her economy as a variation of a cent or two in the price of sugar: thus, if there were sugar exports of three million tons, a one cent variation up or down made a difference of $M60 in Cuba's receipts.[75]

The Cuban sugar industry therefore in 1958 remained as dominant in the country's economy as it had always done since the collapse of coffee over a century before. Yet it was an old-fashioned industry, unable or unwilling to take advantage of an expanding world demand. Partly this was because of the very character of the world sugar condition, and partly also because the severity of the depression in Cuba had brought a protective series of laws which in the interests of humanity had sanctified both an archaic system of growing cane (the *colonia*) and a highly restrictive labour situation. Foreign investment was in decline and though this was welcomed for political reasons it expressed a lack of faith in an industry now apparently in its old age. Whereas in the 1850s Cuba had been the first to seize upon new ideas, in the 1950s she was the last.

What then should be done? No revolutionary leader in 1959 had any proposals for the sugar industry. In 1953, Castro had spoken of even more reforms to benefit the already pampered *colonos*; afterwards, silence. Enlightened economists such as Pazos or López Fresquet were primarily concerned with the industrialization of other sectors of the economy. In so far as the international sugar market was concerned, there was, in fact, little that Cuba could do within the boundaries of the existing system.

A resolute and united policy by all the cane-growing countries of the West Indies and South America could perhaps have secured slightly more progressive terms from the consumer countries. But the chances of such unity and of such resolution were remote. Cuba and Jamaica were almost within sight of one another, but their relations were negligible. There was no chance of Castro and Trujillo or of Cuba and Peru meeting to discuss common sugar policy. There were political rivalries based on generations of social and cultural differences. Politics apart, there was no precedent, before the UNCTAD conference in Geneva in 1965, for a group of primary producers to decide common policies. Had they been able to do so, the cane producers might have sought a settlement whereby the beet growers of the north at least did not expand

[75] *Ibid.,* 52.

their production. The cane producers might have argued that if the advanced countries really desired to assist unselfishly those less well off, they should in this, as in other ways, try to cease competition with tropical or sub-tropical countries in the crops that are those countries' life blood. The U.S. or the Soviet Union can grow wheat as well as beet; the Caribbean cannot.

But of course strategic fears of reliance on foreign trade in wars dictate European sugar policy, even though during and after both world wars the Great Powers of Europe needed Cuba more than she needed them. The difficulties of reaching a common agricultural policy even in the European Economic Communities suggest the complication likely to be met by Cuba and her cane-growing partners. Yet this would still have been the most creative policy for a Cuban government in 1959.

A second alternative seemed to be to accept things as they were: to sell between a third and a quarter of the harvest to the U.S., this proportion fractionally increasing over the years as the U.S. population rose, at the same time doing all possible to get the reversions from failures by other countries, within the U.S. league, to fulfil their quotas. Such failures might, however, have become rarer, and over the years other sugar producers of the Caribbean, such as the Dominican Republic would be bound to covet greater slices of the U.S. market. Still, if this policy had been accompanied by a really ruthless attempt at diversification of agriculture and industrialization, it might have been effective.

The third alternative for Cuba in these conditions of 'monoculture' was to seek to join another of the international sugar leagues: the English, the French or the Russian. The first two of these were out of the question, because of their limited size, and because of internal or imperial arrangements in England and France, not to speak of the English and French political arrangements with the U.S. The only possible new league, therefore, was the Russian. This was a desperate and, in the circumstances of 1959, apparently unreal plan. Russia, if not self-sufficient in sugar, was after all, herself a very large sugar producer. No one in Cuba had really thought of the Russian alternative in 1958 or 1959. Even the Cuban Communists seem to have presumed, even hoped, that somehow or other existing sugar marketing arrangements would be preserved.

Cuban radicals' inclination in 1959 was not to spend too much time on sugar, rather on diversification of agriculture and on industrialization. The great aim was to escape from the monoculture. The song of the 1950s of Carlos Puebla described sadly how

> The roads of old Cuba
> Lead nowhere.

Sugar had taken Cuba to an *impasse*. The revolutionary aim was to bring new roads, to rework the nickel mines, to grow tomatoes or avocados, to become self-sufficient in steel, to sell cigars to China: anything to avoid the production of sugar on the existing scale, much less an increased one.

Thus no one on the Left had a sugar policy. The sugar mills and estates were to be dragged into politics in the wake of the revolution's land reform and not as a part of sugar policy. Few stopped to think that one crop might work more effectively with one type of land reform than another: and that, doubtless, the concern should be first with the industrial structure of sugar, afterwards with the agricultural side. Quite apart from the gloomy long-term state of the international sugar market, the Cuban sugar industry needed reform. The low priority given to research; the static nature of an industry whose main capital investments, whatever the ownership, had been made over thirty years before; the incredibly complicated relations between *colonos* and mills; the nature of existing state involvement in the industry, quota-controlled and restricted, with regulations down to the last sugar bag – a state structure which really foreshadowed nationalization, though without any of its advantages; the fact that, with the restrictions and control which carried over even in years when harvests were theoretically 'free', competition between mills had virtually ceased; and the decline in the average yield per acre of Cuban sugar cane since 1938; all these facts suggested the need for reorganization.

The choice lay between greater freedom of mills to compete, and to modernize themselves, and the nationalization of the industrial side of the industry which would have been the logical continuation of the existing situation. The latter would have enabled the state to carry directly the responsibilities for welfare of large communities now borne by the sugar mills, and the closure where necessary of small or unproductive mills. It would have made possible the setting aside of at least 1% of annual income for research which in its turn might have led to the discovery of some non-edible use for sugar which would (and still may) alter radically the lives of sugar producers.[77] It would have enabled modernization and mechanization to be brought in with maximum understanding between worker and employer. Given the uneasy state of relations between U.S.-owned sugar mills and workers, it would probably have improved labour relations. The large U.S. *centrales* dotted about Oriente and Camagüey undoubtedly had a debilitating effect on the country whatever their economic value. Nationalization, too, would have given the government direct responsibility for sugar policy in place of what had been anyway admitted for

[77] This is not so far fetched as it might seem, since sugar ($C_{12}H_{22}O_{11}$) is 99·9% chemical.

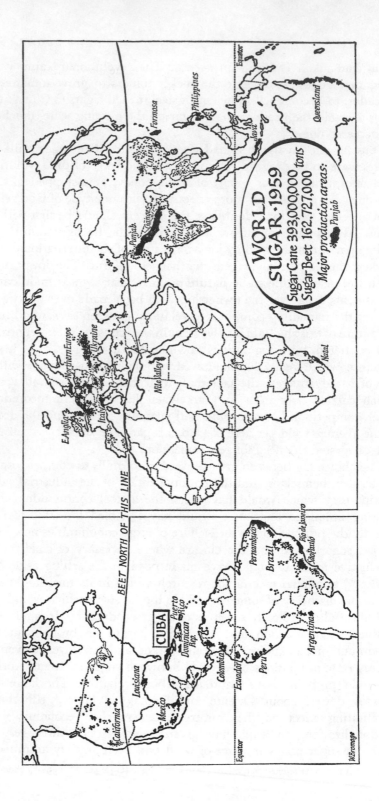

WORLD
SUGAR · 1959

Sugar Cane 393,000,000 tons
Sugar Beet 162,727,000 tons

Major production areas:

● Punjab

BEET NORTH OF THIS LINE

Queensland

Equator

Philippines

Java

Formosa

China

Punjab

Ganges

India

Natal

Northern Europe

Ukraine

Nile Valley

Italy

E. Anglia

California

Louisiana

Mexico

CUBA

Puerto Rico

Dominican Rep.

Colombia

Ecuador

Peru

Pernambuco

Brazil

Rio de Janeiro

São Paulo

Argentina

Equator

W. Bromage

years to be indirectly theirs. It would give the government a control over the commanding heights of the economy with the minimum trouble. The industrial side of a sugar industry lends itself well to governmental direction. Combined with a flexible policy towards the sugar-growing estates, it might have been possible to get through the first years of a revolution without social upheaval and without the flight to Havana or abroad of administrators and technicians on the sugar mills. Nationalization of the mills (though not of the plantations) would have avoided the great customary temptations of favouritism, perhaps inevitable in the existing system. The possibilities indeed of corrupt practice were so great as to make state control desirable almost on those grounds alone. Nationalization might also have strengthened the hand of the government internationally by enabling Cuba to be represented by a delegation who did not represent a combination which included U.S. interests.

Such a policy towards the industrial side of the sugar industry could not have been adopted without consideration of the land where cane was grown. Thus perhaps the aim should have been to encourage a reduction of the surface on which sugar was grown, credit being given for the import of cane cutters, with much national instruction for farmers about growing cane, while increasing yields through better drainage, fertilization and more frequent planting, and the national adoption of Lobo's rationalizing policies in Matanzas.

This policy, however, was not followed. When nationalization came, it came, like the treatment of agricultural lands, in the wake of other policies. In the early days of 1959, the revolutionary government desired to shake free of sugar rather than to saddle itself with running the industry; hence many follies and much frustration.

CHAPTER 30

Tobacco and other Industries

The Cubans remained the greatest cigar-smokers in the world. A seventh of their cigars only were exported. The rest – 350 million or so in 1957 – were smoked by Cubans: fifty a head in the year, women and children included. But these were only half the cigars smoked in Cuba in 1918 when the figure reached well over 100 a head.[1] Cubans also smoked cigarettes in vast numbers.

There had been for many years now five well-defined tobacco-producing regions: of which Vuelta Abajo, the golden area at the west end of the island, was far the most important.

Tobacco had fallen behind cattle and beef products as the second biggest industry of the country, though it remained the second biggest export. Between two-thirds and three-quarters of Cuban tobacco was exported, mostly as leaf. Exports of cigars had greatly declined since the beginning of the century: 256 million cigars were exported in 1906; only about 40 million in the 1950s.[2] Still, the *douceur de vivre* so far as a good Havana cigar is concerned certainly ended in 1914. For tobacco growers in Cuba, this had been compensated by the increase in domestic demand, yet an immense quantity of cheap U.S. cigarettes was imported, perhaps 50% over and above 20,000 packets legally.[3] There was room of course for home manufacture of cheap cigarettes.

Tobacco production under Batista was consistent; a record production level of ninety million pounds in 1957 was the third highest ever (the highest was in 1950). But even here higher figures had been recorded (in 1926 the total reached ninety-five million pounds). Cubans were smoking slightly more cigarettes and cigars than in the past, but the difference was small.[4] Tobacco was grown on a quarter of Cuban farms, but was a primary source of income on only 14%, or between 20,000 and 25,000 farmers, who employed another 60,000 workers.[5] Three per cent of the cultivated area (110,000 acres) was

---

[1] *Estudio*, 499.

[2] Even this was better than in the 1940s when the figure dropped to 14 million. 1954 saw an export of 110 million cigars thanks to the relaxation of controls. But the figures soon slipped back.

[3] World Bank, 860–3. In 1958 there were only 15 cigarette factories.

[4] All figures here from *Anuario*, 1957, 147 ff.

[5] *Cf.* Núñez Jiménez, 322.

planted in tobacco.[6] Three-fifths of all tobacco farms were cultivated by sharecroppers[7] who, however, often owned some livestock and farm equipment. They got their tobacco seedlings and food on credit, many small farmers being thus perpetually in debt to shopkeepers.[8] Tobacco farms were, of course, small: the average was about 15 acres, except for the coarser region of Remedios, where it was 40 acres.[9]

The owners of tobacco land were often companies, sometimes North American such as the Cuban Land and Leaf Tobacco Company in Vuelta Abajo. This company for instance let land to eighty share-croppers,[10] who together employed over 3,000 wage workers. The company provided houses, irrigation, outhouses, a doctor, nurse and clinic, water, and allotments for vegetables. To producers of shade tobacco (grown under the artificial shade of cheesecloth on poles) the company also gave free manure and free credit for wages; they paid a third of all expenses such as fertilizers; and in return received half the crop.[11] Producers of sun tobacco – the biggest number – only gave to the company a quarter of the crop, but sharecroppers here had to pay more expenses – three-quarters of manure costs, and so on.[12] Other owners administered a part of their estates themselves and levied a variation of these charges on their tenants. The variations of holding were indeed infinite.[13] Thus often the wage workers grew tobacco themselves on land which they were allotted to grow vegetables or to keep cattle, thereby getting an extra income; and sometimes owners were exacting, demanding a full year's interest for the credit of a few months.

There seems to have been little change on these generally prosperous farms. On instances noted by Lowry Nelson, the same families had remained in the same place for over thirty years. Widows might take over active management from dead husbands.

A critical and controversial change had recently affected the cigar factories of Havana. These were still grouped together in Havana, great names well-known throughout the world (particularly at good dinner tables) – Romeo y Julieta, Ramon Allones, Larrañaga, Partagás, Montecristo, Menéndez Garcia (the biggest) – though there were about one thousand factories in the whole of Cuba.[14] These factories had always depended on hand labour. Elsewhere, cigar-rolling machines had been in

[6] 1949 figures (World Bank, 857), as estimated by U.S. Embassy, Havana.
[7] Seers.
[8] In 1950 90% of small farmers in the Remedios area were found to pay interest rates of 20% on loans from shopkeepers (World Bank, 593–4).
[9] Again these were 1946 figures.
[10] *Partidarios*.
[11] Shade tobacco might be necessary for say two-thirds of the wrappers of cigars.
[12] This instance was described by Nelson, 130–1.
[13] In Remedios there were sub-tenants of sharecroppers too (*cuartarios* and *tercedarios*), cf. loc cit.
[14] Núñez Jiménez, 322; *Investment in Cuba*, 82.

use for a long time. The Cuban cigar-makers, tightly organized and exclusive, had successfully resisted the introduction of machines since the first attempt to bring them to Cuba in 1925. This caused some lesser factories to incur losses and some had even moved to Florida, where they could supply the U.S. customer more cheaply – a bizarre event in a semi-developed country. But in 1950 a decree by Prío had permitted machine-made cigars. $40 a month was also provided for 900 workers who were consequently unemployed: this might not compare very satisfactorily with their previous $5 a day – $50 a fortnight – but was still a benevolent step, rare in the history of both North and South American labour relations.[15] Nor did this mean that all cigars were machine-made; the best cigars continued to be hand rolled. The number of cigars remained much the same. The number of different brands by now passed belief: Fernando Ortiz saw nearly 1,000 different types of cigar in a collection belonging to a Havana factory.[16]

The workers in tobacco factories in the 1950s numbered 35,000, compared with over 24,000 in 1899. In addition there were some 50,000 tobacco selectors and 8,000 twisters of leaf. Selection and stripping was seasonal work, lasting only a few weeks. 3,000 workers were occupied in Cuba's fifteen cigarette factories.[17] Probably 130,000 were working in the tobacco industry either on the agricultural or industrial side.[18]

The tobacco industry was better organized than sugar. It had a long tradition of honesty. One writer recalled in the old days 'seeing Negroes meet the train running from Villanueva to Batabanó on Thursdays with wheelbarrows loaded with sacks of gold doubloons, which were unloaded at Punta de Carta, Bailén and Cortés, and then carried on muleback through the tobacco country, leaving payment for the crop at each *vega*'.[19] Two commissions looked after the industry, one for prices, one for marketing. The former had an experimental station distributing better types of seed, compiling statistics and so on.

---

[15] *Cf. H.A.R.*, August 1951. It was partially paid for by a tax of $5 on each 1,000 machine-made cigars. The government had initially to suspend this law due to workers' protests.

[16] *Cuban Counterpoint*, 43. fn.

[17] Núñez Jiménez, 322.

[18] *Estudio*, 1103. Principal cigar factories in 1958 (*loc. cit.*):

Menéndez, García & Co.	$M2·58
Cifuentes & Co.	$M1·21
Tabacos Rey del Mundo	$M1·01
J. Palacio	$M0·97
Tabacalera Moya	$M0·74
Romeo y Julieta	$M0·59
José L. Piedra	$M0·48
Larrañaga	$M0·43

[19] 'Recuerdos Tabacaleros del Tiempo Viejo', in *Horizontes*, Havana, August 1936, qu. Ortiz, *Negros Esclavos*, 38.

The desirable reorganization in the tobacco industry was in agriculture. The sharecropping system led often to injustice; and most growers would have been more efficient had they been owners of their own land.

Fernando Ortiz, the chief chronicler of the Afro-Cuban tradition, contrasted sugar and tobacco, the two most noted Cuban products: the value of tobacco lay in its leaves, of sugar in its stalk; cane lived for years, tobacco for months; cane sought sunlight, tobacco shade; cane was without scent, could look after itself for months; tobacco was aromatic and needed constant care from skilled men. Above all, cane demanded seasonal mass labour, tobacco constant attention from a few experienced men. Cane was grown on large estates, tobacco on small holdings. All sugar was the same in the end, beet and cane sugar even producing the same element; no cigar is alike. Finally, sugar spelled slavery, tobacco freedom, and therefore Ortiz suggested Cuba should escape from sugar into tobacco production.[20]

Alas, despite the supreme quality of Cuban cigars, such an escape was not possible. Cuba can produce an indefinite amount of good tobacco. But so can every other island in the Caribbean, and many other countries. There was no chance that Cuban cigarette tobacco could ever displace the favourite suppliers of the main consumers. Her cigars were admittedly the best in the world. But the world cigar market has dropped sadly since the beginning of the century. Further, the great Cuban cigar came from tobacco which was grown only in a very small region of Cuba, the Vuelta Abajo, along the River Cuyaguateje. Here climate and soil combined, as along the great wine rivers of France, to produce the perfect conditions for the production of the great cigar. But the area was not large and in the nature of things could not be expanded to form an industry on which the whole island could live.

Cuba's railways and roads had been for many years better than in any country of the Americas save for the U.S. – perhaps even better than Canada's. But out of Cuba's 11,000 miles of railway, nearly 8,000 miles were private sugar lines; even the remaining 3,000 miles of public railway were dictated by the insatiable needs of the sugar industry, which was responsible for four-fifths of the freight tonnage in Cuba.

Four-fifths also of the public railways in Cuba belonged either to the U.S.-owned Consolidated Railways, operating east of Santa Clara, or to the Western Railroads of Cuba, bought in 1953 by the government from the English United Railways. Hershey & Co. ran a 100-mile railway in Matanzas. There were also sixteen small railways, chiefly in the east, with an average of under thirty miles each.

The Cuban roads were mixed. Those between big towns were

[20] Fernando Ortiz, *Cuban Counterpoint, passim.*

excellent; farm-to-market roads were bad. In 1955 the U.S. Embassy thought that only a fifth of Cuban farms had all-weather roads or railways to them.[21] Still, their general condition was so good that the decline of railway freight, since the opening of the Central Highway in 1931, had been as marked as it had been in the U.S. This did not make Cuba necessarily a modern country: it was simply another instance of the influence of a U.S. model. Bus transport similarly competed with railways, as did, in the 1950s, private cars on a popular scale. At the end of the 1940s, the government began a big new four-lane highway between Havana and Matanzas (the Vía Blanca), as well as other improvements on the Central Highway. Another highway linked Havana to the airport. In Havana in the 1950s, three modern tunnels eased the traffic flow. The Central Highway was, however, in need of improvement, since it was too narrow,[22] and had no shoulders.

The number of cars rose nearly 13% a year in the 1950s – from 70,000 in 1950 to 160,000 in 1958.[23] An extraordinarily high proportion were taxis or cars for hire.[24] There were also an amazing number of Cadillacs and Oldsmobiles, but much inter-city traffic was still by bus, all owned by private companies. The largest was the Omnibus Aliados, with over half the buses, partly with rural services, mostly urban; and the Autobuses Modernos, founded in 1950–1 in Havana, after the removal of the old Havana Electric Railways, by William Pawley, the North American businessman (in Latin America) and ambassador (to Peru and Brazil).[25] The new company did not prosper. The government bought it out but sold it back to private enterprise in 1958. The bus service on the Central Highway was admirable, ten buses leaving Havana for Santiago every day, with good connections to towns on the north and south coasts.

Nineteen towns had airfields, and there were about a hundred other landing fields, many on sugar mills. North-east Oriente, with bad roads and railways, was almost as dependent on the air as was Alaska. The chief company was Cubana, a subsidiary of the U.S. Pan American Airways to begin with after its foundation in 1930, but bought[26] by a Cuban syndicate in 1953 headed by José López Vilaboy, a newspaper chief. Cubana flew to twenty places inland, and to Miami, Madrid, and other places abroad. Havana airport was also bought by Cubana at the same

[21] *Investment in Cuba,* 106.

[22] 21⅓ feet.

[23] UN Statistical Yearbook, 1963, 380. Mexico, Argentina, Brazil and Venezuela had more in South America.

[24] 22,000 compared with 10,000 in 1954. *Investment in Cuba,* 112. Lorries and commercial vehicles increased less fast, from 30,000 in 1950 to 50,000 in 1958.

[25] It was he who had been selected by the CIA to ask Batista to leave Cuba in December 1958.

[26] Pan American kept 25% of the shares.

time. Cubana had a fleet of chiefly English aeroplanes but was about to buy Boeing 707s at the time Batista fell.

There were still thirty shipping lines though, in the Cuba trade; they included regular sailings from New York and New Orleans and less frequent ones from Europe. With Palm Beach and Key West there were ferries. Havana accounted for two-thirds of the imports of Cuba but the sugar areas of the east exported more. Cuba's merchant marine was small: only about eighteen ocean-going ships out of a total number of 2,300 vessels.[27]

Cuba had been a leader in the scramble for instant communications. Havana was the first city in the world to have an automatic multi-exchange telephone. Wireless and television were also developed early. The telephone service became a permanent monopoly of the Cuban American Telephone Company, owned chiefly by IT & T, partly by the American Telephone and Telegraph Company.[28] It was, therefore, another utility entirely owned by North Americans.

Criticism of the telephone company had been persistent not only because of foreign control but because of bad management. There were still many unfilled orders.[29] The World Bank even reported that the company paid to its shareholders 'a good dividend on capital at expense of maintenance and replacement of equipment'.[30] The company, on the other hand, had wished for years to secure the revision of its contract so that it could raise rates which had remained the same since 1909. This was finally done in March 1957, the day after the attack on the palace, and with the customary distributions of bribes. The company then embarked on an expansion programme, with a huge new issue of stock, promising to install 60,000 new telephones by the end of 1960. This work was begun and, in 1958, there were just under 200,000 telephones, nearly all automatic. However, the telephone company had been marked from its birth by shady dealings by some of its personnel and was never free from corruption.[31]

The Cubans used the telephone phenomenally. The average Cuban subscriber seems to have made no less than fourteen to fifteen calls a day, compared with eight to nine in other parts of South America and five in the U.S. The load on existing equipment was thus heavy. Cubans also used the telephone a good deal for calls to the U.S.: 'Call up Miami for a spare wheel, and get it over by the next plane.'

---

[27] See *Cuba: The Pursuit of Freedom,* Appendix XII, for fisheries.

[28] The Cuban Telephone Company with the Cuban American Telephone and Telegraph Company, the Puerto Rico Telephone Company, and others, formed the basis of IT & T.

[29] The number of telephones, 60,000 in the 1920s, dropped to 30,000 in the depression and had risen again, to 110,000 in 1950 and 150,000 in 1955.

[30] World Bank, 340.

[31] López Fresquet, 26.

There were 160 wireless and four television stations, bringing messages of hope or gloom to over a million radio sets and nearly 500,000 television sets (all bought since 1950), and all made in the U.S.[32] These broadcasting companies were all Cuban, but the towns at least often gave the impression of being deluged with cheap North American music. There was one station for 'good music'. Already Cuba was dominated by television almost as much as the U.S. (at least in towns), more so than most European countries. No one had yet used it to effect for politics, though Chibás had shown the possibilities of wireless in 1949–51. Batista rarely appeared.

The Cuban industrial scene – excluding sugar and tobacco – had much changed since the depression and the tariffs of 1927. The last few years had shown a high rate of investment by foreign firms. Many new plants were begun. There was more diversification at the end of Batista's rule than at the start, though this was due partly at least to the industrial or agricultural bank founded under Prío.

Though many North Americans came to Cuba to found businesses in order to escape taxes at home, labour presented a serious problem. Recollection of the 1930s helped to keep workers organized, and made them terrified of further change. Industrialists thus customarily met 'a most insurmountable resistance to modernization'.[33] In 1950 the World Bank thought 'it is not easy to see how further investment in . . . Cuban industry could be made *less* attractive'.[34] Workers' resistance to mechanization of the cigar industry might be understood as an exceptional obstacle in a special business though, even there, costs had so risen as almost to price Cuban cigars out of their old markets. But some textile mills had been forced out of business and others had been saved only by government intervention. Where new methods had been successfully introduced, with the agreement of the workers, there had usually been a stipulation that the same size of labour force would be used as before; even that the new equipment should turn out no more products than the old.

All governments since 1945 had done what they could to encourage new industries; there were three-year exemptions from customs dues on new machinery or equipment, six-year exemptions from taxes on loan interests, ten-year exemptions from customs dues on imported raw materials; depreciation costs could be deducted, and so on. The trouble was that though several new industries were indeed set up, few of them used Cuban raw materials.

[32] *Investment in Cuba*, 116–18; *Estudio*, 1178–9.
[33] World Bank, 134–5.
[34] *Ibid.*, 135.

Under Batista, several of these hindrances were destroyed, by fair means or foul. The government made dismissals of labour possible and cut away red tape, and there is no reason to think that corruption in industry, though considerable, was on a larger scale than under Prío and Grau. (On the other hand, the corrupt practices of the army were much greater and often affected industry indirectly.) The Agricultural and Industrial Development Bank greatly helped too. The result was the expansion of the mid-1950s, causing industrial production to increase between 1955 and 1958 by 3·4% a year. Total investment perhaps increased from about $M2,800 in 1955 to $M3,300 in 1957.[35] In 1957 manufacturing was up by 12%, electricity by 30%, building by 25%: mining only was down, by 20%.[36] Even so, industrialization depended on imports of raw materials and many of the ridiculous sides of the Cuban economy survived: thus out of 11 million kilos of tomatoes exported annually, 9 million probably came back as sauce.[37] Further, the end of the negativeness of labour policy had only been achieved by the further implication of the leaders of trade unions into the system, and the corruption of some of them.[38]

One-third of the capital invested in Cuba was in sugar, followed in order of value by transport and communications, by mining and metallurgy, and by electricity.[39] The largest non-sugar plant in Cuba was the cotton-spinning Textilera Ariguanabo at Bauta, a few miles west of Havana, with 72,000 spindles, 2,000 looms, and employing 2,500. It had been founded in 1931 (before when all Cuban textiles had been imported) by Dayton Hedges of New York.[40] In 1948 Hedges founded a large and efficient rayon works at Matanzas, which employed 1,200. The Hedges's concerns dominated the Cuban textile business till 1958 when Burke Hedges, jr, after his father's death, sold the rayon business for a lavish sum to the state corporation, BANDES.[41] Ariguanabo had had incessant labour troubles in the late 1940s, when Hedges had desired to mechanize, and in fact actually laid off a third of its workers (with compensation), but the rayon works was from the beginning more modern

[35] *Estudio*, 1098.
[36] See Index of Industrial Activity, qu. *ibid.*, 1143.
[37] Industrialization was also slow in relation to human resources, and did not keep pace with the domestic savings and the possibilities offered by the general economy.
[38] Between 1945 and 1951, inclusive, annual industrial consumption of electricity hovered between 130,000 and 155,000 million kilowatts; between 1952 and 1956 it went faster, nearly by 10%. But the largest increase was, however, residential use, increasing between 1945 and 1956 from 77,993 million kilowatts to 383,544 million. In August 1957 residential consumption of electricity was nearly seven times what it had been eleven years before. (See *Anuario*, 1957, 205-9.)
[39] See 'Capital invested in Cuba', in table, *Investment in Cuba*, 116
[40] See above, p. 332.
[41] The Economic and Social Development Bank.

with mechanical innovations, and there was no serious labour resistance to mechanization.[42]

After the Hedges's concerns the next largest non-sugar industrial plant was the Bacardí rum business at Santiago, which also made beer, and employed about 2,000. This manufacture was the only Cuban product about whose management the generally critical World Bank Mission reported that it 'could suggest no improvement'.[43] Strong cane brandy (*aguardiente*), and a little rather unsuccessful wine was made, from tropical fruits, and also some cheap domestic gin. There were five large modern breweries, including Bacardí's, producing excellent popular lager-type beers, demand for which (as in Europe at the same time) was rising fast. These manufactures employed some 10,000.[44] Coca-cola, Pepsi-cola, Canada Dry and Orange Crush, had Cuban dependencies.[45] Also in Cuba were three paper mills, with good chances of producing newsprint from bagasse in a fourth, opening experimentally in 1958, and ordinary paper from a fifth also from bagasse (W. R. Grace & Company).[46] Cuba had a rather advanced chemical sector producing, especially, sulphuric acid (from imported sulphur); and about forty good pharmaceutical laboratories, some of them U.S. owned. Annual sales of pharmaceutical goods were high – between $M60 and $M70 at retail prices – and indeed the World Bank found 'literally hundreds of Cuban enterprises producing patent medicines, home remedies, lotions, pomades, etc.'[47] About half the drugs and medicines sold were made in Cuba. Other plants – all developed since the depression – included canners, pasteurizing and cheese plants, butter factories and fifty-nine ice-cream plants.[48] The U.S.-owned Burrus Flour Mill at Regla opened in 1952 to lessen Cuba's reliance on imports of flour, which by 1955 had dropped to about 60% of total production.[49] There were some vegetable oil plants, chiefly U.S.-owned (Proctor and Gamble in 1931 had bought the old-established Sabatés & Co. and the Hershey Corporation's oil plant), but none made any impact on the Cuban demand for fats, which was almost entirely met by the U.S.[50] North Americans were also in the lead in other businesses – for example, paint, fertilizers and rubber (particularly tyres). The leather industry, on the other hand, was a contrast, being still a conglomeration of old small-scale concerns, providing, in the

[42] World Bank, 962.
[43] *Ibid.*, 979.
[44] Census of 1953.
[45] *Estudio*, 1110–13.
[46] Grace & Co. had been making paper from bagasse successfully in Peru since 1939.
[47] World Bank, *loc. cit.*
[48] *Investment in Cuba*, 76.
[49] *Ibid.*, 78.
[50] *Ibid.*, 81–2.

mid-1950s, about 7½ million pairs of shoes, coping with all but fancy demand.[51]

Cuba had no coal, few hydro-electric possibilities (because of sluggish rivers), and as yet inadequately developed oil resources. The main domestic fuel was bagasse.[52] Cuba's electricity consumption ranked high among countries of the Americas after the U.S.[53] The sugar mills made their own electricity, and all but a small percentage of the rest was distributed by the Cuban Electric Company, a subsidiary of the American and Foreign Power Company (itself a subsidiary of the vast Electric Bond and Share Company of New York) which had had a virtual electrical monopoly since the Machado days: Machado had himself sold his own smaller electrical supply business to Cuban Electric before being president of Cuba, and his chief financial backer, Henry Catlin, had been its president.[54] Most of Cuba had had electricity since the 1920s, at least in towns and large villages. Cuban Electric had an excellent record of growth, especially in the 1950s, as more and more businesses and private people modernized their lighting and air-conditioned their rooms. There were, however, many shortcomings: much equipment was old; there were frequent power shortages in the countryside; and rates were higher than those in the U.S.,[55] partly due at least to the need to bribe officials, from the president down. Scandals in the past had proliferated: government officials paid bills only when they felt like it; Havana city was years behind;[56] and in the industry there had been numerous semi-political strikes.[57]

The last years before the fall of Batista had been attended by numerous new projects: the French Compagnie Générale d'Enterprises Eléctriques had received a $M20 contract to construct a plant for the new development at East Havana; a hydro-electric project in Las Villas made use of the Habanilla river: such developments, admirable as they were, were however too late to save the tattered flag of private enterprise.[58]

Ever since a small strike at Bacuranao in 1914[59] a little oil had been known to exist in Cuba. An oil boom during the First World War had

[51] Shoe imports averaged 115,000 pairs between 1947 and 1953. Cf. Investment in Cuba, 97 and fn.

[52] The waste left behind after the sugar cane had been ground and the juice extracted.

[53] 103 watts of installed capacity per capita per year.

[54] See Cuba: The Pursuit of Freedom, p. 570. For a description of Cuban Electric's remarkable adventures in 1933–4 see Problems of the New Cuba, 400.

[55] The company said that they were not high in comparison with 'cost to consumer of generating his own power' and Cuban costs generally (Investment in Cuba, 105).

[56] Phillips, 126–7.

[57] Cuban Electric also operated the one small gas company.

[58] Estudio, 1169–72.

[59] Actually the Motembo oil field near Colón had been discovered in the late 1800s, Bacuranao in 1864, another near Cárdenas in 1890.

attracted some seventy companies, but only one well was found with commercial possibilities. The major oil companies began, however, to seek oil on a large scale after the Second World War, after the new boom in Venezuela. All save one had given up by 1954. In that year a rich strike was made at Jatibonico by the Tarabuca Group.[60] From May 1954 onwards 250 barrels a day flowed. Further exploration followed, backed by a generous credit policy by the Batista government which proclaimed it would pay up to 50% of oil exploration. Another important strike followed at Jatibonico in 1956, and yet another at Yayajabos in Pinar del Río. In October 1957 the Pan American Land and Oil Royalty Company, with Texan interests, announced that they had bought three million acres in Cuba along with certain shares in other development projects. Between 1954 and 1958, investment in Cuban oil leapt from $M3 to $M44, producing from 57,000 to between 300,000 and 400,000 barrels.[61]

Thus the revolution found Cuban domestic oil quite promising though no clear knowledge existed of the size of the reserves. Meantime, most of Cuba's needs were met by imports. Rising use of cars greatly increased demand. Three-quarters of the petrol was imported from the U.S. or the British West Indies, and one-quarter was produced in local refineries from imported crude oil. Shell had just finished a big plant at Regla, with a capacity of 80,000 barrels. Also in 1956 Texaco finished a plant with 20,000 barrel capacity at Santiago.[62] Total new investment in the mid and late 1950s was about $M75.[63] A plan also existed to pipe oil from Campche in Mexico to South Cuba and thence to Florida.[64]

Cuba still had rich mineral resources, the large lateritic ore reserves of North Oriente being potentially one of the world's largest sources of nickel and of iron, an important producer of chrome, cobalt, copper and manganese, as well as some other minerals in small amounts – zinc, gold, silver and lead. 287 mines were open in Cuba in 1958, including 84 petrol explorers; the U.S. took 96% of the output.

That Cuba had iron, mostly in northern Oriente, some in the south, had been known for centuries.[65] The latter began to be developed in the 1880s, the former in 1908 by Pennsylvania and, later, Bethlehem Steel. The south coastal operation persisted till 1945 (by then Bethlehem Steel controlled that too), the north only till 1917, but during the Second

---

[60] *H.A.R.*, June 1954.

[61] *Ibid.*, June 1958.

[62] *Ibid.*, April 1956.

[63] *Investment in Cuba*, 95.

[64] *H.A.R.*, October 1957. Edwin W. Pawley, a friend of Truman's, was involved in this.

[65] Columbus said in his diary, 25 November 1492, 'I saw on the beach many iron-coloured stones.'

World War the U.S. government, through the Freeport Sulphur Company, worked the iron at Mayarí in pursuit of nickel. All but 15 % or so of the iron-producing regions were owned by U.S. companies and they or their parent companies had other and more easily worked sources of supply. For these companies, their Cuban sources were merely reserves. This was potentially inflammatory so far as Cuban interests were concerned but, in practice, resentment was confined to a few economists and to people who, like Castro, lived near the disused mineheads with heavy unemployment. There was not much public interest in iron or indeed any mineral resources in Cuba. The U.S. had been responsible for nearly all the exploration and mapping of resources (done chiefly because of shortages in the war). The World Bank Mission criticized Cubans as too often relying 'on future wars to stimulate further mineral development'.[66] But it was commercially out of the question for Cubans to work the small quantity of ore not controlled by U.S. interests: any expenditure of capital on mineral resources would so easily vanish with U.S. competition. Even so, the first Cuban steel plant had just been built at Cotorro in Havana in 1958 by the U.S. Republic Steel Company.

Nickel raised the question of Cuban mineral resources in its most acute form. Before the Second World War, all Cuban nickel resources were owned by Bethlehem Steel, and nothing was done. During the war the U.S. government built a large plant at Nicaro, fifteen miles east of Mayarí on the Bay of Levisa, at the huge cost of $M33·5. Employing 1,800 people, and therefore becoming the third largest industrial plant in Cuba in terms of workers[67] (with a payroll reaching $M13),[68] the Nicaro plant was operated by a subsidiary of the Freeport Sulphur Company (Nicaro Nickel). It began to work in 1943. In 1946 Cuba produced almost 10 % of the nickel in the world. But the mill was closed in 1947.

Nicaro, still owned by the U.S. government (through a company in which the Administration held all the shares), was reopened in 1952 during the Korean War and kept open. It was now operated for the U.S. government by the Nickel Processing Corporation, a firm specially founded for the purpose by the National Lead Company (60 % of the shares) and the Cía de Fomento de Minerales Cubana (Cuban shareholders, with 40 % of the shares).[69] The Freeport Sulphur Company still retained an interest, since it provided most of what was used in the plant (through *its* subsidiary, Nicaro Nickel). An ex-U.S. ambassador, Robert Butler, was involved in this transaction, along with Inocente

[66] World Bank, 202.
[67] After Bacardí Rum and Dayton Hedges's textile mill at Ariguanabo, Nicaro was the most valuable plant in Cuba.
[68] World Bank, 998.
[69] But *cf. H.A.R.*, April 1952.

Alvarez, an Auténtico lawyer and Grau's foreign minister, to whom in fact Butler had been accredited,[70] which gave it a certain air of scandal. But rather more serious criticism attended the appointment of the General Service Administrator, Edward Mansure, an insurance man who, it turned out, allotted insurance to various political friends in Chicago who had recommended his appointment.[71] This return to the age of Mark Hanna did not, however, come out into the open till four years later, and meanwhile Mansure had announced a $M34 expansion programme at Nicaro: even this was attended by several serious doubts, since it later turned out that the Frederick Share Corporation gave $8,510 to the Republican party while seeking the contract which they afterwards gained.[72]

Nicaro having reopened, the Freeport Sulphur Company (which held a long-term contract to supply the U.S. government with nickel) announced that they were proposing to work the large nickel and cobalt deposits at Moa Bay, also on the Cuban north coast, about fifty miles east. The chairman of the Freeport Sulphur Company, Moa Bay, John Whitney,[73] said that Moa represented the best new source of nickel in the world. Once again all taxes were exempt for this U.S. concern. In March 1957 a processing plant costing $M120[74] was announced for Moa Bay, a result of a contract with the U.S. (government) General Services Administration by which the latter undertook to take all the nickel and cobalt which the company could produce till June 1965 – up to 270 million pounds of nickel and 29 million pounds of cobalt.[75] In the same month the Nicaro expansion project was completed.

Copper was the oldest and largest mining operation in the past history of Cuba, dating from 1530 at El Cobre, named after the mine.[76] The English ran the mine in the nineteenth century, selling out in the 1890s to a German-U.S. firm. In the twentieth century, however, the biggest and most efficient copper mine was at Matahambre, in the west of Pinar del Río, discovered in 1912, and after 1921 with a majority of stock owned by the U.S. Metal Company Ltd, the ore being refined by the U.S. Metal Refining Company, of Contact, New Jersey. The U.S. Metal Company withdrew in 1943 after labour troubles and low prices, and Cubans took over control. Matahambre had large deposits.

[70] *Fortune*, June 1953.

[71] *H.A.R.*, March 1956. Mansure (b. 1901, Chicago), chairman of E. L. Mansure Co.; president of Crime Prevention Inc., Cook County.

[72] *H.A.R.*, November 1956. Randall Cremer, ex-official of the company, told a committee of the House of Representatives that he felt 'naturally bound' by an agreement with the Republican party chairman, Hall.

[73] John Whitney (b. 1904), gentleman and financier; educated Oxford and Yale; owner of *New York Herald Tribune* and U.S. ambassador in London 1957–61.

[74] *H.A.R.*, February 1958.

[75] *Ibid.*, April 1957.

[76] See above, for nineteenth-century operations.

El Cobre had closed in 1918, but copper was found in all Cuban provinces. In 1950 the value of copper production exceeded that of all other metallic resources, though by the late 1950s it was overtaken by nickel. Nickel from Cuba still represented 40% of North American importation and Cuba was fourth among Latin American copper producers.[77] About 1,000 workers toiled away in Matahambre, the mine being connected to the little port of Santa Lucía by an aerial tramway.[78] The U.S. shareholders mostly sold out to Cubans after 1945. El Cobre was being exploited again in a small way.

Manganese and chrome also played a part. Cuba produced over half the world's chemical grade manganese, all being bought by the U.S. This metal, controlled, like iron, by Bethelehem Steel, had been mined since 1888 by U.S. companies and, as with other Cuban minerals, had had its best times during the world wars, when carriage was specially difficult between the U.S. and her normal providers in Africa or India. Rearmament in the 1950s kept the mines open and production in 1952–7 was about the same as during the Second World War.[79] Cuba was thus second to Brazil as manganese producer in the western hemisphere. She had been the major chrome producer for a while in the Second World War, but dropped a long way afterwards, though deposits remained large. Operations were partly in the main mineral areas, Mayarí to Baracoa, partly in north Camagüey. The old Caledonia mine at Mayarí, like Matahambre, had recently passed from Bethlehem Steel to Cuban interests.[80] Production in the 1950s was only about a third of what it had been in the four war years.

Non-metallic minerals such as marble, limestone or salt employed more than these mines and, of course, made a greater impact on the economy, since the effect of the former was nil. Limestone was found in nearly every province, and was extensively used in building and to make burned lime, to process sugar. Marble was the outstanding product of the Isle of Pines.

To be a 'reserve country' in all these ways was clearly infuriating. The mines were only worked when North America was waging war. Peace brought inactivity. It was the same story as in the sugar industry. U.S. ownership of the mineral fields meant that the Cuban economy could never be seen as a whole. Even those minerals which were exported were left unprocessed. On the other hand, those who believed that nickel

[77] Núñez Jiménez, 219.
[78] See *The Explosives Engineer* (Hercules Powder Company, Wilmington, Delaware), March-April 1955.
[79] Núñez Jiménez, 219–20; Jenks, 26; World Bank, 211, 980–3; *Investment in Cuba*, 64–5. *Cf.* Charles F. Park Jr., *The Manganese Depository of Cuba* (U.S. Department of the Interior (mimeographed), 1941); *Estudio*, 1077–9.
[80] See *Estudio*, 1079–81.

could be greatly developed reckoned without the knowledge that substitutes for it would be increasingly found in the 1960s.

The importance of Cuba to the U.S. will not be fully understood without realizing that the U.S. companies engaged in Cuba read 'like a *Who's Who* of American business': total U.S. investment stood at over $1 billion;[81] shareholding and commercial-political interest was widespread. Any action in Cuba which affected these interests would be bound to have widespread consequences. 160,000 workers, over 90% Cubans, were employed in North American firms in Cuba, and North American firms spent $M730 in Cuba, of which $M70 was in taxes – almost 20% of the Cuban budget. Many of these firms were Cuban subsidiaries of U.S. companies, dependent on the parent company for supplies. Any radical party in Cuba would have been driven to affect these interests since the U.S. business community dominated Cuban trade and even an outstanding Cuban capitalist like Julio Lobo was inclined to abdicate political responsibility to the U.S.[82]

[81] That is $M1,000. Estimates vary considerably of the exact amount invested in Cuba by the U.S. in 1959. Thus the U.S. Department of Commerce named investment in industry and public utilities as $M879 in 1957. J. Wilson Sandelson in Plank, *op. cit.*, 101, gave a total including agriculture of £M1,500. *Cuba Socialista* September 1962 had $M965.

[82] Lobo to the author (November 1968) complained that the U.S. should have alerted Cubans earlier to the realities of Castro's movement.

CHAPTER 31

The Economy: Labour

The history of labour in Cuba had been curious. Before 1933, there had been a workers' accident compensation law only and certain social security measures for railway men and mineworkers. The government always took the side of employers in disputes with labour; under Machado, labour leaders had been murdered, strikes crushed by force, labour organizations banned. But the movement survived and, from the late 1930s, labour, because of its earlier struggles, was a major force. Successive governments, during Batista's first period of power, sought to placate labour with a series of advanced laws – providing an eight-hour day; a 44-hour week (with pay for 48 hours); a month's paid holiday; four further official holidays with pay; nine days' sick leave with pay; women workers to have six weeks' holiday before and after childbirth; some wages to be tied to the cost of living; and employers to be unable to move factories without government permission. Employees could only be dismissed with proof of cause. In *The Political and Social Thought of Fidel Castro*, a booklet published with Castro's approval in 1959, it was pointed out 'since 1933 Cuban distributive policy has (as the result of wage increases, the introduction of the eight-hour day, paid holidays, social insurance and so on) brought about a juster distribution of the national income [which] . . . used to flow into the pockets of the few and now reaches the hands of many.'[1]

It seemed indeed that the government almost intervened on the side of labour. By the 1950s in fact labour had almost a stranglehold over the government; and it would not be an exaggeration to say that Batista, during his second period of power, ran Cuba by means of an alliance with organized labour. In return for the support of labour, Batista underwrote the vast number of restrictive practices, the limitations on mechanization and the bans on dismissals, which were such a characteristic of the Cuban labour scene. The leaders of the union movement, such as Mujal, Hirigoyen and Linares, were Auténticos, once closely connected with that parliamentary party; there was also the dissident Communist leadership, which had run the central union structure from the time of its organization as a fairly respectable part of society about 1938 until 1948. They had left behind a tradition of

[1] English edition published Havana, 1959, 153.

étatisme which the Auténticos, being the party in the government as well, were happy to carry on. Thus organized labour was becoming an official trade union. Labour disputes were almost always settled by government decree. Collective bargaining was almost unknown, for one law provided that all disputes had to be discussed under the auspices of the Ministry of Labour if a majority of workers in the firm so desired. The Ministry of Labour had, however, only political appointees: and in the 1940s the unions packed the ministry with friends.

This situation was negative. 'Harder to get rid of a worker than of a wife' was a common joke by Cuban businessmen over daiquirís at the Havana Biltmore Yacht Club; 'Easier to get a new wife than a new job' the worker would doubtless have replied. Both workers and their leaders were obsessed with the past; they recalled not only the depression but how only recently the mill owner had power of life and death over the sugar worker (a mill owner might have a worker whipped or even killed by the rural guard); the memory of slavery, abolished only sixty-five years before, hung about the island like a dark cloud. Many union leaders, despite their friendship with Auténtico politicians, seemed motivated by revenge. But there was also insecurity about the future. Who knew how long the time of *vacas gordas* would last? Perhaps the 1950s were a mere interlude of calm before a new hurricane returned to blow away the forty-hour week, the holidays with pay, the social legislation, as if they had been unprotected coffee trees in a time of storm. If investors, industrialists and businessmen felt themselves gamblers, Cuban workers were a prey to all the anxieties which resulted from

the instabilities, the stagnation and the chronic unemployment of the Cuban economy. They see all about them the fearsome consequences to workers and their families from loss of jobs. They lack confidence in the will or ability of employers, investors and the government to create new enterprises and new employment.[2]

There was the possibility of appeal to the courts over the Ministry of Labour. But this would be expensive, lengthy and perhaps settled ultimately by bribery, in which both employers and unions steeped themselves. Good friendships were anyway always at least as important as a good case (and such friendships ensured jobs, much more than did the themselves underemployed labour exchanges). The law was not always clear and was therefore much debated. Nor were the economic facts ever quite beyond dispute; how many were really unemployed, who were they, were any statistics honest? Different groups of workers developed into rigid, jealous, exclusive, essentially conservative castes of privilege, jobs passing from father to son.

[2] *Ibid.*, 358.

The tragedy was that, for all the enlightened labour legislation, there remained a large unemployed section of the population and an even larger partially employed one. Neither was usually incorporated in the union structure. The minimum unemployed during the five months of sugar harvest was about 8 % of the labour force; the maximum unemployed during the rest of the year might have been 32 %.[3] Probably in fact in an average year about one quarter of the labour force worked less than half the year, a tenth not at all. Thus the economy swung annually from a highly unsatisfactory but controllable situation (where a benevolent State might have been able to afford reasonably therapeutic measures) to a tragic one which in European or other advanced countries would have been regarded as intolerable: the only time that the U.S. approached such levels of unemployment was in 1933,[4] when there was doubt whether the State would endure. The Cuban State was not benevolent in the sense of providing unemployment benefits, and the Cuban unions turned a blind eye to unemployment much of the time – in the sugar mills, union power lay with the workers who had all-the-year-round jobs at the mill. The situation was partly saved in many families by the fact that it was unusual for all members to be out of work at the same time; many of those out of work were from the class of the 50,000 to 60,000 young men who annually reached the age of work, and perhaps most people by the age of thirty or so had found some solid all-the-year-round job. Many nominally unemployed sugar workers also had small plots of land which enabled them to grow something between harvests. The province with least unemployment was, not unexpectedly, Pinar del Río, which had the most diversified agriculture. The sugar areas on the other hand had the most unemployment.[5] These problems had also been specially acute since the depression, since, as has been seen, Cuba had a substantial increase in population between 1933 and 1958.

The fear of falling back into this melancholy group of the unemployed or underemployed naturally gripped the imaginations of all who had good jobs protected by unions and laws. Some labour leaders, for instance, favoured mechanization but, like labour leaders in most countries in such circumstances, they feared the inadequate creation of new jobs. Town workers, particularly casual ones who had come in from the country, sought to stay with a single employer for six months:

[3] The 1953 census found 173,811 during the 1953 harvest who were not working. See *Investment in Cuba*, 23, where this question is perceptively if conservatively discussed. *Cf. Estudio*, 804 ff. Felipe Pazos (*Cambridge Opinion*, February 1963) put the unemployment figure at 'seldom below 15%' and, in his speech to the Club de Leones, San Juan Puerto Rico, (29 March 1961) put the figure as between 300,000 and 400,000, never below the first.

[4] 12·8 million out of 51·8 million or 24·6% (*Historical Statistics*).

[5] *Estudio*, 815.

if they accomplished that, they would qualify for insurance protection and would be impossible to dismiss. Many failed, and did odd jobs washing cars, selling lottery tickets or begging: among all these categories there were internal social divisions, the better parts of Havana being most sought after, and so on, in reverse order.

These conditions made many labour leaders reactionary: the fact that workers could not be dismissed had a debilitating effect on them, depriving them of initiative; they had little to do except negotiate with a friendly Ministry of Labour. Driving around in ducktailed Cadillacs, the labour leaders, many of whom were involved in the graft and gangsterism associated with all pre-Revolutionary politics, made a deplorable impression on nearly all sections of society, particularly on the often nearly starving unemployed for whom they were supposed to be responsible. One example of corrupt practice related to the building of the Havana Hilton Hotel, which belonged to the pension fund of the Restaurant workers. So much money was wasted or stolen that even when going very well the hotel could not yield 1% return to the pension fund.[6]

The labour question obsessed businessmen in Cuba. Cuba's remarkable stagnation was attributed to it, though this was chiefly due to the prolonged crisis in the sugar industry. Many employers had constant and (in comparison with conditions of the past) unwonted trouble due to the overmanning of their enterprises. One employer made sixty appearances before the labour courts without one favourable decision. One company filed 200 applications for permission to sack workers for justifiable causes and failed each time. There was a famous instance of a disgruntled hosiery worker who became 'insubordinate'. On being warned, he wantonly cut up masses of cloth with his shears. He was dismissed and appealed. While waiting for the law to take its course, he came regularly to the factory and, according to the defence lawyers, 'outraged the female employees with depraved exhibitions'. The labour court supported the employer and the man found other work. Eight years later he appealed to the final Labour Court of Appeal, which decreed that the first factory would have to reinstate him and pay him back wages of $16,000. The employer appealed to President Prío who, acting for once like Solomon, cancelled the payment but ordered the worker reinstated.[7] These things contrived, with the existence of a large unemployed pool of labour, to give the impression to unthinking businessmen and others, not entirely falsely, that capitalist laws of supply and demand did not apply to Cuba. Some New York businessmen thought Cuba a country where an undesirable revolution had

[6] López Fresquet, 18.
[7] World Bank, 149.

already occurred. Certainly North American capital had often considered Cuba for new projects and had turned away because of the labour laws.[8]

In 1958 most cane cutters earned \$3 to \$4 a day.[9] In cane-cutting areas, wages were usually greater per household since every four households usually had seven workers – some, of course, being teenagers. The average industrial wage usually gave an income of about \$1,600 a year.[10] All these wages were high – for those who received them – in comparison with what usually prevailed in Latin America, but they were only about half U.S. levels in 1950–1, although the average U.S. wage for all industries had been as low as \$1,600 as recently as 1941–2.[11] Of course, Cuban prices were not directly comparable with those of the U.S. but the fact that U.S. manufactured goods could compete effectively with Cuban, often at higher prices than in the U.S., suggests the relative costs in the two countries. On the other hand, Cuban big estates were not feudal in character and were worked as large capitalist enterprises serving a national or world market and employing paid labourers. All big sugar estates had, of course, to collaborate with the state in respect of quantities of cane cut and even wages paid.

The rigidity of the Cuban labour scene was severely criticized in the World Bank's report on Cuba in 1951; partly in consequence, some successful efforts were then made to breach its reactionary side without, however, providing any compensating reorganization of society. Most important was the famous surrender by the cigar workers, enabling the mechanization of that industry.

Batista's government grasped the nettle of revising the right to dismiss workers, stopping short of it in terms of legislation but allowing it in several individual cases. Most labour leaders accepted this: for they had, like Mujal, transferred their loyalty directly from the Auténtico government to Batista's as if they had been impeccable civil servants. The consequences were, as has been seen, the late 1950s' rush of investment from abroad and a slight rise in unemployment, to something like 28 % in the dead season in late 1958;[12] this was despite such progress as had been made in agricultural diversification, particularly in rice and coffee – crops which are complementary to sugar, with harvests at different

---

[8] *Cf. H.A.R.*, May 1954.

[9] The average wage for ordinary or semi-skilled industrial labour was from \$6 to \$7 a day; builders got \$7·50; crane operators \$8·40; samplers in the sugar industry, \$4·67; weighers, \$7·15 to \$7·69; general mechanics \$10·71; welders, \$11·12; foundrymen, \$15·57; shop foremen, \$12·47; chief electricians, \$23·35 (W.B., 142). To each of these sums, 9·09% was added to convert their 44-hour week into one of 48 hours.

[10] Oshima's estimate.

[11] *Historical Statistics*, 94.

[12] *Primer Estudio Provisional del Balance de Recursos de Trabajo*, 23 July 1962.

times. This meant that fewer and fewer young people reaching fourteen found employment quickly. Still, the tendency gave alarm, scarcely affected by the increase in the minimum wage in February 1958 to $85 a week in Havana, $80 in other cities, and $75 in the country.[13]

The 1953 census suggested that a quite high percentage of Cubans – 25 % of the labour force or about 450,000 – could be regarded as skilled. But Cuba always seemed short of foremen and inspectors. The census also showed that a sophisticatedly high proportion of the labour force was occupied in service activities, many with the railways and highways. A North American study of the Cuban economy published in July 1956[14] described the Cuban worker as having 'wider horizons than most Latin American workers and [expecting] more out of life in material amenities than many European workers ... His goal is to reach a standard of living comparable with that of the [North] American worker.' His imagination, that is, had been roused – he knew from television, films, or personal observation the kind of life lived by North Americans. At the same time it was clear that, unless a striking change occurred both in the sugar industry and in the place of sugar in the economy, this goal might move further away, not nearer. The workers feared that mechanization and improved methods of production would assist the capitalist, not the worker, and that neither government nor private initiative could create an expanding economy.

A million workers, or half the total labour force, belonged to a union in 1958.[15] The unions had been grouped together in the national confederation, the CTC, in 1938, which from then till 1947 had been run chiefly by the Communists, with the mulatto, Lázaro Peña, as secretary-general. The Auténticos had bludgeoned their way into control in 1947. First, Angel Cofiño, then Eusebio Mujal, was secretary-general. Almost half the total membership of the CTC consisted of the sugar workers who, under leaders such as Conrado Bécquer and Conrado Rodríguez, were much the most influential union for nearly all sugar workers, both

[13] *H.A.R.*, March 1958. These figures were not all fulfilled.

[14] *Investment in Cuba*, 24.

[15] Maybe up to 1,500,000, possibly only 800,000. In 1943 the labour force reached 1,520,851 or 46·84% of the total population over thirteen. Agriculture, including fishing and mining, accounted for 41·9% of the population – a drop of 7·2% since 1919. Ten years later, the Cuban labour force was estimated at just over two million (53·8% of those over fourteen); 60% of the labour force lived in places classified as urban (including the *bateys* of sugar mills); 17% of the labour force were women. Women only, as would be expected, were found more often in the town than the country – especially Havana, where over half the working women were (Census of 1953, xl–xli, 153 ff.). Over half the women (65%) who worked carried out various forms of 'service' jobs. The average age of the working force was 33·8, and of those seeking employment it was only 28·9. The economically active of these, 31%, lived in Havana province. 41% were in agriculture, and 18% lived as artisans or by helping operate machines (*ibid.*, xlii). This shows a surprising absence of drift from the land since 1943: in most developing countries the index of wealth is indeed the proportion of the working population who are not on the land.

in the mills and in the fields, were organized in the unions. There were, however, thirty-two industrial federations in all, with union organization, as might be expected, weak or non-existent in the very many smaller farms (other than those connected with sugar) and on cattle ranches or on coffee farms. Unions, like student politics, often led to political advancement – being obvious means of such for ambitious working-class men, especially Negroes or mulattoes. Most big unions had special committees on Negro questions. The Cadillac-mounted leaders of Mujal's group talked a lot about the class struggle, but few knew much about daily problems of workers. Mujal was believed to have accumulated a fortune of several millions. The port workers were the most obstructive union of all: though they had to cope with unemployment between October and January, they had secured laws which raised port costs in Havana so high as to discourage commerce. Communist-controlled even under Batista, they were the highest-paid workers in Cuba. Most were Negroes or mulattoes. They were backward, reactionary and lawless. Many were part-time smugglers, pimps or male prostitutes (the famous *negros bugarrones del muelle*). They were headquarters of *santería* or ñáñiguismo; the most famous Communist dock labour leader Aracelio Iglesias, murdered in 1948 in a brawl, was himself a santero.

It is clear, then, how at the same time friends of the old regime in Cuba were able to argue that the country had the most advanced labour laws and its enemies could say that the people were neglected. It is equally plain how the apparently strong institution of the Cuban trade unions was later incapable of providing resistance, moral or physical, to the pressure of revolution. The Cuban working class was in many respects exactly what Fanon called organized labour in the Third World in *Les Damnés de la Terre* – the 'pampered proletariat'.

CHAPTER 32

The Economy: the Central Neurosis

Old societies out of joint usually demand overall solutions:

[A reformer might] teach a farmer to grow tomatoes . . . twice as big as his neighbour's, but then . . . they lie rotting in the field because there is no market . . . or because there are no lorries to take them to market or no roads. If the tomatoes . . . get to market, it is so controlled that the farmer gets only a small return on his effort. When he seeks credit to invest in fertilizer . . . he finds it . . . non-existent. Once he has made his land useful, he may well find that his ownership is disputed and some faraway urban landlord may try to take it away from him. His local political representative is more than likely in cahoots with the urban landlord.[1]

In Cuba, the interlocking nature of the political and economical problems was at least as strong as elsewhere. There were two main economic anxieties: first, the anxiety of Cuban workers about employment generally, due to the memories of the 1930s, meant that costs of production were high, that efficiency was lowered and that foreign investment was discouraged. In 1950 the World Bank wrote:

Unless this vicious circle is broken, all efforts at economic betterment in Cuba will be severely handicapped. Cubans of all classes will suffer by lower incomes, by fewer and inferior job opportunities and perhaps even by internal dangers to their cherished political freedoms.[2]

The warning was clear, and some slight changes for the better were introduced between then and 1952, when the 'cherished political freedoms' were indeed subverted. The Batistiano government afterwards attempted, like many other dictatorships, to seize the nettle of labour costs and, with the connivance of the corrupt unions, enabled manufacturers to cut costs by letting them lay off labour. After that, foreign investment increased considerably, but it did so, of course, in the unnatural scenery of Batista's arbitrary rule.

The second economic anxiety was also well described by the World Bank.

---

[1] G. C. Lodge, 'Revolution in Latin America', *Foreign Affairs*, January 1966.
[2] World Bank, 359.

Cuba enjoys a level of income and a standard of living among the highest in Latin America and probably the highest in any tropical country. However, the productive basis for this was mainly established before 1925 [that is, the industrial structure of the sugar industry]. Since then, the Cuban economy has made relatively little progress. Cuban incomes have fluctuated with the world market for sugar, [have been] affected strongly by trade cycles, tariffs, quotas and wars, but have shown little ... overall tendency to advance. At the same time, the Cuban economy suffers from a high degree of instability. Every year there is a long dead season when most of the sugar workers are unemployed and the most extensive capital equipment in the country lies idle ... instabilities from booms and depressions and political crises in the outside world quickly raise or lower the Cuban economic [picture] ... A stagnant and unstable economy with a high level of insecurity creates resistance to improvements in productive efficiency. And yet improvements in productive efficiency are the key to creating a more progressive, more stable economy ... [This is] the 'master circle' of all vicious circles that needs to be attacked.[3]

This 'master circle' lasted throughout the 1950s. The Sugar Agreement of 1953 inaugurated an era of permanent restriction of Cuba's main product. Apart from some changes in ownership of the mills, sugar remained stagnant. This affected much of the economy, despite the investment and building boom. Such efforts at diversification as the mechanization of rice-growing had brought small but not fundamental changes. It still seemed that diversification was 'almost beyond capitalist laws'. The spirit of lottery remained: for the grand capitalist, whatever might be won in the unpredictable international sugar market outshadowed all possible profits from less striking but constructive ventures of agricultural change.

The further problem was that Cuba had become a 'marginal supplier' in both the U.S. and the world markets. Except during the world wars and for some years afterwards, these markets had been so protected that further growth in sugar, the main industry of Cuba, seemed improbable. Thus the Cuban economy had lost the main expanding force which had impelled it since the late eighteenth century. Cuba produced 5·2 million tons of sugar in 1925; in 1955, 4·4 million tons. During that time the population had increased 70%, from 3½ million to 6 million,

---

[3] World Bank, 361. Felipe Pazos, Prío's Director of the National Bank (and Castro's), wrote in 1954: 'at bottom the major economic problems of Cuba in the last thirty years and many of the social, political and even moral problems, derive from this lack of growth in the basic industry.' (Felipe Pazos, *Dificultades y posibilidades de una política de industrialización en Cuba, Humanismo*, No 24, Mexico, 1954.)

giving an increase in the labour force of some 800,000. Of course, not all these men were out of work all the time, but 'the pressure of a growing population on a stagnant economy' continued to be the most severe problem.[4]

The word 'diversification' had therefore been on the lips of economists and politicians since the 1920s. Not much had really been done. Most capitalists were engaged in sugar. Available technology related to sugar. Sugar was so easily and effectively grown in Cuba. Until 1950 agricultural credit was only available for sugar or tobacco: the absence of farm-to-market roads hindered the development of other crops, but sugar had its own railways. Marketing facilities were good for sugar but for little else. Until 1950 governments had tried to keep down the prices of crops other than sugar to avoid rises in the cost of living. Freight rates too had favoured sugar till about 1950. True, since 1927 tariffs had stimulated home production, industrial and agricultural. But some government efforts had been self-defeating. Thus a law of 1942 obliged sugar mills to plant subsidiary crops such as beans or maize. This meant that at least part of non-sugar crops thereafter lay in the hands of those financially best equipped. But, by other legislation, sugar wage rates were to be paid for this activity. U.S. foods and manufactured products also entered Cuba only too easily. Hence, to secure diversification, sugar-men and cattle-men would have had to cooperate far more than they had ever showed any signs of being able to do.

The aim should have been clear: the expansion or creation of export industries or crops unconnected with sugar; and the concentration on sugar by-products for exports and the domestic market. But this could hardly be done without an economy planned more carefully than in the past and in more detail than, say, had been found possible in England or France.

One problem was that though Cuban capital had always been plentiful, there had been little desire to invest it in domestic industrial activity. There were definite improvements in this respect in the mid-1950s, partly due to the Agricultural and Industrial Development banks. In 1950 the World Bank argued that the 'investment atmosphere had become so unpleasant that foreigners did not care to bring industrial capital in . . . and Cubans themselves prefer to send theirs outside or to put it into real estate'.[5] Of course, conditions for a successful capital market cannot be created overnight and did not fully exist in any South American or Caribbean country. The Havana Stock Exchange,[6] the only Stock Exchange in Cuba, had only eighty members, and a

---

[4] Pazos, *loc. cit.*

[5] *Ibid.*, 136. Even during the prosperous days of 1947–9, the gross capital accumulation by Cubans absorbed only about 5% of the Gross National Product.

[6] Founded 1884.

small number of private shares were listed – less than sixty, and only about twelve actively traded. Few new issues came up. Most medium-sized enterprises were family companies in which outside shareholders were unwelcome. The money needed to expand a business was usually found among friends and relations. There were few brokers. The law governing the Stock Exchange was an old Spanish one. There was little supervision over market activities and high fees were paid to get securities onto the market. The consequence was that a small percentage only of the savings of Cubans went into new ventures. Saving as a proportion of the GNP was considerably less in the 1950s than in the 1940s. Repair, maintenance, acquisition and installation of capital equipment absorbed what savings there were, and in the 1950s a quarter went to building.

Recollection of past crashes, such as that of 1920 and that of New York in 1929, played a part. Cubans were very reluctant to invest in government issues, which were chiefly bought by banks, insurance companies and pension funds. In fact, most Cubans with money were interested first and foremost in having cash available. The nature of the economy made this necessary to meet the customary sudden swings of fortune. Available short-term funds were often put in New York or in bank deposits, sometimes (as in the case of many of Batista's associates) in U.S. currency in Cuban bank safety deposit boxes. Secondly, savers were interested in property, either in Havana or perhaps in Miami and New York City. In the 1950s building represented nearly 30 % of capital formation, higher than between 1947 and 1949. Others with money invested in ordinary U.S. stock. Cubans had 'at least' $M150 invested in the U.S. in 1955,[7] probably over two-thirds in Florida. Prominent among these were Grau's crooked ex-Minister of Education's investments in the Alsina Corporation and Batista's large Florida investments.[8] The World Bank in 1950 found that a 'startling amount' of the larger denomination dollar bills returned to New York for collection from Florida had clearly originated in Cuba.[9] At least $M250 in the 1950s was deposited as nominally short-term assets in U.S. banks. Maybe in the mid-1950s Cuban investment in the U.S. had fallen off but by 1958 it had gone back at least to its former figure.[10] Again thanks to the improved financial conditions existing after the establishment of the National Bank, capital investment by Cubans increased during the 1950s.[11] Some investments by Cubans had been made

[7] *Investment in Cuba*, 15.
[8] World Bank, 519.
[9] *Ibid.*,
[10] *Cf. Investment in Cuba*, 15, fn. 25.
[11] According to the National Bank, investment between 1952 and 1957 was 12% of the gross product, fairly high, that is.

in Canada, Europe and some parts of South America (especially Venezuela).[12]

Foreign investment in Cuba greatly contrasted with Cubans' own investment. In 1900 foreign investment probably totalled $M50.[13] By 1913 it had risen to about $M400, of which about $M220 was U.S., the rest being English, French, Spanish or Canadian.[14] By 1929 U.S. investments reached about $M1,000,[15] the largest quantity of U.S. investment in Latin America – mostly in sugar mills, but also in utilities and tobacco. This figure fell during the depression and the Second World War, but rose again afterwards, to reach perhaps $M1200 in 1958.[16] By the 1950s utilities – electricity, telephone, railways – totalled more than their agricultural or sugar interests: about $M300 compared with $M270.[17] The rate of 'increase' of U.S. investment in Cuba had been slower than in any other Latin American country; but $M3,000 had been invested in Latin America by U.S. citizens in the first ten years after the Second World War, a third of that in oil.

English investment had dropped, and in 1958 consisted chiefly of a Shell refinery and a number of insurance companies. Canada had an important bank and some other minor businesses. France still had a sugar mill and the West Germans a supermarket chain, opened in 1955. Spaniards still had extensive holdings of property, while Cuban Spaniards sent home at least $M5 from Cuba.[18]

Cuba had about fifty banks with nearly two hundred branches, as well as the Postal Savings Bank and the National Bank, which had been moderately successful and remained the most prestigious economic body on the island, though its director under Batista, Martínez Sáenz, the old ABC leader, was inferior as an economist to Pazos, the director under Prío. But some good economists, such as Julián Alienes, had remained in Cuba throughout the *Batistato*.

As in the sugar industry, Cubans were gradually recovering control of banks since 1945. In 1939 foreign banks held over 80% of all deposits; in 1959 Cuban banks owned 60%. Still, the Royal Bank of Canada, the

---

[12] Even if a high figure of $M400 for total Cuban investment abroad is taken, this represents only a small percentage of the total amount of Latin American capital invested abroad— between $M5,000 and $M10,000 in 1963 according to Sir George Bolton (*Annual Review of BOLSA*, 1962–3, qu. *Manchester Guardian*, 8 April 1963), or between $M8,000 and $M10,000, according to *H.A.R.*, XV, 1174, in 1962. See also Dumont's figures, as described above.

[13] W. J. Clark, *Commercial Cuba: a book for business men* (1899) (excluding Spanish).

[14] Winkler, 275.

[15] Winkler had $M1,500, Paul Dickens $M1,000, Jenks $M1,150.

[16] Herbert Matthews in the *New York Times*, 26 April 1959, speaks of $M800, but in 1960 U.S. investments were reckoned at about $M1,000 (*New York Times*, 5 November 1962). Núñez Jiménez, *Geografía*, 294, speaks of $M800, following Matthews. See also figures of Sanderson, quoted above p. 1172.

[17] *Investment in Cuba*, 10.

[18] *Ibid.*, 120.

Bank of Nova Scotia, the National City, Chase Manhattan, and the First National Banks remained prominent and probably decisive. These and the other foreign banks (and for a long time the Cuban banks too) were marked by great reluctance to back anything but riskless ventures. Where labour remembered the depression, banks recalled the 'Dance of the Millions' of 1920. In contrast with most Latin American countries, banks were therefore a passive element in the Cuban economy. After 1950 the Cuban recovery was partly due to slightly less conservative attitudes to borrowing, to the influence of the National Bank, and to the change in 1951 from a monetary system based on the interchangeability of dollar and *peso* to one based on the *peso* alone (the *peso* remained however equal to the dollar). Bank deposits increased throughout the 1950s, showing no decline as the civil war continued, save for a brief drop in 1958 from 1957 levels, themselves high chiefly because of the successful harvest.[19]

The 1950s also saw the creation of new government credit institutions: to the Agricultural and Industrial Development Bank (BANFAIC) of 1951 was added a Mortgaging Insurance Institute in 1955, a National Finance Agency in 1953, the Cuban Foreign Trade Bank in 1954 and the Economic and Social Development Bank (BANDES) in 1955, all autonomous subsidiaries of the National Bank. BANFAIC had had much success, lending money for rice development, small credit associations, a Hanabanilla hydro-electric plant, and so on. The Mortgage Insurance Institute had the east Havana low cost housing project to its credit. The National Finance Agency had partly financed the expansion of Cuban Electric, a new Havana waterworks, and Marianao sewage. The Cuban Bank of Foreign Trade had carried out a sugar railway equipment arrangement with West Germany and had partly financed the Havana Hilton Hotel and the Havana harbour tunnel.

Taken as a whole U.S. capital had of course contributed greatly to Cuba's general development, though it had partly been responsible for the excessive emphasis on sugar. It had certainly brought living standards which could only be satisfied with plentiful supplies of American goods. As early as 1927, Leland Jenks had said that the U.S. had brought expensive techniques and heavy overhead charges and sought to compensate the consequent loss in personal relationships by housing improvements and welfare work. 'It finds that engineers from the [United] States will fill managerial positions more satisfactorily for $500 a month than Cubans for $250 . . . It has made it possible for irrevocable decisions affecting most of the Cuban population to be taken in Wall Street . . .'[20] These comments were as valid in 1958 as thirty years

[19] *Cf.* World Bank, 566; *Investment in Cuba*, 124; *Estudio*, 916.
[20] Jenks, 301–2.

before. Cuba might be the most highly capitalized tropical country[21] – that is, it had more capital per head than similar countries. But the phrase meant that it was more linked than any other country to the international capitalist system, however that itself might be changing, and the proximity of the north-east of the U.S., the richest region in the world, undoubtedly had a debilitating effect on the development of Cuban industries: goods from that area could be taken to Cuba cheaper than to Texas or California.

The tax system in Cuba meantime was full of contradictions, and for many years had been crying out for reform. Customs and purchase taxes gave half the total tax. Direct (income) taxes provided a mere quarter of total revenues. Nevertheless this fraction was much higher than it had been twenty years before. Budgetary revenues were anyway low – about 14% of the national income – since public works were usually financed out of loan issues, not taxation. Most of the taxes (64%) went on salaries. Throughout Batista's second period, a high proportion of revenues went to the armed forces, but in 1955 (before the beginning of the civil war), the proportion was perhaps about one quarter.[22] The provincial governments and municipalities lived from hand to mouth, depending on the national government.

Public debt increased throughout the 1950s. The debt outstanding in 1950 derived from past floating indebtedness and from various settlements of public works bills dating from the Machado era. In 1950 the Cuban government floated its first domestic issue of bonds. Between then and 1955, $M400 was raised, almost twice as much as Cuba had altogether previously borrowed. About a quarter was held by banks, a quarter by the Currency Stabilization Fund on behalf of U.S. banks, and the rest by other big insurance companies or pension funds. Between 1956 and 1958 the cost of political upheaval became evident. In 1958 total debt reached about $M800;[23] this, though high in comparison with what it had reached before, was hardly unbearable reckoned against the wealth of the nation, though some of the methods used in raising the money to pay it were questionable. But the bond issues almost all maintained their value at par.

In 1958 Cuba imported far more agricultural products from the U.S. than any other Latin American country did.[24] Of these most were goods which could have been grown at home – vegetables, oil, lard (the largest

[21] The phrase is H. C. Wallich's, *Monetary Problems of an Export Economy* (1950), of 1948. But it applies to 1958–9 too.

[22] Figure taken from *Investment in Cuba*, 121, adding 'National Defence' to 'Security and Justice'.

[23] Cf. *Estudio*, 850. The revolutionary regime accused Batista of leaving behind a debt of $M1,200. Batista's bank president, Martínez Sáenz, defended himself from gaol in *Por la Independencia de Cuba* (Havana, 1959).

[24] *Statistical Yearbook of UN, 1959*, qu. *Estudio*, 1145.

5   Peasants come to Havana to support the agrarian reform

4. Interrogation of the prisoners after the Bay of Pigs: Luis Gómez Wangüemert (editor of *El Mundo*), leaning

agricultural item). This figure was fairly constant.[25] But Cuba exported more or less twice the volume of agricultural goods that she consumed herself.

In the past Cuba had had an unfavourable balance of trade only rarely. This gave her a good name in international monetary circles. In the 1950s, however, there was usually a deficit in the balance of payments because of a fall in sugar prices and the increased import of North American goods. In the last months before the fall of Batista there was a considerable flight of capital, though it was difficult to know how large, for during the last years before 1958 Cuba lost much of her monetary resources for other reasons. To counteract the economic restrictions on sugar production, the government had embarked on a public works programme, backed by bonds. These expenditures further stimulated a demand for imports which (along with other expenses such as services, remission of profits, etc.) could not be met. Thus the resources in 1958 were actually below those of any year since 1947[26] and, in real terms (after subtracting further loans in foreign money etc.) were lower than any year since 1942. Even so, Cuba remained among the countries of Latin America with the largest gold reserves.[27]

Tourism developed considerably in the 1950s. In 1957 about 350,000 tourists[28] visited Cuba, bringing in $M62, compared with the 160,000 who arrived, on the average, ten years before, and who had brought only about $M17. Until 1956, however, the money that tourists spent in Cuba did not balance what Cubans spent abroad.[29] By 1958 there were many places apart from Havana and Varadero which offered good opportunities for the pleasure-bound traveller.

The importance of exports for the Cuban economy remained; so did the pattern. Exports made up between 30% and 40% of the national income, but the rest of the economy was still built up round exports. Between 1902 and 1945 four-fifths of Cuban exports went to the U.S., and after 1945 most Cuban exports still did, but the percentage nevertheless dropped to just over two-thirds in the 1950s due to increased sugar demand by other places.[30] This partly derived from a changed attitude to tariffs: before the Depression the Cuban government used the tariff primarily for revenue; afterwards, they used it to stimulate

[25] Cf. the rather confusing figures in Estudio, 1146–7.
[26] Estudio, 924.
[27] Ibid., 931; cf. H.A.R., February 1959, which quotes the National Bank as saying that the reserves had fallen $M424 to about $M373 between 1952 and 1959.
[28] Including excursionists who only stopped off there on a cruise.
[29] Estudio, 1126. Cubans abroad spent $M37·5 as tourists in 1958; there were about 33,000 Cubans supposed to be living abroad then. It is highly probable that the figures for tourist spending in Cuba was an underestimate. Certainly whole zones of Havana seemed laid out for tourist satisfaction on a bigger scale than these figures would suggest.
[30] Investment in Cuba, 135.

agricultural and industrial development, along with diversification, which gathered momentum after the Second World War.[31] From 1908 until the Depression Cuba had, incidentally, exported more to the U.S. than any other Latin American country. Since then, she was always second to Brazil.[32] What diversification there had been had not yet affected exports. Sugar represented the same proportion of exports after the Second World War as it did before the Depression,[33] in 1948 90 % of exports, falling back afterwards towards 80 %.

The decrease in Cuban exports to the U.S. had surprisingly little effect on Cuban imports from the U.S.; the U.S. supplied two-thirds of Cuban imports between 1911 and 1940, and about three-quarters since 1950. As ever since the eighteenth century, the most important import was food – nearly 30 % of the whole between 1948 and 1954. How absurd that a country so promising for horticulture – no winter to speak of, good rain supply, good soil – should be importing from the U.S. nearly half its vegetables and fruit!

It is not easy to explain the remarkable debility of Cuban society in the middle of the twentieth century, to balance the considerable prosperity on the one hand against the psychological weaknesses on the other, the stifling labour laws and the stagnation, the reliance on sugar and the world market and the increased diversification. The weaknesses derive partly from the consequences of a long and destructive war of independence, in which most of the best men of the generation of 1895 died and in which the old Cuban society of the nineteenth century, already in decay, received a mortal blow. Afterwards, while Cuban politicians sought only personal profit from power, both Spaniards and Negroes, at the top and bottom of the social scale, in their separate ways chose to withdraw from responsibility; Spaniards remained Spaniards even in the second generation, they busied themselves with commerce and private life and, though for years economically dominant, they were politically inactive; Negroes recovered slowly from slavery, found criollo politics too hispanic to take an active part in them, and derived the most comfort from re-enacted African memories. Into the vacuum thus left strode the North Americans who, not always with enthusiasm, directed the economy and the foreign policy of Cuba for much of the twentieth century. In the 1920s Cuba had a per capita income about half that of the U.S. or two-thirds that of Britain, since she was an integral part of the U.S. economy. There was full employment. Naturally, patriotic Cubans worried about the political price paid for these benefits

---

[31] A general summary of the tariffs in Cuba in the mid-1950s can be seen in ibid., 136.
[32] Historical Statistics of the U.S.
[33] Investment in Cuba, 140.

but that they were material benefits for the majority cannot be questioned. Cuban men of business came to regard the U.S. as 'the godfather of the island',[34] to whom they were ready to hand over responsibility. Though the Cubans had a currency of their own after 1914, the U.S. dollar bill was the only paper currency in general circulation until 1934.

The Depression and the Revolution of 1933 marked the political, social and economic system indelibly. As a consequence of her close relations with the U.S., Cuba probably suffered more from the former event than any other country. The Revolution of 1933 was conceived not simply as a means of overthrowing Machado but as a way of reconstructing a new world, worthy of Martí's patriotic dreams. In the event, the Revolution and what followed brought many important changes. The power of private capitalism was bridled. Much enlightened social legislation was introduced. The sugar planters received a new deal. Diversification of agriculture was encouraged. The Platt Amendment was abolished and the role of the U.S. in the economy reduced. Labour organized itself. A new constitution was prepared. But no political system was achieved and, instead of the 'decent men' of the Auténticos being responsible for these improvements, it was in fact Batista and the Communists. Further, the political life of the country remained feeble. The social changes did not prevent, indeed they increased, the stagnation in the country's main industry. Neither exports nor imports, nor educational figures, attained in the post-1945 world the levels of the 1920s. Both the population and the unemployed increased. Intellectuals sought scapegoats. The U.S., anyway partly responsible, was at hand.

Corruption and frivolity were doubtless the characteristics of old Cuba but it is pompous to condemn every manifestation of the latter as harshly as the former; the castle in the style of the Black Forest belonging to the Abreus, in the midst of the canefields of Matanzas, may shock Puritans but its absurdity is also an enchantment. Such follies may doom classes who construct them, but they nevertheless themselves survive to delight even those whom a more earnest purpose later dispatches there.[35]

[34] A remark to the author of Julio Lobo, 10 November 1968.
[35] This castle is now a workers' home.

BOOK FOUR

The Clash
1959-62

'In our revolution there are elements of the gunman
and of Saint Francis.'
CARLOS FRANQUI TO CLAUDE JULIEN, 1960

CHAPTER 33

Castro in America

In the spring of 1959, the contenders for power in Cuba had already, it seemed, been reduced essentially to three groups: Castro and the rebel army; the Communists; and the liberal men of good will. The contenders did not, however, all recognize each other as such. The contenders did not as yet contend, nor were they so unified as they seemed: were the rebel army officers all so loyal? Had the liberals decided upon the determining point of their liberalism? What, after all, did it really mean to be loyal to Castro? In the battle for power, which, with hindsight, seems to have been inevitable, some never fought, however their loyalties may really have lain.

The reason lay partly in Castro's personality. A month after Batista's flight, Castro had established a personal hold over the Cuban masses such as no Latin American leader had ever had. Not even Perón at his peak had been so obviously and so universally loved. To those who had dreamed hopelessly for many years for a settled wage, for schools and medicine for their children, Castro represented a hope brighter than Grau in 1933 or 1944. Already he was the champion to whom multitudes desired to surrender their will, confident that he would not betray such expectations. After his return from Venezuela, Castro appeared so often on the television screen (the State Department was already beginning to curse the salesmen of those 400,000 sets) that he resembled less a De Gaulle or a Kennedy (others who used television to effect) than a kind of permanent confessor or a resident revolutionary medicine man. He roused the expectations of masses who, until January, had been torpid, despairing, cynical, lost 'ragged-trousered philanthropists', and anti-political. To the masses Castro, with his known unpunctuality, his volatility, his distrust of convention and law, his improvidence and talkativeness, seemed the most typical of themselves.[1] To the middle class he already seemed suspect: psychiatrists noted how he often spoke with two watches on his wrist.[2]

Television and radio were, of course, in private hands, including the two powerful national television networks, Channel 2, owned by

[1] Cf. Dewart, Christianity and Revolution, 33.
[2] See an attempt at a psychiatric explanation of Castro's behaviour and character by Oscar Sagredo Acebal, in Bohemia Libre, 17 September 1961.

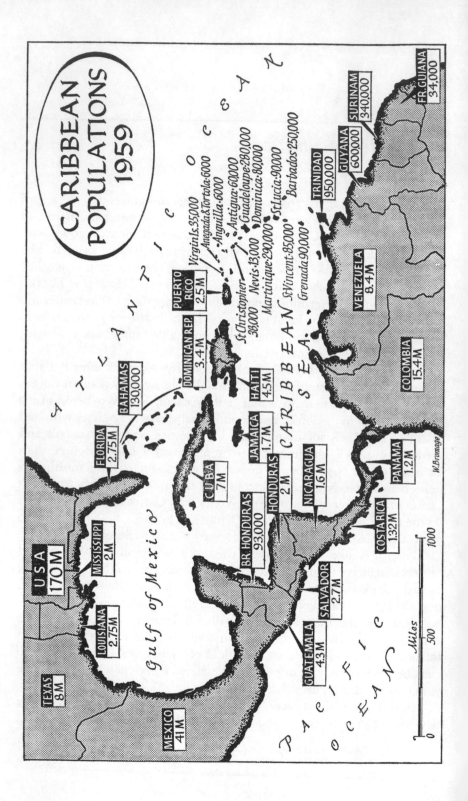

CARIBBEAN POPULATIONS 1959

TEXAS 8M
USA 170M
MISSISSIPPI 2M
LOUISIANA 2.75M
MEXICO 41M
FLORIDA 2.75M
BAHAMAS 130,000
CUBA 7M
DOMINICAN REP. 3.4M
PUERTO RICO 2.5M
HAITI 4.5M
JAMAICA 1.7M
BR.HONDURAS 93,000
HONDURAS 2M
NICARAGUA 1.6M
GUATEMALA 4.3M
SALVADOR 2.7M
COSTA RICA 1.32M
PANAMA 1.2M

Virgin Is. 35,000
Anegada & Tortola: 6000
Anguilla: 6000
Antigua: 60,000
Guadeloupe: 280,000
Dominica: 80,000
St. Christopher: 38,000
Nevis: 13,000
Martinique: 290,000
St. Lucia: 90,000
Barbados: 250,000
St. Vincent: 85,000
Grenada 90,000

TRINIDAD 950,000
GUYANA 600,000
SURINAM 340,000
FR. GUIANA 34,000
VENEZUELA 8.4M
COLOMBIA 15.4M

ATLANTIC OCEAN
CARIBBEAN SEA
Gulf of Mexico
PACIFIC OCEAN

Miles
0   500   1000

W.Bromage

the newpaper *El Mundo*, and CMQ Radio TV, belonging to the Mestre Brothers, but Castro never had any difficulty in appearing when he wanted, and several small stations, such as the Havana television company Channel 12, Radio Rebelde, Unión Radio and Radio Mambí, were from the beginning unconditional supporters of Castro.

Castro himself must always have had in his mind the suspicion sown by Guevara (with his experience of Guatemala) and by Raúl Castro that only an extreme solution could be victorious: either a dictatorship of the proletariat or the ruin of the revolution. To those of the middle class whose imaginations, from worthy motives or from base, were dominated with a vague desire for revenge on the U.S., Castro represented already, by the mere fact of his astounding victory, the spirit of challenge. *'Gracias Fidel'* was the placarded cry of thousands at public meetings throughout the spring: 'thanks' as yet for conquest and for further conquests ahead. Beyond Havana lay Latin America, her eyes on Cuba almost for the first time; beyond Cuba, the world. No Cuban had been so famous as Castro. Already shepherds in Spain and wool workers in Yorkshire had heard of 'Fidel'; he, a keen student of the international press, knew that they knew.

The speeches which Castro made now and which became so important part of his tenure of power were never carefully prepared. He would naturally consider the points which he wished to emphasize but found that

If you try to give a definite shape to your ideas, to give them a prior form, when you begin to speak, you lose one of the finest influences that the public can exercise over the person who speaks, which is to transmit its ardour, its enthusiasm, its force, its inspiration through him. Often my speeches are conversations . . . with the public.[3]

The machinery of retribution against Batista's henchmen meantime ground on, imprisonments, trials and executions being reported from all over the island, with gory accounts being published of Batistiano tortures, along with documentary proof of the despoliations practised by the old regime.[4] The harvest ground on too, the 130th since Cuba first became the world's greatest sugar producer. The President decreed the 1959 sugar harvest should be 5·8 million tons, of which 350,000 tons were for the home market, 2·2 million tons for the U.S., 500,000 tons for the U.S. reserve, 1·5 million tons for the world market, the rest for various reserves.

[3] Lockwood, 178.
[4] It is curious to note that this ultra-nationalist regime should have employed as its chief executioner, at La Cabaña, a North American who joined Guevara in the Escambray, the farouche Captain Herman Marks, a native of Milwaukee with a criminal record.

But there were already discordant voices. In Washington, Wieland, still at the Caribbean desk in the State Department, wrote a memorandum arguing that 'if we strengthened the moderates in Cuba, Fidel could see that his own survival depended on the moderate wing and dissociate himself from the extremist wing'.[5] But the U.S., regardless whether they knew who or what that 'extremist wing' was, had little power to do anything just now. More important, inside Cuba, 6,000 employees of the Cuba Electric Company declared a slowdown in order to achieve a 20% rise in wages, while 600 workers who had been dismissed by the company in 1957–8 began a strike in part of the presidential palace, demanding reinstatement. There were also hunger strikes by railway workers who had been left unemployed and by workers of a closed paper mill near Havana. 3,000 building workers left Moa Bay. The restaurant workers threatened to strike unless the casinos reopened. Twenty-one sugar mills were delayed in the harvest by wage demands. The revolution had aroused expectations, how were they to be satisfied? Castro spoke of his sympathy with the demands but appealed against strikes. In a speech to the Shell Oil workers he promised: 'We did not carry out the Revolution to defend the interests of the mighty but of the humble. Now it is the right strategy to avoid major conflicts, even if a sacrifice must be made, because a sacrifice now will be compensated by greater returns at another time.'[6] Yet it was obscure how these aims would be achieved.

More pointedly still, perhaps, Castro became involved in a dispute with the humorous paper *Zig Zag*, the *Canard Enchaîné* of Cuba. *Zig Zag* made fun of him. Castro threatened to have it suppressed. Was the time for humour past? It began to be wondered, in intellectual circles only, to be sure, whether all had been solved. To the world Castro might seem a man of destiny. To intimates he seemed already more 'lost in the labyrinths of power'.[7] To the Shell workers Castro announced that the only sacrifice he would never make for the revolution would be 'to use force to carry through the revolution'. For the moment, he was believed.

On 7 February the cabinet had approved what was called a fundamental law of the Republic, a major abrogation of the Constitution of 1940. Legislative power was to be vested in the cabinet, which alone could change the fundamental law. Thus, even while liberals were still at least nominally in power, an autocratic measure perpetuated power in a self-perpetuating cabinet. It is difficult to believe that this was really, to democrats, justified by the 'exigencies of the Revolutionary

[5] Wieland, 649.
[6] *Discursos para la Historia*, 52.
[7] Casuso, 202.

Period', as President Urrutia put it.[8] Urrutia, however, was pre-occupied by one thing only: the suppression of gambling. Urrutia proposed compensation of employees. Castro on television slightingly said that 'from an air-conditioned office it is very easy to take bread from the mouths of casino employees'.[9] Urrutia wished to resign. He was persuaded to stay. This was Castro's first clash with the government which he had himself set up.

The next clash was not long in coming. The prime minister, the eminent lawyer, Dr Miró Cardona, had found his position false from the beginning. Like President Urrutia, he had already tried once to resign, in January, over the question of restoring the death penalty and making legal penalties retroactive.[10] But his lack of real power and Castro's lack of real responsibility, combined with his middle age in comparison with the youth of Castro and his friends, caused him now to resign absolutely, and to recommend that Castro should become premier in his stead.[11] Castro went to Urrutia with Luis Orlando Rodríguez. The latter, the ex-Auténtico youth leader, and now Minister of the Interior (though by no means an intimate of Castro's), told Urrutia that Castro should now become prime minister, since in that way 'the revolution would gain unity'. Castro said that 'he would accept the post of Prime Minister but, since he would be responsible for the policy of the Government, he would need sufficiently broad powers to enable him to act efficiently.'[12] That is, he did not want Urrutia to preside at cabinet meetings or even to be present at them. Urrutia said that he 'would be glad to have him become Prime Minister . . . with the broad prerogatives he required', and added that he, Urrutia, wanted to 'leave the Presidency to enter the Supreme Court'. Urrutia tendered his resignation to the cabinet, but several ministers, as well as Castro, begged him not to do so. The Minister of Public Works, Manuel Ray, was among them: 'Doctor, don't resign, you are the Revolution's last hope.'[13] Again, Urrutia agreed to stay; he was not thereafter present at cabinet meetings and retained only a nominal veto over decrees.

These were critical surrenders by the liberals. Miró wrote later: 'I resigned. Cuba did not protest; it accepted, it applauded.'[14] For Urrutia too, it was the beginning of the end. Had he been a man of greater energy, resolution and imagination, he might have done much. Unfortunately, he was no politician. He had been too long in the law

[8] Even when writing in exile (Urrutia, 35).
[9] *Revolución*, 1 February.
[10] *Diario de la Marina* (Miami), 12 November 1960.
[11] Lockwood, 176.
[12] Urrutia, 38.
[13] This is Urrutia's account, and Castro's account to Lee Lockwood initially confirms it (176) except of course for Ray's remark.
[14] *Diario de la Marina*, 12 November 1960.

courts. He was keen on having capital letters in the right places. He got up too late in the mornings. He never insisted that a day for elections should be swiftly announced.[15]

On assuming the prime ministership, Castro went out of his way to emphasize his moderation; he spoke of his 'lack of personal ambitions, loyalty to principles, unshakeable and profound democratic convictions'. He denied having ever wished a lowering of rents; and promised that the standard of living in Cuba would soon be raised above that in either the U.S. or Russia.[16] On the other hand, he also announced on 23 February that 'it would not be correct to organize elections now. We should get a crushing majority. It is in the public interest that elections are delayed till political parties are fully developed and their programmes clearly defined.'[17] Was this a declaration of intention, or a deception? If the latter, was it self-deception as well? Probably it was more valid a statement than Castro himself would have admitted later. By this time Castro had already appointed his 'more radical' brother Raúl as commander-in-chief of the armed forces. This meant evidently a step further to the Left in the army, for the Minister of Defence was Martínez Sánchez, Raúl Castro's advocate-general in the Sierra; the 'Second Front Frank País' appeared to control the army.[18]

On 16 February, the day that Castro attained the prime ministership, the national coordinator of the 26 July Movement referred to the revolution now 'under way' in somewhat mysterious terms as 'not an act, but a process' which would be characterized by a long series of socially conscious laws. These were summarized in sixteen points, which Castro himself did not formally acknowledge.[19] He did, however, often repeat the word 'process' in somewhat mystical style; and, in his first address to the cabinet, he said that it was necessary to 'begin . . . the

[15] In this paragraph I have benefited from discussion with Urrutia's secretary, Antonio de la Carrera.

[16] *Discursos para la Historia*, 32.

[17] *Revolución*, 24 February 1959.

[18] The other commanders were now Majors Cienfuegos (commander-in-chief); Belarminio Castilla, Hubert Matos, Ramiro Valdés, Calixto García, Antonio Duarte, Dermitio Escalona and Eddy Suñol, in command respectively of the military districts of Oriente, Camagüey, Las Villas, Matanzas, Havana, Pinar del Río and Holguín. Castilla shortly gave way to Manuel Piñeiro. Others of importance in the Army were Waldo Reina, commanding the infantry, Filiberto Oliviera, chief of the San Antonio air base, Abelardo Colomé, at the campamento de Managua, Demetrio Montseny, who was deputy to Guevara at La Cabaña, Antonio Lussón, director of operations, William Gálvez, inspector-general of the Army, Osmani Cienfuegos, head of army education, and René León, chief of the logistical section. Of these commanders, Suñol, Oliviera, Colomé, Montseny, Castilla, and Lussón had all been in Raúl Castro's column and, with the exception of Hubert Matos, all remained in prominent places during the whole of the 1960s. Piñeiro, Valdés, Calixto García, Suñol, Castilla, Oliviera, Colomé, Lussón and Osmani Cienfuegos were, along with Raúl Castro, members of the central committee of the (new) Cuban Communist party in 1965.

[19] *Revolución*, 16 February. See Suárez, 46–7, for a discussion of this stage of the evolution of Castro's thought.

revolution';[20] at the same time, he had begun to buy arms, light rifles and grenades from Belgium, ostensibly for fear of invasion by Trujillo.[21]

Many minor quarrels flickered between Communists and members of the 26 July Movement. Thus the chiefly 26 July police did nothing to prevent ex-saboteurs of the Civic Resistance from breaking into the offices of the Communist newspaper *Hoy*. Carlos Rafael Rodríguez, who had become the editor, remarked, 'If Fidel thinks that now the insurrection has won, we communists are going into a monastery he is making a mistake. The Revolution has not yet begun, and if he chooses the right road one day we shall all meet. But if not, it will be neither the first nor the last time that we shall go underground.'[22]

Castro's cabinets (which soon became weekly rather than almost daily occurrences) were, from the beginning, unusual gatherings. The cabinet might be due to assemble at three. Castro might not appear till three or more hours later, perhaps accompanied by Celia Sánchez and Guevara. At that point, the ministers would try to get the 'leader and guide' to speak to them on a special project. Castro might say that he needed sleep, since he had gone to bed at three, four or five the night before, and the meeting might be further delayed.[23]

There might be discussion, restricted to two or three people, at greater length on a subject dear to a particular minister's heart: such as Manuel Ray's plans for the much-needed secondary roads, opposed by Castro's preference for great highways. Ray himself had taken over in January, on his own initiative, all heavy equipment (steamrollers, bulldozers) which might be needed for development, and was probably the most active of all ministers in these weeks. His first plan was to finish all Batista's projects which were already begun. Castro agreed. But Ray disliked the East Havana project, which he thought involved too great an investment in housing. In such conversations, Ray, ex-leader of the underground in Havana, who had, however, only met Castro twice before 1 January, began to have doubts about Castro. Was Castro playing with them? On the other hand, Castro also impressed his colleagues as a good listener. His charm remained compelling, whether among two or three people, or two or three thousand.

At one of these meetings in February, Castro came up to a group of ministers and said: 'I have received an invitation from the American newspaper editors[24] to go to the U.S. Should I go?' 'Of course,' replied Pazos, the Bank Director, who, though not strictly a minister, was present. 'But suppose Eisenhower invites me to the White House?'

[20] López Fresquet, 47.
[21] *Ibid.*, 82–3. 25,000 F.A.L. light rifles, 50 million rounds and 100,000 grenades.
[22] Evidence of Guillermo Cabrera Infante, who was present when these remarks were made.
[23] This description derives from ministers now in exile: Elena Mederos, Pazos and Ray.
[24] ASNE – the American Society of Newspaper Editors.

'You should go,' said Pazos. Castro was evidently worried lest he lose prestige as a revolutionary leader, fearing that his Latin American admirers might suppose that he had sold out to North America, as so many other putatively radical leaders of Latin countries had done before; once more Castro and the slender cause of good Cuban-U.S. relations were the victims of the historic weaknesses of so many past leaders of the continent.[25]

Meantime, a new U.S. ambassador to Havana arrived: Philip Bonsal, with long experience of Spanish countries and of turbulent times with the Telephone Company in the 1920s. He had laid telephones through hundreds of Andalusian villages when the Spanish traditional Right regarded the telephone as the source of all their troubles. Latterly, he had been ambassador in Bolivia and Colombia. He had, too, been briefly vice-consul in Havana. The son of Stephen Bonsal, a journalist in the war of 1898, to experience he added a generally progressive and happily Whiggish frame of mind. 'On the basis of abundant though contradictory evidence' in Washington he had concluded before arriving that 'Castro was not a Communist'.[26]

The Cuban upper classes made things hard for Bonsal. Castro himself was obsessed, like many of those around him, with the recollection of Sumner Welles in Cuba in 1933; he later referred to the arrival of Bonsal as if in fact he had been Welles. The upper classes, he told an audience in 1961:

... never ceased to talk of the day when Bonsal would arrive. Three days before the radio and television ... began to talk about Bonsal's arrival, as if it were a really great event. The publicity was such that it began to be shocking for all revolutionaries or all men of honour even if not revolutionary ... Bonsal was treated as a proconsul.[27]

As a result, Castro avoided Bonsal for some time without a formal interview: doubtless he was actually uncertain as to what policy he wanted to follow towards the U.S. Anyway, while avoiding the U.S. ambassador, he nevertheless accepted the invitation to visit the U.S. newspaper editors in April.

Hitherto the revolution had been marked more by a mood, than deeds which positively alleviated the condition of the people. In March, however, the government took several overtly progressive steps: rents

[25] Pazos's evidence.

[26] Bonsal, 'Cuba, Castro and the U.S.', in *Foreign Affairs*, January 1967, 266. Philip Bonsal (b. 1903) educated St Pauls, Concord, and Yale. In Spain, Chile and Cuba with ITT, 1926–35. Vice-Consul, Havana, 1938, chief of division of American Republics, in State department, 1942–4, First Secretary, Madrid, 1944–7.

[27] *Obra Revolucionaria*, 46 of 1961, 24. Castro made the same allusion to Bonsal elsewhere. e.g. in the interview with Lee Lockwood: 'he came with the demeanour of a proconsul .. ; the reactionary press received him almost as if the Saviour had come' (p. 141).

for those who paid less than $100 a month were cut by half, raising thereby the purchasing power of the majority in the cities by perhaps a third (tenants who paid more had rents cut by 30% or 40%). Owners of vacant sites would have to sell, either to the newly set up National Savings and Housing Institute (INAV) or to anyone who wanted to build and buy a house. INAV also took over all funds from the Lottery and, instead of lottery numbers, in future issued bonds: if these were kept for five years, they could be redeemed at 110%, if before at lesser rates. The government also took over the Telephone Company – nominally for the time being, it is true[28] – and cut its rates also, by means of an 'intervention', a tactic previously used by both Batista and Perón. Almost all labour contracts were re-negotiated between January and April, 1959. Licences and letters of credit would henceforth be needed for the import of about two hundred luxury goods. López Fresquet had already introduced measures to insist on less tax evasion, and a compromise had been reached whereby pre-1956 evasion was forgiven on condition of part repayment of 1956–8 taxes.[29] The property of Batista, of all his cabinet ministers since 1952, of all officers of the armed forces who had participated in the civil war, of all members of both houses of parliament, opposition and government, during the 1954–8 sessions, and of all who had sought any of these offices, all mayors and all provincial governors, was declared confiscated and was to pass to the State. In practice, this decree was not fully carried out. Thus Grau San Martín was permitted to live on in Cuba without interference, despite his collaboration in Batista's elections, perhaps because he was old, perhaps because he had known Castro in the past.

On 1 March Castro launched a large land distribution project in Pinar del Río, signing cheques himself, handing over land to peasants as if he were (though no one noticed the similarity) Machado or even Mussolini.[30] 25,000 acres had been bought up by the old Agricultural and Industrial Development Bank; 8,000 were handed out for pasture, 8,000 for tobacco. The government also announced that they were

[28] The Federation of Telephone Company Workers had undergone a palace revolution in February when the old leaders, headed by Vicente Rubiera, had been thrust aside by the 26 July Movement. (See Rubiera's evidence in James Monahan and Kenneth Gilmore, *The Great Deception*, 20–22.)

[29] López Fresquet, 86–7.

[30] 'I remember him, one day, during military manoeuvres, walking through a vast bare plain of yellow stubble surrounded by distant green hills . . . peasants came running from all sides, red-faced, panting, to see him, touch him, shout to him. One of his Secretaries followed him with a leather envelope, the exact size of 1,000 lire bills to hand banknotes to the more miserable with the gesture of a gambler dealing out cards . . . Nobody who saw it will ever forget the sight of city squares filled with mosaic, all eyes turned to one focal point, the balcony or stand from which he was speaking.' As this quotation about Mussolini from Barzini's *The Italians* (1964), 147, suggests, charismatic leaders have more in common with each other than with their own peoples.

going to develop the marshy and crocodile-ridden territory in the central south of the island, Cienaga de Zapata.

These measures increased the money supply without, however, much increasing production. Foreign trade fell off after the decree necessitating the licensing of luxury goods. People who in the past had lived by speculation in land prepared to abandon the country. More importantly, anxiety about the nature of the revolution was beginning to be widespread in Catholic circles. Andrés Valdespino, president of Juventud Católica, and Under-Secretary at the Treasury, wrote in *Bohemia* on 22 February that the radical reforms needed in Cuba could be enacted without Communism. Some young Catholics, such as Artime and González Corzo in the Ministry of Agriculture, were already, by March 1959, contemplating conspiracy.[31]

The trials of Batistianos were still going on, and on 3 March came a new and what seems, in retrospect, a decisive test of the regime's integrity. Forty-four Batista airmen, accused of war crimes, were found innocent in Santiago. The defence had argued that the pilots had not killed civilians but, on the contrary, that some had even dropped their bombs on unpopulated places. They claimed to have falsified their reports to their commanders. The bombing of Sagua de Tánamo was also found not to have occurred. The court found that the evidence was inadequate to prove the pilots' guilt and, despite speeches on the wireless by the prosecutor, acquitted them. This caused a storm of protest in Santiago. The pilots were not released. Then Castro announced on television in Havana that the acquittal had been an error and called for a re-trial. The Minister of Defence, Martínez Sánchez, no less, replaced Lieutenant Sánchez Cejas as prosecutor, and a new court composed of safe revolutionaries was appointed. The president of the first court, Major Félix Peña, was found dead in his car in Campamento Columbia: suicide was presumed, but this death was never cleared up. He was replaced by a more reliable revolutionary, Major Piñeiro, who had been on Raúl Castro's staff and was now military commander in Santiago.[32] At the second trial all the airmen were convicted and sentenced to thirty, twenty or two years' imprisonment. The prosecutor concentrated on insulting the defence and produced no new evidence. Castro announced, 'Revolutionary Justice is based not on legal precepts, but on moral conviction . . . Since the airmen belonged to the air force of former president . . . Batista . . . they are criminals and must be punished.' The point, of course, was not that the men may have been guilty and the first judgement wrong; nor that all who served Batista in

---

[31] *Dos Héroes y un Ideal* (1962), 15.
[32] The other members of the new court were Majors Belarmino Castillo, Carlos Iglesias, Demetrio Montseny and Pedro Luis Díaz Lanz.

the air force were indeed more or less guilty men; but that the verdict of the first court was set aside for political and vengeful reasons. Several witnesses who had testified favourably to the defence were also goaled, and the defence lawyers lost their jobs.[33]

This proceeding was deplorable, but it did not, perhaps, in itself, mean that the regime was already committed to a permanently arbitrary path. Comparable events in France in 1944 did not in themselves doom the Fourth Republic. The political atmosphere was very heated. At all events, a crisis followed. The Minister of Health, Elena Mederos, one of the most principled of Cuban women, told Castro that she wished to resign: 'You don't want me in your government. I'm of a different generation to you and your friends. We are quite opposed to each other in spirit. I must resign.' Castro charmed her successfully: 'No, no,' he said, 'I need you. This train,' he added expansively, referring to the Revolution, 'knows where it is going. Your time to get off will be later.'[34]

But it was still doubtful whether the train did know where it was going. Even *Revolución* protested against the continuance of the trials. Castro told visiting U.S. newspapermen in mid-March that elections were going to be delayed for two years to enable the opposition to develop. On 6 March he told the national association of bankers that he desired their collaboration and added, to the correspondent of *U.S. News and World Report*, that he had no intention of nationalizing any industries. Castro held two large meetings of cabinet members, leaders of the 26 July Movement and army officers, to 'create a uniform policy'; but these were complete failures, the first ending in a riotous altercation as to who had been more effective in the struggle against Batista, the Sierra men or those of the city, the second discussing nepotism and the spread of bureaucracy.[35] On 4 March U.S. Ambassador Bonsal lunched with the Cuban Foreign Minister, Agramonte, and Castro, and had a 'very agreeable talk'. 'I thought there was a chance of working with him,' Bonsal later commented.[36] But then the pendulum seemed to swing back once more; on 13 March, at a ceremony to commemorate the dead killed two years before at the famous attack on the palace, both Castro and the old Directorio leader, Faure Chomón, made strong left-wing speeches, Chomón more extreme than Castro, suggesting even that the remains of the Directorio Revolucionario might be found to the left of the 26 July. The Directorio never again formally demanded elections as

---

[33] See 'The Case of the Airmen', in *Cuba and the Rule of Law* (International Commission of Jurists), 181–91.

[34] Evidence of Elena Mederos. After this event, it becomes harder and harder to know the truth of many things which have occurred in Cuba and perhaps this is where History may be said to have ended and contemporary politics begins.

[35] López Fresquet, 48–9.

[36] Bonsal to the author.

it had in January. Castro said that, were he not prime minister of Cuba, he would like to lead an expedition against Trujillo. It was also noticeable that the Communists took part in this rally as a participating sponsor, on the same level as the two other 'revolutionary organizations', the 26 July Movement and the Directorio. When, a few days later, on 22 March the ex-president of Costa Rica, José Figueres, a progressive friend of the Cuban opposition in the past, visited Cuba, this trend in Castro's speeches was repeated. At a great rally in Havana, Figueres allowed himself to give a lecture to the Cubans about representative democracy and to say that, in the event of war, Cuba should certainly stand with the U.S. and the West. David Salvador, the union chief of the revolution, an ex-Communist and anxious to work himself into membership of the revolutionary leadership, pulled the microphone away from Figueres and shouted that under no circumstances would Cuba support the U.S. in a new war. Within a few days, Castro was accusing Figueres of being a false friend; he added that the great trusts in their selfishness had killed ten times more Cubans than had the tyranny of Batista. The Revolution, he remarked, was confronted by an international conspiracy of vested interests. A significant conversation seems to have occurred in the cabinet, now, during discussion of the price of meat, which was usually raised in the dry season, when demand exceeded supply. Castro opposed the rise; the Minister of Commerce, Cepero Bonilla, said that the consequence would be the slaughtering of young steers and added that even the studs might be killed; Castro replied that that would not matter, since such a policy would leave him with a reputation of having given food to the people while if others took over they would have to raise prices. 'If we stay in power, we will import new studs.' Castro's attitude was approved, and his critics thought he was genuinely apprehensive of elections, for which surviving Auténticos such as Varona were calling vehemently.[37]

Still, not all Castro's accusations and anxieties were baseless. The first wave of exiles from Cuba, Batistianos and rightists, were already plotting. Even Colonel Artigas, lottery chief to Prío, called on Wieland in Washington with a plan to overthrow Castro by force. Wieland said firmly that Castro was not a Communist; there was no need at all to try to overthrow him.[38] Castro's ex-brother-in-law, Díaz Balart, Batista's youth leader, began in Miami to organize an opposition movement, the White Rose, to invade Cuba. Cubans never keep secrets and Castro was soon able to accuse the 'enemies of the Revolution' of buying arms in Miami, while apparently the U.S. authorities were not stopping them. Suddenly Castro's mood again changed – perhaps because of a change

---

[37] López Fresquet, 165.
[38] *Communist Threat*, 860.

in the advice of Guevara or Raúl Castro, perhaps out of conviction, perhaps from vacillation. He made another very calm speech. On 25 March came his first major allusion to the wish of the revolutionary government to end such racial discrimination as there was in Cuba, in jobs and in places of recreation; a speech which caused some anxiety among Conservatives in Cuba, but had no effect on foreign policy.[39] The alarm was confined to old Spanish white families, who saw in it a ghost of a slave revolt of the past. About the same time, the Minister of the Economy, Regino Boti, told his old economics master, Pazos, that the two of them, with the Finance Minister, López Fresquet, would be accompanying Castro on his visit to the U.S. the next month. Pazos said to Boti: 'This means negotiation?' Boti replied, 'Of course.' Pazos then said that the question of the amount of economic aid should be discussed. Boti, who was not an intimate of Castro's, said that Cuba should ask for $M500 worth of aid. In the following weeks, Pazos worked out various programmes for education, sanitation, housing, and so on, which might allow for this sum to be spent without definite strings attached. But there was no discussion between Pazos, Boti and Castro on the subject – nor, indeed, on any subject, except vaguely on the political one of whether Cuba should or could be neutral and what neutrality meant.[40] This vagueness was in line with Castro's response to a hint by the State Department in February, that they would be fully prepared to give economic help to Cuba: this message was communicated to Justo Carrillo, the new vice-president of the National Bank, and José Antonio Guerra, on a visit to the IMF in February. On return, Carrillo went to a meeting of economic advisers, at which Castro was present: Castro received the good news and Carrillo was left waiting for further instructions, which never came. The impression was left with the economic advisers that Castro was simply uninterested in serious negotiations with the U.S. Publicly, however, Castro told a Cuban television audience on 2 April that he was going to the U.S. to secure credits perhaps from the World Bank, perhaps from the Export-Import Bank that 'will defend Cuba and the Revolution'.[41] Castro then authorized the dispatch of a memorandum to Washington listing themes for negotiation in economic matters.[42] BANFAIC, meantime, announced a plan for some forty new industries: a copper tube plant; a plastic plant; a light bulb plant. All these would secure cooperation from U.S. private business. Rhetoric and promises were thus not only the occupation of the govern-

---

[39] See comment by René Depestre, *Casa de las Americas*, vol. vi, No. 34, January 1966. This was Castro's first allusion to the racial question, and also, as Suárez points out (p. 50) the first occasion that the Communists published Castro's speech in full in *Hoy*.

[40] Pazos's evidence.

[41] *Revolución*, 3 April 1959.

[42] Justo Carrillo Memorandum.

ment. Still, the Cuban middle class was not comforted. On the contrary, Mrs Ruby Hart Phillips of the *New York Times* wrote in mid-April that they felt 'seriously hurt' by the reductions in rent, as well as by the forced sale of vacant sites. 'Nothing convinces them that this is not due to Communist influence.[43] The value of the *peso* also had fallen substantially since January, with world sugar prices at their lowest point since 1945. Nevertheless the measures enacted in March, along with the wage increases since January, did mean that the national income had been seriously and visibly redistributed, with real wages increasing perhaps over 15%, and the incomes of rentiers and entrepreneurs dropping accordingly. This remarkable political achievement, which gave such a large section of the populace a big stake in the Revolution, was accomplished by a drop in imports and by the reluctance of capitalists to invest or to increase prices.[44]

With Castro due to arrive in Washington on 15 April, a bizarre conference was now held by U.S. ambassadors in the Caribbean area. Nothing shows more clearly the extent to which the colossus of the north was uncertain as to how to react to the new phenomenon to its immediate south. There were clashes between Bonsal from Cuba, Robert Hill from Mexico, and Whiting Willauer from Costa Rica. Willauer, appointed ambassador to Honduras in 1954, because of 'years of experience in fighting Communism' (by his own account), had been one of the paladins of the defeat of the revolution in Guatemala.[45] The meeting of ambassadors turned out, in the view of Hill, to be 'designed to set the policy of patience and forbearance in dealing with Mr Castro. I took issue,' Hill later testified, 'with Ambassador Bonsal because I felt, despite his excellent presentation ... that patience and forbearance with a Communist would lead to disaster to the U.S.' Hill told the conference that 'the time to deal with Castro was there and then ... We had the instruments, if we wanted to resort to the Organisation of American States, to deal with the problem ... I believed that all evidence of Communism should be submitted to the OAS and that the U.S. request appropriate action ... I was unable to get that language adopted ... The only ambassador who supported me was Ambassador Willauer ...'

> Mr Bonsal's position [Hill went on] was that Castro was in power; that he had tremendous popular support; that there was considerable support in the hemisphere for Castro and Castroism, and that we ought to go slow in dealing with him ... despite the fact that he was

[43] *New York Times*, 24 April 1959.
[44] See Felipe Pazos, *Cambridge Opinion*, February 1963.
[45] See Allen Dulles's telegram congratulating him on his work over Guatemala, described in *Communist Threat*, Part 13, 865.

constantly insulting the U.S. and our President ... But Bonsal felt
that eventually Castro would see the light and return to the family of
Latin American nations. He said Cuba needed a revolution and Cuba
would then start to prosper and make its contribution to the Latin
American family ... The Ambassador pointed out that of course
Castro had Communist associates. However, he [thought] that Castro
made the decisions.[46]

Bonsal privately indeed told Ambassador Willauer that Castro 'wasn't
such a bad fellow; that he was, of course, eccentric, that he ... thought
he could probably be handled and he, Bonsal, could handle him if he
were left alone ... Castro was a terrific person, physically and mentally,
he was far from crazy, he was not living on pills [as some newspapers
had alleged] and he was not a Communist.'[47]
As always on such diplomatic occasions, the critical discussion was
about the communiqué. Hill and Willauer desired a firm statement of
U.S. criticisms of Castro. Bonsal thought that 'anything in the communiqué which cast any reflections upon Castro would make his job
very difficult'. Hill said, 'You are going to discourage every country in
Latin America that fears the Castro menace ... I cannot go along with a
communiqué that whitewashes Castro.' Bonsal said, 'If you cannot be a
team player why not resign?' Bonsal got his way, but both Willauer and
Hill made reports to Washington in dissent.[48] At the same time, it has
since become known that, on 26 March, two weeks before these exchanges, President Eisenhower was informed by the CIA that 'the
Castro regime was moving more and more towards an outright dictatorship'.[49]
The U.S., then, was essentially undecided about her policy. Some
diplomats, like some soldiers, wanted 'action'. But what sort of action
and on what grounds? Since Castro's own views seemed somewhat undecided, it was hard for the U.S. government to reach any decision
themselves. Could they not have acted differently so as to ensure that, if
and when Castro made up his mind, he would do so in such a way as not
to harm what were conventionally supposed to be U.S. interests – the
strategic balance in the Caribbean and the freedom of investment and
commercial exchange in Cuba itself? It is, perhaps, appropriate to
point out that while there were two opinions in Washington over
Castro, there were apparently two views inside the Communist party of
Cuba on the same subject; the one headed by Blas Roca, the party's

[46] Hill testimony in *Communist Threat*, Part 12,803.
[47] Willauer testimony, *Communist Threat*, 871.
[48] Hill testimony. Hill got no answer from Assistant Secretary of State, Rubottom (*ibid.*,
816).
[49] Eisenhower, 523.

secretary-general, the other by Carlos Rafael Rodríguez, the editor of *Hoy*. From March 1959 onwards, the latter seemed unable to contain his admiration for Castro, many articles testifying to Castro's integrity and patriotism and also attempting to prove that the Communists had done something for the rebel cause.[50]

The divisions in the U.S. were raised acutely during Castro's visit there in April. Before the expedition began, Ambassador Bonsal, whose optimistic and benign character can be observed clearly in the insults of his enemies, gave a reception which Castro attended. All was smiles. Grau San Martín took the opportunity of coming out of his ambiguously contrived retirement to demand elections. Elections were the only source of power. Castro had to reply. Elections, he replied, would follow when an Agrarian Reform was complete, when all could read and write, when all children went free to school and all had free access to medicine and doctors.

Castro left Havana for Washington on 15 April as the private guest of the U.S. newspaper editors. The Cuban ambassador in Washington, the worthy Ernesto Dihigo, had asked whether Castro required an official invitation from the U.S. government, and he had replied that he did not.[51] Still, maybe he would not have refused such an invitation had one been proffered. Had matters come to such a pass that the difference between an official invitation and a private one could decide the relations of nations? Such matters had done so in the remote past, but this, after all, was the age of rational man.

The public relations of Castro's journey to the U.S. were to be organized by Bernard Relling of New York. Relling proposed several alterations in the plans for the journey; Castro accepted all except the one that the men in his entourage should have their hair cut and another that those soldiers who went should, if possible, be those of a university background and should speak English.[52] North American institutions and clubs, meanwhile, sent innumerable invitations to Castro to include them on the journey. Unofficial North Americans indeed stretched out their hands to embrace a hero whom they had partly created, because of their own ardent demands for heroism.

About seventy people set off with Castro in two aeroplanes. Neither Raúl Castro nor Guevara went. Almost for the first time since January, Castro was wholly surrounded by people of social democratic instincts; almost for the first time, too, such people could get at him. Castro, however, made no concession to convention for the journey: he arrived

[50] Andrés Suárez (59) draws attention to the naming by Roca, in early April, of a new secretariat (himself, Luzardo, Aníbal Escalante) which did not include Rodríguez.
[51] Casuso, 207.
[52] *Ibid.*, 211.

at the airport two hours late 'in a worn and wrinkled uniform'.[53] On the aeroplane Castro passed the time talking to Pepín Bosch of Bacardí, who had been Prío's Finance Minister: Castro was arguing how much he thought the State could do for the economy, Bosch was describing the merits of private enterprise. Pazos, also on the aeroplane, had given Castro his list of projects for possible development and aid. But there was no discussion of these matters. Pazos did not insist. He regarded himself as a technician, not a politician.[54]

Castro was met at Washington Airport by Under-Secretary Rubottom. He broke away from guards to greet a large cheering crowd. At his first press conference in the U.S. he was asked if he came to seek foreign aid. Castro replied: 'No, we are proud to be independent and have no intention of asking anyone for anything.' Pazos, surprised, later asked Boti the meaning of this. Boti said, 'Yes, we have no intention of asking now, during Castro's visit, for aid, but you, Pazos, will return in a fortnight to make a request';[55] and, indeed, this theme was maintained throughout the visit: no economic discussions, no concessions to the U.S. Pazos and López Fresquet had discussions about money at the State Department and the International Monetary Fund. The State Department asked after the Cuban economy. It was magnificent, said López Fresquet. Did Pazos agree? Yes, replied the Bank Director, except that we have more *pesos* than dollars. No one asked for money and no one really offered it. No doubt, had it been asked for, it would have been offered; had it been offered, it might just possibly have been accepted. The progressive Rubottom went the furthest in asking about foreign aid saying that the U.S. was very interested in Cuban projects. But each side, proud and suspicious, held back.[56]

The country, however, gave Castro a warm enough welcome. Everywhere he was followed by crowds. Everywhere his words were given close attention. To the newspaper editors at Washington, to Harvard and Princeton, at New York, he gave long and successful speeches,

[53] *Ibid.*

[54] Pazos's evidence; López Fresquet (106) has a similar account.

[55] Pazos's evidence; Castro had made the same point himself to López Fresquet. See López Fresquet, 105–6.

[56] Pazos's evidence; *cf.* López Fresquet, 108. To this frozen attitude Senator Kennedy alluded when, a year later, he publicly wondered whether 'Castro would have taken a less radical course' had the U.S. 'given the young rebel a warmer welcome in his hour of triumph, especially during his trip to this country' (J. F. Kennedy, *Strategy of Peace*, 1960). The view was often expressed by others more forcefully. Thus Dumont: '*Cette décade d'avril 1959, les Etats-Unis ont laissé passer une occasion inespérée dans leur histoire, de réviser leur politique vis-à-vis du sud de leur continent . . . Admettre la révolution cubaine, c'était en quelque sorte accepter une forme de décolonisation poussée . . .*' (*op. cit.*, 31). He added: '*Les chances d'établir un régime socialiste humaine assez indépendent de l'URSS, s'effondrent.*' Goldenberg is no doubt right in saying that the U.S. should have offered aid, and publicly, even if Cuba did not ask for it.

impressing his audiences by making jokes in English. Publicly, the visit was an unexampled success. Security guards, on the other hand, were put to great trouble.

There were other personal encounters: with Henry Luce of *Time* magazine; with Frank Bartholomew, president of United Press International; and with the Foreign Affairs Committee of the Senate. At some of these intimate meetings Castro appeared less confident than in the larger gatherings. Apart from a lunch with the Acting Secretary of State, Christian Herter, the only official meeting that Castro had with the U.S. government was with the vice-president, Richard Nixon. President Eisenhower was in Carolina, playing golf – a tactical and, perhaps, a tactless error, for Eisenhower could have seen Castro without losing dignity. Castro, like everyone else, might have found Eisenhower, the private man, more appealing than the public one.

On the other hand, according to Pazos, Castro had no desire to meet Eisenhower: a meeting could only have embarrassed him, while Eisenhower was 'more than irritated' that Castro was coming at all and would have liked to have refused him a visa.[57]

Nixon saw Castro at his office. Castro went there though he had previously demurred, thinking it too grand. The two men met alone. Nixon immediately took against Castro, apparently because the Cuban showed no interest in the files which the vice-president produced on Communism among Castro's supporters. Nixon also spoke of the bad impression made in the U.S. by the executions in Cuba. 'I simply confined myself', Castro said later, 'to ... explaining the realities of our country, which I believe were similar to those of the rest of Latin America, and to demonstrating that the measures we were going to take, some of which affected North American interests, were just.'[58] Afterwards, Nixon wrote: 'I was convinced Castro was either incredibly naïve about Communism or under Communist discipline and that we would have to treat him and deal with him accordingly.'[59] He also immediately suggested to his colleagues in the U.S. administration that a force of Cuban exiles should be armed immediately to overthrow Castro.[60] Nixon, that is, joined those Republican ambassadors for whom Castro was already an enemy, and one or two others, such as J. Edgar Hoover of the F.B.I. and Eisenhower's experienced trouble-shooter, William Pawley. Whilst hardly noticing it, therefore, the U.S. administration was falling back into an almost nineteenth-century position, echoing that of Polk's administration or Buchanan's, whereby active intervention from the U.S. mainland could not be excluded.

[57] Eisenhower, 523.
[58] Lockwood, 186.
[59] R. M. Nixon, *Six Crises* (1962), 351–2.
[60] See Draper, *Castro's Revolution*, 62.

Castro's reaction was different. He returned after his discussion with Nixon to the Cuban Embassy, where he slept in a room next to Ernesto Betancourt, an economic adviser, and Boti. He was noticeably reticent about his talk with Nixon, but thoughtfully said à propos of nothing in particular, 'What we have to do is stop the executions and the in-filitrado'[61] – that is, the infiltration of Communists. This was, no doubt the high point of Castro's democratic phase. He later remarked that the North Americans whom he had met in the U.S. were unlike the planters and businessmen whom he had known in Cuba.[62] About the same time, Castro said to López Fresquet, 'Look, Rufo, I am letting all the Communists stick their heads out, so that I will know who they are. And when I know them, I will do away with them.'[63] López Fresquet thought that Castro had spoken 'with such frankness and honesty' that it had to be true.[64] Even more bizarre, Castro was prevailed on to meet the C.I.A.'s chief expert on Communism in Latin America, a Central European named Droller: the two talked privately for three hours, and afterwards Droller told López Fresquet, 'Castro is not only not a Communist, he is a strong anti-Communist fighter.'[65] Castro himself, in the U.S., was publicly explaining that he was not a Communist; nor, he said, were Raúl Castro or Vilma, his wife, Communists. If there were any Communists in the Cuban government (and he personally knew of none), they had no influence. Castro's heart was with the West in the cold war. Foreign investments would not only be respected, but encouraged. Yet the constant and obsessive concern of North Americans, public and private, with the single question of Communism irritated Castro and indeed others in his entourage: it was as if the U.S. did not care what Cuba was, provided it was not Communist. At the same time, it also seemed – no doubt the impression was erroneous – that the U.S. did not, for all its single-minded fear, quite appreciate what Communism was. An instructive and clearly well-informed article appeared on 26 April in the New York Times;[66] some U.S. officials thought that Cuba ought to be left to meet their economic difficulties before being forced to turn to the U.S. for help. Others believed that to wait too long risked a collapse of Castro's government, which would be followed either by a new right-wing dictatorship or, worse, the Communists. Such men

[61] Ernesto Betancourt's evidence. Betancourt later coined the phrase 'Alliance for Progress' (Schlesinger, 175). Castro later explained that the interview with Nixon was conducted in English, without an interpreter. He added 'My personal impressions were good' and said that Nixon never asked an impertinent question 'nor one that might have been regarded as any kind of inquisition about our politics' (Hoy, 16 May 1959, 4).

[62] At Princeton, to Betancourt.

[63] López Fresquet, 110.

[64] López Fresquet to James, ibid., 124.

[65] Ibid., 110. Droller later directed Cuban exile activities against Castro, under the name of Bender.

[66] By E. W. Kenworthy in Washington.

wanted the U.S. to take the initiative to help Cuba. But, in the face of conflicting views, there was indecision.

Yet, even while in North America, Castro was still under call from other voices. Raúl Castro, it seems, telephoned him tauntingly, saying that the Cuban press was reporting that the public success of his visit meant, in fact, a surrender to the U.S.[67] It was certainly a critical moment for the Communist cause in Cuba. On 15 April Hubert Matos, the rice grower who, as a commander, had led the advance into Santiago and who was now military governor of the province of Camagüey, made a speech which violently attacked Communism.[68]

Castro was due to go to Canada after the U.S. He also accepted a sudden invitation to go to Brazil and Argentina. Pazos argued that he should have refused, since there was so much to be done in Cuba. Boti told Pazos that it would be best to go, for otherwise Castro would be in Cuba on May Day, when he would be certain, if there, to make a violent speech. He added that Guevara would soon be sent off on a long journey and then receive an ambassadorship – a frequent consolation prize for Latin American extremists.[69]

The journey to Canada was a repetition of that to the U.S. But on the way from there to South America, Raúl Castro flew suddenly to meet his brother at the inappropriate rendezvous of Houston, Texas. It is not known what transpired then. It has been said that the beardless commander of the army adjured his elder brother to maintain his revolutionary integrity. It seems equally probable that the main discussion was about the theme of the speeches that Raúl Castro and Guevara would make on 1 May in Cuba; and they spoke, when the day came, of the need for 'unity'.[70] But afterwards, even on the journey south, Castro seems still to have kept up the moderate and confiding *persona* which he had shown in the U.S. To an old friend, José Ignacio Rasco, a leader of Cuba's few Christian democrats (he was a professor at the Catholic university of Santo Tomás de Villanueva and had been secretary of the 1957 National Liberation Movement), Castro confided, on the aeroplane, that he was not a Communist because 'Communism is the dictatorship of a single class and I . . . have fought all my life against dictatorship'; because 'Communism means hatred and class struggle and I am opposed to any form of hatred'; and because Communism 'Clashes with God and the Church and although I do not practise religion the way I learned it at secondary school, neither do I wish to have a quarrel with the Church'. He promised Rasco that, when he

[67] López Fresquet., 112–13, describes.
[68] See *Revolución*, 17 April, 1959.
[69] Pazos's evidence.
[70] On 22 March Castro had suggested that he would be making a speech on 1 May. In these circumstances, of course, this promise could not be fulfilled.

returned to Cuba, he would 'change, talk to businessmen, give up insulting the Nuncio'.[71] To another old friend, Conte Agüero, he admitted that 'you can't confide in the Communists'.[72]

The visits to Buenos Aires, Rio de Janeiro and Montevideo were also successful. At the former, Castro spoke at the second meeting of the committee of twenty-one Latin American countries.[73] There he proposed that the U.S. should give aid worth $M30,000 in public capital to Latin America over the next ten years. This proposal was dismissed in the U.S. as a ridiculously large sum, though when it came to the point the Alliance for Progress in the era of Kennedy spoke of $M20,000 of aid being needed.[74] Castro's speech reads as if sincerely intended: it pointed out that the U.S. had helped Europe on this scale, and that this sort of aid would actually benefit the U.S. in the long run. In this, of course, he was right. But actual economic contact between Cuba and the U.S., on 2 May, was confined to a U.S.-Cuban agreement under the Point 4 programme, concluded for technical cooperation in the development of agrarian reform.

Castro returned to Cuba on 7 May. He was met at the airport by Ambassador Bonsal, still the advocate of conciliation. The two men had a friendly talk. That, however, was the last that Bonsal was to see of Castro till June;[75] and between then and June decisive changes occurred.

Certain political shifts had, anyway, happened while Castro was away. The potentially dangerous Colonel Barquín had been ordered abroad as military attaché. Raúl Castro had appointed an old friend from the Moncada and *Granma* days, Ramiro Valdés, until now military commander in Matanzas, to the important post of chief of intelligence (G2) under the army. This post, which in the end made him head of Cuba's political police, had previously been filled by the less amenable Major Sanjenís. Attacks in *Revolución* and elsewhere had begun on the right-wing newspaper *Avance*. Some erstwhile traditional supporters of the revolution, such as Major Lorié, resigned. The outspoken Major Matos was certainly in contact with Díaz Lanz, the head of the air force, fearing and criticizing the Communist influence in the

[71] Rasco to James, James 131.

[72] Conte Agüero, *Los Dos Rostros de Fidel Castro*.

[73] This committee of the OAS had been set up in September 1958 in order to consider how 'Operation Panamerica', as proposed by President Kubitschek of Brazil, to try and raise the Latin American rate of economic growth, might be put into effect.

[74] Javier Pazos (*New Republic*, 12 January 1963), a Cuban delegate at the Buenos Aires conference, later recalled that Castro 'was very enthusiastic about his private Alliance for Progress scheme of $30 billion [i.e. English $M30,000]. My impression was that he was contemplating the possibility of staying on the American side of the fence as a sponsor of this . . . and as the leader of a Nasser-type revolution.' Castro also visited his uncle, Gonzalo Castro, an immigrant to Argentina.

[75] Bonsal to the author; see also Bonsal, *Foreign Affairs*, January 1967.

army. Meantime, sugar prices had fallen to their lowest point since 1944. The fall was at least partly due to Castro's airy talk of producing as much sugar as possible and of selling it below prevailing world market prices. On the other hand, the harvest for 1959 was nearly complete, and it was already clear that it would be higher than recent years. From North America, trumpets of alarm were beginning to blow: *Time* magazine on 11 May said: 'Fellow travellers work on the commission for the Revision of Cuban History Books'; in a television programme entitled 'Is Cuba going red?', a CBS correspondent, Stuart Norris, said that Cuba was becoming a Communist beachhead, a totalitarian dictatorship. There was a chorus of protests from Cubans in the U.S., headed by the respectable and elderly ambassador, Dihigo.[76]

The facts, however, were still ambiguous: Castro had, apparently, promised Major Matos that he would soon dismiss Communists or near-Communists such as his brother Raúl, Guevara, his old friend Alfredo Guevara (who had become head of the new film institute) and the geographer Núñez Jiménez, (Che Guevara's old aide at Santa Clara who had been helping to draft the agrarian reform law).[77]

In a speech on 9 May Castro continued to repeat the democratic phrases of his visit to the U.S.: the Cuban revolution, he said, was 'entirely democratic', and he explicitly denied that he had anything to do with Communism, for 'not only do we offer people food, but we also offer them freedom'.[78] So far so good: but about the same time, on 11 May, the University of Havana (having been closed since December 1956), finally reopened; and the first event of the new term was the setting up of a committee to purge the university of anti-revolutionaries. This news was less comforting. Some time early in May the journalist Cazalis met the Minister of Agriculture, Sorí Marín, who warned him, 'Fidel is going to take everything for himself. He knows no limits and it is impossible to know where we are going.'[79]

In the face of these conflicting pieces of dubious evidence, the only conclusion that it is possible to reach in respect of Cuba in May 1959 is that Castro was still vacillating between several tactics. Such 'intransigence' as the U.S. displayed could only have played a very small part, though the persistent questioning of whether Castro was or was not a Communist was more than an irritant, since it implied that, though Cuba was independent, she was not free to choose Communism.

[76] Bonsal, *loc. cit.*
[77] Daniel James, 150–1.
[78] *Revolución*, 10 May 1959.
[79] Cazalis, *La República* (Caracas), 4–10 February 1966.

CHAPTER 34

Agrarian Reform: Politics and Crisis

A few days after his return from his travels Castro appeared before his cabinet in his Cojímar house with a draft agrarian reform law. The cabinet wanted, naturally, to read the law before promulgation, but Castro insisted it must be accepted as it was.[1] Otherwise, he said, the details would leak out and assist the opposition. Eventually, a sub-committee of three (headed by Castro's ex-adjutant-general, Sorí Marín, the Minister of Agriculture) examined the law. Sorí Marín (who despite his portfolio had hitherto had nothing to do with the law) showed the draft to the distinguished sugar economist, José Antonio Guerra, general manager of the National Bank, and Felipe Pazos, its director. Some amendments were suggested, but these were never accepted by Castro, because at the crucial moment Sorí Marín could not be found.[2] On 17 May the Agrarian Reform law was promulgated, in a formal ceremony in the Sierra Maestra, with all the cabinet attending.

This law was aimed less at the improvement of agriculture than at a change in the structure of land-holding. It had been mainly written by Guevara's aide, the geographer and economist Núñez Jiménez, with various others such as the economic editor of *Revolución*, Oscar Pino Santos, a man always associated with the Communists or the extreme left, though he had, nevertheless, till December 1958, been public relations director of Batista's National Economic Council. Núñez Jiménez, though always associated with the Left in the past, had decided to join Guevara from the University of Las Villas very late in the civil war – on 24 December 1958, to be precise: in consequence his beard was still less than perfect on the day of victory.

The first article of the law reflected the Constitution of 1940: the proscription of estates larger than 1,000 acres.[3] This maximum did not, however, apply to those sugar or rice plantations where the yields were more than half larger than the national average; in these instances, the maximum was 3,333 acres.[4] Foreign companies might hold land even over that limit, if the Cuban government deemed it in the national interest. The law affected directly only about 10% of the farms in the

[1] Evidence of Elena Mederos; López Fresquet (114) confirms.
[2] Evidence of Elena Mederos, Felipe Pazos and José Antonio Guerra.
[3] 30 cabs or 402·6 hectares.
[4] 100 cabs or 1,342 hectares.

country at the normal maximum of 1,000 acres (or 12,000 properties),[5] and much less than that at the special maximum. On the other hand, the law affected about 40% of the total land in farms. The law emphasized the role of the state and of collective undertakings much more than had been supposed likely; hence Castro's coyness to the cabinet the previous day. Even the Communists had supposed, if only as a tactic, that all land confiscated would be divided up; but by May they had accepted that the 'vigour of the Revolution and the support for it from the masses . . . made possible more radical measures.'[6]

Property over these limits would be expropriated, compensation being promised in twenty-year bonds, bearing an annual interest of 4·5%. Payments, as in the case of the agrarian law in republican Spain and in eastern European countries after 1919, would be on the assessed value of the land for tax purposes. Land expropriated would either be made into agricultural cooperatives, to be run for the time being by an Institute of Agrarian Reform (INRA), or would be distributed as individual holdings of 67 acres – the size of farm which was considered a 'life-providing minimum' for a family of five. *Precaristas*, sharecroppers and renters would have the first claim on the land which they had previously been working. If this turned out to be less than 67 acres, the rest of the plot would be made up as soon as possible, in so far as land was available. If cultivation were afterwards neglected, the land was supposed to be handed back to the state. Land once distributed could only be sold to the state, or with the state's agreement. It could not be divided.

The law also set out to free the sugar *colonos* from the mills. Companies would not, after the harvest of 1960, be allowed to run sugar plantations unless their shares were both registered and owned by Cubans; nor would anyone be able to have shares in sugar plantations if they were employees or owners of, or shareholders in, sugar mills. Land not given over to sugar could also be owned only by companies with their shares duly registered. Further, in future, land could be bought only by Cubans.

This law differed considerably from that promulgated in November 1958 by Law 3 of the Sierra Maestra. By that document, land was to be given to those who cultivated it. But now redistribution would form only a small part of the programme. Castro later explained that he 'already understood . . . that if you take, for example, a sugar plantation of 2,500 acres, where the land is good for sugar cane . . . and you divide it into

[5] There were probably a few more than 12,000 farms bigger than 1,000 acres, out of a total of 185,000.

[6] Carlos Rafael Rodríguez, *La Revolución Cubana*, Folleto II, 53.

two hundred portions of $12\frac{1}{2}$ acres each, ... the new owners will cut the production of sugar cane in half ... and ... raise for their own consumption a whole series of new crops.'[7] He added that his experience in the Sierra Maestra had suggested that, if large herds were divided up, the cows would be quickly eaten by their new owners, rather than kept for milk. 'This naturally fortified my conviction that the land of *latifundistas* should not be divided, but should be organized.' Still, the reform had more links with democratic models than, say, those of postwar eastern Europe. While no Cuban private estates could now be larger than 1,000 acres, in Poland and Bulgaria the maximum was between 50 and 120; and indeed many eastern European reforms of the 1920s went further than the Cuban ideas of 1959. The cooperatives presented a great contrast with Russian experience. The rates of interest proposed on the bonds were higher than General MacArthur's Agrarian Reform in Japan, and the time of repayment was shorter than the reform instituted in Formosa. The law was also obviously ambivalent in some ways: thus a tenant tobacco farmer in Pinar del Río would be doing much better, by the redistribution of land, than a tenant on the swamps of Las Villas. Further, the reform was in fact really political in intent rather than strictly economic, since it gave to the government a powerful instrument by which it could arbitrarily impoverish or ruin its enemies; and perhaps the reform was intended from the beginning as a first step towards further expropriation.[8]

INRA, the Agrarian Reform Institute, became quickly the main agency of the new government, for its task was not only to expropriate and redistribute land, but to organize road-building, health, education and housing in the country. INRA was also given a credit department, and it absorbed the old Sugar, Rice and Coffee Stabilization Institutes. It became, indeed, a kind of shadow government of its own. Under it, the country was divided into twenty-eight zones of different sizes, each commanded by an officer of the rebel army, who was responsible for carrying out the law, and who had much freedom in the interpretation of orders. Castro was the president of INRA, but the director in charge of day-to-day operations was the part-author of the law itself, Dr Núñez Jiménez. This appointment explained some of the errors of judgement committed in the next two years: Núñez Jiménez was, according to Professor Dumont (who was generally sympathetic to revolutionary Cuba), 'better fitted to organize a meeting or ride a horse, banners in the wind, to occupy the territory of the United Fruit

[7] Lockwood, 89.

[8] See for instance the doubtless sensationalized account of the second national congress of the Institute of Agrarian Reform by the then second-in-command of the district of Manzanillo, and future exile commander at the Bay of Cochinos, Manuel Artime (*Traición*, Miami, 1960, 53–63).

Company, than to organize, rationally, the socialist sector of agriculture.'[9] The assistant director, Oscar Pino Santos, had also helped draft the law but he was nevertheless a journalist by profession who had no experience of administration. Another odd appointment was Eduardo Santos Ríos, once Communist party leader in Oriente, who had been Batista's sub-director in BANFAIC, the Agricultural and Industrial Development Bank. The chief of the legal department was Waldo Medina, a judge sacked by Batista.

The co-operatives constituted the most unexpected part of the new law. Most people had expected simply the *reparto*, the division of land among the landless, the age-old, if vain, dream of all agricultural workers in Spain and Hispanic America. But in fact the co-operatives from the start did not ever signify what that word usually means; INRA appointed the manager of the enterprise, sometimes from among the workers. The workers were paid about $2·50 a day all the year round, supposedly an advance on the co-operatives' profits which would be added up at the end of the year. Any further profit, theoretically, would then be distributed. (Castro later explained that the idea of co-operatives had only been decided upon at the last minute, in the aircraft on the way to the signing of the law in the Sierra Maestra.[10])

INRA also had from the start some farms to run directly – the estates of Batista, his supporters, or others who had either fled, were dead or in prison. These were the prototypes of the state farms which later became the chief means of agricultural organization in revolutionary Cuba.

When the agrarian law was promulgated, the immediate consequence was a fall in the quotations of sugar companies on the New York Stock Exchange. Other Cuban stocks, such as utilities, unconnected with sugar, also dropped. In Cuba, the Sugar Mill Owners Association argued that the law would have 'grave economic repercussions' and asked Castro to postpone its enactment. They said that sugar cane could not be adequately prepared for harvest if the big land holdings were broken up while, if the *centrales* lost their administration cane, they would be unable to give credit to the *colonos*. The curious system of harvesting which had pertained since the 1880s was thus threatened at the roots. Tobacco growers in Pinar del Río also protested, though they did not seem to be much affected. The last of the Rionda family to have estates in Cuba, a Cuban-American now president of the Francisco Sugar Co., told his shareholders that he had made representations to

[9] Dumont, *Cuba*, 47. In view of this judgement it is entertaining to read the judgement before the U.S. Senate Internal Security Sub-Committee of an ex-Auténtico policeman, Silva, that Núñez Jiménez was a 'very dangerous man owing to his great talents' (*Communist Threat*, 534).
[10] *Revolución*, 22 December 1961.

MISSILE-READY TENT

LAUNCH POSITION

MISSILE ERECTOR

7 U.2 photograph of missile base at San Cristóbal, West Cuba

The withdrawal of the missiles:

8a The Soviet vessel *Fizik Kurchatov* at sea, showing six canvas-covered missile transporters with missiles on deck (7 November 1962)

  b The U.S. navy radar ship *Vesole* (left, foreground) alongside the Soviet vessel *Volgoles*, outbound from Cuba, with missiles on deck (11 November 1962)

the U.S. government over the law.[11] The Vertientes Sugar Co., with its huge mill, thought that its activities might soon be limited to the industrial side of sugar.[12] George Braga of the Manatí Sugar Co. sent a similar letter to his shareholders. A storm thus arose against the Agrarian Reform law and, because of the nature of land-holding in Cuba, it arose in New York as much as on the island. The theme of Communism in Cuba began more and more to appear in the U.S. press,[13] though most companies were merely uncertain of what provisions were applicable to them, and when.

Had such commentators looked closely, they would have observed that a clash between the revolution and the Communists seemed now to be under way in Cuba. Thus, on 8 May, the 26 July Movement's newspaper *Revolución* had denounced the Communist secretary-general, Blas Roca, for seeking to divide the Movement, 'that same Blas who made an agreement with Batista [in 1938] now denies the validity of Fidel's power'. The day before the launching of the Agrarian Reform law, *Revolución* denounced the Communist party as deviationist. Since Castro went to *Revolución* almost daily to check personally what was put into the paper, these attacks were obviously printed with his agreement. Perhaps in the quarrel between *Hoy* and *Revolución* in the middle of 1959 Castro merely let *Revolución* have its head in order to disprove accusations by U.S. journalists that the two papers were publishing identical headlines.[14] On 16 May *Revolución* anyway criticized a joint statement by a member of the 26 July Movement and the Communist party as an 'underhand political pact', which ignored both the 26 July national directorate and Fidel Castro. On 21 May Castro, in an interview on television, explained that his aim was a revolution different from capitalism ('which kills by hunger') and from Communism (which suppresses those liberties 'so dear to man'). The Cuban Revolution would be as autochthonous as Cuban music, and, being characterized by humanism, would be neither Left nor Right but 'one step forward'. It was, in colour, not red but olive green, the olive green of the rebel army uniform. As for the Communists, they were showing themselves 'anti-revolutionary' in their agitation for wage increases, and there were indeed certain coincidences between Communists and counter-revolutionaries. Were not the Communists responsible for

[11] Bernardo Rionda Braga, *ibid.*, 8 June, qu. Scheer and Zeitlin, 95–6. Bernardo Rionda was the nephew of Manuel and though, like him, born in Asturias, was now almost completely North American.

[12] Vertientes-Camagüey Company, Annual Report, January 1960 (*loc. cit.*).

[13] Scheer and Zeitlin (319) in their excellent analysis of the U.S. press of 1959–60, say that *Time* and *Newsweek* had only one article on the theme of Communism before 17 May. One can assume, therefore, that henceforth the public relations officers were very busy.

[14] See Lechuga's article in *Diario de la Marina*, 17 May 1959, in which he draws attention to the accusation and to the controversy.

unrest in San Luis, where peasants armed with stakes had attempted a spontaneous seizure of land?[15] On 22 May Castro appeared again on television: extremists, he said, had no place in the Cuban revolution. He also said – a hint, presumably, to his companions on his Washington journey – that soon Guevara would embark on a journey to Africa, Asia and Europe as his representative. The Communists' executive committee replied that they were appalled at Castro's 'unjust and unjustifiable attack',[16] while the secretary-general, Blas Roca, accused Castro of endangering the revolution by 'unleashing an anti-Communist campaign'.[17] But there was more trouble for them to come.

On 24 May the non-Communist union leaders formed a new labour alliance (the Frente Obrero Humanista) to support the 26 July Movement against Communism. Despite the short notice, this alliance successfully beat the Communists in all the major labour elections at the end of the month. The sugar workers, after re-electing by an immense majority (855 to 11) the ex-Senator Conrado Bécquer as their secretary-general, rather than the Communist Ursinio Rojas, denounced *Hoy* as propagating 'unfounded, defamatory and counter-revolutionary' statements against Bécquer. Bécquer himself pointed out that the 'Communists never helped the 26 July Movement before the 26 December 1958', that is, five days before Batista fled.[18] The Communist newspaper *Hoy* was censured by the Sugar Workers' Congress.

Thus, at the end of May all seemed to be going well for the liberal cause in Cuba. The law of Agrarian Reform, on analysis, turned out to be as modest as many other such laws in democracies. López Fresquet was bringing in a moderate tax reform law.[19] But, unfortunately, the liberals of Cuba themselves did not know how to direct their cause. They had no organized political following. Faced with the increasing evidence of Castro's immense talents as an orator and leader and his extraordinary popularity, those within the government felt themselves isolated. Elena Mederos at the Ministry of Health told her friend, the bank director Pazos, that they were both wasting their time, that they were simply being used, and that 'nothing was working'. Pazos assured her that 'things were going much better' and that he had recently secured that Castro came regularly week by week to the National Bank.[20] But, of course, such things were trivial in comparison with the importance of building a national movement to support the liberal cause. Further,

---

[15] *Revolución*, 22 May 1959. San Luis is a small town in Oriente, 15 miles north of Santiago. In 1961 Castro was to say that on this subject he had been misinformed (see speech of December 1 1961).

[16] *Hoy*, 23 May 1959.

[17] *H.A.R.*, xx, 266.

[18] Ruby Hart Phillips, *New York Times*, 30 May 1959.

[19] López Fresquet, 118.

[20] Elena Mederos's and Pazos's evidence.

even the liberals, including men such as Rufo López Fresquet, the Finance Minister, who later abandoned the revolution, were still many of them as mesmerized by Castro as was the nation itself.

The National Co-ordinator of the 26 July Movement was still Marcelo Fernández, who had filled this central position ever since the failure of the general strike in April 1958, in succession to Faustino Pérez. To him, presumably, and to others nominally in the direction of the 26 July, mostly ex-leaders of the Civic Resistance, would have fallen the task of its reorganization as a political party. Marcelo Fernández, though regarded in the university in the mid-1950s as a 'fellow traveller' (his candidacy for the presidency of the engineering school had been backed by the university Communists), was politically a moderate if an opportunist. The explanation why he did not, during 1959 establish a constitution and programme for the 26 July Movement, was simply that he could not get a clear directive from Castro. He seemed 'infuriated and worried that he never saw Fidel and that he never knew where he was'.[21] The 26 July Movement, of course, had evidently to depend on Castro, but Castro consistently refused to define its purpose. No doubt men such as Fernández, in the Movement's lower echelons, could have made some progress on their own. But they, like many others, were loyal to Castro. A word from him and their work, had they done it, would have been annulled. Thus their potentially powerful organization throughout the country remained a skeleton. The 26 July Movement seems to have had numerous interesting ideas about protecting Cuban industry from the U.S. Atlantic seaboard, nationalizing minerals, creating a hundred thousand new peasant proprietors who, in the tradition of the French Revolution rather than the Russian, would have been the backbone of a genuine national if limited revolution. But, as everyone really knew, the idea of Fidelismo without Fidel, or the 26 July Movement without Castro, was always fanciful.[22] Since Marcelo Fernández had been the organizer of the Movement since before January 1959, there could have been no question of his special appointment in order to destroy the Movement through inaction or ineptitude. Still, as in the years before the victory, the most anti-Communist group in the 26 July – Faustino Pérez, Carlos Franqui, Marcelo Fernández – was at the same time resolutely anti-American: dislike of the old Communists derived from memories of their persistent enthusiasm for the orthodox Communist line, not because of its violence or its revolutionary quality.

The Communists were now stronger than in January, with tentacles or sympathizers in every part of the state organization, especially in the new Agrarian Reform Institute (INRA), and with Guevara and Raúl

[21] The comment of Elena Mederos.
[22] See Javier Pazos, *Cambridge Opinion*, February 1963.

Castro, who were at least Marxists, as Castro's closest advisers. The controversy between *Revolución* and *Hoy* had been halted on Castro's explicit orders to *Revolución*.[23] In a country without political organization and without institutions the attractions for Castro of turning to the Communist party must have been strong, quite apart from his general alignment with the Communists on the subject of nationalism and on the U.S. On the other hand, the Communists had also shown, from their extremely prudent balance between articles in their press dealing with China as well as Russia that they too had their internal problems; not least because in respect of 'permanent revolution in the hemisphere', they were already outflanked by Guevara.[24]

At the end of May the Communists met again and worked out a theoretical basis for their policy towards Castro and the revolution. Blas Roca evidently had to contend with criticism not only from Carlos Rafael Rodríguez, the strongest supporter among the Communists of Castro's revolution (and therefore theoretically on the Right of the party), but also from among the Left. The consequence was a very moderate statement indeed, allocating a place in any revolution to the *petit bourgeoisie* as well as to the workers and peasants, and saying that, since the aims of the revolution were independence, land for the peasants, industrialization and 'strengthening democracy', it did not matter if Castro gave the name 'humanist' to the Movement which he directed. Blas Roca also denounced 'any leftist extremist tendency, any exaggerated measures', which reflected the dependence of Cuba upon imports and upon the geographical fact of proximity to the U.S.[25] This moderation was intended not only to pave the way towards permanent understanding with Castro, as Carlos Rafael Rodríguez desired, but also even to restrain him and Guevara.

With Castro vacillating, the latent forces of the opposition began to gather more coherently than they had done before, and perhaps it was this that decided him. The National Association of Cattlemen of Cuba thus declared firmly that the maximum limit of private property to 3,333 acres was inadequate to make business profitable. Caiñan Milanés, the cattlemen's president, pointed out that the land reform was more radical than the Communists' programme as it had been announced in 1956 – an accusation which, curiously, was confirmed by Carlos Rafael Rodríguez to Ruby Hart Phillips, though he said that the Communists were naturally participating in the revolution. Though there was some

[23] Private information.
[24] See description in Suárez, 55-7.
[25] *'Conclusiones del pleno del Comité Nacional del PSP, realizado en los días 25 al 28 de mayo de 1959'*, *Hoy*, 7 June 1959. It is true that these conclusions had an appendix which described how the peculiarity of the Cuban revolution was supposed to be that the peasants, not the working class, were the chief factor in the overthrow of Batista.

coincidence between the Communists' programme of 1956 and Castro's, he thought that Castro was going too fast in providing for the take-over of administration caneland away from the sugar mills.[26] Landowners, meanwhile, bought time on the private radio stations to attack the law, and held rallies; it transpired that the Cattlemen's Association voted a fund of $500,000 to bribe newspapers to denounce the Reform.[27] Mgr Pérez Serantes, Castro's old friend at Santiago, had at first praised the Agrarian Reform law as 'necessary and human'; but he then changed his tune and cryptically said that 'certain groups in Cuba suspect that the authors of that law and the Communists have been drinking at the same spring'.[28] But the opposition did not, could not, rally round the Church, which was now divided, just as it had been in Batista's time: Mgr Evelio Díaz, for instance, had recently spoken of the agrarian law as fundamentally just.[29]

Nor could the opposition rally around any good Liberal either, since the good liberals were still in the government. The spokesman of protest thus became 'Tony' Varona, Prío's prime minister in 1950–2. Prío, on the other hand, publicly backed the law of Agrarian Reform. Varona's criticism of the law was to argue that the government should not distribute cultivated land and that state lands should be distributed first. Once again he called for elections.

On 11 June the U.S. government dispatched an official Note to Cuba on the subject of agrarian reform. This expressed 'concern', though it admitted both that Cuba had a legal right to expropriate foreign property and that land reform was a step towards social progress. The U.S. would insist, of course, on 'prompt, adequate and effective compensation', though they did not insist on specific amounts or valuation methods.[30] Some North American sympathizers of Castro later argued that this Note was of 'great significance in moulding the suspicions and arousing the ire of the Cuban revolutionaries'.[31] This is a little difficult to believe; no Cuban could have expected, realistically, that a law confiscating broad acres of property belonging to the United Fruit Company, the Pingree Ranch, or the King Ranch of Texas, could have been passed without protest in the U.S.

The point at issue was when compensation would be paid – 'promptly' or by bonds over twenty years – a serious matter, and one which would arise everywhere in Latin America after a land reform, for no country is

[26] Phillips, *The Cuban Dilemma*, 83.
[27] *Revolución*, 25 June 1959.
[28] *H.A.R.*, xii, 320.
[29] *Bohemia*, 29 May: 'Our present Land Reform in its noble purpose fully enters into the spirit and sense of Christian justice.'
[30] *New York Times*, 12 June 1959.
[31] Scheer and Zeitlin, 96.

ready to pay vast sums for compensation on the spot. The question was further complicated by the casual and wasteful manner in which the actual expropriations were carried out: thus when the Pingree Ranch was turned into a cooperative, a $20,000 breeding bull was killed by the army for a barbecue.[32] The expropriations were almost everywhere carried into effect by relatively inexperienced officers of the rebel army, who often simply took over what they thought worth confiscating. Only rarely were inventories made or receipts given. Thus in practice the details of the law were rather unsatisfactory in suggesting what actually happened.

Before the U.S. Note had in fact been delivered, Castro made a public proposal to the U.S. that they should increase purchase of Cuban sugar from three million tons a year to eight million.[33] Ultimately, no doubt, like the other advanced countries, the U.S. could have bought more tropical products if they had set about it generously; but an immediate increase of nearly 200 % could not have been straight away practical. Soon after this, Bonsal saw Castro who agreed that:

[A big speech] was not the best way of attaining his expressed objective of underlining Cuba's ample and flexible historic potential as a supplier of sugar to the American market. He agreed with me that if he were to find it desirable to make this point again, he would exchange views with me as to the best way of doing so without indulging in empty gestures which could only discredit his awareness of the sugar situation ... These [Bonsal added later] were indeed the halcyon days of our relationship'.[34]

Bonsal did not, however, see Castro again till September.[35] In the meantime, the political situation radically changed. The day after the U.S. Note on Agrarian Reform, a cabinet meeting was held. Castro, as usual, was very late. He immediately made it clear that he proposed to dismiss several of the more moderate members, including Elena Mederos, who had reluctantly stayed 'on the train in March'.[36] Castro took a long time to come to the point and only indeed came into the open when Elena Mederos challenged him. She was succeeded as Minister of Social Welfare by her under-secretary, Raquel Pérez, a girl of no political experience. The Minister of the Interior, Luis Orlando Rodríguez, who had proved ineffective, was succeeded by the governor of Havana Province, José Naranjo, an ex-medical student who, though he had

[32] Lazo, 188.
[33] *Revolución*, 10 June 1959.
[34] Bonsal letter to Arthur Schlesinger, November 1962.
[35] Bonsal to the author.
[36] See above, p. 423. This description of this cabinet meeting derives from Dr Mederos; see also Lopéz Fresquet, 50–1.

been with Echevarría in the Directorio, had also fought with Raúl Castro in Oriente. Due to their old friendship Castro promised Rodríguez a new job by letting him publish *La Calle* again. Dr Serafín Ruiz de Zárate, who had been doctor with Guevara in Las Villas, became Minister of Health. Angel Fernández, at the Ministry of Justice, was succeeded by his deputy, Yabur, a lawyer who had once been a friend of Manolo Castro in the university, of Syrian origin, an old enemy of Fidel Castro, but now an unconditional friend. Sorí Marín, the Minister of Agriculture who did not see the Agrarian Reform law before it reached the cabinet, was replaced by Pedro Miret, who had been with Castro at Moncada and in Mexico. Finally, Agramonte, the safe but ineffective Foreign Minister, was replaced by Dr Raúl Roa, for a long time Dean of the faculty of Social Sciences at the university, and since January ambassador to the OAS. All the outgoing members were known to oppose the Agrarian Reform in some particulars.

Roa was a characteristic example of a Latin American intellectual. At the university he was one of the first generation of revolutionary students, a law student associated with Mella, Martínez Villena, and De la Torriente Brau. He followed Mella into the Communist party in 1927[37] but later left. From his writings of the 1930s it is clear, however, that he was still close to Communism. But afterwards, his left-wing friends dead, he entered academic rather than political life; he married into a well-established commercial family of Syrian origin, the Kouris, became estranged from the Communists and, by the 1950s, seemed entirely literary, though not without occasional nostalgic articles about the heroic days of his youth. In 1955, when in Mexico on behalf of the Congress of Cultural Freedom (of which he was the Cuban representative), he had refused to meet Castro, on the grounds that he was a gangster.[38] In 1956 he had denounced the 'brutal methods of the Soviet army to repress the patriotic rising of the Hungarian people' by 'the lackeys of Moscow', and also 'the brain-washing and systematic engrossing of the sensibility' to which all are subject under 'Marxist Caesaro-papism'.[39] In 1959 he had adhered to the revolution, though during that summer he republished his denunciations of Communism with the introduction that the Cuban revolution had 'its own roots, programmes and course. It does not derive from Rousseau, George Washington or Marx'.[40]

Roa was thus an ambiguous minister. Ambiguous he remained, though remaining also Foreign Minister in a government whose leader

---

[37] Nicolas Guillén, himself a Communist, mentions Roa as a member of the party, in an interview with Joaquín Ordoqui, in *Hoy Domingo*, 14 August 1960.
[38] Casuso, 115. Llerena MSS, 33–4, also refers.
[39] Reprinted in 1959 in Havana, in *En Pie*, 217.
[40] Preface to *ibid.*

and some of whose ministers were twenty years younger than him.[41]

The spectre of opposition caused Castro to become more radical. Need he have done so? Was the fear in his mind the product of overworking fancy or were real enemies preparing machetes, guns and manifestos? Certainly he was meeting opposition, not only from the Cuban upper class and U.S. business interests, but also from the U.S. government. The situation was dangerous. Many remembered Guatemala. The counter-revolution might be weak but behind it, in the haunted minds of the reformers in Cuba, loomed the cloud of the U.S. with its hundreds of unofficial agencies and pressures, its power and its tradition-al reactions to defiance in the Caribbean region. Castro desired, any-way, to tease the U.S.[42] Doubtless he went a little further in anticipating a vigorous response before it had actually been aroused, and it seems that the leaders of the Revolution, from Guevara to Carlos Rafael Rodríguez, believed that the hostility of the landowners and the North American companies to the Agrarian reform was a fundamental reason forcing the Revolution towards more radical steps.[43]

On 13 June Castro violently attacked as traitors the critics of the Agrarian Reform law, saying that not a comma of it would be changed, and that the opposition was only preoccupied with their 'vested in-terests'. To the small group sitting in the television studio he rhetorically asked if they wanted elections. No, they hastily replied. Two days later Cuba formally rejected the U.S. Note of 11 June, saying that 'prompt' compensation was out of the question; the landowners would have to accept the bonds with $4\frac{1}{2}\%$ interest. The Cuban reply was, however, moderate in many ways, clearly being drafted in the Foreign Ministry. It conceded that the U.S. was a sincere supporter of land reform and had, in the past, helped Cuban economic growth; and it pointed out that, though the Constitution of 1940 had indeed provided for com-pensation for any expropriation in cash, Batista had ruined the Treasury and there was an unfavourable balance with the U.S. 'Powerful reasons'

---

[41] He is still Foreign Minister (1970). One of those law students who had known Roa well all his life wrote of him that he was intellectually a 'colonist', either of Sánchez Arango, or of his wife Ada Kouri, and ultimately of Castro (Carrillo MSS).

[42] See Betancourt conversation above, 1090. Carrillo, the old political warrior, who was now the vice-president of the National Bank, resigned on the ground that the INRA destroyed the autonomy of the National Bank. This was refused by Castro.

[43] See Carlos Rafael Rodríguez, La Revolución Cubana etc., Folleto II, 'the Revolution had to advance in order to survive'. Guevara said much the same in his speech in Algiers in late 1963: 'The great landowners, many of them North Americans, immediately sabotaged the law of Agrarian Reform. We were therefore face-to-face with a choice which comes to you more than once in your revolutionary life: a situation in which, once embarked, it is difficult to return to shore. But it would have been still more dangerous to recoil since that would have meant the death of the Revolution . . . the most just and the most dangerous course was to press ahead . . . and what we supposed to have been an agrarian reform with a bourgeois character was transformed into a violent struggle . . .' (As quoted Révolution (Paris), October 1963.)

justified the form of indemnities. This moderate response surely demanded a moderate counter-reply. At the same time, however, ominously, a series of bombs were exploded in Havana – three during Castro's speech of 13 June. Was it possible that the old cycle of violence was about to begin again? Certainly the government feared so. Immediately came a number of arrests, chiefly of ex-members of the Batistiano armed forces. The Constitution of 1940 was quickly amended to permit a death penalty for 'counter-revolutionaries', and a prominent right-wing lawyer, Enrique Llaca Ortiz, was spirited out of his home by agents of the Rebel Army intelligence, the DIER, and held for several days.

This event, reminiscent of happenings under so many Cuban governments, brought a quick clash between the government and the judiciary. The Audiencia of Havana ordered Llaca's release. The DIER was ordered to obey Castro. Castro then ordered the Ministry of Justice to proceed against the judges of the Audiencia (Gómez Calvo, Peñate and Paprón). The Supreme Court stepped in. Mr Justice Alabau (the same who, in 1958, had indicted Ventura and Laurent for the murder of four boys) found that the judges had not exceeded their functions; he added, 'neither the Revolution nor the Revolutionary Government can repudiate *habeas corpus*,' since *habeas corpus* had been the banner of the revolution and 'only tyrants and despots discard *habeas corpus*.'

The Llaca case was an indication to Castro of how far he could legally go against the opponents of the regime with the existing Constitution; press further and he would have to jettison it. Yet while he was beginning to act within Cuba – by instinct, impatience or ill-judgement – dictatorially (though there are democratic countries where people are held a week without trial), internationally Castro still seemed the persecuted outlaw in travail. He spoke as a man surrounded by enemies, struggling among nameless conspiracies, as if still spiritually in the Sierra Maestra with a handful of men, fighting his lonely battle against tyranny. From a position of government, he remained a rebel. Other roles did not attract him, or rather, he could not fill them and many Cubans, with their long ambiguous unaroused hostility to the U.S., their memories of Wood and Sumner Welles, their regard for their new leader, seem scarcely to have wished him to. From this time onwards, Castro never repeated the anti-Communism which had occasionally cropped up in his speeches or in private conversation. Henceforth, he reserved his criticism for those who were anti-Communists. While allowance should be made for the irritation of Castro and his colleagues at being persistently questioned by U.S. and other journalists as to whether they were Communists or not (with the assumption that they had no right to be so in the Americas), it is difficult not to conclude that some critical decisions must have been made now by Castro, Guevara and his brother

– and perhaps no one else; not necessarily the Cuban Communists themselves.

At this time, López Fresquet produced his comprehensive Tax Reform law for Castro to sign; he did so laughing, saying, 'Maybe when the time comes to apply the Law there won't be any tax-payers.'[44]

The Llaca case, meantime, would perhaps have been noticed more had it not been for its coincidence with an unsuccessful sally into foreign affairs. Many exiles from other Latin countries were now in Havana. An abortive attempt had already been made on Panamá. A force of volunteers was assembled to attack Trujillo, recalling the attack of 1947 on the Dominican Republic. Castro had always attacked Trujillo in his speeches; now he would do so physically, though not in person. Possibly the imminence of the invasion was a reason for Castro's evident decision in early June to reach a rapprochement with the Communists, whom he seems to have criticized in May.[45] There had been abortive plans for other attacks on nearby dictatorships – including Nicaragua and Guatemala – perhaps without the government's support. Now, with Castro's blessing, about two hundred Dominicans, with ten Cubans under a rebel army Officer, Delio Gómez Ochoa (who had gone to the Sierra in May 1957 from Santiago and had been an anti-Communist representative of the 26 July Movement in Havana in mid-1958), landed in two waves on the north coast of the Dominican Republic. Most were killed, however, immediately on landing. A few, including Gómez Ochoa, struggled inland, and were eventually captured. Most of these were tortured and shot, though not the commander. Afterwards, a group of young Dominicans formed a political movement inspired by the memory of the dead: the 14 June Movement, a group of generous young men who were brutally treated by successive regimes in the Dominican Republic, but nevertheless endured.

The Dominican invasion, intentionally or not, avoided extra attention being paid to what, with the Llaca affair, was a decisive turn for the revolutionary government. No doubt Castro had specifically desired the resignation of the liberal ministers before the take-over by the army, on behalf of the Agrarian Reform Institute as part of the Agrarian Reform law, of 131 large cattle ranches in Camagüey. Technically, the state 'intervened' in the running of the farms, just as they had in respect of the telephone company and as Prío had done in respect of the western railways. But intervention now meant permanent state direction. The total involved was between 250,000 and a third of a million acres. The

---

[44] López Fresquet, 164.

[45] This is argued by Andrés Suárez (66–7) not entirely convincingly, though it is clear that the idea of a venture against Trujillo did clash with their 'May conclusions'. Suárez's argument also is that the failure of the Dominican invasion led Castro to realign his entire politics.

ranches which were seized included North American estates such as the 26,000 acres recently bought by King Ranch of Texas and the Manatí Sugar Co., and other North American companies, along with large estates owned by the Betancourts, Agramontes and other famous Camagüeyan families. The army was meant to leave to each ranch 3,333 acres (100 cabs), though this stipulation was not always fulfilled.

The consequences were to give the government control of the beef supply. The ranchers, passing into open hostility to the revolution, predicted accurately that there would be excessive slaughtering and afterwards a beef shortage. This indeed had always occurred in revolutions.[46]

The cattle ranches of Camagüey were in fact the heart of counter-revolutionary Cuba, the home of conservative interests, whose predictable denunciations of agrarian reform alienated those members of the liberal centre, who were still attached to the regime. Meantime, the U.S. had officially still not answered the Cuban Note of 15 June. But, privately, U.S. businessmen were beginning to use the famous metaphor of the water melon: 'The more the Revolution is sliced, the redder it gets',[47] and on 22 June *Time* magazine told its seven million readers that Núñez Jiménez, the director of INRA, was 'a longtime Communist-liner', and prepared its readers for the news that Cuba's agrarian reform was inspired by the Devil. But this interpretation had not yet been decided by the Church in Cuba: a meeting of sixty-two representatives of the religious congregations inconclusively met at Belén at the end of June to discuss the matter.[48]

Within a week of the intervention of the large ranches, the government found itself under attack from another not unexpected quarter. The head of the air force, Díaz Lanz, had been increasingly fretful. Son of an army officer imprisoned by Machado and still only thirty-two, before the revolution he had been a commercial air line pilot for Q Airways. He had flown arms and ammunition to the Sierra Maestra from Florida. A good pilot, he was a man of limited intelligence. Though he had been a member of the notorious Second Tribunal which tried the Batistiano pilots at Santiago in March, he had refused to fly to Santo Domingo with the unsuccessful Dominican Republic expedition.[49] He had been for some time a conspirator against Communist influence in Cuba. In June he had complained at the 'indoctrination classes' in the air force, given by instructors sent by the commander-in-chief of the armed forces, Raúl Castro. This 'indoctrination' consisted of nationalistic versions of Cuban history, justification of governmental plans,

[46] e.g. in Spain when the anarchists took over in 1936.
[47] *Wall Street Journal*, 24 June 1959.
[48] See report in *Bohemia*, 4 July 1959.
[49] Evidence to Senate Internal Security Sub-Committee, 417.

particularly agrarian reform, and some elementary Marxism. The level of sophistication was low.

During June Díaz Lanz had, in fact, been ill with typhus. On his return to duty on 29 June, he gave a press conference, denied that, contrary to rumour, he had been kept a prisoner, and added, 'I am against every type of dictatorship, Trujillista, Batistiano, Communist ... especially the Communist system.' Castro immediately summoned him, upbraided him for giving such a declaration without his authorization and told him not to return to the air force. Díaz Lanz went home, prepared a letter of resignation and in the afternoon fled in a small boat with his family to Miami. In Havana Juan Almeida, the mulatto veteran of Moncada and the *Granma*, temporarily took Díaz Lanz's place.

Díaz Lanz was next attacked by Castro as the Benedict Arnold of the Cuban revolution. Even Felipe Pazos accused him of opportunism and of flying in the civil war as a mercenary. A purge of the air force followed. Officers thought to have been friendly with Díaz Lanz were dismissed, and a number of Venezuelans and Costa Ricans were brought to Cuba as replacements.

Next followed the final act in the political education of President Urrutia. Urrutia had already appeared in public with Major Matos with an anti-Communist speech in Camagüey of 8 June and had angered Castro by so doing. Having failed to resign with the liberal ministers on 12 June, Urrutia kept quiet until the end of the month when he was interviewed by Luis Conte Agüero in a television programme. Conte Agüero asked for his comments on the already weary question, were there Communists in the government? Urrutia said:

> In the ... Council of Ministers I know of no Communists. Dr Fidel Castro, you may be sure, is no Communist, and neither am I ... The Communists are fighting for the dictatorship of the proletariat, in which I do not believe ... It is essential that we prevent the frustration of the Revolution, this humanist Revolution of ours.[50]

Desperately, Urrutia was trying to use Castro's own language to attempt to describe his position. The Communists responded. On 30 June, Aníbal Escalante, for many years a member of the Communist leadership, denounced Urrutia: the president had abandoned his neutrality, had disloyally insulted the Communist party, thereby attacking the 'solidarity of the revolutionary camp in a difficult moment'.[51]

[50] Urrutia, 46. This was on 27 June.
[51] *Hoy*, 30 June 1959.

Castro now intervened. Alluding both to Urrutia and Díaz Lanz, he made this somewhat ambiguous reflection:

I consider it not entirely honourable that if we are to avoid being called Communists, we must embark on campaigns against them and attack them ... This is not done by self-respecting men. We ... proclaim everyone's right to write as he thinks, from the *Diario de la Marina* to *Hoy*.[52]

The newspapers still continued, after all, though none now received a government subsidy, and some, having been always used to that assistance, found it, as a result, difficult to survive.

The next few days passed comparatively peacefully. Ominously, however, Guevara returned from his journey to the Middle East. Elsewhere, the clouds continued to mount; on 30 June, in Washington, a report prepared by 'the intelligence Community' under the chairmanship of the CIA argued that Castro was 'pro-Communist and his advisers either Communist or pro-Communist'.[53] The newspaper *Avance* meanwhile accused Urrutia of buying a luxurious villa, while *Revolución* published an affecting story whereby Castro made clear that he himself did not have enough money for a cabin even in the Zapata Swamp: 'Personally I neither have nor am I interested in having anything. Disinterest is a garment I wear everywhere', he remarked sententiously. On 12 July *Prensa Libre* hinted that Urrutia ought to follow Castro's example. On 13 July Conte Agüero again interviewed Urrutia (who in the meantime had issued a writ for libel against *Avance*). What were these rumours about Urrutia's difficulties with Castro? The president answered, 'I have absolutely no disagreement with Fidel Castro ... [who] sides with humanist democracy as do I.' But later he said: 'I believe that the Communists are inflicting terrible harm on Cuba ... The Communists in Cuba want to create a second front against the Cuban Revolution ... a front consisting of all those who side with Russia against the free world. I believe that this is criminal and harmful.' He recalled that the Communists in the time of Batista had criticized 'our policy of insurrection'; he recalled the Communists' curious behaviour in the Second World War; and he even ventured on a critique of Soviet society based on Marxist texts.[54]

Urrutia thus tried to drive a wedge between Castro and Communism, and he let it be known that he would continue his attacks on the latter. The next day, Díaz Lanz, the defecting air force commander,

[52] *Revolución*, 2 July.
[53] Raymond Leddy to Senate Internal Security Sub-Committee, *Communist Threat*, 849.
[54] See Urrutia, 49–53.

appeared in Washington at, no less, the Internal Security Sub-Committee of the U.S. Senate. Before Senators Eastland, Dodd, Olin, Johnston, Hruska and Keating, he gave a series of hair-raising if incoherent and inaccurate[55] accounts of life in Cuba, which greatly titillated these worried legislators – gossip, rumour, private speculation, some true statements, some false.

The achievement of Díaz Lanz, however, was to drive public and official opinion in the U.S. further into distrust of Cuba, and to weaken the liberal opposition in Cuba.[56] If the opponents of Castro were going to the U.S. to testify before a sub-committee known for its intemperance, then they would become traitors immediately, even in the eyes of moderate men. If Díaz Lanz acted thus, why should not Urrutia? Were all moderate men potential witnesses before the Senate? Further, how was it possible that the Senate Internal Security Sub-Committee should receive evidence from the defecting chief of the air force of a presumably friendly foreign country? Surely this suggested that the Senate did not regard Cuba as a foreign country. It followed, therefore, that if there were a persistent revolution in Cuba, the Senate would regard this as rebellion and recommend action accordingly.

The Senate, of course, was not the executive (as Castro acknowledged later), and the executive could not answer for what the legislature did (Eisenhower and Herter pointed out that they were not involved). But perhaps what the legislature thought today the executive might think tomorrow? In fluid political situations small things matter. The 'Díaz Lanz affair' had precisely the opposite effect to what Díaz Lanz probably wanted: the prevention of further radicalization of the regime. It gave Castro another opportunity to head leftwards with impunity.

Even Urrutia had to denounce Díaz Lanz, but it did not save him.[57] On 17 July he woke up to find that Castro had resigned. Going downstairs in the National Palace, he found the cabinet waiting, not knowing what to do. Urrutia tried unsuccessfully to telephone Castro. The cabinet assembled, Castro did not arrive, the ministers dispersed full of rumours. Conrado Bécquer, the sugar workers' leader, one of the many Vicars of Bray of the Cuban revolution, meantime publicly called for Urrutia's resignation. That night, Castro spoke on television. In a long and extraordinary speech he destroyed the president. It was less a speech than an execution. Urrutia 'complicated' government. Urrutia's appointments had been most disturbing. Then there was

[55] For instance, he called the Cuban Labour leader, Salvador, a Communist when he was plainly not.

[56] T. Szulc and K. E. Meyer, *The Cuban Invasion: the Chronicle of a Disaster* (1962), record one minister (perhaps Ray) as telling them, 'This shut us up.'

[57] He retracted this later. See his book, p. 67. On the 16th he had been due to speak again on television but he was told that the space had been sold.

Urrutia's house. There was Urrutia's salary of $40,000 a year, which, unlike that of ministers, had not been reduced; but most important was the blackmail of Communism. Urrutia was fabricating a legend of Communism in order to provoke aggression from abroad; he planned to abandon Cuba to return later and rule it along with a few North Americans. Urrutia was even responsible for removing the name of God from the fundamental law of the Republic. Castro then described himself as 'impotent' and 'defenceless'; 'even now we are hardly able to do any work, having been exhausted since Monday due to the fevered anti-Communist declaration that forced us into our present international position'. The purge of the judges was 'supposed to restore calm among the judiciary but because of rivalries and personal difficulties with a judge who was also his friend, Urrutia had decided on a guillotine'.

While Castro was speaking, messages in support of him began to arrive at the television station, while crowds gathered round the presidential palace, demanding Urrutia's resignation. All the ministers in the cabinet assembled and were prevented from leaving by Martínez Sánchez, the Defence Minister.[58] Urrutia's aide, Captain Aníbal Rodríguez, suggested a desperate resistance. Urrutia, however, thought better of it. He resigned, for the fourth time since January. This time no one stopped him from doing so. He left the palace.[59]

What moral is to be drawn? The assassination of Urrutia's character was merciless. But for thousands of Cubans, for the masses who supported the revolution tooth and nail, an obsessive interest in Communism seemed to involve an alignment with the U.S., the enemies of the revolution, and the friends of the old *status quo*. From now on in Cuba, the expression of anti-Communist views rendered the speaker liable to suspicion and even ultimately to arrest, trial and long-term imprisonment. By this time at least Castro must have decided, whatever sentimental views he may have had earlier, that, as he told Herbert Matthews four years later, the Cuban Communist party 'had men who were truly revolutionary, loyal, honest and trained. I needed them'.[60]

[58] López Fresquet, 125.
[59] Urrutia went to a friend's house, spent some time under house arrest and then took refuge in the Embassy of Venezuela, being permitted afterwards to leave the country with difficulty.
[60] Matthews, *Return to Cuba*, 11.

CHAPTER 35

The Eclipse of the Liberals

Cuba now had no president and technically no prime minister. But Castro retained his hold on public opinion, the armed forces and INRA, and within hours a new president had been sworn. Castro had intended that Miró Cardona, the first premier after January 1959, should be asked to become president, but both Raúl Castro and Guevara thought that such an appointment would merely cause a new crisis within a few months.[1] A more amenable figure was Osvaldo Dorticós, the minister for law revision. He was abler than Urrutia, but of an equally *bourgeois* background: he came from one of the first families of Cienfuegos and was connected with the great Tomás Terry, who had married a great-aunt of his father's. For a time he had been a Communist and secretary to the president of the party, Marinello,[2] but afterwards he had sunk back into middle-class habits, becoming a prosperous lawyer, legal adviser to the Cienfuegos waterworks and commodore of the Cienfuegos Yacht Club. He discreetly worked with the 26 July Movement in Cienfuegos, though his Uncle Pedro, an old member of ABC and a senator, had worked for BANFAIC under Batista; he was now in prison.

Dorticós's colleagues regarded him as 'moderate'. Elena Mederos who sat next to him recalled that, in cabinet meetings, he would sweat with nervousness when Castro launched into an attack on the U.S.[3] Yet Dorticós was to prove invaluable as a nominal leader of the Cuban revolutionary regime. He gave it stability, continuity and formality on the occasions that such things were needed; 'bowing to Castro's every thought', he acted as secretary of the cabinet in an effort to find something to do. He became swiftly known as the one member of the Cabinet to keep office hours, and the only one indeed who was used to regular work.[4]

Castro, meantime, had announced that his political future would be submitted to 'all the people' on 26 July at a big meeting at the Plaza Cívica to commemorate the sixth anniversary of the storming of the

---

[1] This is Pazos's recollection based on contemporary hearsay.
[2] He had stood for the Communists in Cienfuegos in 1950.
[3] Evidence of Elena Mederos.
[4] López Fresquet, 52. Dorticós (b. 1919. Graduated Law School, 1941) remains (1970) president of Cuba.

Moncada barracks. In the intervening days peasants swarmed into Havana, many organized by INRA, many of their own volition. On 23 July a general strike organized by the CTC called for Castro's return to power. On the 26th came the great meeting in the Plaza Cívica, the *concentración campesina*. There was a public holiday. The army paraded. Residents of Havana fought with each other to lodge the countrymen. The huge audience, on the day, of countrymen and townsmen treated the occasion as one of entertainment. President Dorticós began the proceedings by announcing that in response to innumerable requests, Castro would resume as prime minister. The great crowd cheered for several minutes, sang, danced and called revolutionary slogans. Castro then spoke for four hours. He began with the sun high, and continued until after it had sunk behind his head. It was the first of many such occasions. The crowd was mesmerized. Castro, as usual, spoke clearly, without notes, often repeating his points to drive them home without ever quite repeating his phraseology. There were interruptions for dancing and singing as well as shouting '*Viva* Fidel!' There were men selling soft drinks, hats, sandwiches. This was 'direct democracy', the immediate communion between the 'maximum leader' and the people.

Castro had already suggested that his government would, at the very least, keep independent of U.S. diplomatic direction. Such a suggestion was irresistible. Idle to think that the unsophisticated or illiterate find such a policy unappealing. It appeals to the sophisticated and the unsophisticated, rich and poor, with consistent force. Only a few can escape the appeal of patriotism. Idle too, to say that patriotism is absurd for a small country demanding foreign markets and dominated by foreign capital. The absurd is often appealing too. Of course, Grau, even Batista, had promised much the same as Castro. Television and radio, however, gave to tens of thousands the impression that Castro was more determined than his predecessors.

By July, however, there seemed to be more positive changes as well. Castro had early announced a public works programme valued at $M134, to ease unemployment, now believed to be running at 700,000, or 10% of the total population. The Agrarian Reform Institute announced that it would spend $M100 in its first year. The Finance Minister, López Fresquet, announced his 3% income tax on all salaries, large and small, to help to finance the public works programme. The government ordered the oil refineries to raise the petrol price by 5 cents per gallon in order to finance a minimum wage of $85 a month for garage workers (as promised by Batista, though not realized by him). Then there was, of course, the agrarian reform itself. In August, some land began to be distributed to a few landless families. 100,000 families were supposed to receive plots of 67 acres within the next four months, all from large uncultivated estates.

But what did this add up to? If beneficial, of course, it mattered less what the process was called: socialism or democracy, Marxism or liberalism; general descriptions are more usually sought by defenders of ailing systems or their bitter opponents, than by their successful practitioners. Castro had launched the conception of humanism, to see it taken up as a banner by those who opposed Communism. He probably had toyed, however, perhaps was still toying, with remaining internationally neutral, a revolutionary nationalist 'Nasserite' position which, though its relations with the U.S. were distant, still remained far from an alignment with Russia.

There was further the question of the Communist party, which had organization, preparation, confidence and, at its back, a powerful if, as all those who had contact with Spanish Communists anyway knew, a not always predictable ally in Russia. Already the Communists had some position in the Cuban State, already they were Castro's followers, though he was not yet their leader. More positively, by July 1959, after years without a clear creed, Castro seems, under the influence of his brother and Guevara, to have felt increasingly drawn towards the idea of a complete explanation of politics, especially if its merits were constantly put to him by close and stern friends. There was the nagging anxiety that, unless he went to extremes, the *bourgeoisie* would spoil the revolution. Though some of the Communist leaders were, as U.S. critics alleged, wooden and without imagination, others were clever men; the central committee had a wide range of talent on which to draw. By this time, Castro might not have been able to dislodge the Communists even if he had tried. If he could not destroy them, perhaps the only choice was to join them.

Who now looked back with longing to parliamentary government? Apparently not even ex-President Prío. Tony Varona and Grau San Martín were still the only advocates of the democratic system and neither commanded much enthusiasm. If Cuba's liberals had been more united, more resolute and more forthcoming, Castro would have had to reckon with them. But liberals adopted Castro's language. For them, too, he was 'leader and guide'. They were devoted to 'the Revolution' which was after all such a personal achievement of Castro's. They could only be said to represent, at the best, the professional middle class – say 50,000 families, including school teachers, of whom many, especially some of the country school teachers, were hardly *bourgeois* people. They in no way represented the rest of the quite large Cuban middle class – the 100,000 businessmen, merchants, bankers, administrators or directors of enterprises and their families, many of whom were actually unable to distinguish social democracy from Communism, and who regarded Felipe Pazos as a man of the same kidney as Blas Roca. With one or two Whiggish exceptions (such as the Bacardí chief, Pepín Bosch, and the sugar baron, Lobo), they had viewed the revolution with distrust from the start. Castro could never count on them as allies in a great progressive democratic movement. He had, after all, in his speeches, already awakened the political imagination of the masses.

The suggestion that Castro had reached a decision on whether or how to work with the Communists by July 1959 may be exaggerated. But it could not have been long delayed.[5] In discussing all revolutions historians seek turning-points, moments of decision: students of Cuba endlessly seek the precise and dramatic point when all was lost for the liberal reforming cause. No simple moment can be so marked, since it was always unclear precisely how Castro did, in fact, work with the Communists. But it is equally evident that, at some time in the summer of 1959, Castro decided that he could afford to be authoritarian as well as radical, and also cast around for arms; thwarted of success in both Europe and the U.S., he began, at least now if not before, to contemplate an approach to the Soviet Union.

Meantime, after the meeting at the Plaza Cívica on 26 July 1959, the *guajiros* were reluctant to go home. Many of them had never before seen Havana. The shops, the girls, the extraordinary buildings, the ostentatious wealth, all the trappings of indolent living were too much for them. The radio and television implored them to assemble at certain points. Eventually they did so, with military help.

August 1959 began passively, with a plea for patience and understanding by Senator Fulbright in the conduct of U.S. relations with Cuba. Anxiety evidently existed in the minds of Cuban Communists because of the announcement of Khrushchev's visit to the U.S.; many times in that summer, the Cuban Communist paper, *Hoy*, assured its readers that Khrushchev's visit would halt the absurd ideological anti-Communism in the U.S. and so enable Cuba to embark peacefully on economic relations with Russia and other 'Socialist countries'. Another difficult moment occurred between the papers *Revolución* and *Hoy* when the latter accused the former of employing a Mujalista, Angel Cuiña,

[5] It is worthwhile noting that the first accusation, from an admittedly second-hand source, that Castro approached the Soviet Union through the French Embassy in Mexico, was dated July 1959. *Cf.* James, 237, who, on the alleged testimony of the ex-military attaché at the Cuban Embassy in Mexico, Captain Manuel Villafaña, says Ramiro Valdés came twice to Mexico this month. However, Valdés had excellent reasons for going to Mexico, since he was married to a Spanish-Mexican. A more likely emissary was the Communist president, Marinello, who returned to Cuba on 28 July after a visit to Russia, Poland and Czechoslovakia. Visitors to China in 1959 included Violeta Casals (July), Aníbal Escalante (October) and Chomón (November).

as labour editor; *Revolución* responded by accusing Marinello of having sent a copy of his poems to Santiago Rey, Batista's Minister of the Interior, and proving the matter by publishing the *dedication*. On 7 August *habeas corpus* was restored in Cuba; it had been suspended after Batista's fall. Lawyers began to file writs to free about five hundred people held prisoner as counter-revolutionaries, many of them arbitrarily arrested and most casually treated when in gaol.[6]

But this was premature. In mid-August, a plot by cattle farmers was unearthed in Las Villas. This had been devised partly by counter-revolutionaries of Camagüey and backed by Trujillo (it is just possible that the CIA were also involved). The conspirators approached Majors William Morgan, the U.S.-born liberator of Trinidad, and Eloy Gutiérrez Menoyo. Morgan had, since January, been running a frog farm near Trinidad. The plotters tried to bribe the two majors to help them, and both pretended to fall in with these schemes, though it cannot quite be excluded that both of them did indeed really side with the counter-revolution and then turn King's evidence.[7]

Morgan assembled fifty men at Trinidad Airport and dispatched a message to Trujillo saying, 'I hold the town and am fighting off government troops. Send me arms.' To maintain the illusion when the arms and men arrived, Morgan called on his men to shout, 'Down with Castro. Death to the Agrarian Reform', while Gutiérrez Menoyo asked Trujillo for a uniform comparable to *El Benefactor's* own. (Trujillo had asked for a country villa belonging to the editor of *Bohemia* as a price for his help.)[8] Morgan and Castro watched the plotters assembling from under a mango tree. All the invaders were then arrested and many others – perhaps as many as two thousand – were detained in other parts of Cuba. It seemed that a provisional government had been planned, with an ex-Labour minister of Prío's (Hernández Tellaheche) as president, the cattle chief Caíñan Milanés as vice-president, and another landowner, Mestre Gutiérrez, as prime minister. All these men and many others were arrested.[9]

That there was a conspiracy appears certain. That Trujillo was involved is equally clear. From this time on, however, the social benefits conferred by the revolution upon the poor and the landless were accompanied by imprisonments, delayed trials, occasional executions, more and more arbitrary seizures of land and overcrowded prisons. Castro's prisons were no doubt to begin with an improvement on those of

[6] For a description, see John Martino, *I was Castro's Prisoner* (1963).
[7] See Paul Bethel, *Cuba y los Estados Unidos*, 77–87, where the Information officer at the U.S. Embassy describes a meeting with Morgan before the failure of the plot.
[8] López Fresquet, 137–8.
[9] Morgan's U.S. citizenship was afterwards revoked. A recent biographer (R. D. Crassweller, *Trujillo*, 349–51) says that Morgan received $500,000 from Trujillo.

Batista. Torture was unusual, but thoughtlessness, overcrowding and humiliations frequent. The numbers in prison were also already higher than under Batista. Indeed, some who had supported Castro at an earlier stage were already now in gaol. Revolution, like Saturn, was beginning to devour its children.[10] As for the agrarian reform, estates of even medium size began to be taken over; cattle, machinery and even personal objects passed to INRA, which often did not give a receipt for what it took, much less compensation; peasants moving onto the land only gained for the time being *vales* or chits negotiable at the so-called people's stores.

Some days later a meeting of the Council of the Organization of American States was held in Santiago de Chile. Dr Roa was present, his first big conference as Cuban Foreign Minister, but at the last minute his thunder (always, it must be said, a pipe not a rumble) was stolen by the appearance of Raúl Castro, who made a curious figure, with his uniform and long hair in a bun, in comparison with the neat gentlemen of the council. His military aircraft arrived at Santiago without permission and was, for a time, held at the airport. He had come, he said, to 'give the boys a trip' and escort Dr Roa home. The only person pleased to see him, however, seemed to be the Chilean Socialist, Salvador Allende, along with crowds of enthusiastic lower-class Chileans. Other Latin American democrats, such as Betancourt, were chilly; Betancourt, indeed, was already telling friends privately that Castro was 'an evil influence in Latin America'.[11]

The conference concerned itself firstly with the problem of the Dominican Republic; the suggestion was made for an American peace commission to go there. Roa agreed; fearful of the precedent, Raúl Castro, however, said that the revolutionary government would certainly not admit any OAS investigation in Cuba. He added that in Cuba there would be a plebiscite within six months to decide when elections would be held. Elsewhere, the U.S. government remained at odds as to how to approach Cuba; for instance, an unedifying quarrel broke out between Wieland, still at his unenviable post on the Caribbean desk in the Department of State, who maintained that Castro was not a Communist, and the U.S. air attaché in Mexico, Colonel Glawe, who called Wieland himself 'either a fool or a Communist'.[12]

[10] Though it would be five years before Castro used this same metaphor and denied its applicability.

[11] Szulc and Meyer, 21.

[12] The whole curious incident can be read in *Communist Threat*, 845, 806–7, 797–98; and Wieland, *ibid.*, 602. This argument occurred in an aeroplane between Mexico and Mazatlán, during a 'briefing' for Dr Milton Eisenhower, the president's brother, a U.S. representative who had become a progressive influence on U.S. policy towards Latin America.

For the time being, however, these gyrations in the U.S. administration were not allowed to affect economic relations. Thus the U.S. Department of Agriculture, when revising the annual sugar quotas, gave Cuba a slightly increased tonnage along with the U.S. mainland producers. This was in the light of the still low sugar prices – world prices reached their lowest point in eighteen years in July (2·55 cents, whereas the minimum price for economic sugar farming in Cuba was thought to be 3·25 cents).

Inside Cuba, a group of small sugar planters petitioned the government to take over about a quarter of the 161 sugar mills, on the ground that they were behind in paying their debts to the *colonos*. But the low prices were of course adding to the mill owners' difficulties too: they could not even afford to pay for repairs. For the time being, the government only took over the *Macagua* mill, in addition to the eleven which they already ran because of their past ownership by Batista or his friends. The sugar industry limped onwards in bad shape, preparing for the second harvest of the revolution, to begin in January. The INRA production director, Pino Santos, comfortingly if meaninglessly, said that Cuba would follow an 'aggressive sugar policy'.

In September the government embarked anyway on an aggressive tariff policy: taxes on imports were laid – up to 30% on food, 40% on typewriters and office machines, 60% on cheap cars and some household items, and 80% on expensive cars. Import permits were henceforth generally required and foreign exchange restricted. The mood was to be one of austerity. Castro attacked alcoholism as 'a vice worse than all others combined', and imposed heavy taxes on drink. Yet at the same time, contradictorily, there was an attempt to revive tourism. Carlos Almoina, the head of the Tourist Institute,[13] announced a crash programme designed to boost investment in hotels, and a new jet airport, and plans were made for a big tourist conference the following month. Since, of course, nearly all tourists came from the U.S., this naturally meant an appeal for good relations.

In September indeed it was as if the regime, on the brink of drastic reconsideration of alliances, drew back, to allow moderate men such as Almoina to propose moderate plans. Euclides Vázquez Candela, the sub-director of *Revolución*, carried on a new polemic with the Communists.[14] Since June Castro had been attending, as prime minister, regular meetings of his economic advisers and economic ministers every Thursday – though he had always hitherto avoided any discussion of

[13] Almoina, a young intellectual of a *bourgeois* Spanish background, joined the U.S. army in the 1950s through disgust at the factionalism of the revolutionaries. (He later joined the opposition to Castro, was captured, condemned to death, reprieved and imprisoned.)

[14] *Cf. Revolución*, 10 September 1959, in which he argued that if Cantillo had formed his junta in mid-1958, the Communists would have supported him.

Cuba's economic relations with the U.S.[15] There was even an amiable meeting on 5 September between Bonsal and Castro. (Bonsal had forced the interview, after waiting since July, by saying that he was off to Washington for 'more than routine consultations'.) This meeting was relaxed and Bonsal left in a moderately hopeful mood; Castro said that the U.S. government should not pay too much attention to 'the propaganda excesses of young people working in an atmosphere of revolutionary enthusiasm'.[16] Relations between the two countries were held, however, at a nervous level by Admiral Burke, chief of naval operations, always one for tough action in the Caribbean: Soviet submarines, he announced, had been sighted in the Caribbean and the whole area was menaced by Communism. The admiral had indeed decided by now that Castro was a Communist, on the grounds that the Russians were interested in control of the world sea lanes such as Indonesia, Egypt, and now Cuba: 'the narrow places of the continents spelled danger.'[17]

In Cuba itself, López Fresquet, the Finance Minister, discussed for a long time with Hubert Matos the question of Communism and the revolution: unlike Burke, Matos did not think Castro a Communist. The Finance Minister and Matos thereupon agreed to work together 'to stop Communism, but devised no concrete plans'.[18] The same month Castro came down with his brother and Cienfuegos to Santa Clara and sacked the 26 July provincial leader (Joaquín Torres) and the heads of the army and of the INRA in the province (Demetrio Montseny and Suárez Gayol), substituting, not so much Communists, as unconditional supporters of themselves.[19] Matos, increasingly isolated in Camagüey, the most prominent and well placed of the army leaders willing to oppose Communism, had indeed done nothing before a new INRA chief, Captain Jorge Enrique Mendoza, was sent at the end of the month to increase the pace of agrarian reform in the province. Mendoza, an ex-law student and Ortodoxo, and a news reader on Radio Rebelde in the Sierra Maestra (who had first been appointed to INRA in Oriente), was, though not an old Communist, clearly not (as events were to show) a man to protest against the direction of the regime.[20]

Castro now, in the early autumn, seems to have tried vaguely to

[15] Evidence of Felipe Pazos.
[16] Bonsal, *Foreign Affairs*, January 1967.
[17] The admiral in conversation with the author, 26 December 1962.
[18] James, 167.
[19] These were, respectively, an old friend of Raúl Castro's, 'Nicaragua' (Carlos Iglesias), Orlando Puertas and Manuel Borgés (evidence of Joaquín Torres). All three of these were in Raúl Castro's column in the Sierra Cristal. Montseny remained in Cuba, Torres went into exile. Suárez Gayol, not the type of revolutionary ever to feel satisfied with the Revolution which he had achieved, went to Bolivia with Guevara where he was killed in 1967. He had been in touch with Matos earlier on.
[20] Mendoza later became editor of the government paper *Granma*, in 1967, and retains that post (1970).

reunite his followers: Cuba, he said, would have elections within four years. But to hold them sooner would only distract the Cubans from their main task of ending unemployment. He added that he would resign as soon as public opinion moved against him. At that time, however, he thought that 80 % of the population was with him. Doubtless there he was right.[21] But there is nothing to suggest the seriousness of his talk of elections. In September, thwarted in the search for arms from the U.S., Cuba asked England for seventeen Hunter jet fighters. Mr Selwyn Lloyd, the Foreign Secretary, was undecided. The U.S. apparently asked her ally not to sell and, after some weeks of further uncertainty, she agreed not to do so.[22] A pattern in Cuba similar to that which had occurred four years before in Egypt seemed about to develop and perhaps this was the really decisive moment for the history of the regime. Guevara, meantime, returned from his Afro-Asian tour, bearing rather unprofitable treaties with Egypt and Ceylon. Guevara praised most of the countries to which he had been except India, whose development, he thought, was kept back by 'cows and religion'. Yugoslavia, he added, was the country advancing fastest: a comment which some people thought significant. One journalist referred to him, prematurely, as a 'Titoist', but there is other evidence to suggest that Guevara had been greatly impressed by non-Communist countries during his tour – even by Japan, whose development he admired.[23] The Cuban Communists were back on a most moderate line: Blas Roca, at another plenary session of the party's central committee, spoke of the dangers of 'leftism', when the Cuban revolution depended more than other revolutions on the international situation and Cuba itself on imports. This was doubtless a reflection of the international mood set by Khrushchev's visit to the U.S.[24]

On 12 October the U.S. replied to the Cuban Note of 15 June on agrarian reform: Whatever the wrong-doings of the Batista regime, U.S. investors should not be penalized for actions for which they had no responsibility, nor did those actions provide the Cuban government with a valid reason for ignoring international law and the basic law of

[21] The last public opinion survey was held in late June. The cabinet was in session when the survey was made and the results were brought to Castro there, showing a decline from a February figure of 91·85% to 78·31%. The ministers seemed alarmed; Castro said 'we are still doing fine; at the end we will have only the children with us' (López Fresquet, 56).

[22] See discussion in the House of Lords, 2 December 1959. The Cuban government asked for a replacement of the 17 Sea Furies sold to Batista by an equal number of Hunter jet fighters. The British government rejected the request on the ground that 'the supply of jet aircraft . . . would introduce a new factor into a still very delicate situation'. The British government explicitly denied that the decision was reached after U.S. pressure.

[23] Luis Simón MSS, 286.

[24] Hoy, 7–8 October 1959. Khrushchev arrived in the U.S. on 15 September and the famous Camp David meeting, the high point perhaps of the era of co-existence, between Hungary and the U2 crisis of 1960, was on 25 September.

Cuba. The Japanese agrarian bonds had been used to pay Japanese landholders (Cuba had alluded to MacArthur's agrarian reform which provided compensation in bonds) and not foreign owners. The U.S. was, therefore, preparing to press her demands.

The exiles were also busy in early October, particularly carrying out flights over Cuba from Florida. On 11 October one aircraft dropped three bombs on a sugar mill in Pinar del Río, the first of many such occasions. Cuba protested to the U.S. Had the hard line won in Washington to such an extent that the government or the CIA were now prepared to help the exiles with arms, as Vice-President Nixon had proposed?[25] Despite the wealth of information which later flowed out of the U.S. on the subject of the administration's relations with the Cuban exiles, no evidence suggests that the U.S. government approved of CIA support for Cuban exiles before mid-March 1960.[26] But what if it did not approve? Agents of the CIA were sometimes prone to self-assertion even against the line of U.S. policy. What if someone in the administration nodded, either in sleep or silent approval, of limited support for the exiles? Possibly the CIA anticipated a decision which it felt certain would come. Among twenty men captured by the government in Pinar del Río two were U.S. pilots; the whole group had been supplied from Florida, no doubt unofficially, as the U.S. government said, but how unofficial was the CIA in Miami?[27] It is not possible yet to say for certain.

On 15 October, Martínez Sánchez, Raúl Castro's old advocate-general who had been Minister of Defence and as such had assisted the reorganization of the armed forces to give the key commands to Castro's faithful supporters, was moved to an equally sensitive post, the Ministry of Labour. Raúl Castro now joined the cabinet as Minister for the Armed Forces. At the same time, the moderate Minister of Labour, Manuel Fernández, dropped from sight, and on 17 October the Cuban ambassador in Washington plainly hinted for the first time in public that if Cuba were thwarted in her demands for arms from the British and the U.S. she might turn elsewhere – perhaps to Russia. On 15 October, too, there occurred the last of the regular Thursday meetings between Castro and his economic advisers and ministers: a recent meeting had spent itself entirely in an attempt by the advisers to persuade Castro to keep a dinner engagement which he had made a month before with a group of powerful businessmen. He excused himself, saying, 'for those people, I have no message';[28] succeeding events suggest that the die was now cast.

[25] Dewart thinks so, Cf. 45–6.
[26] But López Fresquet (136–7 and 168–9) says that the so-called Double Checker Corporation of Florida, which was used for the employ of U.S. pilots in the Bay of Pigs invasion and which had been incorporated on 14 May 1959, was already a CIA cover, and had been involved even in the Trujillo plot of June 1959. See Miami Herald, 5 March 1963.
[27] See Time, 26 October 1959.
[28] 'Es que para estos señores yo no tengo mensaje' (Carrillo MSS).

The first major crisis in the regime since the scandal over Urrutia in July now came with the resignation of Matos, the military governor of Camagüey, on the ground that the revolution was being infiltrated by Communists. In his later trial he agreed that he had been talking of the need for a 'National Directory' of the 26 July Movement. Fourteen officers resigned with him. Matos took his decision because of Raúl Castro's appointment. He wrote on 19 October to Castro:

I do not want to become an obstacle to the revolution and believe that, before choosing between adapting myself and resignation to avoid doing harm, it is honest and 'revolutionary' to leave. I think that, after the substitution of Duque[29] and others, whoever has had the frankness to speak to you of the Communist problem should do so. . . . I can conceive of the revolution's triumph only with the nation united. It is right, however, to recall to you that great men begin to decline when they cease to be just. I only organized the Cienaguilla expedition [in the Sierra] . . to defend the rights of the country. If after all, I am held to be ambitious or conspiratorial, it would be a reason not merely for leaving the Revolution but for regretting that I was not one of the many comrades who died in the struggle. I hope you will understand that my decision (which I have considered a long time) is irrevocable. Also I request you, speaking not as Major Matos, but simply as one of your comrades of the Sierra – you remember! – as one of those who set out determined to die in carrying out your orders, that you will agree to my request as soon as possible, allowing me to return home as a civilian, without having my sons afterwards learn in the street that their father is a traitor or a deserter. Wishing you every kind of success for yourself and in your revolutionary efforts for the country . . . I remain ever your comrade, Hubert Matos.[30]

This somewhat passive challenge (coinciding with another mysterious air raid from Florida) infuriated Castro, who denounced Matos in public. Perhaps Matos hoped to force Castro to make a clear declaration of his political aims. He apparently believed that Castro was unaware of the Communist conspiracy directed by Raúl Castro, who, he had told the Finance Minister, was ready to kill his brother, if need be.[31] The next day, anyway, Castro ordered the occupation of the city of Camagüey by the armed forces of the province. He perhaps feared an

[29] Mendoza's predecessor as INRA commander in Camagüey.
[30] Text in Guilbert, 127–8. The letter was published in *Prensa Libre* at the end of the month.
[31] López Fresquet, 130; López Fresquet and Matos had met on 5 September and Matos repeated the same to Andrés Valdespino on 6 September. On 29 September he had complained directly to Castro of the influence of communism. (B. Viera, *Bohemia Libre*, 11 December 1960.)

immediate U.S. invasion. Matos, sitting at his home, waited calmly for the storm. He penned another delphic communication, to be delivered to the country after his arrest:

> The risk I run does not matter. I believe that I have the courage and the serenity to face all contingencies . . . it is preferable to die rather than turn one's back on the values which animate the cause of truth, reason and justice. You spoke yesterday of my being in league with Díaz Lanz and God knows who, trying to stab the Revolution in the back . . . Very well, Fidel, I await calmly what you decide. You know I have the courage to pass twenty years in prison . . . I shall not order my soldiers . . . to open a single burst of fire against anyone, not even against the cut-throats you may send. I hope that History will give them their recompense, that History will judge, just as you once said that History will judge you too, Fidel . . .[32]

The courage of Matos was admirable, though his passivity well expresses the weakness of the liberal opponents of the new course. They could not bring themselves to desert the revolution; therefore, they could not desert Castro since Castro was the revolution.

On 20 October Castro came down to Camagüey with a group of followers to arrest Matos in person, as a 'traitor who had obstructed Agrarian Reform'. A great number of people came into the city that day as if to a carnival. Castro began speaking into a microphone the moment that he arrived at the airport, and marched towards Matos's headquarters. A crowd collected behind him. They arrived at the gates of the headquarters. Matos, waiting with his officers, could no doubt have shot them down. He did not do so. He went into captivity without a struggle. His officers followed too, though one, Manuel Fernández, later killed himself in despair.

Castro and Matos returned to Havana; Camilo Cienfuegos remained to take over Matos's command and broadcast a fiery denunciation of him. The following day the whole 26 July Movement executive in Camagüey resigned. The provincial coordinator, Joaquín Agramonte, was arrested. In the evening, apparently unconnected with the events at Camagüey, the ex-commander of the air force, Díaz Lanz, flew a two-engined B25 bomber from Florida over Havana and dropped thousands of leaflets signed by him, claiming that Castro was a Communist. A Cuban aircraft was sent up to shoot him down. Some bombs were thrown on the ground. In the confusion, it was thought that these had been dropped from the air. This is improbable. A Cuban frigate fired at the aircraft. Two people were killed, forty-five wounded, all no doubt as a result of the Cubans' own actions. Díaz Lanz's aircraft was one of several origin-

---

[32] This document was secretly circulated and is published in Guilbert, 128.

ally bought by Batista in the U.S. but never handed over to him; later it had been delivered by a U.S. sheriff to a Batistiano captain. The U.S. government afterwards admitted that it was a military aeroplane, though they argued that bombs could not be dropped from it. This, however, was never ascertained.[33] The Cuban Government published a pamphlet entitled *Havana's Pearl Harbor*, with a photograph on the title page purporting to show an air battle over the capital; this proved to be a *photomontage* and in fact it depicted U.S. C.54s over New Jersey in 1947.

Castro himself was in Havana at this time, addressing the Travel Agents' Conference. He went immediately to the television station to denounce the U.S. for at least passive complicity. A drunkard, Roberto Salas Hernández, tried unsuccessfully to kill him with a knife. Castro banned all night flights to Cuba, suspended *habeas corpus* once more and announced a plan to gather a volunteer army of workers – the origin of the later famous revolutionary militia. The travel agents remained at the Hilton Hotel, regally entertained. The president of ASTA, however, said: 'It is absolutely . . . no use to offer . . . tourists, splendid hotels, casinos, sumptuous night clubs, entertainments of all sorts . . . unless [he] . . . feels that he is coming to a place where he will be welcome.'[34] It was indeed hard to believe that this was the case when on 23 October *Revolución* came out with headlines as large as those which might have proclaimed a world war: 'THE AEROPLANES CAME FROM THE U.S.A.'

That day was one of travail for the surviving liberals in the cabinet. Felipe Pazos, the director of the National Bank, calling on President Dorticós for other reasons, said that, if Matos were being arrested for opposing Communism, so should he be; and was not too much fuss being paid to the pamphleteering raids? Dorticós replied that it might seem so, but they had to think of the rest of the world. Pazos said that he was not interested in the rest of the world but in Cuba. He also wished to resign. Dorticós said that he would raise the question in the cabinet.

Dorticós told the cabinet that Pazos had tried to recruit him to rebel against Castro. All the prominent Fidelistas thereupon demanded vigorous action against Pazos; Raúl Castro was in favour of execution. Pazos's supposed friends, the economists Boti and Cepero Bonilla, were silent. Eventually, on López Fresquet's initiative, it was decided to summon Pazos to the cabinet.[35] Pazos was undecided what to do. He

[33] See *New York Times*, 10 November 1959. The charge of bombs seems disposed of by the knowledge that, while they were supposed to be falling, Raúl Castro and Dorticós were watching a beautiful grass-skirted Hawaiian doing a belly dance in the Havana Hilton Hotel as part of the Travel Agents' Conference (see *Spectator* (London), 4 December 1959).

[34] *H.A.R.*, xii, 545.

[35] López Fresquet, 60–1.

thought of resigning due to ill-health and went to his doctor, who gave him a typhoid injection to give the appearance of fever.[36] In the cabinet, Matos's execution was also proposed. The leading moderates still in the cabinet – Ray, López Fresquet, Faustino Pérez – opposed this scheme. Castro insisted to the cabinet that he was an anti-Communist, and virtually succeeded in persuading his hearers that that was so. At least they did not resign. Castro put his arm round Ray's shoulders and said, 'Have confidence in me';[37] and, indeed, they did. Everyone contrived to confide in Castro. They believed him to be the arbiter, for he said different things to different people. Thus, to the board of the newspaper *Revolución* he said, 'What Che and Raúl have done in the Army [i.e. favouring Communists] borders on treason.'[38] Castro had by now got to know everyone's personal views and friendships so that he was able to play upon their sensitivities. On the other hand, cabinet meetings now became much more infrequent; indeed, there seem only to have been two more between November and late March 1960.[39] Decisions were taken elsewhere.

On 25 October Castro addressed half a million people brought by the labour unions to the front of the Presidential Palace: 'What reason have they for attacking Cuba? What crime have we committed? What has the Cuban people done to merit such attacks? . . . I ask the people if we have not achieved the most honest government in Cuba's history? . . . if they approve the execution of the war criminals . . . the abolition of sinecures?' . . . And so on. The cumulative effect of this rhetoric was overwhelming. The 'moderates' quivered. Pazos remained undecided, reflecting with Halifax that 'the angry buzz of a multitude is one of the bloodiest noises in the world'. But before a decision came on his fate, there was a new sensation: Camilo Cienfuegos, the man best loved in Cuba after Castro, the romantic cavalryman, the commander-in-chief of the army, the most loyal of the loyal, who had taken over from Matos in Camagüey, was lost over the sea in a flight to Havana. The country ceased work while an abortive search was carried out, but Cienfuegos was never found. Foul play was immediately suspected. Was not Cienfuegos anti-Communist? Had he been killed by Raúl Castro personally in a fit of jealousy? For these allegations, no evidence has been forthcoming. Castro certainly seemed upset and surprised when his brother brought the news to a cabinet meeting,[40] but then he was an excellent actor, and one observer who accompanied Castro on a search for Cienfuegos by air later recalled that Castro seemed in fact in no way

---

[36] All this derives from Pazos.
[37] Ray's evidence.
[38] *Ibid.*
[39] López Fresquet, 59.
[40] *Ibid.*, 58 and private information.

upset by the course of events and spent no time at all in the actual search. Cienfuegos had vigorously supported the arrest of Matos, at least in public. There is no evidence to suppose that he had any strong political views of any kind.[41] Indeed, Cienfuegos appears, on the contrary, to have been the leading member of that group of ex-officers of the Sierra who, without ideology and without any specially marked social origins, would always be loyal to Castro as a man through all his intellectual changes and accidents.

The search for Cienfuegos lasted several days. On the second day, false news came that he had been found. There was wild enthusiasm, and a holiday was proclaimed. But by early November the search was called off. Cienfuegos was presumed lost. He became a new martyr of the revolution. It was meantime understood that Matos would soon be tried. Revolutionary tribunals were reinstated and it was made clear that Pazos would be allowed to leave the bank for an embassy abroad.

The government of the U.S. had observed these developments with perplexity. It was no doubt harder for them to control flights to Cuba from Florida than Castro thought, though it was certainly easier than they had themselves at first said, as became clear when, on 27 October, they caused it to be a criminal act to leave the U.S. to further civil strife in any other nation and sent to Miami an extra hundred immigration agents. The Florida authorities sympathized generally with the exiles; and, though Díaz Lanz was soon arrested, a Miami judge refused to extradite him. At Havana, Bonsal and the embassy were still behaving with maximum caution, exchanging Notes with the Cuban foreign ministry over flights from Florida, Bonsal seeing Dorticós, though not Castro. On 27 October Bonsal had delivered a Note to Dorticós charging Cuba with deliberate efforts to 'replace traditional friendship with enmity'.[42] But this was a vague accusation. In Washington no one quite knew what to do: 'What is eating Premier Castro?' Eisenhower was asked at a press conference on 28 October. The president replied with no doubt genuine uncertainty:

I have no idea of discussing possible motivations of such a man . . . certainly I am not qualified to go into such an abstruse and difficult

[41] Speculation about Cienfuegos' death has continued. The chief argument of those who allege foul play is that Cienfuegos's aide, Major Naranjo, was shortly afterwards killed and *his* assassin, Major Beatón, also killed in 1960. A nurse, later found insane, said in Miami in 1960 that she had nursed Cienfuegos in a Havana clinic. Roberto de Cárdenas, captain of the base from which Cienfuegos was supposed to have taken off, suggested that the flight was a put-up job, that no one saw Cienfuegos in the aeroplane, and that several others either killed themselves or were overpowered (see *La Vanguardia* (Lima) 16 August 1960). No doubt this is one of the many matters that history will elucidate, though, judging from such mysteries as to who killed General Prim in 1870 it is entirely possible that it will get no further than journalism.
[42] Department of State Memorandum, 27 October.

subject as that . . . here [after all] is a country that you believe, on the basis of our history, would be one of our real friends. . . . It would seem to be a puzzling matter to figure just exactly why the Cubans would now be, and the Cuban Government would be, so unhappy when, after all, their principal market is right here. . . .'[43]

By this time, the U.S. administration was already beginning to wonder whether to continue the sugar quota.[44] But a week after this press conference by Eisenhower, General Cabell, deputy director of the CIA, testified firmly to the Senate that the CIA gave evidence that

Castro is not a Communist . . . the Cuban Communists do not consider him a Communist party member or even a pro-Communist . . . It is questionable whether the Communists desire to recruit Castro into the Communist party, that they could do so if they wished or that he would be susceptible to Communist discipline if he joined.[45]

Though this comfortable news was not made generally known, on 13 November, Cuba, replying to the U.S. Note of 27 October, amicably described her desire to live in peace with the U.S. but adjured the U.S. not to identify herself with the financial interests of a few unrepresentative U.S. citizens and to stop the counter-revolutionary activities; the economic problem between Cuba and the U.S. was not just a matter of land reform: the 'historical reality of the present Revolution' had to be recognized and, in return, Cuba would recognize the historic reality of her links with the U.S.

The Note does not seem to have been answered. Had in fact the U.S. made its decision to oppose revolutionary Cuba *coûte que coûte*? Not yet. After all, there remained in Cuba many redoubts of *bourgeois* values. The most prominent, curiously enough, was the labour organization.

The condition of the Cuban unions had not changed during 1959; the leaders had consistently backed the government, but had boycotted those men known to be Communists. The unions were not, however, likely to make a vigorous challenge on behalf of the free system. The credit of many of the leaders was low because of past collaboration with Mujal or Batista. Some had only narrowly escaped being tried as Batistianos. Others were anxious through some new display of zeal to work their passage back to what now passed for respectability. The whole history of Cuban labour made such men likely to react defensively, selfishly and uncreatively to demands made on them by any progressive

[43] Qu. Szulc and Meyer, 39.
[44] D. D. Eisenhower, *Waging Peace* (1966), 524.
[45] *Communist Threat*, 162-3. General Charles Cabell (born 1903), director of plans, U.S. Strategic Air Force, 1944; director of operations, Mediterranean Allied Forces, 1944–45; deputy director of CIA since 1953.

government. If they had handed themselves over *en bloc* to Batista in 1952, it was not surprising that, despite their apparently strong position, they should, in 1959, be a rather easy prey for the Communists.

On 18 November 1959, the CTC held its Tenth Congress. Out of 3,000 delegates only about 260 were formally Communists. At the first session three Communists were included by the secretary-general, Salvador, on a list of thirteen nominees for the Executive Committee. Fights broke out everywhere. Castro had to be brought to restore order. No doubt this was contrived, though no one could have foreseen that the CTC would react quite like the madhouse to which Castro compared it. The Communists shouted 'Unity, Unity!', while the 26 July Movement replied with the accusation '*Melones, Melones!*' ('Melons'), the suggestion being that the Communists were pretending to be like the water melon, olive-green on the outside, the colour of the Fidelista uniforms, but red inside.[46] Castro explained that the Communists were included because of 'the needs of unity', But afterwards the CTC voted overwhelmingly against the three Communists, though Salvador supported them. Castro then instructed Salvador to draw up another list in the name of 'Unity'. The known Communists were excluded, but so too were well-known anti-Communists such as Reinol García, the Catholic Youth leader who had been international secretary of the CTC since January. The old Communist trade union leader of the 1940s, Lázaro Peña, reappeared in the corridors of the Congress and he and Raúl Castro did their best to discredit another secretariat member, Octavio Louit Cabrera, by privately showing around an old letter in which he asked Batista's police for release on the grounds that after torture he had adequately cooperated with them. Manolo Fernández, the anti-Communist secretary-general of the actors' union, was similarly discredited by the rather obvious trick of showing a photograph of him with a group of Batista officers.[47] Louit (who remained on the executive) was thus replaced as organization secretary by Jesús Soto, whose anti-Communism was later shown to be only skin-deep, and Gonzales, the international secretary, by Odón Alvarez de la Campa, a man similarly placed intellectually. Both these men appear to have been mesmerized by Raúl Castro.[48] The newspaper *Revolución*, the organ of the 26 July Movement, changed over and for good, during the course of these events, from a cautious hostility towards the Communists to an even more circumspect approval of their

[46] Two years later (both in 1959 and 1961), the Minister of Labour Martínez Sánchez, boasted, 'we will continue to be "*melones*" since we shall continue to be green outside and red within' (*Revolución*, 27 November 1961).

[47] Rodríguez Quesada, *Salvador*, 16. (Rodríguez Quesada was a delegate to the Congress.)

[48] The Executive was now composed of Octavio Louit, Conrado Bécquer, and José Pellón (thought to be all anti-Communists); and Soto, José María de Aguilera and Alvarez de la Campa, thought to be intellectually neutral. Aguilera, an opportunist, had always presented himself as 'a devout Catholic' (Andrés Valdespino, *Bohemia Libre*, 4 December 1960).

activities, and of the principle of 'revolutionary unity' with them. Castro seems himself not to have made any more hostile comments about them.

For the time being, however, it seemed that the Communists had been kept out. Indeed, the *New York Times* published its report of the Congress under the headline, 'Reds Frozen Out by Cuban Unions'. As a result, the Congress was ready to make a number of concessions to the Communists' point of view, an attitude anyway urged by Salvador in the name of nationalism. Thus the CTC withdrew from the American Labour Confederation (to which the AFL-CIO was affiliated), and proposed the creation of a new 'revolutionary confederation of Latin American workers'. This resolution was generally popular and strongly advocated by Salvador. Though few realized it at the time, the CTC was now half way towards recapture by the Communists, despite the fact that the party withdrew its delegates from most of the discussions and despite the castigation of the new executive (including 'such notorious Mujalistas as Octavio Louit Cabrera') by Lázaro Peña.[49] In fact, the executive excluded the stronger characters among the anti-Communists in the CTC and included a number of easily subornable bureaucrats.

At the end of the Congress, on 25 November, several more liberal ministers were dismissed from the cabinet, the issue really being the still unresolved matter of Hubert Matos, despite the fact that the minister involved, Faustino Pérez, denied it. Both Pérez and Manuel Ray had violent quarrels with Castro at the cabinet meeting, the latter saying that he doubted the truth of the accusation leading to Matos's arrest.[50] Manuel Ray then gave way at the Ministry of Public Works to Camilo Cienfuegos's brother Osmani (who had been chief of military education and was certainly very close to the Communist party), and went first to teach architecture at the university, afterwards to open opposition. Faustino Pérez, one of Castro's oldest followers, was replaced at the Ministry of Stolen Property by an ex-naval captain, Díaz Aztaraín, who had been discharged for conspiracy by Batista and whom Castro had made a captain of corvettes. He had married a sister of Raúl Castro's wife Vilma Espín de Castro, though nepotism could not be suspected as a cause of his promotion: at this moment the eldest of Castro's brothers, Ramón, who now ran the family estate, was engaged in a public quarrel with the regime. On 25 November, he had written a letter to *Prensa Libre*, denouncing the government and defending *Prensa Libre* itself, which had been accused of 'counter-revolutionary' views.

[49] *Hoy*, 25 November 1959.
[50] López Fresquet, 150–1, has an account. According to Ray (*Bohemia Libre*, 26 November 1960), Raúl Castro on this occasion said that the 26 July Movement had fulfilled its task in the fight with Batista and that there was no more need for it.

This third reorganization of government also confirmed the disappearance of Pazos from the National Bank to take up a nominal appointment as ambassador to the European Economic Community, and his substitution by Guevara, no less, who, since his return from his travels abroad, had directed the Industrial Development section of INRA. This change caused a financial panic and a run on the banks. Guevara announced, however, that he would follow Pazos's policies, and Castro blandly assured López Fresquet that Guevara would be more conservative than Pazos. But the consequences of Pazos's resignation were more serious for the regime than Castro could have imagined. Most of Pazos's best assistants, such as José Antonio Guerra and Ernesto Betancourt (the 26 July Movement's man in Washington before 1959), also left. (The vice-president, Justo Carrillo, Pazos's contemporary, had already gone.) Several of these officials stayed to hand over to Guevara and his aides, but their resignation – not all left Cuba – meant the disappearance of the liberal wing of the revolution, the genuine reformers who were also respected in Washington. For these and other reasons, it was now that Bonsal concluded that 'we could not expect to reach any sort of understanding' with Castro.[51]

The loss of so many technical advisers became immediately a source of anxiety to the government. After all, for Castro and his friends it was not a matter of running an existing society successfully but of changing society. A number of socialist or progressive advisers were brought in from the rest of Latin America, among them many Chileans, such as the economist, Jacques Chonchol, a Christian Democrat economist who acted as U.N. adviser to INRA, and Alban Lataste, a social economist who worked in the industrial section of INRA. But this was not enough, and the shortage of skilled administrators and planners was evidently an extra reason for a turn towards the East in search of aid.

Contact to this end must have been made in mid- or late November, for the Russian vice-president, Mikoyan,[52] was then in Mexico and was apparently called on by the sub-secretary of External Commerce, Héctor Rodríguez Llompart.[53]

On the surface, Cuba still had in late November 1959 several moderate ministers. Thus, of those appointed in January 1959, Boti was still at the Ministry of Economy, Hart at the Ministry of Education, López

[51] Letter to Schlesinger, previously cited.

[52] Anastas Ivanovich Mikoyan (b. 1895). Member of the Communist Party since 1915, and of the Central Committee of the Soviet Communist party since 1923. Member of the Praesidium 1935–66. In 1959 First Deputy Chairman of the USSR Council of Ministers.

[53] James, 249. Since Mikoyan arrived in Havana in February to conclude a commercial treaty, it is obvious that some negotiations with Russia must have been opened about two months earlier and this is the most suggestive occasion: at the time, indeed, *Revolución* made two pointed proposals for a visit by Mikoyan to Havana on 3 November and 17 November.

Fresquet at the Finance Ministry, Oltuski at the Ministry of Communications, Camacho at Transport, Luis Buch secretary to the cabinet and Cepero Bonilla at the Commerce Ministry. The Ministry of Justice was held by Alfredo Yabur, no revolutionary, and several of the other ministers such as Raquel Pérez de Miret (social welfare), or Serafín Ruiz de Zárate (health), could scarcely be regarded as dangerous by even the most suspicious. But ministers counted for little. Thus some of them, like Hart or Yabur, Dorticós or Raúl Roa, despite middle-class backgrounds, would follow Castro all through the 1960s. There were too other ministers more obviously revolutionary, apart from the Castro brothers, such as Guevara, Naranjo (the new Minister of the Interior), Martínez Sánchez, Miret and Osmani Cienfuegos.[54] The political police, the hated G.2, now almost as feared in *bourgeois* circles as Batista's SIM had been, was headed by Ramiro Valdés, of Moncada and the *Granma*, an intimate of Guevara's with whom he had been in Las Villas. The ordinary police was still under Ameijeiras, Castro's enthusiastic admirer. Of the even nominally leading members of the government, only López Fresquet now had serious qualms about the direction being taken by the regime, yet he was still as Castroist as Castro. Others were able to adapt themselves with surprising ease to the revolution and its consequences, even for instance to accept that at the end of November *habeas corpus* should finally and indefinitely be suspended; and there were many new arrests on suspicion of conspiracy at both ends of the island.

At the same time a number of new laws were directed against foreign firms. Foreign oil concessionaries thus had now to drill on their properties and not hold them against a distant future. Sixty per cent of their earnings had to go to the government (that is, slightly more than was the case in the Middle East). More cattle lands were seized. The King Ranch's big properties were triumphantly converted into a co-operative. Cattle feed was impossible to get except through INRA, so cattle had to be sold. Another law of November 1959 empowered the state to take over firms which found themselves in difficulties or tried to cut their losses by reducing production; this enabled the government to carry out many nationalizations, in particular of hotels. Land belonging to Bethlehem Steel and to International Harvester was also seized. Most of these seizures were outside the dictates of the agrarian reform, though the first land titles were handed out by Castro to the deserving small peasants on 9 December. Early in December, Núñez Jiménez was in Europe trying to negotiate a $M100 loan; he failed, perhaps because of U.S. pressure.[55] Perhaps had he been successful the pace of change in

---

[54] All these save Martínez Sánchez (who resigned after attempting suicide in 1965) were members of the Central Committee of the new Cuban Communist party in the late 1960s.

[55] *New York Times*, 5 December 1959.

Cuba might have slowed down. Among those upon whom he called in Europe was General Franco who, on being told that the Revolution was meeting difficulties because of the desire of the U.S. to be compensated for the expropriated *latifundios*, adjured him several times, 'Don't pay them a penny, not a penny'.[56] On 10 December Secretary of State Herter made vague threats as to what the U.S. 'might do to the Cuban sugar quota if Cuba doesn't calm down'.[57] In mid-December a Russian official, Alexander Alexayev, arrived in Havana as representative of the Tass agency.[58] Following five months of simple hostility to anti-Communism, the regime was now moving into a stage when preparations were being made for the complete realignment of her national and international posture.

[56] As reported by Núñez Jiménez on his return to Cuba, in the newspaper *Revolución* offices.

[57] *Wall Street Journal*, 11 December 1959.

[58] *Revolución*, 15 December 1959. Alexayev (b. 1913) had been First Secretary at the Russian Embassy in Argentina 1954–8 and in 1960 became head of the 'Latin' department of the Soviet Foreign Ministry. Alexayev became Russian ambassador to Cuba in 1962.

CHAPTER 36

A Sword is Drawn

The trial of Hubert Matos and his brother officers, for 'uncertain, anti-patriotic and anti-revolutionary conduct' which, with their resignations was said to have provoked alarm and sedition in the forces under their command, began on 11 December. This trial later became of supreme importance for an evaluation of the integrity of the revolutionary government.

Matos was tried by a tribunal whose president, Major Sergio del Valle, was at the time commander-in-chief of the Cuban air force; Del Valle, a doctor in the Sierra Maestra, second-in-command to Cienfuegos in the journey west, later became chief of staff to the army and Minister of the Interior,[1] as well as a founder member of the central committee of the new Cuban Communist party. Other members of the tribunal were Dermitio Escalona, the military commander in Pinar del Río, Guillermo García, famous as the 'first peasant' to join Castro in the Sierra Maestra, and Juan María Puertas. The prosecutor, Jorge Serguera had been in Raúl Castro's column in the Sierra Cristal and, after being on the war crimes tribunals in Oriente was now Judge Advocate of the army, being previously a law student. Afterwards he was to become military commander in Matanzas province, Cuban ambassador to Algeria and finally director of radio and television in the late 1960s. As can be imagined, therefore, legal procedures did not play a decisive part in this trial. Both Raúl Castro and Fidel Castro made speeches at the trial, both full of irrelevant detail about the activities of Matos in the Sierra Maestra and the premier engaged in a series of undignified clashes with Matos and his counsel, Dr Lorié Bertot, who had had the misfortune not only to have been an attaché at the Cuban Embassy in Madrid under Prío but to have written a letter to Batista's secretary to ask if in 1952 he could keep his appointment, a fact which came out during the trial (Lorié Bertot had also written a fulsome article in praise of Batista in the Mexican press). All these circumstances militated against the possibility of Matos receiving a fair trial. No evidence against him was presented save reports of conversations during early 1959 that he had been critical of Communist influence in the revolution. A major argument of Raúl Castro's was that Matos received $120,000

[1] He retained this office in 1970.

from ex-President Urrutia; but in reply Matos claimed that this had been used for normal expenses and the presumed charge of corruption was not pursued. Possibly Matos had indeed done his best after mid-summer to slow down the process of agrarian reform in Camagüey (as argued by César Selema, the 26 July representative in the province in succession to the arrested Joaquín Agramonte); and doubtless he was indeed an anti-Communist in touch with others of similar views in the leadership of the revolutionary government. Perhaps too Matos had attempted to appoint non-Communist officials in Camagüey but that was not a crime. Both Matos and Napoleón Bécquer, another officer tried with him, were incidentally free-masons and members of the Manzanillo lodge.[2] Matos's speech in his own defence at the end of the trial had to be made at six o'clock in the morning and lasted till almost eight o'clock; the text of this was not published in the revolutionary newspaper.[3]

In the end Matos received a sentence of twenty years and another twenty-one officers who had resigned with him received seven, three and two years of prison, respectively (the prosecutor had demanded the death penalty and the rumour was that Matos would have received this had it not been for the arguments of Faustino Pérez.[4] At all events one may be sure that the tribunal was not uninfluenced by the presence of the prime minister and the Minister of Defence as witnesses).[5]

Several other more genuine counter-revolutionaries, such as Rafael del Pino, were tried about the same time. Del Pino, for all his old friendship at Bogotá with Castro, received thirty years for trying to assist Batistianos to leave illegally. A number of North Americans received sentences too or were imprisoned indefinitely, for a variety of offences, some genuinely subversive, some not. Two men were executed for armed rebellion in Pinar del Río, many gaoled. Fifteen sailors were arrested in Santiago in connection with a plot to kill Castro. The atmosphere in Havana was one of suspicion and foreboding. Tourism had fallen off to a fifth of what it had been in 1958 and five major steamship lines cancelled their stops in Havana Bay. On 17 December Castro predicted that next year his followers would have to defend the revolution with weapons in hand, for a tremendous campaign against the revolution had been mounted; workers in bars, servants in private houses, should denounce to the police all remarks against the revolution; all ordinary

---

[2] Evidence of Manuel Bermúdez at the trial (*Revolución*, 15 December 1959, 12).

[3] See *Revolución*, 14, 15, 16 and 17 December 1959. The first two days of the trial were well reported, but not the last. Castro's speech was republished in a pamphlet, '*Y la luz se hizo*'.

[4] S. Casalis, *La República* (Caracas), February 1965.

[5] Matos remains in gaol (1970) but several of his fellow prisoners made a sensational escape from La Cabaña in 1960. In 1967, General Barrientos, the president of Bolivia, agreed to exchange Régis Debray, the French revolutionary, for Matos – an offer of which Castro did not take advantage.

men should become soldiers of the revolution: this was a step towards the creation of a militia.

The month of December 1959 therefore marks a critical stage in the revolutionary development of Cuba, when the government made plain that its enemies would not secure a fair trial. Matos's trial naturally shook the 26 July Movement to its roots – such as they were.

The consequent atmosphere of suspicion, however, did not yet extend beyond the upper-class suburbs of the big towns, though a mild sensation was caused by the arrival at Miami of two priests, Fr Ramón O'Farrill and Fr Eduardo Aguirre, saying that they had fled Cuba, since it was becoming Communist. The priests' superior, Mgr Díaz, confined himself to saying that the priests had left without his permission. Every visitor to Cuba meantime testified that Castro's popularity seemed in no way diminished among the majority of the population and, since North American democracy had itself degenerated into a popularity contest, this left Castro's critics with little to argue about. For the Cuban masses, Castro still represented not only hope, however, but achievement. The co-operatives on the land were exciting novelties. Some land was being distributed. The cuts in rents, telephone and electricity rates had increased purchasing power, and as yet the ensuing inflation had not at all caught up with wages. The tariffs against imports from the U.S. and the cuts in the travel allowance had hit the rich, not the poor. There had not been much change in rural unemployment, but free education and health for all was evidently now within reach, reducing the need for essential outlays by those who could least afford it. The law rumbled on ineffectively but at least, for the first time in Cuban history, not corruptly. The unfairness of treatment to counter-revolutionaries or suspected counter-revolutionaries seemed to the majority either justifiable, in an emergency, or perhaps a fair *quid pro quo* for generations of negligence, unthinking or conscious. The regime had already begun to make a special point of insisting on fair shares for Negroes, after Raúl Castro's speech commemorating Maceo's birthday in early December. This insistence later went further than the facts justified, a wary eye being cast towards the U.S. South. But as a rallying cry it could not fail to be popular and, even after the Matos affair, Castro retained his hold on nearly the whole population, apart from the upper class.

One remarkable occurrence in December 1959 was the abolition of Santa Claus. Santa Claus had been imported, along with Christmas trees, into Cuba during the 1930s, from the U.S., probably in consequence of the exile there, during the Machadato, of so many members of the *bourgeoisie*. This Protestant fantasy was abolished as 'imperialist'. Instead, there appeared the somewhat artificial figure of Don Feliciano, wearing a *guayabera*, a straw hat, a beard. This typical Cuban small farmer failed, however, to excite much affection or respect. Christmas trees were also banned from import. But the revolutionary government made a great fuss of the need to celebrate, and to give thanks, above all, of course to Castro. Prices for the traditional Christmas pig were cut. Money for the poor was collected in large quantities. Here, as before, the only people who were annoyed were the upper classes, who, in the last twenty-five years, had looked increasingly to the U.S. for their standards. The Church was not best pleased either, but many isolated Catholics still backed the regime: near the end of 1959 Fr Ignacio Biain was still praising the revolution in the pages of his journal, *La Quincena*, and he was still ready to criticize those who opposed it – even a man such as the Finance Minister, López Fresquet, who was voicing private doubts.[6] But a large Catholic layman's congress in Havana at the end of November became in effect a protest against Communism. Choruses of '*Caridad!*' (Charity) had been heard in the same rhythm which characterized the revolutionaries' cries of '*Paredón!*' (To the execution wall).

Each week brought a new vacillation and a new uncertainty between Cuba and the U.S., and between Cuba's internal politics and U.S. diplomacy. On 29 December President Dorticós thus called for a new commercial agreement with the U.S. to lead to better relations. This olive branch took Ambassador Bonsal back to Washington on 6 January 1960 for consultations. Would he return? Various anti-U.S. measures were decreed in his absence. Due to an increasing foreign exchange crisis, U.S.-owned sugar mills were banned from borrowing from Cuban banks and instructed to go to Wall Street. Cuban citizens who earned U.S. dollars were henceforth to convert them into *pesos*. Roa, the Foreign Minister, had recently said that foreign investment was welcome. But did these measures suggest that Roa could be discounted? Admittedly, Castro on 4 January declared publicly that he hoped relations with the U.S. would improve during 1960, while the Cuban Tourist Institute was still trying to find U.S. tourists, but by inviting Joe Louis as a guest for New Year they were evidently beginning to think now of black or poor North Americans rather than the old rash of businessmen. On 8 January INRA took over another 70,000 acres of U.S.-owned property, maybe worth a total of $M6. Bonsal, back in Havana by 10 January, protested, without receiving more than the usual reply that owners would be paid in bonds over twenty years with $4\frac{1}{2}\%$ interest. But as yet no one had seen any of these tantalizing documents. Did they exist at all? *Some* compensation, admittedly, had been paid: thus on 19 December INRA had taken over six U.S. sisal

6 López Fresquet, 164.

plantations for which it paid 50% in cash – $M1·3, promising the rest in bonds.[7] Still the U.S. government, in formally replying on 11 January to the most recent Cuban Note (of 13 November) on agrarian reform and related subjects, merely repeated its old position: cash compensation on the nail. The next day 'a spokesman for the Hershey sugar mill said that an unidentified plane dropped incendiary bombs on seven sugar cane fields north-east of Havana'.[8] The two events were, no doubt, unrelated in their inspiration; in their interpretation, they could, in Cuba, only be linked.

Two further campaigns were conducted by the government in January. The first was against alleged Mujalistas in the trade unions. After the December Congress, a purge committee had been set up composed of Salvador (increasingly doubtful now about the course upon which he was engaged); Soto, the ambiguous textile workers' leader, who seems to have willingly accepted the orders of his minister, Martínez Sánchez, to gain control of the union; Aguilera, the equally ambiguous bank employees' chief, a personal rival of Salvador's ever since being replaced by him in control of the 26 July Labour Front in 1957; and the doubly amputated Alvárez de la Campa. These men had an easy time discrediting several prominent union leaders such as the builders' leader (Rafael Estrada), the tobacco workers' leader (Luis Moreno), and the hardware workers' leader (Martínez Leiva). Their method was brutally simple; Luis Moreno, for instance, was summoned to a meeting to which only Communist members had been asked. He was denounced as a Mujalista, expelled and a new committee elected in his place. His successor, Faustino Calcines, had been a Communist for many years. On other occasions the democrats arrived at meetings half an hour after the Communists to find that all the decisions had been taken. This technique had been followed by Communist parties with equal success in eastern Europe, and was the main contribution by the Cuban Communists to the establishment of totalitarian government in Cuba; Blas Roca may have been correct when he pointed out in 1965 that the significance of the Cuban revolution was that 'socialism' had been achieved without the Communists being in the central place. But their role in destroying the old unions was very helpful.

The most prominent union leader of all did not have to be so treated. This was Conrado Bécquer, the secretary-general of the sugar workers. Either under pressure or because he saw which way the tide was flowing, he crossed over to the Communist group. He was a bureaucrat willing to work under Castro as under Prío, though he had, it will be remembered, carried out a hunger strike in 1957 against Batista's strike-breaking. Other unions were dealt with piecemeal. Thus the

[7] *New York Times*, 20 December 1959.
[8] *Ibid.*, 13 January 1960.

Theatre Artists dismissed Manolo Fernández as a counter-revolutionary (he took refuge in a foreign embassy) and replaced him by Violeta Casals, a well-known Communist actress though also a Radio Rebelde news reader in the Sierra. Armando Hernández, the Metallurgical Workers' Federation leader, was similarly replaced. The same process went on all over the country. One who complained about the Communists was (according to herself) Castro's sister Juana, until recently a strong backer of the revolution. Castro allegedly replied, 'Look, Juanita, we must use these people; we must be politicians. One must have a left hand.'[9] The CTC secretary-general, David Salvador, also complained to Castro, who replied that if it were not for the conflict with the U.S., he would get rid of the Communists, by February at latest. Word of this was purposely leaked to the 26 July Movement and the press. Salvador himself apparently believed that 'the only way the U.S. would accept the Cuban revolution' was 'international blackmail'; he accepted Castro's argument that the danger of a Communist capture of power was necessary for Cuba 'to have a lever' against the U.S. He was also still apparently transfixed, as were so many who afterwards entered opposition, by Castro's extraordinarily powerful personality.[10] Meantime the new labour leaders made appeals for the freezing of prices and for the abolition of the right to strike – appeals which the cabinet saw fit to answer immediately with legislation to those ends.

The difficulty now was that anyone who opposed this process indeed became a counter-revolutionary so far as Castro was concerned. Further, the only means of resisting was by force of arms. Small groups of people met, sought to get in touch with friends already in the U.S., perhaps tried illegally to go to the U.S., and finally were captured: if they had committed some act against the regime with arms they might be shot or would certainly be imprisoned for many years. Even those who were caught in the conspiratorial stage would be imprisoned – indefinitely, like most political prisoners, for the sentences were no guarantee of being either freed at the end of their term or of being kept till then. These proto-rebellions were never severe threats. But to Castro they no doubt seemed so. He continued to live in a disorganized way, to resist all suggestions for the formalization or institutionalization of the government or of his movement, rarely sleeping in the same house but sometimes in Cojímar, or in Celia Sánchez's apartment in Vedado or in the Havana Hilton. But even so, still he showed himself incessantly.

These matters were not allowed to remain without criticism from the

[9] In her sensationalist article published by *Life* and the *Sunday Telegraph* (London) in 1964.
[10] Rodríguez Quesada, *David Salvador*, 18. This must have been written after discussions later with Salvador himself.

non-revolutionary press. Throughout 1959 the *Diario de la Marina*, *Prensa Libre*, *Avance* and others had attacked the revolution or given space to its opponents. The government had been able to ignore such protests since they came from organs which had always been lukewarm towards the revolutionary experiment before 1 January and were consequently easy to discredit. The government also could rely on its own newspaper *Revolución* and the Communist paper *Hoy*. No controversy had shaken these papers or their relations with each other for months. But a crisis had been reached after the support given to Matos by the 26 July Movement's newspaper in Camagüey, *Adelante*. By January 1960 the old papers of Cuba were at full blast in denunciation of the revolution, led by the *Diario de la Marina*. At the same time both the College of Cuban journalists and the Union of Graphic Arts (that is, the printers) had been prepared to curry favour with them.[11] On 11 January, Castro gave the order that news cables should be accompanied by statements of 'clarification', put in by the printers' union, and nicknamed *coletillas* (little tails) by *Prensa Libre*. The newspapers in question denounced *coletillas* but were unable to prevent them. On 18 January Jorge Zayas, editor of *Avance*, sent down an editorial which the printers refused to set. Instead, the 'free press committee' demanded that the government take over *Avance*. A gang from the Graphic Arts Union invaded the building, led by its new Communist secretary-general, an old Communist newly appointed, Dagoberto Ponce. Zayas, who must have foreseen this clash (he had already sent his family to the U.S.) swiftly took asylum in the embassy of Ecuador. In a few days he left for Miami by aeroplane, where he later founded an exile newspaper, *El Avance Criollo*, with which to rouse the exiles to impotent fury for some months against the government of Castro. The Rivero family's *Diario de la Marina* and *Prensa Libre* – still run by that old revolutionary of the 1930s, Carbó – and some other lesser papers, continued to attack the government and to publish news discreditable to it. But since the government controlled the printers and the College of Journalists, it was quite clear that the days of these free journals were numbered; and at the same time, the regime was laying its hand over the remaining independent radio and television stations. Thus José Pérez, director of the second most important national television channel, Channel 12, was persistently obstructed by 'revolutionaries' on his staff and finally left his office to an 'intervenor' appointed by the government.

Two days after the collapse of *Avance* Castro once more appeared on his favourite television screen. His words were familiar:

[11] These were Baldomero Alvarez Ríos, Jorge Villar, and Tirso Martínez who became respectively President, Vice President and Secretary of the College of Journalists, and Pedro Souret, Dagoberto Ponce and Jesús Pullido of the Union of Graphic Arts.

International plot . . . insolent threats . . . war criminals . . . international oligarchies . . . state of siege . . . the only hope all counter-
revolutionaries have ever had: to destroy the national revolution
with the help of foreign forces . . . we are a small nation fighting
alone . . . a small nation robbed of its reserves. . . . There is the threat
to take away the sugar quota, to hold back part of the price of sugar,
for they have begun giving the name of subsidy to the difference in
price between the world market and that of the U.S. [which] . . . of
course, is the result of U.S. sugar interests, who cannot produce at
world market prices.

Castro then violently attacked both Ambassador Bonsal and the Spanish
ambassador, Juan Pablo de Lojendio, Marqués de Vellisca, for helping
counter-revolutionaries in Cuba, particularly Lojendio for helping
Spanish priests (curas falangistas). It later transpired that, in fact, a
meeting of all religious superiors (except that of the Christian Brothers)
had been held in the Spanish Embassy to concert action against the
regime.[12] Lojendio, however, immediately drove like one innocent to
the television station, broke into the studio and demanded the microphone. Castro, who was still there, was for a moment taken aback and
for once a Cuban television audience saw a genuine quarrel. The studio
crowd shouted 'Fuera!' 'Out', the picture faded, but the radio audience
plainly heard the ambassador's imprecations, 'I have been slandered.'
Castro then gave Lojendio twenty-four hours to leave Havana, which he
did.[13] Next day, mobs paraded outside the Spanish Embassy and
Revolución proclaimed: 'How debased are those who confide in Bonsal.
What an inconceivable alliance – Bonsal, Lojendio, the war criminals,
the great landowners, the thieves.' Bonsal had already, however,
returned to the U.S. The argument that he should never return was
pressed even harder. There had been no Cuban ambassador in Washington since November when Ernesto Dihigo had been withdrawn for
indefinite consultations.

In succeeding days, it seemed that, at the least, diplomatic relations
would be broken between the U.S. and Cuba. Senator Styles Bridges,
chairman of the Republican party's policy committee, called for review
of the sugar quota. Senator J. M. Butler said that the U.S. should re-
examine Cuban policy, 'paying special attention to [Theodore] Roosevelt's . . . "Big stick".' For good measure in Havana, meantime,
Amadeo Barletta, the proprietor of another opposition newspaper,
El Mundo, was charged as a Batistiano; there was, perhaps, some truth

---

[12] See Fr G. Sardiñas, in Bohemia, 21 May 1961.
[13] He was not disgraced in Spain, for he went on to become ambassador to Switzerland.
Lojendio (b. 1906) had been Ambassador in Havana since 1952.

in this allegation, for Barletta, an Italian by birth, had indeed a rather dubious international past. He owned forty-three businesses in Cuba, including until now Channel 12. But though he had not attacked Batista, he had not hitherto much criticized Castro and if he had indeed been a Batistiano, why had the government waited a full year before accusing him? At all events, *El Mundo* was taken over outright by the government on 22 January and after a while began to appear under the editorship of Luis Gómez Wangüemert, a journalist of Curaçao origin who had been working for Barletta for a number of years without previously having shown strongly radical views.

For those who desired a *rapprochement* between the U.S. and Cuba, some slight hope remained. On 26 January, Eisenhower made a fairly conciliatory speech on Cuba. By the end of the previous year, he said, the administration had indeed been 'discussing a change in the law that . . . [required] the U.S. to buy half of Cuba's sugar crop annually at premium prices'.[14] He was also being secretly advised to embark on other plans: Nixon and the chiefs of staff still wished 'to build up an anti-Castro force within Cuba itself. Some thought we should quarantine the island, arguing that if the economy declined . . . Cubans themselves might overthrow Castro'. But before the administration finally committed themselves to these tunnels of adventure, they did make one more effort to reach a compromise. The same day as Eisenhower's conciliatory speech, the U.S. minister in Havana (Bonsal still being away) called on the ambassador from Argentine, Julio Amoedo, and asked him to try to negotiate between the U.S. and Castro. The suggested basis for a compromise would be: an end to the campaign of television and press insults; Castro should receive Bonsal on his return and genuinely seek a way for differences to be solved; in return, the U.S. would finance Castro's agrarian reform as well as other economic and social problems.[15]

Amoedo saw Castro at midnight at the house of Celia Sánchez. Castro was at first negative and spoke of an editorial in the following day's *Revolución* which 'categorically and brutally' rejected the conciliatory message of Eisenhower of 26 January. This was, as it chanced, a critical moment in the Cuban revolution. A Soviet exhibition (which had also visited New York and Mexico) had opened in Havana.[16] Anastas Mikoyan was due to visit Cuba in early February and, though that fact

---

[14] Eisenhower, 524–5. Castro had also suggested in a speech at the national meeting of sugar workers that if the U.S. were to cut the quota, Cuba would nationalize the industry, (*Revolución*, 16 December 1959).

[15] For this and following, see letter from Amoedo in *New York Times*, 13 April 1964; article by T. Draper in the *New Leader*, 27 April 1964; and article by Amoedo, *ibid.*, 8–12. What 'finance' meant is obscure; presumably compensate the expropriated.

[16] This had been announced on 15 December.

was not generally known, it was known to the U.S. government:[17] Mikoyan indeed dined with Dulles on his way to Cuba and told him and Robert Murphy that he hoped to set up a trade mission. The State department 'kremlinologists' concluded that the trade mission would be a cover for 'clandestine and subversive operations throughout the hemisphere'.[18] Perhaps it seemed, in the long run, better to go out of the way to haul Cuba away from an alliance with Russia while risking the accusation of appeasement, than be held responsible, in this election year, for the loss of the island to Communism. No doubt, too, Eisenhower shrank from aggressive action against Cuba; apart from the objections on moral grounds which he may possibly have felt, if such action went wrong that also would scarcely enhance Republican electoral chances in November, for once again, as in 1956 over the Suez crisis, democratic electoral preoccupations cast a shadow over the integrity of diplomacy.

At all events, Castro relented; he permitted Amoedo to speak and cancelled the bitter editorial, ordering *Revolución* to call off the attacks on the U.S. (He thereby demonstrated himself to be in complete control of the press.) The next day, President Dorticós announced that differences between Cuba and the U.S. could be resolved by diplomacy, that the traditional friendship of Cuba and the U.S. was indestructible, and that the Cuban people desired to tighten diplomatic and economic relations with the U.S. The newspaper attacks ceased. Mgr Evelio Díaz, still coadjutor in Havana, chose Martí's birthday on 28 January to reaffirm support for the revolution – the last gesture, as it turned out, of a bishop towards the regime. Mikoyan's visit was, nevertheless, announced on 31 January.

Perhaps this was a moment when the drive towards open war between Cuba and the U.S. might have been avoided. Eisenhower did nothing about the plans for backing the counter-revolutionaries. Instead, he went on a short journey 'to see South America for himself'. But incendiary raids by exiles from Florida continued. The day after Dorticós's speech, incendiary bombs fell in Puerto Padre and upon several canefields in the north. There were other raids, one by a U.S.-built aircraft of Moroccan registration flown by an individual who was in the employ of Masferrer.[19] Then Mikoyan arrived in Havana.

The Russian attitude towards Cuba and towards Latin America was unclear. Did they even have a policy? They had given some support, often grudging, to the Communist parties of Latin America over the last

---

[17] Herter said that the Mikoyan visit had been arranged 'quite a long time ago' (*New York Times*, 1 February).
[18] Robert Murphy, *Diplomat among Warriors*, 537–8. (Murphy says the date was 1958 but this must be wrong.)
[19] *Bohemia*, 7 February 1960; see *New York Times*, 30 January 1960.

thirty-five years or so. Bombastic statements had exploded from Soviet publications from time to time: 'Latin America is a seething volcano. As in one country, so in another, outbursts are taking place which are sweeping away reactionary regimes and loosening the nooses which U.S. monopolies have thrown over their economies.'[20] Such exclamations did not necessarily mean that the Soviet government as such, preoccupied with problems of world power and survival, was enthusiastic about the capture of power by Communist parties in the New World. Clearly such achievements would embarrass the U.S. and presumably hinder any *modus vivendi* between the U.S. and the Soviet Union, which seemed then an important diplomatic aim. Stalin had a similar problem over Spain in 1936–9: a successful new Communist state in Spain would render more difficult any *rapprochement* with England and France, at the time the main drive of his diplomacy. A Communist Cuba was not, in short, a goal specially to be desired by the Soviet Union in the winter of 1959–60.

Russia had then only three diplomatic missions in Latin America – in Argentina, Mexico and Uruguay – though it had also consular or commercial representatives in Bolivia, Brazil, Chile and Colombia. China, North Korea and North Vietnam had no representation. Some eastern European countries had commercial agents. Tass had men in the three countries where there were Soviet embassies, while the Czechs had representation in Argentina. Quite recently, in December 1959, Russia had made a trade agreement with Brazil to buy $M200 worth of coffee – much their largest commitment in the New World.

Mikoyan had been to Mexico – the first Latin American visit by any major Russian politician – but in Cuba he found a different situation. Met at the airport by Castro and by the Cuban Communist leaders, he inaugurated the Soviet scientific exhibition and placed a wreath on Martí's statue – an intelligent gesture somewhat marred by the removal of the wreath by a group of Catholic students from the University of Villanova (Mgr Boza, the Rector, denied, somewhat half-heartedly, that he had cancelled lectures that day to permit this demonstration). Mikoyan toured Cuba and praised the agrarian reform. A concert was given in his honour at the auditorium of Havana at which, on his entrance, Raúl Castro and Guevara led the audience to clap: all save the Ministers of Finance and Agriculture, López Fresquet and Miret, did so.[21] Finally, an economic agreement was signed; Russia would buy 425,000 tons of sugar from Cuba in 1960 and a million tons a year in the next four years. Russia would also lend £M100 to Cuba for twelve

[20] *Kommunist*, October 1958.
[21] Evidence to Draper of Andrés Suárez, who was in López Fresquet's box. Miret stayed in Cuba, however, to become a member of the central committee of the Communist party in 1965.

years at $2\frac{1}{2}\%$ – the same sum which Núñez Jiménez had failed in December to raise in Europe. This would be used for new machinery and buildings. Russia would supply Cuba with crude and refined petrol and a variety of other products, such as wheat, pig iron, rolled steel, aluminium, newsprint, sulphur, caustic soda, and fertilizer. There would also be technical aid to build new factories and to drain swamps. Cuba would export fruit, juices, fibres, and hides to Russia. The agreement, signed with a flourish, was vague on many points, particularly on how much of each commodity Cuba was to import, what factories would be built and how many of what kind of technicians would come. It is not known whether, as seems likely, the question of arms was touched upon at this meeting; perhaps Castro put the question and perhaps Mikoyan referred it to Moscow.

So began the era of Cuban–Soviet economic arrangements. Other decisions were taken at this time, too – such as to establish a board for revolutionary propaganda for the rest of Latin America, the Asociación de América Latina Libre. Maybe too the establishment on 20 February of a central planning board under the Ministry of Economics owed something to Mikoyan's visit. Cuba began to be referred to in propaganda as *Territorio Libre de América*. The secretary of the Chinese journalistic association visited Havana and announced that a new Chinese daily would be set up, the type to come from Peking and the editorial offices to be at the Communist newspaper *Hoy*. These developments cannot all be exactly traced to the visit of Anastas Mikoyan, but they marked a change in the international status of Cuba. Admittedly, neutral countries such as Egypt had even closer relations with Russia, but the strategic geographical position of Cuba made it much less easy for her to remain neutral even with less close bonds with Russia. Further, it was evident that the new relations with Russia would be followed by elaborate dealings with other members of the Soviet *bloc*: even while Mikoyan was still in Cuba, an East German delegation arrived to reach a financial and commercial agreement.

The U.S. Embassy in Havana dutifully pointed out that Russia would now be buying Cuban sugar at world market prices, while the U.S. bought three times more at special prices. It was not the size of the Russian agreement but its style and accessories (and its promise o political arrangements) which gave it importance. The money involvec for Russia was actually half that in the Brazilian coffee undertaking Still, a commercial agreement with the USSR, even a military agree ment, did not necessarily mean the acceptance of a Marxist or Marxist Leninist ideology, with all the internal and external consequences whicl that involved. Russia perhaps would have preferred a neutral Castro to committed one. If the latter did eventually occur, it was something whicl at all events cannot be attributed solely to Russia–perhaps not at all–and perhaps chiefly to Castro rather than the Cuban Communists. At the cabinet meeting which discussed the Mikoyan visit, Armando Hart had said, 'We don't need Russian Communism. If Marx and Engels had not existed, Fidel would have invented Communism anyway.'[22] The commercial agreement, on the other hand, was desirable, even essential, for, if Cuba were to achieve an outright break with the U.S., the Communist countries could provide an alternative market large enough to accept as much sugar as the U.S. customarily did.[23] Cuba had, after all, sold sugar to Russia in the past – over a million tons between 1955 and 1958.[24] The market was familiar to Cubans, and so were its opportunities. In November 1959 Russia had bought another 330,000 tons of sugar, but at the end of 1959, with sugar prices low, Cuba had a sugar surplus reaching to $1\frac{1}{2}$ million tons; while Russia had experienced a drought which harmed her own sugar beet crop.

What then had been the significance of Castro's calm in replying to the U.S. offer as transmitted by the Argentinian ambassador? As 'a dilatory tactic to diminish tension . . . while waiting for Mikoyan's arrival', as the ambassador himself thought? As something to fall back on if Mikoyan's visit proved a failure? It is unclear. Mikoyan's visit sharpened divisions in Cuba. 'Thank you,' said the *Diario de la Marina*, 'your visit has . . . defined the camps.' On 29 February Cuba sent a Note to the U.S. suggesting that negotiations should begin through diplomatic representatives with the one condition that, while these were going on, neither the U.S. government nor Congress should adopt any unilateral measures which might prejudice negotiations or cause damage to Cuba, her people or her economy. An *ad hoc* commission had already been appointed, ready to go to Washington, with full powers. On the 29th the U.S. said that the condition could not be accepted; the U.S. 'must remain free, in the exercise of its sovereignty, to take whatever steps it deems necessary'.[25] Viewed with the serenity that is possible in historical understanding, this reaction seems too strong; the condition seems reasonable, on the assumption, remote though it might be, that Cuba was sincere; on the other hand, Cuba could have spun out the negotiations indefinitely and insisted on the condition being upheld. Still, this was simply a matter to be tested, if negotiations were really desired.[26] Possibly, in Eisenhower's absence in South America, the mood

[22] López Fresquet, 162–3.
[23] Thus the *Wall Street Journal*, 5 February 1960: 'European and U.S. credit sources are cracking down on Cuba and the Cubans will have no other place to go than to Russia.'
[24] *Sugar y Azúcar*, April 1960.
[25] *New York Times*, 1 March 1960.
[26] It is unclear whether President Eisenhower was consulted in this matter: he had left Washington on 24 February for Brazil and was thereafter, till 29 February, in Argentina. His memoirs make no mention of the issue.

in Washington hardened against a *rapprochement*. Eisenhower himself was receiving some practical education in Latin American matters and, inasmuch as he had received a letter from the president of the Chilean students denouncing the U.S. as the friend of the rich and of the *status quo*, Eisenhower was beginning to realize that, as he himself put it, 'the private and public capital which had flowed bounteously into Latin America had failed to benefit the masses and . . . upon my return . . . I determined to begin planning . . . for all the people of Latin America.'[27] Perhaps in consequence, the U.S. did nothing to alter its sugar legislation for six months.[28] Interestingly, Castro himself seemed relaxed and fit during such foreign contacts as occurred at this time – notably the visit of Jean-Paul Sartre and Simone de Beauvoir in late February and early March.

Whatever the U.S. had replied, and however unyielding they may have seemed, it is likely, nevertheless, that they had lost the friendship of Cuba by the end of February 1960. The Cuban government had, on 24 February, denied an anti-Communist demonstration the right to meet in Central Park, Havana and the old Communist president, Marinello, had explained that 'whoever raises in Cuba the flag of anti-Communism raises a traitor's flag'. Earlier in the month, 104 people, including the son of Batista's ex-mayor of Havana (Luis Pozo), were sentenced to between three and thirty years' imprisonment for their part in the Trujillo plot of 1959. The evening newspaper, *El País*, collapsed when its editor, Guillermo Martínez Márquez, resigned after refusing to print a *coletilla* at the foot of an anti-Communist article. INRA took over another fourteen sugar mills in February. A national militia, led by the youthful Captain Acevedo, was already being organized to replace some of the activities of the army whose loyalty was suspect.[29] (Acevedo, still under twenty-one, was typical of those on whom the Castro brothers were now increasingly relying: he had fought with Guevara in Las Villas and afterwards became instructor of the army recruits from secondary schools.) The last U.S. employee of the telephone company had been expelled. All commercial advertisements of foreign origin were banned on television or on the radio. All foreign-made chemical products were henceforth to be repackaged in Cuba before sale. The Church, too, was hardening its hostile position. The radical Mgr Díaz was in mid-February replaced as coadjutor to the archbishop in Havana by a tough anti-Communist, Mgr Boza Masvidal,

---

[27] *Waging Peace*, 530.

[28] Scheer and Zeitlin, 149, say that the U.S. administration had already decided to cut the quota. This is not borne out.

[29] Acevedo became (1965) a founder member of the central committee of the new Cuban Communist party.

who thereupon assumed the role of spokesman for the sick cardinal and sometimes for the hierarchy as such. The new bishop of Pinar del Río, Rodríguez Rozas, made one final declaration for the revolution. Afterwards, silence.[30] But still, however, the Communists were far from being on the most militant wing of the revolution; in a new report on 28 February Blas Roca denied that 'imperialism' was likely to launch an actual invasion of Cuba. Economic aggression was possible, but the U.S. needed Cuban sugar. It is true that this report did mention the 'increasing aggressiveness of the enemy and that the Revolution was advancing', but these statements were rather perfunctory.[31] It is difficult to see, therefore, that the Communist party, as such, could have been privy to Castro's private thoughts at this time.

On 3 March, *Revolución* announced that the U.S. reluctance to negotiate on the Cuban terms signified 'economic aggression', and the next day all chance of *rapprochement* between the U.S. and Cuba ended, probably by an accident. A French freighter, the *Coubre*, bringing 76 tons of war material (light rifles and grenades) from Belgium exploded in Havana harbour, in a manner reminiscent of the *Maine*. 75 Cuban dockers were killed and 200 injured. Many harbour installations were destroyed. A second munition ship was taken out of the danger zone. In one of his most memorable speeches, grave, resolved, but, as usual, in control of anger, Castro blamed the U.S. (though he admitted that he had no proof) for this 'sabotage', proclaimed twenty-four hours of mourning, and finally hurled at the U.S. the challenge of conflict: 'You will reduce us neither by war nor famine.' Secretary of State Herter naturally denied the accusation of responsibility. But immediately thereafter in the Cuban government press the attacks on the U.S. broke out anew.

As in the case of the *Maine*, the truth about this explosion has never been discovered. Cuban longshoremen and dock workers believed that it was an accident. Had inexperienced soldiers helped to unload, had dockers been seen smoking, or was it sheer incompetence? (Castro himself said that the dockers had been searched for matches.) Of course, the U.S. administration and, even more, the exiles in Miami, had a motive in preventing arms from reaching Cuba but, as in the case of the *Maine*, or the death of Prim, the accusation was not proven. One expert from Belgium, Dessard, admittedly, said that there was sabotage, but it was obscure how this could be so.[32] Meantime, Jean-Paul Sartre listened to this speech of Castro's about the *Coubre* and 'discovered the hidden face of all revolutions, their shaded face: the foreign menace

[30] Dewart, 158.
[31] *Hoy*, 1 March 1960.
[32] López Fresquet, 83.

felt in anguish. And I discovered the Cuban anguish because suddenly I shared it'.[33]

The administration in the U.S. had not even now decided what action it should take. On the other hand, they had introduced a bill into the Senate which gave President Eisenhower power to cut the Cuban sugar quota if there should be need. Eisenhower, on the 15th, said airily that this had not been intended as a reprisal against Cuba but as 'a way of assuring that the U.S. would get the sugar that it needed'. As some measure to appease the situation in Florida, a flight information centre had been set up at Miami to try to control pilots leaving from Florida, Alabama or Georgia. The Customs said that they would pay $5,000 for information leading to seizure of arms and the arrest of the guilty. Was this a last sop to Castro or a first step to ensure that what activity there was from the exiles was under effective U.S. organization? There was at least one more sop, however: in the first few days of March, the last of the liberals in the cabinet, Rufo López Fresquet, the Finance Minister, was approached by Mario Lazo, legal adviser to the U.S. Embassy and for years also to several large U.S. firms in Havana.[34] Lazo said that he believed that he could offer to Castro, on behalf of the U.S. government, new military planes and technical assistance (such as radar) to prevent exile aircraft coming from Florida. The U.S. would, perhaps, also be prepared to apologize for being unable to stop such incursions due to the many isolated airports. The gesture would mean 'an end to the quarrelling' and a new opening for talks.[35]

López Fresquet told Castro of this on 15 March at a reception at the Egyptian Embassy, supposing that it was a direct U.S. offer. Castro was 'curious'. 'What an interesting thing this international chess game is,' he commented and said that he would give an answer in forty-eight hours. But it is evident that the first two weeks of March had been of great moment for the regime. Thus on 1 March it had been announced by Blas Roca that 'imperialism' seemed unlikely to be going to invade Cuba; but on 16 March a resolution (said to have been adopted on 28 February) by the Communist party said that the Cubans needed arms from the friendly socialist countries, not just aid.[36] It seems possible therefore that Castro had seized on the *Coubre* disaster in order to justify an appeal to Russia for arms, an appeal which the Communists themselves, perhaps reluctantly, were now agreeing to support. Thus Lazo's

[33] J. P. Sartre, *Sartre on Cuba* (1961), 145. It is clear that Sartre accepted unquestioningly that the explosion was caused by sabotage; on the anniversary of the explosion on 4 March 1961, Castro also explicitly blamed the U.S. for the 'murder of these Cuban workers and soldiers' (*Obra Revolucionaria*, 4 March 1961, 10).

[34] Mario Lazo (born 1895), educated Pennsylvania and Cornell.

[35] López Fresquet to Draper, *New Leader*, 27 April 1969; *cf.* Lazo, 211, where Lazo implies this initiative was his own. See Andrés Suárez, 90, for further comment.

[36] *Hoy*, 16 March 1960.

idea came really too late. But, before any decision could be reached, the Cuban government made an apology for the remark of Castro's on 22 January suggesting that Bonsal was implicated in counter-revolutionary activities. The U.S. *chargé d'affaires*, Daniel Braddock, was also permitted to talk over problems of compensation with INRA. Ambassador Bonsal returned to Havana.[37] But on 17 March López Fresquet was summoned by President Dorticós, who said that Castro and he had decided not to accept the U.S. offer of the 15th. 'We don't trust the U.S.; we think that what they want us to do is to contradict ourselves. Once we admit publicly that they are on the level and that they are friendly to us, they will give Cuba nothing.' López Fresquet then told Dorticós that if Castro thought that no reconciliation with the U.S. was possible, he would himself resign; and that day he did so, later leaving for the U.S. He was the last of the liberal ministers,[38] and the last minister to defect from the Cuban revolutionary government, though many were later dismissed or transferred.

That same day in Washington, by chance, President Eisenhower accepted a recommendation of the Central Intelligence Agency to begin to arm and to train Cuban exiles.[39] This, of course, had for almost a year been pressed by Vice-President Nixon and by others such as Admiral Burke. The mind of the CIA was fixed on its successful operation in Guatemala five years before. Although for a long time only a 'support of [Cuban] guerrillas was envisaged',[40] the administration had now committed itself. Perhaps they thought that they could still draw back if need be, though President Eisenhower himself explained that the reason for the comparatively moderate size of operations was only because 'the Cubans living in exile had made no move to select . . . a leader whom we could recognize as the head of a government in exile'.[41] The U.S. sword was nevertheless now drawn against Cuba, the culmination of fifteen months of vacillation and of at least as many years of ambiguous feelings; and at the same time, appropriately, Blas Roca left Cuba for a visit to the Communist countries, doubtless to discover what his brother Communist leaders really thought of these developments.

[37] *New York Times*, 19 March.
[38] All this derives from a letter from López Fresquet to Draper, published in the *New Leader*, 27 April 1964.
[39] Eisenhower Press Conference at Cincinnati, 12 June 1961 (*New York Times*, 13 June 1961). Eisenhower confirms in his memoirs, *Waging Peace*, p. 533.
[40] The CIA Director of Plans, Richard Bissell, to the author, 14 January 1963.
[41] *Waging Peace*, 533. It would seem from Bonsal's article in *Foreign Affairs*, January 1967, 272, that he was not apprised of this decision.

CHAPTER 37

The End of Capitalist Cuba

Yet having drawn a sword on 17 March, the U.S. had still not withdrawn the sugar quota. This now became the gauge in the conflict between the U.S. and Cuba. Agents of other countries interested in taking Cuba's sugar quota were active in Washington. Others still hoped that the U.S., by proceeding with kid gloves, could stave off or delay disaster in Cuba; among these was poor Ambassador Bonsal. But how far prized was the sugar quota in Cuba? On 21 March Guevara, the president of the National Bank, inaugurating a 'University of the Air' on television, denounced the quota as 'economic slavery' along with the U.S. premium which gave Cuba 5 cents per lb, or 2 cents above the world market. This premium had, he said, the effect of stimulating sugar to the point of enslaving Cuba with a permanent single crop economy, while forcing her to spend $1·15 on imports from the U.S. for every $1 earned.[1]

At the same time, Guevara also gave his listeners some inkling of his own philosophy:

> To win something you have to take it away from somebody. . . . This something is the sovereignty of the country: it has to be taken away from that somebody who is called the monopoly, although monopolies in general have no country they have at least a common definition: all the monopolies which have been in Cuba which have made profits on Cuban land, have very close ties with the U.S.A. In other words, our economic war will be with the great power of the North.[2]

The U.S. government not unnaturally suggested that, if the quota was indeed 'enslaving', Cuba should renounce it. But other Cubans argued that any scheme to withdraw the quota was, in effect, 'a new Platt Amendment'. Bonsal, back in Havana, on 21 March tried to find out what in fact Cuba desired to do. This was difficult, since the

[1] Mario Lazo recounts a conversation with Guevara at this time in which the latter said, 'The higher sugar prices in the American market, limited by a unilaterally imposed quota, were a fiction'. Once the American quota is eliminated, he argued, 'and the sooner the better', Cuba would be master of the world market, able to dictate prices (*Dagger in the Heart*, 241). This conversation went on as Guevara's did later with Julio Lobo: 'The Castro regime and Yankee imperialism are engaged in a death struggle and we both know that one of the two must die.'

[2] *Revolución*, 22 March 1960.

Cuban government as a corporate unit itself did not know. Guevara probably wished to force a showdown with the U.S., hence his speech. But this did not necessarily apply to Castro – particularly at that moment while his position was still not impregnable at home.[3] Further, the U.S. did not really desire to cut off the quota (and so risk being accused of economic aggression by other countries of Latin America), Cuba would, perhaps, have preferred the U.S., by rough action, to appear in the ranks of aggressors.

The regime was still being attacked in several leading Cuban newspapers. Castro's old friend, the ex-secretary-general of the Ortodoxos, Luis Conte Agüero, violently denounced the government on television for its arbitrary behaviour but, on 25 March, he was physically prevented by an armed mob led by the deputy chief of the security police (G.2), Major Piñeiro ('Barbaroja'), from reading 'an open letter' to Castro on the main CMQ station.[4] On 27 and 28 March he received the full brunt of personal denunciation, first by Raúl Castro at an open-air meeting (with cries of '*Paredón*') and then by Fidel Castro on television, the new scourge of liberty. Conte Agüero wisely left for asylum at the Argentinian Embassy. This was a good example of the use of force to prevent free speech. On 28 March the chairman of the Havana hair-dressers' association, Raúl Ramón Proenza, was sentenced to three years' imprisonment for writing anti-Communist slogans on walls.

Such incidents led to the decision by the government to take over the CMQ station, the most important television centre in Havana. This occurred in a farouche manner. The bank accounts of about 400 Cubans were suddenly frozen on charges of collaborating with Batista: they were given fifteen days to prove their innocence or to accept the seizure of their accounts. Among those so effected were Abel and Goar Mestre, the owners of CMQ. Abel Mestre went on 30 March (the day after Conte Agüero's eclipse) to the bank with a number of salary cheques to be paid. But the clerk said that the bank employees' union did not wish to honour these. The following day, Abel Mestre entered the television studio just before the start of a popular programme, *Ante La Prensa* (on which Castro himself often appeared), locked the door behind him, announced that this week he himself would be the guest and delivered a tirade against Castro. Afterwards he went immediately into exile. Thereafter CMQ was a government station. There

[3] He alluded to the matter in a television speech in June 1960 and said of Guevara's declaration, 'We do not have to give any explanation.' (*Obra Revolucionaria*, 11 June 1960, 17.)

[4] Piñeiro, married to a North American, had been in Raúl Castro's column and afterwards became chief of the army in Oriente. He was one of the most faithful supporters of Castro and had entered the Ministry of the Interior in the course of the autumn of 1959.

had been several disputes between the government and the directors, because of the latter's reluctance to pay back salaries to employees who had gone to the Sierra. The only effective vocal opposition to the government could now come from the old newspapers, *Diario de la Marina* and *Prensa Libre*, and from the pulpit, since Channel 12, the other big television network, was under a government intervener and since all the small radio stations had by force or intimidation been grouped together in a new government-inspired corporation ironically known as FIEL (*Frente Independiente de Emisoras Libres*), under the virulent-voiced commentator Pardo Llada.

The unions by this time had their fangs drawn. The famous purge committee was still trying to expel all union officials who had voted against Communist candidates at the last Congress. But the purge committee itself was falling apart. Salvador, secretary-general of the Labour Confederation, was accused by his more militant comrade, Soto, of inadequate zeal, especially after the builders had refused to get rid of their leader Luis Peñelas and accept those proposed by the purge committee. Then Soto and the Minister of Labour dismissed Peñelas while Salvador was abroad in France to deliver compensation to the families of the French seamen killed in the *Coubre* disaster. Salvador went angrily to Castro who feigned surprise and denounced the Minister of Labour to his face. The latter refused to resign. Later Salvador learned that this scene had been a hoax and that the Communist executive had been ratified. Salvador then resigned, though for a time the matter was not made public.[5] Further, the extent to which he had often enthusiastically supported the government from the beginning of 1959 made it difficult for him to begin to contemplate joining the opposition – or even to imagine that he would be welcome there. The Ministry of Labour was anyway taking from the unions most of their *raisons d'être*; it alone negotiated with employers and it received authority to settle the labour controversies. In mid-April a new law required registration of all employers, employees and self-employed. Workers would not in future be able to seek work save through the ministry's offices and lists. Control of labour and relief of unemployment were conceived as irredeemably combined. The newly organized unions 'asked' their members for a loan of 4% from their salaries for the government's industrialization programme and kept also the old 1% membership fees, despite the fact that they no longer did their work.

There continued, at the same time, to be real rebellion in Cuba, explaining at least the severity of the measures undertaken by the regime against its enemies. About twenty men, including members of their chief's family, were for instance believed to be in the Sierra Maestra

[5] Rodríguez Quesada, 19.

under the ex-rebel, Captain Manuel Beatón. Beatón, whose talents were slight, had been passed over for good government positions in 1959, had taken to drink and, apparently in a personal quarrel, had murdered Major Cristóbal Naranjo, who had been charged to investigate Cienfuegos's disappearance. Beatón escaped from La Cabaña and set up as a bandit, raiding farms for food. Another little group was doing much the same in the Sierra Cristal, under Captain Higinio Díaz (Nino), an old but always undisciplined member of Raúl Castro's column, though he was a more serious opponent, being probably helped from Guantánamo (with which contact was still open) by the CIA.[6]

Díaz was also a member of a new group, the Movimiento de Rescate Revolucionario (MRR),[7] formed by several former followers of Castro, among them, Jorge Sotús, the 'prosperous warehouse owner's son' of Santiago who, after taking part in País's almost successful rising in that city on 30 November 1956, had led the first main group of reinforcements to Castro in March 1957; Sergio Sanjenís, who, after skirmishing about Matanzas in 1958 with Víctor Paneque, had been for a short while chief of military intelligence in Havana in 1959; and Manuel Artime, a professor at Havana Military Academy till November 1958, who, after a little fighting in the Sierra, had been for a while a zone chief of INRA. All these had abandoned the revolution because of its apparently Communist affiliations. Artime was a Catholic of a Spanish Conservative background.[8]

Artime was to be a specially important opponent of Castro. After the revolution he, with several others of similar views, had been in the Ministry of Agriculture under Sorí Marín.[9] He and the director of Agriculture, Rogelio González Corso, had begun to conspire against Castro as early as March 1959, and apparently made contact with Matos before his arrest. By April 1960 the MRR were Castro's best organized opponents, with a great many followers in the island, a clandestine newspaper, *Rescate*, and excellent connections in the U.S. After Eisenhower gave the CIA authority to support the exiles, the MRR was for a time the CIA's chief hope. Artime went on a speaking tour of Latin America, whilst Sanjenís and González Corso remained in Havana and Nino Díaz in the Sierra Cristal. The CIA (whose director in the anti-Castro operation was Frank Droller, the central European known to Cubans as 'Frank Bender', who had met Castro with such enthusiasm the previous year) busied itself with negotiating a centre for

[6] Szulc and Meyer, 59, suggest so.
[7] Movement of Revolutionary Rescue.
[8] See his political testament in *El Mundo* (Miami), 29 April 1961, and his somewhat hectic memoir, *Traición* (Mexico 1960).
[9] On 10 January 1959 he was found in charge of postal cheques and statistics at the Ministry of Posts, Telegraph and Radio.

training Cuban exiles in Guatemala (with the permission of the Guatemalan president, Ydigoras) at the coffee ranch Helvetia, near the Pacific coast, belonging to Roberto Alejo, brother of the Guatemalan ambassador to the U.S.[10] At the same time, a political front to this group began to be organized around the persons of Justo Carrillo, José Ignacio Rasco, professor at the university and a leader of the Cuban Christian Democrats, and Aureliano Sánchez Arango. All these were still in Havana, though living as private persons.

There were still, however, opponents of the revolution who were not connected directly or indirectly with the U.S. The most publicly active had been for some months a group of Catholic students led by Alberto Müller, a nephew of the bishop of Matanzas. His last protest had been an attempted demonstration at the doors of the CMQ television station during the Conte Agüero affair. In April his news sheet, *Trinchera*, was publicly burned, his friends mobbed by revolutionary students, and he himself forced to leave the university and take to underground activity. Other opposition was also being organized by Manuel Ray, until November Minister of Public Works, now teaching architecture at the university. Since he had been head of the underground against Batista not much more than a year before, he was returning to an activity which he knew well. By April he had already made contact with other progressive critics of the regime, including the Labour leader, Salvador, whose disillusion was setting in fast.[11]

Castro and the Cuban revolutionary government did not take long to discover the commitment of the U.S. to the exiles. The revolution had effective intelligence in Miami, and Cubans, Right as well as Left were bad at keeping secrets. Perhaps in order to forestall overt U.S. action with the exiles, as early as the end of March, Castro combined a warning to the U.S. that 'Cuba is not another Guatemala' with an offer to send back Ambassador Dihigo to Washington 'if they are readier to discuss things on a friendlier basis' – an allusion, no doubt, to López Fresquet's abortive offer of 17 March. There were other signs of a modification of Cuba's foreign policy in April: President Dorticós offered to send help to President Betancourt to put down a military rising in Venezuela – an offer which was refused. On 19 April Castro told a North American reporter, Richard Bates, on CBS television that:

---

[10] According to D. Wise and T. B. Ross, *The Invisible Government* (1965), 23, the CIA in Guatemala was represented by R. Kennard Davis. The CIA director of plans (Bissell), Droller's superior, denied to the author in 1963 that the CIA offered Ydigoras a *quid pro quo* of support for Guatemala's ambitions against British Honduras. But Ydigoras said in December 1961, and repeated in October 1962, that the 'U.S. had promised him assistance in his dispute over British Honduras in return for permitting the U.S. to use Guatemala as a training base for the invasion of Cuba' (See *New York Times*, 14 October 1962).

[11] Evidence of Ray.

Some similarity exists in the policy of the [U.S.] Government to that of Hitler and Mussolini in swearing that the revolution is a Communist plot: as Prime Minister I have been faithful to the Revolution. Cuba is going through a profound and genuine revolution and this is the main reason for the misunderstanding, which is due to many interests that will never be in agreement with a genuine and just revolution.

On 22 April he accused the U.S. of trying to create an international front against him. The next day President Ydigoras of Guatemala, who had already agreed to the use of the Helvetia coffee plantation for such dubious purposes, blandly accused Guevara of financing a revolution against Guatemala. But something of the truth about the CIA's activities quickly began to be known, since the Cuban news agency, *Prensa Latina* (run by an Argentinian protégé of Guevara's, Jorge Masetti), announced shortly that Ydigoras had made a secret pact against Cuba with his fellow dictator, Somoza, in Nicaragua, and that the proposed invasión had the backing of the State Department. Roa accused Ydigoras of planning a seaborne invasion in conjunction with the United Fruit Co. A breach of diplomatic relations followed on 25 April – the first with any country except the Dominican Republic. *Time* castigated Castro's concern with invasion by the adjective 'wacky';[12] but *Time* nevertheless itself had said on 29 February: 'Thoughts of Monroe and of intervention in Cuba were inevitably voiced in Washington.'

Cuba, however, still had many sympathizers, particularly in Europe, among the many intellectuals of the Left, who found no existing institutional framework but also no Utopia in Europe to satisfy them. Similarly, North American intellectuals, headed by such veteran globe-trotters as Carleton Beals and Waldo Frank, founded the Fair Play for Cuba Committee. A seven-column advertisement charged that the U.S. had over-dramatized Soviet–Cuban relations; 'many American republics, including the U.S., traded with Russia; the Communists [in Cuba] only numbered 16,000; give the reformers of Cuba "a fair hearing".' Controversy raged through the western hemisphere. After the Chilean students' letter to Eisenhower and his reply, there came a Chilean letter to Dorticós and his answer. Pablo Neruda finished a *Canción de Gesta* about Cuba in April. Cuba became for a time a catalyst of nationalistic emotions in several countries. The publication of a handbook on guerrilla warfare[13] by Guevara in April had an intoxicating effect on the articulate far Left throughout South America. Even in Spain students talked of taking to the hills, at the end of the summer term. Castro's

12 *Time*, 23 May 1960.
13 *La Guerra de Guerrillas.*

success in the Sierra, combined with the resolution of his revolutionary programme, thrilled students everywhere, loosening the bonds of young Communists with old party leaderships, creating in universities spontaneous alliances incongruous in all save the desire for action, struggle and gunfire. Nor was the enthusiasm confined to intellectuals. When Eisenhower went to Río de Janeiro he was greeted with signs saying 'We Like Ike, We Like Fidel, too'. The same happened during a visit to Latin America by Stevenson. An English film maker with a beard, even in Puerto Rico, was enthusiastically cheered, '*Viva* Fidel'.

In the U.S., apart from the Fair Play for Cuba group and other intellectuals, public and covert enmity was increasing. A baseball team decided not to play in Havana. A Foreign Aid bill passed with the provision that there should be no help to Cuba, unless conceived in the 'national . . . or hemisphere interest'. Farewell then to the third proposal in the compromise put to Castro through the ambassador of Argentina during the winter. In Havana, the U.S. Embassy delivered protest after protest at the arrest of U.S. citizens (many of them Cuban Americans), and note after note: and since the revolution was bringing not peace but a sword to the Caribbean, there could be no question of the sale of U.S. helicopters to Cuba. Cuba continued to protest about bombing raids, some bogus, some real, from Florida. But two events overshadowed local political responses: the imminence of the U.S. presidential election of 1960 and of the Summit Conference with Russia at Paris.

The fate of the latter was comic. Richard Bissell, the CIA director of operations, and an ex-Marshall Aid economist, who was now supervising the administration's scheme for setting the Cuban rebels at Castro, had, some years earlier, devised the incomparable U.2 photoespionage aircraft. The Russian destruction of the U.2 flown by Gary Powers (and his capture) wrecked any chance of an immediate thaw in diplomatic relations between the U.S. and Russia. Thereafter until the end of Eisenhower's administration, Russia was busy criticizing the U.S. with as much vituperation as in the days of Stalin. It may be that had it not been for this crisis with the U.S., Russia would have responded with less alacrity to the blandishments of Cuba, and Russian leaders would have thought more carefully about the consequences of sponsoring a close ally in the Caribbean.

The presidential election also cast its shadow on Cuban-American relations, though the matter played no part in the 'primaries'. Senator Kennedy treated the question with his customary wariness. Vice-President Nixon knew of the plan to arm the exiles; indeed, it was in a sense his plan, since he had urged it since April 1959. That made it hard for him to talk.

On 1 May a large parade of workers, brought as usual to Havana by free transport, assembled in the Plaza Cívica. There were also official representatives from Russia, China and eastern Europe. Fidel Castro once more addressed them. He denounced the electoral system, alleged that 'direct democracy' (such as he believed himself at that moment to be practising) was a thousand times more pure than 'these false democracies which use all means of corruption and fraud to betray the will of the people'. There were well publicized cries of '*Elecciones para qué?*' 'Elections what for?' It was noticeable that David Salvador, still nominally secretary-general of the CTC, was not present. Castro also told the crowds about 'invasion plots' from Guatemala. On this occasion the chant '*Cuba sí, Yanqui no*' was apparently first heard; it shortly became the chorus of a slight but entertaining jingle sung and played on gramophones all the summer, indeed until the records wore out.

Two days later, the Senate Internal Security Sub-Committee in Washington committed the imprudence of hearing evidence from Batista's ex-chief of staff, General Tabernilla, and from Colonel Ugalde Carrillo, who had commanded against Castro in the Sierra; the latter testified, on flimsy grounds, that a Soviet base was being built in the Ciénaga de Zapata for launching missiles.[14]

Despite the delusion of the colonel, the mere fact of his interrogation caused fury in Cuba. 'Flagrant intervention,' denounced Dr Roa. Nor was anyone in Cuba pleased by an AFL-CIO statement the next day that Castro was turning Cuba into a Russian outpost. Conrado Bécquer, the sugar leader, eager now to prove his staunchness, told his followers that AFL-CIO was directed by gangsters and that their views could be discounted.

On 7 May Cuba finally resumed diplomatic relations with Russia, and the Directorio leader Faure Chomón, who in the last year had moved at least as leftwards as Castro, was dispatched to Moscow as ambassador. Blas Roca, after visiting China and being enthusiastically received by Mao Tse-tung, was in Moscow in May and met Khrushchev for the first time; he wrote back a message of good cheer: 'Cuba cannot be blockaded economically by the U.S. imperialists. Our factories will not be paralysed from lack of oil, neither will our wives run short of bread if the U.S. monopolies decide to reduce the sugar quota and refuse to send what we need for our normal life.'[15] The first Russian ambassador to Cuba was Sergei Kudryatsev who had been prominent before in western circles as the director of the famous Canadian spy ring in the late 1940s; since he had diplomatic status, he had been expelled from Canada, not imprisoned.[16]

[14] See *Communist Threat*, 393.
[15] *Hoy*, 24 May 1960.
[16] Sergei Mikhaylovich Kudryatsev, b. 1915, Minister in France, 1959–60, Ambassador in Cuba 1960–62.

These moves merely met frontally the rumour of new U.S. measures against Cuba. Meantime, other travellers from Cuba followed Roca: the inspector-general of the army Major William Gálvez, to Peking, the director of agrarian reform, Núñez Jiménez, to Moscow. As yet no Russian arms seem to have been either promised or delivered, but it can be assumed that the question of arms must have been already in the air, and probably Núñez Jiménez discussed both sugar and oil with Russia. (Russian oil began to arrive in Cuba on 19 April.) In April Cuba had signed a major trade agreement with Poland; again, this was hardly open to complete condemnation – as Tad Szulc admitted in the *New York Times* on 2 April: 'Cuba's shortage of dollars . . . and the refusal by U.S. and most Western European exporters to grant credits leaves her with virtually no alternative.'

May saw the end of the free press. The *Diario de la Marina* had criticized the revolution with courage and consistent venom. On 11 May an article calling for free elections was organized and signed by 300 of the 450 employees. But the remaining minority brought in the strong men of the Graphic Arts Union under Dagoberto Ponce and the Journalists' Association under Tirso Martínez, who together broke up the plates from which the employees' letter was going to be printed. The secretary of the journalists who worked on the *Diario*, Pedro Hernández Lovio, called the police, but the local police captain said that he saw no sign of disorder: 'Show me a dead man and I will take action,' he said.[17] The editor, José Ignacio Rivero, protested and fled to the Peruvian Embassy. The *Diario de la Marina* was closed down. The following day *Prensa Libre*, the last of the free newspapers, with a circulation of 120,000, denounced the seizure of the *Diario* as a despoliation, an act of coercion and violence and a crime against freedom of expression. The same day, 12 May, Catholic students symbolically buried the *Diario* in a knoll at the university. On the 13 and 14 May *Prensa Libre* continued to denounce the government. A *coletilla* to a brave article by Luis Aguilar León boasted that for those who did not like 'totalitarian unity' there was always *paredón*, prison, exile or contempt. On the 15th, 80% of the employees at *Prensa Libre* signed a statement supporting the paper in 'these most burning controversies'. The following day, the signatories were taken before the CTC, presided over by David Salvador, who must have been in a difficult position, since he was already himself in contact with enemies of the revolution such as Ray. The employees were persuaded to recant and, in reward, they had an interview at one o'clock in the morning of 16 May with Castro. After further disturbances, the sub-editors Medrano and Ulises Carbó left the building and took refuge in the Embassy of Panamá. On the 16th *Prensa Libre* was taken

[17] Baran, 23.

over by the government on the grounds that it, like the *Diario de la Marina*, was attacking 'truth, justice and decency'. There did still remain one or two free independent newspapers of small circulation, which, however, refrained from criticism of anything, as well as two anarchist papers (*El Libertario* and *Solidaridad Gastronímica*) and a Trotskyist one (*Voz Proletaria*); while the weekly journal *Bohemia, Time*, the *New York Times* and other North American papers continued for the time being to be sold on news stands. The views of the government continued to be given in *Hoy*, *Revolución* and the new-style *El Mundo*, while the Directorio still nominally controlled an evening paper, *La Calle*, and there were several government papers in the provinces.

The fall of the free press in Cuba would have been more difficult to explain (or to bring about) had it not been for the fact that, like the union leaders, all these papers had not only collaborated with Batista but in many cases had actually received financial help from his government and those of his predecessors. This subsidization of the press had become so customary (as in Mexico still) that several newspapers completely relied on it.

About this time, the remaining non-Communist staunch and liberty-loving members of the 26 July, under its nominal leader Marcelo Fernández, seem to have met and drawn up an ultimatum to Castro demanding that he publicly reaffirm his hostility to Communism. The ultimatum was not presented, apparently because of the intervention of Carlos Franqui, the editor of *Revolución*. But Castro, as usual, got to know of these moves, and might perhaps have responded even so, had it not been for an opportune intervention by the Tass correspondent, A. Alexayev, a diplomat more than a journalist. Alexayev apparently gave Castro a direct message from Khrushchev, telling him that 'the Soviet Government wishes to express to you that it does not consider any party as an intermediary between it and you. Comrade Khrushchev ... considers you to be the authentic leader of the Revolution'.[18] This suggested that Khrushchev was hoping to place Castro in the same position as Nasser or any leader of the third world, but not in that of a Gomulka or a satellite leader. He was helping Castro to assert himself as an individual leader without concern about the Cuban Communist party – a judgement presumably reached after he had talked matters over with Blas Roca. But to Castro, the letter had other implications: that he could take over the Communist party him-

[18] Casalis, *La República* (Caracas), 4 and 10 February 1966. S. Casalis was then a prominent journalist writing daily articles for *Revolución* and close to Guevara and Castro at this stage. His evidence may very well seem open to question, but the result nevertheless seems to give it much credence. Nicolás Rivero, who worked in the Foreign Ministry, thought that Alexayev did his best to persuade the Castro brothers to make fewer anti-U.S. rodomantades. (*Castro's Cuba*, 54.)

self and use it as if it were his bureaucracy. Thus the Cuban and Russian leaders were, for many months, at odds, paradoxically on the precise question of whether the Communists should take power in Cuba. For reasons of international politics, Russia probably would have desired a friendly neutral in Cuba more than a satellite: for reasons of national as well as international politics, and even psychological reasons, Castro himself seems to have preferred a more committed status. The Cuban Communist party probably believed that the U.S. would almost certainly intervene in Cuba rather than let them capture power. Javier Pazos, then still working under Boti in the Ministry of Economics, said later that many Communists 'privately admitted' that they hoped that this would occur, causing Cuba to become a kind of 'Hungary of the West', with repercussions throughout the continent.[19]

The destruction of the free press marked the beginning of a campaign against the revolution by the Church. Early in May a Mass held in the cathedral of Havana to commemorate the victims of Communism was broken up by militiamen singing the International. On 16 May, Mgr Pérez Serantes, archbishop of Santiago, finally laid aside neutrality and issued a pastoral letter denouncing the restoration of diplomatic relations with the Soviet Union: 'It can no longer be said that the enemy is at the gates, for in truth he is within, as if in his own domain.' He went on: 'The true Christian cannot live without freedom . . . it has always seemed better to us to lose all, even to shed blood, than to renounce liberty.' Every home should, therefore, be turned into a domestic catechism class. But since there were few homes where the leaders of the family were qualified to fulfil this duty, he appealed to those who were to take the lead.[20] Too late, perhaps fifty years too late, the archbishop could do little: his warnings that Communism led to materialism caused a hollow laugh in such a city as Havana where capitalism had been more material than anywhere else. Still, the pastoral was read in the churches of Oriente and Havana, and published without comment in the two remaining independent papers, *Información* and *El Crisol*. The Communist Carlos Rafael Rodríguez replied in *Hoy* that nobody in Cuba was stopping anyone from the practice of religion: were there not hundreds of Catholics among the revolutionaries? Castro refrained from comment for the time being, reluctant for a full-scale clash when the tide of conspiracy seemed to be flowing high in the universities and among his old supporters. According to the *New York Times,* half the students were now neutral to the revolution – that is, potentially hostile. Perhaps against the will of the hierarchy, cautious against Castro as they had been cautious against Batista, the Catholic Church became

[19] Javier Pazos, *Cambridge Opinion*, February 1963, 25.
[20] A translation appeared in *Catholic Mind*, (January–February 1961), 1153.

inevitably a stronghold of opposition to the regime once the private schools began to be closed and independent youth and other organizations started to be banned.

It is difficult not to suppose that the government had this in mind when they dispatched 800 third-year students in May to the Sierra Maestra to help teach the peasants. Meantime, one of the few professors who still spoke openly, the ex-Auténtico minister, Sánchez Arango, already in contact with MRR, the exiles' political organization, was publicly accused of converting his classes into a counter-revolutionary political forum, and escaped to Miami through the embassy of Ecuador.

In Miami the CIA had by now practically persuaded the exiles' organizations to form themselves into a 'united front'. With the arrival of Sánchez Arango, this curiously named group became at last a reality, taking the title of Frente Revolucionario Democrático. This included the Auténtico prime minister under Prío, Tony Varona, who from the first had criticized Castro for his failure to hold elections; Rasco; Manuel Artime of the MRR; Justo Carrillo, the ex-chief of BANFAIC; and Aureliano Sánchez Arango. Artime was the military representative and the link with the CIA, but there were also connected with these men other Cuban soldiers, such as Colonel Martín Elena, an officer who had resigned his commission in 1952, when in command at Matanzas, in protest against Batista's *golpe*. A number of other Cubans, including various ex-officers of Batista's army, many of them linked with Barquín and his plot of April 1956,[21] had already set off for secret training in Guatemala and for a while some were at the U.S.'s own counter-guerrilla school at Panama. But this side of operations was still in an early stage. There were certainly under a hundred Cubans in training. The CIA was also active among other actual insurrectionaries in Cuba.

These new Cuban warriors were not precisely apprised of the fact that they were soldiers of the U.S., being told variously that their activities were paid for by 'a group of private U.S. businesses' or by 'a Cuban millionaire'. Few were deceived by this unsubtle posturing. But once these men had undertaken to work with the U.S. espionage organization they really surrendered freedom. So too did the politicians. Over the months these men, though they quarrelled with each other and with their benefactors, became in effect North Americans, relying on the U.S. to help them when things went wrong and regarding the U.S. president as their chief.

A steady flow of emigrants continued to come to the U.S., businessmen, ranchers, men of conspiracy, men with families, families without

---

[21] These included Manuel Blanco, Alejandro del Valle, Roberto, José and Miguel Pérez San Román, Miguel Orozco, Hugo Sueiro, Ramón J. Ferrer, 'Chiquí' García Martínez, Osvaldo Piedra and Alfonso Corsi.

fathers. The ease with which they were permitted to leave Cuba and to enter the U.S. was one of the factors which debilitated the opponents of the regime, causing almost each one of them to arrive in Miami, as it would seem, the leader of some new political organization, known by bombastic initials, but consisting of little more than the immediate family of that single exile. In this way Castro lost manpower but also many potentially dangerous opponents.

In Cuba the sugar harvest was now once more drawing to an end. A total of 5·8 million tons had been produced. But the harvest itself was less important than the fact that it had been the last one under the system of free enterprise which, with all its wastefulness and injustice, had made Cuba what she was. Immediately the harvest came to an end nearly all sugar land belonging to the mills, 2·7 million acres, was taken over by INRA. A thousand co-operatives were created on the plots thus made. Included in this immense seizure were the 275,000 acres belonging to the Cuban Atlantic, Cuban American, and the other grand U.S.-owned companies. In compensation, Cuba offered twenty-year bonds at 4½%, but in the case, for instance, of United Fruit, there was much doubt about the value: the company claimed its land was worth £M32, the government, £M6. With the estates there went, of course, machinery, shops, many buildings and labour: INRA ran many old shops as they were and opened new ones, so that by midsummer there were over 2,000 'people's shops', *tiendas del pueblo*. The mills themselves were not as yet touched and theoretically they could look forward to a harvest in 1961 where, outposts of private business, they would buy cane from co-operative planters as well as from the surviving *colonos*. Many mills doubted whether this arrangement could last. They were right to do so, since the whole system of private enterprise in Cuba was now menaced.

This train of events began when on 23 May the three large oil refineries in Cuba – Texaco, Royal Dutch and Standard Oil – were told by the government that a large consignment of Russian oil, in pursuance of the agreement of February, would soon arrive and that they would henceforth be asked to process 6,000 lbs of Russian crude oil a day. The capacity of the refineries was 85,000 lbs. These companies were already owed $M16 by Cuba for oil imports. The Cuban requirement would be detrimental to Venezuela. The companies hesitated. They were told that a fifth of Cuba's annual crude oil consumption would be supplied by Russia. This oil was anyway cheaper than that of Venezuela. The companies again hesitated.

Meantime, there was considerable coming and going in Havana. Sukarno paid a visit and according to one account took a careful look around Cuba and then, not entirely in jest, said to Castro, 'And you call this an under-developed country!' Dorticós went on a three-week tour of South America and, at the same time, Cuba invested in powerful short-wave radio equipment to broadcast to South America: and one observer dates Dorticós's journey as the beginning of the campaign by Castro to 'export his revolution to South America'.[22] Núñez Jiménez in Russia arranged for the purchase of some thirty new factories, along with technicians to run them in order to manufacture everything from steel to pencils. They would cost $M8o of which half would be paid for in goods. Castro tauntingly said that Cuba could produce more sugar were it not for the U.S. quota – his first apparent acceptance of Guevara's hard line of March.[23] In early June he formally abandoned the drive to bring in U.S. tourists. The State Department had recently said that all economic aid to Cuba would soon cease. But this was already limited anyway to two small programmes – six technicians at the agricultural experimental station and some others training Cubans in civil aviation – an annual cost of below $200,000. There was some tension in Havana over notices – prepared by the U.S. Embassy, for the use of businesses in the city – saying, 'This is the property of the U.S.', as if an invasion were about to follow. Bonsal, in a situation of increasing unhappiness as ambassador, being made to bear the brunt of humiliations intended for his predecessors, continued to send Note after Note criticizing slanders of his country, without avail. He did not know of the arming of the exiles; had he done so he could hardly have remained. In Cuba itself a group of students from the University of Santa Clara took to the hills; their leaders were captured and Plinio Prieto, a rebel army major, Porfirio Ramírez Ruiz (president of the Students' Federation of Las Villas) and Sinesio Walsh were shot, the first execution of students since January 1969.[24] David Salvador, still nominally the secretary-general of the unions, had gone underground in June, forming, with the ex-26 July leader in Camagüey, Joaquín Agramonte, the 30 November Movement – named after the day that Frank País had risen in 1956 in Santiago.[25] The wheel was indeed full circle. These students were regarded by the regime as much as bandits as Batista had regarded the men of the 26 July. They had not received much help from the peasants, and the leaders were in fact cornered in small towns buying food. More serious was the movement into active clandestine politics of Manuel Ray, the

[22] Tad Szulc, 'Exporting the Cuban Revolution', in Plank, op. cit., 81.
[23] Hoy, 29 May 1960.
[24] Plinio Prieto had been in 1950 a teacher at a Havana night school and in 1952 he had joined Sánchez Arango's Triple A organization. In 1957 he joined the Directorio Revolucionario. He ran arms to Cuba from Florida in 1958 and on one occasion was lost in the Gulf of Mexico, spending ten days in an open boat without food.
[25] Rodríguez Quesada, 19.

ex-Public Works minister. By midsummer he had founded a new secret organization known as the Movimiento Revolucionario del Pueblo (MRP) which, unlike the MRR, had to begin with no relations with the U.S. Ray tried to gather all the old supporters of Castro who had now withdrawn their approval, inside and out of Cuba. Salvador joined him, the movement gained some followers, but it steadfastly refused collaboration with the CIA who, occupied with their own leaders, thought Ray was too far to the Left for them. Ray's slogan '*Fidelismo sin Fidel*' could, however, appeal only to the sophisticated, and to few even of them. To the masses, the phrase seemed an absurdity, as indeed, in a sense, it was. Meantime, rumours of invasion reached even the U.S. press: the well-informed *Wall Street Journal*, for instance, in early July published an article saying that 'there are government officials already engaged in considering just how Mr Castro's downfall might be hastened by promoting and discreetly backing opposition to him within Cuba if . . . his prestige . . . should . . . wane'.[26]

In the middle of 1960 freedom in the University of Havana was finally destroyed. That centre of learning had a long tradition of being domineered by a group of tough, often somewhat elderly students not averse to the use of firearms and kidnapping for the achievement of modest aims such as the presidency of the law students or the sub-secretaryship of the union. The students who engineered the collapse of university autonomy were in one sense therefore the apotheosis of an old if discreditable tradition. The men concerned – Rolando Cubela, a major in the Directorio; José Puente Blanco, one of Echevarría's successors; Angel Quevedo; and Omar Fernández – were to the government of Castro what the MSR of Manolo Castro had been to Grau San Martín: a *bonche*, prepared to use every means to secure mastery, which in this instance meant state control of the university. These four men, incidentally, had military ranks, and Omar Fernández, already administrator of customs, soon became Minister of Transport. Among some of these leaders, the policy demanded meant, as in the case of Cubela and Puente, a complete break with their past democratic political attitudes; others, such as Ricardo Alarcón (even as 26 July coordinator in the university in 1958), had always been in favour of collaboration with the Communists.[27] In 1959 these men had established themselves in the student federation, by political pressure, though even so Cubela had only beaten Pedro Luis Boitel, an opposition candidate for the Presidency of the FEU, by a narrow majority in an election in which intimidation was used. Similarly, Alarcón had only taken over the presidency

---

[26] Philip Geyelin, in *Wall Street Journal*, 11 July 1960.
[27] Fausto Masó (to Draper), who adds that Alarcón was used by Guevara as a '*punta de lanza*' within the 26 July Movement.

of the Law School by the 'promotion' of his chief rival, Amparo Victoria, to the post of Secretary of Embassy in Holland.[28]

The University was finally subverted by means of a carefully prepared incident in the Faculty of Civil Engineering. The professor of Hydraulics and one other teacher were quite unjustly denounced by a group of Fidelista students as being in breach of examination proceedings. The faculty board refused to dismiss these men. But the students then nominated two engineers as successors to them, one a brother-in-law of Guevara. The University Council backed the faculty board. On 15 July 1960 a large meeting of students (doubtless however a minority of the student body) and some teachers denounced the University Council and 'appointed' a new board of governors to direct the university: four professors and four students. The board then dismissed the council and the faculty boards.

Castro and Raúl Castro came to the university in pursuit of these demands; professors such as Portell Vilá, seeing how things were going, quickly made arrangements to leave the country. Two-thirds of the teachers at the university refused to accept the new board of governors and were dismissed by it. Dr Miró Cardona, ex-prime minister and still nominally an ambassador, a member of the law faculty, protested, but without success, before President Dorticós. The Rector of the University, Clemente Inclán, an opportunist of many years' standing, was after some months replaced by Dr Juan Marinello, for many years the president of the Cuban Communist party, a poet and well-known man of letters of the Left, though something of a figurehead; and, on 4 August, the government endorsed the board of governors as a policy-making body and approved a committee of University Reform to change the curriculum, the administrative procedures and policies of the University.[29]

The manner in which this ancient university lost its liberties was deplorable. Nevertheless, those liberties in the past had led so often to licence, its institutional fabric was so rotten with politics and gang warfare, that mere reform could arguably never have altered the fundamental disequilibrium. The political stranglehold over the FEU and its sub-committees held by perpetual students and the corruption and inefficiency of many teachers had given the University a terrible name. Like the press and the unions, this bastion of liberty had been often in disrepair. It is distressing to note that, after the radical revolution in the university, the new student leaders such as Cubela rode about in large cars, living the good life and bringing discredit even to the puritan revolution in which they had played an important part. The new board

[28] Professor Portell Vilá, in *Bohemia Libre*, 6, 13 and 20 November 1960.
[29] *Cuba and the Rule of Law*, 249–50; *Revolución*, 5 August 1960.

of governors began to scour the world for replacements for the dismissed academics, while admitting that for a time education would suffer. Meantime, other safeguards of political liberty were disappearing. Thus on 5 July a group of left-wing lawyers, some in militia uniform, entered the headquarters of the Havana Bar Association and took possession of its offices.

The great oil companies in mid-June at last replied that they would not process Russian oil, on the ground that this step would damage Venezuela.[30] The Cubans' case derived from a law of 1938 providing that foreign refineries were required to process Cuban crude oil – which the companies defined as oil taken from the Cuban soil. It seems that the secretary of the U.S. Treasury had strongly urged a refusal by the companies to process the oil, despite the companies' own reluctant inclination to agree.[31]

For a few days the Cuban government delayed its answer. Doubtless this situation necessitated a hasty consultation with Moscow. Raúl Castro left for Prague, presumably to discuss arms. The Havana Hilton and the Nacional hotels were taken over by the government. Nico Beatón and others of his gang in the Sierra Maestra were caught and shot. Two U.S. diplomats were expelled as counter-revolutionaries. U.S. policy specifically changed. 'Patience and forbearance' were openly dropped. A 50-kilowatt radio station on Swan Island, 400 miles southwest of Cuba, was built by the CIA to cover the Caribbean, first to attack Trujillo (the Church had turned against the 'benefactor' and the end of his evil regime was approaching) and then to attack Castro.[32] On 22 June Herter, Secretary of State, appeared before the Senate to plead for a bill authorizing Eisenhower to cut the sugar quota. The bill had been lying unattended since earlier in the month. 'This would be an appropriate time,' said Herter, 'for the U.S. to seek ways to diversify its sources of supply and reduce the dependence of its consumers on Cuban sugar.' This change of line was against the advice of Ambassador Bonsal who, despite his unexampled gloomy position in Havana, believed that the U.S. 'should have continued our policy of restraint longer than we did'.[33]

On 25 June came Castro's response: Herter's action proved everything that he had been saying. It was a declaration of economic war.

[30] 'Unexpectedly', *Wall Street Journal* stated on 13 June.

[31] Bonsal, *Foreign Affairs* (January 1967), 272, says that a Havana oil company representative present at the crucial meeting, so told him.

[32] Eisenhower, 534. Swan Island was set up under the cover of being the Gibraltar Steamship Corporation, owned by three prominent New York financiers, Thomas Dudley Cabot Walter G. Lohr and Sumner Smith. The first of these had been president of the United Frui Company.

[33] Letter to Schlesinger, 2.

Cuba must be prepared for months, even years, of hardship because of the policies undertaken by the U.S. Cuba would not starve, but even necessities would be lacking. There would no doubt be an armed attack. For every cut in the quota, however, a U.S. sugar mill would be expropriated.

The immediate consequences of these exchanges were that world sugar prices dropped to 2.85 cents a pound with the fear that excess Cuban sugar would be dumped on the market at a low price. Castro fixed his selling price of sugar hastily at 3 cents and the world price rose uneasily ten points to 2.95 cents. On 28 June the U.S. House of Representatives Committee on Agriculture, after a brief and, even to its undemanding members, unsatisfactory discussion, unanimously approved the bill on the sugar quota which enabled Eisenhower to reduce the quotas in 1960 or eliminate them altogether. The same day Castro signed the order saying that the Texaco oil refinery in Santiago had to refine Soviet crude oil or be expropriated. On 29 June, Cuban petroleum officials arrived at Texaco, Santiago, with two barges loaded with Soviet oil. The U.S. directors had already left. They had known what was coming. On 30 June the Esso and Shell refineries were taken over in Havana. The U.S. Senate passed the bill on 3 July, again scarcely without discussion.

Eisenhower delayed his signature on the sugar bill for a week. The State Department urged that, instead of a cut in the quota itself, the premium should be abolished, so that Cuba would thereafter simply be ranked with other producers without bonuses.[34] The ambassador in Cuba, Bonsal, still desired a small cut,[35] but Eisenhower decided to go the whole hog. On 6 July he reduced the quota for Cuba by 700,000 tons, the remaining unfulfilled slice of the Cuban share for 1960, and also by another 156,000 tons, the quantity that Cuba could have sent to the U.S. to make up for other countries' deficits. 'This action,' Eisenhower reflected, as he signed, 'amounts to economic sanctions against Castro. Now we must look ahead to other moves – economic, diplomatic, strategic.'[36]

Castro accused the U.S. of economic aggression and, for the first time, announced that arms would soon be available for the militia: presumably Raúl Castro had already reached an agreement in Czechoslovakia. On 9 July, over 600 U.S.-owned companies in Cuba were ordered to present sworn statements showing raw materials, spare parts, files, and so on, which were then in stock. This was an obvious foreshadowing of a complete nationalization of U.S. property. Perhaps they were not taken over there and then, for lack of technicians to run them rather than for

[34] According to Szulc and Meyer.
[35] Letter to Schlesinger.
[36] Eisenhower, 535. The total quota for 1960 had been 3,119,655 tons, of which over three-quarters had already been fulfilled.

any other reason, or perhaps because they relied primarily on importing raw materials from North America. Possibly, too, the Communist party attempted to draw Castro back. The same day, Khrushchev announced publicly that 'artillerymen' could defend Cuba, if need be with rockets.[37] Russia also would be prepared to take the 700,000 tons of sugar that the U.S. had spurned. Khrushchev added that the Monroe Doctrine was dead and 'the only thing you can do with anything dead is to bury it so that it will not poison the air'. Guevara remarked contentedly that Cuba was now defended by 'the greatest military power in history'; nuclear weapons were standing in the way of imperialism.[38] In the rising tide of charges and counter-charges, provocation and retaliation, neither side saw the end of the tunnel. A new attempt to mediate by the president of Argentina, Frondizi, met with no success.[39] The real significance of these events was that any idea that the Cuban Communists may have had that the U.S. could be provoked into a military intervention in the style of Hungary, in 1956, had now to be abandoned; Russia had given what passed for a guarantee; and therefore the party had no choice before them except to try and bring order and stability to the Cuban economy, which was now so disturbed by many arbitrary measures.

The regime in Cuba intended now to diversify her agriculture so that in a very short time – maybe by following the dicta of Professor Dumont – she need no longer rely on sugar. But this could not be achieved overnight. Meantime, the huge quantity of sugar which had previously gone to the U.S. had to be sold. For this reason alone Cuba would have wished to turn to Russia. By this time, too, Castro seems to have decided that for him freedom meant freedom to choose Communism if it could be arranged, or at the least freedom for close relations with the Soviet *bloc*,[40] and while these decisions were being taken, old comrades such as Marcelo Fernández, the national coordinator of the 26 July Movement, and Oltuski, the Minister of Communications, who had so impressed Sartre, dropped out from the government. The new line had need of new men.[41]

Having decided to escape from the sugar quota, Cuba's problem was

[37] 'In a figurative sense, if it became necessary, the Soviet military can support the Cuban people with rocket weapons.' Castro, commenting on this development from a hospital bed, but on television, said that the rockets were real not figurative and added insistently that the Russian offer had been 'absolutely spontaneous'. See Khrushchev's remarks to Carlos Franqui, in November 1960, quoted below, 1316 fn 17.

[38] Speech, 10 July 1960, *Obra Revolucionaria*, 26 July, 49.

[39] See *New York Times*, 6 July 1960, and *Hoy*, 30 July 1960; *cf.* Andrés Suárez, 95.

[40] The argument by Albert and Pearl Wohlstetter that Castro's motives towards the U.S. can be explained by his equally ambivalent relations towards his father seems ingenious if far-fetched.

[41] Both Fernández and Oltuski nevertheless stayed in Cuba and remain prominent servants of the Castro regime though both have had their difficulties with the security police, Oltuski even passing some time in gaol.

to derive the maximum benefit from U.S. abrogation of it. It was therefore desirable that the abrogation should have been unilateral and like an act of aggression. Eisenhower and Herter fulfilled these necessities to the letter. The abrogation caused much international sympathy for Castro. For years afterwards, ill-informed, if well-intentioned Liberals justified Castro's Communization of Cuba as a response to Eisenhower's sugar policy. But that policy enabled Castro to respond with a series of counter-measures which might not then have occurred (or just possibly might never have occurred) and anyway would have been more difficult to justify, even to the Cubans. These counter-measures led to the eclipse of all U.S. and most large Cuban private concerns within a few months, so weakening what chance there was of these giving backbone to further opposition. Thus apparently on Castro's own initiative alone and probably against both the wishes and the expectations of all his followers and of the Communists, on 6 August the Cuban Telephone Company, the Cuban Electric Company, the oil refineries and all the sugar mills which previously had only been 'intervened' were formally expropriated.[42]

No doubt these and other expropriations were carried out too quickly for economic success. Russian production had dropped in the early 1920s, partly because of the hasty nationalizations and the departure of technicians; China, learning this lesson, had proceeded in the late 1940s and 1950s at a slower pace. Seven years after the Chinese revolution a third of industry, two-thirds of commerce and most of agriculture were still in private hands.[43] Chinese production in consequence rose in the early years of the revolution. These lessons were lost on Cuba. Even some firms willing to collaborate with the regime were taken over. Certainly it would have been wiser to delay intervention until it was certain that the new responsibilities could be effectively borne.

These points of view were clearly put at the time by members of the Cuban Communist party: Blas Roca immediately explained that 'private enterprise that is not imperialistic... is still necessary', and that some of the interventions 'could possibly have been avoided'.[44] Escalante urged at the eighth Congress that the revolution should try to keep the national *bourgeoisie* 'within the revolutionary camp'.[45] It does not seem, however, that Castro kept in close touch at this time with these sensible if elderly Communists.

During midsummer 1960, there were many statements of redefinition of what had occurred in Cuba: 'There are many similarities between

[42] See strong arguments to this effect by Andrés Suárez, 97.
[43] *Cf.* E.T. Luard and T.J. Hughes, *Economic Development of Communist China*.
[44] Blas Roca's report (English ed.), Eighth National Congress of PSP (1961), 105.
[45] Aníbal Escalante's report, *Hoy*, 19 August 1960.

the Cuban and the Chinese revolution,' remarked Odón Alvarez de la Campa, the armless trade unionist, to an audience in Peking; the unions themselves had acquired a 'revolutionary philosophy' as an organ of revolutionary indoctrination.[46] Cuba had now sold over 2½ million tons of sugar to Communist countries in 1960, and only just over 2 million to the U.S. In August, the blunt-spoken Guevara, at the First Congress of Latin American Youth (whose mission was to rally the youth of Latin America against Yankee imperialism), said: 'If I were asked whether our Revolution is Communist, I would define it as Marxist. Our Revolution has discovered by its methods the paths that Marx pointed out.' A commercial and technical agreement had recently been signed with China. The Chinese State Opera as well as the Georgian Ballet made ceremonial visits. The important tenth Congress of the Cuban Communist party in August gave what seemed at least full support to the revolutionary government, though as usual Blas Roca spent much time castigating what he took to be a Leftist position, an even greater danger than imperialism. But he seemed completely to have passed over to the position held by his lieutenant, Dr Carlos Rafael Rodríguez, since in the course of his report to the Congress he gave full backing to Castro as the leader and guarantor of 'maximum unity'.[47] The editor of *Bohemia*, Miguel Angel Quevedo, who in June had published articles denouncing Hungary, Stalinism and concentration camps in Siberia, and who had been one of Castro's oldest supporters, sought asylum and suspended his journal saying:

> The deceit has been discovered. This is not the Revolution for which over 20,000 Cubans died. In order to carry out a purely national Revolution there was no need to submit our people to the hateful Russian vassalage. To carry out a profound social revolution, it was not necessary to install a system which degrades man to the condition of the State. ... This is a revolution betrayed.[48]

He was followed into exile by Antonio Ortega, editor of *Carteles*. Several officials went at the same time, including the ex-Prime Minister, Miró.

But if Cuban society was being transformed along controlled and socialist lines, Castro remained a *caudillo*, a familiar figure in Latin America, but also an eccentric one, who remained restless, as it were on the run, still a rebel, still in jungle green uniform. Much depended upon him. In early July he was ill for a while, with an intestinal infection complicated by pleurisy in one lung. But by 26 July he was fit enough,

[46] The relations of Cuba with China as opposed to Russia are explored below, in the Epilogue to this book. Alvarez de la Campa defected from Cuba in 1964.

[47] See Blas Roca, Report, *op. cit.* The comments of Andrés Suárez, 101–2, are useful.

[48] He committed suicide in Caracas in 1969, leaving a note blaming the Revolution for his death.

along with perhaps not quite a million others, to 'rededicate the nation to the goals of the Revolution'. He also dedicated at this time the Camilo Cienfuegos mountain boarding school for children of peasants in the Sierra Maestra who lived in places too scattered for normal day school attendance to be possible. Belgian and Czech rifles were being bought to arm the new militia, which was now, he claimed, 200,000 strong.[49] But his main pledge was to make Cuba 'an example that can convert the Cordillera of the Andes into the Sierra Maestra of the Hemisphere'.

These thunderous cries were daily noted in Washington. So too was the fact that dealers in imported goods were now almost eliminated; in rural areas free enterprise was almost at an end, since the *tiendas del pueblo* sold goods at low prices with liberal credit. The upper classes had received increases in income tax and there were now much stricter regulations against evasion. Meantime, U.S. banks were refusing to change *pesos*, black market exchanges gave only 60 U.S. cents for a *peso* and in mid-July a Caribbean Rescue Committee was set up to assist and receive Cuban refugees into the U.S. (as well, technically, as refugees from the Dominican Republic, though there were many fewer of these).

In mid-August a special meeting of American foreign ministers of the OAS was held at San José, Costa Rica, on the proposal of both Cuba and the U.S. Christian Herter (who had succeeded Dulles) sought to persuade the conference to condemn Cuba for endangering the hemisphere. Many South Americans were prevented from agreeing, less by their consciences than by their knowledge of Castro's popularity among the public in their own countries. The Cuban representatives expressed themselves angry at having to leave their revolvers in the waiting-room. A committee was finally named to mediate between Cuba and the U.S., but the Cuban delegation had formally withdrawn. Castro, in Havana, predictably denounced the OAS as an organization in the pay of the U.S., and described President Eisenhower's recent proposal for a $M600[50] Latin American aid programme with contempt. But Eisenhower's proposal was the genuine plan of a perplexed president: 'We knew . . . that we could not indefinitely support governments that refused to carry out land and social reforms. We needed new policies that would reach the seat of the trouble.'[51] In the end, however, the U.S. were disappointed by what happened at San José; a resolution was passed which condemned all intervention in the Americas by non-American states and declared totalitarian states to be inconsistent with the continental system. But the

[49] *Revolución*, 27 July 1960.
[50] Of which $M100 was for earthquake relief in Chile.
[51] Eisenhower, 537.

State department had hoped for a condemnation of both Castro and Cuba, and neither were named.

Cuba's links with the U.S. were steadily growing fewer. No country was now supposed to buy Cuban sugar even with money lent by the U.S. Business consultants were busy trying to work out how credit terms abroad could be made to limit Cuban imports of spare parts. Companies predictably were trying to get their losses in Cuba written down as losses for tax purposes. The Standard Oil Co. sought to get oil tanker owners to refuse to carry Russian oil to Cuba. The Senate cut mutual security appropriations to any country which supplied military or even economic assistance to Cuba.

Cuban imports from the U.S. in the first five months of 1960 were thus 30 % below 1959, and it was evident that for the last half of the year the pattern of trade would change completely. Meantime, the State Department were carefully removing those of their members who had been implicated in their time in softer relations with Cuba: Rubottom thus left Washington on 30 July to become ambassador in Argentina; Thomas Mann, a conservative Texan, took over as Assistant Secretary of State for Inter-American Affairs.[52] In Guatemala training continued, though on a small scale. Hatreds between ex-supporters of Castro and ex-Batistiano army officers smouldered. In Miami also there were quarrels. Manuel Artime, the CIA's choice as military commander, was unpopular. Meantime, on the other side of the sea several hundred Latin American students remained in Cuba after what was termed the First Latin American Youth Congress, in order to study not only farm techniques but also guerrilla and revolutionary activity.[53] The ranks in the Americas were closing.

In August a new pastoral letter, this time signed by Cardinal Arteaga and all the other Cuban bishops, formally denounced the Cuban regime. Mgr Díaz told the secretary to the presidency that the Church would be closed unless there were guarantees against riots; Dorticós gave them, 'despite all the provocations'. Castro responded more harshly against 'systematic provocations' by the Church, saying that 'whoever condemns a revolution such as ours betrays Christ and would be capable of crucifying Him again'. In the third week of August, six members of Juventud Católica, together with a Spanish Jesuit, Fr Manual Deboya, were captured after a gun battle in which two policemen were killed and the priest wounded. Deboya was charged with running an underground opposition cell. Finally, 2,000 members of Juventud Católica met at the Colegio Lasalle in Santiago, where the Castro brothers had

---

[52] Thomas Mann (b. 1912), had been a lawyer and since 1952 had been deputy chief of mission in Mexico.

[53] Tad Szulc, 'Exporting the Cuban Revolution', in Plank, 82.

been educated, and vigorously endorsed the pastoral letter, shouting 'Cuba sí, Comunismo no'.[54]

Thus Castro seemed once more surrounded by trouble. In one of his most successful oratorical performances, on 2 September, he responded to the OAS 'Declaration of San José' with his new 'Declaration of Havana'. Cuba would accept Russia's offer of rockets in order to repel U.S. invasion. She would recognize Communist China. 'What have we done to deserve the Declaration of San José?' he demanded; the answer, 'Our people have done nothing more than break their chains.' He also issued a clarion call to the miserable of Latin America to throw off their chains too. This Declaration was said to have been approved by the National Assembly of the Cuban people – that is, the large crowd in the square. On 5 September the Economics minister, Boti, represented Cuba as the OAS's committee of 21, and denounced Eisenhower's aid plan: at least $M30,000 was necessary, as Castro had said in 1959 at Buenos Aires. Cuba would not sign the Declaration of San José and thereafter would cut herself off from all U.S. aid programmes for Latin America. Finally on 18 September Castro with a large entourage went to New York to attend the United Nations.

This second visit of Castro's to the U.S. contrasted with his first. This time there were no cheers. At best, there was silence, at worst, hostile demonstrations and sporadic brawls, in one of which a nine-year-old girl was killed. Squalid quarrels occurred over where the Cubans were to stay; having arrived at the Hotel Shelbourne, on the east side of New York, the delegation left in a hurry on the grounds that it was too expensive, and went to the Hotel Teresa in Harlem. Castro kept out of sight much of the time, visited the U.N. only twice, and was once a guest at the Russian delegation. His speech to the U.N. lasted four and a half hours, twenty-six minutes, the longest which had been delivered there. It was well-delivered, eloquent as usual, and dramatic, but failed to impress the U.S. press, who found it absurd and full of lies. But since this was the occasion of Khrushchev's public quarrels and table hitting, no friend of Russia could expect a good hearing – despite the fact that Khrushchev's motives should be interpreted in terms of his own struggles for power in Russia.[55] Castro left for Cuba on 28 September, on a Soviet airliner hastily borrowed when his own aeroplane was impounded under writs of attachment obtained in Miami against Cuban debts. He left behind over half his delegation. The visit had served little purpose.

While Castro was in New York, Cuba had begun to cast a shadow

[54] During August 1960, the North American sociologist, Wright Mills, was in Cuba to write the most famous of the early defences of the Revolution, Listen Yankee, (published in England as Castro's Cuba).

[55] See M. Tatu, Power in the Kremlin, trans. H. Katel (1969).

over the presidential election. Senator Kennedy for the Democrats began to speak of this issue as if it were yet another Republican failure. He once began to discuss the subject with his staff and said, 'All right but how would we have saved Cuba if we had the power?' Then he added, 'What the hell, they never told us how they would have saved China.'[56] In that spirit, he certainly succumbed to the temptation to use the matter very often. Thus on 23 September (Castro being still in New York) Kennedy said that he would have treated Cuba very differently during the last years of the Batista regime, 'but that now we must make clear our intention . . . to enforce the Monroe doctrine . . . and that we will not be content till democracy is restored to Cuba. The forces fighting for freedom in exile and in the mountains of Cuba should be sustained.' Nixon, who of course knew about the training of the exiles already under way, could not sound so vehement: 'We must recognize that there is "no quick or easy solution" to Castro's threat'; but 'given the opportunity and time the people of Cuba will find their own way back to freedom.'

Just at that moment, as it happened, the CIA's pursuit of that opportunity was heading for trouble: they now found the political front which they had constructed was turning out badly and desired, instead, a single leader. Richard Bissell had discovered the Cubans to be 'incorrigible, completely incapable of forming a front behind a single leader'.[57] One leader of the CIA's front, Sánchez Arango, admittedly a difficult man with whom to work, resigned with the accusation that the CIA had embarked on 'an incessant series of pressures and rebuffs'.[58] Justo Carrillo resigned from the Frente on 30 September on the grounds that 'the most sinister interests predominate'.[59] By this he meant that ex-Batistianos were receiving support within it. 'Tony' Varona became the formal coordinator of the exiles, but Artime remained the military leader (though staying in Miami).

The U.S. Embassy in Havana, an increasingly gloomy and solitary building, advised all nationals to leave Cuba as soon as possible. Castro made no bones about his troubles with the opposition: in the Sierra de Escambray about 1,000 rebels had gathered during October, now secretly supported by Castro's old friend, the North American Major Morgan, and by others who had fought in that district during the war with Batista. Strong forces of militiamen were moved into the foothills of the Escambray under Castro's own command, the peasants of the region being methodically evacuated to prevent them making food available. In Havana, and other cities, Ray's MRP also began to be active.

[56] Schlesinger, 202.
[57] Bissell to the author, 14 January 1963.
[58] Memorandum, qu. Draper, 71.
[59] Carrillo letter to Dr Miró Cardona.

In Escambray the fighting, which for a time seemed ominous, lasted a shorter time than had been thought likely. Starved of food, the rebels risked skirmishes and several of their leaders, ex-students or rebels, were killed or executed. Morgan and another Major, Jesús Carreras, of the Directorio, were captured (and executed some months later).[60] Some prisoners were condemned to twenty or thirty years' gaol. This important challenge to Castro was not apparently given much help by the CIA, who regarded the *guerrilleros* as lacking good security.

On 6 October at Cincinnati Kennedy specifically accused Eisenhower of creating in Cuba 'Communism's first Caribbean base'; the administration should have listened to Ambassadors Smith and Gardner (whose testimony to the Senate Internal Security Sub-Committee had just been released). Kennedy accused Eisenhower's administration of letting Castro get all the arms he needed for victory, while repeating his denunciation of the regime's support of Batista: 'We did nothing to persuade the people of Cuba and of Latin America that we wanted to be on the side of freedom.'

Perhaps as a result of these charges,[61] Eisenhower announced on 13 October a complete ban on all U.S. exports to Cuba, except medicine and some foodstuffs. The Secretary of Commerce, Muller, glibly said, 'If it pushes them into trade with the Communist *bloc*, that's just too bad. After all, we've been the ones that have been pushed around lately.'

The response in Cuba was swift. During the weekend of 14–15 October, Captain Núñez Jiménez at the head of INRA took over 382 large private enterprises in Cuba, including all the banks (except two Canadian ones), all the remaining private sugar mills, eighteen distilleries, sixty-one textile mills, sixteen rice mills, eleven cinemas and thirteen large stores. A second Urban Reform law followed which provided that no one should own more than one residence. Lessees of rented property became tenants of the state and, after a certain number of years, would become outright owners, while landlords would be compensated, though never at more than $350 a month.[62] On 25 October Castro nationalized another 166 U.S. enterprises. The Nicaro nickel plant and Woolworth; Sears Roebuck and General Electric Westinghouse; International Harvester, Remington Rand and Coca Cola; hotels and insurance companies: all the proudest names of U.S. international capitalism were silently and almost without protest overwhelmed. On 29 October Ambassador Bonsal was withdrawn for an

---

[60] See Martino, *I was Castro's Prisoner*, 142, an eye-witness description of Morgan's execution in La Cabaña.

[61] As suggested by the *Economist*. Eisenhower is silent on this topic in his memoirs.

[62] The cost of the building would be paid to the owner according to a specific value over a period of years, less the rent already paid. Mortgagees would receive 50% of their debt paid by new owners, the rest being paid to the government.

'extended period of consultation'. He never returned, though the U.S. Embassy itself remained in Havana till January 1961, when Castro told the Cubans that a U.S. invasion would occur before Eisenhower left the presidency on 20 January; he ordered a general mobilization, explaining that the excuse for the invasion would be the false accusation that Cuba was constructing rocket pads on her territory. He therefore demanded that the U.S. reduced their staff in the embassy to eighteen. Eisenhower then broke diplomatic relations. On neither 15 nor 25 October were the Communists any too pleased, Blas Roca and Carlos Rafael Rodríguez refraining from comment in *Hoy*. No doubt they had not been consulted.

One incident remains to be related marking the end of a stage in Cuban history. On 11 October 1960 Che Guevara, president of the National Bank, sent for Julio Lobo, the great sugar king, who had remained in Cuba despite disillusion with Castro for almost a year. He had lived quietly on his plantation, making plans for the emigration of his family. Up till then his sugar mills had functioned normally, though he had lost his land. When Guevara sent for him he supposed that he wanted to talk with him about certain moneys owing to him from the National Bank in connection with his building of the Hotels Capri and Riviera. But Guevara, with his customary candour, explained to Lobo that he and his aides had been examining Lobo's past accounts with morbid attention to detail and that they had not found any instance of irregularity. For this reason, Lobo had been 'left till the last', but now his time had come. 'We are Communists,' Guevara said, 'and it is impossible for us to permit you, who represent "the very idea" of capitalism in Cuba, to remain as you are.' Lobo had therefore to disappear or to 'integrate' with the revolution. Lobo pointed out that Khrushchev surely believed in the peaceful coexistence of two systems of production and peaceful competition between them. Guevara replied that that was all very well between nations but such a thing could not happen within the same one. Lobo asked how he could integrate himself with the revolution. In reply, Guevara proposed that he, Lobo, should become the general manager of the Cuban sugar industry under the revolutionary government, dealing with commerce, agriculture and industry. Guevara added that Lobo would, of course, lose his estates but he would be permitted the usufruct of *Tinguaro*, his favourite mill. Lobo, who in the past would have much liked the opportunity of rationalization and modernization that such an appointment could have given him, asked for time to consider the offer. Guevara agreed and Lobo undertook to tell his answer to Guevara or one of his aides (since Guevara was leaving shortly for Moscow) within a week. Lobo returned home and made immediate plans for flight. He instructed his secretary to take all she could from the banks and bury it in the old secret passage beneath his office in old Havana. But the next day his house was sealed and guarded. Lobo left for Miami on 13 October, leaving behind all his vast enterprises, his palaces, his El Greco and other splendid paintings, and his locks of Napoleon's hair.[63]

[63] Evidence of Julio Lobo, Madrid, 9 November 1968. Most of his skilled employees afterwards left Cuba but his general manager, Tomás Martínez, remained to direct the sugar industry of Cuba under the revolution, along with others who stayed, as usual, for a mixture of private and public motives.

CHAPTER 38

The U.S. Prepares for Battle

During the culminating weeks of the campaign for the presidency of the U.S. in 1960, Cuba became for a few days the central topic. On 18 October, Nixon told an audience in Miami that the new Cuban regime was an intolerable cancer. 'Patience,' he said, 'is no longer a virtue.' The administration, he hinted broadly, was even then planning several steps to destroy this 'economic banditry'.[1] On 20 October Kennedy's staff put out a provocative statement about strengthening Cuban fighters for freedom. Nixon was annoyed. He had understood, he said later, that Kennedy had already been informed about the CIA's schemes during a general briefing on foreign affairs by Allen Dulles. But he was apparently misinformed.[2] Nixon assumed Kennedy was upbraiding the administration for not doing what in fact he knew they secretly were doing. Hence the somewhat bizarre discussion on the subject of Cuba in their fourth television electoral debate together; Nixon, to guard the security of his clandestine operations, accused Kennedy of 'dangerous irresponsibility' and of jeopardizing all U.S. friends in Latin America. Nixon said, 'What can we do? We can do what we did with Guatemala. There was a Communist dictator . . . the Guatemalan people themselves eventually rose up and they threw him out. . . .' Kennedy replied by arguing that mere economic quarantine was too little and too late.

This peculiar discussion led to even more peculiar results. Liberal editorials praised Nixon; columnists of the Right such as George Sokolosky praised Kennedy as speaking in the tones of Theodore Roosevelt and being closer to the national attitude of the Republican party than to the muddy internationalism of the Eisenhower administration. This would have an effect on Kennedy's Cuban policies later on.

There were, however, different democratic voices, notably that of Adlai Stevenson, then campaigning in North Carolina. On 25 October he made a speech which contradicted Kennedy's position, even attacking the economic embargo which, he thought, would drive Cuba further into the Soviet *bloc*. He also telephoned Kennedy to express his concern over the hard line which he had been employing and, probably in consequence, Kennedy for a time left the subject of Cuba alone,[3] definitely

[1] See Nixon, *Six Crises*, 352–3.
[2] *Cf. ibid.*, 354, fn; Schlesinger, 204; T. C. Sorensen, *Kennedy* (1965), 205.
[3] Adlai Stevenson to the author, 6 February 1963.

withdrawing from his most militant stand, to the relief in particular of the *New York Times*.

What was the reality? In Cuba, all believed an invasion inevitable. Castro talked of it all the time. But no one knew what type of invasion, above all what size, was likely. Florida, too, was in the same state of near ignorance as Havana. Miami might be full of Cuban refugees. Street signs and shops might have begun advertising in Spanish. But only a few people had friends or relations actually being trained in Guatemala, even though by November 1960 perhaps 60,000 people had already left Cuba since the coming of Castro, mostly by regular air flight, some by small boat, nearly half of them tourists without papers – probably half the whole professional group of the past in Cuba.

By now there were still only between 400 and 500 Cubans under training in Guatemala.[4] Yet the secret was out. On 30 October a Guatemalan paper, *La Hora*, published a front-page editorial by an eminent journalist, Clemente Marroquín Rojas, explaining that an invasion of Cuba was 'well under way, prepared not by our country, which is so poor and so disorganised, but implicitly by the U.S.A.' The Guatemalan Foreign Minister denied this, but the opposition demanded investigation. Few North Americans might read Guatemalan papers, but some did, among them Ronald Hilton, editor of an admirable monthly, the *Hispanic American Report*. He wrote an editorial in his November issue, explaining that Castro knew about the invasion plans even if public opinion in the U.S. did not.[5]

The purpose of the training in Guatemala was still to organize a guerrilla movement on the lines of what was already going on in the Escambray. Arms and supplies would be flown in from outside to assist guerrilla bands. Eisenhower had allotted $M13 to this scheme in August.[6] But already it had been proposed that it should be abandoned and in its place an invasion should take place, with air cover in U.S. planes (as in Guatemala in 1954) piloted by Cubans. This major change of policy had been agreed by early November. For it had been found more and more difficult to support what guerrilla activity there was; movement of information in and out of Cuba was increasingly complicated; and above all the Cubans had very bad security: this was 'the biggest single reason for this major policy decision'.[7] Apparently this decision was not put to the president, who later specifically said that no

---

[4] Schlesinger, 207. *Cf.* Haynes Johnson, *The Bay of Pigs* (1964), 55.
[5] It is curious that the only U.S. journal to pick up what was published in a Guatemalan paper was this semi-academic one.
[6] According to Schlesinger, 206.
[7] Bissell's evidence. (Bissell put this decision as early as December, but I think he must have made a mistake: *cf.* Haynes Johnson, 54; Schlesinger, 207; and Sorensen, 295.) Cuban exiles thought the major reason was the CIA's dislike of the guerrillas in Cuba, because these could be controlled.

plan for an invasion had been elaborated whilst he was in office.[8] Actually there was such a plan, but in the middle of the election it was not thought worthwhile telling him. Anyway, the CIA's guerrilla instructors left Guatemala and in their place came trainers for a conventional attack, with tanks, artillery and air support. Only some sixty *guerrilleros* continued, in the Counter Insurgency School in Panama. Recruiting for the Cuban operation began in Miami on a more sustained basis. But the invasion was envisaged as still requiring only about a thousand men at most.[9]

This was a strange decision. Partly, it rested on the assumption that the assault force had only to land for an army to spring up around it from the discontented people. In Guatemala in 1954, the CIA's aeroplanes had indeed merely arrived over the capital for the Arbenz regime to melt away. The CIA certainly had their success in Guatemala at the back of their minds, though they might perhaps have learned something from the erroneous Anglo-French anticipation of what would occur in Egypt in 1956, and from the fact that there were three clear differences between Cuba and Guatemala: firstly, the revolutionary regime in the latter country had never established its hold over the people to anything like such an extent as Castro had; secondly, Castro had destroyed the traditional army whereas Arbenz had not; and thirdly, Cuba was an island therefore more easily defended against a Duke of Brunswick than was Guatemala.

'The aim of the invading brigade,' Bissell said later, 'was specifically to establish a bridgehead . . . and *thereafter* to destroy Castro's air force [i.e. from an airstrip which they would have captured]. A government could have been established, which the U.S.A. could have recognised . . . We did not expect the "underground" to play a large part.'[10] It is difficult therefore to avoid the conclusion that the CIA hoped this government would be the recipient of substantial and open aid from the U.S. Indeed, the only logical explanation for a scheme to attack Cuba with about 800 to 900 men was that this would soon give the U.S. an opportunity to intervene.

There were, of course, further alarms. In November, just after Kennedy's election victory, a revolt in Guatemala nearly occurred, the very place where the new rebels were being trained. Eisenhower resolved 'that if we received a request from Guatemala for assistance, we would move in without delay'[11] – apparently the first clear decision by a

[8] Eisenhower said in 1962, 'We were more or less thinking of guerrilla type of action until we could get enough forces to do more . . . There was no specific strategical or tactical plan developed before I had left.' (H.A.R. v, xii, 33.)
[9] Recruits were paid up to $400 a month, additionally $175 for a wife, $50 for a first child, $25 for other children.
[10] Bissell to the author.
[11] *Waging Peace*, 612

government of the U.S. to intervene with its own troops since 1933. The administration also feared an attempt by Cuba to overthrow the Guatemalan or Nicaraguan governments, and, as a result, patrolled the Guatemalan and Nicaraguan coasts by sea and air, for some weeks.[12]

In November 1960 Manuel Ray escaped from Cuba, having left behind his MRP well organized and with its morale raised by a daring rescue from La Cabaña of several officers condemned at the same time as Matos. Ray's plans in Miami were the same as those which he had had in Cuba: to overthrow Castro from within Cuba and to continue politically the reforming work of the revolution as the liberals had envisaged it in 1959. But the CIA continued to distrust the Cuban underground, Bissell chiefly because of the Cubans' bad security arrangements, 'Frank Bender' perhaps because of their progressive aspirations. Ray's error doubtless was to have anything to do with the U.S. But the trouble was, as in the case of every revolt against authority in Cuba since the nineteenth century, that no Cuban rebel could bring himself to admit this. As it was, even Ray began to find himself increasingly expectant of the CIA, even though ranking himself as really in opposition among the exiles in Miami. Nor was Ray, though personally brave and appealing, able to establish himself as a major political leader of international importance.

On 17 November[13] Kennedy, president-elect, was for the first time told by Allen Dulles and Bissell about the plan for the invasion. Kennedy said that he was 'astonished by its magnitude and daring',[14] as well he might be, since it almost exactly reflected what he had demanded, perhaps with less than complete seriousness, during the electoral campaign. On 29 November, Allen Dulles gave Kennedy a more 'detailed briefing';[15] the president-elect listened with attention and then told Dulles to carry the work forward. 'The response was sufficiently affirmative,' says Schlesinger, 'for Dulles to take it as an instruction to expedite the subject.' But at the same time Kennedy 'had grave doubts from that moment on'.[16] Thus Kennedy, Hamlet-like, encouraged what he in fact mistrusted, perhaps already caught up by the dilemma between the policy which he had advocated during the campaign and what he thought wise – a dilemma which was to haunt him all the time in office. On 6 December Kennedy had his first meeting with Eisenhower, but, though Cuba was on the proposed agenda, the project of invasion does not seem to have been discussed.[17] Kennedy did not see Eisenhower

[12] *Ibid.*, 613.
[13] Or 18 November (*cf.* Schlesinger, 148, 210).
[14] Sorensen, 295.
[15] Schlesinger, 211.
[16] Sorensen, 295.
[17] See Eisenhower memorandum, *Waging Peace*, 712 ff.

again till 19 January, the day before his inauguration, and does not seem to have occupied himself with the matter before then.

In the meantime, much had happened. In early December the CIA's plans for invasion were presented to 'the secret inter-departmental committee charged with special operations', but apparently not formally approved.[18] The U.S. chiefs of staff as yet knew nothing of what was planned.[19] The fact of the forthcoming change of administration caused a certain confusion. Decisions took longer.

> The outgoing administration were reluctant to take responsibility for what they were not going to do themselves [recalled Bissell] and the people coming in were reluctant to take decisions before they saw the papers. And this was important because the situation in Cuba was getting more and more difficult.[20]

On 10 December, Willauer, the ambassador to Costa Rica and, as has been seen, one of the architects of the attack on Guatemala in 1954, was told by Secretary of State Herter, 'There are quite a lot of doubts whether this plan is correct, what the timing should be, various problems about putting the thing together.' Willauer was to investigate. With Under-Secretary Thomas Mann, he was convinced that the project 'should not be . . . undertaken unless there was practically no chance that it would fail'.[21] Eisenhower, meantime, was busy with political considerations; he wanted the Cuban exiles to elect a leader who would be recognized by the U.S. as the legal government of Cuba, if possible before the inauguration of Kennedy.[22] He had also made available $M1 for the resettlement of Cuban refugees, now numbered at 100,000.

By this time the news of the training at Guatemala was no longer secret. Following the *Hispanic American Report*, the *Nation* and then the *Los Angeles Mirror* and *St Louis Dispatch* were speaking of the secret camps. In Miami all Cubans knew where the recruiting centres were, especially after a visit at Christmas time by a group of the Guatemalan Cubans on a recruiting drive. These got on very badly with the politicians of the Frente, and indeed the Frente themselves were still squabbling. The CIA still desired to have no truck with Ray's group. Several of the latter were refused permission to join in the expedition, including at least one of the officers of Matos's group who had been rescued from La Cabaña in October. Recruitment was in the hands of Joaquín Sanjenís, brother of the MRR leader in prison in Cuba, and nephew of José Miguel Gómez's secretary; he seems to have favoured right-wing

[18] Schlesinger, 211.
[19] See Lazo, 251.
[20] Bissell to the author.
[21] Willauer to Senate, *Communist Threat*, 873–5.
[22] *Waging Peace*, 613–14.

recruits. Nor was he careful about the recruitment of Batistianos. The ensuing antagonisms seemed worse when they began to be generally known, as they did by 6 January, when *Time* reported that Ray was getting no funds from the U.S., while the Frente under Varona was being amply supplied – $135,000 a month regularly and $500,000 on occasion; on 10 January the *New York Times* even published a map of the Guatemalan base.

Eisenhower decided to do nothing about this. The rumours led Castro to a full general mobilization, enabling him to encourage the Russians to send yet more arms. Meantime the Guatemalan government announced that the camps were for training men to resist an impending Cuban attack. A group of U.S. reporters visited the Alejos coffee plantation base. The Cuban pilots were bidden for the visit.[23] In Europe such revelations as these about a government's intentions would have caused a storm. In the U.S. the constitutional organization of opposition was harder. Similarly, those who were prepared to criticize publicly an attack on Castro were few. They certainly could not be supposed to include Kennedy. From his television statements on 20 October, Nixon even might have been supposed the liberals' champion. But Nixon had his own problems at that time.

There were troubles too at the base in Guatemala. Some new arrivals from Miami were considered by the old commanders to be conspiring. These resigned, taking with them 230 men out of what was still only about 550. A CIA chieftain harangued the little army and persuaded all but forty to continue training. Twelve men considered incorrigible were held prisoner in a remote part of North Guatemala. But the mutiny rumbled on.[24]

It was in these circumstances that Kennedy took up the reins as president, on 20 January. Two days later, Allen Dulles and General Lemnitzer, representing the joint chiefs of staff, reviewed the invasion plans for members of the new administration – Rusk, McNamara and Robert Kennedy.[25] By this time the chiefs of staff had already become concerned with the Cuban plans, after having 'tacitly questioned' the prohibition on U.S. participation earlier in the month. CIA planners, however, were already looking at maps of south Cuba for possible sites for landing. On 26 January Kennedy had his first meeting on the subject of the invasion: he was 'wary and reserved'.[26] He allowed the CIA to continue its preparations, himself, meantime, being preoccupied with the articulation of the general plan for Latin American development of which he had already spoken in his campaign speech – an 'Alliance for

[23] Szulc and Meyer, 91.
[24] Haynes Johnson, 61.
[25] Schlesinger, 216; Willauer, 876, refers.
[26] Schlesinger, 216.

Progress'.[27] Had it not been for the Cuban issue, doubtless such a scheme would never have received any backing. At the same time the question of Cuba had revived for the first time for twenty-five years the controversy about U.S. intervention. One or two meetings were held in Washington in early February, and at least one of the people put to work on the project by the previous administration (Willauer) was unceremoniously dismissed.[28] But nothing more precise was done. Artime (taken out of his guerrilla training at Panamá), Varona and Antonio Maceo visited Guatemala, had various disputes with the officers there, patched them up and returned. A bigger recruiting drive began. Young men in Miami went to the recruiting base to avoid being left out of 'a major event' in their country's history. Not all went to Guatemala. Not all were accepted. Enquiries would be made about their political activity and background. Some were still taught guerrilla activity, since there were plans for diversionary work. One group of *guerrilleros* trained in Louisiana (some complained and said that they wanted 'a conventional war').[29]

Kennedy was undecided whether to go ahead with the invasion. One of his advisers, Schlesinger, advised against it on the simple grounds that it 'would fix a malevolent image of the new administration'.[30] The CIA leaders were, however, strongly in favour of going ahead;[31] Allen Dulles asked what could be done with the trained Cubans if not sent to war? Was there not a 'disposal problem'?[32] They would return disconsolate to Miami to complain, and U.S. prestige would be diminished; so would the cause of democracy. Bissell was an equally strong advocate: the morale of the brigade was high and had to be tested. Kennedy agreed that the 'simplest thing might be to let the Cubans go where they yearned to go to: Cuba', with the minimum risk to the U.S. There should, however, be no U.S. military intervention. Air strikes were too risky. The idea of landing at Trinidad, canvassed by Bissell, was rejected by Kennedy as too spectacular; the CIA suggested the Bay of Cochinos (or Bay of Pigs) as an alternative and the chiefs of staff agreed, though preferring Trinidad.[33] On 15 March Kennedy told the CIA to continue to plan on the assumption that the invasion would occur, but in such a way that it could still be called off twenty-four hours before it

[27] The phrase was apparently the joint responsibility of a Cuban liberal economist Ernesto Betancourt, and Karl Meyer of the *Washington Post*.

[28] *Communist Threat*, 875.

[29] Evidence of Antonio Campiña, Washington, 1962.

[30] Schlesinger, 218.

[31] 'Allen and Dick didn't just brief us . . . they sold us on it,' said a 'White House Adviser' to Stewart Alsop.

[32] Dulles appears to have first used this famous phrase on 11 March (Schlesinger, 219).

[33] This was a wily choice for it could give a well-defended beachhead, on which a provisional government could be easily landed.

was due to begin:[34] a somewhat desperate expedient, it would seem, by any standard. It now seemed that Kennedy was being persuaded to go ahead by the senior advisers inherited from Eisenhower, although he personally was against it.[35] But he was also caught up by the ideas which he had himself proposed the previous autumn. How could he abandon a policy which he had previously upbraided the Republicans for not embarking upon? There were, of course, risks to his general policies, with the Soviet Union, Latin America and Europe, interwoven with this scheme. But Kennedy seems to have made the curious error of supposing that this *amour* of his with the exiles could still be kept a secret from his bride, U.S. public opinion.

Kennedy compromised by telling the CIA to try to make the exile organization more liberal. They did this by bringing Manuel Ray's group into the Frente. On 18 March, the Frente chose Dr Miró Cardona, first premier under Castro, to be 'provisional president of Cuba' (he had reached Miami from Havana in the winter) out of a list of six presented by the CIA. The exiles' relations with the U.S. indeed increasingly resembled those of the Spanish kings with Rome over the election of bishops. On 22 March Ray signed an agreement with his old antagonist Varona, permitting Miró to found a 'Cuban Revolutionary Council' which would become the provisional government of Cuba after the success of the invasion. This body would retain most of its members in Cuba. It should give maximum priority to the aid of combatants already in Cuba. No one with 'a responsible position' under Batista would be able to join the new Cuban army. An agreement on the 'effective way of treating *latifundia*' was to be reached within two weeks.[36]

The council was merely the old Frente together with Ray. Droller-Bender insisted that Artime should be military commander. Prominent exiles rallied to support the council. Ray, according to Bissell, 'was quite eager to settle down after March'.[37] Back in Washington, Schlesinger prepared a white paper to prove that Castro had betrayed the revolution: the theme was to be that 'our objection', as Kennedy put it, 'isn't to the Cuban Revolution, it is to the fact that Castro has turned it over to the Communists.'[38]

There was, however, now a marked difference of view between the White House and the chiefs of staff on the one hand, and the CIA on the other. Both the former supposed that the latter was counting on the

[34] Schlesinger, 220.

[35] 'I used to come home from meetings supposing that only two persons – me and the president – were against the idea of invasion,' Schlesinger told the author (7 September 1962).

[36] Document qu. Draper, 96–8.

[37] Bissell to the author.

[38] Schlesinger, 222.

invasion being supported by large-scale risings inside Cuba, while the
latter was thinking much more of 'an Anzio concept'. No special effort
was being made to coordinate the movements of internal guerrilla
forces, though the CIA apparently thought that there were then in
Cuba 2,500 active militants in the army, 20,000 supporters in the
towns and behind them a quarter of the Cuban population. The intelligence branch of the CIA did not know of the planned invasion, and the
CIA failed to back up their own operators in Cuba.[39] The reason, as
ever, was the lack of proper security among the Cubans. But this lack of
faith in the Cuban guerrillas was not apparently communicated to
Kennedy, who seems at best to have avoided knowing too much of the
details and anyway seemed to be growing 'steadily more sceptical' as
time went on. When Schlesinger gave Kennedy the text of his white
paper, he asked, 'What do you think about this damned invasion?' 'As
little as possible,' said Kennedy.[40]

A decision had now to be reached: should the invasion go on or not?
Adlai Stevenson came to Washington and

> Expressed alarm at the press reports and asked [Kennedy] specifically
> what was going on . . . [Kennedy] said I could rest assured that
> whatever was being planned there would be no question of U.S.
> involvement. I said I was very greatly relieved at this . . . I think
> at that time I did sense a very considerable degree of anxiety in
> Kennedy's mind as to whether he was in fact doing the right thing or
> not.[41]

A little afterwards, according to Stevenson, 'Tracy Barnes of the
CIA came up and briefed us here on the Delegation [to the UN] . . .
he assured us that this was simply a question of helping the exiles and
that this was not in any way a U.S. operation. In the light of what happened, I suppose this can be regarded as less than candid.'[42] Others less
loyal would perhaps have put it less politely.

The doubts voiced by Stevenson were put also by Senator Fulbright
in a memorandum on 30 March: to let the exiles overthrow Castro
would be generally denounced as an example of imperialism; the U.S.

[39] Szulc and Meyer, 125, report that the 'national co-ordinator' of the Cuban underground
about 12–15 April was smuggled out of Cuba (?through Guantánamo) and sent back after
discussions with Miró's group, with two tons of C4 plastic explosive. But he was in Miami
when the invasion began.

[40] Schlesinger, 233.

[41] Stevenson to the author, 6 February 1963.

[42] *Ibid.* I imagine that this was the conference of 8 April referred to by Schlesinger, 245–6,
though Stevenson did not mention Schlesinger's presence at it to the author. According to
Schlesinger, Stevenson afterwards said he disapproved of the plan but would make out the
best case for it.

would inevitably be tempted, if things went wrong, to use their own armed forces; he argued instead for containment: 'The Castro regime is a thorn in the flesh . . . not a dagger in the heart.'[43] On 31 March Chester Bowles, Assistant Secretary of State, opposed the invasion plan in a memorandum to Dean Rusk.[44] But, perhaps unfortunately, Kennedy spent Easter in Palm Beach, closer to the influence of the exiles and of his old friend, ex-ambassador Earl Smith. He returned more militant. On 3 April, Schlesinger's white paper was published: 'The present situation in Cuba confronts the western hemisphere and the Inter-American system with a grave and urgent challenge . . . [and] offers a clear and present danger to the authentic and autonomous revolution of the Americas.' On 4 April a decisive meeting was held. Dulles and Bissell repeated their well-known views in favour of action, with some new arguments. It was now or never to crush Castro; if the U.S. delayed Castro would have Soviet MiGs and trained pilots.[45] Provided the expedition was fully 'Cubanized' it would not matter much even if it failed. The survivors could quickly get to the Sierra Escambray – though, as no one apparently realized, those hills were nearly 100 miles away from the beachhead. Dulles had said that he thought the success would be easier than in Guatemala in 1954. A CIA emissary from Guatemala reported the brigade to be in good heart.[46] As for the Department of State, Rusk, who apparently distrusted the project, did not speak forcefully. His more forthright assistant, Thomas Mann, said that he would have opposed the plan at the start but now that the matter had proceeded so far, it should continue. McNamara favoured the invasion; he was swayed by the positive views of the joint chiefs of staff. A. A. Berle, jr, desired 'the men to be put into Cuba but did not insist on a major production',[47] whatever that may have meant. Only Fulbright openly opposed the invasion. Schlesinger, also fundamentally hostile, was too overawed to speak. How was he, 'a mere college professor', to intervene when the chiefs of staff and the secretaries of State and Defence approved? But, afterwards, he told Kennedy what he thought, and later said the same in a memorandum. Kennedy nevertheless decided to go ahead – apparently assuming that it was less an amphibious invasion than a large infiltration. Perhaps he too was overawed by his senior

---

[43] *Fulbright of Arkansas*, ed. Karl E. Meyer (1963), 194–205.

[44] Evidence of Chester Bowles, November 1962.

[45] This point of view was forcefully put by Allen Dulles in an interview in 'Meet the Press' on TV on 31 December 1961. Reston in the *New York Times* on 4 April said that between 100 and 200 Cuban airmen were in Czechoslovakia learning to fly MiGs and that this addition to Cuban air forces meant that only a full U.S. invasion could oust Castro. One can guess that this tale came from the CIA.

[46] Haynes Johnson and Bernard Gwertzman, *Fulbright the Dissenter*, London, 1969, 175; Sorensen, 296.

[47] Schlesinger, 228.

advisers – a sadly familiar development in the relation of politician and bureaucrat in democracies.

The Cuban Revolutionary Council was meantime preparing to return to Havana, though, to escape the feverish and reactionary attitude of Miami, they went first to New York. Two scholars from Harvard, Doctors John Plank and William Barnes, did their best. Schlesinger tried to persuade the Cubans to understand that the U.S. could not overtly support the invasion in any way. Kennedy publicly stated on 12 April that the U.S. would never intervene in a Cuban conflict. Whether the CIA chiefs thought this was the case seems unlikely; for Bissell was arguing strongly in favour of giving air cover, even though this might have led to U.S. intervention.[48] Afterwards the CIA kept the Cuban Revolutionary Council uninformed of their plans. Miró believed that the U.S. would one day intervene. A. A. Berle assured Miró that the U.S. would support the invaders with arms but not with any reinforcement of men.[49] Miró remained incredulous, though Kennedy had him told that, if he did not accept that there would be no U.S. intervention, there would be no invasion at all. Meanwhile, a U.S. marine colonel made a special report to Kennedy after a visit to Guatemala that the rebels were in a high state of elation, which he shared.

The atmosphere in Guatemala was indeed one of confidence. But this was at least partly because the officers had been led to believe that the U.S. would back them up in every way, including air and sea cover. Several CIA officers committed themselves to this effect.[50] Varona, for instance, was apparently told by a U.S. colonel that the Cubans would receive full air cover, and Ray was left with the same impression.[51] None of the leaders was told of the plan to head for the Escambray if things went wrong. All assumed that the sixteen B.26s which the CIA placed at the disposal of the exiles would be adequate to crush the – as it was assumed – disorganized and incompetent Cuban air force. The commanders in Guatemala had only a 'brigade' but they were apparently misled into thinking other units would be involved. They thought that their task was to establish a beachhead to which the provisional government would quickly come to ask help from the U.S. and elsewhere if need be.[52] The CIA advisers were so keen on the invasion that they urged the Cubans to go ahead even if it was cancelled in Washington. To do this they would even make a show of imprisoning

[48] Bissell to the author. See below, p. 590 fn 38.
[49] Schlesinger, 239.
[50] See Haynes Johnson, 68.
[51] *H.A.R.*, V, xvi, 33; evidence of Ray.
[52] This was no doubt a reason for selecting the landing place at Girón and Cochinos Bay since it was easily defendable, given air superiority, by a small number of men; there were only three approach roads over the swamps.

the advisers,[53] including the operational chief, 'Frank'.[54] With this strange qualification the men of Brigade 2506 – so named after the serial number of one of its members who had died accidentally during training – were taken to Puerto Cabezas in Nicaragua. They set off on 14 April by sea, being seen off by Luis Somoza, the dictator of Nicaragua who asked them to bring him back some hairs from Castro's beard.[55] Like Narciso López's expeditions a hundred years before, they set out to fight for freedom, but under odd and ambiguous auspices; and the figure of the angry Somoza shaking his fist on the quayside was an appropriate mascot for them.

[53] Haynes Johnson, 76.
[54] His name was apparently William Freeman. His predecessor was William McQuaring – according to an exile in testimony in April 1961 (*Playa Girón, Derrota del Imperialismo*, 4 vols (1961), IV, *Los Mercenarios*, 333).
[55] Haynes Johnson, 77.

CHAPTER 39

Cuba Socialista: I

As it happened, and as such zealous students of history as President Kennedy and that self-effacing 'college professor' Schlesinger must have realized, the very thing now needed by Castro to consolidate his regime was an unsuccessful attack from without, backed, though not to the hilt, by the U.S. Both the French and the Russian revolutions had been consolidated by invasions by exiles. Castro, like the Committee of Public Safety and the Bolsheviks, feared an invasion; Castro, like Miró Cardona (the Duke of Brunswick of Miami) could hardly believe that the 'illiterate millionaire', as he elegantly described Kennedy, would not, if it came to the pinch, back his protégés; but at least there would be a struggle, which surely would unite Cubans patriotically around the government against the old, and no doubt the final enemy, the Colossus of the North. At the time of the invasion, the Cuban revolutionary regime was in full economic crisis, characterized by confusion in both industry and agriculture, and Castro had had to admit in harsh contradiction with earlier boasts, 'for a country at the outset of such a fundamental revolution, it is particularly dangerous . . . to think that living standards can be substantially and immediately improved'[1].

But Castro made no concessions to try to avoid the dangers of invasion. Indeed, many passages in many speeches suggest that he was relieved that the last gloves, such as they had been, were off: 'The struggle of great interests is set forth, the inflamed struggle between Revolution and Counter-Revolution . . . war to the death between the forces was inevitable and in a revolution, the struggles are to the death'; and 'What is a Revolution? Is it perhaps a peaceful and tranquil process? Is it perhaps strewn with roses? Revolution is of all historic events, the most complex and convulsive.'[2] The prospects of actual gunfire would stimulate Castro on 16 April 1961 to his first public admission that Cuba was socialist: 'That is what they cannot forgive – that we should here . . . under their very nostrils, have made a socialist revolution.'[3] A month

[1] *Obra Revolucionaria*, 11, 26 March 1961.

[2] Speech, 4 January 1961 (*Obra Revolucionaria*, No. 1 of 1961, 22 and 24).

[3] Playa Girón, I, 75. This was of course a well-planned statement: Raúl Castro later said (*Revolución*, 24 July 1961) that the statement meant that the Revolution had fulfilled its national liberating phase (*etapa nacional liberadora*) as well as its anti-imperialist and anti-feudal agrarian stage.

earlier Faure Chomón, the olive-skinned ambassador to Russia, had, in Castro's presence, spoken of the revolutionary leaders as 'we Communists' at a ceremony commemorating the death four years before of his old leader, Echevarría (who had been far from being a Communist). At the time of the formation of the Directorio, Chomón had customarily been referred to by the university Communists as a gangster and he in turn had denounced them as 'patio revolutionaries'; while he had refused to agree in the Sierra Escambray to Guevara's demand that they should both ally with the local Communists under Torres. Now, doubtless through opportunism, he was the most zealous philo-Communist of all.[4] A month before that Castro, in an interview in the Italian Communist paper L'Unitá, had said of the Cuban Communists that they were:

> The only party that has always clearly proclaimed the necessity of a radical change in the structure of social relationships. It is also true that at first the Communists distrusted me and us rebels. It was a justified distrust, an absolutely correct position . . . because we of the Sierra . . . were still full of *petit bourgeois* prejudices and defects, despite Marxist reading . . . Then we came together, we understood each other and began to collaborate.[5]

One month previous even to that Aguilera, the propaganda secretary of the CTC, and Castro's chosen instrument in the trade unions, though another opportunist, had announced: 'It is time to state without fear, with unshaking knees, with untrembling voice and with our heads held high, that we are marching inexorably towards socialism in our Fatherland.'[6] The relations of Castro and his Communist allies were, however, still ambiguous, though the youth movement of the 26 July had merged with the Communist Youth. Castro himself made all the main decisions,[7] sustained probably by his personal backing from Khrushchev, and it is impossible to avoid the conclusion, judging from what happened later, that Castro was primarily interested in using the Communists, almost as Batista had used them, as a kind of bureaucracy to control the Labour movement and as much of the economy as he captured from private hands.

In December, nevertheless, Castro set up indoctrination schools of

[4] Manuel Ledón, one of Chomón's old comrades in the Directorio, recalled bitterly that in 1958 Chomón had tried to get help from the U.S. Embassy in Havana: his anti-imperialism, he commented, was indeed, 'eloquently modern'.

[5] L'Unitá, 1 February 1961. As Draper points out, this speech marked the beginning of an era of humbleness on Castro's part before the ideological purity of the Communists.

[6] Revolución, 7 November 1960. Andrés Suárez, 115, points out that Hoy did not publish this.

[7] e.g. the critical question of the establishment of State farms in place of co-operatives. Cf. Dumont, 57.

'revolutionary instruction' under his old Communist friend at the university, Leonel Soto, 'to train cadres for a united party'.[8] Soto was the first Communist party member to receive a major appointment under the regime and for a time he was alone. These schools (twelve in the provinces) gave courses lasting nine months, with students from the 26 July, the Communist party and some from the Directorio Revolucionario. They studied Marxist–Leninism in a primitive fashion; and the first course ended in April 1961. The national school was established in the Ministry of the Interior, in a large salon of the old Jesuit school of Belén which had been taken over for that branch of the administration. Here classes began at three in the afternoon, and continued till half-past ten at night; Blas Roca's *Fundamentos del Socialismo en Cuba* was the usual textbook in 1961. 'From three o'clock till five, Professor Carlos Rodríguez lectured on this work. At 5.15, after a coffee break, the group, of twenty-eight, divided into four seminars. At 7.30, there was a general discussion and Professor Rodríguez gave a final talk at nine o'clock'.

On the surface, Cuba seemed now firmly within the Communist alliance. On 1 January 1961 a parade in Havana had exhibited Russian tanks and other weapons, though not, as yet, MiGs. On 4 March, Castro had explained that he could draw on 'mountains on mountains of Communist arms' to defend Cuba if need be; the U.S. calculated that $M50 worth of Soviet weapons had arrived by April.[9] Even before the end of 1960, it had also become clear that Cuban embassies in South America were being used to deliver money to local Communist parties; and on 4 October 1960 the Cuban ambassador in Lima, Luis Ricardo Alonso, was discovered to have handed over $30,000 to various Peruvian Communists.[10] Similar occurrences were reported from El Salvador. Peru broke relations with Cuba in December. Prensa Latina offices were also closed, both there and in the Argentine. Cuba in November withdrew from the World Bank, arranging for the repurchase of her old shares of capital. Meantime, an ambassador had arrived in Havana from China, and from all the Communist countries. The western embassies on the other hand had become isolated oases of *bourgeois* society, eating black beans off gold plate. Internationally, Cuba was already recognized more as a part of the international Communist *bloc* than even of the nationalistic neutral world.

[8] *Cuba Socialista*, February 1963. Castro clearly was aware of the loaded nature of this activity, as can be seen from his speech of November 1961 when he explained, 'To indoctrinate is not a pleasant word . . . it makes you think that you are impressing knowledge on someone by force of repeating it innumerable times' (*Revolución*, 11 November 1961, 9).

[9] *White Paper on Cuba*, 22.

[10] The letter was discovered by anti-Communist Cubans who broke into the Embassy in November. Alonso later became ambassador in London, defected in 1965 and published an anti-revolutionary realistic novel.

Towards South America the Cuban leaders regarded themselves as having provided a 'catalyst';[11] for them, the Andes remained the Sierra Maestra of the continent, as Castro had described it in late 1960.

But from the very beginning of Cuba's relationship with the Communist world, Castro, Blas Roca and the others had to take into account the two factors of the development of the Chinese quarrel with Russia and the reluctance of Russia to make an explicit treaty committing her to defend Cuba if attacked. The Communist party of Cuba attempted a policy of neutrality in the Chinese dispute, thereby obliging itself to print both sides of every argument from the moment when the matter became acute after the meeting of the World Federation of Trade Unions in Peking and the Bucharest conference during June 1960. This neutrality was hard to maintain, particularly since there were evidently differences between Blas Roca, secretary-general of the party for so long, the representative of orthodoxy, and Carlos Rafael Rodríguez and those younger party members who sympathized more with Castro. This did not mean, however, that they were necessarily less extreme. On the contrary, though Rodríguez himself was by temperament and habit an anti-Stalinist, and a Khrushchevist first and foremost, many younger members of the Communist party, like some Fidelistas, were very favourably inclined towards the Chinese. In 1960 several Fidelistas, such as William Gálvez, the inspector-general of the army, visited China, while José María de la Aguilera and Vicente Cordero, for the CTC, were present in Peking during the first public clash there between China and Russia. Aguilera, as has been seen, seems to have been a person without any ideological foundation before 1959: yet the Cuban trade unionists in Peking gave general support to the Chinese position in July 1960.[12] The same month China and Cuba signed a commercial and tariff convention while, in September, Cuba and China entered upon diplomatic relations. These events were not much liked by either Blas Roca or Carlos Rafael Rodríguez, despite their own differences, and during the winter of 1960–1 therefore the Cuban-Chinese links on a governmental level were much superior to those between the Cuban and Chinese Communist parties. The 'international chess game' thus had its obscurer moments even on the left side of the Iron Curtain.[13]

The Cuban Communist party as such, however, made up its mind as to its general course of action in November and December 1960. Blas Roca, it will be recalled, had visited Mao in April with some approval. But in the early winter he and the rest of the party took a decisive turn

---

[11] Guevara, in honour of Guiterás, 15 May 1961, *Obra Revolucionaria*, 44.

[12] *Hoy*, 3 August 1960.

[13] These matters are discussed in Andrés Suárez, 104–6.

towards Moscow and this decision was rendered final at the meeting of Communist parties in Moscow in December. This occurred almost at the same time as Guevara (who a little earlier, after a successful commercial expedition to Prague, had stayed in Moscow several weeks without achieving much), was being received with enthusiasm in Peking. The enthusiasm was well-placed: at a banquet, Guevara had said that 'the great experience of the Chinese people in their twenty-two years of struggle in the backward countryside had revealed a new road for the Americas'.[14] In reply, Chou En-lai had spoken of the Cuban experience in glowing terms; and at the end of November, Cuba and China concluded an agreement whereby the Chinese would buy a million tons of sugar in 1961 and grant a credit of $M60 for equipment and technical aid. On leaving China, Guevara said: 'In general there was not a single discrepancy.'[15] Thenceforward, China spoke only of Castro, never of the Cuban Communists,[16] and Castro had for some years the backing of China as well as, through the Communist party and the Russian Embassy, of Russia.

For Chinese approval did not yet endanger that of Russia. In mid-December a new Russo-Cuban agreement was also signed. Russia would buy 2·7 million tons of sugar in 1961 at 4 cents a pound. Cuba expressed her fervent satisfaction. Russia expressed her willingness to defend Cuba 'against unprovoked aggressions', but made no new mention of missiles. Possibly Russian willingness to go even as far as this in a formal document would have been less easy to secure had it not been for China. Thereafter vessels sailed regularly to Cuba from the Communist ports of the old Hanse, and articles describing the beauties of East Europe appeared frequently in Cuban magazines such as the now revolutionary *Bohemia*, the army magazine *Verde Olivo*, or more glossy propaganda papers such as *Cuba* or *INRA*. Khrushchev gave another public promise to defend Cuba in case of aggression (but he admitted that the rockets which he had mentioned in July were 'symbolic').[17] In January Castro announced that 1,000 young Cubans would study agrarian collectives in Russia. In the spring of 1961 visitors to Cuba were received in Russian style with bouquets of flowers.

Cuba had already recognized Albania, Hungary, Outer Mongolia and North Vietnam, and embassies from these nations trundled across the world with great enthusiasm to Havana, which they found, with

---

[14] New China News Agency, 18 November 1960, qu. Andrés Suárez, 116.

[15] *Revolución,* 9 December 1960.

[16] This is Andrés Suárez's point, 117.

[17] Carlos Franqui (editor of *Revolución*): 'The imperialists contend that the statement of the Soviet Government concerning the possibility of rocket weapons in the event of an armed aggression against Cuba is purely symbolic. What do you think?' Khrushchev: 'I should like such statements to be really symbolic.'

surprise, enjoyed a living standard somewhat higher than they themselves aspired to. Fraternal solidarity was also pledged by Dr Núñez Jiménez in October with the FLN in Algeria and with Sekou Touré during his visit to Havana in October.

Cuba retained some non-Communist connections. Though she had withdrawn from the World Bank, Cuba naturally remained a member of the International Sugar Council[18] and of course of the U.N. Cuba exchanged sugar with Egypt in return for rice. She also remained on commercial terms with Canada, whose Conservative prime minister, Diefenbaker, bluntly refused to impose any embargo on Cuba. Through Canada, Cuba received some spare parts for cars, as for electrical and industrial appliances. Canadian businessmen were able to divest themselves of ideology more easily than those of the U.S. Canada was not a member of the OAS, and she was therefore excluded from the main institution through which the U.S. hoped to act. In return, Cuba compensated the Canadian banks (taken over in December) in cash, rather than in non-existent bonds.[19] There were still non-Communist 'technicians' in Cuba. Some Japanese for instance were making valiant efforts to grow rice in the impenetrable Zapata swamps, and an Irish company had been contracted to build a jute factory in Santa Clara.

In January 1961 too there even seemed a remote chance of reopening relations with the U.S. Both Castro and Blas Roca suggested in speeches that President Kennedy might in this respect be an improvement on President Eisenhower. On 21 January Castro said, 'For our part we are going to begin anew.' On 7 March he even proposed that 'if some day the U.S. wishes again to buy sugar from Cuba then we can discuss . . . indemnification'. Did the Cubans really now wish for an improvement? It is quite possible. Castro had purged at least something of his personal, national resentment against the U.S. But the sort of agreement which was remotely attainable with the U.S. would have been one to live and let live, leading eventually to U.S. acceptance of the regime, maybe to a certain modification of the most objectionable traits of the Cuban revolution, so far as the U.S. was concerned; and with the quarrelsome exiles swarming in Miami and Cuba's own inevitable identification with the – as it seemed – swelling revolutionary tide in Latin America, such a development was barely conceivable, even if the U.S. had been prepared to accept the humiliation of a socialist Cuba next door to them.

[18] The Mexico meeting of the Sugar Council in December concluded that in 1961 sugar available for the world market would be 16% above needs. As early as November Russia was in fact dumping Cuban sugar in the world market at less than prevailing prices.

[19] According to one unconfirmed source, the Royal Bank of Canada was enabled to withdraw its capital, unlike all the other banks.

What Russia thought of all this was still not clear, perhaps even to Russians. The Cuban revolution had not been planned by Russia. The swift developments there had taken the Russian government by surprise. Perhaps, as Khrushchev's letter transmitted through Alexayev seems to have suggested, Russia would still have preferred a neutral Cuba to a satellite one. But the Cuban cause had struck a definite note of enthusiasm in the Russian public. Poets and intellectuals thought that Cuba was enacting a genuine revolutionary struggle such as would perhaps give them new faith in their own system. Cuba had to be assisted and maintained now as well as ultimately to be made use of. Cuba represented a cause to which Khrushchev clearly responded and of which, once committed, he had to take care in his relation with his rivals. Thus Soviet (and eastern *bloc*) aid came in 1960 and 1961 in many ships, apparently without the cost being counted. Evidently Cuba could serve too as a centre of international Communist activity in South America, as well as a propaganda victory with which to taunt the U.S. (and perhaps China), and, who knew, giving some sort of military benefit as well. But this side of the matter seems not yet to have been discussed.

In return Russian technicians impressed Cubans as hard-working, but often 'their technical knowledge' seemed 'mediocre'. Many of them 'drank like Cossacks.' They lived in isolation, spent evenings on the beach playing basketball, never talking of politics, seeming 'a generous, watched-over, hard-working but poor people', a far from satisfactory representation of a 'future full of promise'. The Cubans found Czech technicians more human, but there were fewer of them. Chinese technicians were mercifully also few, and incomprehensible.[20]

Along with these international friendships, the old Communist leaders were certainly now always in public, at saluting bases and addressing workers and other groups, though they had no official status. Lázaro Peña, the old Labour chief, was to be seen at every gathering of the union but, apart from being referred to as the 'founder', he had no discernible profession. In the press the Communists were simply referred to as *dirigentes revolucionarios*, revolutionary leaders, a bland title with which however no one else was favoured. Of course, these men were not usually popular among the intimates of Castro. None of them as yet were members of the cabinet and, though they evidently had influence in some departments of State, their control over the army and INRA has been exaggerated. After January 1961 they never again made any pronouncement as a party upon any event in Cuba.

[20] *Cf.* the judgments in Casalis's articles, *La República* (Caracas), February 1966.

Between Fidelistas and Communists also there lurked one major antagonism: over the devious and far from heroic role that the party had played during the civil war. Even Guevara seems to have treated the Communist leaders personally with some scorn.[21] There also lurked scandal: thus among the old leaders of the Directorio Revolucionario such as Chomón (despite his identification of himself as a Communist), there still lurked the disagreeable affair of the betrayal of the four students in Calle Humboldt in 1957. Recently the presumed traitor, Marcos Armando Rodríguez, a young Communist, had been arrested in Prague and returned thence to Cuba;[22] he was under guard and interrogation in prison, but still protected by Communists such as Joaquín Ordoqui, a member of the Central Committee, and his *compañera*, Edith García Buchaca, once wife of their comrade Carlos Rafael Rodríguez.[23] At this time the old members of the Directorio were unable to force any action by the Communists to assist their pursuit of this enemy and this grumble behind the scenes was symptomatic of the anxieties within the revolution. Meanwhile the only effective group remotely opposed to the Communists from within the government seemed still those around Carlos Franqui and the newspaper *Revolución*, though Franqui himself had evidently undergone a serious change of mind since 1959.

There was, however, as yet no ideological identification between Castro and the Communists. The furthest that any of Castro's friends had gone in this direction was Guevara's argument that the Cuban revolutionaries were discovering Marxist laws by the practice of government: 'We, practical revolutionaries, initiating our struggle, merely fulfil laws foreseen by Marx the scientist.'[24] But Guevara, in conversation with René Dumont, had also said that his aim above all was to give workers 'a sense of responsibility', not of property, and Guevara was already critical of the Soviet Union's new emphasis on material encouragement to hard work. He refused to 'participate in Cuba in the creation' of 'a second North American society'.[25] Guevara envisaged thus already the perfectibility of man, a reliance only on loyalty to society, even before the second year of revolution was out. This, of course, suggested that Cuba was about to embark on all the difficulties, starting at the beginning, previously met in the socialist countries. Where the two groups, Fidelistas and Communists, could agree was in respect of the struggle against imperialism, assumed to be identical with

[21] See Luis Simón MSS.
[22] On 1 January 1961. He had been pursued consistently by Fructuoso Rodríguez's widow.
[23] All this came out in Rodríguez's trial in 1964.
[24] *Verde Olivo*, October 1960.
[25] Dumont, 54.

the counter-revolution; after all, even alleged leftist counter-revolutionaries such as Ray and Miró Cardona were now throwing in their lot with the CIA. For Castro and the Communists, to a slightly lesser extent, the 'Cuban national struggle' could now be seen primarily in terms of the struggle against the U.S.

One category of Cubans demands note though it elusively avoids analysis. These were those who, like Luis Orlando Rodríguez (ex-Minister of the Interior in 1959 and editor of *La Calle*, Grau's Director of Sports and leader of the university *bonche* in the 1940s), Marcelo Fernández (the old national co-ordinator of the 26 July Movement), José Pellón and Octavio Louit, had until 1959 been reckoned as not only non-Communists, but even '*enragé* anti-Communists',[26] and who now remained in Cuba, without breaking with the regime and indeed continuing to play minor parts in government. All these cases differ when it comes to the point; Luis Orlando Rodríguez apparently took the line of least resistance, having always perhaps been a little superficial, anti-Communist when it was fashionable and pro-Communist when that line too became profitable.[27] Others were bureaucrats prepared to serve anyone, particularly in the union movement. Others like Marcelo Fernández and Faustino Pérez are in perhaps the most interesting position of all: serious anti-Communists (despite a flirtation by the former with Communism when at the university), they lost their jobs in 1959 or 1960 for their hostility towards the old Communist party in Cuba. But they remained in Cuba, either mesmerized by Castro, or convinced that on balance it was wiser to remain and attempt in the long run to try to influence the regime towards what they conceived as moderate courses from within, or perhaps believing that whatever name was given to the practices of the government they were right. There were others such as Efigenio Ameijeiras or Juan Almeida, men of limited intellect but loyal to Castro as a leader and willing to follow him anywhere under any circumstances. Others still stayed because their families or friends desired to stay or because they themselves knew and loved the island too much to think of changing residences for mere political reasons. Others, again, found in the version of Communism applied in Cuba by Castro a surprisingly safe intellectual harbour after years moving from Catholicism to Ortodoxia to either García Barcena's or Aureliano Sánchez Arango's minor action groups; many had already shifted their political position so often that one more shift, even from liberalism to Communism, was a mere extra change almost as superficial as the others. Others still believed that with Castro

---

[26] As *El Mundo* (Miami Beach), 3 June 1961, put it about Luis Orlando Rodríguez.

[27] Rodríguez published anti-Communist articles in *La Calle* after it had been revived in 1959–60; the newspaper was closed and he became ambassador in Venezuela.

probably the choice of the Communist path was the final statement of freedom away from the U.S.: to replace the angry liberal father, the U.S. near at hand, with a distant one, however autocratic and narrow, appears to have been for many Cuban intellectuals an act of will second to none; and once Castro had personally established his control over the local Cuban Communist party, all their anxieties, such as they were, were at rest.

In its military organization Cuba was not yet a Communist state. After the Matos crisis the rebel army, with its doubtfully revolutionary and loyal political leadership, had been run down and re-organized. In its place now stood the militia, a volunteer army of about 150,000 men and women who, supporting the revolution, put on uniform and took up guns after their daily work, for about eight hours a week, and guarded public buildings and other installations of importance from the attacks of counter-revolutionaries. These amateur soldiers seemed everywhere in Cuba in 1961, sometimes obtrusive and officious, often lazing in rocking chairs in verandahs, their loaded rifles across their knees: 'We Cubans are an army people,' a heavily armed boy of fifteen remarked[28] in July 1961; it was true. The illusion of a nation in arms could not have been stronger under Carnot. Yet there remained among these dedicated gunmen a certain frivolity as well as charm which would have troubled Carnot or Trotsky. Perhaps this militia really embodied a return to the old national supposition that a regular army was pointless, since anyone could take up a rifle or a machete to defend his rights. The militia of course was organized by the army and army officers ran it, the commander being still the youthful Captain Rogelio Acevedo.[29] The head of the militias in the provinces was often the head of military intelligence, the so-called G.2, as well.

G.2 was now the main organization for the detection of counter-revolution being still under the direction of Castro's old *Granma* and Moncada colleague, Ramiro Valdés. Valdés organized (probably under Russian supervision) an efficient political police, though as yet it was in its early stages with, interestingly enough, prominent assistants being men of the supposedly once non-communist Directorio Revolucionario.[30] In the winter of 1960-1, some counter-revolutionaries captured in the Escambray had been tortured by the holding of their heads under water to get information and others were taken out to the execution wall and fired at with blank cartridges. Castro ceased this on the representations of some of his old followers. But in fact conditions in Cuban

[28] To the author.
[29] The militia was really the focus of the national defence effort until new 'revolutionary' officers' schools had produced a fully socialist generation.
[30] For instance Julio García Oliviera, José Abrahantes, Carlos Figueredo.

prisons from 1960 onwards once again, as under Batista or Machado, beggar description.[31]

Another disturbing development still had been a civilian branch of the militia, the Committees for the Defence of the Revolution (CDR), local citizens organized frankly as militant informers against possible counter-revolution.[32] The commander of these committees was an unknown, José Matar, a man without personal experience of command in the Sierra, and a young Communist of the old guard. Their activities extended to checking upon people who suddenly started disposing of their furniture: this would suggest that these people had decided to abandon Cuba and, being forbidden to take their possessions with them, wished to hand them over, for safe-keeping till counter-revolution or for ever, to friends, relations or western diplomats. These acts were illegal since a penalty for safe emigration was the gift to the State of all possessions save one suit of clothes and a few small objects (one ring, for instance).

The Agrarian Reform Institute (INRA) had by now absorbed all the old autonomous economic institutions such as the Coffee, Sugar, and Rice Stabilization bodies, and BANFAIC, the Bank for Economic and Social Development. Through INRA, indeed, the State controlled all the main capital equipment of the nation including, pre-eminently, sugar. The harvest of 1961 was the first *zafra del pueblo*, the people's harvest. Of course, this harvest had been sown in the bad old days and there had as yet been no reorganization whatever of the sugar mills – even though they had mostly been renamed, chiefly after heroes of the revolution or great dates in the international revolutionary tradition.[33] International revolutionary feast days indeed were now as many as those of the Church.

The harvest was successful, the figures by early April 1961 suggesting that the total would reach as high as any good average year before 1959. But the expressed goal of the revolution was still to enable the nation to escape from sugar. Work on this escape had been begun, so much so that, unless indeed diversification were quickly successful, the economy would inevitably decline, since a failure to replant in 1960 meant a fall

[31] See accounts in e.g. Martino, *I was Castro's Prisoner*, and *Cuba and the Rule of Law*. I have also benefited from discussions with several ex-prisoners among them Dr Joaquín Martínez Sáenz.

[32] *Revolución*, 29 September 1960.

[33] There were also some Communist heroes such as the sugar workers' leader, Jesús Menéndez, murdered in 1947, who gave his name to what used to be the proud *Chaparra*; *España* became *España Republicana*; the first Communist to act as a go-between with Castro in the Sierra Maestra (and killed in early 1961 in an air crash), Osvaldo Sánchez, received in memory, Arango's *Providencia*; the United Fruit Company's *Preston* mill became *Guatemala*, after the abortive revolution; and *Natividad* became *7 November* (1917).

in sugar production in 1963. By the spring of 1961, 33,000 peasants had become owners of land which they had previously cultivated as squatters, sharecroppers or tenants; just under a million acres had thus been 'distributed', nearly half in Oriente.[34] This accounted for between a third and a quarter of the farmers who in the past had suffered under this form of tenure. The land involved was not large; thus what was distributed even in Oriente amounted to only about 6% of the farmland (by 1946 estimates). Julio Lobo alone had this amount of land. But then, these farmers had in the past only held a small percentage of the total farm area. For those involved it nevertheless meant a revolution, less in their way of living, than in their view of society and their relations with it. It meant a freedom from indebtedness as well as from living outside the law. The agricultural co-operatives numbered about 900,[35] of which about 550 were devoted to crops, a few to livestock alone and 120 to mixed crops and livestock. Most were between 500 and 800 acres. They aimed to avoid the economic losses which would have followed had this land been divided up. But INRA never issued regulations for the management of the co-operatives, and their construction was loose. On the other hand, INRA did appoint managers, often members of the co-operative, who were supposed to keep in touch with the INRA zone chiefs. Co-operative members were usually paid $2.50 per eight-hour day, though there was no national scale. Wages were still held to be an advance on eventual profits to be divided at the end of the year, but these were not distributed either in 1959 or in 1960.

At the end of 1960 these co-operatives were about to die. The system seemed inequitable: some farms did well (for instance, forest co-operatives, because of the heavy demand for wood) and some badly, according to the wealth of the farm, rather than according to the deserts or the work of the labourer. However fair this might seem under capitalism where labour could be cut down or increased, it seemed unjust under socialism. The confusion was also unbelievable. Accounts were not kept properly. Even a sympathetic observer[36] noted: 'Everything happened *por la libre*. The most conscientious peasants in the co-operatives would fight against anarchy but the individual efforts were drowned in the

[34] Ownership titles granted and land distributed in Cuba, June 1959 to February 1961:

	Number of Titles	Hectares
Pinar del Río	5,536	53·4
Havana	2,669	37·7
Matanzas	3,057	33·1
Las Villas	4,508	58·3
Camagüey	2,524	27·1
Oriente	14,529	173·2
Total	32,823	382·8

[35] 881 in August 1960.
[36] Ania Francos, *La Fête Cubaine* (1962),

mass. It was often necessary to go to Havana to settle the smallest question.' Such errors were admitted by Castro: 'Certain administrators, with a vague conception of the Revolution . . . believed that the more goods they could hand out to farmers, the more revolutionary they were being.'[37] Another weakness was that very large pig and chicken farms were built, exposing the animals to epidemics. Castro himself seemed obsessed by hatred of *marabú* (the thorny tropical acacia which grows as a weed in the south) and had vast stretches cleared, while ignoring other places capable of producing much more at less cost.[38]

In the summer of 1960, after the harvest, sugar cane co-operatives were also set up and, by the spring of 1961, there were rather over 600 of them.[39] Most of the 120,000 members had previously been full-time agricultural workers at the sugar mills. Run with the same expectation as the other co-operatives (that they would eventually become commercially self-sufficient), they were in fact similarly under INRA, but more formally organized. There was thus a general assembly of all members of the co-operative able (though usually not anxious) to elect a directing board of seven to aid the manager, who was himself appointed by INRA. Their finances were centrally organized, with regional headquarters, technical staff accounts, machine repair workshops, and so on. INRA usually set up a *tienda del pueblo*, people's shop, where basic goods could be bought at reduced prices, perhaps 12 % cheaper. Since rents were also abolished, these workers (paid $2.50 a day as were their colleagues in the other co-operatives) were in many respects a good deal better off than in the past – while there were any goods to buy. But on some occasions it is clear that co-operatives were founded against the desire of the workers concerned, who might be more interested in more wages than the sacrifices needed for the Revolution.[40] In late 1961 Castro himself complained that the small farmer of Mantanzas was 'allergic to co-operatives. He does not want to hear them mentioned. He is frightened by the mere word'.[41]

These 'pseudo-co-operatives',[42] however, afforded scant help in the amelioration of unemployment, even though seasonal workers could still be brought in for harvests, and they might one day be made permanent, providing diversification made it possible. Eventually it

[37] Castro, *Revolución*, 11 November 1961, 6.

[38] Dumont, 44–5.

[39] 622 to be precise. These figures were given in May, but they no doubt apply to March too. There had been 604 in August 1960. They covered 80,000 *caballería* (Castro, in speech, 10 November 1961, *Revolución* 11 November, 10.)

[40] See Agustín Souchy, *Testimonios sobre la Revolución Cubana*, Buenos Aires, 1960, 32.

[41] Castro, speech, 10 November 1961. Goldenberg (*op. cit*, 237) recalled an instance when former tenant farmers appeared before a dispossessed landlord and offered, out of fear for the future, to go on paying rent. Blas Roca, in a speech to the heads of schools for revolutionary instruction, made similar admissions.

[42] As Dumont called them, 44.

was expected that the manager would be elected, and that all profits would be distributed (though during the first five years four-fifths of profits were to be invested for schools, housing, roads, and so on). Diversification meant the cultivation of pangola grass, maize, rice and other crops on about a quarter of the total. The pangola would be used for feeding new herds of cattle. But most of these diversification areas (300,000 acres) were old cane ones and, by accident or inexperience, much good cane land was uprooted (by Castro among others), while bad land was often left to bear cane. The use of this excellent land was justified as a short-term measure to avoid the cost of clearing quite new land, but it brought trouble in the future. Nor to begin with were great efforts made to reap what could have been a great advantage of these arbitrary acts: there was no new scientific planting, little rationalization of the agricultural side of the industry. On the other hand, these measures did of course confirm the disappearance of all large *colonos* of the past, making possible improvements in the future.

The errors in administration partly derived from the fact that there were simply fewer men doing the work of management. In 1961 there was additionally a long drought. Weeding was ill-done, and drainage sometimes not kept up. On very many sugar estates, the precise character of diversification was left to the local manager, who did what he wished at his whim or his regional boss's. There was also a labour shortage, for better wages were to be had elsewhere, particularly in the new State farms which gave a chance of better housing. With other factors, these errors caused production in the cane co-operatives to be 10% lower in 1962 than in the surviving private plantations.[43] Planting was generally ignored in 1960 and 1961. In an historically comprehensible (if economically unwise) obsession to escape from sugar, the Cuban revolution neglected in fact the only crop which, like it or not, they could live on in totalitarian conditions; for sugar can be cut by an army or by machines and it is ground by an industrial proletariat, even though they may live in the country; and planting of course requires only the most modest agricultural knowledge.[44]

INRA had always since January 1959 administered some estates confiscated from Batistianos. After the Agrarian Reform others were added. By May 1960 INRA ran over 500 farms covering over two million acres. These had begun with the cattle estates, chiefly in

[43] See Carlos Rafael Rodríguez's speech to sugar workers, 18 July 1962. He said that land producing 40,000 to 50,000 *arrobas* of cane had been torn up, while some producing half this was left standing. (See comments in Seers, 130.)

[44] For this reason, the Cuban experience cannot be much of a guide for the agricultural development of other socialist countries nor, of course, for other Latin American territories, despite the Chilean Communist Juan Noyola's remark, 'I am one of the numerous Latin Americans who consider the Cuban Revolution as our common patrimony.' (Qu. Dumont, 18.)

Camagüey, and were later extended to rice plantations. Castro later explained:

> When we came to the case of the great cattle ranches, vast extensions of land where a few men managed thousands of head of cattle, the question arose, what should be done? Organize a co-operative ... with very few people ... rich [people]? I reached the conclusion that it was necessary to search for a superior form of social ownership of those lands.[45]

The decision not to divide up the rice plantations after the 1960 harvest was indeed a decisive one for the future of the regime. The state farms which were the result were, as it happens, not provided for under the agrarian reform but, by late 1960, they began to be regarded as the easiest method of running Cuban agriculture in the totalitarian circumstances then unavoidable. As early as August 1960 Castro told René Dumont that he desired to create large state farms for all agricultural production except sugar properties.[46] The following January, all the old non-sugar co-operatives were converted into state farms, and they and the cattle ranches were thenceforth known under the more resounding title of *granja del pueblo*.[47] This meant little more than the formalization of existing reality, since the co-operatives had not been allowed to work properly as such. By April 1961 there were 266 state farms, covering over five million acres, or an average of 20,000 acres[48] embracing every crop and being found all over the island – though Oriente and Camagüey together accounted for over half the total acreage. Many farms were divided into separated parcels of land, sometimes separated by miles, thus directly reproducing some aspects of the old system which were most in need of reform. These farms were administered directly by the State, without, as in the case of the still surviving cane co-operatives, any regional or local headquarters. They employed nearly 100,000 workers, mostly seasonal (70,000) and paid $2.11 a day (with free housing, medical care and education).

These farms bore obvious resemblances to the Russian *sovkhozy*. But the actual circumstances of Cuban agriculture helped to dictate the decision. Workers on the co-operatives were unused to taking individual

---

[45] Lockwood, 90.

[46] Dumont, 56. Dumont criticized them from the start, foreseeing some of the difficulties which they later encountered. He also thought that Castro had been too excessively influenced by his reading of Soviet literature, where the co-operative was described as an 'inferior form of property' and points out the personal nature of Castro's decision: Castro alone took the decision.

[47] However, the farms previously directly run by INRA continued to be so under different administration.

[48] The *Granma* farm in Oriente was over 100,000 acres, and there later came to be a farm of even over 250,000 acres.

initiatives, and the co-operatives themselves worked badly from the start. It seemed that a straightforward state system would assist both the diversification and the supply of food regularly to the cities. Sociologically, this had some success. Some workers on these farms for a time were happy to regard themselves as civil servants, serving a state which they themselves controlled; and Castro argued the system meant that land could be used 'in an optimum way, absolutely rationally, determining at each moment that whatever crop benefits the nation shall be produced'.[49]

But within a few months of their foundation, the sheer size of these state farms began to cause difficulties. The dispersion of the different parcels was another reason. The farms seemed, as Dumont had foreseen, to be little confederations, rather than a single unit. There was much disorganization, much folly: an observer in Pinar del Río found that the administrator of INRA for the province 'depended on the zone representatives who in turn depended on the co-operative administrators. The system was operating from the bottom upwards . . . I doubt if any zone representative knew what he was responsible for.'[50] Passing by Santa Clara in May 1960 the French agronomist, Dumont, called on the provincial director of INRA, Luis Borges, an ex-student of dentistry. 'He vaunted himself before us to sign a little document every time he needed to acquire such and such an installation, factory, shop . . . Clearly he carried out these expropriations without preconceived plan, on a whim, without seeing if it was really useful and above all if INRA was capable of running it.'[51] In the headquarters of INRA 'you could see . . . not the prim, old-line functionaries . . . but bearded rebels in uniform carrying arms. The working hours were not the 9 to 5 of the ordinary government workers [but] the irregular . . . nocturnal hours . . . of the guerrilla'.[52] Whether this was beneficial was doubtful. Meantime, no one thought of indemnification and everyone who coveted this was therefore driven to dream of, or plot, a change of government. Few received receipts for property which had been taken over. Many workers even on state farms sold goods privately and no one really knew how much land the state controlled or was supposed to.

Agricultural wages had probably gone up about a fifth since 1958. The people's shops, *tiendas del pueblo*, on the co-operatives had cut prices and increased buying power in the country. INRA claimed that meat consumption had gone up two-thirds in comparison with 1958; but this had been caused by extra slaughtering (made possible by increased demand in the towns) which soon led to shortages. In the early summer of

[49] Lockwood, 90.
[50] I. Pflaum, *American Universities Field Staff Reports Service*, V, No. 4, 38.
[51] Dumont, *Cuba*, 37.
[52] E. Boorstein, *Economic Transformation of Cuba* (1968), 48.

1960 Castro made several speeches in which he told workers in well organized unions such as the builders' or waiters' that the revolution was
not for them primarily but for the unfortunate: workers too would have
to make sacrifices for the revolution.[53]

Many, therefore, were the difficulties attendant on progress.

The most sympathetic criticism of the development of the agricultural
programme of the revolution made in 1960 was that by Professor René
Dumont, of the Sorbonne, who on 20 May gave a press conference
giving constructive comment of several sorts, urging reflection, order
and discipline.[54] No one, Dumont pointed out, had insisted that the co-
operatives should keep accounts. The Agrarian Reform law had charged
INRA to prepare the statutes of the co-operatives. But even here nothing
had yet been done. The weaknesses of Dr Núñez Jiménez as chief of
INRA were already patent but he nevertheless remained loaded with
the full responsibility, rather than the Minister of Agriculture, Pedro
Miret (preoccupied by reafforestation). Further, Dumont pointed out,
on the large farms communications between plots might be non-existent. Difficulties of administration found in the cane co-operatives were
redoubled. The manager was often merely a farmer with little or no
experience of such large-scale farming, sometimes illiterate and ignorant
of new crops and scientific training, often chosen because of his political
reliability.[55] For this reform to have been successful, he should have
been a master-farmer of vast knowledge. The state farm as constituted
in April 1961 was not yet the answer to Cuban agriculture – though it
had not yet been proved to be a failure.

These drawbacks to the state farms had not indeed been understood
or admitted as early as the spring of 1961. The drive of Cuba's agricultural policy was in fact now in the direction of more and more of
such large concerns. Few land titles were now granted to private peasants – only 200 new titles affecting 6,000 acres were distributed between
February and December 1961.[56] The need for planning had now been
generally admitted. Castro confessed at a later meeting that he had
been 'one of the great promoters of action by impulse' but had been
weaned away to 'planning' by Guevara, Carlos Rafael Rodríguez and
Boti.[57]

[53] e.g. 'A pesar de ser la Revolución un proceso cuyo objetivo fundamental es la ayuda a los sectores
más humildes del país, a los más necesitados, ocurrirá a veces de que alguna medida revolucionaria afectará
también algún sector humilde . . .' (Obra Revolucionaria, 16 June 1960, 5).

[54] His report was partly published in the Études 1962 de Tiers Monde. René Dumont (b.
1904) is Director of Research at the Institut National Agronomique in Paris. His most
famous book was False Start in Africa.

[55] Carlos Rafael Rodríguez, qu. Seers (from F. Castro, O. Dorticós, 68–72).

[56] No new titles at all were granted in Pinar del Río, Matanzas and Camagüey.

[57] 'I want the works begun "at will" to end, I want such haphazard ideas as works "by impulse" to end because they are now the antithesis of planning. Before, everything was "at
will", but now everything must be planned.' (Obra Revolucionaria, 30 August 1961, 6).

By the spring of 1961 a little over a third of the farmland in Cuba was probably run by the State. Of the area now administered by the Agrarian Reform Institute, only 27% had actually come to it in consequence of the original agrarian reform of May 1969; 7% had come from gifts; 13% from 'voluntary' sales; and 50% derived from decrees of expropriation issued in the struggles of 1960, in July and October, land taken from great sugar mills and cattle estates as a result of political action.[58] The errors made in consequence of the State's capture of this large slice of the economy were many, since it was an unprecedented situation. Planning was inadequate in respect of seeds, fertilizers, insecticides, transport, and so on. Agricultural workers drifted into Havana or other cities to become semi-employed bureaucrats, while a labour shortage grew up behind them. Minor decisions continued to be referred to Havana. Too many tractors were bought, too few less sophisticated implements. INRA ceased, after the lyrical first days, to work in harmony with the armed forces. Transport became disorganized, because of the disappearance of spare parts, because of the new managers' inexperience, and because inadequate provision had been made both for the shipment of material and then for essential supplies. It was indeed extremely difficult to change fast from a system whereby many farms, some big, some small, produced a few individual crops, to one where a limited number of huge government estates tried to produce many crops. No individual had of course any economic interest in the success of these farms. There were bad estimates of the likely increase of demand for food caused by the rise in incomes after the earlier achievements of the revolution (such as cuts in rents and utilities). Estimates of production were also wildly wrong.[59] Accounts in the co-operatives were apparently not kept, and so prevented effective planning.[60] The Cubans had no traditions of sound book-keeping anyway. In this sense, they showed themselves an ex-colonial people who had left for too long to others their initiative and their invention. Used to extensive cultivation, all farms, big and small, found it hard to take full advantage of irrigation and drainage, even if these were established.

These vast changes in land tenure were also undertaken without even many of those trained and experienced managers who had existed in Cuba in the past. For by now the exodus to Miami included technicians from all over Cuba. Although many such persons were inevitably hostile to the new order, many more would have stayed if the regime had merely attempted one thing at a time. A breach with the U.S. was not necessary for a diversification of agriculture. It would doubtless have

[58] Gutelmann, qu. Dumont, 60–1.

[59] See Severo Aguirre, in *Cuba Socialista*, May 1962.

[60] Socialism cannot work without adequate statistics, for capitalism a guess is often as good (*cf.* Dumont, 100).

been wiser had it been possible, to have avoided the 'international chess game' while enacting agrarian reform.

Even without considering these matters, the government neglected all the large number of farmers still independent. True, farmers with estates smaller than 160 acres (as a result of the revolutionary redistribution or not) had begun since December to be linked together for purposes of planning, giving credit, machinery, distribution of output, in a new national co-operative association – Asociación Nacional de Agricultores Pequeños (ANAP).[61] By May 1961 about 85,000 farmers, with enterprises totalling about six million[62] acres and responsible for a quarter of the entire farmland, were part of ANAP and well within reach of INRA and the State.[63] Confusion, lack of wisdom and uncertainty of direction however took many of these farmers into the ranks of active counter-revolution and there were, in the winter of 1960–1961 many parts of Cuba where in consequence the writ of the government did not run.

A little over 40% of the land, almost 10 million acres, remained outside ANAP and in private hands, more than any single other category;[64] these were all now farmers with estates of between 150 and 1,500 acres, with probably few estates above 1,000 acres; that is, they were not exactly *latifundistas* though they nearly all employed several men. Maybe there were over 10,000 of them, and the total number of independent ones numbered 175,000, or far more than there had been in 1946.[65]

This whole category of private farmer was ignored by the regime. Banks being nationalized, transport and distribution being disrupted and INRA given all the advantages, they found it hard both to get supplies and to deliver their goods. These difficulties inevitably led many to a sulky reluctance to co-operate in any way with the new

---

[61] This had a general administrator appointed by INRA (José Ramírez, an old Communist and Raúl Castro's messenger in the Sierra), a network of people's stores, regional bureaucrats, etc. Farmers with larger estates could join providing they had a proved 'revolutionary background'. ANAP was, of course, a politically committed society. It had 1,400 tractors, or rather less than 10% of the total in Cuba.

[62] INRA'S 1961 report gave a total of $3\frac{1}{2}$ million hectares in the hands of ANAP, obviously too high, as Seers says (p. 128), but his calculation that this is because there were 2·2 million hectares only in farms less than 67·1 hectares in 1946 does not take into account the increase in the number of small farms between 1946 and 1959.

[63] Within ANAP there were several other associations of peasants, devised to link the small private farmer to the national economy. By means of the Credit and Services Cooperative, farmers joined together to get credit and machinery and sell crops but cultivated land independently. These appear to have been confined to Las Villas and Oriente and to have numbered 220 or so by 1962. These were genuine co-operatives. Dumont, a strict critic, was impressed by one which he visited near Ciego de Avila in 1963. The president was elected by the members for a year, and an elected four-member council planned production (see Dumont 89–90).

[64] Though over 40% of the land had been expropriated, including the land divided up.

[65] *Cuba Socialista*, May 1963, 15.

society, and to an increase in food shortages, especially in the towns (where over 60% of the population lived), as well as to the beginning of a black market. The only exception was among the sugar *colonos* who naturally took their cane to the mill as they had always done. The fact that the mill was now a state business made little difference. They continued to be paid in the same way, by *arrobaje*. But even some of them – perhaps 1,000 – refused in December 1960 to attend a pre-harvest rally, despite an attempt to persuade them to do so by Castro's brother Ramón, who opportunely seemed by now to have changed his views about the desirability of revolution.[66] It would seem unlikely that the regime wished to take over the properties of these farmers, but its policies were already, in early 1961, leading it to a position where it might have to do this in the name of simplification. Fear of this understandably was in the minds of many of these farmers, and exacerbated their plight.

In April 1961, if these farmers and those in ANAP are linked together, about 65 % of Cuban farm land was in private hands, including about two-thirds of the land in cane, three-quarters of the head of cattle, and most of the tobacco and coffee:[67] only rice among important crops was entirely in State hands.

The effects of the agricultural reform were by early 1961 hard to see, since reliable statistics were not published and, despite the appearance of some encouraging figures from the Government, it is doubtful if anyone really knew the truth. The production of the still surviving large private agricultural sector was quite impossible to know. Black market production was inestimable. One truth, however, was evident, whether it was a consequence of bad distribution or bad management or reluctance of private farmers to sell their produce: food was short from November 1960 in Cuba and became very short from the Spring of 1961 onwards.

On the other hand, in 1961 the main crop, sugar, gave a production of 6·8 million tons or higher than that of any year since the record-breaking crop of 1953 – in fact the second highest ever;[68] but the steps taken in 1960 meant that the crop for 1962 and thereafter would probably be down.[69] Cuba was obviously growing more cotton than before 1959, even if the 100,000 acres which the state claimed to be under cotton was probably an exaggeration. Among other crops, rice

---

[66] HAR *xiii*, 879.

[67] See calculations in Seers, 128.

[68] Of course, the *zafra del pueblo* was not finished till May–June but the signs were clear by the end of March that it would be a bumper year. This was partly because rainfall in 1960 had been exactly right.

[69] Also in 1961 the government decided for the first time to cut all the cane that had grown, not leaving any unharvested, as was usual: so 94% of cane was cut.

was stagnant[70] in 1961, but, so far as can be seen, every major crop, except coffee, returned higher figures in 1961 than in 1958.[71] Even rice was higher in 1961 than 1958. Any verdict on these figures is difficult; but if they were correct, it simply suggests that distribution must have been even worse than was usually admitted. The cattle situation somewhat resembled that of sugar: in the first quarter of 1961, 40,000 were slaughtered in Las Villas in place of 18,000 in the same months of 1959, that is, an increase of almost 40%. Havana's demands were three-fifths up in 1960 on 1958.[72] Similar increases existed in other provinces.[73] This meant a major reduction in beef reserves, so that from 1962 onwards the pinch would be severely felt. These inroads into reserves of food could have been prevented, since they were predictable.

While the land which was devoted to sugar, coffee and tobacco remained much as before, large tracts of new territory – over 440,000 acres, as reported in August 1961[74] – had been reclaimed from idleness or scrub, and planted with the crops of diversification, particularly rice, and also cotton and potatoes. This increase meant an increase in employment, though no doubt a less substantial one than that claimed by the Ministry of Labour. In all these crops there was also a substantial rise in the use of fertilizer and a modest increase in investment in agricultural machinery.[75] In 1959 and 1960, many landowners, including some who were later expropriated, tried to extend or to intensify their areas of cultivation, hoping thereby perhaps to postpone or (if Castro should change his mind or was overthrown) avoid reform.[76] Up till July 1960, after all, there had been relatively few expropriations. The increase of ownership among coffee and tobacco growers – mostly old tenants or share-croppers – helped morale in those departments. Meantime, the enthusiasm roused by the revolution stimulated farm managers to attempt impossibly high targets and even made workers, in 1959 and 1960, at least, in private estates, insist to their employers that high targets

---

[70] *Cuba Socialista,* May 1962, 57. INRA told Bianchi in 1962 that production fell but it did not give the magnitude.

[71]

	1957	1958	1959	1960	1961
Tobacco	41·7	50·6	35·6	45·3	52·3
Rice	256·8	225·9	282·1	304·2	230·0
Coffee	36·7	43·7	29·5	55·2	38·5
Potatoes	94·9	79·3	71·6	97·6	101·4
Maize		134			198

[72] INRA, *Un Año de Liberación Agraria.*

[73] *Cf.* Seers.

[74] *Obra Revolucionaria,* No. 30 of 1961, 78.

[75] *Cf.* Seers, 118. INRA said that $M81 had been spent on agricultural machinery by May 1961, of which $M35 had been spent in socialist countries. But had it arrived? According to the Banco Nacional Memorial for 1958 only $M17 had been spent on agricultural machinery between 1953–8. But of course the real value of these things had all changed. Much old machinery was falling apart.

[76] See comments by Felipe Pazos, in *Cambridge Opinion,* February 1963.

be named and pursued, on pain of denunciation before the INRA chief of the locality.[77] Cuba might pride herself on being the only country to have an agrarian reform and at the same time to raise production: but, as Dumont pointed out, even if this was true the comparison could only be made in comparison with socialist countries. Japan and Israel had enjoyed much more notable increases of production.[78]

Production and land tenure were not, of course, everything. Agrarian reform in addition meant better conditions of all sorts. Rural unemployment had almost ended. INRA's housing department had built by the end of 1960 fifty new small hospitals, sixty new schools, as well as the famous Camilo Cienfuegos primary boarding school in the Sierra Maestra, and about 10,000 new houses or apartments.[79] INRA also built many other new buildings, such as shops, clinics, clubs, warehouses, libraries – but, of course, no churches. There were about 2,000 *tiendas del pueblo* built by April 1961. No doubt some of these investments were economically rash; the quality of some of the new houses was much too high for mass production. Further, the Urban Reform of October 1960 not only ended private renting but virtually halted all private building. Castro said in 1962 that the Revolution could not in future build more than 10,000 to 12,000 houses a year, though 400,000 were needed.[80] Some roads which were built were also unnecessarily wide.[81]

The State's industrial reorganization had been at first under a department of INRA – the industries, that is, which had been confiscated from Batista's supporters. This department was run by Guevara for some weeks between his return from his travels and becoming president of the Bank. By July 1960 wholesale nationalization gave to this industrial department sixty companies worth $M800, including twenty sugar companies, the telephone and electric companies ($M80 and $M300 each) and three oil companies. In October INRA received a further 300 industrial establishments, including the remaining sugar mills and all the banks. By late 1960, INRA controlled over half the industrial structure of the island; and by February 1961 nearly three-quarters. In that month, the industrial undertakings were detached from INRA and made into a separate Ministry of Industries, under Guevara, with vice-ministries running different sections.[82]

[77] *Cf.* Felipe Pazos, '*Comentarios a dos Artículos sobre la Revolución Cubana*' (typescript).
[78] Dumont, *Cuba*, 62.
[79] 19,000 new houses a year were built in the period 1959–61, compared with 10,000 before 1958 (*ibid.*, 74, fn. 2). Most of these were in the country. In a number of speeches in 1961 Castro explained that housing would be far from a priority in revolutionary spending (e.g. speech at First Production Congress, 30 August 1961, *Obra Revolucionaria*, 6).
[80] *Revolución*, 22 June 1962.
[81] René Dumont and Julien Coléou, *La Ràforme Agraire é Cuba* (1962), 11.
[82] INRA kept the canneries and some other industries concerned with food.

Guevara's new empire employed 150,000 of whom 60,000 were in the sugar industry (at the mills or on its commercial side).[83] The ministry was highly centralized. All concerns sent to the ministry the proceeds of their sales, and were sent by the ministry the sums needed for their operation, though for the time being each business was responsible for its budget and its targets. No money was kept by separate enterprises. Credit was available at three months' call from the Finance Ministry. Guevara began to regroup the different industries[84] according to purpose, regardless of their success or efficiency: a fantasy of centralization which Guevara thought could be made to work, because of Cuba's small size, by telephone or aerial communication – 'a perfect mechanism of horology'.[85] Alas, the perfect mechanism, like the perfect socialist man, had not yet been found. Guevara, like King Ferdinand VII, found it impossible to keep even his clocks chiming in time with each other. As in agriculture, bureaucracy raised its head.

The problems incurred in the mere running of this ministry, with its multitudinous activities, were innumerable. Everyone underestimated the difficulties which Cuba would have in trying to organize herself alone, having been for so long an economic appendage of the U.S. However brilliant an economic imagination Guevara and some of his assistants might have, they had no experience of commercial administration. Guevara was then aged thirty-two. Some of his aides, such as the Chilean, Albán Lataste, the director of planning, or Angel Gutiérrez Paz, were older but they also had no experience of direction of industry.

[83] Ministry of Industry source in 1961
[84] These were:

Sugar mills	105
Distilleries	18
Manufactures of alcoholic drinks	6
Soap and scent factories	3
Factories of milk derivatives	5
Chocolate factories	2
Flour mills	1
Packaging or container factories	8
Paint factories	4
Chemical products factories	3
Basic metallurgy undertakings	6
Paper mills	7
Lamp factories	1
Textile and clothing factories	61
Rice mills	16
Food plants	7
Oil and grease plants	2
Coffee roasting plants	11
Printing presses	1
Building concerns	19
Electric plants	1
Total	287

[85] Guevara, *Révolution* (Paris), October 1963.

The only claim to fame indeed of the sub-secretary of the ministry, Orlando Borrego, was to have served with Guevara on the court which sentenced the BRAC commander, Captain Castaño, in 1959. Guevara complained of the difficulty of finding manpower to run these enterprises: 'we have to think hard where we can find 500 factory managers, and not a day passes when we don't have to sack one of them for incompetence'.[86]

It is difficult not to admire the energy, resolution and audacity with which Guevara and his companions faced their impossible task: impossible, since of course they had not only to run existing industries, or merely to raise their productive capacity – itself difficult in the unprecedented circumstances – but to lay down the lines for the further industrialization of Cuba, for those industries which would in the future, it was hoped, take over the burden of earning Cuba's international living from sugar. Thus elaborate plans were made to exploit the mineral deposits of Oriente, for making Cuba self-sufficient in steel, for shipyards capable of building large fishing boats, for machinery of all sorts, including mechanical cane cutters, for a new petrol refinery, for new electrical installations, for chemical expansion, for the production of paper from bagasse, hormones from cane wax, rubber from butane; indeed, many of Guevara's ideas derived from making the most use of the many rich by-products of the sugar industry. Since Cuba had such large reserves of nickel, should she not take her place as the second world producer? There were also projects for technological education – classes in statistics and lathe-turning, in industrial management and accountancy. A new plant might be needed and new refining methods might have to be learned. If the standard of living could be raised in the country, could not those who lived there be persuaded to buy things made in the towns?

Was this all a dream? In 1961 it did not entirely seem so. The first Cuban five-year plan had been presented in December. But serious problems were being met in running existing industry, much less expanding it; the spare parts which machines needed, like new slaves in the nineteenth century, had been brought across the sea – from Miami. No stocks had been kept in Cuba. Further, many existing industries had depended on the import of raw materials, all from the dollar area, to get started at all. Some factories, such as the Hedges's rayon factory, had for a while to be closed. Canada was a possible source of supply, but even there commerce needed foreign exchange. By the Spring of 1961, however, Guevara's ministry concentrated less on repairing machinery bought in the U.S. than on buying new stock from Russia or east Europe, and buying also ersatz raw materials from the same suppliers;

[86] Guevara, *Obra Revolucionaria*, 6 January 1961.

thus in May 1961 Guevara would inform Cuba that contracts for over a hundred factories had been signed with the eastern *bloc* including one for a steel mill, a petroleum refinery, and a motor car factory. There would be new flour mills from East Germany. Over a hundred technicians from the East were already in Cuba, apart from Chileans and other Latin Americans. The difficulties however of harnessing the country to a quite new technology were legion.

There were also, of course, difficulties about the possibility of expansion on the scale envisaged. Cuba still lacked indigenous sources of power. This meant a perpetual oil import and, unless the 'friendly countries of the East' changed their usual methods of commerce, a continuing challenge to the balance of payments. Food and other necessities would indefinitely have to be imported. All the essentials which Cuba had previously bought in the U.S., if not the luxuries, would have to be found from elsewhere. In December Russia had announced that she would buy in 1961 four million tons of sugar at 4 cents a pound; but would this continue? The central point was that, in order to escape from the sugar monoculture, Cuba would have to industrialize. But to industrialize she needed foreign currency, which could be earned, now as in the past, most easily by selling sugar. Cuba might have earned currency by selling market produce on a grand scale; would it be fanciful to see Cuba selling avocados as Israel did? But the obvious market for such expansion was the now closed North American one.

There were also difficulties with labour. Cuban workers often seemed to think that the revolution entitled them to work less, or at least to do so at their own pace.

The new state in industry, as in agriculture, ignored the surviving private sector and no effort was as yet made to organize within the State system the army of shoemakers, carpenters, small tobacco factories, garages, which probably exceeded 50,000 separate undertakings. The proprietors of these businesses were told by the government that there was no plan whatsoever for their capture by the State, but many were not reassured: they knew that governments break promises.[87]

The swift economic transformation of Cuba was, uniquely in the history of revolutions, brought about without a struggle. The State captured a series of concerns in prosperous working order. There was no problem of post-war reconstruction, as there had been in post-1945 Europe. Maybe peaceful transition actually hampered the success of socialism, since old ways and personnel had merely to be converted, not defeated.

[87] This did not happen till early 1968 in this instance.

The problems of organization and planning, combined with the co-ordination of town and country, led, in early 1961, to the formation of regional planning boards – *Juntas Unificadas de Coordinación Económica y Industrial* (the JUCEI). They marked the extinction of the revolution *por la libre* administered by optimistic ex-students. They were a praiseworthy attempt, inspired by Raúl Castro, to escape from excessive centralization. If they placed greater power in the hands of local bureaucrats, perhaps these would have a better chance of knowing what was happening than bureaucrats in Havana. These boards expressed the extent to which the old Communists (as they began to be known) expected to contribute to the new society. Thus in the JUCEI of Oriente, founded in March 1961 with Raúl Castro as its president, the secretary-general of the old Communist party of the province, Ladislao González Carvajal, appeared as the JUCEI secretary-general; and this identification of an established unofficial bureaucracy with a new official institution would be repeated throughout the island.[88] Of these Communists, only those who had chanced to be in Las Villas during Guevara's campaign there – such as Arnaldo Milián, secretary general of the Las Villas JUCEI – had done much in the fight against Batista.

Cuban Labour, the federation controlled by old Communists, had only one role to play in the development of the economy: to follow orders. In early 1960 Luis Simón, working in the State Electricity Company, had suggested to the minister, Martínez Sánchez, a new Labour charter; the latter had replied that 'the State imposes, it does not make contracts'.[89] Since then, the nationalization of the labour force had proceeded apace. In September 1960 the Ministry of Labour devised a 'crime against production', against persistent absentees – the only method of protest, now that strikes were unthinkable. During 1961 absenteeism would become a major problem for the revolution. A law in November 1960 enabled the Ministry of Labour to 'intervene' in any company where a labour dispute threatened production. In March 1961 new laws provided that workers should register with the ministry to qualify for a work permit, and gave the ministry authority to settle all labour disputes by means of a decree. Some degree of freedom of responsibility remained at a lower level: workers could elect advisory councils of their own which sometimes had limited local influence. But henceforth there were no disputes, only inarticulate hostility – particularly towards Lázaro Peña, the founder and now again secretary-general of the CTC(R). Nor was unemployment wiped out: if it

[88] Thus Ladislao's brother, José Luis, became secretary in Pinar del Río, Silvio Quintana in Havana, Leonides Calderio in Matanzas, Felipe Torres in Camagüey, and Arnaldo Milián in Las Villas.

[89] '*El estado impone, no convenia*' (Simón MSS, 299).

had decreased in the country (perhaps the average working year had increased from about 160 to 200 or 240 days,[90] it survived in the cities where there were perhaps 200,000 unemployed, excluding the under-employed who had increased because of the absence of tourists and North American goods to sell. Many hours were lost in military parades, meetings of all sorts and 'campaigns'.

As it was, economic breakdown was avoided by the challenge of invasion.

Note on statistics in Cuba 1959–61

During this time, the Cuban state took over very quickly much of the nation's means of production and services. Most trained Cuban statisticians, however, had gone into exile. The collection of statistics, therefore, in the first years of the Revolution was done in the most rudimentary way, despite the fact that in an economy which is to be planned, accuracy in this field is almost more important than anything else. In addition, many errors were made by officials who were both incompetent and anxious to please by exaggeration. The statistics of production from the (until 1963) large private agricultural sector were and, indeed, are still, very difficult to estimate. Finally, from 1960 onwards the Government itself was wont to regard statistics themselves as one more weapon in the fight against counter-revolution and 'imperialism'. Hence, with the best will in the world, it is impossible to regard the published figures for production between 1959 and 1961 as any more than 'indicative' (to use the graceful description of Professor Bettelheim). After 1961, other problems arise in respect of Cuban production figures, some of which are discussed in the Epilogue to this book. This whole matter has been explored in a masterly manner by Carmelo Mesa-Lago in his pamphlet, *Availability and Reliability of Statistics in Socialist Cuba*. Occasional Paper no. 1 (January 1970) of the Centre for Latin American studies at the University of Pittsburgh.

[90] Unemployment was in 1960–61 probably substantially higher than 1958 in industry, transport and building, lower in agriculture.

CHAPTER 40

Cuba Socialista: II

1960 had been labelled as the 'year of agrarian reform', just as 1959 had been the year of 'liberation'. 1961 would be the year of 'education'. This meant not the expansion of education in general but a campaign against illiteracy. It was thought that there were nearly a million illiterates in Cuba, comprising half the rural population. Martí had said: 'To be literate is to be free.' This campaign, which (no doubt correctly from the point of view of strict economic priorities) had been given a low place in a list of necessities presented by Blas Roca at the Communist conference in August, represented the last fling (for the time being) of the romantic side of the revolution. Castro had promised at the U.N. that illiteracy would be stamped out within a year. Thousands of Cubans, whose faith in the revolution might otherwise have wavered, prepared in the spring of 1961 to throw themselves into a great campaign which would start in April. First, the illiterates would be found and named; by February 1961 412,000, by April 546,000.[1] In the towns volunteers who could read would teach those who could not. In the remote country districts teaching would be a full-time job. Who better for this task than secondary school children – by the nature of things, many of them middle class – who might, after all, learn from the experience of staying a few months in the poorer parts of the country? All secondary schools therefore would be closed after 15 April. Volunteers – and naturally the pressure to be a volunteer would be strong – would enrol as *brigadistas alfabetizadores* and, after instructions at Varadero beach, set out for the remote parts of their island, armed with a uniform, a hammock, a blanket, a paraffin lamp, a flag, a portrait of their patron, Conrado Benítez (a militiaman killed by the counter-revolution in the Sierra de Escambray) and two manuals: *¡Venceremos!* and *¡Alfabetizemos!*

The character of these manuals was scarcely objective: thus, exercise A of *¡Alfabetizemos!* began: 'We are going to read *Organ-ización de Estados Americ-anos*.' Illustrations showed happy labourers with their produce and children. *¡Venceremos!* contained useful words and phrases such as 'Friends and Enemies'; 'The Revolution wins all battles'; and 'International Unity', as well as detailed instructions for the

[1] By August, when the campaign was well under way, 985,000 had been identified.

teacher. In the glossary at the end of *¡ Venceremos!* among the ten or so words or phrases beginning with B we hear of Bloqueo Económico: 'State of siege imposed by imperialism [which] . . . we have conquered thanks to the countries which trade with us.' Better no doubt a lively prejudice than a glum neutrality if one is going to learn to read fast. On the other hand, there was more rhetoric than sense in the incidental knowledge picked up during the illiteracy campaign.

Established now in Campamento Columbia, Batista's old military headquarters, Armando Hart, the Minister of Education, member of a Catholic but firmly revolutionary family – his father had recently become president of the Supreme Court – had also embarked on the reorganization of education. The Under-Secretary, Dulce María Escalona, a Communist, had been director of the Escuela Normal under Prío and Batista; she was a mathematician of intelligence, humanity and ability, who had been once interested in Dewey. The achievements of the revolution in education by 1961 were considerable: whereas, before 1959, over 40% of children between six and fourteen did not go to school, by 1961 probably all but 20% did. There were still however many who dropped out in the last two grades between eleven and fourteen. This achievement in primary education had been made possible by the increase of teachers in rural areas (about 5,000), in response to an appeal for volunteers. But enrolments had been faster and, partly due to the rise in population, the number of children per teacher was 37 in 1960–1, compared with 35 in 1956.[2] Most new teachers had been rather hastily trained at San Lorenzo in the Sierra Maestra. The old one-room primary school with several grades studying together naturally continued. The Camilo Cienfuegos City School in the Sierra was not yet ready for more than a handful of pupils. In addition, the formation of a children's revolutionary movement, socialist Boy Scouts and Guides, for children between seven and thirteen, the Unión de Rebeldes Pioneros,[3] based on the Russian youth movements of the same nature, headed by the 'youngest volunteer in the Sierra', Captain Joel Iglesias, gave the zealous something new to think about.[4] Most barracks had been turned into schools, but many schoolboys nevertheless seemed to be almost soldiers.

There was also some reorganization of secondary schools. Thus the old five-year *bachillerato* was abolished and replaced by courses designed specifically to increase the numbers of university students. University

---

[2] Seers, 114.

[3] Organized 10 May 1960. It merged with Juventud Socialista, the Communist Youth, October 1960.

[4] Iglesias, who was chief of the 10th police station, Havana, in January 1959, when aged hardly twenty, became a founder member of the Central Committee of the Cuban Communist Party in 1965.

entrance standards radically dropped. Most secondary schools remained in cities, while children who did not live there stayed in hostels, and many new boarding schools and technical colleges were established on nationalized estates or in luxury houses. Enrolment of pupils apparently increased by a third.

In the spring of 1961 all private schools had not been nationalized, though many had closed through lack of support. Some schools, such as Castro's old school, the Jesuit Belén, had been taken over. Foreign schools, such as the admirable Ruston's Academy of Havana, had also closed. Those private schools which did remain were unenthusiastic at the prospect of having to shut down on 15 April for the illiteracy campaign. They rightly realized that they had little chance of reopening. In March there had been riots, especially in Santiago and at Guantánamo, against the prospect of closing, but 15 April found all private schools, except a few nursery schools, ready to accept the inevitable.[5]

The universities, on the other hand, had not yet been formally reformed. But they were changing. Many teachers were in exile or had been removed. Heads of departments were all safe revolutionaries. In many departments foreign teachers had been recruited. In practice, the universities were Marxist-Leninist in bias by the spring of 1961. There had as yet been no radical revision of faculties to harness higher education to the needs of the economy (such as by abolition of arts courses) but the matter was already in the air. Students were far more strictly disciplined than ever before. Attendance at lectures was virtually compulsory, and those who did not wish to join the militia were in difficulties. 1,700 students had been sent in 1960 by the Ministry of Industries to study in the Soviet *bloc*. Teacher training colleges had been founded at Batista's old tubercular centre at Topes de Collantes in Escambray and in the Sierra Maestra at Minas del Frío. There were other educational projects, ranging from language courses to schools for sewing for peasants, schools for taxi drivers, shoemakers' classes, or rehabilitation classes for prostitutes.

The weakness of all these projects was the shortage of teachers. Many of those who taught were scarcely more than students or otherwise unqualified.

The revolution doubtless had increased the quantity of education; the quality of teaching had as probably declined. But access to education perhaps matters more than the wisdom of the educators. Even here, however, there had been much waste. Scholarship students were not all up to the work they were expected to do. Some did not work enough. There were still in 1961, as there were to be several years later, too many

---

[5] The education budget in 1961 was probably twice that of 1958, even taking into account the collapse of the value of the peso.

lawyers and artists and too few technicians. Standards in general were lowered at the university to meet the demands of new entrants.

The regime ran theatres, cinemas, television centres and musical activities, and sent the Havana state orchestra around the country. But the newspapers were now very dull. *Revolución* and *Hoy* differed only in that the latter presented a more solid and economically informed picture of events, under the editorship of Carlos Rafael Rodríguez, and the former, still under Carlos Franqui's editorship, with many of its staff secretly wretched at the way things were going, concentrated more on Castro's doings in the Sierra. The lively and heterodox literary supplement, *Lunes de Revolución*, had already excited the enmity of the orthodox communists. *Bohemia* under its new editors played the same role among magazines, while the army magazine, *Verde Olivo*, sold only a little less than *Bohemia* and remained the most dogmatically Communist.

ICAIC, the film institute of Cuba, directed by Castro's old Communist contemporary at the university, Alfredo Guevara, ran the cinemas, made new Cuban films, and dealt with the import of foreign films. Since the U.S. blockade in the autumn of 1960 and the shortage of foreign currency, few new U.S. or European films were shown, though some old ones were, of no special orthodoxy.[7] New films from the 'friendly countries' of the East also appeared, such as *A week in the Soviet Union* and *Life and Death of Ernst Thaelmann*.[8] The effort of two young filmmakers, Orlando Jiménez and Saba Cabrera, to shoot a specifically nonrealist film, *Pasado Meridiano* or *PM*, an impressionistic picture of an afternoon in January 1961, later brought up the whole question of commitment in the arts, leading in July to a famous discussion between Castro and selected intellectuals, afterwards to a cultural congress in August.[9] The ultimate consequence was the establishment of a Writer's Union directed by officials.

The revolutionary government also reconstructed the old National Council of Culture which eventually came under the direction of Edith García Buchaca, a veteran Communist, now *compañera* of Joaquín Ordoqui. This embarked on an ambitious sponsorship of painting and sculpture, concerts, music, dancing and theatre. These activities were dominated by insistence on a 'revolutionary conscience'. This did not necessarily mean a lowering of standards, since the best theatre company, Studio Theatre, run by Vicente Revueltas and his sister, was

---

[7] *The Sun also Rises, The Great Dictator*, etc. etc.

[8] The German Communist leader who died in Buchenwald.

[9] The film was not publicly shown; one reason was that it gave a free and easy impression of life in Havana at a time when the whole city was supposed to be alert and expecting an invasion. The only reviewer to praise it, Néstor Almendros, was sacked from his job on *Bohemia*. For a description, see Nicholas Wollaston, *Red Rumba*, 220.

already, even before 1959, Marxist in outlook; this flourished in 1960 and 1961, bringing Brecht and other European playwrights to the Cuban theatre for the first time with great success.

Publishing houses were now under the government, even though there had been none of any substance before. The difference no doubt was that in 1959 it would have been possible to publish, at one's own expense, a book attacking the regime in Cuba, whereas in 1961 it would not. The Imprenta Nacional directed by Alejo Carpentier had embarked on a vast expansion, mainly comprising speeches by Castro, Lenin, Marx, and Blas Roca's *Fundamentals of Socialism in Cuba*, but also more digestible wares, such as Jenks's *Our Cuban Colony*, along with Ramiro Guerra's *Azúcar y Población*, Tolstoy, *Don Quixote* and Voltaire. The Council of Culture published García Lorca and Cirilo Villaverde in large numbers. There was no purge of libraries: Orwell was still to be found in the National Library, though a new imprint of *Dr Zhivago* from Buenos Aires was apparently seized in early 1961 as counter-revolutionary literature.[10] Foreign newspapers and journals were by this time no longer sold and literature criticizing the regime or the system would usually not be displayed in bookshops. Much depended on who made the decisions: thus the director of the National Library, María Teresa Freyre de Andrade, an ex-Ortodoxo, and in the 1930s a member of the Jóvenes Revolucionarios Cubanos (in the 1950s she had taken refuge in the Mexican Embassy to avoid persecution), was a woman of intelligence and humanity.

Both television and radio continued to serve as a perpetual means of projection for the government. Even when there was no public occasion to celebrate, a record of one of Castro's speeches could be heard at one o'clock every day on the radio. Both mediums sounded, with their syncopation, as if they were revolutionary parodies of the U.S. system: '*Aquí Radio Progreso – la On-da de la Alegría.*'[11] The techniques of Madison Avenue (and the operators had themselves in some cases worked in New York or at least for New York companies) sold the revolution, the illiteracy campaign, and the struggle against the blockade. In the streets the revolutionary songs still, almost continuously, blared from gramophones, and, above all the *Hymn of the 26 July*, still jingled to their seaside rhythm. One of the best known voices of the revolution, however, Pardo Llada, the chief of the radio and television corporation FIEL, nicknamed the 'Minister of Hate', defected to Mexico late in March, screaming 'betrayal' in the same voice as he had until then screamed 'imperialism'.

[10] Fritz Allemann, *Der Monat*, April 1961. See discussion in Draper. The author saw an isolated copy of *Dr Zhivago* in a bookshop in Obispo Street in mid-1961.
[11] The Wave of Happiness.

Whether or not this government could be effectively labelled Communist, its achievements guaranteed it, even without the compelling oratory of Castro, the support of the vast majority of Cubans. The militant and conformist side of the regime, permanently on a war footing, troubled surprisingly few. The insistent intrusion of government into private lives, the call for volunteers for the militia, afterwards for the illiteracy campaign, a happy marching throng on the way to 'Unity', though intolerable to the *bourgeoisie,* caused at least a break from the unbelievable tedium which had marked many Cubans' lives in the past. Though Batista and the Auténticos had used propaganda, the Cubans had never experienced the massive doses of national propaganda that had been the lot of European nations during the World Wars. The majority, too, believed that for the first time the government, if intolerant, was at least not corrupt. It is tempting no doubt to dismiss this as an achievement comparable merely to Mussolini's in making Italian trains punctual.[12] But the break from corrupt officials, corrupt judiciary, corrupt politicians, corrupt unionists and corrupt men of business was, in the minds of the majority, a stark, extraordinary, maybe baffling but wonderful contrast. The sleazy world of prostitution, police protection rackets and clip joints had also almost vanished, and only prostitutes wholly regretted the disappearance of Uncle Sam. Gambling still continued, and sometimes on a grotesque scale: opponents of the revolution, many with passages booked to the U.S., knowing they could not take their money out of the country, went nightly into the still glittering and new casinos at the Havana Hilton (Habana Libre), the Riviera, the Nacional or the Capri hotels, sometimes placing counters on every square of a roulette board; in the background, behind the croupier's head, a huge notice proclaimed that 'To Save is to Make the Revolution'. Another, above the cashier, announced 'Lumumba will live for ever in the hearts of all free peoples'!

The anomaly of such gambling in a puritanical revolution was explained by the reluctance to increase unemployment by dismissing the croupiers. But it also served to keep some possible counter-revolutionaries from other temptations. These great hotels of Havana, built only two or three years previously, with their air-conditioning beginning to falter, the service and the food in decline, seemed like splendid ruins of a past civilization amid a new discordant one as yet unclearly defined. The Habana Libre presented the greatest contrast, since with its paintings by Wilfredo Lam, its ballroom, swimming pool and tinkling music, its several casinos, it had become the main international conference centre, the hotel for delegations from friendly socialist nations, for sym-

[12] As M. Leo Sauvage did, in an article in *The New Leader,* 8 November 1965, which criticized a review by the author in the *New York Times.*

pathetic Communists from the western hemisphere and fellow travellers from Europe. A bookstall in the foyer sold the latest revolutionary literature and the works of Marx and Martí. Through its revolving doors during 1961 would come delegation after delegation, revolutionary leaders of all generations, from all countries, from Ludwig Renn to General Lister, Francisco Juliao from Brazil, and the Leftist Perónist Cooke from ʿArgentina, not to speak of journalists, cartoonists, spies, militiamen and militia girls, black, white, mulatto, in olive green uniforms, rifles at the trail, cigars in their mouths, as ready for a murderous attack as for the cha-cha-cha.

The majority of Cubans admittedly did not visit the Habana Libre, though from time to time whole floors of this and other palaces were given over to country people for courses in sewing or domestic hygiene. There would have been no difficulty in anyone going there if they had wished. Roof-top bars were now for the first time open to Negroes. This sense of social freedom was a further reason why, as all observers agreed, the majority backed the government, or rather were fascinated, even mesmerized by it. Most Cubans felt at least free from their landlord and the prejudices of the old master class. Social and national freedom went together. Cuban nationalism had been so aroused by Castro's speeches and the events of the last two years that the satisfaction at having shaken off the yoke of the U.S. went deep, among non-Communists as well as Communists. The government told the people so often that for the first time they could truly say 'This is my own, my native land' that, whether or not they required propaganda to make them think so, they believed it. Such reflections, on the other hand, were probably not shared by the old organized working class in the cities, whose standard of living dropped with the coming of the revolution.[13]

Much depended on Castro. His faults were evident: verbosity, carelessness of human life, xenophobia, egotism, a reluctance to delegate authority. But so too were his positive qualities: his energy, his audacity, his obsession to know what was going on, to see for himself the reality of how reforms were enacted. No one could accuse him, as Fanon in Les damnés de la terre did so many leaders of new states, of retiring to a palace and never visiting the country. On the contrary, Castro seemed never to be in the capital, always travelling by helicopter or jeep or Oldsmobile, always looking at some new project, always speaking, encouraging, threatening, denouncing, never indifferent. Simple and

[13] As admitted by Guevara: 'It is not a secret to anyone that our friends in petrol, for example, or of the telephone and electric companies, have not been directly benefited economically by the Revolution.' (Revolución, 29 November 1961, 3). For contrasting views of travellers to Cuba in the winter of 1960–61, see Warren Miller, The Lost Plantation, London 1961 (published in New York as Ninety Miles from Home), a sympathetic diary of a North American; and Nicholas Wollaston's Red Rumba, London 1962, 13–91, and 209–31.

sophisticated people alike still believed in him as their guide. How could he respond other than by dazzling them with his qualities? Castro had convinced his countrymen that he was a political genius and was recognized as such throughout the world. He had great talents. He was a superb orator. He was a dangerous enemy. Cubans and Latin Americans had been taught to respect force for too long under unjust governments of a different kidney for them to refuse admiration to a man of force of the Left.

Nationalism of course does not exist in the void but customarily springs from over-close experience of another nation which even xenophobia cannot quite shake off. To hear the literacy campaign pressed with jingles which were devised by advertising agents was to realize that North American habits had stretched far into the mind of the nation. In pursuing North America with such special venom, Cuba was now pursuing part of herself, as the continued counter-revolutionary activities during the winter of 1960–1 suggested all too bluntly.

Communism, like Catholicism, owes its strength where it exists to a flexible adaptation to national character. Just as East Germany under Ulbricht has a Prussian priggishness, so Cuba under Castro retained a gaiety and even a superficiality which helped to make the revolution acceptable. Songs and jingles swept the island as much as ever, though now busloads of schoolgirls might be heard singing:

> *Somos Socialistas,*
> *Marxistas, Leninistas,*
> *Mañana seremos*
> *Tremendos Comunistas.*[14]

Even the shouts mechanically called by obedient throngs at mass meetings had sometimes a childish note:

> Pim – Pan – Pum
> Mao – Tse – tung.

A long speech by Castro might be interspersed by cheering, shouting, clapping and dancing, which would afford both the crowd and Castro a chance of rest though there would also be the more alarming cries of *Paredón, Paredón* (that is, to the execution) *Paredón* to the imperialists and the priests, though even this might turn into a bloodthirsty rumba

---

[14] I may have antedated this jingle somewhat; I heard it for the first time in July 1961. Another version runs:

> *Somos socialistas*
> *lo dijo el caballo*
> *y al que no le guste*
> *que lo pa·ta un rayo.*

Castro figures in both revolutionary and counter-revolutionary myth as *caballo* (the horse).

(*Para los Curas, Paredón*). (Guevara once boasted that the Cuban Revolution was Revolution with Pachanga; but it also spelled execution, with the rumba.) Partly these effects were contrived, but they were really more spontaneous. Even to visitors who found the huge portraits of Marx and Castro unappealing, along with the posters of strong and sober workers with shovels poised, the strident cries of exhortation to unity, to patriotism, to work, Castro's appeals to the Cubans to become Spartans[15] and above all the ubiquitous guns, Cuba retained in 1961 some of its extraordinary charm, though most foreigners were as much excited by its paradoxes as by its achievements.

A major cause for anxiety was the law. Until the winter of 1960–1 the Supreme Court had remained much as it had been since the fall of Batista. The judges observed with dismay the increasing number of arbitrary arrests, the long sentences, and the political trials to which all opponents of the regime were subject, but this was not the concern of the ordinary judiciary; the revolutionary tribunals were outside their jurisdiction, just as the Urgency Courts first set up by Machado and used latterly by Batista to try political offenders fast, had also been.[16] Still, many of the judges were out of sympathy with the revolution. On 17 November 1960 the president of the Supreme Court, Emilio Menéndez, and his colleague Judge Morell Romero suddenly fled to the Argentinian Embassy. Their colleagues of the Court named them traitors, though nine of these dissented: within the week, these nine were themselves in exile. Menéndez was succeeded by Judge Enrique Hart, father of the Education minister and, as everyone thought, a good democrat and Catholic. But in December came a further purge of the court, now reduced to fifteen members. A government spokesman argued that the old Supreme Court included too many members pledged to un-revolutionary philosophies: in several cases involving the valuation of confiscated property, the court had even ruled in favour of plaintiffs. Castro explained that there was no need to have so many judges in Cuba, since litigation was no longer necessary. Henceforward, as this declaration might suggest, the revolution was a factor in all judicial procedure. It was not that, in the majority of criminal cases, guilt or innocence was prejudged but that, if guilt were decided, the services to the revolution of the person accused would exert a decisive influence over the sentence. Further, statements of the character and career of the accused were now

---

[15] '*Nosotros tenemos que ser un pueblo espartano . . . un pueblo luchador.*' (Speech to Milicias, *Obra Revolucionaria*, 20 January 1961, 16.)

[16] The thirty-two judges of the Supreme Court, which had been purged in January 1959, had, normally, life tenure and presided over five separate chambers. These dealt with civil and criminal appeals, administration and disputes over judicial and municipal appointments. The Court also dealt with such questions as the constitutionality or removal of local government officials, and in those and certain other circumstances sat all together.

made before the verdict. This politicization of law was doubtless inevitable in the unfolding violent revolutionary situation. The old legal system before whose tangles Generals Wood and Crowder had confessed themselves baffled, at long last snapped, like an old and rotten tree, the ancient rooks' nests still visible when it reached the ground.

There was also war in Cuba in 1960-1. All through the winter there had been small infiltrations, by the CIA and the exiles, rumours of invasion, emergencies, conspiracies and acts of violence. Militiamen had often to be kept from work, thereby adding to economic difficulties. Exile sources believed that 1,330 people had been shot by the government by October 1960, and by March more. The struggle in the Escambray between the counter-revolution and the government persisted all winter, but the latter gradually won by wearing down the *guerrilleros*, who lacked food and supplies and were not effectively sustained by the U.S. from the air. Many were shot, while among the dead on Castro's side was his personal physician, Luis Fajardo. The fighting continued till the spring, though more and more sporadically. Guevara thought that there were still 200 in arms in the Escambray in early 1961.[17] Several expeditions from Miami on the Cuban coast were broken up as soon as they arrived. The most serious failure was the escape of ex-captain Jorge Sotús, of the MRR and leader of Castro's first reinforcement in the Sierra; he escaped from the Isle of Pines in December 1960 by reaching a telephone in the prison, impersonating a superior officer in Havana and ordering his own release.[18] There was an attempt on Castro's life outside the Italian Embassy the same month, and occasionally militiamen were mysteriously murdered, one hanging on a tree, with the notice: 'Take this one down, we need the tree for others.'

In the winter of 1960, Rogelio González Corzo of the MRR directed a powerful campaign of sabotage and terrorism in Havana; many bombs were laid, letter boxes blown up, water mains destroyed, sugar and tobacco plantations set aflame. Mysterious posters assured Castro that his days were numbered. Ray's MRP also claimed responsibility for some of these acts, though Ray himself left secretly for Miami (MRP was thereafter directed in Cuba by Antonio Viciana, an accountant). A new companion, the ex-secretary-general of labour, David Salvador, founder of the 30 de Noviembre Movimiento was caught with Joaquín Agramonte as they tried to sail out of the River Jaimanitas near Havana in a yacht; Salvador was sent off to La Cabaña.[19] A bomb exploded on

---

[17] Ricardo Rojo, *Che Guevara*, Paris 1968, 91.

[18] He was, however, later killed by accident when embarking in Miami on a clandestine journey.

[19] He had $13,000 with him and he was at first accused of being in possession of foreign currency and of trying illegally to leave the country. See Rodríguez Quesada, 19-20. He was not tried till August 1962 when he was sentenced to thirty years.

6 December in the church of Our Lady of Charity, with the note '*Viva Khrushchev* – Down with priests' – probably a fraud. Sixteen people were later dispatched to gaol for periods of up to thirteen years. Seventeen students of *Juventud Católica* were arrested for placing a bomb at the University of Havana. Farm machinery was destroyed. The Havana–Santiago express was derailed near Santa Clara. Bands of rebels under Clodomiro Miranda and Benito Campa, both ex-combatants against Batista, roamed Pinar del Río and Matanzas. There was occasional hi-jacking of aeroplanes, bomb attacks on crowds, while big fires were lit, at the former Esso refinery in March and at the Hershey sugar mill, and the big Havana store of El Ecanto was destroyed in April.

One aim of the MRR and MRP was to stimulate government repression in the manner undertaken two years before by Batista. In this they were not successful. The consequence was more to drive the population apart into two increasingly hostile groups – the minority against the regime, the majority still for it. Among liberal intellectuals who had supported the regime in the beginning, a terrible crisis of conscience arose: should they not join the underground? Should they return to the life of sabotage and conspiracy. To try and dissuade them, there was a continuous parade of executions, including, in March, that of the North American Major Morgan and his old companion Major Carreras, who had tried to prevent Guevara from reaching the Sierra Escambray in 1958. On 18 March 1961 many of the most prominent leaders of the underground, including González Corso, were betrayed, arrested and later shot.[20] Among these were Sorí Marín and Rafael Díaz Hanscom who had tried to unite all the anti-Castro forces in Cuba.

Protests still admittedly occurred from within the regime, though the only open one was that emanating from the old thorn in the flesh of Batista, the Electrical Workers' Union, whose leader, Amaury Fraginals, had remained untouched by the purges. On 9 December a number of Cuban Electric employees[21] gathered in their headquarters at the Prado and marched to the Presidential Palace, shouting '*Cuba Sí, Rusia No*'. Fraginals was finally admitted to see Dorticós. He made his complaint. But four days later he went into hiding, and was immediately

[20] Lazo, 289.
[21] U.P. said 2,000; the Cuban Press, 200. Fraginals, aged 31, began to work for Cuban Electric in 1947. In 1956 he joined the 26 July Movement in Havana and worked for the action and sabotage group under Aldo Vera. He was in gaol from November 1957 until January 1959. He then was elected provisional secretary-general of his union, and confirmed in this position in May (Interview, *El Mundo*, Miami, 8 April 1961). Fraginals said: 'On 12 December we received an emissary who brought us an ultimatum: either we make declarations against the men who had taken part in the demonstrations or we would be put before the *paredón* . . . There was only one traitor, Abrahantes. The rest fled to different embassies and some of us stayed hidden.'

accused by Castro of organizing terrorism. The Electrical Workers' Union then expelled Fraginals dishonourably.[22] What seems more curious than these acts of defiance were acts of submission: how was it possible that an old Auténtico, anti-Communist trade union leader like Conrado Bécquer, senator even under Batista and collaborator of Mujal should be permitted to remain as secretary-general of the all important FNTA (sugar workers' union), or should permit himself to do so? Such anomalies can only be explained by the cynical opportunism built into the Cuban union system for so long: Bécquer moved from treasurer of the FNTA before 1959 to secretary-general afterwards.

The Church remained a privileged centre of opposition, since Castro and the Communists had decided to avoid meeting it head on. In August 1960 Blas Roca, the Communist secretary-general, had explained that, though the Church's influence was based on an existing division of classes, there were many Catholic workers who understood the desirability of social change. But in October, Mgr Boza Masvidal had attacked the government for 'passing the just limits of aid and vigilance' and of reaching for 'absolute control', making the individual into a mere piece of state machinery. Blas Roca in *Hoy* compared the bishop's article with the 'imperialistic' propaganda emanating from Swan Island. A priest who favoured the revolution, Father Germán Lence, denounced the hierarchy. In November a third pastoral by Mgr Pérez Serantes praised the U.S. for its stand against Communism, though added that it took an ideology to beat an ideology such as Communism; the real battle was between Rome and Moscow, not Washington and Moscow. The new United Youth Movement tried to prevent the reading of the pastoral in the cathedral of Santiago by singing revolutionary songs. On 4 December the hierarchy issued a final joint pastoral letter enjoining Castro to reject Communism, adding 'the Lord will illumine you'. Castro replied saying that the government did not have to answer the clergy, and committed himself to the view that to 'be anti-Communist is to be counter-revolutionary', explaining it was also 'counter-revolutionary to be anti-Catholic, anti-Protestant or anti-anything which divides Cubans'.[23] But there was little more protest. The churches remained open, if scarcely full, and Castro occasionally gave speeches criticizing, though not attacking, the Church.[24] The Church magazine *La Quincena* (the last independent paper) ceased. (The smaller independent papers such as *Información* and *El Crisol*, which had not suffered the political onslaught met by the *Diario de la Marina* and

[22] Fraginals was later captured but escaped to the U.S.

[23] *Revolución*, 17 December 1960.

[24] *Cf.* speech of 6 March 1961, where he alluded to the Indian Chief Hatuey's reluctance (in 1510) to go to the same heaven as the Spaniards.

Prensa Libre, had been forced out of circulation by the collapse of advertising, as well as by the absence of any government subsidy.)

In April 1960, just after Eisenhower had given his first blessing to the CIA's adventures, a reasonably fair poll – the last one up till this time – found that most Cuban town dwellers had believed themselves better off than in the past and that three-quarters of them thought that they would be even better off in another five years. Nearly half those living in towns were fanatically in favour of the regime, thinking Castro had 'the same ideas as Jesus Christ', and were longing 'to kiss the beard of Fidel Castro'. (Of these, half had had either no education or had not gone further than elementary school, while nearly half were in their twenties.) When asked about their desires, three-fifths of them said that they coveted above all an improved standard of living, one-third wanted jobs for all, one-third merely 'the success of the Revolution' as such. A quarter hoped for national unity and no more hatred. Few people apparently longed for a democratic government, measured by electoral processes – much fewer than those who demanded an honest government. Few feared Communism. When asked the question: 'What really matters in your own life, what are your wishes and hopes for the future, what would your life look like if you are to be happy?', somewhat over half[25] replied that they wanted good or improved health either for themselves or their family; when asked what were their worst personal fears, just under half[26] said ill-health. Public fears almost all concentrated on fear of a return to past conditions, of tyranny, police crime or oppression, violence, chaos.[27] These reactions were from town-dwellers, who probably by now numbered over 60% of the population; and no doubt the government of the revolution was even more popular in the countryside.

The worst side of the regime was, however, already its prisons. By this time there may have been 10,000 political prisoners in Cuba. Some had had something of a trial, some had not. Treatment by guards, food, sanitary arrangements, were all bad. There were far more prisoners now than Batista ever had and conditions were very bad. Some were held in old fortresses such as La Cabaña, or the Príncipe, and all the prisons were overcrowded. The revolutionary government fell back in this matter upon traditional Cuban authoritarian reactions. Many accounts of life in the prisons of Cuba under Castro were no doubt sensationalist, whilst other writers were driven to exaggerate. Still, the

[25] 52%.
[26] 49%.
[27] This derives from a public opinion survey conducted by Lloyd Free, Director of the Institute for International Social Research at Princeton, New Jersey, making use of a private Cuban research organization which was actually anti-government.

evidence suggests that the new regime was hardly an improvement on that of Batista in the matter of the treatment of enemies. The interrogation rooms of the G.2 might be more sophisticated than the torture chambers of Batista's SIM, but they were scarcely less vile.

The unhappiness, already the despair, of the Cuban middle or upper classes, was by this time undeniable, even supposing that they were not themselves in prison or conspiring, or closely related to those who were. Most of those who had anything to lose had by now lost their old confidence that society, being run by themselves, was on their side, however rotten it might be. All the predictable grooves of old Cuban behaviour were wearing down. Of course, one reason why the revolution was winning was that these grooves were in Cuba more superficially cut than elsewhere. Still, even under Batista, there had always been an established order of things of a certain kind, visits to clubs and hotels, cocktails and banquets, speculations and celebrations, journeys to the U.S.; now all those things, though not yet impossible, were difficult. Over most middle-class people brooded the question whether they should leave Cuba for the U.S., abandoning house, wealth, possessions, maybe for ever, or remain and become drawn into either the politics of counter-revolution or at least the contemplation of it. Long used to the acceptance of authority because they or their friends controlled it, it was impossible to accept that sanction when represented by a revolutionary group of wild, passionate, untidy, young, gun-happy soldiers.

For the majority, for nearly all the country-dwellers and for most of those who lived in towns, the reverse was true. For the first time they knew that authority was on their side, that justice could not be bought by their landlord or their employer; already they knew that, though unemployment might continue and that their lot might still be otherwise hard, the class which had bullied and patronized them was seriously menaced. Castro's tourist board, INIT, had taken over hotels, clubs, and, most important, beaches, and made them available to the general public. The Varadero International Hotel now cost $15 a day instead of $50, the marvellous sands and translucent blue water at the Havana Biltmore Yacht Club was open to all at 50 cents. Along miles of coast public bathing places were established. All this was done at great cost and within an arbitrary time fixed by Castro. The revolution had already increased opportunities for women and for the black or mulatto minority. The organizations of Cuban women played an essential part in co-ordinating mass support for the regime, even mass activity. (The illiteracy campaign of 1961 would be about half run by women or girls, and the cotton crop of 1962 harvested by women.)

Among the middle class, attitudes to the revolution were based chiefly on age: the young were mostly in favour, the old mostly against.

By now most of the well-known liberals had left the regime, and some had even left the country. But these good men were not willing to collaborate with disgruntled *rentiers* either in thought or in action. Curiously, almost for the first time in Cuban history, the only real contact between classes, between the old Cuba sliding away and the new one struggling to be born, was the Church, still somewhat undecided, though the hierarchy and the majority of priests and of leading laymen were now hostile to the government. But while two years before no detectable class interpretation could have been put upon the battle against Batista, there was now a class struggle in full spate in which both sides showed themselves intolerant.

The regime remained government by oratory. Castro's speeches and the size of his audiences were something new to the Americas, if not perhaps to Europe: Sartre wrote that 'this pedagogic eloquence, a little heavy sometimes, at other times vivid, gives the French listener the barely perceptible impression of listening to Péguy speak'.[28] Others recalled Mussolini. Castro himself, however, later argued:

> There is a great difference between our multitudes and the Fascist mobs . . . Our multitudes are not fanatical. Rather, very firmly-based convictions have been created on the basis of persuasion, of analysis, of reasoning. The Fascists brought together multitudes who seemed content. [But] their organisation and mobilisation of the masses was done by typically military means. They never had the character of spontaneity and, much less, the enthusiasm and the magnitude that our public meetings have . . . we offer facilities so that they can be brought to the meeting but absolutely nobody is required to come.[29]

By the time this remark was made – 1964 – there were certainly some classes of the population – the secondary school children for instance who were indeed required to go. But in 1960–1 enthusiasm was clearly real.

The contradictions and contrasts in Cuba in April 1961 were not well known in the U.S., despite the lavish sums spent on intelligence. Cuba was a country with just over a third of its agriculture and about a half of its industry in state hands, with political power concentrated in one man and his adherents. Castro's new allies, the Communists, and their powerful friends across the Atlantic had definite but ambiguous influence. Such was the challenge presented to Kennedy's U.S., a nation which, like Cuba, also fretted at mistakes of the previous ten years, but whose solid political structure could hardly be more different. Usually, the more men differ, the less they fight. In this instance, the two societies

[28] Sartre, *Sartre on Cuba*, 34.
[29] Lockwood, 179.

seemed incapable of living together. An invasion had indeed been mounted by one against the other which in its turn had done what it could to injure its rival's interests elsewhere in the Americas. They seemed about to fight for the simplest of reasons: they were enemies. It is therefore curious to recall not only that the U.S. base at Guantánamo Bay continued to employ daily some 2,000 Cubans from the city of the same name but that every day, even in April 1961, two aeroplanes filled with exiles, flew out of Havana to Miami in very large numbers considering that the air fares had to be paid for abroad. Perhaps 100,000 people had already left Cuba by the end of March 1961, mostly to the U.S. but also to Spain, Mexico and the rest of South America.[30] It remained indeed possible to telephone Miami from Havana and *vice versa*, and many calls were made, some concealing messages of espionage, most of affection; the international struggle between the U.S. and Cuba, and at its back that between the U.S. and Russia, was thus, at a personal level, simply a Cuban civil war, with the tragedy and inconvenience that faction customarily causes.

[30] The International Rescue Committee of New York estimated at the end of 1960 that as many as 30% were labourers and another 30% employees of one sort or another (Quoted Goldenberg, 210).

CHAPTER 41

Battle of Cochinos Bay

'During the early hours of 15 [April 1961],' Castro later recalled,[1] 'because of certain news received from the province of Oriente we did not sleep. All the signs from one moment to another were that the invasion was going to take place. We were on guard.' He thought that the invasion would be in Oriente. Twelve battalions and batteries were sent to reinforce that coastline, though the most likely landing places – those which gave access to mountains – were already defended as well as possible. Castro had always assumed that the invasion would begin with an attack on his air force and, unlike Nasser in 1956 or 1967, he had dispersed his few planes, camouflaged them and surrounded them with batteries. For Cuba had then only a very small air force – fifteen B.26s, three T.33s, and six Sea Furies; the promised Russian MiGs had not yet arrived. These aircraft were separated one by one, while out-of-service aeroplanes were grouped together as bait to fool the attackers. Castro then went to military headquarters and ordered a general alert.

At 6 a.m. two B.26s with Cuban markings flew over the headquarters, dropping bombs. Six other B.26s bombed three other Cuban airfields (Santiago, San Antonio de los Baños, and Baracoa). The B.26s were, of course, U.S. aeroplanes, painted by the CIA, and flown from Nicaragua by exile pilots under the orders of Captain Villafaña who, a year previously, had still been military attaché in Mexico representing the government whose airfields he was now bombarding. At this time, the invasion fleet from Nicaragua had been twelve hours at sea and had another forty hours to go before it could reach Cuba itself. The rumour of landings in Oriente was a deliberately contrived feint by the U.S. navy, save that, near Guantánamo, a force of 168 Cuban exiles under Captain Nino Díaz was intended to land, though it failed to do so.[2]

The bombing caused much public panic in Havana and in the other cities. Apart from minor disturbances in the 1930s, Cuba like the

---

[1] In speech of 23 April.

[2] B.26s were chosen because, though they were old, slow Second World War survivals, they were possessed by many countries. The CIA thought that this would prevent identification with the U.S. (Sorensen, 301). Flying time between Nicaragua and Cuba meant that these machines on each flight could only have an hour at most over Cuba.

U.S. itself, had never previously been under the attention of this sophisticated warfare. The panic was natural, coming on top of months of
rumours (*bolas*). But the military damage done was slight. There were no
military aircraft at Havana. None of those was much damaged, though
some decoys on the ground were blown up. At San Antonio de los
Baños, one combat plane was destroyed; at Santiago, two. A few other
aircraft were damaged. The other combat aircraft took to the air. The
rebel aircraft made several sweeps over their targets, machine-gunning
after they had dropped their bombs, before giving up when the anti-
aircraft fire became too heavy. None of the attacking aeroplanes were
shot down. On the ground seven people were killed, forty-four wounded,
including two women.

Castro immediately struck against the underground. The police, led
by Ameijeiras, ironically a strong anti-Communist though a devoted
adherent of Castro, rounded up, during 15 April, all persons remotely
suspected of hostility to the government, guilty or innocent, saboteurs
and priests, men and women. The Blanquita Theatre, the moat of La
Cabaña, the Príncipe Castle and the baseball park in Matanzas were all
filled with detainees. The unsuccessful bombing raid gave Castro the
occasion to smash all chances that the opposition underground might
have to assist in the invasion. This did not matter to the CIA, who
had discounted the importance of the underground and who did not
even trouble to communicate effectively with their own paid agents.[3]
During the day, exhortations were broadcast. Guevara ironically proclaimed: 'Our great master who teaches us most has always been
imperialism. Every time that our soul flags, or that we think of resting,
imperialism shows us, as today, that in a Revolution one can never
rest.'[4]

Meantime, in Miami, a B.26 flown by Captain Mario Zúñiga had
landed direct from Nicaragua; his aeroplane had been carefully dotted
with bullet-holes to give the illusion of combat. He released the untruth
that, being then a member of Castro's air force, he had decided to
rebel, had bombed some Cuban airfields, and had flown to safety.
His story was confused by the unplanned earlier arrival at Key West of a
B.26 which had taken part in the bombing and which had made for
Miami, not Nicaragua, after developing engine trouble. The story was
further weakened by Zúñiga's refusal to give his real name; had his
story been true, the Cuban government would presumably have

---

[3] Bissell told me: 'Our operations were *not* hampered by the arrest of so many people in
Havana after the raids . . . we did not expect the underground to play a large part.' (Interview, January 1963.) Nevertheless, *cf.* the contradictory remark of Lyman Kirkpatrick,
The Real CIA, 197, who says that these detentions were 'the first catastrophic blow to the . . .
operation.'

[4] *Playa Girón*, I, 19.

quickly discovered the identity of the defector. But he was photographed. His wife in Miami recognized him and naturally wanted to get in touch, for she had not seen him since he had left, months ago, for Guatemala. Some sophisticated journalists also noticed that while Cuba's B.26s were known to have plexiglass noses, the Miami ones had opaque ones.[5] It seemed in addition curious that Dr Miró Cardona and the Cuban Revolutionary Council should be able to talk excitedly in the press in New York as if they knew all about what was going on: 'The Council has been in contact with and has encouraged these brave pilots,' said Miró, after asking reporters to gaze 'into these revolutionary eyes that have known little sleep at night'. Alas, poor Miró could not even in the teeth of reaction resist claiming that he was a revolutionary. Finally, the Cuban government announced that machine-gun ammunition used over Havana was made in the U.S.

The Cuban government were also internationally active. The diplomatic corps in Havana was summoned to the Foreign Ministry and shown some evidence of the foreign origins of the attack. The Foreign Minister, Roa, successfully raised the question of aggression at the U.N. Adlai Stevenson repeated the undertakings of Kennedy that the U.S. would not participate in action against Cuba and said that the pilots who arrived in Miami must be Cuban and that their aeroplanes were Cuban; he showed a photograph of these aeroplanes with the Cuban star upon them. The Guatemalan representative untruthfully denied that Cubans had been trained in his country. Stevenson's second-in-command, Harlan Cleveland,[6] had been assured by the CIA that the pilots who arrived in Miami were genuine defectors. Apparently, as it happened, Secretary of State Rusk confused the men of Miami with two genuine defectors, Roberto and Guillermo Verdaguer, air force officers who had arrived in Florida the previous day.[7] In fact, however, it was becoming clear that the 'cover story' would not hold either in the U.N. or in the eyes of an interested U.S. public opinion. Stevenson was later furious when he discovered that he had been lured into deceiving the world. It is odd that he did not resign.

At the same time, on board the attacking ships, the brigade was briefed by its officers. The officers were told by their CIA trainers that the bombing missions had been successful and that Castro's air force had been virtually destroyed.[8] That night the decoy mission under Nino

[5] Szulc and Meyer, 121.

[6] James Harlan Cleveland. Rhodes scholar and, when working on the Marshall Plan, inventor of the phrase 'Revolution rising expectations'.

[7] Schlesinger, 246. It is unclear from his excellent account whether the CIA deliberately lied to other sections of the government or whether the Intelligence Branch was itself ignorant.

[8] San Román to Johnson, in Haynes Johnson, 94.

Díaz off Oriente again failed to land, despite the direction of a CIA man on board.[9] The invaders sailed on oblivious that they would now land in very different circumstances to those which they had earlier contemplated.

It had been intended by the CIA that two further air strikes of B.26s would finish off the work done by the first, to coincide with the landings (to be at dawn on 17 April). They were to fly to an airstrip on the beach which would, it was hoped, then be occupied.[10] But Kennedy cancelled these further air attacks. The CIA directors, Bissell and General Cabell, were 'deeply disturbed', though not so much so that they insisted on seeing the president personally.[11] They merely gave the orders to their underlings in Nicaragua. Meantime, Kennedy had previously (at noon on Sunday, 16 April), authorized the expedition to continue to the beaches.

In Havana Castro addressed a large crowd at the funeral of the seven victims of those killed by the air attack the previous day. He recalled the incident of the *Coubre*, whose destruction he again attributed to the U.S. He alluded to the air attacks on canefields by aeroplanes based in the U.S.; and to Pearl Harbor, and how outraged the U.S. had been. He ironically read out dispatches by the United Press which had given the orthodox U.S. version of events. He ridiculed Kennedy and Stevenson. Cries of *Fuera*, Assassins, Cowards, *Patria o Muerte, Paredón*, interrupted the oration, as well as the jingles:

Pa'lante y Pa'lante	Forwards, forwards
Y al que no le guste	Let him who doesn't like it
Que tome purgante!	take a strong dose!
and *Fidel! Jrushchov!*	Fidel and Khrushchev
Estamos con los Dos![12]	We are with you both!

The first of these was shouted when Castro for the first time referred to the Cuban revolution as Socialist.

> Comrades, workers and peasants,
> This is the Socialist and Democratic Revolution of the humble, with the humble, for the humble . . . The attack of yesterday was the prelude to aggression by the mercenaries. All units must now go to their battalions . . . Let us form battalions and dispose

[9] Evidence of Antonio Campiña.
[10] General Cabell and Bissell to Mario Lazo (*Dagger in the Heart*, 256) confirmed that three air strikes were planned, not two as suggested by Schlesinger.
[11] They were partly misled by the belief that the first strike had destroyed more aircraft than in fact it had. Kennedy later decided this cancellation was an 'error, but not a decisive error' (Schlesinger, 266). Here he was probably wrong. See Lazo, 273 ff., and Lyman Kirkpatrick, 198 (who says that CIA representatives considered the change of plan 'criminally negligent').
[12] *Revolución* had formally rejected the U.S. spelling of Khrushchev in October 1960.

ourselves to sally out facing the enemy, with the National Anthem
... with the cry of 'To the fight' ['*Al combate*'], with the conviction that to die for our country is to live and that to live in chains
is to live under the yoke of infamy and insult ... *Patria o Muerte,
venceremos.*[13]

With these words, Castro prepared for battle.

In the evening the invasion fleet made rendezvous thirty miles south
of Cienfuegos with landing craft dispatched from the U.S. naval air
base at Vieques.

The Revolutionary Council, the shadow organization referred to by
Castro as the 'Council of Worms' (*gusanos*), was meantime conferring in
New York. The council members, already shadow ministers of this and
that, Transport and Telegraphs, Education and Reconstruction, were told
by the CIA that they should prepare to return to Cuba, and accordingly
were flown to Miami under Bender-Droller, where they were given
dinner and uniforms. They waited. Their masters told them nothing.
Were they in fact prisoners? They went to bed in ignorance of the fact
that the expedition over which they were nominally in command would
begin while they were sleeping: the reason being 'security', the old
excuse which, often justifiably, the leading partners in any alliance give
to justify a deception of their allies.[14] The detention was not known to
Kennedy.[15]

The brigade was now ready to land. Its political chief was Manuel
Artime, the Catholic ex-inspector of INRA; the military commander
was José Pérez San Román. He and all the six battalion commanders –
the battalions were only 200 men each – had been army officers before
1959,[16] along with the second in command (Erneido Oliva), the chief of
staff (Ramón Ferrer), and the air force commander (Manuel Villafaña),
though many of these officers, being young, had had little to do with the
civil war. Several of them, including Pérez San Román and his brother,
had been vaguely associated with the *puros*, the rebel group of officers
who, under Colonel Barquín, had tried to overthrow Batista in 1956,
and were indeed held prisoner for a time in late 1958.[17] San Román, like
Artime, Oliva, Varela Canosa and Villafaña, had held jobs under

[13] *Playa Girón*, 1, 450–77. The penultimate sentence was a quotation from the Cuban
national anthem.
[14] Szulc and Meyer, 122; Schlesinger, 249.
[15] *Ibid.*, 257.
[16] Alejandro del Valle: 1st paratroop battalion
   Hugo Sueiro: 2nd infantry battalion
   Valentín Bacallao: 3rd armoured battalion
   Roberto Pérez S. Román: 4th heavy gun battalion
   Ricardo Montero Duque: 5th infantry battalion
   Francisco Montiel: 6th infantry battalion
[17] Suárez Núñez, 112.

Castro in 1959,[18] though Montero Duque, commander of the 5th battalion, had led a battalion fighting Castro in the Sierra Maestra and thus had fled the country in January 1959.[19]

The brigade was composed of predominantly middle-class and upper-class men, though there were too a hundred or so working-class Cubans. The average age was about thirty, though one man was sixty-one. There were about fifty Negroes and a few more mulattoes, including Oliva, the second-in-command. About 250 had been students and 135 had been soldiers at one time or another. Most of the brigade were Catholics and there were three priests among them, all Spaniards, one of them having been an officer in Franco's army in the civil war. The invaders wore shoulder patches in the shape of a shield bearing in the centre a Latin cross. The political views of the brigade varied from extreme right to centre. It did not include apparently anyone so far to the Left as Manuel Ray, or any member of his organization (the MRP). One or two people (such as Felipe Rivero,[20] of the family of the editors of the *Diario de la Marina*) regarded themselves as nationalists of the third position – Nasserites. One or two (such as José Manuel Gutiérrez) were there almost by chance, since their friends were joining in, others since they desired work. The sons of Miró Cardona, of Varona, of Raúl García Menocal, of 'Millo' Ochoa and of Alonso Pujol,[21] were there, as were Batista's president of the Assembly, Cándido Mora, uncle of the then Cuban minister for Foreign Trade, once a member of Masferrer's MSR, and brother of the dead leader of the attempted assassination of 17 March 1957; Batista's ambassador in Japan (García Montes); and, foolishly, both from the brigade's point of view and their own, several well known killers of Batista's time, including Ramón Calviño (nominally on the naval side) who had murdered personally twenty people after having been once a member of the 26 July Movement; José Franco Mira; Rafael Soler Puig, who personally had killed the Dominican exile, 'Pipi' Hernández, and the Communist dockers' leader, Aracelio Iglesias; and Jorge King Yun who, a common criminal, had murdered a militiaman in escaping from Cuba in 1960. This group had been allotted a sinister role if the invasion were to succeed: to deal with political opposition.[22] Castro's accountants later

---

[18] The two latter had been naval and air attachés in the Cuban Embassy in Mexico until early 1960. The pilots (operating from Nicaragua) included Captain Farias who had, when in command of the Camagüey air base, carried out an investigation into the death of Camilo Cienfuegos.

[19] His evidence when captured. *Cf. Playa Girón*, IV, 418. Other officers of Batista's army in the brigade were Captain Morales and Major Montero Díaz.

[20] Unfortunately for him his wife was a niece of Batista's minister Morales del Castillo, and had hidden his stamp collection in late December 1958.

[21] Prío's vice-president.

[22] Kennedy and his advisers at Washington seem not to have known of the inclusion of these men, which indeed was specifically against his orders. There were also several others with

reckoned that the 1,500 men of the brigade once had owned in Cuba a million acres of land, 10,000 houses, 70 factories, five mines, two banks, and ten sugar mills.[23] In fact, the invasion force contained a remarkably representative cross-section of those opposed to Castro.

The training of these men varied considerably. Some had had only one week, and some none at all. Others had been tramping the jungles of Guatemala for nearly a year. The majority could not have had more than two and a half months. Of the 160 or so who with Nino Díaz were supposed to land in Oriente and to stage a diversion and embark on guerrilla war, half had had only one week's training.[24]

In the baggage of one priest, Father Ismael de Lugo, a manifesto was later found proclaiming:

> We come in the name of God, Justice and Democracy . . . We do not come out of hatred, but out of life . . . The Assault Brigade is composed of thousands [sic] of Cubans who are completely Catholic and Christian . . . Catholics of Cuba: our military might is crushing and invincible and even greater is our moral strength, our faith in God and in His protection and His help. Cuban Catholics: I embrace you on behalf of the soldiers of the liberating Army. Families, friends and relatives . . . soon you shall be re-united. Have faith, for victory is ours because God is with us and the Virgin of Charity cannot abandon her children. Catholics! Long Live Cuba, free, democratic and Catholic. Long live Christ the King!

Cheered by these and other statements, the invading army anchored 2,000 yards offshore, Pérez San Román off Playa Girón in the *Blagar* and the *Caribe*, Oliva off the Zapata swamp in the *Houston*, a sadly appropriate name for a Cuban exile troopship, with the *Barbara J*. Frogmen marked the landing places, the first men on shore, also appropriately, being North Americans: at Playa Girón, a CIA officer who went under the name of 'Gray'; at Playa Larga, at the top of the Bay of Cochinos, another agent known as 'Rip'. The frogmen mishandled the landing, and began to exchange shots with a patrolling jeep, while intense firing began on both beaches long before any substantial forces had landed. Landing was complicated by ignorance of the coral reefs lying offshore, which destroyed or delayed several landing craft. The *Blagar* began to pound the darkness with 75 mm shells. The pilot of the landing craft assigned to Oliva fell into the water. The landing craft engines themselves failed. Landing therefore was spread over

[23] *Playa Girón*, IV, 14.
[24] Evidence of Antonio Campiña.

---

dubious pasts, such as Rosendo Valdés, who had been a 'vigilante' at a notorious police station, and Mario Freyre, a landowner from Bayamo of a controversial reputation.

about six hours. At dawn, the supplies, the ammunition reserves and the whole 5th battalion were still on shipboard. One group, the so-called 3rd battalion, which was led by Valentín Bacallao, landed at Playa Girón and set out for the Girón airstrip. When they reached it they began to clear it ready for aircraft. Both Pérez San Román and Oliva, the commanders, also reached Playas Girón and Larga respectively.

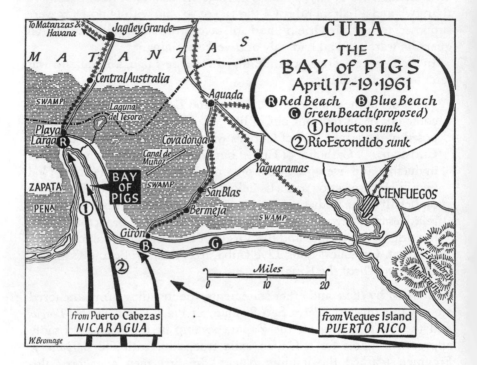

Castro heard of the invasion at 3.15 a.m. as a result of micro-wave transmission from militia units at Playas Girón and Larga, which were silenced about 4 o'clock. At this time, a battalion of the rebel army under Osmani Cienfuegos (Camilo's brother), the Minister of Public Works, was at the *central Australia*, twenty miles inland to the north of Playa Larga; there were platoons of armed charcoal workers in and around this very swampy land, based on Cayo Romano, north of Girón, to the south-west of Playa Larga and Buenaventura next to it. It was an area which had not been regarded as a likely point for invasion, because it was far from mountains and communications were difficult. Behind the woody region of hard soil stretching ten kilometres from the shore lay an impassable swamp, crossed, before the Revolution, only by two narrow-gauge railways, one a sugar line from Cochinos Bay to the *central Australia*, the other from Girón on the coast to the *central Covadonga*. It was an area where the revolution had certainly brought change to the 3,000 to 4,000 charcoal burners who previously had worked there as tenant farmers. Three roads had been built across the swamps, and tourist centres were being constructed at Girón, Larga and the Laguna del Tesoro. The standard of living in the region must have radically risen in the previous two years. Further, the region was actually being now used as a pilot for the great illiteracy campaign, and 200 adult teachers were at work there. 300 children from the swampland on the other hand were studying various trades in Havana – ceramics, tanning, carpentry.[25]

It would have been hard indeed to have found a region in Cuba in which a rebellion could have been less easily inspired among the local people. But then such a thing was not part of the CIA's purpose. Once established, however, the invaders would be hard to dislodge, for they could only be approached on land down three roads and not at all across the swamps. A provisional government could quickly have been established after the bridgehead. The swampland militia, further, was well equipped, particularly with the critical micro-wave radios. Castro was also assisted by luck and by the last-minute decision of Kennedy to abandon the second air strike.

Castro's first move was to place his air force on the alert and to order Cienfuegos's battalion at the *central Australia* to move south against the enemy. The militia of Matanzas province was mobilized to move south too. Castro himself flew to the *central Australia*. An able ex-regular officer Major José Fernández, 'el Gallego', was placed in overall field command. He showed himself much the coolest of Castro's officers in the following days, though little was made of him in heroic myth afterwards. He certainly seemed infinitely more competent as a commander than 'Major' Flavio Bravo, the young Communist contemporary of Castro's at the University, who was given command of the militia.[26]

At dawn, two Cuban Sea Furies, two T.33 jet trainers (quite forgotten by the U.S. planners) and a Cuban B.26 began to attack the landing craft and ships in Cochinos Bay. The B.26 was shot down but the confusion and damage caused at the last stage of the disembarkation was enormous. When the invading paratroops began to arrive at Playa Girón, their confused comrades fired on them as they made their drops. The 5th battalion, still in the *Houston*, the least experienced and least well-trained of the invading forces, then refused to disembark. The confusion was not staunched by the arrival of an invading B.26 from Nicar-

[25] Castro speech of 23 April, in *Playa Girón* 47.
[26] Evidence of a war correspondent on Castro's side who desires to remain anonymous. See also Ania Francos, *La Fête Cubaine*, which has an attractive picture of the fighting from the Cuban side.

agua – 3½ hours' flying time away – to provide cover for the invaders. Both the ships *Houston* and *Barbara J* were now under attack from the T.33 jets and a Sea Fury. The *Houston* was hit by a rocket from one of the former, and began to sink, laden with ammunition and oil supplies. The 5th battalion leapt into the sea, about thirty drowning, the rest gathering disconsolately on the beach looking for their commanders. Meantime at 9.30 a.m. in front of Playa Girón, the *Río Escondido*, with the main bulk of ammunition, oil, food and medical supplies, as well as the communications equipment, was also hit by a rocket from a Sea Fury. It blew up immediately, with a big explosion.[27] The remaining ships withdrew out of danger from the battle zone, their commanders promising the invading commander, Pérez San Román, that they would return at night to land the rest of the supplies. But for the rest of the day the brigade was left with little. The paratroops had lost most of their equipment in the swamp. Tanks had been effectively landed at Girón but they had not yet begun to establish contact between the two groups of invaders, under Pérez San Roman and Oliva respectively.

At ten o'clock in the morning Oliva's forces at the head of the Bay of Cochinos at Playa Larga were in combat with the battalion of militia from the *central Australia*, though the strength of the paratroops was not adequate to force them to retreat far. In the east, at Girón, brigade paratroops had established road blocks on two of the roads across the swamp, while San Román protected the coast road from Cienfuegos. Within this perimeter, the invaders had captured two *pueblos*, San Blas and Girón, where a number of people threw in their lot with the invaders, helping them with food and water, five joining in as fighters.[28] Meantime, the Matanzas militia, accompanied by a well-trained and equipped force from the militia leaders' training school, was advancing southwards from *central Covadonga* towards the paratroop road blocks, and a battalion of infantry from Cienfuegos was also moving west along the coast road. About 150 militia had been taken prisoner, of whom a number – 50, according to the brigade – joined up with the invaders.

Back in the U.S. the Cuban Revolutionary Council had been surprised to hear at dawn the news of the invasion rhetorically issued in their name by a New York public relations firm, Lew Jones, which, as Arthur Schlesinger tells us sardonically, had once been used by Wendell Wilkie. They were furious. In Washington, at a press conference, Dean Rusk avoided direct questions on Cuba, on the grounds that a debate on the subject was being held at the U.N. There, Roa,

[27] The U.S. commission on the causes of the failure of the expedition (General Maxwell Taylor, Robert Kennedy, Admiral Burke, Allen Dulles) gave special emphasis to this (Sorensen, 297).
[28] Haynes Johnson, 115.

backed by Russia, was castigating the U.S. at the Security Council for countenancing aggression. Stevenson, very unhappy, did the best he could.

Castro was now moving against all opposition throughout the island in the most thorough and decisive fashion. Between the raids on 15 April and the evening of 17 April, perhaps 100,000 were arrested, including all the bishops (Pérez Serantes at Santiago was under house arrest), many journalists and the vast majority of the real underground, including most of the CIA's 2,500 agents and their 20,000 suspected counter-revolutionary sympathizers. Many North American journalists were held in overcrowded prisons. A number of imprisoned leaders of the counter-revolution such as Sorí Marín,[29] the advocate-general in the Sierra and Minister of Agriculture in 1959, Eufemio Fernandez, Prío's police chief and ex-commander of Acción Revolucionaria Guiteras (ARG), Arturo Hernández Tellaheche, Prío's Labour minister and a leader of the 'Trujillo conspiracy' of 1959, and González Corso, the MRR saboteur, were shot. In these days what chance there was of any internal uprising in Cuba was ruined irreparably, perhaps for ever; but then the CIA had no regard for such a development. They had remained insistent that only invasion could lead to counter-revolution. Even men who had been sent in recent months into Cuba by the CIA as infiltrators were left without instructions. Some had heard mysterious messages broadcast from Radio Swan Island: 'Look well to the Rainbow' or 'The fish will rise very soon' or 'The fish is red'; but no one had been told what these meaningful words signified. One man reported, perhaps over-optimistically, that his 'men were in constant contact with one another and always ready for action but, unbelievably, they had never received the agreed signal from the U.S.'[30] In the late afternoon, the Lew Jones Agency issued an appeal in the name of the Revolutionary Council (still in virtual prison in Miami) for 'a coordinated wave of sabotage and rebellion'; by then there was almost no opponent of the regime left free in Cuba to answer either this spirited call or other more secret ones.

Back on the beaches, however, Oliva's battalions for a time held their own against their immediate opponents. The column of militia leaders from Matanzas coming along the road from the *central Australia* was badly damaged by the first coordinated air and land attack by the invaders.[31] At this time the Cuban forces had no air support, all available aeroplanes being occupied with attacking the invaders' ships. But in a few minutes the exile aeroplanes were shot down by a T.33 and a

[29] He had apparently made two efforts to kill Castro, on the first occasion being reprieved.
[30] Lazo, *Dagger in the Heart*, 26.
[31] Haynes Johnson implies that nearly all the 900 men in this battalion were killed. This was certainly an exaggeration.

Sea Fury. The T.33 jet trainer, far faster than the brigade's B.26s, was evidently becoming the major factor in the fight. Yet on both fronts the brigade had survived. They needed now their supply ships. But these had been pursued so successfully by the Cuban T.33s that they were already far away and reluctant to return. The *Caribe* had fled 218 miles south, the *Atlántico* 110 miles; the flagship *Blagar* and the *Barbara J* had also fled. The Cuban crew of the *Blagar* refused to go back unless the U.S. navy intervened, which of course they did not, though the U.S. officers on board wanted to return and doubtless had it not been for telecommunications and other modern equipment they would have done so: 'Nelson would never have won a victory if there had been a telex' an English admiral once remarked.[32]

The brigade was thus deserted by its supply ships, and so, instead of the night of 17–18 April being the occasion for reinforcement, it was one for renewed attack by the Cuban government forces who, under the able Major José Fernández, attacked first on the San Blas front with a consolidated advance of armoured cars and tanks. This was halted with bazookas and mortar fire by the invaders' paratroopers under Del Valle. Still, behind the tanks came four infantry battalions with howitzers and more tanks. They too were held up. A heavy attack was also mounted against the western, Playa Larga, position, using first 122 mm howitzers. The artillery fire caused alarm. When it ceased, Oliva attacked with brigade tanks. This coincided with a counter-attack by Castro's tanks, and brought no progress. Castro's forces, being inside the swamp, began to attempt an encircling movement on to Cape Ramona, at the same time pressing on remorselessly as far as possible with tanks by the direct route. Some 2,000 men were involved in Castro's attack – 1,600 militia, 300 regular soldiers, 200 police, 20 tanks. Both sides found their weapons equipped with surprising power, both sides believed they were fighting like heroes. But when day came and the Stalin tanks of the Government kept pressing on, the 2nd battalion of invaders panicked, though they were later rallied again by Oliva, who showed himself a competent and brave commander.

Now that the air-raids of 15 April had been shown to have failed utterly, the second strike (cancelled on Sunday) was reinstated. The B.26s of Nicaragua were supposed at dawn to strike again at San Antonio de los Baños, the airfield where the T.33s, so fatal to the *Houston* and the other B.26s themselves, were believed to be based; but fog prevented this. The pilots flew back to Nicaragua, disconsolate. An hour or so later, at 8.45 a.m., Oliva, commander of the Playa Larga section of the invasion, proposed at a meeting with the other commanders that, in

[32] Admiral Durnford-Slater in 1956. See Hugh Thomas, *The Suez Affair*, London, 1967, 158.

view of the large attack massing on his wing, the whole brigade should regroup and make for the Escambray mountains along the Cienfuegos road. This, the U.S.'s alternative scheme, was rejected by Pérez San Román, who had not heard of it before, as being too far, and since he supposed that the U.S. would, in the last resort, help the brigade out of their difficulties: in this illusion he was reinforced by a conversation with 'Gray' of the CIA[33] by radio telephone. 'Gray' assured him that 'We will never abandon you', offered to evacuate the force if need be and said that the 'jets are coming'. The illusion spread that the U.S. would in fact soon be intervening. Throughout the afternoon the brigade waited, once being cheered by the arrival of two U.S. Sabre jets which flew over the battlefield, but apparently did nothing.[34]

Meantime Castro's forces hesitated to strike a decisive and crippling blow due to their confusion about the numbers of their attackers. Only at about 6 p.m. did artillery begin to fire again, this time aiming at Girón and San Blas, followed by further attacks on land.

At about the same time, U.S. B.54s dropped supplies over Girón but, as an extra frustration, the wind blew these into the sea or the jungle. Much of them, however, was recovered, partly with the help of townspeople from Girón.[35] Meantime, the ships *Blagar*, *Barbara J* and *Atlántico* were some fifty miles south of the Bay of Pigs struggling with problems of their own: what was the U.S. government going to do? Would the crews return to the shore without adequate air cover? The CIA apparently cancelled the instructions to return to unload once more without consulting Washington.[36]

In Washington the recriminations had begun. In the morning Kennedy had had a letter from Khrushchev promising the Cubans 'all necessary assistance'. At midday Kennedy privately regretted that he had kept Allen Dulles as head of the CIA.[37] Neither Kennedy nor his advisers were deceived by Lew Jones's optimistic communiqués – 'peasants, workers and militia are joining the freedom front' – nor by the enthusiastic news in Miami newspapers (and even in one English paper) that Santiago had fallen and the Central Highway had been crossed at Colón. In the afternoon he and his advisers replied to

---

[33] Johnson, 142–3.
[34] This point is unclear. Castro said that U.S. jets at a great height attacked a column of his men and caused great damage and one of the invaders told Johnson that he saw signs of an attack. The jets might have come from the aircraft carrier *Essex*. But they had no orders to undertake this flight. 'Gray' of the CIA told San Román that the aircraft were specifically there to give protection against Cuban aircraft (*cf. ibid.*, 148). 'Gray' also implied to San Román that a large quantity of other aircraft was overhead.
[35] *Ibid.*, 149.
[36] Sorensen, 295.
[37] Schlesinger, 250.

Khrushchev's protest of the previous day with as much verve as they could summon: 'The great revolution in the history of man . . . is the revolution of those determined to be free.'

That night, as it became clear that the brigade was surrounded by 20,000 troops with artillery and tanks, large sections being already across the swamps into the hard forest land by the shore, Kennedy went to a ball. But he was interrupted. At midnight he was urged strongly by Bissell and Admiral Burke to make an air strike from the aircraft carrier *Essex* lying off Cuba, to knock out the T.33s and so free the tired pilots of the B.26s at Nicaragua to deal with Castro's tanks. These men were anxious to expand the conflict in order to save the brigade.[38]

This was the critical moment of the invasion. Had Kennedy agreed to let loose the aircraft from the *Essex*, the future might have turned out differently. But he only authorized six unmarked jets on the *Essex* to fly over the Bay of Cochinos at dawn the next day to cover a B.26 attack from Nicaragua and to help cover the landing of supplies from the *Blagar* and *Barbara J*. These aircraft were not to seek air or ground targets, a curiously ambiguous instruction which was rendered futile by a confusion over time with Nicaragua. The B.26s, two flown by U.S. pilots, arrived an hour early and were mostly shot down before the naval cover arrived. Some Cuban pilots in Nicaragua had refused to sally out again on what seemed to them a foolhardy mission. Four U.S. airmen were killed.[39] In these circumstances the *Essex* jets never set off at all and the ships never approached the beach even to try to unload their supplies.

At Miami in the morning the furious exiles' Revolutionary Council at last met Schlesinger and Berle, two members of Kennedy's administration upon whom they could at last pour out their anger and frustration. They had heard of the disasters from the front, they themselves wanted (they said) to go to the beaches, or at least to Nicaragua, they demanded air strikes and reinforcement. Alas, by the time that Schlesinger and Berle could retire to consult, the news from the beaches was too bad even to contemplate evacuation.

Ever since dawn Castro's forces had been closing around the beleaguered invaders. The paratroopers organized a counter-attack with the 3rd battalion, which faltered and became a retreat. At ten o'clock in the morning Castro's troops took San Blas, and at eleven reached the

---

[38] The author asked Bissell, 'In the end were you in favour of giving U.S. air cover?' Bissell: 'Yes, I was. Very strongly. When I saw that there would otherwise be a disaster I argued very strongly in favour of U.S. air intervention.' Hugh Thomas: 'Could this have led to U.S. [general] intervention?' Bissell: 'Yes.' (Discussion in Washington, 14 January 1963.)

[39] They were Wade C. Gray, Thomas Willard Ray, Riley W. Shlamberger and Lee F. Baker, the only U.S. casualties at Cochinos, though some other CIA men had taken part, e.g. 'Gray' and 'Rip' the frogmen. *Cf. New York Times*, 27 February 1963; *Birmingham* (Alabama) *News*, 4 May 1961; *Examiner* (Birmingham), 3 February 1963.

defences of Girón with tanks and militia. Both at Playa Girón and at Playa Larga the invaders were now falling back, becoming separated from each other. Pérez San Román was in contact with his battalion commanders only by messenger on a jeep, though he remained in desperate radio contact with 'Gray' of the CIA on the *Blagar*. But there was still no help forthcoming. For the time being the brigade had superior firepower but, after a while, the mere weight of numbers began to count. Castro's infantry persistently advanced, and the brigade mortars eventually used up all their ammunition. In the mid-afternoon the U.S. navy was permitted by Kennedy to approach the beaches to try to evacuate survivors, in company with the other invading ships. Of course they were too late. San Román explained by wireless that the Cuban tanks had reached Girón by 4.30 p.m. and announced that they were taking to the swamps. Between 4 and 5 o'clock on 19 April the invading forces destroyed their heavy equipment and dispersed as best they could, some[40] taking to the sea in small boats in the hope of rescue by the U.S. navy, most[41] taking to the swamps. The U.S. navy did not, however, take off survivors but, at the last, turned away, either given pause by artillery or by the knowledge that the invading forces had been dispersed. The disappearance of these ships caused anger: one invading soldier remarked, 'In the wake of that ship goes two hundred years of infamy.'[42]

Lew Jones in New York sought to save face, and announced: 'The recent landings in Cuba have been constantly although inaccurately described as an invasion. It was in fact a landing of supplies and support for the patriots who have been fighting in Cuba for months.' It was also put abroad that most of the invaders had successfully reached the Escambray.

Kennedy had by this time received the Cuban Revolutionary Council, and charmed them into acceptance of his decision not to salvage the invasion, whatever they or the actual fighters supposed that they had been told by the CIA. If the U.S. moved against Cuba, would not the USSR move against Berlin?[43]

Kennedy was thus wise to refuse to send in the full weight of U.S. military might at this point; no doubt a weaker or a more rash president would have done so.[44] Whatever the truth, or the constitutional position of the CIA's encouragement of the invaders to expect full U.S. aid, the

[40] Among them the paratroop commander Del Valle and the C-in-C's brother, Roberto.

[41] Including Artime, Peréz San Román, Ferrer, Oliva, the last separately, supposing that the first three had deserted.

[42] Haynes Johnson, 171.

[43] This obsession troubled Kennedy throughout his term.

[44] Nixon in *Readers' Digest*, November 1964, said that his advice to Kennedy on Cuba at this point had been to 'find a proper legal cover and . . . go on'.

U.S. government conducted itself badly in sending off a handful of men on a badly planned expedition to fight against overwhelming odds. Of course, the invaders deceived themselves, and no doubt difficulties of language and interpretation confused communications; maybe they made in their own minds explicit what had in those of others been either implicit or simply an encouragement. Perhaps the CIA thought that the brigade would fight better if they imagined that the U.S. would save them from disaster, even if it were not true. If so, they showed scant knowledge of psychology. It would seem certain that had the leaders of the invaders known the reality of U.S. policy – in so far as it had been defined – they would have planned a different battle in maybe a different place. But when Kennedy had said on 10 April that no U.S. forces would be involved in their attack, they imagined that this was for external consumption only. North American society seemed so bruised with advertisement and journalistic misinformation that it was impossible for even relatively honest politicians to be believed.

The U.S. government had also shown itself divided, ill-informed and careless of detail. Kennedy, like Eden over Suez, seems to have accepted the view of his advisers that his principal opponent was 'a hysteric'[45] and therefore incapable. Kennedy should have cancelled the scheme and listened to Fulbright and Schlesinger, the only men among his advisers who opposed it;[46] in allowing it to continue, though with his heart not in it, he showed himself less a man of destiny than a Hamlet, a prince whose courtiers were out of control. Meantime, waves of protest swept Latin America, doing more for the cause of Castro than all his propaganda campaigns and secret disbursement of money and pamphlets put together.

Castro's forces captured the surviving invaders in groups. Eventually there were 1,180 prisoners (1,297 had landed), including most of the leaders, disillusioned, bewildered and, as they thought, betrayed. One man at least, who had the brigade banner, reached Havana and the sanctuary of an embassy. The brigade lost 80 men in fighting and perhaps 30 to 40 in the disembarkation. Nine had died while *en route* to Havana in an overcrowded lorry; apart from these men, all the prisoners were well treated; Castro announced that his losses had been 87,[47] but the implication of his speech on 19 April was that the losses were greater than this: the chronicles of the invaders from the estimate of an unnamed Cuban doctor reckoned Cuban revolutionary losses as 1,250, with another 400 dying of wounds, and 2,000 wounded.[48] It is

[45] Schlesinger, 266.
[46] Apart from Chester Bowles, who had not been closely involved in the discussions. Schlesinger alone had opposed on the ground that it would not work, not that it was wrong.
[47] Speech of 23 April.
[48] Haynes Johnson, 129.

in fact hard not to believe that the Cuban revolutionary government did not lose many more men than they announced. The prisoners were not shot[49] but held, after public interrogation by Castro, Carlos Rafael Rodríguez and others, to be tried on television, imprisoned in distressing circumstances, and finally exchanged for medical supplies one and a half years later:[50] Oliva, Artime, Pérez San Román, were ransomed at $500,000 each; the others at $25,000, $50,000 and $100,000. Over half the brigade, including San Román and Oliva, later joined the U.S. army. The CIA estimated in early May that the invasion had cost $M45, a sum which they had not had to ask or account for to any authority.[51]

For Castro the defeat of the invasion was a triumph. After the defeat came the celebrations, the parading of prisoners on television, the jubilant announcement on 1 May, Workers' Day, that Cuba was a socialist state and that there would be no more elections. The revolution, he explained, was the direct expression of the will of the people; there was not an election every four years in Cuba but an election every day. Revolution, he added, had not given a vote to each citizen, it had given each citizen a rifle. The constitution of 1940 was too old and antiquated.[52] Castro placed special blame on Spanish priests, and only those who were not 'counter-revolutionary' would be allowed to stay in Cuba. All private schools would be nationalized. The prisons of Cuba remained full.

Kennedy, licking his wounds, blamed no one but himself, admitted himself in the wrong, and defiantly stated: 'The complacent, the self-indulgent, the soft societies are about to be swept away with the debris of history. Only the strong, only the industrious, only the determined, only the courageous, only the visionary, who determine the real nature of our struggle, can possibly survive.'[53] Ironically, the only other politician who might have made such a remark at this time was the one for whom Kennedy felt such special animosity: Castro. Kennedy went on quickly to approve the project of the U.S. Space Agency to land a man on the moon 'before this decade is out'; perhaps a victory for the U.S. in Cuba might have deprived mankind of that achievement in 1969.

[49] Except the Batista thugs, Calviño, Soler Puig and Jorge King Yun.

[50] Castro's original proposal for their exchange for 500 big tractors fell through after curious negotiations in the U.S. which reflected little credit on anyone; cf. Haynes Johnson, 229 ff., the brigade chronicler who blames domestic U.S. politics for the fact that the brigade was not exchanged in June 1961 for $M28 in credits, tractors and cash but for $M62 in December 1962.

[51] Their estimate in the Senate Foreign Relations Sub-Committee on Latin American Affairs (*New York Times*, 9 May 1961). To this might be added the $M62 which was eventually gathered to pay the prisoners' ransom.

[52] *Obra Revolucionaria*, 1 May 1961, 19–20. Russia, more circumspect, still officially referred to Cuba on 1 May as a sympathizer not as a member of the Socialist bloc. Castro's use of 'Socialism' was no doubt in the Russian sense of the word – a society *en route* to the perfect, but as yet unachieved, Communist society.

[53] *New York Times*, 21 April 1961.

CHAPTER 42

Between the Crises

After the defeat of the invasion Cuba was driven towards full membership of the Communist alliance. Undecided Cubans, who had before April hesitated as to whether to join the underground or not, now naturally chose to support Castro rather than the right-wing invaders based in Florida. Castro himself remained the conductor of events, the resilient and indefatigable orator, apparently still the decisive voice in all political activities. The main nation-wide activity of 1961, the illiteracy campaign, was a project to which the Communists had given low priority and one which most evidently bore on it the marks of the earliest, original stage of the revolution – the redemption of Castro's promise to the U.N. in 1960. But, beneath Castro, his old followers of the early months dropped away from the limelight; in their place the Communist chiefs, familiar names in Cuban politics since the 1930s, middle-aged or even elderly men, came into their own, dogmatizing, explaining, directing: one wave of leaders was giving way to another. The Communist party, the Directorio Revolucionario, the 26 July Movement, the United Youth Movement and the Young Pioneers, casually began to be referred to as *organizaciones revolucionarias integradas*; then these words appeared in the press with capital letters – ORI; then by July it began to appear, without announcement, that the old Communist leaders (and only they) were always referred to as 'leaders, *dirigentes*, of the ORI'. Much play was made with the idea of a 'united movement'; indeed, to hear the enthusiasm at the ideas which were forthcoming at the great meeting, the 'Asamblea General Nacional', on 26 July 1961, in the presence of the cosmonaut, Major Yuri Gagarin, to commemorate the eighth anniversary of Moncada, it would have been supposed that that was indeed the magnificent prize an anxious nation was longing for. Castro, having worked up the crowd with his customary skill, rhetorically asked: '*Que levanten la mano los que apoyan la unión de todos los revolucionarios en el Partido Unico de la Revolución Socialista* (Will all who support the union of all revolutionaries in the united party of the Socialist Revolution raise their hands!).' 'At which everyone present including Dr Castro raised their hands giving cries of "Unity".'[1]

But no united party appeared. In his speech on 26 July Castro

[1] *Revolución*, 27 July 1961. The author was present.

limited himself to saying that the integration of the revolutionary parties would begin from below. On 6 November he explained that the 'true revolutionaries' would be 'a select and small party of the masses', while the masses, though they could support the revolution, could not call themselves revolutionaries.[2] Were there problems between the surviving Fidelistas and old Communists? If so, nothing appeared in the press. Aníbal Escalante, whose work as a Communist had begun even before the fall of Machado, began assiduously to organize the ORI as a model for this united party. An office of the ORI was set up in nearly every town, in fact merely the headquarters of the old Communist Party.[3] Its provincial secretaries were simply those who already had become secretaries of the planning boards (JUCEI)[4] and who had been in some cases for many years secretaries of the Communist party. Blas Roca said that there could be no better secretary-general of a future united party than Castro. Who could believe it? Castro's qualities were not secretarial. How long would he last? President Dorticós travelled to Belgrade to a conference of neutral countries, to Russia and to China, but seemed to resolve nothing. Nor did Blas Roca's visit to Moscow to the 22nd Congress of the Russian Communist party make clear to what extent the Cuban Communist party was abreast of events.

In early December some of these questions seemed to have been answered. Castro, hard pressed among his new bland allies, had to survive in order to conquer. On 2 December he explained to a somewhat surprised nation in a television speech that he had been for many years an apprentice Marxist–Leninist at least, even at the university, that he and his comrades had in the 1950s consciously disguised their radical views in order to gain power, and that, having become progressively more experienced, he had become a better Marxist and would be so until the day of his death.[5] It is not clear, however, whether the Communists or even Russia really relished the idea of Castro's socialism. It is improbable that Castro was telling the truth, and it is most likely that, being still rejected from full membership of the Communist *bloc*, he was making a bold bid for admission by battering on the front door while also claiming the leadership both of the Cuban and the Latin American Communist movement. So far as Cuba was concerned, government would in the future be by 'collective leadership'.

[2] Speech of Castro to the 1st National Congress of Responsables del Trabajo de Orientación Revolucionaria (*ibid.*, 11 November 1961, p. 9).

[3] Escalante said in October that the ORI had headquarters in 100 out of the 126 townships of the island (*Bohemia*, 6 October 1961).

[4] These were set up along the lines previously described (see above, p. 559) in all provincial capitals by the end of July.

[5] There are several versions of the speech: two published in the first and second editions of *Revolución* on 2 December, one in *Bohemia* (abridged) on 10 December: one in *Obra Revolucionaria*.

Three months passed. The economic situation grew worse. The good figures for agriculture in 1961 were now seen to have been due to unrepeatable favourable factors. The lack of ordinary household goods caused much discontent. Houses were in short supply. There seemed to be much waste everywhere, especially in the ubiquitous armed forces. The National Conference of Production in August had revealed an 'infinite number of instances of bad management'. The U.S. market had been completely closed to Cuban goods since April and, in June, all U.S. goods had ceased going to Cuba – including lard and butter, basic food for Cubans. Public transport (on which so many depended to get to work) declined. Disorganization of production and distribution drove those with cars to travel many miles to find food in the country. INRA's sub-department, ACOPIO, received a monopoly of food distribution, but it lacked lorries or rolling stock to do this adequately. Professor Dumont thought that in 1961–2 only half the fruit and vegetables of the island were gathered.[6] Small farmers were supposed always to sell to ACOPIO, but this organization often could not organize the collection. Nor did ACOPIO make, to begin with, any distinction as to quality – which therefore, as might be expected, did not improve. Prices were held the same also all the year round. All decisions still depended on Havana. Even according to official figures, agricultural production fell in 1962. Cane replanting was 17% behind – as much as 30% in the cane co-operatives. Rice production would fall in 1962 from 300,000 tons to 200,000, the yield per hectare from 17 to 14 quintals. Yield also fell in respect of maize. The state farm production fell faster than that of the surviving private farms. 'The little *paysans routiniers* of Rancho Mundito [Pinar del Río] without irrigation or tractors, with poor soils on eroded hills, still harvest nearly seven tons of *taros* per hectare. On richer soils, with tractors and irrigation, the state farms only obtain a third of that, two to four tons.'[7] The State bought up most pigs belonging to small farmers; many died, chiefly from being too congested. The 'socialist chicken' was not a success either. Huge differences occurred in the produce of State farms according to the competence of the administration.

Industry was reorganized in about fifty consolidated businesses (*empresas consolidadas*), but Guevara did not give full direction to future development. Raw materials and equipment were bought by Guevara sometimes without much consideration of how they were to be used. He was, however, candid enough to admit that 'salaries cannot be raised; now we must simply work.'[8] Soviet and other Communist *bloc* aid amounted to $M570 in 1961–2, or $40 a head; in comparison U.S. aid

---

[6] Even in 1961, the author can remember seeing avocados lying uncollected under trees in Matanzas.

[7] Dumont, 70. But see note on p. 560. Taros are cheap food plants.

[8] 'There are years of work ahead of us,' he went on (*Revolución*, 29 November 1961, 3).

to the rest of Latin America attained only about $2 a head. This $40, as Dumont pointed out, corresponded to the average total income of many parts of Africa. Yet the only bright spot in late 1961 was the successful end to the literacy campaign; and even there it seemed certain that much money had been lavished on a scheme of little immediate economic help and that some who had allegedly been taught to read would really not last as readers. Official statistics claimed that the percentage of illiterates had been reduced to 3·9% of the population, with at the end only 250,000 unable to read and write.

There was still no overt sign of the dissension in the State, though a speech by Castro revealed that he knew that there had been innumerable unnecessary arrests, with people being held for weeks without trial, and then returning to their houses to find their property had been stolen. He also said that after a speech of his in which he had adjured the nation to attack the *lumpenproletariat*, a police chief in Matanzas had given an order to arrest the *lumpenproletariat*, with the result that 200 homosexuals had been arrested in a single city.[9] The prolonged disappearance of Castro in February 1962 suggested that he was ill or even dead. He had told his audience on 2 December that as a student he had got to page 370 of *Das Kapital*: was he finishing it? His only sign of life were two pronouncements on foreign policy, in one of which he seemed to differentiate himself markedly from the Russian policy on coexistence between States of different social systems.[10] At the end of January Castro responded to the suspension of Cuba from the OAS (decided upon at Punta del Este[11]) by a most violent and revolutionary speech known thereafter as 'the Second Declaration of Havana', in which he appealed to the peoples of Latin America to rise against 'imperialism': 'the first and most important thing to understand is that it is not right or correct to distract the people with the vain and convenient illusion that they can triumph by legal means over the power that monopolies and oligarchies will defend with blood and fire'. Latin Americans should therefore adopt guerrilla warfare on the Cuban model. This speech may not have been very carefully thought out, but it certainly had resonance throughout the world. It was cheered as a call to permanent insurrection by China and

[9] *Revolución*, 11 November 1961.
[10] See interview with Russian editors in *Revolución*, 30 January 1962. *Cf.* the *Pravda* version reprinted in *ibid.*, 29 January 1962, and Andrés Suárez's comments, 144. The other pronouncement was 'Tres Años de Revolución', in *Cuba Socialista*, January 1962. To the editors he said: 'It is impossible for peaceful coexistence to exist between the exploited masses of Latin America and the Yankee monopolies . . . As long as imperialism exists international class war will exist between the exploited masses and the monopolies.'
[11] The U.S. once again sought a condemnation of Cuban communism but the conference merely resolved that Cuba had voluntarily placed herself outside the inter-American system. No measures against Cuba were specified and no sanctions taken, while the biggest Latin American countries, Brazil, Argentina, Mexico and Chile abstained from voting, along with Bolivia and Ecuador.

used by the militant wings of all revolutionary parties in Latin America as a manifesto. But it was not popular in Russia, though the Russian government did praise it as an expression of the intention of Cuba 'to base its relations with all nations on the principles of peaceful coexistence'.[12]

The disputes about the organization of the new united party in Cuba came to a head in January, but nothing was done. Aníbal Escalante gave tongue frequently and dogmatically about the future of the party. There were some foolish expropriations of peasants as a result of apparently real counter-revolutionary plotting, particularly in south Matanzas and south-east Las Villas.[13] Nunez Jiménez was dismissed as executive chief of INRA, Castro himself abandoned the presidency of that organization, and that major post as well as Núñez's was given to Carlos Rafael Rodríguez, the most flexible of the old Communists, Castro's oldest friend among them and a long-time critic, from within the party, of Blas Roca. This was the first important formal government post obtained by the Communists in Castro's regime. But the trouble in agriculture with the independent farmers, who still controlled over half the land, was such that a disaster was only avoided, according to Rodríguez, because of the 'prestige of the revolution' (or, should he have said, its power) and some small farmers' continued 'faith' in Castro. With this prestige strengthened rather than weakened by the events of the winter, Castro could decide that his quarrels (as they turned out to be) with the old guard of the Communists ought to come out into the open. Perhaps he was assisted in his now half-overt struggle against the Communists by the news, angrily communicated by Guevara in the March issue of *Cuba Socialista*, that henceforth Russian and east European raw materials would have to be paid for in foreign exchange earnings, not by Russian gifts or loans.[14] Nor, as can be imagined, despite Castro's intervention in their favour, were all the small-holders reconciled to the revolution; many 'drew back on themselves',[15] helping towards the decline of production in 1962. Guevara in addition had no love for the sort of disciplined party which seemed to be being built up by Escalante. For him it was already becoming a 'party of administration, not pioneering, a new élite which sought an easy life, with beautiful secretaries, Cadillacs, air-conditioning'.[16]

On 9 March the first official 'directorate of the ORI', evidently, as Escalante had said, a prototype for the future 'united party', was announced, a balanced compromise between old Communists and Fidelistas: in addition to Castro and his brother, there were thirteen Fidelistas

[12] *Revolución*, 19 February 1962.
[13] As explained by Carlos Rafael Rodríguez in *Cuba Socialista* May 1963, 14.
[14] *Cuba Socialista*, March 1962.
[15] Dumont, 87.
[16] Guevara in interview to *Al Thalia* (Cairo), published April 1965.

and ten old Communists. There was also Chomón, the sole representative of the Directorio, and President Dorticós. Admittedly the relations between at least four of the Fidelistas[17] and the old Communists before 1959 remained ambiguous. Still, there were on the list other Moncadistas or Granmaístas,[18] or veterans of the Sierra Maestra,[19] including three who had played some part in the 26 July Movement underground.[20] Of the Communists, eight had made their name before 1945,[21] one represented the Communist group who had been at the university with Castro,[22] and one had been until recently the Communist Youth leader.[23] Only one of the Fidelistas was a mulatto (Almeida), though three[24] of the rest were either mulatto or Negro.

There was too a greater crisis to come: in fact these nominations really only seem to have registered relative positions of power. The National Directorate was rarely heard of again. On 12 March Castro announced the formal beginning, on 19 March, of food rationing: Cubans were now entitled to two pounds of fat, six of rice and one and a half pounds of beans a month. In Havana and other cities, meat, fish, eggs, and milk were also rationed. Adults received three pounds of meat, one of fish, a quarter of a pound of butter, one of chicken meat and five eggs also each month. Children got a litre of milk a day. Malanga and other vegetables were also rationed. Ration cards were only issued to those who could prove that they had paid their rent. On 13 March, Castro gave a speech at the university commemorating the fifth anniversary of the attempt to kill Batista, in 1957. The testament of José Antonio Echevarría (president of the students, killed instead) was read out by a certain Ravelo. Then Castro spoke: 'And we,' he said, using the plural which he now always affected, less regally, presumably, than fraternally:

And we, while he was reading, were following the testament in a book ... We noticed that he skipped the fourth paragraph ... Out of curiosity we began to read what he had skipped and we saw what it said ... *'We trust that the purity of our aims will attract the favour of God, to allow us to establish the rule of justice in our country.'* Now that is very interesting, 'I thought: "Caramba!" Did he intentionally omit these

[17] Raúl Castro, Osmani Cienfuegos (a rapidly rising star after the Bay of Pigs), Augusto Martínez Sánchez, and Guevara.
[18] Almeida, Ramiro Valdés, Haydée Santamaría and Guevara.
[19] García, 'the first peasant to join Castro'; the head of the air force, Sergio del Valle; and Osmani Cienfuegos.
[20] Hart, Emilio Aragonés, and Dorticós.
[21] Roca, C. R. Rodríguez, the Escalante brothers, Lázaro Peña, Severo Aguirre, Ordoqui and Manuel Luzardo, the only 'old Communist' already formally in the cabinet.
[22] Flavio Bravo.
[23] Ramón Calcines.
[24] Lázaro Peña, Ramón Calcines and Severo Aguirre.

three lines?' When he finished reading, I asked him. And he said: 'At the entrance they gave me instructions. I described what I was going to read and they told me to skip those three lines.'

Is this possible, comrades? Are we, so cowardly, so bigoted in mind, that we have to omit three lines from the testament of José Antonio Echevarría simply because . . . he believed in God? What sort of faith is this in truth? . . . And the tragedy is that the comrade who received the order to omit those lines is a poet, and in his own little book of verses (which I have here) is one which is entitled 'Prayer to the Unknown God'.[25]

Castro ended his speech with some mysterious allusions to the dangers of sectarianism – a word which was not often off his lips for months – and cited Lenin's pamphlet on left-wing Communism: 'an infantile disorder', a text often used by orthodox Communists when hectic dreamers of the Left are to be condemned. He also explained that the Young Rebels would soon be re-christened Young Communists – an event which occurred without much celebration in April.

On 16 March Guevara, who must have been specially close to Castro at this time, made a blistering attack on the revolutionary union leadership, concluding that the achievements of the revolution were 'confined to the establishment of a few small consumer goods factories and the completion of some factories begun under the dictatorship. He asked why it was that under the Revolution shoes lost their heels after one day's wear, and why the Revolution's Coca-cola tasted so vilely.' Does that sort of thing happen under capitalism? No. Then why should it happen under socialism? Because of the nature of socialism? No, that is a lie. It happens because of our own shortcomings, our lack of revolutionary vigilance, the inadequacy of our work.[26] On 17 March Castro told 'revolutionary instructresses' at the Conrado Benítez school that ORI secretaries up and down the country had imposed despotism on the country and were 'almost indistinguishable from Batista and his henchmen'.

Another ten days passed. Castro had clearly made a calculated bid for what affection he still could excite among what little remained of old Catholic Cuba and of the 26 July Movement; they would see surely that there was still a gap between himself and the Communist party of old. On 22 March the National Directorate of the ORI named a 'secretariat' which clearly would do all the work in the formation of the projected, 'united party'. It included Blas Roca but not Escalante, and the other members were Fidelistas. Roca himself took over as editor of

[25] *Obra Revolucionaria*, 1962 No. 13.
[26] Guevara, *Trabajo*, reported Goldenberg, 257.

Hoy, the party newspaper. On 24 March an old Communist, Manuel Luzardo, was brought into the cabinet as minister of (internal) Commerce, and Chomón, the one surviving Directorio leader, was brought back from Moscow as Minister of Communications. On 25 March the new INRA chief, Carlos Rafael Rodríguez, explained that the Russian and east European advisers had become critical of the economic administration of Cuba, while Raúl Castro was named vice-premier. On 27 March, finally, in a major television speech, Castro made a violent criticism of Aníbal Escalante, national organizer of the ORI, who had been dispatched the day before to Prague, being succeeded in his job at ORI by President Dorticós.

'Aníbal Escalante,' Castro told his listeners and watchers, 'was a Communist for many years:

> In our opinion he was a true Communist, an honest Communist . . . but Aníbal Escalante erred. Aníbal Escalante, a Communist, committed grave errors. The fact is that Communists also make mistakes! They are men, after all. Is this the only time that the Communists have made a mistake? No, Communists have made many mistakes. The history of the international Communist movement is studded with mistakes. Many apply Marxism wrongly. A man, after all, and only a man, and like every human being exposed to the temptation of error, Aníbal Escalante erred.

There followed specific charges: of organizing a party which would be in effect an apparatus following Escalante's own leadership; of creating a 'nest of privilege, of benefits, of a system of favours of all types'. Meantime, inside the Cuban administration, it had become impossible for a minister to remove any individual from one post to another without first asking the permission of the ORI. Things had got to such a pass that 'if a cat gave birth to four kittens, the ORI secretariat would have to be consulted'. *Sectarismo,* 'implacable, insatiable, incessant', had sprung up in every corner of the peninsula.

Castro turned to other instances of misbehaviour. There was Fidel Pompa, secretary of the ORI in a group of farms in Oriente: when the list of the national leaders of the ORI had been published, Pompa, 'with the mentality of a *gauleiter* rather than of a Marxist', had made insulting remarks about several Fidelistas (among them Guillermo García, the famous first peasant to join the revolution; Haydée Santamaría; Sergio del Valle; and Emilio Aragonés). How indeed, continued Castro, was Fidel Pompa to know who these people were and how much they had done in the civil war when, at the time, he had been hiding under his bed?

Castro finally asked: 'What should be our attitude towards the old

Communists? One of respect and recognition of their merits, and recognition for their past militancy. In my escort there are many old Communists and I am not going to dismiss them, since I have confidence in them. What on the other hand should be their attitude to us? One of modesty.'[27]

Castro chose to make this frank speech not discreetly, to a select body of the faithful (as Khrushchev had made his speech attacking Stalin), but before all the nation, on television screens – on no doubt 80% of the 500,000 Cuban television screens.

A few days later Castro went to Matanzas and spoke again, this time to the Provincial Committee of ORI in the town. The theme of his speech was advertised as being to 'complete and make precise' his remarks of 26 March.[28] He explained that rumours and suspicion had forced him to bring the whole Escalante affair into the open. He repeated the various charges against Escalante, though in harsher terms: Escalante had created a personal shrine, simply to satisfy his own desire for power. He had created a veritable parody of government; and 'it is not only Aníbal's fault – we have to distinguish between the things which are Aníbal's fault, those that are our own, and those that are the fault of five hundred Aníbals going free. The result anyway has been to create a divorce between masses and party.' He added: 'the masses saw all these problems: the transgressions of power, the arbitrary arrests, the wilfulnesses, the excesses, the whole policy of contempt towards a people!'

Castro then turned to the rules that ought to guide the revolution in future. The revolutionary caucus (núcleo) in factory or farm, office or anywhere else, must henceforth be composed of people who had gained this position through merit, not simply because they were old Communist militants. At the same time there should be no more arbitrariness, bureaucracy, anarchy, and no more drunkenness: 'Anthems, songs, we can have but no more congas for drunken dancing.'

In these two speeches Castro sought to make clear to the Cubans that he and not the old Communists were the masters of the Cuban revolution. But what now was he? He had taken the trouble to differentiate himself from the Communists. He continued to refer to himself as a Marxist–Leninist. But he remained an unusual one. Escalante was to be the scapegoat for the terror, as for the economic difficulties. The revolution over which Castro presided remained volatile. Partly this was

---

[27] *Obra Revolucionaria*, No. 10, 1962.

[28] No complete version of this statement was published, but an abbreviated version eventually appeared in the May issue of the small circulation monthly, *Cuba Socialista* and in *El Mundo* on 10 May. (This was the first time since 1959 that a major speech of Castro's was not published the day afterwards in the leading Cuban papers. The reason for this reticence was that the unabridged text was a good deal too personal.)

because of the threats from the exiles, the rumours of wars, the explosions and the landings, the arrests of spies and traitors. But even so the elusive united party of the revolution took a long time to appear. During the summer of 1962, workers in different enterprises made selections from among their members of 'model workers' from whom ultimately party members would be selected. This normally very democratic procedure had the effect of delaying the formation of the party indefinitely. Relations in the ministries and other organizations between the old Communists and the men of 1959 were very bad. Castro, not the old Communists, now made all the important theoretical speeches. Blas Roca, the theoretician of 1961, dropped back from the public eye in 1962, his main organizer over thirty years, Escalante, being in exile. Carlos Rafael Rodríguez kept to agrarian reform in place of his previous wide-ranging lectures on general policy and later in 1968 he would report to the central committee of the new Communist party that in his opinion in 1962 Escalante had been 'more abnormal than wicked' (this was at the time of Escalante's second bid for power in Cuba, in the mid 1960s). The only two other old Communists to retain national positions of the first importance were Manuel Luzardo at the Ministry of Commerce and Leonel Soto, Castro's old friend, at the school of revolutionary instruction. Many old Communists who had secured good positions through Escalante's backing were replaced, though César Escalante, Aníbal's brother, remained as theorist and intellectual director of the ORI, which itself remained in being as a shell for the 'new party'.

Russia accepted, doubtless without enthusiasm, the destruction of Escalante and, possibly in panic at the thought of losing Cuba to China, had greeted Cuba on 1 May as next in importance after the socialist *bloc* and before Yugoslavia: Cuba had evidently been promoted. In mid-May a new commercial treaty was signed between Cuba and Russia: by this, commercial exchange between the two would increase to $M750, and now apparently Russia agreed to buy two to three million tons of Cuban sugar in 1962.[29] Kudryatsev, the Soviet ambassador, left Cuba hastily, without being seen off at the airport; Castro later said that he had asked him to leave, but it is evident that he was the spokesman of an older stage of Cuban–Russian relations.[30] Castro himself remarked in the hearing of several people in the offices of *Revolución*, 'This Kudryatsev bores me more than Bonsal did'.[31] He was succeeded by Alexayev, who had been in Cuba off and on since 1959 and who had

---

[29] *Revolución*, 15 May 1962. Andrés Suárez's comments are interesting (155).

[30] Lisa Howard, *War/Peace Report*, September 1963. Chomón left Moscow on 5 May. His successor, Carlos Olivares, took some time to arrive. So both embassies had no heads of mission for a time.

[31] *Este Kudryatsev me tiene ya más cansado que Bonsal* (Evidence of Guillermo Cabrera Infante, then editor of *Lunes de Revolución*.)

once been in the Russian embassy in Buenos Aires. The Cuban newspapers were full of old stories of the Sierra (of the time, that is, before
overt Communist support for Castro), and leaders until then discredited
(such as Faustino Pérez, who had resigned over the Matos affair) were
now once more favourably mentioned. Blas Roca in *Hoy* described
Castro unequivocally as 'the best and most effective Marxist–Leninist of
our country'.[32] In agriculture, a number of farms which had been
wrongly expropriated in the February crisis were handed back to their
owners by the new directorate at INRA. It was as if Castro had once
more exhausted the usefulness of another wave of followers and was
seeking out a new one still, perhaps composed of the flotsam of the past.

Diversification of agriculture and industrialization meantime went
forward very slowly, though there were a number of further collec-
tivizations – bakeries, clothing and bedding factories, distilleries –
without apparently any special legislation. The consequences of the
neglect of the sugar industry during 1960 and 1961 now became
apparent. The 1962 sugar harvest was clearly falling behind all recent
years, due to the rash cutting down of cane in the drive for diversification. 'We must simply recognize,' said Guevara who, as Minister of
Industries, was still responsible for the manufacturing side of sugar, 'that
this is a bad harvest.' He admitted there had been sabotage, bad work,
indolence and shortage of hands.[33] He did not, however, admit that the
'volunteers, though unpaid, often cost more through their expenses of
transport or errors of cutting than the regular day's pay of workers.'[34]
Communications all over the island were breaking down for lack o
spare parts. Food supplies were more and more irregular. ACOPIO, the
monopoly food-purchase body, wallowed in disorder, peasants not
knowing whether their produce would be bought or not. The shops were
empty. Middle-class Cubans and now many from the working class
also filled the Pan American flights to Miami; in this way more and
more technically trained people left Cuba. Everyone complained:
Russian and east European technicians about Cuban waste and inefficiency, a Polish journalist that he was longing to get back to the
beaches of *bourgeois* Belgium;[35] Cuban officials complained about Russian intransigence and bad workmanship, and the reluctance of Russian
technicians to leave their air-conditioned offices.[36] Cuban and Russian
relations were very bad. There were some signs that Castro was anxious

[32] *Hoy*, 22 April 1962.
[33] At Asamblea Plenaria Azucarera Nacional, *H.A.R.*, XV, 318–19.
[34] Dumont, 81.
[35] To the author, in July 1962.
[36] This was certainly not always justified. In the summer of 1961 I stayed several days on a
state farm near Manzanillo upon which four young Russian agronomists were working.
They rose daily at 6.30 and returned at 4.30 p.m., sweating more, and more exhausted
than any workers I have ever seen.

to start playing off Moscow against China which had also greeted the denunciation of Escalante with approval[37] and themselves like Russia concluded a new commercial treaty. Only with great difficulty, in addition, did the Polish Foreign Minister, Rapacki, secure mention of the word 'co-existence' in the joint communiqué with Cuba after his visit in May, while Raúl Castro gave a big speech on the North Korean national day – an occasion which customarily passes without enthusiasm in Warsaw or Budapest. Cuba also studiously avoided public condemnation of Albania, China's only ally in Europe. On 3 June Khrushchev gave a reply to these implicit criticisms and upbraided Cuba at a celebration bidding goodbye to about a thousand Cubans who had been training in Russia. Khrushchev compared Cuba's economic position with that of Russia after the civil war. He said that Lenin had then brought in the New Economic Policy which made concessions to capitalists within Russia, in order ultimately to strengthen socialism. Such things might be necessary in Cuba (*Hoy* said much the same for a time, without avail). It would take more than arms and heroism to get over the food shortages. Khrushchev promised to send 'arms and other things' to Cuba, but the road to socialism meant a high degree of consciousness, intelligence and work.[38]

After this lecture a *rapprochement* began. With his old knapsack and rifle, Castro went first for a new tour of the Sierra Maestra telling Cuban Communists that he had 'once more raised the banner of rebellion' – against whom was left unexplained.[39] At the end of June, however, Castro, with unusual humility, at another celebration, bade goodbye this time to Soviet technicians with the words:

> We know our deficiencies, we know of inexperienced administrators who in some cases lack political intelligence and in others lack a sense of hospitality. We know that a [Russian] technician who went to a state farm run by an experienced and hospitable comrade . . . would be very well treated. But we know that there was no lack of places where the administration received them coldly or with indifference . . . or when the administration did not make use of the knowledge of the technicians . . . [Some] thought that the way to treat the technicians well was to take them out, or even to offer them girls.

He ended up with a sudden new enthusiasm for 'the Soviet people, led by the at all times glorious Communist party of the Soviet Union . . . and by the great and dearly loved friend of Cuba, Nikita Khrushchev'.[40] Blas Roca made a speech in Montevideo which accepted blame for

[37] Andrés Suárez, 156.
[38] *Revolución*, 4 June 1962,
[39] *Ibid.*, 16 June 1962.
[40] *Ibid.*, 1 July 1962.

having not seen earlier that guerrilla war was the correct means of struggle against Batista.[41] But it was clear that something else had occurred which made it worthwhile, even necessary, to mend matters with Russia. This was partly of course the knowledge that now Cuba could not do without Russian economic aid. China might be a heroic example but still only Russia could provide Cuba with cane-cutting machines, credit, technical assistance, and, above all, a market for her sugar: the Chinese could have eaten the sugar but could not have paid for it. It had become obvious that the harvest would not top five million tons. This marked a return to the figures of the controlled low harvests of the mid 1950s, so that Cuba would not even have been able to deliver the $4\frac{3}{4}$ million tons contracted to Russia.[42] Meantime, nearly 3,000 Cubans a week were leaving their country for exile, mostly for the U.S., but many also for Spain or the rest of South America: by midsummer over 200,000 exiles had left the island since the beginning of 1959, or almost 3% of the population – already one of the largest exoduses on record. Further, they were from all sections of the community, with the exception of the countryside.[43] Many of these were people who had previously sympathized with the Castro regime. The climax of disorder in the Cuban economy after the revolution was probably attained in mid-1962. In the face of these economic and social difficulties it seems evident that a military decision of the first importance had been taken by the Cuban and Russian governments.

[41] *Cuba Socialista*, July 1962.
[42] As agreed under their 1961 economic pact.
[43] R. R. Fagen, R. A. Brody and Thomas J. O'Leary, *Cubans in Exile: Disaffection and the Revolution* (1968), 17; see also *The Cuban Immigration 1959–1966 and its impact on Miami-Dade County, Florida* (Coral Gables, Florida, 1967).

CHAPTER 43

The Missile Crisis: I

In the months since the humiliation at Cochinos Bay, the government of President Kennedy had had many matters to treat of other than Cuba: the Congo; the steel magnates; the Alliance for Progress; Laos and Vietnam; the Negro question; Berlin; and Khrushchev at Vienna. Kennedy had travelled. But Cuba had remained a dominant (though not a predominant) concern. Cuba had been suspended from the OAS in January. Personally, Kennedy felt responsibility for the still imprisoned members of Brigade 2506: those men were in confinement because of his personal decisions or indecisions a year before – the first clear intimation of the bitterness of power to one who previously had only known of its delights.[1] Publicly, he was not allowed by his Republican opponents to forget Cuba. A new electoral campaign, the half-term legislative elections of November 1962, was at hand. Kennedy would no doubt be reproached for allowing Cuba to remain Communist, just as he had himself reproached the Republicans in 1960. Further, there were still the Cuban exiles, still the Cuban Revolutionary Council, still the latter's president, the ex-prime minister, Miró Cardona. The shadow president of Cuba and the actual president of the U.S. met several times and, on 10 April 1962, Miró took away the impression that Kennedy was anxious to re-form an exile army: 'I left the White House with the assurance that the liberation of Cuba would follow soon with Cubans as the vanguard in the battle.'[2] But Kennedy merely expressed the hope that one day soon Cuba would be free and, knowing that whatever he said would be passed quickly to Miami, did not make any pledge. Miró had misunderstood A. A. Berle in the week before Cochinos Bay; once again he was confused.[3] But at all events during the spring of 1962 the enthusiasm of the exiles, dampened after Cochinos, began to mount. The U.S. press published articles about the size of

---

[1] The prisoners of the Bay of Pigs were not tried until March 1962 (except for five executed as war criminals for their part during the struggle against Batista and a few others condemned for political crimes apart from the Cochinos battle). At the trial, only Ulises Carbó, son of Sergio, and Alonso Pujol, son of Prío's vice-president, denounced the U.S.

[2] Miró Cardona's article, published in *S.P.* (Madrid), 1 May 1963.

[3] Evidence of Richard Goodwin in letter, 12 May 1969. Perhaps also Miró was involved in a justification of his own authority and continued working relations with the U.S. government.

forces required to overthrow Castro: six divisions, a figure which Miró said Kennedy had mentioned to him, were thought necessary.

Doubtless these rumours reached Castro. The Cubans in Miami were less discreet even than usual when they scented victory. During the trial in March of the men of Cochinos Bay, a message had been passed to Castro through President Goulart of Brazil, by Richard Goodwin, that if the invaders were shot, opinion in the U.S. would be so roused as to make invasion inevitable.[4] During late April a huge marine manoeuvre was carried out by the U.S. in the Caribbean, followed by further raids by exile groups – notably 'Alpha 66'.[5] Such Miami rumours and the general atmosphere of hostility and tension must have caused Castro to fear an invasion.

In Cuba itself, meantime, while the economy slackened, discontent clearly grew. On 16 June demonstrations occurred in the city of Cárdenas. Housewives marched into the streets beating pots and pans. Tanks were dispatched by the heavy-handed Major Jorge Serguera, the provincial military commander, to overawe them. Dorticós arrived to make a speech, blaming the 'imperialist blockade' as well as 'our errors' for shortages and denouncing the housewives' protest as 'a miserable and counter-revolutionary provocation'.[6] Afterwards, demonstrations occurred at Santa Clara[7] and at El Cano near Havana, where one young militiaman was killed and another wounded by the police in a confused incident. The government reacted as if terrified by what further crises they might encounter: the shops at El Cano were confiscated, the inhabitants lost all their cars, telephones and lorries, and were forced into unemployment and submission.[8] The local militia, which had proved notably inadequate in this trial, was purged and reorganized.

These events, combined with the economic dislocation, made Castro more nervous than ever of the effects of a possible invasion, which he began to regard as more difficult to withstand than at any previous time. Was the militia loyal? How would it react if faced with the marines?[9] Surely, as the U.S. election campaign continued, there would be greater call for the U.S. to 'solve' the Cuban question, if need be by force? What, after all, if Miró really had a commitment from Kennedy as he, Miró, himself believed – and as Castro doubtless by this time had learned? There were other suggestions of invasion, some

[4] Haynes Johnson, 274–5.
[5] Cf. Le Monde, 11 May.
[6] See Revolución, 17 June and 18 June 1962.
[7] As the author discovered, in the course of a visit there in July.
[8] El Cano later became the site of an experimental farm.
[9] Those over forty years old were really no more than a reserve; those under forty were used to guard public buildings etc.

false, such as Rusk's routine interviews with Latin American ambassa-dors.[10]

Thus on 1 July, only a few days after the El Cano incident, Raúl Castro set out for Moscow to secure a promise of more protection for Cuba from Russia. As a result of the discussions between Raúl Castro and Khrushchev and others, Russia agreed to send an increased military force to Cuba, modern equipment, a number of short-range surface-to-air (SAM) missiles used for defence, similar to those which had been given by Russia to Indonesia and Iraq, and also some medium- and intermediate-range missiles capable of delivering nuclear and thermo-nuclear warheads on the U.S. and other targets in the Americas.

There seems, however, little doubt that the decision to send missiles to Cuba must have been taken by the Russians some time before this, possibly in April,[11] at all events before Khrushchev's lecture to the returning Cubans on 2 June. If the decision were taken in April, at, for instance, as seems likely, the Soviet Party Praesidium meeting held between 22 and 25 April, it may not have been communicated to the Cubans before mid-June, though perhaps there was some preliminary discussion during Khrushchev's talks with the Cuban Minister for Public Works, Osmani Cienfuegos, and the Cuban ambassador to Moscow on 28 April and 5 May, respectively. Perhaps the visit to Cuba of Rashidov, a Soviet Praesidium Alternate and secretary-general of the Uzbek Communist party, at the head of the delegation to 'study irrigation problems', was important; Rashidov spent an unusually long time is Moscow on his return before going back to Uzbekistan.[12] Doubt-less, at an early stage of their decision-making, in April or May, the Russians kept their ideas very much to themselves.

The reason for the decision to send missiles to Cuba, however, is not entirely clear. Cuba, fearing invasion, had a desire for extra defence against the U.S. Superficially missiles would afford this. Cuba also had a

[10] See *Política Internacional*, No. 1, 181–2, and Joxe, *loc. cit.* It is possible that Castro also learned of a second planned 'manœuvre' for late October in which the marines were supposed to overthrow a tyrant named Ortsac in a Caribbean island.

[11] This is the argument of Michel Tatu, *Power in the Kremlin*, 233, on the basis of analysis of hardening statements by Russians from then on, and from changes in the command structure of the Russian armed forces. Castro himself in a speech in 1963 spoke of conversations begin-ning on the matter in June (*Revolución*, 20 April 1963), and this is the interpretation of Roger Hillsman, *To Move a Nation* (1967), 159. A contrary view is expressed by H. M. Pachter, *Collision Course* (1963), 6–7, where it is suggested that the decision was not taken till Guevara's visit to Moscow in August. Good Cuban sources have described to me what sound without doubt to have been equipment connected with the missiles as having been transported by road at night by heavily guarded Russian lorries on 22 May.

[12] Tatu, 335. Andrés Suárez, 160, also points to Rashidov's visit as important. Sharif Rashidovich Rashidov (born 1917) had been chairman of the Uzbek Writers' Union before becoming chairman of the Praesidium of the Uzbek Republic. He had headed the Soviet delegation to the Cairo conference on Afro-Asian solidarity in 1957 and was to be Russia's representative at the famous Tricontinental Conference in Havana in January 1966.

desire that Russia should be 'highly compromised' in her fate. But this extra security could probably have been afforded by extending the guarantees under the Warsaw Pact to Cuba, or by a more explicit and formal commitment by Khrushchev to declare war in case of aggression against her ally. Yet for Russia the installation of, say, sixty missiles, some with the range of 1,000 miles,[13] a few of 1,500 to 2,000 miles,[14] would in fact have doubled the capacity of Russia to strike the U.S. This would still have left Russia with only half the means of striking her enemy that the U.S., with its bombers and missiles, had to strike Russia. But these weapons placed in Cuba would (because of their approach from the South) escape the U.S. early warning system, thus upsetting plans for retaliation. So the missile installation would have been naturally a move which would have been pressed vigorously by some Russian military chiefs – though possibly not by all of them: thus perhaps Marshal Moskalenko, who in the spring of 1962 was in charge of strategic rockets, may have been unhappy at shipping such valuable weapons to so exposed a situation, for he was replaced in April.[15] But legally or illegally, right or wrong, the installation of missiles would evidently have political consequences out of proportion to the strategic advantage gained. Of course, Khrushchev did not desire to use the weapons. But he knew that, if successfully established, they could be a means of exerting diplomatic pressure on Kennedy: either, as the U.S., and indeed most commentators, have assumed, over Berlin; or in order to achieve a guarantee against a U.S. invasion of Cuba. Khrushchev's own position was at that time exposed within the Communist camp so far as Berlin was concerned and he coveted a prestigious victory.[16]

If Cuba had agreed or had asked for offensive missiles, Russia was of course legally entitled to send them. But this was an affair outside legality. It was not clear how the U.S. would react. Yet the legal rights of Cuba would not determine that reaction. So much must have been clear to Khrushchev, who naturally realized that the U.S. knew that Russia had never before established missiles in the territory of an ally, and that the tradition of Russian diplomacy had always been to refuse to over-extend her lines of communication. Khrushchev must therefore have expected the U.S. to be surprised at this new move.

On the Communist side, those involved in this drama have told various and contradictory stories. Thus Khrushchev, in a television interview in 1967, said, 'When we learned that a new socialist state had appeared not far from American shores, I understood that it would not last long if we didn't help it . . . And so I decided, after consulting my

[13] Medium range missiles (MRBM).
[14] Intermediate range (IRBM).
[15] Tatu, 23.
[16] See *ibid.*, 232 ff.

colleagues, to send some rocket units to Cuba.'[17] This indeed cuts a long story very short. For in 1962 itself Khrushchev told both Kennedy (in his letter of 27 October) and the Supreme Soviet:[18] 'we carried weapons there at the request of the Cuban government ... including ... twenty Russian IRBMs[19] ... These were to be in the hands of Russian military men ... Our aim was only to defend Cuba.'[20] But those who establish bases abroad customarily say that they do so at the request of the governments concerned. Russia would gain strategically from setting up missiles in Cuba providing that Khrushchev and the Kremlin were indeed able to maintain control of the situation, that Castro would not be able to force events, and that the local Soviet technicians would always under all circumstances, even a U.S. invasion of Cuba, be able to communicate with home. If the U.S. were to invade Cuba, the missiles would have failed, so far as Cuba was concerned; and Russia would have to go to war with the U.S. But the central Russian gain by which the whole matter would be judged was the change it would make in the global balance of strengths. This was so considerable as to make the idea tempting for that reason alone. After all, it seems likely that Russia had always desired a neutral in Cuba more than a satellite; but if satellite she had become, with all its consequent risks, then one *quid pro quo* would be to make her a strategically profitable satellite.

For President Kennedy and his Secretary of Defence, McNamara, had sought to maintain superiority of nuclear weapons and systems of delivery on a scale sufficient to destroy Russia's nuclear striking power at all known or suspected bases,[21] hopefully leaving enough force left over to threaten all large Russian cities with destruction if there chanced to be any nuclear striking force left intact – for example, in submarines. Even after a surprise attack by Russia, the U.S. hoped to be able to bring to bear as much as, or more, destructive power than Russia had been able to use first. The U.S. second strike was to be as great as the Russian first strike.[22] McNamara had explained, in a speech at Ann Arbor (University of Michigan), that this apparently wasteful policy enabled him to escape from the doctrine of massive retaliation against Russian cities advocated by Dulles and Nixon in the 1950s. Of course, 'counterforce', as McNamara's policy was known, could theoretically be employed in reply to a nuclear attack against cities, but it would be more likely to be used as a first strike aroused by a major conventional attack. The policy necessitated a vast stockpile of nuclear weapons.

[17] As reported, verbatim text, in *Sunday Times* (London), 16 July 1967.
[18] On 12 December 1962.
[19] Intermediate range ballistic missiles.
[20] Speech of 12 December.
[21] U.2 photographs had made all Russian missile bases generally evident.
[22] Gilpatrick at Hot Springs, 21 October 1961.

Thus the U.S. in November 1962 had probably between 200 and 220 ICBMs, while Russia probably had only between 50 and 75. By 1964, when the programme would be complete, the U.S. would have 1,000.

Russia had pursued a less grandiose policy. In 1962 she had probably five times fewer nuclear delivery weapons than the U.S. She had about 350 to 700 shorter-range missiles, but these could not reach the U.S. from Russia, only Europe.[23] Russia had only 200 intercontinental bombers compared with 600 U.S. They had about 1,000 medium-range bombers each. About 130 to 150 missiles were established on U.S. Polaris submarines. It is possible, therefore, that during early 1962 Russian planners were desperate, especially if a U.S. invasion of Cuba was liable to force them to redeem Khrushchev's pledge to defend that (to them) remote island. After all, the world balance of nuclear power had recently been upset. If anything could be done to prevent an invasion and therefore to neutralize Cuba, enabling it to survive, the opportunity should be seized.

Cuba was, of course, an attractive advertisement for the world Communist movement. But militarily speaking Cuba must have been an embarrassment for Russia. The best thing to do, in the face of a Cuban desire for protection, would be to guarantee Cuba completely against U.S. invasion, while retaining all power of military decision in Cuba for the Russian command. Though the Warsaw Pact guarantees would have formally given Cuba security, they would not do so if war actually came: for it could not be defended by conventional means. In one sense, therefore, the installation of missiles in Cuba was a more conservative step than it seemed to North Americans. Since 1961 there had been no equilibrium, only uneasy imbalance. Khrushchev himself apparently explained to Kennedy in his 'secret' letter of 26 October that the missiles had been sent to Cuba because of the Bay of Cochinos, when Cuba had been attacked.[24]

[23] This was a received view in Washington in 1963: cf. Mark Frankel, in the *New York Times*, 13 December 1963, quoting from a Rand information analysis which criticized the idea that the missiles were put into Cuba to defend the island; and Arnold L. Horelick, 'The Cuban Missile Crisis', in *World Politics*, April 1963. It is impossible to agree with his view that medium-range missiles would alone have served the Russo–Cuban purpose, since, though they would have hit southern U.S. cities, the real point of the 'deterrent' is to expose the capital to fire; quite apart from the fact that the U.S. missile sites in Montana or North Dakota were also outside the range of either T.1s, T.2s or T.4s established in Cuba. The Wohlstetters appear wrong ('Controlling the risks in Cuba', *Adelphi Papers* (1965)), 12, in suggesting that 2,200 miles could cover all the U.S. from Cuba. Half Montana, for instance, would be out of range.

[24] As summarized by Elie Abel, *The Missiles of October* (1967), 180. See below, 634. fn. 31 For this paragraph, see Sir Basil Liddell Hart, in *Quick* (Germany), 11 November 1962, who pointed out that Khrushchev's 'best chance of destroying the nuclear balance was to put a large number of IRBMs into Cuba, the only place from which such intermediate-range weapons could reach the principal targets in the U.S.' He concluded, however, that the adverse change in the nuclear balance was a 'basic curb to Russian cold war activities' since it hindered (them) pressing threats to near the brink.

Castro later gave several explanations for the installation of the missiles in Cuba. He told the Cubans (in January 1963) that the Russians had desired them, and repeated this explanation to Claude Julien of *Le Monde*: 'We had thought among ourselves of the possibility of asking Russia for missiles. But we had not reached any decision when Moscow proposed them. It was explained to us that in accepting them we would reinforce the Socialist camp.'[25] To Lisa Howard, a sympathetic listener from the American Broadcasting Company, Castro explained (in May 1963) that the decision involved 'simultaneous action on the part of both governments'. To Herbert Matthews, Castro (in October 1963) said that the Cubans asked for the missiles from Russia; he and his friends in early 1962 'felt almost sure that the U.S. were preparing a military invasion of Cuba'. They had been strengthened in this belief after Aleksei Adzubei, Khrushchev's son-in-law and editor of *Izvestia*, had reported to that effect after an interview with Kennedy – a judgement which, like Miró's conclusion, seems to have been erroneous.[26] Castro added that Russia thought that the U.S. would attack him and that 'the idea of installing the nuclear weapons was his, not [that of] the Russians''.[27]

But, soon after, Castro changed his tack again. To another Frenchman, Jean Daniel of *L'Express* (in November 1963), he said: 'Now, I'll tell you something that nobody knows about. I have never spoken of it before[!][28] But . . . the world has a right to know the true story of the missiles.' Six months before the crisis, at the time of Miró's interview with Kennedy, Castro explained, Cuba received the news that the CIA was preparing a new invasion. Castro and his advisers were uncertain what Kennedy personally was thinking. Adzubei then visited Kennedy and, as Castro told Matthews, derived the impression that the president believed that the balance of world forces had been disrupted by the Communist capture of Cuba: 'Kennedy reminded the Russians that the U.S. had not interfered in Hungary.' Though Adzubei apparently did not then think that the U.S. was about to attack, he and Khrushchev decided that that was possible when they heard of Castro's earlier information. (According to Pierre Salinger, Kennedy had mentioned Hungary on this occasion but not 'in the context' that Castro placed the remarks.)[29] Russia, said Castro, was after this 'reluctant to install

[25] *Le Monde*, 22 March 1963. The interview was in January.

[26] The State Department denied it. The subject is ignored by both Schlesinger and Sorensen.

[27] Herbert Matthews, *Return to Cuba* (1964), 16.

[28] *Cf.* the version in *L'Express*, 14 December 1963. The versions in the *New York Times*, *Observer* (London) and *New Republic* are all shorter, and the *Observer*'s version is badly transcribed.

[29] *New York Times*, 13 December 1963. Adzubei asked Kennedy directly whether there would be an invasion of Cuba and Kennedy said no. If Adzubei desired to know the import-

conventional weapons' since the U.S. might then still risk an invasion, and then Russia would have to retaliate and a world war would be inevitable. So, in June, Raúl Castro and Guevara went to Russia to discuss the installation of missiles. . . .' Jean Daniel said further that Castro told him:

> The only thing we asked the Russians to do was to make it clear to the U.S. that an attack on us was an attack on the Soviet Union. We had extensive discussion before arriving at the proposal of installing guided missiles, *a proposal which surprised us at first and gave us great pause.*[30] We finally went along with the Soviet proposal because, on the one hand, the Russians convinced us that the U.S. would not let itself be intimidated by conventional weapons and secondly because it was impossible for us not to share the risks which the Soviet Union was taking to save us.[31]

But oddly enough, even this was not Castro's last account. On 7 January 1964 Castro told Matthews that Daniel's 'journalistic version' was inaccurate; it had been the Cubans who had put forward the idea of missiles. He repeated this to Matthews 'at least four times'.[32] Castro suggested to another correspondent[33] that he personally had desired the missiles so that the U.S., if they invaded Cuba, would have to confront the possibility of thermo-nuclear war. In October 1964 Castro did not answer adequately a question on this subject when put to him by another representative of the *New York Times*, Cyrus Sulzberger: 'Both Russia and Cuba participated,' he tautologically replied. Again, in July 1965, Castro said that 'we made the decision at a moment when we thought that concrete measures were necessary to paralyse the plans of aggression of the United States and *we posed this* necessity *to the Soviet Union.*'[34] Finally, in 1967 Castro gave yet another account to Herbert Matthews: 'we felt ourselves in danger from the U.S. We consulted with the Russians, when they suggested the missiles, we immediately said "Yes by all means".'[35]

Of these differing accounts, that given to Jean Daniel was the most complete but also the most troublesome. If the minor errors are ignored as deriving from Daniel's or Castro's bad memory (Raúl Castro and Guevara did not go to Moscow together, neither went in

[30] Author's italics.
[31] *New Republic*, 21 December 1963.
[32] Herbert Matthews, *Return to Cuba*, 16.
[33] B. Collier, *New York Herald Tribune*, 17 August 1964.
[34] To Lee Lockwood, 200.
[35] Herbert Matthews, *Castro*, 196.

ance of Cuba to the U.S. he could compare it to the importance of Hungary to the USSR: an unfortunate parallel from which Khrushchev may have drawn an obvious moral. Karol (*op. cit.* 263) argues that Khrushchev knew all along that the U.S. would not invade Cuba.

June), there would seem one major discrepancy of timing: Adzubei's discussion with Kennedy in Washington was on 30 January 1962, while he is supposed to have gone some time *after* the reports about the CIA's new invasion activities. Yet these were said to have come only six months before the installation of the missiles, that is, in April 1962 – a likely date, since it was then that Miró Cardona left the White House for Miami with the 'certitude' that Cuba would soon be freed.

These accounts by Castro should not, however, obscure two central points: first, that however honestly the Cubans and the Russians may have believed that the U.S. were planning an invasion of Cuba, they were wrong: Kennedy, like Theodore Roosevelt in 1906, did not desire a military occupation of Cuba. Secondly, whether or not Castro took the initiative over the missiles – a most improbable eventuality, in the direct sense of the word – he must have been delighted to have them and probably had always coveted them, at the very least since Khrushchev's first mention of the matter in 1960 when it will be recalled that the Russian leader first announced that 'in a figurative sense' his artillery-men could support Cuba with rocket fire. Guevara, it will be recalled, immediately gave a very tough, Cuban interpretation of these words, even claiming that in consequence, Cuba was, by force of circumstance, 'the arbiter of world peace'.[36] Perhaps Castro had been scheming, as one impressed above all from the earliest age by weapons, to lay hold of missiles ever since 1960 and that he had seized on the apparent U.S. threat, however genuine he judged it to be, as an excuse to get what he wanted.[37]

Doubtless Kennedy's inaction, which had led to the defeat of Cochinos Bay persuaded Khrushchev (who had met Kennedy in Vienna) that he would not now act. Maybe some Russians thought that the brazen display of Communist might in the American hemisphere would bring home to Latin America not only the possibility of an open challenge to the U.S. but the clear advantage of Russian over Chinese policies.[38]

So much for the origins of this celebrated gamble by Russia in the Caribbean. In practice the plan provided for, first, the protection of Cuba by a powerful ring of defences – twenty-four batteries of surface-to-air missiles, with 25 miles' radius, a hundred MiG fighters, nuclear defence missiles and ship-to-ship missiles. Ilyushin 28 bombers and ballistic missiles would also be established, along with four battle groups of special ground troops with tactical nuclear weapons. The ballistic

[36] Guevara, *Hoy*, 12 July 1960.
[37] Andrés Suárez (163–4) argues this strongly.
[38] Leon Lipson, 'Castro and the Cold War', in Plank, 194.

missiles were to be at San Cristóbal (3 battalions of MRBMs), Guana-jay (2 battalions of IRBMs), Remedios (2 battalions of IRBMs) and Sagua la Grande (3 battalions of MRBMs). All these needed many special vehicles and personnel. Over a hundred ships were needed to bear this material to Cuba:[39] as lavish an armada as had ever set off across the Atlantic for an armed encounter in the Caribbean.

[39] Hillsman, 159.

CHAPTER 44

The Missile Crisis: II

The crisis which now unfolded was a drama in the course of which the population of the northern hemisphere was closer to extinction than at any previous time. Cuba, the agent of the crisis, at last dragged her ambitions and anxieties to be free to inspire for the first time in 200 years a world conflict and also the risk of cataclysm. Yet, in the course of the crisis, the island of Cuba itself slid from view: the protagonists became the United States and Russia. Cuba observed events with impatience from the wings.

On 26 July 1962, at the annual celebration of the foundation of his movement, Castro explained to the thousands gathered at Santiago that a direct U.S. invasion was now all that Cuba need fear. As he spoke, Russian arms and men in large numbers began to arrive at the small harbour of Mariel and other ports. At this time survey work was certainly being done for the future missile sites. In August Cuba took several steps more away from romantic agriculture to Russian methods; a 'labour book', which all had to have to obtain work, was introduced; rises in wages were prohibited; the cane co-operatives became state farms, on the vote, it was said, of all but three of the 1,380 *cooperativistas* gathered at the conference: the *cooperativistas* had complained that they received only half the wage of state farm workers, and that there had been no attempt to convert the co-operatives into genuine or self-sufficient concerns.[1] The *cooperativistas* themselves had apparently been unable to make any attempt whatever to reproduce in Cuba the self-reliant and successful co-operative societies of Israel or even of North America. Many workers had left agriculture for the towns. The cane co-operative had produced less in 1962 than in 1961.[2] The government seems to have concentrated its energies on the state farms. This rationalizing move, of course, did not solve the problem of agriculture. Carlos Rafael Rodríguez remarked, 'The negative factors still outweigh the positive.'[3]

That same day in the U.S., 23 August, the director of the CIA, McCone, was telling President Kennedy that, from exile reports and

[1] According to Dumont, *Cuba*, 52, the three were the only co-operatives to have made a profit in the last two years.

[2] *Hoy*, 21 September 1962.

[3] *Ibid.*, 23 August 1962. These *granjas de la caña* were not merged with the *granjas del pueblo*, so that, with the farms directly run by INRA since 1959, there were now three separate types of state direction.

aerial photographs, he thought that Russia was preparing to place 'offensive missiles' in Cuba.[4] Perhaps the French intelligence officer, Thiraud de Vosjoly, the celebrated hero of Leon Uris's thriller *Topaz*, brought him eye-witness information. No one believed McCone, though it seems he had first put forward the idea as early as 10 August.[5] It was anyway a presentiment of his, not a judgement.

On 24 August Kennedy at his press conference stated firmly: 'I am not for invading Cuba at this time.' The sentence, while it did not satisfy those in the U.S. who pressed for 'Action', was scarcely reassuring in Cuba either. The same day Roger Hillsman, director of Intelligence at the State Department, told the Washington press corps 'off the record' the news that the recent armaments which had been observed to have arrived in Cuba might include surface-to-air missiles (SAM).[6] On 29 August a U.2, flying over Pinar del Río, discovered evidence of SAMs in position.[7] McCone rightly calculated that this meant that offensive missiles would be installed, on the argument that the only use for SAMs would be to protect offensive missiles; but he was on a honeymoon in France.[8] Two days later, possibly in consequence of leakage of information from the CIA, Senator Keating announced that the Russian build-up was 'deliberately designed' to enable Russia to build missile sites.

On 2 September, meantime, a Russian communiqué at the end of Guevara's discussions in Moscow announced that Cuba had asked for more military help and that Russia would supply it because of threats from the U.S. Russia would also build for Cuba a new steel mill and a $M13 fishing port. Two days later, Kennedy publicly announced that the U.S. had seen the Cuban SAMs. He added that the U.S. would have to act if 'offensive ground-to-ground missiles' were introduced into Cuba. He thus clearly distinguished between SAMs and MRBMs, both of which were in reality already being provided for in Cuba; both had either already arrived or were on the way there. Thus while Kennedy was committing his prestige to the maintenance of one position, Russia and Cuba were already committed to another.[9]

[4] Abel, 18. Hillsman, 172, confirms. Maybe, as Abel says (40), Kennedy was still distrustful of the CIA because of its role in the previous Cuban fiasco. Anyway there remained in Washington a general belief that Russia would not take this step, and McCone did not press his opinion.

[5] See Arthur Krock, *Memoirs* (1968), 378, and Patrick Seale and Maureen McConville, 'Is there a "Philby" near de Gaulle?', *Observer*, 14 April and 21 April 1968.

[6] Hillsman, 170. These were the weapons which had brought down the U.2 of Gary Powers.

[7] Sorensen, 670. These were missiles similar to the U.S. Nike. Of course, all U.2 flights over Cuba were technically an illegal violation of Cuban airspace.

[8] *Ibid.*, McCone sent three telegrams on 7, 10 and 13 September, to the CIA giving his views but these were not distributed to Kennedy.

[9] Robert Kennedy, 'Thirteen Days', *Sunday Times*, 27 October 1968, suggests that this statement was made on his advice, itself tendered after a talk with the Soviet ambassador, Dobrynin, on that day.

On 7 September Kennedy formally asked for, and Congress agreed to, the mobilization of 150,000 reserves. This was evidently a request made with one eye on the Cuban situation. Castro's reaction was typical: Cuba did not require instructions from Washington about the steps which it would take to defend its sovereignty. Raúl Castro said that an attack on Cuba would mark the demise of imperialism. Construction work meantime on the Guanajay IRBM site would doubtless have been begun by then.[10] It was incidentally also on 7 September that Khrushchev had his famous conversation with Robert Frost and suggested that the western democracies were too old to fight – a clear indication of a new hard Russian line.[11] A statement by Tass on 11 September attacked the U.S. almost hysterically, and said: 'One cannot now attack Cuba and expect that the aggressor will be free from punishment,' though this document misleadingly added that there was no need to shift nuclear weapons 'for the repulsion of aggression . . . to any other country, for instance, to Cuba.'[12] Some time in the next few days, however, Khrushchev sent a personal message to assure Kennedy that under no circumstances would surface-to-surface missiles be sent to Cuba – a directly false message.[13] What Castro had called, two years before, the 'international chess game' was thus already far advanced in early September. It is fair to add that this summer and autumn of 1962 were characterized by further radical measures of liberalization and destalinization in Russia; this was the time when Khrushchev assured Bukharin's widow that her husband had been innocent and when Yevtushenko's *Stalin's Heirs* and Solzhenitsyn's *One Day in the Life of Ivan Denisovich* were published: Khrushchev was in fact pressing ahead on all fronts ambitiously.

On 8 and 15 September respectively two large Russian freighters, the *Omsk* and the *Poltava*, built for the lumber trade, with large hatches, riding high in the water, arrived in Havana, with lorries on the top deck, and a number of medium-range ballistic missiles beneath.[14] They were apparently unloaded at night by Russians and moved out by convoys between 9 September and 20 September.[15]

The die was now cast.

[10] Hillsman, 184.

[11] Not 'too liberal', as Frost later said. See discussion in Schlesinger, *A Thousand Days* (London edn.), 702, fn.

[12] *Pravda*, 12 September 1962. The jumbled wording of this statement suggests that it was written by Khrushchev. See Tatu, 240. The Cubans treated this as an explicit commitment to defend Cuba if attacked. Thus *Revolución* had huge headlines afterwards announcing 'Rockets for the U.S. if Cuba is attacked.'

[13] Robert Kennedy, 'Thirteen Days', *Sunday Times*, 27 October 1968.

[14] Hillsman, 184. The arrival of these odd vessels was noted by the U.S. but it was thought that a shortage of ships had led to their use. *Cf.* Abel, 42, and Hillsman, 187.

[15] *Ibid.*, 184. *Cf.* Roberta Wohlstetter, 'Cuba and Pearl Harbor: Hindsight and Foresight', *Foreign Affairs*, July 1965, qu. McNamara press conference.

On 13 September Kennedy, however, again stated that if Cuba were to gather an 'offensive military capacity for the Soviet Union', the U.S. would do 'whatever must be done'. This far from explicit statement was intended for U.S. opinion at home as much as for Castro and Khrushchev, perhaps mostly for Senator Keating, who was making strong speeches up and down the U.S. in the Republican interest alleging that offensive missiles were already established in Cuba and denouncing any exchange of 'Berlin for Cuba'.[16] But there had been so many rumours about missiles in Cuba: even in 1959, when the Russians had yet to send any weapons at all to Cuba, the U.S. government's Cuban missile file was five inches thick.[17] The government of the U.S. had so firmly decided that it would be both foolish and against all expected Russian behaviour to send this war material to Cuba that hints from exiles, agents in Cuba and others were neglected.[18]

By 18 to 21 September secret reports began to arrive of mysterious activities in the San Cristóbal area, a thickly wooded, mountainous and beautiful region about half-way between Pinar del Río and Havana.[19] But these were not reliable reports, and despite the fact that construction on the San Cristóbal and Remedios missile sites was almost certainly begun between 15 and 20 September, this was not noticed by the U.2 flight of 17 September.[20] On 19 September the U.S. Intelligence Board formally concluded that Russia would not send offensive missiles to Cuba.[21] Even so, a report reached the CIA two days later from an agent inside Cuba that sixty-foot missiles, twice as large as SAMs, were in the island.[22] But this news was taken even by the CIA with a pinch of salt, out of 'pure scepticism', according to Hillsman.[23] 'Wolf' had been cried too often by too many people. Construction on the fourth Cuban IRBM site seems to have been begun at Sagua la Grande between 25

[16] New York Times, 10 September 1962.

[17] Hillsman, 169.

[18] Cf. Roberta Wohlstetter on this, in Foreign Affairs, July 1965.

[19] Secretary of Defence McNamara, in testimony, 7 February 1963, to the House Appropriations Committee. The author remembers a climb in this region as late as July 1962 to a mountain top from which an endless landscape of royal palms stretched to the horizon and to the sea, the beauty of the scene disturbed only by an occasional vulture.

[20] According to Sorensen, 672, flights were held up after 5 September because of bad weather. This is incorrect; see Hillsman, 171, McNamara (qu. Roberta Wohlstetter (op. cit.)) and Schlesinger, A Thousand Days, 684. The flight on the 5th over west Cuba had been negative, according to McNamara. Some caution was shown because the U.S. lost a U.2 over China on 9 September. The U.2s could cover all Cuba in one flight, given normal weather but usually two were used.

[21] Hillsman, 170; Robert Kennedy, 'Thirteen Days', op. cit. McCone was still away and still thinking differently but according to Arthur Krock (op. cit) his views were cut out of the report by his deputy, General Carter.

[22] Abel, 24; confirmed by Hillsman, 174–5, who says that the report referred to movements on 12 September.

[23] Hillsman, 186.

September and 30 September,[24] and on 28 September, meantime, the Cuban Student Directorate in exile circulated a mimeographed letter stating that fifteen guided missile sites were being built.[25]

The arms increase in Cuba had meantime inspired xenophobia of rare proportions in the U.S. press. The *U.S. News and World Report* in its first September issue[26] specifically said that Cuba was getting 'Soviet rockets with a range of up to 400 miles'. The arrival of Russian troops in Cuba appeared to be the first time that a non-American power had established itself in the Americas since Napoleon III's ill-fated expedition to Mexico. Cuba became consequently the central issue in the congressional election campaign, with Republican politicians upbraiding the president for his inaction. In their issue of 21 September *Time* published a portrait of President Monroe on the cover and described the details of his doctrine, forgetting that, whatever its validity, it did not apply to Cuba, but arguing nevertheless that Russian action in Cuba called for U.S. action under it.[27] In an issue of the *U.S. News and World Report*, dated 17 September a retired general described the military methods of crushing the Cuban regime: a sea blockade and a land invasion. Six divisions, he confirmed, would be needed.

Of course, there were dissentient voices, but not in politically critical places. The Department of Defence announced that Cubans enrolled in the U.S. army could be used against Cuba. The *U.S. News and World Report*[28] then published another excitable article headlined, 'Is Blockade of Cuba on the Way?'. It added: 'A decision to blockade, if made, will have to follow a fuller build-up of Soviet power in Cuba.' A week later, Mrs Henry Luce wrote a long article in *Life* pointing out the contrast between Kennedy's toughness on Cuba during the elections of 1960 and his current 'calm'. She was full of dire if fashionable predictions: 'Time is running out in Latin America and the cold war is still being lost there.' She demanded action: 'What is now at stake in the decision for intervention or non-intervention in Cuba is the question not only of American prestige but of American survival.'[29] In the first week of October Richard Rovere, in the *New Yorker*, published an ominous article about 'a war party' in Washington, which he argued was no less active than the group which engineered war in 1898.[30]

All this meant pressure on the administration at an election time. Even so, there was no suggestion that Kennedy was going to surrender

[24] *Ibid.*, 184.
[25] *New York Times*, 24 October 1962.
[26] Dated 10 September.
[27] The conclusion of the article put the case negatively by destroying the administration argument against direct action to oust Castro.
[28] In an issue distributed 24 September – 1 October.
[29] *Life*, 5 October 1962, 56.
[30] *New Yorker*, 10 October 1962.

to it, as McKinley had done sixty years before. U.2 reconnaissance flights were made over east Cuba on 5 and 7 October and revealed nothing. On 10 October Senator Keating said that he had '100% reliable' evidence from exiles that six intermediate-range missile sites were under construction.[31] Two days earlier it seemed that President Dorticós of Cuba almost admitted the truth when, at the U.N., he had said that the threat of U.S. invasion had led Cuba to acquire armaments which 'it had not wanted and [which it] hoped it would not have to use'.[32] On 10 October Kennedy authorized a new U.2 flight over west Cuba.[33] This was carried out on Sunday 14 October by the U.S. air force (not the CIA), the flight having been delayed a day or two by Hurricane Daisy. Photographs showed that, in an area not covered by U.2 flights since 5 September, sites for a battalion of mobile medium-range 1,000-mile ballistic missiles were being constructed at San Cristóbal.[34] From other excavations it seemed that hard permanent sites for IRBMs of 2,000-mile radius were also being prepared.[35] McCone of the CIA, therefore, as Kennedy later had to admit, was 'right all along'.[36]

Between 16 October and 21 October, the U.S. government confirmed this information. Much time was spent on determining the reasons for the Soviet-Cuban action. Prominent among the theories put forward was that Khrushchev, after the U.S. elections in November, would at the U.N. personally reveal the existence of the missiles and propose the exchange of Berlin for withdrawing the missiles.[37] Others thought that Khrushchev might wish to trade the Cuban missiles for the U.S. ones in Turkey and Italy,[38] or that he desired to prove that the U.S. was too weak to risk nuclear war, thereby permitting further Russian penetration into South America and encouraging even European allies to make

---

[31] After the crisis he said that he had secured this remarkably precise information from a government official, doubtless from the CIA. For discussion of this claim, see Hillsman, 177–9.

[32] *Revolución*, 9 October 1962. Dorticós met Gromyko at New York and it is of course likely that they exchanged views on the major problem about to engulf their two nations.

[33] Schlesinger, *A Thousand Days*, 684. Sorensen, 672, says 9 October. The plan was suggested on 4 October, according to both Schlesinger and Hillsman (p. 175), because (according to Hillsman) of U.S. naval photographs of Soviet ships at sea on 28 September – which seemed to suggest that Russia was sending Ilyushin bombers to Cuba. (Hillsman, 167.)

[34] *Ibid.*, 166.

[35] See Chronology in the *New York Times*, 6 November 1962, which says that Ilyushins were observed in a photograph taken on 28 September. These bombers had a range of about 900 miles, a speed of 500 mph. But the photographs were not evaluated properly until 9 October, the information made available on the 10th.

[36] Krock, 380. It will be remembered that, according to Krock, McCone had guessed that offensive missiles were being placed in Cuba as early as 5 August.

[37] This view was taken by the U.S. ambassador in Moscow, Thompson (Abel, 48; *cf.* Sorensen, 677, on 'Theory 4'). Khrushchev had said earlier that he would postpone bringing up the Berlin question until after the U.S. elections. It is also the basic argument in Tatu's *Power in the Kremlin*.

[38] Actually they were due anyway to be removed by the U.S., as will be seen.

accommodation with Russia.[39] Others speculated that, to disprove the Chinese view, Russia desired the U.S. to invade Cuba – thereby dividing the west and enabling Khrushchev incidentally to move in Berlin.[40] Some certainly thought that the missiles were merely for the defence of Cuba, as well as that the new deployment doubled Russian first-strike capacity – which if it did not really alter profoundly the strategic balance, might nevertheless seem to do so. It seemed to others that whatever the precise reason or reasons for the Soviet action, Khrushchev must have gambled that the U.S. president would be unable to decide on a firm course of action so close to the time of the election.

Kennedy in the end reached the rather lame explanation that Khrushchev's conduct could be explained by a desire to prove the U.S. weak before the world, believing that the defence of Cuba and an increase of missile power were 'likely but insufficient' causes of this new Russian action.[41] The information obtained on 14 October was confirmed by more U.2 flights: twenty (in place of two) occurred in the next six days. Three incomplete IRBM fixed sites and six actual mobile MRBM sites were discovered.[42] All were guarded and manned by Russians, not Cubans. The U.S. counted 30 to 35 missiles, though there were apparently 42.[43]

What was to be done? Complete inactivity was ruled out as being likely to confirm 'the fears of De Gaulle and others that the U.S. could not be depended upon to meet threats even farther from our shores', while in Latin America a 'failure to intervene would bring a Castro-Communist trend', even in countries where non-intervention was a 'religion'.[44] McNamara nevertheless 'pointed out . . . we had long lived within range of Soviet missiles, we expected Khrushchev to live with our missiles nearby, and, by taking this addition calmly, we could prevent him from inflating its importance'.[45] Kennedy rejected this

[39] Apparently the view of the U.S. Ambassador to France, a Russian expert, Charles Bohlen (Sorensen, 677), as well as to some extent that of the president.

[40] Sorensen, 677

[41] In conversation with Schlesinger, on 21 October, Kennedy however attributed the Russian action to a desire to draw Russia and China together or at least to strengthen Russia's name in the international revolutionary movement by standing up for Cuba; to a desire to develop a stronger position in Berlin negotiations; and simply to 'deal the U.S. a blow' (Schlesinger, 693).

[42] They could be dismantled and reassembled, within six days. They were really movable rather than mobile, being about 55 to 60 feet long and liquid-fuelled (cf. Washington Post, 26 October 1962, 48).

[43] 'We never knew how many missiles were brought to Cuba. The Soviets said there were forty-two. We counted forty-two going out. We saw fewer than forty-two going in.' (R. Gilpatrick, on ABC Television, 11 November 1962.) But Russia probably intended 48 MRBMs and 16 IRBMs. None of the latter seems to have arrived.

[44] Sorensen, 681.

[45] Loc. cit., Hillsman, 195. See Abel, 52, for confirmation. Incidentally most of those involved in the decisions changed their position, sometimes several times, in the course of the discussions.

policy because of the international political effects – not, apparently, because of the strategic consequences. He thought that 'the Soviet move had been undertaken so swiftly, so secretly and with so much deliberate deception . . . that it presented a provocative change in the delicate *status quo*'. He considered too that missiles on Soviet territory or submarines were different from missiles in the western hemisphere, particularly because of their political and psychological effect on Latin America. Such a step, if accepted, he thought would be clearly followed by further steps. His September pledges of action had clearly regarded this step as unacceptable. 'He was not willing to let the U.N. debate and Khrushchev equivocate while the missiles became operational.'[46] He 'knew he would have to act' just as if he had been slapped in the face: it was a challenge more than a threat[47] and, given his vulnerable position in U.S. politics over Cuba, he believed that he had to respond.

Thus Kennedy had also, in rejecting the 'do nothing' approach, rejected any idea for mere diplomatic action as argued by some of his advisers.[48] This decision also seems to have been taken more because of national than international politics (as perhaps Khrushchev's had been as well). In retrospect, however, it is curious that Kennedy did not choose first to present the Russians with his evidence in secrecy. The president chose to react strongly and outside existing methods of arbitration and existing alliances: partly from fear that once, for instance, the English or French governments were told, leakages were more likely.[49] If the European allies had been told, the countries of South America, who believed themselves entitled by treaties to close consultation where American events were concerned, would have also to be be brought into the story. But in addition to the problem of keeping the secret, the European allies might make light of the crisis: 'Most Europeans cared nothing about Cuba and thought we were over-anxious about it. They had long accustomed themselves to living next door to Soviet missiles. Would they support our risking a world war (for such seemed to be the case even at the beginning) . . . because we now had a dozen hostile missiles nearby?'[50] Further, the British and French might

---

[46] Sorensen, 683. Dillon told Abel that Kennedy's first reaction 'was that one simply could not accept the fact of Soviet missiles in Cuba trained on the U.S.' (Abel, 48).

[47] This is the reading of Robert Kennedy's record (*Sunday Times*, 27 October 1968). Kennedy later thought that he 'would have been impeached' if he had not acted in some way. See also Ronald Steel, 'Endgame', *New York Review of Books*, 13 March 1969.

[48] Abel, 53. Bohlen, Stevenson and Bundy seem to have thought diplomacy best.

[49] A point impressed on the author by Bundy in conversation (January 1963).

[50] Sorensen, 681. The same point was in Nitze's mind: 'We could expect the British to take a different view. The Allies generally had failed to appreciate why the presence of missiles in Cuba [if they were placed there] . . . would be intolerable to the U.S.' (Abel, 33). Pachter, 16, bluntly commented that the reason 'above all' why the Allies were not consulted was 'the doubt whether they would go along with the chosen style of action'. This was to be an American showdown with the Soviet Union and it had to be carried out by the American president in his own way.

point out with bitterness how generous the U.S. had been in the past with advice to them as to how to cope calmly with nationalism.[51]

The U.S. government thus advanced into the crisis distrusting their allies but willing nevertheless to embark on a policy which might bring ruin, even if victory, to them all.[52] For though NATO was not informed or consulted as such, NATO bases in Italy and Turkey were fully prepared. Kennedy was not prepared to allow Harold Macmillan or General de Gaulle to play the restraining role played over the Suez crisis by General Eisenhower in 1956. The idea of consulting the U.N. was indeed as abhorrent to Kennedy as it had been in 1956 to Eden; for, as a Chilean long ago pointed out, so far as the rest of the Americas was concerned, the U.S. cared 'as much about international law as about a radish'.[53] No doubt the OAS could be brought into the picture, as indeed it later was, but the OAS were told, not consulted, as were the U.N. and NATO.[54]

This failure to consult the Allies was scarcely commented upon at the time, since the Allies concerned felt it wiser not to give the impression that they had been slighted: this neglect was later criticized, however, in Europe and, curiously, defended by the leading U.S. political commentator, Lippmann: 'The command of nuclear power to balance Soviet nuclear power cannot be shared . . . only one can sit at the wheel.'[55]

By 17 October Kennedy and his government were divided on the comparatively simple choice as to whether to instigate an immediate attack by air on the Cuban missile sites or whether to blockade Cuba roughly along the lines proposed three weeks before in the *U.S. News and World Report*. Dean Acheson and the chiefs of staff favoured the former policy;[56] it was ultimately rejected, since it was thought it would expand the conflict and kill thousands of Cubans and Russians, in a surprise attack resembling Pearl Harbour, so blackening 'the name of the U.S.

[51] As Raymond Aron pointed out in his article, 'A European Perspective', in Plank, 141.

[52] Ormsby Gore, the British ambassador, was told of the crisis at noon on 21 October, before any other ally.

[53] Manuel Foster Recabarren; I am indebted to Mr Raymond Carr for this quotation.

[54] The U.S. Congress was also in the dark, as was the cabinet formally until 4 p.m. on 22 October. Kennedy was acting by executive order, presidential proclamation and 'inherent powers . . . He had earlier rejected all suggestions of reconvening Congress' (Sorensen, 701–2). He even seems to have been annoyed that congressional leaders (whom he met at 5 p.m. that day) should argue the toss with him.

[55] Address to the Anglo-American Association in Paris, qu. *New Republic*, 22 November 1962. The leading French political commentator, Raymond Aron, replied, '*Must we have blind faith?* When Lippmann asks Europeans to hand over the wheel of the car, he is really asking them to abdicate after a fashion . . . the combination of an American/nuclear/monopoly and non-consultation with its allies reduces the European countries . . . to the status of protectorate nations.' De Gaulle criticized Kennedy, in his press conference of 14 January 1963.

[56] Robert Kennedy, *Sunday Times*, 27 October 1968.

in the pages of history', leading to 'our indictment in the court of history'.[57]

A decision was therefore ultimately made to establish a naval blockade to prevent the further arrival of offensive weapons, missiles or bombers. The advantage of this was that it began the 'escalation' of the crisis at its lowest rung – it left a large number of possible alternatives open for the future, and it did not in itself risk anyone's death. Kennedy was probably strengthened in making this decision by intelligence reports that Russia was not at all ready for a nuclear war and perhaps the information of Russian unreadiness given by the spy, Penkovsky (arrested incidentally in Moscow on 22 October), played a part here.[58]

While the implications of this recommendation were being worked out by Kennedy's advisers, Kennedy was personally assured in Washington by the Russian Foreign Minister, Gromyko, that Russia would never give offensive weapons to Cuba.[59] This assurance amazed and angered Kennedy and probably contributed to the bitterness of his first public speech on the missiles. Khrushchev had assured the U.S. ambassador in Moscow of the peaceful nature of his intentions on 16 October.[60] But Gromyko perhaps supposed that the U.S. had already discovered the existence of missiles in Cuba and was already speculating about Russia's response.[61] It remains odd that Kennedy did not tax Gromyko directly with the U.S. discoveries in Cuba: Robert Kennedy suggested that this was because U.S. policy had not been quite decided.

The impending crisis had been well concealed, though the British Embassy got wind of matters by 17 October.[62] Troop and aircraft movements to Florida had been remarked by the press, though on Kennedy's

[57] The words of Robert Kennedy (Sorensen, 684–5; cf. Schlesinger, A Thousand Days, 689); he told his brother, 'I now know how Tojo felt when planning Pearl Harbour.' For all this, see Sorensen, and Robert Kennedy, 'Thirteen Days', op. cit. The decision for the blockade was made on 18 October, but some discussion of alternatives continued, for the joint chiefs of staff still preferred an air strike or an invasion. An invasion would however have been much more difficult then than in 1961. Thus, Cuba now had probably 22 anti-aircraft guided missile bases, and two more being built (guide line missiles); surface-to-surface 'cruise' missiles, comparable to the U.S. Maces and Matadors; 100 MiG fighters; 20 Ilyushin 28 light bombers; and some Komar class, Russian P.T. boats carrying missiles (Washington Post, 26 October 1962, 18). At the same time the commander-in-chief of the tactical air force told Kennedy that even a major surprise air attack could not have eliminated without fail all the offensive missiles.

[58] Oleg Penkovsky, The Penkovsky Papers (1965), 323.

[59] Most of their talk was about Berlin. Kennedy later made much of this apparent deception by Gromyko but though (unlike the Russian ambassador in Washington) it must be assumed Gromyko knew of the existence of missiles in Cuba, doubtless he regarded himself within his rights as calling them 'defensive' just as Rusk would have referred to the U.S. Jupiters in Turkey by that useful adjective. Given the tortuous and unsatisfactory nature of international diplomacy, Gromyko's remarks do not now seem specially heinous.

[60] Hillsman, 166.

[61] Cf. ibid., 167.

[62] General Strong, director of the Joint Intelligence Bureau, noticed signs of unusual activity in the Pentagon on this day (Abel, 60).

request the *New York Times* did not publish an article on the subject.[63] Long-prepared naval manœuvres off Vieques caused both Moscow and Havana to become apprehensive.[64] Even so, Kennedy's announcement

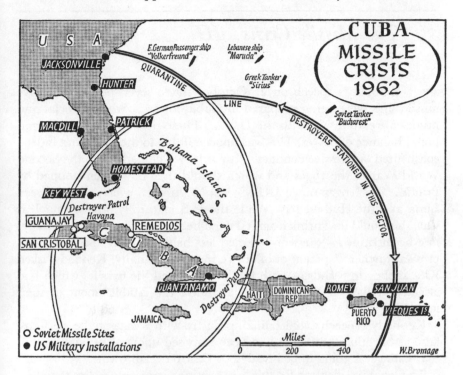

of his decision was delayed until 22 October, to give time to his advisers to inform the Allies in Europe and South America, not to speak of Congress. The little criticism there was from Congress was that an air strike or an invasion of Cuba would be more appropriate: even the often pacific Fulbright supported this idea on the grounds that a blockade would pit Russian ships against U.S. armed forces and hence risk war more easily.[65]

---

[63] Schlesinger, *A Thousand Days*, 692. Sorensen, 698, describes the incident in a different style. Abel says the *Washington Post* also 'patriotically abandoned its metier'. Hillsman says the *New York Times* simply kept quiet.

[64] See *Revolución*, 19 October.

[65] Johnson and Gwertzman, 182; Robert Kennedy, *Sunday Times*, 27 October 1968.

CHAPTER 45

The Missile Crisis: III

Kennedy's speech on 22 October made seven points: offensive missile sites were being prepared in Cuba, an area 'with a special and historical relationship with the U.S.A.' These sites altered the international balance of power. This was unacceptable to the U.S., and indeed constituted 'aggressive conduct' of the sort which had led to the Second World War in the 1930s and which should then have been stopped by Britain. The longer-range IRBMs would threaten everything between Lima and the Hudson Bay. While the U.S. naturally opposed nuclear war, she would not shrink from it if need be. A 'quarantine' would therefore be instituted – the word seemed less bellicose than 'blockade' – to prevent further shipment of offensive material. Finally, Kennedy asked Khrushchev to withdraw both the bombers and the missiles which had already arrived in Cuba and to abandon the establishment of their launching sites.[1]

Kennedy's speech avoided linking Castro with Russia on the, perhaps, false assumption that Cuba had been imposed upon; there was no hint that Cuba was going to be invaded or Castro overthrown.

The legal justification for this 'quarantine' was formally less the U.N. Charter than the Charter of the OAS, which entitled member states to take 'collective measures to guard the security of the Americas'. The approval of the OAS was sought on 23 October and obtained by 19 votes too, with Uruguay abstaining, though only because her ambassador in Washington had received no instructions. All the other ambassadors were overawed by the solemnity of Dean Rusk's appeal to them. A U.S. resolution to the U.N. Security Council also called for the dismantling of the offending sites and the removal of both the missiles and the jet bombers, and for the establishment of a U.N. Observer Corps to visit Cuba in order to guarantee this.

The quarantine itself comprised sixteen destroyers, three cruisers, an anti-submarine aircraft carrier and six utility ships[2] disposed in an arc from Florida to beyond Puerto Rico,[3] with orders to inspect, stop and, if

---

[1] *New York Times*, 23 October 1962.

[2] Sorensen, 708.

[3] The line was drawn 500 miles from Cuba, rather than 800 as at first envisaged, on the suggestion of the English ambassador to give more time to Russian ships actually approaching to get instructions (Schlesinger, *A Thousand Days*, 699, and Robert Kennedy, *op. cit.*).

necessary, disable (rather than sink) those Russian vessels *en route* for Cuba which were capable of carrying nuclear warheads, air-to-surface or surface-to-air missiles, bombers, or any equipment to support that material. By including surface-to-air weapons, Kennedy was extending the quarantine to cover the most dangerous sort of defensive weapons. Kennedy also told his ambassadors in Guinea and Senegal, where Russian aircraft stopped on their way to Cuba, to ask the governments of those countries to refuse landing rights to Russia during the crisis, so as to avoid the dispatch of warheads by air; both agreed – even Sékou Touré, a friend of Castro's, on the grounds that he opposed bases on foreign soil.[4]

The world then waited with some apprehension for the Russian response. From the U.S. there was general though not unanimous approval. The *New York Times* showed a certain lack of enthusiasm by saying that Kennedy 'could not have done much less'.[5] The *New York Post* criticized the lack of consultation of the U.N. and OAS. On succeeding days the *New York Times* published critical letters. In London, Macmillan told Kennedy that Europe, used to living under the 'nuclear gun', might wonder what all the fuss was about; his view was that Khrushchev would try to 'trade Cuba for Berlin'.[6] Adenauer seemed initially 'rather agitated'.[7] Gaitskell in England questioned the legality of the quarantine and urged Macmillan to fly to Washington.[8] Diefenbaker in Canada wavered. The English government, like other allies, nevertheless gave support, though (a fact which passed unnoticed) this was the first time that England had given formal approval to someone else's blockade at sea. The torch had indeed passed on.[9] As some of Kennedy's advisers had predicted, the English newspapers were the most critical. Thus *The Times* wondered if there really were missiles in Cuba, *The Guardian* thought that Khrushchev was showing to the U.S. 'the meaning of U.S. bases close to the Soviet frontier', and even the *Daily Mail* called the blockade an 'act of war' and suggested that Kennedy was being led by 'popular emotion'. *The Daily Telegraph* was also critical. Bertrand Russell announced to the world in general: 'Within a week you will all be dead to please American madmen,' and telegraphed Kennedy: 'Your action desperate. Threat to survival.' He appealed as well to Khrushchev to be cautious.[10]

[4] Abel, 136–9.
[5] *New York Times*, 23 October, 36.
[6] Schlesinger, *A Thousand Days*, 698.
[7] Abel, 128.
[8] Statement by Labour Party National Executive, which also deplored the lack of consultation.
[9] Lloyd's suspended fixed insurance for risks in shipping to London.
[10] Lord Russell, *Unarmed Victory* (1963), 29. On 23 October over six million shares changed hands in the U.S. (*Washington Post*, 24 October 1962). Prices for 'commodity futures' recorded

Bad news also came from the east where the Indo-Chinese border quarrel had burst out again. On 23 October China (who had presumably been informed by Russia of her Cuban action) lifted all restraints on invasion in North India and authorized her troops to advance as far as they could: she was taking advantage of an opportunity – not, of course, coordinating an attack, though Russia gave her full support for a week.[11]

In Cuba itself, two medium-range missiles were ready to operate by 23 October.[12] There were about 20,000 Russian troops in Cuba in four units of about 5,000 men each – two units near Havana, one in central Cuba, one in the east. They had modern Russian ground fighting armaments including rocket launchers like the U.S. 'Honest John'.[13] These facts were not yet publicly admitted in Cuba, though Kennedy's speech had been listened to and most of it was published by *Revolución*.[14] The general supposition was not only that Cuba was about to be invaded but that it would be subject to nuclear bombardment. This, of course, was irrational, though obviously, in a full war, Havana might very well have been destroyed, by conventional or other means. Castro, however, must have known that his most likely danger was a U.S. invasion by sea or an aerial bombardment of the missile sites. On 23 October, anyway, he called for general mobilization. Red posters depicting a man holding a machine-gun called the population to arms. Raúl Castro moved down the island to take command in Santiago, and we catch a glimpse of him on 25 October surrounded by old comrades such as Calixto García, Armando Acosta, Faustino Pérez, Luis Mas Martín and Abilio Cortina (secretary of the Oriente JUCEI) under the slogan *Listos para Vencer*, ready to conquer.[15] According to one observer: 'It was as if a long-contained tension relaxed, as if the whole country had said as one, "at last". The long wait for the invasion, the war of nerves, the sneak attacks, the landing of spies, the blockade. All this was past.'[16] The discipline, the absence of panic and the dedication were impressive. Castro himself spoke

[11] China was later reproached for this advance, by Suslov at the plenum of the Central Committee of Russia on 14 February 1964, published April 1964.

[12] Sorensen, 709.

[13] According to Wohlstetter, *Foreign Affairs*, July 1965, these were not seen by the U.S. U.2s, only by the low level photography which followed.

[14] *Revolución*, 26 October.

[15] *Ibid*.

[16] Adolfo Gilly, *Inside the Cuban Revolution* (trans. Félix Gutiérrez, 1964), 48. Gilly was a Trotskyist who later turned against Castro. Ironically, precisely similar words could be found among U.S. reporters. Thus: 'A sense of relief from frustration has rolled across the Mid-Western prairies following the President's action [*sic*] on Cuba.' (*New York Times*, 25 October 1962, 22, New York edn.)

their biggest jump since the Korean war – including curiously sugar which exceeded the daily limit of ½ cent per pound on 23 October. On 24 October Khrushchev's reply to Bertrand Russell led to a buying spree.

briefly (one hour and twenty minutes) to the Cubans on 23 October condemning Kennedy's 'piracy', and said that anyone who wished to inspect Cuba should come prepared to fight. 'We refuse all inspection: Cuba is not the Congo . . . Our arms are not offensive.' He compared Kennedy to the pirate Sir Henry Morgan, in contrast to Drake, who 'had undoubted qualities'. Did the satiated shark, the U.S., really think Cuba a little sardine?[17] But the 'international chess game' was now at last out of Castro's hands. He was in the dark as to what would happen. He was apparently not consulted by Khrushchev but, like De Gaulle, merely informed. For Castro, too, his alliances were never the same again. For ordinary Cubans, however, the most important part of the crisis was the indefinite suspension of flights by Pan American to Miami: this twice-weekly air service, which had carried perhaps 250,000 refugees to the U.S., was not resumed till 1965 and then under quite different conditions.

The Russian response to the demands of Kennedy was, like Kennedy's own decisions, made in the dark so far as their opponents' real intentions were concerned. Russia seems to have seen the quarantine as intended to prevent the coming of the IRBMs. But the jet Ilyushin bombers had been in Cuba for some time. Was the U.S. merely seeking to avoid the arrival of 'offensive' weapons or were they in fact hoping to crush Castro too? Of course, reaction in the Moscow press was violent: 'America's ruling class has at last dropped its mask . . . seldom has any country committed so uncouth and treasonable an aggression.' The first official Russian response, like Castro's, was to announce on 23 October that all their weapons in Cuba were defensive and that the quarantine was an act of piracy. At the U.N. the Russian ambassador, Zorin, left presumably without instructions, unwisely accused the U.S. of inventing the evidence. Contrariwise, the Russian press officer at the U.N. told his U.S. colleague that New York would probably be blown up the next day.[18] Dobrynin, the Soviet ambassador in Washington seemed, like Zorin, without instructions and out of touch.[19] Khrushchev then wrote Kennedy a letter echoing the public messages, and was promptly answered with a private restatement of the U.S. public position.[20]

It was known in Washington from aerial reconnaissance that twenty-five Russian cargo ships, five of them with large hatches (and therefore suitable for carrying missiles), were then heading for Havana.[21] On the evening of 23 October U.S. newspapers proclaimed: 'Showdown can come

[17] Text in *Revolución*, 24 October. He did not actually admit the existence of missiles.
[18] Abel, 133.
[19] Schlesinger, *A Thousand Days*, 699; Kennedy, *Sunday Times*, 27 October 1968, confirms.
[20] Sorensen, 709.
[21] *New York Times*, 24 October 1962, 1.

tonight.'[22] This was an exaggeration, for the quarantine did not come into being until the following morning, Wednesday, 24 October, when at 10 a.m. Russian submarines were reported to be following the cargo ships, like the long sharks which for so many years used to pursue slave ships on the same route. 'Sea Clash Near' was then the headline of the *Washington Daily News* on 24 October. This was for most people, including for Kennedy and his government, a harsh moment.[23]

During the course of the morning the Russian ships altered course or drew to a halt at sea: 'Some Red ships turning back', the *Washington Evening Star* announced prematurely. The news came to Kennedy and his advisers at a morning meeting. The Pentagon thought that the ships might be aiming to rendezvous at sea with the submarines behind them and so force their way through. At the same time Khrushchev, answering Bertrand Russell in a publicly announced missive, suggested a new summit conference, and pledged that his government would not be reckless and would 'do everything in our power to prevent war'.[24] The use by Khrushchev of the aged Russell in his house in North Wales as an intermediary was the most bizarre aspect of these days. It caused what now seems to have been the first step backwards in the Russian position to be somewhat overlooked. U Thant, a more conventional go-between, proposed a Russian suspension of arms shipments and a U.S. delay in imposing the quarantine. But Kennedy brushed this aside to say that the missiles already in Cuba had to be removed before the quarantine could be suspended.[25] Khrushchev, on the other hand, in his answer to U Thant, showed his willingness to accept negotiation, even with the blockade – a further sign of a retreat.[26] In the afternoon Khrushchev saw a U.S. businessman, William Knox of Westinghouse International.[27] The conversation was ambiguous. Khrushchev seemed weary: the missiles, he said, were defensive; Kennedy was risking a world war; and Russian submarines would soon be sinking U.S. ships if they tried to halt Russian ships. Some in the U.S. administration saw in Knox's report of this talk a Russian desire to negotiate and a need to give Khrushchev a way of escape.[28] At the least, he had now admitted it was true, though privately, that the missiles in Cuba existed. In the Pentagon, meantime, McNamara was quarrelling with the chief of naval staff, Admiral Anderson, about the precise physical consequences of stopping a Russian ship: the admiral, a brave successor to Admiral

[22] *Washington Daily News.*
[23] Robert Kennedy, *Sunday Times*, 27 October 1968.
[24] Qu. *Washington Evening Star*, 24 October (Stocks Final), 1.
[25] Sorensen, 709–10.
[26] Tatu, 265.
[27] Schlesinger, 702–3.
[28] *loc. cit.*

Schley, said that he needed no guidance, since the navy had 'always known how to conduct a blockade'.[29]

On 25 October, a Russian tanker (the *Bucharest*) and an East German passenger ship (the *Völkerfreund*) were allowed through the quarantine without being searched, on the grounds that they could not possibly be carrying missiles or other equipment similar. Twelve of the Russian ships on the way to Cuba had by then halted.

The blockade or quarantine seemed therefore to have worked. There remained the U.S. demands for the removal of existing missiles and bombers. The medium-range missiles were now believed to be ready for use within a few days and the intermediate-range ones within a month. Kennedy and his advisers discussed the possibility of extending the blockade to cover oil, of further low-level flights, of a direct approach to Castro, and again, as before the crisis, at an air strike or an invasion. U.S. newspapers began to publish lists of 'approved fall-out shelters'. There were, meantime, more signs of Russian concern to avoid war. Gromyko made a speech in Berlin without mentioning Cuba. Russian diplomats tried to persuade intermediaries everywhere to try to tempt allied governments to intercede.[30] Adlai Stevenson in the U.N. was making the best publicity out of the Russian representative's obvious lack of knowledge and instruction, while Zorin still denied that any Russian missiles were in Cuba, a point of view which Stevenson found easy to ridicule with a famous public show of the photographs, thereby making up for some of the ignominy which had come to him in 1961. U Thant, ignored the previous day by Kennedy, sent a further plea to both parties to avoid 'confrontation' in the Caribbean.

On Friday, 26 October, there was no change in the Russian or Cuban position and Kennedy ordered a 'crash programme on civil government in Cuba . . . after the invasion'. Work on the missile sites seemed indeed to be continuing apace. The inspection at sea was enacted for the first time on the *Manuela*, a Panamanian vessel, bound for Cuba under Russian charter. The boarding party allowed it to sail on. But *Pravda*'s headline that morning had been remarkably pacific and, in the middle of the day, the Russians made their first positive proposal for a compromise, through the curious intermediary of Aleksander Fomin of their Washington Embassy (doubtless an intelligence officer) and a well-connected Washington television reporter, John Scali of ABC News: would the U.S. be interested in a promise not to invade Cuba in return for a Russian withdrawal of the missiles under U.N. inspection? Scali consulted Hillsman and Rusk and reported later to Fomin that the U.S. saw 'real possibilities' in the idea. A little afterwards, a letter for Ken-

---

[29] *Cf.* description in Abel.
[30] Including grotesquely the ill-fated Stephen Ward of the Profumo case.

nedy arrived from Khrushchev making much the same proposal in evidently sincere though confused terms, while Zorin made the same proposal to U Thant, with the Cuban delegation in New York in support.[31] This letter was emotional, apparently in Khrushchev's own style, being full of recollections of the horrors of war. Russia, said Khrushchev, had sent missiles to Cuba because of the Bay of Cochinos; they were defensive; and a U.S. pledge not to invade Cuba would remove the need for them.

Before Kennedy had time to reply to this letter, another one from the Kremlin on Saturday, 27 October, altered the thrust of the bargain by taking up an idea launched by *The Times* (of London) and echoed by Walter Lippmann[32] in the *New York Herald Tribune* on 25 October, for the evacuation of the U.S. missile bases from Turkey.[33] Khrushchev also assured Kennedy that the missiles already in Cuba were completely under Russian control.[34] This letter confused the U.S. (though in it Russia publicly admitted that there were missiles in Cuba), while the proposal contained in it was not acceptable to Kennedy.[35] Was Khrushchev still in control? The two letters resembled the different telegrams sent from Berlin to Vienna in the crisis of July 1914 which had led to the First World War. 'Who rules in Berlin?' had asked General Conrad von Hötzendorf; and indeed there was doubtless serious dissension at this time between the Russian leaders as to the course to be followed.[36]

The arrival of the second letter was followed by the news that a U.2 aeroplane had been shot down over Cuba by a SAM missile and that another U.2 had accidentally strayed over Russia in the far east, maybe,

[31] Sorensen, 712; Schlesinger, *A Thousand Days*, 706-7. Schlesinger implies that the bargain offered in it was more categorical than does Sorensen. Unlike Khrushchev's other letters, this important one was not published in Moscow. It was thought by some that this suggests that Khrushchev wrote it behind the praesidium's back. Abel quotes a passage from it (181), but it has not otherwise been made public.

[32] Lippmann had written that in both World Wars the U.S. 'suspended diplomacy when the guns began to shoot. In both wars as a result we achieved a great victory but we could not make peace. There is a mood in this country today which could easily cause us to make the same mistake again.' Thus, Kennedy had suspended diplomacy when he had seen Gromyko, when he should have given him a chance to save face. He also suggested that Turkey was comparable to Cuba and an exchange over the two might be a 'way out of the tyranny of automatic and uncontrollable events.' (*Washington Post*, 25 October 1962.)

[33] Marshal Malinovsky had alluded to Cuba and Turkey in the same breath on 23 October. The Russians may have thought that Lippmann was speaking for Kennedy.

[34] The Russians may have had electronic locks, possibly even controlled in Russia, on these missiles, as the U.S. had over their overseas missiles since July of the same year. (Roberta and Albert Wohlstetter, 8, suggest that the real reason for the 20,000 Russian troops was to guard the missiles from the Cubans, not from the marines.)

[35] Although U.S. plans had already been made for the removal of the missile sites from Turkey, already obsolete, as Khrushchev no doubt knew.

[36] Tatu, 270, suggests that Khrushchev was out-voted that day in the praesidium and was not responsible for any of the actions taken then, but later gave (on 21 December 1962) to the Supreme Soviet, a speech describing not what did happen but what should have happened.

as Khrushchev later said, risking confusion with a nuclear bomber. 'Would the Russians view this as a final reconnaissance in preparation for a nuclear attack? . . . There was a moment of frightening grimness.'[37] Castro has since maintained that it was he who was responsible for bringing the U.2 down, suggesting that the missiles in Cuba were not all under central Moscow control.[38] Though Kennedy did not order (as had been provided for) any response to the destruction of the U.2 over Cuba, all the U.S. nuclear and conventional forces throughout the world were now made ready for action, while a huge invasion force was massed in Florida: 'Our little group seated around the Cabinet table in continuous session that Saturday felt nuclear war to be closer on that day than at any time in the nuclear age.'[39] Perhaps Russia desired a war. The chiefs of staff once again recommended an air strike, to be followed by an invasion: both to occur on the Monday.[40]

On the brilliant, rather feminine suggestion of his brother, President Kennedy decided that his most promising line of action would now be to ignore the most recent of Khrushchev's letters and to reply to the penultimate one, by accepting a direct exchange of a promise not to invade Cuba for a withdrawal of the missiles.[41] The withdrawal of the missiles, however, would have to be under U.N. observation. It does not seem as if anyone considered that this was a substantial concession, for none seriously desired to invade Cuba. Robert Kennedy personally took a copy of this letter (which he and Sorensen had drafted) to the Russian ambassador in Washington and added that, unless the U.S. 'received assurances within twenty-four hours', the president would take 'military action' on 30 October.[42] An invasion of Cuba would have probably followed on that day. 'If the Russians were ready to go to nuclear war over Cuba, they were ready to go to nuclear war, and that was that,' Robert Kennedy said afterwards.[43] The Russian ambassador, however, had told Robert Kennedy that he personally thought that Khrushchev was too deeply committed to his present policy to accept Kennedy's letter. Meantime, the Cuban exiles in Miami and elsewhere

[37] Schlesinger, A Thousand Days, 708.

[38] Castro in 1964 Hoy, 2 May 1964, qu. Andrés Suárez, 70.

[39] Sorensen, 706.

[40] Robert Kennedy, The Times, 30 October 1968.

[41] Ibid., 31 October 1968. Hillsman, 223, refers to this as 'the Trollope ploy' after a scene in Barsetshire where the girl interprets a squeeze of hand as a proposal of marriage. See also Sorensen, 714, and Schlesinger, A Thousand Days, 709; Pachter, 67–8, argued that the 'first' letter had been written second but, since it was more personal and probably Khrushchev's unaided work, arrived first. Sorensen dismisses this interpretation (712, fn); Schlesinger seems to accept it.

[42] Robert Kennedy, The Times, 31 October 1968, has a longer account. He added that he thought the missiles in Turkey would anyway soon be removed though not under duress. Schlesinger, A Thousand Days, 709; Sorensen, 715.

[43] Schlesinger, A Thousand Days, 710.

all supposed that the moment of liberation of Cuba was at hand. They were, needless to say, not consulted by the Kennedys in the new plan.

While Washington slept – 'Saturday night was about the blackest of all'[44] – Russia had to react. He had 'received information', Khrushchev later told the Supreme Soviet, 'that the invasion would be carried out in the next two or three days . . . Immediate action was necessary.'[45] Despite, probably, opposition from Kozlov and perhaps Brezhnev, during the night of 27–28 October, Khrushchev confirmed that his 'first letter' contained a real plan by which he was prepared to stand. He gave immediate orders for the cessation of work on the missile sites, for their dismantlement and their return to Russia. Washington discussed the news in the early morning. Kennedy, with magnanimity, welcomed Khrushchev's 'statesmanlike decision', and discouraged any mention of 'capitulation' or 'humiliation', as well he might, since, of course, the promise not to invade Cuba was a *quid pro quo*, if a slight one so far as Russia was concerned. Castro was not consulted by Khrushchev and heard the news while talking with Guevara; he swore, kicked the wall and broke a looking glass in his fury.[46]

So ended the famous crisis over Cuba of October 1962, in the course of which the world was acutely threatened. Yet, like most dramas, this event had a muffled ending. Khrushchev, Kennedy and the world relaxed, but many North Americans and nearly all Cuban exiles thought Kennedy should have gone further, while the Cuban government and many Cubans, at least, were furious with Russia. 'They betrayed us as [they did] in Spain', was one typical reaction.[47] In a famous 'private' speech at the University, Castro accused Khrushchev of lack of *cojones* (balls) and the meeting ended with the students singing a new song,

Nikita, Nikita!	Nikita, Nikita,
Lo que se da	What you give away
No se quita.	You shouldn't take back

The notion of a private bargain between Kennedy and Khrushchev was repugnant to Castro. Publicly, Carlos Rafael Rodríguez drew parallels with Munich, and Castro himself spoke of a 'certain displeasure' after 'misunderstandings' which had arisen with Russia. Castro's own terms for ending the crisis were more elaborate: they included an end not only of the blockade, but of all harassments, raids by exiles, and overflights, as well as a U.S. withdrawal from Guantánamo. These conditions were not accepted by the U.S. In this way Castro formally avoided the conclusion of any bargain binding him. The

---

[44] *Ibid.*

[45] See Tatu, 269, for a convincing explanation of the ambiguities of this speech of 12 December.

[46] Guevara to Ricardo Rojo, in Rojo, *Che Guevara*, 130.

[47] Gilly, 54.

Russians, admittedly, dismantled the missile sites and returned both the missiles and the jet bombers to Russia, demurring, since these last were now supposed to be Cuban property. The Cuban government, however, refused to permit any U.N. observation. China backed Cuba: Khrushchev, they said, had followed his 'adventurism' by 'capitulationism'. But still, as Faustino Pérez found out in a mission to Peking in December, China could offer little in the way of credits.

Since the withdrawal of the missiles occurred without U.N. inspection, the government of the U.S. (though withdrawing the quarantine) did not in the end give a public promise never to invade Cuba. They were able to check that the Russians had indeed done what they said they would do by means of the U.2. Yet, despite their formal freedom to do so, the U.S. did not invade Cuba and it seems that, in further exchanges with Russia, they did give Russia an assurance that they had no intention of doing so. Kennedy, however, felt strong enough to promise the assembly of returned veterans from the Bay of Cochinos, on 30 December 1962, that one day a free Cuba would be restored by force of arms.

It thus seemed to many that Kennedy had gained a great victory, and even those who had doubted his wisdom during the testing time turned afterwards to felicitate him, if only for the restraint which he showed in not pressing his advantage to the point of humiliating Khrushchev or overthrowing Castro. For several years afterwards, Russian foreign policy was reserved and unadventurous. Khrushchev, it is true, also claimed a victory and told the Supreme Soviet on 12 December that socialism in Cuba had been preserved by his skill. Nevertheless, this was evidently a statement directed at the First Secretary's enemies in Russia, and it is clear that in internal Russian policy the Cuban crisis was a turning point. Khrushchev had to face serious difficulties in early 1963, and these contributed to his fall in October 1964. Against a modest gain obtained in respect of Cuba itself, Khrushchev had lost much internationally. He had lost much internally also, and from then on the 'liberal' cause in Russia and the cause of destalinization declined. This was an unexpected and unwelcome consequence of Kennedy's sternness.

Kennedy's motives in the crisis, despite the quantity of information published about them, are still not quite clear: was he perhaps not more concerned by the apparent increase in Russian power, and its political effects, or by the challenge apparently made personally and politically to his administration, than by real military considerations? He was concerned with the line which he had drawn on 4 September and 13 September between offensive and defensive missiles. Of course, he might not have made those statements if it had not been for the election campaign and the pressure of the Republicans. Once they had been made, he clearly had to act if the line was crossed, so as to avoid another humiliation over Cuba.[48] The trouble was that the Russian decision to cross the line had already been taken by the time the statements were made. Kennedy appreciated that the establishment of the missiles in Cuba would assist the Russians though, unlike McNamara, he did not seem to measure their precise significance in doubling the Russian striking force; had he done so, he might have noticed the provocative character of the U.S.'s own missile policy under his rule. Indeed, it is difficult to see why Kennedy and McNamara, having reached a point so far ahead of Russia, were not prepared for precisely this response. Many of the things said by Kennedy, as by Khrushchev, during the crisis were intended primarily for propaganda: in this way must be judged the president's allusion to the cities of Lima and Mexico as becoming within range of nuclear attack: for they were, and are, of course, within range of attack by long-range Russian missiles. Kennedy's appeal to Khrushchev to 'abandon this course of world domination' is more ambiguous; was he talking now to Khrushchev genuinely or to his own public opinion? Thus, puzzles remain.

Kennedy was admirably concerned in the crisis with details, down to the lowest level of administrative action, to ensure that the force used was no more than he had intended and that nothing might get out of control.[49] It is possible to take issue with the policy, and indeed a European might well be tempted to suppose that McNamara's policy of inaction or Stevenson's diplomatic approach would have been wiser. A less proud statesman than Kennedy might have first taken the question to Russia or Cuba, secretly, and left a public challenge to a last resort. But one can only compare Kennedy's mastery and knowledge of his resources, and the subtlety and sophistication with which he approached the 'appalling risks' which he was taking (in the words of the *New Statesman*), regardless of principles, with the hectic way in which Sir Anthony Eden conducted the Suez affair in 1956.

Kennedy acted during the crisis with restraint but afterwards used the power his restraint had given him with some freedom; for instance, he abruptly told Macmillan at Nassau that England could not have a missile of her own at U.S. expense. Europe, shortly afterwards, was admonished; Canada humiliated; and the Western Alliance has never been the same again. To save his position over Cuba, Kennedy therefore began the dismantlement of U.S. links with Europe – a dismantlement likely, under his successors, to go much further. On the other hand, the test ban treaty, implying Russian acceptance of U.S. nuclear

[48] Pachter commented (p. 13): 'Were he humiliated for a second time over Cuba, Kennedy would lose all hopes for a stable world peace'.

[49] *Cf.* Senator H. M. Jackson, *Los Angeles Times*, 29 January 1963; and *Administration of National Security*, published in 1963 by the Senate.

supremacy was one undoubted consequence of Kennedy's restraint during and after the crisis.

Kennedy's action was taken in the full understanding that despite any favourable intelligence assessments that he might have received, nuclear war might be the consequence. The chances that Russia would 'go all the way to war', he later said, seemed to him 'somewhere between one out of three and evens'.[50] McNamara, a scarcely sentimental politician, at one point wondered 'how many more sunsets he was destined to see'.[51] Other advisers to Kennedy made plans for the evacuation of the capital. Before Kennedy spoke on 22 October, all U.S. missile crews had been placed on 'maximum alert', 800 B.47 bombers were prepared, with their bomb bays closed, and dispersed, along with 550 similarly loaded B.52s and 70 B.58s (Hustlers). 90 B.52s carrying 25 to 50 megaton H-bombs were in the air over the Atlantic, while 100 Atlas, 50 Titan and 12 Minutemen ICBMs were ready on their launching pads. All missiles and bombers were also ready on land bases abroad, on aircraft carriers and on submarines. The smaller, though similar, forces available to Russia were doubtless also primed. James Reston in the *New York Times* on 23 October stated authoritatively[52] that the government would use all means necessary to force a withdrawal of the missile sites, and that if this led to Soviet retaliation such as a counter blockade of Berlin, 'the U.S. is prepared to risk a major war to defend its present position'.[53] Nervous jokes about the chances of survival were recorded by members of the U.S. administration as by most ordinary men; Robert Kennedy spoke of the possible 'end of mankind'.[54] Cuban reactions were apparently not dissimilar: Guevara was busy writing an article which (published posthumously six years later) evidently took the question of nuclear war in its stride: 'What we affirm is that we must proceed along the path of liberation even if this costs millions of atomic victims'; he envisaged the Cuban people 'advancing fearlessly towards the hecatomb which signifies final redemption'.[55]

[50] Sorensen, 705. He evidently repeated this assessment to several people, as the author learned at the time.

[51] Abel, 201.

[52] 'On the highest authority' was his source. No doubt this was Kennedy himself.

[53] *New York Times*, 23 October 1962, 1. All major commands were in a state of 'DEFCON 2', the symbol for the last step short of DEFCON 1, war. *Cf. Newsweek*, 28 October 1963.

[54] Robert Kennedy, *Times*, 27 October 1968.

[55] *Verde Olivo*, 6 October 1968. It would seem that it was Castro's apparent willingness to take the risk of possible nuclear war that so greatly impressed Guevara and is the explanation of his otherwise somewhat mysterious comment in his letter to Castro of 1965: 'At your side I have felt the pride of belonging to our people during those radiant yet sad days of the Caribbean crisis. Not often has a statesman acted more brilliantly than you did during those days and I am also proud of having followed you unhesitatingly ...'

The Cuban missile crisis, or the Caribbean crisis, as it has been called by the Cubans, brought to an end exactly two hundred years of often intimate relations between North America and Cuba. At first, from the time of the English expedition until the end of the Napoleonic Wars, Anglo-Saxon businessmen sought commerce in Havana. From the 1820s until the 1890s, far-sighted North Americans supposed that in the long run Cuba would follow Texas, California and New Mexico, into the Union. Between the 1890s and 1962, the Government of the U.S. had, for a variety of political, strategic and economic reasons, regarded the complexion of the Cuban administration as ultimately her affair. But in 1962, President Kennedy, though gaining a propaganda victory over Cuba's new ally, Russia, acquiesced in the *fait accompli* of a Cuban nationalist Communist regime which had been constructed out of, and driven by, virulent hostility towards the U.S. and her part in two hundred years of Cuban history. Was this acquiescence caused by the fact that U.S. economic and even strategic interests in Cuba were slighter than they once had been; that a stagnant Cuban sugar industry was becoming more and more a Cuban concern in the 1940s and 1950s, while nuclear weapons were rendering archaic U.S. preoccupations with the Caribbean and the approach to the Panamá Canal (and indeed the Panamá Canal itself)? At all events, the crisis of 1962, the most severe one in the history of the world, was certainly primarily a matter of prestige, propaganda, and politics, rather than a test of economic and strategic interests.

In 1962 Cuba had a newly established and still somewhat unstable totalitarian government, which controlled all the heavy industry and two-thirds of the agriculture of the country. The economy was in a state of great confusion and civil liberties as understood in North America and Western Europe were non-existent. Most Cubans who believed in the liberal virtues were either in gaol or in exile. But the Cuban Government was nevertheless popular among the masses, either because they admired what the Government had already done, because they coveted what it was promising them for the future or simply because they were spellbound by Castro. It was natural that President Kennedy and his circle, reared in the lap of a supremely self-confident and successful society, should find Castro's arbitrary, inefficient, often cruel and always rhetorical regime utterly intolerable. But Castro had created in Cuba a system which was deliberately the very opposite of everything which the U.S. stood for, or at least of what he thought the U.S. stood for. If there is to be blame for 'what happened in Cuba', the fault lay at least as much in Washington and New York as in Havana or Santiago. Some years later, a historian from North America remarked complacently, 'If our performance in Cuba had been flawless, it might still have proved futile because of Cuban unwisdom'.[56] True, no doubt, but there was such a long record of North American unwisdom in Cuba as to render the comment absurd; leaving aside matters of recent history, during the second Batistato, it is obvious that the recognition of Grau San Martín by Roosevelt in 1933 would have saved Roosevelt's heirs no end of trouble. The folly of the Platt Amendment was made clear by Senator Foraker before it was made law.[57] The dispatch of General Crowder to Havana in 1921 without consultation with the Cuban Government was an act with few parallels even in the history of British imperial relations with the decrepit Moguls of Delhi. It would also have been better if General Leonard Wood had kept his scorn for the Latin race as a whole to himself and if both he and General Crowder had brought themselves to learn a little Spanish. Indeed, it is still difficult not to believe that if the U.S. were going to exert the sort of political control over Cuba that they did between 1902 and 1933, it would have been better if they had taken over the island altogether.

Had the crisis of 1962 turned into the Third World War, as indeed it might have done, these matters would perhaps already be being analysed by those historians who would have survived it. Some, no doubt, would quite ignore the role of Cuba in the development of the drama of 1962. Others might regard the crisis as the final showdown between the Anglo-Saxon and Latin races, with Cuba an appropriate firing point of a most destructive international conflict. It is indeed in some ways fitting that Cuba, for so long the victim of the policies of the great rich powers and their sugar-eating populaces, should have one day almost got her own back and threatened to drag the great powers down with her. In the end, however, both Cubas were in 1962 deceived: Kennedy did not liberate the island from Castro and Khrushchev took away the missiles. Small powers can often begin a world crisis, great powers always end them.

[56] Henry Wriston, in John Plank, *Cuba and the U.S.*
[57] See *Cuba: The Pursuit of Freedom*, p. 453.

Epilogue

'At first sight, a very correct country.'
MAYAKOVSKY, ON A VISIT TO CUBA IN 1924.

NOTE TO EPILOGUE

Events in Cuba since 1962

1963	April–May	Castro's first visit to Russia
		Change back to emphasis on sugar
	October	Second Agrarian Reform
	November	Compulsory Military Service
1964	January	Castro's second visit to Russia
		Russo–Cuban sugar agreement
		Leyland bus agreement
	March	Trial of Marcos Armando Rodríguez
	November	Havana conference of Latin American Communists
	December	Attempted suicide of Martínez Sánchez
	December–March (1965)	Guevara's tour of Afro-Asian countries
1965	March	Castro's attack on Sino–Soviet dispute
		Guevara disappears
		Drive against homosexuality in the University
	April	Civil war in Santo Domingo
	June	Castro's speech emphasizing agriculture
	October	Formation of Cuban Communist party and central committee
		Gromyko's visit to Cuba
		Renewal of emigration to the U.S.A. at first by boat then by air
1966	January	Tricontinental conference
		Formation of AALAPSO
	February	Castro's row with China
	March	Cubela case
		Quarrel between Venezuelan communists and guerrillas
1967	January	Publication of Debray's *Revolution in the Revolution*
	June	Kosygin's visit to Havana
	August	OLAS conference Havana supports armed struggle
	October	Guevara killed Bolivia
1968	February	Escalante and microfaction trial
	March	Revolutionary offensive closes 50,000 small businesses
	October	Padilla Case
1969	July	Opening of the ten million ton harvest.

CHAPTER 46

The Utopians

The purpose of the Revolution in Cuba was put most clearly by Guevara: 'we are seeking something new which will permit a perfect identification between the government and the community as a whole, adapted to the special needs of socialism and avoiding to the utmost the commonplaces of bourgeois democracy (such as houses of parliament) ... We have been greatly restrained by the fear that any formalization might make us lose sight of the ultimate and most important revolutionary aspiration: to see man freed from alienation.'[1]

These designs were admittedly not mentioned as being the purpose of the Revolution in the late 1950s or even in the early 1960s, but no one should be surprised that the policies of revolutionary governments, like those of more orthodox administrations, should change. The reason why these radical plans came to dominate the Revolution has been discussed earlier. They are ambitious, if not entirely new, schemes, and, since ten years is a short time to judge a social upheaval such as that caused by the Revolution in Cuba, it would scarcely seem odd if they have not yet been achieved. Nor are they self-evidently correct: Guevara's contempt for bourgeois democracy seems to be obsessive; his use of the word 'socialism' suggests a single body of revealed truth, whereas by now it should be obvious that there are as many types of, as there are roads to, that dogma. Nor is the word 'alienation' free from ambiguity, particularly when many of those held to be alienated are agricultural rather than city workers. Nevertheless, it is legitimate now to ask to what extent these grand plans have been realized in the years since the missile crisis of 1962, and how far they are likely to be achieved in the immediate future. Perhaps the extent of their fulfilment so far will throw light not only on their validity as a programme but also on their wisdom and justice.

Since 1962 many changes have occurred in the health, education, and in the way of living and thinking of the whole population in Cuba; and a large new bureaucracy and political movement have been constructed to persuade, cajole and, on occasion, force the people to carry out the policies which are expected to further and to finance the social

---

[1] Guevara, *El socialismo y el hombre en Cuba*, Havana, Ediciones R, 1965. This essay has often been reprinted and translated.

changes: for it is certainly not yet possible to identify government and community completely, despite the fact that there is virtually no work other than for the community and despite propaganda which persuades many people that they are living an epic and are, if not always materially better off, at least much more virtuous than they were before.

Cubans now probably all have enough to eat, but only just enough. The strict rationing means that cereals, sugar and fats provide two-thirds of the calories in most people's diet: in 1964, a Czech economist, Selucky, thought that the Cubans received about 'the same quantity of fats, oils, rice, beans, sugar and beef as we got in the last years of the war'[2] – and the year 1964 was a better time than five years later. The queues for items temporarily off the ration (such as – in early 1969 – bread) and outside restaurants suggest that most people would like to eat much more than they do. The distribution of food has been erratic. Still, few die of malnutrition and, in the country, particularly in Oriente province, the very poor peasants must be fed better and more regularly than before the revolution: and nearly everyone has better meals than they did during the terrible years of the depression which lasted so long in Cuba.[3]

Two qualifications must be made: first, high officials, foreign technicians (not to speak of foreign visitors) and all persons in power are able to live better than ordinary people; they have the right to go to special shops where goods can actually be bought. There may be no discrimination against Negroes in the old grand hotels, but none save the powerful get, for instance, into *La Torre*, a restaurant in Havana where there is always excellent food. Most of the leaders of the Revolution seem quite austere and simple men but many officials have not been able to resist the pleasures of power, and enjoy themselves. It should also be recalled that during the twentieth, and indeed the nineteenth, century, Cuba was not a country of famine (nor, since 1900, of plague). For this reason, as for many others, Cuba in the past resembled an unequally developed province of a rich country, a West Virginia, more than a typical part of the under-developed or third world.

The shortages have an effect on the quality of life for all but the highest officials. When the day's work is over, much time has to be spent on queueing for food and other essentials. Militia or other voluntary service for the state also occupies time. It must be said that the Cubans,

---

[2] Radoslav Selucky, Spotlight on Cuba, *East Europe*, v. 13, No. 10, October 1964, quoted Mesa-Lago, *Labour Sector and Socialist Distribution in Cuba*, p. 159.

[3] Rationing seems (1969/1970) to be: *meat*, ¾ pound a week in Havana, ½ pound outside *fish*, ¼ pound a week; *butter*, 2 ounces a month; *eggs*, 3 a week; *coffee*, 1½ ounces a week; *bread* 4 ounces a day; *rice*, 3 pounds a month; *sugar*, 6 pounds a month; *cooking oil*, 12 ounces month; *chicken*, offered only to minors or aged on production of a medical certificate. Othe items such as *clothes* (two pairs of trousers and one shirt a year) and *toothpaste* (one tube month per family) are also rationed.

who are by nature cheerful, seem to accept these things with remarkably good grace, even if they criticize them.

The strict rationing is caused by, first, the absence of the large amount of food imported before 1960 from the U.S.; second, the decline in agricultural production in the early years of the Revolution[4]; and third, the very high percentage – perhaps 30% to 35% – of the national production which is 'saved or invested'.[5] Most traditional Cuban products, such as fruit, vegetables and beef, are shipped off to East Europe and Russia to help pay for Cuba's debts in those countries. Efforts to get the Cubans to change their traditional diets – to eat more fish, for example – have not been very successful. Cubans with memories therefore must recall with cynicism Castro's promise, when food began to be short in November 1960: 'Remember what I am telling you! The foodstuffs which will be available once more by December will never disappear again.'[6] The provision of a network of ice cream restaurants with fifty-four flavours scarcely compensates for the disappearance of regular square meals. Other consumer goods such as minor pharmaceutical or stationery articles are also lacking.

To balance this, unemployment has undoubtedly fallen, despite the new use in the economy of many once housebound women and girls. This is partly because of the emigration of such a large percentage of the population[7]; partly because of the drift to the cities during the first years of the Revolution, in particular to government, party agencies and the armed forces[8]; and partly because of the increase in the number of children who go to school or colleges. The gangs of children hanging around doing nothing, which was such a characteristic of old Cuba, have almost disappeared, except in parts of Havana, along with the 'dead season'. Many former sugar cane cutters have been absorbed in one capacity or another in 'revolutionary tasks' in the ministries or on

[4] Recent figures are not conclusive, but FAO statistics up to 1965 suggest a per capita decline in agricultural production since 1958 of 31% (FAO *Monthly Bulletin of Statistics*, April 1965 pp. 17–20). Since 1965 agricultural production has doubtless increased but not for the benefit of the consumer.

[5] Estimate of Wassily Leontief, 'A Visit to Cuba', *New York Review of Books*, 21 August 1969.

[6] *Obra Revolucionaria* no. 28, 9 November 1960.

[7] See below, p. 708.

[8] It is difficult to know for certain what this rural population which drifted into the cities actually did. Goldenberg (who left Cuba in July 1960) thought that 'many factories employed more workers than they really needed; the civil service was greatly inflated; there were many ways of getting a state scholarship to some school or other; although militia service was unpaid for, it was sometimes possible to live on it; finally the system of *botellas* had reappeared' (Goldenberg, 260). *Bohemia* (2 March 1962) commented 'Cuba has a sector called supplementary reserve. Here we have thousands of men and women who do nothing except receive a salary from the state . . . They sit at home and wait till they can collect their cheque at the end of the month. Many would like to do something with their time, others fill their heads with bad ideas.'

the state farms, which have been too inefficient to organize their workers economically. There has even been a shortage of skilled labour, particularly in the sugar industry. But observation suggests that there is substantial underemployment even in sugar mills. This may increase if the present programme of mechanization is successful. It also seems that the 'revolutionary offensive' of 1968[9] which closed so many small businesses, from bars to fruit-sellers, must have led to much unemployment, particularly in Havana and among both the owners of, and workers in, the many surviving small factories and workshops (*chinchales*), employing two or three people, and shops, even though emigration has accounted for some of them.

The Revolution has in many ways improved Cuban health. The general teaching hospitals, the specialist hospitals and the specialist institutes are well maintained by a new generation of Cuban doctors with 'a high level of understanding and ability'.[10] Everywhere there has been a marked increase in hygiene and sanitation. The availability of medicine has been much more fairly spread throughout the country. Preventive medicine has been much emphasized and many clinics have been established in rural areas. Deaths from tuberculosis, malaria and typhoid have been much reduced and as elsewhere polio seems to have been eliminated by mass vaccination. One admirable achievement is the Mazorra lunatic asylum, imaginatively directed by Doctor Bernabé Ordaz, once an establishment of nightmares, today serene – it has become deservedly a part of every approved tour of the country for foreign visitors.[11] On the other hand, doctors, though now slightly more numerous than in the past, have probably been less well trained.[12] Some of the best doctors in Cuba have emigrated. Medicine and other equipment has often been lacking or irregularly supplied, since most of it comes from Russia or East Europe. Prejudice, masquerading as ideology, has perhaps sometimes hampered the best treatment: one doctor in Santiago refused to use North American equipment on Cuban patients even if he had none other.[13] Nurses and dentists remain short. Gastroentiritis, syphilis and hepatitis seem to have increased recently.

[9] See below, p. 669.

[10] The comment of Dr David Spain, director of the department of pathology at Brookland Hospital Centre, Brooklyn, qu. Leo Huberman and Paul Sweezy, Socialism in Cuba, *Monthly Review Press*, New York, 1969, 58.

[11] I could not help wondering, during a visit to the asylum in 1969, how many of the well-kept patients whom I saw were there in direct or indirect consequence of political events since 1959.

[12] There are now about 8,000 doctors in Cuba, in comparison with 7,200 in 1958. Of these about 2,500 left Cuba between 1959 and 1965, and they are still leaving at the rate of four a month. See Willis Butler, 'Cuba's Revolutionary Medicine,' *Ramparts*, May 1969. Taking into account the increase in population, doctors per head probably number much the same as in 1958.

[13] To the author, in 1961, admittedly a tense time.

Infant mortality, at forty per thousand live births seems at the very least to have remained static and, if still low in comparison with the rest of Latin America, remains higher than for most of the Caribbean and is almost double that of the U.S. and Western Europe.[14]

Cuba has no population policy and no worries about population. Her growth rate, at about 2·7%, is lower than that of most of her neighbours and, as Castro himself suggested, Cuba could, if her economy were well organized, feed a population three times her present size. On the other hand, Cuba's food production since 1959 has not kept pace with the population increase and the annual rate of population increase is going up. Her present density of population of about seventy per square kilometre is thus likely to be double that within thirty years or less. That will bring her not far short of the congestion on the smaller Caribbean islands. There are admittedly birth control clinics in most large Cuban hospitals and the *anillo*, a variety of intra-uterine loop, is offered free to all women after their first child (if they are in hospital, which most now are) but, despite advertisements drawing attention to this service, it does not seem to be much used, probably because of male opposition on the grounds that it would make infidelity easier. In these important respects, therefore, socialist Cuba is rather less 'revolutionary' than, say, capitalist Japan, which halved its birth rate in ten years between 1947 and 1957.

Education in Cuba has undergone a rebirth since the Revolution, though some qualifications are necessary. In numbers, the changes seem immensely beneficial: half the children of primary school age had no education before 1959. Today they all receive some teaching, so that primary schools have nearly 1½ million pupils instead of 720,000 in 1958. There are 50,000 primary school teachers in place of scarcely 17,000 before 1958. A much bigger percentage of children also go as state scholars (*becados*) to secondary schools than in the past – about 180,000 out of 400,000 of the appropriate age group; while, since 1967, nearly all infants go to kindergarten (*círculos infantiles*) from their 45th day onwards under the administration of an old Communist, Clementina Serra. In 1964–5 the Ministry of Education reported an enrolment in adult education of 484,000.[15]

Many children, however, are taken away from home to go to the secondary boarding schools against their wills, and all teaching is

[14] The figure of 40 per thousand was given in a speech by the Minister of Health, Helidoro Martínez Junco, at the close of the first national forum for paediatric standards, November 1969 (*Granma*, 23 November 1969). Government investment in health, though evidently high, is hard to estimate, given the ambiguous value of money. Thus, on paper, the Government spent ten times in 1967 what was spent ten years before ($M260 in place of $M20) but this takes no account of what was spent on private medicine in the past nor of the complete and incalculable change in the value of money.

[15] Leo Huberman, 'A Revolution Revisited' *Nation*, 2 August, 1965.

carried out under the shadow of the regime's slogan for youth – *Estudio, Trabajo, Fusil* (Study, Work, the Rifle). Children from six years upwards have to play a part in 'productive labour' in some branch of agriculture during the week-ends and in the holidays, as a part of 'socialist education'. From the names of schools to the examples given in learning grammar, much attention is paid to revolutionary heroes, in particular to Guevara, the model revolutionary without fear and above reproach. Religion, of course, plays no part. There also remain serious shortages of books, of teachers and of school rooms, so much so that, as the Minister of Education, José Llanusa, explained in 1968, these shortcomings probably would not be overcome until 1980. Finally, the content of education in revolutionary Cuba seems, despite a veneer of modernity, to be old-fashioned: there is learning by rote, and rules and examples; while the emphasis given to physical fitness in recent years (particularly under Llanusa, a former national director of Cuban tourism and of sports) is curiously reminiscent of the English public school, the 'team spirit' being, in Cuba as in Wessex, a good corrective to suspect 'intellectualism' and the spirit of inquiry. Also, as a North American favourable to the Revolution remarked, 'Pictures, slogans, the names given to state farms . . . all teach young Cubans to think of their lives as intimately related to Revolution elsewhere:'[16] an imperial education through the looking-glass.

These qualifications apply even more strongly to higher education. At first sight, the achievements have been remarkable. There were 30,000 technical school pupils and 40,000 full-time students in 1969, compared with 6,250 and 25,000 respectively in 1958 and, if the increase of university places has been relatively slight, it is obviously salutary in an agricultural country to increase technical education at the cost of law students and historians. There have also been some magnificent achievements, such as Ricardo Porro's splendid if unfinished school of Fine Arts in the old Country Club golf course.[17] On the other hand, all students have to take a year's course in dialectical materialism; spend fifteen days a year in a military camp; play their part, like school children, during the vacations, in 'productive labour'; and serve a number of hours a week in the militia. Most available textbooks are direct translations of Russian texts. The teaching in some departments is mostly done by last year students. University autonomy has come to an end and, though students nominally participate in the running of the institutions in which they work, these are in all important respects tied to the needs of the economy, not the desires of the student. The Communist

---

[16] Elizabeth Sutherland, *The Youngest Revolution, a Personal Report on Cuba*, New York, 1969, p. 59.

[17] Porro afterwards went into exile, in Paris.

Party of Cuba, here as in other sections of society, plays the decisive part: for instance, it was certainly not spontaneous disgust but national politics that caused a national assembly of students in 1967 to insist that homosexuals should publicly confess their shortcomings,[18] and in 1965 to demand a purge of all students suspected of a lack of enthusiasm for the Revolution.[19]

Long-term prospects for the Universities in Cuba are scarcely encouraging. After observing in December 1966 that university students had less 'revolutionary consciousness' than middle-grade agronomists, Castro denounced 'the wall of theory and abstractionism', and two years later, in December 1968, was found looking forward to a time when all Cuban universities could be abolished, since only a few exceptional activities would then require higher studies. Normal education would always include technical education in the last years and most people would then enter agriculture or industry as trained technicians: 'in future, practically every factory, every agricultural zone, every hospital, every school will be a university'; and, it might be added, looking at the children marching to meals in military formation, and at the proliferation of uniforms (grey shirts and green trousers for secondary school pupils – becados, pink shirts and blue trousers for girls doing domestic or technical training), every school a regiment.

Already there have been a number of minor troubles in the university: some students have disliked the undemocratic organization of the students' union, the compulsory militia service, the occasional unequal treatment of men and women, the forty-five days of agricultural work and the disapproval of tight trousers and miniskirts. The possibility of active dissent is, of course, closed, and Llanusa has told students 'we shall not have a Czechoslovakia here'.[20]

The revolutionary regime, needing the labour and the enthusiasm of the young, has given them in return benefits and rewards. The proportion of the population below fifteen years old must be close to the world average of 45%. Visitor after visitor to Cuba marvels at young Cubans' dedication, vitality and sense of responsibility at an early age. The Isle of Pines was in 1966 renamed the Isle of Youth, and became the centre for experimental agriculture carried out without pay and without expenses by an ever increasing number of Cubans from the age of twelve

[18] See below, p.657. According to one account to me, one student was expelled from the University on this occasion on the ground that he had not lifted up his hand to vote with the majority.

[19] See an account by C. K. McClatchy, Cuba Revisited, 1967, McClatchy Newspapers, Sacramento, California. McClatchy was told by one student that only devoted revolutionaries should be permitted to get a university education, regardless of academic ability.

[20] The Ministry of Education at one point decreed that skirts should be two inches above the knee.

to twenty-seven.[21] Will this new generation be ready in the future to hand over the torch to fresh generations? Or will, as happened with the first generation of Komsomol enthusiasts in Russia and East Europe, the present generation of youth leaders turn with the passing of the years into apparatchiks, suspicious of new changes, the 'conservative' target therefore for criticism or hatred by a new wave of 'liberals', 'abstractionists', or 'humanists'?

The latter eventuality is surely the more probable, as is suggested by a 'hippie' cult and its repression in late 1968, and from the high percentage of young people among criminals in the crime wave of 1968–9[22] and among those who would clearly like to leave Cuba but cannot do so except illegally.[23] Unless the community and the government are indeed one by that time, more and more people in future will regard with scepticism Castro's paternalistic dictum 'Work is Youth's best pedagogue' and begin to question the theory that 'taking part in agricultural tasks will not only deepen the revolutionary conscience of the young but will serve to give them new human values'. Indoctrination is 'a double-edged sword'.[24] After Savanarola, the Medicis returned; and, in the end many people, perhaps most people usually come round to the view that private ease and entertainment are worth more than all the creeds in the world and that scepticism is more productive than enthusiasm.

The Revolution's treatment of health and education gives several hints as to the real character of this regime: we see dedicated men working with bad equipment, children evidently enjoying themselves marching to the adult sound of trumpets, uniformity parading as patriotism. But nothing is quite as clear cut as it sounds in the speech, say, of a Cuban delegate to UNESCO. Such ambiguity also appears when the status under the Revolution of both women and of Negroes is considered.

'The true feminine struggle,' a Cuban girl in her late twenties told Elizabeth Sutherland, an astute North American observer, 'is the rejection of all those childhood teachings, all those family pressures during

---

[21] For a description see (inter alia) James Higgins, 'The New Men of Cuba', Nation, 12 February 1968. The Isle of Youth now has a population of perhaps 50,000 in place of 8,000 in 1953. It is a kind of permanent summer camp for voluntary workers, with all essentials provided free.

[22] See below, page 683.

[23] At present no young man between 14 and 28 – that is, potentially of a military age, is permitted to apply for an exit visa to emigrate from Cuba. The most famous escapee to get round the law in recent years was Armando Socorrás Ramírez who, aged 22, successfully stowed away in June 1969 in the wheel carriage of a jet aircraft travelling between Havana and Madrid; the youngest, Rafael Sánchez Reinel, who swam to the U.S. base at Guantánamo aged 13.

[24] Remark by Josué León Fuentes, a graduate of the Casa Blanca secondary school, Havana, who later went into exile (Paul Bethel, Terror and Resistance in Communist Cuba, Citizens' Committee for a Free Cuba, 1964, 20).

adolescence and even the dominant social thinking which affects her as an adult . . . the ideal of femininity, of womanhood, as meaning the dedication of one's life to finding and keeping a companion, generally at the price of being his satellite.'[25] Though this battle is not yet over, the role of women has certainly much changed since the Revolution. First, the family has altered considerably. Civil marriages are free (held in marriage palaces, on the Russian model, such as that in Havana in the old building of the Spanish Club) and honeymoon couples get reduced rates and priority treatment at what used to be smart hotels at beaches or in the country.[26] Children are encouraged to go to kindergartens from very early in their lives, so leaving women free for 'productive work'. The consequence has been that, whereas before 1959 women were only exceptionally involved in agriculture (as, for example, in the cane-fields of Pinar del Río) in the late 1960s much of the coffee-planting, particularly in Havana province, was done by women, and women have also directed cane collection centres.[27] In late 1967, the Labour Minister Jorge Risquet (an old Communist who had been education officer in Raúl Castro's column in the Sierra Cristal) explained that in future 'the chief task of women will be to replace in the factories those workers who have gone off (voluntarily) to the sugar harvest'. An injunction by the Cuban Federation of Women, at the time of Castro's destruction of small businesses, adjured women to maintain a 'militant combative attitude everywhere: at home, at school, in the neighbourhood, at work, in recreation centres, in shopping queues and on buses'[28]: an indication of the large number of activities with which women are supposed to be able to juggle. Certainly, women played a large part in the Committees for the Defence of the Revolution. The proportion of girls among university students has increased, girls have taken over as traffic police in Havana, while the sewing schools and other handicraft courses of peasant girls have doubtless been genuinely revolutionary in their effects.

On the other hand, the goal of incorporating a million women into economic activity will probably not be reached by 1970. The new independence of women has not always commended itself to men, however radical they may otherwise be, and women have evidently borne the brunt of rationing and shortages of ordinary goods, from clothes to soap. They often now work as well as keep house. Even in 1962 women were noticeably more hostile than men to the revolution,[29]

[25] Sutherland, p. 90.
[26] They also seem to be virtually compulsory for those living together in consentual unions.
[27] *Bohemia* of 29 March 1968 described a cane collection centre run by women as a 'tribute to the revolutionary activity of womankind'.
[28] *Granma* weekly edition 20 March 1968.
[29] Zeitlin, pp. 126–7.

and probably over half of those who have gone into exile since 1959 have been women. Women have not really been prominent in politics[30] and it is possible to doubt whether they have truly been happier with their publicly committed status in modern Cuba than they were in the past. The cult of virility or *machismo*, may have almost vanished, along with prostitution (and sexual habits have somewhat changed too) but in most Cuban households in the past women in fact reigned supreme. Outside the house men rode about in Oldsmobiles or Buicks with machine guns, became gangsters, spoke of Liberty and Destiny, frequented bars, brothels and casinos, but perhaps that was all only theatre and in real life women ruled. Now the gap between reality and imagination has closed but possibly real feminine power is less, given that in personal relations Cubans still seem conservative: thus, though both marriage and divorce have much increased, in 1967 a survey in *Juventud Rebelde* suggested that 50% even of *habaneros* thought virginity a prerequisite to marriage.

As with women, so with Negroes: if material conditions are alone considered, at first sight both Negroes and mulattoes must be better off in Cuba today than before the Revolution. The provision of title deeds to squatters, the increase of attractive rural housing, the illiteracy campaign, the increase of education, sanitation, hygiene and health in the countryside (particularly in Oriente province) must have benefited Negroes and mulattoes in particular. In 1962, in the last reasonably independent survey of opinion made in Cuba, the North American sociologist Maurice Zeitlin found that 80% of Negroes were wholly in favour of the Revolution, as opposed to 67% whites.[31] Perhaps many Negroes still see Castro as a kind of national *santero* in an Afro–Cuban ritual, the strong man who is exorcising evil (many had the same view of Batista and Machado). Yet some Negroes suffer from greater self-consciousness now and the Afro–Cuban fiestas, symbols of continuing separate loyalties, have, because of the difficulty of getting cocks and other items necessary, became less frequent. Yet they survive, whites attending as in the past, and doubtless *santería* and *ñáñigo* will outlive Castro as they have outlived other captains-general of Cuba[32]: 'Abakuá will last in Cuba as long as there are drums'.[33] In addition, older racial

[30] Out of 100 central committee (or central committee commissions and politburo) members in 1965, five only were women, and of these, four must have owed their importance to their proximity to male leaders of the revolution – Celia Sánchez being Castro's secretary since the Sierra Maestra, Elena Gil being secretary to Dorticós, Vilma Espín (President of the Federation of Women) being wife to Raúl Castro and Haydée Santamaría being wife to Armando Hart, the party's Secretary of Organization. The other woman, Clementina Serra, an old Communist, is Director-General of Infant schools.

[31] Zeitlin, *Revolutionary Politics and the Cuban working class*, Princeton, 1967, p. 77.

[32] See my article on a Congolese *fiesta de palo* in January 1969 (*The Times* 1 March 1969).

[33] '*Hay abakuá pa rato! Habrá abakuá mientras haya tambor*', said in 1959 the Cuban composer Ignacio Pineiro.

prejudices and habits, attitudes of subservience by Negroes as of arrogance by whites, seem to continue. Neither Marx nor Martí, the two prophets of the Revolution, understood race as it is apprehended in the second half of the twentieth century, and the works of neither seem adequate to resolve the anxieties that evidently characterise Cubans as well as other 'Afro–Americans': are they to support assimilation or integration, hispanization or assertion of Africa, and will old myths (of black sexual superiority, for instance) disappear, along with blond dolls?[34]

All these issues were brought into the domain of controversy by a black Cuban communist, Carlos Moore, in a famous article in *Présence Africaine*, a Paris Maoist journal, in 1965. He argued that the Cuban revolution was simply a victory of the white national bourgeoisie, that prejudice continued, that the size of the Negro population in Cuba continued to be falsified in statistics, along with the contribution of Negroes to the history of Cuba, and that Cuban Negroes played no greater part in Cuban politics than they had before 1958 – if anything less.[35] It is true that only a tenth of the central committee of the Cuban Communist party as constituted in 1965 seems to have black blood, and that the regime has evidently laboured its tolerance towards Negro susceptibilities in order to contrast itself with North American practice (Castro, it will be remembered, never mentioned the Negro question in any speech or statement of intentions before he came to power). The advantages gained by the Cuban Negroes since 1959 at Castro's hands have certainly been less far-reaching than those obtained in the last ten years of Spanish colonial rule by mulatto publicists such as Juan Gualberto Gómez or Martín Morúa Delgado.

It is possible that Castro's overt support for the black power movement in the U.S. (particularly since the visit of Stokely Carmichael to Havana in 1967) will cause difficulties in Cuba itself. Thus Walterio Carbonell, a Negro Communist who, in 1953, defended Castro's policies against the orthodox Communist Party in Cuba, has already spent some time in a camp of rehabilitation[36] on the ground that his folkloric investigations had racist overtones. Some exiled North American Negro militants from Robert Williams to the Black Panthers have

[34] See an excellent chapter by Elizabeth Sutherland, *The Youngest Revolution*, pp. 62–78. Jan Carew, a Guyanan, asked in 1963 a Negro from Oriente 'what it's like to be a Negro in revolutionary Cuba', to receive the answer 'we are still black and a minority and the Revolution does not invent soap to wash you white . . . they free us on paper but there is a lot of separateness in our lives still . . . and we're not like the Yankee Negro, we're not trying to be like the white Cuban . . . the white Cuban is one of the most boring human beings God ever made, they're heroic . . . they will defy the white world and you will applaud them and admire them but you'll never like them . . . I wouldn't want [my daughter] to get involved with one of those dull sanctimonious bearded white idiots' (*Topolski's Chronicle*, vol. XI, Nos. 17–20, 1963).
[35] Carlos Moore, *Présence Africaine*, October 1965.
[36] See below, p. 685.

encountered what they have taken to be prejudice,[37] and several counter-revolutionary guerrilla leaders, such as 'Cara Linda' and 'Machetero', were Negroes.

Cuba is still, of course, the largest and most populous of the islands of the Caribbean, even though, for reasons of language, the Revolution has had little effect upon the English, French and Dutch islands and only a limited effect on Puerto Rico (save, perhaps, for the contra-productive one of the arrival there of some 15,000 Cuban exiles). Castro has affirmed Cuba's cultural Spanish and Spanish–American links, rather than her economic Caribbean ones and in many respects the Cuban Revolution is primarily cultural. Yet in the long run it is hard to see how any of the islands of the Antilles can ever achieve political freedom unless they do so in common with each other, and here the black and African tradition in Cuba is certain to be the most resilient, in contrast with the endless rhetoric of the Spanish-American revolutionary heritage.

Social revolution as complete as that which has occurred in Cuba usually frees people from many crusty habits, however little that may have been the original aim of the social reformers. But Cuba was always one of the freest places so far as sex was concerned and the Revolution has had a strong puritanical element. The consequence has therefore been ambiguous.

Thus as before 1959 *posadas*, or *casas non-sanctas*, for brief encounters at a modest cost, continue despite attempts to suppress them in the first, liberal years of the Revolution.[38] There is evidently in Cuba, in consequence of the Revolution, an inquisitive mood of experiment affecting all sides of personal and family behaviour – with one qualification: the experimenters must be heterosexual. Homosexuals have been less favoured; and there is no reason to suppose that the Cuban homosexual population is any less than in the rest of the world, indeed under persecution it may be growing.[39] In 1965, a national campaign was

---

[37] Carlos Moore was Williams' interpreter. Williams, after several years of exile in Cuba (where he ran a radio station named Radio Free Dixie), went to China and from there denounced the Cuban Revolution in his newsheet, *Crusader*: 'The Negro is becoming again a pathetic victim to race prejudice and discrimination . . . Afro–Cubans are beginning to feel the pinch of subtle but fast returning racism' (*Crusader*, Vol. 8 No. 43, March 1967). Later, he argued that the Cuban counter-espionage police (G2) was infiltrated by the CIA (*Ibid*, May 1967). Williams wrote a long letter to Castro in August 1966 complaining of his treatment. In mid 1969, the Black Panthers, including Eldridge Cleaver, in Havana, were encountering difficulties and even arrests. (*See International Herald Tribune*, 26 June 1969.)

[38] In the first months of the Revolution César Blanco, an ex-Lutheran minister, chief of public order to the first Minister of the Interior, used to go to *posadas* in Havana and surround them with lights and loudspeakers. He would then announce on the latter, 'You have five minutes from now to abandon these vicious antics'. But this period of puritanism did not last and the *posadas* were nationalized by Llanusa when director of tourism. Blanco left Cuba for the U.S. in October 1960.

[39] See José Yglesias, Cuban Report: their hippies, their squares, *New York Times Magazine*, 12 January 1969.

launched against this minority, homosexuality being declared incompatible with revolutionary attitudes. Several prominent homosexuals lost their jobs, in, for instance, the film institute ICAIC, and in the university they were made to confess publicly their 'vices', were expelled from their courses and in some cases dispatched to work on the land. Though this disagreeable campaign was afterwards abandoned – on Castro's initiative, it was said, though the whole affair could not have been begun without his encouragement – an English writer could still find in 1968 a boy who, believing that he was homosexual, wished that he had died at birth, since in Cuba 'homosexuals are regarded as worse than beasts'.[40]

The regime has other phobias. Thus, after various attacks in earlier years of the Revolution on those who sought a soft life, Castro, on 28 September 1968, in a speech commemorating the 8th anniversary of the foundation of the Committees for the Defence of the Revolution, denounced young Cubans who had taken to living in an 'extravagant manner': long hair and fancy clothes, he said, spelled moral degeneracy and would ultimately lead to political and economic sabotage. A week later, a well-known commentator, Guido García Inclan, denounced not only exotic clothes and long hair but those who played guitars, smoked marijuana and 'danced madly to epileptic music'. These were the sort of people who 'hung about listening to imperialist jukeboxes' in small bars but (after so many of these had been closed) were now organizing themselves in 'bands of schizophrenics' with names like 'los Beats' or 'los Chicos Melenudos' (the long-haired boys), with special initiation ceremonies and oaths of loyalty. This had led to such 'incredible acts' as the desecration of the national flag and of portraits of Guevara. There followed mass shavings of long-haired men and the departure of miniskirted girls, who were said to have made 'passionate love in their school uniforms', to forced labour camps in the countryside. The campaign is bizarre in a country supposedly 'liberated' by bearded men ten years before.

[40] Michael Frayn, *Observer*, 12 January 1969.

CHAPTER 47

The 'Ten Million Ton Harvest' and its Implications

The political revolution following the capture of power in 1959 was to have been accompanied by, first, an immediate increase in standards of living; second, a rapid industrialization; and third, a switch away from that emphasis on sugar which had played for so long such a large and, as many thought, destructive part in Cuban society. None of these things occurred: Guevara in 1960 spoke of a future in which Cuba would be self-sufficient in steel, while by 1965 industrialisation had been indefinitely postponed: in 1960 Castro was explaining how improvements in living standards would come faster than in any other country which had undergone a revolution but two years later the standards of life in the cities had collapsed while at the end of the 1960s most Cubans were living in a very Spartan manner. Finally, while between 1960 and 1962 the role of sugar in the economy was denigrated, sugar has if anything since 1963 played a larger part than before 1959.[1] The 'year of the Decisive Endeavour', 1969–70,[2] was indeed specially geared to the production of ten million tons of sugar, a goal which, because of the innate unwisdom of relying on the production of a large quantity of an already far from scarce commodity, would once have seemed so foolish as to be absurd. In order to expand the capacity of the sugar industry to produce ten million tons of sugar, it was necessary to invest a new \$M1,000, a figure which exceeded the total assets of the sugar industry in 1965.[3] With a rigidly controlled economy, however, and the emigration of many technicians, it was obviously easier to concentrate all energies upon this well-tried crop than to launch successfully into other enterprises, at least as a matter of central concentration. In this

[1] It was on 10 August 1963, before the Institute of Hydraulic Resources, in the Havana Libre Hotel, Havana, that Castro announced, 'we are going to develop the cane fields primarily and then the cattle. These are going to be pillars of the economy until 1970.'

[2] The years since 1959 have each received a name from the government to suggest the national theme. Thus, 1959 was the year of Liberation, 1960 of Agrarian Reform, 1961 of Education, 1962 of Planning, 1963 of Organization, 1964 of the Economy, 1965 of Agriculture, 1966 of Solidarity with the Underdeveloped World, 1967 of Heroic Vietnam, 1968 of the Heroic Guerrilla. As with many things in Cuba, the labelling of years was systematized, not invented, by Castro: thus the year 1953 had been described by Batista as the 'year of the centenary of the Apostle' (that is, of Martí's birth).

[3] Michel Gutelman, *L'Agriculture Socialisée à Cuba* (Maspero, Paris 1967, 205).

respect, the Revolution has been fundamentally regressive, and it must have occurred to many Cubans to ask whether it would not have been more beneficial to have achieved a less profound social change if thereby it had been easier to achieve economic diversification.

Despite the special and grand emphasis laid on sugar since 1964, however, harvests have usually been well below the figures achieved in the 1950s and the yield from the cane has also been smaller.[4] These failures are partly attributable to bad weather, but bad management, delay in getting the cane from the field to the mill,[5] neglect of the industry in the early years, sabotage, shortage of machinery, and even shortage of labour have also been responsible. For a variety of reasons, (among them retirement) the professional cane cutters of the 1950s have almost disappeared and voluntary labour, however energetic, has often been less satisfactory. The harvest of 1969 was described by Castro as 'the country's agony', and totalled $4\frac{1}{2}$ million tons only. But the goal of reaching ten million tons in the harvest of 1970 was proclaimed for such a long time and such stress had been laid on this goal in propaganda ('What are you doing towards the ten million?') that it almost seemed as if the regime would stand or fall by the extent to which this target was fulfilled.

Nevertheless, in the middle of May 1970 Castro bitterly admitted that this target could not after all be achieved and that nine million would be the maximum possible. Even this, however, represents less of a real achievement than it will seem at first sight, since much of the sugar came from cane left over from 1969 or prematurely cut from the harvest of 1971. It is also unfortunately conceivable that the figures were falsified and, providing that Russia assists in the deception (by, for instance, announcing she has bought from Cuba seven million tons), there is no means of checking the truth of the announcement.[6] Further, even if the ten million tons had been achieved, Cuba would still have been producing less sugar per head of population than she was in 1925, while the long-term costs of this grand Potemkin-type harvest cannot easily be measured.

It was a bizarre undertaking: the news that this harvest of 1970 would

[4] The yield from the cane averaged 10·85% in 1969 in comparison with 12·62% in 1958. In 1969 Castro was speaking of a yield of 12·05% as quite exceptional (interview, 20 December 1969, published *Granma* weekly edition, 28 December 1969).

[5] Cane loses sucrose by easily calculated percentages if there is a prolonged delay between canefield and mill. Cane which reaches the mill seven days after being cut has lost 25% of the sugar it would have had if it reached it immediately. In the first part of the harvest, of 1969–70, this seems to have happened quite often.

[6] It is true that the faking of statistics is a little more difficult than it might seem, particularly when the separate achievements of the individual mills are all announced and indeed followed by the press during the course of the grinding. But since 1964 Cuba has followed a policy of secrecy about sugar statistics to 'impede . . . enemies of the Revolution'.

begin on 26 July 1969 (with a *zafra chica*) and that Christmas Eve 1969 would be celebrated, because of the activities on the cane fields, in July 1970, are among the most notable surrealistic contributions to Cuban political life. Meantime, a delegation from North Vietnam, not to speak of the Soviet Minister of Defence, Marshal Grechko, and the entire Cuban cabinet have all done their time in the canefields, while government propaganda has spoken of the harvest as if it were a military challenge: 'Every worker should act as he would in the face of an enemy attack, should feel like a soldier in a trench with a rifle in his hand.'[7]

A commercial agreement with Russia signed in January 1964, and the International Sugar Agreement of 1968 (in force for five years from 1 January 1969), assures Cuba of markets in the short term: the Russians agreed to buy an annually increasing amount of Cuban sugar at 6 cents a pound up to 7 million tons by 1970, though in fact Cuba was on a number of occasions unable to meet her part of the bargain.[8] The International Sugar Agreement gave Cuba a quota of 2·15 million tons.[9] But even leaving aside the political consequences of so close a commercial friendship with Russia,[10] the long-term consequences of reliance on sugar in a world able to produce increasing quantities of it are discouraging, particularly when the Cuban sugar industry seems less efficient and competitive than it was even in the 1950s – not to speak of the last century, when it was in the van of technical experiment (Cuba was even overtaken by Brazil as the largest sugar cane producer in 1966).

There is, however, one important recent development: the beginning of mechanization of the sugar harvest. There were admittedly many early difficulties. Thus despite the construction with the help of Czech and Russian technicians, and parts, of 100 cane-cutting and stripping machines from Russia in 1965 and about 5,000 machines for lifting the cane when it is cut, most of the harvest of sugar in 1969–70 was still being both cut and loaded by hand.[11] For the Russian machines, the *Libertadoras*, often broke down, could only work eight hours a day and when there was

[7] Castro's speech at the opening of the main stage of the harvest, 27 October 1969 (*Granma* weekly edition, 2 November 1969).

[8] Russia agreed to take 2·1 million tons of sugar in 1965, 3 million tons in 1966, 4 million tons in 1967 and 5 million tons in 1968–9. China blamed Russia for forcing Cuba to continue to emphasise sugar in her economy (See *People's Daily*, 22 February 1966).

[9] The total sugar available for sale on the 'free market' was conceived as 9·4 million tons, of which 7·7 million were basic exports and 1·65 re-exports from the Communist countries (some Cuban sugar included, doubtless). Other large quotas included Australia, 1·1 million; British West Indies and Guyana, 200,000 and Brazil, 500,000.

[10] See below, page 698.

[11] See P. Sakun, *URSS*, July 1968, figure for imported cane-cutters. The most frequently used variety of cane, incidentally, remains that used before 1959 – the Javanese POJ 2878, but recently successful experiments have been made with a Barbados variety.

no dew, and were useless in the rain or on bumpy ground. In 1968, Castro nevertheless explained that mechanization would be complete by 1975, when the Revolution would 'have secured one of its most humane achievements, having changed over for ever from working conditions fit for animals to those which are truly humane' – that is, to complete mechanization.[12] In the following years, several new combine cane harvesters, of Cuban manufacture, for cutting cane, were used, and the harvest of 1969–70 will apparently use over 200 of these *Hendersons* (called after Robert Henderson, its English-American inventor who had been before the Revolution general manager of the United Fruit Company's mill, *the Preston* – a curious hero for the Revolution but undoubtedly a real one).[13]

Since 1962, the structure of agriculture, industry and labour have all been transformed, so that the still partially bourgeois society which was threatened in the Missile Crisis no longer exists.

In October 1963, a second agrarian reform nationalized all private holdings larger than 167 acres (five *caballería*). Many of these larger proprietors who had been left out of the earlier agrarian reform were said to be leaving their land uncultivated, presumably since they did not see the point of producing anything if they were only able to sell at the low prices offered by the Institute of Agrarian Reform (INRA). But the private sector of agriculture generally had fulfilled its obligations in respect of production more efficiently than had the state farms or co-operatives, so that the second agrarian reform law was a political rather than an economic measure. Many of these private farmers in the middle range were among the opponents of the regime and had taken to the hills, particularly in the Escambray, Matanzas and the north of Las Villas, during mid-1963, in sporadic revolts.[14]

Some 11,000 farms were thereby added to the state domain, which was in consequence responsible for a little over two-thirds of Cuban agriculture.[15] Though the actual acts of state intervention were often carried out callously, there was no widespread fighting, and no deaths seem to have been reported. All expropriated farmers who were not actual opponents of the regime were compensated, at the rate of $15 a month per

---

[12] Speech, 5 July 1968.

[13] The *Hendersons* are cutters assembled (apparently at Santa Clara) on top of bulldozers imported from Russia. They need a cane collection centre where the leaves of the cane are stripped off before being dispatched to the mill. Some 300 of these were planned for 1971.

[14] Carlos Rafael Rodríguez, *La Revolución Cubana y el Periodo de Transición*, Folleto 2, 12.

[15] The second agrarian reform expropriated 6,062 farms between 5 and 10 *caballería* (a total of 608,000 hectares), 3,105 between 10 and 20 *caballería* (610,000 hectares), 1,456 between 20 and 30 *caballería* (508,000 hectares) and 592 larger than 30 *caballería* (377,000 hectares).

caballería confiscated, up to a total of $250, for a period of ten years. In addition, some private farms remain with up to about 900 acres, mostly estates farmed by a single family.

Even after this reform, however, there remained between 150,000 and 200,000 small farmers in Cuba, or almost 80% of the farmers of the country before the Revolution.[16] These, despite alarms, remained in being at the beginning of the 1970s. About a quarter of these farms, or 40,000, are so small that they produce only for the farm family, with no surplus for sale. These include many of those 35,000 who received title deeds of land shared out under the terms of the unfulfilled first agrarian reform.[17] Some of these farmers remain relatively rich men. But all private farmers are free only up to a certain point. Thus they are members of the state-directed Association of Private Farmers,[18] are allowed to grow certain crops only, and can sell their produce only to the state purchasing agency (ACOPIO). These farmers can also only sell their estates, if they wish to do so, to the state, and the regime apparently thinks that in the long run, all these private estates will by sale come into state hands.[19] Not unnaturally, therefore, there has been considerable anxiety, particularly among those farmers who might seem to come within the next category, 100 to 150 acres.[20]

The small farmers still make a big contribution to the revolution's agricultural programme. They grow most (70%) of the fruit in Cuba, nearly all the coffee and tobacco (90%), own almost half of the livestock and still grow about 25% of the cane. (Tobacco is grown by about 40,000 private farmers, though the manufacture of cigars and cigarettes is controlled by the government.) It would be a serious mistake if ideological preconceptions were to cause any further state intervention in a department of the economy which, despite many discouragements, is still very productive.

Since 1964 agriculture has been the centre of the regime's attention and has naturally benefited substantially. 25% of the Gross National Product is invested in agriculture.[21] There have been huge imports of tractors from Russia and Czechoslovakia, many irrigation projects, the building of fertilizer plants – one by the English firm of Simon-Carves, costing £M14 near Cienfuegos[22] – several experimental cattle projects

[16] According to the Agricultural Census of 1946 – and there is no later source – farms smaller than 150 acres constituted over 80% of the farms in Cuba.

[17] Only 35,000 deeds were distributed under the terms of the regime's promise in 1959 to give 100,000 land titles.

[18] *Asociación nacional de agricultores privados*.

[19] Castro's speech to the 3rd congress of ANAP, May 1967.

[20] Dumont, p. 87.

[21] There were 35,000 tractors in 1967 in comparison with 9,200 in 1960 (Castro speech of 2 January 1968).

[22] Simon-Carves of Stockport had built chemical or fertilizer plants in other Communist countries before (see Ian Ball, *Daily Telegraph*, 3 February 1967).

(including an Institute of Animal Science[23]) to increase the quality of animals, directed by the English agronomist, Dr Thomas Preston of Aberdeen, greater care of grasses, and much greater use of fungicides and pesticides. Castro's own interests in agriculture have been continuous. The nationalization of most of the cane land, though it has carried with it familiar disadvantages, has at least made possible on a national scale the rational planning of planting and harvesting. The large investment which the Revolution has made in agriculture could certainly assure Cuba of being one of the most modern and prosperous agricultural countries in the world by 1975–80, assuming that wise decisions are made politically. In particular, the future of Cuban rice and of cattle, especially beef cattle, seems promising. Livestock figures are now apparently well over those of 1959, despite the heavy slaughtering which went on during 1959–60.[24] Land under cultivation is said to have increased by 50%.[25] Except for wheat, fats and oils, Cuba could supply all her basic foods, and, in the long run, home-grown cotton and other fibres could presumably supply the domestic clothing industry. But there are dark sides to the situation. Thus, despite efforts to decentralise since 1965, there remains much inefficiency, and the planning powers of JUCEI, the planning boards, and INRA, though much reduced in functions, continue to hamper local managers, even if it is no longer the case, as occurred before 1965, that small items such as nails had to be ordered from Havana. Castro's own obsession with agriculture and his unchallenged position in the country is not an unmixed blessing for agricultural administrators. Thus since 1965 special farms have been assigned to the personal attention of Castro and these have received absolute priority in respect of equipment, often to the cost of other farms. These farms have so multiplied since 1968 that René Dumont, after a prolonged visit in 1969, described the Cuban countryside as 'now divided up in a series of special giant enterprises given over to single crops'.[26] This is a complete reversal of what occurred before 1965, when each People's Farm diversified and grew twenty-five to thirty-five different crops.

There have also been continuous difficulties with the agricultural workers. In 1966 there had to be a nationwide campaign against the

[23] See the *Informe Anual* of the *Instituto de Ciencia Animal*, 1966.

[24] According to one (Cuban) estimate, cattle numbers about 7 million head of cattle, well above the 1959 figure of 5·8 million. The aim is to raise numbers of cattle to 12 million by 1975, permitting an annual slaughter of 4 million and the daily production of 30 million litres of milk (Gutelman, *L'Agriculture socialisée à Cuba*, 79). However, it is fair to doubt whether these targets will be achieved and whether Castro is right in predicting a rice surplus by 1970. Russia, it will be remembered, has not fulfilled a single one of her agricultural plans since 1929.

[25] According to Castro, on 2 January 1968, land cultivation in 1958 in Cuba was 2·3 million hectares. In 1967 this had risen by 56% to 3·7 million hectares.

[26] René Dumont, Les Cubains trouvent le temps long, *Le Monde*, 9 December 1969.

withholding by workers on state farms of small plots of land for themselves; 'even the paths between state farms' had been privately sown, state irrigation had been diverted to secret private plots and private cultivation and the keeping of livestock around state workers' houses had begun at an alarming rate. In precisely the same way, the slaves of the past had developed their own *conucos* around their barracoons. It does not seem as if the twentieth-century authoritarian state has in the long run been any more successful than the nineteenth-century private capitalist in preventing agricultural labourers from self-help. How much agricultural time and labour is 'wasted' in this way is impossible to predict.

Finally, agricultural production, particularly if it is intended to be internationally competitive, is increasingly the consequence of a huge combined economic system in which efficiency depends upon industry, science and commerce as much as upon the farmer. Most competitive agricultural countries, such as Denmark or Britain (since 1945), are serviced by a large number of 'para-agricultural workers'.[27] Thus it is not really feasible to concentrate on agricultural development regardless of its implications, and it must be a matter of serious doubt whether Cuba's continued reliance on Russian and East European industry for the tools of her agricultural undertakings promises well, since this in dustry has in the past been so unsuccessful in serving her own agricultures.

There is also a black market. As early as 1963 the black market was supposed to give food prices at between three and ten times the official figures. For a long time, the regime turned a blind eye to the large number of townspeople who would drive out of the cities at week-ends to buy food direct from peasants and indeed, with the rationing of petrol from the beginning of 1967, and the lack of buying power of all money, along with the virtual disappearance of all goods from the shops, this activity has more or less come to an end. It was replaced by a system of barter, by which hats, for instance, would be exchanged for chickens, or coffee for a barrel of beer, though one instance was reported in 1969 of a pig for a party being bought for $600.

It is fairly clear that agriculture will dominate Cuban life for the foreseeable future, perhaps forever. Castro appears to bank on likely world food shortages to secure for Cuba permanently a market for increased agricultural production.[28] On the other hand, Castro's politics have changed often and other Cuban leaders still seem to expect more tradi-

[27] René Dumont and Bernard Rosier, *The Hungry Future*, André Deutsch, London, 1969, 38.
[28] Perhaps this at least he has learned from Professor René Dumont, many of whose other suggestions have been unwisely spurned.

9   Castro speaks in the Plaza de la Revolución, 1964

10 a Castro cuts cane, 1965
    b Castro explains a new dam

tionally that agriculture in the long run will 'create exports so as to allow us to enter upon industrialization'.[29] In either event, the social consequences are likely to be considerable, since the Cuban regime evidently hopes, at the moment, to reverse the customary drift of labour into the cities characteristic of the rest of the world and preserve, or even expand, the rural population – so attempting to disprove the conventional wisdom that progress and industrialization are synonyms. This romantic plan is not likely to succeed.

The control of the immense bureaucracy created by the Revolutionary intervention in every sphere of the national life, in all departments, but particularly in agriculture, has been one of the government's most difficult tasks. This began to be appreciated at least as early as 1963. Castro's speeches in the following twelve months were full of scorn for many of the cogs in the machine which he had created: 'the place where I was born and brought up, which was a latifundia, had one or two office clerks; now it is a state farm and has twelve clerks';[30] 'We have accomplished nothing if previously we worked for the capitalists and now we work for another type of person who is not a capitalist but who consumes much and produces nothing';[31] 'capitalists threw away money in luxuries, in entertainment, but did not waste money in the work centres and managed their businesses well. And we, the socialists, are we going to stop the capitalist waste and still throw away the fruits of the peoples' labour? The people benefit not at all if the money that the capitalists spent in one way we socialists spend in another . . . what difference is there between a stingy rich man and a squandering revolutionary? That the former impoverishes some to enrich himself, while the revolutionary impoverishes everybody without enriching anybody';[32] and 'a spendthrift in an important position equals the harm done by 10,000 counter-revolutionaries.'[33]

In 1966 'the struggle against bureaucracy' had become a 'prime task' for the Cuban Communist Party. Sometimes, the regime insisted that bureaucracy was an unpleasant residue of capitalism and by no means a fault inherent in socialism. But Castro was found complaining, in a speech to the Cuban women's federation in December 1966, that even

---

[29] Dr Carlos Rafael Rodríguez, in an interview to the author in January 1969, said 'we hope that whereas sugar now accounts for 80% of Cuban exports, the percentage will drop to some 25%, with coffee, beef and minerals accounting for some 70%: in particular, coffee, in the past a derisory export, should account for 25% of Cuban exports in the future.' Castro made the same prediction in a speech on 4 November 1969, but in an earlier speech (27 October 1969) promised that production of sugar cane would be doubled again by 1980. (*Granma*, 2 November 1969.)

[30] Fidel Castro, *Obra Revolucionaria*, September 1964 No. 23, pp. 9–20.

[31] Fidel Castro, at Matanzas, *Revolución*, 15 November 1964.

[32] Fidel Castro, *Obra Revolucionaria*, October 1964 No. 28, p. 33.

[33] Fidel Castro at Matanzas, *Revolución*, 15 November 1964.

the 'struggle against bureaucracy committees' had become 'bureau-cratized' and admitted that they would continue to be so for 'several more years'. Many workers in banks and offices, meantime, were 'rationalized' or dismissed and, in a speech in early 1967, Castro regretted that he had not in 1959 transferred the capital from Havana to the small town of Guáimaro.

CHAPTER 48

The New Men

Industry has also undergone a structural change since 1962, for in March 1968 the government destroyed the last vestiges of private enterprise, during the so-called 'revolutionary offensive' which closed without compensation 50,000 small businesses, from fruit sellers in the street to cockpits, pawn shops, music schools, laundries and garages. This campaign evidently owed much to the example of the cultural revolution in China and was certainly embarked upon only after much deliberation. Since then, apart from fishermen and farmers, the only private undertakings in Cuba are a few medical practices. Many famous bars and restaurants were closed, some for good, some to open sporadically thereafter on the initiative of the local Committee for the Defence of the Revolution.[1] For seven years, the small businessmen had in fact lived in a twilight society, constituting more a safety valve than an economic enterprise, since the state was the only big customer (for the manufacturers, for example, of machinery or clothing) and the only provider of raw materials. As early as 1962, many shops, restaurants, and groceries had been taken over without special decrees and, in December of that year, most enterprises using hired labour were nationalized. This revolutionary offensive was described by Dr Carlos Rafael Rodríguez as the 'logical consequence of the deepening of the Revolution', which until then had 'left behind in the cities a still large *petit bourgeoisie* of small traders and speculators. This . . . was a persistent threat to the type of socialist man whom we desire to create. In practice it became a centre of opposition . . . [giving] special favours to the remains of the rentier class . . . who thereby received the best of what was being produced by the community.'[2] In a speech at the time, when opening a school at Boca de Jaruco, Castro argued that private business is basically immoral and that material incentives of any sort mar the character of the new man. Castro described the bar owners, hot-dog stallholders and night club proprietors whom he was destroying, as 'drones in perfect physical condition who put up a stand and earn fifty dollars a day while they watch the lorries go by filled with women on their way to work in Havana's Green Belt' (95·1 % of hot dog stallholders, he assured the

[1] See below, p. 681.
[2] Interview, 13 January 1969.

country, with surely an excess of precision, were counter-revolutionaries or 'small spongers').

In the succeeding months, Castro began to develop at greater length the concept of the free 'new man' who would, as Guevara had hoped, be no longer alienated from society, unsullied by contact with the profit motive, but conscious, like Alain's peasant, of the country rather than the corrupt city, and living for the community from the cradle to the grave. (Castro seems first to have spoken of this at length at the congress of small farmers – ANAP – in May 1967; he described how in the future 'we shall do away with the vile intermediary, money' and how then men would work from habit, though there would be an abundance of everything and a free distribution of goods.)[3] But even in 1965 he was saying that 'from an early age [man] must be discouraged from every egotistic feeling in the enjoyment of material things, such as the sense of individual property',[4] though he had avoided taking sides in the controversy over material incentives for labour, sometimes seeming to favour moral rewards, as did Guevara, and sometimes material ones, as did the more traditional old Communists. Indeed, some of Castro's remarks on this matter conflict as strongly with his later views as any other change of face; for instance, in the summer of 1965, the year of Guevara's disappearance from the Cuban political scene,[5] he is found telling a meeting of cane cutters that 'we cannot choose idealistic methods that conceive all men to be guided by duty, because in actual life, that is not so . . . it would be absurd to expect that the great masses of men who earn their living cutting cane will make a maximum effort just by being told that it is their duty, whether they earn more or less. That would be idealistic.'[6]

At all events, Cuba in the late 1960s was committed to an industrial attitude long since discarded in Eastern Europe. Overtime pay was abolished. So too was 'socialist emulation', the scheme whereby, as in Russia, workers receive extra pay for more work and a penalty for failing to fulfil their targets. (This had been used in various forms between 1962 and 1967; abolition was doubtless a relief to all, since some first-prize workers had shown an embarrassing preference for material goods – a refrigerator or a motor bicycle – rather than a holiday in Russia.)[7] National work heroes in the style of Stakhanov were also

[3] Speech at the conference of small farmers, May 1967.

[4] Lockwood, 126.

[5] See below, p. 693.

[6] Fidel Castro, '*Discurso en el Acto de Entrega de diplomas a las Trabajadores que mas se distinguieron en la V zafra del pueblo*', El Mundo, 25 July 1965.

[7] The first 'festival of socialist emulation' was held in April 1962, and later that year 45 prize houses were distributed to the first winners – fourteen, incidentally, to soldiers. In 1965, 1,500 refrigerators and 100 motor cycles, 500 journeys to Russia and East Europe and 2,000 holidays at Varadero beach were offered, but only 80 journeys to Russia were taken up. In

abolished, since it was found that they caused jealousy, not admiration. (There were also doubts: did the National Hero of Labour for 1964, Rafael Cuevas, really lay 2,190 bricks in four hours, and did his predecessor in 1963, Reinaldo Castro, really cut a daily average of 1,280 *arrobas* of cane – a figure which certainly compared well with the 150 *arrobas* which was the daily average for the cane cutter before 1959?)

In place of these discredited methods, Castro since 1968 attempted to institute 'Communism and yet more Communism'.[8] He repeatedly said that in the long run he desired to abolish money completely, and indeed by 1969 several things, such as sport, cinemas and local telephone calls, were available in 'a Communist way', that is, free. An article in the government daily newspaper *Granma* put the matter clearly: 'since we were small we were taught to ask "how much have you got? How much are you worth?" Then we learned that money was unnecessary... already in Cuba those six letters (*dinero*) mean less. The new generation does not believe in all the old myths about money.' Further, voluntary labour or voluntary overtime has become more and more the typical solution of the regime to labour problems, though it is hard to make a true estimate of the value, or cost, of this to the economy. Castro was thus attempting to create, from above, a gigantic kibbutz, as it were, out of Cuba, though at the same time seeking the target of a monstrously big sugar crop in 1969–70.

Doubtless in some ways this new policy seeks to make, and indeed successfully makes, a virtue out of necessity, seeking a philosophical justification for economic hardship. There is little point after all in material incentives in the form of money if there are no goods to buy. On the other hand, it seems that this attempt to achieve the stage of Communism at the same time as building socialism, to differentiate Cuba from the more comfortable regimes of Eastern Europe and Russia (lands at least mildly responsive to the 'philosophy of the full shop window', which Castro has mocked), responds to a puritanical, anarchic and individualistic strain in Castro's own character and also in the character of Cuban society which, in the past, knew so much about money and so much more than the previously largely agrarian Communist countries already in existence.

Moral incentives have not yet triumphed entirely. In September 1969, wages for sugar workers were raised by a third, specifically in order to try and avoid a further drift of experienced men from the

[8] Castro, speech, 19 April 1968.

1966,100 private cars were among the prizes. Meanwhile, César Escalante, secretary for the 'commission of revolutionary orientation' of the PURS, had complained that 'very few workers actually participate in emulation . . . only a third of workers attend emulation meetings . . . brotherly competition has not yet been understood by the masses' (*Hoy*, 18 October 1964).

industry.[9] There remains much absenteeism – the Cuban workers' only effective protest and occasional sabotage – and it is doubtful whether what the then secretary-general, Miguel Martín, described in 1967 as a 'morass of indiscipline, irresponsibility and superficiality' (to characterize labour attitudes) has really much changed,[10] and whether, despite such experiments as the Isle of Youth (where a moneyless society has got further than on the main island), these policies have really brought Cuban workers nearer to ideal Communism than the more tolerant policies of, say, Dubček or Tito. Can Communism as defined by Marx, after all, triumph in an atmosphere of 'liberalism, no, softening, no'?[11] Is not the disappearance of the state also a necessity?[12] And, despite the understandable revulsion felt by many Cubans, after four centuries of corruption, from the seamier side of the money economy, is that revulsion quite so strong as to cause Cubans as a whole to react in a quite different way from the rest of humanity? It is impossible to believe it, or even to think that what Leo Huberman and Paul Sweezy call the 'de-automobilization' of Cuba is much liked.[13] Societies have to take into account good and bad people alike. What if the perfect man were to turn out to be a tragic delusion? It is indeed difficult to believe that these ideas would last long were it not for Castro's unique skill in presenting them in their most attractive light.

The increasing emphasis on sugar in Cuba since 1964 has meant that there has scarcely been any new industrialization. On the other hand, serious efforts have been concentrated on various existing undertakings, particularly nickel, where the two old U.S. plants at Moa and Nicaro, on the north shore of Oriente province, on top of one of the largest nickel deposits in the world, have pressed ahead, with production well above that of the 1950s.[14] Nickel has now surpassed tobacco as the country's second most valuable export, after sugar.

Batista's regime was sustained in the 1950s by an alliance of the Army with the highly organized and powerful trade unions. Both were

[9] Speech by Jorge Risquet, Minister of Labour, 6 June 1969. He added that it was 'logical' for a worker, even 'of complete revolutionary outlook', to be concerned about the family budget.

[10] *Bohemia* (12 September 1969) published an inquiry into labour difficulties at a railway workshop at Camagüey. This showed that in April 1969 only five men out of 1,600 had responded to an appeal to cut cane without pay, that each worker did less than half an hour's voluntary overtime, and that 4,611 man days were lost through absenteeism.

[11] Castro, speech, 28 September 1968.

[12] In an interview on 13 January 1969, I suggested to Dr Rodríguez that Marx had thought that the Communist society could not be achieved until after the disappearance of the state (scarcely a possibility at the moment in Cuba). He replied sharply: 'Marx wrote little about the nature of Communist society.'

[13] Sweezy & Huberman, *Socialism in Cuba*, 95. Anyone who has seen those Cubans who still drive cars look after these prized possessions would doubt it.

[14] Production of nickel reached 35 million tons in 1967, in comparison with 18 million in 1958.

corrupt, and the unions were also restrictive, preventing the modernization of agriculture and industry – in particular of the sugar industry.

The Revolution, by converting the unions basically into a department of state, had smashed both the corruption and also the past restrictive hostility to change which characterized this system. A number of
unproductive sugar mills have thus been abandoned and, as has been
seen, a beginning has been made to both mechanization and the
rational planning of the sugar crop, along the lines vainly advocated by
Lobo in the 1950s (carried out, ironically, by Tomás Martínez, the
Revolution's chief sugar manager, and Lobo's general manager in the
past). Bulk handling of the sugar crop at the ports has also been possible
with the end of the old union of dock labourers. Some, doubtless, would
hesitate before regarding these activities as among the benefits of the
Revolution, but they are so nevertheless, despite the troubles and even
misery which they have actually brought to certain well-established
working-class communities.

But there is nothing else very imaginative about the Cuban labour and
industrial scene under the Revolution. There is no workers' control. A
sugar mill, for instance, is run by an Administrator appointed by the
state, advised by chemists and technicians as in the past – often the same
men who did the job before 1959 and who have remained in Cuba for a
variety of reasons, some idealistic, some personal. The cane is cut, and
carried, by the same men who worked for Lobo or Gomez Mena –
apart from the armies of voluntary workers, whose activities are perhaps
less economic than educative or political in intent. Except that there is
no chance to protest save by absenteeism, sabotage or exile, and that
even on the dirtiest wall there are likely to be posters adjuring patriotism, there has been less change in life at the mill than would have been
thought possible: and as late as 1969 the Minister of Labour, Risquet,
was admitting that there was still a 'marked difference' between the
income of workers during the harvest and after it.[15]

The unions, reduced to fourteen in 1966, and with free elections un-
heard of since 1961, are now primarily methods of organization. In
September 1963 there seems to have been a major challenge to the
regime by the old Construction Workers, but it was heavily repressed.[16]

[15] Speech of 6 June 1969. He added that, in the dead season, some workers still looked elsewhere than in the sugar industry for employment and, if they found it, would not come back.

[16] According to exile sources, at the meeting of the equipment union (a constituent of the
Construction Workers' Federation) on 11 September 1963, resolutions were passed demanding
full pay for 'lay-offs' when equipment was being repaired (a frequent occurrence), regular
hourly wages for heavy equipment workers when re-assigned to common labour during break-
downs in machinery, and publication in the press of a manifesto incorporating the union's
demands. Lázaro Peña, the secretary-general of the CTC(R), tried to address the meeting
but he was drowned by shouts of 'we are hungry! we want freedom! we want work!' The
leaders of this protest were afterwards punished. (Paul Bethel, *Terror and Resistance in Communist Cuba*, 41.)

In June 1968, the secretary-general of the Labour confederation, Miguel Martín (who had succeeded the 'founder' Lázaro Peña), gave a regional meeting in Camagüey the familiar explanation that since 'the working class is in power', the general collective interest as defined by the government was 'the criterion for all judgements'. New faces may now be seen among the union leaders, but none of them is an independent spirit, and indeed their manner of election precludes any but 'vanguard workers' or 'exemplary workers'. From August 1969, every Cuban worker has had to possess a 'control card' and a 'labour dossier' upon which all absences and other shortcomings are marked.

The economic planning of Cuba has stayed much the same since the early 1960s. Thus the JUCEPLAN, the Cuban version of the Russian GOSPLAN, remains, despite reforms, as do the local boards, the JUCEI, founded in 1961 as rough equivalents of the Russian regional Economic Councils. In industry, all plants producing the same item are integrated in a single combined *empresa* or corporation while, in agriculture, state farms are grouped regionally under INRA. Domestic trade is controlled by the Ministry of Internal Trade, foreign trade by its respective ministry. The methods, of course, closely resemble Russian practice, as do the economic plans; and the first Cuban Five Year Plan was reduced to a four-year one so that it would end at the same time as those in other socialist countries. In Cuba, the JUCEPLAN prepares the national plan, which is then referred to the Ministries, then to the *empresas* and finally to the farms and factories, where production meetings are held and where, in theory, workers can propose alterations. The plan then retraces its steps upwards to JUCEPLAN to be approved by Ministers, being thereafter sent back down the channel of production in the form of definite goals for definite plants. The consultative process is an illusion; to the workers, one reporter quite sympathetic to the Revolution wrote, the whole process is a 'complete abstraction'; they showed 'little interest in discussing it'.[17] In November 1968, a new secretary-general of the CTC(R), Héctor Ramos Latour,[18] boasted how a million workers had discussed a new social security law, in a 'parliament of the working masses', but he presented no news as to whether or not a single amendment had in consequence been introduced.

The Cuban Revolutionary Government, like all socialist administrations, has also had persistent difficulties in establishing standards. Thus some years ago it was said that the 'establishment of the *norms system* has brought to light deficiencies in the work of the local trade unions, who

[17] Adolfo Gilly, *The Monthly Review*, October 1964. See also the remarks of Lázaro Peña, then secretary-general of the CTC(R) in September 1962, quoted Mesa-Lago.
[18] He succeeded Miguel Martín as secretary-general in November 1968.

do not yet understand the importance of production and baulk when faced with any measure of reorganization which may change old working habits, the remains of capitalism'.[19] Wages in Cuba are paid according to skill, and fairly wide differences still exist in consequence between eight separate grades in four occupational sectors,[20] though some information on this subject has been kept secret. There is a minimum wage of $85 a month and a maximum one of $450. Pensions are $60 a month. These rules mirror Russian practice, though the ratio between the highest paid technician and the lowest paid industrial worker is higher than in Russia,[21] while leading technicians in Cuba as elsewhere in the Communist world get all sorts of advantages such as free cars, special meals and journeys.

For those who find the demands made upon them under the present system of labour organization excessive, there is 'labour justice'. This copes with such matters as nonfulfilment of schedules, absenteeism, damage to state machinery and negligence, and imposes a variety of penalties, including deduction of wages, transfer from place of work, dismissal and also commitment to forced labour camps; thus among the thirty-two reasons in 1962 for committal to the camp at Guanahacabibes in West Cuba were 'negligence or ignorance which causes a standstill in production and hampering output standards'.[22]

Apart from the isolated incident of the builders' protest in 1963, there is, however, little overt evidence of hostility of workers towards the revolutionary regime. In 1962 far more workers told the sociologist Zeitlin that they thought that they had more influence on the government than before 1959 while most workers believed that there was no call for any election. Quite obviously most workers thought that nationalization meant that they now worked for themselves and not for the boss.[23] Skilled workers seemed more inclined to support the revolution than unskilled ones. On the other hand, there has been no serious inquiry since. No one knows to what extent, for instance, Escalante and the old Communists enjoyed support in 1968.[24]

It is impossible to say precisely to what extent the low productivity of the Cuban economy since the Revolution is due to poor wage scales, and to what extent it has been the consequence of bad management, lack of spare parts, absence of technicians, the U.S. blockade, excessive

[19] Martínez Sánchez, La implantación del sistema salarial, 16, qu. Mesa-Lago, 71.
[20] Agricultural labourers, administrative employees, industrial workers, technicians and executive officials.
[21] The ratio in 1968 was 1:11 in Cuba and 1:6.8 in Russia.
[22] 'Reglamento del Centro de Rehabilitación de Uvero Quemado', Nuestra Industria, March 1962.
[23] Zeitlin, Revolutionary Politics, 38, 206. The figures were in the first matter 170 to 8 with 17 thinking that they had the influence as before 1959 and 7 having no opinion; Zeitlin's sampling method is open to question.
[24] See below, p. 693, for the Escalante affair.

expenditure on the social services and so on. Nevertheless, it is clear that, quite apart from failing to increase production in the more important sectors of the economy such as, in particular, sugar, the mixture of material and moral incentives has not increased the quality of products: in the early years of the Revolution, glue did not dry, matches broke their heads, toothpaste turned to stone after a few months. There were numerous conferences on 'quality' but in 1966 President Dorticós was still describing the matter as 'alarming'. Cursory inquiries in 1969 (rendered difficult by the almost total absence of material goods in the shops) suggest that this has certainly not much changed, and productivity per working day, although greater than in 1963–4, is still probably lower than before the Revolution.

The shortage of statistics and the unreliability of those that do exist naturally make it difficult to speak of general production figures for the years between 1960 and 1970 in Cuba. But it seems likely that whereas between 1959 and 1961 there was probably a rise in Gross National Production, and between 1961 and 1963 at least nothing worse than stagnation, since 1963 there has been a drop amounting to at least an average of 0.5% a year.[25] Considering that the Government has, according to its own statistics, failed to ensure much more than an average four-hour day of work from its citizens,[26] it is perhaps surprising that the fall of production has not been greater still.

[25] See Mesa-Lago, *Availability and Reliability of Statistics in Socialist Cuba*, Centre for Latin American studies, University of Pittsburgh, 1970, p. 51.

[26] As quoted K. S. Karol, *Les Guérrilleros au Pouvoir*, Paris 1970, 424.

CHAPTER 49

The Guardians

If Cuban society is as yet far from the Utopia coveted by Guevara, and now by Castro, the political machine constructed to create it has become elaborate. Castro himself, it is true, remains the curiously described 'maximum leader', prime minister, first secretary of the Cuban Communist Party, commander-in-chief of the armed forces, and Minister–President of the Institute for Agrarian Reform. It is evident that, even more than in the years during which the Revolution consolidated its hold, he takes all the decisions, gives what emphasis and explanations he judges right for the policies undertaken and, by the continuing use of television, press and radio, as well as personal appearances before both large and small crowds, sustains and justifies the regime, at the same time upholding the enthusiasm of his own followers.

The main political change since 1962 has been the eclipse of the old Communist leaders who, because of their many years of experience both of political organization and of the world Communist scene, played such an important part in the establishment of the 'socialist' character of the Cuban Revolution in the years 1960 and 1961. The surviving members of Castro's 26 July Movement are in power, though nevertheless they call themselves formally Communists. Aníbal Escalante's ORI (*organizaciones revolucionarias integradas*), which set out to be an amalgamation of the 26 July Movement and the old Communist Party, on the latter's terms, disappeared during 1963 without ceremony, while its successor, the PURS (*Partido Unificado de la Revolución Socialista*), appeared without inauguration. This movement was soon recognized by the Russian Communists as a 'fraternal party' but, in 1965, the PURS in its turn gave way to a new 'Communist Party of Cuba'.

This, as usual in communist states, was controlled by a central committee with a politburo and a secretariat superior to it, which, totalling a hundred members in all, remained, despite a few expulsions and deaths much the same until the end of the 1960s.[1] Of this one hundred,

[1] Efigenio Ameijeiras, Armando Acosta, Ramón Calcines and José Matar were expelled in 1966, 1967, 1968 and 1969 respectively. Three members of the 1965 central committee were killed with Guevara in Bolivia in 1967 – Major Juan Vitalio Acuña, Antonio Sánchez Díaz and Captain Eliseo Reyes.

sixty-eight were formally military men, although the actual military role of some of them in the Sierra or elsewhere was slight.[2] (Provincial committees of the new party were also from the start full of army men.) Twenty-one of the hundred were apparently members of the old Cuban Communist Party before 1959, ranging from men grown grey in the service of the party (such as Fabio Grobart, Blas Roca and Juan Marinello) to younger contemporaries of Castro at the University (such as Flavio Bravo and Leonel Soto)[3]. Nevertheless, no old Communist was on the politburo or on the secretariat,[4] which was dominated by the two Castros and their followers from the first days of the struggle against Batista.[5] The fact that the ideological director of the Revolution (*Responsable Nacional de Ideología*) is the ex-Catholic, ex-Minister of Education, Armando Hart, a man more of ambition than of intellectual distinction, means that the ideological director of the regime is firmly under the control of the Castros. Though only ten of the central committee and its bodies had been at the Moncada or on the

[2] Thus Major Flavio Bravo, an old Communist of Castro's generation at the University, is not known to have fought much; while *Comrade* Marcelo Fernández and *Comrade* Armando Hart probably did as much as Major Faustino Pérez. The military contingent in the Central Committee formally consisted of 58 majors, 9 captains and a lieutenant, major being still the highest Cuban army rank.

[3] This was in contrast with the old party representation on the 24-member national committee of the PURS. There, the old Communists had 11 members, with the 26 July Movement 12 and the Directorio Revolucionario 1. Old party members were in 1965 Blas Roca, Carlos Rafael Rodríguez, Armando Acosta, Severo Aguirre, Flavio Bravo, Ramón Calcines, Joel Domenech, Fabio Grobart, Secundino Guerra, Manuel Luzardo, Isidoro Malmierca, Juan Marinello, Miguel Martín, José Matar Franye, Arnaldo Milián, Lázaro Peña, José Ramírez, Ursinio Rojas, Clementina Serra, and Leonel Soto. Blas Roca was chairman of a commission to draw up a constitution for Cuba, a project of which nothing much has been heard. Carlos Rafael Rodríguez, though no longer President of the Institute for Agrarian Reform (a post he held from 1962 to 1964), has remained on the central committee's economic commission and, as a frequent spokesman for the regime both in Cuba and abroad, exerts more influence on policy-making than any other old Communist – possibly, at times, more than anyone else, apart from Castro (with whom he seems to be on excellent terms) a remarkable career for an ex-member of Batista's cabinet during the Second World War.

[4] Perhaps it is worth adding that all save three of the Communist Party presidium elected at its last independent congress in 1960 were in 1965 members of the central committee or its branches (the three were Aníbal Escalante and Joaquín Ordoqui, who were disgraced, and César Escalante, who was dead). Two out of six members of the National Committee elected in 1960 also found places in 1965 (Arnaldo Milián and Felipe Torres, but not Ladislao and José Luis González Carvajal, Leonidas Calderio and Silvio Quintana), along with the youth leader of 1960 – Isidoro Malmierca, who became first editor of the new party newspaper, *Granma*.

[5] Thus of the eight men who constitute the politburo and the secretariat, four were both in the Moncada attack and on the *Granma* (the two Castros, Ramiro Valdés and Juan Almeida). Armando Hart was a prominent organizer of the 26 July Movement from early on, and Guillermo García was the 'first peasant to join Castro' in the Sierra (one may doubt whether his presence in such a high political role in 1965 is much more than honorific, despite his military responsibilities). Sergio de Valle, chief of the army staff and afterwards Minister of the Interior, succeeded Guevara as chief doctor in the Sierra in 1957. The eighth member was Osvaldo Dorticós, the President of the Republic, whose role in the struggle against Batista was slight.

Granma[6] and only four seem to have been ex-members of the Directorio Revolucionario,[7] most of the military members, and therefore a majority of the whole committee, must have been in the Sierra Maestra in one role or another.

The regime has sought to ignore all these old differences, and the Revolution has often depended on even newer men: the ex-shop assistants, clerks and factory workers of 1958 who perhaps trained as teachers were, within months, found to be 'able, dynamic and revolutionary', and so became directors of sugar mills by 1961 – a living suggestion of the lack of opportunity in the old society.[8] These opportunists of the system were typified by Captain Jorge Enrique Mendoza and Major Jorge Serguera, who by 1969 were in charge respectively of the national newspaper *Granma* and of the mass media; by Major Piñeiro, the head of counter-espionage, Major Acevedo, the first commander of the militia, and Major Iglesias, the first commander of the united youth movement. Equally interesting has been the continuing adherence to the regime of men such as Major René de los Santos, chief of army intelligence (DIER) in 1959, and described even by Manuel Artime as 'non-Communist and above reproach',[9] yet he remained in Cuba to be a founder member of the central committee of the new Cuban Communist Party in 1965.

Most of these men, who are often courageous, energetic and dedicated, were still at the end of the 1960s only in their thirties and may consequently be expected, in default of a counter-revolution, to want many more years of power. Leaving aside the old Communists, the average age of the central committee of 1965 could scarcely have been more than thirty-six. On the other hand, at lesser levels, the Revolutionary government has been much assisted by the survivors of other important generations in left-wing Cuban politics; survivors on the one hand from the political gangster age of the late 1940s[10] and, on the other, from the old Left generation at the University in the 1920s and 1930s. True, many of these ex-students were even by 1944 far from radical, as the experience of Dr Grau San Martín's administration showed. But others, such as those who had sided with Ala Izquierda Estudiantil in their

[6] The two Castros, Almeida, Ramiro Valdés, Calixto García and Jesús Montané were both at Moncada and on the *Granma*; Pedro Miret and Haydée Santamaría were in addition at the first, but not on the second, and Efigenio Ameijeiras and Faustino Pérez were on the *Granma* but not at Moncada.

[7] Chomon, José Abrantes, Julio García Olivera and José Naranjo.

[8] *Bohemia* 15 January 1961, quoted Goldenberg, 212.

[9] (*Hombre intachable y no comunista*, Artime, 78).

[10] Thus of those who were with Castro at Cayo Confites in 1948, Carlos Franqui was for a long time editor of the 26 July Movement's newspaper *Revolución* (and afterwards was understood to have been working on Castro's 'memoirs'); Eduardo Corona and Enrique Rodríguez Loeches have been ambassadors; and Feliciano Maderne a deputy judge of the Supreme Court.

youth, had remained so, at least nominally, and could be counted upon to support revolutionary action in the 1960s, which they had long advocated without perhaps ever thinking (or perhaps in the end desiring) that it would actually happen.[11]

Castro has, in short, been uniquely able to harness to revolutionary nationalism a contrasting galaxy of energies, including not only reformers and idealists but also the 'social outcasts always in the van of every revolution or counter-revolution'.[12] Many who in the late 1960s worked as bureaucrats went through the most diverse political, and politically active, experiences in the late 1940s and 1950s, and now at last have found an intellectual or emotional haven.[13] Castro was able brilliantly to profit from the incandescent situation in Cuba in the 1940s and 1950s, to create a single movement from several 'generations' of men who were idealistic, frustrated and willing to commit violence. (Perhaps this had its drawbacks once the Revolution was firmly in power, since the brave señorito does not always make a good manager; thus Castro complained in 1963 that there were 3,000 candidates to be diplomats, only 100 to be agronomists). But it is with some relief that a liberal historian must note that none of those primarily responsible for the destruction of the free press, such as Dagoberto Ponce or Tirso Martínez, for the subversion of the university, such as Rolando Cubela or Omar Fernández, or the conversion of the unions into a department of state, such as Jose María Aguilera or Octavio Louit, has done particularly well under the regime which they did so much to establish.

The Cuban Communist Party was in 1969 about 70,000 in size, proportionally the smallest per head of the population among Communist countries.[14] The process of selection of members was original: after a purge of the ORI (and the expulsion of those old Communists who took part in the elections of 1958), the central committee of the ORI appointed commissions to select new members. These commissions analysed all places of work and arranged for the selection of certain 'exemplary workers' as party members, who further had to meet general assemblies of workers. This method, devised for the old PURS between 1962 and

[11] For a 'generational' interpretation of the Cuban Revolution, see Roberto Retamar's 'Les Intellectuels dans la Révolution', in Partisans (Paris), April–June 1967.

[12] See Dennis Mack Smith, Italy, A Modern History (Ann Arbor 1959), 16; those who in Italy 'from the condottiere to the Carbonari and the fascist squadristi have been the most combustible and explosive elements in Italian society'. Perhaps General Wood, for all his New England priggishness, was right when he said of Cuba in 1900, 'generations of misrule and duplicity have produced a type of man whose loyalty is always at the disposal of the man on top, whoever or whatever he may be' (Hagedorn, vol. 1, 282).

[13] For instance, the chief of the Foreign Press department of the Foreign Ministry during my visit to Cuba in 1969 had been before the Revolution an accountant at the big department store, El Encanto.

[14] In 1951, there were allegedly about 50,000 members of the then Communist Party.

1965, seems also to have been put into effect for the Communist Party since then. Most party members attended one of the schools of revolutionary instruction set up in 1961 to make sure that revolutionaries learned the principles of Marxism–Leninism (though these were closed in 1968). The first congress of the Cuban Communist Party, despite Castro's assertions that it would be in 1966, 1967 and so on, has been indefinitely postponed. There have also been inordinate delays in the selection of party members in the Ministries.

As important as the Party in organizing the country and stimulating the public have been the neighbourhood 'Committees for the Defence of the Revolution' (CDRs). Every street has one and everyone may join, so that it is not surprising that on paper there are over three million members (out of a total Cuban population, including children, of about eight million), organized hierarchically (with a central committee in Havana), not only for vigilance and snooping but for putting educational, medical or other campaigns into national effect, and holding regular seminars on 'revolutionary instruction'. The CDRs report on suspicious counter-revolutionaries, list possessions of those who have asked to leave Cuba, organize everything from fiestas to volunteers to work in the country, and interfere in all private life for the public good– ensuring the 'life of the open book', as José Yglesias put it in his sympathetic study of life in Mayarí in Oriente.[15] The anniversary of their foundation, on 28 September 1960, is one of the main revolutionary feast days, accompanied by dancing, poetry reading, beauty contests and a mass rally in the Plaza de la Revolución, with a speech by Castro. Being organized on a geographical basis the CDRs are the centre of 'revolutionary activity' for many who do not work in factories or farms, and hence have a high percentage of women among their membership. One of their campaigns, the Social Rehabilitation Front, was launched in September 1969 with the broad aim to 'counteract all behaviour detrimental to the social system'. These committees are really the core of the new Cuban society, creating a new culture of propaganda, participation, conformity and labour in a country which in the past was such a curious mixture of private endeavour and private suffering. But the precise measure of participation is quite slight and all major matters of, for instance, town planning or economic policy are decided at the summit, and not at the roots, of the political structure.[16]

The Party, the Committees for the Defence of the Revolution and, of

---

[15] José Yglesias, *In the Fist of the Revolution*, 274–307. The now extinct theoretical journal *Cuba Socialista* described the CDRs as 'system of collective revolutionary vigilance, in which everyone knows who everyone is, what each person in each block does, what relations he had with the tyranny . . . . whom he meets . . .' Qu. Zeitlin, 100.

[16] For a study of the CDRs see Richard R. Fagen, *The Transformation of Political Culture in Cuba*, Stanford University Press (1969), 69 ff.

course, the armed forces control the country. Besides them, the 294 municipal councils of Cuba rather surprisingly survive, but their power is slight and candidates for those bodies have to fulfil Party conditions, while the Party appoints the presidents. In an effort to reinvigorate local life and escape the most stultifying bureaucratism, 'local government delegates' were elected with much fanfare in 1967–8 by public assemblies, but once again 'safe revolutionaries' dominated among those successful, and in many respects their essentially parish pump activities duplicated those of the CDRs.

The armed forces, with (since 1 March 1964) their two and a half to three years of compulsory service and their $259M. expenditure, total 200,000[17] – by far the largest military undertaking in Latin America. The Cubans have 300 tanks and 165 combat aircraft, with 24 surface-to-air missile installations. Most of the regular soldiers, including officers, have been recruited since 1959. Since many of them were previously unemployed members of the lumpenproletariat, bootblacks or washers of cars, they owe everything to the Revolution and, apart from the curious occasion in 1967 when certain unnamed senior officers were supposed to be showing themselves susceptible to 'Chinese propaganda', their loyalty seems to have been absolute. Among the top commanders, many served under Raúl Castro in the Sierra Cristal in 1958, and Raúl Castro has throughout remained Minister of Defence (though he once was absent for several months, taking a course in Russia). The armed forces, it should be added, are the backbone of the regime in more than one way, since they spend a great deal of time in agricultural tasks, for which the government has to pay only the military wage of $7 a month rather than the national wage. In 1969–70, the armed forces were 'mobilized for the sugar harvest as they would have been in case of war', with about 80,000 men from the forces involved, being responsible for an estimated 18 % of the harvest.[18]

Justice in revolutionary Cuba is a part of the governmental system, as in other Communist countries. This means that with conventional crimes or misdemeanours the law works adequately, relatively quickly and free from bribery, if often brutally or arbitrarily. In the case of political crimes, there is no rule of law. *Habeas corpus* has not existed since 1959 and people can be, and are, held for interrogation for weeks or indefinitely without trial. There is no way of appealing against, or even drawing attention to, these abuses.

At major political trials, such as those of Matos in 1959, Marcos Armando Rodríguez in 1964 and of Aníbal Escalante and his friends

[17] Separate services total: Army 175,000; Navy, 7,000; Air Force, 12,000. Reserves total 85,000. Military services can be extended beyond three years, even more if needed for agricultural tasks.
[18] Castro, speech of 4 November 1969 (*Granma* 16 November 1969)

in 1968[19], Fidel Castro and other revolutionary leaders have played important parts, Castro acting as prosecutor as well as witness and judge.[20] The speech of the public prosecutor, Dr Santiago Cuba, initiating the judicial term of 1961–2, set the tone by criticizing 'ancient themes about the separation of powers and about the independence and political neutrality' of the judiciary.[21] Political trials have all been marked by irregularity of procedure; this began during the trial of the Batistiano pilots in March 1959 and of the 'Trujillo conspirators' in June of the same year (when the noise was such that the defence could not be heard). In the trial of Rodríguez only the confession of the accused proved guilt; and in the case of Escalante, the accused were merely found guilty of a pro-Russian political attitude which, if inconvenient to Castro, had been virtually government policy a year or so before.[22] Other trials of those accused of counter-revolutionary activities or espionage have been similarly unfair. Some trials have had admittedly to occur in conditions close to war. But neither that fact nor the frequent guilt of the accused excuses the indignity which has characterized these occasions. In the early days, defence lawyers and witnesses were themselves arrested. Latterly, defence lawyers have been appointed by the government and defence witnesses have not given evidence.

At lower levels and in non-political trials, reasonably serious efforts seem to be made to establish the guilt or innocence of accused persons but, when sentences are delivered, these are likely to be heavy or light in respect of the 'revolutionary qualities' of the persons concerned. There is clearly much casualness in minor cases, particularly in the *Tribunales Populares*, the grass roots courts which meet in the evenings to deal with brawls, minor labour disputes and problems of public order. On these, which numbered 366 at the end of 1968,[23] legal training by judges is limited to a ten-day course; they only have to be 'good Communists' and to have reached the sixth grade in education. They are the Cuban Revolution's version of English justices of the peace. These judges – three sitting together – can impose $500 fines, six months' gaol, house arrest, or internment in a 'rehabilitation farm'.[24] More serious offences are dealt with by the *Audiencias*, as in the past. In 1968–9, there was a big crime wave, apparently a consequence of the 'revolutionary offensive' of March 1968: and, in the spring of 1969, a number of exemplary sentences were imposed. Sergio del Valle, the ex-doctor of the Sierra

[19] See below, page 692.
[20] The speeches of Raúl Castro and Fidel Castro in the Escalante case were in fact at the Central Committee of the Party, but they were nevertheless judicial in effect.
[21] Quoted *Cuba and the Rule of Law*, p. 65.
[22] See *Granma* (weekly edition) 11 February 1968. There seems, however, no reasonable doubt that Marcos Armando Rodríguez was guilty. See below, 691.
[23] *Verde Olivo*, 10 November 1968.
[24] See an account by Michael Frayn, *Observer*, 10 January 1969.

and second-in-command to Camilo Cienfuegos in 1958, who had become Minister of the Interior, explained that crimes against property had recently risen (after a big drop since 1959), that the use of the death penalty for a wide variety of crimes would be desirable, and that inveterate criminals should be 'eliminated mercilessly'. (Death penalties for robberies had occasionally been invoked in 1962.)[25] He was especially alarmed that over half the murders in Havana should have been carried out by members of religious (particularly Afro–Cuban) sects.[26] On the whole, however, the crime rate has dropped by half since before the Revolution, though it is still four times the English rate.[27] There is practically no drunkenness and very little prostitution.

Numbers of persons killed or imprisoned under the Revolution are impossible to estimate fairly: Castro himself admitted the existence of 20,000 political prisoners in 1965;[28] a pessimist might well suspect the figure to be closer to the 40,000 named by the exiles, if those in forced labour or 'rehabilitation' camps are included. The total number of executions by the Revolution probably reached 2,000 by early 1961, perhaps 5,000 by 1970.[29] But who can be certain of figures in this realm? Further, accounts by ex-prisoners of appalling conditions during interrogation or in Cuban political prisons in La Cabaña, the Príncipe or (until 1965) the Isle of Pines are too numerous to be discounted.[30] It is true that most accounts of inhumanity date back to 1960–61, when invasion was daily expected, but no good regime should be capable, even under any provocation, of such malign behaviour to its opponents. The history of other totalitarian states suggests that such conditions might recur if there are no safeguards against them. As it is, malevolent operators of the Ministry of the Interior live like successful bull-fighters, in silk suits and grand houses, and showing themselves no improvement on

[25] Lieut. Pedro Pupo Pérez, Deputy Minister of Public Order, on Channel 6 of the national television network, 5 May 1969. The death penalty has also been applied for rape of minors, and to people guilty of trying to sabotage the harvest.

[26] Speech during the National Forum on Internal Order, 24–9 March 1969.

[27] In 1960 there were 198,107 crimes; in 1968, 96,693; in 1960 there were 230 murders; in 1967, 88 – or 1·14 per 100,000 inhabitants. This is still about four times the English murder rate and four times the English crime rate.

[28] Interview with Lee Lockwood, Lockwood, 205. Castro said then that 'at least half' of these prisoners were in 'some form of rehabilitation plan'.

[29] In 1963 the Cuban exile newsheet, *Cuban Information Service*, with an accuracy that does not command confidence, estimated that 2,875 people had been executed by order of Revolutionary Tribunals, 4,245 executed without trial, 2,962 killed fighting against Castro forces and 613 missing (*Cuban Information Service*, 1 June 1963). A later estimate, by a Spanish diplomat in Havana, with access to cemetery statistics, was 22,000 Cubans killed or died in gaol; 2,000 drowned attempting to escape; 24,000 Cubans now in concentration camps, 7,000 in gaol, 7,200 on penal farms and 17,231(!) held by the security police. (Jaime Caldevilla, Spanish information officer in Havana, as reported in *The Daily Telegraph*, 28 April 1969.)

[30] For the descriptions of Cuban prisons, admittedly in the early years, see Carlos Rodríguez Quesada, *David Salvador*, 20; John Martino, *I was Castro's prisoner*, passim; *Cuba and the Rule of Law* (International Commission of Jurists); and Haynes Johnson, *The Bay of Pigs*.

Colonel Ventura or Pilar García, while in gaol the long list of political prisoners is headed by Hubert Matos, David Salvador, Alberto Müller, Pedro Luis Boitel, Gustavo Arcos and Carlos Almoina, all 26 July men of the early days, of whose condition nothing for certain is known.[31]

For several years perhaps the most odious creation of the Revolution was the rehabilitation camps known as Military Units for Aid to Production (UMAP). These camps were set up to house large numbers of civil servants, homosexuals, ex-members of the bourgeoisie or potential, rather than overt, opponents of the regime. Many officials suspected of leading a soft life in Havana were dispatched to the camps on suspicion and the Committees for the Defence of the Revolution also sent unenthusiastic revolutionaries there. There they worked in the fields for often many months in prison conditions. These camps were ultimately brought to an end but they seem to survive in a different form.

For all except a few prisoners there is, however, a 'rehabilitation' programme, by which those willing to be 'rehabilitated' move progressively from one stage of re-education to another, until their conditional release, when the ominously named Department for the Prevention of Social Evils allocates them to a suitable centre of work. But dangerous enemies of the state are not offered these choices and many resilient prisoners have refused to take advantage of them.

The Cuban government has never deigned to answer the requests for information about political prisoners put by, for instance, Amnesty International or other international bodies. Few political trials have been observed by foreign journalists or outsiders and while, in the late 1960s, Castro has acknowledged many errors of economic policy, he has yet to admit a single mistake in the treatment of his opponents. The regime, like those of Eastern Europe, thus has on its conscience the bloody character of its establishment, innumerable searches of houses without warrant, thefts of property of suspected persons, lengthy interrogations in secret police buildings and callous infliction of indignities on prisoners and their visitors ('Go away and wear a black dress since you are a widow,' Major William Gálvez briefly told one visitor to the Isle of Pines).[32] In 1968, Castro refused the proposal of the Bolivian President, Barrientos, to exchange Hubert Matos for Régis Debray, and offered in reply '100 counter-revolutionaries' for the bones of Guevara: but the latter were already consumed.

[31] Nor indeed whether these men will not suffer in consequence of any publicity given internationally to their cause.

[32] *Cuba and the Rule of Law*, 225. Gálvez, a prominent army officer in the early 1960s, was Inspector-General of the Army in 1960. His sense of humour was always macabre: as military governor of Matanzas in 1959 his first act was to polish the shoes of the bootblacks in the Parque Marta Abreu, the city's main square.

On the other hand, conditions in ordinary prisons for common criminals have certainly improved since 1959, with serious efforts being made at re-education.

The instruments of control used by the government have, of course, included censorship, but also the positive use of television, radio, films and the press, the first of these in a truly revolutionary way, sombre presage perhaps of tyrannies of the future, not only enabling Castro to destroy his enemies in the first years of the revolutionary regime but also sustaining the new system during its many difficulties and changes of policy. Much is made of the years of revolutionary struggle against Batista and the average Cuban who has remained in the island must have a very curious view of the old days by this time, whatever attitude he may have to the Revolution. Street and city names have not been changed, nor have statues been built to living men; however, this is not the age of stone or marble, but of celluloid, and there are everywhere pictures of Castro, along with Martí, Marx and Lenin, while Guevara's dour but stirring visage has been seen even more often now that he has reached Parnassus. The names of hospitals and sugar mills, schools and factories, usually commemorate some dead hero of the recent past, such as Abel Santamaría (killed at Moncada), Conrado Benítez (the young literacy teacher killed in mysterious circumstances in early 1961), or Camilo Cienfuegos. Older heroes, of the 1930s, such as Guiteras or Martínez Villena, are also commemorated. The innumerable epigrams of Martí, some good, some bad, are written in huge letters on hoardings to prove some point or another for a political system of which he would doubtless have fallen foul. The whole propaganda projects of the Revolution are, indeed, a good example of Sorel's myth in action – 'a complex of remote goals, tense moral moods and expectations of apocalyptic success'[33] – sustained by memories of past skirmishes extravagantly made epic, as well as by regular mass rallies on national holidays such as the anniversaries of the flight of Batista, of the attack on Moncada barracks and of the foundation of the Committees for the Defence of the Revolution. The propaganda of the Cuban regime has consistent aims: to replace the mentality of the lottery with that of nationalism, in order to make sacrifices bearable;[34] and to distort the real history of the recent past. One young architect described a hard day's work in the canefields and then saw how a few hundred yards away a cutting machine had done the same work in a few minutes; 'it was then,' he said, 'that I realized what it meant to be underdeveloped, how close, in spite of Havana's modernity, we were to Africa.'[35]

[33] E. A. Shils' introduction to Georges Sorel, *Reflections on Violence* (Glencoe, The Free Press, 1950), 20–21.

[34] Cf. Goldenberg, 301.

[35] André Schiffren, *The New Republic*, 29 June 1968.

A more inaccurate description of Cuba's predicament could scarcely be imagined.

Newspapers are in consequence tedious. *Granma*, the 'official organ of the central committee of the Communist Party of Cuba', is less a newspaper than an exhortation sheet, reporting Castro's speeches in full, with little news and occasional snippets of inspiring history. Its editor, the mulatto, Jorge Enrique Mendoza, who was once the chief of agrarian reform in Camagüey who clashed with Matos, is best known for his curious assertion in 1967 that the Israeli army in the Six-Day War was commanded by Nazis. There are no other national daily papers except for an evening version of *Granma*, *Juventud Rebelde*. The director of television and broadcasting, Major Jorge Serguera, also curiously has a link with the Matos case since he was then, as a Judge-Advocate of the Rebel Army, the chief prosecutor. He was for a time military governor of Matanzas, a post he lost after unwisely sending for tanks to use against housewives in the bread riot of Cárdenas in 1962. The last columnist who ventured a joke about the Revolution, Segundo Cazalis, was savagely attacked by Castro in March 1964 and his column, *Siquitrilla*, was abruptly brought to an end. Compared with the Cuban press, that of Spain might be considered sparkling. Any cartoon such as that which appeared in 1900 in *Discusión*, during the U.S. military occupation, depicting poor Cuba crucified between two thieves, would doubtless earn the artist more than the twenty-four hours' gaol intemperately handed out by General Wood.

The censorship has been candidly defended by Castro: 'The Revolution is the first to lament that individual guarantees cannot be granted – . . . the Revolution explains that to concede those guarantees would serve that powerful enemy who has tried to destroy the Revolution and to drown it in the blood of the people.'[36] During the *Siquitrilla* affair, Castro explained: 'These gentlemen who write "truth never hurts", I don't know whether they conceive of truth as an abstract entity. Truth is a concrete entity in the service of a noble cause.' (So, it might be added, is untruth, from time to time.) Cazalis, the journalist in question, incidentally, had earlier received an order not to attack in his column the government of Spain, with whom Cuba was then undertaking commercial relations.

The history of the arts under the revolution has naturally been unsteady and, in innumerable personal instances, tragic. Thus the first flush of national self-confidence which was a characteristic of 1959 and expressed in particular by the Monday supplement to the newspaper *Revolución*, was succeeded by increasing disillusion during the years

[36] Speech at 1st national congress of *Responsables del Trabajo de Orientación Revolucionaria*, *Revolución*, 11 November 1961.

1961–62, particularly during the months when Aníbal Escalante was busy setting up the ORI. *Lunes de Revolución* was banned, films such as the famous PM (which had no revolutionary content) were attacked, the main means of self-expression came under the control of men who worked safely for the regime: thus Alfredo Guevara, an old Communist (if relatively young), took over the direction of the promising film institute (ICAIC); and Nicolás Guillén, an admirable poet but politically an instrument of the Communist Party, became President of the Writers Union. Even before the missile crisis, independent spirits began either to abandon Cuba, or to keep silent, or to take jobs as cultural attachés in Cuban embassies abroad; while others made their peace with the regime, reached compromises, and either allowed themselves to be censored or censored themselves; others still, moving into positions of cultural power, began to regard as part of their job the passing of judgement on the works of their contemporaries. Some work of note continued to be done and, in terms of quantity of output (novels, plays, films, poems), the Revolution's achievement has been remarkable, but the most distinguished Cuban artists are still those who, like the novelists Alejo Carpentier (now Cuban cultural minister in France)[37] and José Lezama Lima, or the painters, René Portocarrero[38] and Wilfredo Lam (who has lived in Paris since the late 1940s), were well established before the Revolution, or those who, like Severo Sarduy or Guillermo Cabrera Infante (once the director of *Lunes de Revolución*), are now in exile. Against this should be set the fact that the regime has spent a great deal on artistic promotion, and it can fairly claim to have brought poetry, ballet, music, travelling libraries and theatre to the countryside of Cuba. Some of the historical work on Cuba in the last century, particularly that by Manuel Moreno Fraginals and Juan Pérez de la Riva, has been of a high standard.[39] The two main literary and artistic magazines, *Unión* and *Casa de las Américas*, are good. But new popular music seems to have died and Cuba which, during the 'bad old days', was for so long a source of new music and dances, from the conga, rumba, mambo and habanera to the chachachá, has not had any new rhythms to which to dance or to export.

Restrictions on liberty have been quite flexibly interpreted so far as painting is concerned despite, admittedly, efforts by Blas Roca and other old Communists to force down the throats of the Cubans the realist standards of their Mexican friends, such as David Alfaro Siqueiros. Thus Castro explained in 1963 that when 'Russia's satellites in Havana' (pre-

[37] Surprisingly, considering the sceptical tone of such books as *The Kingdom of this World*.
[38] Portocarrero enjoys a favoured position since, though he lives and works in Cuba, he is able to exhibit and sell abroad, and spends what he wants.
[39] Moreno Fraginals is known for his excellent study of the nineteenth-century sugar mill, *El Ingenio*. Pérez de la Riva is editor of the scholarly *Revista de la Biblioteca Nacional*.

sumably Escalante) had asked him to ban an abstract painting, as Khrushchev had done in Russia, he had replied: 'Our enemies are capitalism and imperialism, not abstract painting.'[40] Guevara in 1965, in *Socialism and Man*, described social realist art rather surprisingly as the 'corpse of nineteenth-century bourgeois painting'. But Castro's 'Address to the Intellectuals' in 1961 had included the aphorism: 'everything within the Revolution, nothing against the Revolution', while the declaration of principles at the foundation of the Union of Writers and Artists included the remark 'we regard it as absolutely essential that all writers and artists, regardless of individual aesthetic differences, should take part in the great work of defending and consolidating the Revolution. By using severe self-criticism we shall purge our means of expression to become better adapted to the needs of the struggle.'[41]

'Our principal idea has been full freedom for those who support the Revolution, nothing for those who are opposed,' President Dorticós remarked rather sourly in 1964[42] and, in 1965, Castro was explaining that his view of art had much in common with his view of Truth: 'Art is not an end in itself. Man is the end. Making men happier, better.'[43] In 1966, admittedly, José Lezama Lima published a major novel, *Paradiso*, which not only had no concern whatever for the Revolution but, in its famous Chapter XI, dealt mainly with homosexual practices. But it turned out that the novel had only passed the censor because it was so long and difficult to read, no second impression appeared and soon a much harder note was set by the editor of the young Communist paper, *El Caimán Barbudo*, Jesús Díaz, in an article entitled *Towards a Militant Culture*.[44] In 1967, a big exhibition of modern paintings was held in Havana: no socialist realist paintings admittedly were exhibited but Castro's own contribution was ominous: an anti-aircraft gun, a bull and seven cows.

The test of the regime came, however, as might be expected, in literature. In 1966, the great Chilean poet, Pablo Neruda, was roundly criticized in a letter signed by many of the Cuban regime's most faithful writers for suggesting, after a meeting with President Belaúnde of Peru, that there could be an end to the 'cold war in culture'. At a conference in 1967, Cuban writers unanimously accepted a proposal by Castro that copyright should no longer be respected and that royalties should not be paid, even to foreigners. One writer, Jaime Suretsky, argued that 'non-payment enabled the author to realize himself as a human being' (though writers have earned royalties abroad which they have not been

[40] Interview with Claude Julien, *Le Monde*, 23 March 1963.
[41] *Hoy*, 23 August 1961, quoted Goldenberg, 254.
[42] Dorticós to Mark Schleiffer, *Monthly Review* April 1964, p. 655.
[43] Lockwood, p. 207
[44] *Para una cultura militante, Bohemia*, 26 September 1966.

able to touch). Finally, in a famous case in 1968, the young poet Heberto Padilla, gained the Writers' Union annual poetry prize from an international jury, but was never permitted to receive it from the Cuban Writers' Union on the grounds that one of his poems, *Fuera de Juego*, was insufficiently committed. In fact, his early criticisms of the stifling atmosphere of the Cuban cultural scene in the Young Communist periodical, *El Caimán Barbudo*, had already caused his denunciation by Lisandro Otero, the editor of *Cuba* and a prominent conformist novelist.[45] In 1969 Haydée Santamaría, the Moncada veteran who had become literary *apparatchik* as President of the Casa de las Americas, explained to the juries who were to judge the latter's annual prize that no artist could remain non-political since that itself implied a political stand,[46] while later in 1969 the Padilla affair was apparently repeated in the case of Pablo Armando Fernández who also won a prize, delivered himself of some critical remarks about the Cuban cultural scene on television, and had the prize withdrawn. (But, in this case, Castro intervened and insisted on the return of the award.)

Perhaps the most disagreeable side of these developments has been the increased role of the armed forces through their organ, *Verde Olivo*, in the establishment of cultural standards: It was *Verde Olivo* which first attacked Padilla and other writers 'whose spinelessness is matched only by their pornography and counter-revolutionism'.[47]

The reason for these events is as much the existence of a by now well entrenched literary bureaucracy (as in all Communist countries) as national political developments. Thus the Union of Writers and Artists (UNEAC) directs the main Cuban publishing house. All writers have to belong to it. The bureaucrats attached to this institution, as to the centre for the dissemination of Cuban culture, the Casa de las Américas, or the 'committee of revolutionary orientation' (or censor-

---

[45] Nevertheless, Padilla afterwards lived peaceably. Associated with Padilla was Antón Arrufat. See *Times Literary Supplement*, 11 July, 22 August and 14 November 1968, *Le Monde*, 5 November 1968, and David Gallagher, *New York Review of Books*, 23 May 1968. Even more disagreeable, Leopoldo Avila, in *Verde Olivo* (8 November, 1968), falsely accused Padilla of having swindled the Cuban foreign trade agency and having been dismissed. The cause for Padilla's explosion in *El Caimán Barbudo* was that journal's inquiry into the attitudes of prominent Cuban writers to Otero's novel *Pasión de Urbino*. Since Otero is a powerful apparatchik, all save Padilla were adulatory. Padilla raised the question of why so much fuss was made about Otero's novel when the brilliant apolitical interpretation of Havana in the last years of Batista, *Tres Tristes Tigres*, by the exiled Guillermo Cabrera Infante, had not been considered. After these exchanges, the editors of *El Caimán Barbudo* were speedily changed, even though one of them, Jesús Díaz, was the author of *Towards a Militant Culture*.

[46] *Bohemia*, 24 January 1969. Not surprisingly, therefore, the novel prize went to *La Canción de la Crisálida* by Renato Prado Oropesa about Guevara in Bolivia and the essay prize to the Peruvian guerrillero, Héctor Béjar. This was a change from Haydée Santamaría's speech in 1968 on the same occasion, when she had said that there was no more reason for a book jacket to have political content than the trousers of the critics.

[47] Quoted 'Commentary', *Times Literary Supplement*, 14 November 1968.

ship board), founded by César Escalante, have undoubtedly used their power to further their own not always distinguished careers, at the cost of less conventional spirits. For the present, admittedly, these things have perhaps scarcely got beyond the condition of scandal and have not yet reached outrage. So far as numbers are concerned, book production has much increased, fifteen million being produced in 1969 – mostly textbooks, and about 70% distributed free.

Since 1962, there have been only a few political crises. Thus the Minister of Labour, Augusto Martínez Sánchez, the lawyer from Holguín who presided over the destruction of the free unions in 1959–60, tried unsuccessfully to kill himself in 1964 when he was dismissed, partly for mismanagement, partly apparently since he sought to flirt with all political groups. Eighteen months later, early in 1966, Rolando Cubela, who, as President of FEU, had done similar hatchet work in destroying the university in 1960, was sentenced to twenty-five years' imprisonment for taking part in an attempted assassination of Castro, in connivance with the CIA.[48] He joined in gaol, therefore, Pedro Luis Boitel, the democratic student leader whom he helped to ruin. At the same time, Efigenio Ameijeiras, Castro's first chief of police in 1959, and at the time a Vice-Minister of the Armed Forces, was imprisoned and dismissed from the central committee of the Cuban Communist Party for 'moral offences' and there was a national purge of corrupted elements. Armando Acosta, for a long time the Communist boss of Oriente, was also dismissed with some fanfare in 1967 after failing with the slogan 'more sugar from less cane' (or, according to one informant, for holding a specially lavish party to celebrate his daughter's fifteenth birthday). But the most serious crises were those which led to the final discrediting and discomfiture of the two most prominent old Communists after Blas Roca and Carlos Rafael Rodríguez: namely, Joaquín Ordoqui and Aníbal Escalante.

Ordoqui – a Communist since 1927 – and his *compañera*, Edith García Buchaca, lost their jobs (as respectively Vice-Minister of the Armed Forces and President of the Council of Culture) when it became known that, in exile in Mexico in 1957–8 and afterwards in Havana, they had protected the young Communist Marcos Armando Rodríguez, who confessed to having betrayed the four students killed by Ventura and Batista's police in Humboldt Street in 1957.[49] Rodríguez was finally shot after his two trials had shaken the unity of the revolutionary

---

[48] Cubela, who had not done very well for himself during the Revolution, was apparently approached by Manuel Artime, the exile leader, on behalf of the CIA, when he was an attaché at the Cuban embassy in Madrid. The plot was unearthed by a skilful Cuban spy in exile circles in Miami. Cubela escaped death only after a 'personal appeal for clemency' by Castro.

[49] See above, p. 147.

government,[50] and Ordoqui and Edith García Buchaca were kept under house arrest indefinitely.

The second instalment of the Escalante affair shook the government even more than the case of Marcos Armando Rodríguez. Aníbal Escalante, the old communist leader who had been main organizer of the ORI and discredited publicly in 1962, returned to Cuba from Prague in 1964. He was given an honorary post as administrator of the farm *Dos Hermanos*. Far from learning from his past errors, however, he apparently re-embarked on an attempt to recover his lost position by playing on the discontents of 'old militants' of the old Communist Party, who, like himself, had failed to establish themselves in the new Castroist party. Among these were two members of the Communist Central Committee constituted in 1965, José Matar, the first chief of the important Committees for the Defence of the Revolution and afterwards Cuban ambassador in Budapest, and Ramón Calcines, the sugar workers' leader from Las Villas, who, after being the Communist Youth leader in 1960, was practically Minister of Foreign Affairs from January 1961 to March 1962 while he was part of the Foreign Relations Commission of the ORI; later, he had run the fruit export section in the Institute of Agrarian Reform. A series of luncheons and dinners were held at *Dos Hermanos* and other places. Heretical speeches were also said to have been made at funerals. Escalante and this 'microfaction' (as he and his friends were described by their enemies) seem to have disapproved of armed struggle in Latin America, and to have considered the guerrilla war in Venezuela an 'adventure'. They allegedly said 'No one understands Fidel: he is mad', and argued that Guevara was a Trotskyist (and that his departure was to be welcomed). The microfaction was accused later of having criticized voluntary labour in agriculture, desired to re-introduce material incentives, suggested that the revolutionary leadership was petty bourgeois and represented a 'leftist adventurist deviation', and that a change of leadership would improve relations with Russia.[51] Escalante was charged with establishing a group of personal followers in several sections of the Cuban communist party and with gathering documents on the economy and passing them to Russian officials; particularly, as befitted one who had spent a lifetime in

---

[50] See *Liborio* (Chile) No. 1, and Hugh Thomas, 'Murder in Havana', *New Statesman*, 29 May 1964. For a semi-fictional treatment of this extraordinary case, see *Utiles despues de muertos*, by Carlos Manuel Pellecer (Barcelona 1969), an ex-Communist from Guatemala who lived for some time in Cuba. The main point never cleared up was whether in fact Rodríguez, as he claimed, had confessed his betrayal to Edith García Buchaca; and how it was that Rodríguez could have been warned, when in Prague in 1961, of his impending arrest, by a Brazilian diplomat.

[51] The microfaction also took a strong line on the question of the elimination of the bus conductor, since they believed this 'would lead to more conflicts in the buses'. (Raúl Castro's speech, *Granma*, 11 February 1968.)

a communist party, to Russian security officials.[52] Needless to say, these activities could not be concealed, the Cuban public began to hear in speeches about the 'microfaction' (depicted in cartoons as microbes) in mid-1967, and eventually Escalante and thirty-six followers were tried. Many curious activities were unearthed: for example, Félix Fleitas, chief of security of the ORI in 1961–2, had recalled to his discredit the fact that he had once run a *bordello* for Soviet technicians; Escalante had approached Russian, East German and Czech officials whom he thought had access to Russian leaders in order to create an opinion in the Soviet Union in favour of his position – among them, Dr Frantisek Kriegel, a Czech adviser to the Ministry of Health,[53] and Emilio de Quesada, an old Communist who openly admitted, in his trial, that 'we came to wish for a certain degree of political pressure to secure changes'.[54]

The consequence was that Escalante and his friends were imprisoned for varying periods, and that Calcines and Matar lost their places on the Central Committee.

Finally, among the major political crises of the regime, Guevara resigned in 1965 from his post as Minister of Industries after what seems to have been a quarrel with Castro,[55] fought in the Congo with the Kinshasa rebels, and died, aged thirty-nine, two years later in Bolivia, betrayed, like the Italian nationalist, Pisacane, in the nineteenth century, by the peasants whom he had hoped to free: killed with him, as has been seen, were several members of the Central Committee of the Cuban Communist Party.[56] Guevara was shot by the Bolivian army after his capture.

Guevara was a brave, sincere and determined man who was also

[52] Raúl Castro explained in his speech to the Central Committee of the Communist Party that 'a very small number of advisers, journalists and secretaries of foreign embassies participated in the activities of the microfaction'.

[53] Kriegel had fought in the Spanish War and in 1968, as a member of the Praesidium of the Czechoslovak Communist Party, became one of the most prominent liberalizers in the Dubček regime. He was arrested with Dubček on 21 August 1968 and has since been discredited.

[54] *Granma* (weekly edition) 11 February 1968 contains speeches.

[55] This is clearly the implication of Ricardo Rojo's life (*Che Guevara*, French edition, 168). Guevara returned from an extended world tour on 14 March 1965, and on 16 March wrote to his mother in Buenos Aires that he was going to spend a month cutting cane and then five years directing a nationalized industry. In fact, for a variety of reasons Guevara left Cuba at the end of July 1965 for the Congo. Castro ordered him to leave the Congo because of the worsening of Cuban–Chinese relations and, in March 1966, Guevara was again in Cuba. He left for Bolivia in September 1966.

[56] See above, p. 677. In addition to these (Juan Vitalio Acuña, Antonio Sánchez Díaz and Eliseo Reyes) ten other Cubans were killed in Bolivia (Major Ricardo Gustavo Machín, Orlando Pantoja, Israel Reyes, Jesús Suárez Gayol, Manuel Hernández, Octavio de la Concepción, José María Martínez, René Martínez, Fernández Montes de Oca and Carlos Coello); three Cubans escaped from Bolivia via Chile (Daniel Alarcón, Harry Villegas and Leonardo Tamayo). Six of these men had been with Guevara on the road to Santa Clara in 1958, and all but two had been members of the 26 July Movement.

obstinate, narrow and dogmatic. At the end of his life, he seems to have become convinced of the virtues of violence almost for its own sake: 'How close could we look into a bright future should two, three or many Vietnams flourish throughout the world with their share of deaths and their intense tragedies . . . [with] imperialism impelled to disperse its forces under the . . . increasing hatred of all peoples of the world.'[57] Hatred, for Guevara, was indeed a praiseworthy emotion which could transform man into 'an effective, violent, selective and cold killing machine'.[58] Guevara became in his last years a man for whom the sweetest music was openly the 'staccato singing of the machine guns and new battle cries of war and victory'.[59] In an article written during the missile crisis but published posthumously, he even remarked 'we must proceed along the path of liberation, even if that costs millions of atomic victims'.[60]

In Cuba, Guevara too had shown other dogmatism: he was worsted in the controversy with Marcelo Fernández, his successor as President of the National Bank as to the extent to which state corporations should or should not be autonomous. Guevara took the narrowest centralist line. His airy predictions in 1960–61 that Cuba would be able swiftly to industrialize came to naught. The many half completed or empty factories, 'standing like sad memories of the conflict between pretension and reality', as the Yugoslav journal *Borba* put it in 1965, were his memorial.[61] He was not a merciful spirit. A Cuban lawyer defending a woman accused of having had relations with the previous government recalled that Guevara had in 1959 said: 'I do not know how you dare take an interest in this person . . . I will have her shot . . . if any person has a good word for the previous government that is enough for me to have him shot.'[62] He seems to have assumed in the most *simpliste* way also that the high wages gained by the European working classes were inevitably paid for by the 'millions of exploited peasants and workers of Latin America, Africa and Asia'.[63] He was dogmatic: in 1961 he was

[57] Guevara's message to the journal, *Tricontinental*, June 1967, published *Granma*, 17 April 1967.

[58] *Ibid.*

[59] *Ibid.*

[60] *Verde Olivo*, 6 October 1968. It is surely impossible that Guevara's elevated thoughts on the dignity of war (reminiscent of Theodore Roosevelt, who also suffered from asthma) would have been ventured by anyone other than a native of a continent which, for all its palace coups and gangsterism, has been less exposed to the consequences of conflict and violence than any other during the last century. Blas Roca incidentally is also 'not afraid of nuclear weapons' (see Anthony Sylvester, Cuba's Lesson for Latin America, *Daily Telegraph*, 11 June 1965).

[61] See Guevara's speech at the first National Production Conference, 1961, pp. 110–12. For a veiled attack on Guevara's economics, see also the speech of President Dorticós, in *Cuba Socialista*, March 1966, p. 26–42.

[62] *Cuba and the Rule of Law* (International commission of Jurists, Geneva, 1962), 158.

[63] Remarks to Marc Schleifer, *Monthly Review* (April 1964), 652.

credited with the old-fashioned view that 'we must arrive at 100% state ownership', since even small properties were unproductive and disturbing to the entire country.[64] Yet he was candid and, on the whole, he deceived neither himself nor others. His quarrel with the Soviet Union and the, as he thought, increasingly *embourgeoisé* Communist parties of East Europe, was expressed without much care for his own future. He believed that both the law of value, which still characterizes even inter-socialist trade, and material incentives, used then in Cuba as in East Europe, were immoral. His influence over Castro, always strong, for good or evil, has grown after his death, for Castro has since taken up many of his views. As in the case of Martí, or Lawrence of Arabia, failure has brightened, not dimmed, the legend.[65]

Since 1962, opposition in Cuba has been sporadic. The last bid by the 'liberals' was a promise by Manuel Ray to land in Cuba with an army of liberation by 20 May 1964. But though he set off from Puerto Rico, he landed in the Bahamas, not Oriente, and his star has since sunk. He and most other prominent anti-Castro Cuban politicians have been integrated into North American life. Manuel Artime apparently organized a new exile army in Costa Rica in 1963-4, with CIA money, but without an invasion.[66] Several assassination attempts, on the other hand, are said to have been inspired in North America, notably that of Rolando Cubela in March 1966, perhaps the last fling of the *señorito* in Cuban politics.[67] Minor guerrilla skirmishing has gone on most of the time in Oriente and other mountainous districts in an unsung war; rumours abound but probably at least 4,000 *guerrilleros* have been killed since 1962.[68] A special 'organization for the struggle against "banditry"'

[64] *Revolución*, 29 November 1961.

[65] Lives of Guevara have begun to appear. For a sympathetic and favourable study by a friend, see *Che Guevara, Vie et Mort d'un ami* by Ricardo Rojo (Paris 1969); and, for a hostile study, see Horacio Rodríguez, *Che Guevara, Mythe ou Réalité* (Paris 1969).

[66] See Al Burt, 'The Mirage of Havana', *Nation*, 25 January 1965. According to Burt, the Costa Rican government brought this adventure to an end on the ground that it was being used as a base for smuggling. Of past Cuban politicians, Batista lives on in Spain in comfort, protected by his millions; Grau San Martín died in Havana in 1969; Prío, Masferrer, Ventura, Varona, Sánchez Arango, Raúl Chibás, Felipe Pazos and Javier Pazos – Batistianos, Ortodoxos, Auténticos, ex-members of the 26 July Movement – live on in the U.S. or elsewhere. Julio Lobo is in Madrid. Other exiles are to be found all over South America and in Paris – a diaspora as large and perhaps in the long run as fruitful as that of the Spanish Republicans after 1939.

[67] The end of those dapperly dressed youths, in the words of Carleton Beals, with 'long fine hands, white skins, sleek plastered black hair, . . . capable of facing the firing squad or directing a Santa Clara sugar plantation' (Carleton Beals, *The Crime of Cuba*, 70) – capable of only these two things perhaps.

[68] Raúl Castro (22 July 1967) spoke of 3,591 'bandits' and 500 Cuban soldiers killed since. He said between $500 million and $800 million had been used solely to destroy 'armed bandits'. In 1965 Fidel Castro had spoken of 2,005 bandits and 295 Cuban soldiers killed (Speech of 26 July 1965).

(LCB) has been founded under an old associate of Raúl Castro's in the Sierra Cristal, Major Menéndez Tomassevich. In 1968 there was a big wave of sabotage, including arson in ships, factories and farms, with several shot or imprisoned in consequence. Of this secret war little has been written – perhaps never will be. One story, however, was published in Cuba of how a Haitian *santero* named Baldomero, aged seventy-five, took to the hills with a group of voodoo followers. The disciples were captured, but Baldomero was never found. Rumours in the Sierra Maestra were that he had made himself invisible, or had changed himself into a serpent, or a stone, or a tree; once, indeed, a peasant, surprised by a snake, shouted, in the hearing of others, 'Quick, quick, kill him, it might be Baldomero'. The legend of Baldomero lives on.[69]

The regime's relations with the Church quietened after the crises of 1960–61. The churches stayed open, and the Papal Delegate, Mgr. Cesare Zacchi (later also Bishop of Havana), has also remained, along with the Cuban diplomatic mission to the Vatican. At one time the police made lists of those who went to church, but this practice has been stopped. On the other hand, religion plays no part in schools and no new rural settlement has a church. Priests and pastors have to do military service. No practising Catholic can become a Communist. Holy Week was in 1965 rechristened 'Playa Girón Week' and devoted to mass manual voluntary labour (it has since become extended to 'Playa Girón Month'). In 1966, streets near churches were turned into play-grounds at the times of services, the noise of children drowning the Mass. Licences to repair churches have, it seems, sometimes been refused and, in consequence, the buildings can be closed as dangerous. In early 1969, there were attacks on religion as such in the magazine of the armed services, *Verde Olivo*. This organ criticized the 'spirit of resignation' implicit in religion, its 'blind faith' in the supernatural and its search for truth through prayer; for 'religion divided the popular forces' and helps to delay the appearance of the New Man, who, of course, should be as free from superstition as from ambition.[70] Jehovah's Witnesses were accused by Castro in 1963 of being a counter-revolutionary sect and, in 1969, their pacifism, their refusal to swear by the national flag, to work on Sundays and 'to give adequate attention to weapons' were all condemned. Two-thirds of the ministers at the Western Baptist convention were also arrested in April 1965, tried, and found guilty of espionage. The Protestant churches have, however, suffered consider-

[69] Orlando Reyes, *Mitos y Leyendas de las Villas*, Colección folklórico Cubano, ediciones de la Universidad Central de las Villas, 1965.
[70] *Verde Olivo*, 2 February 1969.

ably since the emigration of so many North American pastors and seem to have retreated into at best political neutrality.[71]

More recently, the Cuban hierarchy appealed in a pastoral letter in the spring of 1969 for an end to the U.S. economic boycott, and the Cuban government applauds the socially conscious Catholics and priests of South America – providing that they are 'militant' like the Camilo Torres Movement, which believes that 'the armed struggle is the duty of the Christian conscience in Latin America' and that the 'guerrilla's love of violence is basically a sublime love of truth'.[72] In 1968 Castro noted the presence of a group of revolutionary priests at the Cultural Congress of Havana and compared the orthodox Communists of Latin America to them: 'When we see sectors of the clergy becoming revolutionary, how shall we resign ourselves to seeing sectors of Marxism becoming ecclesiastical?'[73]

[71] See C. Alton Robertson, *The Political Role of the Protestants in Cuba*, in Occasional Bulletin of the Missionary research library, New York, Vol. xviii, Nos. 2 and 3 (February and March 1967).

[72] *Punto Final*, Santiago de Chile, 25 February 1969. Camilo Torres, a radical Colombian priest, was killed by the Colombian army in 1966.

[73] Castro's closing speech to the Congress, 1968.

CHAPTER 50

New Friends and Old

The extent to which the Cuban Revolutionary Government has allowed its internal policies to be dictated since 1962 by the desires of its main commercial and military ally, Russia, is naturally still obscure. But it is obvious, on the one hand, that, despite the close relations between the two countries, Castro, because of his own temperament and because of Cuba's geographical position, has often been at least verbally an unsteady ally; on the other hand, that in a number of matters of real importance to Russia, he has had to follow Russian ideas most closely. Thus Castro, unlike, for instance, the Communist Party of Italy, supported the Russian invasion of Czechoslovakia in 1968; and Russian influence probably secured that Cuba turned her main economic attention back from the heady ideas of swift industrialization to continued emphasis on the production of sugar. By the Russo–Cuban sugar agreement of January 1964 Cuba indeed agreed to sell to Russia, at the fixed price of 6 cents a pound (then well above the world market price), increasing proportions of her sugar crop between then and 1970. Russia, therefore, is the father of Cuba's continuing monoculture – though, despite Khrushchev's talk about an 'international division of labour' within the socialist world, both Russian and Czechoslovak sugar beet production has continued to increase and Russia has re-sold much Cuban sugar on the world market.

Leaving aside military assistance, which appears to be free, Russia and the East European communist countries must be owed by Cuba many hundreds of million dollars on both current and capital account. Thus between 1965 and 1969, Soviet civilian aid seems to have amounted to $M300 a year, and maybe more than that in 1969–70.[1] Of Cuban

[1] In 1968 the rough equivalent of $M327 was an estimate of the figure. For 1965, see P. J. Wiles *Communist International Economics*, Basil Blackwell, Oxford, 1969, p. 403. Wiles estimated this as follows:

sugar subsidy	95 M roubles
exports to Cuba f.o.b.	338
imports from Cuba f.o.b.	277
balance	61
freight services rendered to Cuba	34
salaries and technical advisers less Cuba contribution	3
	808 M roubles

i.e. approximately $M308

Revolutionary Diplomacy:
11a Castro in Russia, 1964: (*L to R*) Mikoyan, Brezhnev, Podgorny, Castro,
   Malinovsky, Khrushchev, Grechko, Alexiev (Soviet Ambassador to Cuba)
 b Castro with the Deputy Prime Minister of North Vietnam, Le Thanh Nghi,
   1967

imports from Russia, oil is doubtless the largest item, apart from machinery, with over 150 tankers arriving from Russia a year.[2] All Cuba's wheat comes from Russia and Cuba has imported from her or from her satellites some 40,000 tractors and 2,000 combine harvesters, not to speak of innumerable spare parts for old North American machines. Cuban exports to Russia were apparently valued at 281 million roubles in 1961, and 372 million in 1968; Cuban imports have also risen consistently.[3] Russia has re-equipped sugar mills, built electricity plants, hospitals, factories, irrigation plants and roads. Numerous Russian technicians are at work in Cuba, and many Cuban students have by now had extensive technical education in Russia. As Castro put it in 1969, Russia's aid has been 'inestimable and decisive'. The U.S. Government guesses that the Cuban capital debt to Russia approaches $1·5 billion.[4] On the other hand, figures mean little in this field: Castro himself in 1967 spoke of his foreign commerce as being 'practically on a barter basis, with so-called exchange money, almost worthless except in the country in which the agreement is held'.[5] Russia has probably done well out of her sugar dealings with Cuba, given the apparently high cost of producing sugar from beet in Russia itself.[6] It is also obvious that the disbursement of a million or so dollars a day to Cuba is not a very large expenditure measured alongside Russia's other spending abroad.

Thus Russia plays almost as great a part in Cuban politics as the U.S. did in the past: she is Cuba's main market for her main product; she supplies Cuba with the weapons (and doubtless the intelligence and espionage technology) without which the regime might not have been able to survive; she takes most of even Cuba's secondary products such as fruit and vegetables; she is her only supplier of both wheat and oil. A Russian embassy official, Rudolf Shliapnikov, apparently told Aníbal Escalante in 1967, referring to Russia's hold over the Cuban economy, 'We have only to say that repairs are being held up at Baku for three weeks and that's that'.[7] Castro has publicly admitted that he knows only too well 'the bitterness of having to depend to a considerable degree on

[2] 167 tankers docked in Havana in 1967, or one every 54 hours (Castro's speech of 2 January 1968).

[3] Sakun P., *URSS*, July 1968. According to P. Sakun, Russian commercial attaché in Cuba from 1960 till 1968, the figures were (in million roubles):

	1959	1960	1961	1962	1963	1964	1965	1966	1967	1968
Total	6·7	160	539	541	508	591	646	689	842	914
Russian exports to Cuba	—	67	258	330	360	331	338	432	507	542
Russian imports from Cuba	6·7	93	281	211	148	260	308	257	335	372

[4] U.S. department of commerce, *Survey of Agriculture in Cuba*, 1969, 15. A good diplomatic source in Havana early in 1969 put this figure much higher.

[5] Castro speech, 10 August 1967 (at the end of the OLAS conference).

[6] See discussion in Gutelmann, 215, where it is suggested that Russian costs must be three times as great as those in Cuba.

[7] Speech of Raúl Castro to the Central Committee, reported *Granma*, February 1968.

things which come from outside and how that can become a weapon and at least create the temptation to use it':[8] at least, the U.S. in the past paid in convertible currency, not in goods of dubious appeal or efficacy. Doubtless, therefore, the desire to escape from Russian economic control was one reason for the imposition of petrol rationing (though only in January 1968), as for the conclusion of a $M30 credit agreement with Rumania for oil drilling equipment in March 1968. Every effort has recently been made to save fuel, even to produce sugar 'without a single drop of oil'. But for the moment, Cuba under socialism could no more do without Russia as a market and as a supplier of essential fuel than she could do without the U.S. under capitalism. It is thus remarkable that Cuba has ventured so often so far away from Russia's policies as she has. Even Castro's support for Russia over Czechoslovakia may not have been so reluctant as might be supposed since, as his speech on the occasion made clear, however much he might deplore the use of force by one big country against another small one, he also much disliked the tolerant character of socialism under Dubček.

The main area where Russia and Cuba have fallen out, however, has been over the question of whether or not the policy of the armed struggle is the only way to achieve revolution in Latin America.

Castro's attitudes to this matter have varied often in the eight years following the Second Declaration of Havana which pledged Cuban support for the 'liberation' of the continent. These changes have occurred partly because of some unforeseeable event in the world outside, such as the retirement of Khrushchev, the Vietnam war and its repercussions within the U.S., partly because of Guevara's expedition to Bolivia, the Russo–Chinese dispute, and difficulties within the Communist parties of South America themselves (in particular the Communist Party of Venezuela). Thus, despite the undoubted annoyance felt by Castro with Russia after the missile crisis in 1962, Cuban–Russian relations remained very good for two years – chiefly because of Castro's close friendship with Khrushchev (to whom perhaps he even felt, after his two visits to Russia in 1963 and 1964, a species of loyalty), partly perhaps because of a reluctance to embark upon any further entanglements while the Cuban Communist Party itself was still far from united. Until late 1965, at least, Castro seemed ready to accept the view, strongly held by Russia and by the orthodox leadership of the Latin American Communist parties, that the question as to whether the road to socialism should be peaceable or by means of an 'armed struggle' (*lucha armada*) was one to be settled by the 'struggling peoples themselves'.[9] Castro also avoided, in his speeches

[8] Castro speech, 13 March 1968.
[9] As stated in the communiqué at the end of Castro's first visit to Moscow in May 1964.

or simply in newspaper reports, any mention, of any sort, of the difficulties between Russia and China, with almost as many articles continuing to appear in the Cuban press about the latter as the former. This cautious attitude was internationally approved in November 1964 at a secret conference of Latin American Communist parties at Havana.[10]

But this caution was never very popular in Cuba, and Guevara (before he disappeared in March 1965) and Raúl Castro went some way to differentiate themselves on the matter from Fidel Castro in some of their statements. Castro began to find himself described by the Chinese as a revisionist, while radical revolutionaries in the rest of Latin America, though still looking to Cuba as the capital of Revolution and knowing that, for the simple reason of having survived, the underprivileged of South America regarded Castro as a saviour, began to doubt the purity of Castro's ideology. 1965 nevertheless was a good time for Russo–Cuban relations. During that summer, after Guevara had left, Castro criticized harshly the ideal of moral incentives which he afterwards adopted, while the conversion of the old PURS (previously ORI) into the Cuban Communist Party, with its militarily-orientated Central Committee, was completed.

Castro's cautious attitude came to an end at the first Tricontinental Conference, held in Havana, in January 1966, when the Afro–Asian Solidarity Organization, previously held together by the Egyptians and the Russians, was turned into AALAPSO (Afro-Asian and Latin American Peoples' Solidarity Organization) and, much to the Russians' surprise, was captured by Castro, who then gave a wild promise that any revolutionary movement anywhere in the world could count on Cuba's unconditional help. AALAPSO established its headquarters thereafter in Havana, and the familiar figure of Osmani Cienfuegos, previously not much known for his international activities or interests, became the new secretary-general. The presence of a remarkable number of radical guerrilla leaders from the rest of Latin America gave drama to the conference, and naturally these men quite overshadowed the representatives of the orthodox Communist parties whom the Russians had hoped would dominate the scene. Admittedly, Castro did treat the conference to a spectacular attack on China which had recently gone back on the terms of its rice agreement with Cuba – an attack which he followed up in March by describing Mao Tse Tung as 'senile, barbarous and no longer competent to stay in office'. The Chinese, he said, had confused Communism with Fascism, and Mao's regime was

[10] See D. Bruce Jackson, *Castro, the Kremlin and Communism in Latin America*, Johns Hopkins University, Baltimore, 1969, 28–31. The conference was a complete success for the Russians. The Chinese, who had expected much of the occasion, were later very angry – perhaps showing Castro the extent of Chinese–Russian rivalry for the first time.

worse than an absolute monarchy.[11] But this did not compensate the Russians for their diplomatic defeat in seeing the Tricontinental Conference endorse the idea of the armed struggle with no holds barred. This change of front by Castro was caused partly by a desire to resume leadership of the world's militant revolutionaries, partly because of increased scepticism about the 'peaceful way' after the failure of the Socialist–Communist alliance in the elections of 1964 in Chile, partly as a result of the deepening of the war in Vietnam, where Cuba had close relations with the North Vietnamese, as befitted, it seemed, two small and isolated countries fighting the U.S.[12]

Cuba's relations with the rest of the Communist world have since that time been dogged by controversy. Castro and the orthodox Communists have violently attacked each other, Castro criticizing in particular the Venezuelan Communists, whom he accused of having betrayed the Venezuelan freedom fighters led by Douglas Bravo. AALAPSO divided, and no new conference has been held, though the Latin American delegates at that conference formed themselves into a new organization – OLAS (Latin American Solidarity Organization) – which held its conference at Havana in August 1967, to 'coordinate and give impetus to the struggle against U.S. imperialism'. Influenced by the reappearance, in Bolivia, of Guevara (who was elected President of the conference in his absence), the meeting unanimously echoed his appeal for the creation of 'many Vietnams' in the Western Hemisphere. Castro used the occasion to launch a specially violent attack on the 'pseudo-revolutionaries' of the bourgeois Communist parties, not simply the Venezuelans: the Yugoslavs, for instance, were by this time almost inured to being referred to by Cubans as 'opportunists and traitors'.

Guevara was killed in October 1967, but despite the consequent failure of his plans, the guerrilla movement in Latin America received much publicity in the world press. Castro felt strong enough therefore to send only a very minor representative to the celebrations in Moscow for the fiftieth anniversary of the Russian Revolution, Dr Machado Ventura, the Minister of Health (he it was therefore who heard Brezhnev give his own attack on 'pseudo-revolutionary theories divorced from life' – by which he meant different people from Castro). The controversy continued in innumerable Communist Party journals, in literary weeklies and in *Pravda*. Guevara began to be attacked by orthodox Communists, on the one hand, as having been a 'Bakuninist' and, on the other, as having refused to accept the leadership of the Bolivian Communist Party. The publication of Guevara's Bolivian diaries, though

[11] Castro speech of 13 March 1966.

[12] Cuba is also the only country to have diplomatic relations with the NLF in Vietnam, the 'Ambassador' being Raúl Valdés Vivó, who before the Revolution was secretary-general of the Communist Youth movement.

exciting interest in his fate, did not enhance his reputation, and the Russian edition of that work contained a long critique of his military tactics. Castro, in an introduction to the Cuban edition, however, accused the Bolivian Communist leadership of having betrayed Guevara, just as he had accused the Venezuelan Communists of having betrayed Douglas Bravo.

Large numbers of South Americans and Africans have meantime received guerrilla training in Cuba. Cuba is reputed to have helped the Republic of Congo (Brazzaville) put down a revolt in 1966, to have advised El Fatah in Jordan and, in 1964, to have helped to overthrow the Sultan of Zanzibar. Cuba continues to broadcast to Latin America many hours of propaganda and encouragement to subversion in Quechua, Aymará, Guaraní and other tongues, as well as in Spanish. The 'armed struggle' itself, however, remains an elusive part of South American life, exaggerated by both the Cubans and also by the South American governments, the latter in order to be in a good position to receive new arms supplies from the U.S. In the Cuban press, the South American continent continues to seem 'one vast battle front', seething with violence, the revolutionaries 'thrashing government troops' and about to enter in triumph the Miraflores Palace in Caracas or, like Zapata's men in Mexico, Sanborn's restaurant.[13]

In 1969 Castro's militancy somewhat declined. Concentrating on the herculean efforts needed to harvest the famous ten million tons of sugar, Castro made little reference to the 'armed struggle' in his speeches.[14] In early 1970 Bravo, the Venezuelan guerrilla leader, publicly broke with Castro, accusing him of being a tool of the Soviet Union.[15] But the old quarrels smoulder and neither revolution nor the principles of the Alliance for Progress have made much headway.

The discussion on the disputed desirability of the armed struggle has distorted Cuban history. The combat urged by Guevara in his last writings (and supported by Régis Debray) somewhat facilely envisaged a battle of *ultras*, with no compromise with the bourgeoisie and none with the liberal establishment in the U.S. Yet Castro's own struggle in the hills was different; he fought as a political leader driven to take up

[13] This criticism was made of the Cuban Press in 1965 by the Guatemalan Communist Manuel Galich (See *Revolución*, 1 April 1965).

[14] A speech of Carlos Rafael Rodríguez to the Central Committee of the Cuban Communist Party in 1968 made clear that the Sino–Soviet controversy was not to be a subject of argument; Manuel Bravo Chapman was indeed attacked for trying to turn the INRA supply department into a centre of political debate on this matter (*Granma*, 11 February 1968). In 1969 a Cuban defector, Orlando Castro Hidalgo, who had worked in intelligence, claimed that in May 1968 Castro made a secret agreement with Russia committing Cuba to a pro-Soviet line in Latin America in return for continued economic aid (*Christian Science Monitor*, 16 July 1969). This apparently did not exclude continued training in Cuba for guerrillas for the rest of the underdeveloped world, for example the Eritrean liberation army.

[15] *Le Monde*, 15 January 1970.

arms but always willing to make concessions and gestures to all. As in previous Cuban civil wars, liberal North Americans helped the Cuban rebels to the best of their considerable ability. By seeking to fight under purer colours, even without compromise with the local Communist parties, the South American rebels of the late 1960s may possibly preserve the integrity of their ideals (though even that is not certain, since desperate circumstances need cynicism as well as heroism); but they will not be fighting as did Castro, who was more economical in lives than Guevara presumably would have been had he achieved his 'two, three or more Vietnams'. Castro is evidently aware of these paradoxes: in 1961 he explained 'Naturally, if we had stood on the top of Pico Turquino when we were only a handful of men and said that we were Marxist–Leninists, we might never have got down to the plain'[16]; and Carlos Rafael Rodríguez once sagely remarked 'who could conceive Matthews' articles in the *New York Times* in favour of a Communist guerrilla?'[17]

The Cubans are in an unusual position in comparison with the rest of Latin America so far as the 'armed struggle' is concerned; the Cuban wars of independence, 1868–78 and 1895–98, were far more destructive in terms of lives and social consequences than the wars of independence of the early nineteenth century in the other parts of the old Spanish Empire. Indeed, those Cuban wars, by completing the ruin of the old Cuban oligarchy, opened the way to the dominance of Cuban society by North America – an outcome which would be the most likely consequence of a long armed struggle in any large Latin American country in the 1970s – an eventuality which is certainly possible. On the other hand, the Cuban revolutionary war of 1956–58 was infinitely milder than say the Mexican revolution or the long period of violence which has characterized Colombia since 1948.

The Cuban Revolution, a Garibaldiesque challenge to North America as much as an attempt to resolve Cuba's own problems, indeed remains perhaps more menacing to North than to South America, for it was to begin with a reproach to the greed of affluence and the standards of North America which, because of improved communications, were introduced into Cuba at so great a pace in the 1950s. The Cuban revolution is thus as much a part of a North American revolution as one of the South: a fact more and more evident as Florida continues to throng with exiles, becoming once more what she administratively was for a time in the late eighteenth century: *la jurisdicción de la Habana ultramar*; while Cuba herself, by a bizarre inverse historical repetition, is now again cut off from the rest of Spanish America as she was before

[16] Speech of 20 December 1961.
[17] Carlos Rafael Rodríguez, *La revolución cubana y el período de transición*, II, 41.

1762, with Russia playing the role of imperial mother once played by Spain.

North American policy has not much changed since the missile crisis. The last statement menacing Cuba by a U.S. president was Kennedy's at the Orange Bowl, Miami, on 29 December 1962, when he welcomed back the prisoners from the Bay of Pigs and promised that, one day, the Brigade's flag (which he agreed to keep safely) would be returned to it in a free Havana.[18] Afterwards, however, Kennedy sought passivity rather than war and it is just possible that his murder in November 1963 prevented reconciliation.[19]

The policy of President Johnson towards Cuba was conservative. Preoccupied by Asia, the administration concentrated on the maintenance of the economic embargo and on the isolation of Cuba from the hemisphere, and largely succeeded. The base at Guantánamo was retained. Cuban adventures abroad, such as Guevara's attempted guerrilla war in Bolivia, were crushed,[20] but Cuba herself was left alone.[21] Meantime, those who lost money in Cuba kept their files open,[22] and private investment in Latin America slowly began to increase again, after the years when it dropped substantially because of fears of revolution.[23] In 1969 there was discussion again of a possible U.S. *rapprochement* with Cuba. Castro told a North American banker that the new U.S. administration seemed more courteous and cautious than its predecessor. Nevertheless, it would seem that during the present stage of his intellectual development Castro has said too often, 'We have no contact with the U.S. and we don't want any' – the embargo notwithstanding – for there to be any real possibility of understanding.[24] The embargo after all, has its political uses and it has probably helped Castro more than it has hurt him.

[18] *New York Times*, 30 December 1962.

[19] See Jean Daniel's article in *New Republic*, 14 December 1963; also William Attwood, *The Reds and the Blacks* (Hutchinson, London 1967), 144.

[20] For an interesting argument that the CIA never lost trace of Guevara (but pretended to), that his re-appearance in Bolivia was immediately analysed in Washington and that the CIA did not desire Guevara killed, see Andrew St George, 'How the U.S. got Che', *True*, April 1969.

[21] To say therefore with Saverio Tutino (*Partisans*, April–June 1962) that in Cuba '*C'est la vie quotidienne qui est directement ménacée*' seems romantic.

[22] The Foreign Claims Settlement Commission fixed U.S. claims to Cuba at $M2,700, of which $M400 were individual claims by separate people and the rest 948 corporation claims (*New York Times*, 24 May 1967).

[23] Private investment in Latin America was estimated at $1 billion in 1957 and dropped to $M200 in 1961 (*New York Herald Tribune*, 10 June 1962, 7). The slump of private investment in Latin America, by Latin Americans themselves and by U.S. citizens, with the transfer of much capital elsewhere (to Europe for instance), was one major consequence of the Revolution in Cuba.

[24] Interview with K. S. Karol, *New Statesman*, 22 September 1967.

After the missile crisis, the U.S. suspended Pan American flights from Havana to Miami and for three years the only flights out of Cuba to the Western world were via Mexico or Madrid. The number of exiles to leave Cuba was therefore small. But since December 1965, an air service has been established whereby 3,000–4,000 'gusanos'[25] leave Cuba each month on airliners chartered by the U.S. Government. This safety valve, both merciful and wise, has since 1965 taken 200,000 Cubans to Florida; but the waiting list at the Swiss Embassy of those who desire to leave is believed to exceed another 200,000, while all males between fifteen and twenty-seven, as well as those who 'will reach that age in the next few years' are banned from leaving. (Many technicians also cannot leave.) With the 300,000 or so who left Cuba between 1959 and 1962, a tenth of the population has abandoned Cuba or desires to do so. The possibility of flight is admittedly a better alternative than the policies practised by Stalin during the 1930s and 1940s, when a similar proportion of the Russian population was in concentration camps.[26] But comparison with Stalin is scarcely the best criterion and the waiting list is itself a cause of terrible chagrin, since an application to leave Cuba opens the would-be exile to difficulties and humiliations, including the loss of professions and possessions. Those who apply to leave Cuba place themselves at the disposal of the Government and, even if all goes well and the applicants are given a place in the queue, the usual practice is that they work on farms for a minimum wage, usually for two years or even more, before they receive their permission to leave, their tickets (paid in foreign currency), and their visas to enter the U.S. or Spain. They live in special constructed barracks, *albergues*, with earth floors, much resembling indeed the *barracones* of slaves in the last century. In consequence, many still seek to leave Cuba illegally, by boat or through Guantánamo, often to die in the attempt, perhaps eaten by sharks, or caught and shot.[27]

[25] *Gusano*, literally maggot or earthworm, the Revolution's name for those who oppose it.

[26] The regime's 'permissiveness' to those who desired to leave Cuba was among the grounds for criticism by Escalante's 'microfaction'. Out of the 38,000 Chinese (that is, born in China) in Cuba in 1953, only about 5,000 remain, according to one investigator. So far as anyone knows, these arrangements will last forever.

[27] Estimates of numbers of Cuban exiles now abroad vary very much. With children born in exile, the total may now be something close to 800,000.

CHAPTER 51

The Pursuit of Freedom

Cuba in the 1960s has thus presented a tragedy for a large minority of her citizens, especially for the many of them who, through no fault of their own but because of the accumulation of social history, seemed previously too frivolous for drama: so many families have been divided or broken, so much personal unhappiness has been caused for political reasons and, leaving aside the leaders, so many also, on both sides, doctors and educationalists in Havana as well as democratic exiles in the U.S., believe that they have acted for the best, yet nevertheless despise and hate each other. Most distressing, perhaps, is 'the internal conflict, almost impossible to convey, of the individual who is convinced of the correctness of his analysis of the "betrayed revolution" and yet is constantly wary of abetting . . . another "enemy camp" that was and still is abhorrent to his values.'[1] There is also the tragedy of a political movement which began by harnessing generous emotions from all kinds of people and has become, at the least, intolerant; and there is the tragedy of innumerable Cubans who die in exile far from the land which they love.

The Cuban Revolution, therefore, gives a lesson in politics. Those who admire the social advances made under the Revolution must consider the brutality of the gaolers, the arbitrary character of an unpredictable but ubiquitous tyranny, the tedium of an inefficient bureaucratic state and the melancholy of a society where eccentricity and private experiment ('the sad colouring of submission,' as Segundo Cazalis put it), much less private enterprise, is damned. Those who abhor the tyranny need to be reminded of the evident integrity of many of the leaders, that a minimum wage, and universal schooling and medicine did not obtain before (but could have done so), and that rural poverty is much reduced. The lovers of the Revolution, sometimes dazzled, as was Columbus, by the beauty of the Cuban vegetation and the charm of the people (as by the restricted view of the country they sometimes get through the windows of the black ICAP car[2]), also perhaps

---

[1] Carlos Luis, *Notes of a Cuban Revolutionary in exile*; see also the novel by the former Cuban Ambassador in London, Luis Ricardo Alonso, *Territorio Libre* (Peter Owen, London, 1966).

[2] ICAP, the Cuban Institute of Friendship with the Peoples is the official body which looks after visitors and ensures that they see the best of Cuba. ICAP's budget is generous and seems always able to afford cigars, daiquiris and good meals to reliable visitors.

need to recall that health and education are only aids to the good life and that in Cuba as elsewhere in the Communist world, where it is often supposed that the ends justify the means, the ends themselves seem forgotten. The end of even Marx's political ambitions was a society where human beings are not regarded as objects or part of an inscrutable historical process and where the smallest minority can dissent even on trumpery matters. The multitudes in uniform are surely supposed to be marching to a spot where they can disband. For a historian, the good life is a society where Truth is not abused and where the study of history, even recent history, can be pursued without interference – a society much like that which Fidel Castro described in his first famous speech, *History Will Absolve Me*, and which he said that Batista had destroyed in 1952: 'Once upon a time there was a Republic. It had its constitution, its laws, its civil rights, its President, a Congress, and law courts. Everyone could assemble, associate, speak and write with complete freedom . . . There existed a public opinion both respected and heeded.'[3] This was rather an exaggeratedly favourable description by Castro of Cuba under Carlos Prío; it bears no relation to life under Castro himself.

Of course, Castro and his government may have been popular, perhaps with most of the people most of the time, though, with the absence of elections or even opinion polls since 1960, there has been no knowing this for sure, and it is impossible to distinguish, in a totalitarian system, between, as Boris Goldenberg put it, 'spontaneous enthusiasm and enforced or opportunistic conformity'.[4] But even if it could be statistically proved that more Cubans still loved Castro than hated him, that would only be one factor. Given the power which autocratic governments can now have over the mass media to control discussion as they like, it becomes less and less interesting to say of such and such a regime that it is popular. Was it ever so? General Crowder was doubtless right when in 1927 he told Secretary of State Kellogg that 'most Cubans favoured a second term for Machado'.[5] Even in relatively free societies, polls are wayward. Maxime du Camp at Naples in 1860 heard people in the streets shout 'Long Live Italy' with enthusiasm and then ask their neighbour what the word 'Italy' meant. Who are they, how many are they, these masses who, throughout the 1960s, have shouted 'Yankees, Remember Girón!', or *'Estoy con Fidel'*, *'Venceremos'*, *'Paredón'*, *'Fuera'*, *'Unidad'*, *'Fidel, seguro a los Yankees darle duro'*, *'Somos socialistas, palant'y palant'y'*, *'Viva el socialismo chachachá'*, *'Ni un paso atrás'*, *'viva la internacional proletaria'*, *'Patria o Muerte'*, or other of the innumerable

[3] *History Will Absolve Me*, 16.
[4] Goldenberg, 236.
[5] Robert F. Smith, 116.

slogans of Revolutionary Cuba? Were some the same men and women who in 1950 suggested, in a poll taken by the Esso Standard Oil Company, that most Cubans would prefer to work for a U.S. company than the Cuban Government[6] – a thought difficult to coordinate with the attitudes of the thousands who cheered Castro's tirades against the 'illiterate millionaire', Kennedy, in the early 1960s? It is doubtless so.

Castro's magnetism and oratory have enabled him to direct Cuban society since 1959 very much according to his own designs. He has successfully persuaded many people that the absence of goods in the shops is a sign of virtue, that the market economy such as exists even in East Europe is an evil, that cities are vicious and that the countryside is noble.[7] His oratory has persuaded many to accept even the ideas of abolishing Christmas and to welcome the fact that the harvest of the year 1969–70 will last eighteen months; similarly, in the past there were eloquent slave owners able to explain why there should be a Sunday only every ten days, and yet still be loved. Castro's elevation of violence, his harping on the theme of conflict, his use of the rifle as a symbol, attracts the nation and probably panders to the latent *macho* spirit which has perhaps suffered a set-back in private life.[8] Strong and intolerant governments are often much more popular than easy-going and tolerant ones, just as war is not universally hated.

Further, Castro has done many things which have been popular even if they have been unjust to minorities or even if they have been at least partly designed to achieve popularity. Revolutionary Cuba has throughout enjoyed a quite new national spirit deriving from the heady experience of social revolution and international adventure. Castro's own personality, undoubtedly fortunate, apparently heroic, certainly indefatigable and formidable, is itself a phenomenon in which many

[6] See *Public opinion survey in Cuba prepared for Esso Standard Oil Company* (Cuba), September 1950, by International Public Opinion Research Inc., of New York. 'About 1 out of 3 people give first preference to an American Company and very few voice a desire to work for the Cuban Government.'

[7] Perhaps here as in so many matters, an epigram of Martí's paved the way: *La ciudad extravía el juicio, el campo lo ordena y acrisola* ('The city distorts the judgement, the country orders and refines it').

[8] Castro's charm also has played a part. From whom else would Jean-Paul Sartre have accepted the remark: 'If someone asked me for the moon it would be because someone needed it'.? After this, Sartre said in 1960, Castro became one of his 'few friends'. It is remarkable how Castro's willingness to use violent language unthinkable in a bourgeois democracy has also enthralled many foreign visitors. The most curious comment is from Clive Jenkins who visited Cuba in 1961 and asked a militiaman: 'Do you want elections?' He looked at me and shook his machine gun, 'We've got these,' he said. At this point in time, I found this a convincing reply.' (The militiaman's remark was an echo of Castro's speech of 1 May 1961.) Introduction to *Cuba and Fidel*, by Norman Lewis, Union of Democratic Control London, 1961.

Cubans can take pride.[9] The educational and health reforms of the Revolution are immensely popular in a nation which coveted them in the past more than formal democracy; the armies of children hanging round the tenement or the bohío were of course in the past a constant reproach to the parents, as well as an anxiety. Finally, the ruin of the old master class, the end of corruption and of *gangsterismo*, the abolition of social discrimination and of the subservient attitudes to North America have certainly given many Cubans much pleasure; while the Revolution's earliest and internationally most famous achievement – the opening of the private beaches to the masses – symbolizes one side of the achievement of the last ten years which the most resolute friends of pure political liberty have to take into account.

The question, therefore, whether these achievements have been worth the candle is likely to be subjective. Depending on temperament as much as on riches or class, there are those, in Cuba as elsewhere, who believe that 'if a more just economic system is only attainable by closing men's minds against free inquiry . . . the price [is] too high'.[10] The facts are clear; there is no constitution in Cuba and, though a commission of the Central Committee of the Communist Party is said to be preparing one, nothing suggests that such a thing would change matters, any more than the Soviet constitution of 1935 did in Russia. Castro's government, therefore, remains what it has been since 1959 – a good example of Halévy's definition of dictatorship – 'a group of armed men, moved by a common faith, seize power, and decree that they are the state'.[11] To some Cubans it must indeed seem as if one of the idealistic political gangster groups of the late 1940s – the most idealistic as well as the most ruthless – had finally seized the public buildings and now monopolize the big cars and the machine guns.

Without doubt, also, this system of government, as well as being oppressive, is also often inefficient. Governments desirous of economic development naturally wish to ride roughshod over local interests. How tedious to have to have an inquiry over the siting of a new airport! But in the long run the discussion of policy before it is decided upon is of course profitable. In Cuba, according to Segundo Cazalis, bad news, in the classic style, is often not taken to Castro, since he associates the bearer with the intelligence.[12] Castro's personality is a complicated one and certainly not fully known even to himself: what is clear is that he does not find it easy to surround himself with constructive critics. 'Yes-men'

[9] It has been assumed that in the event of a free election Castro would win (see for example the assertion to this effect by Professor Roger Fisher, Professor of Law at Harvard, in *The New Republic*, 15 June 1963). How anyone can know this is obscure.

[10] Bertrand Russell, *The Practice and Theory of Bolshevism* (Allen & Unwin, London 1920), 8.

[11] Élie Halévy, *The Era of Tyrannies* (Allen Lane, The Penguin Press, 1967), 215.

[12] Cazalis, *La República* (Caracas), 14 February 1965.

clearly abound. A free press in Cuba might have prevented the neglect of the sugar industry during 1960–63, the numerous wasteful industrial projects, the still controversial coffee campaign of the late 1960s, or the sad neglect of the beautiful city of Havana (which, whether Castro likes it or not, is one of Cuba's prides), and even the Ten Million Ton harvest of 1969–70. Is it necessary to point out, so late in the day, that Liberty is a convenience as well as a principle? There is also, in an arbitrary system always the possibility of further distortion, as occurred in Germany under the stress of war in the early 1940s, or in Russia under that of agrarian change in the 1930s; whereas parliamentary democracy, for all its faults, has the virtue of being a good way of settling internal disputes without violence.

The Cuban Revolutionary Government is hence an experiment whose moral, not whose example, needs to be borne in mind by others: Cuba's standard of living measured by most gauges was always higher than most countries of the so-called underdeveloped world. Cuba's social misery in the past was due to an extreme form of that public meanness and private affluence that characterizes North America as well as South. Cuba, before 1959, certainly needed reform and more than most countries. It should be possible to stand back and welcome such changes that are incontestably benevolent; to question those which seem of uncertain merit; to denounce those which have been unjust or mistaken; to criticize tyrannical methods even if these have resulted in some good being done; and not to despair that, in other circumstances or in other countries, the means may match the ends. Socialism, after all, was intended by those who first thought of it to be a system of society in which not only the common good was given priority but in which each individual would be treated with the respect that human beings deserve.

Castro in 1963 expressed surprise that North Americans should seek to differentiate Castroism and Communism,[13] and at first sight Revolutionary Cuba clearly owes much to the Communist system as practised in Russia or East Europe. The organization of the party, of labour, and of planning, reflects orthodox Communist ideas as practised in well-established Communist states; in particular, of the party within the Army and the police.

There are obviously characteristics of the Cuban system which distinguish it from the 'friendly socialist countries', as they are known in Havana. These include some institutions (if that is not perhaps too strong a word) such as the Committees for the Defence of the Revolution and the militia. It also seems that, despite the frequent incompetence of

[13] '*No sé por que establecén esta diferencia*', *Hoy*, 24 February 1963. '*Entre esos mil milones,*' Guevara once remarked, the Cuban Communists were '*una gota pero uno gota diferenciable* (a drop but a recognizable drop).

the huge bureaucracy that the state has bred in Cuba, the functionaries carry out their duties with somewhat greater respect for individuals than has been the case in other Communist countries. The state is still able to count on the enthusiasm of many, particularly children and young people. Perhaps, however, this also is a subjective judgement, since many with experience of Cuban prisons would think differently.

The national temperament and climate of Cuba, along with the most recent historical experience of Cuba, has most affected the character of the system. For example, Castro on the one hand had no tradition of competent officialdom to assist him, as was the case in Communist countries of Eastern Europe and in Russia; nor was the Cuban Communist system built, as was the case in every other country where the theory has caught hold, upon a people which had suffered the ravages of a prolonged and bloody war. The Cuban civil war which brought Castro to power was quite modest in its scope and the dictatorship of Batista, although vulgar and brutal – and the brutalities were specially easy to publicize – cannot be compared with the tyranny of the Nazi new order in Europe and in West Russia in the early 1940s.

It is also obvious that any dictatorship in a country with an equable climate such as Cuba, where there is no need for winter fuel nor for winter clothing, is easier to bear and therefore itself assumes a somewhat more benevolent identity. Thus it is possible to excuse some of the abuses of Communism in Russia by the explanation that it is Russian; and some of the attractions – for so they are to many – of Communism in Cuba by the explanation that it is Cuban.

The Cuban revolutionary state is also to be differentiated from other Communist systems because of Castro's own claims to be able to decide for himself the direction and the timing of his interpretation of Marxist–Leninism. Castro's temperament, the manner in which he came to power – through his own efforts, like Mao or Tito, that is, and not on the coat-tails of the Red Army – and Cuba's geographical situation, have given him an independent position. Castro has used this to argue that it is possible to build Socialism and Communism at the same time (Lenin and Marx would have considered this view heretical, superficial, infantilist or Bakuninist) and that 'battle is the best school of Marxism'. Castro supports 'revolutionaries, with or without parties', or any revolutionary process in any Latin American country – even if those who have prompted that revolution are a group of military leaders, considering that 'in most countries the [orthodox] Communist movement is too narrow and dogmatic to contain all . . . revolutionary energies'.[14]

[14] These remarks were made by Castro respectively to K. S. Karol (*New Statesman*, 22 September 1967), on 29 August 1969, *à propos* of the 'pseudo-revolutionary' Venezuelan Communist party; on 14 July 1969, at Puerto Padre, in respect of the Peruvian military government; and again, to K. S. Karol, in 1967.

Never has Castro admitted that war is an evil. Once again, in 1970, as in 1959, it would seem that the name of his first political group, the UIR (*Unión Insurreccional Revolucionaria*) which he joined as a student, is in many ways the best label for his political position.

Perhaps this is just to say that Castro, a revolutionary before he was a Communist, had a temperamental preference for youth and for heroic, action rather than for age, study (of Marx or anyone else)[15] and caution and is therefore inevitably critical of the older generation of Communist party leaders in Latin America – the old contemporaries of Blas Roca, Escalante, or Ordoqui. On the other hand, perhaps this, like the view that it is possible to build Socialism and Communism at the same time, is a transient, not a firmly worked out, philosophy. Once the fashion in Cuba was for material incentives, now (when there is nothing to buy) it is for moral ones; but will this last for ever? The 'new man' may turn out to have old passions. Castro's views on the armed struggle were less heroic between 1962 and 1966 (and, indeed, have been slightly less heroic since 1969). It is reasonable enough to suppose that Castro will always prefer 'the most competent, the most able, the most audacious' people, as he told the North American, Lee Lockwood[16], but in those terms the perfect revolutionary sounds much the same as the perfect capitalist. Castro and the railway builder, Percival Farquhar, probably would see eye to eye.

When it comes to the point, Castro's changing moods more than any firmly organized body of principles seem most characteristic of him; thus there was a remarkably short space between the time he was saying with, as some of his later enemies would admit, apparent sincerity, 'Neither I nor the movement are Communist' (on 13 January 1959) or 'the only sacrifice which I am not prepared to make . . . would be to use force to further the revolution' (6 February 1959) to the famous remarks of 1961: 'I shall be a Marxist–Leninist for the rest of my life' (on 2 December 1961). What, therefore, characterized the Cuban Revolution is that on top of a familiarly organized Communist system, there has been an elevation of Castro's role as 'maximum leader', and the articulation of this personal power through frequent and skilfully managed personal appearances, culminating in great speeches. All major decisions have been taken in Cuba since 1959 by Castro, sometimes paying heed to those pressure groups which exist even in a closed society (such as the

[15] Castro must be the first Marxist–Leninist leader who had scarcely read much of the works of the Master and who scarcely allows more than a few words and few expressions taken from Marxism to enter his vocabulary. In his speech on 4 November 1969, encouraging the armed forces to do their best in the great sugar harvest of 1969–70, he announced that he and his followers were to be the standard bearers of '*the best* of Marx's ideas and of the best of Lenin's ideas' – which, of course, might mean anything.

[16] Lockwood, 190.

Army or the old Communists), sometimes not. In public, 'the Revolution', that irresistible movement of men and spirits towards Utopia, is made to resemble an African deity, whose needs, sometimes wayward and inscrutable, are interpreted by Castro as *santero*, a worthy successor to others who aspired to fulfil this role in Cuba, from Carlos Manuel de Céspedes and Martí onwards. (Grau San Martín was, of course, a false prophet, but, is it permissible to say, a prophet all the same?) The waywardness of Castro can be seen in his odd admission that 'capitalism digs two graves – one for itself, one for the society which comes after capitalism'.[17]

It is tempting to compare the distinctive colouring which Castro has given to Cuban communism with fascism[18]; there is Castro's evident belief, with Chibás but also with Mosley or Hitler, that political power lies in 'the response of a large audience to a stirring speech'.[19] There is the willingness of large sections of the population, including intelligent and humane people, to surrender their individuality to Castro as men did to Fascist leaders. There is the persistent elevation of the principle of violence and the appeals to martial reactions in the regime's propaganda; and there is the cult of leadership, the emphasis on physical fitness in the education system, and the continual denigration of bourgeois democracies. The very statement of Guevara's in *Socialism and Man* which defines the drives of Cuban socialism shares with fascism, as with expressionism, 'the urge to recapture the "whole man" who seems atomized and alienated by society',[20] a man who could not find himself among the 'commonplaces of bourgeois democracy', as Guevara put it. The 'New Man', held to be typified by Guevara, a hero, and man of action, will and character, would have been admired by French fascists such as Brasillach or Drieu or by D'Annunzio, of the wild demagogic epoch of the Republic of Fiume, who himself has seemed to at least one commentator to have been Castro's intellectual precursor.[21] Castro's moralizing and his desire to break with all material aims reflects fascist regenerationism; and his presentation of himself as the thoughtful and benevolent father resembles Mussolini. In fact, of course, the fascist revolutions of the 1930s cannot be understood (any more than Castro's can) if observed wholly negatively, or if it is forgotten that even the Nazi revolution 'satisfied a deeply felt need for activism combined with identification [with] . . . a classless society'.[22] Fascism was a heresy

[17] Speech in Camagüey, *Hoy*, 15 May 1962.
[18] See above, pp. 255, 269, 304–5.
[19] R. Skidelsky's phrase in referring to Mosley, in *European Fascism*, ed. by S. J. Woolf (1968), 236.
[20] George Mosse, 'The Genesis of Fascism', in *Journal of Contemporary History*, No. 1, 1966.
[21] Cf. Richard Lowenthal, 'Unreason and Revolution', in *Encounter*, November 1969.
[22] Mosse, *loc. cit.*

of the international socialist movement and several fascist leaders had once been men of the Left: it is possible to imagine Castro moving in time (or, more probably, at a certain time) from extreme Left to what passes for extreme Right. The charismatic leader, both left and right, after all, lives against an artificial background. As George Kennan put it, 'He creates [the background] for himself; but he believes in it implicitly and in part he generally succeeds in making it seem real to others as well. And his role, as he plays it, may be none the less heroic and impressive for this artificiality of the scenery.'[23] Of no one is this percipient comment more true than of Castro who is also, of course, the heir of the Latin American continent's tradition of *caudillismo*.

But the main deviations from the international Communist movement which have characterized the Cuban Revolution have really derived from the history of Cuba itself. Revolutionary governments are driven by pictures of the past as much as by visions of the future. For at least a generation Cuban politicians have been passionately in love with the word 'Revolution'.[24] The abuses of capitalism in Cuba created the Revolution in its own image. Cubans have also been equally in love with the word 'liberty'; slaves sought liberty from masters, merchants from Spanish laws, romantics from the Spanish Army, twentieth-century intellectuals from the strait-jacket of sugar. Now Castro considers that he has redeemed these past desires by creating the first *territorio libre* of America, though several hundred thousands of Cubans have defined freedom as exile.

Castro frequently described the Revolution as a 'process', beginning with the first Cuban war of independence, and the propaganda of the regime always so depicts it. Thus 1968 was celebrated as the culmination of a 'hundred years of struggle': 'the Revolution of 1868,' wrote the novelist, Lisandro Otero, in the glossy propaganda magazine *Cuba* of which he is the editor, 'was continued in 1895, rendered more profound in 1933, reborn in 1953, and was triumphant if not consummated in 1959' (the history of Cuba might also be written as the history of the prisoner in La Cabaña, or the exile of Miami, where the statue of José Martí stands next to that of Bolívar and where Maceo's grandson in 1961 formed part of a council to overthrow Castro). Though history has been distorted since 1959, Castro's Revolution was the culmination of three generations of 'revolutionary activity', verbal violence, extravagant hopes of redemption and further embroidery on the idea of

[23] George Kennan, *Russia and the West under Lenin and Stalin.*
[24] See above, pp.271–5. But this is true even of exiles: thus Castro's sister, Juanita,, in her attacks in the U.S. and elsewhere on her brother, still speaks of the need for a 'true Revolution' to create 'a totally new Cuba . . . a Cuba which has nothing to do with the past or the present' (Interview in Miami, 21 October 1969, on Radioemisora WFAB).

freedom: 'When the news reached my encampment . . . it provoked an unimaginable delirium . . . we considered ourselves definitely free,' wrote Orestes Ferrara, a colonel in the rebel army in 1898.[25] The news in question was that of the intervention of the U.S. who then seemed to proffer freedom, just as in 1960 it seemed proffered by Russia.

Yet the obsession with freedom creates its own bondage, and is there not doubt whether in any real sense even Castro is a free man? He imposes his personality on Cuba but, like all Cuban rulers, he is at the mercy of the sugar markets as of the twenty-year relative stagnation in the Cuban economy which he has not arrested. In part, too, he is the creation of the dreams of Cubans for a revolutionary leader of epic stature, just as he is the articulate expression of a nation whose 'authentic qualities' include what is usually known as 'gaiety' – such as, for instance, responsiveness to rhythm – as well as cruelty: a country which, if it has never had a good civil service, has usually had a bloody police. The long shadows of past habits stretch across the most radical reforms, either blacking them out or giving them quite different colours. In 1959, Castro was in much the same position *vis-à-vis* the U.S. as was the Spanish prime minister Sagasta in 1898 at the beginning of the Spanish–American war. But Castro could call Russia into the lists to sell him arms (and to buy his sugar) where Sagasta could not call on, say, Britain or Germany: the cold war, that is, 'provided Castro with alternatives denied previous rulers of Cuba'.[26] It is possible that the 'liberals', the only alternative in 1959 to Castro and the Communists, would in effect have repeated, if they had had the chance, what their grandfathers did in 1898 (denying it, of course, with a show of nationalistic rhetoric) and swung Cuba into an ever closer alliance with the U.S., the island benefiting from U.S. aid and technology, so as to make Cuba materially better off than she could ever have been under Castro, though culturally submissive. Castro has in contrast created a strong, ruthless but original and popular despotism, with many remarkable social reforms to its credit and which, whatever label is given to it, represents a serious challenge to the liberal society. It would be an even more serious one if the totalitarian side of the system were dismantled and if free discussion and criticism were to be encouraged. This, however, is not likely since the regime depends so much on fanaticism and dogmatism, and fanatics are seldom humane.

In the two centuries since the English captured Havana in 1762, the Cuban population increased fifty-fold, from 150,000 to over seven million. As in the case of the U.S. the growth derived from immigra-

[25] In a letter to me sixty-six years later from Rome, 28 April 1964.
[26] Ruiz, *Cuba, The Making of a Revolution*, 5.

tion, rather than natural increase. So big a change in population meant that the island, including scenery and even climate – because of the felling of the great forests – has changed. But 'authentic Cuban' situations repeat themselves: American presidents under electoral pressure – Polk, McKinley, Kennedy – adopt strong measures; exiles gather in Miami (especially in the 1890s, the 1930s, the 1950s, but never so much as in the 1960s); revolutionary 'bandits' raise the flag of liberty in the hills and are shot as thieves; and, as Castro should be warned, political rebellions occur at economically prosperous times – in 1868, 1895 and 1956. The next rebellion will probably occur after, not before, the Revolutionary Government has achieved its economic goals, and the population has time to speculate on their purpose.

The history of Cuba since the late eighteenth century, when the country began to produce sugar on a lavish scale for the world market, has been like the history of the world seen through the eyes of a child: an invention in Silesia, a plague in Africa, a war or a prosperous time in England or in France – these apparently unconnected events beyond Cuba's control have determined the lives of Cubans who, despite their tropical innocence, were the only links between them. The island was never isolated. All great events, from the Napoleonic wars to the Suez crisis, dictated to Cuba; and the history of the Revolution of Castro is the history of what was itself self-consciously a great event whose purpose was to escape the bondage of geographical as well as economic circumstances. But iron historical laws, which are a limitation even on the greatest powers and the greatest men, naturally impose themselves on Cuba and Castro: starting out in 1959 like Talleyrand at the Congress of Vienna, representative of small states wishing to be heard, she desired to be exemplary. But, alas, 'poor Cuba always hopeful, always deceived!'[27] The future of Cuba continues to depend on circumstances beyond her control. Dr Grau San Martín told Sumner Welles that 'Cuba could get along without the regulation of foreign powers and even without foreign commercial interchanges'; Eddy Chibás wanted Cuba 'free from the economic imperialism of Wall Street and the political imperialism of Moscow, Rome and Berlin.' But still the only alternative market to Russia in 1970 for Cuba's sugar production is the U.S. just as Russia was the only alternative in 1960 to the U.S. With economic diversification further away than ever, and the whole island turned into a single sugar plantation, Cuba has no hope of escaping the politics of its customers or its investors. The eighteenth-century problem of obtaining slaves from across the sea from other countries has been exactly reproduced by the problem of obtaining oil; the Russian embassy official

[27] Luis Estévez y Romero, *Desde el Zanjón hasta Baire*, 41.

Shliapnikov who boasted how a delay at Baku could strangle the Cuban economy is a twentieth-century South Sea Company factor. Perhaps even Cubans for all their gifts, cannot escape Goethe's dictum: 'In vain will undisciplined spirits strive to achieve pure freedom. For the Master first reveals himself in limitation and only Law can give us liberty.'

Index

From the Reviews

"This is a remarkable book. . . . It
is not simply that it is monumen-
tal, virtually encyclopedic; it can
also be fairly described as balanced, thoroughly researched,
and insightful. For the narrative
of the decade from 1952 to 1962
it might be considered definitive.
This study goes far toward clari-
fying the colors in the confused
kaleidoscope that is contemporary Cuba."
— *American Historical Review*

"Both an incisive analysis and a
moving evocation of a diverse
and tragic history. If possible,
Hugh Thomas has excelled his
brilliant book on the Spanish
Civil War."
— ARTHUR SCHLESINGER, JR

"An encyclopedic work that is
immensely readable. . . . His
prose blends language and fact
so as to make everything —
economic statistics, art styles,
agricultural techniques — not
merely accessible but absorbing
His language is witty but never
mocking, crisp but never harsh."
— *The New Yorke*

ISBN 0-06-014277-